DATE DUE

			PRINTED IN U.S.A.

Literature Criticism from 1400 to 1800

Guide to Gale Literary Criticism Series

When you need to review criticism of literary works, these are the Gale series to use:

If the author's death date is: **You should turn to:**

After Dec. 31, 1959
(or author is still living)

Contemporary Literary Criticism

for example: Jorge Luis Borges, Anthony Burgess,
William Faulkner, Mary Gordon,
Ernest Hemingway, Iris Murdoch

1900 through 1959

Twentieth-Century Literary Criticism

for example: Willa Cather, F. Scott Fitzgerald,
Henry James, Mark Twain, Virginia Woolf

1800 through 1899

Nineteenth-Century Literature Criticism

for example: Fedor Dostoevski, Nathaniel Hawthorne,
George Sand, William Wordsworth

1400 through 1799

Literature Criticism From 1400 to 1800
(excluding Shakespeare)

for example: Anne Bradstreet, Daniel Defoe,
Alexander Pope, François Rabelais,
Jonathan Swift, Phillis Wheatley

Shakespearean Criticism

Shakespeare's plays and poetry

Antiquity through 1399

Classical and Medieval Literature Criticism

for example: Dante, Homer, Plato, Sophocles, Vergil,
the Beowulf Poet

Gale also publishes related criticism series:

Children's Literature Review

This series covers authors of all eras who have written for the preschool through high school audience.

Short Story Criticism

This series covers the major short fiction writers of all nationalities and periods of literary history.

Poetry Criticism

This series covers poets of all nationalities and periods of literary history.

Drama Criticism

This series covers dramatists of all nationalities and periods of literary history.

ISSN 0740-2880

Volume 17

Literature Criticism from 1400 to 1800

Excerpts from Criticism of the Works
of Fifteenth-, Sixteenth-, Seventeenth-, and
Eighteenth-Century Novelists, Poets, Playwrights,
Philosophers, and Other Creative Writers,
from the First Published Critical Appraisals
to Current Evaluations

James E. Person, Jr.
Editor

 **Gale Research Inc.** · *DETROIT* · *LONDON*

STAFF

James E. Person, Jr., *Editor*

ıc, Thomas Ligotti, Zoran Minderovic, Joann Prosyniuk,
Sandra L. Williamson, *Associate Editors*

John P. Daniel, David J. Engelman, Judy Galens, Tina N. Grant, Eric
Priehs, Linda M. Ross, Debra A. Wells, Allyson J. Wylie, *Assistant
Editors*

Jeanne A. Gough, *Permissions and Production Manager*

Linda M. Pugliese, *Production Supervisor*
L. Mpho Mabunda, Maureen A. Puhl, Jennifer VanSickle,
Editorial Associates
Donna Craft, Paul Lewon, Camille Robinson, Sheila Walencewicz,
Editorial Assistants

Maureen Richards, *Research Supervisor*
Paula Cutcher-Jackson, Robin Lupa,
Mary Beth McElmeel, *Editorial Associates*
Amy Kaechele, Julie Karmazin, Tamara C. Nott, *Editorial Assistants*

Sandra C. Davis, *Text Permissions Supervisor*
Maria L. Franklin, Josephine M. Keene, Denise Singleton,
Kimberly F. Smilay,
Permissions Associates
Rebecca A. Hartford, Michele M. Lonoconus, Shelly Rakoczy,
Shalice Shah, Nancy K. Sheridan, Rebecca A. Stanko,
Permissions Assistants

Margaret A. Chamberlain, *Permissions Supervisor (Pictures)*
Pamela A. Hayes, *Permissions Associate*
Karla A. Kulkis, Nancy M. Rattenbury, Keith Reed, *Permissions
Assistants*

Mary Beth Trimper, *Production Manager*
Mary Winterhalter, *External Production Assistant*

Arthur Chartow, *Art Director*
C. J. Jonik, *Keyliner*

Contents

Preface

Literature Criticism from 1400 to 1800 (LC) presents criticism of world authors of the fifteenth through eighteenth centuries. The literature of this period reflects a turbulent time of radical change that saw the rise of drama equal in stature to that of classical Greece, the birth of the novel and personal essay forms, the emergence of newspapers and periodicals, and major achievements in poetry and philosophy. Much of modern literature reflects the influence of these centuries. Thus the literature treated in *LC* provides insight into the universal nature of human experience, as well as into the life and thought of the past.

Scope of the Series

LC is designed to serve as an introduction to authors of the fifteenth through eighteenth centuries and to the most significant interpretations of these authors' works. The great poets, dramatists, novelists, essayists, and philosophers of this period are considered classics in every secondary school and college or university curriculum. Because criticism of this literature spans nearly six hundred years, an overwhelming amount of critical material confronts the student. *LC* therefore organizes and reprints the most noteworthy published criticism of authors of these centuries. Readers should note that there is a separate Gale reference series devoted to Shakespearean studies. For though belonging properly to the period covered in *LC,* William Shakespeare has inspired such a tremendous and ever-growing corpus of secondary material that the editors have deemed it best to give his works extensive coverage in a separate series, *Shakespearean Criticism.*

Each author entry in *LC* attempts to present a historical survey of critical response to the author's works. Early criticism is offered to indicate initial responses, later selections document any rise or decline in literary reputations, and retrospective analyses provide students with modern views. The size of each author entry is intended to reflect the author's critical reception in English or foreign criticism in translation. Articles and books that have not been translated into English are therefore excluded. Every attempt has been made to identify and include the seminal essays on each author's work and to include recent commentary providing modern perspectives.

The need for *LC* among students and teachers of literature was suggested by the proven usefulness of Gale's *Contemporary Literary Criticism (CLC), Twentieth-Century Literary Criticism (TCLC),* and *Nineteenth-Century Literature Criticism (NCLC),* which excerpt criticism of works by nineteenth- and twentieth-century authors. Because of the different time periods covered, there is no duplication of authors or critical material in any of these literary criticism series. An author may appear more than once in the series because of the great quantity of critical material available and because of the aesthetic demands of the series's *thematic organization.*

Thematic Approach

Beginning with Volume 12, roughly half the authors in each volume of *LC* are organized in a thematic scheme. Such themes include literary movements, literary reaction to political and historical events, significant eras in literary history, and the literature of cultures often overlooked by English-speaking readers. The present volume, for example, focuses upon Fifteenth-Century English literature. Future volumes of *LC* will devote substantial space to the English Metaphysical poets and authors of the Spanish Golden Age, among many others. The rest of each volume will be devoted to criticism of the works of authors not aligned with the selected thematic authors and chosen from a variety of nationalities.

Organization of the Book

Each entry consists of the following elements: author or thematic heading, introduction, list of principal works (in author entries only), annotated works of criticism (each followed by a bibliographical citation), and a bibliography of further reading. Also, most author entries contain author portraits and other illustrations.

- The **author heading** consists of the author's full name, followed by birth and death dates. If an author wrote consistently under a pseudonym, the pseudonym is used in the author heading, with the real name given in parentheses on the first line of the biographical and critical introduction. Also located here are any name variations under which an author wrote, including transliterated forms for authors whose native languages use nonroman alphabets. Uncertain birth or death dates are indicated by question marks. The **thematic heading** simply states the subject of the entry.

- The **biographical and critical introduction** contains background information designed to introduce the reader to an author and to critical discussion of his or her work. Parenthetical material following many of the introductions provides references to biographical and critical reference series published by Gale in which additional material about the author may be found. The **thematic introduction** briefly defines the subject of the entry and provides social and historical background important to understanding the criticism.

- Most *LC* author entries include **portraits** of the author. Many entries also contain illustrations of materials pertinent to an author's career, including author holographs, title pages, letters, or representations of important people, places, and events in an author's life.

- The **list of principal works** is chronological by date of first book publication and identifies the genre of each work. In the case of foreign authors whose works have been translated into English, the title and date of the first English-language edition are given in brackets beneath the foreign-language listing. Unless otherwise indicated, dramas are dated by first performance, not first publication.

- **Criticism** is arranged chronologically in each author entry to provide a useful perspective on changes in critical evaluation over the years. For the purpose of easy identification, the critic's name and the composition or publication date of the critical work are given at the beginning of each piece of criticism. Unsigned criticism is preceded by the title of the source in which it appeared. All titles by the author featured in the critical entry are printed in boldface type. Publication information (such as publisher names and book prices) and parenthetical numerical references (such as footnotes or page and line references to specific editions of works) have been deleted at the editors' discretion to provide smoother reading of the text.

- Critical essays are prefaced by **annotations** as an additional aid to students using *LC*. These explanatory notes may provide several types of useful information, including: the reputation of a critic, the importance of a work of criticism, the commentator's individual approach to literary criticism, the intent of the criticism, and the growth of critical controversy or changes in critical trends regarding an author's work. In some cases, these notes cross-reference the work of critics within the entry who agree or disagree with each other.

- A complete **bibliographical citation** of the original essay or book follows each piece of criticism.

- An annotated bibliography of **further reading** appears at the end of each entry and suggests resources for additional study of authors and themes. It also includes essays for which the editors could not obtain reprint rights.

Cumulative Indexes

Each volume of *LC* includes a cumulative **author index** listing all the authors that have appeared in *Contemporary Literary Criticism, Twentieth-Century Literary Criticism, Nineteenth-Century Literature Criticism, Literature Criticism from 1400 to 1800,* and *Classical and Medieval Literature Criticism,* along with cross-references to the Gale series *Short Story Criticism, Poetry Criticism, Children's Literature Review, Authors in the News, Contemporary Authors, Contemporary Authors Autobiography Series, Contemporary Authors Bibliographical Series, Dictionary of Literary Biography, Concise Dictionary of Literary Biography, Something about the Author, Something about the Author Autobiography Series,* and *Yesterday's Authors of Books for Children.* Readers will welcome this cumulative author index as a useful tool for locating an author within the various series. The index, which includes authors' birth and death dates, is particularly valuable for those authors who are identified with a certain period but whose death dates cause them to be placed in another, or for those authors whose careers span two periods. For example, F. Scott Fitzgerald is found in *TCLC,* yet a writer often associated with him, Ernest Hemingway, is found in *CLC.*

Beginning with Volume 12, *LC* includes a cumulative **topic index** that lists all literary themes and topics treated in *LC, NCLC* Topics volumes, *TCLC* Topics volumes, and the *CLC* Yearbook. Each volume of *LC* also includes a cumulative **nationality index** in which authors' names are arranged alphabetically under their respective nationalities and followed by the numbers of the volumes in which they appear.

Each volume of *LC* also includes a cumulative **title index,** an alphabetical listing of the literary works discussed in the series since its inception. Each title listing includes the corresponding volume and page numbers where criticism may be located. Foreign-language titles that have been translated are followed by the titles of the translations—for example, *El ingenioso hidalgo Don Quixote de la Mancha (Don Quixote)*. Page numbers following these translated titles refer to all pages on which any form of the titles, either foreign-language or translated, appear. Titles of novels, dramas, nonfiction books, and poetry, short story, or essay collections are printed in italics, while individual poems, short stories, and essays are printed in roman type within quotation marks.

A Note to the Reader

When writing papers, students who quote directly from any volume in the Literary Criticism Series may use the following general forms to footnote reprinted criticism. The first example pertains to material drawn from periodicals, the second to material reprinted from books.

T. S. Eliot, "John Donne," *The Nation and the Athenaeum,* 33 (9 June 1923), 321-32; excerpted and reprinted in *Literature Criticism from 1400 to 1800,* Vol. 10, ed. James E. Person, Jr. (Detroit: Gale Research, 1989), pp. 28-9.

Clara G. Stillman, *Samuel Butler: A Mid-Victorian Modern* (Viking Press, 1932); excerpted and reprinted in *Twentieth-Century Literary Criticism,* Vol. 33, ed. Paula Kepos (Detroit: Gale Research, 1989), pp. 43-5.

Suggestions Are Welcome

In response to various suggestions, several features have been added to *LC* since the series began, including a nationality index, a Literary Criticism Series topic index, thematic entries, a descriptive table of contents, and more extensive illustrations.

Readers who wish to suggest new features, themes, or authors to appear in future volumes, or who have other suggestions, are cordially invited to write to the editor.

Acknowledgments

The editors wish to thank the copyright holders of the excerpted criticism included in this volume, the permissions managers of many book and magazine publishing companies for assisting us in securing reprint rights, and Anthony Bogucki for assistance with copyright research. We are also grateful to the staffs of the Detroit Public Library, Wayne State University Purdy/Kresge Library Complex, and the University of Michigan Libraries for making their resources available to us. Following is a list of the copyright holders who have granted us permission to reprint material in this volume of *LC.* Every effort has been made to trace copyright, but if omissions have been made, please let us know.

COPYRIGHTED EXCERPTS IN *LC,* VOLUME 17, WERE REPRINTED FROM THE FOLLOWING PERIODICALS:

Acta Litteraria Academae Scientiarum Hungaricae, v. XVIII, 1976. Reprinted by permission of the publisher.—*Annuale Mediaevale,* v. 6, 1965 for "Sentimental Comedy in the 'Franklin's Tale,'" by Alfred David. Reprinted by permission of the author.—*Assays,* v. IV, 1987. Copyright © 1987, University of Pittsburgh Press. All rights reserved. Reprinted by permission of the publisher.—*The Chaucer Review,* v. 6, Fall, 1971. Copyright © 1971 The Pennsylvania State University, University Park, PA Reproduced by permission of The Pennsylvania State University Press.—*CLA Journal,* v. XX, December, 1976. Copyright, 1976 by The College Language Association. Used by permission of The College Language Association.—*Essays and Studies,* n.s. v. 21, 1968. © The English Association 1968. All rights reserved. Reprinted by permission of the publisher.—*The Huntington Library Quarterly,* v. 36, February, 1973. © 1973 by The Henry E. Huntington Library and Art Gallery, San Marino, CA 91108. Adapted by permission of The Henry E. Huntington Library.—*Massachusetts Studies in English,* v. 3, Fall, 1971. Copyright © 1971 by *Massachusetts Studies in English.*—*Papers on French Seventeenth-Century Literature,* v. XIII, 1986. © 1986 PFSCL. Reprinted by permission of the publisher.—*Spencer Studies: A Renaissance Poetry Annual,* v. V, 1985. Copyright © 1985, AMS Press, Inc. All rights reserved. Used by permission of the publisher.—*Studies in the Literary Imagination,* v. XI, Spring, 1978. Copyright 1978. Copyright 1978 Department of English, Georgia State University. Reprinted by permission of the publisher.—*Tennessee Studies in Literature,* v. VI, 1961. Copyright © 1961, renewed 1989 by The University of Tennessee Press. Reprinted by permission of The University of Tennessee Press.—*Western Humanities Review,* v. 23, Spring, 1969. Copyright, 1969, University of Utah. Reprinted by permission of the publisher.

COPYRIGHTED EXCERPTS IN *LC,* VOLUME 17, WERE REPRINTED FROM THE FOLLOWING BOOKS:

Aers, David. From *Chaucer.* Humanities Press International, Inc., 1986. © David Aers, 1986. All rights reserved. Reprinted by permission of Humanities Press, Inc., Atlantic Highlands, NJ 07716.—Axton, Richard. From "The Morality Tradition," in *Medieval Literature: Chaucer and the Alliterative Tradition, Vol. I.* Edited by Boris Ford. Revised edition. Penguin Books, 1982. Copyright © Boris Ford, 1982. All rights reserved. Reproduced by permission of Penguin Books Ltd.—Barney, Stephen A. From "An Evaluation of the 'Pardoner's Tale',"in *Twentieth Century Interpretations of 'The Pardoner's Tale': A Collection of Critical Essays.* Edited by Dewey R. Faulkner. Prentice-Hall, 1973. Copyright © 1973 by Stephen A. Barney. Reprinted by permission of the author.—Barthes, Roland. From *Critical Essays.* Translated by Richard Howard. Northwestern University Press, 1972. Copyright © 1972 by Northwestern University Press. All rights reserved. Reprinted by permission of the publisher.—Blake, Norman. From "William Caxton," in *Middle English Prose: A Critical Guide to Major Authors and Genres.* Edited by A. S. G. Edwards. Rutgers University Press, 1984. Copyright © 1984 by Rutgers, The State University. All rights reserved. Reprinted by permission of the publisher.—Carr, Francis. From *Ivan the Terrible.* David & Charles, 1981. © Francis Carr 1981. All rights reserved. Reprinted by permission of the publisher.—Cigman, Gloria. From an introduction to *The Wife of Bath's Prologue and Tale and The Clerk's Prologue and Tale from the Canterbury Tales.* By Geoffrey Chaucer, edited by Gloria Cigman. University of London Press Ltd., 1975. Introduction copyright © 1975 Gloria Cigman. All rights reserved. Reprinted by permission of the publisher.—Cook, Daniel. From an introduction to *Troilus and Criseyde.* By Geoffrey Chaucer, edited by Daniel Cook. Anchor Books, 1966. Copyright © 1966 by Daniel Cook. All rights reserved. Used by permission of Doubleday, a division of Bantam Doubleday Dell Publishing Group, Inc.—Cooper, Helen. From *The Canterbury Tales.* Oxford at the Clarendon Press, 1989. © Helen Cooper 1989. All rights reserved. Reprinted by permission of Oxford University Press.—Coote, Stephen. From *English Literature of the Middle Ages.* Penguin Books, 1988. Copyright © Stephen Coote, 1988. All rights reserved. Reproduced by permission of Penguin Books Ltd.—Daiches, David. From *A Critical History*

PHOTOGRAPHS AND ILLUSTRATIONS APPEARING IN *LC,* VOLUME 17, WERE RECEIVED FROM THE FOLLOWING SOURCES:

Mr. A. H. Carter: **p. 217;** Sovfoto/Eastfoto: **p. 369;** H. Roger Viollet: **p. 382.**

William Caxton

1421?-1491?

English printer, translator, and editor.

Renowned as the founder of the first printing press in England, Caxton made important contributions to the development of English literature through his publication of significant works by English authors, including Geoffrey Chaucer's *Canterbury Tales* (1478?), Thomas Malory's *Le morte d'Arthur* (1485?), and through his translations of French, Latin, and Dutch manuscripts. In selecting works to be made widely available to English readers, Caxton strongly influenced his country's literary tastes and styles while furthering the codification of the English language. In addition, Caxton's translating and editing shaped a number of important texts, and scholars regard his numerous prologues and epilogues as invaluable resources in illuminating Caxton's approach to those texts.

Information about Caxton's early life is scarce. The precise place of his birth is unknown, though Caxton indicates in the preface to *The recuyell of the historyes of Troye* (1473?) that he was born in "Kent in the Weald," or the woods of Kent. His approximate date of birth has been deduced primarily from the record of his apprenticeship to the cloth merchant Robert Large, which began sometime around 1438. Biographers have speculated that Caxton came from a family of some importance, since Large was a highly successful businessman who also served as Lord Mayor of London during Caxton's tenure with him. After Large's death in 1441, Caxton moved to the city of Bruges, which was at that time the burgeoning commercial and cultural center of the powerful duchy of Burgundy. Caxton remained in Bruges for nearly three decades, enjoying a successful business career which culminated in his appointment in 1468 to the position of Governor of English Merchants.

In 1469, Caxton began translating a French manuscript concerning the history of Troy, but soon afterward abandoned the project. However, as he relates in the prologue to *The recuyell of the historyes of Troye,* he later showed the manuscript to Margaret, Duchess of Burgundy, who suggested revisions of Caxton's translation and "commanded" that he finish the work. In the midst of this undertaking he traveled to Germany, where he completed his translation and learned the art of printing. In 1473, he began his printing venture, with *The recuyell of the historyes of Troye.* Returning to England around 1476, Caxton established a printing press in the precincts of Westminster Abbey. From his workshop, he translated, edited, and published books in English, producing nearly one hundred works during the next twenty years. The majority of the publications were histories or romances in the chivalric tradition, although he also published various religious pieces, selections from the poetry of John Gower and John Lydgate, as well as philosophical and instructive works. Critics have argued that Caxton could not have produced

Portrait long thought to be Caxton; however, recent scholarship has raised doubts regarding its authenticity.

such a volume of work without significant help from scribes and technicians, suggesting that he spent most of his time translating and editing rather than working in the print shop. Caxton continued to prosper throughout his lifetime; after his death in 1491, his achievements were commemorated with a stained glass window at St. Margaret's Church in Westminster.

The diverse nature of the works Caxton published has led to much speculation regarding his intent. Critics agree that while he sought to meet the demands of his commercial market, his reliance on patronage necessitated the publication of certain specific works. For example, *The recuyell of the historyes of Troye* was published, according to Caxton, at the behest of Margaret, Duchess of Burgundy, while Anthony, Earl Rivers requested editions of *The dicts or sayings of the philosophres* (1477?), and *Th'istories* of Jason (1477?). Caxton's prologues indicate that most of his publications were supported by patrons, but this backing did not necessarily preclude the printer's responding to a larger, more popular audience. Scholars believe that in many cases Caxton may have sought out benefactors after he had chosen to undertake a particular project, using these individuals to endorse his product rather than dictate his selection of it. In this way, Caxton achieved the more aesthetic goal of spreading what he considered to be Europe's finest literature throughout England. Critics have noted Caxton's insightful identification of works that remain important today, including a translation of Vergil's *Aeneid* entitled *Eneydos* (1490?), several of Chaucer's works, Malory's *Le morte d'Arthur,* various philosophical works, and the poetry of Lydgate and Gower.

Beyond the desire to expand the range of England's literary models, Caxton states in his prologue to *Le morte d'Arthur* that his reasons for printing were in part didactic. He reveals that his purpose was "that noble men may see and learn the noble acts of chivalry, the gentle virtuous deeds, that some knights used in those days, by which they came to honor; and how they that were vicious were punished and often put to shame and rebuke; humbly beseeching all . . . that shall see and read in this said book and work, that they take the good and honest acts in their remembrance and follow the same. . . . " This sentiment is restated throughout the prologues and epilogues to his other publications, including *Game and Playe of the Chesse* (1474?) and *Godfrey of Boloyne* (1481?), two particularly instructive works. Caxton's comments also reveal a second motivation. Repeatedly, the publisher expressed his love of the French language and literary style, often submitting this as a reason for his choice of particular works. Indeed, critics have observed a pattern in the selection of the works produced by Caxton's press. He seems to have preferred works that were in the French metrical style rather than alliterative in the fashion of much English poetry, and works that were in the French chivalric or courtly tradition. Often the degree of Caxton's literary intervention has been attributed to the extent to which given works met these criteria. Some scholars have, for example, linked his selection of a French rather than a Latin source for the translation of Vergil's *Aeneid* to these preferences.

Critics have examined with particular interest Caxton's treatment of *The Canterbury Tales* and *Le morte d'Arthur.* When he printed Chaucer's *Canterbury Tales* in 1478, he emphasized his respect for Chaucer in the prologue and demonstrated this esteem by making only minor alterations to the text. Upon his discovery in 1484 that his edition had been taken from one of the many unreliable copies of *The Canterbury Tales,* in which "wryters have abrydgyd it and many thynges left out, and in somme place have sette certayn versys that he never made ne sette in hys booke," he immediately published a second edition from a more complete source. In the case of Malory's *Le morte d'Arthur,* Caxton made significant editorial alterations to the work, almost doubling its size. Although these changes overwhelmingly centered on syntax and word choice, Caxton did manipulate the plot as well. However, the variations Caxton imposed on Malory's

original transformed the work from an alliterative to a metrical piece and strengthened its chivalric undertones; hence the work was adapted to Caxton's French model. Some scholars have censured the editor for his modifications of *Le morte d'Arthur,* but recent arguments have been made in Caxton's defense which suggest that the revisions were intended not as a commentary on Malory's literary competence but rather to update the work to reflect the developments taking place in literature on the European continent, particularly in the Burgundian court.

Critical commentary regarding Caxton and his publications began on a defamatory note in the sixteenth century, when Gawin Douglas, the printer's earliest recorded critic, castigated Caxton's *Eneydos* as "na mare like [*Aeneid*] than the Deivil and Sanct Austyn." Negative reaction was also expressed in the eighteenth century by Edward Gibbon, who detested Caxton's selection of works. Gibbon did, however, excuse Caxton by concluding that he was simply an unlearned businessman pandering to an aristocratic audience with an underdeveloped sense of classical literature. Supporting Gibbon's view, Isaac Disraeli stated that "as a printer without erudition, Caxton would naturally accommodate himself to the tastes of his age . . . mindful of his commercial interests . . . . [He] left the glory of restoring the classical writers of antiquity, which he could not read, to the learned printers of Italy." However, during the nineteenth century, critics began to view Caxton in a more favorable light. William Blades began the trend in 1863, when he published a biography of Caxton which has become the definitive source for information on the life of the printer. In this book, Blades answers the objections raised by earlier critics regarding Caxton's selection of works as well as doubts cast on his credibility as a man of letters which had been perpetuated, Blades contended, by critics who took Caxton's self-deprecating remarks too seriously. Blades argued that Caxton deserved recognition for his informed and educated choice of material for publication. He also introduced the notion that Caxton was strongly influenced by the Duke and Duchess of Burgundy in his literary taste and would shape his publications so that the Burgundian style would be perpetuated in English literature. Throughout the rest of the nineteenth century and into the twentieth century, commentators followed Blades's lead, defending Caxton as an educated and qualified judge of literature. In the latter half of the twentieth century, critics have moved away from viewing Caxton as exclusively a bibliophile or entrepreneur, recognizing that he successfully combined traits of both roles and concluding that he achieved an effective balance of pleasing his customers and exercising true literary foresight in the selection of his publications.

PRINCIPAL WORKS*

The recuyell of the historyes of Troye (legend) 1473
Game and Playe of the Chesse (allegory) 1475
The dictes or sayeings of the philosophres (philosophy) 1477
Th'istories of Jason (legend) 1477

Boecius de Consolacione philosophie (philosophy) 1478
The Book of Curtesye (poetry) 1478
The Canterbury Tales [by Geoffrey Chaucer] (poetry) 1478-85
Chronicles of England (history) 1480
The historye of Reynart the Fox (legend) 1481
The mirrour of the world (history) 1481
The siege and conqueste of Jherusalem by cristen men, or *Erascles,* or *Godfrey of Bologne* (legend) 1481
Polychronicon (history) 1482
Confession Amantis [by John Gower] (poetry) 1483
The legende of sayntes (legend) 1483
The book of the ordre of chyvalry or knyghthode (prose) 1484
The book of the subtyl hystoryes and fables of Esope (fables) 1484
The booke whiche the knyght of the toure made (prose) 1484
Royal Book (prose) 1484
The lyf of the holy & blessid vyrgyn saynt Wenefryde (legend) 1485
Le morte d'Arthur [by Thomas Malory] (legend) 1485
Th'ystorye and lyf of the noble and crysten prynce, Charles the grete (history) 1485
Th'ystorye of the noble, ryght valyaunt & worthy knyght Parys and of the fayr Vyenne (legend) 1485
The myrroure of the blessyd lyf of Jhesu Cruste (legend) 1486
Book of Good Manners (prose) 1487
The boke of the fayt of armes and of chyvalrye [by Christine de Pisan] (prose) 1489
Doctrinal of Sapience (prose) 1489
Of the victoryous prynce Blanchardyn, sone of the noble kyng of Fryse, and of Eglantyne, quene of Tormaday (history) 1489
The Right Pleasaunt and Goodly Historie of the Foure Sonnes of Aymon (legend) 1489
The arte and crafte to knowe well to dye (prose) 1490
Eneydos (legend) 1490

*The works listed here were printed at Caxton's press and were compiled, edited, and in some cases translated by Caxton. Most contain prefaces, prologues, or epilogues written by Caxton. All dates are approximate.

William Blades (essay date 1877)

[*An English scholar and printer, Blades published several important studies of the history of printing in England. His work on Caxton,* The Biography and Typography of William Caxton, England's First Printer *(1863), is still considered among the most authoritative sources of information about Caxton's life and career. In the following excerpt from that work, Blades praises Caxton's linguistic facility as well as his skills as a translator, editor and author.*]

As a linguist, Caxton undoubtedly excelled. In his native tongue, notwithstanding his self-depreciation, he seems to

have been a master. His writings, and the style of his translations, will bear comparison with Lydgate, with Gower, with Earl Rivers, the Earl of Worcester, and other contemporaneous writers. Many of his readers, indeed, thought him too "ornate" and "over curious" in his diction, and desired him to use more homely terms; but, since others found fault with him for not using polished and courtly phrases, we may fairly presume that he attained the happy medium, "ne over rude, ne over curious," at which he aimed. When excited by a favourite subject, as the *Order of Chivalry* he waxed quite eloquent; and the appeal of Caxton to the knighthood of England, has been often quoted as a remarkable specimen of fifteenth-century declamation. With the French tongue he was thoroughly conversant, although he had never been in France; but Bruges was almost French, and in the Court of Burgundy, as well as in that of England, French was the chief medium of conversation. With Flemish he was also well acquainted, as shown by his translation of *Reynart;* indeed, this language, after so long a residence in Bruges, must have become almost his mother-tongue.

Caxton's knowledge of Latin has often been denied or underrated; but as governor of the English nation in Bruges, and as ambassador, he must have been able to read the treaties he assisted to conclude, and the correspondence with the king's council. Moreover, he printed books entirely in the Latin tongue, some of which were full of contractions, and could only have been undertaken by one well acquainted with that language. These were the "Infancia Salvatoris," three editions of the "Directorium Sacerdotum," a "Psalterium," "Horæ," "Tractatus de Transfiguracione," and several "Indulgences." To "ordain in print" a Latin manuscript of the fourteenth or fifteenth century required a knowledge of the language on the part of the workman as well as of the master; for, as the letters *n* and *u* were identical in shape, and as *m* and *i* varied only in the number of strokes, the latter being without a dot, it was impossible to read some words—for instance, mınımum (minimum), where fifteen parallel strokes distract the eye—apart from their context. We have, however, in the English translation of the *Golden Legend* positive evidence on this point; for, in the "Life of Saynt Rocke," the printer says, "which lyff is translated oute of latyn in to englysshe by me wyllyam Caxton."

As translator, editor, and author, Caxton has not received his due meed of praise. The works which he undertook at the suggestion of his patrons, as well as those selected by himself, are honestly translated, and, considering the age in which he lived, are well chosen. Romances, the favourite literature of his age, were Caxton's great delight—and that not merely for the feats of personal prowess which they narrated, although no quality was more desirable in the fifteenth century, but rather, as he himself says, for the examples of "courtesy, humanity, friendliness, hardiness, love, cowardice, murder, hate, virtue, and sin," which "inflamed the hearts of the readers and hearers to eschew and flee works vicious and dishonest." In Poetry Caxton shows to great advantage, for he printed all the works of any merit which then existed. The prologue to his second edition of the *Canterbury Tales* proves how anxious he was to be correct, and at the same time shows the difficulty he had in obtaining manuscripts free from error. The poetical reverence with which Caxton speaks of Chaucer, "the first founder of *ornate* eloquence in our English," and the pains he took to reprint the *Canterbury Tales* when a purer text than that of his first edition was offered to him, show his high appreciation of England's first great poet. In History the only available works in English were the *Chronicle of Brute* and the *Polycronicon;* the latter Caxton carried down, to the best of his ability, to nearly his own time. It was, indeed, as a writer of history that Caxton was best known to our older authors, some of whom, while including his name among those of English historians, have overlooked the far more important fact that he was also England's prototypographer. (pp. 88-90)

William Blades, in his The Biography and Typography of William Caxton, England's First Printer, *1877, Reprint by Frederick Muller Ltd., 1971, 383 p.*

Alice D. Greenwood   (essay date 1908)

[*Greenwood was an American critic and poet. In the following excerpt, she provides a brief overview of Caxton's major translations and comments on his significance in the development of English literature.*]

Although the introduction of printing brought about no sudden renascence, it accelerated and strengthened, under the direction of Caxton, the drift of the current of our fifteenth century literature; and this places our first printer in a position wholly different from that of his more mechanical successors. Caxton was quick to discern the direction in which taste was tending and, himself helping to direct that taste, he ignored the old metrical romances, favourites for long, preferring to satisfy the chivalric-romantic fashion of the times by prose translations from French works of already established repute. That romances of the kind of *The Four Sons of Aymon,* or *Paris and Vienne,* were destined to disappearance early in the next century in no way neutralises their importance as a step in English literature. They handed on material not disdained by Spenser, they formed a link between medieval and modern romance, and from among them has survived an immortal work, Malory's *Morte d'Arthur.*

We might have supposed Caxton's publication of Chaucer to have been epoch-making, had it not had to wait for long before kindling any fresh torch; but there is no evidence that it roused in others the enthusiasm felt by its editor. In truth, the men of that age, who had but just emerged from a long and sordid war, were not, and could not be, poetical; and, save for the poems of Chaucer and Lydgate, Caxton held firm to prose.

His publications, excluding church service-books and practical manuals, fall into three groups: didactic works, romances and chronicles. Of the last—large and, doubtless, costly—three proved sufficient; of romances, he issued ten or eleven, probably for the courtly class of readers; while, of moral and didactic works, for the most part small and cheap, he provided no less than twenty-nine, not

counting *Reynard the Fox,* and *The Golden Legend,* which partake of the entertaining element at least equally with the instructive. As several of these books and tracts went into two editions, they were, evidently, in considerable demand with the general public; but the tinge of utility is upon them, and they have not the literary interest of the larger works.

As has been observed already, the greater part of Caxton's output was translated. Tudor prose, like that of the earlier period, was chiefly fashioned on French models, to which we owe nearly all the prose masterpieces of the epoch, and a proportionate debt of gratitude. But Caxton found another quarry in fifteenth century prose, and in the case of both English and French material he acted as editor, translating with the same freedom as his predecessors, and "embellishing the old English" of Trevisa or of *The Golden Legend.*

Caxton had lived so long abroad that he probably found more difficulty than other writers in selecting the most suitable words to employ; and it is difficult to believe that one hand alone turned out so large a mass of literature as he did, any more than it manipulated the printing-press unaided. Nevertheless, his translations must, like his press, be reckoned as having the stamp of his authority, though others, probably, helped. A comparison of his editions of *The Golden Legend, Polychronicon* and *The Knight of the Tower* with the original English versions leaves the older prose easily first. Again and again, the modern reader will find the word rejected by Caxton more familiar than its substitute; again and again, Caxton's curtailments, inversions, or expansions merely spoil a piece of more vigorous narrative. This is particularly evident in *The Knight of the Tower,* which Caxton seems to have translated entirely afresh, unaware of the older version, whose superiority is remarkable. And in his original and interesting prefaces we may, perhaps, see how it was he went wrong. He appears to have been desirous of avoiding the colloquially simple manner of earlier writers, and to have felt his way towards the paragraph, working out, in those prefaces for which he had no French exemplar, a somewhat involved style. He is fond of relative sentences, and sometimes piles them on the top of each other without finishing the earlier ones: "Which thing when Gotard had advertised of and that he bare so away the bread, but he wist not to whom ne whither, whereof he marvelled and so did all his household." He mixes direct and indirect speech; he uses the redundant *which:* "I fynde many of the sayd bookes, whyche writers have abrydged it and many thynges left out." Only when he has plain statements to convey, as in his continuation of the *Chronicle,* or an anecdote to relate, such as the tale of the dean and the poor parson in the epilogue to Aesop, does he become direct; but then he is, sometimes, almost as vigorous as Latimer himself. In this power of writing with a naïve vivacity, while deliberately striving after a more ornate manner, Caxton belongs to his age. He provides, as it were, a choice of styles for his readers.

The mannerisms of the Middle Ages are still noticeable in Caxton's work: in his irrepressible moralising, his quotations from old authority, his conventional excuse for writing a book (to keep himself from idleness, which is the nurse of sin), his arrant inaccuracy as to names, his profession of incapacity "to smattre me in suche translacions"; but his definite claim to have embellished the older authors, his quiet pride in his own authorship and the interest taken therein by his noble patrons, his conscious appreciation of language, are of the new world, not of the old. The days of anonymous compiling are over; and, henceforth, not the substance, alone, but its form will challenge attention. Prose is no longer to be merely the vehicle of information, but conscious literature.

Caxton's largest and most popular book, *The Golden Legend,* is, also, the most medieval in kind. It may almost be called a cyclopaedia of traditional sacred lore, comprising not lives of the saints only, but explanations of the church service and homilies upon the feast days, as well as a shortened but complete chronicle, Lombard in origin, to A.D. 1250. The public decidedly preferred it to Malory or Chaucer, and it went through edition after edition. For one thing, it was a long-recognised classic; for another, it presented the favourite mixture of morality combined with entertainment. Many of the lives are copies from earlier English versions, more or less "mollified" by their editor. Those of French saints are a new, and often slipshod, translation. Others are compiled from the three renderings (Latin, English and French) and from further sources such as *Polychronicon* and *Josephus,* and practically form a new version. With regard to the merit of these, opinions will differ. It may be true that Caxton's *Becket,* for example, presents a more compact story than the original; on the other hand, the incessant curtailment has spoiled the charming incident of the Saracen princess. Caxton, moreover, altered the usual arrangement of the *Legend* to insert a series of lives of Old Testament heroes, and it is a vital question in estimating his rank as a prose writer whether these lives are to be reckoned his own or not. They are so far superior to the mere translations that one of his critics takes it for granted they must be his own; another, that they must come from an earlier English version now lost. The MSS. of the old version now remaining to use contain none of these Old Testament lives save *Adam,* from which the Caxtonian version differs entirely. The earlier *Adam,* except for the usual legendary interpolations, is strictly Biblical in language, adhering closely, at first, to the revised Wyclifite version, afterwards to the first Wyclifite version; whereas Caxton's *Adam* is, in the main, a sermon, and the succeeding lives, though they follow the Bible closely as to incident, are much shortened as to wording, and not distinctively reminiscent of the Wyclifite versions; indeed, they afford more points of resemblance to the later phraseology. If it can be supposed that Caxton actually rendered them into English himself, his literary powers here rose to a pitch far higher than he attained at any other time. (pp. 377-80)

Alice D. Greenwood, "English Prose in the Fifteenth Century: Caxton, Malory, Berners," in The Cambridge History of English Literature: The End of the Middle Ages, Vol. II, *edited by A. W. Ward and A. R. Waller, G. P. Putnam's Sons, 1908, pp. 377-86.*

Nellie Slayton Aurner   (essay date 1926)

[*An American scholar and critic, Aurner was the author of several publications on early English letters, including* Caxton: Mirror of Fifteenth Century Letters. *In the following excerpt from that book, Aurner discusses Caxton's role in the development of English literature.*]

After a survey of Caxton's books as an outgrowth of his life and the life of those about him, one feels that he really was significant to an extent that has not been generally recognized in the history of English literature. The influence which he introduced and extended over an ever-widening circle of readers was not imposed from outside, nor from above, but sprang from the very heart of the most vital force of fifteenth-century England. As Governor of the Merchant Adventurers abroad, Caxton was for years the central figure of that company, remarkable for its vivid life, which made successful war against the monopoly of the staple and fostered the spirit of initiative in civic and commercial affairs.

This spirit of initiative Caxton carried over into his activities as editor and printer. Other countries might follow the laws laid upon them by the revival of learning, but he, although he learned the new art by working on a Latin book, made use of it immediately in the service of his native tongue.

Too simple-minded and humble to dream of reforming the taste of his countrymen, or of remoulding their ideas according to some foreign pattern, he made use of the wonderful new invention to express and preserve what seemed to him best in the literature of his time. A very large amount of this literature was available only to the limited number of Englishmen who knew French and Latin. Caxton's translations, together with those he obtained from others, revolutionized English literary prose. Both in quantity and quality the contribution of his press in this field is so remarkable that it is worthy of a study in itself, not merely for its effect upon the language, but for its significance in the general development of English literature.

An interesting parallel might be drawn between the literary work of Caxton and that of King Alfred. Both were pre-eminently translators and diffusers of knowledge. One brought into existence the first body of written prose in the English tongue; the other first put into print, and enormously extended the possibilities of, English prose with the effect of greatly increasing both writers and readers. Both were popularizers in the best sense of the term. They were eager to extend knowledge beyond the limited circle of nobles and scholars "to thende that many myght come to honoure and worshyppe". Both took books which they thought "most needful for the people to know", and made them intelligible and interesting to the ordinary individual.

As King Alfred in compiling his laws did not feel that he could include novelties of his own, but exercised his judgment in choosing the best and dropping out what his own experience and that of his ancestors had shown useless or harmful, so Caxton with like conservatism printed what his own judgment and that of the friends and patrons he admired regarded as best in the letters of his time.

In their spirit of devout reverence for religion and humble devotion to their Church in its forms and ceremonies, the two men were alike. They shared, too, a passionate love for the brave deeds of heroes remembered in the songs of the people. The loss of the book in which King Alfred treasured his collection of popular tales is one of the tragedies of literary history. Fortunately the romances that Caxton loved have not met a similar fate, though we must remember that such would have happened, but for Caxton's printing, to the greatest of them all, Malory's *Morte Darthur*.

Modesty, simplicity, and almost childlike absence of affectation or striving for effect, are characteristics of both men. Awkwardnesses of expression and lack of logical connections they have, too, in common. Neither had received the conventional training for a literary career, and both carried on their work of translation in the midst of distractions inevitable to a life of administrative detail. King Alfred's pathetic "gif wē ðā stillnesse habbað" (if we have the leisure) might well have been echoed by Caxton.

Of course there were differences. The great King had more dignity and his writings are more marked by elevation of thought and style. On the other hand, Caxton had spontaneity and a vein of humour which his royal predecessor lacked. The **"Epilogue to Earl Rivers's *Dictes*"** (treating of the Earl's omission of Socrates's sayings "towchyng women") and the anecdote of the pompous prelate, related at the close of *Æsop,* are given in a manner not unworthy of Chaucer himself.

A point not sufficiently recognized in considering the influence of other nations on English literature is Caxton's transfusion of a new element into the literary spirit of England—the Burgundian. Probably because the works he translated were in the French language, it has been generally taken for granted that Caxton's work merely carried on what had long been the dominant Court element— French. This is a superficial view. Burgundy, a powerful rival of France, differed from the latter kingdom as distinctly and in as many respects as did other nations. And Caxton was as familiar with the Flemish as with the French section of it—witness his *Reynard the Fox.* The researches of William Blades showed that every one of Caxton's books drawn from a source outside of England can be traced to the libraries of Bruges. This close connection with the Netherlands may have had some influence in linking England with the Germanic centres so important during the Reformation. (pp. 203-06)

Even from the narrower view-point of service rendered to the Renaissance, he is not entirely without claim to gratitude. He referred with special warmth to lovers of the new learning, as in his lament over the death of John Tiptoft, Earl of Worcester. And in his books themselves may be found distinct foreshadowing of that love for classical antiquity which was to become the literary passion of the succeeding generation. Not only did he give the stories of Troy, Jason, Æneas, and Ovid's *Metamorphoses,* but he

published several editions of Cato's distichs, Cicero's *Old Age* and *Friendship* (translation) and the *Dictes and Sayings of the Philosophers.*

But the most important service he rendered to the revival of learning was the systematic way in which he proceeded to enlarge the reading public in various directions. To be sure, his romances and books on chivalry were "not for every rude and uplandish man", but he published other books which he tells us were specially designed for use "emonge the people" and for the "erudicion of the ygnorant". Books for children and for old people, and special books for women were also provided. And he took pains to make these books interesting.

Who can doubt that the creation of a public capable of understanding and responding to genuine literature was of more importance at this time than a supply of Greek and Latin texts? It was the soil thus prepared that enabled the native genius of England to develop so that it assimilated the mass of material brought in by the new learning, and was stimulated by it to fuller expression of native themes and indigenous ideas, instead of being overwhelmed and content to imitate classic models.

Lecturing on the first century of the English Press, Professor A. W. Pollard recently suggested that "the general slowness of our intellectual advance may perhaps be regarded as the price we paid for Shakespeare and the other Elizabethan dramatists and song writers." Could there be found a critic with vision so narrow as to regret this price?

After granting all the defects that carpers have discovered in the father of English printing—that he did not immediately give England a position of leadership in the new learning, that he was not an artist in types or in illustrations, that he did not print the Bible in English and thus make England a leader in the Reformation, that he was one of the people and not a scholar and reformer—there still remain ample grounds for gratitude that it was he and "not Launcelot, nor another", that was called to the kingdom of English letters for this important task. "Homeliness", it has been said, "best expresses the qualities of his work and of his press." In its best sense this can be accepted and echoed as a tribute by any one who grows to love and respect him through the fuller knowledge that careful study gives.

The perspective of time has shown in many cases that it is not always the intellect which turns the human soul into new fields of development, nor is it the scholar alone who renders great service to his race. Was it not Richardson rather than Fielding who first gave the novel its modern form, and is it not Shakespeare rather than Jonson or Bacon who represents to us most truly the Elizabethan age?

It is hard to see how any student of English literature today who takes the trouble to become really acquainted with Caxton's work and the period it represents can fail to recognize how much the later development of this literature owes to his sound judgment and instinctively right critical sense. For Italy, for France, for Germany other influences led to different results, no doubt better for them; but fortunately the lines of growth for English letters followed a distinctively national design. And it is only fair that those who take pride in thinking that their native tongue has made them share in the priceless inheritance of a literature unlike all others should realize the importance of William Caxton, not only because he gave to England printing, but because he considered the new invention merely as a means of expression for the best in the life of his time and his people, and thus promoted that natural growth which has given English literature its character and distinction. (pp. 206-08)

> *Nellie Slayton Aurner, in her* Caxton, Mirrour of Fifteenth-Century Letters: A Study of the Literature of the First English Press, *Philip Allan & Co. Ltd., 1926, 304 p.*

A. T. P. Byles   (essay date 1934)

[*An English scholar and clergyman, Byles has edited Caxton's versions of* The Ordre of Chyvalry *and* The Fayttes of Armes *for the Early English Text Society and published articles on Caxton in various literary journals. In the following excerpt, Byles elucidates Caxton's contributions to English literature as a translator and author, suggesting that his critical faculties were more refined than was generally acknowledged by early commentators.*]

Caxton's influence as a man of letters was exerted not only in his choice of books for publication, but also by his work as a translator and as an original author. In his translations he shows that curious mixture of diffidence and boldness which characterizes much Renaissance literature. Although he is acutely conscious of his deficiencies in both French and English, he does not hesitate to 'embellish' the old-fashioned English of Trevisa and bring it up to date. In the same spirit Spenser, while deprecating comparison with Chaucer and Langland, prophesies that his *Calendar*

> shall continue till the world's dissolution.

The **'Prologue to *The Recuyell*'** is of the greatest interest in its revelation of Caxton's beginnings as a translator. Desiring to turn this notable romance into English he impulsively

> toke penne and ynke, and began boldly to renne forth as blynde Bayard in thys presente werke. . . . And afterward whan I remembryd myself of my symplenes and vnperfightnes that I had in both langages, that is to wete, in Frenshe and in Englissh, for in France was I never, and was born and lerned myn Englissh in Kente in the Weeld, where I doubte not is spoken as brode and rude Englissh as is in ony place of Englond, and haue contynued by the space of xxx yere for the most parte in the contres of Braband, Flandres, Holand and Zeland; and thus whan alle thyse thynges cam tofore me aftyr that y had made and wreten a fyue or six quayers, y fyll in dispayr of thys werke and purposid nomore to haue contynuyd therin, and the quayers leyd apart, and in two yere aftyr laboured nomore in thys werke.

It was only at the 'dredefull comandement' of the Duchess of Burgundy that the translation was completed in 1471. Caxton's long residence abroad had probably caused him to lose touch to some extent with contemporary English idiom, and it is not surprising that the Duchess 'fonde a defaute in myn Englissh whiche she comanded me to amende'. The structure of the sentences is quite foreign to the English idiom, and bizarre words and mistranslations abound. In *The Historie of Jason,* 1477, Caxton feels that his safest course is to be piously literal,

> folowyng myn auctor as nygh as I can or may, not chaungyng the sentence ne presumyng to adde ne mynusshe ony thing otherwyse than myne auctor hath made in Frensshe.

The greatness of his task in translating *The Golden Legend,* 1483, had made him 'halfe desperate to haue accomplissd it' when the Earl of Arundel came to his aid with kindly encouragement. The Prologues to Caxton's later translations show that he was troubled by the growing preference of his public for ornate and rhetorical prose, a taste which he did not feel himself competent to satisfy.

> . . . Pardone me of the rude and symple reducyng, and though so be there no gaye termes ne subtyl ne newe eloquence, yet I hope that it shall be vnderstonden. (*Charles the Great,* 1485).

> . . . Pardoune me of the rude and comyn Englyshe, whereas shall be found faulte. For I confesse me not lerned, ne knowynge the arte of rethoryk, ne of such gaye termes as now be sayd in these dayes and vsed. But I hope it shall be vnderstonden of the redars and herers. (*Blanchardyn and Eglantine,* 1489.)

The fullest discussion of Caxton's difficulties as a translator is found in the **'Prologue to *Eneydos'*,** one of his last works, published in 1490. Some gentlemen had blamed him for using 'ouer curyous termes whiche coude not be understande of comyn peple, and desired me to vse olde and homely termes in my translacyons'. 'Fayn wolde I satisfye euery man', says Caxton; so he began to read an old book, but found the language so rude and broad that he could not understand it. Further, the Abbot of Westminster showed him an Old English (or perhaps early Middle English) manuscript, which was more like Dutch than English. And what is 'common English'? 'For that comyn Englysshe that is spoken in one shyre varyeth from another.' His point is illustrated by the anecdote of the merchant called Sheffield, who is taken for a Frenchman because he asks for 'egges' in Kent, instead of 'eyren'. Another set of critics 'desired me to wryte the most curyous termes that I coude fynde. And thus bytwene playn rude and curyous I stande abasshed.' Caxton rejects the older English as out of date, and also seeks to avoid the highly rhetorical style. He tries to steer a middle course, aiming above all at clearness of meaning.

> In my judgemente, the comyn termes that be dayli vsed ben lyghter to be vnderstonde than the olde and auncyent Englysshe . . . . Therfor in a meane bytwene bothe I have reduced and translated this sayd booke in to our Englysshe,

not ouer rude, ne curyous, but in suche termes
as shall be vnderstanden by Goddys grace accor-
dynge to my copye.

Caxton's liberal use of pairs of synonymous words is partly the development of a tendency that can be traced to Old
English prose, and is partly due to his desire to 'satisfy
every man' by giving him an alternative. In the earlier
stages of the language the use of pairs of words was adopted to give greater balance and dignity to prose, a use which
is also exemplified in the familiar phrases of the Prayer
Book of Edward VI. So in the Alfredian translation of
Bede's *Ecclesiastical History, conclusit* is translated as
betÿnde ond geendode, decessus as *gewiteness ond forpför,*
and *videretur* (it seemed) as *pühte ond gesawen wære,* the
second phrase a conscious Latinism. Trevisa uses a great
many pairs of words, such as *domesmen and juges, tempest
and tene, wondres and merveillis of dyuerse contrees and
londes* (Higden, *miranda locorum*), in his translation of
the *Polychronicon,* 1387. The 'augmenting' of the English
language, of which Professor Chambers speaks in *The
Continuity of English Prose,* has its roots in a more distant
past than the early fifteenth century. As the century went
on, however, English prose became more imitative, and
began to adapt French constructions and to introduce
large numbers of French words. It is Caxton's desire to
please all tastes that explains his lavish use of synonyms;
the modernist can take the Frenchified 'curyous' word,
while the old-fashioned reader will find his 'rude, brood
termes', in a larger proportion than is generally imagined.
An investigation of the synonyms in *The Fayttes of Armes*
yielded the following results:

> There are about 300 separate pairs of synonyms
> in *The Fayttes of Armes,* many of them occurring
> again and again (e.g. hurt and damage, due or
> capitaine, socoure and helpe, dyuers and many,
> wylis and subtyltees, myght and power, reputed
> or taken, barat and deceyte). About 42% consist
> of the anglicized form of the word of the origi-
> nal, followed by the native English equivalent
> (e.g. poys or weyght); in 15% this order is re-
> versed (e.g. to ploughe and laboure the lande);
> 26% consist of a pair of native English words
> (e.g. thou felest and knowest); the remainder
> (about 17%) consist of a pair of French words
> (e.g. his culpe and deffawte). So it appears that
> out of every 100 words used in these synony-
> mous pairs, about 55 are of native English ori-
> gin, while 45 are anglicized French words.
> Moreover, the latter differ greatly from the fan-
> tastic French borrowings found in *The Recuyell;*
> nearly all of them survived in general use for
> more than a century (cf. *cautelous* in Shake-
> speare, *Coriolanus,* IV. i. 33), and many are in
> use at the present day. [Byles, in his introduction
> to *The Booke of Fayttes of Armes,* by Christine
> de Pisan, 1932]

That there is some difference of opinion among critics as
to the literary value of these synonyms is indicated by the
following comments by reviewers of my edition of *The
Fayttes of Armes.* Mr. W. J. B. Crotch, writing in the *Review of English Studies,* October, 1933, thinks that many
will disagree with my view that the excessive use of pairs
of synonymous words is a chief cause of tautology in all

Caxton's works. 'It should be remembered', he writes,
'that although Caxton's circle of distinguished readers was
largely bi-lingual, the printing press was even then making
its appeal to other social grades, who may have had no
such facility of language; indeed he was but following the
practice of his favourite author, Chaucer, by whom the use
of synonyms has been hailed as enriching the language and
welding two great strains into one.' On the other hand,
Mr. J. P. Oakden, of St. Andrews, writes in the *Modern
Language Review* of the same date:

> Even at its best, Caxton's work is marred by the
> inordinate use of tautological synonyms, a trick
> of style which is seldom effective. In the musical
> prose of the *Book of Common Prayer,* which
> abounds in examples of this stylistic feature, the
> repetition is often quite effective in its emphasis
> and sonority. There is no such justification for
> it in Caxton's work, and the use of no less than
> 300 pairs of synonyms in *The Fayttes of Armes*
> is unpardonable.

My own opinion is that these synonyms are a defect inherent in the prose of the time. Their occurrence can be explained by the uncertain state of the English vocabulary,
and they are an exaggerated development of a venerable
form of ornament; but judged according to the canons of
absolute art, in the profusion with which they are used by
Caxton, they are, as Mr. Oakden says, indefensible. It can,
however, be said in their favour that they helped to enrich
the vocabulary of English for subsequent authors.

Both as translator and as original author Caxton makes
use of more than one style. He consciously endeavoured,
however, to model his style on that of contemporary
French prose, with its long, complex sentences and abundance of subordinate clauses. Pecock had the skill to write
this prose with success. Dr. Chambers tells us that the first
sentence of *The Donet* fills 31 lines, and the first sentence
of *The Folewer,* 40, but both sentences are quite grammatical and well-formed. Caxton's grasp was less firm. Too
often in place of intricate but logical French constructions
we find constant transgressions against the unity of the
sentence. In the following passage from *The Order of Chivalry* the French infinitive is represented by a different construction at each occurrence.

> *Caxton.* Chastyte and strengthe . . . surmounte
> hit, *by remembraunce* of his commaundementys,
> and *for to remember and wel to vnderstonde* the
> goodes and glory that God gyueth to them, . . .
> and *by wel to loue God.*

> *Royal MS 14 E ii, Brit. Mus.* Chastete guerroye
> et sourmonte luxure, *par remembrer* dieu et ses
> commandemens, et *par bien entendre* les biens et
> la gloire que dieu donne a ceulx, . . . et *par bien
> amer dieu.*

From the Old English period English had showed itself ill
adapted to a complicated sentence structure, and it is interesting to find in the Alfredian translation of Bede faults
similar to Caxton's; the redundant *pæt,* synonymous pairs
of words, long and sometimes incoherent sentences, and

constructions borrowed direct from the Latin original, such as the passive use of *sēon* to correspond to *videri* (= to seem). Even when he is translating, however, Caxton is capable of writing an essentially English style.

> Than the kynge demanded his counceyll of what deth they had deseruyd to dye that had so doon and wrought agayn the wylle of hym. Some sayd that they shold ben hanged, and some sayd thay shold ben slayn. And other sayd that they shold be beheedid. Than sayd the kynge, By the lord that made me, they ben not worthy to dye, but for to haue moche worship and honour. For they haue ben trewe to theyr lord.

'Had he written often thus', as Johnson said of Gray's *Elegy*, 'it had been vain to blame, and useless to praise him.' In his unfortunate desire to please every man, however, he neglected his natural gifts in direct narrative, and cultivated the French sentence-paragraph. Dr. Leon Kellner, who made a detailed analysis of Caxton's syntax in *Blanchardyn and Eglantine*, considers [in his introduction to *Blanchardyn and Eglantine*, 1890] that

> there is no ground whatever for supposing that he slavishly sacrificed the genius of his native language to Latin or French . . . . Caxton's syntax is essentially English, as much so as that of Chaucer and Gower; his arrangement of words is, in spite of his original, truly Saxon; and even in his introduction of foreign words, he only continued what the preceding centuries had begun.

He mentions as Gallicisms the phrases *the his, the two,*

Caxton's imprint.

placing of adjectives after the noun, the use of the definite article with the vocative case, and some isolated examples of French constructions with verbs, such as "He demaunded to the stywarde'. Dr. Kellner speaks with the greatest authority within the limits of his thorough investigation, but this was practically confined to *Blanchardyn and Eglantine, The Four Sons of Aymon* (both printed *c.* 1489) and (for purposes of comparison) *Morte Darthur.*

It has to be kept in mind that the comments of editors on Caxton as a translator are usually based upon a single text. His style differs in works written at different periods. The great inferiority of *The Recuyell* to the remainder of his work has already been noted. His style varies also according to his subject. Dr. Kellner's analysis was based on narrative writing, in which Caxton keeps most closely to the simpler English idiom, and there is no reason to doubt the accuracy of his findings, which were published as long ago as 1890. My own study of *The Order of Chivalry* and *The Fayttes of Armes*, expository rather than narrative works, leads me to the opinion that in this type of writing Caxton was strongly influenced by the French structure of sentences. Very occasionally he renders the French word for word, as in *The Recuyell*, with a total disregard for natural English expression. Thus he translates

> lesquelles choses, pour example de se confermer a yceulx, se bon semble, sont a oyr propices et expediens.

as

> the whiche thynges for example to be conformed to theym yf they seme good ben for to be herde propyce and expedyent.

French conjunctions and prepositions, too, are very awkwardly translated,

e.g.   *to purpoos of* for *a propos de.*
   by trauers of for *au trauers de.*
   sayd that   for *puisque* (= since).
   what that   for *quoyque* (= although).

On the whole, however, Caxton wrestles fairly successfully with Christine de Pisan's French, and shows a firmer control of sentence structure than in 'The Order of Chivalry', translated about five years earlier. If we compare two consecutive sentences from Christine's Prologue to *The Fayttes of Armes* we can estimate the difference between a successful rendering of a long French sentence and a less happy effort.

First sentence

> *Christine de Pisan.* Maiz comme il affiere ceste matiere estre plus excecutee par fait de diligence et sens que par subtilitees de paroles polies, et aussy considere que les excerceans et expers en lart de Cheualerie ne sont communement clercz ne instruis en science de langage, Je nentens a traittier ne mais au plus plain et entendible langaige que je pourray, a celle fin que la doctrine donne par plusieurs aucteurs, qui a laide de dieu (je) propose en ce present liure declairer, puist estre a tous cler et entendible.

Caxton. But as it apperteyneth this matere to be more executed by fayt of dyligence and witte/than by subtyltees of wordes polisshed/ and also considered that they that been excersyng and experte in tharte of chyualrye be not comunely clerkys ne instructe in science of langage/I entende not to treate/but to the most playn and entendible langage that I shal mowe/to that ende that the doctryne gyuen by many auctors/whiche by the helpe of god I purpose to declare in this present boke/may be to alle men clere and entendible.

In this sentence the relation between the clauses is correctly maintained, Caxton's punctuation helps the sense, and the only Gallicisms are the placing of the adjective after the noun in *wordes polisshed* and the use of *considered that* as a conjunction.

Second sentence:

Christine de Pisan. Et pour ce que cest chose non accoustumee et hors vsage a femme, qui communement ne se seult entremettre ne mais quenouilles filasses et choses de mesnage, Je supplie humblement audit treshault office et noble estat de cheualerie que, en contemplacion de la soye dame minerue, nee du pays de grece, que les anciens pour son grant scauoir reputerent deesse, laquelle trouua, selon que dient les anciens escrips, sy comme autrefois (je) ay dit et que mesmement le recite le poete bocace en son liure des femmes cleres, et semblablement le recitent autres plusieurs, lart et la maniere de faire le harnois de fer et dacier, quilz ne veuillent auoir a mal se moy femme me suis chargee de traittier de si faitte matiere, ains vueillent ensuiure lenseignement de senecque, qui dit, Ne te chault qui die, mais que les parolles soyent bonnes.

Caxton. And by cause that this is thyng not accustomed and out of vsage to wymen/whiche comynly do not entremete but to spynne on the distaf and ocupie theim in thynges of houshold/I supplye humbly to the said right hie office and noble state of chyualrye/that in contemplacion of theyr lady mynerue born of the contre of grece/whom the auncyents for hir grete connyng reputeden a goddesse the whiche fonde lyke as olde wrytyngis sayen/and as I haue other tymes sayd/And also the poete boece recyteth in his boke of clere and noble wimmen/and semblably recyten many other/the arte and manere to make harnoys of yron and steel/whyche wyl not haue ne take it for none euyl/yf I a woman charge my self to treate of so lyke a matere/but wyl ensewe thenseignement and techyng of seneke whiche saith/retche the not what they saye/soo that the wordes be good.

Caxton is here dealing with a very complicated sentence, and his omission of a punctuation mark after *fonde* (*Caxton,* 1. 6 above), and his mistranslation of *quilz ne veuillent auoir a mal* (*Christine,* 1. 9), show that he has not grasped its structure. A strong anacoluthon begins at 'And also the poete boece' (MS. bocace), while Seneca's maxim is turned into nonsense by the mistranslation of *qui* (= *who*) as *what*. The sentence is so complex that even in the original

French it requires a grammatically redundant *que* (in *quilz ne veuillent*) to make the meaning clear. If Caxton had rewritten the sentence or had simplified it by omitting some of the subordinate clauses, he would probably have escaped the pitfalls which beset him. This example shows, therefore, how seriously he is hampered, even in his latest and best work as a translator, by his too close adherence to the sentence structure of his original, and particularly by his method of translating a complex sentence piecemeal without grasping the true relation of the component parts.

Caxton's style in his Prologues, Epilogues, and other original writings was very serviceable from the beginning of his literary career, and later became capable of considerable eloquence. The Prologues and the Epilogues to *The Recuyell* reach a much higher level than the translation itself. In his original writings he was less hampered by the overconscientious attention to friendly criticism which always made him a 'Mr. Facing Both Ways' as a translator. Like Wordsworth and other distinguished theorists, he wrote more naturally and more successfully when he involuntarily put on one side his theories about 'ornate' and 'rude' terms, and wrote as the spirit moved him. These writings are invaluable for an understanding of Caxton's character, for we have no letters or other personal documents of his, and legal records are a poor substitute when we wish to revive a figure from the past. Some of his phrases are purely conventional; such are the humble addresses to royal and noble patrons, the excuse that work is undertaken 'in eschewyng of ydlenes, moder of all vices', and the frequent apologies for his inefficiency, though in his earlier works this customary expression of the author's modesty expresses a genuine feeling. Behind these conventions, however, and sometimes transforming them, there is the artless revelation of a generous and enthusiastic soul. In the **'Prologue to *Eneydos'*,** the hackneyed excuse about avoiding idleness is expressed with a freshness and truth that give it new life.

After dyuerse werkes made, translated, and achieued, hauyng noo werke in hande, I sittyng in my studye, whereas laye many dyuerse paunflettis and bookys, happened that to my hande cam a lytyl booke in frenshe, . . . whiche booke I sawe ouer and redde therin.

Here is the nucleus of the personal essay; it suggests Montaigne, or Lamb, pleasantly chatting 'On Books and Reading'. In his allusions to English poets, too, there is a note of keen and genuine appreciation which raises them far above the conventional eulogy. In speaking of Lydgate and Skelton, he confines himself to the language of compliment, and does not embark upon detailed appreciation. In several places, however, he states the grounds for his admiration of Chaucer, and these are found to be his enlargement of the vocabulary and power of expression of English poetry, and his gift of concise and rapid narrative.

I desire and require you that of your charite ye wold praye for the soule of the sayd worshipful man Geffrey Chaucer, first translatour of this sayde boke into Englissh, and enbelissher in making the sayd langage ornate and fayr, whiche shal endure perpetuelly, and therfore he ought eternelly to be remembrid. (**'Epilogue to** *The Consolation of Philosophy'*.)

And so in all hys werkys he excellyth in myn oppynyon alle other wryters in our Englyssh. For he wrytteth no voyde wordes, but alle hys mater is ful of hye and quycke sentence, to whom ought to be gyuen laude and preysyng for hys noble makyng and wrytyng. For of hym alle other haue borowed syth and taken, in alle theyr wel sayeng and wrytyng. (**'Epilogue to** *The Book of Fame'*.)

Caxton's praise of Chaucer in the 'Prohemye' to the Second Edition of *The Canterbury Tales* seems to provide a somewhat ironical commentary on the printer's own style.

He comprehended hys maters in short, quyck and hye sentences, eschewyng prolyxyte, castyng away the chaf of superfluyte, and shewyng the pyked grayn of sentence, vtteryd by crafty and sugred eloquence.

It is easy to show, however, that Caxton was capable of writing a concise style. There is a notable economy of words in the anecdote of the good parson and the worldly dean, added by Caxton to his translation of Aesop. The exchange of question and answer is admirably written, and the significant details are briefly but surely stated in such a way as to make both the characters remarkably life-like. The rich dean 'of a grete prynces chappel' came riding into a good parish, 'with a x or xij horses, lyke a prelate', and found in the church 'a good symple man, somtyme his felowe' at college. The dean, supposing that his humble old friend was not beneficed, greeted him casually and 'toke hym sleyghtly by the hand'. On finding, however, that he was the incumbent of a good living, 'that other aualed his bonet', and asked him with more respect what was the value of the benefice.

"Forsothe," sayd the good symple man, "I wote neuer, for I make neuer accomptes therof, how wel I haue had hit four or fyue yere." "And knowe ye not", said he, "what it is worth? It shold seme a good benefyce." "No, forsothe", sayd he, "but I wote well what it shalle be worth to me." "Why," sayd he, "what shalle hit be worth?" "Forsothe," sayd he, "yf I doo my trewe dylygence in the cure of my parysshens in prechyng and techynge, and doo my parte longynge to my cure, I shalle haue heuen therfore; and yf theyre sowles ben lost, or ony of them, by my defawte, I shall be punysshed therfore. And herof am I sure." And with that word the ryche dene was abasshed, and thought he shold be the better, and take more hede to his cures and benefyces than he had done. This was a good answere of a good preest and an honest.

I know of no other passage that shows so clearly the kinship between Caxton and Chaucer; the quiet satirical humour, the concise narrative style, the vivid characterization in the space of a few lines, the sentiment of admiration for simple goodness, all these show how truly Caxton entered into the spirit of his greatly loved master.

Probably Caxton's most celebrated piece of prose is his ex-

hortation to the knights of England in the **'Epilogue to** *The Order of Chivalry'*. It is interesting to notice that it belongs to the same period as 'Aesop' (*c.* 1484), for it shows the same economy of words, combined here with a deep indignation that finds expression in rhetorical figures, such as Caxton usually avoids.

O ye knyghtes of Englond, where is custome and vsage of noble chyualry that was vsed in tho dayes? What do ye now, but go to the baynes and playe atte dyse? And some, not wel aduysed, vse not honest and good rule, ageyn alle ordre of knyghthode. Leue this, leue it, and rede the noble volumes of saynt graal, of Lancelot, of Galaad, of Trystram, of Perseforest, of Perceual, of Gawayn, and many mo . . . . There shalle ye see manhode, curtosye, and gentylnesse . . . . Allas! what do ye but slepe and take ease, and ar al disordered fro chyualry. I wold demaunde a question yf I shold not displease. How many knyghtes ben ther now in Englond that haue thuse and thexcercyse of a knyghte? That is to wete, that he knoweth his hors, and his hors hym? I suppose, and a due serche sholde be made, ther shold be many founden that lacke, the more pyte is.

The variety of subject and of treatment in Caxton's original writings is remarkable. His continuation of *Polychronicon* is written in a straightforward but not very distinguished narrative style, but in the introductory essay on history we come upon sentences worthy of Bacon in their sonority.

Other monymentes, distributed in dyuerse chaunges, enduren but for a short tyme or season. But the vertu of hystorye, dyffused and spredd by the vnyuersal worlde, hath Tyme, whiche consumeth all other thynges, as conseruatryce and kepar of her werke.

In the **'Epilogue to** *Eneydos'* he takes the reader into his confidence with regard to his difficulties as a translator; he prefixes to *Morte Darthur* a discussion on the authenticity of Arthur; in the **'Epilogue to** *The Dictes or Sayengs'* he humorously conjectures the reasons for Earl Rivers's omission of Socrates' sayings about women. He was, indeed, an unconscious pioneer in the essay form, and as such he is beginning to gain popular recognition. (pp. 10-23)

It was fortunate for England that her first printer was not a mercenary trader, but a man of vision and high ideals. He had a typically English respect for rank, but he reserved his truest devotion for the aristocracy of the mind, the poets and thinkers whose works he multiplied in the hands of his readers. In his original writings he shows the quiet strength, the modesty, the insistence on the highest standard of excellence, that characterize a great man. As the variety, sincerity, and intrinsic merit of his writings are more fully appreciated, there will come, I believe, a wider recognition of his rightful place in the illustrious company of English Men of Letters. (pp. 24-5)

A. T. P. Byles, "William Caxton as a Man of Letters," in The Library, *Vol. XV. No. 1, June, 1934, pp. 1-25.*

H. S. Bennett (essay date 1947)

[*Bennett was an English educator, author, and critic known for his publications on fifteenth-century English literature. In the following excerpt, he discusses Caxton's audience and analyzes his prose style.*]

As our first printer Caxton is worthy of our undying regard. The sneers of Gibbon and Disraeli, and any modern attempts to write down his services to English literature, must be regarded as ignorant and unworthy. Except that he omitted to print *Piers Plowman,* Caxton showed a real understanding of what was best in the available literature of his time. The printer of the first editions of the *Canterbury Tales, Troilus and Criseyde, Confessio Amantis, Morte Darthur,* to say nothing of various smaller works of Chaucer and Lydgate, deserves our warmest praise. But Caxton's services to literature were not confined to one class of writing. He showed an admirable catholicity of taste, while retaining a preference for certain kinds of books. The works of the great writers of antiquity he did not attempt to print in their original languages. That was being done by countless continental presses, and Caxton preferred to translate afresh, or use the translations of others. Prose romance was represented by *Godfrey of Boulogne, Charles the Great, Paris and Vienne, Blanchardyn and Eglantine, The Four Sons of Aymon,* and *Morte Darthur.* The *Recuyell of the Histories of Troy, The History of Jason,* and *Eneydos* contained much classical myth and story, while the favourite beast fable was represented by *Reynard the Fox* and *The Fables of Aesop.* Other instructive works of a more austere nature were to be found in the translations of Boethius and Cicero. Morality and piety were the informing qualities of another large group of which the work wrongly attributed to St. Bonaventura and translated into English by Nicholas Love as *The Mirror of the blessed life of Jesu Christ,* the *Dicts or Sayings of the Philosophers,* and the *Golden Legend* are outstanding examples. *The Book of Good Manners, The Moral Proverbs* of Christine de Pisan, *The Curial* of Alain Chartier, *The Book of the Knight of the Tower* were among works published by Caxton which have a didactic purpose, and so, in a different fashion, has *The Governal of Health.* Books of a more informative nature were not neglected: Trevisa's translation of Higden's *Polychronicon,* as well as a *Description of Britain, The Chronicles of England,* and an encyclopaedic work, *The Mirror of the World;* books on chivalry and war, *The Order of Chivalry* and *The Book of the Feats of Arms and Chivalry;* and books of elementary grammar and vocabularies. In addition to works in these categories Caxton also published service books, indulgences, statutes of the Realm, and other minor pieces.

This was an impressive body of work for a pioneer printer to have accomplished between 1475 and 1491. We may well discount any denigration of Caxton's services to literature so far as quantity, range, and quality of his output is concerned. Nor is it fair to say that he 'purveyed to his aristocratic English public a selection of the books, French or English, from a former generation, when time and public preference had winnowed them from the mass'. He certainly had an aristocratic public, but equally certainly he had (and knew he had) a more general public. The size,

variety, and literacy of this public is only slowly becoming clear, but sufficient is known about it for us to be able to say that Caxton was doubly lucky in the moment of his commencing to print. He found a considerable reading public available, and he found that the public had been accustomed for half a century at least to reading matter of every possible kind. Caxton had only to reap what others had sown.

This is not to deny that he followed custom centuries old by which authors sought for recognition and recompense by dedicating their work to some rich patron. Caxton had many such: Edward IV, Richard III, Henry VII, Margaret of Burgundy, Mary Beaufort, and Elizabeth of York, are all mentioned by him, as are the Earls of Warwick, Rivers, Oxford, and Arundel. To these he was indebted for encouragement when the burden of translation or publishing seemed overwhelming. Thus the Earl of Arundel promised to take 'a good quantity' of copies of the *Golden Legend* at a time when Caxton found himself 'halfe desparate to have accomplished it', and it was Margaret of Burgundy's 'dredefull commandment' which set him to work again on the *Recuyell.* But in addition to these aristocratic patrons, Caxton looked to a wider public, and was quick to respond to their needs. William Pratt, mercer, and 'my synguler frende and of olde knowlege', brought him a French *Book of Good Manners* and begged him to translate and publish it. Similar requests were made by other London friends and merchants: William Daubeny, a royal treasurer, asked Caxton to translate the romance of *Charles the Great,* while the popular encyclopaedia *The Mirror of the World* was the outcome of 'the request, desire, coste and dispense of the honourable and worshipful man Hugh Bryce, Alderman & Cytezeyn of London' who wanted to make a present to the Lord President Hastings.

In response to commands and requests such as these Caxton could reasonably expect a good sale for his works. One of the secrets of his success was the skill with which he judged the nature of his potential patrons. He knew that some of his books would have only a limited appeal, while others were of a general interest. This is clear from many of his invaluable prologues. In them he indicates the nature of the book and the kind of audience to whom it should appeal. *Tully of Old Age* or *Eneydos,* for instance, are not for every 'rude and vnconnynge man to see, but to clerkys and very gentylmen that vnderstande gentilnes and scyence'. Others are for 'ladies and gentilwymen', others for 'every gentilman born to arms, and all manere of men of werre, captains, souldiours, vytallers'. Some of his books, however, he hoped would have a wider public: 'All men' or 'every man livyng' are invited to read such works as the *Recuyell* or *Boethius;* and the *Golden Legend* he hopes will profit all those who read, or hear it read. Again, he says that he has 'translated and reduced out of ffrensshe in to englysshe *Godfroy of Bologne* to thende that euery cristen man may be the better encoraged tenterprise warre for the defense of Cristendom'.

The truth seems to be that Caxton satisfied a special and a general demand. He undoubtedly gratified his own tastes, and at the same time satisfied those of a growing public whose eagerness for literature had been steadily increasing through the earlier years of the century. For long they had been forced to accept what chance brought their way. Only the most energetic and well-to-do could hope to collect what they wanted. Even so ardent a collector as Sir John Paston was sometimes defeated as his unsuccessful attempts to get the books of Sir James Gloys, the family chaplain, witness. The Pastons were rich enough to employ a copyist, W. Ebesham, to satisfy their needs, and we may note that among other works which remained in quires as they were written were Cicero's *De Senectute* and *De Amicitia*. If they had waited a few years they could have purchased in Caxton's edition the Earl of Worcester's translation of these two works. We know that within ten years of Caxton's starting to print in England they had a copy of the *Game and Play of the Chess,* and there can be no doubt that many others were ready to respond to the advertisement which Caxton issued telling anyone who wanted his wares to 'come to Westmonester in to the almonesry at the reed pale and he shall have them good chepe'.

From the time that he first began to translate the *Recuyell* Caxton was constantly at work turning into English books in French, Dutch, or Latin. Within some twenty-three years no less than twenty-four books had to be translated by him before they could be printed. This involved a very considerable intellectual and physical effort, and the results of this part of his work fill some 5,600 pages of print. Caxton is very modest about his abilities, both as a translator and as a writer of English. With regard to the first, we need not take his protestations too seriously. His school and commercial education had given him a sound working knowledge of the languages which he used, and while he was not a finished scholar, the imperfection in his translations may often be ascribed to haste rather than to ignorance. His knowledge of French, in practice, was good: in the *Mirror* we are told that there are only ten mistakes in translation, and editors of other works of his make similar statements. He worked quickly—the *Mirror,* a work of 200 folio printed pages, was translated in ten weeks, and *Godfrey of Boulogne,* which ran to 288 folio pages, took twelve weeks—often turning his French into English with little attempt at making a good English sentence of it, and at times transferring French words bodily where no English equivalent was to hand. As might be expected, he improved as he went on. His sentences in the *Recuyell* are those of an amateur, and we must not judge him on his earliest efforts. Yet it must be admitted that he rendered his original in too piecemeal a fashion, with the result that his sentences are often very unEnglish in their flow, and complicated in structure. Thus he allows himself to write sentences such as 'a moche meruyllous dragon and ferdful', or 'the whyche thynges for example to be conformed to theym yf they seme good ben for to be herde propyce and expedyent'.

Any discussion, however, of his merits as a translator must involve the wider consideration of his merits as a writer of English. In forming a judgement we have, in addition to his translations, the invaluable prologues and epilogues which he attached to some of his works, and these give many precious indications of his hopes and fears as a writer. 'Rude and simple' is his favourite way of describing his powers of writing English, and almost every piece of original work by him harps upon his ignorance, inexperience, and lack of skill. To some extent these protestations were common form, but Caxton was genuinely concerned about his limitations as a writer. To begin with he lacked any training in the use of 'the art of rhetoric or of gay terms'. Eloquence he regarded as 'soo precious and noble that amooste noo thyng can be founden more precious than it'. In common with most people of his time, he sincerely believed in the 'polysshed and ornate termes' for which he praised Skelton, and made attempts to follow what he thought to be the most elegant current English. But innumerable difficulties beset him, for he could get no one to advise him where the best English was to be found. Almost at the end of his life we find him still uncertain. In the **'Preface to *Eneydos'*** (1490) he tells us how he wrote a few pages, but when he came to look it over he saw that it was full of 'fair and strange terms'—the very thing that recently he had been told to avoid, since such terms, it was said, perplexed the common reader. On the other hand, the old and homely terms he was asked to use instead were difficult to employ, and when he sought the advice of the Abbot of Westminster, and was shown a book written in Old English, he found it 'more like Dutch [i.e. German] than English'. He comes to the heart of the matter when he says that 'comyn Englysshe that is spoken in one shyre varyeth from a nother', and he illustrates this by his story of the merchant who asked for *egges* and not for *eyren,* and was thought to speak in French. He finally decides to use 'Englysshe not ouer rude, ne curyous, but in suche termes as shall be vnderstanden by Goddys grace'. The whole of his writings prior to this, however, show them generally erring on the side of 'fair and strange terms'. Here he followed a tradition nearly a century old which held it necessary to augment the language in a variety of ways . . . . The practice of using pairs of synonymous words was especially cultivated by Caxton. This was no new practice, and may even be seen in Old English prose, but in Caxton it has become a stylistic trick. No doubt it enabled him to use both an English and a French word, 'so that if he missed his reader's understanding with one barrel he might hit with another', but for modern readers this is merely tiresome. Another common feature of Caxton's style is his tendency to make use of a French word such as *occision* without bothering to translate it. (When he was called on to use the word again in another book he realized the weakness of this practice and wrote 'slaughter or occision'.) Similarly we get 'spider or spyncop'; 'worldy or terryen'; 'sourded or rose up', but frequently we are left with the French word only—'consomme' (complete), 'corrempe' (break), 'escimuz' (prickly), 'excusacion' (excuse), or 'musarde' (vagabond).

In addition to this uncertainty about diction, Caxton was even more uncertain about his writing of prose. The major part of his life had been spent out of England, and the Duchess of Burgundy, no doubt, had good reason to find 'defaut in myn englysshe'. Much reading of French literature had accustomed Caxton's ear to the long, involved sentences, but had failed to instruct him in their grammatical and logical construction. Caxton, therefore, attempted throughout his literary work to use the long sentence, without success. His average sentence length is between two and three times that of modern prose, and is full of faults. The excessive length is made the more unpleasing by the number and variety of subordinate clauses and phrases employed. Relative and substantival clauses are the most frequently used—running to great lengths, as may be seen in one sentence of 136 words in the **'Prologue to the *Golden Legend'*** where 'and' and 'that' are each used *six* times. This lack of variety is constant in Caxton's prose; connectives such as 'which', 'wherefore', 'and', 'but', 'while', and 'that' are continuously overworked and give a monotonous and clockwork effect. Other constantly recurring stylistic features are the free use of anacoluthon, of the pleonastic pronoun, of the omission of the subject or verb, and the careless use of connecting words.

Writers upon Caxton's prose have taken these and other characteristics into account, and have given widely differing verdicts as to its merits. Most, it is true, have based thier views on one particular volume of his works, and have looked no farther. Thus Oscar Sommer finds little that is pleasing from his study of the *Recuyell,* while Kellner ranks Caxton as a great writer of prose on the evidence of *Blanchardyn and Eglantine.* Craik says that he has a style of 'admirable clearness', but Krapp declares that 'he has only one device for elevating his style, and that is in the multiplication of words . . . . For form and structure his feeling is rudimentary.' We must allow that Caxton lacked any sensitive feeling for prose, and only stumbled on a good sentence by accident. The reader of Caxton is fortunate if he does not find himself in difficulties on every page, difficulties which arise from an inability to see how the sentence is planned. It is not that his prose has an archaic flavour which is unpleasing, but rather that it is often involved and confused in sentence structure. Malory can use archaisms, but his cadence and movement carry us successfully through his sentences. The great seventeenth-century users of the long sentence had a fundamental logical control of their periods: however majestic and laden with image and reference, all was at the service of the main idea.

Caxton humbly followed his original for the most part: if it was a good French prose that he was translating something of its merits came out in his versions, and vice versa. When he departed from his original it was seldom for the better. His own prologues and epilogues show how limited were his powers as a writer of prose, although those written in his later years show an increasing mastery of the art of prose composition. Their value is for the insight they give us into the problems which beset Caxton as a translator and printer, [and] for their many personal touches. (pp. 205-12)

H. S. Bennett, "Fifteenth-Century Prose," in his Chaucer and the Fifteenth Century *1947. Reprint by Oxford at the Clarendon Press, 1958, pp. 177-218.*

Donald B. Sands   (essay date 1957)

[*Sands, an American educator and critic, was the editor of Harvard's publication of Caxton's* Reynard the Fox *and author of several essays exploring the development of English literature through the Medieval and Renaissance periods. In the essay below, he argues that Caxton's selection of works for publication displayed not only good business sense but also sound critical ability.*]

This paper endeavors to show that William Caxton when faced with a situation that allowed him to make a choice among a number of literary works displayed sound critical ability. It does not ignore the possibility that Caxton's business sense prompted the publication of numerous works. It assumes that a hard business head and critical ability are not incompatible. Some evaluations of Caxton would have us believe that they are.

English printed books in Caxton's lifetime can be divided into two groups—those printed by command or at least under the protection of a patron, and those, as works of a factual, devotional, or edifying nature, printed to fulfill a particular need. A number of Caxton's publications do not fall into either of these two groups. Examination of them reveals that they were probably financial risks and also that they were, for the most part, of an enduring or unusually effective literary nature, one that another printer-publisher without Caxton's qualifications would probably have overlooked. Realization of this distinction reveals Caxton not only as a shrewd businessman but also as an eclectic critic well in advance of his age.

First, an *ad hoc* definition. Here we shall assume that a critic is one who chooses the valuable and permanent from a number of literary works, good, bad, and indifferent, and that a man is no critic at all if he does not possess the opportunity to choose. In other words, if a patron or if an obvious public need determines what a man chooses, then he does not exercise his critical judgment. He may remain an excellent editor or publisher, but he is not a critic. Now let us see how a checklist of Caxton's works conforms to this scheme.

Here the seventy-seven individual works published by Caxton are broken down into ten categories. The number seventy-seven may appear low, but omitted are works printed in French, works belonging to a second issue or second edition, doubtful works, works printed in Caxton's type but published after his death, and works apparently produced for Caxton by another printer. The categories were suggested by H. B. Lathrop [see Further Reading]; the titles within categories are those in E. Gordon Duff's *Fifteenth Century English Books.*

First I count ten titles that would satisfy the needs of clergymen. Such sacerdotal pieces as *Quatuor Sermones, The Doctrinal of Sapience,* and John Mirk's *Liber Festivalis* are of a practical nature, for a ready market awaited them and hence little financial risk was involved in their production. It is significant that no patron seems to have backed any of these titles. None was done by aristocratic command.

Next I find two language texts: one is Donatus, which in Caxton's day had no serious rival; the other is *The Vocabulary in French and English.* Neither text had a patron;

neither perhaps involved financial risk since one met the need for instruction in Latin and the other for instruction in the great commercial vernacular of the day.

A third category contains works for private devotional ends—death-bed prayers, ruminations on the four final things, lives of saints, and similar pieces possessing a strong subjective appeal to a devout reading public. I number twelve works here of which, to be sure, four were produced under patronage. Here again Caxton could have been certain of his public, just as sure perhaps as a modern publisher would be when producing good Western or detective novels. The four works produced under patronage can be explained away—or nearly so. *The Fifteen Oes* was printed at the command of Lady Margaret and Queen Elizabeth; it is Caxton's attempt at a *Prachtausgabe,* a rather poor one since its ornamental borders and woodcuts are clumsy and primitive. *The Golden Legend,* finished only when the Earl of Arundel promised Caxton a buck in summer and a doe in winter and further implied he would take a certain number of copies when it was printed, is a tremendously ambitious work containing 449 leaves. Clearly the expense both in time and physical labor involved in the production of this work is so much greater than that needed for other devotional works that some sort of financial support would seem inevitable. The third devotional work that appeared under patronage, *The Book of Divers Ghostly Matters,* was done at the desire of "certain worshipful persons." It contains three separate tracts and was apparently printed on order. No second edition of it appeared. The fourth work, the English version of the *Cordyale,* seems to have been foisted on Caxton by Earl Rivers, who had recently undergone "great tribulation and adversity" and hence wished religious doctrine to "go abroad among the people." Devotional works, in other words, if small and plain, probably sold well; if they were large, elaborate, or somewhat anomalous, then patronage was needed.

A fourth and also financially safe category is made up of nine official publications such as indulgences and statutes. Such subliterary work is the mainstay of small printing houses; it is surprising that Caxton did so little of it.

Moral and didactic works without sacerdotal or devotional emphasis make a fifth category, to which several works of a financially risky nature belong. I number thirteen pieces here and find that six were produced under patronage. For example, *The Knight of the Tower* was produced at "the request of a lady"; *The Dicts or Sayings* at the command of Earl Rivers, and *The Book of Good Manners* at the suggestion of a wealthy mercer of London by the name of William Pratt. Here, however, the works Caxton produced on his own are important. They are *The Game and Play of the Chess,* Chaucer's translation of *Boethius, Cato,* Cicero's *De Amicitia* and *De Senectute,* and Aesop's *Fables.* All but the first of these might easily be included in a reading list of a Great Books course in a modern college. All appeared without any indication of financial or aristocratic backing.

A sixth category made up of practical pieces on the art of war and on the principles of health numbers three works, two of which had backers. The one which Caxton produced on his own is the medical text *The Governal of Health.*

A seventh category, numbering six pieces, covers historical and political works, three of which were patronized. The three which Caxton produced independently have definite factual if not literary value. They are *The Description of Britain,* Ranulph Higden's *Polychronicon,* and *Godfrey of Boloyne.*

Both the sixth category, that containing practical pieces, and the seventh, containing historical and political pieces, were apparently safe, for several recent scholars have pointed out the diversity in secular fifteenth-century manuscripts, a diversity that indicates that the late medieval Englishman was far more interested in straight factual information of all kinds than had for long been supposed.

An eighth category numbering eight pieces contains the romances of the day, and it is significant that five of the eight romances were patronized; as was, for example, Malory's *Morte d'Arthur,* desired, it seems, by "many noble and divers gentlemen." Modern novels are risky things, and such works as *The Four Sons of Aymon* and *Blanchardyn and Eglantine* were probably risks in Caxton's day. Of the three works Caxton produced on his own, two—*The History of Jason* and *The Eneydos*—have classic prototypes; they can be counted as preferences altogether in his favor.

The ninth category, containing the works of the finest English poets up to Caxton's day, numbers thirteen pieces, five by Chaucer, seven by Lydgate, and one by Gower. All of these Caxton produced on his own, and numerically they make up the largest category of the ten. There is no patronage here, and presumably their production involved financial risk simply because Caxton had no way of knowing just who would buy them, as he did with the sacerdotal and official publications; or how popular they might be, since he was the person who was printing them for the first time. Here, it seems to me, Caxton's literary sense must have been his guide. He did not, to say the obvious thing, *have* to publish these pieces.

The tenth and last category contains one work, Caxton's translation of *Die Historie van Reynaert die Vos.* It is, if you wish, a satiric piece. It is significant in that there had been up to 1481 nothing at all like it in English literature. It is, of course, the habit of literary historians to point to the Aesopic fable, the beast *fabliau* of "The Fox and the Wolf," and Chaucer's "Nun's Priest's Tale." The truth is, however, that Caxton's *Reynard* is altogether different from any of these. It is a comic epic and not a fable. Its incidents derive more from the Germanic *Märchen* than from the Aesopic tradition. Here Caxton introduced something new into English literature, and did so without patronage or any assurance (other than the intrinsic appeal of the piece) that it would succeed. That it did so in his particular age is evidenced by the three editions that appeared before the close of the century.

The implications of this study—namely, that Caxton was first a good businessman and then, given the opportunity, a good critic—run contrary to three evaluations of Caxton that are accepted in the usual reference works. The dilettante approach would have us believe that Caxton, being a wealthy man, published merely to please a cultivated audience, and consequently took literature chiefly as a hobby. In the **"Prologue to *Charles the Great*,"** he tells us he made his living from printing; his printing of so many works of so many kinds indicates a serious desire to reach the book-buying public.

A second approach, one almost at the opposite pole, is that which postulates a predominantly religious and patriotic urge behind Caxton's activities. It imputes to Caxton as a man the religious nature of works which were produced in all likelihood to supply a ready market. It interprets the lip-service given to patrons as profoundly moving, and ignores the relatively commonplace nature of the literature produced by patronage. Finally, it fails to see anything significant in the value of the literature Caxton chose to print when he was not satisfying practical needs or producing for a patron.

Finally, there is the approach that treats Caxton as the product of his age. In the body of reputable Caxton criticism it is the most formidable because the most recent and the best documented. Henry Stanley Bennett poses the question [in "Caxton and His Public," *Review of English Studies* XIX, No. 74 (April 1943): 113-19], "Did Caxton form the taste of his age or did he reflect it?" Bennett accumulates much evidence to show that fifteenth-century England wanted to read pretty much what Caxton printed. It is an easy transition to conclude that Caxton merely rode the crest of the wave or, in Bennett's equally metaphorical words, "Caxton had only to reap where others had sown." In this light, Caxton is a middleman and presumably his rewards should be those of a middleman.

It seems to me that it is unfair to Caxton to assume that he could be a Dr. Johnson or a T. S. Eliot and then to condemn him for not being so. First of all, there is the evidence of Caxton's successors. Wynkyn de Worde and Richard Pynson, for example, produced reprints and when not, then works under patronage and works of little or no value. To return to the question of choice with which this paper began: Caxton had no choice at all when producing for the Queen, Earl Rivers, or William Pratt. Nor was his ability to choose put to test in his production of sacerdotal, devotional, or purely factual works because here he was supplying a need. The market was certain. But with the tales derived from classical antiquity, with Cato and Cicero, with *Reynard the Fox,* and with Chaucer, Gower, and Lydgate—all published on his own—the situation was different. How different, is shown by his successors who merely followed in their master's footsteps, simply because Caxton had already produced the very best literature available in his day. (pp. 312-18)

Donald B. Sands, "Caxton as a Literary Critic," in The Papers of the Bibliographical Society of America, *Vol. 51, 4th Quarter, 1957, pp. 312-18.*

N. F. Blake   (essay date 1968)

[*An English biographer and critic, Blake is among the foremost scholars of Caxton's life and career. He has written numerous books and essays on Caxton, including two biographies, and has edited a volume of Caxton's original writing entitled* Caxton's Own Prose *(1973). In the following essay, Blake discusses the influence of fifteenth-century cultural and literary trends on Caxton's original prose, his translations, and his selection of books for publication.*]

In this paper I should like to consider how Caxton reacted to contemporary trends in literary English and what information this yields us about the development of fifteenth-century English prose. Those who have commented on Caxton's attitude to the literary language have usually been content to review the opinions found in his **'Prologue to *Eneydos.*'** But *Eneydos* was one of the last books he printed, and the prologue represents the culmination of his views about English which had been developing over the previous twenty years. Consequently a juster appreciation of Caxton's attitude towards English may be obtained by examining his prologues and epilogues in the order in which they were written, for not only are his final views of interest, but also the influences which caused his opinions to change in the way they did are important for an understanding of the fifteenth century. So I shall commence by tracing briefly the development of his opinions.

We must naturally start with the *History of Troy,* the first English book to be printed. In his various prologues to this work, Caxton claimed that he took pleasure in the 'fayr langage of Frenshe' for the original was written 'in prose so well and compendiously sette and wreton, whiche me thought I vnderstood the sentence and substance of euery mater'. When he had completed some of his translation he showed it to Margaret of Burgundy who found fault with his English. What criticism she made is not revealed, though it is more than likely she thought the style not sufficiently ornate. As it was, Caxton claimed that he followed the original as closely as he could, but nevertheless the result was a 'rude werk' containing 'rude Englissh'. The impression one gets is that Caxton followed the French closely in order to share the merits of its style which was so 'compendious' and intelligible, but that unfortunately something was lost in the process of translation. No doubt some of this attitude is conventional for it was traditional to decry one's own merits by employing the humility formula. But both the praise of French style and the words used to express that praise are important. Caxton praises French prose, but mentions no English prose as being comparable. Yet the word 'compendious', which he uses to describe French prose style, was a favourite one with Lydgate, as a few examples will show:

> Undir a stile breeff & compendious (*Fall of Princes* I. 90)
> Compendiously this mateer for to declare (ibid. VIII. 2647)
> Withoute frute he was compendious (*Troy-Book* Prol. 351)
> Now must I ful besy ben a whyle . . .
> Myn auctor folwe & be compendious (ibid. V. 2315-19).

Conciseness was not in fact a virtue of the French original or Caxton's translation, or even indeed of Lydgate. But it was evidently considered a necessary virtue of style. The term was used by Lydgate to describe his own poetic style. It was adapted by Caxton to the French prose style of his original in order to show that it had the same stylistic features as English poetry. It was these features which he wished to give to his own prose by close translation. The quotations from Lydgate's *Troy-Book* are important for Caxton knew this work, to which he refers in his prologue. But he refers to it in tones of the greatest respect. His own translation, he writes, cannot in any way be compared with Lydgate's poem though it covers much of the same ground. Caxton completed his translation only because his own was in prose.

After his return to England Caxton printed the *Dicts of Philosophers* translated by Earl Rivers and his own translation of *Jason*. While the latter repeats that Caxton's translations have little in the way of elegant prose, in the prologue to the former Caxton wanted to pay Rivers a compliment on his translation. To us today there seems little difference stylistically between the two, though Caxton speaks of them in quite different ways. The one has no 'beaute or good endyting of our Englissh tonge', the other is 'right wel & connyngly made & translated into right good and fayr Englissh'. The important thing to notice is the paucity of Caxton's critical vocabulary. He has neglected to use 'compendious' and there is no reference to rhetoric. He has not yet learned how to praise a work. This he was to do by printing Chaucer's *Boethius,* for through this work he became aware of the critical opinions about Chaucer common in the fifteenth century. There is a significant enlargement of Caxton's critical vocabulary in the prologue to this book. Chaucer was the 'first translatour of this sayde boke into Englisshe & enbelissher in making the sayd langage ornate & fayr'. The 'langage' appears to mean English in general rather than the prose of the translation, for Chaucer is also called 'the worshipful fader & first foundeur & enbelissher of ornate eloquence in our Englissh'. It has been shown that Caxton took these phrases from other works about Chaucer which were known to him. Caxton is absorbing the fashion current at the time, in which the two words 'ornate' and 'embellisher' appear constantly. Nevertheless we should not forget that Chaucer is also praised for following the Latin 'as neygh as is possible to be vnderstande'. The same point is made in *Of Old Age*. The Latin text, in which matters are 'specyfyced compendiously', is difficult, but 'this book, reduced in Englyssh tongue, is more ample expowned and more swetter to the reder, kepyng the iuste sentence of the Latyn'.

Trevisa's translation of Higden's *Polychronicon* was treated differently. Although made within ten years of Chaucer's *Boethius,* this translation was considered by Caxton to be outdated, though good. Consequently he has 'chaunged the rude and old Englyssh, that is to wete certayn wordes which in these dayes be neither vsyd ne vnderstanden'. Trevisa evidently did not have quite the same stylistic reputation as Chaucer and therefore his language wanted modernization. As a close translation of Higden it was estimable, but it wanted some embellishment.

With his second edition of *Canterbury Tales* Caxton repeats many of the critical comments he had made about Chaucer in his prologue to *Boethius.* Chaucer embellished English and made it ornate. But Caxton now also mentions what had been characteristic of English prior to Chaucer. Then the English language was 'rude' and 'incongrue, as yet it appiereth by olde bookes'. Whether these old books were in poetry or prose is not revealed. But there is a clear indication that Chaucer polished English by making it rhetorical and ornate as one can see by comparing his writings with older books. Caxton goes on to praise Chaucer for his conciseness and his 'sugred eloquence', the sentiments and the words being alike borrowed from Lydgate. Caxton has become more deeply involved in the current critical fashions about Chaucer and court poetry.

At this stage his involvement begins to affect his descriptions of his own prose. He has become aware of what is expected in a good style. In *Charles the Great* he uses the critical vocabulary of rhetoric to comment on his own translation for the first time. He is still, as usual, apologetic for his style which he calls 'rude & symple reducyng'. But he goes a step further by commenting on the lack of rhetoric: 'though so be there be no gaye termes ne subtyl ne newe eloquence, yet I hope that it shal be vnderstonden'. His association with the court and his knowledge of Chaucerian criticism must have made him conscious of what was fashionable. Yet he still attaches importance to comprehension as well as to decoration, a point to which he returns: 'And yf in al thys book I haue mesprysed or spoken otherwyse than good langage substancyally ful of good vnderstondyng to al makers and clerkes, I demaunde correxyon and amendement'. It seems as though a good style and comprehensibility go hand in hand. From now on an apology for the absence of the gay terms of rhetoric 'as now be sayd in these dayes and vsed' is a constant feature of his prologues. It is found particularly in *Feats of Arms* and *Blanchardyn and Eglantine.* Quotation from these hardly seems necessary. Yet he still goes on insisting that he has followed his French source closely and uttering the hope that his works are comprehensible.

The discussion of rhetoric in the **'Prologue to *Eneydos'*** is the natural culmination of the other prologues. In some ways Caxton has not changed. He still translates because of the style of his French original: 'in whiche booke I had grete playsyr by cause of the fayr and honest termes & wordes in Frenshe, whyche I neuer sawe to fore lyke ne none so playsaunt ne so wel ordred'. The difference is now that he has a greater stock of words with which to express his pleasure. He admits, however, that there are some gentlemen who have taken objection to his translations because he used 'ouer curyous termes whiche coude not be vnderstande of comyn people' and they wanted him to use 'olde and homely termes'. This fact is interesting in showing that Caxton's opinions were influenced by the fashion of the court and also that there was an anti-rhetorical faction at court. Caxton goes on to say that he read an old book which he found difficult to understand because of its 'rude and brood' English. Similarly at the request of the Abbot of Westminster he looked at some old documents whose language was more like 'Dutch' (i.e. Low German)

A page from The Recuyell of the Historyes of Troye.

than English so that he was unable to understand it. This leads Caxton on to the everchanging nature of the English language, an opinion which he may well have picked up from the poets of the courtly tradition. The implication of his argument is that those who wish for the old and homely terms are foolish, for English has progressed beyond that state whether they like it or not. He prefers modern terminology since his books are designed for a cultivated and educated audience. However, he will try to maintain a middle position between the extremes of old and homely terms and over-refinement. But significantly he refers those who fail to understand his language to Virgil and the *Epistles* of Ovid, from which one can assume that he was on the side of the educated, Latinate clientele and that he thought his rhetorical embellishments were based on Latin. Finally, Caxton praises the work of John Skelton extravagantly. Since Skelton was one of the most prominent aureate writers of the time, it confirms that Caxton was in favour of rhetoric and embellishment and it suggests that he wanted his own work to be judged by such standards.

Now that this survey of Caxton's views is complete, it is time to evaluate the points arising from it. The most important is the evidence that at the start of his publishing career he had little critical vocabulary, but that he enlarged this vocabulary over the years. The two major in-

fluences contributing to this increase were the critical opinions surrounding the works of Chaucer and the opinions of his fashionable clientele from the court. The greatest impetus within the former influence came undoubtedly from the works of Lydgate, since Lydgate followed what he thought was the Chaucerian poetic tradition and wrote many lines in his praise. Indeed there is much to suggest that Caxton looked at Chaucer through the works of Lydgate. But the Chaucerian criticism was directed more to the poetic language than to English in general. Caxton was forced to follow the poetic model even though he was writing in prose, because the new poetic style had such prestige and because there was no English prose in the courtly style which he could emulate. To some extent the absence of such a prose style was beginning to be rectified at the end of Caxton's life by the works of Skelton, and clearly a court which contained such an aureate writer as Skelton as tutor to the Prince of Wales could hardly avoid being concerned with rhetorical fashion. This in its turn would influence Caxton. But in general the absence of a native prose style was overcome by translating from Latin or French and by following the original style closely. This is why Caxton constantly refers us to the French and Latin originals. Their style has those features which English prose lacks, but which could be found in English poetry. At the same time there was in existence in English an older prose style, which was not considered a satisfactory model, just as there had been an older poetic style which had been outmoded by the Chaucerian revolution. That style could be seen in old books. Exactly what this style consisted of is not clear, since Caxton never discusses the matter in detail, though the general history of late medieval English literature leads me to accept that it was the alliterative style. For Caxton the disadvantages of this old style were its vocabulary and lack of rhetorical refinement. Old books used an obsolete vocabulary, they used words no longer fashionable. Presumably they were words of Anglo-Saxon or Norse origin instead of being modern words coined from French or Latin. Similarly the old books followed the native stylistic traditions instead of following the rhetoric found in French or Latin models.

So far I have been considering Caxton's developing attitude to style and rhetoric, and the influences which caused that attitude to change. Now it is necessary to consider to what extent Caxton's own style was influenced by the fashionable acceptance of rhetoric. Wendelstein, [in *Beitrag zur Vorgeschichte des Euphuismus,* 1902], for example, has pointed to some minor rhetorical flourishes in Caxton's *Charles the Great.* Thus he notes the repetition of the suffix *-ly* at the end of clauses: 'and dyd do paynte the hystoryes after somme poyntes of our crysten fayth moche ryche*ly* and repayred the places ryght delycyous*ly.* And on that other he dyd do ordeyne & founde chirches autentyk*ly,* & compose baptyzatoryes & frentes conuenab*ly*'. He also singles out the pointing of clauses by the use of rhyming words: 'Whan thys was de*maunded,* it was com*maunded*'. But Wendelstein omitted to mention that these rhetorical tricks are taken over directly from the French *Fierabras,* which Caxton was translating: (i) 'puys a paindre histoires selon aulcuns poins de nostre foy cristienne moult riche*ment* et les places reparer tres delicieuse*ment,* et d'aultre part il fist ordonner et fonder es-glises auctentique*ment* et composer baptitoires conuen-able*ment*'; 'Cecy estre de*mandé,* il fut com*mandé*'. Here we should recall that one of Caxton's major theses was that English prose style was at its best when it kept as close as possible to a French or Latin original. He insisted on this because it was intended that some of the fine French or Latin style would show through in the English transla-tion. It should not, therefore, be a matter for surprise that this did in fact happen from time to time. It does not of course follow that Caxton was aware of all the places where this had taken place. And it is certainly true that his own original compositions cannot be shown to have been influenced by foreign models. No rhetorical flourish-es have been pointed out in his own compositions, which are more notable for their clumsy style than for their bal-anced or rhythmical sentences. His style becomes very loose when he has no guide. His appreciation of rhetoric is superficial: he was unable to practise what he preached. The one exception could be his use of doublets, which was a type of embellishment. This feature had been used by Chaucer, and is largely confined in Caxton to passages which demand a more elevated style. They allow Caxton to use French loanwords and thus to give his work a more fashionable appearance. The French content of Caxton's vocabulary depends likewise on whether the passage is translated or original. Original passages contain far fewer loanwords than translated ones, though they do not have words from the alliterative style. His own prose uses a lim-ited vocabulary, though he does use words which were no doubt fashionable such as 'noble'. Neither his style nor his vocabulary was particularly affected by French when he made an original composition. Furthermore we should re-alize that his policy of translating closely from Latin or French was one which he probably adopted because it was the fashion of the time to do so. He did it, he says, to trans-fer the elegances of French and Latin style to English. Yet he also translated closely when he translated from Flem-ish, as in *Reynard the Fox,* which meant he imported many Flemish loanwords. Yet since in his **'Prologue to Eneydos'** he stated that the older English, which he was trying to avoid, and Low German had much in common, one might have supposed that he would have avoided imi-tating Flemish style and introducing Flemish loanwords. He did not; and once again we see that Caxton did not carry out in his own work what he claimed as desirable. This inability to carry out his own stated preferences is im-portant in confirming that his opinions reflect contempo-rary ideas rather than his own observations and practice. This is why his evidence is so valuable.

Even though Caxton may not have been able to provide much in the way of rhetorical embellishment in his indi-vidual compositions, one would expect contemporary prejudices to manifest themselves in his choice of texts for he would have to sell them to his fashionable clientele. Al-though my subject is prose rather than poetry, the evi-dence from the poetry is important and I shall deal briefly with that first. The major poets printed by Caxton are Chaucer, Gower and Lydgate, and these three represent the triumvirate of the courtly tradition. Their names were constantly linked by fifteenth-century and early sixteenth-century writers who commented on the new poetic fash-ion. All the other poetry printed by Caxton may be said to be part of this new tradition. Benedict Burgh was Lyd-gate's pupil and finished some of his work; the *Court of Sa-pience* was often attributed to Lydgate himself; and the poet of the *Book of Courtesy* looks back to Chaucer, Gower and Lydgate as the three great poets and thus re-veals his allegiance. All the poems use stanza or couplet, a markedly French vocabulary and many rhetorical expe-dients. On the other hand, Caxton has often been blamed for not printing *Piers Plowman.* Since so many manu-scripts of this poem circulated in the fifteenth century, and since some of them were connected with London, it seems likely that Caxton knew of its existence. We cannot be cer-tain about this, but we can imagine that if he did know of the poem he would not have printed it, for it must have represented to him the older poetic tradition from which Chaucer had broken away. It uses the old alliterative metre with old words arranged in the traditional English manner. In terms of poetry Caxton must have meant the alliterative poems when he referred to 'old books'.

It would be natural to assume that Caxton and his con-temporaries were affected by the current fashion towards poetry in their attitude to prose. As far as Caxton is con-cerned, this would mean that we would expect him to pub-lish work in the courtly stylistic tradition and to avoid the alliterative or native prose. This assumption may be tested firstly by considering what type of prose work Caxton chose to print and secondly by examining how he edited the books before printing them. The characteristic feature of the prose printed by Caxton is that it consists either of translation or of work based on foreign models. I must em-phasize that I am not here concerned with Caxton's own translations, but only with those works which already ex-isted in an English version before coming into Caxton's hands. Such works include Earl Rivers's two translations, *Dicts of Philosophers* and *Cordial;* Chaucer's translation of *Boethius;* Worcester's translations, *Declamation of No-blesse* and *Of Friendship;* the earlier English translation of *Of Old Age;* Trevisa's translation of Higden's *Polychroni-con,* with which we may include the *Description of Britain;* and Malory's *Morte Darthur.* This book we today tend to think of as a re-creation rather than a translation, but to Caxton it was 'take oute of certayn bookes of Frensshe and reduced' to English. The above list is in no way compre-hensive, for it excludes many of the more specifically reli-gious works, such as *Mirror of the Life of Christ* and *Pil-grimage of the Soul.* All these are translations as well, ex-cept for Mirk's *Festial* which is a re-telling of the *Legenda Aurea* rather than a straightforward translation. Of all the publications issuing from the press only one can properly be said not to be a translation, namely the *Chronicles of England.* And this work, which originated as a translation and for which there were foreign models, is closely associ-ated with London and the court. It has no trace of the al-literative style. What is noticeable, therefore, about Cax-ton's choice of books is that he did not print anything by an Englishman written in what we may call the native tra-dition. Such authors as Rolle, Hilton and the author of the *Cloud of Unknowing* are completely passed over, even though their works were popular and many manuscripts survived. Though sometimes modelled on foreign sources, the works of these authors can hardly be thought of as translations. And more importantly they belong stylistically to the native prose tradition. Furthermore, even such original English compositions as there were in the fifteenth century were not printed by Caxton. There can consequently be no doubt that Caxton favoured translated works and that this prejudice was shared by many members of the court. The most cultivated and respected men of the time, such as Rivers, Worcester, Skelton and later Berners—to name only a few—made translations rather than original compositions. It is significant that the only works by Skelton which Caxton referred to are all translations: 'For he hath late translated the Epystlys of Tulle, and the boke of Dyodorus Syculus, and diuerse other werkes oute of Latyn in to Englysshe'.

It is not difficult to understand how this prejudice came about. In the fifteenth century the distinction between poetry and prose was not so great as it is now. It was accepted that poetry had broken out of the old mould by using foreign models. Chaucer had modelled his poems on French or Italian ones, and Gower had made good use of Ovid. Lydgate had made many poetic 'translations', of which his *Troy-Book* is perhaps the outstanding example. Though we today tend to highlight Lydgate's statements that he was writing in the Chaucerian tradition, we should not forget that he also in the *Troy-Book* pays many fulsome tributes to Guido's style. It was natural that prose should follow the lead set by poetry; that it should emancipate itself from the native tradition by following foreign models. But there was one important difference. In poetry there had been Chaucer; in prose there was no English model of comparable stature. Therefore while Lydgate and other fifteenth-century poets could claim to be writing in the Chaucerian manner, although more often than not they were imitating foreign models, the prose writers could not claim to be following any English model. Hence they were thrown back on their sources which they tended to follow slavishly. It is of course easier to be more literal in prose, and we may notice that even poets such as Chaucer and Skelton made literal prose translations. But it is the great misfortune of late medieval English prose that neither Skelton nor Chaucer established himself as a model. This meant that there was no English model which could curb the worst excesses of translation and make the translator lift his eyes from his source.

We must now consider the other aspect of Caxton's publishing activity, namely to what extent he altered the texts he had decided to print. In many cases it is not possible to come to any decision since his version is the only one that survives. But from what he wrote in his prologues it would seem unlikely that he altered the translations by, say, Rivers or Worcester. Similarly he did not materially change Chaucer's *Boethius*. These translations were not touched because Caxton had too much respect for the translators. There are, however, two works which Caxton did alter considerably, Malory's *Morte Darthur* and Trevisa's translation of Higden. The reasons which led Caxton to adapt these works differ; but it is better first to discuss what the changes were before considering what caused them.

From even a glance at Vinaver's edition of Malory, it is evident that Caxton altered Book Five most. This is the book which is based upon the English alliterative poem, *Le Morte Arthure,* and Malory took over much of the vocabulary and alliteration. Let us consider a short passage from this book together with Caxton's adaptation:

> *Malory:* Than the kynge yode up to the creste of the cragge, and than he comforted hymself with the colde wynde; and than he yode forth by two welle-stremys, and there he fyndys two fyres flamand full hygh. And at that one fyre he founde a carefull wydow wryngande hir handys syttande on a grave that was new marked. Than Arthur salued hir and she hym agayne, and asked hir why she sate sorowyng. 'Alas,' she seyde, 'carefull knyght. Thou carpys over lowde! Yon is a werlow woll destroy us bothe.'

> *Caxton:* And soo he ascended up in to that hylle tyl he came to a grete fyre, and there he fonde a careful wydowe wryngynge her handes and makyng grete sorowe, syttynge by a grave new made. And thenne kynge Arthur salewed her and demaunded of her wherefore she made such lamentacion. To whom she ansuered and sayd: 'Syre knyghte, speke softe for yonder is a devyll; yf he here the speke, he wyll come and destroye the.'

In the Caxton passage we may note the avoidance of alliterative groups: *creste of the cragge, comforted . . . colde, fyres flamand, sate sorowyng, carefull knyght.* Some of the alliteration may have been eliminated incidentally through the attempt to modernize the vocabulary. It is interesting to see how often this modernization takes the form of introducing French words: *ascended (yode up), demaunded (asked), lamentacion (sorowyng);* though in other cases it merely involves using a less specific word for the forceful older word: *devyll (werlow), speke (carpys).* Caxton also uses vague adjectives such as 'great' as in '*grete* fyre' and '*grete* sorowe'. The tone of the conversations has become more elevated in Caxton, for not only does the lady address Arthur as 'Syre knyghte', but her speech is also more subdued from the brusque tone it has in Malory. In general Caxton's version is more courtly and less specific. Finally we may note the use of repetition in 'wryngynge her handes and makyng grete sorowe', in which the latter phrase has been added by Caxton. The use of the doublet may have been an attempt by Caxton to heighten the pathos by using a rhetorical figure. The changes I have pointed to show how Caxton adapted the text. It is significant that the passage should be from the fifth book. The remaining books, which are for the most part based on French sources, are generally only modified rather than rewritten.

Trevisa's translation was different from Malory's. It was an older English translation of a standard Latin work by a man who had achieved some eminence as a translator. Caxton, for example, also mentions his translations of the Bible and *De Proprietatibus Rerum.* Nevertheless, Caxton felt that Trevisa's language should be modernized. As with Malory, these changes often involved the introduction of French words: *embelysshers (hizteres), encrece (eche), doctryne (lore), obedient (buxom), disposed (icast),* though in many cases we find the replacement of one Germanic word by another: *calleth (clepeth), after (efte), dyches (meres), right (swipe).* Yet there is a difference in Caxton's attitude towards these two authors. Trevisa made use of alliteration in his translation, but more often than not the alliteration is confined within a doublet. Caxton has not altered these doublets as a general rule so that such expressions as *halkes and huyrenes* and *wayes and wrynclis* remain. The reason for this is twofold. Trevisa's alliteration is a stylistic ornament superimposed upon the basic sentence pattern, which is solidly based on Higden's Latin. In Malory's Book Five, on the other hand, the alliteration is an integral part of the sentence structure and any recasting of the sentence results in destroying the alliteration. But in Trevisa the alliteration, being decorative, occurs in doublets and the revision of any sentence would not necessarily lead to its elimination. And Caxton, as we have seen, was partial to doublets. Indeed one of the notable features of his adaptation of Trevisa is the increase in their number. Furthermore, doublets had been used by Chaucer and other courtly writers, so that in Chaucer's *Boethius* we find such pairs as *commoevynge and chasynge, duskid and dirked, felonyes and fraudes.* Thus Trevisa must have had many stylistic virtues in Caxton's eyes, even though his vocabulary was not sufficiently modern. It would seem as though Caxton thought Trevisa, though an older writer, less old-fashioned than Malory.

Certainly Caxton would also have considered Malory more old-fashioned than Chaucer. But how would he have regarded Trevisa in relation to Chaucer? Both men were translating at approximately the same time. Yet Caxton claimed that Trevisa's language was no longer up to date, whereas he has nothing but praise for Chaucer's. In so far as the matter has been studied, it would seem that Caxton made few alterations to Chaucer's prose. Caxton allows such words as *yclepid* and *apayed,* which he frequently altered for his printing of Trevisa, to remain in Chaucer's text. There are not, however, many such words in Chaucer, for his language is definitely more Latinate and his style more ornate than Trevisa's. This difference is attributable to the different areas in which they lived and possibly the tastes of their patrons. Chaucer's association with the court and London no doubt influenced his style. Trevisa wrote his work in the West Country which was less affected by courtly fashions. It would seem as though Caxton viewed Chaucer, Trevisa and Malory in that descending order of stylistic excellence. This order also represents the extent to which he modified their translations. Furthermore, he did recognize the differences between various styles, and he considered style sufficiently important to justify his rectifying what was not fashionable.

The preceding survey has necessarily been brief, but it has shown that Caxton attempted to print works written in what he considered to be the courtly style and that when a book was not written in that style, he altered it to make it conform. There can also be little doubt that he acted in this way because he was attempting to follow the fashion of the court. This conclusion leads to some further observations. Today we tend to think that modern prose style originated with Malory. To Caxton and the fifteenth century it must have seemed as though Malory was the culmination of the old, alliterative style: he represented the end of one style rather than the beginning of another. It is time now that we reconsidered the position of the fifteenth century in the history of English prose, for we have hitherto failed to recognize that the authors of the time were trying to break new ground. Consequently their achievement has been undervalued. They could see that poetry had made a new start and they wished to do the same for prose. But since they had no English model and were forced to rely on foreign ones, it is only to be expected that their attempts to fashion a new style should seem naïve to us. But this does not mean that the fifteenth-century translator 'had seldom any interest in English style' [I. A. Gordon, *The Movement of English Prose*]. On the contrary, he was intensely conscious of it and tried to improve it. Naturally the first steps were uncertain, but the fifteenth-century translators paved the way for the achievements of the sixteenth century. And if Berners is the first to write modern English prose, it was only because many before him had shown him the way. But this does not mean that there was such a straight line of descent from early medieval English prose to Renaissance prose, as some writers on Middle English prose have suggested. Of course, the translators were influenced by the alliterative tradition which they were trying to supersede. And we have seen that some alliteration was acceptable. But the fifteenth century was trying to make a definite break with the prose of the past, and they were to a large extent successful. Modern scholars have tended to minimize this break because insufficient attention has been paid to the works and aims of fifteenth-century translators.

Finally, I should like to consider whether the attitudes to prose I have traced in the fifteenth century might have any bearing upon our views of the Alliterative Revival, though here I can do no more than make one or two general suggestions. There is a tendency to link the revival with the north and west of the country, and even to suggest that it might have been fostered by baronial opposition to the central monarchy. For Caxton and the fifteenth century the alliterative style in both prose and poetry represented the old English style for the whole country. Chaucer had broken away from it in poetry and many fifteenth-century disciples had followed in his footsteps. Similarly prose writers had tried to adapt his stylistic revolution to prose by basing their work on foreign models. The new style was associated with London and the court. Yet even there in the fifteenth century there were still people who favoured the old alliterative tradition and who wanted Caxton to follow that style. Wynkyn de Worde did in fact revert to the older style by publishing the works of such authors as Rolle. These two facts show that the old style was still popular in London and elsewhere, and that it was the Chaucerian style which was new and trying to break away. For many in London the alliterative style must still have been the accepted one. Chaucer and his followers were the innovators, not the alliterative writers. This, I suggest, is how the fifteenth century saw the relationship of the two styles. And if they saw it in this way, it could well be that this was what in fact had happened. Certainly it seems unlikely that, if the alliterative style was characteristic only of the North and West, there would have been sufficient adherents of the style in London to make Caxton give it serious attention.

I hope I have shown that Caxton can tell us a great deal about contemporary literary fashion. Caxton is important because he is one of the few people who discuss what they are trying to do. Too many other fifteenth-century authors have merely left translations without giving us any insight into their method of working. Caxton tells us why he produced certain works and at the same time, as he is not himself a literary innovator, he reveals what others were thinking as well. This evidence has been overlooked in the past, but I would venture to suggest that it is of crucial importance for an understanding of the development of fifteenth-century English prose. (pp. 29-45)

N. F. Blake, "Caxton and Courtly Style," in Essays and Studies, *n.s. Vol. 21, 1968, pp. 29-45.*

Robert L. Montgomery (essay date 1973)

[*Montgomery is an American critic and educator. In the following excerpt, he compares Caxton's concept of the purpose of literature with that of critics in the Tudor period.*]

Caxton's place in the history of English criticism is not large. Apart from Atkins' suggestion [J. W. H. Atkins, *English Literary Criticism: The Medieval Phase*] that his rejection of aureate style anticipates the rhetorical concerns of the sixteenth century, there is scarcely any mention of him. Such reticence is understandable. In the modern sense of the term he was no critic. Those critical propositions which he uses and mentions are simple and easy and would seem to amount to no more than the common attitudes toward literature of the late Middle Ages. And, so far as one can tell, he had no influence over later developments. But in spite of such handicaps, there are two sufficient reasons for lending his remarks some greater attention: his unpublished translation of Ovid's *Metamorphoses* is prefaced by a genuine, though brief, poetics; and the attitudes he reflects derive from concerns which continued to inform the criticism of the English Renaissance. Indeed his is one of the few English voices in the late fifteenth century with anything at all to say about literature.

The most obvious of Caxton's concerns is his attention to style, and since on the whole this side of his importance in the history of English criticism has received adequate attention, I offer only a few summary comments. We need no longer subscribe to the exaggeration in Donald L. Clark's notions that in "the late middle ages rhetoric had come to mean to all intents and purposes nothing more than style," that style was never seen "as being engaged in any useful occupation," and that poetic itself was absorbed into rhetoric. But there were tendencies in this direction, and Caxton's enthusiasm for Chaucer, though balanced by his respect for the poet's wisdom and sententiousness, reflects the contemporary delight in the mastery of language. Caxton praises "his ornate wrytyng in our tongue," and asserts that his craft is evident in "short, quyck, and hye sentences, eschewyng prolyxyte, castyng

away the chaf of superfluyte, and shewyng the pyked grayn of sentence utteryd by crafty and sugred eloquence." In qualifying ornateness by the virtues of efficiency and sententiousness Caxton is on the side of the angels, but we should notice that in this prologue at least he approaches the question of the value of poetry through his interest in style.

This interest generally expresses itself as a mixture of almost naïve wonder at the beauty and skill which "eloquence" can achieve and recognition that it must serve civilized ends. In the **"Prohemye"** to *Polycronicon* (1482), Caxton says that "eloquence is soo precious and noble that almooste noo thyng can be founden more precious than it. By Eloquence the grekes ben preferryd in contynuel honour to fore the rude barbares. Oratours and lerned clerkes in like wise excelle unlerned and brutyssh peple." Unspecified but firm associations bind eloquence, learning, and philosophy in these remarks, and in his second edition of *The Canterbury Tales* (1484) Caxton suggests that "we ought to gyve a singuler laude unto that noble & grete philosopher Gefferey Chaucer the whiche for his ornate wrytyng in our tongue may wel have the name of a laureate poete. For to fore that he by hys labour enbelysshed, ornated, and made faire our englisshe, in this Royame was had rude speche & Incongrue." The marriage of civilized learning and ordered, pleasing expression was to become a point of doctrine for the humanists of the sixteenth century, and well before the end of that century the point had been fully argued out. Caxton is content with celebrating the union.

He does, however, exhibit a continuous interest in the didactic status of all kinds of writing, and this interest modifies his attitudes toward imaginative literature. From his remarks in a variety of contexts it is clear that he was aware of generic differences distinguishing kinds of discourse, and it is also clear that on the whole these differences were not matters for interested or searching speculation. The one point which appears to be of concern is the gap between fact and fiction, but this, as we shall see, takes its importance only from its relationship to the larger matter of didactic effectiveness.

At its simplest Caxton's point of view is summed up in his phrase that the fables of *Reynart the Foxe* (1481) will provide "nede prouffyte of alle god folke," but although this might well stand as his acknowledged rationale for everything he printed, there emerge from his prefaces, prologues, and epilogues some particular matters of emphasis. The fables have the special property of instructing in "subtyl deceytes" so that we may be defended against them. This does not tell us much, but if we turn to *Blanchardyn and Eglantine* (1489) and observe Caxton listing the standard features of chivalric romance, it is evident that he regards this form as almost identical with epic, and epic in its turn is identical with history in the quality and significance of the deeds it records: we "rede in Auncyent historyes of noble fayttes & valiaunt actes of armes & warre which have ben achyeved in olde tyme of many noble prynces, lordes & knyghtes." In *Godefroy of Bologne* (1481) and in his edition of Malory's *Morte D'Arthur*

(1495) the values of notable historical events receive full praise, and it is worth noting that Caxton makes a lengthy argument for Arthur's status as a historical rather than a fictional or mythical figure. The preface to *Godefroy of Bologne* begins: "The hye courageous faytes and valyaunt actes of noble, illustrious, and vertuous personnes ben digne to be recounted, put in memorye and wreton to thende that there may be gyven to them name immortal by soverayn laude and preysyng." Recalling the tradition of the Nine Worthies, he mentions "the incredible, chevalrous prowesse of the noble and valyaunt Hector of Troye, whos excellent actes wryten Ovyde, Homer, Virgyle, Dares, Dictes, and other diverse." What we would call epic or legend Caxton takes to be history.

He thus seems to prefer history over other forms of narrative, and he argues that the actuality of event and character is more likely to offer a convincing lesson to the reader. He makes this point in his rejection of the view that Arthur is a creature of fiction:

> And I accordyng to my copye have doon sette it in enprynte to the entente that noble men may see and lerne the noble actes of chivalrye, the Jentyl and vertuous dedes that some knyghtes used in tho dayes, by whyche they came to honour, and how they that were vycious were punysshed and ofte put to shame and rebuke, humbly besechyng al noble lordes and ladyes and al other estates of what estate or degre they been of, that shal see and rede in this sayd bok and werke, that they take the good and honest actes in their remembraunce and to folowe the same, wherein they shalle fynde many joyous and playsaunt hystoryes and noble & renomed actes of humanyte, gentylnesse, and chyvalryes. For herin may be seen noble chivalrye, Curtosye, Humanyte, frendlynesse, hardynesse, love, frendshypp, Cowardyse, Murdre, hate, vertue, and synne.

Epic history offers exemplary and exalted virtue and vice as models for behavior and understanding, and Caxton seems to believe that this literary form offers such qualities in the purest state. His emphasis on the signal act, upon deeds and events which exhibit moral attributes, places him in the mainstream of Renaissance critical thinking. The concern is not with literary character but with patterns which reveal the temper of worldly life. In the **"Prologue to *Charles the Grete*"** (1485), he echoes his French source in endowing the nature and use of all "wrytyng" with a reason for being: "the thynges passed dyversly reduced to remembraunce engendre in us correction of unlauful lyf. For the werkes of the auncient and olde peple ben for to gyve to us ensaumple to lyve in good & vertuous operacions digne & worthy of helth in folowyng the good and eschewyng the evyl." Example fixed in the memory draws the mind to virtuous behavior. So, apparently, does doctrine embodied in action:

> And also in recountyng of hye hystoryes the comune understondyng is better content to the ymagynacion local than to symple auctoryte to which it is submysed. I saye this gladly, for oftymes I have ben excyted of the venerable man messire henry bolomyer, chanonne of lausanne,

for to reduce for his playsyr somme hystoryes as wel in latyn & in romaunce as in other facion wryton: that is to say of the ryght puyssaunt, vertuous, and noble charles the grete, kyng of fraunce and emperour of Rome, Sone of the grete Pepyn, and of his prynces & barons, as Rolland, Olyver, and other, touchyng somme werkes haultayne doone & commysed by their grete strength & ryght ardaunt courage to the exaltacyon of the crysten fayth and to the confusyon of the hethen sarzyns and myscreaunts, which is a werk wel contemplatyf for to lyve wel.

Narrative supplies the mind with doctrine exhibited in place, event, and hero. This argument, supported by rudimentary reference to standard psychology, anticipates the point that Sidney was to make more decisively a century later: unadorned precept or authority cannot excite the imagination and move the reader to virtue half so readily as figures brought before the mind's eye. So far as I am aware Caxton is the first English writer to mention the imagination in a context similar to that invoked by Sidney when he describes poetry as a speaking picture. For Caxton, interestingly, it is actual, historical event which has the power of enforcing conviction; for Sidney the poetic image is more compelling than history because the poet's imagination (which does not concern Caxton) can fashion images which are not only vivid but ideal. Implicit in Caxton's brief account of narrative is an imitative principle. In his comments on *Reynart the Foxe* he assumes that the reader will make inferences, learning from the fables how deceit and trickery work and thus how to avoid becoming their victim; more elevated stories, "hye hystoryes," encourage mimetic behavior and speak to such responses as forcefully as they do to the moral understanding.

Caxton appears to be sensitive to rough generic differences defined according to the effects of several kinds of discourse: hence he can distinguish between precept and narrative, parable or example, history, and fable. But those which deal in concrete events and characters require a kind of veracity: verisimilitude seems to be as much on Caxton's mind as true doctrine. Witness the manner in which he comments on *Reynart:*

> Now who that said to yow of the ffoxe more or lesse than ye have herd or red, I holde it for lesynge. But this that ye have herd or red, that may ye byleve wel & who that byleveth it not is not therfore out of the ryght byleve. How be it ther be many yf that they had seen it, they shold have the lasse doubt of it, for ther ben many thynges in the world whiche ben byleved though they were never seen. Also ther ben many fygures, playes founden, that never were don ne happed. But for an example to the peple that they may the better use and folowe vertue.

Caxton's strategy is first of all to insist that his version of the fables is the correct one and then momentarily to pretend that the stories of the fox are true, using the argument that things which are unfamiliar may nevertheless be believed. But if that argument is unsatisfactory, we have the assertion that what is invented may serve as instructive example. The matter may consist of "japes and bourdes" but it is nevertheless full of "wysedom and lernynges." As one might expect, the imaginative vehicle is important only as a vehicle; Caxton really wants to stress its credibility, and in his epilogue to the second edition (1489) he mentions the fox as if he were someone whose biography might be of interest: "it is not written ony where what did hereafter befalle hym nor how he dyde, but I weene he was hongid for he hyely desrvyd it, for he was a shrewde and felle theefe and deceivyd the king with lesingys." Caxton then moves on to describe the hot justice that awaits people like the fox after death: "they goo to hell when they dye and the Deviles pull them by their beardes and brenne their erses with hote Irons." Caxton's sense of humor relieves the dogged pursuit of the relevance of the fables and of their essential closeness to life, but these are nevertheless the main issues.

Herschel Baker has underlined the concerns of Renaissance historiography by mentioning "a pair of ancient commonplaces that underlie most Renaissance discussions" of the topic:

> One is that the historian, unlike other writers, has a special obligation to ascertain and state the truth of things. The other is that such truths are exemplary: they are paradigms of moral and political behavior, which, authenticated by famous men's experience, provide patterns that can shape our own response to perennially recurring situations. Thus history, unlike more imaginative kinds of literature, was thought to be both true and useful.

Caxton is quite comfortably within the set of attitudes Baker summarizes. If a choice is to be made between works of the imagination and history as sources of morally useful example, he will choose history, as a passage in his preface to *Polycronicon* (1482) reveals:

> And thus the pryncipal laude and cause of delectable and amyable thynges in whiche mannes felycyte stondeth and resteth ought and maye wel be attributed to hystoryes, which worde historye may be descryved thus: Historye is a perpetuel conservatryce of thoos thynges that have be doon before this presente tyme and also a cotydyan wytnesse of beinfayttes, of malefaytes, grete Actes, and tryumphal vyctoryes of all maner peple. And also yf the terryble feyned Fables of Poetes have moche styred and moeved men to pyte and conservyng of Justyce, how moche more is to be supposed that Historye, assertryce of veryte and as moder of alle philosophye, moevynge our maners to vertue, reformeth and reconcyleth ner handle alle thoos man whiche thurgh the Infyrmyte of oure mortal nature hath ledde the mooste parte of theyr lyf in Ocyosyte and myspended theyr tyme passed ryght soone oute of Remembraunce. Of whiche lyf and deth is egal oblyvyon. The fruytes of vertue ben Inmortall, specyally whanne they be wrapped in the benefyce of hystoryes.

It is not so remarkable that Caxton summons history to reconcile men's lives, but it is worth our notice that he

places it above poetry, whose power to affect the emotions he readily acknowledges. History is the radical discipline, the mother of all philosophy and the supplier of the memory, and it seems to be such because it lies closest to the truth of human experience, especially to that sort most central to our moral health. One senses that Caxton has chosen the term "feyned" not simply as the usual description for fiction but as an emphatic counterpoise to "assertryce of veryte." History has the further power of being instructive in the events of the past. He suggests repeatedly in this preface that the record of the past ties human events into a unity and gives them constantly renewed and perpetual meaning. The man who has direct experience of a fundamental sort, "by the taste of bytternes and experyment of grete jeopardyes," possesses the kind of wisdom history passes on to someone "syttynge in his chambre or studye," and such wisdom consists in knowing rightly "the polytyke and noble actes of alle the worlde as of one Cyte, and the conflyctes, errours, troubles & vexacions done in the sayd unyversal worlde in suche wyse as he had ben and seen them." Caxton's view of history is much more than the familiar notion that history exists for the uses of the present. Not even a process leading to the present, the past is undifferentiated. No age or person has any peculiar status: they are without chronology and individuality—"one Cyte" or a "unyversal worlde," figures in a single immense canvas framed and composed to exhibit only those moral attributes common to the experience of all ages.

The knowledge thus acquired by the studious man suggests the continuity of human experience, and it is seldom very far away from moral practicality of the most manageable sort. A shortcut back to the significant experience of predecessors, history for Caxton gives emphatic priority to the actual over the invented, so that in such a context there is no easy welcome to theories of fiction, perhaps because the brand of fiction with which he is familiar is more fabulous than verisimilar. Imaginative literature may be emotionally effective, it may be awesome or terrible, it may move men to pity and to the "conservynge of Justyce," but it takes second place. Even in the midst of his praise of eloquence as the medium by which some men excel, Caxton remarks that some writers (poets) "have taken another waye for tenflamme more the courages of men by fables of poesye than to prouffyte." This doctrine embraces a basic and rather obvious mimetic principle, though why words which do not represent actual events should be more arousing than other kinds is not clear. Caxton may be implying that the historian is more likely to avoid rhetorical emotionalism, and perhaps he has inherited an attenuated echo of Platonic theory. In any case he assumes that certain events are to be defined by their moral attributes and that historians have selected such events precisely because they exhibit such qualities. It is not style itself which produces the desired moral effect upon the reader, though eloquence works, as we have seen, to civilize as well as to arouse.

Caxton's only "poetics" is remarkable both because it is his and because it advances the cause of poetry in a somewhat grudging way which is consistent with the reservations and biases we have already noted. This poetics, the **"Prohemye"** to the recently discovered first half of the manuscript of his edition of the *Metamorphoses,* has not yet been published. In general demeanor this prologue, rather lengthy for Caxton, is a traditional defense of poetry. It appears to owe a good deal to the fourteenth and fifteenth books of Boccaccio's *Genealogia Gentilium Deorum,* though it lacks the argumentative vigor of that work and does not approach Boccaccio's full and reasonably independent effort to define the nature of fiction.

At first Caxton's argument turns on two familiar uses of anecdote about poetry. References to Solon, Cyrus, Euripides, and Sophocles testify to the power of verse to move people to action. (Curiously Orpheus and Amphion, the most usual illustrations of this commonplace, are not mentioned.) The initial set of anecdotes argues that metered language in itself is the motive force in poetry:

> Also Cyrus Emperor of Lacedomone that was poete of Athenes when the Lacedomonyens for cause of adversytees that they hade in the batayles [with] the messynniens wold wythdrawe the route of theyr host to thende that theyre infortune torned not to more sclaundre myght fal to theire publique wele, he composed some metres and recyted them to hys knyghtes, by whyche they were so espryed with right grete love martial that they wold not retorn but unyed with one corage attones at the first stroke they veynqushhed & overcame theyre enemyes and broughte & put them in perdurable servytude.

This is consistent with what we have previously understood of Caxton's view of the emotional uses of style. Another anecdote, the story of Alexander's visit to the tomb of Homer, is part of a brief section testifying to the respect paid by eminent rulers to poets.

Such remarks are *pro forma.* For the most part Caxton regards poetry with tender wariness, even though he begins his **"Prohemye"** with an attack on the enemies of poetry. The real motive of the piece appears in the following remarks:

> But for as moche as some poetes be eygrely blamed of many whiche have made vayne & garylous processes in hye style & profunde eloquence, therfore it is necessarye to shewe bryefly how & in what facion or in what ordre & maner Christen men ought to rede & understond the poetes and theyr subtyl werkes.

In other words, a good Christian has to pick and choose, for poets are not always to be trusted. Caxton employs the figure of the ruminating and selective bee "whiche nothynge gadreth of the floures but the colour and savour out of whiche only he can draw out the honey." Citing Basil the Great, he urges the praise of poets "when they treate not of debates or discensions," or when they do not "touche scurilite, followynge, or dronknes, or whan they preyse not rych ne glotonous table." Moreover he is suspicious of accounts of the pagan gods, and "also when they telle of them in suche wyse that dyvers expositours discorde." Generally, he continues, "late us only gyve . . .

preysynge to the Oratours when they enhaunce vertu, and put doun & blame vyces."

In such a literary universe the fictive quality of poetry is superficial or secondary, except when mistaken for the truth. Certainly it is insufficient reason to value literature or to consider it distinctive. Caxton's partial model, Boccaccio, had managed to transcend the limits of a poetic so stubbornly preoccupied with right doctrine, and he represents the common medieval method of finding a way around the temptations offered by the poets when he argues, as Augustine, Basil, Jerome, and countless others had done, that what may appear to be a frivolous or impious departure from the truth is in reality a metaphorical construct which may be translated into sober and useful verity. This is also Caxton's approach, but he embraces it with less rigor and persistence than the "compiler" of the French version from which he translated. Colard Mansion surrounds his text with nearly a hundred folio pages of allegorical readings of the myths, symbolic meanings of various pagan dieties, and other trappings which have the cumulative effect of suggesting a more learned and esoteric Ovid than Caxton understood. Mansion, too, lacks a genuine theory of fiction, but he makes the most of the conventional patristic and Boccaccian tradition.

Caxton presents his Recuyell of the Historyes of Troye *to his benefactor Margaret, Duchess of Burgundy.*

Caxton, by contrast, is almost apologetic: "And thenne emong the Latyn Poetes Ovyde of Salmonence is to be preysed and honoured hyely, how be it in some of his dittes he is or semeth to be sorrowfull and in other delyryous, nevertheles his werke is ryghte excellent and notable. Of whyche bycause of the perycye [preciousness] & subtilte of the fables wherin is conteyned grete and prouffitable wysedom to them that knowe & understande theme." One might conjecture that Caxton never published his version of Ovid because he felt its sententiousness was insufficiently obvious without an apparatus of commentary, or because his labor may have been intended for a private patron, one of those able to know and understand the profit and wisdom to be yielded by the fables. Without further information the matter cannot be settled. But what is apparent is Caxton's firm belief that fables are justified only by their capacity to deliver useful truth and are suspect insofar as they record extreme or painful emotions.

Such a view of fiction imposes strict limitations. There is behind it no theory of the imagination that allows for the creation of fictional images which are instructive in any way other than the allegorical, and even here Caxton drastically simplifies that aspect in his source. So it would seem that his poetics advances only a very small distance beyond the terms in which he praised "Oratours" in his **"Preface to *Polycronicon.*"** The poetic fable, like eloquence, may be a vehicle for wisdom. When it is not, it is to be avoided. In the same preface Caxton gives history and epic a definitively superior place to fable and fiction, and a touch of that bias remains in his remarks on Ovid. First of all he reads the title as if it meant "transmutacion of one fable into another or interpretation of theym." Ovid is a conscious rationalizer of his predecessors in the genre, "ffor he seeng as wel the latyn poetes as the poetes of Grece that hade ben to fore hym and hys tyme had touched in wrytyng many fables and them passed superfycyelly without expressynge theyr knowledge or entendement." Furthermore Ovid's weaving the separate myths together is seen as an achievement of "gret subtyltee," and even more to Caxton's taste he "tyssued & medled with fable and hystorye togidre." The intrusion of history guarantees a validity that fables by themselves would lack: "And his dictes or sayeings ben not to be reudyed ne reproched ther as they ne conteyn but fable only."

In some ways these comments would appear to anticipate Castelvetro's notion that poetry ought to be founded in history or in the imagining of events like history, but Castelvetro was concerned that fictive writing be made credible for the enjoyment of a public of meager intelligence. Caxton, on the other hand, believes that fables should have a foundation in true doctrine, and here we may recall his conviction that history imitates the significance of human experience more accurately and impressively than other forms of writing. Now he adds:

> For over & above the eloquence whiche is right swete, under veyle or shadowe hyd, he compryseth the scyence & advertysement of grete partye of thingis comen, or at leste by possybylyte ben for to com. And yf the cronyclers of hystoryes hade wryten by so cler & lyght style the gestes & feates of the noble & valyaunt men or of

thinges possible to come, thenne eche man might at the first sight have conceyved & comprised theym where the hade be holden theme more for Phylosophers than for poetes.

The passage is not entirely lucid, but what I wish to stress in it is Caxton's insistence on Ovid as a prophet of the possible. This is not the same concept as Aristotle's doctrine of probability or possibility as conditions on which to structure an action; it is rather an assertion that the possible is an element of subject matter and would appear to be one more effort to value Ovid as somewhat more than a poet. In the same vein he praises Ovid for intelligibility and for having given order to the fables he has compiled, "reservyng that whiche serveth not and ampled that whyche was to shorte to understonde." This is not to say that the reader is exempted from all effort at interpretation. "For who so can discovre and take away the veyle or shadowe fro the fables he shal see clerly somtyme poetrye & somtyme right hye phylosophye under other scyence of Ethyque, under other yconomyque, under other polytique. Under other he shal fynde geste or hystorye comprysed, yf he wil entende and employe hys tyme by aspre diligence." And Caxton argues quite sensibly that Ovid was well aware men could not literally be turned into beasts: these metamorphoses are a means of condemning those who are "lad and conduyted by theyre sensyble appetyte" and of showing the difference between reasonable creatures and brute beasts.

Caxton is thus very much a man of his age: he accommodates fiction by the convenient method of allegorical interpretation, but I have sought to underscore another and less expected side of his attitude toward literature, his preference for historical fact. This preference reveals itself not in an outright dismissal of poetry but in a reluctance to give poetry as a genre the same unequivocal value as history. Of the two, history is the more complete, more reliable teacher. Caxton admires neither Chaucer nor Ovid as "makers" but for other virtues. It is this attitude, I think, which differentiates his position from those developed later on the Continent and in England—though in many respects, of course, his views are quite consistent with the broader concerns of Renaissance critical thinking. He has two related motives: his persistent effort to make various kinds of books available to an audience unlearned in Latin and his equally steady insistence that what is read be morally profitable. The second motive is one that dominated later English Renaissance criticism far more absolutely than it did companion developments in Italy and France. Later and more sophisticated English critics did not, of course, share Caxton's fondness for history over fiction, but in other respects his biases would appear to be fundamentally consistent with theirs. One need only add as a footnote to the history of criticism that Caxton deserves a place in it for much more than his few remarks on style or his admiration of Chaucer. (pp. 91-103)

Robert L. Montgomery, "William Caxton and the Beginnings of Tudor Critical Thought," in The Huntington Library Quarterly, *Vol. 36, No. 2, February, 1973, pp. 91-103.*

Frieda Elaine Penninger   (essay date 1979)

[*Penninger is an American educator and critic specializing in the study of medieval and Renaissance literature. In the following excerpt, she discusses Caxton's prose and verse narratives as exemplifications of his editorial methods and linguistic goals.*]

The Medieval mind, as it is reflected in the books from Caxton's press . . . , sought wholeness but experienced multeity. It sought truth through fact, it often denied the value of the nonfactual; it nevertheless cherished the nonfactual, and it frequently and ironically mistook fiction for fact. It paid homage to edification and instruction, but it often engaged in merely entertaining itself. William Caxton apparently shared in these paradoxical views. As a culminating, ultimate, and certainly unintended paradox, he made his most significant contribution as translator, editor, publisher, and critic through the fictional narratives in prose and verse that he presented to his public. More than a third of the total number of titles printed by Caxton are fictional narratives, and a very high proportion of the works published by him which continue to hold reader interest are narratives. Caxton himself recognized the value of the fictional narrative, as his prologues and epilogues testify, though this recognition may, in fact, have been more intuitive than conscious.

What the fictional narrative at its best can accomplish is the creation of a reality which at once transcends the contradictions and imperfections of temporal reality and reduces time and space to a patterned and measurable whole. It enables the human mind to grasp and understand its own particular relationship to the universe—exactly the value which the Middle Ages sought in nonfiction. Fiction can provide an avenue into human personality and into the full dimensions of life which direct experience does not always provide. Fiction can approach a truth about the human condition which subsumes partial truths. The prose and verse narratives published by Caxton, many of them translated by him, sometimes do and sometimes, perhaps more often, do not achieve this kind of perception. Caxton's inferior narratives, however, are instructive through their shortcomings, for rough or imperfect narratives may enable us to examine the craftsman's work before the ultimate finish of perfection produces the art which conceals its artistry under the cover of inspiration.

The first of Caxton's prose narratives is also his first independently printed book. Its very name, *The Recuyell,* or collection, *of the Historyes of Troye* [1475], is a warning that the book contains a mixed genre, part history and part fiction, and that the plot will be long and winding. It has, however, a basic structure in being developed around three destructions of Troy. The author-compiler of the French text which Caxton translated, Raoul Lefèvre, sees an additional structural pattern in the fact that each book has a chief hero—Perseus, Hercules, or Hector. Book I, centered, more or less, in Perseus and his marriage, contains only a small proportion of Trojan episodes, but it ends with Hercules's destruction of the city's walls: The Trojans had refused to pay the gods for building the walls, and they lost their city as a result.

Book II contains a second destruction of Troy, this time in vengeance for the inhospitality shown the questers after the Golden Fleece; but the hero, Hercules, having destroyed the city a second time, goes to his own death and destruction. Book III relates the rebuilding of Troy and then its third destruction after Priam's son carries off Helen, the story made famous by the *Iliad.* The formal elements of a balanced plot are present in the large outlines of the story, but they are so heavily overladen with detail that the structure is obscured. Although *The Recuyell* attempts to record life, both author and translator lacked the gift of selectivity which would have enabled them to keep the significance of the material in focus.

The Recuyell is treated in this discussion as a fictional narrative, but Lefèvre and Caxton might have classified it among historical accounts. Although Lefèvre cites his sources and clearly considers them to be authoritative, Caxton is aware that all the sources do not agree. He warns his reader that Dictes, Dares, and Homer tell different versions of the story and that the names of the characters are given in various forms, but, says Caxton in his Epilogue,

> all accord in conclusion, the general destruction of that noble city of Troy and the death of so many noble princes, as kings, dukes, earls, barons, knights, and common people, and the ruin irreparable of that city, that never since was re-edified, which may be example to all men during the world how dreadful and jeopardus it is to begin a war, and what harms, losses, and death followeth. Therefore th'apostle saith "All that is written is written to our doctrine," which doctrine for the common weal I beseech God may be taken in such place and time as shall be most needful in increasing peace, love, and charity, which grant us He that suffered for the same to be crucified on the rood tree. And say we all Amen for charity.

Raoul Lefèvre furnished Caxton with a second narrative, *The History of Jason* [1477], in which the plot is put together in the simple fashion that is sometimes called the "clothesline technique" because one episode after another is attached, like clothes hung on a washline, to the plot line and the time sequence involves simple chronological time. Although Lefèvre demonstrates more selectivity in the choice of his materials in *Jason* than he did in *The Recuyell of the Historyes of Troye,* the characters are not developed with much insight, and no significant theme focuses the episodes. The material is capable of an archetypal rendering which would give it psychological significance, but it receives no such development here. Perhaps the link to Troy, the fictive original home of the Britons, together with the romantic and gory fascinations of the plot, led Caxton to translate and print *Jason.*

Most unfortunately, the Classical world also yielded Caxton another book, *Eneydos.* Caxton used a French prose text derived from the *Aeneid* as the basis for his own translation, and his Prologue offers an account of how he selected his text:

> After diverse works made, translated, and achieved, having no work in hand, I sitting in

my study where as lay many diverse pamphlets and books, [it] happened that to my hand came a little book in French which late was translated out of Latin by some noble clerk of France, which book is named *Eneydos,* made in Latin by that noble poet & great clerk Virgil, which book I saw over and read therein. . . . In which book I had great pleasure by cause of the fair and honest terms & words in French. Which I never saw to fore [before] like, nor none so pleasant nor so well ordered, which book as me seemed [it seemed to me] should be much requisite to noble men to see as well for the eloquence as the histories.

Caxton admired his French book, but it is a poor representation of the *Aeneid.* The plot has been reorganized along chronological lines, its proportions have been altered, and the style of Caxton's translation, with its incessant synonyms, does nothing to speed the tedious narrative. In fact, one of Caxton's earliest critics has remained his most virulent and eloquent. Gavin Douglas, a Scots poet (1474?-1522), is as famous for his wrath with Caxton as for his own translation of the *Aeneid.* Douglas begins his Prologue with praise of Virgil:

> Laud, honor, praisings, thanks infinite
> To thee and thy sweet, ornate, fresh writing,
> Most reverend Virgil, of Latin poets prince,
> Gem of ingenuity and flood of eloquence,
> Thou peerless pearl, patron of poetry. . . .

Douglas says of Caxton:

> William Caxton, of the English nation,
> In prose has printed a book of English gross,
> Calling it Virgil's *Aeneid,*
> Which that he says from French he did translate,
> It has nothing to do therewith, God knows;
> They are no more alike than the devil and Saint
> Augustine.

Douglas has a good deal more to say in the way of the particulars of Caxton's transgressions, for the Scots poet exclaims, "I spitted for despite [contempt] to see so spoilt" Virgil's "ornate, golden verses."

A close comparison between Virgil's *Aeneid* and Caxton's translation is impossible for the reason that Caxton is not close to Virgil. What has happened to the Latin epic can be glimpsed, however, by looking at Caxton's opening in comparison to Virgil's. Caxton begins:

> For to hear, open, and declare the matter of which hereafter shall be made mention, it behoveth to presuppose that Troy, the great capital city and the excellentest of all the cities of the country & region of Asia, was constructed and edified by the right puissant & renowned king Priamus, son of Laomedon, descended of th'ancient stock of Dardanus by many degrees, which was son of Jupiter & of Electra his wife, after [according to] the fictions poetic, and the first original beginning of the genealogy of kings. And the said Troy was environed [surrounded] in form of seige and of excidion [destruction; this occurrence in Caxton is the only example of "excidion" in English cited in *The Oxford English*

Dictionary], by Agamemnon, king in Greece, brother of Menelaus which was husband to Helen. The which Agamemnon, assembled and accompanied with many kings, dukes, earls, and great quantity of other princes & Greeks innumerable, had the magistration [command; again, this occurrence is the only example cited in *The Oxford English Dictionary* of "magistration" in English] and universal goverance of all th' excersite [exercise, drill] and host to-fore [before] Troy.

Virgil begins in quite another way:

> Arma virumque cano, Troiae qui primus ab oris
> Italiam fato profugus Laviniaque venit
> litora, multum ille et terris iactatus et alto
> vi superum, saevae memorem Iunonis ob iram,
> multa quoque et bello passus, dum conderet urbem
> inferretque deos Latio; genus unde Latinum
> Albanique patres atque altae moenia Romae.

Douglas's translation does not correspond line for line with Virgil, but it is quite close:

> The battles and the man I will describe
> From Troy's bounds first that, fugitive,
> By fate to Italy came and the coast of Lavinia.
> O'er land and sea driven with great pain
> By force [power] of [the] gods above, from every stead [place],
> Of [by] cruel Juno through [because of] old remembered wrath.
> Great pain in battle suffered he also
> Before he his gods brought into Latium
> And built the city from which, of noble fame,
> The Latin people taken have their name,
> And also the fathers, princes of Alba,
> Came, and the wall-builders of great Rome also.

The pedestrian quality of Caxton's text and its great distance from Virgil are apparent from these samples. As Douglas exclaims, "He runs so far from Virgil in many place,/In so prolix and tedious fashion."

The matter of Rome served Caxton somewhat poorly. But at the least he recognized the value of the Trojan and Roman stories. He admired language. He was diligent as a translator, making available to English readers what no other translator had done. He is not the last translator who has failed to do justice to Virgil. Caxton's *Eneydos* cannot be admired; but perhaps Gavin Douglas grew more wroth with the printer than was deserved.

Higden's *Polychronicon,* in its zeal to advocate historical truth, condemns works which tell one feigned thing by way of another. Caxton, however, not only modernized, extended, and printed Higden's *Polychronicon;* he also translated the *Fables of Aesop* (specifically drummed out of the corps of philosophers by *Polychronicon*), *The Metamorphoses of Ovid,* and the anonymous *Reynard the Fox.* The *Fables of Aesop* as Caxton translated and printed it (1484) begins with the life of Aesop, who was born deformed and speechless but who was granted speech and wisdom because of an act of hospitality. Aesop, who was sold into slavery by a jealous and wicked steward, served his masters well and wittily, but he was finally unjustly executed. The true Aesopian fables are chiefly concerned with animals—"The Cock and the Precious Stone," "The Fox and the Grapes," "The Dog in the Manger"—but the Caxton collection also includes "The Fables of Avyan," "The Fables of Alfonce," and "The Fables of Poge the Florentyn." In these various additions the characters are often human; in "Poge the Florentyn" they are monsters—a two-headed cat, a two-headed calf, a cow which gives birth to a serpent, and the like—quite enough to rouse Higden's displeasure. Scholars credit to Caxton's own composition two brief, untitled stories which conclude the *Aesop* collection. The first, which begins "There was in a certain town a widower wooed a widow . . . ," twists the Medieval injunction to scorn temporal life and seek eternity into a justification for rushing headlong into death through the pursuit of sensual pleasure. The second, embedded in Caxton's Epilogue, begins "Now then I will finish all these fables with this tale that followeth . . . that there were dwelling in Oxford two priests . . . " In the tale, a poor priest shows his old friend who has become a rich dean that the true measure of success in life is the attainment of heavenly reward.

The Metamorphoses of Ovid, translated by Caxton in 1480 but apparently never printed by him, is concerned with the transformations—metamorphoses—by which persons in some dire strait are turned into various animals, plants, or trees. In a not altogether logical way, these transformations are explained as reflections of the many changes to which the world is subject: Seasons change; skeletons of sea creatures are found where there is now only dry land; water may be sometimes fresh and sometimes salt. Since the French translator had greatly expanded the fragments of the Troy story found in Ovid, *The Metamorphoses* as Caxton translated it has become another Troy book.

Ovid relates not only to Troy but to another matter close to Caxton's heart: Geoffrey Chaucer. One of the changes on which the French Ovid comments is the fact that fame alters and distorts the records of what a man has done, and to this statement Caxton adds the observation that Chaucer demonstrates this fact in his *Book of Fame. The Metamorphoses of Ovid* was frequently a source book for Chaucer. Indeed, it almost appears that Caxton chose his books for their connection with Chaucer—Cicero, Cato, *Reynard,* Ovid, Virgil, Gower, Lydgate, and all the Troy material in various ways, bear on the understanding of Chaucer.

Caxton printed *Reynard the Fox* twice [1481, 1488]. These charming stories of the sly fox, the noble lion, and their various companions in adventure and scheming have been endlessly reprinted and read, if not, as their Dutch Prologue, translated by Caxton, recommends, for profit, at least for pleasure.

Caxton's versions of Classical stories and his fables relate in some respects to the novel, which is usually not considered to have emerged as a formal genre until the eighteenth century in England. All of Caxton's narratives have some degree of the complex inter-relationship of plot episodes which is generally taken as the hallmark of the novel. Two prose romances, *Paris and Vienne* (1485) and *Blanchardin and Eglantine* [1488], are even more clearly

in the general form of the novel, and Caxton himself translated as well as printed both works.

In *Paris and Vienne,* the title personages are young lovers separated by Vienne's father, who wishes to secure for her a profitable match. Her long and ingenious resistance to various suitors, together with Paris's great services to her father, finally unites the true lovers. The story is undistinguished in plot, characterization, or style; but the narrative demonstrates the interest readers have always taken in true love, particularly when its course contains disguise, intrigue, parental cruelty, and other such ordeals.

Much the same criticism may be made of *Blanchardin and Eglantine;* its narrative style is not lively, and its plot is long and tedious. Blanchardin, the son of a king and queen who had thought themselves destined to be childless, is not reared to perform deeds of war; but when he sees a tapestry of the Trojan War, he aspires to fight and consequently runs away from home. He is soon knighted by a man whose mortal wound and stolen lady he vows to avenge. Blanchardin does kill the villain and recover the lady, but she promptly dies of grief upon discovering that her knight is dead. Blanchardin is so moved by the sight of her collapse upon the stomach of her lover that he breaks into a long declaration of his intention to pursue love himself and attaches his affections to Eglantine, a lady who has many suitors and a reputation for scorning them. Blanchardin finally wins both on the battlefield and in the lady's heart.

Although the plot is not strong, it can almost be said that in *Blanchardin and Eglantine,* episode is all. The characterization is often improbable and usually unimportant, and no significant statement issues from the events. The book's appearance in repeated editions testifies to its popularity, but the popularity of such a book is no tribute to the general taste. More important than either *Paris and Vienne* or *Blanchardin and Eglantine,* however, is what Caxton says about the value to be derived from such reading. In the **"Prologue to *Blanchardin and Eglantine,*"** he asserts that reading fiction can be commended:

> [I] knew well that the story of hit was honest & joyful to all virtuous young noble gentlemen & women for to read therein as for their pastime; for under correction, in my judgement, it is as requisite other while [sometimes] to read in ancient histories of noble feats & valiant acts of arms & war which have been achieved in old time of many noble princes, lords, & knights, as well [as] for to see & know their valiantness for to stand in the special grace & love of their ladies, and in likewise for gentle young ladies & damoiselles for to learn to be steadfast & constant in their part to them that they once have promised and agreed to, such as have put their lives oft in jeopardy for to please them to stand in grace, as it is to occupy them and study over much in books of contemplation.

While neither *Paris and Vienne* nor *Blanchardin and Eglantine* has the qualities of plot, theme, and character necessary to make it a great book, the recognition of the value of such reading "to pass the time" constitutes a step toward the acceptance of fiction in its own right—a step for which Caxton has been as much praised as he has been criticized for his unfortunate translation of *Eneydos.*

Caxton had no need to translate the story of King Arthur, for a fifteenth century prose narrative of Arthur and his knights was readily available. Caxton's **"Prologue"** to Sir Thomas Malory's *Le Morte d'Arthur* (1485) tells how he decided to print it:

> After that I had accomplished and finished diverse histories as well of contemplation as of other historical and worldly acts of great conquerors & princes, and also certain books of examples and doctrine, many noble and diverse gentlemen of this realm of England came and demanded me [asked me] many and oftentimes wherefore that I have not do made & enprint the noble history of the Saint Grail and of the most renowned Christian king, first and chief of the three best Christian and worthy, King Arthur, which ought most to be remembered among us English men tofore [before] all other Christian kings. For it is notoriously known through the universal world that there been ix worthy & the best that ever were.

Caxton then explains the Nine Worthies, three pagan—Hector, Alexander, and Julius Caesar; three Jewish—Joshua, David, and Judas Maccabaeus; and three Christian—Arthur, Charlemagne, and Godfrey of Bouillon (Caxton's spelling is Boloyne). He had already printed Godfrey's story, and

> The said noble gentlemen [Caxton does not further identify them] instantly required me to emprint the history of the said noble king and conqueror King Arthur and of his knights, with the history of the Saint Grail, and of the death and ending of the said Arthur, affirming that I ought rather to enprint his acts and noble feats than of Godfrey of Boloyne or any of the other eight, considering that he was a man born within this realm and king and emperor of the same, and that there been in French diverse and many noble volumes of his acts, and also of his knights.

> To whom I answered that diverse men hold opinion that there was no such Arthur and that all such books as been made of him been but feigned and fables, by cause that some chronicles make of him no mention nor remember [of] him no thing nor of his knights, whereto they answered, and one in special said that in him that should say or think that there was never such a king called Arthur might well be aretted [counted] great folly and blindness. For he said that there were many evidences of the contrary. First ye may see his sepulcher in the monastery of Glastonbury; and also in *Polychronicon,* in the v book, the sixth chapter, and in the seventh book, the xxiii chapter, where his body was buried and after found and translated to the said monastery. Ye shall see also in the history of Bochas [Boccaccio] in his book *De casu principum* [*De casibus virorum illustrium*] part of his noble acts and also of his fall; also Galfrydus in his Brutysshe book [Geoffrey of Monmouth in his British book, *Historia regum Britanniae*] recounteth his life; and in diverse places of En-

gland many remembrances been yet of him and shall remain perpetually, and also of his knights. First in the Abbey of Westminster at Saint Edward's shrine remaineth the print of his seal in red wax closed in beryl, in which is written *Patricius Arthurus, Britannie, Gallie, Germanie, Dacie, Imperator.* Item: in the Castle of Dover ye may see Gawain's skull & Cradok's mantle; at Winchester the Round Table, in other places Lancelot's sword and many other things.

> Then all these things considered, there can no man reasonably gainsay but there was a king of this land named Arthur. For in all places Christian and heathen he is reputed and taken for one of the ix worthy and the first of the three Christian men, and also he is more spoken of beyond the sea, more books made of his noble acts, than there be in England, as well in Dutch, Italian, Spanish, and Greek as in French. And yet of record remain in witness of him in Wales in the town of Camelot the great stones & marvellous works of iron lying under the ground, & royal vaults which diverse now living hath seen, wherefore, it is a marvel why he is no more renowned in his own country, save only it accordeth to the word of God, which saith that no man is accept[ed] for a prophet in his own country.

> Then all these things foresaid alleged I could not well deny but that there was such a noble king named Arthur and reputed one of the ix worthy & first & chief of the Christian men; & many noble volumes be made of him & of his noble knights in French which I have seen & read beyond the sea, which been not had in our maternal tongue; but in Welsh been many & also in French & some in English, but nowhere nigh all.

> Wherefore such as have late been drawn out briefly into English, I have after the simple cunning that God hath sent to me, under the favor and correction of all noble lords and gentlemen enprysed [undertaken] to enprint a book of the noble histories of the said King Arthur and certain of his knights, after a copy unto me delivered, which copy Sir Thomas Malory did take out of certain books of French and reduced it into English. And I according to my copy have done set it in print, to the intent that noble men may see and learn the noble acts of chivalry, the gentle and virtuous deeds, that some knights used in those days, by which they came to honor; and how they that were vicious were punished and often put to shame and rebuke; humbly beseeching all noble lords and ladies and all other estates of what estate or degree they been of, that shall see and read in this said book and work, that they take the good and honest acts in their remembrance and to follow the same, wherein they shall find many joyous and pleasant histories and noble & renowned acts of humanity, gentleness, and chivalries. For herein may be seen noble chivalry, courtesy, humanity, friendliness, hardiness, love, friendship, cowardice, murder, hate, virtue, and sin. Do after the good and leave the evil, and it shall bring you to good fame and renown. And for to pass the time this book shall be pleasant to read in; but for to give

faith and believe that all is true that is contained herein, ye be at your liberty; but all is written for our doctrine and for to beware that we fall not to vice ne sin, but t'exercise and follow virtue, by which we may come and attain to good fame and renown in this life, and after this short and transitory life to come unto everlasting bliss in heaven, the which He grant us that reigneth in heaven, the blessed Trinity. Amen.

Caxton equates the value of Arthur's story to its historicity; he states that the evidence alleged by his gentlemen-visitors persuaded him to print the book. But the **"Prologue"** expresses a remaining skepticism about the full historicity of the accounts of Arthur. Caxton also knows that a printed book ought to be edifying; he knows that not all the stories about Arthur and his knights are moral; and so he resorts to advising his readers to follow the good examples and to shun the bad ones, despite the fact that "all is written for our doctrine," a biblical quotation which Chaucer before him had used to excuse naughty stories. Finally, the stories can be read for entertainment, "to pass the time" pleasantly.

Insight into the significance of *Le Morte d'Arthur* can be gained through a comparison of the group of books which Caxton printed on the subject of the three Christian worthies: *Godfrey of Boloyne* (1481), a straight historical account in which fact is only moderately tempered by the author's point of view; *Charles the Great* (1485), a loose, rather aimless assortment of traditional materials assembled with some sense of dramatic development and coherence but lacking any distinct plot or theme; *Four Sons of Aymon* [1488], another Charlemagne romance which is somewhat more tightly constructed than *Charles the Great;* and *Le Morte d'Arthur.* It is useful to examine these four books in the order here given so as to observe the development of the prose narrative from factual history to fiction in the romance tradition which comes close to constituting the novel.

William of Tyre, whose dates are about 1130 to about 1190, became archbishop of Tyre in 1175. He wrote a Latin history which begins with the First Crusade, 1096-1099, and its immediately antecedent history and which is still regarded as a standard and reliable account. Caxton translated from a French version, somewhat modified, of William's *Historia rerum in partibus transmarinis gestarum,* concerned with Godfrey of Bouillon (1061?-1100). Caxton's translation is called by various titles: *Godfrey of Boloyne* or *Siege and Conquest of Jerusalem* or, for the Roman Emperor Heraclius, *Eracles.* The first of these titles seems most clearly indicative of Caxton's intention to relate the story to one of the Christian worthies.

In Caxton's translated portion of the history, William develops the story of the crusade through its various sieges, negotiations, and trials; and he finally comes to the crowning of Godfrey as king of Jerusalem. William deals bluntly with the difficulties of the crusaders. At the siege of Antioch, the scarcity of food, the high prices, and the prevalence of rain and death cause many to desert. Christians eat camels, asses, horses, dogs, and cats; and even cannibalism is reported. At Jerusalem, things are no better: heat, dust, and lack of water cause anguish as great as the hunger at Antioch. Beasts die, rot in the sun, and add the stench of their carcasses to the crusaders' grievous pain of thirst.

The valor and nobility of Godfrey contrast with the shame and suffering experienced during this crusade. The eldest of four valiant brothers, Godfrey is a devout man; and he honors good and religious men, keeps his word, scorns vanity, and is generous and kind. Although small in stature, he is remarkable for his strength and for the ease with which he bears his armor. In battle, he delivers a mighty blow which cuts an armor-clad Turk into two pieces, one of which falls to the ground while the other remains in the saddle. When it appears that Godfrey's chief vice is a too great love of going to church, he is elected king of Jerusalem; but his meekness and humility cause him to refuse to wear a king's crown in the city where Christ wore the crown of thorns. Godfrey lives to rule only a year.

Although William of Tyre's history is the result of conscientious, intelligent reporting, he is clearly so impressed by the contrast between the ignominious conduct of some of the crusaders and the virtue of Godfrey that he plays up the difference. In Caxton's translation, *Godfrey of Boloyne* is given focus and continuity because it isolates from William of Tyre's longer account a single central hero who is engaged in a single central action. Such selection can be part of the process by which fiction shapes unity from the diversity of life; but *Godfrey of Boloyne* remains historical and biographical, not fictional; for intelligence, sympathy, and judgment, but not imagination, have worked upon the material.

Caxton's Charlemagne stories are less factual than his *Godfrey,* less flattering to the hero, and generally less focused in plot. In Caxton's *Charles the Great,* which is divided into three books, the character of Charles is not favorably presented. He blusters and threatens, but his peers Oliver and Fierabras perform in a more creditable fashion. In Book I, the founding of the kingdom of France is traced back to one of Aeneas's companions, a man named Francus; the text names the holders of the French throne from Francus to Charles, and it then tells of Charles's succor of Jerusalem, whither he is led by a bird and whence he returns with miracle-working relics. Book II concerns a battle between Oliver, one of Charles's peers, and Fierabras, a gigantic and noble pagan who is eventually converted to Christianity, in a loose narrative which includes many attendant circumstances. Book III deals with Charles's being led by a vision to emerge from retirement to rescue the shrine of St. James of Galicia from the Saracens. During his return to France, he loses Roland through the treachery of Ganelon, the story made famous in a different version in *The Song of Roland.* The sequence of events from book to book is governed by no discernible purpose.

In *Four Sons of Aymon,* Charles is even less great than in *Charles the Great.* In *Four Sons of Aymon,* which is one of the "rebel vassal" stories, the four sons—Reynawde, Alarde, Guichard and Richarde—fall into enmity with Charles and engage in a blood feud which sets father against sons. Charles's pettiness is best illustrated in the episode in which Reynawde surrenders his horse Bayard to Charles. When Charles has a stone fastened about Bayard's neck and casts him into a river, the narrative directs our response to the episode by its description of the grief of Charles's men at such cruelty. The compiler of *Four Sons of Aymon,* whoever he may have been, has escaped from the reverence for heroes that has often been dictated by history, but he has created a contradictory, not a complex, character. The extended length of *Four Sons of Aymon* and its prosaic style render it dull in manner and detail. In translating and in printing this story, Caxton contributed more to the history than to the grandeur of the chivalric romance.

Without Caxton's stories of Godfrey and Charles the Great, fifteenth century English literature would be different, but different chiefly in bulk. If Caxton's final reply to the "diverse gentlemen" who came to his shop to persuade him to print Malory's *Morte d'Arthur* had been "no," the shape of English literature would have been radically altered. We would have a heritage of Arthurian stories, to be sure, but not the long prose cradle-to-grave English narrative which *Le morte d'Arthur* supplies. For four hundred and forty-nine years no fifteenth century text of Malory was known except Caxton's printed edition, and all subsequent editions of Malory were based on Caxton's.

Then, in 1934, W. F. Oakeshott discovered a fifteenth century Malory manuscript. Called the Winchester manuscript from the place of its discovery, it is judged by scholars to be neither a manuscript directly from Malory's hand nor one which he supervised. But even though the Winchester manuscript is not a definitive text, it offers an opportunity for comparing Caxton's version with that of another independent copy. Caxton's edition itself is extant in one perfect copy in the Morgan Library in New York City and in one damaged copy in the John Rylands Library in Manchester, England; these two copies contain a number of different readings. One of the miracles of modern printing has brought facsimile editions of both Caxton's Malory from the Morgan copy and the Winchester manuscript within reach of scholars.

Readers have known from the beginning that Caxton exercised his judgment in editing *Le morte d'Arthur;* for he states, in both Prologue and Epilogue, he has done so. The Epilogue reads:

> Thus endeth this noble and joyous book entitled *Le morte d'Arthur,* notwithstanding it treateth of the birth, life, and acts of the said King Arthur, of his noble knights of the Round Table, their marvellous enquestes [knightly ventures; *The Oxford English Dictionary* cites Malory and Caxton in *Blanchardin and Eglantine* as its first examples of this usage] and adventures, th' achieving of the Sangreal, and in th' end the dolorous death and departing out of this world of them all, which book was reduced into English by Sir Thomas Malory, knight, as afore is said, and by me divided into xxi books, chaptered and enprinted and finished in th' Abbey [of] Westminster the last day of July, the year of Our Lord MCCCClxxxv.

> *Caxton me fieri fecit.*

Comparison enables us to see how Caxton's printed text differs from the Winchester manuscript; although it does not enable us to determine precisely what Caxton's own manuscript contained, we can examine with profit some of the differences between the Winchester and Caxton texts. Caxton's comment in the Epilogue that *Le morte d'Arthur* embraces the whole life of Arthur and his knights suggests that the narrative is a continuous if somewhat episodic whole. The Winchester manuscript contains eight *explicits,* or end notes, which bring the work to a series of conclusions. Warm debate exists among scholars over the question of whether Malory meant to provide one unified work or a series of separate tales. It is evident that Caxton, if he worked from a manuscript with the full eight explicits and their possible implication of the division of the text into separate tales, chose to treat the matter as one tale.

Turning eight tales into one would constitute a major editorial decision, one well beyond the division of the material into books and chapters. A comparison of a short passage from the two versions shows also the frequent small differences which exist between the two editions. The passages quoted come from folio 148, v, in Winchester and from Book VIII, Chapter 1, in Caxton. The "W" in the left margin indicates the Winchester text; the "C," the Caxton:

W	Here begynnyth the fyrste boke of Syr Tristrams
C	Here foloweth the viij book the which is the first book of sir Tristram
W	de lyones and who was his fadir and hys modyr and how he
C	de Lyones/& who was his fader & his moder/& hou he
W	was borne and fostyrd and how he was made knyght of Kynge Marke of Cornuayle
C	was borne and fosteryd / And how he was made knyghte
W	There was a kynge that hyght Melyodas and he was lorde
C	Hit was a kyng that hyghte Melyodas / and he was lord
W	of the contrey of lyones and this Melyodas was
C	and kynge of the countre of Lyonas And this Melyodas was
W	a lykly knyght as ony was p^t tyme lyvyng and by fortune
C	a lykely knyght as ony was that tyme lyuynge / And by fortune
W	he wedded kynge Markis sist of Cornuayle and she was
C	he wedded kynge Markys syster of Cornewaille / And she was
W	called Elyzabeth that was called bothe good and fayre and
C	called Elyzabeth that was callyd bothe good and fair And

W   at that tyme kynge Arthure regned and he
       was hole kynge
C   at that tyme kynge Arthur regned / and he
       was hole kynge

W   of Ingelonde. Walys. Scotlonde and of
       many othir realmys
C   of England / walys and Scotland & of many
       other royammes

W   how be hit p^r were many kynges that were
       lordys of many
C   how be it there were many kynges that were
       lordes of many

W   countreyes But all they helde p^r londys of
       kynge Arthure
C   countreyes / but alle they held their landes
       of kyng Arthur/

W   ffor in Walys were •ii• kynges and in the
       Northe were many kynges
C   for in walys were two kynges/and in the
       north were many kynges/

W   and in Cornuayle and in the weste were•ii•
       kynges. Also
C   And in Cornewail and in the west were two
       kynges / ¶Also

W   in Irelonde were •ii• or •iii• kynges and all
       were undir the
C   in Irland were two or thre kynges and al
       were vnder the

W   obeysaunce of kynge Arthure so was p^e
       kynge of ffraunce
C   obeissaunce of kyng Arthur / So was the
       kynge of Fraunce

W   and the kyng of Bretayne and all the lord-
       shyppis unto Roome /
C   and the kyng of Bretayn and all the lord-
       shippes vnto Rome /

Caxton's text is slightly more modern than the Winchester: Winchester uses the old character þ (thorn) where Caxton prints *th*. It uses contractions such as p^r for *there* or p^e for *the*. Neither is heavily punctuated, but Caxton's virgule (/) provides a useful clue to syntax. The spelling in the two versions differs, but the twentieth century reader would find it difficult to choose between them for spelling preferences. Caxton cannot resist the impulse to use doublets: "lord" becomes "lord and king."

In studying the two versions of Malory, however, it becomes apparent that the essential change which Caxton makes is not in details: lordys, lordes; helde, held; londys, landes. Rather, it is in Caxton's large excisions in the account of Arthur and the Emperor Lucius. The extent and nature of these changes—ones too extensive to quote—can be most readily perceived by examining the Emperor Lucius story in the edition by Eugène Vinaver which gives the Winchester text at the top of each page and the Caxton version on the lower portion. Caxton has clearly exerted a great editorial effort in compressing the material.

The editor's duty of fidelity to a text sat somewhat lightly upon Caxton as he edited Malory, perhaps because he had reservations about the book. Caxton's various prologues and epilogues indicate that he valued factuality, edification, diversion, and style. His **"Prologue to *Le morte d'Arthur"*** asserts that he had been persuaded that Arthur is an historical figure, but his full belief in the stories clustered around Arthur can hardly be asserted. The **"Prologue"** directs attention to the possible moral profit to be gained from reading *Le morte*—if the reader follows the good examples and not the evil ones. Caxton recommends the book for pleasure reading; but on the subject of fair language, his **"Prologue"** is silent.

The case can also be made that Caxton's alterations of *Le morte d'Arthur* are in harmony with Malory's own efforts. Malory's explicits indicate that he wished to make the vast body of Arthurian lore conveniently available to English readers, and he was concerned with controlling the mass and shape of his materials. In his punctuation and spelling, designed to give recognizable shape to words and sentences, in his divisions of material into books and chapters, and deletions, Caxton seems to have had the same goal of forcing the material into comprehensible form. A twentieth century editor who uses modern spelling and punctuation and who divides sentences and paragraphs in conformity to contemporary practice is doing precisely the same thing that Caxton did, and for the same reason.

Although Malory's *Le Morte d'Arthur* is composed from a great body of disparate materials, it achieves a central focus: a group of peers sworn to a common goal gather in a circle around a common table and serve a central and peerless leader. When Arthur takes unworthy actions, as in the begetting of Mordred, who eventually kills his father, and when, for the peerless but mortal leader Arthur, the knights substitute the peerless and immortal quest of the Grail, the temporal circle of the Round Table is broken. Arthur is a hero, but he is not the ultimate hero, and the fact that he can be equaled or bettered by deeply flawed Lancelot demonstrates that lack. There is an archetypal, unified, and significant theme in *Le Morte d'Arthur.* We cannot claim preternatural perceptions for Caxton; but when he called Malory's book *Le Morte d'Arthur,* he made no mistake. The book is not *King Arthur and His Knights of the Round Table;* it is *The Death of Arthur,* the end of a temporal ideal, the death of chivalry.

Le Morte d'Arthur has the simple and incontrovertible evidence of a host of readers to testify to its success, despite the failure of Malory and Caxton to make it a perfect book. It is better than *The Recuyell of the Historyes of Troye* because it has its materials under better control; better than *Jason* or *Charles the Great* because it has found a more significant theme; better than *Four Sons of Aymon* because it draws less fixed and arbitrary lines between good and evil—Malory can work with amphibologies. It is better as a story, though not as history, than *Godfrey of Boloyne* because the storyteller can select and shape material as the historian must not.

LeMorte d'Arthur is too long; too many knights trase and traverse and foyne too many times. But it is an effective story; it is, as Caxton knew, a story of "the knowledge of good . . . involved and interwoven with the knowledge of evil" and redeemable only in death; a story with a moral;

perhaps a story made from history; but a story. (pp. 86-102)

Frieda Elaine Penninger, in her William Caxton, *Twayne Publishers, 1979, 175 p.*

Norman Blake (essay date 1984)

[*In the following excerpt, Blake emphasizes Caxton's use of prologues and epilogues as promotional pieces for his publications.*]

[The] problem of publishing printed books is how to sell multiple copies of the same work. To give his texts appeal to his audience Caxton included prologues and epilogues. These are not found in all his printed books, because not all of them needed to be promoted in the same way. As a general rule he did not include promotional material in editions of English poets because their works were usually well enough known to be sold without this support. The poets he printed were in the courtly tradition and most had been dead for some time; he did not produce the works of living poets. One work that was provided with a prologue is the second edition of the *Canterbury Tales.* This example is significant because it reveals that the market for works of this kind was limited and that Caxton had to persuade people who already had one edition to buy another. It does not follow that what he wrote in this prologue reflects the truth, though it has often been taken at face value by modern scholars. The prologue is worth looking at in depth.

He opens with a rhetorical flourish, "Grete thankes, lawde and honour ought to be gyven unto the clerkes, poetes and historiographs," which is modelled upon the opening of his own prologue to the *Polychronicon* which he had borrowed earlier from the prologue to the *Historical Library* by Diodorus Siculus. The opening is not as suitable as it might be because it is more concerned with the writing of history than of poetry, though Chaucer is described as a philosopher. Among the noble writers Chaucer is especially to be praised, Caxton continues, because he embellished English "eschewyng prolyxyte, castyng away the chaf of superfluyte, and shewyng the pyked grayn of sentence utteryd by crafty and sugred eloquence." These sentiments are borrowed from Lydgate's praises of Chaucer—and Lydgate was a poet Caxton knew well and whose output he may have imitated. In other words the opening sentences of the prologue are modelled by Caxton on other works so that he can praise Chaucer in a suitable rhetorical way. The potential purchasers needed to be impressed by the style to understand that the work itself was of some literary excellence. Caxton continues by turning to the *Canterbury Tales,* which contains accounts of the pilgrims and tales "whyche ben of noblesse, wysedom, gentylesse, myrthe, and also of very holynesse and vertue, wherin he fynysshyth thys sayd booke." Unfortunately people had tampered with the text so that it contained parts that were not genuine. Six years previously Caxton had himself been brought a poor text of the poem which he had printed, supposing it to be satisfactory. These were then sold to gentlemen. However, one of them visited him to complain about the text and said that his father had a good manuscript which he would try to get his father to let the publisher have, if he agreed to print a sound text. Caxton accepted this proposal and the new text was produced.

The important thing to notice is that Caxton stresses the superiority of the second edition as compared with the first; it is said to have an authentic text. In actual fact the text of the second edition is if anything worse than that of the first, because it represents an amalgam of the first edition with the second manuscript. It was clearly important for Caxton to persuade his clientele that they were reading a better text, even though they were not. This behaviour is common enough in sales promotions. It is also significant that he does not mention who the gentleman in question was; he remains conveniently anonymous. Similarly the gentleman's father is not identified. Both are probably fictitious. Caxton invented the gentleman and his father to underline the request by the gentleman and the unwillingness of the father to part with the volume. In this way he is able to suggest that there is a demand for a new edition, while at the same time he can show that the text he is using is so valued by someone it was not easily relinquished to allow the printer to publish the second edition. By this story he is able to show how attractive his edition is so that all those with a first edition can be encouraged to get the second as well.

Window commemorating Caxton in St. Margaret's, Westminster.

Reprints, however, represent a special case. For the most part Caxton included prologues and epilogues to the translated works, for they were new to the English audience and therefore needed introducing to them. Often, these works had prologues and epilogues in their French versions, and on many occasions he adapted what he found there. The result is an amalgam between a translation of the French prologue and pieces added by Caxton, though he did sometimes include two prologues, one by the original author and his own. In the *History of Troy* he included a preface before the prologue, because there was one in Lefèvre's version. In it he refers to Lefèvre's work and to his dedication of that work to Duke Philip of Burgundy before he introduces details about his own translation and its dedication to Margaret. The preface is followed by the translator's prologue. In this he refers to the French version which contained "many strange and mervayllous historyes wherein I had grete pleasyr and delyte as well for the novelte of the same as for the fayr langage of Frenshe." The book contains excellent stories and is written in an approved style. He therefore decided to make a translation which he gave up in despair because of his faulty style. It was then that Margaret encouraged him to continue, provided he made some improvements in his style. After his own prologue he included a translation of Lefèvre's prologue. In the epilogues he refers to Lydgate's poem about the Troy story, which may have prompted him initially to make a prose translation, and to the fact that he had been asked for copies of his translation by so many gentlemen that he was forced to print it. All these details are included to attract attention and hence custom. The book was originally made for a duke of Burgundy; the translation was approved by and dedicated to Margaret, duchess of Burgundy. The story was exciting and written in a good French style. The account of Troy as found in Lefèvre's version is mostly new in England, though parts of it had been covered by Lydgate who was one of England's great poets. The translation has both novelty and tradition in its favour. Finally it was in demand among gentlemen and so it is implied it ought to be acquired by all gentlemen.

We can see from this work that Caxton needed to emphasise patronage, novelty, style, and demand among the characteristics of his books. These features reappear constantly in the prologues and epilogues, though they are supplemented by others such as the good quality of the second edition of the *Canterbury Tales.* However, although he had a formal dedication in *History of Troy* which was expressed in the preface, this was dropped in later works. It was important simply that the book be associated with someone fashionable, not that it should be formally dedicated to him or her. For the most part he liked to have a story about the translation's genesis, as here, for that helped to underline the book's attractiveness, but he was quite prepared to invent the details when necessary. To start with, the prefatory matter was rather long partly because he had not learned to amalgamate his own comments with those of the original author, but this changed as he gained in experience. Much of what we today know about Caxton and the contemporary taste for literature was introduced into the prologues and epilogues

which were part of the promotional side of his business; it therefore needs to be interpreted with care.

As a final example of the way he set out his prologues and epilogues we may consider the prologue to his edition of Malory's *Morte Darthur,* a work peculiarly associated with Caxton. The prologue was probably written after the rest of the work had been set up in type, and so it may be later than the epilogue in which Caxton says briefly that the book is about Arthur and his knights, that it was translated by Sir Thomas Malory knight, and that it was divided by Caxton into twenty-one books. The prologue, however, is lengthy and was designed to make this version of King Arthur better known to potential purchasers by relating it to the general history of Arthur. The prologue opens with an impressive sentence which refers first to other books published by Caxton of a historical or didactic nature and then to a visit which "many noble and dyvers gentylmen of thys royame of Englond" paid to him to complain that he had never printed anything about King Arthur who was the most famous of all English kings. In this way Caxton is able to begin his prologue with a rhetorical sentence, to refer to other works he had published, and to imply that he produced his version of King Arthur's deeds because there was a great demand for the book from unnamed gentlemen. He then goes on to refer to the theme of the Nine Worthies, consisting of three pagans, three Jews, and three Christians. The three Christians were Arthur, Charles the Great, and Godfrey of Bouillon. Caxton had published the deeds of Godfrey and was to publish those of Charles. The gentlemen demanded to know why he had not published anything about Arthur who was an Englishman seeing that he had printed the deeds of Godfrey. Caxton's reply to this question was that many people considered Arthur to be fictitious and not historical.

The gentlemen replied that it was absolute madness not to believe in Arthur's historicity—and at this stage in the discussion one of the gentlemen present was most vociferous in the debate about Arthur's genuineness. This gentleman is not named. The historical proofs of Arthur's existence are listed. Caxton then goes on to say that he has read many accounts of Arthur in French, and that other accounts exist in Welsh and English though these are not complete. He has therefore decided to print a version translated by Malory from French from "a copye unto me delyverd." Finally he gives a very generalised account of the contents and says that he presents the book "unto alle noble prynces, lordes and ladyes, gentylmen or gentylwommen, that desyre to rede or here redde of the noble and joyous hystorye of the grete conquerour and excellent kyng." Thus although he claims he had been asked to publish the work by certain gentlemen, he dedicates it to all gentlemen and gentlewomen rather than to those who had asked for it or to the one who was most vociferous in proving Arthur's historicity. He does not even say how he acquired the manuscript, although the implication is that he was lent it by a gentleman. It seems likely that most of what is found in this prologue is fictitious and that it was included to arouse interest in Arthur. Doubts about his historicity are raised and stilled; accounts of Arthur in other languages are mentioned; Arthur's place as a king of England and as one of the Nine Worthies is brought up; the demand for a work about Arthur by members of the aristocracy is specified; and the general moral and historical nature of the work is stressed. It all adds up to clever propaganda to promote the book.

Several points emerge from this discussion of Caxton's prologues and epilogues. He imitated the models found in his sources and was able to develop them to answer his particular needs. They formed a vehicle for his sales propaganda. As part of this promotion he needed to refer to the demand for each book by members of the gentry and to its wider appeal because of its links with French culture. At the same time he did not shrink from inventing stories that created an interest in his books and that introduced some apparent controversy. The whole approach is sophisticated, and this needs to be borne in mind when assessing Caxton's overall contribution to literature and publishing. It might be claimed that Caxton is the first English critic because he is forced to evaluate a book critically in contemporary terms in order to try and sell it. From his comments we can gauge how people responded to literary works and what qualities they expected to find in them. (pp. 400-03)

> *Norman Blake, "William Caxton," in* Middle English Prose: A Critical Guide to Major Authors and Genres, *edited by A. S. G. Edwards, Rutgers University Press, 1984, pp. 389-412.*

Joseph M. Levine   (essay date 1987)

[*Levine is an American educator and historian who has written several studies on the development of English letters. In the excerpt below he considers the historical perspective of Caxton's publications, noting particularly the practice of blending fact and fiction.*]

It was just three weeks before the battle of Bosworth Field, on July 31, 1485, that William Caxton finished printing his version of Thomas Malory's *Morte Darthur.* It is certainly one of his most impressive efforts, and for the student of historiography it remains his most absorbing. To be sure, it has not always been of much interest to modern historians, whose concern must be with the present value of medieval sources and who have generally found medieval narrative wanting, except perhaps for the contemporary portions of medieval chronicles. If, however, we prefer to know what the Middle Ages made of the past, rather than what we make of past medieval politics, it becomes necessary to cast a wider net. And here Caxton and his publications offer an unusual opportunity. As the first of the English printers, he seems to have set himself deliberately to selecting and editing all that he thought best and most representative in the literature of his time. This included chronicles, of course, but it also embraced some other characteristic representations of the past— romances and saints' lives, for example, which he deliberately placed alongside the more sober narratives. For Caxton, they were all "histories," good stories but also true and useful descriptions of past times.

No doubt this is a little disconcerting to the modern reader—sometimes even to the professional medievalist. For most of us, the distinction between history and fiction is fundamental, although we cannot always make out the precise boundaries; and we insist upon a sharp separation between the novels and the histories that lie on our bookshelves and in our libraries. In the Middle Ages, manuscripts abound in which poems and chronicles, romances and saints' lives, are jumbled together without apparent distinction. Medieval chroniclers invariably, and often deliberately, tell imaginary stories, while medieval storytellers almost always give sources for their inventions about the past. There is only a little theory for either history or fiction, and nothing much to keep them apart, so that the writer of whatever kind promises faithfully to follow his authority, whether or not he has one and whether or not it is reliable, and the reader is in no position to tell the difference. If the medieval historian often appears to be writing fiction, the medieval writer of fiction invariably pretends to be writing history.

As we shall see, the difficulty was compounded by the relative indifference of the medieval reader to the literal meaning of a narrative, which he accepted as only one, and that not always the most important, way to decipher a text—or to read the past. No doubt everyone, then as now, knew that there was a difference between a lie and the truth, between a faithful description and a fanciful one, but it was quite another thing to come to value that distinction above any other and to find out how to establish it in practice. In short, it was necessary to devise some explicit criteria for recovering the historicity of an event, and a practical method of proceeding, before it could become possible to define the modern ideas of either history or fiction, much less to defend their autonomy. It was first necessary to invent a new idea of fact, a notion that the liberal representation of past or present could be interesting in and for itself, or for some present purpose, and that it could and should be radically distinguished from a spurious or imaginary description. For this, new motives as well as new means were required. But nothing of this was done, nor was it much attempted, as far as I can see, until well after Caxton's time. Meanwhile, the modern reader continues to be baffled by the confusing mixture of history and fiction that he finds everywhere in medieval narrative and is often at a loss to understand both the intentions and the reassurances of his author.

Take Caxton's first published work, the *Recuyell of the Historyes of Troye* (1474). Here is a tale that begins with the rivalry of Saturn and Jupiter, recounts at length the exploits of Hercules, and culminates in the eventual destruction of Troy by the Greeks. Hercules is introduced as the flower of medieval knighthood; he displays his chivalry at a great tournament before a resplendent audience of lords and ladies who look on from a grandstand. Stranger still, the legendary Callisto takes the veil and enters a cloister while Jupiter must disguise himself as a nun in order to take advantage of her. The ancient gods are in this way each "euhemerized" and brought up to date; as Caxton explains (following his source), it was the custom in those times to exalt all those who did great deeds or served the commonwealth and to turn them into gods. So poetry was turned—or returned—into pseudohistory.

Caxton, as always, follows his authorities and appears to accept their stories without question.

Caxton's immediate source was a recent French romance by Raoul Lefevre, chaplain to the Duke of Burgundy. The influence of the culture of Burgundy upon Caxton (who grew up in it) and upon his English contemporaries was profound. Caxton had originally intended, he says, to stop with a translation of the first part of Lefevre, since he knew that the English poet John Lydgate had already written about the fall of Troy. However, his patroness, the Duchess of Burgundy, persuaded him to complete his story, since Lydgate had written in verse "and also peradventure had translated some other author than this is." Different writers, Caxton explains, have different tastes and tell different stories.

Typically, Caxton did not worry much about the differences. When he had finished his translation, he added an epilogue asking his readers not to be concerned about the subject matter of his book, "though it accord not to the translation of other which have written it." Divers men, he repeats, have made divers books, and they do not all agree about what the ultimate sources—Dares, Dictys, or Homer—report. Nor was this surprising, since Homer favored his Greek countrymen, while Dares supported the Trojans, and everyone was likely to mistake the proper names. What did it matter, since on the main point all agreed? All reported the terrible destruction of Troy and the deaths of many great princes, knights, and common people, "which may be ensample to all men during the world how dreadful and jeopardous it is to begin a war and what harms, losses and deaths followeth." In short, the moral of the tale was unimpeachable, irrespective of its literal veracity, and the moral justified the telling and retelling of the story.

Of course, Caxton was only a printer, at best a translator, and one must be careful not to generalize too easily. Nevertheless, he was an intelligent reader at the least, publishing for a sophisticated audience, and we may be sure that his indifference to fact was not unusual. For us, everything in our history depends upon the sources, and our first instinct (as historians) is to work backward in time through each version of the tale and every recension of the text to the originals, which we then try to evaluate and weigh as evidence. For Caxton, it was enough to find a recent authority and to concentrate on rewriting and translating it into a contemporary prose and setting. This appears to have been the ordinary method of both romance and chronicle. For the first two books, Caxton and Lefevre were content with Boccaccio's *Genealogy of the Gods,* and encyclopedic handbook of classical mythology that had already digested the ancient legends and retailed them as history. They did not know and apparently did not care anything about Boccaccio's sources, which were in fact a mixed bag of ancients and moderns also treated without much discrimination. For the third book, they settled on a long and pedestrian work of the thirteenth century, the *Historia destructionis Troiae* of Guido della Columnis. They did not know, since Guido did not say, that he had relied in his turn largely on a twelfth-century poem by Benoit de Sainte-Maur, the *Roman de Troie.* What they did

notice was that Guido's work had been based ultimately on two purported eyewitness accounts by the ancient writers, Dictys Cretensis and Dares Phrygius. Caxton did not realize that Lydgate's poem had also depended on Guido (and so eventually on Benoit) and was thus based ultimately on the same two spurious authorities. Had he known this, he might possibly have worried a little more about their differences, though it is very doubtful that he would have known how to resolve them.

As for Dictys and Dares, we now believe that both were composed early in the Christian period in Greek and translated into Latin, the first probably in the fourth century, the second about two hundred years later. Dictys purports to be a Greek; Dares pretends to be a Trojan. Dares' work is prefaced with a letter in which "Cornelius Nepos" explains to his friend "Sallust" how he had discovered the lost history on a visit to Athens and then translated it. Dares was particularly admired in the Middle Ages as the first of the secular historians (preceding Herodotus) and for his Trojan bias, since all the Western nations, from ancient Rome to modern Burgundy, France and Britain, liked to trace their ancestry back to one or another of the fallen heroes of ancient Troy. It was not an impressive narrative, but it was preferred to Homer, who presumably wrote long after the events, had a Greek bias (so it was thought), and in any case could only be read during the Middle Ages in a meager Latin epitome. It was only after Caxton's time that the two spurious works came under suspicion and only much later that they were decisively exposed as frauds. It was not easy to discard what had been so long accepted as the first beginning and foundation of all Western secular history.

Of course, neither Dares nor Dictys portrayed a medieval Troy. That was left to Benoit and his followers, who visualized it in contemporary chivalric terms. On the whole, the Middle Ages did not share our sense of the past and was untroubled by anachronism; the past was rarely differentiated from the present, however distant. In this respect, Lydgate's *Troy Book* was no better than Lefevre's, though it may have been a superior piece of literature. Like Caxton and Lefevre, Lydgate accepted his authority without question and devoted his own efforts simply to versifying the tale, elaborating its contemporary setting and adding long didactic passages to point the moral. The function of the storyteller, he says, is to enliven the work "with many curious flowers of rhetoric to make us comprehend the truth." Lydgate no doubt thought of himself as a historian, and when his poem was published in the sixteenth century, it was accordingly proclaimed as the *Auncient Historie and onely Trewe and Syncere Cronicle of the Warres betwixte the Grecians and the Trojans* (1555). Guido was applauded then for his faithful digest of Dares and Dictys ("by due conference found wholly to agree") and Lydgate for his Chaucerian verse. Caxton on the other hand was derided for his "long tedious and brainless babbling, tending to no end, nor having any certain beginning." The criticism was not altogether inappropriate, but it had almost no historiographical significance. The only glimmer of something new was the notion in the preface that to print an old text faithfully, like Chaucer or Lydgate, it was first necessary to collate all the manuscripts.

Of this neither Caxton nor anyone else in the Middle Ages seems to have had any inkling, though here, if anywhere, lay the future of modern historiography.

Caxton went on publishing romances for the rest of his life, and there is no sign that he ever wavered in his belief that they were historically true. In 1477 he published his *Historie of Jason,* also from Lefevre by way of Dares and Guido, with the story of the Golden Fleece as a pendant to the story of Troy. The opening scene, where Hercules and Jason joust before the court of Thebes, is visualized carefully in a way that sounds just like the modern courts that Caxton knew in Burgundy and Britain. It appears that the more Lefevre or Caxton strove for historical verisimilitude—that is, the more they tried to persuade their audience of the reality of their stories—the more they made their narratives seem contemporary. When Jason is knighted for his prowess, he asks his prince only "that it please you to assign me a place where I may do feats chivalrous and knightly." When Caxton wanted to know about Jason's later career, he turned once again to Boccaccio's *Genealogy of the Gods.*

In 1481, Caxton translated *Godfrey of Bologne* from a French version of William of Tyre's Latin history of the first Crusade. Here was one of the best written and most reliable chronicles of the Middle Ages, though despite William's best efforts its history was soon turned into legend. (For Caxton, the work was "no fable, nor feigned, but all that is therein is true.") In the prologue Caxton remembers the "nine worthies"—the nine greatest heroes in human history—three pagans, three Hebrews, and three Christians: Hector, Alexander, and Julius Caesar; Joshua, David, and Judas Maccabeus; Arthur, Charlemagne, and Godfrey. By the end of the fifteenth century this canon of heroes had long been established and was familiar in chronicle and romance, painting, pageantry, and tapestry. Caxton singles out Hector, whose deeds were described by Ovid, Homer, Virgil, Dares, and Dictys, "each better than other rehearsing his noble works." They made Hector seem "as new and fresh as yet he lived." And he recalls Arthur with the "great and many volumes of Saint Grail, Galahad, and Lancelot de Lake, Gawain, Perceval, Lionel and Tristram." He also picks out Charlemagne for special notice, as though he was already thinking of the two works he was going to print in 1485: the *Morte Darthur* and *Charles the Great.* For the latter he translated another French work, a prose adaptation of a romance that told how the Saracen giant, Fierabras, who was defeated by Oliver, was baptized and sent to heaven. "The works of the ancient and old people," Caxton repeats, "ben for to give us ensample to live in good and virtuous operations." Unfortunately, Caxton does not say anything about the completely fictional love tale *Paris and Vienne* that he also published in 1485, but of the romantic fantasy *Blanchardyn and Eglantine* that he printed a few years later (1489), he recites the now familiar commonplaces: "In my judgment, it is as requisite other while to read in ancient histories of noble feats and valiant acts of arms and war which have been achieved in old time . . . as it is to occupy them and study over much in books of contemplation." As always, the chivalric ideal, timeless and exemplary, meant more to Caxton and his contemporaries than the literal reality of any of the tales they read, and the concrete example, historical or fictional, more than any philosophy.

The historical fictions of medieval romance had an almost exact counterpart in the historical fictions of medieval hagiography. The lives of the saints offered an alternative array of Christian heroes whose ascetic lives and marvelous deeds were also meant to encourage the reader or listener to emulation. Here also fact and fiction intermingled in subtle and sometimes surprising ways, although the details of Christian narrative, like those of romance, were rarely disputed. Caxton's proudest work may well have been his own version of the *Legenda aurea,* that vast compilation of hagiographical material that so delighted the later Middle Ages. His original was a Latin volume written sometime in the middle of the thirteenth century by an Italian bishop, Jacobus da Varagine. In nearly two hundred chapters, it recounted the festivals and saints of the church calendar, drawing on sources and a tradition that stretched back over a millennium, though characteristically, it reproduced much of its material—often verbatim—from the recent encyclopedia of Vincent of Beauvais. The role of the hagiographer was to compile and rewrite, and Jacobus was industrious and facile. He produced what was undoubtedly one of the most popular of all medieval works, extant still in over a thousand manuscripts and imitated and translated into most of the European languages. Caxton knew the Latin original but relied for the most part (as usual) on a French version as well as on a previous English translation. These he freely altered, adding several new lives and a great deal of fresh historical material drawn from the Bible, turning it into English either on his own or from another unknown source. The result was the most comprehensive version of the *Golden Legend* yet, some four hundred and fifty leaves and six hundred thousand words, an enormous labor that cost him more than a year to print (1482-83) but won him an annual gift from the Earl of Arundel of a buck in summer and a doe in winter.

Caxton hoped that the *Golden Legend* would give "profit to all those that shall read or hear it read and may increase in them virtue and expel vice and sin that by the example of the holy saints amend their living in this short life." His source, Jacobus, was no more concerned than any contemporary romance writer with evaluating the evidence and winnowing truth from fiction. If anything, Caxton was less so, even to the extent of expunging some of the occasional criticism that he found in the original. In this he followed the usual course of medieval hagiography. The modern Jesuit scholar Hippolyte Delehaye, writing from the vantage point of three hundred years of Bollandist scholarship, reminds us that the hagiographer is a poet, not a historian; that he cheerfully disregards facts, prefers general types to real individuals, and is willing to borrow indiscriminately to fill out and color his story in order to sustain interest. His one main concern is to edify. As a result, the saint's life is part biography, part panegyric, part moral lesson. It is true that there is often a historical element which it is the task of modern "scientific" history to detect. But sometimes the whole saint's life is a fiction invented or made up of entirely borrowed elements, like Lydgate's St. Amphibalus, accidentally transformed from the cloak (*amphimallus*) of St. Alban. Caxton knew there was a problem with his life of St. George—discrepancies in the sources about place names and chronology—and for once he, or rather Jacobus, sets them out plainly, but neither he nor the Italian had the faintest notion what to do about it. It never occurred to either of them that there might be no reliable source whatever for the fictional saint who, Caxton points out, was not only the patron saint of England and the cry of men of war, but who had given his name to the Order of the Garter and to the Chapel at Windsor Castle, and whose very heart presently rested there, "which Sigismund the Emperor of Almayn brought and gave for a gift and precious relic to King Harry the fifth."

The parallel between hagiography and romance has often been remarked. From the first appearance of the chivalric tales in the twelfth century, there is evidence that clerics read them and sometimes wrote them. Jongleurs, we know, were often entertained in religious houses. "The figures of romance," we are reminded, "invaded the churches themselves, creeping into the carvings of the portals, along the choirstalls, and into the historiated margins of the service books." Preachers used them to illustrate their sermons and their manuals of vices and virtues. Chrétien de Troyes, who did more than anyone in the twelfth century to invent and refurbish the Arthurian legends, seems to have been a cleric, as was John Lydgate, the monk of Bury, two hundred years later. (On the other hand, Robert de Boron, who was the first to try to make a coherent scheme of the cycle, and Thomas Malory, who was the last, were probably both knights.) At the same time, saint's life and legendary were directed more and more at the laity and turned into the vernacular, as with the *Golden Legend* or its English counterpart, the *Nova legenda Anglie*. Occasionally, the heroes of romance were transformed into saints, while romance writers and chroniclers drew heavily on hagiography. But the fusion was less than perfect, for the church remained perpetually on guard against the subversive morality of chivalry. The Grail romances that early entered into the Arthurian cycle and were retold by Malory in the *Morte Darthur* were one undoubted response, an attempt to Christianize the knight and turn his military ardor to religious purposes. "There are no knightly deeds so fine," exclaims the author of the *Perlesvaus,* "as those done for the adornment of the law of God." But for some, including Malory himself, it was the combative, adulterous Lancelot who remained the hero, even though it was Galahad who was chosen to win the Grail. Either way, and despite this persistent "clash of ideologies," it was legend, not history, that mattered, and no one in the Middle Ages seems to have wanted it any other way. (pp. 19-28)

> *Joseph M. Levine, "Caxton's Histories: Fact and Fiction at the Close of the Middle Ages,"* in his Humanism and History: Origins of Modern English Historiography, *Cornell University Press, 1987, pp. 19-53.*

FURTHER READING

Antin, David. "Caxton's *The Game and Playe of the Chesse.*" *Journal of the History of Ideas* XXIX, No. 2 (April 1968): 269-78.
> Examines Caxton's aims in translating and publishing *The Game and Playe of the Chesse* by analyzing the rules of the game and comparing them with Caxton's manuscript. Antin concludes that Caxton's purpose was to teach morality rather than the rules of chess.

Blake, N. F. *Caxton and His World.* London: Andre Deutsch, 1969, 256 p.
> Authoritative twentieth-century biography containing an exhaustive listing of Caxton's publications.

———. *Caxton's Own Prose.* London: Andre Deutsch, 1973, 187 p. Collection of Caxton's prologues and epilogues with an introduction providing information and critical commentary on Caxton's original writing.

———. "William Caxton Again in the Light of Recent Scholarship." *Dutch Quarterly Review* 12, No. 3 (1982): 162-82.
> Re-evaluation of Caxton's works arguing that the Burgundian influence on Caxton's choice of works for publication was less significant than had been previously held.

Bornstein, Diane. "William Caxton's Chivalric Romances and the Burgundian Renaissance in England." *English Studies* 57, No. 1 (February 1976): 1-10.
> Argues that Caxton was an integral part of a fifteenth-century "Burgundian renaissance" in England. Bornstein specifically notes Burgundian influences in Caxton's romances, chivalric works, and his prologues and epilogues.

Bühler, Curt F. *William Caxton and His Critics.* Syracuse, N.Y.: Syracuse University Press, 1960, 30 p.
> General overview of Caxton's contributions to English literature which asserts that the influence Caxton has exercised over the centuries has been due to his printing and wide dissemination of works rather than a superior writing ability.

Childs, Edmund. *William Caxton: A Portrait in a Background.* New York: St. Martin's Press, 1976, 190 p.
> Concise biography providing facts about Caxton in the context of European society in the fifteenth century.

Colvile, K. N. "William Caxton: Man of Letters." *The Quarterly Review* 248, No. 491 (January 1927): 165-78.
> Examines Caxton's choice of works for publication.

Crotch, W. J. B. *The Prologues and Epilogues of William Caxton.* London: Oxford University Press, 1928, 115 p.
> Complete collection of Caxton's original writings containing a substantial biographical introduction.

Duff, E. Gordon. *William Caxton.* New York: Burt Franklin, 1905, 118 p.
> Critical biography of Caxton which focuses on general descriptions of the works he translated and published, with special attention given to those the author judged as under-represented in other texts.

Gibbon, Edward. "An Address, &c." In *The English Essays of Edward Gibbon,* edited by Patricia B. Craddock, pp. 534-45. London: Oxford University Press, 1972.

Disparages Caxton's contribution to English literature on the basis of his seemingly unsophisticated choice of works for publication. Gibbon's remarks, made in 1793, set the tone of criticism until William Blades offered a countering view in the late nineteenth century.

Goodman, J. R. "Malory and Caxton's Chivalric Series, 1481-85." In *Studies in Malory,* edited by James W. Spisak, pp. 257-74. Kalamazoo: Medieval Institute Publications, Western Michigan University, 1985.

Examines Caxton's version of Malory's *Morte D'Arthur* in the context of the chivalric socio-political climate of fifteenth-century England. This essay also contains significant discussion of *Godefroy of Boloyne, Book of the Ordre of Chyualry,* and *Charles the Grete.*

Hall, Louis Brewer. "Caxton's *Eneydos* and the Redactions of Vergil." *Medieval Studies* XXII (1960): 136-47.

Compares Caxton's *Eneydos* with its medieval predecessors: *Excidium Troiae, Roman d'Eneas, Ilias Latina, Primera Crónica General* (the legend of Dido and Aeneas), and Chaucer's "Legend of Dido." Hall concludes that Caxton's version of Vergil's work is a transitional piece between medieval and Renaissance literature.

Hellinga, Lotte. *Caxton in Focus: The Beginning of Printing in England.* London: British Library, 1982, 109 p.

Examines the evidence for dating Caxton's books in order to establish an accurate chronology of the development of printing in English.

Howorth, Henry H. "The Importance of Caxton in the History of the English Language." *The Athenaeum* 104, No. 3500 (24 November 1894): 715-16.

Overview of Caxton's career in which Howorth praises his contributions to the English language and asserts that no one better reflected "the best English of his time."

————. "The Importance of Caxton in the History of the English Language II." *The Athenaeum* 105, No. 3514 (2 March 1895): 284.

Correction of the essay cited above. Howorth clarifies a miscommunicated point regarding Caxton's use of the highest standard of English in his translations, noting: "What I wished to say was that, contrary to a good deal of common prejudice, Caxton was not a provincial person, speaking an uncouth dialect, but that from his life and training he was very happily circumstanced for acquiring and for using the best standard English of his time."

Jeremy, Sister Mary. "Caxton's *Golden Legend* and Varagine's *Legenda Aurea.*" *Speculum* XXI, No. 2 (April 1946): 212-21.

Considers the "relationship between the plan, content and detail" of Caxton's *Golden Legend* and Varagine's *Legenda Aurea.*

————. "Caxton's *Life of S. Rocke.*" *Modern Language Notes* LXVII, No. 5 (May 1952): 313-17.

Suggests that Caxton's "Life of S. Rocke" in *The Golden Legend* was drawn from a Latin original.

Knight, Charles. *William Caxton: The First English Printer.* 1844. Reprint. London: William Clowes & Sons/Hardwick & Bogue, 1877, 158 p.

Detailed biography offering full account of Caxton's life and work.

Lathrop, H. B. "The First English Printers and Their Patrons." *The Library* III, No. 2 (1 September 1922): 69-96.

Addresses the criticism of Caxton's selection of seemingly unsophisticated works for publication by emphasizing the relationship between Caxton and his patrons.

Lucas, F. L. "Honest Ovid Among the Goths." In his *Authors Dead and Living,* pp. 39-45. New York: Macmillan Company, 1926.

Contrasts Caxton's translation of Ovid's *Metamorphoses* with the original. Lucas expresses disappointment with Caxton's version because of the simplicity and non-melodic nature of the language.

Markland, Murray F. "The Role of William Caxton." *Research Studies* XXVIII, No. 2 (June 1960): 47-60.

Explores various interpretations of available historical and autobiographical evidence to determine Caxton's own view of his role in relation to English letters.

Matheson, Lister M. "Printer and Scribe: Caxton, the *Polychronicon* and the *Brut.*" *Speculum* 60, No. 3 (July 1985): 593-614.

Argues that Caxton was indeed the author of portions of *The Chronicles of England* and the *Polychronicon,* using detailed comparison of the original sources and Caxton's versions as evidence of his claims.

Matthews, William. "Caxton and Malory: A Defense." In *Medieval Literature and Folklore Studies: Essays in Honor of Francis Lee Utley,* edited by Jerome Mandel and Bruce A. Rosenberg, pp. 77-95. New Brunswick, N.J.: Rutgers University Press, 1970.

Contends that Caxton's editorial practices were less arbitrary than many critics have claimed and specifically defends Caxton's edition of Malory's *Morte D'Arthur.*

McCarthy, Terence. "Caxton and the Text of Malory's Book 2." *Modern Philology* 71, No. 2 (November 1973): 144-52.

Examines Caxton's liberal editing of Book 2 of Morte d'Arthur.

Painter, George D. *William Caxton: A Quincentenary Biography of England's First Printer.* London: Chatto & Windus, 1976, 227 p.

Detailed biography of Caxton which seeks to clarify confusing information which was recorded by Blades, Duff and Crotch.

Plomer, Henry R. *William Caxton.* New York: Burt Franklin, 1925, 195 p.

Biography in which Plomer argues that Caxton's literary career was wrought from his unusual foresight, wisdom, and patriotic altruism.

Roberts, W. Wright. "William Caxton, Writer and Critic." *Bulletin of the John Rylands Library* 14, No. 2 (July 1930): 410-22.

Discusses Caxton's choice of works for publication and his influence on the development of English literature. Roberts views Caxton as a pioneer rather than an expert in the evolving English language.

Robinson, Grace Louise. "A Great-Grandfather Wordbook." *The Catholic World* CXVII, No. 701 (August 1923): 607-16.

Surveys Caxton's *Dialogues in French and English,* praising it as an "ancestor of the legion of modern texts for language" as well as a "forerunner . . . of twentieth-century works in the field of economics, industry, politics, and social and religious life."

Rutter, Russell. "William Caxton and Literary Patronage." *Studies in Philology* 84, No. 4 (Fall 1987): 440-70.
    Explores the various theories regarding Caxton's reliance upon patrons and how these theories affect the assessment of Caxton's achievements and career. Rutter also posits his own theory that Caxton was partially supported through patronage but that his success was due at least in part to his own business skills.

Stuart, Dorothy Margaret. "William Caxton: Mercer, Translator and Master Printer." *History Today* X, No. 4 (April 1960): 256-65.
    Concise biographical summary which integrates information about Caxton's literary pursuits with other significant personal and social events.

Geoffrey Chaucer

1340?-1400?

English poet, prose writer, and translator.

Widely regarded as the "father of English poetry," Geoffrey Chaucer is the foremost representative of Middle English literature. His *Canterbury Tales* (1478) is one of the most highly esteemed works in the English language, and its "General Prologue" is often acclaimed by critics and readers alike as "the most perfect poem in the English language." Notable among his other works are the *Book of the Duchess,* the *Parlement of Foules,* the *House of Fame, Troilus and Criseyde,* and the *Legend of Good Women.* Familiar with French, English, Italian, and Latin literature, Chaucer was able to meld characteristics of each into a unique body of work which affirmed the ascent of English as literary language. Chaucer's works, which reflect his consummate mastery of various literary genres, styles, and techniques, as well as his erudition, wit, and insight are regarded as classics of European literature.

Born into a family of London-based vintners sometime in the early 1340s, Chaucer had a long and distinguished career as a civil servant, serving three successive kings—Edward III, Richard II, and Henry IV. He first appears in household records in 1357 as a page in the service of Elizabeth, the Countess of Ulster and wife of Prince Lionel, the third son of Edward III. By 1359 he served in Edward's army in France and was captured during the unsuccessful siege of Rheims. The king contributed to his ransom the following year and Chaucer shortly thereafter must have entered the king's service, where, in various capacities, he would serve for the rest of his life. By 1366, Chaucer had married Philippa Pan, another courtier who had attended the Countess of Ulster. She was the sister of Katharine Swynford, who became mistress and subsequently wife to John of Gaunt, Edward III's fourth son and the primary power behind the throne. John of Gaunt appears to have become Chaucer's patron, because the pair's fortunes are linked for the next three decades—rising and falling together. Chaucer traveled to Spain in 1366 on what would be the first of a series of diplomatic missions to the continent over the next decade. In 1368, the death of John of Gaunt's first wife, Blanche, occasioned Chaucer's composition of the *Book of the Duchess,* which was circulating by the time he went to France in 1370. He traveled in Italy in 1372 and 73, visiting Genoa to negotiate a trade agreement and visiting Florence concerning loans for Edward III. He returned to England and was appointed a customs official for the Port of London, a post he would hold until 1386. Chaucer's career as a civil servant continued to flourish; he visited France and Calais in 1376 and 78, Italy again in 1378, and gained additional custom responsibilities in 1382. By 1385, he was living in Kent, where he was appointed a justice of the peace. The following year he became a member of Parliament.

The next few years were difficult ones for Chaucer. Linked

with the royal family, he suffered when the aristocracy became the dominant political force. In 1386, he either resigned or was removed from his duties as a customs official; his wife had died by 1387; and, although he had been reappointed as a justice of the peace, he was not returned to Parliament. His fortunes rose again in 1389 when John of Gaunt returned from the continent and the young King Richard II regained control of the government from the barons. Chaucer was appointed a clerk of the king's works, responsible for the repair and maintenance of various royal buildings. However, he was removed from this office in 1391, and the next few years were dismal for him. By 1396, records suggest, he had established a close relationship with John of Gaunt's son, the Earl of Derby, who as King Henry IV later confirmed Chaucer's grants from Richard II and added an additional annuity in 1399. In December of that year, Chaucer leased a house in the garden of Westminster Abbey where he lived the remainder of his life. When Geoffrey Chaucer died on 25 October 1400, he was accorded the honor of burial in the Abbey (then traditionally reserved for royalty) and his tomb became the nucleus of what is now known as Poets' Corner.

It is thought that Chaucer translated the *Roman de la*

Rose (1230-1275?) and composed some of the early "Complaints" during the 1360s. What survives of Chaucer's rendition of the *Roman de la Rose* is extant in the Middle English poem, the *Romaunt of the Rose.* Chaucer translated the first 1705 lines, following the original of Guillaume de Lorris fairly closely. Scholars agree that the *Roman de la Rose* is the most significant of all of the literary influences on Chaucer.

In his first major work, the *Book of the Duchess,* Chaucer attempts to soothe the grief of John of Gaunt, whose wife, Blanche, died in 1368. At the beginning of the poem the narrator is overcome by sleep while reading the story of Seyes and Alcyone. In a dream, he meets a Black Knight, who is mourning. The narrator then inquires about the Knight's grief, and the Knight is consoled as he relates his story. Although most of the lines have parallels in the *Roman de le Rose* and other French court poetry, it never reads like "translation English," instead surpassing the French models by converting the insincere language and sentimental courtly romance imagery of dying for love into a poignant reality—a beautiful woman is dead, and the Knight mourns her. Critical opinion on the *Book of the Duchess* is mixed; many critics deride the narrator's obtuseness, while others praise Chaucer for his skillful manipulation of generic conventions.

Critics believe that Chaucer next wrote the *House of Fame* and the *Parlement of Foules.* The exact sequence cannot be determined, but both are thought to comment upon the efforts to arrange a suitable marriage for the young Richard II; the *Parlement* on the unsuccessful efforts to gain the daughter of Charles V of France, and *Fame* to celebrate the actual betrothal of Richard and Anne of Bohemia in 1380. A dream-vision, the *House of Fame* appears to be an examination of the function of poets, the nature of poetry, and the unreliability of fame. Critics have detected the influences of Dante's *Divina Comedia* (1307-21) in this 2,158–line poem and have noted certain autobiographical references. Chaucer provides a detailed description of his life during the period he was controller of the customs, and this is the only work in which he names himself. The *Parlement of Foules,* a 699–line poem, also takes the form of a dream-vision, and betrays the influence of Italian Renaissance literature. The work is an allegorical disputation about love. As critics have noted, *fine amour* was the prerogative of the nobility, whereas sexuality symbolizes the lower classes.

Sometime during the early 1380s Chaucer translated Boethius's *De consolatio philosophiae,* (524), one of the seminal books of the Middle Ages. The *Consolatio* explores, among other topics, two major philosophical dilemmas of medieval Christianity: how human freedom of choice can exist alongside of divine omnipotence, and how a just God could permit the suffering of the righteous. Chaucer's prose in this translation, commonly known as *Boece,* has been less well received than his verse treatments of Boethian themes: *Troylus and Criseyde,* the "Knight's Tale," the "Nun's Priest's Tale," and a number of his shorter pieces.

Troylus and Criseyde, a 8,239–line adaption of Boccaccio's *Il Filostrato* (c. 1338) was long considered by some critics to be Chaucer's finest poetic achievement. A tale set against the backdrop of the Trojan War, the work is marked by a symmetry, decorum, and metaphorical quality lacking in Boccaccio's story. Chaucer's adaptation adds depth and changes the depiction of the main characters. His Criseyde is more refined and elegant than Boccaccio's capricious heroine, making her final defection difficult for some readers to understand. Chaucer's treatment of her is sympathetic, and this is the first version of the tale in which she is not degraded after making her decision to accept the political betrothal to Diomede rather than marry Troylus. Criseyda's irresponsible cousin Pandarus becomes her guardian uncle, and his betrayal of her confidence to Troylus has given the English language the term "pander." Troylus himself is reduced to an impotent passivity that modern readers find hard to accept in a Trojan warrior, although he formulates many of the primary concerns of the story. Critics note the tension between the erotic and the intellectual spheres, interpreting the poem in one of three general ways: as the first novel in English, due to the characterizations and the work's concern with manners and morals; as the epitome of courtly love romances; or, as a religious and philosophical allegory expressing Boethian concepts.

The "Prologue" to the *Legend of Good Women* indicates that it follows *Troylus* in the chronology of Chaucer's works. The last of his dream-vision poems, it relates the traditional stories of such faithful women as Dido, Cleopatra, and Lucrece. The *Legend* remains unfinished, and most critics consider it dull and perfunctory, finding its prime importance as an example of Chaucer's structuring of a long poem as a collection of interconnected stories.

The *Canterbury Tales,* started sometime around 1386, is considered Chaucer's masterpiece. Organized as a collection of stories told by a group of travelers on pilgrimage to the shrine of Thomas à Becket in Canterbury, the *Canterbury Tales* reflects the diversity of fourteenth-century English life. The pilgrims depict the full-range of medieval society, and the tales they relate span the medieval literary spectrum. Chaucer's artistry manages to bring each character to life and create truly memorable individuals. Within the framework of the *Canterbury Tales* there are ten parts, which appear in different order in different manuscripts. Critics believe that Chaucer's final plan for this work was never realized: he either died before he could place the sections in sequence or stopped work on it, and modern editions follow the arrangement of one of two medieval sources, that of the Ellesmere manuscript, or that of the Hengwrt manuscript. Both are dated to within a decade of Chaucer's death.

The *Canterbury Tales* begins with the "General Prologue" introducing the pilgrims with short, vivid sketches. They are presented by rank, with the knight and his entourage first, followed by the ecclesiastics and representatives of the lower classes. Interspersed between the twenty-four tales are short dramatic "links" presenting lively exchanges, usually involving the host and one or more of the pilgrims. The stories told are generally indicative of class and personality, though scholars have noted some discrepancies between the teller and the tale. The social variety of the pilgrims is highlighted by the diversity of the tales and their themes: courtly romance, racy *fabliau,* allegory, sermon, beast fable, saint's life, and, at times, an amalgam of these genres. The work contains what many readers feel is a realistic depiction of Chaucer's world, from the social mix of the pilgrimage to the intellectual curiosity which characterized medieval Christianity. For many, the work as a whole points to the vast and diverse knowledge of the poet and conjures up the complexity of the fourteenth-century European mind.

The final two works assigned to Chaucer, the *Treatise on the Astrolabe* and the *Equatorie of the Planets,* are dated about 1391-92. Both are prose introductions to the use of scientific instruments and, if authentic, as many scholars believe, demonstrate that his prose could be even better than in the translation of Boethius's work, although it is still less appreciated than his verse. These works further illustrate the variety and depth of the poet's erudition.

Chaucer's genius was recognized in his own time and his works have since attracted a vast body of criticism. Praised by French and English contempories alike for his technical skill, he was revered as a master poet and his contributions to the English language were especially lauded. In the fifteenth century, William Caxton judged Chaucer to be "the worshipful fader and first foundeur and embellisssher of ornate eloquence in our Englissh," a judgment which has since become traditional. Praise such as Roger Ascham's assessment of Chaucer as "our Englishe Homer" and Edmund Spenser's pronouncement in *The Faerie Queene* (1596) that he was a "well of English vndefiled," have remained the standard opinions. From time to time, critics have appeared who find Chaucer's language incomprehensible and obscene, but such reactions are uncommon. Puritan critics in the sixteenth century raised such objections, as did the English Romantic poets in the early nineteenth century. Dissenting from his Romantic counterparts—including Lord Byron, who thought Chaucer "obscene and contemptable"—William Blake maintained that the *Canterbury Tales* contain a fundamental truth when he wrote, "The characters of Chaucer's Pilgrims are the characters which compose all ages and nations." For such later nineteenth-century critics as Robert Southey, Chaucer remained a poet unmatched. "Chaucer is not merely the acknowledged father of English poetry," Southey stated, "he is also one of our greatest poets. His proper station is in the first class, with Spenser, and Shakespeare, and Milton; and Shakespeare alone has equalled him in variety and versatility of genius." The twentieth century has seen studies in Chaucer's versification, language, and prosody proliferate, and scholars continue to find Chaucer an immensely talented poet of style, substance, humor, humility, and ultimately, humanity. "Of all writers of genius," Emile Legouis has written, "Chaucer is the one with whom it is easiest to have a sense of comradeship."

The outstanding English writer before Shakespeare, Geoffrey Chaucer brought Middle English to its full efflorescence. The originality of his language and style, the vivacity of his humor, the civility of his poetic demeanor, and the depth of his knowledge are continually cited as reasons for the permanence of his works. His poems continue to draw the interest and praise of readers and critics centuries after his death and are among the most acclaimed works throughout the English-speaking world. "Chaucer is neither a Homer nor a Dante, but his position in regard to English literature is analogous to that which they occupy towards the literature of their respective countries," according to Richard Garnett. "Each was the first poet of his nation, not indeed the first who had ever written poetry, but the first who had so written poetry as to command the attention of contemporaries and of posterity."

* PRINCIPAL WORKS

The compleynt of Anelida; The compleynt of Chaucer; Th'envoye of Chaucer unto the kinge [edited by William Caxton] (poetry) 1477

† *The temple of bras; A tretyse which John Scogan sente unto the lordes and gentilmen of the kynges hows; The good counceyl of Chaucer; Balade of the vilage without peyntyng; Th'envoye of Chaucer to Skegan* [edited by William Caxton] (poetry) 1477

Boecius de consolacione philosophies [translation of Boethius's *De consolatione philosophiae;* edited by William Caxton] (prose) 1478

The Canterbury Tales [edited by William Caxton] (poetry) 1478

The double sorow of Troylus to telle [edited by William Caxton] (poetry) 1483

The book of Fame made by Gefferey Chaucer [edited by William Caxton] (poetry) 1484

Book of the tales of Cauntyrburye [edited by William Caxton] (poetry) 1484

Complaint of Mars; Complaint of Venus; Envoy to Bukton [printed by Julian Notary] (poetry) 1499-1502

Chaucer's Works [printed by Richard Pynson] (poetry) 1526

The Workes of Geffray Chaucer newly printed, with dyuers works which were neuer in print before [edited by William Thynne] (poetry and prose) 1532

The Workes of our Ancient and lerned English Poet, Geffrey Chaucer, newly Printed [edited by Thomas Speght] (poetry and prose) 1598

The Works of Geoffrey Chaucer compared with the former editions, and many valuable MSS. out of which, three Tales are added, which were never before printed [edited by John Urry] (poetry and prose) 1721

The Canterbury Tales of Chaucer. 5 vols. [edited by Thomas Tyrwhitt] (poetry) 1775-78

The Poetical Works of Geoffrey Chaucer. 6 vols. (poetry) 1845

The Complete Works of Geoffrey Chaucer. 7 vols. [edited by Walter W. Skeat] (poetry and prose) 1894-97

The Book of Troilus and Criseyde by Geoffrey Chaucer [edited by Robert K. Root] (poetry) 1926

The Works of Geoffrey Chaucer [edited by F. N. Robinson; revised edition, 1957] (poetry and prose) 1933

The Text of the Canterbury Tales, Studied on the Basis of All Known Manuscripts. 8 vols. [edited by J. M. Manly and Edith Rickert] (poetry) 1940

The Canterbury Tales [edited by Nevill Coghill]   (poetry) 1951

The Equatorie of the Planetis [edited by Derek J. Price] (prose) 1955

The Parlement of Foulys [edited by Derek S. Brewer] (poetry) 1960

Troilus and Criseyde [edited by Nevill Coghill]   (poetry) 1971

Chaucer's Lesser Poems Complete in Present-Day English [translated by James J. Donohue]   (poetry) 1974

The Complete Poetry and Prose of Geoffrey Chaucer [edited by John H. Fisher; revised edition, 1989]   (poetry and prose) 1977

A Variorum Edition of the Works of Geoffrey Chaucer [general editor Paul G. Ruggiers] (poetry and prose) 1979-

The Riverside Chaucer [general editor Larry D. Benson] (poetry and prose) 1987

*Exact publication dates of Chaucer's works published before 1500 are uncertain.

†This volume consists of separate fascicles; these works are now known as the *Parlement of Foules,* the "Envoy of Scogan," "Truth," "Fortune," and "Lenvoy de Chaucer a Scogan," respectively.

Eustace Deschamps   (poem date c. 1386)

[*A disciple of the poet and composer Guillaume de Machaut, Deschamps was a notable and enormously productive French court poet. He held various offices in the court of Charles V and also composed prose and dramatic pieces. In the following poem, which scholars date to approximately 1386, Deschamps lauds Chaucer's translation of the* Roman de la Rose, *comparing the English poet to Socrates, Ovid, Seneca, and Aulus Gellius.*]

> O Socrates full of wisdom,
> Seneca in morals, Aulus Gellius in practical affairs,
> Ovid great in thy poetics,
> Concise in speech, experienced in rhetoric,
> Lofty eagle, who by thy science
> Dost illumine the kingdom of Aeneas,
> The isle of giants (those of Brutus), and who there hast
> Sown the flowers and planted the rose-tree;
> Thou wilt enlighten those ignorant (of French),
> O great translator, noble Geoffrey Chaucer;
>
> Thou art a mundane god of love in Albion;
> And *of the Rose* in the Angelic land—
> Which from Lady Angela the Saxon has since become
> England, for from her this name is taken
> As final in the etymology—
> Into good English *The Book* thou hast translated;
> And a garden, for which thou hast asked plants
> From those who poetize to win them fame,
> Now for a long time thou hast been constructing,

> Great translator, noble Geoffrey Chaucer.
>
> Of thee therefore from the Heleian spring
> I ask to have an authentic draught,
> For the spring is entirely in thy keeping,
> To assuage therewith my feverish thirst,
> Who in Gaul shall be as one paralyzed
> Until thou shalt make me drink.
> An Eustache am I, and thou shalt have a plant from me;
> But treat with favor the writings of a novice
> Which by Clifford thou shalt receive from me,
> Great translator, Geoffrey Chaucer.

L'envoy

> Excellent poet, glory of squiredom,
> In thy garden I should be but a nettle,
> In comparison to what I have just spoken of—
> Thy noble plant, thy sweet melody;
> But, for my information, I beg thee an official verdict,
> Great translator, noble Geoffrey Chaucer.

(pp. 952-53)

Eustace Deschamps, in a poem in The Complete Poetry and Prose of Geoffrey Chaucer, *edited by John H. Fisher, Holt, Rinehart and Winston, 1977, pp. 952-53.*

Geoffrey Chaucer   (poem date c. 1386-1400)

[*In the following excerpt known as Chaucer's "Retraction" from the* Canterbury Tales, *the poet lists his works revoking those which deal with "worldly vanitees," instead offering his moral and philosophical pieces as truly representative of his mind. Of the works listed, the* Book of Leon *has not been preserved and the* Book of the Five and Twenty Ladies *is better known as the* Legend of Good Women. *The approximate composition date for the entire* Canterbury Tales *has been used to date this excerpt.*]

Now praye I to hem alle that herkne this litel tretis or rede, that if ther be any thing in it that liketh hem, that therof they thanken oure Lord Jesu Crist, of whom proceedeth al wit and al goodnesse. And if ther be any thing that displese hem, I praye hem also that they arrette it to the defaute of myn unconning, and nat to my wil, that wolde ful fain have said bettre if I hadde had conning. For oure book saith, "Al that is writen is writen for oure doctrine," and that is myn entente. Wherfore I biseeke you mekely, for the mercy of God, that ye praye for me that Crist have mercy on me and foryive me my giltes, and namely of my translacions and enditinges of worldly vanitees, the whiche I revoke in my retraccions: as is the ***Book of Troilus;*** the Book also of ***Fame;*** the ***Book of the Five and Twenty Ladies;*** the ***Book of the Duchesse;*** the ***Book of Saint Valentines Day of the Parlement of Briddes;*** the ***Tales of Canterbury,*** thilke that sounen into sinne; the ***Book of the Leon;*** and many another book, if they were in my remembrance, and many a song and many a leccherous lay: that Crist for his grete mercy foryive me the sinne. But of the translacion of Boece *De Consolatione,* and othere bookes of legendes of saintes, and omelies, and moralitee, and devocion, that thanke I oure Lord Jesu

Crist and his blisful Moder and alle the saintes of hevene, biseeking hem that they from hennes forth unto my lives ende sende me grace to biwaile my giltes and to studye to the salvacion of my soule, and graunte me grace of verray penitence, confession, and satisfaccion to doon in this present lif, thurgh the benigne grace of him that is king of kinges and preest over alle preestes, that boughte us with the precious blood of his herte, so that I may been oon of hem at the day of doom that shulle be saved. *Qui cum patre et Spiritu Sancto vivis et regnas Deus per omnia saecula. Amen.*

> Geoffrey Chaucer, "Chaucer's Retraction," in The Norton Anthology of English Literature, Vol. 1, edited by M. H. Abrams, fifth edition, W. W. Norton & Company, 1986, p. 226.

John Gower   (poem date c. 1390)

[*A friend of Chaucer's, Gower was a learned poet who wrote in French, Latin, and English. His works are often unfavorably compared with those of Chaucer, but are noted for their admirable lucidity and stylistic achievement. In the excerpt below from his major English-language work, the* Confessio Amantis, *the earliest version of which scholars date to about 1390, Gower attributes comments on Chaucer's popularity to Venus. The reference to the* Testament of Love *is often taken as an allusion to the* Legend of Good Women.]

'My poet and disciple greet,
Chaucer I mean, when ye shall meet;
For in his youthful flowery days—
As well he could, in many ways—
Where'er I go, I find the land
All filled with joyful ditties and
With songs that he composed for me.
And, therefore, him especially
Do I with gratitude behold.
But now that he is growing old,
This be the message thou convey:
That he, in this his latter day,
Being my own most faithful clerk,
On his last work shall now embark,
And write his **Testament of Love**
As thou hast done thy *Shrift,* above.'

(pp. 283-84)

> John Gower, "Book Eight: Lechery," in his Confessio Amantis (The Lover's Shrift), *translated by Terence Tiller, Penguin Books, 1963, pp. 260-86.*

William Caxton   (essay date c. 1484)

[*Caxton introduced printing into England in 1476 and published numerous translations which exerted considerable influence on the development of fifteenth-century prose. Among the roughly one hundred books he published were the majority of the English literature available to him at the time, including: Chaucer's* Canterbury Tales *(in 1478 and 1484) and other works, John Gower's* Confessio Amantis *(1483), Sir Thomas Malory's* Morte Darthur *(1485), and much of John Lydgate's poetry. In the following excerpt from the preface*

to the second edition of the Canterbury Tales, *he praises Chaucer's style, providing some information on the textual history of the poet's masterpiece.*]

Grete thankes laude and honour / ought to be gyuen vnto the clerkes / poetes / and historiographs that haue wreton many noble bokes of wysedom of the lyues / passions / & myracles of holy sayntes of hystoryes / of noble and famous Actes / and faittes / And of the cronycles sith the begynnyng of the creacion of the world / vnto thys present tyme / by whyche we ben dayly enformed / and have knowleche of many thynges / of whom we shold not haue knowen / yf they had not left to vs theyr monumentis wreton / Emong whom and inespecial to fore alle other we ought to gyue a synguler laude vnto that noble & grete philosopher Geffrey chaucer the whiche for his ornate wrytyng in our tongue may wel haue the name of a laureate poete / For to fore that he by hys labour enbelysshyd / ornated / and made faire our englisshe / in thys Royame was had rude speche & Incongrue / as yet it appiereth by olde bookes / whyche at thys day ought not to haue place ne be compared emong ne to hys beauteuous volumes / and aournate writynges / of whom he made many bokes and treatyces of many a noble historye as wel in metre as in ryme and prose / and them so craftyly made / that he comprehended hys maters in short / quyck and hye sentences / eschewyng prolyxyte / castyng away the chaf of superfluyte / and shewyng the pyked grayn of sentence / vtteryd by crafty and sugred eloquence / of whom emonge all other of hys bokes / I purpose temprynte by the grace of god the book of the tales of caun tyrburye / in whiche I fynde many a noble hystorye / of euery asta te and degre / Fyrst rehercyng the condicions / and tharraye of eche of them as properly as possyble is to be sayd / And after theyr tales whyche ben of noblesse / wysedom / gentylesse / Myrthe / and also of veray holynesse and vertue / wherin he fynysshyth thys sayd booke / whyche book I haue dylygently ouersen and duly examyned to thende that it be made acordyng vnto his owen ma kyng / For I fynde many of the sayd bookes / whyche wryters haue abrydgyd it and many thynges left out / And in somme place haue sette certayn versys / that he neuer made ne sette in hys booke / of whyche bookes so incorrecte was one brought to me vj yere passyd / whyche I supposed had ben veray true & correcte / And accordyng to the same I dyde do enprynte a certayn nombre of them / whyche anon were sold to many and dyuerse gentyl men / of whome one gentylman cam to me / and said that this book was not accordyng in many places vnto the book that Gefferey chaucer had made / To whom I answered that I had made it accordyng to my copye / and by me was nothyng added ne mynusshyd / Thenne he sayd he knewe a book whyche hys fader had and moche louyd / that was very trewe / and accordyng vnto hys owen first book by hym made / and sayd more yf I wold enprynte it agayn he wold gete me the same book for a copye / how be it he wyst wel / that hys fader wold not gladly departe fro it / To whom I said / in caas that he coude gete me suche a book trewe and correcte / yet I wold ones endeuoyre me to enprynte it agayn / for to satysfye thauctour / where as to fore by ygnouraunce I erryd in hurtyng and dyffamyng his book in dyuerce places in settyng in somme thynges that he neuer sayd ne made / and leuyng out

many thynges that he made whyche ben requysite to be
sette in it / And thus we fyll at accord / And he ful gentyl-
ly gate of hys fader the said book / and delyuerd it to me
/ by whiche I haue corrected my book / as here after alle
alonge by thayde of almyghty god shal folowe / whom I
humbly beseche to gyue me grace and ayde to achyeue /
and accomplysshe / to hys laude honour and glorye / and
that alle ye that shal in thys book rede or heere / wyll of
your charyte among your dedes of mercy / remembre the
sowle of the sayd Geofferey chaucer first auctour / and ma
ker of thys book / And also that alle we that shal see and
rede therin / may so take and vnderstonde the good and
vertuous tales / that it may so prouffyte / vnto the helthe
of our sowles / that after thys short and transitorye lyf we
may come to euerlastyng lyf in heuen / Amen (pp. 90-1)

> *William Caxton, "Canterbury Tales," in* The
> Prologues and Epilogues of William Caxton,
> *edited by W. J. B. Crotch, Oxford University
> Press, London, 1928, pp. 90-1.*

William Webbe   (essay date 1586)

[*Webbe was an English tutor, translator, and critic. In
the following excerpt from his theoretical and practical
critical study of English poetry, which was originally
published in 1586, he praises Chaucer, remarking that
although his "stile may seeme blunte and course," one
sees in him a true poet.*]

Chawcer, who for that excellent fame which hee obtayned
in his Poetry was always accounted the God of English
Poets (such a tytle for honours sake hath beene guien
him), was next after if not equall in time to *Gower,* and
hath left many workes, both for delight and profitable
knowledge farre exceeding any other that as yet euer since
hys time directed theyr studies that way. Though the manner of hys stile may seeme blunte and course to many fine
English eares at these dayes, yet in trueth, if it be equally
pondered, and with good iudgment aduised, and confirmed with the time wherein he wrote, a man shall perce-
iue thereby euen a true picture or perfect shape of a right
Poet. He by his delightsome vayne so gulled the eares of
men with his deuises, that, although corruption bare such
sway in most matters that learning and truth might skant
bee admitted to shewe it selfe, yet without controllment
myght hee gyrde at the vices and abuses of all states, and
gawle with very sharpe and eger inuentions, which he did
so learnedly and pleasantly that none therefore would call
him into question. For such was his bolde spyrit, that what
enormities he saw in any he would not spare to pay them
home, eyther in playne words, or els in some pretty and
pleasant couert, that the simplest might espy him. (p. 241)

> *William Webbe, "A Discourse of English Poe-
> trie," in* Elizabethan Critical Essays, Vol. I,
> *edited by G. Gregory Smith, Oxford University
> Press, London, 1904, pp. 226-302.*

Henry Peacham   (essay date 1622)

[*An English writer and tutor, Peacham is chiefly remembered for his* Compleat Gentleman *(1622), a text-
book of manners and polite learning which stresses the
Puritan sentiment of duty. In the following excerpt from
that work, Peacham praises Chaucer's style.*]

Of English Poets of our owne Nation, esteeme Sir *Geoffrey
Chaucer* the father; although the stile for the antiquitie
may distast you, yet as vnder a bitter and rough rinde
there lyeth a delicate kernell of conceit and sweete inuention. What Examples, Similitudes, Times, Places, and
aboue all, Persons with their speeches and attributes, doe,
as in his **Canterburie-Tales,** like these threds of gold the
rich *Arras,* beautifie his worke quite thorough! And albeit
diuers of his workes are but meerely translations out of
Latine and *French,* yet he hath handled them so artificially
that thereby he hath made them his owne, as his **Troilus
and Cresseid.** The **Romant of the Rose** was the Inuention
of *Iehan de Mehunes,* a French Poet, whereof he translated but onely the one halfe; his **Canterburie-Tales** without
question were his owne inuention, all circumstances being
wholly English. Hee was a good Diuine, and saw in those
times without his spectacles, as may appeare by the
Plough-man and the **"Parsons Tale"**; withall an excellent
Mathematician, as plainly appeareth by his discourse of
the Astrolabe to his little sonne *Lewes.* In briefe, account
him among the best of your English bookes in your librarie. (p. 132)

> *Henry Peacham, "Of Poetry, from 'The Com-
> plete Gentleman' (1622)," in* Critical Essays
> of the Seventeenth Century: 1605-1650, Vol.
> I, *edited by J. E. Spingarn, Oxford at the Clar-
> endon Press, 1908, pp. 116-33.*

Michael Drayton   (essay date 1627)

[*A prolific English poet and dramatist, Drayton was
deemed in his day a poet worthy of comparison with his
contemporaries William Shakespeare, Edmund Spenser, and Ben Jonson. A master in a variety of verse styles,
including pastoral, sonnet, classical ode, and epic, Drayton is today considered competent and occasionally inspired. In the following excerpt from the "Epistle to
Henry Reynolds, Esquire, of Poets and Poesie," written
in 1627, Drayton praises Chaucer's skill.*]

> That noble *Chaucer,* in those former times,
> The first inrich'd our *English* with his rimes,
> And was the first of ours that euer brake
> Into the *Muses* treasure, and first spake
> In weighty numbers, deluing in the Mine
> Of perfect knowledge, which he could refine,
> And coyne for currant, and as much as then
> The *English* language could expresse to men,
> He made it doe, and by his wondrous skill,
> Gaue vs much light from his abundant quill.
>   (pp. 135-36)

> *Michael Drayton, "Epistle to Henry Reynolds,
> of Poets and Poesy," in* Critical Essays of the
> Seventeenth Century, 1605-1650, Vol. I, *ed-
> ited by J. E. Spingarn, Oxford at the Claren-
> don Press, 1908, pp. 134-40.*

John Dryden (essay date 1700)

[*Regarded by many as the father of modern English poetry and criticism, Dryden dominated literary life in England during the last four decades of the seventeenth century. By deliberately and comprehensively refining the English language in all his works, he developed an expressive, universal diction which has had immense impact on the development of speech and writing in Great Britain and North America. Recognized as a prolific and accomplished dramatist, Dryden also wrote a number of satiric poems and critical works, some of which are acknowledged as his greatest literary achievements. In the former, notably* Absalom and Achitophel *(1681),* Religio Laici *(1682), and* The Hind and the Panther *(1687), he displayed an irrepressible wit and forceful line of argument which later satirists adopted as their model. In his critical works, particularly* Of Dramatic Poesy *(1668), Dryden effectively originated the extended form of objective, practical analysis that has come to characterize most modern criticism. In the following excerpt from the preface to his* Fables Ancient and Modern *(1700), Dryden comments on the strengths and weaknesses of Chaucer's poetry, emphasizing his greatness and finding "God's plenty" in the characters and stories in the* Canterbury Tales.]

As [Chaucer] is the Father of *English* Poetry, so I hold him in the same Degree of Veneration as the *Grecians* held *Homer,* or the *Romans Virgil:* He is a perpetual Fountain of good Sense; learn'd in all Sciences; and therefore speaks properly on all Subjects: As he knew what to say, so he knows also when to leave off; a Continence which is practis'd by few Writers, and scarcely by any of the Ancients, excepting *Virgil* and *Horace.*

Chaucer follow'd Nature every where; but was never so bold to go beyond her: And there is a great Difference of being *Poeta* and *nimis Poeta,* if we may believe *Catullus,* as much as betwixt a modest Behaviour and Affectation. The Verse of *Chaucer,* I confess, is not Harmonious to us; but 'tis like the Eloquence of one whom *Tacitus* commends, it was *auribus istius temporis accommodata:* They who liv'd with him, and some time after him, thought it Musical; and it continues so even in our Judgment, if compar'd with the Numbers of *Lidgate* and *Gower* his Contemporaries: There is the rude Sweetness of a *Scotch* Tune in it, which is natural and pleasing, though not perfect. 'Tis true, I cannot go so far as he who publish'd the last Edition of him [Thomas Speght]; for he would make us believe the Fault is in our Ears, and that there were really Ten Syllables in a Verse where we find but Nine: But this Opinion is not worth confuting; 'tis so gross and obvious an Errour, that common Sense (which is a Rule in every thing but Matters of Faith and Revelation) must convince the Reader, that Equality of Numbers in every Verse which we call *Heroick,* was either not known, or not always practis'd in *Chaucer*'s Age. It were an easie Matter to produce some thousands of his Verses, which are lame for want of half a Foot, and sometimes a whole one, and which no Pronunciation can make otherwise. We can only say, that he liv'd in the Infancy of our Poetry, and that nothing is brought to Perfection at the first. We must be Children before we grow Men. There was an *Ennius,* and in process of Time a *Lucilius,* and a *Lucretius,* before *Vir-*gil and *Horace;* even after *Chaucer* there was a *Spenser,* a *Harrington,* a *Fairfax,* before *Waller* and *Denham* were in being: And our Numbers were in their Nonage till these last appear'd. I need say little of his Parentage, Life, and Fortunes: They are to be found at large in all the Editions of his Works. He was employ'd abroad, and favour'd by *Edward* the Third, *Richard* the Second, and *Henry* the Fourth, and was Poet, as I suppose, to all Three of them. In *Richard*'s Time, I doubt, he was a little dipt in the Rebellion of the Commons; and being Brother-in-Law to *John of Ghant,* it was no wonder if he follow'd the Fortunes of that Family; and was well with *Henry* the Fourth when he had depos'd his Predecessor. Neither is it to be admir'd, that *Henry,* who was a wise as well as a valiant Prince, who claim'd by Succession, and was sensible that his Title was not sound, but was rightfully in *Mortimer,* who had married the Heir of *York;* it was not to be admir'd, I say, if that great Politician should be pleas'd to have the greatest Wit of those Times in his Interests, and to be the Trumpet of his Praises. *Augustus* had given him the Example, by the Advice of *Mæcenas,* who recommended *Virgil* and *Horace* to him; whose Praises help'd to make him Popular while he was alive, and after his Death have made him Precious to Posterity. As for the Religion of our Poet, he seems to have some little Byas towards the Opinions of Wickliff, after *John of Ghant* his Patron; somewhat of which appears in the Tale of *Piers Plowman:* Yet I cannot blame him for inveighing so sharply against the Vices of the Clergy in his Age: Their Pride, their Ambition, their Pomp, their Avarice, their Worldly Interest, deserv'd the Lashes which he gave them, both in that, and in most of his **Canterbury Tales:** Neither has his Contemporary *Boccace,* spar'd them. Yet both those Poets liv'd in much esteem, with good and holy Men in Orders: For the Scandal which is given by particular Priests, reflects not on the Sacred Function. *Chaucer's Monk,* his *Chanon,* and his *Fryar,* took not from the Character of his *Good Parson.* A Satyrical Poet is the Check of the Laymen, on bad Priests. We are only to take care, that we involve not the Innocent with the Guilty in the same Condemnation. The Good cannot be too much honour'd, nor the Bad too coursly us'd: For the Corruption of the Best, becomes the Worst. . . . [Chaucer] must have been a Man of a most wonderful comprehensive Nature, because, as it has been truly observ'd of him, he has taken into the Compass of his **Canterbury Tales** the various Manners and Humours (as we now call them) of the whole *English* Nation, in his Age. Not a single Character has escap'd him. All his Pilgrims are severally distinguish'd from each other; and not only in their Inclinations, but in their very Phisiognomies and Persons. *Baptista Porta* could not have describ'd their Natures better, than by the Marks which the Poet gives them. The Matter and Manner of their Tales, and of their Telling, are so suited to their different Educations, Humours, and Callings, that each of them would be improper in any other Mouth. Even the grave and serious Characters are distinguish'd by their several sorts of Gravity: Their Discourses are such as belong to their Age, their Calling, and their Breeding; such as are becoming of them, and of them only. Some of his Persons are Vicious, and some Vertuous; some are unlearn'd, or (as *Chaucer* calls them) Lewd, and some are Learn'd.

Even the Ribaldry of the Low Characters is different: The *Reeve,* the *Miller,* and the *Cook,* are several Men, and distinguish'd from each other, as much as the mincing Lady Prioress, and the broad-speaking gap-tooth'd Wife of *Bathe.* But enough of this: There is such a Variety of Game springing up before me, that I am distracted in my Choice, and know not which to follow. 'Tis sufficient to say according to the Proverb, that here is God's Plenty. We have our Fore-fathers and Great granddames all before us, as they were in *Chaucer*'s Days; their general Characters are still remaining in Mankind, and even in *England,* though they are call'd by other Names than those of *Moncks,* and *Fryars,* and *Chanons,* and *Lady Abbesses,* and *Nuns:* For Mankind is ever the same, and nothing lost out of Nature, though every thing is alter'd. May I have leave to do my self the Justice, (since my Enemies will do me none, and are so far from granting me to be a good Poet, that they will not allow me so much as to be a Christian, or a Moral Man) may I have leave, I say, to inform my Reader, that I have confin'd my Choice to such Tales of *Chaucer,* as savour nothing of Immodesty. If I had desir'd more to please than to instruct, the *Reve,* the *Miller,* the *Shipman,* the *Merchant,* the *Sumner,* and above all, the *Wife of Bathe,* in the Prologue to her Tale, would have procur'd me as many Friends and Readers, as there are *Beaux* and Ladies of Pleasure in the Town. But I will no more offend against Good Manners: I am sensible as I ought to be of the Scandal I have given by my loose Writings; and make what Reparation I am able, by this Publick Acknowledgment. If any thing of this Nature, or of Profaneness, be crept into these Poems, I am so far from defending it, that I disown it. *Totum hoc indictum volo.* *Chaucer* makes another manner of Apologie for his broadspeaking, and *Boccace* makes the like; but I will follow neither of them. Our Country-man, in the end of his Characters, before the **Canterbury Tales,** thus excuses the Ribaldry, which is very gross, in many of his Novels.

> But first, I pray you, of your courtesy,
> That ye ne arrete it nought my villany,
> Though that I plainly speak in this mattere
> To tellen you her words, and eke her chere:
> Ne though I speak her words properly,
> For this ye knowen as well as I,
> Who shall tellen a tale after a man
> He mote rehearse as nye, as ever He can:
> Everich word of it been in his charge,
> *All speke he, never so rudely, ne large.*
> Or else he mote tellen his tale untrue,
> Or feine things, or find words new:
> He may not spare, altho he were his brother,
> He mote as well say o word as another.
> *Christ* spake himself full broad in holy Writ,
> And well I wote no Villany is it.
> Eke *Plato* saith, who so can him rede,
> The words mote been Cousin to the dede.

Yet if a Man should have enquir'd of *Boccace* or of *Chaucer,* what need they had of introducing such Characters, where obscene Words were proper in their Mouths, but very undecent to be heard; I know not what Answer they could have made: For that Reason, such Tales shall be left untold by me. You have here a *Specimen* of *Chaucer*'s Language, which is so obsolete, that his Sense is scarce to be understood; and you have likewise more than one Ex-

ample of his unequal Numbers, which were mention'd before. Yet many of his Verses consist of Ten Syllables, and the Words not much behind our present *English:* As for Example, these two Lines, in the Description of the Carpenter's Young Wife:

> Wincing she was, as is a jolly Colt,
> Long as a Mast, and upright as a Bolt.

                                                        (pp. 481-86)

Chaucer, I confess, is a rough Diamond, and must first be polish'd e're he shines. I deny not likewise, that living in our early Days of Poetry, he writes not always of a piece; but sometimes mingles trivial Things, with those of greater Moment. Sometimes also, though not often, he runs riot, like *Ovid,* and knows not when he has said enough. But there are more great Wits, beside *Chaucer,* whose Fault is their Excess of Conceits, and those ill sorted. An Author is not to write all he can, but only all he ought. (p. 486)

I prefer in our Countryman, far above all his other Stories, the Noble Poem of **"Palamon and Arcite,"** which is of the *Epique* kind, and perhaps not much inferiour to the *Ilias* or the *Æneis:* the Story is more pleasing than either of them, the Manners as perfect, the Diction as poetical, the Learning as deep and various; and the Disposition full as artful: only it includes a greater length of time; as taking up seven years at least; but *Aristotle* has left undecided the Duration of the Action; which yet is easily reduc'd into the Compass of a year, by a Narration of what preceded the Return of *Palamon* to *Athens.* I had thought for the Honour of our Nation, and more particularly for his, whose Laurel, tho' unworthy, I have worn after him, that this Story was of *English* Growth, and *Chaucer*'s own: But I was undeceiv'd by *Boccace;* for casually looking on the End of his seventh *Giornata,* I found *Dioneo* (under which name he shadows himself) and *Fiametta* (who represents his Mistress, the natural Daughter of *Robert* King of *Naples*) of whom these Words are spoken. *Dioneo e Fiametta gran pezza cantarono insieme d'Arcita, e di Palemone:* by which it appears that this Story was written before the time of *Boccace;* but the Name of its Author being wholly lost, *Chaucer* is now become an Original; and I question not but the Poem has receiv'd many Beauties by passing through his Noble Hands. Besides this Tale, there is another of his own Invention, after the manner of the *Provencalls,* call'd **"The Flower and the Leaf "**; with which I was so particularly pleas'd, both for the Invention and the Moral; that I cannot hinder my self from recommending it to the Reader. (p. 490)

> *John Dryden, "Preface to the Fables," in his* Dryden: Poetry, Prose and Plays, *edited by Douglas Grant, Cambridge, Mass.: Harvard University Press, 1952, pp. 471-93.*

Samuel Johnson   (essay date 1755)

[*Johnson is one of the outstanding figures in English literature and a leader in the history of textual and aesthetic criticism. Popularly known in his day as the "Great Cham of Literature," he was a prolific lexicographer, essayist, poet, and critic. His lucid and extensively illustrated* Dictionary of the English Language *(1755)* and Prefaces, Biographical and Critical, to the Works of the English Poets *(10 vols., 1779-81) were new departures in lexicography and biographical criticism, respectively. In the following excerpt from the former, Johnson acknowledges Chaucer's place in English literary history but declares that "he does not . . . appear to have deserved all the praise he has received, or all of the censure that he has suffered."*]

The history of our language is now brought to the point at which the history of our poetry is generally supposed to commence, the time of the illustrious Geoffry Chaucer, who may perhaps, with great justice, be stiled the first of our versifyers who wrote poetically. He does not however appear to have deserved all the praise which he has received, or all the censure that he has suffered. Dryden, who, mistaking genius for learning, in confidence of his abilities, ventured to write of what he had not examined, ascribes to Chaucer the first refinement of our numbers, the first production of easy and natural rhymes, and the improvement of our language, by words borrowed from the more polished languages of the continent [see excerpt dated 1700]. Skinner contrarily blames him in harsh terms for having vitiated his native speech by *whole cartloads of foreign words.* But he that reads the works of Gower will find smooth numbers and easy rhymes, of which Chaucer is supposed to have been the inventor, and the French words, whether good or bad, of which Chaucer is charged as the importer. Some innovations he might probably make, like others, in the infancy of our poetry, which the paucity of books does not allow us to discover with particular exactness; but the works of Gower and Lydgate sufficiently evince, that his diction was in general like that of his contemporaries: and some improvements he undoubtedly made by the various dispositions of his rhymes, and by the mixture of different numbers, in which he seems to have been happy and judicious. (p. 46)

> Samuel Johnson, "Gower, Chaucer, John the Chaplain, Thomas Hoccleves, or Occleve, Lydgate," in his A Dictionary of the English Language, Vol. I, *second edition, Longman, Rees, Orme, Brown, and Green, 1827, pp. 45-55.*

William Blake   (essay date 1809)

[*Critics view Blake, the English artist and poet, as one of the most important literary figures of the nineteenth century. His works are esteemed for their dense thematic texture, for the compression and allusiveness of his style, for the original system of mythology he created, and for the impassioned prophetic tone which characterized all his works. Blake's early poetry demonstrates the influence of the Swedish theologian Emanuel Swedenborg, but the poet later rebelled against those teachings and against all forms of quantifying and systematizing reality. Since all reality is a mental construct, Blake believed, the only path to achieving salvation lies in the full awakening of the imagination. Blake stressed this theme in all his works, emphasizing that, because he was a visionary, his drawings were copied from and his poetry dictated by a higher power. Virtually unknown and often dismissed as a lunatic in his own time, Blake is considered*

the most extreme of the English Romantic writers, but today critics acknowledge his stature as one of the greatest poets of his age. In the following excerpt from his 1809 Descriptive Catalogue *of his paintings and drawings, he describes Chaucer's Canterbury pilgrims as examples of "universal human life."*]

The characters of Chaucer's Pilgrims are the characters which compose all ages and nations: as one age falls, another rises, different to mortal sight, but to immortals only the same; for we see the same characters repeated again and again, in animals, vegetables, minerals, and in men; nothing new occurs in identical existence; Accident ever varies, Substance can never suffer change nor decay.

Of Chaucer's characters, as described in his **Canterbury Tales,** some of the names or titles are altered by time, but the characters themselves for ever remain unaltered, and consequently they are the physiognomies or lineaments of universal human life, beyond which Nature never steps. Names alter, things never alter. I have known multitudes of those who would have been monks in the age of monkery, who in this deistical age are deists. As Newton numbered the stars, and as Linneus numbered the plants, so Chaucer numbered the classes of men. (p. 567)

The Knight and Squire with the Squire's Yeoman lead the procession, as Chaucer has also placed them first in his prologue. The Knight is a true Hero, a good, great, and wise man; his whole length portrait on horseback, as written by Chaucer, cannot be surpassed. He has spent his life in the field; has ever been a conqueror, and is that species of character which in every age stands as the guardian of man against the oppressor. His son is like him with the germ of perhaps greater perfection still, as he blends literature and the arts with his warlike studies. Their dress and their horses are of the first rate, without ostentation, and with all the true grandeur that unaffected simplicity when in high rank always displays. The Squire's Yeoman is also a great character, a man perfectly knowing in his profession:

> And in his hand he bare a mighty bow.

Chaucer describes here a mighty man; one who in war is the worthy attendant on noble heroes.

The Prioress follows these with her female chaplain:

> Another Nonne also with her had she,
> That was her Chaplaine, and Priests three.

This Lady is described also as of the first rank, rich and honoured. She has certain peculiarities and little delicate affectations, not unbecoming in her, being accompanied with what is truly grand and really polite; her person and face Chaucer has described with minuteness; it is very elegant, and was the beauty of our ancestors, till after Elizabeth's time, when voluptuousness and folly began to be accounted beautiful.

Her companion and her three priests were no doubt all perfectly delineated in those parts of Chaucer's work which are now lost; we ought to suppose them suitable attendants on rank and fashion.

The Monk follows these with the Friar. The Painter has

also grouped with these the Pardoner and the Sompnour and the Manciple, and has here also introduced one of the rich citizens of London: Characters likely to ride in company, all being above the common rank in life or attendants on those who were so.

For the Monk is described by Chaucer, as a man of the first rank in society, noble, rich, and expensively attended; he is a leader of the age, with certain humorous accompaniments in his character, that do not degrade, but render him an object of dignified mirth, but also with other accompaniments not so respectable.

The Friar is a character also of a mixed kind:

> A friar there was, a wanton and a merry.

but in his office he is said to be a "full solemn man": eloquent, amorous, witty, and satyrical; young, handsome, and rich; he is a complete rogue, with constitutional gaiety enough to make him a master of all the pleasures of the world.

> His neck was white as the flour de lis,
> Thereto strong he was as a champioun.

It is necessary here to speak of Chaucer's own character, that I may set certain mistaken critics right in their conception of the humour and fun that occurs on the journey. Chaucer is himself the great poetical observer of men, who in every age is born to record and eternize its acts. This he does as a master, as a father, and superior, who looks down on their little follies from the Emperor to the Miller; sometimes with severity, oftener with joke and sport.

Accordingly Chaucer has made his Monk a great tragedian, one who studied poetical art. So much so, that the generous Knight is, in the compassionate dictates of his soul, compelled to cry out:

> "Ho," quoth the Knyght,—"good Sir, no more
>   of this;
> "That ye have said is right ynough I wis;
> "And mokell more, for little heaviness
> "Is right enough for much folk, as I guesse.
> "I say, for me, it is a great disease,
> "Whereas men have been in wealth and ease,
> "To heare of their sudden fall, alas,
> "And the contrary is joy and solas."

The Monk's definition of tragedy in the proem to his tale is worth repeating:

> "Tragedie is to tell a certain story,
> "As old books us maken memory,
> "Of hem that stood in great prosperity,
> "And be fallen out of high degree,
> "Into miserie, and ended wretchedly."

Though a man of luxury, pride and pleasure, he is a master of art and learning, though affecting to despise it. Those who can think that the proud Huntsman and Noble Housekeeper, Chaucer's Monk, is intended for a buffoon or burlesque character, know little of Chaucer.

For the Host who follows this group, and holds the center of the cavalcade, is a first rate character, and his jokes are no trifles; they are always, though uttered with audacity, and equally free with the Lord and the Peasant, they are always substantially and weightily expressive of knowledge and experience; Henry Baillie, the keeper of the greatest Inn of the greatest City; for such was the Tabarde Inn in Southwark, near London: our Host was also a leader of the age.

By way of illustration, I instance Shakspeare's Witches in Macbeth. Those who dress them for the stage, consider them as wretched old women, and not as Shakspeare intended, the Goddesses of Destiny; this shews how Chaucer has been misunderstood in his sublime work. Shakespeare's Fairies also are the rulers of the vegetable world, and so are Chaucer's; let them be so considered, and then the poet will be understood, and not else.

But I have omitted to speak of a very prominent character, the Pardoner, the Age's Knave, who always commands and domineers over the high and low vulgar. This man is sent in every age for a rod and scourge, and for a blight, for a trial of men, to divide the classes of men; he is in the most holy sanctuary, and he is suffered by Providence for wise ends, and has also his great use, and his grand leading destiny.

His companion, the Sompnour, is also a Devil of the first magnitude, grand, terrific, rich and honoured in the rank of which he holds the destiny. The uses to Society are perhaps equal of the Devil and of the Angel, their sublimity, who can dispute.

> In daunger had he at his own gise,
> The young girls of his diocese,
> And he knew well their counsel, &c.

The principal figure in the next groupe is the Good Parson; an Apostle, a real Messenger of Heaven, sent in every age for its light and its warmth. This man is beloved and venerated by all, and neglected by all: He serves all, and is served by none; he is, according to Christ's definition, the greatest of his age. Yet he is a Poor Parson of a town. Read Chaucer's description of the Good Parson, and bow the head and the knee to him, who, in every age, sends us such a burning and a shining light. Search, O ye rich and powerful, for these men and obey their counsel, then shall the golden age return: But alas! you will not easily distinguish him from the Friar or the Pardoner; they, also, are "full solemn men," and their counsel you will continue to follow.

I have placed by his side the Sergeant at Lawe, who appears delighted to ride in his company, and between him and his brother, the Plowman; as I wish men of Law would always ride with them, and take their counsel, especially in all difficult points. Chaucer's Lawyer is a character of great venerableness, a Judge, and a real master of the jurisprudence of his age.

The Doctor of Physic is in this groupe, and the Franklin, the voluptuous country gentleman, contrasted with the Physician, and on his other hand, with two Citizens of London. Chaucer's characters live age after age. Every age is a Canterbury Pilgrimage; we all pass on, each sustaining one or other of these characters; nor can a child be born, who is not one of these characters of Chaucer. The Doctor of Physic is described as the first of his profession; perfect, learned, completely Master and Doctor in his art. Thus the reader will observe, that Chaucer makes every one of his characters perfect in his kind; every one is an Antique Statue; the image of a class, and not of an imperfect individual.

This groupe also would furnish substantial matter, on which volumes might be written. The Franklin is one who keeps open table, who is the genius of eating and drinking, the Bacchus; as the Doctor of Physic is the Esculapius, the Host is the Silenus, the Squire is the Apollo, the Miller is the Hercules, &c. Chaucer's characters are a description of the eternal Principles that exist in all ages. The Franklin is voluptuousness itself, most nobly pourtrayed:

> It snewed in his house of meat and drink.

The Plowman is simplicity itself, with wisdom and strength for its stamina. Chaucer has divided the ancient character of Hercules between his Miller and his Plowman. Benevolence is the plowman's great characteristic; he is thin with excessive labour, and not with old age, as some have supposed:

> He would thresh, and thereto dike and delve
> For Christe's sake, for every poore wight,
> Withouten hire, if it lay in his might.

Visions of these eternal principles or characters of human life appear to poets, in all ages; the Grecian gods were the ancient Cherubim of Phoenicia; but the Greeks, and since them the Moderns, have neglected to subdue the gods of Priam. These gods are visions of the eternal attributes, or divine names, which, when erected into gods, become destructive to humanity. They ought to be the servants, and not the masters of man, or of society. They ought to be made to sacrifice to Man, and not man compelled to sacrifice to them; for when separated from man or humanity, who is Jesus the Saviour, the vine of eternity, they are thieves and rebels, they are destroyers.

The Plowman of Chaucer is Hercules in his supreme eternal state, divested of his spectrous shadow; which is the Miller, a terrible fellow, such as exists in all times and places for the trial of men, to astonish every neighbourhood with brutal strength and courage, to get rich and powerful to curb the pride of Man.

The Reeve and the Manciple are two characters of the most consummate worldly wisdom. The Shipman, or Sailor, is a similar genius of Ulyssean art; but with the highest courage superadded.

The Citizens and their Cook are each leaders of a class. Chaucer has been somehow made to number four citizens, which would make his whole company, himself included, thirty-one. But he says there was but nine and twenty in his company:

> Full nine and twenty in a company.

The Webbe, or Weaver, and the Tapiser, or Tapestry Weaver, appear to me to be the same person; but this is only an opinion, for full nine and twenty may signify one more or less. But I dare say that Chaucer wrote "A Webbe Dyer," that is, a Cloth Dyer:

> A Webbe Dyer, and a Tapiser.

The Merchant cannot be one of the Three Citizens, as his dress is different, and his character is more marked, whereas Chaucer says of his rich citizens:

> All were yclothed in o liverie.

The characters of Women Chaucer has divided into two classes, the Lady Prioress and the Wife of Bath. Are not these leaders of the ages of men? The lady prioress, in some ages, predominates; and in some the wife of Bath, in whose character Chaucer has been equally minute and exact, because she is also a scourge and a blight. I shall say no more of her, nor expose what Chaucer has left hidden; let the young reader study what he has said of her: it is useful as a scarecrow. There are of such characters born too many for the peace of the world.

I come at length to the Clerk of Oxenford. This character varies from that of Chaucer, as the contemplative philosopher varies from the poetical genius. There are always these two classes of learned sages, the poetical and the philosophical. The painter has put them side by side, as if the youthful clerk had put himself under the tuition of the mature poet. Let the Philosopher always be the servant and scholar of inspiration and all will be happy. (pp. 567-72)

> *William Blake, "A Descriptive Catalogue," in his* Blake: Complete Writings, *edited by Geoffrey Keynes, Oxford University Press, London, 1966, pp. 563-85.*

William Hazlitt   (lecture date 1818)

[*One of the most important commentators of the Romantic age, Hazlitt was an English critic and journalist. He is best known for his descriptive criticism in which he stressed that no motives beyond judgment and analysis are necessary on the part of the critic. Characterized by a tough, independent view of the world, by his political liberalism, and by the influence of Samuel Taylor Coleridge and Charles Lamb, Hazlitt is particularly admired for his wide range of reference and catholicity of interests. Though he wrote on many diverse subjects, Hazlitt's most important critical achievements are his typically Romantic interpretation of characters from William Shakespeare's plays, influenced by the German critic August Wilhelm Schlegel, and his revival of interest in such Elizabethan dramatists as John Webster, Thomas Haywood, and Thomas Dekker. In the excerpt below from a lecture on Chaucer and Edmund Spenser originally given in 1818, Hazlitt emphasizes Chaucer's powerful realism, depth of feeling, and ability to balance pathos and humor.*]

There are poets older than Chaucer, and in the interval between him and Spenser; but their genius was not such as to place them in any point of comparison with either of these celebrated men; and an inquiry into their particular merits or defects might seem rather to belong to the province of the antiquary, than be thought generally interesting to the lovers of poetry in the present day.

Chaucer (who has been very properly considered as the father of English poetry) preceded Spenser by two centuries. He is supposed to have been born in London, in the year

1328, during the reign of Edward III., and to have died in 1400, at the age of seventy-two. He received a learned education at one, or at both of the universities, and travelled early into Italy, where he became thoroughly imbued with the spirit and excellences of the great Italian poets and prose-writers, Dante, Petrarch, and Boccacio; and is said to have had a personal interview with one of these, Petrarch. He was connected by marriage with the famous John of Gaunt, through whose interest he was introduced into several public employments. Chaucer was an active partisan, a religious reformer, and from the share he took in some disturbances on one occasion, he was obliged to fly the country. On his return, he was imprisoned, and made his peace with government, as it is said, by a discovery of his associates. Fortitude does not appear at any time to have been the distinguishing virtue of poets. There is, however, an obvious similarity between the practical turn of Chaucer's mind and restless impatience of his character, and the tone of his writings. Yet it would be too much to attribute the one to the other as cause and effect: for Spenser, whose poetical temperament was as effeminate as Chaucer's was stern and masculine, was equally engaged in public affairs, and had mixed equally in the great world. So much does native disposition predominate over accidental circumstances, moulding them to its previous bent and purposes! For while Chaucer's intercourse with the busy world, and collision with the actual passions and conflicting interests of others, seemed to brace the sinews of his understanding, and gave to his writings the air of a man who describes persons and things that he had known and been intimately concerned in; the same opportunities, operating on a differently-constituted frame, only served to alienate Spenser's mind the more from the "close-pent-up" scenes of ordinary life, and to make him "rive their concealing continents," to give himself up to the unrestrained indulgence of "flowery tenderness."

It is not possible for any two writers to be more opposite in this respect. Spenser delighted in luxurious enjoyment; Chaucer, in severe activity of mind. As Spenser was the most romantic and visionary, Chaucer was the most practical of all the great poets, the most a man of business and the world. His poetry reads like history. Everything has a downright reality, at least in the relator's mind. A simile or a sentiment is as if it were given in upon evidence. Thus he describes Cressid's first avowal of her love.

> And as the new abashed nightingale,
> That stinteth first when she beginneth sing,
> When that she heareth any herde's tale,
> Or in the hedges any wight stirring,
> And after, sicker, doth her voice outring;
> Right so Cresseide, when that her dread stent,
> Open'd her heart, and told him her intent.

This is so true and natural, and beautifully simple, that the two things seem identified with each other. Again, it is said in the **"Knight's Tale"**:

> Thus passeth yere by yere, and day by day,
> Till it felle ones in a morwe of May,
> That Emelie that fayrer was to sene
> Than is the lilie upon his stalke grene;
> And fresher than the May with floures newe,
> For with the rose-colour strof hire hewe:

I n'ot which was the finer of hem two.

This scrupulousness about the literal preference, as if some question of matter of fact was at issue, is remarkable. I might mention that other, where he compares the meeting between Palamon and Arcite to a hunter waiting for a lion in a gap:

> That stondeth at a gap with a spere,
> Whan hunted is the lion or the bere,
> And hereth him come rushing in the greves,
> And breking bothe the boughes and the leves:

or that still finer one of Constance, when she is condemned to death:

> Have ye not seen sometime a pale face
> (Among a prees) of him that hath been lad
> Toward his deth, wheras he geteth no grace,
> And swiche a colour in his face hath had,
> Men mighten know him that was so bestad,
> Amonges all the faces in that route;
> So stant Custance, and loketh hire aboute.

The beauty, the pathos here does not seem to be of the poet's seeking, but a part of the necessary texture of the fable. He speaks of what he wishes to describe with the accuracy, the discrimination of one who relates what has happened to himself, or has had the best information from those who have been eye-witnesses of it. The strokes of his pencil always tell. He dwells only on the essential, on that which would be interesting to the persons really concerned: yet as he never omits any material circumstance, he is prolix from the number of points on which he touches, without being diffuse on any one; and is sometimes tedious from the fidelity with which he adheres to his subject, as other writers are from the frequency of their digressions from it. The chain of his story is composed of a number of fine links, closely connected together, and riveted by a single blow. There is an instance of the minuteness which he introduces into his most serious descriptions in his account of Palamon when left alone in his cell:

> Swiche sorrow he maketh that the grete tour
> Resouned of his yelling and clamour:
> The pure fetters on his shinnes grete
> Were of his bitter salte teres wete.

The mention of this last circumstance looks like a part of the instructions he had to follow, which he had no discretionary power to leave out or introduce at pleasure. He is contented to find grace and beauty in truth. He exhibits for the most part the naked object, with little drapery thrown over it. His metaphors, which are few, are not for ornament, but use, and as like as possible to the things themselves. He does not affect to show his power over the reader's mind, but the power which his subject has over his own. The readers of Chaucer's poetry feel more nearly what the persons he describes must have felt, than perhaps those of any other poet. His sentiments are not voluntary effusions of the poet's fancy, but [are] founded on the natural impulses and habitual prejudices of the characters he has to represent. There is an inveteracy of purpose, a sincerity of feeling, which never relaxes or grows vapid, in whatever they do or say. There is no artificial, pompous display, but a strict parsimony of the poet's materials, like the rude simplicity of the age in which he lived. His poetry resembles the root just springing from the ground, rather than the full-blown flower. His muse is no "babbling gossip of the air," fluent and redundant: but, like a stammerer or a dumb person, that has just found the use of speech, crowds many things together with eager haste, with anxious pauses, and fond repetitions to prevent mistake. His words point as an index to the objects, like the eye or finger. There were none of the common-places of poetic diction in our author's time, no reflected lights of fancy, no borrowed roseate tints; he was obliged to inspect things for himself, to look narrowly, and almost to handle the object, as in the obscurity of morning we partly see and partly grope our way; so that his descriptions have a sort of tangible character belonging to them, and produce the effect of sculpture on the mind. Chaucer had an equal eye for truth of nature and discrimination of character; and his interest in what he saw gave new distinctness and force to his power of observation. The picturesque and the dramatic are in him closely blended together, and hardly distinguishable; for he principally describes external appearances as indicating character, as symbols of internal sentiment. There is a meaning in what he sees; and it is this which catches his eye by sympathy. Thus the costume and dress of the Canterbury Pilgrims, of the Knight, the Squire, the Oxford Scholar, the Gap-toothed Wife of Bath, and the rest, speak for themselves. (pp. 26-31)

The Serjeant at Law is the same identical individual as Lawyer Dowling in *Tom Jones,* who wished to divide himself into a hundred pieces, to be in a hundred places at once:

> No wher so besy a man as he ther n'as,
> And yet he semed besier than he was.

The Frankelein, in "whose hous it snewed of mete and drinke;" the Shipman, "who rode upon a rouncie, as he couthe;" the Doctour of Phisike, "whose studie was but litel of the Bible;" the Wif of Bath, in

> All whose parish there was non,
> That to the offring before hire shulde gon,
> And if ther did, certain so wroth was she,
> That she was out of alle charittee;

the poure Persone of a toun, "whose parish was wide, and houses fer asonder;" the Miller, and the Reve, "a slendre colerike man," are all of the same stamp. They are every one samples of a kind; abstract definitions of a species. Chaucer, it has been said, numbered the classes of men, as Linnæus numbered the plants [see excerpt dated 1809]. Most of them remain to this day: others that are obsolete, and may well be dispensed with, still live in his descriptions of them. Such is the Sompnoure:

> A Sompnoure was ther with us in that place,
> That hadde a fire-red cherubinnes face,
> For sausefleme he was, with eyen narwe,
> As hote he was, and likerous as a sparwe,
> With scalled browes blake, and pilled berd:
> Of his visage children were sore aferd.
> Ther n'as quicksilver, litarge, ne brimston,
> Boras, ceruse, ne oile of tartre non,
> Ne oinement that wolde clense or bite,
> That him might helpen of his whelkes white,
> Ne of the knobbes sitting on his chekes.

> Wel loved he garlike, onions, and eklekes,
> And for to drinke strong win as rede as blood.
> Than wolde he speke, and crie as he were wood.
> And whan that he wel dronken had the win,
> Than wold he speken no word but Latin.
> A fewe termes coude he, two or three,
> That he had lerned out of som decree;
> No wonder is, he heard it all the day.—

> In danger hadde he at his owen assise
> The yonge girles of the diocise,
> And knew hir conseil, and was al hir rede.
> A gerlond hadde he sette upon his hede
> As gret as it were for an alestake:
> A bokeler hadde he made him of a cake.
> With him ther rode a gentil Pardonere—
> A voys he hadde as smale as eny gote.

It would be a curious speculation (at least for those who think that the characters of men never change, though manners, opinions, and institutions may) to know what has become of this character of the Sompnoure in the present day; whether or not it has any technical representative in existing professions; into what channels and conduits it has withdrawn itself, where it lurks unseen in cunning obscurity, or else shows its face boldly, pampered into all the insolence of office, in some other shape, as it is deterred or encouraged by circumstances. *Chaucer's characters modernised,* upon this principle of historic derivation, would be an useful addition to our knowledge of human nature. But who is there to undertake it? (pp. 33-4)

Chaucer's descriptions of natural scenery possess the same sort of characteristic excellence, or what might be termed *gusto.* They have a local truth and freshness, which gives the very feeling of the air, the coolness or moisture of the ground. Inanimate objects are thus made to have a fellow-feeling in the interest of the story; and render back the sentiment of the speaker's mind. One of the finest parts of Chaucer is of this mixed kind. It is the beginning of the **"Flower and the Leaf,"** where he describes the delight of that young beauty, shrouded in her bower, and listening, in the morning of the year, to the singing of the nightingale; while her joy rises with the rising song, and gushes out afresh at every pause, and is borne along with the full tide of pleasure, and still increases, and repeats, and prolongs itself, and knows no ebb. The coolness of the arbour, its retirement, the early time of the day, the sudden starting up of the birds in the neighbouring bushes, the eager delight with which they devour and rend the opening buds and flowers, are expressed with a truth and feeling, which make the whole appear like the recollection of an actual scene. . . . There is . . . no affected rapture, no flowery sentiment: the whole is an ebullition of natural delight "welling out of the heart," like water from a crystal spring. Nature is the soul of art: there is a strength as well as a simplicity in the imagination that reposes entirely on nature, that nothing else can supply. It was the same trust in nature, and reliance on his subject, which enabled Chaucer to describe the grief and patience of Griselda, the faith of Constance, and the heroic perseverance of the little child who, going to school through the streets of Jewry,

> Oh *Alma redemptoris mater,* loudly sung,

and who after his death still triumphed in his song. Chaucer has more of this deep, internal, sustained sentiment than any other writer, except Boccaccio. In depth of simple pathos and intensity of conception, never swerving from his subject, I think no other writer comes near him, not even the Greek tragedians. I wish to be allowed to give one or two instances of what I mean. I will take the following from the **"Knight's Tale."** The distress of Arcite, in consequence of his banishment from his love, is thus described:

> Whan that Arcite to Thebes comen was,
> Ful oft a day he swelt and said Alas,
> For sene his lady shall he never mo.
> And shortly to concluden all his wo,
> So mochel sorwe hadde never creature,
> That is or shall be, while the world may dure.
> His slepe, his mete, his drinke is him byraft.
> That lene he wex, and drie as is a shaft.
> His eyen holwe, and grisly to behold,
> His hewe salwe, and pale as ashen cold,
> And solitary he was, and ever alone,
> And wailing all the night, making his mone.
> And if he herde song or instrument,
> Than wold he wepe, he mighte not be stent.
> So feble were his spirites, and so low,
> And changed so, that no man coude know
> His speche ne his vois, though men it herd."

This picture of the sinking of the heart, of the wasting away of the body and mind, of the gradual failure of all the faculties under the contagion of a rankling sorrow, cannot be surpassed. Of the same kind is his farewell to his mistress, after he has gained her hand and lost his life in the combat:

> Alas the wo! alas the peines stronge,
> That I for you have suffered, and so longe?
> Alas the deth! alas min Emilie!
> Alas departing of our compagnie;
> Alas min nertes quene? alas my wif!
> Min hertes ladie, ender of my lif!
> What is this world? what axen men to have?
> Now with his love, now in his colde grave
> Alone withouten any compagnie.

The death of Arcite is the more affecting, as it comes after triumph and victory, after the pomp of sacrifice, the solemnities of prayer, the celebration of the gorgeous rites of chivalry. The descriptions of the three temples of Mars, of Venus, and Diana, of the ornaments and ceremonies used in each, with the reception given to the offerings of the lovers, have a beauty and grandeur, much of which is lost in Dryden's version. For instance, such lines as the following are not rendered with their true feeling:

> Why shulde I not as well eke tell you all
> The purtreiture that was upon the wall
> Within the temple of mighty Mars the rede—
> That highte the gret temple of Mars in Trace
> In thilke colde and frosty region,
> Ther as Mars hath his sovereine mansion.
> First on the wall was peinted a forest,
> In which ther wonneth neyther man ne best,
> With knotty knarry barrein trees old
> Of stubbes sharpe and hidous to behold;
> In which ther ran a romble and a swough,
> As though a storme shuld bresten every bough.

And again, among innumerable terrific images of death and slaughter painted on the wall, is this one:

> The statue of Mars upon a carte stood
> Armed, and looked grim as he were wood.
> A wolf ther stood beforne him at his fete
> With eyen red, and of a man he ete.

The story of Griselda is in Boccaccio; but the Clerk of Oxenforde, who tells it, professes to have learned it from Petrarch. This story has gone all over Europe, and has passed into a proverb. In spite of the barbarity of the circumstances, which are abominable, the sentiment remains unimpaired and unalterable. It is of that kind "that heaves no sigh, that sheds no tear;" but it hangs upon the beatings of the heart; it is a part of the very being; it is as inseparable from it as the breath we draw. It is still and calm as the face of death. Nothing can touch it in its ethereal purity: tender as the yielding flower, it is fixed as the marble firmament. The only remonstrance she makes, the only complaint she utters against all the ill-treatment she receives, is that single line where, when turned back naked to her father's house, she says:

> Let me not like a worm go by the way.

(pp. 36-40)

The story of the little child slain in Jewry (which is told by the Prioress, and worthy to be told by her who was "all conscience and tender heart") is not less touching than that of Griselda. It is simple and heroic to the last degree. The poetry of Chaucer has a religious sanctity about it, connected with the manners and superstitions of the age. It has all the spirit of martyrdom.

It has also all the extravagance and the utmost licentiousness of comic humour, equally arising out of the manners of the time. In this too Chaucer resembled Boccaccio, that he excelled in both styles, and could pass at will "from grave to gay, from lively to severe;" but he never confounded the two styles together (except from that involuntary and unconscious mixture of the pathetic and humorous, which is almost always to be found in nature), and was exclusively taken up with what he set about, whether it was jest or earnest. The **"Wife of Bath's Prologue"** (which Pope has very admirably modernised) is, perhaps, unequalled as a comic story. The **"Cock and the Fox"** is also excellent for lively strokes of character and satire. **"January and May"** is not so good as some of the others. Chaucer's versification, considering the time at which he wrote, and that versification is a thing in a great degree mechanical, is not one of his least merits. It has considerable strength and harmony, and its apparent deficiency in the latter respect arises chiefly from the alterations which have since taken place in the pronunciation or mode of accenting the words of the language. The best general rule for reading him is to pronounce the final *e,* as in reading Italian.

It was observed in the last Lecture ["On Poetry in General"] that painting describes what the object is in itself, poetry what it implies or suggests. Chaucer's poetry is not, in general, the best confirmation of the truth of this distinction, for his poetry is more picturesque and historical than almost any other. But there is one instance in point

The Ellesmere portrait of Chaucer.

which I cannot help giving in this place. It is the story of the three thieves who go in search of Death to kill him, and who, meeting with him, are entangled in their fate by his words without knowing him. In the printed catalogue to Mr. West's (in some respects very admirable) picture of Death on the Pale Horse, it is observed, that

> In poetry the same effect is produced by a few abrupt and rapid gleams of description touching, as it were with fire, the features and edges of a general mass of awful obscurity; but in painting, such indistinctness would be a defect, and imply that the artist wanted the power to portray the conceptions of his fancy. Mr. West was of opinion that to delineate a physical form, which in its moral impression would approximate to that of the visionary Death of Milton, it was necessary to endow it, if possible, with the appearance of superhuman strength and energy. He has therefore exerted the utmost force and perspicuity of his pencil on the central figure.

One might suppose from this, that the way to represent a shadow was to make it as substantial as possible. Oh no! Painting has its prerogatives (and high ones they are), but they lie in representing the visible, not the invisible. The moral attributes of Death are powers and effects of an infi-

nitely wide and general description, which no individual or physical form can possibly represent but by a courtesy of speech, or by a distant analogy. The moral impression of Death is essentially visionary; its reality is in the mind's eye. Words are here the only *things,* and things, physical forms, the mere mockeries of the understanding. The less definite, the less bodily the conception, the more vast, unformed, and unsubstantial, the nearer does it approach to some resemblance of that omnipresent, lasting, universal, irresistible principle, which everywhere, and at some time or other, exerts its power over all things. Death is a mighty abstraction, like Night, or Space, or Time. He is an ugly customer, who will not be invited to supper, or to sit for his picture. He is with us and about us, but we do not see him. He stalks on before us, and we do not mind him: he follows us close behind, and we do not turn to look back at him. We do not see him making faces at us in our lifetime, nor perceive him afterwards sitting in mock-majesty, a twin-skeleton, beside us, tickling our bare ribs and staring into our hollow eye-balls! Chaucer knew this. He makes three riotous companions go in search of Death to kill him; they meet with an old man whom they reproach with his age, and ask why he does not die, to which he answers thus

> "Ne Deth, alas! he will not han my lif.
> Thus walke I like a restless caitiff,
> And on the ground, which is my modres gate,
> I knocke with my staf, erlich and late,
> I say to hire, 'Leve mother, let me in.
> Lo, how I vanish, flesh and blood and skin,
> Alas! when shall my bones ben at reste?
> Mother, when you wolde I changen my cheste,
> That in my chambre longe time hath be,
> Ye, for an heren cloute to wrap in me.'
> But yet to me she will not don that grace,
> For which ful pale and welked is my face."

They then ask the old man where they shall find out Death to kill him, and he sends them on an errand which ends in the death of all three. We hear no more of him, but it is Death that they have encountered! (pp. 42-5)

> *William Hazlitt, "On Chaucer and Spenser," in his* Lectures on the English Poets, and the English Comic Writers, *edited by William Carew Hazlitt, George Bell and Sons, 1894, pp. 26-57.*

Samuel Taylor Coleridge   (essay date 1834)

[*One of the greatest poets and critics in English literature, Coleridge was a leading representative of the English Romantic movement. He is known for such poetic masterpieces as "The Rime of the Ancient Mariner" (1798) and "Kubla Khan" (1816). As presented in his* Biographia Literaria *(1817), Coleridge's critical ideas reflect his interest in German idealistic philosophy. In the following excerpt from a segment dated 1834 in his* Table Talk *(1835), he offers praise of Chaucer and defends the poet's language against charges of being antiquated.*]

I take unceasing delight in Chaucer. His manly cheerfulness is especially delicious to me in my old age. How exquisitely tender he is, and yet how perfectly free from the least touch of sickly melancholy or morbid drooping! The sympathy of the poet with the subjects of his poetry is particularly remarkable in Shakespeare and Chaucer; but what the first effects by a strong act of imagination and mental metamorphosis, the last does without any effort, merely by the inborn kindly joyousness of his nature. How well we seem to know Chaucer! How absolutely nothing do we know of Shakespeare!

I cannot in the least allow any necessity for Chaucer's poetry, especially the ***Canterbury Tales,*** being considered obsolete. Let a few plain rules be given for sounding the final *è* of syllables, and for expressing the termination of such words as *ocëan,* and *natiön,* &c., as dissyllables, or let the syllables to be sounded in such cases be marked by a competent metrist. This simple expedient would, with a very few trifling exceptions, where the errors are inveterate, enable any reader to feel the perfect smoothness and harmony of Chaucer's verse. As to understanding his language, if you read twenty pages with a good glossary, you surely can find no further difficulty, even as it is; but I should have no objection to see this done:—Strike out those words which are now obsolete, and I will venture to say that I will replace every one of them by words still in use out of Chaucer himself, or Gower his disciple. I don't want this myself: I rather like to see the significant terms which Chaucer unsuccessfully offered as candidates for admission into our language; but surely so very slight a change of the text may well be pardoned, even by black-*letterati,* for the purpose of restoring so great a poet to his ancient and most deserved popularity. (pp. 294-95)

Samuel Taylor Coleridge, in an excerpt in his The Table Talk and Omniana of Samuel Taylor Coleridge, *Oxford University Press, London, 1917, pp. 294-95.*

Ralph Waldo Emerson   (lecture date 1835)

[*Emerson was one of the most influential literary figures of the nineteenth century. An American essayist and poet, he founded the Transcendental movement and shaped a distinctly American philosophy which embraced optimism, individuality, and mysticism. In the following excerpt from a lecture delivered in 1835, he places Chaucer in the English literary tradition, finding that he "possesses the most authentic property of genius, that of sympathy with his subjects."*]

Geoffrey Chaucer in the unanimous opinion of scholars is the earliest classical English writer. He first gave vogue to many Provençal words by using them in his elegant and popular poems, and by far the greater part of his vocabulary is with little alteration in use at this day. He introduced several metres which from his time have been popular forms of poetic composition until ours. Moreover he either is the author or the translator of many images and fables and thoughts which have been the common property of poets ever since; and more or less exist in the common speech of men so that the reader of Chaucer finds little in his page that is wholly new. He is struck everywhere with likeness to familiar verses or tales; for, he is in the armoury of English literature. 'Tis as if he were carried back

into the generation before the last, and should see the likeness of all his friends in their grandfathers.

The single fact that he continues to be read by his countrymen now for near five hundred years, might well draw our attention to him. It is more remarkable in the present case as our poet set out with competitors whom his own age did not think of inferior merit. In the first hundred years of his fame, it was common to speak of Lydgate, Gower, and Chaucer as the English poetical triumvirate. By and by Lydgate was dropt; but the stern verdict of Time has now sentenced Gower also to silence and the name of Chaucer remains alone. In literature, one is ever struck with the fact that the good once is good always, the excellent is brand new forever. The average physical strength is so fixed, that among thirty jumpers the longest jump will be likely to be the longest of three hundred; and a very long jump will remain a very long jump a century afterward. Not less stable are intellectual measures. Richard Hooker wrote good prose in 1580. Here it is good prose in 1835. There have not been forty persons of his nation from that time to this who could write better. Often the superiority of the bard whose writings go down to posterity over the bard who is forgotten, is not very great. What Shakspear says of Coriolanus,

> I think he'll be to Rome
> As is the osprey to the fish, who takes it
> By sovereignty of nature,

is a good account of the successful poet in whom sometimes a skilful analyst could hardly show the immediate causes of his popularity and first decided claim of preference to his rivals. But having once secured that preference, having had the good fortune to survive from his age, he now receives a hundredfold additional honor as the representative of the entire humanity of that period. Like the Chickasaw chosen on slight grounds to act for his tribe at Washington, he there is the object of attention from distinguished men of all nations not at all proportioned to his personal merits but he monopolizes the curiosity which his tribe excite.

But the poems of Chaucer have great merits of their own. They are the compositions of a man of the world who has much knowledge both of books and of men. They exhibit strong sense, humor, pathos, and a dear love of nature. He is a man of strong and kindly genius possessing all his faculties in that balance and symmetry neither too little nor too much which constitute an individual a sort of Universal Man and fit him to take up into himself without egotism all the wit and character of his age and to stand for his age before posterity. He possesses many of the highest gifts of genius and those too whose value is most intelligible to all men. The milk of human kindness flows always in his veins. The hilarity of good sense joined with the best health and temper never forsakes him. He possesses that clear insight into life which ever and anon perceives under the play of the thousand interests and follies and caprices of man the adamantine framework of Nature on which all the decoration and activity of life is hung.

He possesses the most authentic property of genius, that of sympathy with his subjects so that he describes every object with a delight in the thing itself. It has been observed that it does not argue genius that a man can write well on himself, or on topics connected with his personal relations. It is the capital deduction from Lord Byron that his poems have but one subject: himself. It is the burden of society, that very few men have sufficient strength of mind to speak of any truth or sentiment and hardly even of facts and persons clean of any reference to themselves and their personal history. But the wise man and much more the true Poet quits himself and throws his spirit into whatever he contemplates and enjoys the making it speak that it would say. This power belonged to Chaucer.

With these endowments he writes though often playfully yet always as a sincere man who has an earnest meaning to express and nowise (at least in those poems on which his fame is founded) as an idle and irresponsible rhymer. He acknowledges in *House of Fame* that he prefers "sentence," that is, sense, to skill of numbers. He would make

> the rime agreeable
> Tho some verse fail in a syllable
> And though I do no diligence
> To show crafte but sentence.

But he felt and maintained the dignity of the laurel and restored it in England to its honor. (pp. 270-73)

No one can read Chaucer in his grave compositions without being struck with his consciousness of his poetic duties. He never writes with timidity. He speaks like one who knows the law, and has a right to be heard. He is a philanthropist, a moralist, a reformer. He lashes the vices of the clergy. He wrote a poem of stern counsel to King Richard. He exposes the foibles and tricks of all pretenders in science [and] the professions, and his prophetic wisdom is found on the side of good sense and humanity.

I do not feel that I have closed the enumeration of the gifts of Chaucer until it is added as a cause of his permanent fame in spite of the obsoleteness of his style (now 500 years old) that his virtues and genius are singularly agreeable to the English mind; that in him they find their prominent tastes and prejudices. He has the English sincerity and homeliness and humor, and his *Canterbury Tales* are invaluable as a picture of the domestic manners of the fourteenth century. Shakespear and Milton are not more intrinsically national poets than is Chaucer. He has therefore contributed not a little to deepen and fix in the character of his countrymen those habits and sentiments which inspired his early song.

The humor with which the English race is so deeply tinged, which constitutes the genius of so many of their writers, as, of the author of Hudibras, Smollett, Fielding, Swift, and Sterne, and which the English maintain to be inseparable from genius, effervesces in every page of Chaucer. The prologue to the *Canterbury Tales* is full of it. A pleasing specimen of it is the alarm in the farmyard in the **"Fable of the Cock and the Fox."** (pp. 274-75)

[A historical feature in the English race is] the respect for women, for want of which trait the ancient Greeks and Romans as well as the Oriental nations in all ages have never attained the highest point of Civilization. A severe morality is essential to high civilization and to the moral education of man it needs that the relation between the sexes should be established on a purely virtuous footing. It is the consequence of the unnatural condition of woman in the East that even life to a woman is reckoned a calamity. "When a daughter is born," says the Chinese *Sheking,* "she creeps on the ground: she is clothed with a wrapper: she plays with a tile: she is incapable of evil or of good." Our venerable English bard fully shared this generous attribute of his nation. I suppose nothing will more forcibly strike the reader of Chaucer than his thorough acquaintance with the female character. He does indeed know its weakness and its vice and has not shunned to show them. I am sorry for it. Well he had observed all those traits that in rarely endowed women command a veneration scarcely to be distinguished from worship. The whole mystery of humility, of love, of purity, and of faith, in woman, and how they make a woman unearthly and divine, he well knew, and has painted better than any other in Griselda and Blanche. The story of Griselda in the *Canterbury Tales,* is, I suppose the most pathetic poem in the language. And the *Book of the Duchess,* though the introduction be long and tedious, seems to me a beautiful portraiture of true love. All the sentiment is manly, honorable, and tender. I admire the description of Blanche who knew so well how to live

> That dulness was of her adrad
> She n'as too sober nor too glad
> In all thinges more measure
> Had never I trowe creature:

(pp. 280-81)

The influence of Chaucer . . . is very conspicuous on all our early literature. Not only Pope, Dryden, and Milton have been indebted to him but a large unacknowledged debt is easily traced. From Chaucer succeeding writers have borrowed the English versions of the celebrated classic mythology. Phebus, Diana and Mars, Priam, Hector, Troilus, Dido, Theseus, Ariadne reign as much in his poems as in those of the ancients, though in quite new costume of manners and speech. Chaucer however did not invent this modern dress for the old gods and heroes. In the year 1260 Guido de Colonna, a native of Messina in Sicily, published a grand prose romance in Latin in fifteen books, called *Historia de Bello Trojano.* This was founded on the apocryphal Greek history of Dares Phrygius and enriched by all paraphrases from Ovid and Statius. This is Chaucer's chief magazine. This is the book which was turned into English poetry by Lydgate at the command of Henry V and translated into English prose by Caxton the printer in 1471. Chaucer's other sources are Petrarch, Boccacio, Lollius, and the Provençal poets. *The Romaunt of the Rose* is translated from William of Lorris and John of Meun. **Troilus and Creseide** from Lollius of Urbino. *The House of Fame* is from the French or Italian. "The Cock and the Fox" is from the Lais of Marie a French poetess. And the extent of Chaucer's obligations to his foreign contemporaries and predecessors is so great as to induce the inquiry whether he can claim the praise of an original writer.

The truth is all works of literature are Janus faced and look to the future and to the past. Shakspeare, Pope, and Dryden borrow from Chaucer and shine by his borrowed light. Chaucer reflects Boccacio and Colonna and the

Troubadours; Boccacio and Colonna elder Greek and Roman authors, and these in their turn others if only history would enable us to trace them. There never was an original writer. Each is a link in an endless chain. To receive and to impart are the talents of the poet and he ought to possess both in equal degrees. He is merely the marble mouth of a fountain into which the waters ascend and out of which they flow. This is but the nature of man, universal receiving to the end of universal giving. (pp. 283-84)

And the nobler is the truth or sentiment concerned the less important becomes the question of authorship. It never troubles the simple lover of truth, said [Moses] Mendelsohn, from whom he derived such or such a sentiment. Whoever expresses to me a noble thought makes ridiculous the pains of the critic who should tell him where such a thing had been said before. For truth is always in the world: "It is no more according to Plato than according to me." Truth is always present; it only needs to lift the iron lids of the mind's eye to read its oracles. But the fact is it is as difficult to appropriate the thoughts of others as it is to invent.

Every great man, as Homer, Milton, Bacon, and Aristotle, necessarily takes up into himself all the wisdom that is current in his time. It is only an inventor [can use the inventions of others]. (p. 285)

The literary man who feels his position and duties should be solicitous to supply men with intellectual light, which he can often do better by direct importation from foreign sources than by the composition of new works, as when Alfred translated Boethius and books of travels for his countrymen or Wicliffe and Luther the *Bible*. Morality is concerned only with the spirit in which it is done; if the writer appropriates the praise and conceals the debt he is a plagiarist. If he generously feel that the thought most strictly his own is not his own and recognizes with awe the perpetual suggestion of God he then makes even the oldest thoughts new and fresh when he speaks them. Chaucer is never anxious to hide his obligations; he frankly acknowledges in every page or whenever he wants a rhyme that his author or the old book says so; and thus is to us in the remote past a luminous mind collecting and imparting to us the religion, the wit, and humanity of a whole age. (p. 286)

> *Ralph Waldo Emerson, "English Literature,"*
> *in his* The Early Lectures of Ralph Waldo
> Emerson: 1833-1836, Vol. I, *edited by Stephen*
> *E. Whicher and Robert E. Spiller, Cambridge,*
> *Mass.: Harvard University Press, 1959, pp.*
> *205-388.*

Henry David Thoreau   (essay date 1849)

[*An American essayist, poet, and translator, Thoreau is considered one of the key figures of the American Transcendentalist movement. His* Walden; or, Life in the Woods *(1854), a record of two years that he spent living alone in the woods near Concord, Massachusetts, is viewed as one of the finest prose works in American literature. Thoreau's aphoristic yet lyrical prose style and intense moral and political convictions have secured his*

place beside Ralph Waldo Emerson as the most representative and influential of the New England Transcendentalists. In the following excerpt from his A Week on the Concord and Merrimac Rivers *(1849), Thoreau finds that Chaucer's verse is "fresh and modern still, and no dust settles on his true passages," and praises the poet's "humanity."*]

Notwithstanding the broad humanity of Chaucer, and the many social and domestic comforts which we meet with in his verse, we have to narrow our vision somewhat to consider him, as if he occupied less space in the landscape, and did not stretch over hill and valley as Ossian does. Yet, seen from the side of posterity, as the father of English poetry, preceded by a long silence or confusion in history, unenlivened by any strain of pure melody, we easily come to reverence him. Passing over the earlier continental poets, since we are bound to the pleasant archipelago of English poetry, Chaucer's is the first name after that misty weather in which Ossian lived, which can detain us long. Indeed, though he represents so different a culture and society, he may be regarded as in many respects the Homer of the English poets. Perhaps he is the youthfulest of them all. We return to him as to the purest well, the fountain farthest removed from the highway of desultory life. He is so natural and cheerful, compared with later poets, that we might almost regard him as a personification of spring. To the faithful reader his muse has even given an aspect to his times, and when he is fresh from perusing him, they seem related to the golden age. (pp. 485-86)

Chaucer is fresh and modern still, and no dust settles on his true passages. It lightens along the line, and we are reminded that flowers have bloomed, and birds sung, and hearts beaten in England. Before the earnest gaze of the reader, the rust and moss of time gradually drop off, and the original green life is revealed. He was a homely and domestic man, and did breathe quite as modern men do.

There is no wisdom that can take place of humanity, and we find *that* in Chaucer. We can expand at last in his breadth, and we think that we could have been that man's acquaintance. He was worthy to be a citizen of England, while Petrarch and Boccaccio lived in Italy, and Tell and Tamerlane in Switzerland and in Asia, and Bruce in Scotland, and Wickliffe, and Gower, and Edward the Third, and John of Gaunt, and the Black Prince were his own countrymen as well as contemporaries; all stout and stirring names. The fame of Roger Bacon came down from the preceding century, and the name of Dante still possessed the influence of a living presence. On the whole, Chaucer impresses us as greater than his reputation, and not a little like Homer and Shakespeare, for he would have held up his head in their company. Among early English poets he is the landlord and host, and has the authority of such. The affectionate mention which succeeding early poets make of him, coupling him with Homer and Virgil, is to be taken into the account in estimating his character and influence. King James and Dunbar of Scotland speak of him with more love and reverence than any modern author of his predecessors of the last century. The same childlike relation is without a parallel now. For the most part we read him without criticism, for he does not plead his own cause, but speaks for his readers, and has that greatness of trust and reliance which compels popularity. He confides in the reader, and speaks privily with him, keeping nothing back. And in return the reader has great confidence in him, that he tells no lies, and reads his story with indulgence, as if it were the circumlocution of a child, but often discovers afterwards that he has spoken with more directness and economy of words than a sage. He is never heartless,—

> For first the thing is thought within the hart,
> Er any word out from the mouth astart.

And so new was all his theme in those days, that he did not have to invent, but only to tell.

We admire Chaucer for his sturdy English wit. The easy height he speaks from in his **"General Prologue"** to the *Canterbury Tales*, as if he were equal to any of the company there assembled, is as good as any particular excellence in it. But though it is full of good sense and humanity, it is not transcendent poetry. For picturesque description of persons it is, perhaps, without a parallel in English poetry; yet it is essentially humorous, as the loftiest genius never is. Humor, however broad and genial, takes a narrower view than enthusiasm. To his own finer vein he added all the common wit and wisdom of his time, and everywhere in his works his remarkable knowledge of the world and nice perception of character, his rare common sense and proverbial wisdom, are apparent. His genius does not soar like Milton's, but is genial and familiar. It shows great tenderness and delicacy, but not the heroic sentiment. It is only a greater portion of humanity with all its weakness. He is not heroic, as Raleigh, nor pious, as Herbert, nor philosophical, as Shakespeare, but he is the child of the English muse, that child which is the father of the man. The charm of his poetry consists often only in an exceeding naturalness, perfect sincerity, with the behavior of a child rather than of a man.

Gentleness and delicacy of character are everywhere apparent in his verse. The simplest and humblest words come readily to his lips. No one can read the **"Prioress's Tale,"** understanding the spirit in which it was written, and in which the child sings *O alma redemptoris mater*, or the account of the departure of Constance with her child upon the sea, in the **"Man of Lawe's Tale,"** without feeling the native innocence and refinement of the author. Nor can we be mistaken respecting the essential purity of his character, disregarding the apology of the manners of the age. A simple pathos and feminine gentleness, which Wordsworth only occasionally approaches, but does not equal, are peculiar to him. We are tempted to say that his genius was feminine, not masculine. It was such a feminineness, however, as is rarest to find in woman, though not the appreciation of it; perhaps it is not to be found at all in woman, but is only the feminine in man.

Such pure and genuine and childlike love of Nature is hardly to be found in any poet.

Chaucer's remarkably trustful and affectionate character appears in his familiar, yet innocent and reverent, manner of speaking of his God. He comes into his thought without any false reverence, and with no more parade than the zephyr to his ear. If Nature is our mother, then God is our father. There is less love and simple, practical trust in Shakespeare and Milton. How rarely in our English tongue do we find expressed any affection for God. Certainly, there is no sentiment so rare as the love of God. Herbert almost alone expresses it, "Ah, my dear God!" Our poet uses similar words with propriety; and whenever he sees a beautiful person, or other object, prides himself on the "maistry" of his God. He even recommends Dido to be his bride,—

> If that God that heaven and yearth made,
> Would have a love for beauty and goodnesse,
> And womanhede, trouth, and semeliness.

But in justification of our praise, we must refer to his works themselves; to the **"General Prologue"** to the *Canterbury Tales*, the account of **"Gentilesse,"** the **"Flower and the Leaf,"** the stories of Griselda, Virginia, Ariadne, and Blanche the Duchesse, and much more of less distinguished merit. There are many poets of more taste, and better manners, who knew how to leave out their dullness; but such negative genius cannot detain us long; we shall return to Chaucer still with love. Some natures, which are really rude and ill-developed, have yet a higher standard of perfection than others which are refined and well balanced. Even the clown has taste, whose dictates, though he disregards them, are higher and purer than those which the artist obeys. If we have to wander through many dull and prosaic passages in Chaucer, we have at least the satisfaction of knowing that it is not an artificial dullness, but too easily matched by many passages in life. We confess that we feel a disposition commonly to concentrate sweets, and accumulate pleasures; but the poet may be presumed always to speak as a traveler, who leads us through a varied scenery, from one eminence to another, and it is, perhaps, more pleasing, after all, to meet with a fine thought in its natural setting. Surely fate has enshrined it in these circumstances for some end. Nature strews her nuts and flowers broadcast, and never collects them into heaps. This was the soil it grew in, and this the hour it bloomed in; if sun, wind, and rain came here to cherish and expand the flower, shall not we come here to pluck it? (pp. 488-94)

> *Henry David Thoreau, "Friday," in his* A Week on the Concord and Merrimac Rivers, *Houghton Mifflin Company, 1894, pp. 441-531.*

James Russell Lowell   (essay date 1871)

[*Lowell was a celebrated American poet and essayist, and an editor of two leading journals, the* Atlantic Monthly *and the* North American Review. *He is noted for his satirical and critical writings, including* A Fable for Critics *(1848), a book-length poem featuring witty critical portraits of his contemporaries. Commentators generally agree that Lowell displayed a judicious critical sense, despite the fact that he sometimes relied upon mere impressions rather than critical precepts in his writings. In the following excerpt from an 1871 revision of an essay which originally appeared the previous year, Lowell compares Chaucer to other great poets, extolling*

Will it *do* to say anything more about Chaucer? Can any one hope to say anything, not new, but even fresh, on a topic so well worn? It may well be doubted; and yet one is always the better for a walk in the morning air,—a medicine which may be taken over and over again without any sense of sameness, or any failure of its invigorating quality. There is a pervading wholesomeness in the writings of this man,—a vernal property that soothes and refreshes in a way of which no other has ever found the secret. I repeat to myself a thousand times,—

> Whan that Aprilë with his showrës sotë
> The droughte of March hath percëd to the rotë,
> And bathëd every veine in swich licour
> Of which vertue engendered is the flour,—
> When Zephyrus eek with his swetë breth
> Enspirëd hath in every holt and heth
> The tender croppës, and the yongë sonne
> Hath in the ram his halfë cors yronne,
> And smalë foulës maken melodië,—

and still at the thousandth time a breath of uncontaminate springtide seems to lift the hair upon my forehead. If here be not the *largior ether,* the serene and motionless atmosphere of classical antiquity, we find at least the *seclusum nemus,* the *domos placidas,* and the *oubliance,* as Froissart so sweetly calls it, that persuade us we are in an Elysium none the less sweet that it appeals to our more purely human, one might almost say domestic, sympathies. We may say of Chaucer's muse, as Overbury of his milkmaid, "her breath is her own, which scents all the year long of *June* like a newmade haycock." The most hardened *roué* of literature can scarce confront these simple and winning graces without feeling somewhat of the unworn sentiment of his youth revive in him. Modern imaginative literature has become so self-conscious, and therefore so melancholy, that Art, which should be "the world's sweet inn," whither we repair for refreshment and repose, has become rather a watering-place, where one's own private touch of the liver-complaint is exasperated by the affluence of other sufferers whose talk is a narrative of morbid symptoms. Poets have forgotten that the first lesson of literature, no less than of life, is the learning how to burn your own smoke; that the way to be original is to be healthy; that the fresh color, so delightful in all good writing, is won by escaping from the fixed air of self into the brisk atmosphere of universal sentiments; and that to make the common marvellous, as if it were a revelation, is the test of genius. It is good to retreat now and then beyond earshot of the introspective confidences of modern literature, and to lose ourselves in the gracious worldliness of Chaucer. Here was a healthy and hearty man, so genuine that he need not ask whether he were genuine or no, so sincere as quite to forget his own sincerity, so truly pious that he could be happy in the best world that God chose to make, so humane that he loved even the foibles of his kind. Here was a truly epic poet, without knowing it, who did not waste time in considering whether his age were good or bad, but quietly taking it for granted as the best that ever was or could be for *him,* has left us such a picture of contemporary life as no man ever painted. "A perpetual fountain of good-sense," Dryden calls him [see excerpt dated 1700], yes, and of good-humor, too, and wholesome thought. He was one of those rare authors whom, if we had met him under a porch in a shower, we should have preferred to the rain. He could be happy with a crust and spring-water, and could see the shadow of his benign face in a flagon of Gascon wine without fancying Death sitting opposite to cry *Supernaculum!* when he had drained it. He could look to God without abjectness, and on man without contempt. The pupil of manifold experience,—scholar, courtier, soldier, ambassador, who had known poverty as a housemate and been the companion of princes,—his was one of those happy temperaments that could equally enjoy both halves of culture,—the world of books and the world of men.

> Unto this day it doth mine hertë boote,
> That I have had my world as in my time!

The portrait of Chaucer, which we owe to the loving regret of his disciple Occleve, confirms the judgment of him which we make from his works. It is, I think, more engaging than that of any other poet. The downcast eyes, half sly, half meditative, the sensuous mouth, the broad brown, drooping with weight of thought, and yet with an inexpugnable youth shining out of it as from the morning forehead of a boy, are all noticeable, and not less so their harmony of placid tenderness. We are struck, too, with the smoothness of the face as of one who thought easily, whose phrase flowed naturally, and who had never puckered his brow over an unmanageable verse. (pp. 291-94)

Chaucer, to whom French must have been almost as truly a mother tongue as English, was familiar with all that had been done by Troubadour or Trouvère. In him we see the first result of the Norman yeast upon the home-baked Saxon loaf. The flour had been honest, the paste well kneaded, but the inspiring leaven was wanting till the Norman brought it over. Chaucer works still in the solid material of his race, but with what airy lightness has he not infused it? Without ceasing to be English, he has escaped from being insular. But he was something more than this; he was a scholar, a thinker, and a critic. He had studied the *Divina Commedia* of Dante, he had read Petrarca and Boccaccio, and some of the Latin poets. He calls Dante the great poet of Italy, and Petrarch a learned clerk. It is plain that he knew very well the truer purpose of poetry, and had even arrived at the higher wisdom of comprehending the aptitudes and limitations of his own genius. He saw clearly and felt keenly what were the faults and what the wants of the prevailing literature of his country. In the **"Monk's Tale"** he slyly satirizes the long-winded morality of Gower, as his prose antitype, Fielding, was to satirize the prolix sentimentality of Richardson. In the rhyme of **"Sir Thopas"** he gives the *coup de grace* to the romances of Chivalry, and in his own choice of a subject he heralds that new world in which the actual and the popular were to supplant the fantastic and the heroic.

Before Chaucer, modern Europe had given birth to one great poet, Dante; and contemporary with him was one supremely elegant one, Petrarch. Dante died only seven years before Chaucer was born, and, so far as culture is derived from books, the moral and intellectual influences to which they had been subjected, the speculative stimulus that may have given an impulse to their minds,—there could have been no essential difference between them. Yet there are certain points of resemblance and of contrast, and those not entirely fanciful, which seem to me of considerable interest. Both were of mixed race, Dante certainly, Chaucer presumably so. Dante seems to have inherited on the Teutonic side the strong moral sense, the almost nervous irritability of conscience, and the tendency to mysticism which made him the first of Christian poets—first in point of time and first in point of greatness. From the other side he seems to have received almost in overplus a feeling of order and proportion, sometimes wellnigh hardening into mathematical precision and formalism,—a tendency which at last brought the poetry of the Romanic races to a dead-lock of artifice and decorum. Chaucer, on the other hand, drew from the South a certain airiness of sentiment and expression, a felicity of phrase and an elegance of turn, hitherto unprecedented and hardly yet matched in our literature, but all the while kept firm hold of his native soundness of understanding, and that genial humor which seems to be the proper element of worldly wisdom. With Dante life represented the passage of the soul from a state of nature to a state of grace; and there would have been almost an even chance whether (as Burns says) the *Divina Commedia* had turned out a song or a sermon, but for the wonderful genius of its author, which has compelled the sermon to sing and the song to preach, whether they would or no. With Chaucer, life is a pilgrimage, but only that his eye may be delighted with the varieties of costume and character. There are good morals to be found in Chaucer, but they are always incidental. With Dante the main question is the saving of the soul, with Chaucer it is the conduct of life. The distance between them is almost that between holiness and prudence. Dante applies himself to the realities, Chaucer to the scenery of life, and the former is consequently the more universal poet, as the latter is the more truly national one. Dante represents the justice of God, and Chaucer his lovingkindness. If there is anything that may properly be called satire in the one, it is like a blast of the divine wrath, before which the wretches cower and tremble, which rends away their cloaks of hypocrisy and their masks of worldly propriety, and leaves them shivering in the cruel nakedness of their shame. The satire of the other is genial with the broad sunshine of humor, into which the victims walk forth with a delightful unconcern, laying aside of themselves the disguises that seem to make them uncomfortably warm, till they have made a thorough betrayal of themselves so unconsciously that we almost pity while we laugh. Dante shows us the punishment of sins against God and one's neighbor, in order that we may shun them, and so escape the doom that awaits them in the other world. Chaucer exposes the cheats of the transmuter of metals, of the begging friars, and of the pedlers of indulgences, in order that we may be on our guard against them in this world. If we are to judge of what is national only by the highest and most characteristic types, surely we cannot fail to see in Chaucer the true forerunner and prototype of Shakespeare, who, with an imagination of far deeper grasp, a far wider reach of thought, yet took the same delight in the pageantry of the actual world, and whose

moral is the moral of worldly wisdom only heightened to the level of his wide-viewing mind, and made typical by the dramatic energy of his plastic nature.

Yet if Chaucer had little of that organic force of life which so inspires the poem of Dante that, as he himself says of the heavens, part answers to part with mutual interchange of light, he had a structural faculty which distinguishes him from all other English poets, his contemporaries, and which indeed is the primary distinction of poets properly so called. There is, to be sure, only one other English writer coeval with himself who deserves in any way to be compared with him, and that rather for contrast than for likeness.

With the single exception of Langland, the English poets, his contemporaries, were little else than bad versifiers of legends classic or mediæval, as it might happen, without selection and without art. Chaucer is the first who broke away from the dreary traditional style, and gave not merely stories, but lively *pictures* of real life as the ever renewed substance of poetry. He was a reformer, too, not only in literature, but in morals. But as in the former his exquisite tact saved him from all eccentricity, so in the latter the pervading sweetness of his nature could never be betrayed into harshness and invective. He seems incapable of indignation. He mused good-naturedly over the vices and follies of men, and, never forgetting that he was fashioned of the same clay, is rather apt to pity than condemn. There is no touch of cynicism in all he wrote. Dante's brush seems sometimes to have been smeared with the burning pitch of his own fiery lake. Chaucer's pencil is dipped in the cheerful color-box of the old illuminators, and he has their patient delicacy of touch, with a freedom far beyond their somewhat mechanic brilliancy. (pp. 321-25)

"Piers Ploughman" is the best example I know of what is called popular poetry,—of compositions, that is, which contain all the simpler elements of poetry, but still in solution, not crystallized around any thread of artistic purpose. In it appears at her best the Anglo-Saxon Muse, a first cousin of Poor Richard, full of proverbial wisdom, who always brings her knitting in her pocket, and seems most at home in the chimney-corner. It is genial; it plants itself firmly on human nature with its rights and wrongs; it has a surly honesty, prefers the downright to the gracious, and conceives of speech as a tool rather than a musical instrument. If we should seek for a single word that would define it most precisely, we should not choose simplicity, but homeliness. There is more or less of this in all early poetry, to be sure; but I think it especially proper to English poets, and to the most English among them, like Cowper, Crabbe, and one is tempted to add Wordsworth,—where he forgets Coleridge's private lectures. In reading such poets as Langland, also, we are not to forget a certain charm of distance in the very language they use, making it unhackneyed without being alien. As it is the chief function of the poet to make the familiar novel, these fortunate early risers of literature, who gather phrases with the dew still on them, have their poetry done for them, as it were, by their vocabulary. But in Chaucer, as in all great poets, the language gets its charm from him. The force and sweetness of his genius kneaded more kindly together the Latin and Teutonic elements of our mother tongue, and made something better than either. The necessity of writing poetry, and not mere verse, made him a reformer whether he would or no; and the instinct of his finer ear was a guide such as none before him or contemporary with him, nor indeed any that came after him, till Spenser, could command. Gower had no notion of the uses of rhyme except as a kind of crease at the end of every eighth syllable, where the verse was to be folded over again into another layer. He says, for example,

> "This maiden Canacee was hight,
> Both in the day and eke by night,"

as if people commonly changed their names at dark. And he could not even contrive to say this without the clumsy pleonasm of *both* and *eke*. Chaucer was put to no such shifts of piecing out his metre with loose-woven bits of baser stuff. He himself says, in the **"Man of Law's Tale,"**—

> Me lists not of the chaff nor of the straw
> To make so long a tale as of the corn.

One of the world's three or four great story-tellers, he was also one of the best versifiers that ever made English trip and sing with a gayety that seems careless, but where every foot beats time to the tune of the thought. By the skilful arrangement of his pauses he evaded the monotony of the couplet, and gave to the rhymed pentameter, which he made our heroic measure, something of the architectural repose of blank verse. He found our language lumpish, stiff, unwilling, too apt to speak Saxonly in grouty monosyllables; he left it enriched with the longer measure of the Italian and Provençal poets. He reconciled, in the harmony of his verse, the English bluntness with the dignity and elegance of the less homely Southern speech. Though he did not and could not create our language (for he who writes to be read does not write for linguisters), yet it is true that he first made it easy, and to that extent modern, so that Spenser, two hundred years later, studied his method and called him master. He first wrote *English;* and it was a feeling of this, I suspect, that made it fashionable in Elizabeth's day to "talk pure Chaucer." Already we find in his works verses that might pass without question in Milton or even Wordsworth, so mainly unchanged have the language of poetry and the movement of verse remained from his day to our own. (pp. 334-37)

I will give one more example of Chaucer's verse, again making my selection from one of his less mature works. He is speaking of Tarquin:—

> And ay the morë he was in despair
> The more he coveted and thought her fair;
> His blindë lust was all his coveting.
> On morrow when the bird began to sing
> Unto the siege he cometh full privily
> And by himself he walketh soberly
> The imáge of her recording alway new:
> Thus lay her hair, and thus fresh was her hue,
> Thus sate, thus spake, thus span, this was her
>   cheer,
> Thus fair she was, and this was her manére.
> All this conceit his heart hath new ytake,
> And as the sea, with tempest all toshake,

> That after, when the storm is all ago,
> Yet will the water quap a day or two,
> Right so, though that her formë were absént,
> The pleasance of her forme was presént.

And this passage leads me to say a few words of Chaucer as a descriptive poet; for I think it a great mistake to attribute to him any properly dramatic power, as some have done. Even Herr Hertzberg, in his remarkably intelligent essay, is led a little astray on this point by his enthusiasm. Chaucer is a great narrative poet; and, in this species of poetry, though the author's personality should never be obtruded, it yet unconsciously pervades the whole, and communicates an individual quality,—a kind of flavor of its own. This very quality, and it is one of the highest in its way and place, would be fatal to all dramatic force. The narrative poet is occupied with his characters as picture, with their grouping, even their costume, it may be, and he feels for and with them instead of being they for the moment, as the dramatist must always be. The story-teller must possess the situation perfectly in all its details, while the imagination of the dramatist must be possessed and mastered by it. The latter puts before us the very passion or emotion itself in its utmost intensity; the former gives them, not in their primary form, but in that derivative one which they have acquired by passing through his own mind and being modified by his reflection. The deepest pathos of the drama, like the quiet "no more but so?" with which Shakespeare tells us that Ophelia's heart is bursting, is sudden as a stab, while in narrative it is more or less suffused with pity,—a feeling capable of prolonged sustention. This presence of the author's own sympathy is noticeable in all Chaucer's pathetic passages, as, for instance, in the lamentation of Constance over her child in the **"Man of Law's Tale,"** When he comes to the sorrow of his story, he seems to croon over his thoughts, to soothe them and dwell upon them with a kind of pleased compassion, as a child treats a wounded bird which he fears to grasp too tightly, and yet cannot make up his heart wholly to let go. It is true also of his humor that it pervades his comic tales like sunshine, and never dazzles the attention by a sudden flash. Sometimes he brings it in parenthetically, and insinuates a sarcasm so slyly as almost to slip by without our notice, as where he satirizes provincialism by the cock who

> By nature knew ech ascensioun
> Of equinoxial in thilke toun.

Sometimes he turns round upon himself and smiles at a trip he has made into fine writing:—

> Till that the brightë sun had lost his hue,
> For th'orisont had reft the sun his light,
> (This is as much to sayen as 'it was night.')

Nay, sometimes it twinkles roguishly through his very tears, as in the

> 'Why wouldest thou be dead,' these women cry,
> 'Thou haddest gold enough—and Emily?'

that follows so close upon the profoundly tender despair of Arcite's farewell:—

> "What is this world? What asken men to have?
> Now with his love now in the coldë grave

Alone withouten any company!"

The power of diffusion without being diffuse would seem to be the highest merit of narration, giving it that easy flow which is so delightful. Chaucer's descriptive style is remarkable for its lowness of tone,—for that combination of energy with simplicity which is among the rarest gifts in literature. Perhaps all is said in saying that he has style at all, for that consists mainly in the absence of undue emphasis and exaggeration, in the clear uniform pitch which penetrates our interest and retains it, where mere loudness would only disturb and irritate.

Not that Chaucer cannot be intense, too, on occasion; but it is with a quiet intensity of his own, that comes in as it were by accident.

> Upon a thickë palfrey, paper-white,
> With saddle red embroidered with delight,
> Sits Dido:
> And she is fair as is the brightë morrow
> That healeth sickë folk of nightës sorrow.
> Upon a courser startling as the fire,
> Æneas sits.

Pandarus, looking at Troilus,

> Took up a light and found his countenance
> As for to look upon an old romance.

With Chaucer it is always the thing itself and not the description of it that is the main object. His picturesque bits are incidental to the story, glimpsed in passing; they never stop the way. His key is so low that his high lights are never obtrusive. His imitators, like Leigh Hunt, and Keats in his "Endymion," missing the nice gradation with which the master toned everything down, become streaky. Hogarth, who reminds one of him in the variety and natural action of his figures, is like him also in the subdued brilliancy of his coloring. When Chaucer condenses, it is because his conception is vivid. He does not need to personify Revenge, for personification is but the subterfuge of unimaginative and professional poets; but he embodies the very passion itself in a verse that makes us glance over our shoulder as if we heard a stealthy tread behind us:—

> The smiler with the knife hid under the cloak.

And yet how unlike is the operation of the imaginative faculty in him and Shakespeare! When the latter describes, his epithets imply always an impression on the moral sense (so to speak) of the person who hears or sees. The sun "flatters the mountain-tops with sovereign eye"; the bending "weeds lacquey the dull stream"; the shadow of the falcon "coucheth the fowl below"; the smoke is "helpless"; when Tarquin enters the chamber of Lucrece "the threshold grates the door to have him heard." His outward sense is merely a window through which the metaphysical eye looks forth, and his mind passes over at once from the simple sensation to the complex *meaning* of it,— feels *with* the object instead of merely feeling it. His imagination is forever dramatizing. Chaucer gives only the direct impression made on the eye or ear. He was the first great poet who really loved outward nature as the source of conscious pleasurable emotion. The Troubadour hailed the return of spring; but with him it was a piece of empty ritualism. Chaucer took a true delight in the new green of the leaves and the return of singing birds,—a delight as simple as that of Robin Hood:—

> "In summer when the shaws be sheen,
> And leaves be large and long,
> It is full merry in fair forest
> To hear the small birds' song."

He has never so much as heard of the "burthen and the mystery of all this unintelligible world." His flowers and trees and birds have never bothered themselves with Spinoza. He himself sings more like a bird than any other poet, because it never occurred to him, as to Goethe, that he ought to do so. He pours himself out in sincere joy and thankfulness. When we compare Spenser's imitations of him with the original passages, we feel that the delight of the later poet was more in the expression than in the thing itself. Nature with him is only good to be transfigured by art. We walk among Chaucer's sights and sounds; we listen to Spenser's musical reproduction of them. In the same way, the pleasure which Chaucer takes in telling his stories has in itself the effect of consummate skill, and makes us follow all the windings of his fancy with sympathetic interest. His best tales run on like one of our inland rivers, sometimes hastening a little and turning upon themselves in eddies that dimple without retarding the current; sometimes loitering smoothly, while here and there a quiet thought, a tender feeling, a pleasant image, a golden-hearted verse, opens quietly as a water-lily, to float on the surface without breaking it into ripple. The vulgar intellectual palate hankers after the titillation of foaming phrase, and thinks nothing good for much that does not go off with a pop like a champagne cork. The mellow suavity of more precious vintages seems insipid: but the taste, in proportion as it refines, learns to appreciate the indefinable flavor, too subtile for analysis. A manner has prevailed of late in which every other word seems to be underscored as in a school-girl's letter. The poet seems intent on showing his sinew, as if the power of the slim Apollo lay in the girth of his biceps. Force for the mere sake of force ends like Milo, caught and held mockingly fast by the recoil of the log he undertook to rive. In the race of fame, there are a score capable of brilliant *spurts* for one who comes in winner after a steady pull with wind and muscle to spare. Chaucer never shows any signs of effort, and it is a main proof of his excellence that he can be so inadequately sampled by detached passages,—by single lines taken away from the connection in which they contribute to the general effect. He has that continuity of thought, that evenly prolonged power, and that delightful equanimity, which characterize the higher orders of mind. There is something in him of the disinterestedness that made the Greeks masters in art. His phrase is never importunate. His simplicity is that of elegance, not of poverty. The quiet unconcern with which he says his best things is peculiar to him among English poets, though Goldsmith, Addison, and Thackeray have approached it in prose. He prattles inadvertently away, and all the while, like the princess in the story, lets fall a pearl at every other word. It is such a piece of good luck to be natural! It is the good gift which the fairy godmother brings to her prime favorites in the cradle. If not genius, it alone is what makes genius amiable in the arts. If a man have it not, he will never find it, for when it is sought it is gone.

When Chaucer describes anything, it is commonly by one of those simple and obvious epithets or qualities that are so easy to miss. Is it a woman? He tells us she is *fresh;* that she has *glad* eyes; that "every day her beauty newed"; that

> Methought all fellowship as naked
> Withouten her that I saw once,
> As a coróne without the stones.

Sometimes he describes amply by the merest hint, as where the Friar, before setting himself softly down, drives away the cat. We know without need of more words that he has chosen the snuggest corner. In some of his early poems he sometimes, it is true, falls into the catalogue style of his contemporaries; but after he had found his genius he never particularizes too much,—a process as deadly to all effect as an explanation to a pun. The first stanza of the **"Clerk's Tale"** gives us a landscape whose stately choice of objects shows a skill in composition worthy of Claude, the last artist who painted nature epically:—

> There is at the west endë of Itaile,
> Down at the foot of Vesulus the cold,
> A lusty plain abundant of vitaile,
> Where many a tower and town thou may'st behold
> That founded were in time of fathers old,
> And many another delítable sight;
> And Sàlucës this noble country hight.

The Pre-Raphaelite style of landscape entangles the eye among the obtrusive weeds and grass-blades of the foreground which, in looking at a real bit of scenery, we overlook; but what a sweep of vision is here! and what happy generalization in the sixth verse as the poet turns away to the business of his story! The whole is full of open air.

But it is in his characters, especially, that his manner is large and free; for he is painting history, though with the fidelity of portrait. He brings out strongly the essential traits, characteristic of the genus rather than of the individual. The Merchant who keeps so steady a countenance that

> There wist no wight that he was e'er in debt,

the Sergeant at Law, "who seemèd busier than he was," the Doctor of Medicine, whose "study was but little on the Bible,"—in all these cases it is the type and not the personage that fixes his attention. William Blake says truly, though he expresses his meaning somewhat clumsily [see excerpt dated 1809],

> the characters of Chaucer's Pilgrims are the characters which compose all ages and nations. Some of the names and titles are altered by time, but the characters remain forever unaltered, and consequently they are the physiognomies and lineaments of universal human life, beyond which Nature never steps. Names alter, things never alter. As Newton numbered the stars, and as Linnæus numbered the plants, so Chaucer numbered the classes of men.

In his outside accessaries, it is true, he sometimes seems as minute as if he were illuminating a missal. Nothing es-capes his sure eye for the picturesque,—the cut of the beard, the soil of armor on the buff jerkin, the rust on the sword, the expression of the eye. But in this he has an artistic purpose. It is here that he individualizes, and, while every touch harmonizes with and seems to complete the moral features of the character, makes us feel that we are among living men, and not the abstracted images of men. Crabbe adds particular to particular, scattering rather than deepening the impression of reality, and making us feel as if every man were a species by himself; but Chaucer, never forgetting the essential sameness of human nature, makes it possible, and even probable, that his motley characters should meet on a common footing, while he gives to each the *expression* that belongs to him, the result of special circumstances or training. Indeed, the absence of any suggestion of *caste* cannot fail to strike any reader familiar with the literature on which he is supposed to have formed himself. No characters are at once so broadly human and so definitely outlined as his. Belonging, some of them, to extinct types, they continue contemporary and familiar forever. So wide is the difference between knowing a great many men and that knowledge of human nature which comes of sympathetic insight and not of observation alone.

It is this power of sympathy which makes Chaucer's satire so kindly,—more so, one is tempted to say, than the panegyric of Pope. Intellectual satire gets its force from personal or moral antipathy, and measures offences by some rigid conventional standard. Its mouth waters over a galling word, and it loves to say *Thou,* pointing out its victim to public scorn. *Indignatio facit versus,* it boasts, though they might as often be fathered on envy or hatred. But imaginative satire, warmed through and through with the genial leaven of humor, smiles half sadly and murmurs *We.* Chaucer either makes one knave betray another, through a natural jealousy of competition, or else expose himself with a *naïveté* of good-humored cynicism which amuses rather than disgusts. In the former case the butt has a kind of claim on our sympathy; in the latter, it seems nothing strange, as I have already said, if the sunny atmosphere which floods that road to Canterbury should tempt anybody to throw off one disguise after another without suspicion. With perfect tact, too, the Host is made the *choragus* in this diverse company, and the coarse jollity of his temperament explains, if it do not excuse, much that would otherwise seem out of keeping. Surely nobody need have any scruples with *him.*

Chaucer seems to me to have been one of the most purely original of poets, as much so in respect of the world that is about us as Dante in respect of that which is within us. There had been nothing like him before, there has been nothing since. He is original, not in the sense that he thinks and says what nobody ever thought and said before, and what nobody can ever think and say again, but because he is always natural, because, if not always absolutely new, he is always delightfully fresh, because he sets before us the world as it honestly appeared to Geoffrey Chaucer, and not a world as it seemed proper to certain people that it ought to appear. He found that the poetry which had preceded him had been first the expression of individual feeling, then of class feeling as the vehicle of legend and history, and at last had wellnigh lost itself in chasing the mirage of allegory. Literature seemed to have passed through the natural stages which at regular intervals bring it to decline. Even the lyrics of the *jongleurs* were all run in one mould, and the Pastourelles of Northern France had become as artificial as the Pastorals of Pope. The Romances of chivalry had been made over into prose, and the *Melusine* of his contemporary Jehan d'Arras is the forlorn hope of the modern novel. Arrived thus far in their decrepitude, the monks endeavored to give them a religious and moral turn by allegorizing them. Their process reminds one of something Ulloa tells us of the fashion in which the Spaniards converted the Mexicans: "Here we found an old man in a cavern so extremely aged as it was wonderful, which could neither see nor go because he was so lame and crooked. The Father, Friar Raimund, said it were good (seeing he was so aged) to make him a Christian; whereupon we baptized him." The monks found the Romances in the same stage of senility, and gave them a saving sprinkle with the holy water of allegory. Perhaps they were only trying to turn the enemy's own weapons against himself, for it was the free-thinking "Romance of the Rose" that more than anything else had made allegory fashionable. Plutarch tells us that an allegory is to say one thing where another is meant, and this might have been needful for the personal security of Jean de Meung, as afterwards for that of his successor, Rabelais. But, except as a means of evading the fagot, the method has few recommendations. It reverses the true office of poetry by making the real unreal. It is imagination endeavoring to recommend itself to the understanding by means of cuts. If an author be in such deadly earnest, or if his imagination be of such creative vigor as to project real figures when it meant to cast only a shadow upon vapor; if the true spirit come, at once obsequious and terrible, when the conjurer has drawn his circle and gone through with his incantations merely to produce a proper frame of mind in his audience, as was the case with Dante, there is no longer any question of allegory as the word and thing are commonly understood. But with all secondary poets, as with Spenser for example, the allegory does not become of one substance with the poetry, but is a kind of carven frame for it, whose figures lose their meaning, as they cease to be contemporary. It was not a style that could have much attraction for a nature so sensitive to the actual, so observant of it, so interested by it, as that of Chaucer. He seems to have tried his hand at all the forms in vogue, and to have arrived in his old age at the truth, essential to all really great poetry, that his own instincts were his safest guides, that there is nothing deeper in life than life itself, and that to conjure an allegorical significance into it was to lose sight of its real meaning. He of all men could not say one thing and mean another, unless by way of humorous contrast.

In thus turning frankly and gayly to the actual world, and drinking inspiration from sources open to all; in turning away from a colorless abstraction to the solid earth and to emotions common to every pulse; in discovering that to make the best of nature, and not to grope vaguely after something better than nature, was the true office of Art; in insisting on a definite purpose, on veracity, cheerfulness, and simplicity, Chaucer shows himself the true father and founder of what is characteristically *English* literature. He has a hatred of cant as hearty as Dr. Johnson's, though he has a slier way of showing it; he has the placid common. sense of Franklin, the sweet, grave humor of Addison, the exquisite taste of Gray; but the whole texture of his mind, though its substance seem plain and grave, shows itself at every turn iridescent with poetic feeling like shot silk. Above all, he has an eye for character that seems to have caught at once not only its mental and physical features, but even its expression in variety of costume,—an eye, indeed, second only, if it should be called second in some respects, to that of Shakespeare.

I know of nothing that may be compared with the prologue to the **Canterbury Tales,** and with that to the story of the **"Chanon's Yeoman"** before Chaucer. Characters and portraits from real life had never been drawn with such discrimination, or with such variety, never with such bold precision of outline, and with such a lively sense of the picturesque. His Parson is still unmatched, though Dryden and Goldsmith have both tried their hands in emulation of him. And the humor also in its suavity, its perpetual presence and its shy unobtrusiveness, is something wholly new in literature. For anything that deserves to be called like it in English we must wait for Henry Fielding.

Chaucer is the first great poet who has treated To-day as if it were as good as Yesterday, the first who held up a mirror to contemporary life in its infinite variety of high and low, of humor and pathos. But he reflected life in its large sense as the life of *men*, from the knight to the ploughman,—the life of every day as it is made up of that curious compound of human nature with manners. The very form of the **Canterbury Tales** was imaginative. The garden of Boccaccio, the supperparty of Grazzini, and the voyage of Giraldi make a good enough thread for their stories, but exclude all save equals and friends, exclude consequently human nature in its wider meaning. But by choosing a pilgrimage, Chaucer puts us on a plane where all men are equal, with souls to be saved, and with another world in view that abolishes all distinctions. By this choice, and by making the Host of the Tabard always the central figure, he has happily united the two most familiar emblems of life,—the short journey and the inn. We find more and more as we study him that he rises quietly from the conventional to the universal, and may fairly take his place with Homer in virtue of the breadth of his humanity. (pp. 350-65)

James Russell Lowell, "Chaucer," in his Literary Essays, Vol. III, *Houghton, Mifflin and Company, 1892, pp. 291-366.*

Matthew Arnold   (essay date 1880)

[*Arnold was one of the most important English literary critics of the nineteenth century. Also a noted poet and social critic, he believed that criticism should inform and liberate the public, thus paving the way for progress. He advocated the "real estimate" of the created object, assessing it according to its own qualities, apart from the influence of history and the limitations of subjective experience. His writings include* On Translating Homer *(1861),* Culture and Anarchy *(1869), and* Literature and Dogma *(1873). In the following excerpt from his introduction to Thomas Humphrey Ward's* The English Poets *(1880), Arnold finds Chaucer's poetry superior— in style and in substance—to the romance poetry of the fourteenth century, but argues that, despite his genius, the English poet "lacks the high seriousness of the great classics, and therewith an important part of their virtue."]*

In the twelfth and thirteenth centuries, that seed-time of all modern language and literature, the poetry of France had a clear predominance in Europe. Of the two divisions of that poetry, its productions in the *langue d'oil* and its productions in the *langue d'oc,* the poetry of the *langue d'oc,* of southern France, of the troubadours, is of importance because of its effect on Italian literature;—the first literature of modern Europe to strike the true and grand note, and to bring forth, as in Dante and Petrarch it brought forth, classics. But the predominance of French poetry in Europe, during the twelfth and thirteenth centuries, is due to its poetry of the *langue d'oil,* the poetry of northern France and of the tongue which is now the French language. In the twelfth century the bloom of this romance-poetry was earlier and stronger in England, at the court of our Anglo-Norman kings, than in France itself. But it was a bloom of French poetry; and as our native poetry formed itself, it formed itself out of this. The romance-poems which took possession of the heart and imagination of Europe in the twelfth and thirteenth centuries are French; . . . Themes were supplied from all quarters; but the romance-setting which was common to them all, and which gained the ear of Europe, was French. This constituted for the French poetry, literature and language, at the height of the Middle Age, an unchallenged predominance. (pp. XXIX-XXX)

But in the fourteenth century there comes an Englishman nourished on this poetry, taught his trade by this poetry, getting words, rhyme, metre from this poetry; for even of that stanza which the Italians used, and which Chaucer derived immediately from the Italians, the basis and suggestion was probably given in France. Chaucer (I have already named him) fascinated his contemporaries, but so too did Christian of Troyes and Wolfram of Eschenbach. Chaucer's power of fascination, however, is enduring; his poetical importance does not need the assistance of the historic estimate, it is real. He is a genuine source of joy and strength which is flowing still for us and will flow always. He will be read, as time goes on, far more generally than he is read now. His language is a cause of difficulty for us; but so also, and I think in quite as great a degree, is the language of Burns. In Chaucer's case, as in that of Burns, it is a difficulty to be unhesitatingly accepted and overcome.

If we ask ourselves wherein consists the immense superiority of Chaucer's poetry over the romance-poetry, why it is that in passing from this to Chaucer we suddenly feel ourselves to be in another world, we shall find that his superiority is both in the substance of his poetry and in the style of his poetry. His superiority in substance is given by his large, free, simple, clear yet kindly view of human life,—so unlike the total want, in the romance-poets, of all intelligent command of it. Chaucer has not their helpless-

The Ellesmere Franklin.

ness; he has gained the power to survey the world from a central, a truly human point of view. We have only to call to mind the **"General Prologue"** to *The Canterbury Tales.* The right comment upon it is Dryden's: 'It is sufficient to say, according to the proverb, that *here is God's plenty*' [see excerpt dated 1700]. And again: 'He is a perpetual fountain of good sense.' It is by a large, free, sound representation of things, that poetry, this high criticism of life, has truth of substance; and Chaucer's poetry has truth of substance.

Of his style and manner, if we think first of the romance-poetry and then of Chaucer's divine liquidness of diction, his divine fluidity of movement, it is difficult to speak temperately. They are irresistible, and justify all the rapture with which his successors speak of his 'gold dew-drops of speech.' Johnson misses the point entirely when he finds fault with Dryden for ascribing to Chaucer the first refinement of our numbers, and says that Gower also can show smooth numbers and easy rhymes [see excerpt dated 1755]. The refinement of our numbers means something far more than this. A nation may have versifiers with smooth numbers and easy rhymes, and yet may have no real poetry at all. Chaucer is the father of our splendid English poetry, he is our 'well of English undefiled,' because by the lovely charm of his diction, the lovely charm of his movement, he makes an epoch and founds a tradition. In Spenser, Shakespeare, Milton, Keats, we can follow the tradition of the liquid diction, the fluid movement, of Chaucer; at one time it is his liquid diction of which in these poets we feel the virtue, and at another time it is his fluid movement. And the virtue is irresistible.

Bounded as is my space, I must yet find room for an example of Chaucer's virtue. . . . I feel disposed to say that a single line is enough to show the charm of Chaucer's verse; that merely one line like this:

> O martyr souded in virginitee!

has a virtue of manner and movement such as we shall not find in all the verse of romance-poetry;—but this is saying nothing. The virtue is such as we shall not find, perhaps, in all English poetry, outside the poets whom I have named as the special inheritors of Chaucer's tradition. A single line, however, is too little if we have not the strain of Chaucer's verse well in our memory; let us take a stanza. It is from **"The Prioress's Tale,"** the story of the Christian child murdered in a Jewry:—

> 'My throte is cut unto my nekke-bone
> Saidè this child, and as by the way of kinde
> I should have deyd, yea, longè time agone;
> But Jesu Christ, as ye in bookè finde,
> Will that his glory last and be in minde,
> And for the worship of his mother dere
> Yet may I sing *O Alma* loud and clere.

Wordsworth has modernised this tale, and to feel how delicate and evanescent is the charm of verse, we have only to read Wordsworth's first three lines of this stanza after Chaucer's:—

> 'My throat is cut unto the bone, I trow,
> Said this young child, and by the law of kind
> I should have died, yea, many hours ago.'

The charm is departed. It is often said that the power of liquidness and fluidity in Chaucer's verse was dependent upon a free, a licentious dealing with language, such as is now impossible; upon a liberty, such as Burns too enjoyed, of making words like *neck, bird,* into a dissyllable by adding to them, and words like *cause, rhyme,* into a dissyllable by sounding the *e* mute. It is true that Chaucer's fluidity is conjoined with this liberty, and is admirably served by it; but we ought not to say that it was dependent upon his talent. Other poets with a like liberty do not attain to the fluidity of Chaucer; Burns himself does not attain to it. Poets again, who have a talent akin to Chaucer's, such as Shakespeare or Keats, have known how to attain to his fluidity without the like liberty.

And yet Chaucer is not one of the great classics. His poetry transcends and effaces, easily and without effort, all the romance-poetry of Catholic Christendom; it transcends and effaces all the English poetry contemporary with it, it transcends and effaces all the English poetry subsequent to it down to the age of Elizabeth. Of such avail is poetic truth of substance, in its natural and necessary union with poetic truth of style. And yet, I say, Chaucer is not one of the great classics. He has not their accent. What is wanting to him is suggested by the mere mention of the name of the first great classic of Christendom, the immor-

tal poet who died eighty years before Chaucer,—Dante. The accent of such verse as

> In la sua volontade è nostra pace . . .

is altogether beyond Chaucer's reach; we praise him, but we feel that this accent is out of the question for him. It may be said that it was necessarily out of the reach of any poet in the England of that stage of growth. Possibly; but we are to adopt a real, not a historic, estimate of poetry. However we may account for its absence, something is wanting, then, to the poetry of Chaucer, which poetry must have before it can be placed in the glorious class of the best. And there is no doubt what that something is. It is the $\sigma\pi o\upsilon\delta\alpha\iota o\tau\eta\varsigma$, the high and excellent seriousness, which Aristotle assigns as one of the grand virtues of poetry. The substance of Chaucer's poetry, his view of things and his criticism of life, has largeness, freedom, shrewdness, benignity; but it has not this high seriousness. Homer's criticism of life has it, Dante's has it, Shakespeare's has it. It is this chiefly which gives to our spirits what they can rest upon; and with the increasing demands of our modern ages upon poetry, this virtue of giving us what we can rest upon will be more and more highly esteemed. A voice from the slums of Paris, fifty or sixty years after Chaucer, the voice of poor Villon out of his life of riot and crime, ahs at its happy moments (as, for instance, in the last stanza of *La Belle Heaulmière*) more of this important poetic virtue of seriousness than all the productions of Chaucer. But its apparition in Villon, and in men like Villon, is fitful; the greatness of the great poets, the power of their criticism of life, is that their virtue is sustained.

To our praise, therefore, of Chaucer as a poet there must be this limitation; he lacks the high seriousness of the great classics, and therewith an important part of their virtue. Still, the main fact for us to bear in mind about Chaucer is his sterling value according to that real estimate which we firmly adopt for all poets. He has poetic truth of substance, though he has not high poetic seriousness, and corresponding to his truth of substance he has an exquisite virtue of style and manner. With him is born our real poetry. (pp. XXXI-XXXVI)

> *Matthew Arnold, in an introduction to* The English Poets: Chaucer to Donne, Vol. I, *edited by Thomas Humphrey Ward, Macmillan and Co., 1889, pp. xvii-xlvii.*

William George Dodd   (essay date 1913)

[*In the following excerpt, Dodd examines Chaucer's conception of courtly love in the* Canterbury Tales, *observing that in "his hands, in some manner which defies analysis, the old love conventions become the poet's own."*]

In the **Canterbury Tales,** two types of love are prominent. One of these, the courtly love of the higher classes, [is] abundantly illustrated in Chaucer's earlier works. The other type is found in those tales in which Chaucer in his masterly fashion portrays the life of the lower classes—the love of the *fabliaux.* This is solely and entirely carnal in its nature. We have seen that the courtly love itself was often sensual; but along with the sensualism, there was found a refinement and often a nobility of sentiment which went far toward lessening the repulsive effect of the baser element. The love of the *fabliaux,* on the other hand, is all grossness without any of the refinement.

With this lower type of love we shall not deal here. We shall take the attitude, for this study, that the courtly classes of the poet's own time would have assumed,—that, although the "hende Nicholas," January and May, and that splendid animal, the Wyf of Bath, dignified their passion with the name of love, they were incapable of experiencing real love, or even of comprehending its nature. We shall confine our discussion to what would have been deemed love by those people for whom Chaucer wrote; that is, . . . we shall direct our attention to the courtly love element in the **Canterbury Tales.**

Of the company of pilgrims pictured for us in the **"General Prologue,"** two are of especial interest to us in the present study; these are the Knight and his son the Squire,

> A lovyere and a lusty bachelere.

Of the Knight it is said that he was worthy, wise, meek, and that he loved,

> Trouthe and honour, fredom and curteisye.

These are the qualities which we have found to be requisite in the model courtly lover back to the time of Andreas Capellanus. The characteristics, indeed, of the knight and the lover in mediaeval times were identical, since every knight was supposed, when young, to be in love; and since the great majority of lovers were knights.

The description of the Squire agrees well with our ideas of lovers as derived from the courtly literature. He is said to be courteous and humble. His love was so "hot" that it kept him awake at night. He had travelled far on military expeditions and had conducted himself well, in the hope of standing high in his lady's favor. He was accomplished in riding, song-making, writing, drawing, jousting, and dancing. He was merry all the day with his singing and his "fluting."

> He was as fresh as is the month of May,

and the garments he wore were a symbol of the freshness of his nature.

It is noticeable that the Squire meets all the requirements with regard to character, behavior, dress, and accomplishments, which the god put before his lover in the *Romance of the Rose.* As for his military expeditions, and his desire to stand well with his lady, this, as we have seen in the preceding part of this study, is in accord with ideas commonly held, that the young lover must perform deeds of prowess, so that his fame may come to his lady's ears, if he wishes to gain her favor.

Two other characters of the Prologue are brought into relation with this study by what the poet says of them; these, strangely enough, are the Prioress and the Monk. The Prioress wore a brooch on which was written the motto, *Amor vincit omnia.* Similarly, the Monk wore a pin, the larger end of which was fashioned like a love-knot. Of course, neither of these characters was a lover; but the devices which they wore show the prevalence of love ideas at this time. [As Thomas Warton wrote in his *History of English Poetry:*]

> Chaucer's Prioress and Monk, whose lives were devoted to religious reflection and the most serious engagements, and while they are actually traveling on a pilgrimage to visit the shrine of a sainted martyr, openly avow the universal influence of love. They exhibit on their apparel badges entirely inconsistent with their profession, but easily accountable for from these principles. The Prioress wears a bracelet on which is inscribed, with a crowned A, *Amor vincit omnia.* The Monk ties his hood with a true lover's knot.

It seems hardly necessary, after showing the large use, by Chaucer, of conventional ideas in his erotic work, to point out such features in the **"Knight's Tale."** Yet, following our usual plan, we may note such employment of the stock ideas of love literature as the poet has here made. In so doing, we shall see once more that Chaucer in his love stories never tried to avoid the conventional ideas. On the contrary, he used them freely; but, as a poet of genius, he managed them and never allowed them to manage him.

Love is conceived as a god whose power is absolute. Nowhere may a better expression of the courtly idea of the god of Love be found than in the words of Theseus:

> The god of love, a! *benedicite,*
> How mighty and how great a lord is he!
> Ayeins his might ther gayneth none obstacles,
> He may be cleped a god for his miracles;
> For he can maken at his owne gyse
> Of everich herte, as that him list devyse.

He has shown his power on Palamon and Arcite, for he has, Theseus says,

> maugree hir eyen two
> Y-broght hem hider bothe for to dye! . . .
> Thus hath hir lord, the god of love, y-payed
> Hir wages and hir fees for hir servyse!

Theseus himself was a servant of the god and had been "caught ofte in his las."

Although the god appears often, Venus is prominent as a love deity. In this capacity, she requires absolute devotion; nothing is of avail against her might:

> wisdom ne richesse,
> Beautee ne sleighte, strengthe, ne hardinesse,
> Ne may with Venus holde champartye;
> For as hir list the world than may she gye.

References to Cupid with his arrows appear in the poem. Arcite complains:

> And over al this, to sleen me utterly,
> Love hath his fyry dart so brenningly
> Y-stiked thurgh my trewe careful herte,
> That shapen was my deeth erst than my sherte.

In the description of the Temple of Venus, too, Cupid is pictured as an attendant of Venus:

> Biforn hir stood hir sone Cupido,

Upon his shuldres winges hadde he two;
And blind he was, as it is ofte sene;
A bowe he bar and arwes brighte and kene.

In fact, in this Temple, everything incidental to the passion of love is pictured on the walls.

Venus in her capacity as the goddess of carnal love is referred to in the words spoken by Palamon while praying in the Temple:

I shal for evermore,
Emforth my might, thy trewe servant be,
And holden werre alwey with chastitee.

The lady in the **"Knight's Tale"** has the characteristics, physical and spiritual, common to ladies in the courtly poetry. Her position with regard to her lovers is the usual one of superiority. Arcite determines to return to Athens,

To see my lady that I love and serve.

Elsewhere he declares:

Only the sighte of hir, whom that I serve,
Though that I never hir grace may deserve,
Wolde han suffised right y-nough for me.

Similarly, Palamon is a servant of Emilia. Theseus says of him, addressing Emilia:

That gentil Palamon, your owne knight,
That serveth yow with wille, herte, and might,
And ever hath doon, sin that ye first him knewe,
. . . ye shul, of your grace, upon him rewe,
And taken him for housbonde and for lord.

The attitude of the lady toward the lovers is the usual one of indifference; at least, it seems to be that to the lovers themselves. Arcite, in praying to Mars, says of Emilia:

For she, that dooth me al this wo endure,
Ne reccheth never wher I sinke or flete.
And wel I woot, er she me mercy hete,
I moot with strengthe winne hir . . .

The lovers themselves are portrayed in accordance with the conventional ideas. They suffer torments and woe, and show all the customary symptoms. The changes in mood caused in Arcite by his love are thus described:

Whan that Arcite had . . .
. . . songen al the roundel lustily,
Into a studie he fil sodeynly,
As doon thise loveres in hir queynte geres,
Now in the croppe, now doun in the breres,
Now up, now doun, as boket in a welle.

And again:

His sleep, his mete, his drink is him biraft,
That lene he wex, and drye as is a shaft.
His eyen holwe, and grisly to biholde;
His hewe falwe, and pale as asshen colde,
And solitarie he was, and ever allone,
And wailing al the night, making his mone.
And if he herde song or instrument,
Then wolde he wepe, he mighte nat be stent.

The touch in the last two lines is interesting, and, so far as I know, it is original with Chaucer. I have not met in my reading with any passage in which weeping at the sound of music was a symptom of love.

Finally, the conventional idea that love is caused by beauty is employed. Beauty wounds the heart of the lover through his eyes. Palamon declares:

But I was hurt right now thurgh-out myn ye
Into myn herte, that wol my bane be.

He is "stung" by the sight of Emilia's beauty:

He caste his eye upon Emelya,
And therwithal he bleynte, and cryde 'a!'
As though he stongen were unto the herte.

Arcite has the same experience:

And with that sighte hir beautee hurte him
so, . . .
And with a sigh he seyde pitously:
'The fresshe beautee sleeth me sodeynly
Of hir that rometh in the yonder place;
And, but I have hir mercy and hir grace . . .
I nam but deed.'

The instances given above are not all the examples of Chaucer's employment of conventional ideas in the **"Knight's Tale."** They will suffice, however, to show that in the framework of his love story he made the same large use of these ideas that he was accustomed to make when he wrote of love elsewhere.

Chaucer's purpose in the **"Knight's Tale,"** it is generally held, is to show the conflict between love and friendship. Indeed, this must have been no small part of Boccaccio's purpose in the *Teseide*. But as he manages his narrative, the friendship of the two cousins is given such prominence, is kept so constantly before the reader as almost to make him feel the possibility of friendship's triumph over love in the long run. Not so in Chaucer, whose aim seems to be to show

that love ne lordshipe
Wol noght, his thonkes, have no felaweshipe.

With this end in view, the English poet has made some significant changes in his original, the most important of which we may note as follows:

1. He has greatly abridged Boccaccio's version of the story.

2. From certain hints in Boccaccio, he has developed the character of Palamon, thus making an extremely effective contrast with the character of Arcite.

3. He has made Emilia almost characterless, though he presents her as a charming picture, the object of the love of the two cousins. [G. G. Coulton in *Chaucer and his England*] says of her: "Emelye is, within her limits, as beautiful and touching a figure as any in poetry; but her limits are those of a figure in a stained-glas window compared with the portrait of Titian's." This is quite true, and in the portrayal of Emilia Chaucer perhaps made his greatest change. (pp. 232-39)

From [a synopsis of Boccaccio's *Teseide*] it is apparent that Chaucer, in his presentation of Emilia, has sacrificed much in his original that is beautiful and attractive. We may feel certain that Chaucer himself appreciated the beauty of Emilia's character as Boccaccio portrays her; we may be sure, too, that as an artist he deemed it necessary to make the sacrifice he did. In fact, it is clear that all three of the changes enumerated above, which the poet has made in his original, and not the least, the change in the character of Emilia, conduce to one end. By the abridgment of the tale, Boccaccio's diffuseness is avoided; by the sharp distinction drawn between the characters of Palamon and Arcite, attention is directed to them; and by leaving Emilia a bright and lovely picture, yet on the whole characterless, the same effect of concentrating the reader's mind on the two cousins is obtained. The total result is that which Chaucer was, doubtless, aiming at: namely, to heighten the impression that the love passion of the two heroes was not only earnest but absolutely genuine.

In this feature it must be acknowledged, I think, that the English poet has improved greatly upon the Italian original. While passion, and that in abundance, is not wanting in Boccaccio's poem, there is about this passion an evenness, a certain lack of warmth, one might almost say a placidity, which make it seem artificial. Such an impression Chaucer has entirely overcome; and in so doing, he has accomplished in a much more effective manner his purpose of showing the conflict between the love and the friendship of Palamon and Arcite.

We have already had examples in this study in which Chaucer employed the conventions of the courtly love poetry for humorous purposes. In the **"Nonne Preestes Tale"** we find the same clever use of these ideas. The poet ascribes to Pertelote those qualities and characteristics which were expected of the lady in conventional love affairs:

> Curteys she was, discreet and debonaire,
> And compaignable, and bar herself . . . faire.

She was also fair, so fair, indeed, that

> she hath the herte in hold
> Of Chauntecleer loken in every lith.

The most interesting use of conventional ideas in the poem is found in the words of Pertelote, in which she tells Chauntecleer what kind of a husband a woman likes:

> For certes, what so any womman seith,
> We alle desyren, if it mighte be,
> To han housbondes hardy, wyse, and free,
> And secree, and no nigard, ne no fool, . . .
> Ne noon avauntour . . .

These were the qualities demanded of courtly lovers from the time of Andreas on. Considering the connotations of the words "secree" and "avauntour" in the courtly love, it is a delightful bit of humor in the poet to have Pertelote demand of her husband (!) that he be *secret* and that he be not a *boaster of favors received*.

In the early part of [the **"Squieres Tale"**] where is described the merriment at the house of Cambinskan, the poet makes some use of conventional love language. For example:

> Now dauncen lusty Venus children dere.

The line contains the idea that Venus is the goddess of Love and of lovers; and "lusty Venus children" means nothing more than "lovers." Reference to the service of the love deity, and to the gaiety which was demanded of a lover, is found in the lines:

> He moste han knowen Love and his servyses,
> And ben a festlich man as fresh as May.

Secrecy in love affairs is hinted at in the lines:

> Who coude telle yow the forme of daunces,
> So uncouthe and so fresshe countenaunces,
> Swich subtil loking and dissimulinges
> For drede of jalouse mennes aperceyvinges?

We have already had instances of Chaucer's portrayal of false lovers; for example, in the **"Anelida and Arcite"** and in several of the individual poems of the *Legend.* In every case the deceiver, who pretends to be in earnest, acts in all respects the courtly lover's part. The **"Squieres Tale"** furnishes one more example of this type. Though he was a hypocrite, yet to the falcon the pretender appeared to be true. She tells Canace of the impression he made upon her when he came a-wooing. He seemed to her a "welle of gentilesse"; he showed "humble chere" and a "hewe of trouthe," "plesaunce," "busy peyne."

> Right so this god of love, this ypocrite,
> Doth so his cerimonies and obeisaunces,
> And kepeth in semblant alle his observaunces
> That sowneth into gentillesse of love.

In the lines quoted it is interesting to note once more, along with the conventional love ideas, the transfer of terms of religion to love.

In the further description of their relations, the falcon tells of the tercelet's "service," of his humility, of his reverence for her, of his obedience, and of his "truth,"—all of which characterized the courtly lover in his position of inferiority before the lady.

Finally, she speaks of the tercelet as being "gentil born, fresh, and gay, goodly for to seen, humble and free," all of which were the regular qualities ascribed to the courtly lover.

The situation in the love affair of the **"Franklin's Tale"** is precisely that of the accounts of many of the troubadours. Here is a woman who is married, and happily married too, to a knight; but her beauty inflames another man with passion. He suffers in silence as long as he can bear it; then he mentions his love to her and begs for her favor. The end of his love is purely physical gratification, and she recognizes the fact and listens patiently to his requests. But unlike the ladies in most of the early stories Dorigen does not grant the desired favors to the importunate lover. This feature may have been in the original "lay" from which Chaucer professes to have taken his story. If it was not, the poet has departed from what may be called the more usual plan of such stories for the special purpose of putting before the reader a picture of the ideal love of man and wife. For the real interest in the tale is not in the love story of Aurelius, or in the wooing of Dorigen by Arveragus, but in the discussion of the question of "sovereignty" which the Wife of Bath had started a short time before.

In those episodes which deal with love the usual conventional ideas are employed. The familiar winged god is mentioned in the lines:

> Whan maistrie comth, the god of love anon
> Beteth hise winges and farewel! he is gon!

The conventional secrecy in love affairs is observed by Aurelius.

> Of this matere he dorste no word seyn.
> Under his brest he bar it more secree
> Than ever dide Pamphilus for Galathee;
> His brest was hool, withoute for to sene,
> But in his herte ay was the arwe kene.

The lover, as usual, is his lady's servant. Arveragus, it is said,

> loved and dide his payne
> To serve a lady in his beste wyse;

and at last, this lady for his "worthinesse" and for his "obeysaunce" had pity on him and accepted him as her husband. Whereupon he swore that he would never take upon himself the "maistrye" over her,

> But hir obeye, and folwe hir wil in al
> As any lovere to his lady shal.

The idea of the lover's fear to speak his love to his lady appears in the lines:

> For she was oon the faireste under sonne,
> And eek therto come of so heigh kinrede,
> That wel unnethes dorste this knight, for drede,
> Telle hir his wo, his peyne, and his distresse.

Similarly, though Aurelius loved Dorigen better than any other creature for two years,

> never dorste he telle hir of his grevaunce;
> Withouten coppe he drank al his penaunce.

As the love of Aurelius for Dorigen was unsuccessful, there are many statements devoted to this lover's woes and sorrows and amorous pains. He made songs, complaints, roundels, and virelays in which he lamented

> that he dorste not his sorwe telle
> But languissheth as a furie dooth in helle;
> And dye he moste, . . .as dide Ekko.

He addresses his lady:

> Madame, reweth upon my peynes smerte
> For with a word ye may me sleen or save.

When she puts on him the task of removing the rocks along the shore, recognizing the impossibility of his performing it,

> He to his hous is goon with sorweful herte;
> He seeth he may nat fro his deeth asterte.
> Him semed that he felte his herte colde;
> For verray wo out of his wit he breyde.

His brother puts him to bed, where

> In languor and in torment furious
> Two yeer and more lay wrecche Aurelius
> Er any foot he mighte on erthe goon.

Here again, in the case of the **"Franklin's Tale,"** the examples quoted do not comprise all the conventions of which Chaucer has made use. But they are enough to show that, as a basis for the love stories involved in the narrative, he has employed nothing but ideas which had been long familiar in love literature. Further comment on the tale seems unnecessary. Working with the courtly commonplaces, the poet has so managed them as to make the story real. Aurelius's passion appears as genuine and earnest as is the grief which Dorigen feels at being forced to be untrue to her husband. (pp. 245-50)

With the **"Franklin's Tale,"** Chaucer's employment of the courtly-love ideas ceases. One question now suggests itself, an answer to which would be very interesting, were it possible to get it: "What was Chaucer's own attitude toward these conceptions, of which he made such a large use in his poetry?" The writer wishes to state frankly that he does not believe it is possible to answer this question finally and definitely. It is difficult to tell what Chaucer's ideas are on any subject, so predominantly dramatic is his poetic work. Indeed, the question just stated would not be raised, were it not that others have felt that they could see in the poet's works evidence of a spirit of irony and satire against the courtly ideas. . . . [For example, according to Billings' *Middle English Metrical Romances,* Chaucer's] "attitude towards the chivalric ideal of love was, upon the whole, a critical one." Still later, certain remarks of Mr. Tatlock [in his *The Development and Chronology of Chaucer's Works*] seem to indicate that he sees in the **"Knight's Tale"** a tendency on the part of the poet to poke fun at the courtly love therein portrayed. But all such statements seem to be unwarranted, and Mr. Tatlock, oddly enough, himself supplies the corrective for them. He says, in the connection just noted: "Satire is easier to suspect than to prove, especially in a poem written when ideas of what is ludicrous and the connotations of words were so different from what they are now." We cannot say that Chaucer did not laugh to himself at some of the vagaries of lovers of his time. But we may suspect that the actions of courtly lovers then were no more ridiculous than are the actions of lovers of our day to people with a lively sense of humor. Extravagant as the courtly love may seem to us, this was the only kind of love there was at that period (except the grosser passion of the *fabliaux* which we do not consider here). Only in so far as love is always a fit subject for satire, was the chivalrous love ridiculous in an age when chivalrous ideas obtained.

But, aside from the question as to Chaucer's inclination to display levity at the extravagance of lovers, the most casual consideration of his poems will show the improbability of his deliberately satirizing the courtly love. In all the early lyric poems, which are purely conventional in both sentiment and language, there is nothing that remotely suggests satire or irony. And the same is true of those later lyric poems, where there is indeed fun in full measure. The *Book of the Duchess* abounds, as we have seen, in the courtly ideas and sentiments. Yet far from satirizing these ideas, the poet uses them to pay a graceful and delicate compliment to his patron. Consider again the *Parlament of Foules.* Here, if anywhere in the whole range of Chaucer's poetry, we might feel justified in saying that the courtly ideas were being satirized—if we judge entirely from the contents of the poem. Nothing can be plainer than that the goose and the duck openly ridiculed the courtly sentiments of the royal tercelet. But are we to identify Chaucer with the goose and the duck? Clearly not. The occasion which the poem was written to celebrate (and scholars agree that it has reference to the courtship of the royal couple) precludes the possibility of any satirical purpose on the part of the author. . . . Levity there may be; of fun there is plenty. But to say that there is irony in the description of the courtly love of Palamon and Arcite is unwarranted by anything in the poem itself.

What then is Chaucer's attitude toward this love, judging from his poetry? All we are justified in saying is that he used the courtly ideas, as he used every element of the life about him, for artistic purposes. If love is ridiculed anywhere, it is done by some one of the poet's characters. And we have no right to say that the sentiments expressed by any character are those of the poet himself. We cannot justly say even, as one writer above quoted has said, that Chaucer's attitude toward the chivalrous love is a critical one. It is enough to say, and it detracts nothing from the glory of our poet, that in treating this material he has maintained the detachment of a poetic artist, and has been unconcerned about giving his own opinions.

A recognition of this makes short and easy the task of summarizing the results of this investigation. . . . [Both] Gower and Chaucer in their treatment of love employed ideas which had been present in erotic literature from the time of the troubadours. These ideas Gower took as he found them, as many another poet did before him, and lacking the ability to impress them with his own individuality he left them unchanged. The language employed to set them forth was conventional throughout. The figures of the lovers whom Gower wishes to portray he does succeed in endowing with some degree of life and human quality. But his lack of imagination impoverishes his poetry, and his tendency to moralize has the grotesque result of making Gower the man elbow out of place Gower the artist. With Chaucer, the opposite of all this is true. In his hands, in some manner which defies analysis, the old love conventions become the poet's own. The language he uses to give expression to the passion of love is clever, forceful, and inevitable. His characters live before us as real people. In his maturity, he shows himself always the poet of genius, under whose magic touch commonplaces are transformed and become alive. In a word, in his use of the courtly-love ideas, as in all his work, Chaucer the artist is brilliantly revealed, even though we see but little of Chaucer the man. (pp. 251-54)

William George Dodd, "The Element of Love in Chaucer's Works" and "Conclusion," in his Courtly Love in Chaucer and Gower, *1913. Reprint by Peter Smith, 1959, pp. 91-250, 251-54.*

George Lyman Kittredge (lecture date 1914)

[*An expert on Chaucer and Shakespeare, Kittredge was an American scholar and a renowned professor at Har-*

vard University from 1888 to 1936. In the excerpt below from a lecture delivered in 1914, he provides an overview of the Book of the Duchess, *praising its poetic beauty and remarking that there "is a haunting charm about it that eludes analysis, but subdues our mood to a gentle and vaguely troubled pensiveness."*]

Four dreadful plagues laid England waste in Chaucer's lifetime. In the third of these, in 1369, died Queen Philippa and her daughter-in-law Blanche, the wife of John of Gaunt, Duke of Lancaster. Chaucer and his wife, also named Philippa, were both attached to the royal household, and they received an allowance of black cloth for mourning.

So far as we know, Chaucer paid no tribute of verse to the memory of the good queen, whom all men loved. Probably none was expected. King Edward had but slight acquaintance with the English language, and no interest at all in English literature. His son John, however, belonged to Chaucer's generation,—they were of almost exactly the same age,—and he doubtless requested the poet to write an elegy: we should rather say "commanded," since we are speaking of a prince of the blood. That the commission was grateful to Chaucer's feelings we may well believe; for the ***Book of the Duchess*** is instinct with sadness. True, Chaucer does not lament this great lady in his own person, but that is due to his exquisite and admirable art. He detaches himself completely, to concentrate our attention on the theme, which is, as it ought to be, the bitter grief of the despairing husband, who has lost the love of his youth, and can think of nothing but her gracious perfections.

This artistic detachment, which becomes from this time forward a marked feature of Chaucer's method, is achieved in the present instance by a skilful use of familiar conventions. The elegy is cast into the form of a vision. The poet tells the story of a dream: how, wandering in a wood, he fell in with a stranger knight in black garments, and asked and received an explanation of his sorrow. The poet expresses the deepest sympathy. Though himself in trouble, as we learn from the prologue, he ignores his own woes utterly in his effort to console the stranger, and does not remember them when he wakes, so profound is the impression of the haunting dream.

> Thoghte I, "This is so queynt a sweven,
> That I wol, by proces of tyme,
> Fonde to putte this sweven in ryme
> As I can best, and that anoon."
> This was my sweven; now it is doon.

Thus, by a delicate and well-imagined fiction, the artist Chaucer can hold his attitude of detachment, so vital to the effect of the composition, while, at the same time, Chaucer the humble friend can suggest, without obtrusiveness, his respectful and affectionate sympathy with the ducal house.

The substance of the elegy, by this adjustment, is spoken, not written merely; and it is spoken by the lady's husband, who can best describe her beauty, her charm of manner, and all her gracious qualities of mind and heart. Thus we have in the ***Book of the Duchess,*** not a prostrate and anxiously rhetorical obituary, from the blazoning pen of a commissioned laureate, but a tribute of pure love from the lady's equal, who can speak without constraint,—from her husband, who has most cause to mourn as he has best knowledge of what he has lost.

Let us follow the course of the story in brief, preserving, if we can, that simplicity of language which is one of its distinguishing traits. The Dreamer is speaking, and he begins his prologue with an ejaculation of artless astonishment:—

> I have great wonder that I am still alive, for I have had no sleep this long time. Hopeless love gives me no rest. It amazes me that a man can live so long, and suffer so much, and sleep so little. I should think he would die. One night, a little while ago, weary from lack of sleep, I bade my servant bring me a book to pass the time away, and I began to read it, sitting up in my bed. It was a volume of old stories, and one of them was Ovid's tale of Ceyx and Alcyone. It told how King Ceyx was lost at sea, and how Queen Alcyone, in anxiety and distress, prayed Juno to vouchsafe her a dream, that she might know whether her husband was alive or dead. And Juno despatched her messenger to the God of Sleep, and he, obeying her command, sent the drowned Ceyx to Alcyone in a vision. He stood at the foot of her bed, and called her by name, and told her of his fate, and bade her bury his body, which she should find cast up on the shore:—

> "And far-wel, swete, my worldes blisse!
> I praye God your sorwe lisse.
> To litel whyl our blisse lasteth."

> Alcyone awoke, and mourned, and died ere the third morrow.

> I was astonished at this tale, for I had never heard of any gods that could send sleep to weary men; and straightway I made a vow to Morpheus, or Juno, or whatever divinity it might be that had such power. Scarcely had I finished speaking when I fell fast asleep over my book, and I had a wonderful dream, which I do not believe even Joseph or Macrobius could interpret. I will tell you what it was.

So ends the prologue, which not only serves as a felicitous introduction to the vision that is to follow, but gives us, in perfection, the atmosphere, the mood, of the piece,—love and sorrow and bereavement. It shows us, too, the Dreamer in complete psychic sympathy with the subject; for what could be more natural than that he should dream of some bereavement or other, when his mind was full of the piteous tale of Alcyone, and the background of his thought was his own suffering for hopeless love? (pp. 37-40)

The first thing that strikes one in reading the ***Book of the Duchess*** is the quality of artlessness or *naïveté,* to which, indeed, the poem owes much of its charm. This challenges instant attention, for naïveté is often rated as one of Chaucer's permanent traits. As such, it holds a conspicuous place in ten Brink's classic inventory of his literary characteristics [see Further Reading], along with "fondness for the description of psychological states or conditions," "effective pathos," and "a tendency to humorous realism."

Now few facts of history, be it sacred or profane, are more solidly established than that Geoffrey Chaucer, in his habit as he lived, was not naïf. Whatever one may think of our American practice in the appointment of diplomatists, it is quite certain that, in the fourteenth century, men were not selected by the English king to negotiate secret affairs on the Continent because they were innocent and artless. And even so, a naïf Collector of Customs would be a paradoxical monster.

Besides, whatever else he may have been, Chaucer was admittedly a humorist, and naïveté is incompatible with a sense of humor. If I am artless, I may make you laugh; but the sense of humor, in that case, is yours, not mine. The source of your amusement, in fact, will be your keen perception of the incongruity between my childlike seriousness and the absurdity of what I have said or done. Hence, if I myself am a humorist, I may assume naïveté, from my own perception of the incongruous, in order to lend my words additional effect. This, of course, is the principle which underlies the rule that a jester must look as grave as he can; or, to put the precept in its crudely familiar guise, "Don't laugh at your own jokes!"

Real naïveté, as everybody knows, gives a person an appearance of innocence and helplessness, and will therefore be amusing, or pathetic, or both at once, according to the subject or the situation. As a trick of art, therefore, we expect to find the ingenuous manner adopted, now for purposes of humor, and now for those of pathos.

I should apologize abjectly for parading these truisms, were it not that they have been so continually overlooked in the literary criticism of Chaucer as to lead to frequent confusion between the artist and the man. And this confusion is exhibited at its very worst in the ordinary appraisal of the ***Book of the Duchess.***

In this elegy, the device, I need not say, is employed to heighten the pathos. It deserves our earnest attention. For we shall immediately discover that certain supposed flaws—not in the main design, which is unassailable, but in this or that detail—are due to Chaucer's use of this artistic expedient, and not to feebleness of grasp or a wavering vision.

In the first place, the effect of artlessness in the poem is produced by extreme simplicity in style and versification. That the simplicity results from lack of skill is, I fancy, a proposition that nobody will maintain, though it has often been taken for granted (may I say *naïvely?*) by critics who ought to know better. Consider the following passage, where Chaucer is describing, with the swift and terse precision of his best narrative art, the apparition of Alcyone's drowned husband:—

> Anon this god of slepe a-brayd
> Out of his sleep, and gan to goon,
> And did as he had bede him doon;
> Took up the dreynte body sone,
> And bar it forth to Alcyone,
> His wyf the quene, ther-as she lay,
> Right even a quarter before day,

And stood right at her beddes fet,
And called hir, right as she het,
By name, and seyde: "My swete wyf,
Awak! let be your sorwful lyf!
For in your sorwe ther lyth no reed;
For certes, swete, I nam but deed;
Ye shul me never on lyve y-see.
But goode swete hert, that ye.
Bury my body, at which a tyde
Ye mowe it finde the see besyde;
And far-wel, swete, my worldes blisse!
I praye God your sorwe lisse.
To litel whyl our blisse lasteth!"

Whoever hugs the delusion that because the diction and the metre are simple, it is easy to write like this, is humbly besought to try his hand at imitating The Vicar of Wakefield, or Andrew Marvell's Song of the Emigrants in Bermuda.

Let us pass to a consideration a little more debatable, but equally certain in the upshot.

There are two characters in the **Book of the Duchess**—the Dreamer, who tells the story, and the Knight in Black. Now the Knight is not naïf at all. On the contrary, he is an adept in the courtly conventions, which have become a part of his manner of thought and speech. He is a finished gentleman of a period quite as studied as the Elizabethan in its fashions of conduct and discourse. All the naïveté is due to the Dreamer, whose character is sharply contrasted with that of the Knight. The Dreamer speaks in the first person. One might infer, therefore, that he is Geoffrey Chaucer, but that would be an error: he is a purely imaginary figure, to whom certain purely imaginary things happen, in a purely imaginary dream. He is as much a part of the fiction in the **Book of the Duchess** as the Merchant or the Pardoner or the Host is a part of the fiction in the **Canterbury Tales.**

The mental attitude of the Dreamer is that of childlike wonder. He understands nothing, not even the meaning of his dream. He can only tell what happened, and leave the interpretation to us. Let us revert to our summary:

> I have great wonder that I am still alive; for I cannot sleep for sorrow and I am ever in fear of death. One night, not long ago, I was reading an old book, and I found a story in it about the God of Sleep. It astonished me, for I had never heard of him before. And so I vowed to give him a feather bed if he would send me slumber. And straightway I fell asleep over my book; and I had a dream which makes me wonder whenever I think of it. I will tell you what it was.

When we come to the Knight in Black and his pathetic history, the Dreamer is true to his nature of gentle simplicity—always wondering and never understanding. He wonders what makes the knight so sad; and when the knight tries to tell him, he still wonders, and still questions. Hints and half-truths and figures of speech are lost upon him, until at last the knight, in despair, as it seems, at his questioner's lack of comprehension, comes out plainly with the bare fact: "She is dead." "No!" says the Dreamer, still with his air of innocent surprise. "Yea, sir," replies the knight, "that is what I have all this time been trying to tell

you. That is the 'loss' I mentioned long ago." Even then the Dreamer has little to say. He can only speak the language of nature and simplicity: "Is that your loss? By God, it is a pity!" And then he dreamt that the hunt was over, and a clock in a tower struck twelve, and he awoke, and there he was—lying in bed, with his book of ancient stories still in his hand. And so he wonders more than ever. He does not know what the dream means, or whether it means anything at all. But it was a strange dream, truly, and full of charm, and he decides to write it out as well as he can, before he forgets it.

This childlike Dreamer, who never reasons, but only feels and gets impressions, who never knows what anything means until he is told in the plainest language, is not Geoffrey Chaucer, the humorist and man of the world. He is a creature of the imagination, and his childlikeness is part of his dramatic character.

For almost half a century, by record, the literal-minded have rehearsed, over and over again, their obvious censure on the construction of this beautiful elegy. Chaucer, they allege, is ridiculously obtuse. He hears the knight composing a dirge on his dead lady, and sees that he is dressed in mourning; yet he keeps asking him "what he has lost," and is thunderstruck at the final revelation. Substitute for "Chaucer," in these strictures, "the Dreamer," and they are half-answered already. For the Dreamer is not merely artless by nature; he is dulled, and almost stupefied, by long suffering. So he tells us at the very first:—"I am, as it were, a man in a maze. I take heed of nothing, how it comes or goes. Naught is to me either pleasant or unpleasant. I have no feeling left, whether for good or bad."

This is not all. The Knight in Black, unaware that the Dreamer has overheard the dirge, takes pains to mystify him at the outset with an allegory of Fortune and the chess-play, and evades his subsequent questions as long as evasion is possible. For the knight, though eager to talk, shrinks from uttering the bare and brutal truth:—"She is dead!" Speech eases his soul. It is a tender joy to describe his lady's beauty, to dilate on his own childish years and his innocent worship of love, to tell of their first meeting among a goodly company, to remember how abashed he was when he tried to reveal his devotion. It is a relief to him that the Dreamer seems not to comprehend.

But what of the Dreamer? Is he really deaf and blind to what he hears and sees? By no means! Artless he is, and unsuspicious, and dull with sorrow and lack of sleep; but the dirge is too clear for even him to misunderstand. "My lady is dead," so ran the words, "and gone away from me. Alas, death! why did you not take me likewise when you took her?" The Dreamer knows perfectly well that the lady is dead. What then? Does Chaucer straightway make him forget? The blunder would be incredible. Chaucer may have been an immature artist when he devised this situation, but he was not a fool; and if, in the haste of writing, he had momentarily entangled himself in such a confusion, all he had to do was to strike out the dirge. The excision of thirteen lines, without the change of a word beside, would have removed the stumbling block—and there are more than thirteen hundred verses in the elegy!

In fact, however, there is no confusion. The Dreamer knows that the lady is dead, but he wishes to learn more, not from idle curiosity, but out of sympathetic eagerness to afford the knight the only help in his power—the comfort of pouring his sad story into compassionate ears. And he tells us as much, in the plainest language.

> Anoon-right I gan fynde a tale
> To him, to loke where I might ought
> Have more knowing of his thought.

He owes his knowledge of the lady's death to overhearing the knight, who was too much absorbed to notice either his steps or his greeting. With instinctive delicacy, therefore, he suppresses this knowledge, and invites the knight's confidence in noncommittal terms, on the ground of pity for his obvious suffering. And when the knight speaks eagerly, though not plainly, as we have seen, and the Dreamer notes that words are indeed a relief, as he had hoped, it is not for him to check their flow. Let him rather hide his knowledge still, and tempt the knight to talk on and on. It is the artless artfulness of a kindly and simple nature.

Thus, by the interplay of two contrasted characters,—the naïf and sympathizing Dreamer and the mourning knight, who is not naïf at all,—brought together in a situation in which the Dreamer, impelled by simple kindliness, conceals his knowledge in order to tempt the knight to relieve his mind by talking, Chaucer has effected a climax of emotional suspense which culminates in the final disclosure. The conclusion is beyond all praise. "Where is she now?" the Dreamer asks. "Oh!" says the knight, coming out at last with the hideous fact that he could not bring himself to utter before, "she is dead." "Is that your loss? By God, it is ruth!" And with that the hunt was over, and a bell struck twelve in the dream castle,—was it a real sound this time?—and he awoke and found his book of Ceyx and Alcyone still in his hand.

This outburst is pure nature: it shows us the Chaucer that is to be when he shall break loose from contemporary French fashions of allegory and symbolism and pretty visions and dare to speak the language of the heart. What can one say in such a case but "Good God, man, I am sorry for you!" The rest is silence.

The ***Book of the Duchess*** belongs to Chaucer's early period, when his technique was almost purely that of the French love-allegory. For his leading conventions, and for a quantity of details, he is indebted to the Romance of the Rose, which he had already translated, and to his distinguished contemporary Guillaume de Machaut. In his use of this material, however, Chaucer shows a high degree of originality, both in applying the dream convention to his specific purpose, and in the imaginative control which he exercises over the traditional phenomena.

Here, for the first time, whether in French or English, we find the standard French conventions—the love-vision, and the lover's lament—turned to the uses of a personal elegy. To discern their fitness for this particular purpose was a considerable achievement; for they are, in fact, quite as well adapted to that end as the pastoral device, with which we moderns are more familiar, and which, as in the Lycidas, we accept without a scruple.

Let us first consider the Prologue, which introduces us to the Dreamer and contains the Ovidian story of Ceyx and Alcyone.

The situation comes from Le Paradys d'Amours, a pretty poem by Chaucer's contemporary, Froissart the chronicler, who was no doubt his personal friend. Here, as in the ***Duchess,*** the Dreamer is a woful lover, whose melancholy will not let him sleep. Froissart also gave Chaucer a suggestion for the mood of gentle sorrow, as well as for what is so essentially bound up with that mood—the Dreamer's artlessness. In the Paradys, however, this trait is not dramatic: it is merely the reflection of the poet's own nature. Froissart was, in deed and truth, the most naïf of men. Intensely susceptible to impressions from without, he reacted with all the grace of infancy and all its innocent and subtle charm. This Chaucer felt when he read the Frenchman's poem. His artistic instinct recognized its appropriateness to his own elegiac subject; and his dramatic power enabled him to comprehend and express. And so he created his Dreamer, and entrusted the story to him to tell.

I have just said that Froissart gave Chaucer a suggestion, also, for the mood of his elegy; but here again it was only a suggestion. For the Frenchman does not sustain the mood, which to him was merely an introductory convention. The Paradys is in no wise elegiac. It begins in a melancholy strain, but sorrow is not its theme. It deals with the joy of love, with the comforts and rewards which the god grants to his faithful servants. In Chaucer, on the contrary, the whole poem is developed out of the Dreamer's mood, which is constant, habitual, and not to be separated from his character.

In Froissart, then, the situation and the mood are alike momentary, external, evanescent,—the only constant element is the writer's own naïveté. In Chaucer, both the situation and the mood are involved in the Dreamer's temperament, which, compulsive in its gentle innocence, unifies the conception, and subdues the whole to a tone of tender and wistful monody.

Chaucer's indebtedness to Guillaume de Machaut has long been recognized, but few critics seem to appreciate his skill in adapting the borrowed material to his main design. Machaut, in the Fontaine Amoureuse, hears a lover's complaint embodying the legend of Alcyone and closing with an appeal to Morpheus:—"Let him take my form, as he took that of Ceyx, and visit my lady as she sleeps, and tell her how I suffer. Then I am sure she will relent. I will reward him with a nightcap of peacock's feathers; that he may sleep the sounder, and a soft bed stuffed with the plumes of gyrfalcons." The singer is not speaking for himself. He had composed the lament for a great lord, into whose presence Machaut is straightway conducted. This lord, who is reclining by the border of a crystal fountain, takes the poet into his confidence. Then they both go to sleep, and have a vision of Venus. She promises the young lord her help, and evokes the figure of his lady, who comforts him with a smile and gracious words, and leaves him full of hope.

This is a pretty fancy, and the use of Alcyone's story in the lament is undeniably ingenious. We may even discover a psychological link of cause and effect between its presence there and the vision vouchsafed to the lover. But the psychology is feeble and the connection somewhat remote.

Froissart, at all events, saw no such link, for when he imitated the Fontaine Amoureuse, as he did in his Paradys d'Amours, he omitted the story of Alcyone altogether. He retained the vow to Morpheus, however, substituting a ring for the nightcap and the feather bed,—which, in his innocence, he thought undignified,—and in one respect he made a felicitous alteration: his dreamer *prays only for sleep,* which falls upon him suddenly. But Froissart employs the dream that slumber brings only to transport himself into the conventional garden, where he encounters certain personified abstractions, and is reassured by the god of love, who grants him an audience, and where he finally meets his lady, with whom he has an eminently satisfactory conversation.

Chaucer's procedure, with these two poems in his mind, is in the highest degree illuminating. Like Froissart, he makes his Dreamer pray to Morpheus, but his sense of humor prompts him to discard the ring in favor of the feather bed. Machaut's story of Alcyone he keeps, recurring to Ovid for some details, but he brings it into vital connection not only with the Dreamer's character, but with the substance of the dream as well. The Dreamer sees the bereaved husband because he has just been reading of a similar bereavement. The lack of precise conformity between the impression made upon his waking mind and the image that recurs in slumber is true to dream-psychology. We do not look for absolute identity in such cases. Here Chaucer, unlike his predecessors, shows himself in immediate contact with the facts and experiences of human life—even with the life of dreams.

Undoubtedly Chaucer meant this carrying over of the waking impression into the dreamstate to be inferred by his readers, though the naïveté of the Dreamer suppressed all mention of the inference. The fact of such transmission was commonly recognized, and Chaucer has adverted to it more than once. In the **"Squire's Tale"** we are expressly informed that Canace's interest in the wonderful mirror was the direct cause of her dream:—

> In hir sleep, right for impressioun
> Of hir mirour, she had a visioun—

and there is a very illuminating case in the ***Parliament of Fowls*** [where the poet describes a dream inspired by Cicero's *Somnium Scipionis*]. (pp. 45-59)

Here the connection between the proem and the story, though formally exact, is imaginatively less close and rather more mechanical than in the ***Book of the Duchess;*** but it is still quite satisfactory. As Africanus once took his grandson out of this world, and revealed to him the future dwellings of the righteous and the wicked, so now he conducts Chaucer to a park-gate with two inscriptions, one indicating "the blisful place of hertes hele and dedly woundes cure," the other the realm of Danger and Disdain. They enter the park, which proves to be a lover's paradise with the regular landscape, and the usual conven-

tions follow. Africanus is heard of no more—which is very like a dream. The rest of the ***Parliament*** does not here concern us.

Passing from the prologue of the ***Book of the Duchess*** to the Dream itself, we find that Chaucer uses his literary models with equal skill, and shows a like felicity in converting the standard forms to his immediate needs. His problem, we remember, was to apply the conventional type of "lover's complaint" to the ends of a personal elegy. Two recent poems by Guillaume de Machaut lay ready at hand, the Judgment of the King of Bohemia and the Remedy for Fortune. Chaucer drew freely from both, as well as from his old favorite, the Romance of the Rose, which he had already translated, apparently entire, and long passages of which he must have known by heart.

The plan of the Judgment of the King of Bohemia shows an obvious similarity to that which Chaucer adopted for the ***Book of the Duchess.*** I may be allowed to repeat a very brief summary which I have used on another occasion.

> On a fine morning in spring, the poet wanders out into a park where there is many a tree and many a blossom. He sits down by a brook, near a beautiful tower, concealing himself under the trees, to hear the birds sing. A lady approaches, accompanied only by a maid and a little dog. She is met by a knight, who greets her politely, but she passes on, without heeding. The knight overtakes her, and addresses her once more. She apologizes for her inattention, remarking that she was buried in thought. They exchange courtesies, and the knight begs to know the cause of her pensive mood, promising to do his best to comfort her. He himself, he avers, is suffering from bitter grief. The lady consents, on condition that the knight will reveal the origin of his own sorrow. Accordingly, they exchange confidences, in the hearing of the poet, whose presence remains unsuspected.
>
> The lady, it appears, has lost her lover by death. The knight's *amie,* on the contrary, is living, but has forsaken him. They dispute as to which case is the harder. William reveals himself, and at his suggestion the question is submitted to the King of Bohemia, who decides that the knight has the best of the argument.

Such general resemblances, to be sure, are of little significance. When, however, we study the details of the Black Knight's story, the obligations of Chaucer to Guillaume de Machaut come out in a way that is almost startling.

The knight, in response to the Dreamer's questioning, goes back to the memories of his boyhood. As long ago as he could remember, he had honored the god of love as his liege lord and submitted his spotless heart to his control. Love was only a sentiment to him in those days,—an aspiration, a vague dream of something beautiful that might come to pass by-and-by. And so, in devout humility, he had ever besought the god to be propitious, and to entrust his heart, at the appointed hour, to the keeping of some lovely and gracious lady. His prayer was answered. He chanced one day to come into an assembly of the fairest ladies ever seen, and one among them surpassed the rest as the summer sun outshines the moon and the seven stars. He "held no counsel but with her eyes and his own heart," and, thus guided, he thought it was better to serve her in vain than to win the favor of any other woman. Long time he worshipped her in secret, afraid to speak; and when at last he took courage to reveal his adoration, he stammered and forgot everything he had to say. She was hard to win, but at length she had pity upon him, and granted him "the noble gift of her mercy." And thus they lived full many a year, in honorable love and perfect harmony.

This part of the poem embodies the famous description of the Duchess Blanche and of her character, which Lowell admired so much and declared "one of the most beautiful portraits of a woman that were ever drawn."

Now there is nothing new in the Black Knight's story, either in form or substance. The experience he describes is typical, and he speaks throughout in the settled language of the chivalric system. Love was the only life that became the gently nurtured, and they alone were capable of love. Submission to the god was their natural duty; in his grace and favor was their only hope; for no man's heart was in his own control. It was the god of love, not the man's choice, that bestowed it, and none could withstand the god's decree. (pp. 60-3)

I have no wish to minimize the indebtedness of Chaucer to his French predecessor. Indeed, there is no temptation to err in that way. For Chaucer uses his borrowings with the power of a master, and nowhere in the poem does his originality appear more strikingly than in the description of the Duchess Blanche,—the very place where his indebtedness is most conspicuous. In Machaut, there is much grace and beauty, but the schematism is complete. The lady utters her lament, and the knight responds. There is no genuine dialogue. In the description, Machaut follows the enumerative method so dear to the middle ages, as if he were, in Hamlet's phrase, "dividing" the lady "inventorially." Hair, forehead, eyebrows, eyes, nose, mouth, cheeks, teeth, chin, and complexion are catalogued in scientific order, with some exquisite touches, but with a total effect of absurd formality. The Elizabethans knew the method well. It was, in truth, inherited from their schematic forefathers, along with many other legacies of thought and style which the sciolists who decry the study of "mediævalism" do vainly misinterpret. Olivia makes merry with such stilted accumulation of details in her "Item, two lips, indifferent red."

But Chaucer knew that one should not "make so long a tale of the straw as of the corn," and, in the very act of borrowing from Machaut, he has avoided this fault, though it is one to which the rapid and garrulous short couplet might well have tempted him beyond resistance. In the Black Knight's description of his lady, we find the same admirable selective art that distinguishes the later work of the poet. Chaucer's knight declares that he cannot describe his lady's face—it passes his ability in expression; but he dwells lovingly on her hair, and lingers over the description of her eyes, which were not too wide open:—

> Were she never so glad,
> Her loking was not foly sprad,
> Ne wildely, though that she pleyde;

> But ever, me thoughte, her eyen seyde,
> 'By God, my wrathe is al foryive!'

This trait, one is surprised to discover, is taken from Machaut. Yet we cannot doubt that it was true to the life in the case of the Duchess Blanche. Apparently it was the fashion for ladies to let their eyelids droop a little, with what used to be called a languishing look. In *his* lady, the knight protests, this was not an affectation:—

> It was her owne pure loking,
> That the goddesse, dame Nature,
> Hadde mad hem open by mesure,
> And clos.

This is not in Machaut, where also we miss the exquisite couplet closing with "My wrathe is al foryive!" The whole description is so broken up, in Chaucer, as to produce precisely that effect of artless inevitableness that the occasion requires. The mourning knight is not describing his lady: he is giving voice to his unstudied recollection—now of her nature, now of her beauty, now of her demeanor, now of her speech—spasmodically, in no order, as this or that idea rises in his agitated mind.

That Chaucer should adopt the fiction of a dream, both here and elsewhere, needs no explanation; for it was one of the favorite devices of his age, as of the age preceding and of that which followed. What challenges attention is the frequency with which he adverts to the philosophy of dreams. Not that he has anything new to say. The subject had been exhausted by the philosophers, and he could merely ponder over their theories and observations, at a loss for a solution of problems that still puzzle some of the best heads amongst us. He deals with the topic in the *Parliament of Fowls,* at the beginning of the *House of Fame,* with extraordinary vividness in the last book of the *Troilus,* and with all his wit and humor in the discussion between Chanticleer and Pertelote. Dreams play as large a rôle in Chaucer as presentiments do in Shakspere. We may guess, if we like, that Shakspere was in his own person susceptible to presentiments and that Chaucer, for his part, had uncommonly vivid dreams. If so, this consideration reduces the amount of convention and increases the proportion of fact in Chaucer's employment of the device. All this not by way of apology, where none is needed, but as an observation worth making, whether it is valid or not—a point that is none the less interesting because it can never be decided. The world is well acquainted with inspiration that comes in sleep; and English literary history does not lack its examples, from Cædmon at Whitby to Coleridge and his Kubla Khan.

Chaucer, then, in casting the *Book of the Duchess* into the form of a dream, was faithful to a prevalent fashion. When, however, we compare his dream-poem with its predecessors, we are at once aware of an essential difference. Their dreams are a mere device to get the reader into a sort of fairyland, a mediæval Arcadia, people by personified abstractions—Hope and Mercy and Desire and Jealousy and Despair—or by typical lovers scarcely more concrete than the abstractions themselves. The dream-machinery is often handled with no little skill, and there is at times an atmosphere of unreality which appealed to our forefathers as a welcome relief from the tumult and ugliness of every day. But there is no attempt to reproduce the actual phenomena of dreams. The author goes to sleep at the beginning of his poem and wakes up at the end. In the interim, he may be in a strange country, perhaps, but he is not in any dreamland that mortals know.

But Chaucer had a strong sense of fact, and his ***Book of the Duchess*** is really like a dream. This effect, which every reader must instantly admit, is partly due to the naïveté of the Dreamer's temperament, which we contemplate, as we read, with something of that tolerant superiority with which we remember, in our waking moments, the innocent faith we have accorded to the irrationalities of dreamland. In part, however, this effect of dreaming is produced by a number of delicate touches, almost too elusive to isolate, but undeniably significant in their total impression.

The first of these touches, perhaps, is when the Dreamer joins the chase. "Who is hunting here?" he asks of a fellow who is leading a hound in a leash. "Sir," replies the huntsman, "it is the Emperor Octavian." "Good enough!" is the Dreamer's only comment, "let us make haste!" This is surely like a dream. There is no surprise at the news—no question who the Emperor Octavian is, or how he happens to be in that vicinity. Another point concerns the Dreamer's horse. What becomes of it after the hunt? We suddenly find the Dreamer on foot, walking away from the tree at which, though he has not said so, he has taken up his station, and he never thinks of his horse again. This, too, is very like a dream. Then there is the little puppy that has followed the hounds in its helpless fashion, and is now astray in the woods. It comes up to the Dreamer, and fawns upon him as if it knew him, but runs away when he would take it in his arms, and leads him down a grassy ride into the depths of the forest. Like the horse, the puppy drops out of the Dreamer's vision as other objects appear. Thus, we all remember, do dreams behave.

I do not contend that Chaucer carried out his dream-psychology in a thoroughgoing and consistent manner. That would have destroyed the continuity required in a narrative. But assuredly, in various details, he brought the experiences of the Dreamer, with admirable art, near to the actual phenomena of the dream-life.

Never was there a more conventional situation—a dream, a paradise of trees and flowers and birds, a lamenting lover, an incomparable lady. We who wander through the middle ages have seen and heard it all a hundred times. Yet somehow the conventions are vitalized. The artificiality of the situation is merged and lost in the illusions of dreamland which here are genuine illusions, since the dream is really like a dream. Two typical figures—the lover who sighs in vain, and he who has loved and lost—have come to life. First, the Dreamer,—innocent, helpless, childlike, a veritable John-a-dreams,—joining a dream-hunt which comes to naught, pursuing a little dog which disappears, and finding under a tree a mourning knight whom he cannot comprehend. And there are greetings, and questions, and half-understood replies. The Dreamer has the curiosity of a child, and a child's yearning to comfort his incomprehensible elders. The knight has sought solitude, but a child has stormed his fortress, a grown-up child, who speaks the language of the knight's own world.

And the knight talks to the Dreamer in transparent riddles, playing with his own sorrow; he can confide in him all the better for not being understood. And the dream behaves like a dream. Things grow clearer and clearer, until there is the shock of perfect revelation: "She is dead, I tell you! Can't you see what I mean?" "Is that your loss? By God, I am sorry for you!" The intrusion of reality marks the moment of waking. "A bell strikes twelve! Do I hear it in my dream, or is it the clock in the tower? Ah! I am awake, and here is my book of Ceyx and Alcyone still in my hand!"

The ***Book of the Duchess,*** with all its defects, is a very beautiful poem. There is a haunting charm about it that eludes analysis, but subdues our mood to a gentle and vaguely troubled pensiveness. The mind is purged, not by the tragedy of life, with its pity and terror, but by a sense of the sadness which pervades its beauty and its joy. Ours is a pleasant world of birds and flowers and green trees and running streams, and life in such a world is gracious and desirable, and nothing is so good as tender and faithful love, which is its own reward. But the glory of it all is for a moment. Alcyone prayed to Juno to send her a dream, that she might know whether her long-absent husband was alive or dead. And the drowned Ceyx came while she slept, and stood at her bed's foot, and bad her bury his body, which was cast up on the shore:—

> And far-wel, swete, my worldes blisse!
> I praye God your sorwe lisse.
> To litel whyl our blisse lasteth!

Now this thought—that life and love and happiness are transitory—is not, with Chaucer, a commonplace reflection, with which he has only a concern that is conventional and impersonal and external. Nor is it, again, a dogma of experience, to which he has dispassionately adjusted his philosophic scheme. It is an element in his nature: it beats in his heart, and flows in his veins, and catches in his throat, and hammers in his head. All men are mortal, no doubt, but seldom do we find one in whom mortality is a part of his consciousness. And such a man was Chaucer— yet so sound of heart, so sane and normal, so wholesome in his mirth, so delighting in the world and in his fellow-creatures, that no less a critic than Matthew Arnold, speaking with limited sympathy and imperfect comprehension, would exclude him from the fellowship of his peers on the strength of a formula, because he "lacked high seriousness" [see excerpt dated 1880]. Whether Chaucer saw life whole, I do not know. One thing I know—he saw it steadily. (pp. 64-72)

> *George Lyman Kittredge, "The Book of the Duchess," in his* Chaucer and His Poetry, *Cambridge, Mass.: Harvard University Press, 1915, pp. 37-72.*

Aldous Huxley   (essay date 1920)

[*Known primarily for his dystopian novel* Brave New World *(1932), Huxley was a British-American man of letters who is considered a novelist of ideas. The grandson of noted Darwinist T. H. Huxley and the brother of scientist Julian Huxley, he was interested in many fields of knowledge, and daring conceptions of science, philosophy, and religion are woven throughout his fiction. In the following excerpt, Huxley lists the poet's acceptance of the natural order, his knowledge of the world, and his brilliant characterization as reasons "that make Chaucer worth reading."]*

There are few things more melancholy than the spectacle of literary fossilization. A great writer comes into being, lives, labours, and dies. Time passes; year by year the sediment of muddy comment and criticism thickens round the great man's bones. The sediment sets firm; what was once a living organism becomes a thing of marble. On the attainment of total fossilization the great man has become a classic. It becomes increasingly difficult for the members of each succeeding generation to remember that the stony objects which fill the museum cases were once alive. It is often a work of considerable labour to reconstruct the living animal from the fossil shape. But the trouble is generally worth taking. And in no case is it more worth while than in Chaucer's.

With Chaucer the ordinary fossilizing process, to which every classical author is subject, has been complicated by the petrification of his language. Five hundred years have almost sufficed to turn the most living of poets into a substitute on the modern sides of schools for the mental gymnastic of Latin and Greek. Prophetically, Chaucer saw the fate that awaited him and appealed against his doom:

> Ye know eke that, in form of speech is change
> Within a thousand year, and wordes tho
> That hadden price, now wonder nice and strange
> Us thinketh them; and yet they spake them so,
> And sped as well in love as men now do.

The body of his poetry may have grown old, but its spirit is still young and immortal. To know that spirit—and not to know it is to ignore something that is of unique importance in the history of our literature—it is necessary to make the effort of becoming familiar with the body it informs and gives life to. The antique language and versification, so "wonder nice and strange" to our ears, are obstacles in the path of most of those who read for pleasure's sake (not that any reader worthy of the name ever reads for anything else but pleasure); to the pedants they are an end in themselves. Theirs is the carcass, but not the soul. Between those who are daunted by his superficial difficulties and those who take too much delight in them Chaucer finds but few sympathetic readers. I hope in these pages to be able to give a few of the reasons that make Chaucer so well worth reading.

Chaucer's art is, by its very largeness and objectiveness, extremely difficult to subject to critical analysis. Confronted by it, Dryden could only exclaim, "Here is God's plenty!" [see excerpt dated 1700]—and the exclamation proves, when all is said, to be the most adequate and satisfying of all criticisms. All that the critic can hope to do is to expand and to illustrate Dryden's exemplary brevity.

"God's plenty!"—the phrase is a peculiarly happy one. It calls up a vision of the prodigal earth, of harvest fields, of innumerable beasts and birds, of teeming life. And it is in the heart of this living and material world of Nature that Chaucer lives. He is the poet of earth, supremely content to walk, desiring no wings. Many English poets have loved the earth for the sake of something—a dream, a reality, call it which you will—that lies behind it. But there have been few, and, except for Chaucer, no poets of greatness, who have been in love with earth for its own sake, with Nature in the sense of something inevitably material, something that is the opposite of the supernatural. Supreme over everything in this world he sees the natural order, the "law of kind," as he calls it. The teachings of most of the great prophets and poets are simply protests against the law of kind. Chaucer does not protest, he accepts. It is precisely this acceptance that makes him unique among English poets. He does not go to Nature as the symbol of some further spiritual reality; hills, flowers, sea, and clouds are not, for him, transparencies through which the workings of a great soul are visible. No, they are opaque; he likes them for what they are, things pleasant and beautiful, and not the less delicious because they are definitely of the earth earthy. Human beings, in the same way, he takes as he finds, noble and beastish, but, on the whole, wonderfully decent. He has none of that strong ethical bias which is usually to be found in the English mind. He is not horrified by the behaviour of his fellow-beings, and he has no desire to reform them. Their characters, their motives interest him, and he stands looking on at them, a happy spectator. This serenity of detachment, this placid acceptance of things and people as they are, is emphasised if we compare the poetry of Chaucer with that of his contemporary, Langland, or whoever it was that wrote *Piers Plowman.*

The historians tell us that the later years of the fourteenth century were among the most disagreeable periods of our national history. English prestige was at a very low ebb. The Black Death had exterminated nearly a third of the working population of the islands, a fact which, aggravated by the frenzied legislation of the Government, had led to the unprecedented labour troubles that culminated in the peasants' revolt. Clerical corruption and lawlessness were rife. All things considered, even our own age is preferable to that in which Chaucer lived. Langland does not spare denunciation; he is appalled by the wickedness about him, scandalised at the openly-confessed vices that have almost ceased to pay to virtue the tribute of hypocrisy. Indignation is the inspiration of *Piers Plowman,* the righteous indignation of the prophet. But to read Chaucer one would imagine that there was nothing in fourteenth-century England to be indignant about. It is true that the Pardoner, the Friar, the Shipman, the Miller, and, in fact, most of the Canterbury pilgrims are rogues and scoundrels; but, then, they are such "merry harlots," too. It is true that the Monk prefers hunting to praying, that, in these latter days when fairies are no more, "there is none other incubus" but the friar, that "purse is the Archdeacon's hell," and the Summoner a villain of the first magnitude; but Chaucer can only regard these things as primarily humorous. The fact of people not practising what they preach is an unfailing source of amusement to him. Where Langland cries aloud in anger, threatening the world with hell fire, Chaucer looks on and smiles. To the great political crisis of his time he makes but one reference, and that a comic one:

The Knight from the Ellesmere manuscript.

So hideous was the noyse, ah *benedicite!*
Certes he Jakke Straw, and his meyné,
Ne maden schoutes never half so schrille,
Whan that they wolden eny Flemyng kille,
As thilke day was mad upon the fox.

Peasants may revolt, priests break their vows, lawyers lie and cheat, and the world in general indulge its sensual appetites; why try and prevent them, why protest? After all, they are all simply being natural, they are all following the law of kind. A reasonable man, like himself, "flees fro the pres and dwelles with soothfastnesse." But reasonable men are few, and it is the nature of human beings to be the unreasonable sport of instinct and passion, just as it is the nature of the daisy to open its eye to the sun and of the goldfinch to be a spritely and "gaylard" creature. The law of kind has always and in everything domination; there is no rubbing nature against the hair. For

God it wot, there may no man embrace
As to destreyne a thing, the which nature
Hath naturelly set in a creature.
Take any brid, and put him in a cage,
And do all thine entent and thy corrage
To foster it tendrely with meat and drynke,
And with alle the deyntees thou canst bethinke,
And keep it all so kyndly as thou may;

Although his cage of gold be never so gay,
Yet hath this brid, by twenty thousand fold,
Lever in a forest, that is wyld and cold,
Gon ete wormes, and such wrecchidnes;
For ever this brid will doon his busynes
To scape out of his cage when that he may;
His liberté the brid desireth aye . . .
Lo, heer hath kynd his dominacioun,
And appetyt flemeth (banishes) discrescioun.
Also a she wolf hath a vilayne kynde,
The lewideste wolf that she may fynde,
Or least of reputacioun, him will sche take,
In tyme whan hir lust to have a make.
Alle this ensaumples tell I by these men
That ben untrewe, and nothing by wommen.

(As the story from which these lines are quoted happens to be about an unfaithful wife, it seems that, in making the female sex immune from the action of the law of kind, Chaucer is indulging a little in irony.)

For men han ever a licorous appetit
On lower thing to parforme her delit
Than on her wyves, ben they never so faire,
Ne never so trewe, ne so debonaire.

Nature, deplorable as some of its manifestations may be, must always and inevitably assert itself. The law of kind has power even over immortal souls. This fact is the source of the poet's constantly-expressed dislike of celibacy and asceticism. The doctrine that upholds the superiority of the state of virginity over that of wedlock is, to begin with (he holds), a danger to the race. It encourages a process which we may be permitted to call dysgenics—the carrying on of the species by the worst members. The Host's words to the Monk are memorable:

Allas! why wearest thou so wide a cope?
God give me sorwe! and I were a pope
Nought only thou, but every mighty man,
Though he were shore brode upon his pan
     (head)
Should han a wife; for all this world is lorn;
Religioun hath take up all the corn
Of tredyng, and we burel (humble) men ben
     shrimpes;
Of feble trees there cometh wrecchid impes.
This maketh that our heires ben so sclendere
And feble, that they may not wel engendre.

But it is not merely dangerous; it is anti-natural. That is the theme of the **"Wife of Bath's Prologue."** Counsels of perfection are all very well when they are given to those

That wolde lyve parfytly;
But, lordyngs, by your leve, that am not I.

The bulk of us must live as the law of kind enjoins.

It is characteristic of Chaucer's conception of the world, that the highest praise he can bestow on anything is to assert of it, that it possesses in the highest degree the qualities of its own particular kind. Thus of Criseyde he says:

She was not with the least of her stature,
But all her limbes so well answering
Weren to womanhood, that creature
Nas never lesse mannish in seeming.

The horse of brass in the **"Squire's Tale"** is

So well proportioned to be strong,
Right as it were a steed of Lombardye,
Thereto so *horsely* and so quick of eye.

Everything that is perfect of its kind is admirable, even though the kind may not be an exalted one. It is, for instance, a joy to see the way in which the Canon sweats:

A cloote-leaf (dock leaf) he had under his hood
For sweat, and for to keep his head from heat.
But it was joye for to see him sweat;
His forehead dropped as a stillatorie
Were full of plantain or of peritorie.

The Canon is supreme in the category of sweaters, the very type and idea of perspiring humanity; therefore he is admirable and joyous to behold, even as a horse that is supremely horsely or a woman less mannish than anything one could imagine. In the same way it is a delight to behold the Pardoner preaching to the people. In its own kind his charlatanism is perfect and deserves admiration:

Mine handes and my tonge gon so yerne,
That it is joye to see my busynesse.

This manner of saying of things that they are joyous, or, very often, heavenly, is typical of Chaucer. He looks out on the world with a delight that never grows old or weary. The sights and sounds of daily life, all the lavish beauty of the earth fill him with a pleasure which he can only express by calling it a "joy" or a "heaven." It "joye was to see" Criseyde and her maidens playing together; and

So aungellyke was her native beauté
That like a thing immortal seemede she,
As doth an heavenish parfit creature.

The peacock has angel's feathers; a girl's voice is heavenly to hear:

Antigone the shene
Gan on a Trojan song to singen clear,
That it an heaven was her voice to hear.

One could go on indefinitely multiplying quotations that testify to Chaucer's exquisite sensibility to sensuous beauty and his immediate, almost exclamatory response to it. Above all, he is moved by the beauty of "young, fresh folkes, he and she"; by the grace and swiftness of living things, birds and animals; by flowers and placid, luminous, park-like landscapes.

It is interesting to note how frequently Chaucer speaks of animals. Like many other sages, he perceives that an animal is, in a certain sense, more human in character than a man. For an animal bears the same relation to a man as a caricature to a portrait. In a way a caricature is truer than a portrait. It reveals all the weaknesses and absurdities that flesh is heir to. The portrait brings out the greatness and dignity of the spirit that inhabits the often ridiculous flesh. It is not merely that Chaucer has written regular fables, though the **"Nun's Priest's Tale"** puts him among the great fabulists of the world, and there is also much definitely fabular matter in the *Parliament of Fowls.* No, his references to the beasts are not confined to his animal stories alone; they are scattered broadcast throughout his works. He relies for much of his psychology and for much of his most vivid description on the comparison of

man, in his character and appearance (which with Chaucer are always indissolubly blended), with the beasts. Take, for example, that enchanting simile in which Troilus, stubbornly anti-natural in refusing to love as the law of kind enjoins him, is compared to the corn-fed horse, who has to be taught good behaviour and sound philosophy under the whip:

As proude Bayard ginneth for to skip
Out of the way, so pricketh him his corn,
Till he a lash have of the longe whip,
Then thinketh he, "Though I prance all biforn,
First in the trace, full fat and newe shorn,
Yet am I but an horse, and horses' law
I must endure and with my feeres draw."

Or, again, women with too pronounced a taste for fine apparel are likened to the cat:

And if the cattes skin be sleek and gay,
She will not dwell in housé half a day,
But forth she will, ere any day be dawet
To show her skin and gon a caterwrawet.

In his descriptions of the personal appearance of his characters Chaucer makes constant use of animal characteristics. Human beings, both beautiful and hideous, are largely described in terms of animals. It is interesting to see how often in that exquisite description of Alisoun, the carpenter's wife, Chaucer produces his clearest and sharpest effects by a reference to some beast or bird:

Fair was this younge wife, and therewithal
As any weasel her body gent and small . . .
But of her song it was as loud and yern
As is the swallow chittering on a barn.
Thereto she coulde skip and make a game
As any kid or calf following his dame.
Her mouth was sweet as bragot is or meath,
Or hoard of apples, laid in hay or heath.
Wincing she was, as is a jolly colt,
Long as a mast and upright as a bolt.

Again and again in Chaucer's poems do we find such similitudes, and the result is always a picture of extraordinary precision and liveliness. Here, for example, are a few:

Gaylard he was as goldfinch in the shaw,

or,

Such glaring eyen had he as an hare;

or,

As piled (bald) as an ape was his skull.

The self-indulgent friars are

Like Jovinian,
Fat as a whale, and walken as a swan.

The Pardoner describes his own preaching in these words:

Then pain I me to stretche forth my neck
And east and west upon the people I beck,
As doth a dove, sitting on a barn.

Very often, too, Chaucer derives his happiest metaphors from birds and beasts. Of Troy in its misfortune and decline he says: Fortune

Gan pull away the feathers bright of Troy
From day to day.

Love-sick Troilus soliloquises thus:

He said: "O fool, now art thou in the snare
That whilom japedest at lovés pain,
Now art thou hent, now gnaw thin owné chain."

The metaphor of Troy's bright feathers reminds me of a very beautiful simile borrowed from the life of the plants:

And as in winter leavés been bereft,
Each after other, till the tree be bare,
So that there nis but bark and branches left,
Lieth Troilus, bereft of each welfare,
Ybounden in the blacke bark of care.

And this, in turn, reminds me of that couplet in which Chaucer compares a girl to a flowering pear-tree:

She was well more blissful on to see
Than is the newe parjonette tree.

Chaucer is as much at home among the stars as he is among the birds and beasts and flowers of earth. There are some literary men of to-day who are not merely not ashamed to confess their total ignorance of all facts of a "scientific" order, but even make a boast of it. Chaucer would have regarded such persons with pity and contempt. His own knowledge of astronomy was wide and exact. Those whose education has been as horribly imperfect as my own will always find some difficulty in following him as he moves with easy assurance through the heavens. Still, it is possible without knowing any mathematics to appreciate Chaucer's descriptions of the great pageant of the sun and stars as they march in triumph from mansion to mansion through the year. He does not always trouble to take out his astrolabe and measure the progress of "Phebus, with his rosy cart"; he can record the god's movements in more general terms that may be understood even by the literary man of nineteen hundred and twenty. Here, for example, is a description of "the colde frosty seisoun of Decembre," in which matters celestial and earthly are mingled to make a picture of extraordinary richness:

Phebus wox old and hewed like latoun,
That in his hoté declinacioun
Shone as the burned gold, with streames bright;
But now in Capricorn adown he light,
Where as he shone full pale; I dare well sayn
The bitter frostes with the sleet and rain
Destroyed hath the green in every yerd.
Janus sit by the fire with double beard,
And drinketh of his bugle horn the wine;
Before him stont the brawn of tusked swine,
And *"noel"* cryeth every lusty man.

In astrology he does not seem to have believed. The magnificent passage in the **"Man of Law's Tale,"** where it is said that

In the starres, clearer than is glass,
Is written, God wot, whoso can it read,
The death of every man withouten drede,

is balanced by the categorical statement found in the scientific and educational treatise on the astrolabe, that judicial astrology is mere deceit.

His scepticism with regard to astrology is not surprising. Highly as he prizes authority, he prefers the evidence of experience, and where that evidence is lacking he is content to profess a quiet agnosticism. His respect for the law of kind is accompanied by a complementary mistrust of all that does not appear to belong to the natural order of things. There are moments when he doubts even the fundamental beliefs of the Church:

A thousand sythes have I herd men telle
That there is joye in heaven and peyne in helle;
And I accorde well that it be so.
But natheless, this wot I well also
That there is none that dwelleth in this countree
That either hath in helle or heaven y-be.

Of the fate of the spirit after death he speaks in much the same style:

His spiryt changed was, and wente there
As I came never, I cannot tellen where;
Therefore I stint, I nam no divinistre;
Of soules fynde I not in this registre,
Ne me list not th' opiniouns to telle
Of hem, though that they written where they
    dwelle.

He has no patience with superstitions. Belief in dreams, in auguries, fear of the "ravenes qualm or schrychynge of thise owles" are all unbefitting to a self-respecting man:

To trowen on it bothe false and foul is;
Alas, alas, so noble a creature
As is a man shall dreaden such ordure!

By an absurd pun he turns all Calchas's magic arts of prophecy to ridicule:

So when this Calkas knew by calkulynge,
And eke by answer of this Apollo
That Grekes sholden such a people bringe,
Through which that Troye muste ben fordo,
He cast anon out of the town to go.

It would not be making a fanciful comparison to say that Chaucer in many respects resembles Anatole France. Both men possess a profound love of this world for its own sake, coupled with a profound and gentle scepticism about all that lies beyond this world. To both of them the lavish beauty of Nature is a never-failing and all-sufficient source of happiness. Neither of them are ascetics; in pain and privation they see nothing but evil. To both of them the notion that self-denial and self-mortification are necessarily righteous and productive of good is wholly alien. Both of them are apostles of sweetness and light, of humanity and reasonableness. Unbounded tolerance of human weakness and a pity, not the less sincere for being a little ironical, characterise them both. Deep knowledge of the evils and horrors of this unintelligible world makes them all the more attached to its kindly beauty. But in at least one important respect Chaucer shows himself to be the greater, the completer spirit. He possesses, what Anatole France does not, an imaginative as well as an intellectual comprehension of things. Faced by the multitudinous variety of human character, Anatole France exhibits a curious impotence of imagination. He does not understand characters in the sense that, say, Tolstoy understands them; he cannot, by the power of imagination, get inside them, become what he contemplates. None of the persons of his creation are complete characters; they cannot be looked at from every side; they are portrayed, as it were, in the flat and not in three dimensions. But Chaucer has the power of getting into someone else's character. His understanding of the men and women of whom he writes is complete; his slightest character sketches are always solid and three-dimensional. The "General Prologue" to the *Canterbury Tales,* in which the effects are almost entirely produced by the description of external physical features, furnishes us with the most obvious example of his three-dimensional drawing. Or, again, take that description in the Merchant's tale of old January and his young wife May after their wedding night. It is wholly a description of external details, yet the result is not a superficial picture. We are given a glimpse of the characters in their entirety:

> Thus laboureth he till that the day gan dawe,
> And then he taketh a sop in fine clarré,
> And upright in his bed then sitteth he.
> And after that he sang full loud and clear,
> And kissed his wife and made wanton cheer.
> He was all coltish, full of ragerye,
> And full of jargon as a flecked pye.
> The slacké skin about his necke shaketh,
> While that he sang, so chanteth he and craketh.
> But God wot what that May thought in her
>   heart,
> When she him saw up sitting in his shirt,
> In his night cap and with his necke lean;
> She praiseth not his playing worth a bean.

But these are all slight sketches. For full-length portraits of character we must turn to *Troilus and Cressida,* a work which, though it was written before the fullest maturity of Chaucer's powers, is in many ways his most remarkable achievement, and one, moreover, which has never been rivalled for beauty and insight in the whole field of English narrative poetry. When one sees with what certainty and precision Chaucer describes every movement of Cressida's spirit from the first moment she hears of Troilus' love for her to the moment when she is unfaithful to him, one can only wonder why the novel of character should have been so slow to make its appearance. It was not until the eighteenth century that narrative artists, using prose as their medium instead of verse, began to rediscover the secrets that were familiar to Chaucer in the fourteenth.

Troilus and Cressida was written, as we have said, before Chaucer had learnt to make the fullest use of his powers. In colouring it is fainter, less sharp and brilliant than the best of the *Canterbury Tales.* The character studies are there, carefully and accurately worked out; but we miss the bright vividness of presentation with which Chaucer was to endow his later art. The characters are all alive and completely seen and understood. But they move, as it were, behind a veil—the veil of that poetic convention which had, in the earliest poems, almost completely shrouded Chaucer's genius, and which, as he grew up, as he adventured and discovered, grew thinner and thinner, and finally vanished like gauzy mist in the sunlight. When *Troilus and Cressida* was written the mist had not completely dissipated, and the figures of his creation, complete

in conception and execution as they are, are seen a little dimly because of the interposed veil.

The only moment in the poem when Chaucer's insight seems to fail him is at the very end; he has to account for Cressida's unfaithfulness, and he is at a loss to know how he shall do it. Shakespeare, when he rehandled the theme, had no such difficulty. His version of the story, planned on much coarser lines than Chaucer's, leads obviously and inevitably to the foreordained conclusion; his Cressida is a minx who simply lives up to her character. What could be more simple? But to Chaucer the problem is not so simple. His Cressida is not a minx. From the moment he first sets eyes on her Chaucer, like his own unhappy Troilus, falls head over ears in love. Beautiful, gentle, gay; possessing, it is true, somewhat "tendre wittes," but making up for her lack of skill in ratiocination by the "sudden avysements" of intuition; vain, but not disagreeably so, of her good looks and of her power over so great and noble a knight as Troilus; slow to feel love, but once she has yielded, rendering back to Troilus passion for passion; in a word, the "least mannish" of all possible creatures—she is to Chaucer the ideal of gracious and courtly womanhood. But, alas, the old story tells us that Cressida jilted her Troilus for that gross prizefighter of a man, Diomed. The woman whom Chaucer has made his ideal proves to be no better than she should be; there is a flaw in the crystal. Chaucer is infinitely reluctant to admit the fact. But the old story is specific in its statement; indeed, its whole point consists in Cressida's infidelity. Called upon to explain his heroine's fall, Chaucer is completely at a loss. He makes a few half-hearted attempts to solve the problem, and then gives it up, falling back on authority. The old clerks say it was so, therefore it must be so, and that's that. The fact is that Chaucer pitched his version of the story in a different key from that which is found in the "olde bokes," with the result that the note on which he is compelled by his respect of authority to close is completely out of harmony with the rest of the music. It is this that accounts for the chief, and indeed the only, defect of the poem—its hurried and boggled conclusion. (pp. 179-89)

Aldous Huxley, "Chaucer," in The London Mercury, *Vol. II, No. 8, June, 1920, pp. 179-89.*

Emile Legouis   (essay date 1924)

[*A French scholar and philologist, Legouis is the author of* Chaucer *(1913),* Edmund Spenser *(1923), and* Wordsworth in a New Light *(1923), and the acclaimed* Histoire de la littérature anglaise *(1924;* A History of English Literature, *1926), written with Louis Cazamian. In the following excerpt from the last-named work, Legouis discusses Chaucer's ability, exemplified by the* Canterbury Tales, *to represent the multi-faceted world of medieval England in an extraordinarily powerful and suggestive poetic synthesis.*]

All the writers of [the fourteenth century] reveal some aspect of contemporary life and of prevailing feeling and thought. The author of *Pearl* shows us the mysticism of refined minds, Langland the anger which was threatening the abuses of governments and the vices of the clergy, Wyclif the ardour for religious reform which already could amount to Protestantism, Gower the fear aroused in the wealthier class by the Peasant Rising, Barbour the break between the literature of Scotland and of England and the advent of patriotic Scottish poetry. Each had his own plan, his dominant and, on the whole, narrow passion, a character which was local and of his time. Each was enclosed within the limits of a restricted experience, if not within those of a dialect incapable of expansion and without a future.

It is Chaucer's distinction that he turned impartial, eager and clear-sighted eyes not only on the past, which his books discovered to him, but also on all the society of his time, on foreign countries and on every class in his own country. His work reflects his century not in fragments but completely. More than this, he is often able to discern permanent features beneath the garments of a day, to penetrate to the everlasting springs of human action. His truthful pictures of his age and country contain a truth which is of all time and all countries. (p. 82)

What is most striking in Chaucer is the interest he took in every one of the different worlds through which he passed and all his heterogeneous occupations. He was at his ease at court, among traders, among clerks, with the people. To observe was as much his joy as to read. It is inconceivable that there was an hour of his life whence he did not extract pleasure. He could bear a heavy burden of work easily, with the air of an idler whose life is all pleasure. The literary work he accomplished is considerable in extent, but far more remarkable for the radiance of his sympathy and the length and breadth of his clear vision.

We know nothing of the work of artistic preparation which is to be presumed from Chaucer's success in poetry, but it was indubitably intense and long. Genius doubtless accounts for the lengths by which his poetry outdistanced Gower's, but something is due to the persevering will of an artist who gave himself unstintingly to the acquisition of necessary technique. Alone among his contemporaries, Chaucer put art first. He did not seek to direct men, to judge events, to reform morals or to present a philosophy. Poetry was his only object. Up to the very end, the task he set himself was to write verses which should have charm and life. To realise the immense effort which this involved it is only necessary to remember the state in which he found the versification and the poetic language of his dialect.

It is hardly possible to exaggerate the part he played as creator of English versification. Save the frail octosyllabic line already in use, he had himself to forge all his instruments. He imported the decasyllabic line from France and, under Italian influence, made it pliable. It became the heroic line which was the surpassing vehicle of the great poetry of England. We [know] that the progress of this poetry was barred by the lack of a verse-form at once ample, ductile, noble and sonorous. Chaucer used the new line alternately in stanzas and in couplets, the stanza for songs and the couplet for narratives. He cast it in moulds unknown to his country—the roundel, the virelay, the ballade. Out of all his essays two came to dominate: the seven-lined stanza (*ababbcc*), to which his name has since

attached, and the couplet. But what fashioning and refashioning, what experiments and doubts, this presupposes! All his youth and part of his maturity must have been mainly dedicated to this labour which, since nearly all his earliest works are lost, cannot be traced.

His immediate choice of his own dialect as the vehicle of his poetry is proof of his decision and of his sure judgment. He did not, like Gower, allow himself to be tempted either by Latin or by French. He risked his whole literary fortune on London English, the King's English, of which it has been said how poor it was. He found it a thing of nought and left it so rich that English poetry had but to add blank verse to it in order to be fully equipped.

Chaucer's first act of faith in the only tongue which was to him a living language, notwithstanding he clearly saw its defects, was to inculcate in it all the delicacy and refinement he perceived in the poetry of France. He disregarded the debased, artificial and prosaic Anglo-Norman, and went straight to the continent to seek masters and models.

To wed the vocabulary of his native land to the courtliness of France was his first and essential task. He recast English words—that is, surviving words of Teutonic origin and acclimatised words of French origin—in the moulds of the French poets. He expressed in English all the graces and refinements he found in the poetry of France.

Unlike the authors of the *Grene Knyght* and *Piers Plowman,* he definitely broke with the Anglo-Saxon literary tradition. His face was turned to the south, and he took the whole of his ideal from the continent.

He might be thought unlucky in his time. There never was a period in which French poetry was apparently more frail and destitute than that which intervenes between Rutebeuf and Villon or between the *Roman de la Rose* and Charles d'Orléans. In this poor, meagre and pretentious garden there was little but artificial flowers to cull. And, because of the accident of date, it was from one of the most debilitated of the French poets, Guillaume de Machaut, that Chaucer took his first lessons. He could learn from him neither animation nor vigour, nor frankness of style, nor strength of feeling and thought. But Machaut was refined, as much a musician as a poet. Although not a great artist he was yet pure artist, and well fitted to give the young Englishman the teaching he needed in the rules of his craft. In France, it was Machaut who chiefly propagated the poems made in fixed forms, the ballades, roundels, *chansons royales,* and it was from him that Chaucer learned to use these forms for his lyrical verses. For his narratives and descriptions he is no less in debt to Machaut's lays. He often also emulates those French pupils of Machaut who were his contemporaries, Eustache Deschamps, Froissart, Otto de Granson. His work is full of details borrowed here and there. He followed with slightly ironic curiosity a tenson on the comparative merits of the Leaf and the Flower. He took part in the symbolic cult of the Marguerite or daisy, which in the second half of this century, out of deference to some great ladies named after that flower, superseded that of the Rose.

Nevertheless, it was above all to the *Roman de la Rose* that he owed his initiation as a poet. At some unknown moment of his life, probably as his youth was ending, he translated the famous *Roman* into English verse. It is not unlikely that he produced the version of which we possess a part, and which is most faithfully and exactly translated. This was excellent practice, calculated to bring discipline into the versification and style of a young poet. If he does not always attain to such fresh colours and sonorous rhymes as Guillaume de Lorris, it is that he was hindered by his interpreter's task and by a language as yet unformed. He is conscious of the fact. He complains that "ryme in Englisch hath such skarsetë," and meanwhile he practised to such good purpose that he brought nearer the day when this difficulty disappeared.

The *Roman de la Rose* did more for him than discipline his style. It was the work which had the most comprehensive and constant hold on him. Its double character, due to the difference, amounting to contrast, between the two poets who composed it, did not shock Chaucer as an interruption of unity, but made this work—this Bible of poetry—doubly attractive to him. According to his mood, he was inspired by Guillaume de Lorris or by Jean de Meung. Guillaume, with his delicate grace and the clarity of his atmosphere of love, caught him first, in his youth. Later it came to pass that the flood of ideas, satire and classical reminiscences, which rolls through the work of Jean de Meung, was better suited to his need of more solid and humorous nourishment, and this poet began and continued to charm him more than any other, so that he borrowed from him again and again, even for his final masterpiece.

The first effect of the *Roman* was, however, in one sense to pervert his genius while it helped to fashion his style. It led him into the sphere of the allegorical and kept him there for many years. Chaucer's reverence for this poem was such that it delayed the flowering of his dramatic genius, which he neglected until after his journey to Italy. Such prolonged restraint would be more regrettable had he not produced some entirely charming works in the form of allegories, and had his art not gained by the slow process of cultivation and ripening to which it was subject when, as it were, he put himself to school. Only after these trials did he risk the hard enterprise, often so dangerous to formal beauty, of representing life directly.

His debt to France goes beyond the many imitations which can be discovered in his work, the reminiscences of the *trouvères* in lines, reflections, descriptive touches, opinions or quips. He owes another debt to France which is vaster, more diffused through his poetry, less easy to apprehend but not less certain. He is no mere recipient of her largess. She has bequeathed to him a whole heritage, not isolated possessions but his very nature. His mind is as French as his name, which is a form of *chaussier*. He is the lineal descendant of the French *trouvères*, one of them in all but language.

It was not that he gallicised his grammar or vocabulary more than his contemporaries. But this first great literary artist of his country attempted to express in his own language the poetic beauty which he felt in the best French verses and which answered to his urgent instinctive need. This ideal, to which he attained, was the very inverse of that of the scops.

As the reader passes from their works to his, he has again, in striking degree, the impression of dawning clarity which he received when he left Anglo-Saxon for old French poetry. The rarefied, white light shed over Chaucer's work, hardly ever touching the violent colours of more southern poetry, is exactly the same in tone as that which shone for the poets of the Île-de-France. A Frenchman may enter Chaucer's country and be conscious of no change of sky or climate.

Like the French *trouvères,* Chaucer has a lightness of heart which is not tumultuous but diffused. It is born of his pleasure in life and is revealed by his taste for the well-lit pictures which call up spring, the month of May, flowers, birds and music. One line, in which he resumes the youth of his Squire, might be the device of all his poetry:

> He was as fressh as is the moneth of May.

This line is entirely French, the essence of the earliest French poetry.

The same may be said of his pitch, neither too high nor too low. His voice, too, has a pure, slightly frail quality. He never forces his tone; rather, he sometimes uses a mute. It is an even voice, made to tell a long story without weariness or jar, perhaps not rich or full enough for the highest lyricism, but wont to keep to the middle tones in which meaning is conveyed to the mind most clearly and exactly.

There is the charm of fluent simplicity, complete correspondence of words and thoughts. Chaucer's best verses merely note facts, external details or characteristics of feeling.

There is constant restraint, alike in expressing emotion and satire. When he touches the pathetic, he stops short of cries and weeping; he tempers his irony with wit, and he provokes smiles rather than unchecked laughter. Everywhere there is undefinable sobriety and good manners which imply that the poet is ruled by intelligence, rather than carried away by passion. In other words, his temperamental and intellectual powers are perfectly balanced.

All these qualities belong, in the same measure, to the old French poets and to Chaucer. His French extraction is proved by his possession of all of them, and by the fact that he goes beyond them only at those rare moments when, under an Italian influence, he rises above both his own nature and French nature. When Chaucer forsakes France he is a little denaturalised.

It should be added that with the virtues of the French *trouvères* he has the faults from which the best of them are not exempt. Like them, he too often does not condense, is garrulous, often charmingly but yet indisputably. There are times when he lacks the sinew and the pace which an occasion demands, when he dawdles instead of hastening his steps, walks instead of flying. His discreet poetry is near the border-line of prose; it has its awkward, slow and platitudinous moments. There is padding at which we smile, but which we must recognise for what it is. Again like the old French poets, Chaucer has, however, a good-humoured, artless way with him, which makes all these manifest defects into an additional attraction. Sometimes he even uses them to point his sharpest quip.

These characteristics do not belong only to his youth, but are permanent in him. Chaucer cannot be said to have had a French period. He is always French, although he sometimes gathered riches abroad, as he marvelled at antiquity or at Italy. Fundamentally unchanged, he acquired from the Italians and Latins a certain adventitious diversity, and ended by using his French manner to paint the society of England. (pp. 83-6)

Up to [the time of the **Canterbury Tales**] Chaucer's work, although he sought inspiration in France and Italy, or rather because he was the too docile pupil of foreign masters, is interesting mainly to the English. He deserves admiration for having civilised his country poetically, but he had spent his strength almost entirely on translating and adapting. He was still no more than the "great translator" praised by Eustache Deschamps [see excerpt dated c. 1386], the word being taken in its wide sense. His part was that of interpreter between the continent and his country. Who could have hoped that, as he neared his fiftieth year, he would suddenly be revealed as himself a master, the painter of English society, and the creator of a work which in this fourteenth century would leave the contemporary poetry of France far behind it, and even, in some respects, that of Italy also?

The genius which was to flower had been his from the beginning. He did not suddenly become an observer. He had already seen and retained much, although hitherto he had not found among his models a mould in which to cast his observations. Without doubt, there was already that rich diversity in his nature which made him curious of the beautiful and the ugly alike, which was compounded of poetry and prose, piety and scepticism, grace and humour. When, however, he wished to house this complexity, he found only literary forms apt to isolate one or other of its aspects. He had been held by allegory or lyrical narrative when his genius was impelling him, irresistibly, towards dramatic and realistic storytelling, the weaving of a web in which the threads would be both comic and sentimental.

So far, he had brought only two considerable poems to completion, the one a mere translation of the *Roman de la Rose,* the other his adaptation of *Il Filostrato,* a poem whose original harmony he disturbed by his efforts to introduce into it matter of his own. He had begun two other important poems, but had been unable or unwilling to finish them. The **Hous of Fame** discouraged him by the factitiousness of its allegorical machinery and the use, or rather abuse, of personified abstractions which its plan entailed; he wearied of the **Legende of Goode Women** because it imposed on him a partisanship, obliged him, by its preliminary conditions, to be unfailingly sentimental and partial, and therefore necessarily monotonous. Did he wonder whether he would ever find a more pliable and wider frame, in which he could fit stories as varied as life and mobile as his changing moods, stories in which he could be lyrical and epical, by turns, which he could tell tenderly, swiftly, poetically, feelingly, humorously or merrily?

It was at this moment that he bethought him of the collections of stories of which several had been made in the Middle Ages, on the plan so awkwardly reproduced by his friend Gower in the *Confessio Amantis.* The *Decameron* would undoubtedly have stimulated him further had he not been, to the best of our knowledge, unaware of it. Yet Boccaccio's example was not such as to fulfil his aim of variety. That society of elegant young gentlemen and ladies, hardly distinct from each other, telling tales while the plague raged in Florence, was not the band of storytellers he wanted. It was strongly individualised narrators, taken from the most diverse classes, whom he wished to interpose between himself and his readers. And at last he had the very simple and yet quite novel idea of a pilgrimage which would unite people of every condition. Since the spring of 1385 he had been living at Greenwich, on the road of pilgrims from every county in England who were constantly drawn to the shrine of Saint Thomas à Becket at Canterbury. Often and often he had watched the progress of their variegated cavalcades, men and women, knights and burghers, handicraftsmen and clerks, mingled in momentary fellowship. One fine day, moved by devoutness or mere curiosity, he may himself have joined one of these troops. No sooner had he got his idea than the work went of itself. He had but to describe his pilgrims, give each of them his individual characteristics as well as the marks of his rank, then put an appropriate tale into his mouth.

Thus the first requisite was to present a band of storytellers clearly. No enterprise could be more difficult at any time, difficult to-day and more difficult at a date when nothing of the sort had yet been attempted. The simplicity of Chaucer's method, its complete lack of any artifice, the sure hand with which he traced portraits to form the prologue of his *Tales,* are surprising. He made his group of pilgrims into a picture of the society of his time of which the like is not to be found elsewhere. Except for royalty and the nobles on the one hand, and the dregs of the people on the other, two classes whom probability excluded from sharing a pilgrimage, he painted, in brief, almost the whole English nation.

There are thirty of the pilgrims, following the most diverse trades. The Knight with his son, the Squire, and the Yeoman who bore the Squire's arms, represent the fighting class. A Doctor of Physic, a Man of Law, a Clerk of Oxford and the poet himself give a glimpse of the liberal professions. The land is represented by a Ploughman, a Miller, a Reeve and a Franklin, trade by a Merchant and a Shipman, the crafts by a Wife of Bath, a Haberdasher, a Carpenter, a Webbe or Weaver, a Dyer and a Tapicer, the victuallers by a Maunciple, a Cook and the Host of the Tabard. The secular clergy provide the Good Parson and the odious Sompnour or summoner of an ecclesiastical court, who are joined on the road by a Canon addicted to alchemy. The monastic orders supply a full contingent—a rich Benedictine Monk, a Prioress with her chaplain Nun, a mendicant Friar, and not far from these religious, a doubtfully accredited Pardoner wends his way.

Chaucer, desiring distinct outlines, first used the easiest and clearest method of differentiation, which is to contrast various callings. This results—especially in those days did it result—in a whimsical medley of colours and costumes which at once catches the eye, and it allows a whole series of habits and tendencies to be suggested by half a word. Only the generic features, the average characteristics of each calling, have to be marked, in order to give a sufficiently definite picture which has its own identity. Thereafter all that is left to do is to make each person talk as befits his station and nature.

The idea looks so simple that all the noise it has made in the world might be thought exaggerated. It was, however, a novelty. It had no precedent outside obscure corners of a rudimentary drama, and it was to mark a turning-point in European thought. It was more than a literary innovation. It was a change of mental attitude. Poetry turned, with tolerant curiosity, to the study of man and manners. For the first time, the relation between individuals and ideas was clearly realised. Ideas ceased to be an end in themselves, and became interesting as revealing him who expressed them, who believed in them, or who was pleased by them. And they acquired therewith an unforeseen value. The ideas which Chaucer had hitherto given to the world could not be called very original. They were less novel and perhaps less powerful than those, for instance, of Jean de Meung. It would be easier to extract some sort of philosophy from Jean de Meung's works than from Chaucer's. When, however, Chaucer's ideas emanate from a man of a given temperament, represent the prejudices of a class or the routine of a trade, they immediately take on youth or fun, become penetrating and sometimes profound, although they themselves are unchanged. It is that dramatic use is made of them. Their value in isolation or abstraction matters as little as ever, but they are richly significant because they fall from the lips of a definite person who reveals or betrays himself by their means.

For such an end it is necessary that the author efface himself voluntarily. Chaucer is fully conscious of the realism to which he obliges himself. He assumes the part of mere interpreter, a chronicler and no more, who relates without altering a word or a tone stories he has heard told. By his grouping of representatives of the different callings, and by his impartiality which allows individuals to speak and never dictates their thoughts or words, he has painted, with minute exactness, the body and soul of the society of his time. He is as truly the social chronicler of England in the late fourteenth century as Froissart is the political and military chronicler of the same period.

Chaucer has collected the descriptions of the pilgrims in his general prologue, which is a true picture-gallery. His twenty-nine travelling companions make almost as many portraits, hung from its walls. They face us, in equidistant frames, on the same plane, all hanging on the line. Chaucer is a primitive, aiming at exactness of feature and correctness of emblem. He is a primitive also by a certain honest awkwardness, the unskilled stiffness of some of his outlines, and such an insistence on minute points as at first provokes a smile. He seems to amass details haphazard, alternates the particulars of a costume with the points of a character, drops the one for the other, picks either up again. Sometimes he interrupts the painting of a pilgrim's

character to put colour on his face or his tunic. It is an endearing carelessness, which hides his art and heightens the impression he makes of veracity:

> Ses nonchalances sont ses plus grands artifices.

Who enters this gallery is first struck by some patches of brilliant colour, dominating one or other of the portraits, the squire's gown,

> Embrowded was he, as it were a mede,
> Al ful of fresshë floures, white and reede,

and near him the yeoman who serves him "in coote and hood of grene." How the Prioress's rosary "of smal coral," its decades, "gauded al with grene," and its hanging brooch "of gold ful schene," stands out against her dress! There are faces as strongly coloured as any of the fabrics or accessories—the pustulous countenance of the Sompnour, "a fyr-reed cherubynes face,"

> With skalled browes blak, and piled berd,

and the Miller, whose beard "as any sowe or fox was reed," with his wart whence sprouts a tuft of red hairs, his wide and black nostrils and his mouth "as wyde as was a gret forneys." There are also duller colours to rest the sight, and to make the cruder hues more brilliant by contrast. The pious and modest Knight was "nought gay,"

> Of fustyan he werede a gepoun,
> Al bysmotered with his habergeoun.

The poor Clerk was "ful threadbare," the Man of Law "rood but hoomly in a medled coote," the Reeve wore a "long surcote of pers," or blue, and the Good Parson is drawn without line or colour, so that we are free to imagine him lit only by the light of the Gospel shining from his eyes.

Essential moral characteristics are thrown into relief with the same apparent simplicity and the same real command of means as the colours and the significant articles of clothing. Mere statements of fact, suggestive anecdotes, particulars relating to calling and individual traits, lines resuming a character—all these make up a whole which stands out upon its canvas. The outline is strong and clear although sometimes a little stiff, in the steady light which is shed on it, and it is unforgettable.

Chaucer was not content to make his pilgrims typical only of their several callings. Sometimes a classification of another kind crosses with that by trades and enriches it. Thus the Squire stands for youth and the Ploughman for the perfect charity of the humble, while in the Wife of Bath there is the essence of satire against women. Nor is this all. Chaucer, by details he has observed for himself, puts life into conventional descriptions and generalisations made by others. He adds individual to generic features; even when he paints a type he gives the impression that he is painting some one person whom he happens to have met. He mixes these two elements in varying proportions and with great although imperceptible skill. His figures, a little more generalised, would be frozen into symbolism, mere cold abstractions, while a few more purely individual features would cause confusion, destroying landmarks and leading attention astray.

Thus English society, which to the visionary Langland seemed a swarming and confused mass, a mob of men stumbling against each other in the semi-darkness of a nightmare, was distributed by Chaucer among a group which is clearly seen restricted in size and representative. Its members pause before us long enough for us to identify each one. Each has his own life and an identity which is for all time, yet together they resume a society.

Chaucer does not only draw frank or delicately traced portraits which give to his characters the immobility of permanence. He also makes each pilgrim step out of the frame in which he first placed him. The artist does not pass straight from portrait to tale. He does not let us forget, on the road to Canterbury, that each storyteller is a living being who has his own gestures and tones. As the cavalcade pursues its course, the pilgrims talk among themselves. The poet shows them calling to each other, approving each other, above all squabbling. They criticise each other's stories, and so betray their preoccupations, feelings and interests. In this way a comedy of action goes through the whole poem, connects its different parts, a comedy which is no more than sketched, yet is adequate, in its incompleteness, to reveal the author's intentions and his dramatic vigour. The persons he has painted are again discovered by their own acts and words. As always happens when an analytical portrait gives place to a direct presentment, some of the pilgrims are found to be more complex, their limitations less discernible, their characteristics more numerous and their outline less definite than had appeared. This is certainly true of the famous Wife of Bath, indubitably the most vigorous of Chaucer's creations, who lives less by her tale than by the immense monologue in which she gives outlet to her feelings as she rides along the road. As she speaks, she seems to be magnified before our eyes, to overflow the exact boundaries which the portraitist set to her personality, and to acquire pantagruelian dimensions. Not until Panurge and Falstaff arrived was there her like in literature. The same is true of the Host of the Tabard, the pilgrims' jovial guide, who is barely sketched in the prologue, but who, little by little and by successive touches, by his various remarks as they journey, is made to tell us much of his temper, his tastes, his dislikes and his private life. He is all the more real and living for never being analysed.

The tales gave Chaucer one means of finishing the portraits of his pilgrims. He found them in every corner of mediæval literature, as diverse and unequal as he could wish. The poet used their lack of originality to impart an added probability to his poem, for his pilgrims are supposed not to invent but to retell stories. Above all, he used the tales to characterise the tellers. He chose for each of them a story suited to his class and character, or, at least, he did this admirably where he had time. His first plan was immense, each of the thirty pilgrims undertaking to tell two tales on the way to Canterbury and two on the way back, so that there would have been one hundred and twenty tales altogether. In fact, Chaucer was not able to allot even one story to each of his travellers, nor, still more regrettably, had he time in every case to adjust story to teller. He was still hesitating about the assignment of certain tales when death surprised him. Enough was, howev-

er, accomplished to allow us to appreciate his design and his executive talent.

In a certain number of cases, the tale is so subordinate to the vast comedy in which it has place that its original form has a little suffered. More often, it is its meaning which is changed. It is possible to consider a story by itself to judge whether the writer has succeeded in his aim of producing the strongest possible impression by his distribution of the parts, his manipulation and unravelling of the plot, and his arrangement of details in view of the surprise of the conclusion. The excellence of a tale then depends simply on the skill with which its thread is followed, and on the grace or liveliness of its writing. But the same story may be told to reveal an alleged narrator. It then behoves the author to conceal himself, to sacrifice his own literary talent and sense of proportion and give place to another, who may be ignorant, garrulous, clumsy, foolish or coarse, or moved by enthusiasms and prejudices unshared by his creator. Chaucer follows this principle to most of its consequences in that part of his work to which he was able to put the finishing touches. He very carefully allows more than one of his pilgrims to reveal themselves by introducing into their stories irrelevances, digressions which break the even course of a tale but which give an opening for the information, the discursiveness or the fads of the speaker. We notice this as we read the tales of the Wife of Bath, the Pardoner and the Yeoman of the alchemist Canon.

Elsewhere, the very fact that a story is assigned to a particular person is enough without any digressions, as when the tale of Griselda, fount of abnegation, is told by the good idealist Clerk, or when the graceful and mincing Prioress tells the story of the little cleric, devotee of Mary, who was slain by the Jews, or the Nun relates the tale of the miracle of Saint Cecilia, with its conventual atmosphere.

Chaucer goes so far as to give us stories which he invites us to think repellent or ridiculous. The Monk recites a litany of lugubrious and monotonous "tragedies," which sadden the Knight's good heart and make the Innkeeper yawn. He is not allowed to tell his funeral beads to the end, and when interrupted relapses into silence. The poet is prevented from finishing the tale of Sir Thopas which he allots to himself. The Host of the Tabard chides him for singing a chivalrous ballad, with rhyme but without reason. In such instances as these, the reader is expected to find his pleasure not in the excellence, but in the very extravagance or tediousness of the stories.

These tales are deliberately exceptional. In general, the poet's gift of life is revealed within the stories as in the frame of the poem. Chaucer's own contribution is of varying importance. In the serious, strictly poetic part of the **Canterbury Tales,** his original work is very slight: he makes only insignificant additions, restrained in detail, to his borrowed material, and his merit is mainly in his style, which is often admirable for simple pathos and gentle humanity. The comic and realistic stories, which have analogies with the French *fabliaux,* are in very different case. These he has so much enriched that he might be called their creator. He deserves this title, at least in part, even when he is compared to the author of the *Decameron,* who put so much heat and red blood into a literary form usually of the driest. While, however, Boccaccio observed the conciseness proper to this form and did no more than paint manners, Chaucer, less condensed and less passionate, addressed himself more and more to the study of character. He repeats within several of his stories that effort to capture individuality which is the glory of his prologue. Boccaccio is on the road to picaresque fiction, but Chaucer is pointing the way for Molière and Fielding. As we read the ***Tales,*** especially those of them which are humorous, we have constantly the impression that a birth is in progress. A leaven of observation and truth is fermenting within these established literary forms, which once had a perfection of their own, but which are narrow and about to be discarded. In this travail, modern drama and the modern novel are showing their first signs of life.

If all this poet's work be regarded together, he is clearly seen constantly to have advanced nearer truth. He found poetry remote from nature, its essence being fiction in the accepted belief, while its task was the ingenious transposition of reality in accordance with artificial rules. In the beginning Chaucer submitted to the received code, dreamt with his contemporaries, like them had visions of allegorical figures and combined imaginary incidents. Or he sought the matter of his poems in books, borrowing his subjects and characters. Then, by degrees, he reached the point of deeming nothing as interesting and as diverse as Nature herself. Relegating his books to a secondary plane, ridding himself entirely of the allegory and the dream, he looked face to face at the spectacle of men and set himself to reproduce it directly. He made himself the painter of life.

It is well known how dry, morose and bitter such reproduction of reality can be. It may breed disgust with life and men. Chaucer, without flattering his model, placed it in an atmosphere which is good to breathe. No one can read him and not be glad to be in the world. Whoever enters through the door he opens feels a healthy air blow on him from all sides. This is partly because Chaucer writes in a dialect still new, uses words which he was the first to put to real literary use. The language breathes a freshness, as when earth is turned in April, such vernal youth as it could never have at another time. Usually this novelty of language coincides with crudity of thought and puerility of art. But Chaucer, who begins English poetry, ends the Middle Ages. It happened that he inherited all the literature of France, rich by three centuries of generous effort, free of speech and fertile of thought, already a little weary because it had produced too much. For Chaucer, a literature in its autumn and a language in its spring combined as they have rarely, if ever, done before or since. He is at once very young and very mature; he unites the charm of a beginning to the experience of a long life. When he repeats a description or an idea which has become a little jaded in its native language, he often gives back to it the grace of novelty by the artlessness of his expression. In his highly skilled verses, English words, frozen by a long winter of waiting, first gave forth their fragrance.

To this advantage, due to exceptional circumstances, Chaucer added natural gifts, the first of them the wide sympathy which is otherwise called indulgence. To this especially his poetry owes the soft, lovable and smiling light which is shed on it. For some of his fellow-men he feels affection or respect; about all the others he has so much curiosity that they interest him. No one is excluded. He is not easily repelled. He loves the world's variety, is grateful to defects for their difference from virtues. He looks at himself without illusions, judges himself without bitterness, is carried away by no desire to excel. He places himself on the average level, and finds all the multitude of men beside him. It is the consciousness of shared failings which makes fellowship among men. Of all writers of genius, Chaucer is the one with whom it is easiest to have a sense of comradeship.

Sympathy of this kind, founded on clear self-knowledge, is a form of intelligence. If it were absolutely necessary to define in a word the novelty of Chaucer's masterpiece, it might be said to show, most of all, the progress of intelligence. It evinces a weakening of the passion which leads to lyricism or satire and is supported by self-confidence and by the energy of desires, hopes, loves and hates; a weakening also of the imagination which transforms and magnifies reality, projecting it on to another more or less arbitrarily chosen plane, and which produces epical, romantic or allegorical poems. In the ***Canterbury Tales*** the element of the poet's personality has been subdued, superseded by pleasure in observing and understanding. Hitherto this degree of peaceful, honourable spectatorship had never been reached by poets. More noble and more essentially poetic works had indeed been written: we have but to name two with different claims to greatness, the *Chanson de Roland* and the *Divina Commedia.* Some of the line of French song-makers, stretching from the twelfth-century romancers to Rutebeuf, and past him to reach its apotheosis, a hundred years after Chaucer, in Villon, were more exquisite than the English poet and sounded more thrilling notes than he, nor did he ever attain to the refinements of feeling and language which Petrarch put into his sonnets. But where, before the ***Canterbury Tales,*** can we find a poem of which the first object is to show men, neither exalted nor demeaned, to display the truthful spectacle of life at its average? Chaucer sees what is and paints it as he sees it. He effaces himself in order to look at it better.

He is the pioneer of that group of spectators who regard with amused indulgence, without seeking to redip it in dye of one colour, the web and woof of variously coloured threads which is the chequered stuff of a society. Doubtless he has judged certain colours to be more beautiful than the others, but it is on the contrasts they afford that he has founded both his philosophy of life and the laws of his art. (pp. 91-8)

> *Emile Legouis, "Geoffrey Chaucer (1340-1400)," in his* A History of English Literature: The Middle Ages & The Renascence (650-1660), Vol. I, *translated by Helen Douglas Irvine, J. M. Dent & Sons Ltd., 1926, pp. 82-98.*

Bertrand H. Bronson (essay date 1935)

[*Bronson was an American scholar and author whose*

works encompassed a wide variety of interests, including folklore, music, and literature. Among his many works are Chaucer's House of Fame: Another Hypothesis *(1934),* Johnson Agonistes and Other Essays *(1946),* The Traditional Tunes of the Child Ballads *in four volumes (1959-72), and* The Ballad as Song *(1969). In the excerpt below, he analyzes the* Parlement of Foules, *observing that the poem reflects both Chaucer's originality and his mastery of the conventions of love poetry.*]

It is worth reiterating . . . that Chaucer is not a naïve writer. It is worth repeating that he is a sophisticated artist writing for a sophisticated society. Most of his work which has come down to us is the work of a mature craftsman. [Lounsbury, in his *Studies in Chaucer,*] finds the **Book of the Duchess** and the **Parlement of Foules** artistically unsatisfying: the poems terminate, he says, "so abruptly as well as so tamely that it can fairly be said of them that they are broken off rather than ended." [Root, in his *Poetry of Chaucer,*] finds the introductory portion of the **Parlement** disconnected and peculiarly maladroit. These things may be so; but we should not be ready to assume the fact. The proper critical attitude before Chaucer, it must be insisted, is one of humility. We ought to start with the assumption that he is an artist who knows what he is doing, and that if we are puzzled the fault is more likely to be in ourselves than in him.

Such an attitude in approaching certain of Chaucer's lesser works leads to a revaluation perceptibly higher than the impression conveyed by scholarly criticism in general. It brings us back to values inherent in the poems themselves. This is particularly important in connection with those works which belong to the category of *love visions,* for nowhere else, perhaps, is Chaucer's unique and original quality more subtly revealed. And nowhere else is it so easy for the modern reader to go astray. There is hardly any more illuminating study in the ways of genius than a careful examination of the varying treatments which the poet accorded to this *genre.* For the traditional pattern was to him by no means sacrosanct, and he used it to embody some of his most startlingly individual work. The subject has by no means escaped scholarly investigation; but the main emphasis of that attention has been upon the bonds of connection which link these poems to the parent type. [Here], I wish to stress the opposite aspect of the matter, to appreciate in some degree the literary artistry and the special quality which give to one of these poems, **The Parlement of Foules,** its rare and individual value.

When a mature poet in a sophisticated society takes up a stereotyped and "naïve" literary form, one or other of two results will naturally ensue, if he have talent. Either he will follow the tradition with a conscious and hence more artificial simplicity, or else he will put it to fresh and untried uses. The latter is preëminently Chaucer's way. His singularly sane and masculine intelligence gave him a hawk's eye for pretence and absurdity. Not that he was insensitive to the charm of a pretty convention. He was able to appreciate the appeal of the artificial love-allegory, without quite accepting it at its face value.

His polished contemporaries and immediate predecessors, the men from whom he learned his craft, were poets of love, cultivating the "amorous vision" as their chief vehicle. The courtly society which formed his audience in a world without printed books—an audience the members of which he could call by name, and to whose prejudices and sympathies he could not have avoided being sensitive—expected love poems if they did not even demand them.

It is therefore not in the least surprising that Chaucer practiced this kind of thing. Nevertheless, it is clear enough that the subject and the *genre* were radically uncongenial to his temperament. "Love is to madness near allied"; and Chaucer had no scintilla of madness in his composition. He never lost his head: he only observed—with humorous sympathy and with keen interest. He married, of course; but possibly the only woman with whom he was ever deeply in love was his own Criseyde—a tragic affair. Whether this is true or not, it is not merely a favorite little joke of his—though it is that, too—that he is an outsider in matters of love. That recurrent disclaimer—however many times he may actually have been in pursuit of a woman of flesh and blood—expresses something fundamental in his nature. Ironic contemplation, not only of himself, but of human life generally, is his most characteristic attitude. So it happens that when he sets himself to the task of writing a *love vision,* his temperamental bias transforms it into something new and different. There was a time when Shakespeare, faced with the writing of comedies, made a wry face and produced comedies which are yet not comedies at all. Somewhat similarly, Chaucer, writing allegories of love, produces poems which, while neither cynical nor bitter, are certainly alien to their kind. Thus it is with the lovely and subtle poem about to be examined, a poem which can be fully appreciated only if one accepts it in and for itself, and, without overemphasizing its literary relationships, subjects oneself to its mood.

The **Parlement of Foules** is suffused with an irony sometimes so delicate as to be almost imperceptible. The poem was written for St. Valentine's Day, ostensibly to celebrate love. But Chaucer's ironic attitude permeates it and gives it its unique tone. This prevailing tone is the medium in which the poem exists—its unifying principle. It is struck at once in the introductory stanzas, and is carried through the divergent elements which go to make up the composition to a conclusion both psychologically and artistically satisfying.

The poet's task is to write a love poem. Love! He knows nothing of it, he declares: he can only stand in amazement before its wonderful power; and he resorts in his first stanza to a rhetorical figure to describe it. He has come often on such testimony to its force that he is lost in an *O altitudo.* But his knowledge, he slyly insinuates, is all at second hand, derived from books. The key has thus been sounded: our business is to hear it in the related harmonies. Recently, he continues, he was perusing an ancient volume in search of explicit information—perhaps on this same subject—which he could turn to immediate account; because (and here a nod is as good as a wink to a blind horse) the last word in knowledge, you know, is derived from old books. He did not find anything approaching the information he was looking for, he tells us: instead he got just the opposite. But at any rate he was so taken with his book, which was Macrobius on Cicero's *Somnium Scipionis,* that he went on reading till the failing light forced him to desist and go to bed. The inappropriateness of the book's subject-matter to what had been in his thoughts was so striking that he is moved to give us a brief outline of its content. For instead of telling about love and the happiness of lovers, it was all about the next world, about heaven and hell, the good life, and the reward of souls after death, and its teaching was altogether at variance with the law of lovers, for whom, indeed, it promised a rather gloomy future:

> Likerous folk, after that they ben dede,
> Shul whirle aboute th'erthe alway in peyne,
> Tyl many a world be passed.

Far from giving the lover any encouragement, it taught that he ought not to take delight in this world, which was itself a kind of death, but rather pin his thoughts on the life to come, and work not for selfish ends, but for "commune profyt." That was the only way to arrive at the bliss of paradise. Now, what becomes of earthly love in the light of such doctrine as this? And what, for that matter, becomes of the poet who is to celebrate it in a Valentine's Day poem? Especially when the Church insists, and one more than half believes, that Scipio Africanus is right?

The dilemma here curiously adumbrates the epilogue of the *Troilus and Criseyde,* suggesting a connection more than casual between the two poems. The passage which Chaucer has lifted out of Boccaccio's *Teseide* to describe Troilus' adventures after death echoes the *Somnium Scipionis* almost verbally, and one cannot doubt that both were in Chaucer's mind while he was writing his two poems. How close the parallel is becomes manifest when one sets the stanzas side by side. Africanus shows Scipio the younger a vision of Carthage from a "starry place":

> Thanne axede he [the latter] if folk that here
>   been dede
> Han lyf and dwellynge in another place.
> And Affrican seyde, "Ye, withouten drede,"
> And that oure present worldes lyves space
> Nis but a maner deth, what way we trace,
> And rightful folk shul gon, after they dye,
> To hevene; and shewede hym the Galaxye.
>
> Thanne shewede he hym the lytel erthe that here
>   is,
> At regard of the hevenes quantite;
> And after shewede he hym the nyne speres,
> And after that the melodye herde he
> That cometh of thilke speres thryes thre,
> That welle is of musik and melodye
> In this world here, and cause of armonye.
>
> Than bad he hym, syn erthe was so lyte,
> And ful of torment and of harde grace,
> That he ne shulde hym in the world delyte.
> Thanne tolde he hym, in certeyn yeres space
> That every sterre shulde come into his place
> Ther it was first, and al shulde out of mynde
> That in this world is don of al mankynde.

The corresponding passage in the *Troilus* reads as follows:

> And whan that he was slayn in this manere,
> His lighte goost ful blisfully is went

Up to the holughness of the eighthe spere,
In convers letyng everich element;
And ther he saugh, with ful avysement,
The erratik sterres, herkenyng armonye
With sownes ful of hevenyssh melodie.

And doun from thennes faste he gan avyse
This litel spot of erthe, that with the se
Embraced is, and fully gan despise
This wrecched world, and held al vanite
To respect of the pleyn felicite
That is in hevene above; and at the laste,
Ther he was slayn, his lokyng down he caste.

And in hymself he lough right at the wo
Of hem that wepten for his deth so faste;
And dampned al oure werk that foloweth so
The blynde lust, the which that may not laste,
And sholden al oure herte on heven caste.

Thereupon Chaucer immediately drives home the lesson for young lovers:

> Repeyreth hom fro worldly vanyte,
> And of your herte up casteth the visage
> To thilke God that after his ymage
> You made, and thynketh al nys but a faire
> This world, that passeth soone as floures faire.

Not only are ideas and even phrases alike in the two passages: it has to be recognized that the same fundamental issues are involved in the contrast between the stanzas and their respective settings. The deeper parallel, in both, lies in the juxtaposition of the same two apparently irreconcilable attitudes. The difference is merely one of pitch and of consequent modification of artistic treatment. In the more serious work, such value and meaning have been given to the human attitude that the poem will easily bear the full weight of the contrasting moral. In the lighter piece, the contrast can only be suggested. In either, no one can doubt that the dualism was real enough in Chaucer's thought, and that he saw no facile resolution of it. Under its impact, in the *Troilus* the life of an individual is suddenly raised, in a moment of imaginative and tragic vision, to a universal, and revealed as the life of all mankind *sub specie aeternitatis.* It is the epilogue of the *Troilus* which in some degree gives the work its universality. The solution here does not depend upon a logical sequence. Chaucer flouts a superficial unity in order to achieve an artistic and emotional effect which stirs profounder depths. He risks the lesser to gain the larger end. The issues involved are too subtle to be explained simply as a deliberate and calculated effort to provide an antidote for the pagan atmosphere of the poem.

The same problem faces us in the *Parlement of Foules,* though on a level far less uplifted. But the artistic treatment of it necessarily differs. An explicit moral from the author's own lips would crush this butterfly. Here the content of the book and the dream are merely set down side by side without comment save to mark the contrast. The exact effect upon what follows is the imparting of a flavor of irony to the fantasy of the vision.

This in itself helps in some measure to unite the two parts. But it is by no means the only thread of connection. To say that the poem is discontinuous at this point is to have missed some of Chaucer's most delicate artistry. The linking is done with extraordinary skill and with rare psychological insight.

Nonplussed with the ironic inappropriateness of Africanus' teaching to what he was seeking, the poet retires troubled in spirit:

> For bothe I hadde thyng which that I nolde,
> And ek I nadde that thyng that I wolde.

With his head full of contradictory thoughts, now of earthly love, now of Cicero's—and then certainly Dante's—account of heaven and hell, the poet falls asleep. And now, by a delicious touch of the topsy-turvy logic of dreams, the moral Africanus appears before him to conduct him, not to a sober view of the future life, but to the lovers' paradise with its conventional landscape, its temple of love, and its personified abstractions! The delightful incongruity of the character and the rôle ought not to be missed: it is fully relished by Chaucer. It is heightened when latent recollections of Dante focus to a point and, like Virgil leading the elder poet to the gates of Hell, Africanus brings Chaucer in his dream to gates which—with a difference!—echo the well-remembered inscription. Heaven and Hell are now one; and the gates invite and threaten at the same time. One half offers bliss, the other misery, for this is the entrance to the land of love. So, beautifully, the dream resolves the contrasting materials of the poet's thought, and Macrobius and Dante and earthly love are united. And the quondam spiritual guide, borrowing something of the conviviality of the porter in the *love vision,* seizes Chaucer as he stands in doubt and shoves him in through the ample gates of this ambiguous country. But not that he may take part in any action: "for thou," as the transformed Africanus expresses it to him—

> For thow of love hast lost thy tast, I gesse
> As sek man hath of swete and bytternesse.
>
> But natheles, although that thou be dul,
> Yit that thow canst not do, yit mayst thow see.

At the moment of entrance into the enchanted land, again that humorous disavowal of personal concern on the part of the poet!

Just before Chaucer launches into his account of the dream, he pauses for a stanza to invoke the goddess of love. This stanza has received more attention, perhaps, than any other in the poem, for it has had to do heavy duty in helping scholars to fix the date of the **Parlement.** It will be best to have the exact words before us:

> Cytherea! thow blysful lady swete,
> That with thy fyrbrond dauntest whom the lest,
> And madest me this sweven for to mete,
> Be thow myn helpe in this, for thow mayst best!
> As wisly as I sey the north-north-west,
> Whan I began my sweven for to write:
> So yif me myght to ryme and ek t'endyte.

Now, from the very commencement of his poem, Chaucer has given one indication after another of his slyly humorous attitude toward love. He has done so by his ironic profession of knowing nothing about the subject save what he has learned out of books; he has done so by following this

with an abstract of a book which is itself a devastating criticism of the lover's philosophy (a speaking example of what one actually learns about love out of books!); he continues to do so by making Africanus his dubious guide to the realms of love through portals which recall the gates of Hell, and finally by reiterating his own detachment. This context is sufficiently ironic to suggest that we need not take the invocation to Cytherea at its face value. It is hardly to oversubtilize the poem to suggest that Chaucer may have his tongue in his cheek when he calls on Venus as his inspiration and aid. "Venus," he says, "who madest me to dream this dream, now grant me power to compose it in rhyme,—so surely as I saw thee in the north-north-west when I began to write it!"

Chaucer was a close student of the motions of the heavenly bodies, and he did not talk loosely about them. Knowing this, scholars have made enquiry as to when, in those years, Venus was in the position described. The answer to the question is, curiously enough, Never! . . . Professor Manly, for example, admitting that Venus can never be seen "north-north-west," concludes [in "What is the *Parlement of Foules*?" in *Zeitschrift für englische und germanische Philologie,* 1913] that Chaucer must have meant merely a position as far north as Venus could attain. "Chaucer," he remarks, "had, of course, some knowledge of astronomy, but he is writing here, not as scientist, but as poet." That assertion is incontrovertible: nevertheless, one may suggest that elsewhere the poet has not found incompatible with his idea of poetry a high degree of accuracy in astronomical allusion. In fact, we seem here to have surprised the sole phoenix. Where else throughout his works does Chaucer . . . take such apparent pains to be exact in a reference of this kind and yet prove himself mistaken? I confess I have not made the search: the responsibility lies with Professor Manly and those who hold the same view. "North-west," if you will, is a layman's phrase: "north-north-west" is the phrase of a scientist, or at least of a layman unusually meticulous. And when the layman who uses it incorrectly is Chaucer, one inclines to suppose that he has a reason for being so meticulously inexact. That, at least, seems an easier supposition than the opposite one, especially when the reason for such exact inexactitude has already suggested itself. (pp. 195-206)

It would be unjust to Professor Manly to ignore a parenthetical suggestion which he makes only to abandon. His words are these: "It is true that Venus can never be seen 'north-north-west,' but—unless this term means only 'in an unpropitious position,' (Ab aquilone omne malum) and is a bit of slang, as in Hamlet's 'I am but mad north-north-west'—this must be an inexact phrase for the extreme northern position of Venus as an evening star." It is that *unless* which seems to hold Professor Manly's most promising suggestion. His proverb, The North-*East* wind brings every ill, is nothing to the point; but it is certainly not far from the truth to assume that a position in which a planet was never seen would be an "unpropitious" one for that planet. The citation from *Hamlet* seems apt, and it would be valuable if we could discover that the phrase was a bit of slang in Chaucer's time. But of course it does not bear the sense of unpropitious or unfavorable in Hamlet's speech: it means simply in one particular and narrowly restricted direction—in other words, *hardly at all.* And this, indeed, is not far from the force of the expression in Chaucer's ironic invocation. We may feel very sure that if he saw Venus in the north-north-west when he began to write his vision, he hardly saw her at all! Which, I think, is what he means to imply. The beginning of the **Parlement of Foules** is, indisputably, far from being conceived under the inspiration of the goddess of love.

Consideration of the address to Cytherea has unavoidably taken a disproportionate amount of space. Following this invocation, Chaucer goes on for some time with his charming description of the garden of love, the elements of which are drawn from various sources, chief among these being sixteen stanzas of the seventh book of the *Teseide* which the poet closely follows. At first glance, he seems to have made no significant changes. Boccaccio's own account is not entirely laudatory, so far as the personified abstractions go, so that it fits neatly enough into Chaucer's scheme. But one notices that he adds to Boccaccio's unpleasant figures "other thre—Here names shul not here be told for me"—for whom there seem no counterparts in the original. And one wonders if it is simply accidental that Chaucer alters the metal of which the temple of love is built from copper (appropriated to Venus, as he well knew) to brass, the much more questionable metal which he elsewhere uses for Aeolus' trumpet of ill fame. It is his own fancy, also, which seats Dame Patience *upon a hill of sand* in front of the temple—apt figure for those who base their hopes of reward in love upon faithful attendance. But the most interesting change in this part of the poem is in the figure of Venus herself. Examination of the two passages reveals the fact that Chaucer has greatly lessened the sensuous appeal of Boccaccio's Venus—has, in fact, nearly stripped her of her glamour. Here are the lines from the *Teseide:*

> e vide lei nuda giacere
> Sopra un gran letto assai bella a vedere.
>
> Ma avie d'oro i crini e rilucenti
> Intorno al capo sanza treccia alcuna;
> Il suo viso era tal che le più genti
> Hanno a rispetto bellezza nissuna:
> Le braccia, il petto e le poma eminenti
> Si vedien tutte, e ogni altra parte d'una
> Testa tanto sottil si ricopria,
> Che quasimente nuda comparia.
>
> Olíva il collo ben di mille odori:
> Dall' un de' lati Bacco le sedea,
> Dall' altro Ceres cogli suoi savori:
> Ed essa il pomo per le man tenea,
> Sè dilettando, il quale alle sorori
> Prelata vinse nella valle Idea.

And here is Chaucer's translation:

> on a bed of gold she lay to reste,
> Til that the hote sonne gan to weste.
>
> Hyre gilte heres with a golden thred
> Ibounden were, untressed as she lay,
> And naked from the brest unto the hed
> Men myghte hire sen; and, sothly for to say,
> The remenaunt was wel kevered to my pay,
> Ryght with a subtyl coverchef of Valence—

Ther nas no thikkere cloth of no defense.

> The place yaf a thousand savours sote,
> And Bachus, god of wyn, sat hire besyde,
> And Ceres next, that doth of hunger boote,
> And, as I seyde, amyddes lay Cypride,
> To whom on knees two yonge folk ther cryde
> To ben here helpe. But thus I let hire lye.

The difference is striking. Boccaccio dwells voluptuously on the idea of her surpassing loveliness: Chaucer does not even say she was beautiful. Boccaccio discovers her lying naked, very fair to see, upon a great bed: Chaucer focuses his attention upon the bed. She had hair of gold that shone untrammeled about her head, says Boccaccio: her golden hair was tied up with a gold thread (though unbraided), says Chaucer. Gone is Boccaccio's moving suggestion of the loveliness of her face—"her face was such that in comparison most have no beauty at all": Chaucer seems unaware of the fact that she even had a face. Boccaccio lingers over her arms, her bosom, the prominent apples of her breasts: Chaucer says briefly that you could see her naked from breast to head—which might mean neck and shoulders—and hastens on (shades of Africanus!) to say that the "remenaunt" was well covered to his satisfaction, if only with a very thin material. Boccaccio says every other part of her was covered with a web so transparent that it was almost as if she had nothing on. Chaucer transfers the fragrance of her body to the surrounding atmosphere. Boccaccio in conclusion recalls the apple which symbolized her victory over Hera and Pallas in the Idaean vale. Chaucer dismisses her abruptly with a phrase proverbially applied to dogs—"thus I let her lye." Without maintaining that our poet is flouting the attractions of the goddess, we may still justifiably feel that she suffers a noticeable diminution of charm in his hands. And this is in keeping with the rest of the poem.

Chaucer does not choose Venus as his presiding deity. Instead, he selects the goddess Nature—a significant preference:

> Nature, the vicaire of the almyghty Lord,
> That hot, cold, hevy, lyght, moyst, and dreye
> Hath knyt by evene noumbres of acord.

This divinity, in fact, is the same "noble emperesse," the poet himself tells us, as that Nature whom Alanus so exalted in the *Playnt of Kynde.* And here, as in the earlier work, she is deliberately uplifted at the expense of the goddess of love.

The rest of the poem—somewhat more than half its whole length—is in large part concerned with the debate among the birds, with Nature as arbiter, over the question, which of three tercels the formel eagle shall take as her mate.

It is upon this part of the work, naturally, that scholarly attention has been chiefly engaged. It is admittedly the part which most clearly displays Chaucer's original genius. Hints for this element or that have been found in earlier writers, but the most exhaustive research has so far failed to find an anticipation of Chaucer's peculiar combination. Professor Farnham [in his 1917 *PMLA* article "The Sources of Chaucer's *Parlement of Foules*"] has collected and classified a large number of variants of a widespread type of folk-tale, which he well entitles "The Contending Lovers," in which the story turns upon different pretensions of equal merit among the suitors, and in which the solution is inconclusive. He has also pointed out the abundant use of birds in folk-lore and in other literary works known to the Middle Ages. The fact that his painstaking search has not disclosed an example of the contending lovers type in which the suitors are birds throws Chaucer's originality into high relief. For the disputing of birds about a bird is the most prominent feature of the **Parlement,** whereas the element of story has been reduced to a single situation.

Moreover, and this is a point of the utmost importance, the whole interest of the debate lies in the contrasting attitudes to which the various birds give expression, and not at all in the problematical merits of the three suitors. In stories of contending lovers, you have some positive differentiation to give an edge to the rivalry: for instance, one lover will have physical prowess, another courtesy and liberality, another wisdom. But nothing of the sort holds true for the present case. Here no equivalence of contrasting excellences is suggested. All three tercels rest their chief claims to the formel's pity on an identical assertion and promise. The assertion—that each loves her best—is as incapable of *a priori* proof as the promise—to serve her

The Ellesmere manuscript portrait of the Miller.

faithfully—is unsure. What other positive pretensions do they bring forward? Well, the first tercel offers nothing else at all save a plea for mercy. The second offers no new differentiating quality, but only pleads length of service. The third scoffs at length of service, and exalts (arrogating it to himself by implication) intensity of feeling instead—a return to the undemonstrable. It has been maintained that this poem is an example of the conventional *demande d'amour,* the object of which was to propound a problem without resolving it, in order to provide a social group with a topic for subsequent discussion and argument. But if this is true, the poem is a delicious *reductio ad absurdum* of the type. One feels certain that the respective merits of these particular birds never gave rise to any heated debate on the part of Chaucer's courtly audience! For no question of differing yet equal merits is thrown into relief: there is really nothing to debate. The only rational basis for a decision in the matter of these suitors lies in external considerations which are never at any time in doubt or subject to argument. The cards are stacked for the royal tercel from the start. Nature, with many compliments, offers him first choice, and the other tercels, like Pandarus, hop always behind. The second is openly designated as "of lower kynde," and one has no doubts about the third's inferiority. The speech of the royal tercel is the only one which has any perceptible effect on the formel: after he ceases speaking she is so sore abashed that she is speechless, and an ineffable blush suffuses her feathers:

> Ryght as the freshe, rede rose newe,
> Ageyn the somer sonne coloured is,
> Ryght so for shame al wexen gan the hewe
> Of this formel, whan she herde al this.

The tercelet thereafter remarks that the formel knows perfectly well which of the three she ought to choose—"for it is light to knowe." And at the end of the debate, to make assurance doubly sure, Nature points out to her that, although she may take her pick, there is but one reasonable choice. After this, on a question of merits, Chaucer's audience would be exceptionally ingenious if they could find anything to dispute about. For it is beside the present point, however delightfully unexpected, that the formel, with her mind all made up for her, elects to use her feminine prerogative in the only way that is left open and refuses to choose at all. That, incidentally, is one of the finest strokes of irony in the poem. But is is not the kind of inconclusive ending that belongs to the Contending Lovers, nor yet to the *demande d'amour.* We can discover here no dubious equation of opposite qualities like the choice between knight and clerk. For this reason, it seems to me, we must acknowledge a fundamental distinction between the typical ending and the one before us. This one is not inconclusive; it is, rather, simply irrelevant. And upon this delicious feminine irrelevancy, of course, the goddess Nature seals her hard consent. "Soth is," says the formel to Nature, slyly, "that I am evere under your yerde."

Much the larger part of the scholarly discussion of the **Parlement** has been concerned with an attempt to find a historical counterpart for the central situation of the poem. The formel, it has been supposed, must represent some particular woman, be it Anne of Bohemia, be it Philippa, eldest daughter of John of Gaunt, be it Marie of

France. Likewise, the three tercels must stand for particular princes, whether Richard II, William of Bavaria, Frederick of Meissen, Charles VI, John of Blois, or whomsoever. (pp. 207-15)

All writers who deal with character take hints from people and incidents within the range of their actual acquaintance. Chaucer, we know, is no exception to the rule: witness the Canterbury Prologue, to mention nothing else. I do not mean to suggest that he could not have had certain individuals in mind when he wrote the **Parlement.** Though, if he did, the whole tone of the work renders such an allusion a very dubious sort of compliment—and the poet knew how to pay compliments when he wished. We must remind ourselves once more that, even as a man, Chaucer was not naïve. But, at any rate, if he borrowed a piece of contemporary history for his poem, the fact is of secondary, not essential, importance. It must be apparent that his interest does not lie in the application of his fable to historical personages and events. He makes no effort to individualize these eagles of his: quite the contrary. They are generalized attitudes. Nor does he care much about their situation in relation to one another. But he cares greatly about the contrast between the general position which they together represent, and its opposite.

Chaucer's meaning is best understood if the symbolism is not pushed beyond its obvious significance. His birds, as every reader recognizes, are types of humanity. They fall into one or other of the two main classes of human beings roughly denominated realist and idealist. This thoroughgoing cleavage, however, is naturally restricted, for the purposes of this poem, to the question of love. The poem, we do not forget, was written for St. Valentine's Day. It now remains to watch Chaucer's ironic and detached mind moving through the debate to the felicitous conclusion. No one's feelings can be offended by his shafts of irony, for we may always fall back upon the comforting assurance that, after all, these are only birds!

The royal tercel is the perfect pattern of the ideal of courtly love. His little speech is the very table book of the code to which Troilus subscribed. The other tercels are imperfect exemplars of the same doctrine, which finds nearly complete masculine expression in these three figures. Since there is nothing to argue with reference to their respective merits except what is predetermined, it is no accident that when the general debate opens it flies off at a tangent from the immediate issue; focusing about a criticism of the whole courtly doctrine—an event obviously welcome to Chaucer. He himself has already relinquished the task of reporting the private altercation *in extenso,* lacking the

> leyser and connyng
> For to reherse hire chere and hire spekyng,

which lasted, he says, from morning till sundown. The consequent outcry among the birds is to the effect that the disputants are beating the air. To bring order out of this confusion, Nature calls for spokesmen to give the opinion of each class. For the birds of prey—a sinister compliment, if the English nobility are intended—the falcon speaks a word of lucid sense: Let her take the royal tercel. Characteristically, the goose, spokesman for the lowest, the waterfowl, seizes the next turn, and says: Unless she

will have him, let him love some one else. Sensible advice from a goose! Then, to show that *gentilesse* does not reside solely among the upper classes, the humble turtledove, speaking for the seed-fowl, proves herself committed to the code: Let him serve her faithfully till death, though she hold herself forever aloof. The duck cannot endure such idealism, and swears by his hat that it is senseless: "Ye quek!" says he. The tercelet calls him down: the duck, he says, is so base that he can have no conception of what love is. But the cuckoo, spokesman for the birds that eat worms and such things, is equally realistic, though in a class above the waterfowl: "So I may have my own mate," he says, "they can go on wrangling till the end of their lives,—I care not." Upon this the merlin pours out a flood of vituperation. And if the turtle proved that the nobility did not possess all the delicate feeling, the merlin demonstrates with equal clarity that the lower classes do not have a corner on all the meanness in the world. With crass effrontery he,

> that payneth
> Hymself ful ofte the larke for to seke,

taxes the cuckoo with his diet of worms, and with being the murderer of his foster parent, the hedge sparrow. Nature thereupon commands peace, and, in manifest confidence of the result, puts the choice to the formel. The latter, till now apparently another Ophelia, pathetic in her helplessness, rises to the occasion and magnificently vindicates her womanhood.

There is irony enough in this debate. Against whom, then, is it directed? One critic says, Chaucer is obviously attacking the low views of the bourgeoisie and the merchants. Another says, The satire is clearly directed against the unreality of courtly love. Both, of course, are right. We shall not mistake the poet's intention if we double and then treble the objects of his satire. The irony which we have watched playing intermittently like heat lightning about the poem from its very commencement, illuminating first this element and then the other, has now gathered to a sharper and more obvious focus, and strikes with inescapable precision and frequency those within its immediate range. Two hundred years before Cervantes, Chaucer anticipated Don Quixote and Sancho Panza in this poem. But it is with this as with the later and doubtless greater work: the satire is double-edged. Pure idealism is ridiculous in a realistic world. But the realists are also mad in their own way: they are likewise sometimes not a little contemptible, which can seldom be said of the idealists. If we must be mad—But, Chaucer (a great master of irony) seems to say, let us be as sane as we can. But, again, it is joy to see downright madness!

Meanwhile, he has his poem to finish. So, with a delicate rondeau, sung by the birds to St. Valentine and the opening year, the vision ends. For a poem in honor of Love, the poet has to acknowledge that it contains extraneous elements and that the spirit in which it is composed is not whole-heartedly devoted to Venus. He is sorry he has not been able to write a better love poem: it started off on the wrong foot because of that book of Macrobius which he was reading. But, as he told us at the beginning, all he knows about love is out of books. So he will keep on reading; and maybe some day he will read something that will cause him to dream a really profitable dream, not one of these things in which all is left at sixes and sevens and nothing is decided.

> I hope, ywis, to rede so som day
> That I shal mete som thyng for to fare
> The bet, and thus to rede I nyl nat spare.

With which apparently guileless remark, the wheel has come round to its starting point, and the poem is done.

With a fresh sense in our minds of the quality of the work, we may turn very briefly to a consideration of its relationship to the typical *love vision*. No one, surely, will deny the striking originality of the **Parlement**. The most remarkable thing about it is that the secret of this originality lies elsewhere than in the elements which compose the poem. No other of Chaucer's *love visions* contains so many of the stock conventions of the type. Of the eleven ingredients which Professor Neilson has listed, in his intensive study of the *genre* [the 1899 *Harvard Studies and Notes in Philology and Literature* article "The Origins and Sources of the Court of Love"], as present in the *Roman de la Rose* and as having been stereotyped in later poems of the same kind, the **Parlement** makes undisguised (though sometimes slight) use of all but one. The **Book of the Duchess** and Prologue F of the **Legend of Good Women** are its nearest competitors; but they do not even approach it in this regard. Yet probably most readers would agree that, with the exception of the **Hous of Fame**—which employs the fewest of the stock elements and which transmogrifies most of those it does use—the **Parlement** is the most highly individualized of all Chaucer's *love visions*. To see this clearly, we need only review its treatment of these conventions.

It was conventional for the poet to confess his subjection to love. In the **Book of the Duchess,** in spite of the fact that the poem is not chiefly about himself, Chaucer preserves this convention as the explanation of his sleeplessness. The **Parlement** introduces the same convention, but turns it to the uses of sly humor and irony in a dozen different ways. For, if the irony of the invocation to Venus be not allowed, there are still the introductory stanzas, the ambiguous paradise, the ousting of Venus to make room for Nature, the mock debate on a question of love, and the ironically evasive conclusion,—and these are only the outstanding points. Again, Chaucer did not dislike the convention of an introductory reading of a book, though it could be one of the most wooden elements of the type. He employed it with delicate psychological truth of perception in the **Book of the Duchess,** left a bare hint of it in the **Legend,** omitted it entirely in the **Hous of Fame.** Here he uses it to the full, in a fashion ostensibly straightforward, but actually with surpassing subtlety, making it serve his ironic attitude toward his subject-matter, and at the same time illustrate his profound understanding of the dream psychology. The conventional discussion of dreams, which looms large in the **Book of the Duchess** and the **Hous of Fame,** he reduces to a single stanza in the **Parlement,** where it serves entirely to assist in the delightful transformation of Africanus from spiritual to temporal guide. A number of conventional elements—the idealized land-

scape, the fountain of love, Cupid's arrows, the personified abstractions which inhabit this country, the temple, and the paintings on the walls—he introduces almost unchanged, letting them take their new tone, with only an occasional assisting touch, from the context. But the setting up of Nature for his chief presiding deity, the transformation of all his leading characters into birds, and the ironic termination, are signal modifications of the conventional elements upon which they are based. Above every formal element in importance, however, is the personal tone which pervades the whole poem—a tone hardly less noteworthy in its revelatory quality than the intimacy of the **Legend's** prologue, and second only to the amazing **Hous of Fame.** It is this which makes the **Parlement** the individual thing that it is.

It would be a happy result if the pursuit of this increasingly confident individuality and independence might enable us to determine with any assurance whether the **Parlement** or the **Hous of Fame** came first in order of composition. And indeed, if it were not for one consideration, we should be forced on this basis to conclude that the **Parlement** preceded the **Hous of Fame.** For the latter is indisputably a far freer and more highly individualized piece of work. Even the use of short couplets, instead of constituting an argument for an earlier date, might just as well make for a later date. For the poet who uses them is obviously conscious of a regression from a loftier style to a "light and lewed," a free and easy manner: he is not concerned, he says, to show craft or "art poetical." His expressions are those of a poet who once again turns his Pegasus earthward, not of one who has yet to soar.

The consideration that makes one doubt is the prologue to the **Legend**—by explicit acknowledgment the last of the extant *love visions*. For the prologue, in either of its versions, is clearly a return to a more formal treatment of the convention, a last effort to test the virtues of the type. It is a display of true originality within the narrow room of the rules which traditionally govern this kind of writing. And when one has read it, one is forced to wonder whether the course of Chaucer's development is not most truly plotted by supposing that the poet, after an earlier burst of confident and youthful exuberance in which he strained the conventions to their utmost limit, came back through a comparatively strict observance of outward proprieties to find his rest in a poem which displayed complete mastery of the convention, and yet gave entire proof, within the prescribed limits, of the unique quality of a mature artist and a supreme poet. (pp. 216-23)

> *Bertrand H. Bronson, "In Appreciation of Chaucer's Parlement of Foules," in* University of California Publications in English, *Vol. 3, No. 5, May 24, 1935, pp. 193-224.*

C. S. Lewis   (essay date 1936)

[*Lewis is considered one of the foremost Christian and mythopoeic authors of the twentieth century. An acknowledged authority on medieval and Renaissance literature, he gained fame as a writer of fantasy literature. In the following excerpt from his acclaimed* The Allegory of Love, *Lewis discusses* Troilus and Criseyde *in the context of medieval love poetry, asserting that Chaucer, despite his indebtedness to traditional literary forms and conventions, treats the subject of love with remarkable originality.*]

For many historians of literature, and for all general readers, the great mass of Chaucer's work is simply a background to the *Canterbury Tales,* and the whole output of the fourteenth century is simply a background to Chaucer. Whether such a view is just, or whether it has causes other than the excellence of the *Tales,* need not here be inquired; for us, at any rate, Chaucer is a poet of courtly love, and he ceases to be relevant to our study when he reaches the last and most celebrated of his works. Nor does he stand, for us, in isolation from his century; he stands side by side with Gower and the translators of the *Romance of the Rose*—of whom, he himself was one—and co-operates with them in the work of assimilating the achievements of French poetry, and thus determining the direction of English poetry for nearly two hundred years.

By considering Chaucer in this light we shall lose much; but we shall have the advantage of seeing him as he appeared to his contemporaries, and to his immediate successors. When the men of the fourteenth or fifteenth centuries thought of Chaucer, they did not think first of the *Canterbury Tales.* Their Chaucer was the Chaucer of dream and allegory, of love-romance and erotic debate, of high style and profitable doctrine. To Deschamps, as every one remembers, he was the 'great translator' [see excerpt dated c. 1386]—the gardener by whom a French poet might hope to be transplanted—and also the English god of Love. To Gower, he is the poet of Venus [see excerpt dated c. 1390]: to Thomas Usk, Love's 'owne trewe servaunt' and 'the noble philosophical poete'. In the age that followed the names of Gower and Chaucer are constantly coupled. Chaucer's comic and realistic style is imitated by Lydgate in the Prologue to the *Book of Thebes,* and by an unknown poet in the Prologue to the *Tale of Beryn;* but this is a small harvest beside the innumerable imitations of his amatory and allegorical poetry. And while his successors thus show their admiration for his love poetry, they explicitly praise him as the great model of style. He is to them much what Waller and Denham were to the Augustans, the 'firste finder' of the true way in our language, which before his time was 'rude and boystous'. Where we see a great comedian and a profound student of human character, they saw a master of noble sentiment and a source of poetic diction.

It is tempting to say that if Chaucer's friends and followers were dunces who treasured the chaff and neglected the grain, yet this is no reason why we should do likewise. But the temptation should be resisted. To grow impatient with the critical tradition of the earliest lovers of Chaucer is to exclude ourselves from any understanding of the later Middle Ages in England; for the literature of the fifteenth and sixteenth centuries is based (naturally enough) not on our reading of Chaucer, but on theirs. And there is something to be said for them.

In the first place, we must beware of condemning them for not working the vein which Chaucer had opened up in the *Canterbury Tales,* lest in so doing we condemn the whole course of English poetry. What they have left undone, their successors have left undone likewise. The *Canterbury Tales* are glorious reading, but they have always been sterile. If the later Middle Ages can offer us only the Prologue to *Thebes* and the Prologue to *Beryn,* we ourselves are not in much better plight. William Morris's discipleship to Chaucer was an illusion. Crabbe and Mr. Masefield are good writers; but they are hardly among the greatest English poets. If Chaucer's *Tales* have had any influence, it is to be sought in our prose rather than in our verse. Our great and characteristic poets—our Spenser, Milton, Wordsworth, and the like—have much more in common with Virgil, or even with *Beowulf,* than with the **"Prologue"** and the **"Pardoners Tale."** Perhaps none of our early poets has so little claim to be called the father of English poetry as the Chaucer of the **Canterbury Tales.**

But even if the first Chaucerians were dunces, it would not be safe to neglect their testimony. The stupidest contemporary, we may depend upon it, knew certain things about Chaucer's poetry which modern scholarship will never know; and doubtless the best of us misunderstand Chaucer in many places where the veriest fool among his audience could not have misunderstood. If they all took Chaucer's love poetry *au grand sérieux,* it is overwhelmingly probable that Chaucer himself did the same; and one of the advantages of keeping the **Canterbury Tales** out of sight, as I have proposed to do, will be that we may thus hope to rid ourselves of a false emphasis which is creeping into the criticism of Chaucer. We have heard a little too much of the 'mocking' Chaucer. Not many will agree with the critic who supposed that the laughter of Troilus in heaven was 'ironical'; but I am afraid that many of us now read into Chaucer all manner of ironies, slynesses, and archnesses, which are not there, and praise him for his humour where he is really writing with 'ful devout corage'. The lungs of our generation are so very 'tickle o' the sere'. (pp. 161-64)

Boccaccio's Cupid, Pleasaunce, Beautee, Peace, Priapus, and the rest are Renaissance allegory, not medieval allegory. They are neither, on the one hand, a mere catalogue (like the abstractions in Chaucer's **Compleynts**); nor are they true incarnations of inner experience, like the characters of the *Romance of the Rose.* They have nothing to do, but each has his little bit of description and his recognizable emblems. They are pure decoration—things to be carved on a mantelpiece, or pulled along the streets in a pageant, 'posed' each in his cart with anchors, scales, and other apparatus. They are pretty enough, but they have given the word 'allegory' a meaning from which it will, perhaps, never recover—with what injustice to certain great poets, it is one purpose of this book to show. And the odd thing is that Chaucer does not seem to be aware of the difference. He is too true a child of the Middle Ages even to resent the alien Renaissance quality in his model. That it is alien to him is proved by his treatment of it, for his omissions and alterations are all in the medieval direction; but he does not reach the point of throwing the Boccaccio over, as he might have done if he had read it with our eyes. In the *Teseide* Boccaccio takes a personified Prayer—readers of Homer will remember that prayers are among the oldest personifications—to the home of Venus. Chaucer goes thither himself. On arriving in the garden, Chaucer follows the Italian closely for two stanzas, because the Italian is here describing what every medieval poet wished to describe—the joyous life of the place. In the next stanza, after two lines on the music heard among the trees, he deserts his model; and where Boccaccio tells us how the Prayer went to and fro admiring the *bell'ornamento,* Chaucer compares the music with the harmonies of heaven, and mentions 'a wind, unnethe hit might be lesse'. He then proceeds to insert a stanza which has no counterpart in the original at all, and in which he explains how 'the air of that place so attempre was', that

> No man may ther wexe seek ne old.

Chaucer is, of course, remembering the garden in Guillaume de Lorris, which 'semed a place espirituel' and the garden in Jean de Meun where there is no time. But while he thus makes his garden more spiritual, with heavenly music and a dateless present, he makes it more earthly too by the mention of his inaudible breeze; he deepens the poetry every way. There is in Chaucer a far fuller surrender of feeling and imagination to his theme than Boccacio was prepared to make. Chaucer was working with 'ful devout corage': Boccaccio, for all his epic circumstance, feels in his heart of hearts that all this stuff about gardens and gods of love is 'only poetry'. And so Boccaccio will include a touch of satire and make his Beautee go by *sé riguardando,* and Chaucer will naturally omit this. Only false criticism will suppose that this superior gravity in Chaucer is incompatible with the fact that he is a great comic poet. Dryden went to the root of the matter when he called him a perpetual fountain of good sense [see excerpt dated 1700]. A profound and cheerful sobriety is the foundation alike of Chaucer's humour and of his pathos. There is nothing of the renaissance frivolity in him.

A firm grasp of this contrast between Boccaccio and Chaucer is the best preparation for reading the **Book of Troilus.** For it is possible to misunderstand *Troilus*. His earlier works require historical explanation, and *Troilus* speaks at once to the heart of every reader. His earlier works have French models, and it is from the Italian; and they have little humour, while it has much. Above all, they easily pass as allegory with readers who do not inquire closely, while it is not allegorical at all. All these facts make it fatally easy to regard *Troilus* as Chaucer's first break away from medieval tradition—to interpret it as a 'modern' poem, with much consequent exaggeration of its comic and ironic elements. In reality, the writing of *Troilus* betokens no apostasy from the religion of Cupid and Venus. Chaucer's greatest poem is the consummation, not the abandonment, of his labours as a poet of courtly love. It is a wholly medieval poem. Let us take one by one the facts which seem to point to the opposite interpretation. It speaks at once to our hearts, not because it is less medieval than the **"Compleynt of Mars,"** but because it deals with those elements in the medieval consciousness which survive in our own. Astrology has died, and so have the court scandals of the fourteenth century; but that new conception of love which the eleventh century inaugurated has been a mainspring of imaginative literature ever

since. It is borrowed from an Italian, and not from a French, source; and the Italian source is, in many respects, a Renaissance poem; but then Chaucer is careful to take from his model only what is still medieval, or what can be medievalized. The effect of all his alterations is to turn a Renaissance story into a medieval story. Again, the **Book of Troilus** is full of humour; but it is medieval humour, and Pandarus, as I have already suggested, is a son of Jean de Meun's *Vekke.* Finally, it is literal, not allegorical; but so is the work of Chrétien de Troyes. Chaucer's **Troilus** is best understood if we regard it as a new *Launcelot*—a return to the formula of Chrétien, but a return which utilizes all that had been done between Chrétien's day and Chaucer's. The reader will remember how, in Chrétien, the story of external happenings and the story (already partly allegorized) of inner experience, proceeded side by side.. . . .[The] two elements fell apart, and . . . .the second element was treated independently in the *Romance of the Rose,* and raised to a higher power. Guillaume de Lorris deepens, diversifies, and subtilizes the psychology of Chrétien: the heroine of the *Rose* is truer, more interesting, and far more amiable than Guinevere, and Chaucer has profited by her. He has profited so well, and learned to move so freely and delicately among the intricacies of feeling and motive that he is now in a position to display them without allegory, to present them in the course of a literal story. He can thus go back again, though he goes back with new insight, to the direct method. He can recombine the elements which had fallen apart after Chrétien, because Chrétien's combination had been premature. Allegory has taught him how to dispense with allegory, and the time is now ripe for the great love-story which the Middle Ages have so long been in labour to produce. It is not strange that the product should seem to us more 'modern' than the travail. In every age the achievements smack less of their own age than the struggles, and speak a more universal language. That is how we know that they are achievements. The best is at home everywhere: but it was first at home, and remains always at home, in its own parish of space and time. *Troilus* is 'modern', if you will— 'permanent' would be a wiser, and a less arrogant, word— because it is successfully and perfectly medieval.

I have tried to show elsewhere [see Further Reading] how Chaucer medievalizes *Il Filostrato.* He is more allusive and digressive than his original; like a true 'historiall' poet, contributing to the 'matter of Rome', he tells us more of the story of Troy than Boccaccio would have thought relevant. Boccaccio's standard of relevance is purely artistic: Chaucer's so far as he has one, is historical or legendary. In style, Chaucer obeys the precepts of medieval rhetoric, as interpreted and modified by his own genius: he inserts *apostrophae, descriptiones, circumlocutiones, exempla,* and the like, which are not found in the original, often with beautiful effect. Finally, he brings the whole story into line with those conceptions of love which he had learned, no doubt, from his own experience and imagination, but which he had learned to see clearly and to express from the *Romance of the Rose.* If anything cannot be so brought into line, he omits it. Passages in which Boccaccio displays contempt for women, are dropped: passages where he shows insufficient 'devotioun' to the god of Love, are heightened. Doctrinal passages on the art and law of love are inserted. The cold cynicism of Boccaccio's *Pandaro* disappears, to make room for the humour of Chaucer's Pandarus. And when the whole tale is finished, where Boccaccio simply draws the ugly moral that had been for him implicit throughout.

> Giovane donna è mobile, e vogliosa
> È negli amanti molti, e sua bellezza
> Estima più ch'allo specchio, e pomposa
> Ha vanagloria di sua giovinezza,

here Chaucer, never more truly medieval and universal, writes his 'palinode' and recalls the 'yonge, fresshe folkes' of his audience from human to Divine love: recalls them 'home', as he significantly says.

I do not propose, in this place, to compare the two poems in detail. An inspection of them will reveal to any open-minded reader the nature of the change that Chaucer is making, and my present concern is rather with the result—with the historical significance and permanent value of the **Book of Troilus** as it stands.

To speak of **Troilus** in the language of the stable as being 'by *Il Filostrato* out of *Roman de la Rose*' would seem to be an undervaluing of Chaucer's creative genius only if we forgot that Chaucer's mind is the place in which the breeding was done. Provided that we remember this, such a description is useful. In the story of Cryseide, and her uncle, and Troilus, Chaucer, by means of episodes borrowed from Boccaccio, brings the personified 'accidents' of the *Roman* out of allegory and sets them moving in a concrete story. The *Roman* begins with a young man, himself still unattached, wandering in the garden; that is, in the world of youth and courtly leisure. Chaucer departs from Boccaccio, whose Troilo has already tried love, and begins with the unattached Troilus in the Trojan temple. In both stories the God of Love is following the wanderer unseen, and his archery (which has become a mere colour in the language of Boccaccio) is adequately dealt with by Chaucer. Shot through with Love's arrows, the Dreamer continues to advance towards the Rosebud, but finds his way stopped by a thorny hedge: similarly, though Cryseide is so gentle that no creature 'was ever lasse mannish', yet her cheer was somewhat disdainful, and

> she leet falle
> Hir look a lite aside in suich manere,
> Ascaunces 'What! may I not stonden here?

At last, when all the arrows stick fast in him, the Dreamer, hearing Love's voice call to him to surrender, yields and kneels, becomes Love's man and awaits his commandments; Troilus likewise says

> O Lord, now youres is
> My spirit which that oughte youres be.
> You thanke I, Lord, that han me brought to this.

In a later passage (which owes nothing to Boccaccio) he beats his breast and asks the god's forgiveness for his former jibes. The commandments which Love gives to the Dreamer are not reproduced by Chaucer, but we see Troilus actually obeying them, and the noble lines which describe the improvement wrought in his character by his service to Love, do not come from the Italian:

> his maner tho forth ay
> So goodly was and gat him so in grace
> That ech him lovede that loked on his face.

As the Dreamer fears to pass the thorny hedge, so Troilus shrinks from telling Cryseide his love—'she nil to noon suiche wrecche as I be wonne'. The Dreamer and the Trojan prince are both visited (though at different phases of the story) by a friend who tells them that the obstacles they fear are not insurmountable; for as Pandarus plays the part of Vekke in his scenes with Cryseide, so he plays that of *Frend* in his scenes with Troilus. And Pandarus' whole aim during the early stages of the wooing is to produce in Cryseide the condition which Guillaume de Lorris calls Bialacoil. Troilus, he tells her, 'nought desireth but your freendly chere'; and the promise he extorts from her is

> only that ye make him bettre chere
> Than ye han doon er this and more feste.

It is thanks to the labours of Pandarus that Troilus finds Bialacoil awaiting him outside the *roseir* and soon ready to lead him in beyond it, into the presence of the Rose; or, to speak in our own way, that Cryseide consents to receive and to answer the letter of Troilus and finally to meet him at the house of Deiphebus. Troilus, like the Dreamer, is grateful for admission, but not content: rather

> This Troilus gan to desiren more
> Than he dide erst, thurgh hope, and dide his
>   might
> To pressen on.

But this is not, or not yet, Bialacoil's intention. He dare not let the Dreamer pull the rosebud, he will only give him a leaf that grew near it; and the Dreamer's request for the rose itself rouses Daunger from his lair. Cryseide's 'bel aceuil' or 'bettre chere' is to be equally limited in its functions: her fair welcome Troilus shall have, but if he and Pandarus 'in this proces depper go', they need look for no grace at her hands—not if they both die for it, she adds: for Daunger is very nearly awake. But Bialacoil, in the one story as in the other, is in a very difficult position. Soon he is more than half on the enemy's side, and explains that he, for his part, would gladly let the Dreamer kiss the rose.

> Thou shuldest not warned be for me,
> But I dar not for Chastite;
> —Agayn hir dar I not misdo.

Cryseide's *bel aceuil* is a similar deserter in intent, restrained by Shame and Daunger. When she is urged to speak to Troilus, as he rides beneath her window, she reflects that

> Considered al thing, it may not be;
> And why? For *Shame;* and it were eek *to sone*
> *To graunten him so greet a libertee.*
> 'For pleynly hir entente', as seyde she,
> Was 'for to love him unwist, if she mighte'.

In both stories Bialacoil has failed to reckon on the activities of *Pitè,* and, still more, of Venus herself.

We must guard against the danger of identifying Cryseide with Bialacoil—an identification which would be meaningless, since the one is a woman (that is, a 'rational substance') and the other is merely 'an accident occurring in a substance'—a way in which a woman sometimes feels and behaves. Cryseide's analogue is the nameless heroine of the *Roman,* not any one of the personifications by whom that heroine is displayed; and those who have followed Chaucer most closely in his devout study of her, will best understand Cryseide. There have always been those who dislike her; and as more and more women take up the study of English literature she is likely to find ever less mercy. Yet none who does not love her and wish 'to excuse hir yet for routhe' is seeing her as Chaucer meant her to be seen. That she is not a wanton, still less a calculating wanton, need hardly be argued. The belief that she saw through the wiles of Pandarus, and only appeared to be led by circumstances while in fact she went the way she had intended from the beginning, can be held only in defiance of the text. Chaucer goes out of his way to tell us that 'she gan enclyne to lyke him first', and afterwards

> his manhod and his pyne
> Made love with-inne hir for to myne.

He tells us that she came to the house of Deiphebus 'al innocent' of Pandarus' machinations; and 'al innocent' she entered the chamber of Troilus; and when she admitted Troilus to hers it was because the story she had been told was so probable and so pitiful, and she was 'at dulcarnon, right at her wittes ende'. If we are determined to criticize her behaviour in the first part of the poem from any standpoint save that of Christian chastity, it would be more rational to say that she is not wanton enough, not calculating enough: that we hear too much of her blushes, her tears, and her simplicities, and not enough of her love: that she is 'cold as ice And yet not chaste; the weeping fool of voice'. This would be an error with some sort of foundation, but it would be an error. In the Cryseide of the first three books Chaucer has painted a touching and beautiful picture of a woman by nature both virtuous and amorous, but above all affectionate; a woman who in a chaste society would certainly have lived a chaste widow. But she lives, nominally, in Troy, really in fourteenth-century England, where love is the greatest of earthly goods and love has nothing to do with marriage. She lives in it alone; her husband is dead, her father a self-banished traitor: her only natural protector, whom she 'wolde han trusted' to have rebuked her without 'mercy ne mesure' at any suspected frailty, is on her lover's side, and working upon her by appeals to her curiosity, her pity and her natural passions, as well as by direct lying and trickery. If, in such circumstances, she yields, she commits no sin against the social code of her age and country: she commits no unpardonable sin against any code I know of—unless, perhaps, against that of the Hindus. By Christian standards, forgivable: by the rules of courtly love, needing no forgiveness: this is all that need be said of Cryseide's act in granting the Rose to Troilus. But her betrayal of him is not so easily dismissed.

Here there is, of course, no question of acquittal. 'False Cryseide' she has been ever since the story was first told, and will be till the end. And her offence is rank. By the code of courtly love it is unpardonable; in Christian ethics it is as far below her original unchastity as Brutus and Iscariot, in Dante's hell, lie lower than Paolo and France-

sca. But we must not misunderstand her sin; we must not so interpret it as to cast any doubt upon the sincerity of her first love. At the beginning of that first love there was some vanity in it: she could not help reflecting that she was 'oon the fayreste, out of drede', and 'with sobre chere hir herte lough'. But Coventry Patmore, who knows about such matters, has told us that a woman without this kind of vanity is a monster: and, as Chaucer asks,

> Who is that ne wolde hir glorifye
> To mowen swich a knight don live or dye?

Such venial self-complacencies are, in Cryseide, but the prelude to a complete abandonment of self. Soon she can ask with perfect sincerity

> Hadde I him never leef? By God, I wene
> Ye hadde never thing so leef,

and in the happy days of their mutual love 'eche of hem gan otheres lust obeye'. When the blow falls and she must leave Troy, she is gone so deep in love that she can feel Troilus' pain more acutely than her own,

> But how shul *ye* don in this sorwful cas,
> How shal *your* tendre herte this sustene?
> But herte myn, foryet this sorwe and tene
> And me also.

There is dramatic irony in the last sentence, but this must not be confused with the irony sometimes falsely attributed to Chaucer in this poem. It is destiny that laughs and Chaucer is far from laughter as he records it: if any grief that poetry tells of was ever sincere, then so was Cryseide's grief at leaving Troilus. And lest, with the end of the story in our minds, we should make any mistake, Chaucer tells us in so many words

> That al this thing was seyd of good entente,
> And that hir herte trewe was and kinde
> Towardes him, and spak right as she mente.

If it be asked how this sincerity and unselfishness in the earlier Cryseide is compatible with her subsequent treachery, we can reply only by a further consideration of her character. Fortunately Chaucer has so emphasized the ruling passion of his heroine, that we cannot mistake it. It is Fear—fear of loneliness, of old age, of death, of love, and of hostility; of everything, indeed, that can be feared. And from this Fear springs the only positive passion which can be permanent in such a nature; the pitiable longing, more childlike than womanly, for protection, for some strong and stable thing that will hide her away and take the burden from her shoulders. In the very opening of the poem we find her 'wel nigh out of her wit for sorwe and fere', alone in Troy, the widowed daughter of a traitor: a moment later we see her weeping and on her knees before Hector, whom she temporarily identifies with the strong defender of her dreams. Hector, who is the noblest minor character in Chaucer, reassures her; but even in apparent safety, even in her jests, there is a significance,

> For Goddes love, is than the assege aweye?
> I am of Grekes so ferd that I deye.

Her playful and trusting affection for her uncle Pandarus, on which so much of her story hangs, is, of course, but one more form of the desire for protection; and the relation between the two is well depicted in the scene where she begs her uncle not to leave her until they have had a talk about business. Women of her kind have always some male relative to stand between them and the terrifying world of affairs. And Pandarus thoroughly understands his niece. Having roused her curiosity by the hint of a secret, almost in the same breath he begins to allay her fears,

> Beth nought agast, ne quaketh nat. Wher-to?
> Ne chaungeth nat for fere so your hewe.

and yet to allay them wholly is not his purpose; a moment later he is threatening her with the death of Troilus and of himself. Few things in the poem are sadder or more illuminating than the burst of tears with which Cryseide receives the news, and the bitter reproach.

> What! Is this al the joye and al the feste?

—wrung from her by the realization that the protector of the moment (i.e. Pandarus) has deserted her, while she is still unprepared to find the new protector in Troilus, and can only pray

> O lady myn, Pallas!
> Thou *in this dredful cas* for me purveye.

For dreadful to Cryseide it is. She knows that 'unhappes fallen thikke alday for love'; she believes that her uncle's life 'lyth in balaunce'; she fears scandal, and she fears love itself, its pains, uncertainties, and anxieties. She fears the anger of Troilus, as well she may, remembering her ambiguous position in a besieged city:

> Eek wel wot I my kinges sone is he;—
> Now were I wys me hate to purchace
> Withouten nede, ther I may stonde in grace?

It may be doubted whether Cryseide herself knows precisely how this form of fear affects her. It may reasonably be asked whether there is not in such a woman (though in no impure sense) a dash of what is now called masochism—whether the prince's power to hurt, which is but the other side of his power to defend, is not the most potent of all the spells that are cast upon her. However this may be, Chaucer makes us to understand that Cryseide's first fears of love and of her lover spring from the same root as her later contentment and confidence. The 'tyme swete' of love, for such a nature, could not be more accurately described,

> Wel she felte he was to hir a wal
> Of steel, and sheld from every displesaunce;
> That to ben in his gode governaunce,
> So wys he was, she was no more afered.

No longer afraid, and no longer unloving; even no longer selfish. Such as Cryseide, once given the shelter they desire, repay it with complete devotion; it is not to be believed that she would ever have been faithless to Troilus, ever less than a perfect lover to him, as long as he was present. What cruelty it is, to subject such a woman to the test of absence—and of absence with no assured future of reunion, absence compelled by the terrible outerworld of law and politics and force (which she cannot face), absence amid alien scenes and voices

> With wommen fewe, among the Grekes stronge.

Every one can foresee the result. No one, not even Troilus, is deceived by those desperate speeches in which Cryseide, with pitiful ignorance of her self, attempts to assume the role of comforter and to become a woman of practical ability, resource, and hardihood, who will arrange everything; because, forsooth, some one has told the poor child that women are like that—'wommen ben wyse in short avysement'. Her attempt to be 'feminine' in this sense is short-lived. The very depth of her love for Troilus facilitates her fall, in so far as it produces in her, when once Troilus is left behind, a desolation that heightens to imperative craving her normal hunger for comfort and protection. The old 'wal and sheld' is gone: the more she misses it, the more she needs a new one, and hardly has she ridden out of Troy gate before the new one is at hand: the first, and the only friendly and protective thing that meets her in the new, homesick life among those 'Grekes stronge' who have been a bogey to her for the best part of ten years. The situation, in itself, is half the battle for Diomede; but Diomede, in any situation, would have been a dangerous wooer to Cryseide. Except for fashion's sake, and for a short time, he is no suppliant like Troilus. With swift, nonchalant cruelty he hammers into pieces all her hopes of any comfort save from himself:

> The folk of Troye, as who seyth, alle and some
> In preson been, as ye your-selven see;
> For thennes shal not oon on lyve come
> For al the gold bitwixen sonne and see
> —Trusteth wel and understondeth me!

The stinging brutality of that last, trochaic line is a masterpiece: we can almost see the handsome, blackguardly jaw thrust out. But while all men, and all good women, will hate Diomede, Cryseide cannot. I spoke just now of masochism 'in no impure sense'; but the descent to hell is easy, and those who begin by worshipping power soon worship evil. Chaucer had better be left to tell in his own words the effect of Diomede's tactics upon Cryseide,

> Retorning in hir soule ay up and down
> The wordes of *this sodein Diomede*
> His greet estat, and peril of the toun,
> And that she was allone and hadde nede
> Of freendes help.

It must be said for Cryseide that she does not reach this point without a struggle: a struggle so intense that she can even propose, or think that she proposes, 'to stele awey by night'. That Cryseide, for whom even flight with Troilus was too terrible, will ever really go out alone, by night, to cross the no man's land between the camp and Troy, is a psychological impossibility; but the fact that she can consider such a project bears witness to her desperate efforts to rise above herself. And yet, such is the cruelty of her situation, that this very effort must speed Diomede's suit. As soon as she has resolved, or striven to resolve, upon it, Diomede becomes, no longer the alternative to Troilus, but the alternative to flight. The picture of herself in Diomede's arms gains the all but irresistible attraction that it blots out the unbearable picture of herself stealing out past the sentries in the darkness. And so, weeping and half-unwilling, and self-excusing, and repentant by anticipation before her guilt is consummated, the unhappy creature becomes the mistress of her Greek lover, grasping at the last chance of self-respect with the words

> To Diomede algate I wol be trewe.

What follows detracts little further from the character whose ruin we have been watching. It is disgusting that she should give Troilus' brooch to Diomede, and her last letter to Troilus is abominable; but these are involved in her fall. Such a woman has no resistant virtues that should delay her complete degradation when once she is united with a degrading lover. The same pliancy which ennobled her as the mistress of Troilus, debases her as the mistress of Diomede. For when she yields, she yields all: she has given herself to the Greek *tamquam cadaver,* and his vices are henceforth hers. Her further descent from being Diomede's mistress to being a common prostitute, and finally a leprous beggar, as in Henryson, cannot be said to be improbable.

Such is Chaucer's Cryseide; a tragic figure in the strictest Aristotelian sense, for she is neither very good nor execrably wicked. In happier circumstances she would have been a faithful mistress, or a faithful wife, an affectionate mother, and a kindly neighbour—a happy woman and a cause of happiness to all about her—caressed and caressing in her youth, and honoured in her old age. But there is a flaw in her, and Chaucer has told us what it is; 'she was the ferfulleste wight that mighte be'. If fate had so willed, men would have known this flaw only as a pardonable, perhaps an endearing, weakness; but fate threw her upon difficulties which convert it into a tragic fault, and Cryseide is ruined.

Pandarus is exactly the opposite of his niece. He is, above all, the practical man, the man who 'gets things done'. It is his delight to manipulate that world of affairs from which Cryseide longs to be protected. Every one has met the modern equivalent of Pandarus. When you are in the hands of such a man you can travel first class through the length and breadth of England on a third-class ticket; policemen and gamekeepers will fade away before you, placated yet unbribed; noble first-floor bedrooms will open for you in hotels that have sworn they are absolutely full; and drinks will be forthcoming at hours when the rest of the world goes thirsty. And all the time, he will be such good company that he can

> make you so to laugh at his folye
> That you for laughter wenen for to dye.

Yet he is no mere comedian: he can talk with you far into the night, when the joking and the 'tales of Wade' are over, of

> many an uncouth glad and deep matere
> As freendes doon, whan they been met y-fere,

and if it is necessary to speak to others on your behalf he can 'ring hem out a proces lyk a belle'. He is faithful, too, once you have won him to your side: a discreet, resourceful, indefatigable man; and if it is unwise to entrust your affairs to him, that is largely because his friendship will lead him to go too far on your behalf. So far the character is easily recognizable, for it is happily not uncommon in life, though rare in fiction. What surprises us is to find in conjunction with this practical efficiency, this merriment, and this warm, not over-scrupulous, affection, all the characteristics of a fourteenth-century gentleman; for Pandarus is a lover and a doctor in Love's law, a friend according to the old, high code of friendship, and a man of sentiment. The 'ironic' Pandarus is not to be found in the pages of Chaucer, and those who approach him with this preconception will be disappointed as they read how he 'neigh malt for wo and routhe' at the sight of Troilus' lovesickness; how 'the teres braste out of his iyen' while he pleaded with Cryseide; and how, while he heard Troilus pleading for himself in the house of Deiphebus, 'Pandare weep as he to watre wolde'. I do not say that he did not in some way enjoy his frequent tears; but he enjoyed them not as a vulgar scoffer, but as a convinced servant of the god of Love, in whose considered opinion the bliss and pathos of a gravely conducted amour are the finest flower of human life. A moment after he has thus wept we are told that

> Fil Pandarus on knees and up his iyen
> To hevene threw, and held his hondes hye,
> 'Immortal God!' quod he, 'That mayst nought dyen,
> Cupide I mene, of this mayst glorifye. . . .

If Pandarus is consciously playing a part at this moment, he is a buffoon of the most odious sort. The whole scene becomes crude and farcical: fitter for a harlequinade than for a romance. Not to such characters does Chaucer entrust the comic element in a great poem; for nothing that I have said must be taken to contradict the view that Pandarus is comic, or even that he represents, in a way, the negative element of common sense amidst the courtly idealisms. But the thing is far more delicate—the comedy more subtle—than the modern reader expects it to be. Pandarus is perfectly serious when he expounds the commandments of Love—or even general philosophy—to Troilus. And Chaucer is serious, too, to the extent that he seriously wishes to include all this erotic, or other, instruction: what would a love-poem be without 'doctryne'?

What is funny—and doubtless intended to be funny—is the contrast between love's victim and love's doctrinaire; the contrast which leads poor Troilus to cry

> Freend, though that I stille lye
> I am not deef.

and again

> Lat be thyne olde ensamples I thee preye.

There is comedy, too, in the prolixity and pedantry of Pandarus—the ease with which he reels off the letter of Oenone, the doctrine of contraries, the rules for a lover's service, and the lover's guide to letter writing—as though he had learned them by heart, as very probably he had. Complacent instruction, when the instructor is willing and the pupil not, is always funny, and specially funny to Chaucer. But the intention of Pandarus is not comic—Pandarus would be less comic if it were—and the content of his instruction is not meant to be ridiculous. Certainly, Chaucer would be ill pleased if we laughed at such a stanza as the following:

> What! Shulde he therfor fallen in despeyr,

Or be recreaunt for his owene tene,
Or sleen himself, al be his lady fayr?
Nay, nay: but ever in oon be fresh and grene
To serve and love his dere hertes quene
And thenke it is a guerdoun hir to serve
A thousandfold more than he can deserve.

Here, and in many similar passages, Pandarus combines with his comic role another function equally necessary in Chaucer's eyes. Chaucer intends to teach, as well as to paint, the mystery of courtly love; and the direct doctrine which Love himself, or Frend, or the Vekke, would have spoken in an allegory, is given to Pandarus. It is not what Pandarus says that is comic, on Chaucer's view: it is the importunity, the prolixity, the laughable union of garrulity and solemnity, with which he says it. And this is only part and parcel of his general officiousness. If by a busybody we mean one who is ineffectively busy, then, to be sure, 'busybody' is the last name we can give to Pandarus. But he has the fussiness of the busybody; even where there is nothing to be done, he must needs do something. When Troilus sinks to his knees at Cryseide's bedside, Pandarus comes bustling forward with a cushion for him to kneel on. This is exquisitely funny if we imagine Pandarus doing it with the anxious and perspiring gravity of an old-fashioned nurse—'he for a quisshen *ran*'; but it is hardly funny at all, it is merely silly, if he does it as a joke. Similarly it is not a knowing leer on the part of Pandarus, it is rather the poor man's despair at finding he can be busy no longer, his sense of anticlimax, which should make us laugh when he says plaintively:

For ought I can espyen
This light nor I ne serven here of nought.

And yet, of course, there is knowing humour, or raillery, in the words that immediately follow; and in the banter with which he greets Cryseide next morning, there is humour of a familiar avuncular or parental type, somewhat now discredited. It is this side of Pandarus—a real and important element in his character, no doubt—which has led, by exaggeration, to misunderstandings of his character as a whole. The old gentlemen who joked about christenings at marriages in the nineteenth century were no doubt being gross and common-sensible at the expense of the devout emotions felt by the bridal pair. To that extent they were playing the part of the Goose, or the Vekke, or Godfrey Gobelive. But you must not suppose that these same old gentlemen repudiated the monogamic idealism and romanticism of their period, or would have been anything but outraged at a serious attack upon it: to that extent they play the part of the eagle, or Troilus, or Grand Amour. They eat their cake and have it too, like rational creatures. If romantic love were not venerable, who but a simpleton would poke fun at it? And so it is with Pandarus. He is inside the magic circle of courtly love—a devout, even a pedantic and lachrymose, exponent of it. But he, like every one else, except the lovers themselves for short moments in 'the fury of their kindness', sees also the hard or banal lineaments of the work-day world showing through the enchanted haze; and that on two levels. On the first, he sees eye to eye with the merry old Victorians, and can tease the lovers' pudency or laugh away their fears; 'she will not bite you', as he says to Troilus. On the second level, like all Love's medieval servants, he sees the fatal discrepancy between the commandments of Love and the commandments of God, and becomes uneasy about the part he is playing. He begins to protest too much. He has never done it before—he will never do it again—he had been half in fun at the beginning—at least he is not being paid for it—it was sheer pity for Troilus that made him do it. But when all is said, he cannot resist the obvious conclusion:

Wo is me that I, that cause al this
May thenken that she is my nece dere,
And I hir eem and traytor eke y-fere.

The character of Pandarus cannot be put in a nutshell: the subtlety of a poet's creation is 'far greater than the subtlety of discourse'. There is fold within fold to be disentangled in him, and analysis, with its multiple distinctions, will never exhaust what imagination has brought forth with the unity of nature herself. But we must not substitute a neat satiric abstraction for the richly concrete human being whom Chaucer has given us.

Troilus, throughout the poem, suffers more than he acts. He is the shore upon which all these waves break, and Chaucer has accurately described his theme as being how Troilus' 'adventures fellen Fro wo to wele and after out of joye'. This is not to say that the character of Troilus is ill drawn, but rather that the drawing of Troilus' character is no principal part of Chaucer's purpose; that about Troilus there still hangs something of the anonymity of the Dreamer, the mere 'I', of the allegories. He can be, to some extent, assumed: he is in one sense unimportant, because he is, in another, all important. As an embodiment of the medieval ideal of lover and warrior, he stands second only to Malory's Launcelot: far, I think, above the Launcelot of Chrétien. We never doubt his valour, his constancy, or the 'daily beauty' of his life. His humility, his easy tears, and his unabashed self-pity in adversity will not be admired in our own age. They must, however, be confessed to be true (intolerably true in places) to nature; and, for their admirableness or the reverse, Chaucer forewarns us,

and wordes tho
That hadden prys, now wonder nyce and
   straunge
Us thinketh hem; and yet they spake hem so
And spedde as wel in Love as men now do.

Of such a character, so easily made happy and so easily broken, there can be no tragedy in the Greek or in the modern sense. The end of *Troilus* is the great example in our literature of pathos pure and unrelieved. All is to be endured and nothing is to be done. The species of suffering is one familiar to us all, as the sufferings of Lear and Oedipus are not. All men have waited with everdecreasing hope, day after day, for some one or for something that does not come, and all would willingly forget the experience. Chaucer spares us no detail of the prolonged and sickening process to despair: every fluctuation of gnawing hope, every pitiful subterfuge of the flattering imagination, is held up to our eyes without mercy. The thing is so painful that perhaps no one without reluctance reads it twice. In our cowardice we are tempted to call it sentimental. We turn, for relief, to the titanic passions and heroic deaths of tragedy, because they are sublime and remote, and hence endurable. But this, we feel, goes almost beyond the bounds of art; this is treason. Chaucer is letting the cat out of the bag.

The odd thing is that ***Troilus and Cryseide,*** despite this terrible conclusion, is not a depressing poem. A curious phenomenon is to be noted here, similar to that in the ***Book of the Duchesse,*** where Chaucer's picture of the lost happiness proved so potent as almost to override the consideration of its loss. It is the same with ***Troilus.*** Chaucer has lavished more than half his work, if we regard mere number of lines, upon the happy phase of his story, the first wooing and winning of Cryseide: he has spent almost the whole of the third book upon fruition. But the question is not one of arithmetic. It is the quality of the first three books, and above all of the third, that counts; that book which is in effect a long epithalamium, and which contains, between its soaring invocation to the 'blisful light' of the third heaven and its concluding picture of Troilus at the hunt (sparing the 'smale bestes'), some of the greatest erotic poetry of the world. It is a lesson worth learning, how Chaucer can so triumphantly celebrate the flesh without becoming either delirious like Rossetti or pornographic like Ovid. The secret lies, I think, in his *concreteness.* Lust is more abstract than logic: it seeks (hope triumphing over experience) for some purely sexual, hence purely imaginary, conjunction of an impossible maleness with an impossible femaleness. So Lawrence writhes. But with Chaucer we are rooted in the purifying complexities of the real world. Behind the lovers—who are people, 'rational substances', as well as lovers—lies the whole history of their love, and all its ardours and dejections are kept well before us up to the very moment of consummation: before them lies the morning and the beautiful antiphonal *alba,* remade from old Provençal models, which they will then utter. Outside is the torrential 'smoky' rain which Chaucer does not allow us to forget; and who does not see what an innocent smugness, as of a children's hiding-place, it draws over the whole scene? Finally, beside them, is Pandarus, so close to them in outlook, and yet so far removed: Pandarus, the go-between, the bridge not only between Troilus and Cryseide but also between the world of romance and the world of comedy.

Thus ***Troilus*** is what Chaucer meant it to be—a great poem in praise of love. Here also, despite the tragic and comic elements, Chaucer shows himself, as in the ***Book of the Duchesse,*** the [***Parlement of Foules***], and the ***Canterbury Tales,*** our supreme poet of happiness. The poetry which represents peace and joy, desires fulfilled and winter overgone, the poetry born under festal Jove, is of a high and difficult order: if rarity be the test of difficulty, it is the most difficult of all. In it Chaucer has few rivals, and no masters. In the history of love poetry ***Troilus*** represents the crowning achievement of the old Provençal sentiment in its purity. The loves of Troilus and Cryseide are so nobly conceived that they are divided only by the thinnest partition from the lawful loves of Dorigen and her husband. It seems almost an accident that the third book celebrates adultery instead of marriage. Chaucer has brought the old romance of adultery to the very frontiers of the modern (or should I say the late?) romance of marriage.

He does not himself cross the frontier; but we see that his successors will soon inevitably do so. In the centuries that follow, poems of secondary importance in the history of poetry acquire primary importance in the history of humanity, because they pour the sentiment which the Middle Ages had created into moulds that the law of Reason can approve. The conflict between Carbonek and Camelot begins to be reconciled. In this momentous change Chaucer and the graver of his predecessors have borne an important part, for it is they who have refined and deepened the conception of love till it is qualified for such sanction. (pp. 174-97)

> *C. S. Lewis, "Chaucer," in his* The Allegory of Love: A Medieval Tradition, *Oxford at the Clarendon Press, 1936, pp. 157-97.*

Bertrand H. Bronson   (essay date 1952)

[*In the following excerpt, Bronson comments on Chaucer's profound understanding of psychology as evidenced by his treatment of grief in the* Book of the Duchess.]

It has been generally agreed that there are glaring faults in Chaucer's elegy for Blanche and that, in spite of occasional beauties, the 'prentice hand is but too apparent. Critics have found the poem tedious, disconnected, and ill-proportioned, languid in its beginning and abrupt in its conclusion, frequently lapsing in taste and in meter, deficient both in humor and in self-fulfilment. Coulton's verdict—"obviously immature and unequal, but full of delightful passages"—would seem, judging by the printed comment, to be that of most sympathetic readers; though many have emphasized the negative rather than the positive half of the judgment. Because I believe that much of the disparagement has arisen from misunderstanding, I invite reconsideration of a work of art that has been rated a good deal lower than it deserves. It may be that characteristic values inherent in the more archaic of Chaucer's writings will reassert themselves in the course of our scrutiny. There have been signs latterly that a truer appreciation is in the making, as in the comments of Wolfgang Clemen [in his *Der junge Chaucer*] and James R. Kreuzer [in his 1951 *PMLA* article "The Dreamer in *The Book of the Duchess*"] and to this impulse I wish to add what force I may. Generally, however, the older critical impatience yet prevails.

What has proved the chief stumbling-block comes up for emphatic restatement in J. S. P. Tatlock's [1950] book, *The Mind and Art of Chaucer.* "Indifference to human reality," Tatlock declares,

> is most marked of all in the dreamer (who is in no sense Chaucer himself). Informed by the overheard soliloquy that the lover's grief is due to his lady's death, to say nothing of his garments of mourning and the loving reminiscence all through his prolonged monologue, at the end the dreamer is astounded to learn that she is dead. Perhaps such forgetfulness is dreamlike. . . . But no explanation of the dreamer's state of mind . . .will persuade most moderns, still less a medieval if he thought about it, to accept the contradiction without question. It is en-

tirely unlike Chaucer's later way . . . here he makes a really inexplicable blur . . .why he should so bluntly at the beginning tell us that the lady is dead, though at the end he is to ignore this, who can say?

There is, I believe, a satisfactory answer to this question, in both its parts, and it will be our main business in the ensuing discussion to find it. It would be true to say that we are bluntly informed because it is important for us to know at once, as the dreamer knows at once, that the lady is dead; because the poem as a whole grows and exfoliates from that central fact, which provides at once the principle of its artistic development, the pivot around which the dialogue revolves, the key to character, and the visible dark that underlies the courtly surface-tissue and gives it poignance—"bright metal on a sullen ground." But so summary an answer is *ignotum per ignotius.* We shall have to explore the poem before it can be truly understood.

Kittredge's solution to the immediate problem has long been familiar [see excerpt dated 1914]. In that classic and brilliant lecture on *The Book of the Duchess,* Kittredge anticipates Tatlock's view that the Dreamer is not Chaucer:

> He is a purely imaginary figure to whom certain purely imaginary things happen, in a purely imaginary dream. He is as much a part of the fiction . . . as the Merchant or the Pardoner or the Host is a part of the fiction in the Canterbury Tales. . . . The mental attitude of the Dreamer is that of childlike wonder. He understands nothing, not even the meaning of his dream. . . . He wonders what makes the knight so sad; and when the knight tries to tell him, he still wonders, and still questions. Hints and half-truths and figures of speech are lost upon him. . . . This . . . is not Geoffrey Chaucer, the humorist and man of the world. He is a creature of the imagination, and his childlikeness is part of his dramatic character. [Moreover,] the Dreamer is not merely artless by nature; he is dulled, and almost stupified, by long suffering.

Kittredge then, with what appears a strange *volte face,* adds a further page of characterization that can hardly be reconciled with the foregoing, however corrective. "But what," he asks:

> is he really deaf and blind to what he hears and sees? By no means! Artless he is, and unsuspicious, and dull with sorrow and lack of sleep; but the dirge is too clear for even him to misunderstand. . . . The Dreamer knows perfectly well that the lady is dead. . . . With instinctive delicacy . . . he suppresses this knowledge [from a desire] to afford the knight the only help in his power—the comfort of pouring his sad story into compassionate ears.

There seems to be a double exposure here. We are first presented with a simpleton who cannot understand anything but the most obvious statements of fact, a childlike dullard stupefied with sorrow and sleeplessness; and then we are asked to incorporate with this conception another character who knows the facts, understands what he hears and sees, and puts his knowledge to use with tact and di-

plomacy, with the kindly purpose of enabling the stranger to ease his heart. If Chaucer drew this psychological paradox, he would seem to be guilty of that "inexplicable blur" of which Tatlock complains; or worse, perhaps, of drawing a character with too little inner consistency to compel our belief. But since the Dreamer is the most complex of all the persons depicted, we shall approach him with more assurance when we have considered the simpler characters in the poem.

It is customary to identify the Man in Black as John of Gaunt and the lady whom he describes, as Blanche the Duchess of Lancaster. In these identifications we have, of course, the support of Chaucer's own title, *The Death of Blanche the Duchess,* in the Prologue to the *Legend of Good Women,* as well as Shirley's subsequent asseveration. But not all of us stop to consider how far such ascriptions are to be carried, or what precisely is implied by them.

Most readers would willingly allow that Chaucer was not engaged upon the painting of realistic portraits of these persons, such as he was later to render of some of the Canterbury pilgrims. The Man in Black and his lady, it would be admitted, are idealizations appropriate to their context in the poem: they are images in a dream. They are distanced from reality, and depicted in conventionalized attitudes, like figures in a medieval tapestry. They are drawn against the formalized landscape of the dream-vision, and stand forth as ideal courtly lovers. No one among Chaucer's contemporaries would have looked for a photographic realism, or have expected, or even tolerated, an accurate correspondence of the pictures and the life. They welcomed and were well acquainted with the conventions of the genre. When an eighteenth-century poet composed an elegy on Addison's death, he gave it the form of a pastoral dialogue between Pope and Steele, in which "Richy" recalls to "Sandy" in the following terms the benefit enjoyed by the reading public from "Adie's" papers on the *Paradise Lost:*

> Mony a time, beneath the auld birk-tree,
> What's bonny in that sang he loot me see.
> The lasses aft flung down their rakes and pails,
> And held their tongues, O strange! to hear his tales.

Ramsay's audience, we surmise, was not greatly disturbed by this poetic refraction of literal truth. Given a sufficient clue in the names, they took pleasure in the ingenuity of the poet's translation of recent event into the conventions of pathetic pastoral. Similarly, it is to be supposed, Chaucer's audience received the description of Blanche's acceptance of Gaunt, couched in the conventional terms of courtly love. Says the knight:

> she wel understod
> That I ne wilned thyng but god,
> And worship, and to kepe hir name
> Over alle thyng, and drede hir shame,
> And was so besy hyr to serve;
> And pitee were I shulde sterve,
> Syth that I wilned noon harm, ywis,
> So whan my lady knew al this,
> My lady yaf me al hooly
> The noble yifte of hir mercy . . .

The self-portrait of the lover, from first to last, is the very image of the same ideal. Years before his affection found its saint, he paid tributary homage to Love as his rightful lord and devoutly prayed for grace to become one of Love's elect. "I ches love to my firste craft"—owing to native disposition. His time as novice is finally recognized with favor by the god, "that had wel herd my boone," and he is granted sight of the nonpareil of women. The sequel is equally orthodox. He worships long without daring to speak. He composes love-songs and sings them, "for to kepe me fro ydelnesse." He is reduced to desperation by the conflict between fear and desire. At last, like Troilus, he utters his stumbling entreaty for "mercy," swearing to be steadfast and true, to love his lady ever "freshly newe," to save her worship, and have no other ladies before her. She at once returns him a categorical No, having none assurance of this stable humility. He mourns and suffers full many a day. In due course—"another year"—he makes a second appeal. She is now convinced of his steadfastness and accepts him for her servant, giving him a ring. He is like a man raised from death to life. Henceforth she takes him under her rule and they live for many a year in perfect accord and felicity. It is part of the idealization that, although he worshipped Love long ere they met, worshipped his lady long ere she accepted him, and lived long in unspeakable happiness thereafter, he is still in the Spring of life when the Dreamer meets him. He looks about twenty-four, his face just beginning to show a beard. He is adept in the fashionably sophisticated language of paradox and metaphor—

> In travayle ys myn ydelnesse
> And eke my reste; my wele is woo . . .
> My pees, in pledynge and in werre.

It is quite irrelevant that Gaunt married Blanche at the age of nineteen, and lost her in the Plague when he was twenty-nine; that he had spent great part of those ten years away from home and was abroad (with Chaucer) at the time of her death. In the poem, the knight is not identified, even covertly, as Gaunt until the punning allusion to his place of residence, fifteen lines from the end, unless through the name of the lady, which he reveals in figurative gloss. Despite the commentators, there is in the poem no overt suggestion that the knight is describing wedded love. The question does not and should not arise—unless we choose to read the gift of a ring as that of a wedding-ring: but we may recall that Troilus and Criseyde "entrechaungeden hire rynges" at their first embracing, where, incidentally, Criseyde's charms are detailed in a catalogue warmer, but closely paralleling the one enumerated by the black knight. Within the terms of courtly love it would have been incongruous to mention marriage; and Gaunt would hardly have been complimented by the suggestion that as husband he was governed by his wife:

> In al my yowthe, in al chaunce,
> She took me in hir governaunce.

Similarly, the lady herself, as seen through her servant's eyes, is a paradigm of feminine excellence. From his ecstatic description we learn that she was the embodiment of goodness, truth, fair dealing, charming demeanor, and perfect physical beauty. James Russell Lowell found the portrait as fresh as the first violets gathered in the dew of a spring morning; and certainly it keeps a vernal fragrance, in spite of scholarly research which has shown it to be a florilegium of passages culled from French love-poetry. If Chaucer's audience were able to recognize the borrowings, they would not have been displeased that the garland was woven of blossoms transported from the courtly gardens of sweet France. That would for them have increased its rarity and enhanced its perfume. Not every woman received a tribute so far-sought and precious. We today are so used to equating realism and sincerity that we instinctively devaluate the forms, however exquisite, 'of hammered gold and gold enamelling,' which belong to an earlier and more studied artifice. We are, moreover, so conditioned to the notion—surely a symptom of the modern critical bias—that Chaucer's artistic progress is gauged inversely by the degree of his dependence on established medieval convention that we lack tongues to praise his mastery of that earlier idiom except as it departs from the norm.

Hence we notice signs of verisimilitude in the lover's meandering course of reminiscent eulogy, in the disordered sequence of thought giving rise to impulsive little bursts of ecstasy over one aspect and then another of his lady's merits, and returning upon itself again. But we should also bear in mind that the poet was working within a tradition and keeping a constant eye on the most esteemed models, and that he expected to be judged by the delicacy with which he composed his appliqué into a fresh design. The garment of praise is like his own Squire's habit, "embrouded as it were a mede." It has the crowded abundance of detail—and sometimes the irrelevance—that strikes us often in medieval textiles:

> I wolde thoo
> Have loved best my lady free,
> Thogh I had had al the beaute
> That ever had Alcipyades,
> And al the strengthe of Ercules,
> And therto had the worthynesse
> Of Alysaunder, and al the rychesse
> That ever was in Babiloyne,
> In Cartage, or in Macedoyne,
> Or in Rome, or in Nynyve,—

or was as brave as Hector or as wise as Minerva; because she was as good as Penelope or as Lucrece, although she resembled neither one of them and was in fact unique— "she only queen of love and beauty."

Coming now to the Dreamer, we confront a problem of far greater complexity. To be truly defined, he must be studied not in isolation but in several different contexts and relationships: as a person outside and inside the dream; in association with the grieving knight of his dream; as he relates to the poet who drew him; and as he bears upon the human connections between Chaucer and John of Gaunt. It will be easiest to consider these aspects of the character one by one.

First, then, for the person who speaks to us directly as narrator throughout the poem. We meet him, first, engulfed in brooding melancholy, sleepless with "sorwful ymagynacioun." It is, we notice, his present condition that he is describing, not a state of mind from which he fortunately escaped. He has suffered thus, he tells us, for as long as eight years, and has no prospect of recovery. The strange dream that he experienced recently, and that he intends to describe, was only an interruption. The dream is thus framed by, or suspended in, the Dreamer's own melancholy, into which he must be understood to have lapsed again upon awaking. He is resigned and passive about his condition, lost in a gentle wonder that he still lives, but not actively seeking death. It is only natural that his attention should have been caught by the plight of another star-crossed lover, when he happened upon it in a book he had chosen with which to while away the sleepless hours. The story concerned the grief of a queen, Alcyone, whose husband was lost at sea, and who could recover no word of his fate, nor get respite from her longing. The Dreamer's heart went out to her in pity, for he found his own sorrow imaged in hers.

Chaucer has been censured for not finding a closer parallel to John of Gaunt's bereavement. The tale of Ceyx and Alcyone, as he tells it, stresses the wife's grief, not the love of a husband bereft. The poet knew better than to set out the accounts, *seriatim,* of three lorn males. Alcyone breaks the sequence without disturbing the mood. She and the Dreamer are akin in their protracted love-longing, and she and the knight are at one in their grief. Deprivation unites us all, men and women, knights and queens. Unvarying repetition is not needed to drive home this truth.

When we look closely at the narrator—the "I" inside the poem—it is surprising how little countenance he gives to the view of him that has come to be generally accepted since Kittredge's essay, of a simpleminded man, incapable of mature observation or intelligent response to experience. No doubt it is perilous to assert, where so much depends on the tone of voice, that after five hundred years we can always detect the nuances originally intended. It is at least clear that the narrator is by no means devoid of humor, and also that his sense of humor includes himself. It is not a very childlike person who can take so objective a view of his own predicament that, even while he poignantly feels it, he can both refer to it and refuse to dwell on it, with the civility and lack of overemphasis here displayed. It might be Pandarus himself who is speaking. Eight years is a long time to suffer for love:

> And yet my boote is never the ner;
> For there is physicien but oon
> That may me hele; but that is don.
> Passe we over untill eft;
> That wil not be mot nede be left.

He will talk of his sleeplessness: that, after all, is what leads him to his proper subject. But as to what causes that condition, the less said—short of downright rudeness—the better. A glancing, good-humored allusion is sufficient: who would wish to harp on his own chronic illnesses?

Obviously, too, the narrator can repeat a story with verve; witness the visit of Juno's messenger to the gods of slumber, "who slept and did no other work." The comic aspects of the episode are by no means lost upon him:

> "Awake!" quod he, "who ys lyth there?"
> And blew his horn ryght in here eere,
> And cried "Awaketh!" wonder hye.
> This god of slep with hys oon ye
> Cast up, axed, "Who clepeth ther?"
> "Hyt am I," quod this messager.

Here is no lack of lively and humorous awareness. Soon after, he declares—"in my game"—that, rather than die for lack of sleep, he would give that same Morpheus, or Dame Juno—or any one else, "I ne roghte who"—a fine reward, if they would only put him to sleep. He had scarcely expressed the wish, when, inexplicably, he did fall asleep.

Any one, of course, who wishes to regard the manner of the narrative just reviewed as unsophisticated or childlike is entitled to that privilege. My present purpose is served if it be granted merely that it is unnecessary so to read it. Up to the point where the narrator falls asleep, it would, I think, be difficult to prove any significant difference in character between him and the narrator of the other dream-visions. If there is naïveté in the tone of the narrative, it is such a naïveté as we find in the *Parlement,* the *Hous of Fame,* the Prologue to the *Legend of Good Women,* and, indeed, woven into the very texture of all this poet's work. It is a simplicity and freshness of statement that continually tricks us into discounting the subtlety of perception and genuine human wisdom behind it.

But the problem of the narrator increases in complexity as soon as we enter the dream. The dreamlike quality of the narrative sequence has not passed unnoticed: due praise has been paid to this aspect of the poet's ordonnance. The way in which one episode opens into another without the logical connections or transitions: the Dreamer awakened *into* his dream by a burst of bird-song, to find himself on his bed with the morning sun making kaleidoscopic patterns through the windows of his chamber, richly stained with the Troy legend, and all the walls painted with the scenes of the *Romance of the Rose;* sounds outside of preparations for a royal hunt; the Dreamer's taking his horse at once and joining the party; the recall from the hunt; the disappearance of his horse ("I was go walked fro my tree"); the appearance and vanishing of the puppy—no hunting-dog, certainly; the flowery path through the woods full of wild creatures; the discovery of the handsome knight sitting against a huge oak and lost in grief—all this has the familiar but unforeseen and strange air of a dream.

We may also note subtle differences between the Dreamer's waking and sleeping states of mind. He does not lose his sense of humor nor his lively awareness: for example, his remarks on the heavenly singing of the birds on his chamber-roof—they didn't just open their mouths and pretend to be singing! Each one of them, without considering the cost to his throat, really exerted himself to show his best and happiest art. The Dreamer takes himself quite comfortably for granted as he is. It does not occur to him to reflect—but *we* notice the fact—that he is no longer carrying any of that load of oppressive sorrow under which he fell asleep. By a wonderful leap of psychological insight, and in strict accord with truth rediscovered in our

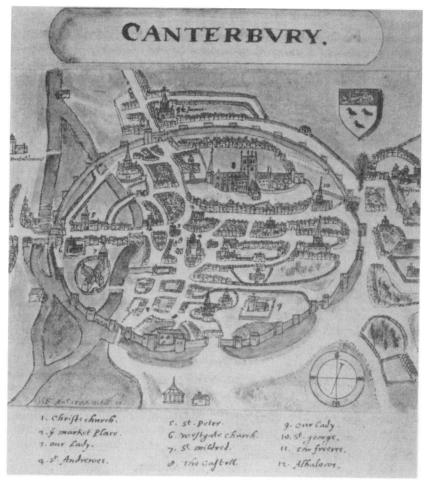

A plan of Canterbury dated 1588.

own century, his private grief has been renounced by the Dreamer, to reappear externalized and projected upon the figure of the grieving knight. The modern analyst, indeed, would instantly recognize the therapeutic function of this dream as an effort of the psyche to resolve an intolerable emotional situation by repudiating it through this disguise. The knight is the Dreamer's surrogate; and in this view it would be significant that the force which keeps the surrogate from his lady is the far more acceptable, because decisive and final, fact of death. The train of analysis would lead us to assume, of course, a kindred connection between the lady of the dream and the fair but cruel "physician" who refuses to work a cure in the Dreamer's waking life. And here it would be noted that the knight's long and rapturous eulogy of his lost lady would serve, in the Dreamer's unconscious, to discharge the latter's sense of guilt for the disloyalty of wishing the death of that Merciles Beaute. The disguise is rendered complete by the surrogate's having perfectly enjoyed his love before death severed them.

Some one will exclaim, ironically, How fortunate for the foregoing argument that Gaunt's Duchess had actually died, so that what the Dreamer desired could correspond with the facts! The taunt, of course, is irrelevant. What we are praising here is a depth of psychological truth that stands scrutiny on the level of basic human nature, making its silent contribution to the strength and consistency of the artifact. The historical Blanche and John of Gaunt and Chaucer await attention; but for the present we are concerned with elements inside the poem—connecting tissues, implicit but latent relations, that work below the surface to establish a convincing artistic unity.

The implied identification between the Dreamer and the knight is confirmed by parallels of repetitive description. Of himself, the Dreamer declares that he marvels he still lives:

> For nature wolde nat suffyse
> To noon erthly creature
> Nat longe tyme to endure
> Withoute slep and be in sorwe.

Of the knight, he says:

> Hit was gret wonder that nature
> Myght suffre any creature
> To have such sorwe, and be not ded.

The vital spirit of each of them has deserted its seat. For himself,

> Defaute of slep and hevynesse
> Hath sleyn my spirit of quyknesse;

and the knight is in the same case:

> his spirites wexen dede;
> The blood was fled for pure drede
> Doun to hys herte, to make hym warm—
> For wel hyt feled the herte had harm.

The Dreamer before falling asleep and the knight when he meets him show a kindred stupefaction, a grief so unrelieved that they fail to make contact with what is passing around them:

> I take no kep
> Of nothing, how hyt cometh or gooth . . .
> For I have felynge in nothyng,
> But, as yt were, a mased thyng,
> Alway in poynt to falle a-doun.

And the knight failed to observe the Dreamer who stood in front of him and spoke:

> throgh hys sorwe and hevy thoght,
> Made hym that he herde me noght;
> For he had wel nygh lost hys mynde.

Both men are hopeless, and the lesson of resignation is one which each has yet to learn. The knight's sorrow is momentarily assuaged by reminiscences, but it keeps recurring, floods back as he ceases to speak, and surrounds the episode of the meeting. The Dreamer likewise has surcease through the dream; but, as we have remarked, the beginning of his narrative, which is also in a sense the ending, encloses the poem with his melancholy. Each has a psychological and as it were biographical relation with Alcyone, and through her with each other. The story of Alcyone is thus a valuable unifying element in the poem as a whole; and, as we shall see, it is much more.

Out of the Dreamer's instinctive sympathy with the knight is developed the mechanism, subtle but with a surface simplicity, that carries the poem through to its conclusion. The Dreamer observes at once that the knight is in mourning and, approaching him silently, receives the sufficient explanation through the knight's overheard lament, that Death has stolen his bright lady. This is information to which, as a stranger, he has no right; but he cannot bear to leave a man in such grief without making any attempt to comfort him. He comes before him, therefore, and greets him quietly, and as soon as his presence is acknowledged, apologizes for disturbing him. He receives a gracious reply, and proceeds to invent conversation on indifferent matters, carefully avoiding reference to the other's state of grief until he has sanction from the knight's own mouth. "The hunt is over," he says; "so far as I can judge, the hart has escaped." "It matters not a whit to me," replies the knight; "my thoughts have been far otherwise engaged." "That is evident enough," replies the Dreamer; "you appear to be sorely oppressed. If you felt like telling me about your trouble, I would do my best to relieve you, believe me; and just to talk might help."

The Dreamer's tact leaves nothing to be desired; his etiquette is unimpeachable. In reply, the knight makes a long figurative statement of his woeful condition, full of rhetorical paradox, but rather unpacking his heart with conventional words than telling his grief directly—partly, perhaps, out of courtesy to a stranger, and partly because he

shrinks from uttering the bare truth. He comes close to it in the avowal that death has made him naked of all bliss. But he prefers to stalk his pain rather than confront it immediately. Yet he is not deliberately concealing his meaning, and certainly expects to be understood. He rails on Lady Fortune in set terms, and says he has played a game of chess with her and lost. She made a sly move and stole his "fers," checkmating him in the middle of the board ("nel mezzo del cammin' ") with an insignificant stray pawn. She has left him destitute of joy and longing for death.

The Dreamer finds his tale so pitiable that he can hardly bear it. He fully apprehends the meaning of the figurative language, which after all only confirms what he has already overheard. To suppose him mystified at this point were to credit him with rather less than the intelligence of a normal dog. Yet some of Chaucer's critics appear to have done just that. They write as if the Dreamer thinks the game was an actual chess-game, that the "fers" was a literal piece on a literal board. How the Dreamer would understand the knight's opponent in a literal sense they do not explain. Fortune in person would be something to see! Obviously, the naming of the knight's opponent forces a figurative meaning upon the game. If the Dreamer fails to understand this, he understands nothing at all. He *must* take "fers" in a figurative sense; and the reason he accepts the figurative term instead of abandoning it is that the knight as yet has given no sanction for the familiarity that a substitution would imply. Decorum, not bewilderment, forbids the Dreamer's referring to the lady in more literal terms.

With all the necessary facts in his possession, the Dreamer realizes that he must try to rescue the knight from this abject submission to misfortune. He sees two possible ways of proceeding. One is to rouse a spirit of endurance in the sufferer; the other, to seek to reduce the proportions of his loss. He tries each of these in turn, not forgetting but taking advantage of the fact that he yet has more specific knowledge than the knight's conversation so far has justified his admitting. At the very least, he must keep the knight talking, to save him from black despair. "You musn't give way like this," he exclaims; "remember how Socrates despised Fortune." "It's no use," says the knight. "Don't say so," insists the Dreamer; "even if you had lost the *twelve* ferses, you would still be guilty of the sin of self-murder if you gave in utterly to sorrow. You would be just as surely condemned as all those other unwise people who ended their lives because of disappointment in love: Medea, Phyllis, Dido, Echo, and Samson. But no man alive in these days would go to such lengths for loss of a fers."

And here we cannot avoid brief discussion of the term "fers," as used by the knight and the Dreamer. Fortunately, we can borrow the assistance of some very learned counsel, of whom the son of Sir James Murray, Mr. H. J. R. Murray, is best of all. Originally, it appears, the piece we now know as the Queen was a masculine figure, in Arabic "firzān," meaning counsellor or wise man—an appropriate and useful companion for a Shah or King on the field of battle. "The fact," says Murray [in his *A*

History of Chess], "that *firz* was adopted and not translated in some of the European languages proves that the meaning of the Arabic name was not understood." This doubtless facilitated the shift in the sex of that piece. An alternative nomenclature arose pretty generally throughout Europe in which the feminine gender of the piece was left in no doubt: *e.g., femina, virgo, domina, dama, frauw, dame, lady.* Also, and apparently commencing earlier, another series: *regina, reina, reine, quene.* But these did not entirely supplant the old term of *fers,* howsoever they may have affected its denotative and connotative significance, until two or three centuries after the time of Chaucer. The power of the piece in Chaucer's game was not nearly so great as the power it acquired later. Chaucer's fers could move only one square at a time, diagonally, and therefore hovered for the most part defensively about the king. The other pieces had much their modern power of movement: hence the rooks, bishops, and knights were all stronger pieces than the fers, and their loss would be relatively more serious. But in giving the fers such importance in the knight's imaginary game, Chaucer may have had in mind the especially close connection between it and the king in actual play, as well as the fact that all the rest were unequivocally male. That the original meaning of the name *fers* was everywhere completely lost at the moment of the game's introduction into Europe, even where chess-men were representatively carved, cannot be proved; and that some traces of that earlier tradition survived alongside the feminizing influence of the newer nomenclature, is surely not improbable. Moreover, the fact that the masculine pawns, on reaching the eighth row, became ferses, would make for further neutralizing of the feminine concept.

This possibility may have a bearing on the meaning of the Dreamer's curious reference to "the ferses twelve." Skeat's interpretation of this phrase [in his edition of *The Works of Geoffrey Chaucer*], adopted by the *Oxford English Dictionary,* is "all the pieces except the king." To arrive at this explanation, Skeat reckons: "pawns, *eight;* queen, bishop, rook, knight, *four;* total, *twelve.*" The King, according to Skeat, does not count, because he cannot be taken; and the bishops, rooks, and knights are counted three instead of six. To justify the latter count, Skeat takes refuge in the game of Shatranj (Chaturamga), out of which chess evolved; and to escape from applying the same principle of *kinds of pieces* to the pawns, he appeals to the old differentiation of individual pawns as shown after Chaucer's day in Caxton's illustrations. This is desperate pleading, in view of the fact that Chaucer's game had, undeniably, two each of bishops, rooks, and knights; that there is no evidence (I believe) of those pieces ever being called ferses; and that the eight pawns however differentiated were all called pawns. The total, with the fers, and without the king, comes to *fifteen* every time, unless we apply Peter's reasoning in the *Tale of a Tub.*

I am tempted, therefore, to suppose that the solution of the crux must be sought outside the game of chess; and, if the concept of the fers was sufficiently heterosexual to permit, I can think of no twelve companions more famous as a king's defenders than the Twelve Peers of Charlemagne, though I cannot prove that "Doucepers" was ever corrupted into "Doucefers." If some one brought forward

twelve equally famous *hetairai* who traditionally went together, I might, I suppose, have to give way. Certain it is, at any rate, that the Dreamer expects his phrase to be understood, that he uses it in a figurative sense, and that the MS. authority never omits the article. "Defy Fortune," urges the Dreamer,

> for trewely,
> Thogh ye had lost the ferses twelve,
> And ye for sorwe mordred yourselve,
> Ye sholde be dampned in this cas . . .

Skeat himself, it may be added, accepts, and goes beyond, the crucial assumption in our conjecture. "As," says he, "the word *fers* originally meant counsellor or monitor of the king, it could be applied to any of the pieces" that is, was not necessarily understood as feminine.

"No man alive," says the Dreamer, "would yield to this suicidal woe, for a fers." Medea, Dido, and Samson, who all died on account of their "ferses," are his comparative cases; and he is not thinking of literal chess-men. He is challenging the knight to justify his extreme grief, knowing well that to do so will force him to recall evidence of his lady's excellence and deflect his self-absorption. The ruse is successful. "Little you know what you are talking about," says the knight: "I have lost more than you suppose." "Then, good sir, tell me the whole story, how and why you have been divested of bliss." "Gladly, if you will give me your undivided attention." "I promise you, there is nothing I'd rather do: I am wholly at your disposal."

As the Dreamer had anticipated, the knight's memorabilia of his love, once stirred, begin to pour out in a flood: her gracious demeanor, her dancing, her laugh, her look, her hair, her eyes, her soft speaking, her fair dealing—on and on, as if he could never stop. He finally does, however, declaring: "This was she who was all my joy, my world's well-being, my goddess; and I was hers wholly and entirely."

The impetuous panegyric has been good for him, as the Dreamer can see. But ecstatic praise without the personal history still leaves the burden undischarged; and it will be yet better if the knight can be got to tell the story of his love, and perhaps be brought to realize it as a treasure that is his to keep, in the teeth of Time and Fortune. "By our Lord," says the Dreamer, "I don't wonder you were wholly hers. Your love was certainly well placed: I don't know how you could have done better." "Done better?" exclaims the knight, forgetting logic at the sacrilege of an implied comparison: "nor could any one have done so well." "I certainly think you're right." "Nay, but you must believe it!" "Sir, so I do," replies the Dreamer, with the reservation in agreement that will keep things going at this critical juncture: "I believe that to you she was the best and any one seeing her with your eyes would have seen her as the loveliest of women." "With *my* eyes? Nay, but every one that saw her said and swore that she was. And had they not, it wouldn't have changed my devotion. I *had* to love her. But *had to* is silly: I wished, I was bound to love her, because she was the fairest and best; it was a free but inevitable offering. But I was telling you about the first time I ever saw her. I was young and ignorant then, but I determined to do my whole devoir in her service. It did me so much good just to see her, that sorrow couldn't touch me the whole day after. She so possessed my mind that sorrow could make no impression."

The Dreamer's reply is charming and adroit. Here is the man who has claimed to be Sorrow himself, the essential personification of that state, describing how the idea of his love could heal him of all sorrow. The Dreamer leads him toward self-realization by suggesting, figuratively, how much he had to rejoice over, since he could still think of her. "You seem to me," says the Dreamer, "like a man who goes to confession with nothing to repent." "Repent!" cries the knight indignantly, rising to the bait: "far from me be the thought of repenting my love. That were worse than the worst treason that ever was. No, I will never forget her as long as I live." The Dreamer does not press the logical victory, but turns back to ask again for the narrative, still not forgetting that the lady's death is a fact that the knight does not know that he possesses. "You have told me," says he, "about your first sight of your lady. I beseech you to tell me how you first spoke to her, and the rest; and about the nature of the loss you have suffered." "Yes," says the knight, "it's greater than you imagine." "How so, sir? Won't she love you? or have you acted in a way that has caused her to leave you? Tell me everything, I pray you."

With this urging, the knight at last abandons indirections and moves straight down the autobiographical road until he reaches the point of perfect felicity. "Al was us oon," he says,

> withoute were.
> And thus we lyved ful many a yere
> So wel, I kan nat telle how.

Too plainly, this is not the end. "For ever after," the storybooks would say. But in life it is not so, and the Dreamer must help him to his conclusion. "Sir," he asks gently, "where is she now?" "Now?" repeats the knight, his grief suddenly overwhelming him. "Alas that I was born! That is the loss I told you of, remember? It was herself." "Alas, sir, how?" "She is dead." "Oh, no!" "She is, though." "So that is it. God, how sad!"

There is nothing in this narrative, nor in the dialogue which punctuates it, that need be taken as insensibility or forgetfulness or egregious simplicity on the part of the Dreamer. To the contrary, it is hard to imagine the situation being handled with more awareness and delicacy by Geoffrey Chaucer, courtier, man of the world, and poet, *in propria persona,* had it confronted him so in actual life. Never presuming on his private knowledge, the Dreamer leads the knight from point to point to disclose everything, and at the knight's own pace and pleasure.

The unwillingness of most critics to accept the narrative on trust, merely because they are not explicitly told that Chaucer knows what he is doing and that he is doing it deliberately, is very churlish. Why must we assume his incompetence, when the contrary assumption points to an explanation both natural and artistically satisfying? To take the intelligence of the Dreamer for granted is to remove the difficulty, for his intelligence and tact dictate his whole procedure.

When we bethink us that the poet would in the first instance be present in person to mediate between his work and his audience, we realize that the critical difficulty must have arisen since his time, as a result of altered relations between author and public, owing to the far-reaching effects of Print.

An author who addresses an *audience,* in the primary sense of the word, and who introduces himself overtly as one of the *dramatis personae* in his work, must naturally expect that his physical presence will color the self-portrait and contribute inevitably to its artistic effect. In fact, he cannot employ the autobiographical method, using the first person but meaning another than himself, without giving unmistakable indications that he is *quoting*—unless his audience is to be sadly misled. This is not to say that he may not present himself, or aspects of his total self, in such fashion as he pleases, and with such emphasis or bias as he wills or cannot avoid. But it is still himself that he is representing, however posed and semi-dramatic; and comparison follows inevitably.

When Chaucer read his poem to the circle for whom it was first intended, he was understood to be referring to himself when he used the first person. His audience, according to their private knowledge or degree of familiarity, might consider that he was distorting facts or truth, deliberately or unconsciously; but they would not leap unaided to the assumption that he was speaking in a fictive personality that had no relation to himself nor any reality outside his poem. When, therefore, Kittredge says that the Dreamer "is as much a part of the fiction in the **Book of the Duchess** as the Merchant or the Pardoner or the Host is a part of the fiction in the **Canterbury Tales,**" we must protest that this is true only as we consider that Chaucer himself is everywhere and throughout an essential "part of the fiction" in the **Canterbury Tales**, and elsewhere; the fiction being Chaucer's Chaucer, meeting and responding to characters and scenes in his work, and being reported on to his audience by that other Chaucer, of flesh and blood, then and there present before them.

In such a sense, therefore, it is necessary to contemplate the first personal representation that meets us in **The Book of the Duchess.** And it is not too difficult to approximate the two, Chaucer and Dreamer, bearing in mind the high and low lighting, the qualifications and emphases and omissions due to the perspective of an accepted literary convention and to the poet's own choice. We do not have to believe that Chaucer was suffering the extremes of unrequited love in actual fact; but we may well suppose that his neglect to present himself in attitudes of abject self-abasement and vermiform humility is a touch of self-definition regarding the love-conventions; and we may read our knowledge of him into the statement that he got more pleasure out of reading than out of backgammon or chess.

The question of identity becomes most acute where it touches Chaucer's relations with John of Gaunt, both within and without the poem. As John of Gaunt, the Man in Black raises delicate considerations with regard to the deportment of the Dreamer as Geoffrey Chaucer. Hitherto, we have been able to limit discussion to the fictive aspects of the two characters. But Chaucer cannot afford to forget that he is dealing with a most sensitive area in his patron's personal life. When we look at the poem as his solution of this human problem, our admiration for the poet's tact and wisdom is greatly increased; and our sense of his artistic skill is much heightened.

Concerning the stroke of genius that prompted Chaucer to put the eulogy into the mouth of the bereaved man, Kittredge has spoken with shrewd appreciation, and of the major artistic contribution which thereby ensues:

> The substance of the elegy, by this adjustment, is spoken by the lady's husband, who can best describe her beauty, her charm of manner, and all her gracious qualities of mind and heart. Thus we have in the **Book of the Duchess,** not a prostrate and anxiously rhetorical obituary, from the blazoning pen of a commissioned laureate, but a tribute of pure love from the lady's equal, who can speak without constraint,—from her husband, who has most cause to mourn as he has the best knowledge of what he has lost. [And again:] The mourning knight is not describing his lady: he is giving voice to his unstudied recollection—now of her nature, now of her beauty, now of her demeanor, now of her speech—spasmodically, in no order, as this or that idea rises in his agitated mind.

Little more need be said. It is worth noticing, however, that there is a special propriety about the charming portrait of Blanche. Although she is described, ostensibly, by her husband, it is actually the poet who has to find the terms in which she is to be described. Chaucer has the problem far more difficult than penning a simple eulogy, of imagining what a husband might say of his deceased wife, and expressing it in such a way as may be neither too intimate nor too reserved and cold. Thus, he really has to speak simultaneously for Gaunt and for himself, to find the precise point at which the husband and the friend may unite in expressive agreement. If Chaucer was the immature artist the critics have usually found him in this poem, he had surely tackled a problem of the last degree of difficulty, both artistic and human. He solves it with a skill and tact beyond praise. The materials employed are nearly all such as could be compiled and uttered by an interested observer who had had opportunity of watching the lady's appearance and bearing and ordinary conduct over a space of time. The elements are objective and external, conventional in kind and expression, the inner qualities being suggested in terms so general that they seem more a statement of the observer's faith, an act of devotion, than a private and intimate portrait. There is no charge of presumption that can be laid against the poet; and yet he has also cast a glow of genuine emotion over the whole picture, partly through its very hyperbole, partly through the disconnected manner of its delivery, which makes it seem the true language of recent bereavement. In its sensitive awareness, its manipulation of literary as well as psychological components, its modulations of tone between reticence and confidence, it is a triumph of controlled artistic intention. C. S. Lewis [in his *The Allegory of Love*] has caught better than any other critic the prevailing mood that it succeeds in establishing: "How fine and fresh

(Chaucer's) treatment is," writes Lewis, "may be judged from the very remarkable fact that though the poem is a true elegy, yet the abiding impression it leaves upon us is one of health and happiness . . . Not because the poem is a bad elegy, but because it is a good one, the black background of death is always disappearing behind these irridescent shapes of satisfied love." In truth, the poet comes not to bury Blanche, but to praise her.

He comes also to offer consolation to the bereaved. And in this aspect of his poem he exhibits possibly his supreme artistry and greatest human wisdom. The poem ends, some critics have felt, too abruptly. "Is that youre los?" asks the Dreamer. "Be God, hyt ys routhe!" It is the last word in the long interchange between himself and the knight. To some it has seemed lame and impotent for a man who earlier gave hopes of so much more comfort.

> But certes, sire, yif that yee
> Wolde ought discure me youre woo,
> I wolde, as wys God helpe me soo,
> Amende hyt, yif I kan or may.
> Ye mowe preve hyt be assay;
> For, by my trouthe, to make yow hool,
> I wol do al my power hool.

But, apart from the fact that sympathy is the only effective kind of help that can be offered directly in the face of bereavement, Chaucer has been offering indirect consolation from the very commencement, and this is one of the unifying elements of his poem. He well knew that the best advice in the world would be inappropriate when served up to his patron as the last word in such a conversation, on such a topic. It would be socially impudent and out of place, as well as ineffectual; also, and inevitably, inartistic. Yet he does have something to convey, if he can, to his grieving friend. And his lesson is the age-old one of resignation and human acceptance of life and death, of thankfulness for past felicity, of the comfort of precious memories, of the dignity of self-mastery in spite of Fortune's "false draughtes dyvers."

At the very opening of his poem, he has sounded the note of resigned acceptance that contains its deepest meaning. "But that is don," he says of his own case: "that wil not be mot nede be left." This truth will be more evident for the knight in the sequel. Here is a foreshadowing: but the fullest statement is the conclusion of the Alcyone episode, where Chaucer conveys by anticipation the human lesson for his patron which he is unable to express at the end directly. Indeed, this is the most important function of the episode, and that which effectually integrates the work when looked at from a formal point of view. The true conclusion has had to be thrown forward from the end to an inconspicuous point where it can insinuate its meaning unobtrusively and without risk of antagonizing, carried as it is not by the poet but by a third spokesman, the figure of Ceyx. Here is the message, put with exquisite and simple beauty, a message from all dead lovers to their bereaved loves, a tender voice from the grave:

> Awake! let be your sorwful lyf!
> For in your sorwe there lyth no red.
> For, certes, swete, I nam but ded:
> Ye shul me never on lyve ysee . . .

And farewel, swete, my worldes blysse!
I praye God youre sorwe lysse.
To lytel while oure blysse lasteth!

"My worldes blysse": It is hardly accidental that the phrase is almost identical with the one that the knight is later to use of his own love:—"al my blesse, My worldes welfare, and my goddesse." The verbal echoes, the carry-over of phrase and idea from one part of the poem to another, the inner harmonies, subtly communicate the underlying relation between its parts, binding it in ways all too frequently ignored. The elements of the work come together and are fused at a level of experience, human and artistic, where likeness melts into a closer unity, and where, in the presence of death, Ceyx and Blanche, Gaunt and Alcyone, the Dreamer and Chaucer and his audience, too, of which we now form a part, are become essentially one. (pp. 863-81)

Bertrand H. Bronson, "'The Book of the Duchess' Re-Opened," in PMLA, *Vol. LXVII, No. 5, September, 1952, pp. 863-81.*

D. S. Brewer   (essay date 1960)

[*Brewer is a prominent English Chaucerian scholar whose works include* Chaucer *(1953),* Chaucer in His Time *(1964), and* An Introduction to Chaucer *(1984). He has also edited* The Parlement of Foules *(1960),* Thomas Malory's *The Morte d'Arthur: Parts Seven and Eight* (1968), *and* Troilus and Croeseyde *(1969). Below, Brewer offers an interpretation of the* Parlement of Foules, *shedding light on the interplay of themes and motifs and providing an explanation of Chaucer's conception of love.*]

In **The Parlement of Foulys** the variety of tone, the brightness of description, the vivid realism of the birds' debate, which are instantly attractive, are matched by the rich significances and subtle complexities of mood which lie beneath the surface of the poem. It appeals on several levels, and is the best of Chaucer's shorter pieces. Yet appreciation of it has varied. It was popular in the fifteenth and sixteenth centuries; among poets Shakespeare echoes it several times, and Spenser partly owes to it the greatness of the "Mutabilitie Cantos." In the eighteenth century it was less regarded, and in the nineteenth and early twentieth centuries it has come to be treated more and more as a historical document, weighed down under a mass of speculation about the identity of the suitors. Only recently has interest in the whole poem, as poetry, revived. A new flexibility in our expectation of what poetry may be, a new assertion of the relevance of medieval poetry, have made it easier for the 'common reader' to submit himself to the controlling power of Chaucer's imagination in a poem that is more unusual than it looks. More information about medieval life and literature has buttressed our new willingness to treat Chaucer as a great poet rather than a great joker. Readers are now in a better position to understand and appreciate Chaucer's artistic purposes than they have been for a couple of centuries. (p. 1)

The variety in the **Parlement** is characteristic of Chaucer and indeed of very much medieval poetry. But in this poem the variety is crucial. There is a brief account of The Dream of Scipio, which touches on heaven, earth, and hell; then the poet wanders in a timeless fertile park, sees gay Cupid, and lustful Venus in her beautiful temple where there is so much suffering; then he sees the surpassing beauty of benevolent, creative Nature, and hears the debate of diverse opinionated birds. All this is in some way concerned with the question of love, but from the conjunction of such various elements spring contradictions. This is the essence of the poem—the existence of a variety of apparently contradictory thoughts and attitudes about love (concretely or dramatically described for the most part), which puzzles the poet and yet brings him delight. At least a partial reconciliation is implicit in the figure of Nature, and the poem ends, if still questioningly, on a note of optimism.

The manner is as important as the matter, and varies accordingly. The style suits the immediate subject equally in the rather plain summary of The Dream of Scipio with its steady onward movement; in the fertile proliferation of names and the livelier metre of the description of the park; in the statelier movement and richer decoration of the descriptions of Cupid and Venus; in the courtly (though not stiff or stilted) diction of the noble birds; and in the livelier cackle of the vulgar birds. The contrasts in style are part of the piquancy of the poem.

For all the variety and the dramatic colouring of some of the speeches the manner is very personal to Chaucer. In this poem he finds for perhaps the first time his characteristic tone, his full range of meaning and richness of implication, combined with his own unique and apparently simple directness. Even after nearly six hundred years the speaking voice comes off the page with its own recognisable personal note. It has a calm assurance, an unforced certainty, a strength and ease and flexibility, which make it seem not only natural but even casual.

The ease and variety are part of the lightness of manner which is important in the poem. The lightness of manner is, like much else in the poem, the product of the sense of piquant contrasts in life.

> Git that thow canst not do, git mayst thow se.
> For manye a man that may nat stonde a pulle,
> Git likyth hym at wrastelyng for to be,
> And demyn git wher he do bet or he.

This is a note struck at the very beginning of the poem:

> I dar nat seyn, 'his strokis been so sore',
> But, 'God save swich a lord'—I sey na moore.

We cannot dissociate manner from matter here, but the dexterity with which the mere tag 'I say no more' is employed to suggest unspoken *nuances* of meaning is an excellent example of colloquial ease and delicacy of touch. This is not to say, however, that the poem is in any way frivolous or flippant in tone. Many passages, if not most, are perfectly serious.

The lightness of tone cannot be dissociated from the simplicity and freshness which everyone notices as one of Chaucer's most obvious characteristics. These qualities, dispersed throughout the poem, come out strikingly in the pure spontaneous joy of such a line as:

> But Lord, so I was glad & wel begoon!

This is delightfully direct and unaffected, as easy to appreciate now as when it was first written. Some of Chaucer's marvellous freshness it is however more difficult for us to appreciate than it was for Chaucer's first audience. In vocabulary, for instance, it is clear that he often used words which were then fresh to the language, though they are not now. He probably did not actually introduce many new words, but he was never afraid of a neologism, and his early critics and followers all praised him for it. Again, his metre was entirely novel, though its novelty was softened for English ears by being based on a familiar feeling for stress. . . . Such a combination of old and new is found everywhere in the poem. One may say, by a simplification which only partly distorts, that while the matter is old, the manner is new. But of course one must add that what is old is given a new twist, and what is new is carefully grafted on to the old. Chaucer was profoundly original and a great innovator; but he worked within the tradition, and was no revolutionary.

All this should suggest that however we may enjoy the freshness and simplicity of much of Chaucer's manner, it is not always as simple as it seems. The freshness, simplicity, and directness are truly there, but they spring from a mind which also shows itself subtle and sophisticated to a degree. It is at home with abstract ideas and is of rather a philosophical cast; and yet is also intensely sensitive to words, and trained to use them in a highly elaborate rhetorical tradition. In the first two stanzas of the *Parlement,* for example, the repetitions, ambiguities, and interjections, all of which have a personal tone and an easy colloquial force, are also figures of rhetoric, deliberately and artfully deployed. . . . Fresh and simple Chaucer may be, at the appropriate time; but there was never a poet less simpleminded.

The mixture of subtlety and simplicity is yet another of the sets of contrasting elements which are at the heart of the poem, and which by their very presence set each other off, and also modify any tendency to extremes. Even the goddess Nature includes within herself something of this sense of opposites, though in her they are reconciled. She is both divine and homely, uniting in herself heaven and earth in easy harmony, yet not glossing over the contradictions inherent in earthly life. She is, in all her complexity and yet simplicity, the dominant image of the poem, and fit symbol indeed for Chaucer's whole poetic achievement.

The method Chaucer follows in the *Parlement* is to lay side by side, as it were, different attitudes to or aspects of love, in such a way as to arouse an implicit or explicit questioning. But the reader is left to draw his own conclusions. The connecting thread between the various sections is partly the poet's own questioning wonder. On first acquaintance the form has a certain dream-like arbitrariness; but this soon resolves itself into the deeper, more suggestive symbolic coherence which can also be the property of dreams, and which is of the essence of the world of the poetic imagination. The poem is governed by what T. S.

Eliot has called 'the logic of the imagination', as contrasted with 'the logic of concepts'.

The first two stanzas are a prologue, in which love is described as a lord of miracles indeed, but also of 'cruel ire'; the pains he gives are great, the joys anxious and transitory. This is a description of love that is hardly friendly; but the confession of Love's supreme power, and the poet's rueful allegiance to him—'God save swich a lord!'—shows him to be a follower of Love, while the tone is lightened with just a touch of half-comic regret. The poet's attitude is complex, with a hint of delicate ironic humour. A sense of opposites, and of tension between them, important throughout the poem, is established in these opening stanzas in both thought and style.

The third stanza changes the style to smoother narrative with the description of the poet's reading habits. He says he reads 'a certeyn thing to lerne'. What the certain thing is, we are never told in so many words. It may be rationalised as 'the nature of love', but it is wrong to press the phrase too hard for its conceptual content. The phrase develops the note of bewilderment in the first two stanzas into a note of inquiry. The poem is to be as it were a quest, with the very subject of the quest precise yet inexplicable—or rather, the whole poem is the explanation. This fourth stanza merges into the first main section of the poem, the summary of the Dream of Scipio, which has as its chief function the suggestion of the 'philosophical' penumbra within which the brighter, more obviously entertaining part of the poem will function. The Dream of Scipio in Chaucer's summary is a survey of heaven and earth in which the triviality, deceptiveness, and harshness of the world in comparison with heaven is emphasised. The poet says he read the book with eagerness, but finished it with disappointment. The trouble with the Dream of Scipio is that it takes no account of the value of the world as God's creation, a creation which, according to medieval thought, sprang from, and was continuously maintained by, God's regulating love. To put it briefly, there is nothing about Nature or love in the Dream of Scipio. There is thus no feeling of release. The poet tells the story of the Dream of Scipio with interest and wonder, but also with a sense of frustration at the end. It is as if the poet can neither agree nor disagree with his authority. The account of the world given in the Dream of Scipio dissatisfies him; not because it is wrong but because it is incomplete.

It may perhaps be asked, what is the Dream of Scipio doing here at all, since it has nothing to say of the chief subject of the poem? The answer must be sought in 'the logic of the imagination'. The Dream of Scipio in brief compass surveys the whole extent of heaven, earth, and indeed hell. It is concerned with the good life, in service of the 'common profit'. It mentions the punishment of the lustful. It is, in brief, a total statement of a point of view that was often dominant in the medieval theory of life— the need to despise the world, and seek only heaven. Any general questioning of the nature of love in the Middle Ages was bound to take into account the ultimate human destiny of heaven or hell, and the total scheme of the universe. Chaucer, writing a poem that must first be entertainment, would not have wished, even if he had felt himself competent, to delve deep into theological matters. But the Dream of Scipio, itself in the form of a story, enabled him to suggest weighty ultimate considerations without overemphasising them, and so capsizing his poem with their weight. There was also another reason. The Dream of Scipio, as incorporated in Macrobius' *Commentary* (cf. **Romaunt,**)), was part of a recognised authority on the truth of certain kinds of dreams. Chaucer uses this authority implicitly to introduce his own dream.

At the end of the Dream of Scipio, in making the transition to the next main section, the poet renews the note of doubt and seeking: he has what he does not want, and has not what he wants. He has Cicero's teaching in the Dream, but has no word of love.

The poet falls asleep and dreams. In his dream his guide is the same as the guide in Scipio's dream. So Chaucer in 'the logic of the imagination' connects the new material of experience with the old material of authority, and the old authority shelters the new experience—not that in the poet's dream there is no use of books, but that everything has a clear relation to experienced life. The poet's dream has a fresh immediacy, contrasting with the reported material of the Dream of Scipio. The development and the change of tempo are marked by the invocation to Cytherea, i.e. under a personification, to the planet Venus, which was thought in sober truth to control fertility, friendship, and love, and also to confer learning and eloquence. Venus is a very suitable planet to be invoked for such a poem as the *Parlement* (the planet is not to be confused with the 'mythological Venus' described a little later).

In his dream the poet is immediately carried to the double gate, with its double message of hope and disaster. The ambivalence here echoes the ambivalence of love in the first two stanzas, and is also a foretaste of more ambivalence of love to come. With this passage the theme of love's ambivalence is repeated and the note of doubt and questioning is sounded again. As in the first two stanzas we are prevented from taking the doubt too sombrely; this time the lightening of tone is achieved by the guide's assurance that no part of the message applies to the poet, who is but a dull fellow. Then for the first time, selfish concern firmly and humorously abandoned, joy comes with the bright, positive description of the park and garden, which is the next main section of the poem—a refreshing contrast to the austerity of the Dream of Scipio. Here nothing is passive or flaccid. The very list of trees is given life and force by the attributes of human usefulness attached to each. And these attributes help also to keep the passage centred on human activity even in natural description. So the passage merges naturally into the description of Cupid and his followers, which itself leads us to the description of Venus and her temple.

The Cupid-and-Venus passage is the next section in the poem, and contrasts with the previous section, as that had contrasted with its predecessor. For though Cupid is surrounded by in the main pleasant qualities, and may be taken as representing fashionable love affairs, some of the qualities about him are evil and treacherous; through Cupid we are led to the miseries and calamities of the temple, with its gross phallic image of Priapus, and the titillat-

ing picture of the all-but-naked Venus. The temple is a hot-house of illicit sensuality; the walls tell stories of disastrous passion, 'withered stumps of time', though there is beauty too. From this hot and spicy atmosphere the poet walks forth to comfort himself with the green freshness of the park. He does not comment on the feelings the place arouses. There is no need; it tells its own tale of love. But his need for comfort here renews the undertone of uneasy doubt and inquiry which had faded in his first contemplation of the park.

In immediate and contrasting juxtaposition the sunlike beauty of Nature eclipses the star of Venus, and all else. Here we enter the last and major section of the poem, the debate of the birds under Nature. Nature is the 'vicar', the deputy, of 'the almighty Lord'. She represents the created energies of the universe, especially those of reproduction, and she also represents, in herself, and through the birds under her care, the beauty, fulness, and orderliness of the creation.

All the birds are met to carry out Nature's will: to choose their mates and to breed. The noble birds are to choose first, and the three noblest all make their claim for the same beautiful formel. The poet expresses his admiration of the speeches of these suitors, but in effect the questions in the poet's mind, felt earlier in his doubt and dissatisfaction and inquiry, are now dramatically expressed in the diverse attitudes of the various other birds to this question of love. At the same time, Nature herself, with her approval of the birds, or of some of them, is at least a partial answer to the earlier dilemma and bewilderment. The complex image of Nature, and the speeches of the birds, contrast with and implicitly correct the wrongful, selfish, and barren sensuality of the temple of Venus; Nature complements and crowns the full, positive image of the park; and she supplements the view of life represented by the Dream of Scipio. At the same time the debate of the birds continues to explore and portray the subtle complexities and conflicts within human love, especially in the relation of *fine amour* to the general necessities of life and of everyday existence.

The birds stand here as representatives of all living species, but especially of mankind. They compose a hierarchy of worth comparable to, though not exactly matching, that of fourteenth-century society, with the hawks and eagles highest, representing the highest, knightly class, and the other groups of birds lower in the scale. Nature, the vicar of God, whose word is law, endorses this hierarchy, and the most worthy birds have the right to choose their mates first. In the mating the initiative 'naturally' rests with the male, but the female has an equal right to refuse his choice. Nature does not deny free will, nor does she constrain love.

Nature stimulates the birds to their duty of procreation by legitimate and natural pleasure. Such pleasure, and its aim, implanted by God's own design, are the elements left out of the Dream of Scipio and found distorted to selfish evil ends in the temple of Venus.

Within this generally satisfactory situation, however, there is still a problem. When the three suitors, vowing eternal fidelity, claim the same mate, they are doing more than merely claim a mate; they express love in the highest, most refined form known to the fourteenth century, *fine amour.* It is necessary to emphasise the noble quality of their love, because it is somewhat different from modern forms, and is therefore sometimes misunderstood. All that is necessary, however, is to take the statements of the suitors at their face value, as accepted by Nature, and as required by the context of the poem. There is no need to look for irony where no hint of it exists. The suitors, by Nature's own decree, are the most worthy of the birds. Each seeks the beloved entirely as his own. There is no indication that their love is against Nature's law, or that it is in any way guilty or immoral. Not even the lower birds, sharp enough critics, dream of its being so. The suitors are simply expressing *fine amour* as understood in dozens of fourteenth-century love poems, and there is no suggestion on any one's part that their love is not genuine and in accordance with Nature's law. The poet in all seriousness greatly admires their noble pleading. The lower birds, however, naturally become impatient. They are too coarse and ignorant to appreciate noble eloquence and fine feeling. To the poet their noise is 'lewedenesse'. But though the poet has a somewhat Shakespearean contempt for the vulgar crowd, he has an equally Shakespearean capacity to present them with humorous toleration. Unrefined they may be, but they have their rights, among which is a right to Nature's ear, and our sympathy. The attitude towards them is not simple.

The superficial problem. . . . has been presented in such a way as to make its solution obvious, granted that the formel is to choose any one at all. But the real interest of the debate is not in the immediate problem, which none of the lower birds discusses (no doubt their irrelevance has its point as a dramatic comment on their ignorance of *fine amour*). What they really discuss is a more fundamental problem, to do with the nature of *fine amour* itself when confronted with the actualities of life. It is clear that if three suitors love the same person, at least two of them must be rejected. Yet they have vowed everlasting love. What shall they do? All the possible solutions to this problem are offered by the lower birds. The solutions are presented dramatically, mostly in terms of impatient, cynical, selfish criticism, such as we should expect from the lower orders. Yet they also show all the reasonable, or at least possible, ways out of the dilemma. The goose says, let the rejected lover love another (as if our feelings were in our own control, and as if it were honourable to go back on one's word). The turtle-dove says, let the rejected lover remain for ever faithful. The duck jeers, and repeats in substance the goose's advice. The cuckoo says, let them *all* remain single.

Neither goose, duck, nor cuckoo are good spokesmen for sense, natural delicacy of feeling, nor honour. We are not expected to admire them. Yet one is bound to have sympathy for what they feel. In truth, doubt or even scepticism about hopeless loyalty in love carried to the length of a life-time's devotion are bound to have a place in every man's mind, ancient or modern, high or low. Pandarus expresses them in the *Troilus,* and Malory makes Dinadan in the *Morte Darthur* express them again. It is important

that they should be expressed. Such lack of fine feeling may well be useful and necessary in certain men, perhaps in most.

But there is no certainty that Chaucer or Malory agreed that such unchivalrous attitudes were proper for their *noble* protagonists—for Troilus, or Launcelot, or for the suitors in the *Parlement.* Indeed, the probabilities are all the other way. To think that Chaucer approves wholeheartedly of the 'perfect reason of a goose' is as if we were to think that Shakespeare was in wholehearted agreement with Falstaff's view on honour. It is impossible to imagine such a thing. That does not deny some truth in what Falstaff says: in some cases a live dog is better than a dead lion. Nor need we deny truth and good sense to some of what the duck and goose have to say (the cuckoo is beyond the pale). It is perhaps natural for modern feelings, untrained in the refined exaltations and ardours of *fine amour,* to respond more easily to the expression of the untutored reflexes of daily life than it was for Chaucer and for the courtly audience for whom the *Parlement* was first written. But certainly the piquancy in this final, rich section of the *Parlement* lies in the residuum of good sense expressed by the coarser birds. It is this residuum of good sense which helps to maintain the delicate ambivalence which is of the essence of the poem.

Nevertheless, it is also clear that the balance of sympathy in the poem is on the whole in favour of the noble birds against the vulgar; in favour also of the loyalty which was essential to *fine amour,* and of which the most explicit spokesman is one of the lower birds themselves, the modest and well-behaved turtle-dove. To remain chaste and faithful did not seem so impossible an ideal in the fourteenth century as it does to some critics who speak on the goose's side in the twentieth. In the 'scale of Nature' in which the graded perfection of the created universe was held to exist, there was a place for chastity as well as for marriage. It was a higher place, a nobler state. Marriage was good, but chastity was better. Chaucer could assume that his audience would naturally believe this commonplace idea. And so divine Nature encourages all three of the tercels, at the end of the inconclusive debate, to continue to 'serve', that is, to love with *fine amour,* for yet another year. Who will actually win the formel is not, in fact, particularly important; the expected solution to the ostensible problem is offered, but it is postponed, and no-one has surely felt in any distress to know the outcome. It is the question about love which is of interest, not the fate of any individuals, for the poem is not about individuals.

For this latter reason we need not concern ourselves with the formel's feelings and motives. The lady's attitude to a lover was conventionally and properly remote. The formel's reluctance to be married is paralleled by that of Emily in **"The Knight's Tale,"** or by Criseyde's immediate response to Troilus's first advances. Like Virginia (in **"The Physician's Tale"**), who is also a prime work of Nature, the formel is not yet ready for love. Her reluctance to choose a suitor is of course the necessary premise of the whole debate.

The debate is concluded with the joyous song of the little birds, so far unregarded, in honour of Nature. This delightful roundel creates a feeling of relief and happy enlargement, a feeling of new life warming old winter's bones, of the world stirring anew with perennial joy. The song corresponds rather to the feelings of joy and loving respect aroused by the contemplation of Nature than to any logical solution of the original problem. We feel 'the agreement of things bound together by the love that governs earth and sea and heaven', even if such love with difficulty binds the hearts of men.

The final stanza of the poem is an epilogue in which the poet, wakened by the joyful song of the birds, turns with refreshed spirit to renew his quest with hope. His implicit questions have not been finally answered. But in the 'logic of the imagination', in the symbolic world of sleep and poetry, the joyous song of the departing birds, happy in the satisfaction of their own modest demands and in their delight in Nature, gives a feeling of release and reassurance, and the final words of the poem are themselves optimistic. Nothing has been resolved—ordinary logic is defeated or unimportant—but we are aware of a completed structure, of opposites balanced if not entirely reconciled. A complex whole of related thoughts, feelings, and experiences has been created, as in some small but elaborate medieval church, not quite symmetrical, but not meant to be, where arch meets springing arch, where a painted side-chapel leads off from the main chancel but is subsidiary and supporting to it, where there is a place for many things in an organised whole, and where are recognised the claims of both heaven and earth. (pp. 13-25)

> *D. S. Brewer, in an introduction to* The Parliment of Foulys *by Geoffrey Chaucer, 1960. Reprint by Manchester University Press, 1972, pp. 1-64.*

Eric W. Stockton   (essay date 1961)

[*In the following excerpt, Stockton praises the "Pardoner's Tale" as an imaginative, suggestive, and poetically wrought sermon on pride.*]

Chaucer's **"Pardoner's Tale,"** which has more than once been called "the best short story in existence," embodies a plot so serviceable that it is still in use. Witness its fairly recent adaptation, for example, in B. Traven's *The Treasure of Sierra Madre,* which makes use of basically the same story quite effectively, both as a novel and a film. **"The Pardoner's Tale"** itself continues to hold extraordinary fascination today, which is no surprise in that the Pardoner himself embodies Chaucer's closest approximation to the Dostoyevskian double man, and in that the tale itself uses something of Faulkner's "cracked lens" technique. All the while the tale remains highly readable. Its ostensible moral, too, that "money is the root of all evil," is as applicable today as in the Middle Ages, when avarice was "the besetting sin." Yet money is not the root of *all* evil. As Melville asks in *The Confidence Man,* "How much money did the Devil make in gulling Eve?" I suggest that pride, the deadliest of the seven deadlies, is the true theme of the tale. "Chaucer, like all great story-tellers, is easy to read rapidly, but when closely examined, he is a difficult writer, sometimes extraordinarily subtle. . . . "

Chaucer hid his deepest meaning, just as death was hidden in the gold the revelers find in the tale.

The psychology of the Pardoner himself has perhaps gotten in the way of the task of interpreting his story's meaning. This is indeed an age of psychology. Fascinating as his psyche remains, however, it is necessary to summarize him here psychoanalytically as a manic depressive with traces of anal eroticism, and a pervert with a tendency toward alcoholism. "Good" as he is as a character, his tale is even better, and it emerges as the clearest revelation of the man's true character. No one but the Pardoner (and Chaucer!) could have told it.

[It is my contention] that the deepest symbolic meaning of the tale shows its three revelers guilty chiefly of *superbia,* pride in its most Satanic form. They blasphemously wish to usurp the role of Christ Himself. This crime far outweighs their other sins, though of these they have plenty: they of course covet money, they associate with loose women in the tavern, they yearn gluttonously for food and drink, they are wrathful toward the Old Man, they envy each other's share of gold, they are tavern-loafers and drunks, and they lie and murder. Far worse than all these sins, however, is their diabolical presumption: just as Satan wished to be second to none, so these three revelers presume, albeit unwittingly, to supplant Christ in His role of killing Death. The story, masterfully told, points up this "moral" in several ways, most notably in the close relationship between the "Homily on the Sins of the Tavern" and the old folktale, "The Robbers and the Treasure Trove."

The Pardoner is asked to tell a story, but first he launches forth into a prologue which tells, among other things, how he *would* preach a sermon if he were preaching. The tale which follows is a sort of demonstration sermon. What truly unifies the **"Pardoner's Prologue"** and [the **"Pardoner's Tale"**] is, in addition to the self-revelation of his character, the fact that both prologue and tale together constitute a sermon-parable on the theme of damnation. The artistic unity of the work centers about this thematic meaning. The story has something of the fable about it, and "The best fiction, at its heart, always is (a fable), of course. . . . " Much in the work points to this inner meaning, while the story also exists for its own sake. The structural bonds between prologue and tale are homiletic and characterizing. The entire prologue and tale operates on two levels simultaneously: the prologue is a boastful self-revelation which establishes the teller's character; it also contains the first two parts of a medieval sermon framework: 1) announcement of theme; and 2) pro-theme or dilatation. These two sermon parts are imbedded in the personal boasting of the Pardoner about his ability as a preacher and his wickedness.

Part 3, the *divisiones* of a sermon, traditionally divided the theme into three divisions or sub-topics. Before beginning Part 3, however, the Pardoner, who is reminded by a restless audience that he is supposed to be telling a tale and not preaching a sermon, makes an attempt to begin a story. These lines . . . constitute what have long been called the "Homily on the Sins of the Tavern." We do not, however, have a separate homily here, but rather the three-fold divisions of the theme of avarice, which are gluttony (including drinking), gambling, and swearing. The fourth major part of this sermon is the major exemplum, the folktale of "The Robbers and the Treasure Trove."

After the major exemplum, which is the tale proper, we have the last two parts of a typical medieval sermon framework: 5) the peroration or application and 6) closing formula. Of these parts, more later. Important . . . is the suggestion that Part 3 (the *divisiones*) furnishes a valuable and essential commentary on Part 4, the major exemplum, which cannot be interpreted fully without it. All six parts of the sermon, indeed, together with their epilogue, form a highly unified and sophisticated work of art, one of mixed genres: self-revelation and demonstration sermon. It will be well to examine at this point the superbly-told tale proper or major exemplum.

The narrative begins with "whilom," the Middle English equivalent of "once upon a time," so the story is timeless. In twenty lines Chaucer sets the scene for the start of the story proper in a tavern or "develes temple." The Pardoner speaks of a "compaignye of yonge folk" generally, not of any three in particular. The young people revel in gambling, drinking, and wenching, and are cursing all the while, as they indulge in their "superfluitee abhomynable." As is well-known, there was a popular belief in the Middle Ages that an oath caused another wound in the body of Christ—a belief used by clerics to discourage swearing (cf. **"Parson's Tale"**). But the revelers are directly intent upon damnation: they deliberately swear because they do not think that the Jews wounded Christ sufficiently. This hell-bent, anti-Christ attitude characterizes them throughout the story.

In his thoughts on their pub-crawling the Pardoner makes an easy and natural transition from his major exemplum, Part 4 of his sermon, back to Part 3, the *divisiones* of the theme:

> The hooly writ take I to my witnesse
> That luxurie is in wyn and dronkennesse.

The Pardoner is so habituated to his usual sermon framework that he cannot escape falling back into it. It is too early in his "sermon" for the major exemplum he has just commenced, which would ordinarily come fourth, just after the *divisiones* of the theme. He therefore digresses, so far as story-telling is concerned, to take up the three *divisiones* of his theme of avarice, which are gluttony (including drunkenness), gambling, and swearing. Or to put it differently, if the Pardoner's tale were only that and nothing more, and not a demonstration sermon, the three *divisiones* would constitute a digression; as it is, the twenty lines which make a false start to begin the tale proper constitute a delaying of the expected *divisiones*. These, however, furnish a basic clue to the meaning of the story.

The Pardoner is medieval, and the Middle Ages usually loved digressions, the more and longer the better. But Chaucer is always the artist who can make a convention, in this case use of digression, serve him, rather than being its slave. The seeming digression from story-telling to sermon indicates that the Pardoner is not quite sure just what he is attempting to do, preach or narrate. The Pardoner *thinks* he is bright, that he is far superior to his audience, but pride is always of limited perception.

In the three parts or divisions, he carefully sets apart one topic from the others by transitions. The first of these is:

> And now that I have spoken of gluttonye,
> Now wol I yow deffenden hasardrye.

The second transition is similarly clear: "Now I wol speke of othes fals and grete." The third division (or third part of the digression), that on swearing, concludes with a firm psychological bridge back to the story proper, in which oaths are of crucial importance. In other words, the transitions are carefully planned, and the next is the finest of all: "Thise riotoures three of which I telle." There has been no mention of *three* rioters in particular, however, but only of a crowd of young people. The Pardoner has departed so long from his story (for some 174 lines) that he has forgotten where he left off. Chaucer has not. He is sure who is rambling, and aware of the ironic contrast of carefully modulated transitions in the midst of a digression which has no place in the story's plot in the first place.

The Pardoner begins his tale almost anew, with an incisive scene of thirty-one lines, a scene which has elicited little comment but which deserves scrutiny. The three revelers are in the tavern, drunk already before 9 a.m. Or, if they are not drunk, they have already achieved their loquacious and quarrelsome state while partly sober (as has the Pardoner himself). Evil as deep-dyed as theirs should not be attributed to temporary inebriation. They themselves are under the misapprehension that their minds are functioning; but the marvelous economy of proportion in the scene, here as elsewhere in the tale (most notably in . . . the scene with the Old Man), reveals the helter-skelter nature of their thinking. One reveler, browbeating a bit, asks his servant boy to make inquiry about the identity of a corpse which is passing by in a funeral procession. But there is no need to send for whom the funeral bell tolls: the boy knows that it was an old companion of his master's, one who was slain last night by a sneaking thief called Death. And Death is one "That in this contree al the peple sleeth." (The use of the plague as background for the tale is original with Chaucer, and is perfect.) The master receives this news about the existence of Death as brand-new information—this after asking about a corpse! The reveling master's mind obviously suffers from deep corruption.

It is worth pausing a moment to characterize the boy. He is one—perhaps the only one—of the children in Chaucer who are life-like, notwithstanding his brief fictional role. Usually, Chaucer's youngsters, whether babes in arms such as Constance's infant son in the **"Man of Law's Tale,"** Ugolino of Pisa's little starvelings in the **"Monk's Tale,"** or the little "clergeoun" of the **"Prioress' Tale,"** are unbearably pathetic. The fact that the boy (as well as the tavern-keeper and the apothecary) possesses at least a modicum of character serves to heighten in contrast the revelers, who in a sense have none. Evil has obliterated their individual natures to the point that they are naught but cunning animals. None earns a name to call his own, none stops to ask the name of the dead man, though the bare fact of his death sends them into a passion. The taverner confirms the lad's reply and repeats his warning, both of which warnings prefigure that of the Old Man.

Rashly disregarding these warnings, the three drunken "riotoures" rush from the tavern in a rage to search out Death and kill him, all the while swearing and thereby wounding Christ. The pace of the story and its immediacy are furthered by the style's breaking out into direct discourse: "Deeth shal be deed, if that they may hym hente!"

"Whan they had goon not fully half a mile," they find "an oold man and a povre." As in the tavern scene, brevity is the soul of the tale. The Old Man is seen for only fifty-four lines. Chaucer here accomplishes an enormous amount in almost no time. This enigmatic figure, who has been exhaustively studied, has been made out to be the Wandering Jew, a hermit or Christian angel (as in several analogues to this tale), and Death himself. He has something of all of these and is therefore more than any one of them. With unerring feeling for "negative capability" Chaucer leaves the Old Man unlabeled and indeterminate, and hence the more universal, the more palpable, as mysterious and true as life itself. The three revelers, however, are sheer evil, and therefore cannot recognize his Christian goodness. They threaten him until he tells them where Death is: down a crooked way to a grove and there under an oak. The symbolism of the setting is mixed, as are the rational powers of the revelers. There is no great difficulty in viewing the wood as an age-old symbol of worldliness and confusion, as in the opening scene of *The Divine Comedy*. The way to it is "croked." The pleasant word *grove* shows the temporary pleasure of worldly evil. The oak, an inevitable fixture of the old folktale, once was sacred to Jove, and its function here is still godly.

The whole tale proceeds in staccato, nervously paced scenes. The first of the two pivotal scenes at the foot of the oak is very short—sixty-eight lines. Upon seeing the eight bushels of gold under the oak, the three men run thither. Indeed, the three run everywhere in this story, including to their doom; and they often run singly, as here. Despite their oaths of brotherhood, they are never united except in evil and death. Their separateness is always apparent.

The structuralism of the oaths in the story has not, to my knowledge, been examined. The Pardoner has entered into the development of his story's plot just after a long stricture against "othes fals and grete," that is, false oaths or perjury and great oaths or blasphemy, both of which kinds of oaths are central in the story. The two kinds of oaths are hateful to God, and are condemned in the Old Testament, as quoted by the Pardoner. The first reveler begins the oaths back in the tavern:

> "Ye, Goddes armes!" quod this riotour,
> "Is it swich peril with hym for to meete?
> I shal hym seke by wey and eek by strete,
> I make avow to Goddes digne bones!
> Herkneth, felawes, we thre been al ones;
> Lat ech of us holde up his hand til oother,
> And ech of us bicomen otheres brother,
> And we wol sleen this false traytour Deeth.
> He shal be slayn, he that so manye sleeth,
> By Goddes dignitee, er it be nyght!"

There are three "grete" oaths here: "Goddes armes," "Goddes digne bones," and "Goddes dignitee." There is also the outrageously false oath of sworn brotherhood, with the irony, which the swearer himself points out, that the others are as evil as he is, in that the three "been al ones." This oath looks forward to and is cancelled out by a second oath of friendship between the two men who remain with the gold. Chaucer a moment later repeats their worst oath: "Deeth shal be deed, if that they may him hente."

This last oath is both false and great. It is false because it is impossible of performance, and such rash vows were sinful. It is also a great or blasphemous oath, for it is the role of Christ Himself to slay Death. In the words of the Easter Preface of the *Book of Common Prayer*, "Jesus Christ our Lord . . . by his death, hath destroyed death, and by his rising again hath restored us to everlasting life." It was a common medieval idea that the first Adam brought death into the world (as the Pardoner himself points out), and that Christ was a second Adam come to banish death. Therefore, the height of sin is the three revelers' oath,

> "And we wol sleen this false traytour Deeth;
> He shal be slayn, he that so manye sleeth,
> By Goddes dignitee, er it be nyght!"

That Death was indeed truly slain "by Goddes dignitee," the Middle Ages never forgot. The three drunken revelers are arch blasphemers, Satanic in their presumption.

The common remedy for swearing was its opposite, prayer. Instead of taking Christ's name in vain, one should name Him piously, for the sake of salvation (**"Parson's Tale"**). The Old Man greets the trio with such a prayer: "Now, lordes, God yow see!" In contrast to them, he abides by God's will in living so long. In what is perhaps the finest, most beautiful, and most Oedipal death-wish since Sophocles, he prays to Mother Earth to let him die. He gently reproves them for their churlishness and ominously hints at its ultimate result:

> "Ne dooth unto an oold man noon harm now.
> Namoore than that ye wolde men did to yow
> In age, if that ye so longe abyde.
> And God be with yow, where ye go or ryde!
> I moot go thider as I have to go."

The revelers miss the allusion to Christ's golden rule, and to the Old Man's hint of an appointment in Samarra. One reveler grows rougher, swears four more blasphemies, and concludes with one ironically false oath:

> "Have heer my trouthe, as thou art his espye,
> Telle wher he is, or thou shalt it abye,
> By God, and by the hooly sacrement!"

This last threat is ironic in two ways: First, the Old Man cannot be made to "pay" for it, since it is God's will that he cannot die. Second, it is the swearer who with his two companions will "abye," and by a holy sacrament, too. For the wine in the bottles is sacramental, in a sense: medieval thought demanded that vice be punished by spiritual forces which were free to use any means available; and wine will be the instrumental cause of two of the revelers' receiving justice.

The Old Man does not escape without telling them where Death is, but then he leaves them with a prayer stressing the infinite mercy of God, mercy which extends to the worst of sinners even to the last moment: " 'God save yow, that boghte agayn mankynde, / And yow amende!' " His farewell is in dramatic contrast with the ten blasphemies specifically uttered by the revelers in the course of the tale.

In the drawing of lots to see who will go to town for bread and wine, all three men lose, since they are gambling against God's omniscient justice. The drawing of lots was placed in the same category as blasphemous swearing by Chaucer's Parson (**"Parson's Tale"**). While his two companions are plotting his death, the "yongeste" reveler proceeds upon his journey to town. (Chaucer purposely makes almost no distinction among the characters of the three.) Again the scene is rapid: all are hurriedly searching for their deaths. The "yongeste" continues the oath-swearing of this story:

> "O Lord!" quod he, "if so were that I myghte
> Have al this tresor to myself allone,
> There is no man that lyveth under the trone
> Of God that sholde syve so murye as I!"

The presumption that he now lives under the throne of God is ironically true, for so he does, even as all men do, but he does not dwell there in the joyous sense he thinks. Now God is moved to permit the Devil to lead him to a still worse thought:

> And atte laste the feend, oure enemy,
> Putte in his thoght that he sholde poyson
>   beye, . . .
> For this was outrely his fulle entente,
> To sleen hem bothe, and nevere to repente.

This last determination rules out divine mercy in advance and guarantees complete damnation as thoroughly as any human action can. An intensification of the earlier oaths sworn deliberately to wound Christ, the oath is defiantly Satanic.

In a more ordinary sermon than this, the Pardoner might well have dwelt at gruesome length upon the sufferings of the two poisoned murderers, as well as their torments in Hell. The focus, however, is upon the swiftness and unexpectedness of death in this world. "What nedeth it to sermone of it moore?" asks the Pardoner, and he kills off all three men in nine more quick lines. Often in the *Canterbury Tales* a story which has been leisurely in getting started achieves a rapid denouement; but in the **"Pardoner's Tale,"** once begun, the pace of the story is swift throughout, thereby accentuating the reckless haste of the sinners. For example, the reveler who goes to town literally runs for bottles, once he has bought poison. He is not shown buying either the bread or the wine. The sharply limited narrative focus conveys the sense of the reveler's thoughts, which dwell upon nothing but the poison. The imagery, too, is at times kinetic: this man's mind does not merely ponder the gold coins, but "rolleth" them up and down in his heart.

There has been mention of the Holy Eucharist at two points in the **"Pardoner's Tale."** Chaucer thus hints subtly at the symbolic significance of this sacrament in the fabric of the story. The first reference occurs in the first of the three *divisiones* of the theme of avarice, as the Pardoner rails against gluttony:

> Thise cookes, how they stampe, and streyne, and
>   grynde,
> And turnen substaunce into accident. . . .

Concerning substance and accident, "Chaucer can hardly have used this phrase without thinking about the current controversy on the Eucharist." The second mention of the Eucharist, again fairly indirect, occurs when one of the revelers threatens the Old Man into telling where Death is to be found:

> "Telle where he is, or thou shalt it abye,
> By God, and by the hooly sacrement!"

The Holy Eucharist has ironically turned into poisoned wine for the murderers. The wine is still symbolically sacramental, in that it is the instrument of God's providence.

Once the two confederates murder the third, they are fated, not by divine predestination, but by their own volition, to die. One of them says,

> "Now lat us sitte and drynke, and make us
>   merie,
> And afterward we wol his body berie."
> And with that word, it happed hym, par cas,
> To take the botel ther the poyson was,
> And dranke, and yaf his felawe drinke also,
> For which anon they storven bothe two.

Chaucer has reduced the number of poisoned bottles from two to only one, thus seeming to increase the odds in favor of the two confederates' selecting an untainted bottle first. (Such gluttons, of course, might well not have stopped until they had drunk all the wine on hand.) Whether the change is intentional or not, there is never lack of intention on God's part. The choice of the poisoned bottle cannot be a matter of "cas" or mere chance. The whole story would indicate that at this point the hand of Divine Providence is again at work, just as it was when the revelers met up with the Old Man, or when God permitted the Devil to tempt the youngest reveler. The religious import of the tale is basic, and cannot be left to accident, for the wages of sin is death.

There remains one last problem, namely, the much-discussed altercation between the Host and the Pardoner. Perhaps it is explainable in part by the Pardoner's previously illustrated homiletic confusion. The Pardoner has now completed the first four parts of his medieval sermon: 1) statement of theme; 2) ante-theme or pro-theme; 3) *divisiones;* and 4) major exemplum. The regular order of the two remaining parts would be 5) peroration or application and 6) closing formula. The Pardoner has previously confused Parts 3 and 4 by digressing after the beginning of Part 4 back to Part 3 to take up the three *divisiones* of his theme. This confusion is understandable, for the Pardoner is not supposed to be preaching a regular sermon in the first place, but that is all he knows how to do. He is like the "worste" reveler who boasts that his "wit is greet" and then shows that it is not. Chaucer achieves a sort of Shakespearean balance by having the Pardoner proceed to confuse Parts 5 and 6. He begins and perhaps thinks he com-

The Merchant from the Ellesmere manuscript.

pletes his peroration or application, and then goes to his closing formula:

—And lo, sires, thus I preche,
And Jhesu Crist, that is oure soules leche
So graunte yow his pardoun to receyve,
For that is best; I wol yow nat deceyve.

This closing formula is surely not the one sincere moment of repentance, as Kittredge would have it, but his crowning infamy [see Further Reading]. For the Pardoner does not believe, any more than do his three revelers, that Jesus Christ is our souls' physician, nor does he truly pray for Christ to save anyone. For all he cares, the souls of his hearers can go blackberrying. As for his not wishing to deceive, the irony is that while attempting to deceive others, he fails, even as he deceives himself into thinking that he is superior to his fellows. His whole effort is a futile attempt to bolster his own ego.

Force of habit (" ' For I kan al by rote that I telle' " ["**Pardoner's Prologue**"]) leads him to his usual closing formula. His confusion now becomes elaborately complex: " 'But, sires, o word forgat I in my tale: / I have relikes and pardoun . . . ' ." He has forgotten he is not really preaching but telling a story; he has forgotten that he has already made his peroration or application—provided

that he *were* preaching; he has forgotten that he has already made sufficient mention of his relics and his pardons all hot from Rome (**"Pardoner's Prologue"**). Since he is not half so clever as he thinks he is, in making a last, concerted effort to sell pardons he picks the wrong man, Harry Bailly, the Host.

The Host is as different as a man could be from the Pardoner, and a fitting object of the latter's subconscious envy. Harry Bailly is a "propre" or virile man, the Pardoner is impotent. The Host is married (**"Prologue to the Monk's Tale"**), the Pardoner can only boast of marrying (**"Prologue to the Wife of Bath's Tale"**). The Host protests that he is a plain, blunt man who "cannot speke in terme," though he is often able to cajole pilgrims of the most diverse kind into doing what he wishes; the Pardoner is mightily proud of his ability to sway minds, yet he is promptly reduced to silence by the Host, even as he was earlier by the Wife of Bath (in her prologue). In the **"Introduction to the Pardoner's Tale,"** the Pardoner has been seen trying at all costs to keep up with the Host—in needing a drink, in swearing by St. Runyon, etc. He will never have done with trying to assert himself; he must boast compulsively, even if it be of his wickedness. Yet he dares to accuse the Host of being the pilgrim "most envoluped in synne." He misjudges his man. There is a limit to Harry Bailly's pleasant disposition, though he good-naturedly likes nearly everyone on the pilgrimage; whereas the Pardoner's psychic unrest is so deep that he hates all men, including himself. It would be a mocking triumph to sell relics after having exposed them as pigs' bones, but only a fool would try to do so.

The Host, on the other hand, is no fool but a keen judge of character. Even if he were obtuse, has not the pardoner crowed openly about how he spits out his venom " 'under hewe / Of hoolynesse to semen hooly and trewe'?" Given the Host's character, it is quite to be expected that he would react fiercely to the Pardoner's accusation. He has understood that portion of the homily which denounces swearing, and knows that he himself is guilty of profanity which approaches a crescendo of virtuosity as the *Canterbury Tales* proceed. The Host also knows the evil wretch who prostituted his talent in giving utterance to the fusion of homily and tale. Indeed, he knows the rascal's shamelessness well enough to twit him so obscenely as to silence the Pardoner' psychotic self-revelation. He can outdo the Pardoner in many things, including crudity.

To recapitulate: the Pardoner's strictures on oaths in his "digression" from his tale underline the structuralism of the oaths in the **"Pardoner's Tale"** itself. The three revelers are guilty not only of avarice and murder, but also of Satanic pride in seeking to kill Death. The entire composition of the tale—its focus, pace, and symbolism—points to pride as the deepest and deadliest sin of the revelers. The psychological make-up of the Pardoner and the resultant homiletic confusion are enough to account for the Pardoner's final effrontery and the Host's consequent profane reaction. The attack upon swearing succeeds in inspiring a marvelously graphic oath.

A good medieval sermon could operate on two levels, and could incite the more intelligent hearers to "guess" where it was going. There could be one meaning for the commons, another and higher meaning for the perceptive elite. In the **"Pardoner's Tale"** perhaps the excellently told story of the three revelers and the sledge-hammer blows of the attacks upon gluttony, gambling, and swearing would have been enough for the groundlings. The keen-witted might also have perceived the underlying meaning of the revelers' blasphemous oath to kill Death. Just how much would the Host have understood of this symbolic meaning? The question admits of no answer. Certainly one can say, however, that the Pardoner himself does not truly understand the symbolical import of what he is saying, or he would not have debased his God-given talent so cold-bloodedly. All his many liturgical and theological references are irreverently made; and in medieval preaching *recta intentio* is more important than *recta scientia.* He can note how "Crist hadde boght us with his blood agayn," but then perversely show that he does not at all believe it, vaunting in the assertion that he remains " 'a ful vicious man' " **("Pardoner's Prologue").** It is the Pardoner, not the Old Man of his tale, whose existence is a living death even as he walks the earth. The Pardoner does not recognize that he speaks his own epitaph:

> —But, certes, he that haunteth swiche delices
> Is deed, whil that he lyveth in tho vices.

(pp. 47-58)

Eric W. Stockton, "The Deadliest Sin in 'The Pardoner's Tale'," in Tennessee Studies in Literature, *Vol. VI, 1961, pp. 47-59.*

Elizabeth Salter (essay date 1962)

[*Salter was a medievalist and the author of* Chaucer *(1962),* Piers Plowman: An Introduction *(1962), and* The Mediaeval Landscape *(1971). In the following excerpt from the first-named work, she provides an overview of the "Knight's Tale," concluding that it is "a measure of the greatness of Chaucer that his imaginative response to a situation in which innocent creatures confront the wilful use of absolute power was strong enough to disturb the overall balance of his work."*]

Chaucer does not mention the source of the **"Knight's Tale"** by name, but there is no doubt that he based it upon the *Teseida Delle Nozze D'Emilia,* a 'romantic epic' in twelve books by his contemporary, the Italian Giovanni Boccaccio (1313-75). Boccaccio's work was dedicated to the lady whom he called 'Fiammetta', and is of two-fold nature; epic material, treated 'con bello stilo', is combined with amatory—a combination of heroic and autobiographical elements which is not entirely successful. Beginning on a high note with the martial exploits of Theseus against the Amazons and Creon, it develops into a romantic narrative, much concerned with the psychology of the Palemone-Arcita-Emilia situation. The author's divided aim results in something which is neither epic nor romance, but which is packed with lavish and stately poetry. Chaucer had recognised the wealth of the *Teseida* from the very beginning of his poetic career and had drawn upon it mainly for its decorative, allusive verse and for its complex analysis of a love-dilemma.

But the Italian poem met changing imaginative needs in Chaucer. When he came to make a complete version of the *Teseida* he worked rather differently. The exact history of the translation is not clear, but it seems, from a reference in the prologue to the *Legend of Good Women,* that well before the planning of the *Canterbury Tales* he had finished a poem which told of

> . . . al the love of Palamon and Arcite
> Of Thebes. . . .

We do not know how far this work resembled the **"Knight's Tale":** what can be said with certainty is that his dealings with the *Teseida* in the poem we have now to consider, reveal him at the outset as an artist of decisive action. The 9896 lines of the Italian are reduced to 2250; several important passages and many details are added. But no numerical reckoning can give a proper idea of how Chaucer remains deeply indebted to the *Teseida*—often following lines of Boccaccio's text faithfully—and yet attempts a large-scale recasting of the work. We are bound to admire his firm grasp of the basic problems set by the *Teseida* and his skill in carrying out some essential changes.

Earlier in his career, in the fragmentary poem **"Anelida and Arcite",** he had thought it possible to copy the *Teseida's* somewhat incongruous mixture of love motif and epic machinery; by now he has abandoned the attempt. Discarding most of the epic pretensions of the Italian, he treats it, predominantly, as a courtly romance. The basic conflict between two entirely different sorts of material is removed: epic invocations are left out, and the rivalry of the two lovers for their lady is made the central theme. To this end, the first two books of the *Teseida,* telling of Theseus's epic conquests, are compressed into less than 200 lines of the **"Knight's Tale":** Arcite's wanderings, after becoming an exile, are similarly rejected, as unnecessary to the main action. The epic catalogue of champions, fighting for Palamon and Arcite in the tournament, is reduced to two splendidly symbolic figures, Lygurge and Emetreus. Even the accounts of fighting, although they keep some of the pseudo-epic similes, move towards the sort of vigorous battle realism mediaeval readers knew well from English romances of the day:

> Out brest the blood with stierne stremes rede;
> With myghty maces the bones they tobreste . . .

All these changes simplify and unify the basic material of the poem.

The minimising of epic elements means, inevitably, some lessening of attention to the character of Theseus, who had played such a large part in the first few books of the *Teseida.* But character generally is strictly subordinated to narrative in the English version. Acting with perfect logic, since the outcome of Boccaccio's story depends upon supernatural, not human, action, Chaucer shows himself far more interested in predicaments than personalities. His lovers, Palamon and Arcite, are distinguishable mainly for their allegiance to differing gods, and the consequences of this—not for their sharply differing characters.

Arcite, who in Boccaccio's work has much more to say than Palamon, and perhaps expresses the poet's own lovesickness for the lady Fiammetta, is approximated much more nearly to his rival in Chaucer's version. Even the formal descriptions of the two are omitted. If, in the English, Palamon emerges as a slightly more attractive figure than Arcite, this is due mainly to Chaucer's handling of his fundamental rôle as 'servant of Venus'—a rôle which is allowed to compare favourably with that of Arcite, the 'servant of Mars'. There is, admittedly, some contrast between the ardent lover who prays to Venus

> 'That if yow list, I shal wel have my love . . . '

and Arcite who asks directly of Mars

> 'Yif me the victorie, I aske thee namoore.'

but it is a contrast which is not developed throughout the poem. Elsewhere he seems anxious to present them in parallel terms, deliberately awarding them similar speeches and actions. The dilemmas in which they find themselves—through little fault of their own—are not used by Chaucer as a means of character study.

Even more marked is his stylisation of the Italian heroine, Emilia. Boccaccio certainly intended her to be an *ideal* representation of all he adored in Fiammetta, who was herself, as he says in his Dedication, a creature 'more celestial than human'. But Emilia has, for all that, some individual features: she is gay as well as beautiful, innocently vain, and she comes to feel deeply about the sufferings of the men who love her. Chaucer's Emelye exists only to provide the immediate cause of the lovers' rivalry. We know little of her feelings and her reactions to the melodramatic scenes in which she is involved; even her physical beauty is conveyed distantly to us, in courtly images. What we *do* know is that she is a prize of inestimable worth: 'up roos the sonne, and up roos Emelye . . . '

In broad outline, Chaucer's adaptation successfully changed what was a mixture of romantic and epic materials into a poem with a unified plot and a consistent, though flat, mode of characterisation. His treatment of the Italian shows in many respects an unmistakable growth of architectonic skill and of self-discipline. Whereas in **Troilus and Criseyde,** for instance, the *Teseida* is still being rifled for 'star' descriptive passages, in the **"Knight's Tale"** that kind of poetry is enjoyed and utilised, but is made to fulfil definite functions. In **Troilus,** Chaucer draws upon and develops further the amorous psychology of the two Italian poems; in the **"Knight's Tale"** he abandons almost completely this 'three-dimensional'' way of regarding human beings, and takes a plainer way with character. In certain basic features, the poem which results has much in common with mediaeval romance—a predominant narrative interest, 'typed' character treatment, and a theme combining chivalry and love.

And yet the **"Knight's Tale"** is not at all a simple poem to define. To describe it as 'remodelled on the lines of a typical chivalric romance' of Chaucer's day would be inadequate. In fact, it makes a far more varied and powerful use of language, is more philosophic and also, perhaps, more enigmatic in the final impression it leaves than any other mediaeval romance. If Chaucer deliberately limits himself in choice of materials and in mode of characterisa-

tion, he allows himself great freedom in other directions, and although some of his procedures are designed to simplify, others, not yet considered, create a new kind of complexity.

The poem has been likened to a tapestry and to a pageant and it is certainly true that Chaucer's wish to shorten the *Teseida* did not lead him to verbal austerity. Richness and formalism of language are features of the **"Knight's Tale"** we first notice: elaborate descriptive detail and high rhetorical address play a significantly large part. For in many ways the poem moves as if it were a set of splendid tableaux: the experience of reading it is sometimes similar to that of turning the pages of an illuminated manuscript, in which the life of saint or secular hero is presented as a series of glittering and stylised episodes. But none of these comparisons—tapestry, pageant, manuscript illumination—do proper justice to the variety of styles the **"Knight's Tale"** contains. This stylistic range is of the greatest interest, since it indicates a range of widely differing themes and attitudes to subject matter: there is no simple generalisation to cover either the whole of the poetry or the total meaning of the tale. One generalisation can be made however about the strongly functional relationship of style and meaning. Even in the more ornate modes of writing, there is no sense of unnecessary luxury. The portraits of Lygurge and Emetreus, for instance, rich as they are in minutiae of physical features, garments, jewels and retinue, and fulfilling no real dramatic need in the story, yet have a vital symbolic significance. For Lygurge fittingly displays the force of Saturn, who, in answer to the plea of his daughter Venus, awards the victory to Palamon. And Emetreus represents the warlike glory of Mars, who sponsors Arcite so powerfully and, as it turns out, so tragically. No detail of their appearance is irrelevant to the conflict being worked out on earthly and heavenly levels: they link human and divine issues emblematically. At the other extreme, the drop into harsh realism of language is not carelessly made, but represents one of the basic themes of the poem—the darkness and suffering which exist at the very centre of this radiant chivalric world.

When we first meet Duke Theseus, he is riding back from his conquest,

> In al his wele, and in his mooste pride . . .

and the theme of worldly magnificence is carried throughout the poem by language which stresses the heightened conventions, the almost ritualistic nature of the life led by man in an elevated and aristocratic society. This, and not lack of inventiveness, explains the frequent use of ordered, formulaic speech and theatrical gesture; the appeal to Theseus by the Theban ladies, is appropriately stiff and dignified in its grief:

> 'I, wrecche, which that wepe and wayle thus,
> Was whilom wyf to kyng Cappaneus,
> That starf at Thebes—cursed be that day! . . . '

and the physical accompaniments—fainting, crying, falling to the ground—are extreme and stylised. So, often, are the initial reactions of the lovers, Palamon and Arcite, to the various strokes of Fortune they have to endure. The poet uses similar emphatic but conventional phraseology to describe Palamon falling in love with Emelye, and Arcite bewailing his exile from Athens: the one cries

> As though he stongen were unto the herte . . .

the other

> The deeth he feeleth thurgh his herte smyte . . .

and their high-set complaints—the one in prison 'everemo' the other free but exiled—are directed along similar lines. Arcite 'wepeth, wayleth, crieth pitously': Palamon declares 'For I moot wepe and wayle, whil I lyve'. Arcite sees a complete victory for Palamon, and states it with rhetorical paradox:

> 'O deere cosyn Palamon,' quod he,
> 'Thyn is the victorie of this aventure.
> Ful blisfully in prison maistow dure,—
> In prison? certes nay, but in paradys!'

Palamon's view of events is only a variation on the same theme:

> 'Allas,' quod he, 'Arcita, cosyn myn,
> Of al oure strif, God woot, the fruyt is
>   thyn . . . '

This deliberate formalising of language imposes a rhythmical pattern upon the **"Knight's Tale"** which is almost musical in its effect. Repetitive formulas, for instance, work as 'leit-motifs'; Palamon's words

> 'That he was born,' ful ofte he seyde 'allas!'

come again, with slight change, from Arcite:

> He seyde 'Allas that day that I was born!' . . .
> 'Allas!' quod he, 'that day that I was
>   bore! . . . '

and although they are not in the least dramatic, comment with dignity upon the sad ironies of the narrative. The recurrent use of long-accepted mediaeval metaphors such as fire, wound, and death for the lover's state serves on the one hand to establish quite clearly the type of idealising passion the poem deals with; it serves also as a constant reminder of the violent implications of love. Arcite's insistent references to love and death—

> 'The fresshe beautee sleeth me sodeynly
> Of hire that rometh in the yonder place,
> And but I have hir mercy and hir grace, . . .
> I nam but deed . . . '

> 'And over al this, to sleen me outrely,
> Love hath his firy dart so brenningly
> Ystiked thurgh my trewe, careful herte,
> That shapen was my deeth erst than my sherte.
> Ye sleen me with youre eyen, Emelye . . . '

have a cumulative power as we move towards the tragic denouement—

> 'Allas, the deeth! allas myn Emelye!'

And so, indeed, have all the recognisably 'stock' expressions of sudden love, sorrow, or anger as a weapon at the heart; individually they are not particularly impressive, but they build towards and enrich the moments when real weapons threaten life. So when we read

> The brighte swerdes wenten to and fro
> So hidously . . .

we remember how many internal conflicts have led to this point:

> This Palamoun, that thoughte that thurgh his
>   herte
> He felte a coold swerde sodeynliche glide . . .

The special importance of substance and physical appearance in this aristocratic life is conveyed by wealthy, though controlled, descriptive detail. The funeral rites of Arcite, for instance, give us, at great length and with great visual appeal, a most elaborately devised spectacle of grief. Cloth of gold, white gloves, horses 'that trapped were in steel al glitterynge', harness of 'brend gold', vessels filled with honey, milk, and blood, meticulously listed trees, garlands, myrrh and incense—all these are a fitting gesture of 'richesse' in honour of one who was born 'gentil of condicioun'. The jewels that are cast into the funeral flames seem to symbolise both the material and emotional extravagance of this society. It is, however, a society which has power to limit and order extravagance; just as the mourning ceremonies for Arcite come to a well-defined end so even the most lavish display of language never gives the impression of mere indulgence. The description of the tournament accumulates vocabulary of strong visual and aural appeal to convey a scene of material splendour:

> Ther maystow seen devisynge of harneys
> So unkouth and so riche, and wroght so weel
> Of goldsmythrye, of browdynge, and of steel;
> The sheeldes brighte, testeres, and trapures,
> Gold-hewen   helmes,   hauberkes,   cote-
>   armures . . .

But it is crowded, not chaotic. The narrator passes rapidly and logically from one object, activity and person to another, even observing social rank, as he moves from 'lordes in parementz' down to 'yemen on foote and communes many oon'. The violent fighting that follows is sharply realised by imitative sound and a particularly vigorous range of verbs:

> Ther shyveren shaftes upon sheeldes thikke;
> He feeleth thurgh the herte-spoon the prikke.
> Up spryngen speres twenty foot on highte;
> Out goon the swerdes as the silver brighte;
> The helmes they tohewen and toshrede;
> Out breste the blood with stierne stremes
>   rede . . .

But involvement in the purely physical zest of the battle, the impact of body and weapon, does not disturb overall artistic patterning. Concrete and vivid language is set to deal with a disciplined series of topics.

The description of the three temples built to Theseus's commands introduces us to an immense show of power manifested in forms of great beauty and terror. Significantly, they . . . 'coste largely of gold a fother . . . ', and whatever symbolic references are later to be taken in, it is clear that, initially, we are meant to be struck with their palpable, visual impressiveness, their 'belle solidité'—carved as they are of marble, alabaster, coral, and 'walled of stoon'. The details supplied about 'the noble kervyng and the portreitures' work always towards a greater sensuous realisation of the object or scene. Though there were literary sources for the passage, Chaucer's love of the visual arts—evident over the whole range of his poetry—surely directs the account of the statue of Venus; aesthetic enjoyment of shape, colour and gesture is strongly felt in the lines which report how it was

> . . .naked, fletynge in the large see,
> And fro the navele doun al covered was
> With wawes grene, and brighte as any glas.
> A citole in hir righte hand hadde she,
> And on hir heed, ful semely for to se,
> A rose gerland . . .

In the temple of Mars, substance is oppressively forced upon our notice: a painted forest, as menacing as any Grünewald landscape, comes to sinister life:

> . . .knotty, knarry, bareyne trees olde
> Of stubbes sharpe and hidouse to biholde,
> In which ther ran a rumbel in a swough,
> As though a storm sholde bresten every bough:

The emphatic alliterative style, used also in the account of the tournament, is interesting; this is the nearest Chaucer ever comes to composing in the old alliterative, accentual measure used by his contemporaries of the west and north of England. Poetry of this tradition had long been famous for its descriptive skill in dealing with battle-narrative and rough landscape, and here we may have Chaucer's own acknowledgement of the special evocative power of blocked alliterative vocabulary. But there are less direct means by which a painted temple can be invested with tangible horror. Patterning of hard single consonants, densely clustered consonant groups, and heavy vowel sounds build up a passage of great force and complexity. Such poetry reminds us of the strain of 'iren tough' in Chaucer's imagination:

> The dore was al of adamant eterne,
> Yclenched overthwart and endelong
> With iren tough; and for to make it strong,
> Every pyler, the temple to sustene,
> Was tonne greet, of iren bright and shene.

As we shall see, this massive embodiment of warlike power is no isolated 'set-piece', but a central illustration of one of the most important themes of the poem. In fact the strong relevance of descriptive material to theme is noticeable throughout the **"Knight's Tale."** These passages just examined express certain values of the society to which Theseus, Palamon and Arcite belong: the store set by brilliant externals, by the translation of the immaterial—pride, joy, fear, grief, animosity—into material ceremonies and rituals. And in their detail, colour, solidity, they give another dimension to the work. What it lacks in depth and subtlety of characterisation, it makes up for in depth and concreteness of setting, and if the figures often seem two-dimensional, the world they inhabit is roundly presented.

The civilisation pictured here in such 'raw and glittering light' is based upon respect for the tangible—the sword, the votive offering, the statue, the gold coin. The grief-stricken cry of the Athenian women, on hearing of Arcite's death, need not be intended ironically, but may express an honest though limited value-judgement:

> 'Why woldestow be deed', thise wommen crye,
> 'And haddest gold ynough and Emelye?'

And we can imagine that such an essentially masculine civilisation with its love of pomp, of fighting, its simple though high code of magnanimity, courage, and piety, would be well understood by the 'parfit, gentil knyght' himself. But there are other elements in the world of the tale, some of them disturbing: correspondingly, other styles interleave the descriptive splendour and the stylised oratory we have just been noticing.

The philosophic material introduced by Chaucer into his Italian source required language of semi-technical, abstract nature: Chaucer's audience would easily have recognised the Boethian Latin behind dignified speeches such as that of Arcite at the beginning of the story:

> 'Allas, why pleynen folk so in commune
> On purveiaunce of God, or of Fortune . . . '

or that of Duke Theseus, towards the end:

> 'The Firste Moevere of the cause above,
> Whan he first made the faire cheyne of love,
> Greet was th' effect, and heigh was his
>   entente . . . '

Comment upon events is not only made, however, in this specialised stylistic mode. It is true that the characters are not given full realistic treatment, and that they more often soliloquise or address each other with rhetorical words and gestures. But there are occasions when the natural speaking voice comes through, using trenchant, dramatic language, and expressing surprisingly pointed opinions. Arcite's initial summing-up of the love dilemma in which he and Palamon find themselves has a crispness of attack and terminology quite unlike his usual mannered delivery:

> 'And therefore, at the kynges court, my brother,
> Ech man for hymself, there is noon
>   oother . . . '

Duke Theseus can also find colloquial words for an unexpectedly common-sense, almost jocular, view of the lovers' duel:

> 'A man moot ben a fool, or yong or oold . . . '

But such language is put to deeper purposes than those of Theseus. For although the poem portrays many aspects of Athenian life with confident exuberance, it also looks intently at the darker implications of divine and human affairs. If we are introduced to warlike violence by the splendid description of the banner of Theseus—

> The rede statue of Mars, with spere and targe,
> So shyneth in his white baner large,
> That alle the feeldes glyteren up and doun . . .

we are later refused the comfort of this protective and glamorous language, and made to feel directly the reverse of the matter. The 'glory' of Mars is conveyed quite as truthfully and savagely by his statue in the temple and by the hideous wall-paintings of non-chivalrous death which we find there. Questions are raised about universal order and justice in words of uncomfortable exactness:

> '. . . O crueel goddes that governe
> This world with byndyng of youre worde
>   eterne, . . .
> What is mankynde moore unto you holde
> Than is the sheep that rouketh in the
>   folde? . . . '

And the crowded, excited activities of the tournament are prefaced by Saturn's revelation of disaster in severest, plainest terms:

> 'Myn is the drenchyng in the see so wan;
> Myn is the prison in the derke cote;
> Myn is the stranglyng and hangyng by the
>   throte . . . '

This movement from images of chivalric ritual and attitudes of extravagant emotion to philosophic analysis, humorous deflation, and pungent, bitter commentary is remarkable on a purely stylistic plane. But we have to consider what this stylistic variety, and, in particular, the dramatic contrast between splendour and harshness, tell us of Chaucer's overall intention in the **"Knight's Tale"**.

Among the many changes which Chaucer worked upon his Italian source, most important for their far-reaching influence are the reflective passages which he gave to the main personages of the tale. Arcite, Palamon and Theseus meditate on death, happiness, providence, turning from personal issues to consider wider metaphysical problems. Arcite's banishment from Athens, Palamon's life-imprisonment, Arcite's death, prompt discussion which restates and then searches to answer the moving question—

> 'What is this world? what asketh men to
>   have? . . . '

And in so far as this material draws substantially upon the *Consolation of Philosophy*—the central theme of which is the relation of providence to man's happiness—its effect is to increase the 'high seriousness' of the poem. By its positioning and varied emphases, however, it encourages the reader to think more deeply about the nature and implications of the narrative, and about Chaucer's attitude to that sequence of events.

As we have seen, he chose to flatten and stylise the characters of Boccaccio's poem, thus allowing the story itself to stand in bold relief. And as if the story were not sufficiently spectacular, he invites us to weigh its larger significance. By reflective additions to the Italian, he forces our attention to a narrative containing elements of extreme cruelty. These elements are 'high-lighted' from the beginning of the poem onwards. Arcite's reaction to the new-won freedom which is, in fact, a new kind of imprisonment, may be initially theatrical—

> He seyde, 'Allas that day that I was born!'

but it develops into something more sober and impressive. Following Boethian reasoning, he admits that the struggle of man towards 'sovereyne good' is all too often confused and misguided: man, he sees, is in some measure responsible for his sufferings:

> 'And to a dronke man the wey is slider.
> And certes, in this world so faren we;
> We seken faste after felicitee,
> But we goon wrong ful often, trewely . . . '

But his submission to the workings of 'God, or of Fortune' stems from despair rather than from respect: it is useless to fight the Omnipotent and Incalculable:

> 'And som man wolde out of his prisoun fayn,
> That in his hous is of his meynee slayn.
> Infinite harmes been in this mateere.
> We witen nat what thing we preyen heere . . .
> Syn that I may nat seen you, Emelye,
> I nam but deed; ther nys no remedye . . . '

The sad truth of this will be borne out by his own experience: he who has already acknowledged his own fallibility and the inexplicable wisdom of God, will be struck down in the moment of greatest triumph. His attempts to come to terms with himself and with heavenly 'purveiaunce' are cruelly rewarded, and he dies questioning, the problem unsolved.

Palamon's words on the same occasion—Emelye is, for him, visible but quite inaccessible—move even more strikingly from conventionally phrased despair—

> Swich sorwe he maketh that the grete tour
> Resouneth of his youlyng and clamour . . .

to a sharp attack upon the arbitrary dispensations of the gods. Some of the sentiments clearly derive from the complaint of Boethius to God, and in its original context, this complaint receives brisk correction from the 'noryce, Philosophie'. In the present context, however, it has an almost uncanny accuracy and relevance: the gods of the **"Knight's Tale"** are to display exactly those qualities Palamon describes—cruelty, malice, indifference. The language he uses is stronger, more incisive than that of the Boethian lament—

> Thanne seyde he, 'O cruel goddes that governe
> This world with byndyng of youre word eterne,
> And writen in the table of atthamaunt
> Youre parlement and youre eterne graunt,
> What is mankynde moore unto you holde
> Than is the sheep that rouketh in the folde? . . .
> What governance is in this prescience,
> That giltelees tormenteth innocence? . . . '

The references to the beast world, though reminiscent of *Ecclesiastes,* stress with greater bitterness and subtlety the helpless condition of man. Constrained in life, he suffers even beyond death:

> 'For slayn is man right as another beest . . .
> And yet encresseth this al my penaunce,
> That man is bounden to his observaunce,
> For Goddes sake, to letten of his wille,
> Ther as a beest may al his lust fulfille.
> And whan a beest is deed, he hath no peyne;
> But man after his deeth moot wepe and pleyne,
> Though in this world he have care and
>   wo . . . '

For the deities who rule the human condition, Palamon has only fear mingled with contempt:

> 'But I moot be in prisoun thurgh Saturne,

> And eek thurgh Juno, jalous and eek wood,
> That hath destroyed wel ny al the blood
> Of Thebes with his waste walles wyde;
> And Venus sleeth me on that oother syde
> For jalousie and fere of hym Arcite . . . '

Though such accusations may be, in terms of Boethian philosophy, 'benighted', they are most germane to the outcome of this particular story. Palamon's rebellious words will find dramatic justification as the narrative unfolds: the final irony will be reached when he, and not the more orthodox Arcite, is awarded the coveted prize.

The theme of divine callousness, even divine injustice, has been introduced: the questions asked by Palamon and Arcite involve the reader in much more than just the immediate love-problem. It comes, therefore, as somewhat of a surprise when the narrator of the tale—Knight or Chaucer or anonymous 'persona'—comments comfortably, even jovially, upon the woes of the lovers:

> Yow loveres axe I now this questioun,
> Who hath the worse, Arcite or Palamoun? . . .
> Now demeth as yow liste, ye that kan,
> For I wol telle forth as I bigan.

We meet, here, a problem which will assume even greater importance later in the poem. By the end of part one, Chaucer has already shown his intention of dealing variously with his material. Consistent, as we have seen, in certain of the procedures he adopts for the **"Knight's Tale"**, he is equally prepared to abandon consistency. In passing so swiftly from powerful expression to comment which is trivial, almost flippant, he seems to be using two voices: one reveals for us the pain latent in the narrative, the other, less sensitive, speaks with imperfect comprehension of that pain. Dramatic verisimilitude, at any rate, is clearly not at stake; if we think back to the original narrator of the tale, the Knight, it is difficult to credit him with the voice of complaint and criticism—although we can, if we wish, imagine that we hear him in the candid, oversimplified appeal to the audience—'Yow loveres axe I now . . . ' This refusal to be limited to any one particular mode of presentation will make for a complex poem, rich in local effects, but not necessarily unified or easy to interpret from a global point of view.

Part two reminds us of this in such a small matter as the description of Palamon's continued imprisonment. The narrator first stresses the miserable conditions in which he lives—

> In derknesse and horrible and strong prisoun
> Thise seven yeer hath seten Palamoun
> Forpyned . . .

and then withdraws from the situation—

> Who koude ryme in Englyssh properly
> His martirdom? for sothe it am nat I;
> Therefore I passe as lightly as I may.

This would not be remarkable—it can be defined, after all, as a well-known rhetorical device, used frequently by Chaucer—were it not that the English poem deliberately chooses to bring Palamon's suffering to our notice, as the Italian source does not. Again, the two voices—one pressing home the 'derknesse' of the story, the other anxious to evade responsibility for it. It is true, however, that on the whole, this section of the poem is comparatively straightforward in approach. It gives some temporary relief from the overpowering sense of pain, of lives clamped down in unalterable misery. The lovers act to change their situations, and sublunary events seem to have taken a vigorous and constructive turn. Arcite's long meditation in the grove gives way to dialogue: Palamon and Arcite quarrel, fight, are dramatically interrupted by Duke Theseus:

> This duc his courser with his spores smoot,
> And at a stert he was bitwix hem two,
> And pulled out a swerd, and cride, 'Hoo! . . . '

The poetry has often to deal with business-like arrangements: the preparations for the first duel, Theseus's plans for his tournament. And the book ends on a note of cheerful anticipation—the knights depart 'with good hope and with herte blithe'.

Warning that such cheerfulness may be under close, even hostile observation by higher powers is occasionally given. Arcite's lament speaks of the 'crueltee' of Juno, the fate of Thebes: he is in no doubt about the 'ire' of the gods—

> Allas, thou felle Mars! allas, Juno!
> Thus hath youre ire oure lynage al fordo . . .

The tyrannical, uncharitable workings of the god of love are twice referred to—once in a passage which is almost wholly Chaucer's invention. Theseus muses upon the compulsions which have brought Arcite and Palamon to the verge of death:

> 'And yet hath love, maugree hir eyen two,
> Broght hem hyder bothe for to dye . . .
> Thus hath hir lord, the god of love, ypayed
> Hir wages and hir fees for hir servyse!'

And yet on none of these occasions are we moved to deep pity or indignation: Arcite turns from accusing the gods to accusing Emelye of being the cause of his death. The idiom is that of the courtly love-complaint—the tone half-desperate, half-detached: 'Ye sleen me with youre eyen, Emelye!' Theseus begins with serious reflection, but soon drops into amused cynicism; he invites our tolerance of the antics of mankind, not our compassion for its suffering. His words are chosen carefully to suggest that we should not take these matters too much to heart:

> 'But yet this is the beste *game* of alle,
> That she for whom they han this *jolitee*
> Kan hem therfore as muche thank as me.
> She woot namoore of al this *hoote fare*,
> By God, than woot a *cokkow or an hare!* . . . '

The robust, even coarse, common-sense of Theseus provides comfortable reading; like the good-temper of the 'narrator', it offsets the unpleasantness of much that has already happened, and much that is likely to happen. When Theseus here invokes the gods, he does so impetuously, almost unthinkingly; neither of his references to 'myghty Mars' sound particularly ominous in their immediate context.

And part three opens with the narrator in optimistic

mood. His tone, as he introduces us to the temples of Venus, Mars and Diana, is light and companionable:

> I trowe men wolde deme it necligence
> If I foryete to tellen the dispence
> Of Theseus, that gooth so bisily
> To maken up the lystes roially . . .

It would be difficult to anticipate, from these words, the spectacle of violence and unhappiness inside the temples. Chaucer's intentions are now by no means comfortable, whatever he has led us to expect. The account of the temple of Venus, greatly shortened from Boccaccio's version, includes, in spite of this, many *fresh* details of the sorrows of love—

> The broken slepes, and the sikes colde,
> The sacred teeris, and the waymentynge,
> The firy strokes of the desirynge
> That loves servantz in this lyf enduren . . .

and fresh instances of wickedness inspired by love—Medea, Circe. The rapturous sight of Venus 'fletynge in the large see' cannot quite dispel the first impression of constricting sadness:

> Lo, alle thise folk so caught were in hir las,
> Til they for wo ful ofte seyde, 'Allas!'

In fact, the sensuous 'colour' of the passage describing the statue of the goddess gives added point to the sombre tableau which precedes it; the disastrous and beguiling aspects of passionate love are sharply juxtaposed.

The temple of Mars, grim enough in the sources from which Chaucer worked, receives new emphatic treatment: it puts before the reader a scene of terror which is half painted image and half allegorical tableau. The abstract power of the originals is preserved—sometimes considerably increased, as when 'il cieco Peccare' deepens, imaginatively and intellectually, into

> Ther saugh I first the derke ymaginyng
> Of Felonye, and al the compassyng;

But an element of startling realism is also introduced: the sterile and destructive nature of Mars is illustrated with cold, almost clinical exactness of observation. We are made to understand the precarious triumph of war—

> Saw I Conquest, sittynge in greet honour,
> With the sharpe swerd over his heed
> Hangynge by a soutil twynes threed . . .

as well as the invasion of ordinary life by accident and death—

> The shepne brennynge with the blake smoke . . .
> The sleere of hymself yet saugh I ther,—
> His herte-blood hath bathed al his heer; . . .
> The careyne in the busk, with throte ycorve; . . .
> The sowe freten the child right in the cradel;
> The cook yscalded, for al his longe ladel.
> Noght was foryeten by the infortune of Marte:

We catch a glimpse of murder—the moment of striking and the ugly sequel:

> The nayl ydryven in the shode a-nyght;
> The colde deeth, with mouth gapyng upright.

And even where the Italian (or Latin) is used, the subject is particularised, brought into clearer focus: allegory leaps to life in 'The smylere with the knyf under the cloke . . . ' and 'Contek, with blody knyf and sharp manace . . . . By comparison, Boccaccio is mild and diffuse.

The aim of the English rendering seems to be confirmed when we reach the statue of the god; a terrible climax has been prepared:

> A wolf ther stood biforn hym at his feet
> With eyen rede, and of a man he eet.

Whatever the origin of this last detail, its function in Chaucer's poem is to impress us with the savage and threatening rôle of Mars: like all the additions and variations we have been considering, it gives concrete form to the 'manasynge of Mars'. In these circumstances it is difficult to gauge the bland comment which closes the episode; the narrator leaves the temple in good spirits:

> With soutil pencel depeynted was this storie
> In redoutynge of Mars and of his glorie.
> Now to the temple of Dyane the chaste
> As shortly as I kan, I wol me haste . . .

Nor does he seem dispirited by what he sees in the temple of Diana. The wall-paintings in this building are wholly Chaucer's invention, and, as we might by now expect, he gives us subjects illustrating the power of the goddess and the suffering of human beings. The capricious vengeance of Diana is the main theme: Callisto, transformed into a bear 'whan that Diane aggreved was with here . . . ', Actaeon devoured by his own hounds 'for vengeaunce that he saugh Diane al naked . . . ', the fateful hunt of Meleager 'for which Dyane wroghte hym care and wo . . . '. In front of the goddess lies a woman in agony of childbirth, calling upon her 'for hir child so longe was unborn'. The summing-up of the narrator is again curiously out of key:

> Wel koude he peynten lifly that it wroghte;
> With many a floryn he the hewes boghte.

In its reminder, however, that these are only *painted* terrors—a fact we may easily, and understandably, have forgotten—it leads on naturally to the enthusiastic description of nobility gathering for the tournament. For the moment we are asked to consider only the brave show of arms, the idealism of those who come to fight 'for love and for encrees of chivalrye'. When we are told that 'the grete Emetreus, the kyng of Inde . . . Cam ridynge lyk the god of armes, Mars' we are clearly meant to recall only one aspect of the martial god. Misery, cruelty, death are obscured by magnificence. Similarly, the honour and privilege of fighting for a lady puts out of mind—for the narrator, at least—the sad and sinister warnings of the temple of Venus: the goddess is now 'blisful Citherea benigne—I mene Venus, honurable and digne'.

But such confidence is to be undermined. Like the optimism of the lovers as they sacrifice to their deities and receive favourable 'signs', it is pathetically inadequate. The intervention of Saturn 'to stynten strif and drede' breaks ominously across the scene, and Chaucer's careful exposition of his nature and sphere of influence (for which his sources give no warrant) does nothing to assure us of a happy or a just outcome. This brilliant and menacing speech by the 'fader of pestilence' brings to a head the poem's insistence upon the pitiful state of man and the revengeful attitude of the gods who shape his destiny. If we needed confirmation of the truth of Palamon's early complaint to the 'crueel goddes', we have it here in most powerful form. Whatever the denouement of the story, it is clear, at this point, that it will involve pain and darkness; we realise, with some sense of shock, that the conflict is not so much between Mars and Venus, War and Love, as between two types of violence: Venus will achieve her ends through 'pale Saturnus the colde'; the lovers are to be united through the workings of the god of 'vengeance and pleyn correccioun'. And, as this part of the poem ends on a threatening note, we know that their happiness will be dearly bought.

Part four shows us the cost of happiness with brutal precision. Arcite is fatally wounded not in the glories of the tournament, but in a humiliating accident—we remember Saturn's claim to 'the derke tresons and the castes olde'. Chaucer lays new emphasis upon the physical details, the pain of his delayed death:

> The pipes of his longes gon to swelle,
> And every lacerte in his brest adoun
> Is shent with venym and corrupcioun.
> Hym gayneth neither, for to gete his lif,
> Vomyt upward, ne dounward laxatif . . .

And the narrator's brusque summing-up—

> Fare wel phisik! go ber the man to chirche!
> This al and som, that Arcita moot dye . . .

by virtue of its heartlessness points to the waste and pathos of the situation. The last speech of Arcite expresses this waste and pathos in a more directly moving idiom; much shorter than the original, it nevertheless manages to review the bitter sequence of events leading up to this moment. The dying man's baffled and, perhaps, ironic questions

> 'What is this world? what asketh men to have?
> Now with his love, now in his colde grave
> Allone, withouten any compaignye . . .'

replace, poignantly, a whole rhetorical series in the Italian. They remind us of many things: his untried stoicism when first in prison, seeing the hand of Saturn in 'this adversitee', but not foreseeing it in his death: his trenchant observation as he becomes further experienced in misery—

> 'Infinite harmes been in this mateere.
> We witen nat what thing we preyen heere:'

—an observation which does not, however, prevent him from 'joye and hope wel to fare' when his prayer to Mars is answered so deceptively with 'Victorie!' It has not been possible for Arcite to learn the full lesson of divine malice; he dies bewildered. But this is a speech of extreme compassion as well as extreme disillusionment. The warm recommendation of Palamon to Emelye—

> 'Foryet nat Palamon, the gentil man . . .'

contrasts vividly with the calculated actions and words of the deities in the poem. Only those who know at first hand that 'in this world greet pyne is' show any capacity for noble intent or deed; if Arcite does not understand the gods and their 'castes olde', he does now understand a virtue which in this poem is an entirely human prerogative—the virtue of charity.

What follows conforms to the pattern we have already noticed. The dignified closing of Arcite's life is treated with scant ceremony by the narrator himself: he does not know where his soul went 'as I cam nevere', nor does he care to speculate. The man is dead: 'Arcite is coold . . .' He has time for a sly joke at the expense of women before he adjusts his tone and style to describe the scene of grief in Athens. And serious indeed is the comment of 'olde fader Egeus', even if it is familiar in language and sentiment; the commonplace and indisputable theme of 'all must die'—transferred from Theseus's speech in the Italian—is imaged afresh, gracefully and mournfully:

> 'This world nys but a thurghfare ful of wo,
> And we ben pilgrymes passynge to and fro.'

The Chaucerian (and Biblical) touch is admirable—except that the next line, 'Deeth is an ende of every worldly soore', meant as a comfort, recalls an earlier moment in the poem, when Palamon refused the comfort of believing that death brings peace.

Clearly, it is not in the interests of the prescribed happy ending that such thoughts should intrude at this stage. But the words have been spoken, for good or ill. A more determined and comprehensive attempt to give comfort and justify events is made by Theseus after the funeral rites, and here again Arcite's happy deliverance from 'this foule prisoun of this lyf' is affirmed. The line draws, for its power, upon our realisation (not necessarily shared by Theseus, one feels) that life has in fact been an imprisonment for Arcite: even freedom shut him away from his love. The argument goes further: it makes an appeal for reconciliation based upon man's acceptance of the power, justice and perfection of the divinity which decrees a natural span of life for all things.

Composing a speech which is new in its most striking features, Chaucer works from Boethius to prove the wisdom and all-embracing love of the 'Firste Moevere of the cause above' and the unceasing flow of life out of what is perfect into what is limited and transitory.

But with the words of Theseus we have arrived at a decisive stage in the poem. Up to this point, as we have seen, Chaucer has taken a rather variable course in the matter of presentation—often appearing to be in two minds about the significance of his story. While he cannot resist drawing out the less attractive implications of the **"Knight's Tale"**, and inviting his audience to attend closely as he does so, he is equally willing to accept what his sources lay down as acceptable. With a boldness ranging from the blunt to the flippant, he can even be found minimising that same seriousness of attitude which he has been at such pains to induce. But now the narrative nears conclusion, and some general statement has to be made which will allow the audience to approve of the 'blisse and melodye' of the last lines. And it is clear that Chaucer felt the need for synthesis: whether prompted by awareness of the difficulties in his poem or not, he gives the speech of Theseus a far wider philosophical scope than it has in the *Teseida*. Arcite's death is to be seen as yet another proof of the 'wise purveiaunce' of God—or, conceding to the original pagan world of the poem, of 'Juppiter, the kyng'. *Our* difficulty does not lie in reconciling the death of Arcite with a divinely ordained plan, but in reconciling the noble account of this plan with the ugly manifestation of divine motives and activities which Chaucer has allowed his poem to give. Theseus's speech is well positioned, but it is, on analysis, an odd conclusion to a story which has admitted so frankly the lack of dignity, pity or love in the deities who interpret the meaning of 'that same Prince and that Moevere'. While the speech alone could persuade us of some just pattern 'to which the whole creation moves', the preceding poem demonstrates with much feeling that

> As flies to wanton boys, are we to the gods;
> They kill us for their sport.

The narrator, who, over the course of the work, has not shown himself sensitive to finer distinctions, gives no sign now that he is disturbed by Theseus's explanation of divine order and benevolence and the negative proof of it in the lives of mortal subjects. For him, the tale is done; the union of Palamon and Emelye cancels out all memory of what has led to it:

> For now is Palamon in alle wele,
> Lyvynge in blisse, in richesse, and in heele,
> And Emelye hym loveth so tendrely . . .

For the modern reader, the conclusion is not so easy. Neither Theseus's speech nor the cheerful valedictions of the narrator can quite rid the mind of the unanswered question—

> 'What governance is in this prescience,
> That giltelees tormenteth innocence?'

The reasoning of Theseus on the subject of mutability is cogent, but he has nothing to offer as an explanation of why the 'Firste Moevere', 'hym that al may gye', should take such unpleasant ways and employ such unpleasant agents to create 'this foule prisoun of this lyf' for human beings noble and potential of good.

The problem is one of balance and emphasis. When we study the use Chaucer made of original materials, there can be no doubt that his imaginative sympathy was called out most strongly by the spectacle of human life subject to cruel and disproportionate strokes of destiny. And, regardless of the dilemma in which he might ultimately find himself, he allowed that sympathy to make strong claims upon him. His portrayal of the sinister gods and their tormented creatures takes in not only the characters and immediate issues of the tale but the whole human condition: we recall the enlarged scope of the paintings in the temple of Mars, and Saturn's cold revelation of limitless power. This portrayal is so memorably done that it becomes very difficult for us to respond uncritically either to a philosophic statement which largely ignores the prominent issue of divine malice or to a happy ending which gives little sign of recognising the unhappiness it builds upon. The reader's predicament is somewhat similar in *The Winter's Tale:* there also a narrative full of extreme and unmotivated cruelty is brought to a 'happy' conclusion, but the reconciliation is hardly sufficient to quieten our uneasiness, even disgust, at the harsh treatment of innocence which makes that reconciliation necessary. Both *The Winter's Tale* and the **"Knight's Tale"** suggest material for tragedy. This material cannot be fully utilised, however, because of the limiting features of the set narrative structure; while the prescribed story is an inadequate vehicle for the emotions so powerfully expressed by the poetry, it cannot be lightly disposed of.

Looking afresh at the **"Knight's Tale"**, it is important to ask ourselves whether the established view of its meaning—'order, which characterises the structure of the poem, is also the heart of its meaning'—is sufficient. Certainly Chaucer is concerned with pattern: the formal, rhetorical layout of the poem has long been recognised—mortal rivalries matched by heavenly, the 'Firste Moevere' matched by Duke Theseus. And, as we have seen, one of Chaucer's directing principles in dealing with the *Teseida* was that of producing a more symmetrical work, even to the point of giving his two heroes similarly phrased speeches. Moreover, life in Athens is shown to be elaborately organised; observance and ritual of all kinds shape experience. But we ought not to confuse rhetorical ordering with imaginative. Chaucer allows the poem to raise imaginative issues which are not resolved by the final philosophic summing-up any more than they are resolved by the bland denouement of the final twenty lines. This is something we have to face in other works of Chaucer. The **"Knight's Tale"** presents us with it in a particularly urgent form. ***Troilus and Criseyde*** is an excellent example of a poem which uses a good deal of philosophic and religious material with an eye to *local* richness rather than to overall thematic consistency. Hence, the kind of statement which is intended, in book three, to sanction and hallow the mutual love of Troilus and Criseyde, and so to release the poet's imagination for its immediate task, stands curiously against the overwhelming homiletic censure of the finale:

> Lo here, of payens corsed olde rites . . .

But at least, in ***Troilus,*** we know from the beginning that the human beings of the story will merit some responsibility for the disasters that overtake them. There is a fall from grace, a betrayal, and if it does not justify the all-consuming fierceness of denunciation which Chaucer ultimately steels himself to deliver, it must be judged adversely by a mediaeval Christian poet. And in ***Troilus*** we are allowed to penetrate the inner lives of the characters so deeply that the tragic course of events seems partially explicable in terms of noble but fallible human nature. In the **"Knight's Tale"** no similar concession is made: the human beings most painfully involved in the narrative are deliberately envisaged as pawns in a game played by the gods—their individuality and freedom of action only apparent when they break through conventional modes of speech and complain with bitterness or despondency about victimisation. The tale confronts us with active malice and passive suffering to an almost unbearable degree: what relief there is—the duel and the plans for a tournament in part two, the tournament itself in part four—also serves to prolong the agony. Chaucer provides for the perceptive reader in the fateful ambiguities of Mercury's words to Arcite—

> . . . 'To Atthenes shaltou wende,
> Ther is thee shapen of thy wo an ende.'

and in Arcite's clear-cut reply—

> 'In hire presence I recche nat to sterve.'

All the brilliance and noise of the tournament cannot shut out from memory the promise of Saturn to Venus—'I wol thy lust fulfille'.

By choosing to lay stress upon these elements in the story, Chaucer considerably widened his range of emotional and descriptive poetry: by choosing also to encourage reflection, even criticism, he made his task of final and total reconciliation much more complex. We may think that we see, in the strange switches of tone and attitude, in the the 'double voice' of poet-narrator, his half-conscious understanding of this fact: on the one hand, he is impelled to re-create the older story with intelligent scepticism, compassion, dramatic insight—on the other, he is reluctant to admit the significance of what he has done. The imaginative advance and withdrawal of the poem is noticeable throughout. And Theseus's speech is, when examined closely, a withdrawal from rather than a solution of the problem. We may be able to accept the lesson of 'false worldes brotelnesse' from the pitiful wreckage of Troilus's love, but we may question whether the proposition that

> ' . . . nature hath nat taken his bigynnyng
> Of no partie or cantel of a thyng,
> But of a thyng that parfit is and stable . . . '

helps us to accept what we have been shown of the sinister dealings of the divine with the human. It is worth considering this speech in some detail, for like the last twenty stanzas of **Troilus and Criseyde,** it moves somewhat arbitrarily among a number of reasons for resignation; its assurance is deceptive, for it relies upon our willingness to put out of mind many of the more uncomfortable aspects of the poem.

Opening with a substantial Boethian addition to the Italian source, [Theseus's speech] sets the death of man in its widest context, and not only states the principle of universal mutability but also implies a benevolent providence:

> 'For with that faire cheyne of love he bond
> The fyr, the eyr, the water and the lond
> In certeyn boundes . . . '

Our comprehension is here invited on the highest philosophic level and in verse of impressive dignity. The eloquence of the passage is beyond doubt: what is debatable is the wisdom of invoking 'the Firste Moevere of the cause above', with its inevitable Christian associations, to cover the activities of Mars, Venus and Saturn in this particular poem. When the succeeding lines draw upon the Italian for their moving images of transitory life—tree, stone, river, man and woman—we cannot help reflecting that Boccaccio gave to Theseus a speech far less ambitious but perhaps more appropriate in the circumstances. A return to Boethian argument is not sustained; Theseus's reasoning descends to a practical sphere. The injunction

> 'To maken vertu of necessitee,
> And take it weel that we may nat eschue . . . '

represents good sense rather than wisdom: it is not simply wrong but 'folye' to rebel against 'hym that al may gye'. A list of useful points takes the speech further and further away from philosophic matters. We are asked to rejoice that Arcite died 'in his excellence and flour' and then that he has escaped 'out of this foule prisoun of this lyf'. The backward-looking reference of this last line has already been discussed; only the confident flow of the poetry disguises the basic illogicality of the appeals. The whole affair is put at lowest rating when we are told that grief is useless since Arcite is now beyond gratitude—

> 'Kan he hem thank? Nay, God woot, never a
> deel . . . '

The conclusion is brisk—perhaps there is even a note of relief as Theseus bids us to cast-off sorrow and 'thanken Juppiter of al his grace'. If we feel the irony of the phrase as a description of Jupiter's ways, we are quickly led on to other things. The speech, which began in so elevated a manner, passes almost without notice into the narrator's soothing voice as he says goodbye to the story.

It is, surely, a measure of the greatness of Chaucer that his imaginative response to a situation in which innocent creatures confront the wilful use of absolute power was strong enough to disturb the overall balance of his work. As it is, the words of Theseus, 'Why grucchen we, why have we hevynesse . . . ', intended as a rallying cry towards cheerful recovery, serve also to emphasise the great gulf which lies between the questions asked by the poet's imagination, and the replies he feels able, in *this* instance, to give. (pp. 9-36)

> *Elizabeth Salter, "The Knight's Tale," in her* Chaucer: "The Knight's Tale" and "The Clerk's Tale," *Barron's Educational Series, Inc., 1962, pp. 9-36.*

Alfred David   (essay date 1965)

[*In the excerpt below, David argues that the worldview presented in the "Franklin's Tale" presages the attitudes depicted in eighteenth-century sentimental comedy.*]

The Franklin is among the most attractive of the Canterbury pilgrims. His tale radiates good sense and good humor, and if he appears to be something of a social climber, he at least expresses genuine respect for the moral superiority that should accompany the privileges of rank and property: "Fy on possessioun, / But if a man be vertuous withal!" It is tempting, therefore, to share Professor Kittredge's wholehearted admiration for the Franklin and to accept his theory that the Franklin happily resolves Chaucer's debate on marriage. "We need not hesitate," Kittredge concluded [in his 1911-12 *Modern Philology* article "Chaucer's Discussion of Marriage"], "to accept the solution which the Franklin offers as that which Geoffrey Chaucer the man accepted for his own part." The Franklin's ideal of marriage, as Kittredge also observed, develops out of his general preoccupation with gentility, so poignantly expressed in his praise of the Squire and his disappointment in his own son. The Franklin, according to Kittredge, tells his story to prove to the company, and especially to the Host, that he knows a thing or two about "gentillesse":

> For the **"Franklin's Tale"** is a gentleman's story, and he tells it like a gentleman. It is derived, he tells us, from "thise olde *gentil* Britons." Dorigen lauds Arveragus' *gentillesse* toward her in refusing to insist on soveraynetee in marriage. Aurelius is deeply impressed by the knight's *gentillesse* in allowing the lady to keep her word, and emulates it by releasing her. . . . And finally, the clerk releases Aurelius, from the same motive of generous emulation.

Is it unfair to feel that the gentleman doth protest too much? Several critics, at least, have in recent years expressed serious doubts that the Franklin's liberal ideas on marriage and nobility would have been as acceptable to Chaucer's audience as they are to us. The Host, a shrewd judge of social credentials, definitely is not impressed, and professor R. M. Lumiansky [in his *Of Sondry Folk*] is surely right that the Host's rude rebuke to the Franklin should be read: "Straw for *your* gentillesse!" Mr. Lumiansky sees the tale as the stumbling effort of a bourgeois gentleman to affect the style and subject matter of courtly romance. Professor Donald R. Howard, basing his critique of the **"Franklin's Tale"** on religious grounds, points out [in his 1960-61 *Modern Philology* article "The Conclusion of the Marriage Group"] that the Franklin's solution to the debate on marriage is a completely worldly one that ignores all the problems regarding the doctrine of the Church on marriage that are raised by the Wife of Bath in her prologue.

The social theories set forth by the Franklin in his tale certainly deserve further scrutiny. The complementary ideals of marriage based on mutual forbearance and of honor based on reciprocal trust and generosity appeal to us because they are so very much our own. It is precisely the modernity of the Franklin's point of view, however, that should make us cautious of accepting it uncritically. He belongs to the class that has since come to rule society, but in the fourteenth century its ascendancy was still very far off. One may at least speculate as to what members of the pilgrim audience such as the Knight and the Squire and what members of Chaucer's own audience would have made of the Franklin's performance.

The **"Franklin's Tale"** replies not only to the other tales in the "marriage group" but also to the **"Knight's Tale"**. The two stories have much in common. Each is set in the romantic past and in a pagan world, each involves a triangle of noble lovers, and each portrays an ideal of the noble life. The Franklin tells his story not merely to describe an ideal marriage but to develop an ideal of conduct designed to govern the relationships between lovers, between husband and wife, and even between debtor and creditor— "gentillesse," that is, in the broadest sense. It aspires to be a tale of "Trouthe and honour, fredom and curteisie," and, therefore, the Knight and his tale provide the models by which the Franklin would wish himself and his tale to be measured. The two tales are linked, moreover, by the Franklin's obvious attempt to compliment both the Squire and his father through the portraits of Aurelius and Arveragus.

Would Chaucer's Knight and Squire have been flattered, or would they have been amused, by this unexpected tribute from a new kind of gentleman? There is good evidence that the Franklin, like most of the pilgrims, does not escape Chaucer's irony. His tale reflects the values of the emerging class to which he belongs, and although Chaucer, who has much in common with the Franklin, may have regarded these values with tolerant sympathy, he makes it plain enough that the Franklin's chivalry is a watered-down version of the old-fashioned kind. It is, therefore, no accident that the **"Franklin's Tale,"** as we shall see, bears a striking resemblance to a species of bourgeois comedy that Goldsmith, nearly four hundred years later, was to call "sentimental."

Before proceeding to the tale itself, let us take a closer look at the portrait of the Franklin in the **"General Prologue."** At first glance, the description of the "worthy vavasour" has only a tenuous connection with the theme of "gentillesse." Nevertheless, if we examine the details of the portrait with a class-conscious eye, they suggest a harmless pretentiousness that is entirely in character for the teller of the tale of Dorigen and Arveragus. The portrait is flattering on the surface, but, as in the case of many of the portraits, the praise of the pilgrim carries with it certain limitations and qualifications. For example, we are left to infer the nature of the Prioress' "conscience" from her tenderness toward mice and lapdogs. We are told of the Franklin, "An housholdere, and that a greet, was he," but his grandeur is measured primarily by the quality of his bread and ale and the quantity of fish and flesh consumed at his table. Like the characters in his tale, he is free with his possessions; yet, his love of good living and conspicuous consumption suggest an aristocratic standard of living divorced from an aristocratic way of life. The Franklin's household is like the Land of Cockayne where fat partridges fly into the mouths of the carefree inhabitants: "It snewed in his house of mete and drynke." Where does all this bounty flow from? Chaucer tells us of his poultry coops and fish ponds; conspicuously absent, in this context, however, is any reference to an activity that with Chaucer is almost invariably an emblem of the noble life— the hunt. Even the lordly monk is devoted to the royal sport. The Knight's favorite pastime, when he is not chasing heathens, is suggested by the fact that the servant who accompanies him is a forester. The only servant mentioned in the Franklin's portrait is his cook.

The note of luxury and softness is sustained in the only details we are given of his costume:

> An anlass and a gipser al of silk
> Heeng at his girdel, whit as morne milk.

An anelace is a dagger or short knife (though it may also refer to a short sword), and a gypcière, an ornamental purse, which probably at one time functioned as a game bag. Planché's history of British costume tells us that under Edward III "the fashion of wearing daggers stuck through pouches became very general amongst knights and gentlemen." The Franklin's dagger and milk-white purse will never be rust-stained like the Knight's gipon. Like the silver-mounted knives of the five guildsmen, they are for ornament rather than for use, and they suggest, like everything else about the Franklin, the symbols of rank no longer serving their old function.

Much as the Franklin dons the badges of nobility in his costume, he adorns his tale with the elevated language of chivalric romance, although he modestly disclaims any skill in the art of rhetoric. I cannot agree with Mr. Lumiansky that the Franklin's affectation of the courtly style is awkward. The Franklin's use of language expresses his personality, but, for all that he is a bourgeois, he is as polished as any of Chaucer's characters. Here and there, he burlesques his own flights of fancy, as in the lines, "th'orisonte hath reft the sonne his lyght,— / This is as muche to seye as it was nyght!" But that does not mean that he is not a true admirer of the courtly style or that he cannot use it skillfully. He finds fault not with the manner but with the conventional matter of courtly romance, and in his tale he ingeniously transforms the aristocratic ideals of love and nobility into something that conforms more comfortably to his own values. The difference may be seen by contrasting the Franklin's treatment of love with the Knight's.

In the **"Knight's Tale,"** love is treated as an over-powering and irrational force that can set the best of friends to fighting like two wild boars over a lady who scarcely knows that they exist. Theseus, an old veteran both in love and in war, views the plight of Palamon and Arcite as the height of folly, but at the same time he regards them with nostalgic sympathy. He accepts the foolishness of passionate love as an inevitable phase in the life of a young nobleman: "A man moot ben a fool, or yong or oold." Whatever else love may be, it is an overmastering passion that drives out every other consideration of loyalty or self interest.

Such stormy emotions are absent from the **"Franklin's Tale."** Arveragus woos Dorigen and suffers, as a courtly lover must, but the Franklin does not dwell upon his trials. The key to the relationship between his lovers is reason, not passion. Each shows awareness of the other's feelings and promises to exercise rational control over his own. Their marriage is a contract under which the rights of each party are recognized and guaranteed. This is not said to detract from the freshness and charm of their agreement—it simply acknowledges the fact that the love of Arveragus and Dorigen is of a different order from the blind passion of Palamon and Arcite.

The same point might be made about the third member of the triangle, Aurelius. He, too, is a "lovyere and a lusty bacheler," and he loves his lady unto the death—or so he believes. The Franklin seems to smile upon Aurelius' "gentillesse" and to find his courtship charming, and he objects to one thing only. Such a delightful young man

The Ellesmere Nun's Priest.

should not lower himself by making love to another man's wife. Dorigen speaks both for herself and for the Franklin in delicately but firmly reproaching her suitor:

> Lat swiche folies out of youre herte slyde.
> What deyntee sholde a man han in his lyf
> For to go love another mannes wyf,
> That hath hir body whan so that hym liketh?

The tenderness and nobility of courtly sentiment touch the Franklin's heart (as later they will captivate Samuel Richardson and Clarissa), but he cannot stomach the immorality. His tale is, therefore, an illustration that one may be noble without being wicked and that noble sentiment may be preserved without the bloody consequences that usually follow in chivalric romance. The tale is one in which all characters behave with such magnanimity that it becomes a moot point at the end which of them has acted most nobly.

"Gentillesse" for the Franklin is not the exclusive prerogative of the nobility. The Franklin's clerk is portrayed so as to compliment another delightful young man of whom the Franklin approves wholeheartedly—the Clerk of Oxenford. Even a clerk may behave nobly, and the **"Franklin's Tale"** teaches, in effect, the same lesson as the tale of the Wife of Bath: anyone may be a gentleman if he behaves like one, or as the old hag in the Wife's tale puts it:

> Looke who that is moost vertuous alway,
> Pryvee and apert, and moost entendeth ay
> To do the gentil dedes that he kan;
> Taak hym for the grettest gentil man.

The Franklin's concept of nobility follows logically from a conviction that all men are capable of reason and virtue and are, therefore, potentially equal. His view of human relationships is profoundly legalistic: it is essentially that of a social contract, and a contract may exist only between free and equal parties. To be noble is to live up to one's agreements, whether in love or in business. Deal fairly with others and they will deal fairly with you. In place of a feudal relationship, based upon the inequality of the sovereign lady and her servant-lover, the Franklin has put an ideal of love that is in essence democratic. The Franklin, it may be recalled, had been a member of Parliament, and while it would be going too far to call his social ideas revolutionary, it is fair to say that they contain the seeds of future revolution. His ideal is honorable, but it does away with the principle of hierarchy, an essential part of the feudal concept of "gentillesse."

Let us go back to the **"Knight's Tale."** Palamon and Arcite are undoubted gentlemen and sworn brothers. Their "trouthe" lasts until they have both seen Emilye. Then there is no more talk of brotherhood until Arcite, on his deathbed, tells Emilye, "Foryet nat Palamon, the gentil man." Is their warfare a flagrant violation of their honor as gentlemen? On the contrary, as Arcite says,

> Wostow nat wel the olde clerkes sawe,
> That 'who shal yeve a lovere any lawe?'
> Love is a gretter lawe, by my pan,
> Than may be yeve to any erthely man;
> And therfore positif lawe and swich decree
> Is broken al day for love in ech degree.
> A man moot nedes love, maugree his heed.

The noble lover accepts a hierarchy even of sworn faith. The laws of reason, of friendship, of self-preservation itself must be sacrificed to the one sacred obligation—the service of one's lady. Two oaths can never be equally binding. The higher one takes precedence.

Yet the Franklin in his tale is attempting to prescribe a law to lovers. One's word of honor is always binding, and so Arveragus tells Dorigen she must abide by her promise. He tells her, "Trouthe is the hyeste thyng that man may kepe." But which truth is Dorigen to keep, her rash promise to Aurelius, or the marital troth she has sworn to Arveragus? The Franklin is, of course, aware of the awkwardness of a man's commanding his wife to dishonor him, and he bids his audience be patient—everything will turn out all right. But the awkwardness is not to be explained away by the happy ending. "Trouthe" is a key word in the tale, and Dorigen uses exactly the same formula in plighting faith to her husband,

> Sire, I wol be youre humble trewe wyf;
> Have heer my trouthe, til that myn herte breste

and in giving her word to Aurelius,

> Have heer my trouthe, in al that evere I kan.

When Dorigen is confronted with this dilemma, she can see only one way out. Her lugubrious catalogue of maidens and wives who have chosen death before dishonor has been criticized as an intrusion upon the tale, but the list serves a very definite purpose—it emphasizes the novelty of the Franklin's solution by suggesting one of the more old-fashioned alternatives to it. Dorigen might kill herself. Or there is another alternative that would surely occur to any gentleman as the natural way out of such an embarrassment: Arveragus should take his sword and challenge his rival. A sure and realistic solution to any triangle situation in fiction is to kill off one member of the triangle. But the Franklin's point is precisely that he will have no such violent solutions. His practical nature and sanguine temperament forbid such irrational and sanguinary methods.

Is it possible to demonstrate nobility without resorting to a sword or an "anlaas"? Clearly it is entirely in keeping with the Franklin's own aspirations to argue that a generous heart may accomplish as much as feats of arms. His solution, therefore, is that generosity and good faith on the part of one gentleman inspire reciprocal generosity and good faith on the part of another. Virtue will be rewarded, and in the pleasant belief that virtue and reason must prevail, the **"Franklin's Tale"** reveals its kinship with sentimental comedy.

Sentimental comedy, as defined in Goldsmith's essay, is "a species of dramatic composition . . . in which the virtues of private life are exhibited, rather than the vices exposed. . . . In these plays almost all the characters are good, and exceedingly generous; they are lavish enough of their *tin* money on the stage; and though they want humor, have abundance of sentiment and feeling." I would add that sentimental comedy usually contains a potentially tragic plot, which is resolved happily through the noble behavior of the characters. A classic example of the genre is Sir Richard Steele's *The Conscious Lovers,* which Steele said in his Preface was written for the sake of a scene in which the hero, Bevil Junior, refuses to fight a duel with an impetuous rival. Steele expressed the hope that the scene might have "some effect upon the Goths and Vandals that frequent the theatres." More modestly, the Franklin presents his conscious lovers as model gentlemen of the fourteenth century.

Sentimental comedy reflects the taste of an audience that at the turn of the eighteenth century was becoming predominantly bourgeois. It is the point of view of this audience that Chaucer has anticipated in his characterization of the Franklin, who is among the first representatives in literature of the class for whom Steele would be writing a new kind of drama. Unlike Steele, however, Chaucer is not writing a problem comedy to present the ideals of the middle class. He is writing a human comedy in which representatives of the various estates and professions take turns expressing their views of life in a series of tales. The Franklin, as it happens, is the man of the future. His ideas are closer to our own than those of the Knight, the man of the past. Whether Chaucer himself possessed the historical foresight to see the change coming, one can only speculate. But he was aware of the difference, and in their portraits and tales he contrasted their ideals of the noble life. On the one hand, we find the fatalism of the chivalric viewpoint, nobly summed up in Theseus' Boethian speech. The **"Knight's Tale,"** too, ends happily, but the happiness of Palamon and Emilye is purchased at the price of Arcite's death. Man must make "vertu of necessitee." On the other side, there is the optimism and relativism of the middle class. No one need suffer because virtue releases man from the bonds of necessity. One point of view is essentially tragic; the other is basically comic. For Chaucer, I do not believe that either is final or complete. Both make part of a procession; they complement one another; and they command our sympathy because of their humanity. (pp. 19-27)

Alfred David, "Sentimental Comedy in the 'Franklin's Tale'," in Annuale Mediaevale, *Vol. 6, 1965, pp. 19-27.*

Paul G. Ruggiers (essay date 1965)

[*Ruggiers is an American scholar who serves as the general editor for the* Variorum Edition of the Works of Geoffrey Chaucer *(1979—). In the following excerpt, he examines the "Nun's Priest's Tale," praising Chaucer's ability to balance the intellectual and poetic content of his work.*]

From many points of view the **"Nun's Priest's Tale"** may be considered a high-water mark of complex thematic statement in the *Canterbury Tales.* Even with its proliferation of exemplary materials (such as we note in the tales of the Pardoner and Franklin), it constitutes a complex of most that is happy in Chaucer's artistic and intellectual equipment: a grasp of form, a subtle ironical tone, cleverness without slavery in the literary allusions, the subjection of high seriousness to the needs of the form, a casual finesse with rhetorical conventions, a sharpening of the theme of marital dissension, a suiting of moral utterance to the narrator, and a delicate balance between the romantic and comic modes. It is, in short, *sui generis.*

Its meaning has to do, in one sense, with the way in which reason and instinct are embattled (a sentiment common to the fabliaux), but it places these firmly against the larger questions of love, the destinal order, and human responsibility, and casts a final vote in favor of self-control. If this shift of balance to the side of reason suggests survival through canniness, we have, I feel, a merely ironical tale. By adducing the more serious questions of a rational universe, Chaucer widens the theological ambience in which his agents live, and tests the familiar triad of love, crucial adventure, and virtue acquired which are the heart of romance.

Coming as it does after the limited range of the Monk, the tale evinces an intellectual complexity which is its characteristic tone; just how far removed we are from the mechanical world of Venus, or Fame, or Fortuna, or from a vague retributive Justice meting out good and ill through apparent caprice is demonstrated by the tale of a cock, hen, and villain fox, all of whom have responsibility in a world they not only must interpret, but create for themselves. It is a world seen not from the point of view of trag-

edy, but of thought and laugh-provoking comedy. It is comedy that comes as a response to the plea of the serious-minded Knight, a man of moderate disposition, albeit a slayer of his foes and a mighty warrior in fifteen battles. The complexity Chaucer attributes to him is not merely a matter of having such a man cry out for gladsome tales. If we compare his character in detail with that of the lugubrious and doleful tale-teller the Monk, we discover new ironies inherent in their actions. The purely physical details of the Monk's hulking figure, his fine horses, his taste for fine food and clothes, his overbearing assertion of service to God outside the monastic world afford a sharp contrast to the figure of the Knight with his meek and maidenly deportment, his restraint of tongue, his avoidance of the signs of wealth, his fruitful activity in defense of the faith. To attribute to the one a limited vision of the meaning of suffering and to the other a preference for tales with a happy ending is to point up in yet another way an expanding complexity of character in the pilgrimage community. Chaucer is, as it were, focusing his own attitudes upon the perplexities of tragedy and comedy in preparation for a new kind of tragi-comic vision far beyond the Monk's limited range.

In the **"Monk's Tale,"** the concept of tragedy, although it does not entirely omit the role of the will, is more mechanical than human, the effect of character upon action being restricted mostly to the defect of "mysgovernaunce" and to the "unwar strook" dealt out by Fortune. We note in it an absence of character development and the tendency to see human suffering only as the result of a fall. The form itself prevents a thoughtful interest in the development of ethos in the agents, in their ability to argue themselves into or out of situations and in the important consideration of the degree of human responsibility which the agents may assume in this life. In all justice to the tales related by the Monk, we must consider that any long treatment of these tragedies would conceivably entail a great deal of thought upon precisely such matters; indeed their defect is their brevity as much as it is the incompleteness of the whole view regarding Fortune and man's lot which they imply.

The interruption by the Knight calls for something more in literature; if not a correction of the view of Fortune in its relations to the law of the Prime Mover such as he himself has already presented in his tale of Palamon and Arcite, at least an amplification of a view of life which allows for quite another way of fictive presentation:

> " . . . whan a man hath been in povre estaat,
> And clymbeth up and wexeth fortunat,
> And there abideth in prosperitee:
> Swich thyng is gladsom, as it thynketh me,
> And of swich thyng were goodly for to telle."

To this the Host gives scolding assent. His point of view may not be that of the Knight, a representative of quite another class of society, but he does know that what he has heard has become a heavy burden to the mind, if not an outright bore:

> "For sikerly, nere clynkyng of youre belles,
> That on youre bridel hange on every syde,
> By hevene kyng, that for us alle dyde,

I sholde er this han fallen doun for sleep,
Althogh the slough had never been so deep."

And so the Knight and Host are united in common intention if not in comprehension of the issue at hand. Both have objected to the performance of the Monk, the Knight we presume because he objects to the statement of a not entirely sound view of life (if we may judge him from the story he has told) and because "litel hevynesse / Is right ynough to muche folk, I gesse." The Host objects because there is "no desport ne game" in these tales, and furthermore the reiterated theme has become monotonous. Both views have their healthy side.

The Monk, however, had had his say and declines to relate a tale of hunting; his natural discretion, which has held him back from engaging in badinage with the Host, again urges upon him the better course of keeping his private life to himself. We turn instead to another religious, the "sweete preest, this goodly man, sir John," who is urged to tell us a happy, cheerful tale. His horse, a jade "bothe foul and lene," offers a contrast to the sleek berry-brown palfrey of the Monk, whom the Nun's Priest now supersedes. But as we read we see that the paucity and poverty of material goods in the Nun's Priest do not preclude a richness of natural gifts and a depth of cheerful goodness absent from the performance of the materially endowed, self-limiting Monk.

For reasons which we can only surmise, Chaucer has not given explicit details about the person and character of the Nun's Priest. In the **"Prologue of the Nun's Priest's Tale"** the Host describes his horse, and in the famous epilogue, regarded by some as a cancelled link, substantially repeats a line and a sentiment which we have already heard him apply to the Monk: "Thou woldest han been a tredefowel aright." We can only conjecture that Chaucer has, by the shift of the line to the previous performance, exhausted one view of the ecclesiastical male and temporarily, at least, abandoned the matter of expanding upon the character of the Nun's Priest. On artistic grounds it seems suitable too to explore the matter of celibacy and marriage (the lives of Monk and Host) immediately following upon the **"Melibee,"** a natural enough movement from the admonitions of Dame Prudence in that tale to the bodily threats of Goodelief in the **"Monk's Prologue,"** and thence to the plight of matrimony in a world from which the best men have escaped. It would seem that Chaucer is by degrees opening the door on the many-faceted subject of marriage, so that when he has finished the **"Nun's Priest's Tale,"** there is little reason for him to revert to the matter of priestly celibacy inasmuch as it diverts attention from the subject of the tale itself and repeats elements now applied to the character of the Monk.

Since Chaucer himself has told us little about the character of the Nun's Priest (some deductions may be made from the tone and attitudes of the tale assigned him), critical opinion has perforce to be conjectural. One commentator describes him as "a handsome, strong, rosy-cheeked youngster, with a sense of humor unequalled in the company," who can "deftly satirize the personal characteristics and the literary style of his predecessor without for a moment arousing the suspicion of his dignified superior."

Another later writer suggests that he is "Scrawny, humble, and timid, while at the same time highly intelligent, well-educated, shrewd and witty," and further that he is "weak in body and fawning in manner." These are tantalizing surmises; in the end, each reader will feel that the personality of the Nun's Priest is best derived from an examination of the story Chaucer chose to assign him.

As we have said, the tale masterfully integrates many elements which we have seen or noted singly or in combinations in other tales. More important perhaps than these elements taken one by one or in combination is the creation of a frame or envelope in which to contain the moral and quasi-mythic structure. This outer frame presents to us those human agents necessary to provide for the reader some ideal of human behavior, some rule of continence and contentment. The old widow, with her little cottage and her careful economy by which she provides for herself and her two daughters, offers by such details as temperance of diet and exercise and a contented heart an image of temperate law, of self-restraint and self-control, of sobriety and reasonable discretion. It is the widow's yard that is the world, apparently safe and secure, for Chauntecleer and his wives; it is into this world that evil intrudes in the shape of the sly fox; it is to this world that the widow wishes to restore Chauntecleer at the conclusion of his adventure, setting in motion the final boisterous attempt at rescue.

But it is Chauntecleer's plight which holds our interest and for which the outer human frame exists. It is Chauntecleer's character and his virtues or absence of virtues, his self-assurance and braggadocio, his pride, his sensuality, his susceptibility to flattery, and his sly intelligence that engage our minds. The opening description of Chauntecleer, replete with instinctive passion and joy, follows immediately upon the associations of poverty and patient, passionless temperance. Style itself echoes the contrast as Chaucer begins to employ the language of the romantic mode, and what is austere or even pedestrian in the opening of the tale gives way to something courtly, perhaps, and descriptively elevated, with even a momentary flight into lyric: "My lief is faren in londe!"

This may be considered the high style, in keeping with the poet's intention to parody the purely tragic view of the Monk and to supply a corrective through the device of comedy. Hence the necessity for enhancing the character of the cock so that he may appear to be regal, hence the fall from good fortune, hence the philosophical rumination about the relation of will to necessity, the elevated speeches, apostrophes and exclamations, the comparisons with figures of classical antiquity, and hence the errors in judgment and the final moral tag. The subjects and mannerisms of tragedy must be present, even in ironical contexts, seen in contrast to the subjects and mannerisms of comedy: the world of love and marriage, of domestic quarreling, of deception and jokes, of personal arrogance and instinctive passions, of personal vanity and wishing to be right at all costs, of wit and hairbreadth escape, of chases and rueful laughter. The result is, in its way, like the relation of the **"Franklin's Tale"** to the **"Merchant's Tale,"** a saner, more humane attitude than the one stated in the previous tale.

A large section of the tale is composed of the debate between Chauntecleer and his beauteous paramour Pertelote on the subject of dreams. Their speeches reveal a great deal of their character; Pertelote's lines beginning "Avoy! Fy on yow, hertelees!" with their repeated exclamations and questions are full of feminine excitability and concern. Her admonitions are purely domestic: "For Goddes love, as taak som laxatyf." Her wisdom is for the most part the wisdom of the home dispenser. Chaucer is clearly enjoying the game. Chauntecleer's long-winded answer, beginning with an elaborate politeness ("Madame, graunt mercy of youre loore.") is a rejoinder of some haughtiness of tone. More than a refutation answering the alleged authority of Cato, the long recital of superior authorities allows us to see Chauntecleer as one of Chaucer's more self-conscious orators, more thoughtful, more playful and sly, more pompous and self-assured. The cock is a narrator of no little skill, constructing his two initial *exempla* with great care as to form and tone and attention to detail. Indeed he is so careful a constructor of plot, with its inevitable conclusions, that the moral statement with which the first one closes tends to overshadow the principal concern with the credibility of dreams:

> "O blisful God, that art so just and trewe,
> Lo, how that thow bewreyest mordre alway!
> Mordre wol out, that se we day by day.
> Mordre is so wlatsom and abhomynable
> To God, that is so just and resonable,
> That he ne wol nat suffre it heled be,
> Though it abyde a yeer, or two, or thre.
> Mordre wol out, this my conclusioun."

But the point is made, first through a reluctant believer in dreams, and then through an actual non-believer who is proved to be wrong. Thereafter Chauntecleer warms to his task, and in a rapid mélange of instances drawn from Biblical, literary, and historical sources, within a space of some 40 lines as compared with the 126 of the first two *exempla*, he rattles off six additional stories to refute his wife's authority. His conclusion is inevitable, a mixture of the tragic assertion with the most bathetic comic statement:

> "Shortly I seye, as for conclusioun,
> That I shal han of this avisioun
> Adversitee; and I seye forthermoor,
> That I ne telle of laxatyves no stoor,
> For they been venymous, I woot it weel;
> I hem diffye, I love hem never a deel!"

And the action that follows upon this long debate, in which each agent has but one major speech, bears out this prediction. But before the action there intervenes his love speech to Pertelote containing its bold and unselfconscious *ludum*, a joke at the expense of his less tutored wife:

> " . . . *In principio,*
> *Mulier est hominis confusio,—*
> Madame, the sentence of this Latyn is,
> 'Womman is mannes joye and al his blis.' "

Whether we cheer or blame him in this joke upon his wife-

paramour, the speech is that of the passionate lover, embellished with sincere regard, expressing gratitude for God's grace, joy and comfort in her companionship, as well as that up-surging confidence that enables him to defy dreams and visions. They have had their quarrel or debate, but their relationship is a happy and a natural one elevated by the poet through the language of love. The jest that Chaucer puts in his beak hints at that double-edged truth to which the Middle Ages were dedicated by tradition on the one hand and by human nature on the other: in the beginning Eve was the source of Adam's fall. And yet, Chaucer's humane and comic realism forbids the dour anti-feminist implications and provides a counterpoise in that other truth, that other affirmation, *Amor vincit omnia.*

> "For whan I feele a-nyght your softe syde,
> Al be it that I may nat on yow ryde,
> For that oure perche is maad so narwe, allas!
> I am so ful of joye and of solas,
> That I diffye bothe sweven and dreem."

We see Chauntecleer here in all his pride, hardly deigning to set his foot to the ground, royal as a prince in his hall, says Chaucer, summoning all his wives with a mere cluck.

Up to this point the narrative has supplied us with a situation which is to be fulfilled in the remaining part of the tale, and with some intellectual attitudes that are to be tested. Chauntecleer's pride has been placed before us not only in the details of his dainty high stepping and his grim lion's look, but in the whole context of his long answer to Pertelote. Chaucer hereafter plays against each other instinct and rational control in much the same way that he assays willfulness and human responsibility in ***Troilus and Criseyde.***

With the return to a purely narrative tone in lines 3187 ff., Chaucer seems to take a deep breath before providing the catastrophe foreseen by Chauntecleer in his dream. In the midst of the beauties of May, when Chauntecleer's heart is full of "revel and solas," he is to discover that the latter end of joy is woe. The Nun's Priest now raises the whole question of destiny and man's freedom as the catastrophe impends, and the fox waits to fall upon the cock. It is a burst of rhetoric in a variety of tones: the extravagant comic sublime ("O false mordrour . . . / O newe Scariot, newe Genylon, . . . o Greek Synon, / That broghtest Troye al outrely to sorwe! / O Chauntecleer . . . ") merges into a more arid statement of simple and conditional necessity familiar to readers of the *Consolatio,* and finally into the traditional indictment:

> Wommennes conseils been ful ofte colde;
> Wommannes conseil broghte us first to wo,
> And made Adam fro Paradys to go,
> Ther as he was ful myrie and wel at ese.

In the mouth of the Nun's Priest, such a statement is a kind of bold impertinence; in Chaucer's mouth it is not less so if we bear in mind the tradition of oral presentation at court. And yet it has a kind of arch humor about it. It can be carried off by welding it fast to the narrative context:

> My tale is of a cok, as ye may heere,
> That tok his conseil of his wyf, with sorwe,

> To walken in the yerd upon that morwe
> That he hadde met that dreem that I yow tolde.

And so the narrator escapes responsibility both for philosophical explanation and for the indictment of women. Just how much involvement we can impute to Chaucer himself, or how much the poet has made the indictment of women a statement assessable only in terms of the priest's character—these are questions that we solve only with a kind of presumption.

And yet there may be a level of artifice here, a trick of narrative in which the artist-writer stands behind his creations and allows some of his own personal attitudes to be expressed through one of his agents, a form of play in which we sometimes discern the remoter *ludum* beyond the situation in which the agents are involved: Chauntecleer has had his intellectual fun in deceiving his wife with a Latin tag; Chaucer has had the Nun's Priest offer us, in Chauntecleer's translation of the Latin, two definitions of love which threaten to cancel each other out: Adam fell through Eve's counsel and bequeathed to their children similar falls without number; yet in the relationship of Chauntecleer and his wife-paramour there is a certain careless and lovely sensuality, a springtime "revel and solas," an overtone of one strong tradition that sees the love of woman as the means by which man perfects himself. It constitutes a perennially perplexing ambiguity which man's mind declines to resolve, even if it could.

We pass out of the romantic and sensual into the mutability theme, into a commentary upon the turn of fortune's wheel, with which we have been bludgeoned in the previous performance. The joke becomes more serious; the sarcasm, faintly antifeminist in the priestly attitude towards women's taste in literature, is kindly enough if it is Chaucer's own view; if it is the Priest's, there is a want of decorum in his speaking even in so veiled a fashion before the Prioress, the Nun, and even the Wife of Bath, who can make a moral point herself, with considerably less ambiguity. But in the familiar lines dealing with the opinions of worthy clerks on the problem of evil and the relation of God's foreknowledge to man's free will, the universal problem of the freedom of all men arises, and one feels that it is not the Priest's reluctance to provide a solution, but Chaucer's own disinclination that is expressed in the line, "I wol nat han to do of swich mateere." It seems strange that this priest should not know what he believes, when all the other clerical tales stand squarely upon the strong base of assertion. It seems less strange that Chaucer should do what writers have always done in the spirit of play: allowed their creations to toy with notions they themselves would decline.

But the context is comic and philosophical. The elevation of Chauntecleer's fortunes to a level we expect of the epic and tragic has the obvious effect of comic incongruity and disproportion. The narrator's special task is to accommodate the mysteries of the destinal order, dreams, Venus, nature, and the rest to a Divine Foreknowing which yet allows to man significant action and a saving self-knowledge. As the subsequent appearance of the fox makes clear, Chauntecleer's original assertion was correct, and Pertelote was wrong: he will indeed have adversity as a result of his dream. Seduced by the confidence which may be the fruit of love, and following his wife's advice so far as to "fly down from the beams," Chauntecleer makes obvious the difference between believing with conviction and acting upon that conviction. No matter how bad the advice of Pertelote, Chauntecleer cannot be exempt from the trials and temptations of his temporal existence. Indeed, the trials and temptations are themselves the means by which the Christian comedy achieves its happy goal, the battlefield upon which the soldier's mettle is put to the test.

The test offered by the appearance of the fox is compounded of flattery and deceit which in some measure balances out Chauntecleer's own towards his wife. In both deceptions there is that curious intermingling of instinctive self-preservation with soothing, blandishing flattery. Both deceptions are successful, the fox's more obviously so inasmuch as Chauntecleer's bird nature itself conspires to supplement the fall: like his father's, and presumably every rooster's before him, Chauntecleer's endeavors to match his parent's singing necessitate the closing of the eyes. "Ah! beware of the betrayal through flattery," cries the Priest, and in an instant, Chauntecleer is caught by his natural enemy.

It is difficult to refrain from pointing up the skill of the rhetorical pattern of complaint beginning with line 3338, "O destinee, that mayst nat been eschewed!" and passing shortly to "O Venus, that art goddesse of plesaunce," then to "O Gaufred, deere maister soverayn," and finally to the capping mock heroics of lamentation in "O woful hennes, right so criden ye," the quadruple outburst drawing into fearful and wonderful juxtaposition comedy of situation with the inflated sublime of exclamatory closet tragedy. Whatever may be lacking in internal unifying factors is more than adequately compensated by the poetic effort to hold in delicate balance the humble matters of comedy with the elevated, the transporting, and the philosophical matters of tragedy.

The poem draws to its closing act in a burst of vividly detailed activity. All that has been restrained, controlled, elevated gives way in style and subject matter to the hectic demands of a chase. The serenity and moderated quietude of the poor widow's household is dissipated in a flash by the spirit of mobilized rescue spreading like wildfire to "many another man," and to the dogs, and in further hectic sympathy, to the hogs, cows, ducks and geese, and a swarm of bees. Then in a sudden move out of the excitement of the chase, the Nun's Priest closes in upon his moral goal in the colloquial and familiar tones of admonition: "Now, goode men, I prey yow herkneth alle."

The reversal of Fortune by which Chauntecleer's native wit brings about his escape gives us some clue as to the relation of man's reasoned actions to the providential plan. The flattery by which he himself deceived his wife was superseded by that of the fox; now again, the laying on of flattery and praise for the sake of personal safety wins the cock his freedom; the fox's last attempt with unctuous and specious humility to win back his loss is deservedly unsuccessful, and Chauntecleer's answer to his enemy is a famous locus in Chaucerian moral statement:

"Thou shalt namoore, thurgh thy flaterye,
Do me to synge and wynke with myn ye;
For he that wynketh, whan he sholde see,
Al wilfully, God lat him nevere thee!"
  "Nay," quod the fox, "but God yeve hym
    meschaunce,
That is so undiscreet of governaunce
That jangleth whan he sholde holde his pees."
  Lo, swich it is for to be recchelees
And necligent, and truste on flaterye.
. . . .
  Taketh the moralite, goode men.

Not only Chauntecleer, but the fox as well has come to a kind of wisdom that goes beyond the use of wit: both of them must observe a law of governance; both of them must come to rueful admissions of their failure to recognize the advantages of self-control. In the famous lines quoted above, both have learned through error.

The **"Nun's Priest's Tale"** thus raises the questions of human responsibility and destiny in the manner of tragedy or the moral romance but dismisses them, as a kind of impertinence, in favor of man's ability to learn from daily experience, in the manner of an ironic comedy. Its subject matter is a weighing of two sides of the ledger of man's serious and comic interests.

A host of questions is set in motion in contexts domestic and destinal. Insofar as the questions can be confronted, they challenge the facile view of tragedy set up by the Monk. The answers, insofar as they are given, are couched in the terms of ironic affirmation: man is responsible for errors in judgment; from the errors flows self-knowledge. And about chance, or love, or destiny, the least said the better.

One level of its meanings can be described by the word "quizzical." They arise out of the complex picture of man seen as willful and self-loving, yet amiable and capable of loving others; created in the divine image but somehow all-too-human; responsible for his actions yet somehow controlled by forces beyond himself. To assert that man is free and at the same time that he is not is in effect to make us accept both assertions as true. To offer the view that love yields joy and then that it offers sorrow, or to hold in balance the philosophy of Boethius and Bradwardine with a world of laxatives and remedies for ague, is in essence to concentrate our gaze upon the disparities in the experience of fallen man and to confess to a certain helplessness in the human condition.

On another more accessible level of meaning we encounter the ironist's pronouncements to those who must pick their way through the obstacles of life: beware of flattery which destroys self-control, blinds us to what we should see, and loosens our tongues when we should be still. The lesson spoken at the close by cock and fox is securely anchored to the real world of expedience in which there are errors in judgment, flattery, negligence, lack of governance, and an uneasy acceptance of another. Whether the promulgator of those pedestrian truths is the inscrutable Sir John pronouncing so knowledgeably on life and love or Chaucer speaking through a mask, a sane hope pervades them: the hope for rational creatures accepting the appalling truth of their day-to-day responsibility within (it is devoutly wished) a rational universe.

The final plight of Chauntecleer demonstrates the relation of instinct to rational control, of thoughtless vanity to presence of mind, of foolish pride to a just humility. The "happy" ending, with the rivals standing hand in hand, so to speak, reciting what wisdom they have achieved, reveals some truths in miniature, truths mundane and pedestrian, but truths nonetheless. (pp. 184-96)

*Paul G. Ruggiers, "The Nun's Priest's Tale,"
in his* The Art of the Canterbury Tales, *The
University of Wisconsin Press, 1965, pp. 184-
96.*

A. C. Spearing   (essay date 1966)

[*In the excerpt below, Spearing analyzes the "Franklin's Prologue and Tale," praising Chaucer's handling of the complex topics of marriage, love, and fidelity, and concluding that the poet has admirably succeeded in creating a work which will provoke endless discussion.*]

In the [**"Franklin's Prologue"**] the Franklin himself has been revealed; the **"Franklin's Tale"** is of interest as a tale, and not merely as a further revelation of the Franklin. But it remains, and most distinctly, the *Franklin's* tale. He tells it to serve certain purposes of his own; and though . . . it in fact escapes from those purposes without his being aware of it, we must begin by considering what they are.

The Franklin intends his tale to be a moral fable, or, to see it in medieval terms, to be an *exemplum* which proves certain general moral principles. The tale possesses three main themes: that of *trouthe,* that of the ideal marriage relationship, and that of *gentillesse.* On each of these themes the Franklin has definite moral teaching to offer, teaching which is not allowed to remain implicit and affect us through our imaginations alone, but which is rendered explicit in the form of aphorisms or *sententiae,* to which we are expected to give our rational assent. His teaching on the subject of *trouthe* is the statement wrung out of Arveragus in the agonizing moment when his wife tells him that Aurelius has succeeded in performing the task which she swore would win her love, and leaves it to him to decide what to do: 'Trouthe is the hyeste thing that man may kepe'. On the subject of marriage, his teaching is contained in his own remarks in the digression suggested by the marriage agreement of Dorigen and Arveragus. These form a whole series of *sententiae,* but perhaps their quintessence may be found in the opening lines of the digression:

For o thing, sires, saufly dar I seye,
That freendes everich oother moot obeye,
If they wol longe holden compaignye.
Love wol nat been constreyned by maistrye.

The last line in particular seems to deserve to have next to it the little pointing hand in the margin that in old texts sometimes indicates the explicit teaching of a work. The third theme of *gentillesse* is one on which emphasis is laid at various points throughout the tale, but we may find the Franklin's doctrine summed up in the remarks made by

Aurelius and the Clerk when each of them decides not to demand fulfilment of a promise:

> Thus kan a squier doon a gentil dede
> As wel as kan a knight, withouten drede

and

> Thou art a squier and he is a knight;
> But God forbede, for his blisful might,
> But if a clerk koude doon a gentil dede
> As wel as any of yow, it is no drede!

Gentillesse is not a matter of rank, but a virtue of spirit belonging to the individual. All this seems clear enough, and if his tale were what the Franklin evidently intends it to be, it would serve merely to demonstrate the truth of these doctrines; though it would be somewhat surprising to find a single *exemplum* proving three such different morals. But when we come to examine each of the three themes in more detail as it is embodied in the actual Tale, we shall find that the matter is less simple than it seems. In each case, the theme will be found to point not towards the clarity of an *exemplum,* but towards ambiguity and dubiety—qualities which are more troubling than simplicity and clarity, but also more interesting and more like life. Let us consider each of the themes separately.

The concept of *trouthe,* meaning 'fidelity to one's pledged word', is certainly a central them in **"The Franklin's Tale",** and one that reflects the legal knowledge and interests that **"The General Prologue"** portrait implied in the Franklin. The suspense that the narrative generates turns on two promises: Dorigen's promise to Aurelius that she will be his if he removes the rocks from the Breton coast, and Aurelius's promise to the Clerk that he will pay him a thousand pounds if he makes it appear that this has been done. *Trouthe* is invoked when both promises are given: Dorigen says

> Thanne wol I love yow best of any man,
> Have heer my trouthe, in al that evere I kan,

while Aurelius declares

> This bargain is ful drive, for we been knit.
> Ye shal be payed trewely, by my trouthe!

The promises thus given are treated as formal and legally binding contracts, and when, through the influence of *gentillesse,* Aurelius releases Dorigen and is in turn released by the Clerk, the releases are performed with due formality and in language which recalls that actually used in legal 'quitclaims' of the Middle Ages. Aurelius says to Dorigen

> I yow relesse, madame, into youre hond
> Quit every serement and every bond
> That ye han maad to me as heerbiforn,
> Sith thilke time which that ye were born,

even though she has given him no written oaths or agreements which he could return to her and she has made him only one promise since she was born. But medieval quitclaims tended to include some such phrase as *a principio mundi usque in diem presencium* ('from the beginning of the world down to this present day'). Similarly, the Clerk says formally to Aurelius 'I release you' and invents a

slightly comic parody of the intensifying phrase to go with it:

> Sire, I releesse thee thy thousand pound,
> As thou right now were cropen out of the
>   ground,
> Ne nevere er now ne haddest knowen me.

The most important invocation of *trouthe,* however, occurs at the point just mentioned, when Arveragus becomes the fourth of the Tale's four central characters to get involved with the theme. Dorigen has promised to love Aurelius if he can perform the apparently impossible task of removing the black rocks which she sees as a danger to her husband. Aurelius tells her that the deed has been done, demands the fulfilment of her promise, and as he does so warns her

> Aviseth yow er that ye breke youre trouthe.

She takes the dilemma to her husband, and he tells her that she must keep her promise, because 'Trouthe is the hyeste thing that man may kepe'. We might well dismiss the incident out of hand by referring it to the Franklin's own legalistic cast of mind. Who but a lawyer or the creature of a lawyer's imagination would think of forcing his wife to keep a frivolous verbal promise to become another man's mistress on condition that he performed a deed which she believed to be impossible? Indeed, the Franklin himself recognizes the oddity of Arveragus's decision, and anticipates protests from his listeners:

> Paraventure an heep of yow, ywis,
> Wol holden him a lewed man in this
> That he wol putte his wyf in jupartie.

If, however, we respond to the human drama of the situation as Chaucer presents it, we shall find that we cannot dismiss it so easily. Arveragus's *sentencia* does not come out pat, as the conclusion of a complacent statement of general principle. It is the last line of a speech in which he is desperately trying to rouse his wife from her misery, by not letting her see his own agony of mind. But as he pronounces the *sentencia,* his agony breaks through, and 'with that word he brast anon to wepe'. He is stretched on the rack of his own principle, and the dramatic moment has an intensity which gives the principle itself a searing force. Once we begin to take the principle seriously, though, a question immediately forces itself on us. What about Dorigen's original marriage promise to Arveragus, in the making of which *trouthe* was also invoked?—

> Sire, I wol be youre humble trewe wyf,
> Have heer my trouthe, til that myn herte breste.

Trouthe may be *the hyeste thing that man may kepe,* but it seems that Arveragus can only make his wife keep her *trouthe* to Aurelius by forcing her to break her *trouthe* to himself. Surely her original marriage pledge has priority and should invalidate the later promise to Aurelius? We ask such questions in vain. They clearly did not occur to the Franklin, and, though they must have occurred to Chaucer, because the theme of *trouthe* is so carefully repeated throughout the Tale, one might well suggest that he did not intend them to occur to his audience. I have argued, however, that it is the very intensity of the human situation from which the *sententia* emerges that forces us to take it seriously and consider all its implications. If we do so, we are surely left with a genuine question—genuine in the sense that no single answer is provided or implied in the **"Franklin's Tale"**—but we are left free to argue about the matter after the tale has ended. And the fact that the tale ends with an explicit question about *gentillesse* suggests that it may imply questions about its other themes too.

The second theme of **"The Franklin's Tale"** is that of marriage. This is in a way an intrusive topic, which the Franklin seems to be imposing on the tale because it relates to interests of his own. The popular story from which the tale is derived, the story of how the heroine escaped from the consequences of her foolish promise, does not require any special emphasis on the ideal quality of her relationship with her husband. We need to know that they truly love each other, certainly, or else his insistence that she should keep her promise would lose all dramatic force; but nothing more than this is strictly necessary. The Franklin, however, is determined to include more than this, and so he explains at some length the unusual agreement they come to about their relationship, and then turns aside in the *diversio . . .* to defend this arrangement on grounds of general principle. The arrangement is that, instead of Arveragus's taking on the dominance (*maistrie*) that usually belonged to the medieval husband, he agrees to obey Dorigen in everything as a courtly lover was expected to obey his mistress. In return, she agrees to obey him, and so each of them becomes servant and each of them master. The defence of this arrangement is that 'Love is a thing as any spirit free', and hence 'wol nat been constreyned by maistrye'. And so it is best for married lovers to be not domineering but patient. During the present century, at least, most readers of **"The Franklin's Tale"** seem to have shared this view of the marriage relationship in the poem, and to have felt that it was Chaucer's own view (which would certainly explain why it is so much insisted on), and that it was presented as the conclusion to a debate on the subject of marriage that was embodied in a number of the other **Canterbury Tales.** These opinions cannot, however, be taken for granted, but must be examined more closely.

The idea that a debate or discussion on marriage is embodied in parts of **The Canterbury Tales** was first put forward by G. L. Kittredge in 1912 [in *Modern Philology*]. It quickly achieved general acceptance, and a reliable more recent survey of the subject can be found in W. W. Lawrence's book *Chaucer and the Canterbury Tales.* The core of the debate is to be found in four tales, those of the Wife of Bath, the Clerk, the Merchant, and the Franklin. Although the manuscripts of **The Canterbury Tales** arrange the various fragments that have come down to us in different orders, there is general agreement that these four tales are intended to follow in the order given. They are all concerned not simply with marriage, but with the question of *maistrie* or dominance in marriage, a favourite topic of both learned and popular discussion in the Middle Ages. The Wife of Bath is an extreme example of the dominance of the wife. She explains in her long prologue how she has had five husbands in her long life and has achieved *maistrie* over all of them, and she then tells a tale in which

a knight has imposed on him the task of discovering what thing it is that women most desire. He is given the right answer—*maistrie* or *sovereignetee*—by an ugly old woman, but only on condition that he marries her. He is disgusted by her ugliness and ignoble birth, but, after she has lectured him at length on the subject of *gentillesse,* he concedes *maistrie* to her, and she at once turns by magic into a young, beautiful, and obedient wife. After **"The Wife of Bath's Tale"** there follow the tales of the Friar and the Summoner, which are not concerned with marriage, but the subject is then taken up again by the Clerk. He tells a story of a peasant girl who is married to a marquis; he submits her to an incredible series of torments and humiliations, all of which she accepts patiently, and at last, when he finds how obedient she is, takes her back into favour. The Clerk says that he tells this tale as a parable showing how we should all bear the tests God sends to us, but he makes specific reference to the Wife of Bath, and to the difference between her heroine and his. **"The Merchant's Tale"** comes next, and this is explicitly linked with **"The Clerk's Tale."** The Merchant has recently married a wife who is the very opposite of the Clerk's patient heroine, and he tells a story of an old knight who marries a young girl after a lifetime of bachelor dissipation, and is at once deceived by her. He is struck blind, and she commits adultery with a young squire in a garden in her husband's very presence.

It will be clear at once that there exist close and complex links between **"The Franklin's Tale"** and the three tales just summarized. In the first place, the Franklin seems to offer a halfway house between the two extremes represented by the Wife of Bath and the Clerk: neither total dominance by the wife nor total dominance by the husband, but a compromise in which both are master and both servant. Moreover, the Franklin seems to be defending marriage itself against the cynicism of the Merchant's attack, by repeating the basic situation of his tale—the marriage of a knight and a lady subverted by the advances of a young squire—but bringing it to an unironically happy conclusion, in which the marriage remains intact, but even the squire does not suffer too much. Again, in linking *gentillesse* with marriage as the subjects of his tale, the Franklin is not merely influenced by the Squire (whose tale comes as an interlude in the marriage debate, between the Merchant and the Franklin), but is returning to **"The Wife of Bath's Tale"**, where the knight had to learn the nature of true *gentillesse* before he could find happiness by conceding *maistrie* to his wife. There are even certain more detailed links between **"The Franklin's Tale"** and the earlier contributions to the debate. The twenty-two *exempla* of Dorigen's lament are all taken from St Jerome's *Adversus Jovinianum,* a book from which many of the Wife of Bath's arguments in her Prologue are borrowed, and which was included in the collection of anti-feminist writings which her fifth husband was in the habit of reading. And certain lines in the Franklin's remarks about marriage seem to echo deliberately remarks of the Merchant. Compare the Merchant's

How mighte a man han any adversitee
That hath a wif ? Certes, I kan nat seye.
The blisse which that is bitwixe hem tweye

> Ther may no tonge telle, or herte thinke

with the Franklin's

> Who koude telle, but he hadde wedded be,
> The joye, the ese, and the prosperitee
> That is bitwixe an housbonde and his wyf?
> A yeer and moore lasted this blisful lyf.

There are echoes both in the language used and in the interrogative form of the statements. The Merchant's rhetorical question was spoken with bitter sarcasm, but the Franklin challengingly repeats it in a literal sense, wishing to substitute for the Merchant's cynicism a more idealistic view of marriage.

It does not follow from this, however, that Chaucer intended **"The Franklin's Tale"** as a solution to the problem of *maistrie* in marriage raised by the earlier tales. In general, Chaucer is not in the habit of offering solutions to problems; his tendency rather is to present human situations as they are (which includes presenting them as moral situations) and to leave us to draw our own conclusions. Let us examine what the Franklin is trying to do in his initial treatment of the marriage relationship of Arveragus and Dorigen. He begins with a situation typical of the kind of chivalric literature to which Breton lays belonged. A knight loves a beautiful lady from a distance; he performs many services to win her; she takes *pitee* on his *penaunce;* and at last she agrees to marry him. So far their relationship has belonged to the convention of courtly love, by which the lady is the dominant partner (the knight's 'mistress' in a literal sense) and her lover is subservient. But this relationship must end with marriage, once the lady has conceded that, for in medieval marriage the husband is dominant. This at least was the medieval theory, though in practice there were of course always Wives of Bath, who had the personal power to reverse this natural order. But in this particular marriage, a completely unusual arrangement is tried. Arveragus promises to go on behaving as a courtly lover; he will 'hire obeye, and folwe hir wil in al', though this situation will be concealed from the outside world. The medieval reaction to the arrangement so far—the reaction that Chaucer would expect from his audience—would no doubt be that this was absurd and unnatural. But in return Dorigen promises to be his 'humble trewe wyf' none the less; so that what is intended is clearly a combination of, or compromise between, the two radically opposed relationships of lover and mistress and husband and wife. At this point the Franklin begins on his *diversio* in defence and explanation of their agreement. The gist of his remarks lies, as I have said, in the *sententia* 'Love wol not been constreyned by maistrye'. The 'debate' about marriage among the pilgrims has been a debate about *maistrie* in marriage. Both sides have agreed that marriage is to be seen as a struggle for power, in which either husband or wife must come out victorious. The Franklin wants to resolve the problem by changing its terms; he wishes to remove the whole question of dominance from marriage, and to present it as something other than a power relationship. Men and women both, he argues, desire liberty; therefore both parties to a marriage must show *pacience* and *suffrance*. Most modern readers, at least in Western Europe and the English-speaking countries, are likely to feel that the Franklin is right about this. We believe that husband and wife should be equal partners in all respects, and that power should have nothing to do with the matter. It is not at all certain, however, that this would be the medieval reaction. The normal medieval view was that a happy marriage relationship would be established, not by trying to get rid of the element of dominance completely, but by both parties agreeing that the husband should be dominant. The natural relationship was as stated in a standard medieval encyclopaedic work, the *De Proprietatibus Rerum* of Bartholomew the Englishman: 'A man is the hede of a woman, as the apostle sayth. And therefore a man is bounde to rule his wyfe, as the heed hath cure and rule of the body.' What Arveragus and Dorigen are trying to do, though their intentions (and the Franklin's) are no doubt good, is to upset the natural order of things. This fact is already reflected perhaps in the confused way in which the Franklin defines their relationship. He tries to get rid of *maistrie,* but only loses himself in paradoxes in which *maistrie* seems to reappear constantly whether he wishes so or not. Thus when he praises patience, it is only as a way of achieving *maistrie* indirectly:

> Looke who that is moost pacient in love,
> He is at his avantage al above.
> Pacience is an heigh vertu, certeyn,
> For it venquisseth, as thise clerkes seyn,
> Thinges that rigour sholde nevere atteyne.

And the Franklin's final statement of their relationship is in terms of a further knot of paradoxes:

> Thus hath she take hir servant and hir lord—
> Servant in love, and lord in mariage.
> Thanne was he bothe in lordshipe and servage.
> Servage? nay, but in lordshipe above . . .

Only in a transcendental world where opposites become one would such an intensity of paradox escape from its own terms of mastery and servitude. But this marriage, like others, has to manage as best it can in the real world.

What happens to the marriage of Dorigen and Arveragus when it is tested by the course of the story appears to demonstrate the confusion and impracticability of the Franklin's ideal. This is quite the contrary of what the Franklin seems to intend, but the story has a human life that frees it from his exemplifying intentions. There can be no doubt of Dorigen's depth of affection for her husband, and she is thoroughly shocked when, in his absence, Aurelius says that he loves her. Nevertheless, she mitigates the force of her refusal by telling Aurelius that if he removes the rocks from the coast of Brittany she will love him in return. In this incident, we are perhaps to see her as acting in accordance with the confused ideals the Franklin has stated: though she is a wife, and has the appropriate feelings, she continues to act as a courtly mistress, setting her suitor a difficult task to perform as the condition of gaining her *pitee*. With the aid of magic, he performs the task, and Dorigen is now in a terrible dilemma. She considers suicide, but at this point her husband returns, and she immediately takes her problem to him. Just as this is a crucial point in the tale so far as the theme of *trouthe* is concerned, so it is with the theme of marriage. In taking her problem to her husband, Dorigen has not acted in accordance with theory, which would evidently have led her to kill herself. She has acted instinctively, and instinct has led her to the submission that in the Middle Ages would have been thought natural for a wife. Arveragus in turn, under the pressure of this crisis, resumes his role as 'head' and instructs her what to do:

> Ye shul youre trouthe holden, by my fay!

(It is perhaps worth recalling that *shul* had a rather strong sense—nearer to 'must' than to the modern 'shall'.) Thus at this crucial point, *maistrie* re-enters the marriage, with an emphasis that gains force from the paradox by which Arveragus uses his *maistrie* to order his wife to keep her promise to become someone else's mistress. From this point on, the theme of *maistrie* in marriage is dropped, and *gentillesse* takes its place as the central theme of the closing stages of the **"Franklin's Tale"**.

I ought perhaps to add that the question of marriage in **"The Franklin's Tale"** is more controversial than most other aspects of the tale, and that the account just given of Chaucer's and the Franklin's intentions would by no means be universally accepted among medievalists. Many modern critics have felt sympathetic towards the Franklin's views on marriage, and, noting that the Franklin and Chaucer belonged to roughly the same social group, and had even held some of the same offices (president of the magistrates' court and knight of the shire), have felt that Chaucer was using him as the mouthpiece for his own views. This may of course be so, and it would be wrong to pretend to certainty in the matter. But it must be remembered that even (perhaps especially) on a topic of such central human interest as marriage, views that now seem enlightened might in the Middle Ages have seemed absurd, and vice versa; and one of the greatest dangers for those with a real admiration for a writer from the past is to be unable to bear to feel that they disagree with him on any important topic.

The third theme of **"The Franklin's Tale"** is *gentillesse,* and the Tale is better adapted to convey this theme than either of the others. . . . [*Gentillesse*] is a topic with which the Franklin is much preoccupied in his Prologue, and that, despite the Host's contempt, he immediately introduces the word *gentil* into the first line of his prefatory remarks about Breton lays. We shall therefore expect the theme to recur in the body of the tale. Once again the crucial point is the scene in which Dorigen takes her dilemma to her husband and he instructs her to keep her promise to Aurelius. In doing so, he is acting according to his conception of *trouthe;* he is also reasserting his *maistrie* in marriage; and thirdly this is the poem's first great act of *gentillesse.* So Aurelius sees it, when Dorigen goes to the garden to keep her promise:

> Madame, seyth to youre lord Arveragus
> That sith I se his grete gentillesse
> To yow . . . ,
> I have wel levere evere to suffre wo
> Than I departe the love bitwix yow two.

Gentillesse is entirely appropriate to Arveragus, for he is a knight; but his *gentillesse* touches off a second *gentil* deed

by Aurelius, a squire, and therefore lower in chivalric status. He releases Dorigen from her rash promise to him, saying

> Thus kan a squier doon a gentil dede
> As wel as kan a knight, withouten drede.

Aurelius in his turn goes to the Clerk to ask for time to pay. The Clerk is outside the order of chivalry entirely, and at first it seems that, like Shylock, he is going to demand fulfilment of the bond. 'Have I nat holden covenant unto thee?', he asks, and again, 'Hastow nat had thy lady as thee liketh?' To the first question the answer can only be 'Yes', but to the second it is a miserable 'No, no'. Aurelius explains what has happened:

> Arveragus, of gentillesse,
> Hadde levere die in sorwe and in distresse
> Than that his wyf were of hir trouthe fals.

He further explains what passed between himself and Dorigen:

> That made me han of hire so greet pitee;
> And right as frely as he sente hire me,
> As frely sente I hire to him ageyn.

The repeated word *frely,* with its sense hovering between 'freely' (applying to Dorigen) and 'generously' (applying to Arveragus and Aurelius), invokes a concept closely connected with *gentillesse. Franchise* (the noun from the adjective *fre*) is one aspect of *gentillesse*—the unselfregarding generosity that is necessary for truly *gentil* behavior. It has been introduced a little earlier in the Tale, in close connexion with *gentillesse,* at the point where Aurelius is first confronted with Arveragus's *gentillesse* and Dorigen's misery, and decides

> That fro his lust yet were him levere abide
> Than doon so heigh a cherlissh wrecchednesse
> Agains franchise and alle gentillesse.

Now, confronted with the *franchise* to which Aurelius's *gentillesse* has led him, the Clerk decides that he too must be *gentil* and release Aurelius from his enormous debt. In doing so he says:

> Leeve brother,
> Everich of yow dide gentilly til oother.
> Thou art a squier and he is a knight;
> But God forbede, for his blisful might,
> But if a clerk koude doon a gentil dede
> As wel as any of yow, it is no drede!

He then rides away, and the story ends. The Franklin himself has the last word, directing the pilgrims' attention towards the ethical theme of *franchise:*

> Lordinges, this question, thanne, wol I aske now,
> Which was the mooste fre, as thinketh yow?

The Franklin's intentions with regard to *gentillesse* are quite clear, and he has been successful in carrying them out. We have seen that his own almost obsessive concern with *gentillesse* is connected with his unease about his relationship to the chivalric class and its virtues. He therefore tells a story which will act as an *exemplum* of *gentillesse,* so as to establish that it is a virtue whose nature he understands, but one which will as far as possible detach the virtue from its class associations. He therefore shifts the emphasis towards the end of his Tale on to *franchise,* an aspect of *gentillesse* which (unlike, say, exquisite manners) has no necessary connexion with aristocratic birth and breeding. And so the Clerk, who has no chivalric status at all, can match the knight and the squire in *gentillesse* by his generosity in the matter of money. In the twentieth century we are likely to feel that the Franklin is entirely right in thus locating the true value of *gentillesse* in virtuous actions rather than in high birth, and this time I think our feelings coincide with Chaucer's. This is precisely the point he makes in his *ballade* called **"Gentillesse"** where he speaks in his own person:

> What man that claimeth gentil for to be
> Must . . . alle his wittes dresse
> Vertu to sewe and vices for to flee.
> For unto vertu longeth dignitee,
> And noght the revers . . .

It is also the point made by the ugly old woman in **"The Wife of Bath's Tale"** when she delivers a sermon to her husband on the subject. In **"The Franklin's Tale"** the second and third acts of *gentillesse* are set off in a chain-reaction by the first and second, and, on a smaller scale, they release generosity in ourselves. The conclusion of the Tale has a genuine and unequivocal warmth.

There remains, however, a certain equivocal quality in the first act of *gentillesse,* which sparks off the others. It makes, indeed, as dubious an *exemplum* of *gentillesse* as it does of *trouthe* and of the avoidance of *maistrie* in marriage. The passage with which Arveragus continues his instructions to Dorigen after his *sententia* about *trouthe* is somewhat surprising:

> 'Trouthe is the hyeste thing that man may
>   kepe'—
> But with that word he brast anon to wepe,
> And seyde, 'I yow forbede, up peyne of deeth,
> That nevere, whil thee lasteth lyf ne breeth,
> To no wight telle thou of this aventure—
> As I may best, I wol my wo endure—
> Ne make no contenance of hevinesse,
> That folk of yow may demen harm or gesse'.

It seems as though Arveragus's emotion is caused as much by the thought of what people would say about *him* if they knew the truth as by his feeling for his wife. This is very natural, of course, and very probable, but somewhat odd as part of an exemplary demonstration of *gentillesse.* But it fits in very well with the Franklin's conception of *gentillesse.* We have seen him in his prologue greatly concerned about social status and reputation, and, though he insists there on *vertu* as the essence of *gentillesse,* he shows a similar concern with reputation in his treatment of Arveragus at the very beginning of his tale. Arveragus has agreed to take on himself no *maistrie* over Dorigen, and this is evidently from the Franklin's point of view an admirable arrangement, yet he seems to think it perfectly natural that Arveragus should not wish it to be publicly known, for his reputation's sake:

> Save that the name of soverainetee,
> That wolde he have for shame of his degree.

His later reaction to Dorigen's dilemma is perfectly in keeping with this. It is true, no doubt, that medieval aristocratic values did depend on external reputation to a greater extent than is likely to seem proper to modern readers; nevertheless, it is difficult not to feel that Chaucer intends us to see in Arveragus an all-too-human *approach* to *gentillesse,* which is taken by the Franklin for the thing itself, but is really somewhat less than that.

Certain other details in the **"Franklin's Tale"** support this interpretation by laying an unexpected stress on reputation or social status. One of these is an afterthought, psychologically very convincing, at the end of the speech by Aurelius's brother in which he introduces the idea of removing the rocks by magic. If this could be done, he concludes,

> Thanne were my brother warisshed of his wo;
> Thanne moste she nedes holden hire biheste,
> Or elles he shal shame hire atte leeste.

Now it seems most unlikely that to humiliate Dorigen would give any satisfaction at all to a man so desperately in love with her as Aurelius is supposed to be. His brother, however, feels indignant at the suffering she is causing him, and would like to punish her for it, and the idea of *shame,* or public humiliation, as a punishment would naturally occur to the Franklin. A second detail occurs when Aurelius is wondering what he will do to pay the Clerk. He decides that he must sell his inheritance and beg for his living, but then he adds the thought that he will have to do it somewhere else so as not to shame his relations:

> . . . heere may I nat dwelle,
> And shamen al my kinrede in this place.

Both of these details suggest thoughts which it would be perfectly natural for someone in the situation concerned to have, but they do help to build up a picture of an excessive and not perfectly *gentil* concern about reputation. *Gentillesse* and *shame,* though far from opposites, are perhaps not quite so closely connected as the Franklin feels, and it is worth noting that the very word *shame* occurs in both the passages just quoted, as it does in line 80 and in line 857 (with reference to the risk Arveragus runs in telling Dorigen to keep her promise to Aurelius).

From our examination of the **"Franklin's Tale"**'s three central themes of *trouthe,* the marriage relationship, and *gentillesse,* it has emerged that in all three cases there is some confusion or ambiguity in the Franklin's treatment of them, with the result that the tale does not function perfectly as an *exemplum* of any of the three. From this it may sound as though the tale ought to be considered a failure; but in fact the very reverse is true. The Franklin intends his tale (it would appear) as a neat moral fable, a machine adapted to convey certain teaching in a clear and unambiguous form. This is not how the tale turns out, but it is surely all the better for it. It is better than the Franklin intends or knows, because it shares some of the confusion and ambiguity of real life. The characters in **"The Franklin's Tale"**, though they begin as ideal types, behave under the pressure of events in a convincingly human (and therefore often unideal) way. They will not be imprisoned by the abstractions they are intended to convey; instead, they go their own ways, and convey a meaning that is more complex and richer than could have been predicted. The Franklin is not aware of this, but Chaucer of course is, and it is part of his intention that we should recognize the gaps between what the teller intends and what the tale conveys. The scheme of *The Canterbury Tales* as a whole is devised to make such subtleties possible; and indeed Chaucer throughout his poetic career had been working towards a freer and more relativistic employment of the narrator in his fictions. (pp. 22-38)

"The Franklin's Tale" [is] found . . . to be full of doubts and ambiguities. The tale ends with a question—which was the most generous of the three men?—to which no answer is given by the Franklin, and which he leaves it to the other pilgrims to settle. It would be a mistake to assume either that this question is merely conventional or that it has a 'right' answer. Medieval courtly poems do tend to conclude with a *demande,* but this convention is genuinely functional. In medieval society, poetry was a pastime, a form of communal entertainment, and if a poem provided matter for discussion after it was ended, so much the better, for conversation was another favourite form of entertainment. "The Franklin's Tale" does indeed provide much matter for discussion; not only the question of *franchise,* but also those of *gentillesse* more generally, of *trouthe,* of the place of *maistrie* in marriage, of the reliability of magic, and perhaps others. On all these topics, the tale offers evidence on more than one side; it incites its audience (whether we think of this as being the Franklin's audience of pilgrims or Chaucer's own audience) to make their own judgements, but it does not tell them what judgements they are to make. A central image in the "Franklin's Tale" is the double-bearded Janus, and he might be taken to stand for the Franklin, offering a double perspective on the convincingly human world of his tale.

Are we to conclude, then, that the total effect of "The Franklin's Tale" is problematic? A comparison with Shakespeare will make clear what is meant. A number of Shakespeare's plays have come in this century to be called 'problem plays', or sometimes tragicomedies; among them are usually included *Measure for Measure* and *All's Well That Ends Well.* In both these plays central characters seem to fit only with difficulty into the roles that romantic stories have ordained for them, and one at least in each play—the Duke in *Measure for Measure* and Helena in *All's Well*—seems to exist partly on a human and partly on a supernatural plane of being. As a result, the very titles of the plays seem to invite questioning: *has* measure been dealt out for measure? and *is* all made well by ending well? These plays do not merely raise separate problems of interpretation, but present a whole view of life which is itself problematic. Is "The Franklin's Tale", with all its unresolved ambiguities, a work of this kind, which we ought to refer to as 'a problem poem'?

The answer to this question is, I think, 'no', and to be able to say this is to go some way towards defining the nature of "The Franklin's Tale". There is an urgency in Shakespeare's problem plays that involves us deeply in their questionings, and their questionings do not merely interest or intrigue, they disturb. On the whole this urgency press-

ing us towards a radical disquiet is not to be found in "The Franklin's Tale," except at one point. That point is Dorigen's speech in which she questions the divine ordering of the universe; a speech which, moving though it is, is a loose end in the poem, asking questions which are not merely unanswered but completely dropped. The contrast between Divine providence and the state of the world was a subject by which Chaucer's imagination was easily stirred, and which he treats in others of his poems with an urgency too great to be fitted into the overall scheme of the work. Apart from this speech, however, Chaucer seems to be careful to keep his work below the level of the disturbingly problematic. It is not that he is unable to reach this level, but that he is aiming at something different. Again and again, when there is a particular danger that we shall become too deeply engaged in the suffering of his characters and the issues that it might raise, he finds some means of drawing us back, reminding us that it is only a tale told by a Franklin, or that the eventual outcome will be happy for everyone. Thus, near the beginning, when Dorigen is left alone by her husband and falls into acute misery, we are warned by a word of patronizing admiration from the Franklin for the nobility of her grief not to take it too seriously:

> For his absence wepeth she and siketh,
> As doon thise noble wives whan hem liketh.

When Aurelius falls into a similarly despairing state, and has to be put to bed by his brother, the Franklin again draws us back from too deep a sympathy with a callous transitional comment:

> Dispeyred in this torment and this thoght
> Lete I this woful creature lie;
> Chese he, for me, wheither he wol live or die.

Dorigen's lament is a large-scale example of how to blunt the cutting-edge of grief by allowing it to become slightly absurd. And, towards the end, when Arveragus seems to be confronted by his wife's confession with as painful and disturbing a dilemma as the choice Isabella has to make in *Measure for Measure* between her brother and her chastity, we are twice given the hint that the outcome will be happy after all. First Arveragus himself expresses a vague hope, in the course of cheering Dorigen up—

> It may be wel, paraventure, yet to day

—and then the Franklin himself intervenes, to warn us not to be too hasty in our responses:

> Paraventure an heep of yow, ywis,
> Wol holden him a lewed man in this
> That he wol putte his wyf in jupartie.
> Herkneth the tale er ye upon hire crie.
> She may have bettre fortune than yow semeth;
> And whan that ye han herd the tale, demeth.

Judgement is to be reserved till we have heard the whole tale; Chaucer's aim is not to press us into judgement by the urgency of separate situations, but to intrigue and interest us until the complete story provides material for endless discussion. In this aim he has admirably succeeded. (pp. 54-6)

A. C. Spearing, in an introduction to The

Franklin's Prologue and Tale from the Canterbury Tales *by Geoffrey Chaucer, edited by A. C. Spearing, Cambridge at the University Press, 1966, pp. 1-56.*

Maurice Hussey (essay date 1966)

[*Hussey is an English scholar who has edited several of the individual tales from the* Canterbury Tales, *as well as Ben Jonson's* The Devil Is an Ass *(1967) and* Criticism in Action *(1969). In the following excerpt from his edition of the "Merchant's Prologue and Tale," Hussey lauds Chaucer's masterful depiction of love and betrayal, observing that the work is so perfectly composed that "it transcends its literary analogues."*]

In the **"General Prologue"** the portrait of the Merchant is unflattering. From it we draw a few well-known phrases:

> His resons he spak ful solempnely,
> Sowninge alwey th'encrees of his winning.

In modern terms this is a bore who insists on discussing his shrewd business deals all through dinner. He also has a vested interest in the freedom of the seas—which makes him even worse—because he has a great deal of traffic on shipboard all the time. Chaucer makes him something of a hypocrite:

> Ther wiste no wight that he was in dette.

Yet being in debt is often the case of an investor, and in modern terms, again, there is provision for such contingencies in the bank overdraft. When Chaucer delivers his concluding snub it is a calculated affront and shows that the portrait is heavily charged with contempt:

> I noot how men him calle.

Most of the pilgrims remain anonymous, but they are not brushed off in this manner. It may be hazarded that Chaucer had his own reasons for disliking the recent operations of the merchant class in his own society. For whatever reason, the Merchant emerges from it as a secretive money-grubber, without attractive qualities.

From being a mere pilgrim each character in turn is built up into a narrator. The pilgrims have all just heard the Clerk's story of the supernaturally patient wife Grisilde as part of the marriage debate when the Merchant suddenly breaks the silence. He loses his original shyness and confesses that he has recently married a woman entirely unlike Grisilde. She is a source of weeping and wailing and it is because he is so disturbed by his reflexions that he now breaks out. Since such abruptness is unexpected, the onset of emotion which causes it is intended as a mark of self-revelation. He is a man of undetermined middle age, and now a disillusioned one. His story is of a man of sixty who wards off disillusion by complete failure to understand what is happening to his marriage. Very recently wed and quickly cuckolded, the protagonist Januarie is in a position hardly preferable to that of the unhappy Merchant himself. It is impossible to say whether or not the Merchant raises some of these issues because he feels the danger of being deceived in the same way, but something like this would explain the weight of masculine emotion in his

narrative. He says as he concludes his prologue that he will not indulge the company any more with his own 'soory herte', but instead he provides them with pages of love, hate, fear, sickness and misery, all made more bitter by an underlying irony which makes the listener squirm, since it is told with such art. Not, we say, Chaucer's own view: rather the narrator's own emotional pressure gives this tale its doom-laden strength.

There is a distinct purpose in returning to the tale that has just closed, if we are to see the architecture of the whole **Canterbury Tales,** enhancing with considered plan the value of the single part. The Clerk told of a Lombard count whose tenants, fearing the hazard of the future under an unmarried overlord, all petition him to marry and secure the future. Their wishes, expressed with dignity and conviction, find favour with him and dissuade him from his intent to remain a bachelor. His sober choice falls upon a country girl, Grisilde, whom he carries away to his palace and marries with suitable ceremony.

The resemblances and contrasts between this and **"The Merchant's Tale"** immediately strike the reader. Sir Januarie is also a resident of Lombardy who suddenly decides in old age that he will marry, even though it is the task of one of his brothers to try to dissuade him. He finds the girl and his wedding is celebrated with splendid ceremony.

From this point the two tales diverge dramatically. To try her patience, Count Walter casts his wife off. He has her children taken away from her, and she submits to being sent back in disgrace to her native village. When Walter is satisfied with her reaction he sends for her again, ostensibly in order to assist at a feigned second wedding; and finally he restores her to her former position and love. The Merchant's narrative, on the other hand, shows the gradual dominance of the bride, who takes a lover and deceives her old husband until the end of the story. Both stories have a degree of allegory about them, but the Merchant's is a great deal more realistic in its handling of a grosser theme.

A further distinction which throws light upon the second narrative is in the difference between the two Lombardys. In the first the background is bleak and austere, conveying the impression of a time before Chaucer; whereas in the second there is a much finer and more colourful society, prefiguring the world of the Italian Renaissance. We might legitimately think of Januarie on a Florentine estate or in a Venetian palazzo if we are familiar with these images of magnificence.

It is possibly as a tribute to his Italian colleagues that the Merchant hints at a populous town in festivity:

> Al ful of joye and blisse is the paleys,
> And ful of instrumentz and of vitaille,
> The mooste deyntevous of al Itaille.

The god Bacchus himself serves the drinks, and Venus too is present, as in a Renaissance painting. Yet in this culture, with its pagan leanings, the Christian religion is neither minimized nor satirized. The priest remains on hand right through the ceremonies and until the blessing of the bridal bed. He returns for the High Mass which is sung on the fourth day to greet the bride on her return to the Great Hall.

Yet, in spite of this, we are forced to accept a certain depravity in Januarie, the master of so much genuine splendour. It is strong enough to make nonsense of all the pretensions of his society, even though he is not typical of their way of life. He is both late and irregular in his manner of marriage, and while every lord will have a Placebo to echo him and act the role of the flattering sycophant, Januarie also has Justinus, who . . . 'places' and judges the whole affair, even if he is not permitted to influence the hero's decision. The world of Pavia contains the seeds of corruption even if it also has the makings of a successful life. After all, wealth was to be the making of the Medici family even if it hastened the fall of the Borgias. The distance between Pavia and London was enough to lend enchantment; for the benefit of the poem's completeness, the 'logic of the poem' as T. S. Eliot might have called it, the world is there: actions do not take place in a vacuum.

Readers of C. S. Lewis's celebrated *The Allegory of Love* will realize how closely **"The Merchant's Tale"** follows the fourfold conditions of medieval romantic love: Humility, Courtesy, Adultery and the Religion of Love. The Humility of Damyan before his master and his lady is plain at his first appearance, but it wears off within the time-span of the story (possibly a year). Courtesy is to be found in the enlightened world of the poem and Adultery made most plain in the first introduction of the lover, at the very wedding-feast of his master. The Religion of Love, a perversion of religion, prescribes a certain ritual in which the lover is in pain in his search for recognition and miraculously cured once it has been noticed.

A perfect guide to this Lombard triangle is to be found in *The Art of Courtly Love* by Andreas Capellanus, not to be confused with Martianus Capella, known as Marcian, author of the book mentioned in lines 521-2:

> that like wedding murie
> Of hire Philologie and him Mercurie.

Marcian's is a heavily abstract work, where Andreas'—which we cannot presume that Chaucer had read—is quite blunt and operates from the proposition 'that one cannot love one's wife, but must love the wife of another man'. Andreas examines all the subsequent steps of romantic entanglement which are the more exciting when for the simpler delights of fornication the lover exchanges the complicated ones of adultery. It has been shown that C. S. Lewis was wrong to give the impression that all courtly love stories are adulterous, since **"The Franklin's Tale"** has for its opening premise a lover whose end is a marriage of rare distinction. On the whole, though, the state arose when wedded love, especially in those of high rank, had nothing at all to do with romance. It was a matter of dynastic arrangements linking two estates quite as much as two individuals, enabling money to beget its percentages quite as easily as the couple did their children. Parents arranged the partners and the dowry often from the childhood of the participants, and all they had to do for their part was to live together. In a mansion this was relatively easy as there was some hope of escape. Love of this type in a cottage could only have been a purgatory.

As soon as the reader confronts **"The Merchant's Tale"** with a prior knowledge of the ideas and idioms of courtly love he notices a significant fact. The events and characters are so close to type that they have little individuality. She is the adored one who slowly comes round to requiting his love, and he is the adorer who has all the pangs of lovelonging to undergo, and all the fears of discovery. He obeys all the rules of the game. His love-letter goes according to type. He is said to be 'gentil', 'servisable' and 'sike'. She, for her part, shows 'pitee and franchise' and she blesses him by bidding him to be 'al hool'. Then at once:

> Up riseth Damyan the nexte morwe;
> Al passed was his siknesse and his sorwe.
> He kembeth him, he preyneth him and piketh,
> He dooth al that his lady lust and liketh.

He has felt the 'fyr', the 'desir' and the 'peyne' but she has shown her 'grace' and they have only to come to terms with their love and arrange the assignation. The vocabulary is as standard and commonplace as the situation itself and Chaucer has no emotion of his own to add to it. It is true that we would prefer to see her married to Damyan, yet she has accepted the contract to Januarie. Seeing the one in his 'sherte' must make her long to see the other instead, but the end of the story offers no solution. She in-

The Pardoner from the Ellesmere manuscript.

deed has her lover, though he is no longer a 'servant'. He is exposed as rapacious and lustful, capable of giving her a short-lived passionate experience and quite as likely to abandon her. Even though the narrator expresses the deepest cynicism towards the marriage he has described in such intense detail he is equally disenchanted by the alternative. There is yet hope for a type of marriage which is outside his experience, and which is to be described in **"The Franklin's Tale"**.

One of the central images of the courtly romance is that of the love garden. It is therefore in accordance with the conventions that Januarie should lay out a garden near his home, a *locus amoenus* (a pleasant place) as it was called.

It is to the well-known *Roman de la Rose* by Guillaume de Loris and Jean de Meun that the Merchant directs us in a reference at line 820, but there are many other related works of European literature that Chaucer and his audience may have known. The earliest that remains is *Le Fablel dou Dieu d'Amors* ('The Fable of the God of Love') in which the ingredients are a garden, a stream, the god of love and the birds congregating to look for mates. In this example there is not only a lock and key but a drawbridge to exclude those who are not wanted. An example of this tradition which we know that Chaucer read was Boccaccio's *Teseide,* the source of **"The Knight's Tale"**. In this love garden Venus and Cupid make their appearance, with Bacchus and Ceres in attendance. The languors of love are portrayed in allegory and the work conveys the authentic spirit of the courtly love vision. There is also Chaucer's own **Parlement of Foules** in which the traditional vision of a spring morning is held on St Valentine's Day.

The Parlement is the poem to look at to gain a pleasing view of the love vision. In it Chaucer is led into a garden by the spirit of Scipio Africanus when he is too old for romantic illusions himself (it is the year 1382):

> For thou of love hast lost thyn tast, I gesse,

says his guide. They look into the park at the vegetation, the allegorical residents and the birds, and they pass through gates with inscriptions in golden letters, telling of the blisses of love, and others in black letters, which contain threats:

> 'Thorgh me men gon,' than spak that other side,
> 'Unto the mortal strokes of the spere
> Of which Disdain and Daunger is the gyde.'

Love is composed of an equal draught of delight and danger, it is assumed, and to enter its world is to accept both aspects. The inscription just quoted is reminiscent of the words written over the portals of Hell and described in Dante's *Inferno,* a visionary poem that Chaucer knew well. In that work the inscription tells only of the dangers:

> Per me si va nella città dolente;
> Per me si va nell'eterno dolore;
> Per me si va tra la perduta gente.

> (Through me is the way to the doleful city, is the way into eternal pain, is the way among the people who are lost.)

Through the more modest *wiket* of Januarie's garden people go to find the adorable qualities of love that are associated commonly with Venus. She had appeared at the wedding and has withdrawn. There is also mention of Priapus (the god of gardens and the god of orgiastic sexuality) and the presiding god is Pluto, whose rape of Prosperpina is one of the greatest of all fertility and vegetation myths. The steady accent upon violence in this garden, as in the whole poem, is familiar enough to the modern reader. There has been Januarie's view of sex as violence inflicted upon the woman; Pluto and Damyan exploit the same characteristics towards their partners; there is a complementary lack of respect and deep affection all round. Thus the power of the scene in the Pavian love garden comes from its inversion of the traditional or conventional order of such things and its lack of refinement and elegance. Even the number of the occupants (three humans) is wrong, and its emphasis upon carnality instead of courtliness quickens the audience's appreciation of the corruptness of this trio.

Chaucer's final comment upon the melody and euphony of tradition comes in the gross image with which the whole story culminates:

> And sodeynly anon this Damyan
> Gan pullen up the smok, and in he throng.

After that there is no time for beholding the rose garden.

Even with all this before us, the image of the garden is not yet exhausted. The one interpretation of it that would spring first to the medieval mind has not yet been mentioned: the Garden of Eden in Genesis. This too is an allegory of the fall of love and the failure of humanity to respond to the opportunities of a Golden Age.

Januarie's walled garden was conceived as a locked paradise for a rich couple to roam about in. Adam and Eve were endowed with far more than earthly riches and their catastrophe was far more terrifying. In Genesis the judgment is expressed thus:

> cursed is the ground for thy sake; in sorrow shalt thou eat of it all the days of thy life; thorns also and thistles shall it bring forth to thee; and thou shalt eat the herb of the field; in the sweat of thy fact shalt thou eat bread, till thou return unto the ground; for out of it wast thou taken; for dust thou art, and unto dust shalt thou return.

Under Chaucer's precise control, **"The Merchant's Tale"** is full of menace, and irony pervades every serious issue. Quite early in the tale Januarie's mind had strayed towards the original Paradise Garden:

> womman is for mannes helpe ywroght.
> The hie God, whan he hadde Adam maked,
> And saugh him al allone, bely-naked;
> God of his grete goodnesse seyde than,
> 'Lat us now make an helpe unto this man
> Lyk to himself '; and thanne He made him Eve.

Unaware of the error of his ways, Januarie grows lyrical, singing of his lot:

> wif is mannes helpe and his confort;
> His paradis terrestre, and his disport.

The most trenchant comment on such a state of mind is available for a modern reader in Milton's *Paradise Lost*: a Hell rather than a Paradise with

> neither joy nor love, but fierce desire.

There is no better description of the reality of that paradise garden: the image stands up in the full horror of its traditional Christian meaning. Januarie and May have before them Damyan, the 'naddre' and 'scorpion', who is the scourge that they each deserve for their unworthiness in promoting neither joy nor love but yielding to fierce desire and calling it by a romantic name. (pp. 1-12)

The richest imagery from the Old Testament that remains to be analysed is to be found in the parody of The Song of Solomon used to welcome May into the walled garden. Januarie greets her in these lines:

> 'Ris up, my wif, my love, my lady free,
> The turtles vois is herd, my dowve sweete;
> The winter is goon with alle his reynes weete.
> Com forth now, with thine eyen columbin,
> How fairer been thy brestes than is wyn.
> The gardyn is enclosed al aboute.'

Our first reference is to chapter IV of The Song of Solomon:

> A garden inclosed is my sister, my spouse;
>   a spring shut up, a fountain sealed.

It is a point that Chaucer does not explicitly make but it helps us interpret his other comments. The garden in the quotation from Solomon is a symbol of fertility and an image of all womankind. May and Januarie are keeping to the spirit of this text since the jealously guarded but cunningly duplicated key allows entry to both men at once. It is as Januarie expected—May is a Paradise in herself, but he had not foreseen the force in Justinus' premonition:

> Paraunter she may be youre purgatorie!

The passage at the head of the last paragraph is a parody of verses from The Song of Solomon. In traditional commentary on the Bible the reference is to a mystical union of Christ and the Church, but in the Merchant's narrative there is only the physical world to portray. Solomon sings in the Old Testament in these words:

> Rise up, my love, my fair one, and come away.
> For lo, the winter is past, the rain is over and
>   gone;
> The flowers appear on the earth; the time of the
>   singing of birds is come, and the voice of the
>   turtle is heard in our land.

Doves, associated with Venus because of their promiscuity, are part of the Biblical imagery as well. Two religious cultures blend perfectly: when one is prepared to think solemnly of Christian love, one is confronted with the face of pagan lust as an alternative.

It has been pointed out that there is reminiscence in this scene of the sharply contrasted story of Susanna and the Elders, so familiar in the Middle Ages. Susanna, a beautiful woman, is, unlike May, a good and virtuous wife, who went into a private garden with her maids to bathe. The Elders are two lustful old men, not entirely different from Januarie, who put an infamous proposition to her. They want her to yield to their senile lusts or in revenge they will swear to her husband that she is in the habit of admitting a young man to the private retreat. Susanna refuses outright and the Elders carry out their threat. The case is heard by Daniel who confounds the old men and has them summarily executed.

The image of Susanna's garden can carry this interpretation for its readers because, although it is an idealized world, it has a lock and key which are prominently displayed in medieval pictorial representations of it. Inside it there are the 'allees' to roam in and the 'laurer alwey grene' of **"The Merchant's Tale"**.

There remains in our imagination, high above our heads, the image of the tree, as powerful an image as any in the poem. It is at first the pear tree of medieval comedy and as such familiar to the original hearers. It is also the tree of the fruit of good and evil in which the serpent took up his abode. Again, it is an image of Januarie himself. Early in the poem he remarks:

> Though I be hoor, I fare as dooth a tree
> That blosmeth er that fruit ywoxen bee;
> And blosmy tree nis neither drye ne deed.
> I feele me nowhere hoor but on myn heed;
> Myn herte and alle my lymes been as grene
> As laurer thurgh the yeer is for to sene.

He is mistaken; he is not an evergreen. He is not living through a midwinter spring, but through the onset of lasting winter itself. When he is taken towards the infamous pear tree he has not realized that every paradise must have such a source of evil. Because he is blind he does not see Damyan in the branches. He stands leaning against the trunk and bending slightly so that his wife can climb upon his back. He is shown, too, pathetically embracing the trunk of the tree as if to prevent anybody from following her up it. His jealousy has been aroused, but he does not realize his precautions are far too late and he is seen clinging to the instrument of his own ruin. He does not see the tree for what it is because he cannot see the evil in his own life. Once his sight returns he still remains blind to the evil he has promoted. The tree is a symbol of so much felt experience and so much complete lack of insight: it is a poet rather than a preacher who can make statements of such a degree of subtlety as this.

Damyan and May have already been dismissed as stock types, perfectly fitted for the role of courtly lovers and without the slightest individuality of character. In this request they throw into relief the only true creation of the Tale, its protagonist. It is quite wrong to reduce him to the abstraction 'Elde' (Old Age) since he is one of the poet's most complex characters.

It is from him that almost all the ironies of the poem originate. In M. H. Abrams's invaluable *Glossary of Literary Terms* (under 'Irony') the following is to be found:

> To keep up a sustainedly ironic document, the
> writer is apt to utilize the device of a naive hero,
> or of a naive narrator or expositor, whose invin-
> cible obtuseness leads him to persist in putting

an interpretation on affairs which the smiling reader just as persistently alters or reverses.

"The Merchant's Tale" has a subtle mind behind the narration, whether this is read as the Merchant or Chaucer himself. The rest of the quotation fits Januarie, the naive hero, to perfection. He is always unaware of the fullest implications of what he says. The long speech on marriage at the opening of the Tale is more appropriate in the mouth of the hero than of the narrator:

> And certeinly, as sooth as God is king,
> To take a wif it is a glorious thing,
> And namely whan a man is oold and hoor;
> Thanne is a wif the fruit of his tresor.
> Thanne sholde he take a yong wif and a
>   feir. . . .

If one stops at that point, there are already many ironies to explain. The first two lines are the declaration of his subject. It is not certain from the tone of the passage whether Januarie recognizes (as the readers do) that he is at that very moment 'oold and hoor'. The word 'fruit' refers the reader forward, all the way to the catastrophe in the pear tree, while the word 'tresor' brings into the poem the financial imagery, the economic motive which is found at every point in Januarie's view of marriage as a financial contract or an animal passion but as nothing of greater value. Ironies such as these run throughout the entire poem and reveal themselves in due order as the present moment sheds a light upon the false security of the past. These are images of return which are completely understood only when their full significance is revealed, but even before, they have enough potential to make the reader smile and flinch at once.

What is so subtle in the presentation of Januarie is the way in which our emotion flows out towards him because he is growing senile, is blinded and betrayed; yet quite as swiftly recoils because of his repulsiveness, his sheer profligacy and the hypocritical remarks he makes concerning the safety of his soul. The bedtime lectures that he gives to a deaf audience of one evoke universal contempt.

There is a great deal more to discuss, however, on the score of the quality Chaucer calls 'fantasye'. Januarie seems to believe that matrimony will make perversions into virtues. He is, as a result, perfectly accurate in his assessment of the possibilities of marriage without realizing that he has none of the qualities needed. This much being granted for a moment, it is natural for him to arrange everything as he does. He is fool enough to see himself as a rebirth of Paris ready to carry off a Helen, when he is more properly a fool of an old husband, a Menelaus, if ever there was one.

His insensitivity emerges in his belief that everything in life has a price ticket round its neck. As soon as he finds his wife he makes ready:

> every scrit and bond
> By which that she was feffed in his lond.

He does not pause to ask why there is no father to give his daughter a dowry. His creation of a pleasure garden is presented to us as an extension of a cashbox in which the key is the all-important possession.

Logically still, a man of his background sees sex as something to snatch, and all relations between the sexes as a kind of war:

> But in his herte he gan hire to *manace*
> That he that night in armes wolde hire *streyne*
> *Harder* than evere *Paris* dide *Eleyne*.

The tale follows him still further but without pornography:

> Allas, I moot *trespace*
> To yow, my spouse, and yow greetly *offende*.

For a time he is so preoccupied with thoughts of his own potency that he does not see it as unnatural, since it has to be fed on a cupboard full of drugs and directed by the reading of a book entitled *De Coitu*.

All this is simple to analyse and to judge, but there is another side to him. His home and estate reflect the good taste of the day; his concern for his servant Damyan, ironic as it is, occupies many lines and is greeted by the rest of his household in terms that are completely unsmiling and unironic:

> And for that word him *blessed* every man,
> That of his *bountee* and his *gentillesse*
> He wolde so *conforten in siknesse*
> His squier.

In the catastrophe of the poem we give him our pity again with his infamous wife crawling on his back to meet a scoundrel aloft in the pear tree. Pluto's sudden kindly action reveals May as she really is, though she is given what may truly be called infernal prompting to evade her husband's just wrath. It is the reader's judgment that the man of her own choice is younger but essentially no better. Damyan is likely to fasten upon her when she is a rich young widow until she (and he for that matter) must look elsewhere again for satisfaction.

All readers recognize the physical comedy of the bedroom scenes:

> And upright in his bed thanne sitteth he,
> And after that he sang ful loude and cleere,
> And kiste his wif.

To use a modern image, the camera has come too close and seen the texture of the skin. In fairness to Januarie, though, it is a good and natural expression of his emotions to sing in such a situation in the dawn's first light; the reader is divided in his attitude.

Care and judgement have gone to the entire presentation of this man. There is no doubt that the reader feels a degree of projection of himself into him: empathy rather than a fellow feeling or full sympathy. He is a man who has not grown up. Although past sixty he still looks for one thing:

> He purtreyed in his herte and in his thoght
> Hir fresshe beautee and hir age tendre,
> Hir middel smal, hire armes longe and sklendre.

He imagines that what attracts him is quite other:

> Hir wise governaunce, hir gentillesse,
> Hir wommanly beringe, and hire sadnesse.

The lady of his hurried choice obeys the first canons of taste but never the second. It is all explained in the subtle image of the mirror:

> Many fair shap and many a fair visage
> Ther passeth thurgh his herte night by night,
> As whoso tooke a mirour, polisshed bright,
> And sette it in a commune market-place,
> Thanne sholde he se ful many a figure pace
> By his mirour.

The language of psychology in these extracts is delicately handled: 'purtreyed in his herte', 'passeth thurgh his herte'; but there is no discrimination in a mirror, which is the symbol of his mind. Mirrors cannot reflect *gentillesse,* which for Chaucer is a Christian quality; they have no power to discriminate in the 'commune market-place' where, by implication, Januarie found May. He brings nemesis upon himself: good wives are not found in the market-place or the brothel. We are unlikely, since we all imagine ourselves basically decent, to sympathize; but we are ready to discuss sexual morality in the light of this vivid story. This is the best assent we can give to the creation of a satirist.

Those who write about Chaucer are often accused of ignoring the native elements in his art and concentrating instead upon his handling of foreign models. The all-encompassing native element is, of course, the use of language; and the reader's wish is not to be deterred by the spelling or the syntax but to try to appreciate what he reads as he would a poem written in later centuries. The editions of Tales in this series aim to make this task lighter by reducing to a minimum the philological information and helping the reader with the task of critical appreciation. (pp. 13-21)

Most considerations of Chaucer's style stem from the fact that his poetry was written to be read aloud and not perused silently in our own manner. Thus the pace of absorption would be slower and the attention more concentrated. The man with the book in front of him can turn back for purposes of clarification but if, as in broadcasting, the text is irrecoverable the greatest virtue in its style is clarity, brevity and discipline. One of Chaucer's later disciples, the printer Caxton, wrote that the poet 'comprehended his matter in short, quick and high sentences, eschewing prolixity' which tells us what was thought a virtue in a poet in his own time.

Occasionally there must be relaxations of attention, passages in which the information-content is low. The effect on those occasions will be emotional and not narrative. Here is an example:

> O perilous fyr, that in the bedstraw bredeth;
> O famulier foo, that his service bedeth;
> O servant traitour, false hoomly hewe.

This passage is entirely of exclamation and many of Chaucer's tales can show pieces to parallel it. The device probably originated in the pulpit, which is very similar to the poet's lectern: each was designed for an artist in the spoken word. The third line in this passage says the same thing twice in different words so that the speed of compre-

hension is allowed to slow down, giving the audience a moment for breath before plunging ahead into the story.

When we encounter the rather pleasing songs that Januarie sings there seems no reason to think that the reciter did not sing them, since we know that singing during sermons was permitted. When the story reaches the idyllic moment in the garden and the verse grows lyrical the poet sings with Januarie:

> 'Ris up, my wif, my love, my lady free,
> The turtles vois is herd, my dowve sweete;
> The winter is goon with alle his reynes weete.'

Similarly since there are six quite distinct characters who speak, the narration must have been a good deal more dramatic than we immediately imagine.

One of the most pregnant forms of oral expression is the proverb. This gives in the fewest possible words the greatest amount of moral wisdom. It is impossible to be dogmatic about what was a proverb and what was not at a distance of six hundred years, but we can say with some certainty that many phrases and lines have a proverbial ring about them. If they were already known they could act as a series of oases for the listener or monitoring stations from which the poem's progress can be judged. Their crispness of sound and movement correspond precisely with the qualities most admired by Caxton and they condition the audience as they are heard in turn. They also invite the reader to assent to a piece of wisdom which is shared by the whole folk.

What is noticeable about the proverbs in **"The Merchant's Tale"** is that they are occasionally inverted and used as a criticism of the speaker. Here is an example:

> 'Bet is,' quod he, 'a pyk than a pikerel,
> And bet than old boef is the tendre veel.'

In these analogies Januarie seeks to justify his marriage with a girl one-third of his age. But it turns marriage into a matter of physical eating, of greed; and is not Januarie 'old boef'? What has been called Chaucer's favourite line also has a proverbial ring to it:

> . . .Pitee renneth soone in gentil herte.

True as this sentiment may be, it is once more restricted in application. It was intended for a nobler scene than the one in which May contrives her forthcoming adultery with Damyan. (pp. 21-3)

[There are many lines] which have the air of being on the way to a proverb:

> Paraunter she may be youre purgatorie!

The final proverb in the Tale is another one inverted through its appearance in an ironical context:

> He that misconceyveth, he misdemeth.

May's words stand out as what we expect of folk-wisdom though the interpretation that we have to put upon them is more complex. Januarie has not misunderstood the message of his senses, but he has been led to doubt it by the persuasion of his wife. He accepts the conventional interpretation without causing further trouble.

The last quotation is an example of the parallelism which is occasionally employed in Chaucer's mature verse. There is a finality and elegance about the expression which is based upon the repetition of the syllable *mis*. The same technique is present in such a line as the second one here:

> And with this word this Justin and his brother
> Han take hir leve, and ech of hem of oother.

It is only a short space from such a construction to a case of perfect antithesis which gives the sense of finish to the line and leaves it memorable and exact:

> Whan tendre youthe hath wedded stouping age.

Anybody who is familiar with the couplet-technique of the eighteenth century will feel that Chaucer had discovered some of its secrets centuries before. What is even more felicitous about this quotation is that when Alexander Pope, the eighteenth-century poet, translated this Tale in his youth under the title *January and May,* he had no need to change the movement of this line, which emerges as:

> When tender youth has wedded stooping age.

A most useful exercise of comparative reading lies in this version by Pope in imitation of Chaucer, a writer he very much admired for a brevity, speed and moral vision so like his own.

The handling of single lines as entities in themselves is often sharp enough without the appendage of the second line. Nowhere in the poem is there a better example than the alliterative:

> Lo, where he sit, the lechour, in the tree

which is brutally exposed and spotlighted as it should be. How completely different is the love-movement which we find in the following line and its echoes:

> He kisseth hire, and clippeth hire ful ofte.

These are a few examples of the writer's sensitivity to language and its qualities of immediacy and swiftness. Nobody could ask for more perfect delineation of the decrepit old man in bed than this:

> He lulleth hire, he kisseth hire ful ofte;
> With thikke brustles of his berd unsofte,
> Lyk to the skin of houndfissh, sharp as brere.

The verse does exactly what it says, it acts out the bristly cheeks which are trying to be tender but are actually sharp and repellent. Such is the range of the verse-movement in **"The Merchant's Tale"**. (pp. 24-5)

It has been remarked that **"The Franklin's Tale"**, the next but one in the series, is Chaucer's corrective for the taste left behind by **"The Merchant's Tale"**. There is indeed a marked resemblance between them, and one would not expect Chaucer to be guilty of repeating his message. In each tale a rich couple has a young man close at hand who offers to destroy their marriage. On the second occasion the husband is absent, not merely unaware of what is taking place, and he thus unwittingly leaves his wife to make the crucial decision. Again a garden is the *locus amoenus* of intended adultery:

> And craft of mannes hand so curiously
> Arrayed hadde this gardyn, trewely,
> That nevere was ther gardyn of swich prys,
> But if it were the verray paradis.

The lover, taking advantage of Dorigen's isolation, is subject to all the complaints of his class:

> In languor and in torment furyus
> Two yeer and moore lay wrecche Aurelius.

The reader also notices familiar terms: 'servant', 'servage', 'peyne', 'grace', 'torment'. This time, however, the lady Dorigen refuses to bid him be 'al hool' again. His only hope is to take a long winter journey to Orleans where a magician is bribed to do the work of celestial 'jogelrye'; the lover acknowledges his help:

> I, woful wrecche Aurelius,
> Thanke yow, lord, and lady myn Venus
> That me han holpen from my cares colde.

For all his expense, Dorigen prefers to destroy herself rather than see him again, and in the end, having achieved nothing, he has the magnanimity to renounce his claim.

Equally interesting is the placing of another definition of the true qualities of marriage at the opening of the tale in which they are to be worthily represented. These lines of definition are couched in the idiom of courtly love, since here Chaucer provides an example in which Adultery is not the end of the affair. True love and marriage are not incompatible when love's servant Arveragus courts Dorigen:

> Thus hath she take hir servant and hir lord,
> Servant in love and lord in mariage,
> Than was he bothe in lordshipe and servage.

She had accepted him as her servant and as her husband where feudal love would have left her without choice. From similar basic situations the two tales reach fundamentally different conclusions about marriage. There are faults and inconsistencies to be exposed, but there is no doubt that the Franklin's perception of the need for mutual trust and respect that should go with happiness is a necessary move away from the Merchant's carnal assessment of married life's possibilities.

To read this Tale after the Merchant's is to explore the standards of human behaviour in all its facets and not to be confined to those of marriage alone. The theme of **"The Franklin's Tale"** resembles that of the Wife of Bath's: 'gentillesse', which emerges from Chaucer's pen (and Dante's prompting of it) as a god-given quality:

> Thy gentillesse cometh from God allone.

And, finally, considering the purpose of the Franklin, one can at last reject the cynicism of **"The Merchant's Tale"** as the prejudice of a disillusioned narrator and not the faith of the controlling poet. Since the group of tales that forms a debate on marriage comes to a halt with the Franklin's contribution, it is of the highest significance that the last of the sequence should dispel the cynicism of the Merchant.

The Merchant finishes his tale, turns to his auditors and prays them all to be glad. Why they should be so is beyond conjecture after such a sordid story. They—and we—would have been glad to have a text on which to base a more satisfactory discussion of matrimony and the moral life. Yet we can be pleased with the great subtlety of the tale. Stating the main themes in extended analysis gives no impression of the conduct of the poem. It remains a matter for admiration that Chaucer had so wide a view of his poetic purpose as to use allegorical characters alongside real ones, to blend paganism and Christianity until one becomes a type of the other and reinforces the overall meaning.

Although the poem is rich and ambiguous, it is not at all confused. A persistent duality in it may seem to leave the meaning open to doubt, but this is not the case. Januarie calls in two counsellors, appears to have two religions, and for his philosophy seems to believe in the principle of eating his cake and still having it. He is sure that religion, which ought to be a normative influence, is sanctioning all his old predispositions and allowing him to remain at heart a whoremaster while ostensibly he is a truly married man. This is *his* confusion, and not the poet's casual permissiveness towards the reader or a general freedom of interpretation of the fable.

A pictorial image, common in medieval calendars, will make the point swiftly, although Chaucer does not himself invoke the image. The month of January is always shown as the time of carousing at the winter feast and often as a man at a table with two or even three faces looking all about him (a reference to Janus, god of doorways, who looks both ways, at the old year and the new). There is also a necessary doubleness about the zodiac sign of Gemini, the twins, under which the catastrophe in the garden is said to take place. Such images of doubleness prepare us for the poem's ending, in which what is genuinely seen is explained as being in conflict with what really happens. May assures Januarie that there was no illict act to be spotted in the tree: it was only 'glimsing' on his part and not true vision. Because the reality is too destructive he is prepared to accept the deception, though everybody else is prepared to destroy him. It is only the surface of the poem that yields this ambiguity: everything is clearly and urgently ethical in intent.

The final work of our literature to which I would compare **"The Merchant's Tale"** is *Othello*. This too is made up of a web of ironies in which the central character is caught. It may be recalled that Iago, who is the supreme example of duplicity, swears by Janus before he destroys his master. In Chaucer's work there is no Iago except fortune itself, and a more guilty but equally characterless Cassio in Damyan. The style of literature to which **"The Merchant's Tale"** should not be compared is the category of medieval comic *fabliau*. This is a type of entertainment suitable for simple people and it is to this category that Chaucer's work has often been relegated. It may be true of any other version of the seduction in the pear tree in European literature but it is not true of this one.

In fact, this is one of Chaucer's masterpieces. If the language is at times fixed and hardened by literary convention, at others it is free and even impressionistic in its images and its sound-effects. The verse-movement is succinct and clear, performing its task with assurance. Landscape, character-portrayal and dramatic outcries are all part of the texture: its irony makes all the laughter uneasy and slightly strained. It looks so perfectly inevitable in its expression, one thinks one might almost have been born knowing it all. This is a sign that it transcends its literary analogues. (pp. 30-4)

> *Maurice Hussey, in an introduction to* The Merchant's Prologue and Tale from the Canterbury Tales *by Geoffrey Chaucer, edited by Maurice Hussey, Cambridge at the University Press, 1966, pp. 1-36.*

Daniel Cook   (essay date 1966)

[*In the following excerpt, Cook comments on the characters of* Troilus and Criseyde, *offering a detailed analysis of the two main protagonists of Chaucer's work.*]

The characters of **Troilus and Criseyde** are shown to us in two ways: they are described and discussed by the poet-narrator and they show themselves forth in their speech and acts. Each exists—for the purpose of analysis—in various strata. Their larger role in the action is determined by the shape of the story as Chaucer received it: beyond certain limits this is unalterable. Each character is, to a degree, conditioned by the literary conventions of Courtly Love. And building upon these strata and employing their materials, the poet has created extraordinary human figures whose movement through the poem exemplifies a deeply felt truth about human experience.

Of these characters the most brilliantly conceived is Criseyde. In important ways she is a Courtly Love heroine. She is of course beautiful, she appears, initially, disdainful and remote and is won with great difficulty, she holds sovereignty over her lover, and she is delicate and fearful for her reputation. These characteristics, while conventional and often conventionally expressed, are yet woven integrally into a figure of astonishing reality, and they become, as well, important elements in the development of the tragedy.

Above all, she transcends her type by a score of delicate touches of femininity illumined by mind and wit. She is playful and gently mocking with Pandarus ("Uncle," quod she, "youre maistresse is nat here"). She has self-respect and dignity, but in surrender is forthright and tender ("Ne hadde I er now, my swete herte deere, / Ben yold, iwys, I were now nought heere"), direct and passionate ("Welcome, my knyght, my pees, my suffisaunce"). Deceived, perhaps not quite unwittingly, by Pandarus, her chiding has a rueful humorousness that is entirely charming ("Nevere the bet for yow, / Fox that ye ben").

But her character is far from a transparent one. Critical opinion of her is so diverse that no judgment is without its defenders. Envious critics have even called Criseyde vain. If this is not groundless malice, one must suppose that they have in mind, for example, her words to herself in the privacy of her chamber: "I am oon the faireste, out of drede, . . . And so men seyn, in al the town of Troie." But to read this as vanity is surely wrong—and what is worse it is humorless naïveté. She is in fact beautiful; she must be so, conventionally, and so the poet tells us and Pandarus and Troilus as well. And a moment's attention to the world of experience, as distinct from that of fiction, will tell us that beautiful women know they are fair, if only because men tell them so. This is not vanity. Criseyde does not court admiration; there is no suggestion anywhere that she makes much of her beauty or uses it for favor or takes unseemly relish from its effect. But beautiful she is and must be, and, as well, direct and unpretentious, of "full humble chere," and "both of yonge and olde / Ful wel biloved." It is importantly this which moves the reader to feel with Troilus his passion in wooing and his bliss in having and his despair in losing.

Just as significant as these features is a basic fact of her nature which is of capital importance to our concept of her whole role in the drama. This is her fearfulness: "she was the ferfulleste wight / That myghte be." Fear is as recurrent a theme in the portrait of Criseyde as is Fortune in that of Troilus. From her introduction in Book I, a widow alone and "sore in drede," to her fear of stealing by night from the Greek camp, and even to the implausible excuse, "for feere," which she offers Troilus in her last letter, her fear—or her deliverance from fear—is mentioned no fewer than twenty times. She fears the Greeks, she fears Pandarus's wild antics, fears to hear his tidings, is terrified of his threats, is pale for fear of Poliphete; she burns in love and dread at the news of her exchange; she would die, but fears to handle sword or dart. Significantly often too, we hear of her dependence upon Troilus: he was her wall of steel; with him she was "al quyt from every drede and tene."

Long ago distinguished critics of the poem saw this timidity of hers as central to a complex character who could, believably, love deeply and sincerely yet, under the pressure of extraordinary circumstances, be guilty of deserting her lover. To perceive this on the most literal level, we need only relate Chaucer's evident emphasis on her fearfulness with the demands which her promise to Troilus put upon her. That such a delicate woman could choose to defy her father and steal at night through a camp full of soldiers across an empty battlefield among unknown dangers to take refuge in a city doomed, as she had been persuaded, to violent destruction need only be phrased to be recognized as absurd. The alternative was the security of her father's care and the protection of a brave leader of a victorious army. The choice was foregone. Her sincerity was beyond question but she was "slydynge of corage."

This is the rationale provided by Chaucer's carefully detailed creation of the fearful Criseyde. Yet it does not tell the whole story. For while we undoubtedly wish—like the poet—to excuse this lovely, tender, loving woman, we do not perhaps quite succeed; our disappointment in her is too great, and there is always that last dreadful and quite unforgivable letter to Troilus. She has by then, we may say, been corrupted by her own expediency, but in retrospect perhaps this too has been prepared for.

Two early passages are relevant. When Pandarus first announces Troilus's love to Criseyde, he threatens that her refusal will be followed at once by his death and his friend's. She nearly died for fear, she felt pity, and she thought

> And if this man sle here hymself, allas,
> In my presence, it wol be no solas.
> What men wolde of hit deme I kan nat seye;
> It nedeth me ful sleighly for to pleie.

(Note that *sleighly* here probably means merely "secretly". . .). The second passage comes some lines later as she reflects upon her new problem. If she were to reject the prince outright, she considers, his ensuing enmity might endanger her already delicate situation in Troy.

> Now were I wis me hate to purchace
> Withouten nede, ther I may stonde in grace?

The conventional reader may find these reflections shocking, but this need not be a necessary view. These thoughts are evidently calculating and ignoble, but in honesty are they so different from the secret, uncensored ignobilities which, we suspect, may sometimes slip unbidden into the mind of all but the severest critics? May this not be another instance of the forthright perceptiveness of this most forthright poet? Whether this be so or not, these very human, though regrettable, thoughts are clearly the product of Criseyde's great weakness, her fearfulness.

In fine, there is ambivalence here. We may understand and excuse—like Chaucer, "for routhe," but calculation in a woman is not pretty, however human it may be, and when the course of Criseyde's decay is seen in retrospect, these speeches take their place in the collected evidence. She was in the last analysis a little too human, too fearful, too weak, too "slydynge of corage." In good fortune we see in her all the virtues that a well-loved and loving woman may have, but in stress she—even she—was flawed with the mutability of earthly things.

Pandarus too is in origin a Courtly Love figure, and like Criseyde he has caught Chaucer's interest and has been transformed into a fascinating and delightful—but more than a little ambiguous—human being. As his Courtly Love role is to play Friend to Troilus's Lover, he must be counselor and confidant, encouraging and optimistic in time of trouble; active and ingenious in advancing the suit. The role naturally suggests the personality which Chaucer's humanizing genius supplies him. He is active, direct, simple and unreflective. He never walks when he can run or leap ("O verray God, so have I ronne! / Lo, nece myn, se ye nought how I swete?"). His emotions are immediate and on the surface. Seeing Troilus in despair, he "neigh malt for wo and routhe." Convinced of Criseyde's final treachery, his reaction is direct and uncomplicated: "I hate, ywys, Cryseyde; / And God woot I wol hate hire evermore!" He is humorously playful both at his own expense and at Troilus's, and his lighthearted pleasure in intrigue is indefatigable. His elaborate stage management of the meeting of the lovers at the house of Deiphebus is both delightful for the pleasure he takes in it and comic for the busy figure he cuts.

But he is in more respects than these the perfect antithesis to Troilus. For, delightful as he may be, he is flawed by an essential shallowness which deprives him of taste and judgment at critical moments. The first clear sight of this, apart from the general lightness of his tone, is his role in the seduction scene in Book III. Even taking into consideration the decidedly forthright medieval attitude toward the bridal bed, one cannot help finding an element of prurience in his extraordinary helpfulness at the bedside. And his tone throughout, while undoubtedly entertaining, is clear enough indication that he is happily, if vicariously, engaged in the eternal chase, no more. Though everywhere in the suit he is superficially sentimental and easily moved to tears of joy by the happiness of the lovers, his perception of the true nature of the love is shallow almost to the point of frivolousness. For at the last, upon learning of Criseyde's impending departure, when he counsels Troilus to abandon her and take another mistress, the advice seems astonishingly insensitive. Suddenly this amusing, gay, sympathetic fellow is an uncomprehending stranger to the very suit he has done so much to further.

Again the ambivalence of our attitude points the way. Pandarus, like Criseyde, though to a lesser degree, is attractive, even lovable. He is entertainingly human and a devoted friend. But the moral flaw is disturbing. Courtly Love convention prescribes his role and presumably puts out of consideration any censure of his part in the seduction. Yet the uncharitable interpretation of his action as an uncle debauching his niece has not escaped him, and it is a mark of his unease that he more than once protests the innocence of his motives. And however selfless his exertions may have been, they have been spent, as we have seen, in support of a liaison which he has not even understood. It all contributes to the growing darkness of the final books: Pandarus's shallow practicality, Criseyde's self-deceiving weakness, and Troilus's helpless despair. Each complements the other in a completed picture of ignorant mortals made defenceless against the strokes of Fortune by their devotion to a false felicity.

[Troilus] is the least individualized of the major characters—most typically the Courtly Lover, fully dependent, as Courtly Lovers are wont to be, on the turn of Fortune. But he, too, greatly perfects and transcends the type. He is, with Hector, holder-up of Troy in war and apparently respected in council. He is handsome, knightly, wholly noble in spirit, sincere and true in love. He is deeply moved by emotion, even beyond the requirements of his literary type, but in an age of unrestrained expression is not unmanly even in excess. His personality is not complex, but its singleness is functional: he alone is unflawed by self-interest or superficiality. Convinced at last of Criseyde's defection, his words are a movingly human testament of his fidelity.

> . . .clene out of youre mynde
> Ye han me cast; and I ne kan nor may,
> For al this world, withinne myn herte fynde
> To unloven yow a quarter of a day!

To this perfection of character is added thoughtfulness, and this too is functional. His reflections upon necessity and free will, as has been seen, are integral to the larger meaning of the poem. In sum, we may see in Troilus a man whose deserts are high, a wholly admirable and wholly undeserving victim of Fortune. Like the Boethius of the *Consolation,* he merits worldly happiness if any do, and his

fall involves us in personal recognition that the end of worldly bliss is woe.

Many elements have contributed to the metamorphosis of character and effect which Chaucer has worked upon his source. He has refined and elevated the love and the lovers, primarily by modifications deriving from the literary conventions of Courtly Love. Drawing upon the strengths of Boethian philosophy, he has universalized a story of passionate love into an exemplification of the vanity of mortal hopes. Most enduringly impressive, however, is the humanizing process that is worked upon his people. The source of this lies nowhere but in Chaucer himself and in his always affectionate and optimistic observation of the world about him. Nothing is so thoroughly Chaucerian as this and no evaluation of the poem should fail to rank highly this feature.

Analysis of the *Troilus* and its characters may have an unfortunate tendency to alter the balance of elements which the poem in fact maintains. Discussion of the relation of the parts to the final tragedy and to the poem's "meaning" tends to produce an emphasis on the weaknesses of the characters and on their melancholy fate, resulting in distortion of the poem's total effect. For if the meaning has to do with the futility of man's commitment to worldly happiness, the poem is also and importantly the means by which that meaning is expressed. Central to these means is the poet-narrator's tolerant and understanding and even humorous attitude toward his people and his action. Though he knows well the imperfections and sorrows of the world and though finally he accepts for us the superiority of the spiritual life, he has also a zestful appreciation of the joys of life, the loveliness of Criseyde, the humorous liveliness of Pandarus, the valor, strength, and sincerity of Troilus, and the beauty and ecstasy of human love. His perception is always acute and his view humane: alert to the potential for comic absurdity in excesses of earnestness and solemnity, consistently sympathetic to love and lovers even when flawed by weakness or failure or self-interest, never harsh or austere, always generous and tolerant. The sincerity of the poem's last stanzas is not to be questioned or underemphasized, but though "al nys but a faire / This world that passeth soone as floures faire," yet in the high solemnity of the conclusion we do not forget that the flowers of the world, though passing, are still passing fair. (pp. xxxii-xxxviii)

> *Daniel Cook, in an introduction to* Troilus and Criseyde *by Geoffrey Chaucer, edited by Daniel Cook, Anchor Books, 1966, pp. vii-xxxviii.*

Matthew Corrigan   (essay date 1969)

[*In the excerpt below, Corrigan examines Chaucer's most famous female characters, Criseyde and Alison, the Wife of Bath. Disagreeing with the prevailing critical opinion, he finds them flawed and unconvincing, maintaining that "Chaucer's conception of woman is as blurred as the image medieval man has of her."*]

If the metaphor of the "unconscious" still holds as a viable means of describing a fact of human existence then it is possible to ascribe metaphorically an unconscious life to literature and art. There are subterranean "problems" in all literature which a later age discovers and discusses, and more often than not these problems represent the penumbral problems of life itself in that earlier age. One such problem—one that has its fullest existence on an unconscious level within an era (and usually on an unconscious level within its literature)—involves the attitude each sex has toward its opposite. Popular mythology and literature have always relied upon and supported the emotional difference between the sexes (presumably because emotion is most easily associated with the obvious biological difference between man and woman), but it is not until the "discovery of the unconscious" that the basic psychic difference between the sexes is asserted, and with Wilhelm Fliess, C. G. Jung and others, set down almost schematically. Jung goes as far as to suggest that the difference between man and woman is the vast and complex difference between two poles; what lies between is an area of rich contention, an area of conflicting fields of force. Phenomenological psychology has expanded upon this to show how the mental outlook which each sex feels peculiar to itself is structured ("structure" here is a metaphor, like "unconscious") along different lines—along different lines of force, if we want to complicate the metaphor; that there are structures of perception, imagination, judgment, etc., which can be understood as preeminently feminine or masculine. Most humans live mythologically anyway, and one of the most complicated myths in man's daily life (perhaps also one of the most necessary) is his conception of what woman is: whether she is a Des-demona in name only, or also in fact—a devil *in deed.* The number of texts turned out today by women explicitly attempting to rectify male misconceptions about the "second sex" indicates on one level the lingering truth of this observation. We should not be so complacent in our acceptance of even the greatest authors as to assume that they did not contribute in their own way to this myth-making. In a sense, the history of man's literature about woman is the history of man's psychological failure with his opposite; if Jung's intuition is valid, it also represents, on one level, a history of man's unconsciousness, or to be more precise, man's awareness thereof. (pp. 107-08)

Surprisingly enough, Chaucer, who—many critics inform us—has given literature two everlasting women, has received little serious investigation along these lines. For my own part, I find Chaucer's two women, Criseyde and Alison, somewhat impure creations, in that neither one has a life all her own. I find each characterization represents Chaucer's own indecisiveness to a marring degree—an indecisiveness which he does not perhaps intend and which is different from the situation where an author purposely characterizes woman's "indecisiveness," or what man has traditionally called her "fickleness." Alison, the Wife of Bath, works as a literary figure for reasons other than her womanliness. She is entertaining, and she is so at the expense of any valid conception of what woman is; and since she is entertaining at woman's expense, our very male culture still encourages us to brook the humor. Alison is, in my terminology, a quite malefic creation. Chaucer's Criseyde, also, I find to be marred. Critics who try to do motivational research on her (and all male critics have done this to some extent) stagger from the task like troops

from a Napoleonic defeat; their pride may be intact and showing, but they are clearly losers all.

Part of the reason Chaucer has received little critical attention with regard to his characterizations of woman has to do with the age in which he wrote and the still obscured view we have of woman in that age. Hardly any two critics are in full agreement on woman's role in the late Middle Ages, and few critics are illuminating or profound on the subject. For some twentieth-century onlookers this period in history represents, somehow, another "golden age of masculinity"—and indeed some very rich male propaganda on the subject of woman as *sexus sequior* is to be found in the times. On the side of the masculine Church, for example, there is the emotional and philosophic argument that accepts woman as second nature to man, as more susceptible of temptation, as a vessel of sin. The misconception is due as much to Aristotle's faulty biology as to a particular reading of *Genesis.* (Aristotle had held that man was the formal or active principle in procreation; that the woman, in adding but *matter* to *form,* was inferior.) Both Bonaventure and Aquinas, writing about a century before Chaucer, consider woman in terms similar to those Aristotle had used: *mas occasionatus,* or "man gone awry"—though Bonaventure seems more willing than Aquinas to redeem her regardless.

One theological dictionary of the early fourteenth century notes:

> A man may chastise his wife and beat her by way of correction, for she forms part of his household; so that he, the master, may chastise that which is his. . . .

Almost three centuries later, a comic Shakespeare is able to put words almost identical with these into the mouth of his Petruchio, but he is able to do so without causing his audience or us any offence. The once serious idea remains but as a comic gesture; archetype has become comic cliché. Chaucer's Wife of Bath provides us with a good summary of the kinds of diatribe against woman that could be heard in the local tavern or from certain pulpits. But behind Alison's words I find a less pure and even suspicious comic instinct, one that smacks somewhat of the original seriousness with which the theological side of the argument was struck.

The late Middle Ages, even on the basic issue of woman, her reality, her rights and status, has its surplus of ambiguity. Woman is not entirely disesteemed as an individual being. Indeed there are many critics who see the age as exorbitantly favorable to woman. Certainly there are some facts which demand a more balanced view than that propagated by the Medieval Church. This is after all the age of courtly love, a phenomenon in which (we are told) the woman figuratively replaces the lord (and Lord) at the apex of the feudal system; an age of such legendary, well-educated figures as Eleanor of Aquitaine, Marie de Champagne, Marie de France. It is also the age of Mariology. In Dante and Petrarch woman becomes one with the poetic muse, thus the chemistry of love becomes the theoretic of the creative process, itself a deeply unconscious thing at this point in time. In the attitudes of each of these poets toward his ideal yet presumably real woman (Beatrice,

Laura) we have something closer to a realization of the feminine principle than we find in the lesser courtly poets, and than in Chaucer; but although it is perhaps the deepest psychological aspect of woman realized by man in the age, it is only one aspect of her possible existence within him—woman herself is not yet realized in the literature (re-realized is perhaps the better word, since we do have the Greek experience of the feminine to look back on).

These, then, are the two almost dialectically opposed views of woman we have to work with in looking at the late Middle Ages. If they are correct in some measure, and not totally misleading, what is remarkable is not that they are opposites, nor that they exist in the first place, but the manner of their existence, their *style*. Though this dichotomy represents one version of what is undoubtedly some kind of a real psychological dialectic within man—it does not, in my terms, represent it very well. In a society where man's natural ambivalence toward his opposite takes the form of movements such as (1) *Frauendienst* (woman-worship in either the Provençal love poem or the Marian lyric), and (2) anti-feminism, we might conclude that there is something close to a psychic misconception of woman innate to the times. This is possibly why the real woman of the Middle Ages is so obscured, especially in its literature. If an author writes in an age of such formulaic psychological attitudes (if that is not too barbaric a way of putting it), he risks merely repeating in some disguised way what his age stands for unconsciously. He is not necessarily condemned to its views—though the risk is great; he is, certainly, in some way influenced by them. For my own part, I find both Chaucer and his age at fault on the issue of woman. I find a certain indolence at work in his treatment of the opposite sex; or to put it another way, I find he has even fewer ideas on the subject than his age might allow. He gives us woman as she exists in the mind of his time. He *describes* her almost from hearsay, even in his two main attempts—Criseyde and Alison. He does not question his own psyche in search of her uniqueness.

It is not that woman—or what I am really suggesting, the female principle—does not exist in the unconscious of the times; she does. It is the nature of that existence, as indeed it is the nature of that unconscious itself, at least as it reveals itself in the literature and art of the times, that is at stake. The writings by women themselves (see for example the memoirs of Margery Kempe or Margery Paston) do not give us a very definite idea of her place in the age; they do not give us what the writings of women give us in so many other ages, namely the complement to man's creative insights, the umbra which sets off his own maleness; about all they suggest is that a strong-willed woman could then, as today, hold her own against man. Though we tremble to put it so drastically, it is almost as though a whole aspect of human nature, namely woman, in herself and in man, is inadequately realized by the age; or is realized but under the careful ratiocination of a celibate psychology, the exact nature of which is lost to us, along with so much else of the age; as a result, perhaps, both art and life "suffer" in some ineffable respects.

To try to put the matter more deliberately, more specifically: there seems to be in Chaucer small sense of the mag-

nitude of woman: she is patient Grisilde, she is shrewish Alison, she is courtly Criseyde; rarely in the text is she possibly something more: nowhere is she mother, at least symbolically; seldom in the text is she significantly ambiguous or ambivalent—an admission on Chaucer's part perhaps that he does not especially find her so; seldom does she assume a psychological reality which acknowledges her peculiar dignity, her unique power, her poetry, or that crucial other thing which Homer, Sophocles, Shakespeare, and so many other writers have tried to link organically with her beauty (in terms that have often disturbed us)—her so-called "evil." Nothing in particular of his own being seems beholden to her for inspiration. We might even say that her tragic along with her symbolic possibilities are lost to him; conjunctively, perhaps even something of the concept of tragic vision itself, at least if tested against the Greek dramatists on the one hand and the Elizabethans on the other.

It is not that Chaucer fails in his portraits of Criseyde and Alison to present us with two pictures of women from his time—his powers of observation and description seldom fail him, and in the long run carry the burden of any inadequacy we might herein posit: it is to suggest that he seldom goes beyond the particular male bias which is entrenched in his audience. At times he relies too much on the previously mentioned dichotomy as a means of characterizing his women. Indirectly, he does parody his own age (and himself) by lampooning the husbands of Alison for their colorful castigations of woman, but he never rises above the mere verbal presentation of the extant arguments on women to provide insight into the system of things which he seems to accept. It strikes me that Chaucer, when he fails to pull himself free from the conventional forces of his age, fails not only as a man who does not, when he could, reasonably vindicate woman, but fails to do so as an artist, as a dramatic poet working beyond the particular sensibility of his audience.

Alison, the Wife of Bath, stands in full opposition to her arch-enemy man. Chaucer makes her aware of the differences—at least on the emotional if not on the psychic level—between herself and man; and she provides us with ostensibly female insights into man's treatment of her sex. I say ostensible because, upon close examination, the insights turn out to be mere Chaucerian reflections in some interestingly rigged mirrors the author manipulates to effect a dazzling perspective. Alison does not at all represent a feminine point of view except in a most contrived way; she comes through, finally, as one of Chaucer's great comic actors, and as such works magnificently. She survives as a garrulous and colorful "character"—not as a woman. In the end, instead of representing an argument against the malefic mythology concerning woman, she becomes, subtly, that mythology's embodiment. But I want to concentrate, here at least, on Chaucer's treatment of Criseyde—an earlier characterization by the poet.

Critics have had, generally, a terrible time with the character of Criseyde. They have interpreted her in every conceivable way, made her conform to every possible notion of the tale's meaning; they have overly humanized her, medievalized her, symbolized her, modernized her. No one, to my knowledge, has examined the text closely to see if possibly Chaucer's own conception of her, even within the terms of medieval psychology and characterization, is not somehow to blame for the confusion. Let me state immediately that I do consider the *Troilus* a masterpiece in almost every other respect. My exception is with the character of Criseyde, or to be more precise, with what critics tell us Chaucer has given us in Criseyde. Too many critics assume that Chaucer has made of Criseyde everything he wanted to make. Criseyde is treated by critics as personally "weak," "impressionable," "ambivalent," "irresolute," "fatal," "self-seeking and vain," "the victim of her own qualities"—in each case as though she is a real and carefully delineated woman. Critics accept the fact of her completeness within the text and are then at a loss to explain her transformation. The fault on their part goes deeper than Chaucer criticism. There is a reluctance on the part of too many critics to entertain the idea that a poet can err or falter in his inspiration—not in terms of some norm or ideal beyond him or beyond his age, but in terms of his own creative intuition. Eliot once cautioned us on this matter:

> Those who expect that any good poet should proceed by turning out a series of masterpieces, each similar to the last, only more developed *in every way,* are simply ignorant of the conditions under which the poet must work. . . .

What he is suggesting cannot help but illuminate the art and the business of criticism. If an author's or an age's treatment of woman is somehow peculiar, then we should not only know about it, we should never forget the fact in approaching the work critically. Our conclusions may as a result be riddled with ambivalences, complementarities, dialectics—but for certain works this may be the only excusable justice.

At the outset, it would seem Chaucer has almost the same chance Shakespeare has to dramatize the reasons why Criseyde acts the way she is supposed to act historically. But this would require one of two clear-cut treatments of character, neither of which is found in *intaglio* in Chaucer's version: he would have to give us what his critics insist he has not given us—an early portrait of a loose woman, one who is destined by her own nature to become unfaithful; or, he would have to account for her change by surreptitiously presenting us, in the early part of the poem, with character traits that might prepare us for her later actions—gestures, words, hesitations would do the trick. Chaucer could not do the first, could not brutalize Criseyde as Henryson would do, making her an approved wanton; he was too good-hearted and he loved his heroine too much. Many critics believe Chaucer chose the second alternative: that he developed Criseyde's character intricately, helping her show early signs of fickleness. Shakespeare's Cressida exemplifies such a detailed and subtle treatment; his is a study of a young woman who, in an atmosphere smelling of licentiousness, will not narrow reason upon her body's desires, will not do her part to make the world and its would-be lovers respect the reasonableness of fidelity. It is not possible to locate two Criseydes or even an ordinarily schizophrenic Criseyde in Chaucer's rendering; if this were so, critical contention could center

about inner characterization rather than concern itself with putting the external pieces together. Chaucer, I am afraid, did not have total control of Criseyde, probably did not feel that it was necessary. Criseyde comes to us not as a complete woman in any sense but as a series of isolated expressions which only obliquely belong more to a woman than to a man in the in the same predicament. The distance between his treatment of her and what we are told she does outside the Trojan world is very nearly impossible to comprehend—at least in terms of the narration.

The place to examine the truth or falsity of such remarks is in the poem itself, particularly in those places where the person of Criseyde (if there is such a thing) is involved in the happenings of her own life. Book I sets the stage for her appearance and presents us with the proper perspective in which to view the kind of love this story entails. Without getting involved in the problem of courtly love throughout the narrative, let me remark only that Chaucer at times insists upon its place as a background to his action, and at other times relinquishes it altogether. Book I devotes much space to the kind of conventions we associate with the courts of love, in particular to Troilus' whole understanding of what love is and how he must conduct himself honorably and swiftly into his lady's service. There is even the suggestion that Troilus' house represents an "order of love," into which he is the last to be initiated; the narrator implies he is smitten by love because he has made such a joke of it heretofore. The courtly references suggest that Chaucer is willing to rely on certain conventions to support aspects of his narrative; we might even treat the use of "fate" as another such convention. This is important because it tells us that Chaucer does not feel he can fall back on life and personal experience to brace his action; at times he is content to let a convention consume the human moment. While he may in places refute the convention he still relies on it to allow himself not to have to deal seriously and at all times with individual emotion and thought.

An important thing to notice from the outset—and few critics make of this what I think they should—is the built-in linear perspective of the narrator. There are few discussions on why Chaucer bothers to make his narrator so much a part of the *Troilus.* Does he mean to give the narrator a personality of his own? I think not. The narrator is simply the reader's (Chaucer's) presence felt on paper. It is not intended to be a *persona* or mask which gives the story a subtle meaning, though it has some mask-like advantages as we shall discover. The tale is probably meant to be narrated, and as such it is the author's purpose to incorporate the narrator into his text. Our reading (and not listening to) the story centuries later means we may find the narrator an obstacle. He is no longer a dramatic part of the reading, but an appendage on paper who prevents the story from achieving realism. He is not an omniscient narrator and he does not know the characters at first hand; he is limited to his source and to second-hand conjecture. Granted the narrator allows Chaucer to leave certain things out (such as a continual awareness of a real war), and to summarize what he *thinks* happens—but he also prevents or obscures the real moments of the human drama. How easy it is for the narrator to avoid giving us all of Criseyde's thoughts and feelings by simply excusing himself and taking us somewhere else in the story. What we are given of the character Criseyde is fabricated from a male point of view, one which is free to decide against dramatizing moments that may strike us as essential to a woman (even a medieval one) in such a situation. We can, I think, even trace a change in attitude toward her from Book II to Book V; it is a reaction that has little to do with any Criseyde we see, and in fact may have to do only with her historical archetype within Chaucer's own consciousness.

Chaucer hides behind his narrator's role, whether consciously or not, whenever he is not willing to follow Criseyde omnisciently into her inner chamber to read her mind. What we learn initially about Criseyde—that is, before we meet her—is not different from her own appearance as she is dramatized through the narrator's words. She is not allowed to rise above the *description* the narrator (Chaucer) gives of her. Her words do not, as in Shakespeare, create the character; they are seldom spontaneous, fresh with the moment's emotion. In Chaucer's version, truly dramatic moments are rare. When Criseyde is expressing her fear in Book II it is very nearly the same as when the narrator tells us she is afraid. Her words do not provide her with a life, a womanliness, beyond the descriptions the narrator makes available to us. Shakespeare's treatment of woman differs on this point: his Cressida reveals herself totally in her words, and no descriptions of her offered by the other characters (or possibly even by ourselves) could match what she herself *is*. Let us examine Chaucer's text for support of these generalizations.

Pandar arrives at his niece's house to tell her of Troilus' love. There are long rhetorical flourishes in which Pandar tries to arouse her interest in what he says should be the best news she has ever heard. The narrator gives us one of those numerous portraits of Criseyde which we would like to question and clarify, because it is simply incomplete. We are told:

> Tho gan she wondren moore than biforn
> A thousand fold, and down hire eyghen caste;
> For nevere, sith the tyme that she was born,
> To knowe thyng desired she so faste;
> And with a syk she seyde hym atte laste,
> "Now, uncle myn, I nyl yow nought displese,
> Nor axen more that may do yow disese."

When Pandar does tell her in grandiloquent terms of Troilus' love for her, Chaucer does what few great dramatists would ever do: he blurs her immediate reaction to the revelation by having Pandar continue his Polonius-like rhetoric. We expect her to respond as a young woman might to such news; instead, we get the beginning of what some critics would rather explain away as the enigmatic or ambivalent Criseyde. The fact is she is simply not there, dramatically or humanly.

We have something of the same inertia when Criseyde sees Troilus for the first time. Troilus' triumphal march is described in full for us before Criseyde goes to her window to be struck with her first emotional reaction to the youth. We do not get a glimpse of Troilus through Criseyde's eyes but through the narrator's; the fact that the description

bears a close resemblance to Pandar's earlier descriptions of the youth shows the difference between Chaucer's narrative technique and an essentially dramatic one. The moment in which Criseyde sights Troilus suggests an attempt to have her absorb everything that the narrator has been telling us about the youth's "fresh, young, wieldy" self. Criseyde does not evaluate emotionally or describe the astral chemistry which works that instant in her blood. Her response, though it gives us one memorable line ("Who yaf me drynke?"), shows us Chaucer's unwillingness to raise Criseyde above the static level of his source.

There is even the feeling, in the way Chaucer expands upon this scene, that he himself is not satisfied with what he has imparted to us about Criseyde. There are listeners among you, he tells us, who will doubt Criseyde's momentary growth of love for Troilus: but does not everything have a beginning? Besides, no ardent love is suggested, merely the faint stirrings; she but *likes* him in the beginning—later his "manhood and his pyne / Made love withinne hire herte for to myne." There are doubtless numerous interpretations of such a line, but one of them, we should note, can be quite ironical and can be so at the momentary expense of Criseyde. We can detect an equal ambivalence in the narrator's description of Criseyde's emotion:

> Now was hire herte warm, now was it cold;

In its suggestiveness this has a good deal in common with those images of fickle womanhood we find in some of the other tales.

Unfair as it is to use Shakespeare as a touchstone for what Chaucer is attempting, it will help to focus our understanding of Chaucer's Criseyde if we quote a speech early in Shakespeare's version. It will show, I think, how Chaucer's narrator occludes any personification of a real woman; and this, not only because the tight, historical narration does not allow an easeful dramatic method, but also for the very reason that Chaucer's concern or talent would not, within the context of his time, allow quite the same investigation of human, feminine motivation. The moment in Shakespeare's play shows us a more brazen Cressida revealing her love to Troilus; what I think is evident is the way in which Cressida reveals herself as a *woman* confronted by the *man* she loves.

Troilus.	Why was my Cressid then so hard to win?
Cressida.	Hard to seem won; but I was won, my lord,
	With the first glance that ever— pardon me;
	If I confess much, you will play the tyrant.
	I love you now; but not, till now, so much
	But I might master it. In faith, I lie!
	My thoughts were like unbridled children, grown
	Too headstrong for their mother. See, we fools!
	Why have I blabbed? Who shall be true to us,

When we are so unsecret to ourselves?
But, though I loved you well, I
  wooed you not;
And yet, good faith, I wished myself
  a man,
Or that we women had men's privilege
Of speaking first. Sweet, bid me
  hold my tongue;
For in this rapture I shall surely
  speak
The thing I shall repent. See, see,
  your silence,
Cunning in dumbness, from my
  weakness draws
My very soul of counsel! Stop my
  mouth.

Shakespeare does not provide his heroine with arguments, clichés, ideas about love or about her predicament—instead he actualizes her state; her words follow and graph the fine, pulsating line of her emotion. We might even suggest that Shakespeare gives us, behind this emotional expression, a psychic superstructure as realistically feminine as man the artist can make it.

Until Book IV Chaucer keeps his Criseyde in situations where little response is required on her part. Much of the action in the interim involves the two men arguing back and forth with regard to Troilus' future plans. It would be salutary to interpret Chaucer's purpose as attempting to provide us with a clandestine Criseyde, and thus to enhance her feminine mystery. But such is not, I am afraid, the case. His treatment of her is haphazard rather than planned. Much of what she does have to say takes the shape of argumentation and debate. Whenever he can he avoids treating her directly. Only in Book IV does Chaucer attempt to bring her to real life—but even then it is not a woman he incarnates so much as an attitude, a pose. Criseyde's womanliness, if it exists in any real way for us, lies beyond anything she says or any action she dramatizes for us. It lies in what we impose upon the story; *it lies perhaps in the image of Criseyde man has within him.*

When Pandar lies to her about Troilus' presence and cajoles her into coming to his house, the narrator avoids Criseyde's reaction, saying: my author does not declare what Criseyde thought at this moment. There are similar instances: their epistles to each other are deleted; the narrator admits he is unsure of her reaction to the kneeling Troilus at her bedside; the Criseyde who hears of her necessary transfer from the city is finally left alone by the narrator because any words he could employ to describe her suffering would surely diminish it. Her long diatribe against Fortune in Book III is taken from Boethius and parallels a later disquisition by Troilus. It does little to make her human in our eyes. When Pandar comes to Criseyde after she has heard of her destiny, she follows convention and lists for him her woes: "Peyne, torment, pleynte, wo, distresse!" The point, once again, is that she does not dramatize her emotion; she describes it, and there is no difference between her description and the narrator's.

Criseyde's most talkative moments are during that final night with Troilus, a Troilus fraught with fatalism and to-

The Parson from the Ellesmere manuscript.

tally without hope. Her remarks, however, amount again to a kind of discourse—on how they should behave in their love from now on. Troilus has lost all will power; even Pandar has had to chastise him for his lack of manliness and decision. Criseyde becomes a momentary well-spring of action. She becomes the converse to Troilus' weakness very much the same way that Pandar had earlier. There is one rich psychological moment at the end of this scene. Criseyde turns Troilus' suspicion back on him, by beseeching *him* not to be unfaithful to her. For a moment it makes Troilus falter. It may do the same to us if we remember that the Wife of Bath, when she was enumerating the deadly wiles of womankind, took a special pride in her ability to offset a husband's suspicion by accusing him of equivocation, thereby disguising her own guilt. While Criseyde is not yet "guilty" in any way, throughout Book IV there is the continual reminder that she must soon fall. Perhaps this affinity with the later conceived Wife of Bath shows an unconscious slip on Chaucer's part, and reveals his inability to get beyond a particular, narrow conception of woman's behavior in such predicaments. Chaucer's conception of woman is as blurred as the image medieval man has of her. Criseyde in fact is a magnificent exemplum of medieval woman: she is at once angel and devil: and man—Chaucer—is unsure what accounts for the transition. There is little in Chaucer's conception of her (little in action, word) to account for her inevitable fall, and he is, in Book V, at a loss to know how to treat her; there is the sense that Criseyde baffles him in the end.

We might conclude that Chaucer's treatment of woman was not totally serious because for him it did not have to be. He fell in with his times perhaps more easily than we would like to believe. Though his poetry is the culmination of most of the poetic activity of his time, as a thinker he was not "beyond" his age in the sense certain artists have insisted on being—seers, "antennae of the race." He was more content to record situations, knowing full well what any great storyteller-poet knows—that this is one of the surest ways of satisfying an audience. His talents along these lines were extraordinary and were developed to their fullest poetic potential. But he does not question seriously the literary or human values of his age. Unlike so many great artists in numerous situations, Chaucer was not compelled to uncover the great human errors of his age—a compulsion, I suspect, which begins, on one level, with man's relationship to woman. He does nothing particularly profound to illuminate an understanding of the psychic, social or biological needs of woman, and in this he reflects the *Zeitgeist* of an age which would not allow an understanding of woman as different from rather than inferior to man. Modern psychology helps us understand how history can evolve such an illusion. In Jungian terms: woman has always represented man's "shadowland"; she "entangles him in his feminine unconscious, the psychical." It might even be argued that the kind of psychic blinders the Middle Ages wore prevented the age from giving rise to a particularly profound image of man himself. Such an age can produce great religious art, and in the case of Chaucer, exceptional poetry, but it cannot supply us with a world-vision that will last beyond its own time.

Perhaps the most worthwhile conclusion of this paper takes the shape of a question: if the Middle Ages could not produce an image of woman, both just and truthful, and if one of its greatest poets could not exceed its restrictions and create such an image—what then are the implications regarding the psychic structure of the times? This is an issue alluded to by Erich Neumann in his treatise on *Amor and Psyche: The Psychic Development of the Feminine,* and one that has yet to be considered by medieval scholars. If woman can be understood only in terms of man's unconscious, in terms of his psyche (remember: Psyche was the bride of Eros) and thus "psychically"—then an age which is warped in its conception of her may be warped in its very psychic makeup. This is not a mere play on words: the issue raises genuine questions about psychology, about consciousness, about unconsciousness, superstition, myth, questions which are for the first time becoming operative in man's total study of the past. Erich Neumann writes:

> It was only after the medieval ban on the feminine-earthly side of psychic life—a ban laid down by a spiritual world one-sidedly oriented toward celestial-masculine values—began to be lifted that the divine in earthly nature and the human soul could be rediscovered. Thus in the modern era a new development of the feminine set in, just as, with the rise of depth psychology,

a new form of psychic development and transformation is beginning to be discernible in the West.

The issue of woman in Chaucer—begun as an investigation of the poet's handling of the female *persona*—has ramifications which lead into the very psychic foundations of the times. But that is an entire study of its own and one, I hope, which will someday be accomplished: I would be content if I have questioned somewhat our easy acceptance of those interpretations of Chaucer's women which make of them something they are not, and which, it seems, neither Chaucer nor the *geist* of the times would let them become. (pp. 109-20)

> Matthew Corrigan, "Chaucer's Failure with Woman: The Inadequacy of Criseyde," in Western Humanities Review, *Vol. 23, No. 2, Spring, 1969, pp. 107-20.*

Phyllis Hodgson   (essay date 1969)

[*Hodgson is an English scholar who has prepared separate editions of "The Franklin's Tale" (1960) and "The General Prologue" (1969) from the* Canterbury Tales. *In the excerpt below from the latter work, she maintains that Chaucer's Christian tolerance, exemplified by the principle of loving the sinner and hating the sin, enabled him to successfully balance the serious and the comic in his work.*]

Nothing in descriptive literature can compare with the 857 lines of the **"General Prologue"** to *The Canterbury Tales.* An introductory essay can do little more than consider some of the elements that Chaucer found ready to his hand, and then assert and illustrate an amazing complexity and originality.

The plan is audaciously simple. Put baldly: lines 1-34 tell of the upsurge of feeling with the renewal of Spring, when folk are stirred to travel. Chaucer describes how, one April evening, he fell in with some twenty-nine men and women met together by chance at the Tabard Inn in Southwark and all in the same mind to set out next morning on a pilgrimage to the shrine of St Thomas à Becket at Canterbury. The closing lines relate how, after supper, they agreed to the suggestion of Harry Bailey, their Host, that in order to shorten their journey they should all compete in story-telling. Every pilgrim should tell two stories on the way out and another two coming back—120 stories in all. The winner should have a supper at the company's expense when they returned to the Tabard. The Host proffered to act as master of ceremonies and adjudicator, and made preparations to accompany the party to Canterbury. When morning came, the pilgrims took to the road. The Host reminded them of their agreement; they drew lots, and it fell to the Knight to tell the first story.

Dovetailed between the opening and final passages is a list of the people involved. Lines 35-41 promise this interpolation, 715-19 round it off. The pilgrims are introduced in succession and, apart from one group of five guildsmen, in single file. Each one is portrayed in a self-contained panel of text which consists of a catalogue of details, closely packed. These panels vary in length from the nine lines given to the Cook to the sixty-one devoted to the Friar. There is no transition from one portrait to the next and no variety from intervening discourse or action. An introductory formula is repeated monotonously, *Ther was* (10), *was ther* (6), *was* (2), *hadde he/she* (2), *they hadde*. The pilgrim poet was proposing merely to describe the way things happened, and what he saw and felt.

Chaucer died, his vast project unfinished, before his pilgrims could reach Canterbury, and with only twenty-three tales told.

One might expect from all this that the **"General Prologue"** would be static, uniform, lifeless and wearisome. The very contrary is the fact. Thanks chiefly to his introduction, Chaucer's pilgrims ride on in the imagination so irrepressible and full of vitality that it is hard to accept that theirs is a journey that never was. We are drawn into their high-spirited company at supper in the Tabard and along the fourteenth-century English road. For nearly six centuries now they have ridden on, as joyously alive as ever. They have inspired music; many of our great poets have fallen beneath their spell; scholars and critics still write about them unwearyingly; recently they have invaded the popular theatre.

The potential energy shown in the **"General Prologue"** springs into animated drama in the links between the tales, where these pilgrims provide their own high comedy, drink, jest and quarrel, reveal their past lives and their prejudices, and exhibit their animosities in their interruptions of each other's tales. Their characterization extends beyond the **"General Prologue"**. The confessions of the Reeve, the Wife of Bath, the Pardoner complete a portraiture as elaborate and subtle as could be expected of later fiction. Some pilgrims, e.g. the Franklin, the Miller, the Knight, disclose more facets of their character by the tales they tell. Harry Bailey, the Host, takes on fuller life as he presides, and controls, and passes comment. The portraits of the Nun's Priest and of Chaucer himself, omitted from the **"General Prologue"**, are eventually supplied. The **"General Prologue"** therefore is certainly not complete without the links.

Nevertheless the metamorphosis has already taken place in the **"General Prologue"**. Long before the end of it the stills have quickened, moved, and escaped from their frames. The magic cannot be explained. It is the purpose of the rest of this introduction briefly to survey that part of Chaucer's material that might be called 'stock' and then to comment on some of the seemingly inexhaustible evidence of the unrivalled manipulation it underwent. (pp. 7-9)

Our interest in the pilgrims is held from the start by our relationship with one of them, the pilgrim narrator who claims to be Chaucer himself, an objective observer yet also involved in the action. He claims our attention with friendly intimacy and soon imparts something of his own enthusiasm and enjoyment. He had set out in a spirit of true devotion, yet now is obviously in a holiday mood, exhilarated by the Spring and by the anticipation of the pleasures of an outing in good company. He is overjoyed at being able to join the fellowship at the Tabard. He has

quickly made the acquaintance of the pilgrims gathered there, and found each of them the best ever. He wants to tell about this luck, and introduces his companions in superlatives, with conversational emphasis and exaggeration.

Already there are two levels of apprehension. First there is that of the reporter, adjusting himself to this nonesuch fellowship with wide-eyed wonder, with a quick eye for unexpected details such as the Knight's soiled tunic, the Wife's wide-spaced teeth, the motto on the Prioress's brooch, and dozens more, but accepting the surface values, ungrudgingly admiring these people for the efficiency they all seem to display, over-ready to like them and agree with them. At the same time there is that of the audience or readers, engaged in this tête-à-tête. Perhaps their suspicion will soon be roused that this gossip is too impressionable, and has missed the point of what he sees? He certainly is too naïve, even obtuse, in praising all and sundry. Equally he appears blind to the distinction between secular and spiritual values in his warm admiration of the Monk, the Prioress, the Friar . . .

The narrator begins by promising to describe his companions fully according to their physical appearance, dress and equipment, social rank and disposition.

> Me thynketh it acordaunt to resoun
> To telle yow al the condicioun
> Of ech of hem, so as it semed me,
> And whiche they were, and of what degree,
> And eek in what array that they were inne.

In what follows very few portraits are developed according to the formula. The order of information and the proportions are seldom alike. The method varies so much from portrait to portrait that one might assume the only standard to be variety. A quarter of the details about the Prioress relate to appearance while nothing at all is said about the Manciple's looks, or the Parson's, and the physical detail about the Cook is limited to an ulcer on the leg. Even where all the promised aspects appear to have been remembered, as in the portrait of the Squire, or Franklin, details of habits, clothes, appearance, nature, experience are jumbled, and items separated that one would expect in sequence. Taken together, the portraits afford an unanalysable mixture of objective physical and psychological description, intermingled with the narrator's comment. Moreover, the focus and the angle of vision are constantly changing as, for example, from the setting of a wide parish or of a large part of the globe to the hairs in a wart on the nose. It is all in keeping with the spontaneity of first impressions and the friendly casual manner in which the narrator engages our attention.

Gradually, and almost imperceptibly, the omniscient poet intrudes. The use throughout of the past tense helps to conceal the introduction of impressions that must be later than those of the first evening. This account, in fact, deals not only with the first encounter, but operates with double time, including both the experiences at the Tabard and also what happened on the road, when the Summoner and the Pardoner sang their duet, the Reeve always rode hindermost, the Miller played his bagpipe and led them out of town. What we are told of their opinion of themselves, their innermost thoughts, their lives at home could have been learnt at the earliest only after days spent in their company. Moreover some of the revelations, such as how the Reeve deceived his lord and privately stocked his own secluded home, how the Shipman murdered and robbed, how the Parson ministered unremittingly to his flock would have been unlikely to be made at all, and certainly not on such short acquaintance.

The omniscient poet, however, is heard most effectively through the chattiness of his involved and fallible pilgrim narrator, who reminds us of his presence by his frequent interpolations in the first person, *I gesse, I trowe, I wot, I seyde, I telle, I sey, as I was war*, etc. But our own awareness is soon stretched admiringly to the poet's exploitation of this fellow, through whose very shortcomings a more acceptable standard of values than his own have begun to emerge. We apprehend more surely than he what sort of men these pilgrims really are. Time and again the apparently casual juxtaposition of statements will give the clue. For example, the generalization about the Prioress, 'And al was conscience and tendre herte', must be understood in the particular context of her sentimentality over a dead mouse or a whipped pet. The deadpan opening comment on her smiles, or the information about the Friar's affability where he could line his own pocket, or about the Wife's deafness, or the supposition from the Pardoner's appearance that 'he were a geldyng or a mare', provides an unmistakable hint of discrepancy in the first, of meretriciousness in the second, of the comic loudness of the third, and of the wretched abnormality of the last. Chaucer turns even his narrator's enjoyment of his own jokes—

> For gold in phisik is a cordial,
> Therfore he lovede gold in special.

> But al be that he was a philosophre,
> Yet hadde he but litel gold in cofre.

into revealing flashes of the Doctor's cupidity and the contrasted disinterestedness of the Clerk. When the narrator repeats his conversation with the Monk and the Friar, adding his own somewhat obsequious agreement in terms which seem to echo the very words of his subjects, he exposes brilliantly the casuistry by which these worldly religious attempt to justify their misconduct. The homely colloquial similes, so appropriate to the narrator's familiar style, express no less some facet of temperament, e.g. of the brutish Miller from whose wart grew

> . . . a toft of herys,
> Reed as the brustles of a sowes erys

or of the gourmet Franklin whose purse was 'whit as morne milk', or of the self-indulgent Friar with a neck 'whit as the flour-de-lys'. The disparate detail, thrown out apparently at random, will often prove to be far more expressive than the single fact it conveys. Hardly any detail is mere decoration. The items of dress and equipment which attract and hold the narrator's wandering eye, the 'bismotered' tunic of the Knight, the Friar's short cloak of double worsted 'that rounded as a belle . . . ', the spurs and red hose of the Wife, the dagger of the Shipman, the rusty blade of the Reeve, all such betray the inner man. Many other apparently external particulars promote

chiefly the recognition of abstract qualities. The Knight's horses were good because it was part of his knightly obligation to provide horses for his lord. The Monk's well-fed mount was round and shining like its self-indulgent rider the disinterested Clerk's horse was lean and its ribs protruded. The Reeve's dwelling

> With grene trees shadwed was his place

pictures its owner's natural secretiveness and unsociability. The bells that jingle on the Monk's harness

> . . . als cleere,
> And eek as loude, as dooth the chapel belle

recall not only the chapel, but also the fact that the outrider ought to be more often there at prayer. Sometimes a final detail neatly sums up the whole person, as the ambivalent motto on the Prioress's brooch, or the twinkling eyes of the accomplished Friar who is remote and cold to all the calls of true charity:

> His eyen twynkled in his heed aryght,
> As doon the sterres in the frosty nyght.

Even the absence of sense impressions can be suggestive. There is no individualizing at all of the 'poure Persoun of a toun', and the question must be asked: Is he an ideal figure too good to be true?

Though the characterization varies in length and depth, each portrait is drawn with the same careful choice of fact. Through such selection the illusion of reality is surely built up. The pilgrim narrator's apparently random, but in effect catalytic, record of his impressions proves far more striking than any merely photographic method. It admits a high degree of individualization, and enormous variety of detail, all with the strictest economy in words. Even the narrator's limited vocabulary of commendation, his repeated compliment of 'worthy' and 'gentil' and his intensifying adverbs 'ful', 'ryght', are exploited pointedly. The epithets only stick where they are deserved. 'Worthy' justly defines the Knight, but the Friar, the Merchant and the Wife of Bath, similarly designated, will not bear comparison with him. The incongruous 'gentil' bestowed with undiscriminating enthusiasm merely exposes the knavery of the Manciple, the ill-bred Summoner and Pardoner.

The company certainly makes a satisfying whole. This is not a predictable conclusion. One must admit that it is a surprising fellowship which contains this particular Prioress and this Wife, this Knight and this Pardoner, and indeed each one of the pilgrims who stands out from the first encounter as strictly himself and no other. Apart from the five guildsmen there is no duplication whatever, but the manner of presentation makes us see double. The portraits, each sharply defined, stretch out in a line, from the Knight to the Pardoner; simultaneously in the mind the pilgrims ride along the road in different order, led by the Miller and with the Reeve coming last. Notwithstanding, the company still appears complete and inseparable. This is the effect of literary art, and to some extent one can trace the contrivance.

The most obvious structural manipulation occurs at 542-4 where, lest the series should seem interminable, the narrator begins to round off:

Ther was also a reve and a millere,
A somnour, and a pardoner also,
A maunciple, and myself—there were namo.

In other words, it will soon be finished. This intervention divides the portraiture into two unequal parts at the same time as it establishes the final group.

Five groupings do in fact emerge.

(1) The Knight with his son, the Squire, and Yeoman— from an aristocratic household of military class, and bound by natural relationship and service.

(2) The Prioress, Monk and Friar, who represent the religious orders, and are also bound by their attitude towards their vocation.

(3) An upper and lower middle-class group (13 pilgrims, 9 portraits), bound by their attitude to material possessions.

(4) The Parson with the Plowman, his brother, bound by consanguinity and by Christian ideals.

(5) A lower-class group of rogues, bound by their adroitness at cheating their employers.

The line of portraits is roughly in accordance with the social hierarchy, with variations in group 3 according to a different principle to avoid the monotony of mechanical arrangement. The Knight ranks highest on this particular pilgrimage. Those of higher status than he would be unlikely to join a common pilgrimage, and so equally would the most lowly. Even with these omissions the representation is so full as to seem a cross-section of medieval English society. All the Three Estates are there. The pilgrims have come from town and country, London and the provinces, from Dartmouth, Oxford and Bath in the west and Orwell (near Harwich) and Bawdswell (Norfolk) in the east. All sorts and conditions of men are included.

The five groups dovetail neatly into each other. The Prioress comes next to the members of that aristocratic society whose manners she would emulate. The Friar precedes the Merchant, but is linked to him by his money-making propensity. The gallery of rogues is introduced naturally by the narrator's humorous inclusion of himself at the end of the list.

Priority too governs the order within four of the groups. The priority might be of birth, position, or defect. The father precedes the son in group 1; the Prioress, head of a religious house, precedes the Monk, who is only potentially able to be head. There is also in group 2 an ascending order of imperfection. The religious vow, delicately balanced against worldliness in the Prioress, is flatly rejected in favour of worldliness in the Monk, and hypocritically exploited by the Friar for worldly gain. The final crescendo of knavery in group 5 is still more marked. The Miller cheats his customers in a small way, the Manciple outwits the superiors who employ him, the Reeve systematically robs a trustful master, the Summoner the church, the Pardoner, by faking forgiveness, God Himself.

The order within the large group 3 is less obvious, but any attempt to alter it is a change for the worse. The thirteen pilgrims here are connected with commerce, industry, the landed gentry, the sea, the university, law and medicine. There are two sub-groups which hold a middle position:

(i) Two friends, the Sergeant-at-law and the Franklin, highest in group 3, the first through office, the other by rank.

(ii) Five guildsmen, who are treated without distinction.

Before the two sub-groups, the disinterested and unworldly scholar, the Clerk, is set between the seemingly prosperous and enterprising Merchant and the worldly-wise self-interested Serjeant-at-law. After the two subgroups the guildsmen's Cook and the Shipman lead down the social scale towards the lower classes to come. The last two pilgrims of group 3, the Doctor and the 'good-wif . . . of biside Bathe', connect easily with group 4. The Doctor ministers to the body, in contrast to the Parson's care for the soul, and his study is but little in the Bible. The 'good-wif', most carnal of all the pilgrims, stands against the 'good man . . . of religioun', the Parson, most spiritual of all. Group 3, moreover, hail from both London and the country; the Franklin and the Serjeant operate in both areas.

All this careful ordering, however, provides only the ground-plan. The impression of three-dimensional togetherness must be given by other means. The balance of sense effects certainly contributes to the unity of presentation and here the visual is the most obvious. A pattern of colours helps to unite the pilgrims. There are bright colours and dull: white and red, black and red, green, coral; against which the garb of the Knight and Clerk is drab. Two tanned faces stand out, and a white neck. There are mixed colours also for contrast: *pomely grey, medlee, motlee, sangwyn and pers.* Red is the dominant colour, *reed as blood, fyr-reed, fyn scarlet reed, sangwyn*—quite a spectrum. There is brightness, too, from silver and gold; eyes twinkle like stars, and a bald head shines like glass. Other patterns will meet the eye—a pattern of beards in different colours and shapes, a pattern of horses bad and good.

For the ear there is a sequence of sounds, heard or remembered: singing and fluting, the jingling of a bridle clear as a chapel bell, a chant intoned through the nose, a merry song to the harp, bagpipes, and an unforgettable duet in a thin treble above a hoarse bass. For the taste there is a range of diet from the Monk's fat swan to the garlic, onions and leeks favoured by the Summoner. Smell is not mentioned, though it might be inferred from the garlic. For the touch there is the supple footware of the Monk and Wife, and the feel of the many different materials, fur, cotton, wool and silk, coarse and fine: e.g. *fustian, faldyng, double worstede, bevere, grys, silk, taffata* and *sendal.*

Each set of variations makes new connections. There is, however, a unifying element stronger still—the omnipresent measure of spiritual values, independent of social order. Representative of all Three Estates, four ideal figures carefully placed, the Knight, the Clerk, the Parson, the Plowman, in turn fix a standard by which numerous relative judgments are sparked off. The Squire, for example, is matched in purpose against the Knight. The holiday jaunts of the Wife, which she called pilgrimages, are set against the Crusades of the Knight and the incessant journeyings of the Parson throughout the length and breadth of his huge parish. In spiritual worth there is no comparison. Even the travels of the Knight himself are no match for those of this priest. The Knight's modest array shows up not only the extravagant dress of his son, but also the forbidden finery of the religious group which succeeds. The simple attendance he requires contrasts with the Prioress's retinue. Similarly, the example of the Clerk serves to expose the exploitation of learning by the Doctor and the Serjeant-at-law. Humble and patient, the Parson and Plowman embody Christian charity and the fulfilment of duty in honest toil. The Parson too is learned. Beside him, the Monk cuts a poor figure and the Friar stands condemned for his ruthless selfishness, as do the Summoner and Pardoner for their unscrupulous fleecing of the poor.

There are scales reaching in all directions—of importance and self-importance, negligence, knavery, ambitions, physical and moral deformity, and much else. When closely examined, each pilgrim is, in fact, defined to some extent by the presence of others. The antithesis between the Prioress and the Wife, for example, brings out the fastidious sensibility of the cloistered virgin and the coarse sensuality of the habitual gadder indulgent in fleshly delights. Hardly less striking is the contrast between the Squire and the Pardoner, both claiming attention by their hair style, their song and their pursuit of the latest fashion in dress. The overwrought gaiety of the Pardoner is the more obvious when opposed to the natural high spirits of the Squire. The gourmet Franklin sets off the gourmand Summoner, the thickset Miller and thin Reeve, the sociable Friar the reserved Merchant, and so on.

A few well-chosen themes are sounded at intervals in different keys. Most of the pilgrims reveal themselves partly by what they value—honour, a lady, fine manners, a fat swan, etc. Cupidity takes different forms in the Monk, Friar, Merchant, Serjeant-at-law, Shipman, Doctor, as well as in the five rascals at the end. The self-importance of the majority of the pilgrims reveals itself under various guises. The pretentiousness of the upstart guildsmen, for example, is clearly manifested through their Cook, brought along, presumably to impress, when even the Franklin had left his at home.

Many more links will suggest themselves—between the Squire and the Monk as horsemen, the Monk and the Franklin as connoisseurs in food, between the two men whose fortunes were bound up with the sea, the Merchant and the Shipman, between the two attendants, the Yeoman and the Cook, etc.

Integration by linguistic means has already been mentioned. Deliberate verbal echoes bring two characters into relationship. Rhyme connects the Friar and Merchant. The rhymes *reverence: conscience* link the Prioress and Parson, but whereas the one wished *to ben holden digne of reverence,* the other *waiteth after no pompe and reverence.* The Doctor, *a verray, parfit praktisour,* recalls the *verray, parfit, gentil Knyght* and loses by the comparison, whereas the Clerk's *sownynge in moral vertu* gains at the expense of the Merchant's *sownynge alwey th'encrees of his wynnyng.* The Friar, like the Squire, is *curteis . . . and*

lowely of servyse (cf. *Curteis . . .lowely, and servysable*), but only where he knew 'profit sholde arise'.

Many devices have thus contributed to the overall effect. But there is a further question relating to the total impression of unity. Why is the joyous mood of the opening not dispelled by the long sequel of shortcomings and even vice, for when Chaucer imposed his moral vision on the social scene few escaped wholly without blemish? Why does the **"General Prologue"** continue to be exhilarating? Let everyone speak for himself. There is obviously a more profound explanation than the picture of a colourful party in holiday mood and the thrill of setting off. For the poet, William Blake, the secret lay in the pilgrims' archetypal nature [see excerpt dated 1809]:

> The characters of Chaucer's Pilgrims are the characters which compose all ages and nations . . . some of the names or titles are altered by the time but the characters themselves remain unaltered; and consequently they are the physiognomies or lineaments of universal human life.

One answer must obviously be sought in the attitude of Chaucer himself and in our relation to him, since, despite their universality, his pilgrims stay within the frame of reference of their professions, and we are not involved personally with them as we are, say, with Hamlet or David Copperfield. It will get nowhere to ask whether Chaucer liked the Friar, the Prioress, or any other, though we may assume that he delighted in them all as precious creatures of his imagination, as any artist would. The pilgrims have validity for us because they sprang from his keen observation of real folk sharpened by his wide reading, from his insight into the ostensible and actual motivations of the human mind, from his enjoyment of incongruity and absurdity—in short from his zest for life and from the fascination which the complex human comedy had for him. These pilgrims still gladden us because of the manner of their introduction. Understanding and humour play round even the basest. The surface remains untroubled by bitter exposure or denunciation. Nowhere in the **"General Prologue"** does Chaucer join with Langland, Wyclif and Gower in frontal attack, demanding moral judgment or instant reform, though it must be remembered that some of the pilgrims make their own charges in the links and tales. Veiling his comment in irony or ambiguity Chaucer stands back in detachment; the tone of his indirect and restrained satire remains urbane and sympathetic. However barbed his shaft, it glances off. That is why on cold analysis the subjects of so many portraits turn out, surprisingly, much worse than expected. Yet Chaucer's sympathy does not necessarily imply approval. His sense of destination is never lost, and from us a moral response is elicited too. We should enjoy the **"General Prologue"** less if this were not so. Each sin is clearly exposed for what it is. Each pilgrim is portrayed in relation to what he ought to be, though the treatment is never heavy-handed. It is left to the audience, or reader, to connect the pieces of information and make an assessment. The opening lines on Spring have given cause for optimism in the divine order of the world. Chaucer's tolerance accords with that of any good Christian, whether medieval or modern, in loving the sinner and hating the sin. In that frame of mind he could reconcile the opening and the sequel, and blend the serious and the comic. (pp. 26-38)

Phyllis Hodgson, in an introduction to General Prologue: The Canterbury Tales, *by Chaucer, edited by Phyllis Hodgson, The Athlone Press, 1969, pp. 7-38.*

E. Talbot Donaldson   (essay date 1970)

[*Donaldson is a renowned American medievalist whose best-known work is his translation of* Beowulf *in the* Norton Critical Edition *(1976). In the following excerpt, he reads the "Merchant's Tale" as a didactic warning against a mercantile approach to marriage.*]

One of the most profound and perhaps most significant of the recent disagreements among Chaucerians concerns the tone of the **"Merchant's Tale"**. Is this story, as Tatlock [in the 1936 *Modern Philology* article "Chaucer's Merchant's Tale"] and many of the older critics have held, a dark one, filled with bitterness and disgust for the human race as represented by January and May and Damian? Or is it, as several recent writers believe, a merry jest, the humour of which is entirely characteristic of the fabliau genre—something that will, as one critic supposes, make us 'glad'? Some years ago at approximately the same time that Professor Bronson [in his 1961 *Speculum* article "Afterthoughts on *The Merchant's Tale*"] was lightly dismissing the tale as just 'another high card in the unending Game between the Sexes', another Chaucerian was writing that in it 'the dam has given way, and the ugly muck that formerly lay hidden beneath the surface'—presumably of the Merchant's personality—'is exposed to the sight of all'. While this is obviously an overstatement, as well as an overwrought statement, I continue to believe in its sense, even though I now deplore the rankness of its rhetorical colouring. Faced with two such divergent opinions, the student who had never read Chaucer but only Chaucerians—dreary fate—might well conclude that Professor Bronson and I were talking about different stories, or else that one or both of us had not read the **"Merchant's Tale"** very well if at all.

This kind of divergency of opinion is doubtless due to our both writing descriptive criticism, which means that while we both pretend to be describing the tale objectively, we are in fact describing our reactions to it: we are casting on its persons and incidents a kind of spotlight, to be sure, but one that takes its colouring from our own preconceptions, and these neither of us has troubled to justify to the reader. Thus Professor Bronson succeeds in making everything about the tale sound extremely funny, although he admits that it takes on a certain amount of bitterness because of the characterization of its narrator as an extremely bilious, misogynistic man. On the other hand, I make the same things sound very grim indeed, although I am careful to say, if not to show, that they are somehow very funny. In this paper I should like to try better to justify my feeling that the **"Merchant's Tale"** is in truth a grim thing by examining some of the passages that form the basis for my feeling.

First let me try to chase away two red herrings that are constantly stealing the bait from those who fish for literary values in the murky waters of this particular narrative. The first is the general problem of the comic as opposed to the serious in literature. Every one is, of course, aware that the fact that a literary work is funny does not rule out its being highly serious—does not rule out its being, sometimes, as profound a commentary on human life as the most overt tragedy. To put it briefly, laughter is not by necessity thoughtless. I have to repeat this truism because any one who tries to emphasize the darker side of a humorous tale becomes a ready victim of the quick *ad hominem* rebuttal which blurs the distinction between *serious* meaning 'solemn' and *serious* meaning 'important'. 'Ho, ho, ho', the opposition chortles, 'the poor fellow doesn't realize that it's all just a joke'—and, of course, to be caught missing a joke is to forfeit one's respectability as a critic: I'm afraid many of us have been guilty at one time or another of demonstrating our critical superiority by finding jokes in Chaucer's text that our opponents have missed—sometimes, indeed, jokes that Chaucer himself may have missed. But I hope in this paper I may be allowed to talk about the **"Merchant's Tale"** without being unduly self-conscious that I am neglecting the obvious fact that it is very funny, in a sad sort of way. In return, I shall apologize to the critic whom I cited rather derisively as having said that the tale is one that will make us glad; any profound work of literature makes one glad, and I am as glad of the **"Merchant's Tale"** as he—though not, I confess, immediately after I have finished reading it, when my feeling is aptly expressed by the Host: 'Ey, Goddes mercy!'

The second point needing preliminary discussion is more limited in scope. Only twenty-three of the fifty-two MSS containing the **"Merchant's Tale"** include the **"Merchant's Prologue"**, in which the Merchant is characterized (for the first time) as an embittered bridegroom. This has led to a good deal of speculation about Chaucer's original intention with regard to the tale, and provides Professor Bronson with one of the bases for his argument that Chaucer wrote it not for a bilious Merchant, but to be told *in propria persona,* from his own mouth, whence it would presumably have come with merry humour devoid of bitterness. Yet when MSS offer several alternatives, one of which characterizes a narrator in a way appropriate to the tale while the others either adapt a link universally admitted to have been written by Chaucer for some one else (in this case, the Franklin) or else make no advance assignment at all, it is only common sense to assume that the more satisfactory alternative represents Chaucer's intention. The frequent absence of the **"Merchant's Prologue"** from the MSS may indeed suggest the possibility that Chaucer added it to an already completed (and circulated) tale, but it by no means establishes a probability that he did so: we simply do not know enough about the early history of the copying of the *Canterbury Tales* to feel secure in the belief that the absence of the **"Merchant's Prologue"** represents a genuine authorial variant as opposed to a mere scribal one. And even if the variant does represent an earlier phase of authorial intention, since it is clear that Chaucer wrote the appropriate **"Merchant's Prologue"** that is preserved in twenty-three MSS, then the variant is important only to a study of Chaucer's method of composition and not to the criticism of the **"Merchant's Tale"** as it now stands. Only if, as a literary fact, the tale failed to fit the narrator as he is characterized in its prologue would the existence of other MS alternatives to the prologue become significant, and only provided that among these alternatives was a more satisfactory reading. But not even Professor Bronson denies the suitability of the **"Merchant's Tale"** to the Merchant as he is characterized in what is an undeniably authentic prologue. He merely seems to regret it because of the preconceptions he entertains about the kind of poetry that witty, urbane, genial Chaucer ought to have written.

Specifically, he believes that the assignment of the tale to the Merchant, as well as the composition of the **"Merchant's Prologue"** (admittedly an unexpected but surely not impossible extension of his portrait in the **"General Prologue"**) took place well after the composition of the tale itself. Here is Professor Bronson's statement of the consequences of his belief:

> . . . what the poet may not at once have realized is that the explanation he had provided [that is, the **"Merchant's Prologue"**] worked an instant sea-change on the story itself. The Merchant's misogyny impregnated the whole piece with a mordant venom, inflaming what originally had been created for the sake of mirth. That Chaucer could have foreseen this effect is very unlikely.

It is not unfair to say that a good deal more bitterness has been let into the **"Merchant's Tale"** by this paragraph, which is near the end of Professor Bronson's article, than one would have expected from his earlier argument. And I will surely allow the point that the 'Merchant's misogyny impregnate[s] the whole piece with a mordant venom'—obviously, that's why the misogyny has been so lovingly presented in the **"Merchant's Prologue"**. But since I do not believe in art by inadvertence, I cannot see how Chaucer could not have been aware of what would happen when he assigned a certain kind of tale to a certain kind of narrator: he was after all a master of the art of manipulating and multiplying fictional contexts. But even though I cannot help gasping at Professor Bronson's wholly unsupported (and unsupportable) statement that it is 'unlikely' that Chaucer foresaw the effect he in fact achieved, it is not my present purpose to defend the poet from inexplicable slanders on his artistic intelligence. What I wish to do is to show that it is idle to speculate, in a complete absence of respectable evidence, about when Chaucer did what with the **"Merchant's Tale"**, since it is a literary fact that it is an intensely bitter story, which, while it suits perfectly its intensely bitter narrator, would of itself, even if it had never been assigned to a specific Canterbury pilgrim, have characterized its narrator as one whose vision was limited almost exclusively to the dark side of things.

The most obvious feature of the **"Merchant's Tale"** is its juxtaposition of the seemingly, or potentially, beautiful with the unmistakably ugly, of the 'faire, fresshe' May with the 'olde' January. This juxtaposition of beautiful and ugly is not static but dynamic, for the ugly constantly casts its shadow over the beautiful or, conversely, the seemingly beautiful ultimately reveals itself to be as ugly, in its own way, as that with which it is juxtaposed. Moreover, the main juxtaposition is reflected in all the story's incidents and throughout the details of its poetic style. If I may use a somewhat metaphysical metaphor, the central situation of the story is like the sun suffering eclipse: during a solar eclipse, every bright patch of sunlight screened through a natural filter such as foliage at each moment exactly reproduces the phase of the sun's darkening, so that the ground under leafy trees is covered with hundreds of tiny eclipses, and every sunny spot suffers the encroachment of the shadow. And everywhere within the tale the shadow encroaches. The narrator's (and narrative's) bitterness is such that it goes beyond the inevitable anti-Platonism of the selfish disillusioned romanticist almost to a complete denial of the possibility of any human value: not only is what is beautiful, and hence what one wants to believe good, actually ugly, but even those things that are generally accepted unquestioningly as valuable are either made to seem fatally flawed or are tainted by the Merchant's poison.

The central juxtaposition and its myriad concomitant reflections are handled with what might be called perfectly bad taste. I'm not sure that this isn't just as difficult an artistic effect to achieve as perfectly good taste, for it often consists, not of a piling up of vulgarities, but of the introduction into a relatively innocuous passage of a single, carefully selected vulgarity that will produce an aesthetic shock upon the reader, destroying a context which seemed fair, or one which he at least wanted to believe was fair. The poem is thus constantly affronting our aesthetic sense, bringing our emotions into play in such a way as to confuse our moral judgment, which finds no safe place to settle. The distinctive tone of the **"Merchant's Tale"** becomes clear when one compares it, in plot summary, with the Miller's: two succulent young females, May and Alison, married to two variants of the type *senex amans,* January and John, and assorted would-be lovers, and, in the plot summary, two vulgar climaxes, with the Miller's potentially more shocking to the reader than the Merchant's. Yet the drunken Miller has in his own way perfect taste, and his narration of a most vulgar event, Absolon's kissing of Alison's rump, is done with a kind of high-poetic awe—almost as if he were exclaiming, 'What hath God wrought?'—that at once heightens the comedy and diminishes offensiveness. On the other hand, the Merchant, excusing with a mealy apology the baldness of his language, succeeds in making a long-anticipated act of coition seem extremely shocking.

'Healthy animality': I detest the patronizing term, but can't think of a better one to describe the **"Miller's Tale"** in its relation to the Merchant's, to which one may apply the modification, 'mere bestiality'. Notice the following lines, January's prospectus for a wife:

> 'I wol noon old wif han in no manere;
> She shal nat passe sixteen yeer certain—
> Old fissh and yong flessh wol I have fain.
> Bet is,' quod he, 'a pik than a pikerel,
> And bet than old boef is the tendre veel:
> I wol no womman thritty yeer of age—
> It is but bene-straw and greet forage.'

Here January, in the guise of a gourmet who knows all about *la bonne cuisine* whether fish, flesh, or female, is already, if unwittingly, seeing his future wife as the young beast he actually gets. And, as so often happens in the tale, the images the speaker uses catch him up in their own truth. Thus in the last line, the *beanstraw* and *great forage* are, of course, foods not for a *bon vivant,* but for what he is unconsciously admitting himself to be: that is, they are coarse, dry fodder for an old beast stable-bound by winter, which is what January is despite his colt's tooth. And even that fish is going to catch up with him later, when he is described making love to May:

> He lulleth hire, he kisseth hire ful ofte—
> With thikke bristles of his beerd unsofte,
> Lik to the skin of houndfissh, sharpe as brere,
> For he was shave al newe in his manere.

Old fish, ineptly razored, painfully embracing tender veal.

There is no need to labour the matter of Chaucer's careful portrayal of the uglier side of the central juxtaposition. This is made rank enough seriously to effect the quality, if not the quantity, of our laughter. Rather more subtle is his handling of that bright beast May. Initially she seems a sort of Galatea created in response to the fantasies of January; but despite the reckless assumption of the aged Pygmalion, the statue when it finally comes to life has no internal qualities to match its outward loveliness. Of course, revelation of what May's qualities really are is postponed as long as possible. Meanwhile the Merchant associates with her—though he does not actually ascribe to her—such thoughts as the romanticist might think she ought to have: he manages to convey without an overt assertion her disgust with January's love-making; and when Damian becomes love-sick for her, the Merchant assures him in a rhetorical outburst that he can never attain her—'She wol alway saye nay'. But finally, on her visit to the squire, May allows him to thrust his letter into her hand, and she hides it in her bosom—her first genuine action in the poem. Thereafter the Merchant relates, with superbly bad taste, how, upon her return to January,

> She feined hire as that she moste goon
> Ther as ye woot that every wight hath neede,
> And whan she of this bille hath taken heede,
> She rente it al to cloutes at the laste,
> And in the privee softely it caste.

In the word *softely* and the object with which it is juxtaposed is the climax of Chaucer's treatment of May, and the microcosm of his treatment of things throughout the poem as a whole. *Softly* had in Middle English as it still has a range of meanings entirely appropriate to May's literal action, 'quietly, surreptitiously', and in this respect it is straightforwardly realistic. But *softly* also has, and cannot help having, another range of meanings that associate it with warm weather, warm May, tender, gentle, alluring womanhood, femininity at its most romantically attractive; and thus the sense of the lines moves backward and forward between May's beauty, May's deceit, and the privy.

May is, however, alone within the poem in being allowed to remain for any length of time unsullied, and the fact that everything else is sullied makes her descent seem inev-

itable even while it is shocking. Indeed, if the narrative had turned suddenly, at a point about halfway to the ending, from the beautiful to the ugly, it might come closer to being the outrageous jest that readers like Professor Bronson want it to be, for a really sudden shock—like Thomas's gift to the Friar in the **"Summoner's Tale"**—is likely to turn realism into fantasy. But the poem has been infected with venom from the very beginning, a venom compounded in part of a most cynical kind of realism. And this venom is no mere overflow from the initial characterization of the Merchant-narrator, but part of the tale's pigmentation. Let us look for a moment at the passage that has been called Chaucer's most daring—or most rash—use of irony. The poem begins with a quick sketch of the bachelor-lecher who in his old age has determined to marry—'were it for holinesse or for dotage I can nat saye':

> 'Noon other lif,' saide he, 'is worth a bene,
> For wedlok is so esy and so clene
> That in this world it is a Paradis.'
> Thus saide this olde knight that was so wis.

After that last line, which is as near to a sneer as poetry can come, the narrator intrudes to say:

> And certainly, as sooth as God is king,
> To take a wif, it is a glorious thing,
> And namely whan a man is old and hoor.

These lines introduce a 126-line passage in which everything that might be said in favour of marriage gets itself said, and a good deal more. Readers have often observed that this passage has nothing in it to show that it is ironical beyond its context, and some have even described it as a perfectly straightforward exposition of the medieval ideals of marriage. But Professor Bronson is right in noting that its sense, whatever its context, is absurd. Indeed, it represents a kind of double distortion of reality: a rebuttal of antifeminism erected on the same bases as antifeminism. According to Jerome, who despite being a saint was not on this subject either clear-headed or fair-minded, the sole motive of a wife is to frustrate her husband. In the Merchant's panegyric, this simple formula is turned upside down with an equally simple-minded result: the sole motive of a wife is to assure her husband's comfort. Both opinions rest on the basic assumption that women were really created to be servile beasts, though according to one they reject their assigned role and according to the other they accept it gratefully. The masculine selfishness latent in the whole antifeminist tradition reaches its clearest expression in the Merchant's praise of matrimony: not 'he for God only, she for God in him', but he for himself, she for him. It is foolish though understandable to suppose, as January did, that May's beauty implies some special virtue, but it is simply absurd to suppose that wives will love their husbands just because they were kind enough to purchase them.

And not even this panegyric is allowed to bask uninterruptedly in the bright sunlight of its own vacuity: the shadow of bitterness falls here too, and in a rather surprising place. Following his source, which is either Chaucer's own **"Melibeus"** or its source, Albertano's endless *Book of Counsel,* the Merchant adduces the creation of Eve in order to establish for his hearers woman's usefulness to man:

> And herke why I saye nat this for nought
> That womman is for mannes help ywrought:
> The hye God, whan he hadde Adam maked,
> And sawgh him allone, bely-naked,
> God of his grete goodnesse saide than,
> 'Lat us now make an help unto this man
> Lik to himself.' And than he made him Eve.

I am unable to read this passage without feeling that in making Eve the Creator is motivated more by a kind of cynical pity than by love for what He has made. The clue to this feeling is that the narrator has substituted for God's statement, 'It is not good for a man to be alone', the action of God's looking at the poor naked thing and seeming to draw from Adam's appearance the conclusion that he had better have some help—there is no *imago Dei* here. 'And sawgh him allone, bely-naked.' Belly-naked is one of those phrases that offer pitfalls to the unwary. In my youth boys used to use it for the way they went swimming when there was no one to see; but it was evidently considered a vulgar phrase, for I don't believe we would have used it before our mothers, or not unscathed in any case; indeed, the word *belly* in any usage was so frowned upon that one still hears the euphemism *tummy* from the mouths of otherwise highly sophisticated speakers. But of course we have all been taught that those good old Anglo-Saxon words—and *belly* is from an Anglo-Saxon word meaning 'bag'—were commonly used in the Middle Ages, and that the vulgarity we associate with them is of relatively recent development. And surely this is sometimes so, but not so often as we think, and not, I think, in the present case. Chaucer only uses *belly* meaning 'stomach' three times in all his works. One of these is in the brilliantly vulgar context of the **"Summoner's Tale",** where it is referred to the highly gaseous churl who is to provide the gift that may be divided equally among thirteen friars. The other is in the Pardoner's sermon, a splendid example of what might be called homiletic shock-treatment, or Pauline hortatory vulgarity. For St Paul is, of course, the great original:

> O wombe, O bely, O stinking cod,
> Fulfilled of dong and of corrupcioun!
> At either ende of thee foul is the soun.

It seems a reasonable supposition that if Chaucer had not meant to have his narrator vulgarize the creation of Adam and Eve he would have chosen another term than *bely-naked*. 'And God saw Adam alone, belly-naked; and then of his great goodness he said, "Let us now make an help unto this man—like to himself"'. And then he made him Eve.' And Eve, another poor worm, is as like Adam as May turns out to be like January. It is a depressing thought.

This sour note, which sounds so often in the poem as to be characteristic of it, sounds again in the wedding of January and May, even more unharmoniously than it does in the Creation. Of course, one is fully aware that no marriage ceremony should be taking place between this ill-matched couple—that January is disobeying Cato's and Nature's precept that man should wed only his similitude. But the marriage ceremony itself is not responsible: it is

not its fault that the bride and groom are unsuited, and it remains a 'ful greet sacrament'. Yet the narrator's 'mordant venom'—to borrow Professor Bronson's phrase again—sullies the ritual because he hates the participants:

> Forth comth the preest with stole aboute his
>   nekke,
> And bad hire be lik Sarra and Rebekke
> In wisdom and in trouthe of mariage,
> And saide his orisons as is usage,
> And croucheth hem, and bad God sholde hem
>   blesse,
> And made al siker ynough with holinesse.

This passage—Mendelssohn on a flat piano—contains at least two dissonances that are worth examining. One is the repetition of the verb *bidden (bad)*, used first in the sense 'command'—he commanded her to be like Sarah and Rebecca—and then in the sense 'pray'—he prayed that God would bless them. That is, 'pray' is the expected sense, but I can never read the passage without feeling that the second use of *bad* has been infected by the first, so that what the words really are saying is, 'And the priest told God to bless 'em'. The phrasing seems abruptly jussive. Indeed, my second translation, while idiomatic, is literally accurate. Moreover, there is some reason for making it, at least as a simultaneous alternate. In Chaucer's works the verb *bidden* occurs 124 times: 104 times it clearly means 'command', and only in twenty uses is the meaning 'pray' either requisite or probable. It occurs just six times with God as the object (*bidden God*), and in the other five the syntax is such as to make it clear that the bidder is making a request of God, not giving Him an order. But here the syntax is bald: 'bad God sholde'. This construction seems to me to reflect the disgusted disillusion of the narrator, who here reduces, with a contempt bred of familiarity, Christian ritual to perfunctory hocus-pocus. The priest is seen as a kind of witch-doctor who presumably controls the Almighty much as Prospero controls Caliban. He dispenses holiness as if it were some sort of magic powder that he can scatter around in order to secure the marriage—an insecticide to ward off the flies of evil. But we know his magic isn't going to work. And that associations with primitive magic are what Chaucer had in mind as he wrote the lines is suggested by something else: when the priest makes the sign of the cross over the bride and groom, the verb used for the action is *crouchen:* 'And croucheth hem'. This Middle English word, common enough to have become part of the name of a whole order of friars, apparently had low associations for Chaucer: the only other time it occurs in his works is in the **"Miller's Tale"**, just before old John recites his ancient night-spell. Shaking Nicholas out of his assumed trance, John exclaims,

> I crouche thee from elves and fro wightes!

Here, too, the background is one of primitive magic.

It is this recurrent action of derogating things-as-they-are, especially those things that we instinctively place value on, that imparts to the **"Merchant's Tale"** its large content of emotional energy. And when one's emotions are being constantly stirred up, one cannot read with detachment—cannot remain uninvolved. The **"Shipman's Tale"**, another study of opportunistic sexual behaviour marital and extramarital, produces an entirely different effect, because no grain of genuine emotion ever scratches its smooth, glassy surface. Even the **"Reeve's Tale"**, a vindictive story told by an angry man, evokes from all but the most squeamish nothing but laughter: the fact that the Reeve believes all millers to be thieves has not jaundiced his view of life as a whole, and under his cool direction the fabliau-machine works effortlessly to show that proud, thieving bullies get their just deserts. But the Merchant's hard-earned conviction that wives are inevitably and triumphantly deceitful and unfaithful so infects his depiction of the world that the reader is made, willy-nilly, to suffer some measure of pity and terror. It is easy enough to laugh at futile, inarticulate wrath, as the pilgrims laugh at the Pardoner when the Host's insult reduces him to silence; but an articulate wrath that keeps wounding our sensibilities necessarily involves us in itself. Detachment only comes to the reader of the **"Merchant's Tale"** at the very end with the culminating outrage, which is an incident of such high and horrible fantasy that it disconnects us from our sense of reality. Yet this detachment comes too late to alter the experience that has gone before, and has, indeed, the paradoxical effect of enhancing its dark values. When May climbs the tree over January's stooping back—tender youth over stooping age—we have to surrender to laughter, but not without some of that sense of sadness we feel when what we have been emotionally involved with moves beyond the point where we can any longer care.

In the meanwhile, between the wedding and the climax there takes place a shift in the emotional balance of the two units in the tale's central juxtaposition. Our natural sympathy for May, evoked by her physical loveliness, and our natural disgust with January reach their respective climaxes in the Merchant's description of their wedding night. Professor Bronson tells us that the mismating of youth and age 'was not the kind of problem that [Chaucer's] generation worried over', but at least one member of his generation, William Langland in *Piers Plowman,* worried over it rather eloquently, and it seems to me that Chaucer took some trouble to make the reader of the **"Merchant's Tale"** worry over it when he quietly shifted the point of view of the narrative so that we see the wedding night through May's eyes rather than January's. But later, when May's female resourcefulness begins to work, some of the disgust we felt for January begins to spill over into our feeling for May: the eclipse is becoming total. And when January goes blind, some of the sympathy we felt for May is displaced and spills over into our feeling for him. Morally, of course, there is little to choose, nor has there been any real exchange of roles, for January is as bad as ever and May is merely revealing herself to be as bad as he. But moral judgment and emotion are not the same thing. We have been led by the Merchant's narrative, especially by his rhetoric, to make some emotional investment in the relationship, the juxtaposition, of January and May, and I for one find it hard immediately to liquidate the investment. The Merchant, by such devices as first defending May's concern for her honour in his rhetorical outburst against Damian, and then shortly afterwards congratulating her on her womanly resolve to be dishonest—

Lo, pitee renneth soone in gentil herte!—

keeps the emotion sloshing back and forth between the weaker and the uglier vessel, frustrating hopes, spoiling values, and maintaining a state of nervousness from which only the most resolutely unflappable reader can free himself.

What seems to me the most triumphant stroke in the Merchant's rhetorical assault on our sensibilities occurs just after May has given Damian a key to the garden of delights and has 'egged' January into asking her to go with him there. The old lecher speaks his invitation:

'Ris up, my wif, my love, my lady free;
The turtles vois is herd, my douve sweete;
The winter is goon with alle his raines wete.
Com forth now with thine yën columbin.
How fairer been thy brestes than is win!
The garden is enclosed al aboute:
Com forth, my white spouse! out of doute,
Thou hast me wounded in myn herte. O wif,
No spot of thee ne knew I al my lif.
Com forth and lat us taken oure disport—
I chees thee for my wif and my comfort.'
Swiche olde lewed wordes used he.

'Such stupid old words he used.' This passage, with its devastating anticlimax, seems to me of itself a sufficient refutation of Bronson's belief 'that there is no intrinsic evidence' that Chaucer wrote the tale 'from a point of view predetermined by such a character' as the Merchant. January's paraphrase of the Song of Solomon comes as close to poetry as the old man ever comes, and at least within hailing distance. Of course the passage has something of his inveterate lust, especially in the final couplet, 'lat us taken oure disport'. But if this were cut off and the rest printed, say, in one of Carleton Brown's collections of Middle English lyrics, I don't think it would shame its company or that any one who did not know would suspect from what context it came. It needs no dedicated patristic critic to point out that in the allegorical tradition the Song of Solomon was taken to represent Christ's love for the Church (or, alternatively, Christ's love for the human soul) and that the love of man and woman, expressed in marriage, was taken to be a mystical analogy of this divine love. Symbolically, the Song of Solomon represented the ideal of marriage. January sullies the symbol in his own way, but the Merchant with his gratuitous sneer wholly destroys its value as an ideal ever to be obtained by human beings. Previously he has dirtied the Creation of Adam and Eve and the rite of marriage, and now he has succeeded in dirtying the theological basis on which marriage was said to rest.

In so doing he has finally allowed the emotional and moral factors of the poem to unite. I dislike moralizing Chaucer's poetry, being persuaded that any work of art that presents an honest picture of existence as seen through any eyes, no matter how jaundiced, hateful, or even wicked the beholder may be, is moral enough of itself. But since I have categorically denied that the **"Merchant's Tale"** is primarily a merry jest, I suppose that I am forced to substitute something concrete for the laughter that I refuse to let take over the poem. It seems to me, then, that the **"Merchant's Tale"** was most carefully written to present the kind of world that can come into being if a man's approach to love and marriage is wholly mercantile and selfish—if he believes he can buy as a wife a domestic beast that will serve his every wish and, somehow, fulfil his most erotic fantasies. When the beast fails to be in its own right anything more than bestial, the purchaser may, like January, settle for an inner blindness which is more complete than physical blindness; or, like the Merchant, he may deliver himself to hatred—of the disappointing beast, of his own romantic dreams, of marriage, of himself. To read this tale without being disturbed by the force and truth of the Merchant's hatred seems to me impossible.

But I'm still feeling worried about my failure to laugh as loudly as others do. Is my sense of humour not robust enough? Perhaps. I prefer, however, to take refuge in the Merchant's own words in his description of the wedding feast of January and May:

> Whan tendre youthe hath wedded stouping age,
> Ther is swich mirthe that it may nat be writen.
>
> (pp. 30-45)

> *E. Talbot Donaldson, in his* Speaking of Chaucer, *W. W. Norton & Company, Inc., 1970, 178 p.*

John Finlayson   (essay date 1971)

[*In the excerpt below, Finlayson examines the "Parson's Tale," finding the Parson less a personification and more a character based on the reality of medieval life.*]

> "For oure book seith, 'Al that is writen is writen for oure doctrine,' and that is myn entente."

This apparent invitation to seek "sentence" in **The Canterbury Tales** (though not in *all,* presumably, since "thilke that sownen into synne" are explicitly retracted, the choice, typically and significantly, being left to the reader) has been vigorously taken up by critics, especially of late. Since, in the words of one of the more influential "sentence" seekers, "**The Canterbury Tales** is not a whole, not an achieved work of art, but rather a truncated and aborted congeries of tales woven about a frame, the Pilgrimage from London to Canterbury," the **"Parson's Tale"** has come to be regarded as the essential key to Geoffrey Chaucer's "doctrine" with the result that we are urged to read the tales backwards or to assume that Chaucer's work has a significant shape (frequently likened to a cathedral), of which the **"Parson's Tale"** is not only the final element but also the key-stone. In either case (and they are both closely connected in the sort of evidence they adduce and the conclusions they reach) what emerges is a new Chaucer, well equipped to meet the approval of Arnold [see excerpt dated 1880]; no longer the comic satirist we thought we knew, but a comedian of almost Dantesque proportions—a moralist who had much more in common with Langland, in terms of intention and technique, than we had hitherto perceived. Most of these and similar interpretations rest on assumptions about art that have acquired the status of articles of faith.

The trouble about any dogmatic approach to an artist so encyclopaedic as Chaucer is that in the desire to order according to the canon, to seek the Castle of Truth which the believer *knows* must be there, the work of art is subjected to the drastic surgery of simplification: the heart is revealed to the eager student, after the lancet of criticism has cut through the enveloping flesh, and is sometimes passed off as the whole man. All art, in such skilled hands, is reduced to the dimensions of the moral fable or, worse, treated as if St. Augustine's preoccupations were sufficient and wholly proper for the literary critic. If one assumes a work of art to be closely analogous to a nut, one will with the exercise of enough ingenuity and misapplied patristic learning inevitably find a pious kernel.

However, it has never seemed to me self-evident that an author's pious retraction of "any thing that displese," of "enditynges of worldly vanitees," necessarily requires that we also should reject the "vanitees" and select only from his work those elements which can be integrated into some narrowly religio-moral statement, on the assumption that the intentions and directions attendant on the process and moment of creation may be retrospectively invalidated. To make such an assumption is to say that only what an author thought or wished he had said at the end of his career is what he truly meant—provided also that it can be demonstrated to be suitably pious. It is not that I would wish to deny Chaucer the validity or importance of the religio-moral "sentence" posthumously ascribed to him, but rather that I would deny that this was clearly his exclusive intention. For me, and possibly for some medieval readers who may now rest in hell, it is not necessarily of primary importance.

His very rejection of those "early" works of his which we now consider of greatest literary merit, and his deliberate ambiguity about the tales themselves, seems an indication that these works were not *intended* in what he himself would have recognized as a pious vein, regardless of what Professors Robertson and Huppé may subsequently have discovered in them to reassure his troubled ghost. It seems to me possible that if one submits oneself to the experience of **The Canterbury Tales,** moral and vain alike, one may arrive at a clearer view of what Chaucer's original intentions were at the moment of creation, however much he may have regretted those intentions at the end of the **Tales** or his life. The uncertain chronology of the retraction and the **"Parson's Tale"** would cause some scholars to be a little wary of building a critical house on such unsettled ground.

In earlier, and some very recent, critics there is a tendency to pass over the **"Parson's Tale"** as rapidly as possible; most translations omit it, as does a well-known college edition of Chaucer by a very eminent medievalist. In other words the **"Parson's Tale"** is a puzzle—it attracts extremes of judgment that starkly illustrate the extremes of critical opinion on **The Canterbury Tales;** to one audience the Parson's dull, long sermon on the Deadly Sins and penance is an unfortunate aberration by the master comedian, sometimes kindly excused as Geoffrey's conventional salute to the orthodoxies of his age—a polite social gesture—or, as a posture unfortunately forced on the author by the nature of his created character. To the other audience, the **"Parson's Tale"** is the coping stone to the whole edifice—not only the key to the *significacio* of the whole, but also the translator into abstract language and doctrinal terms of the continued metaphor of *The Canterbury Tales.* The terms of the debate are implicitly so medieval that the *Owl and the Nightingale* and the *Parlement of Foules* spring unbidden to mind.

In a similar situation Sir Roger de Coverley remarked that "much might be said on both Sides." While it is evident to everyone, whatever their critical persuasion, that the **"Parson's Tale"** is no tale, but a long, prosy, and unleavened sermon, totally devoid of comedy, irony, character or narrative interest, it is also evident that we cannot easily throw it off, as we might the **"Manciple's Tale"**, because of its position and its narrator. It is the last tale, of whose position in the scheme there is no doubt, and it is explicitly told to "knytte up wel a greet mateere." While its presentation of the Seven Deadly Sins may not provide the unifying theme of the tales because it is too wide and general in reference, it is equally evident that we cannot dismiss the moralities of the **"Parson's Tale"** from the meaning of the work, from what is made by the author, simply because "there is no book written whose characters could not be said to exemplify something described by the Parson." While, as Bloomfield points out [in his *The Seven Deadly Sins*], the tale is composed of a "section on the Sins not organically . . . connected with the main body of the tale, which is a treatise on penance," it is part of the world Chaucer created. It is not something to be cast off lightly because it "lacks the appeal of Chaucer's best work," because it is assumed to be an early draft that would have been improved by the author, or because it has been attributed to someone else to release Geoffrey from the charge of bad art. . . . As part of that created world, however, our attitude toward it, our sense of its place in the whole, will to a large extent depend on the preceding matter and the manner of its presentation.

In other words, it seems to me impossible in a work with an explicit linear structure (and, whatever the disputes about the ordering of the tales, we do know that *The Canterbury Tales* has a fixed beginning, a sequential arrangement of tales, and a precise ending) to deny that the events in their ordained sequence, the values they imply and the tone of their presentation, focus our vision and form our attitudes to the end. While in a tragedy it is true that our foreknowledge of the end invests all the preceding events with a special significance, it is also true that the interest and significance of these events is not entirely dependent on the end; indeed, it is the *nature* of the *praxis,* the complete, purposeful action, which makes a work tragic. Few forms of art, other than the bare-bones detective novel, have even the degree of dependency of beginning and end that is observable in tragedy. It is the nature of the events in their sequence and the manner of their presentation which, in most cases, forms the significance of the end of most works.

I would suggest, therefore, that it is the events and created values of the *whole* of *The Canterbury Tales* which decide the significance of the **"Parson's Tale."** Furthermore, I should like to propose that in *The Canterbury Tales* it is the *manner* of presentation which controls our attitude to events, that our approach to the sentiments of the **"Par-**

son's Tale" is dependent on the perspective created by the style of the whole work, that the only valid guide to the artistic significance of the **"Parson's Tale"** is our impression of the dominant mode of expression as we progress in linear fashion from the **"General Prologue."** In short, before we can decide what the tone and significance of the end is, we must come to some sort of conclusion about the purpose and art of the preceding matter.

What that purpose and art are may be illuminated by a consideration of Chaucer's beginning of *The Canterbury Tales,* the **"General Prologue,"**

> For everi wight that hath an hous to founde
> Ne renneth naught the werk for to bygynne
> With rakel hond, but he wol bide a stounde,
> And sende his hertes line out fro withinne
> Aldirfirst his purpos for to wynne.

Whatever may be disputed in Chaucer criticism, we can probably safely assert that the **"General Prologue"** is largely comic-satiric in intention. I use the term "comic-satiric" deliberately, not only because of the difficulty of distinguishing the comic from the satiric, but also because of Chaucer's deliberate variation of tone and intention—the differences in the satiric tones applied to the Prioress, the Monk, and the Friar, for example, not only distinguish them as characters, but also witness to different attitudes to what they represent. Again, because of the identity of their estate, the religious characters quite clearly provide an implicit scale of judgment on one another; because of their human frailty they also provide a satiric comment on clerical abuses and, less directly, on the common human frailty which is initially in social intercourse hidden by the garb of profession and estate. Most satire, as distinguished from complaint, works through an implicit comparison of the object satirized with a certain ethical, intellectual or social standard, usually generally accepted. While the satirist must rely to a large extent on his audience providing this norm for themselves, it is also fairly common for him to provide within the framework of his fantasy a number of normative statements or some device which will function as a moral touchstone. To a large extent the satiric-comic effects of the **"General Prologue"** depend on the audience's recognition and application of this implicit norm which is, in its larger outlines, as readily accessible to the modern reader as to the medieval.

However, just as Langland provides the remarks of Piers in the *Visio* and Pope provides those of Clarissa in *The Rape of the Lock,* so also does Chaucer provide his own internal voices of mortality. The figures of the Knight, the Plowman and the Parson (with the possible addition of the Yeoman and the Clerk) provide not only the ideal social framework of feudal theory, against which the contemporary social actuality may be judged, but are also a reminder of the moral norms of that social structure. In *Piers Plowman,* of course, this interconnection of social structure and moral values is the dominant matter of the *Visio,* but this is religious allegory with little (except for incidental) comedy; the goal of the work is overtly didactic.

The comic element of Chaucer's work is, on the other hand, one of its dominant parts and the satire, as a consequence, works in a very different way. What is important to remember in reading Chaucer for his doctrine is that not only is the satirical voice indirect, but it is also shifting and multiple. The **"General Prologue"** cannot be said to contain a direct moral voice: the creation of the plain, guileless, humble narrator forces the reader to become the moralist, to assign the *significacio*. While the narrator may indirectly direct the satiric statement by what he records and the order in which he relates the observations, he has not the status of an unequivocal voice of truth, as has Piers in Langland's work. The narrator here is rather close in performance and function to Gulliver in Book I of *Gulliver's Travels:* he is a recognizable *persona* of middling sensibility and mediocrity who observes in detail but does not comprehend very deeply; where he makes simple judgments, they are almost always banal and wrong. Just as in Swift the function of the narrator varies from book to book and sometimes from moment to moment—he is the vehicle through which the thing satirized is presented, the object of the satiric attack and, at times, a purely, nonironic comic figure—so also does the function of Chaucer the narrator vary: he is the simple recorder; he occasionally judges what he sees, but it is entirely up to the reader to decide whether the comments of this recorder are simply naive, like those of Gulliver, or whether their deep irony is to be seen as part of the personality of the narrator.

Just as the shifting function of the narrator makes it impossible to locate in him the moral guide to this satiric universe, so also is it inadvisable to assume that any one part of, or element in, **The Canterbury Tales** can unequivocally be taken as the center of values. For example, while the idealized figures of the feudal structure, the Knight, the Plowman and the Parson, provide a norm for evaluation of the society of the pilgrimage, it is important to remember that "Although there is always at least a suggestion of some kind of humane ideal in satire . . . this ideal is never heavily stressed." This particular ideal is provided in fragments and as such is almost drowned in the scene of satire itself, the "felde ful of folke". The fact that the vigorous and captivating presentation of vice and folly overwhelms the bare depictions of the ideal is, of course, part of the satiric statement, but only *part.*

The difference in tone between **The Canterbury Tales** and *Piers Plowman* in their use of the ideal feudal structure points differing satiric intentions: in the *Visio* section of *Piers Plowman* the gradually developed presentation of the feudal structure, the depiction of its actual corruption, its temporary re-establishment in its ideal form, and its subsequent disintegration provide a bitter comment on society and the failure of human social morality. It is a comment that works by stressing the ideal and its relationship to the actual quite heavily, that does not allow the reader any doubt or qualification about the moral position: the condition of humanity is depraved, degenerate, and disgusting; the ideal is shining and beautiful and God-given.

The matter is not quite as simple in Chaucer. To begin with, the ideal of feudal structure is alluded to rather than propounded: the pieces of the structure are dropped into the picture almost haphazardly. Moreover, the actualities of this society do not correspond very well to the outline

of social structure which has thus been invoked. This dichotomy can be taken as the sort of statement that Langland appears to be making—that society has departed from its ideal form and the result is moral and social corruption. Given that the pre-occupation of the satirist is to remind his audience of its failure to live up to the agreed ideals of the age, this is an entirely legitimate interpretation of Chaucer's purpose also. It is, however, only a partial explanation, for the tone of the work within which this ideal is inserted is clearly very different from that of *Piers Plowman*. While the pilgrims have vices, they clearly are not Vices; while the delineation of their characters is controlled by concepts of types, few of them could be described as personifications or one-dimensional caricatures. It is a commonplace to observe that, while the vividness of the pilgrims is directly linked to the vanities they embody, the vitality of what is created seems to make the question of moral judgments less than pressing.

In some satires there is a close conjunction between the moral judgment being made and the kind of satisfaction the satirist offers his reader. For example, in *Macflecknoe* the entertainment resides in our participating with the writer in the pleasure of relating the evident stupidity of the victim, in our being, in fact, able to identify ourselves directly with the poet-judge. The heavy irony of the style does not permit us for one moment to doubt that we are engaged in a work of ridicule which does not allow the object of its attack any personal dignity or life other than that created for it so that it may be attacked. It is this aspect of satiric art that Sutherland is discussing [in his *English Satire*] when he says,

> The satirist proceeds characteristically by drastic simplification, by ruthlessly narrowing the area of vision, by leaving out of account the greater part of what must be taken into consideration if we are to realise the totality of a situation or a character. In its extremest form we usually call this process caricature. It is fatal to satire if the reader or spectator should reflect that much might be said on both sides, or that if we knew all we might forgive all.

This process of caricature provides a direct link of poet, reader, moral judgment and entertainment, and in Chaucer is observable in the treatment of the Pardoner and the Summoner especially. But it is not possible to contain all satire within this narrow limit—only certain aspects of *The Rape of the Lock* or *Gulliver's Travels,* for example, correspond to this satiric method. Many satires work in quite different ways. Some satirists create a fantasy in which the object of attack is not always or immediately self-evident, or in which the object presented is at times the object of the satire and at others not. Belinda and her actions are a notable example of the flexibility of satire— she is ridiculous, but also an object of beauty whose contemplation does not always involve the reader in laughter. The tea-ceremony, as a substitute for the epic feast, is ludicrous, but in itself has a certain comfortable pleasure and elegance. Similarly, contemplation of the Squire, the Prioress, and the Wife of Bath involves both laughter and appreciation.

For want of a better term, we tend to label this sort of effect as Horatian, but this will not quite do if we assume, as has been assumed from the Renaissance onwards, that the object of this sort of satire is corrective. How many Belindas have been reformed by the *Rape,* how many Prioresses have given up dogs and how many Wives given up the quest for yet another husband? The relationships here between the work of art, the reader, and moral judgments are much less simple than in the previous cases. While the reader can and, to some extent, undoubtedly does gain his pleasure from a largely implicit recognition of the distance between the ideal and the actual, between aspiration and achievement, the lack of personal identification of the poet with what he relates allows, and to some extent creates, a suspension of the need to make moral judgments. Since the poet does not provide a direct, personal judgment either by direct statement or by the employment of a style which creates the sensation of moral indignation or scorn, the reader's only immediate identification is with the pleasure or pain directly elicited by the spectacle, the satiric scene.

If the scene is not uniformly ludicrous or disgusting and no overt moral indicators are presented, then the possibility of ambiguity or complexity of response arises. The moral will be implicit in the selection of the details which make up the scene, but I should like to suggest that this implicit moral may not necessarily form the dominant or only impression created by the scene. It is possible that the reader may be involved in a delicate balance of recognition and appreciation: recognition, first, of the veracity of the *mimesis* and, second, of the aberration from the ideal which the created object represents; appreciation of the skill which created the object and of the vitality which the object embodies. In such a response, the need to elicit the *significacio* is hardly more pressing than the need to recognize the artistic form of the creation. Likewise, the recognition of the *significacio* will not necessarily seem to be the center or the essence of the thing created. It is a commonplace that in satire of the Horatian sort the writer is moved to amusement rather than indignation at the spectacle of human folly, but that the laughter, nevertheless, is a weapon and has a reformative purpose. It is this assumption of reformative purpose which tends to direct the critic's attention to what is only one element in the effect—the exposure of the vice.

Focus on this element can and does lead to a distorted view that, in its simplification, does considerable injustice to the complexity of works of the comic-satiric sort, the greatest of the distortions being the tendency to assume that all statements within a work which may be called moral are necessarily those of the author or are univalent. Clarissa's remarks in *The Rape of the Lock* clearly represent the voice of good sense and the ignoring of this voice by the *beau monde* is undoubtedly a satiric comment on that part of society, but is she really the moral center of the work? Are her dictums the climax to which the work has moved? Do these generalities represent the essence of Pope's vision? Possibly to those who feel that the essence of a work lies in some more or less direct moral statement this may be the "meaning" of *The Rape of the Lock,* but most of us will find it a thin summation of that creation. We will, I think, move to a more complete understanding

The Wife of Bath as pictured in the Ellesmere manuscript of the Canterbury Tales.

of comic satire if we allow that Horatian satire is not necessarily reformative, that "the emphasis is not on laughter as reformative but as psychologically necessary. . . . There is implied the understanding that its public efficacy may be elsewhere than in reform. . . . It is the Augustans (not Horace) who put their faith in the creed of utility."

We will, I think, move to a better understanding of the complexity of **The Canterbury Tales** if we allow that comic satire may derive only part of its effect from, and be only partly concerned with, moral judgments. In reading **The Canterbury Tales** I assume the pilgrimage to be the frame it clearly is, the excuse for the Tales. I assume also that the pilgrimage has some symbolic significance, that by using this device, rather than the enforced retreat used by Boccaccio, Chaucer is suggesting some overall spiritual significance for his work, such as that we are to be involved in a journey to some sort of Truth; but since Chaucer does not say so, I do not assume that it is, therefore, an allegory of the Way to Truth or that the spiritual significance of pilgrimage is the dominating preoccupation of the work. Medieval works in which spiritual, moral or theological preoccupation are dominant—from Dante to Chaucer's contemporaries—manifest this concern most directly, as if they had little faith in their audience's ability to discern the sentence beneath the matter. From the variety of characters and satiric tones in the **"General Prologue"** I assume a variety of preoccupations and intentions, and a complexity of vision. From the deliberate withdrawal of the artist and the creation of a naive observer-guide, I assume that preaching, complaint and reformation are not necessarily the dominant intentions of the author.

It seems to me, therefore, that the obvious variety and complexity of comic-satiric vision in the **"General Prologue,"** combined with the deliberate withdrawal of the poet and the consequent pseudo-objective narrative mode may provide a fairly reliable clue to the "significance" of the **"Parson's Tale."** The Parson, as I stated earlier, is part of the ideal feudal structure which is evoked by an apparently haphazard intrusion of idealized portraits into a gallery otherwise given over to portraiture which gives the impression of realism through its concern with follies, vices, and individualizing details of dress and mannerism. These idealized portraits are noticeable because they contrast so obviously with their surroundings, and their effect is not, I think, a simple one. To begin with, they are so idealized that they are immediately less impressive than the caricatures, like the Pardoner, or more "rounded" characterizations, such as that of the Wife. They lack identifiable humanity, since they are little more than personifications of their social roles. The effect they create, therefore, is rather similar to the position of Christ in the York "Crucifixion"—they are the *loci* of moral value, its physical embodiment in the world of the pilgrimage, but they lack the artistic dynamism that is attendant upon the "immoral" characters. The vices and follies of humanity, not simply personified, as in *Piers Plowman,* but embodied in people whose vice is an aspect, though not the totality, of their being, almost overwhelm its ideals. They are not, however, obliterated; their position, on examination, seems less haphazard than one had thought.

The Knight's position at the beginning of the gallery is, of course, due to his social position; it also, however, serves to isolate and subtly emphasize the fusion of social responsibility and moral uprightness which he represents. As a beginning it states an ideal of life which is gradually eroded as we move through the sequence of portraits. The Parson's and the Plowman's position, sandwiched between two of the most vivid secular portraits, the Wife and the Miller, and followed by the caricatures of the Summoner and the Pardoner, again serves to emphasize their idealization and at the same time contrast them with the vitality of folly and vice. The satiric tensions of ideal and actual are obvious enough here, but due consideration must also be given to the balance of tone: the human vitality of the Wife and the Miller vastly overshadows the two idealized characters. Yet the tone is not that of bitter denunciation of vice.

While the positioning of the ideal three in the **"Prologue"** has no architectural shape, it has some significance for the satiric comment and the overall tone. Chaucer has not grouped them together as a stark antithesis to the rest of the pilgrims, nor has he positioned each one as the local, normative standard for specific groups of pilgrims; they are of and among the pilgrims. This grouping has consequences for the satiric tone. It is a way of suggesting, not that the whole world is rotten and corrupt when compared with the medieval social-moral ideal, but rather that this world is a curious *mélange* of folly, vice, and virtue and that, while there are ideals readily available, the color and variety of life not infrequently reside in what, by comparison with an ideal standard, we recognize as human folly. I am aware of the argument that medieval man would react to the idealized characters differently—that they would evoke in him pious responses which are no longer automatic in twentieth century man—but it seems to me that the definition of medieval man is too frequently weighted by reference to medieval ecclesiastical scholarship. This medieval man posited should really be called medieval pious man, Firm-of-Faith and not a little unlearned in patristics.

Social history tends to indicate that there were other types of medieval man: *Pearl, Piers Plowman,* and sermon literature suggest that medieval religious writers were not so certain that medieval man recognized or responded properly to Christian truths; the satire of **The Canterbury Tales** seems to suggest that recognition of an ideal does not necessarily involve emotional engagement in it and a consequent rejection of the non-ideal. It is possible that some medieval men were capable of accepting the validity of certain ideals, using them as ways of ordering experience, but at the same time being more engaged by the vitality of the flawed life which surrounds them than by the pale abstractions of a social-ethical code. The Parson, and his companions, the Knight and the Plowman, therefore, seem to me *part* of a comic-satiric work—points of reference but not, because of their position, the style of their treatment and the overall Horatian tone of the satire, the unequivocal voices of Truth and the controllers of the total statement of the work.

The Parson, then, is part of the varied intentions of the **"General Prologue"**: a representative of a profession in what is clearly intended as a fairly full cross-section of society; an instrument in a fairly intricate series of indirect social and moral comparisons; the butt of a little piece of dramatic business (see the endlink to the **"Man of Law's Tale"**); and the evoker of the commonplace medieval moral system. His tale renders explicit what was at best only implicit in his dramatic position and idealized depiction. Coming where it does, the **"Parson's Tale"** can be seen as re-establishing explicitly the satiric norm that, though established initially through the presence of the idealized characters, is only fitfully implicit in some of the tales. While not the unifying theme of the work or the unequivocal guide to individual tales and tellers, the sermon on penance and the Seven Deadly Sins clearly functions as a generalized, retrospective guide to the moral matter of the whole work.

"Medieval man," wrote C. S. Lewis [in his *Studies in Medieval and Renaissance Literature*], "was not a dreamer, nor a spiritual adventurer; he was an organizer, a codifier, a man of system." And the categories provided by the Parson undoubtedly serve as an aid to allow the reader to order his impressions, to assign praise or blame in a fiction which at times must appear woefully unordered. Very little in Chaucer is, however, without ambiguity or ambivalence. The description of the Seven Deadly Sins can be taken simply as a guide to the vices of the pilgrims and thus as a retrospective denunciation. Tupper's articles provide abundant evidence of the ramifications of vice which can be discerned in the pilgrims and their tales with the aid of the Parson's illuminating sermon. But as Lowes has pointed out [in his 1915 *PMLA* article "Chaucer and the Seven Deadly Sins"], while all the sins are undoubtedly present in the tales and tellers, they are not coterminous with any one tale or teller; indeed, any number of sins may be found in one pilgrim and his tale (see Lowes' article for a demonstration of just how complex sin-defining can become). The Seven Deadly Sins motif, then, does not point a neat, defining finger of denunciation, but the schematized abstractions nevertheless illuminate something very important about vice and folly in *The Canterbury Tales,* namely that the pilgrims are not personified vices, but men in whom various aspects of vice may be discovered. More than that, it illumines the extent to which what we call vices and virtues are inextricably part of the individual's *persona.* But it is (if I may be allowed a mixed metaphor) a double-edged illumination, since the embodiment of vices in the individual pilgrims throws into relief the very dryness of the abstractions.

"The Wife of Bath is prideful, inobedient, and 'likerous', a prattler and a scold. All these traits are castigated by the Parson." This statement is obviously valid, but the analysis in no way accounts for the Wife. The very business of describing the more vivid pilgrims in terms of the Parson's dull catalogues demonstrates the inadequacy of the schematization to capture the essence of those characters. The description of Sporus as a gilded bug is not adequately represented by the critic's conclusion that he is satirized as a parasite. The Parson's catalogue of sins, in effect, represents a way of seeing the world. It is not an invalid way—it has the authority of the medieval religious tradition; but, like any ordering or cataloguing, it is necessarily an abstraction from a vast amount of data, a selection which, while it may accurately relate to a given set of premises, cannot by its nature pretend to be the whole. One could, for example, use part of the Parson's catalogue to give *auctoritee* to the satire implicit in the visual presentation of the Wife:

> And, as seith Seint Gregorie, that 'precious clothyng is cowpable for the derthe of it, and for his softenesse, and for his strangenesse and degisynesse, and for the superfluitee, or for the inordinat scantnesse of it.' Allas! may man nat seen, as in oure dayes, the synful costlewe array of clothynge, and namely in to muche superfluite, or elles in to desordinat scantnesse?

The Wife is clearly a glaring example of the sin of "superfluitee" and "strangenesse" in clothing, but an analysis which contended itself with thus defining her sin would be inadequate. Definition by sin does not, indeed cannot, take adequate account of the details from which the abstraction is drawn, and yet these details often control the tone of the whole description. For example, the details that her "coverchiefs ful fyne weren of ground" and "they weye-

den ten pound" can be subsumed under the headings "precious clothyng" and "superfluitee," but the tone here is outright laughter: the Wife has become not simply an example of one of the divisions of *Superbia,* but a comically ludicrous figure whose impact resides not in our realization of her moral position but in the exaggeration into which her typical female vanity leads her. When we see her sisters today in church with their Easter bonnets, I doubt that our reaction has much to do with our recognition that "the synful costlewe array of clothynge" is derived from one of the Seven Deadlies, but it may in those with a literary education have something to do with the sheer joy of recognition of the unfailing continuity of manifestations of female vanity. It is not that the application of the Parson's observations are mistaken—both clearly play a part in our reactions—but exclusive concentration on this sort of judgment and reaction would ignore other relevant data and reactions and, thus, be a distortion of the whole.

It has been suggested that just as the Parson's sermon is the essential guide to the sins to be observed in the Pilgrims, so also is it the key to the corresponding virtues. While it is true that the Parson carefully delineates the *remedium* for every sin, the correlation between virtuous doctrine and the pilgrims is even less certain than that established with the vices. Lowes has demonstrated that the symmetries of vice and virtue discovered by Tupper rest on very special interpretations. And yet, of course, it is difficult to rid oneself of the feeling that these plain antitheses of the sermon must have some relationship to the whole matter of Chaucer's work.

While many of the most interesting tales seem to lend themselves ill to overt moral statement, a number of tales quite clearly depend artistically on the presence of some *moralitas.* Tales such as those of the Pardoner, the Monk, the Manciple and the Canon Yeoman have a moral cautionary intent. A more positive morality is presented in the tales of the Prioress, the Physician, the Second Nun and Chaucer. These tales are devotional-didactic in tone, characterization and intent, but a glance at their tellers will indicate that no easy conclusions are to be drawn from their presence in the work. The **"Prioress's Tale"** is suitable to her role, but not—except indirectly because of her naïveté—to her character. There is no relationship of any sort between the Physician and his tale—hence an immediate impression of unsuitability, a lasting awareness of Truth issuing forth from out of the mouth of a medieval quack. The Second Nun's story is completely suited to her role, but the question of suitability to character never arises, since she is not described in the **"General Prologue"** or created in her own prologue. Chaucer's **"Tale of Melibee"** could, of course, be taken at face value as another piece of unequivocal doctrine, though it is more common, given its position after **"Sir Thopas"** and its framing within the Host's remarks, to see it as yet another of Chaucer's attempts to create for himself a simple, dense, dull *persona.*

Virtue, then, does not proceed solely from the mouths of the virtuous in *The Canterbury Tales,* nor is it to be found neatly juxtaposed with its appropriate vice. This very lack of uniformity may distress those who seek in Chaucer the moral symmetries of the **"Parson's Tale,"** yet it seems to be an essential part of his indirect mode of procedure. The very fact that virtuous statements, direct and indirect, are to be found scattered apparently at random—now where one would expect them, now where by all the laws of "character consistency" one would expect them least—constitutes a powerful but indirect comment both on the place of virtue in human lives and on the "surprising" quality which makes human beings and literary characters live.

We are somewhat surprised at the **"Prioress's Tale"** because her characterization had led us to expect something about "cheere of court," yet the deliberately sentimentalized tale of the martyred child with its strong vein of superstitious faith and simple-minded fascination with miracles does flow quite naturally from her character. It is, finally, a moral tale suitable to the Prioress and the irony which is attendant upon her characterization cannot be said to have completely disappeared in the overt morality of the tale. That is, attention only to the "character" of the teller and the "matter" of the tale will not infrequently lead us into false or over-simple conclusions. The Physician's recounting of a tale lauding virginity seems explicable only in terms of the dramatic impression to be created by such a strikingly inappropriate juxtapositioning. In terms of character and matter the arrangement is clearly ironic—God works in mysterious ways—and yet here too the style of the telling adds a complicating factor to this conclusion. It is a pathetic tale of an archetypal martyr story kind, reduced to its essential features, exhibiting no imagination, no appreciation of the dramatic realities inherent in the matter—a pious tale told badly, the little attempt at dramatization sorely muffed. How appropriate this all is, in its indirect way, for the Physician! Like most physicians in the Middle Ages (and much later) he is a conventional butt of satire, a man exploiting human misery for money and, like all of his type, anxious to maintain his façade of professional knowledge and moral uprightness. It is fitting that virtuous statements should issue so uncomprehended from a man whose "studie was but litel on the Bible"; fitting also that the virtue exemplified is illustrated in such a sensational, absolute fashion that it could hardly be said to have much to do with any of the daily dilemmas of the Christian.

In other words, the literary critic should be a little wary of drawing conclusions from a simple correlation of matter and teller (or of assuming that pious matter is a sufficient *explanation* of a plain or limping style of presentation). The irony of the relationship of the **"Pardoner's Tale"** to the Pardoner is clearly intended by Chaucer, but the tale also has its own life as a tale. It has, therefore, its existence as a tale; it directly conveys a moral message, and it is also a comment on its teller. The teller himself is, of course, a shifting character—the ludicrous object of the **"General Prologue"** and the smooth persuader of the prologue to his tale provide two quite different perspectives on, and attitudes to, the Pardoner. Both are aspects of the man, contrasting but not mutually exclusive, and the deliberate nature of these changes of focus is emphasized by the reduction of the Pardoner to his ludicrous aspect by the Host's crude reminder of the Pardoner's prob-

able sexual status: "I wolde I hadde thy coillons in myn hond." The humor lies, of course, not simply in the crudity of the response, but also in its reminder of that aspect of the Pardoner which has been overwhelmed by the skill of his prologue and the fascination of the *exemplum:* "I trowe he were a geldyng or a mare."

The Parson's exposition of the *remedia* of sins cannot, therefore, be taken as providing the *significacio* of spots of virtue which are to be discerned scattered throughout the work, because their presentation is too complex for his rigid categories and interests. Any relationship is of a most general sort. What emerges from an examination of "pious" tales, however, is a growing suspicion that these tales, while containing irrefutable moral matter, like the **"Parson's Tale,"** are not necessarily exempt by their matter from the complex satiric vision we quite happily admit to be operating in the secular tales. It is perfectly true that one can read these tales purely for their piety or morality or whatever, and it is undoubtedly true that many of Chaucer's readers would take them in this way, just as many readers today, until instructed by academics, can read *Gulliver's Travels* as a weird travel-adventure story, akin to space-adventure novels. But readers familiar with the range of styles and complexities of vision present in the **Book of the Duchess,** the **House of Fame** and **Troilus and Criseyde** will hesitate to ascribe tedious prose, unimaginative narration, and inappropriate ascription to the fact that the author "could no better." Professor Lawlor [in his *Chaucer*] is right to caution that "We must not, then, be in a hurry to assume that the audience was composed of the sensitive and the discerning," but at the same time we must beware of assuming that the limited perceptions of the less sensitive and discerning are total or even correct perceptions, for the satirist plays as much with his audience as with his creations.

It has been demonstrated that the Parson, while a moral ideal, is also a functioning "character" within the comic-satiric framework—a part of the artistic "house" which Chaucer has created, but not its sole support or chief embellishment. While the Parson and his tale can be seen as an important element in providing a retrospective summary of normative values, an examination of the usefulness of his categories of sin and remedy indicates that the tale is far from a complete or necessary key to the work, especially since the satiric values emerge *in process* and are not dependent on looking first at the **"Parson's Tale"**. The "key" to *The Canterbury Tales,* if one is needed, lies in the dominant comic-satiric mode of the presentation, in which no one character or set of statements is the Truth, but all characters and statements qualify and modify each other and provide a comprehensive complex which, in its *wholeness,* may be a sort of truth.

This flexible satiric mode which we have distinguished in *The Canterbury Tales* has obvious consequences for our reading of the **"Parson's Tale"**. Since an examination of the other religious and their tales has revealed a complexity of attitudes and functions, it is legitimate to inquire whether the Parson and his tale, while being less central to the conception of the whole than has been assumed, may not be more complex in their nature and function than has hitherto been allowed, even by their devotees. The Parson and his tale, while considerably less complex in function than the Pardoner, his prologue, and tale, is not quite as divorced from the methods of the rest of *The Canterbury Tales* as is commonly imagined. Its style is not totally neutral—it betrays evidence of its teller. Its vision, for example, is a generalizing, dogmatic one—the vision of his profession. He talks for the most part in abstract language about vice and virtue and the way to salvation, the very things Piers talks about, but which Langland felt the need to relate to the actual life of men.

While Chaucer's immediate source or sources for the tale have not been discovered, close analogues exist and the relationship to the Parson's sermon has been examined sufficiently to demonstrate that it is a faithful rendering of orthodox matter. It has also been firmly established that the structure of the work corresponds to recommendations of the *artes praedicandi*. These investigations leave us in no doubt that the tale is a thoroughly respectable piece of medieval preaching, both in matter and in the larger elements of style, eminently suitable to the teller and, in its own right, a worthy pice of doctrine. Scholarly investigation seems to have stopped at this point, on the assumption that doctrine is doctrine and further analysis is unnecessary, there being no shell here, only kernel; or that the doctrine is dull and "un-Chaucerian," but that this dullness is forced on Chaucer by the matter. However, a closer look at the undoubtedly long-winded sermon brings to light a number of stylistic features which would allow us to see the **"Parson's Tale"** not simply as the undramatized moral product of an idealized *persona* who represents the medieval religious truths in the pilgrimage, but also as being the product of a distinct personality.

A paradigm of the arrangement of the matter gives us no hint that all elements are not treated with equal balance. For example, the Parson waxes eloquent on Pride, Anger, Avarice and Lechery: examples and ramifications proliferate, and his simple paratactic arrangements gather an accumulative force which betrays an emotional involvement. Curiously enough, in the light of the pilgrims' personalities and tales, common vices such as Gluttony and Envy do not seem to excite him (Gluttony occupies 817-30, whereas Avarice has 739-802). The more intellectual sin of *Accidie*, while given more space than Gluttony or Envy, shares their stylistic features, that is, it is little more than a catalogue of abstractions with very few supporting patristic quotations, in marked contrast to the rest of the sermon, and none of the homely similes which enliven the other accounts of vices. In other words, in his account of the Seven Deadly Sins, one can observe imaginative weightings; the Parson's imagination, and hence the reader's interest, seems to be stirred more by some sins than by others. It is, of course, the elaborations on the model which allow us to distinguish one medieval writer's style from another and, within a work, one *persona* from another. The amount of amplification given to each part of the matter is, on its own, insufficient to permit us to assign a specific individuality to a character whose traits are, for the most part, rigorously non-individual, but within the more amplified sections certain elements of style strike one forcibly. Though much of the sermon is descriptive and

emotionally low-keyed, every now and again the Parson betrays indignation and the language slides from judicial abstractions to the plain-speaking level of the Hell-fire preacher, or the Miller:

> . . . but for youre synne ye been wroxen thral, and foul . . . and yet moore foul and abhomynable, for ye trespassen so ofte tyme as dooth the hound that retourneth to eten his spewyng. / And yet be ye fouler for youre longe continuyng in synne and youre synful usage, for which ye be roten in youre synne, as a beest in his dong.

> O goode God, ye wommen that been of so greet beautee, remembreth yow of the proverbe of Salomon. He seith: / "Likneth a fair womman that is a fool of hire body lyk to a ryng of gold that were in the groyn of a soughe." / For right as a soughe wroteth in everich ordure, so wroteth she hire beautee in the stynkynge ordure of syne.

> . . . forthwith the superfluitee in lengthe of the forseide gownes, trailynge in the dong and in the mire, on horse and eek on foote, as wel of man as of womman, that al thilke trailyng is verraily as in effect wasted, consumed, thredbare, and roten with donge. . . .

> And moore fooles been they that kissen in vileynye, for that mouth is the mouth of helle; and namely this olde dotardes holours, yet wol they kisse, though they may nat do, and smatre hem. / Certes, they been lyk to houndes; for an hound, whan he comth by the roser or by othere [bushes], though he may nat pisse, yet wole he heve up his leg and make a contenaunce to pisse.

> Of this brekynge comth eek ofte tyme that folk unwar wedden or synnen with hire owene kynrede, and namely thilke harlotes that haunten bordels of thise fool wommen, that mowe be likned to a commune gong, where as men purgen hire ordure.

While such excremental allusions are not unique in the medieval preaching tradition, they are also not obligatory. Their use, therefore, can be taken partly as a sign of the Parson's professional competence—strong, earthy comparisons universally have the effect of making the audience pay attention—and partly as an indicator of personal emotional engagement. The Parson has not only an ear for the fashionable popular song of the day ("wel may that man that no good werk ne dooth synge thilke newe Frenshe song, *'Jay tout perdu mon temps et mon labour'* "), but also a keen eye for contemporary fashion and a sharp sarcastic tongue for its sexually titillating excesses. If the Parson is a satiric norm, he is also at times a savagely humorous satirist:

> Allas! somme of hem shewen the boce of hir shap, and the horrible swollen membres, that semeth lik the maladie of hirnia, in the wrappynge of hir hoses; / and eek the buttokes of hem faren as it were the hyndre part of a she-ape in the fulle of the moone. / And mooreover, the wrecched swollen membres that they shewe thurgh disgisynge, in departynge of hire hoses in whit and reed, semeth that half hir shameful privee mem-

bres weren flayne. / And if so be that they departen hire hoses in othere colours, as is whit and blak, or whit and blew, or blak and reed, and so forth, / thanne semeth it, as by variaunce of colour, that half the partie of hir privee membres were corrupt by the fir of seint Antony, or by cancre, or by oother swich meschaunce. / Of the hyndre part of hir buttokes, it is ful horrible for to see. For certes, in that partie of hir body ther as they purgen hir stynkynge ordure, / that foule partie shewe they to the peple prowdly in despit of honestitee, which honestitee that Jhesu Crist and his freendes observede to shewen in hir lyve.

It is possibly noteworthy that there is no balancing attack on the revealing or scanty nature of women's clothing. Ironically, the tone here and in the passage on infanticide is reminiscent, in its prurient fascination with that which it condemns, of the Pardoner's "O wombe! O bely! O stynkyng cod, / Fulfilled of dong and of corrupcioun!" While the Parson's sermon, therefore, may be largely an orthodox statement of the doctrine of penance and salvation and a catalogue of the sins and their remedies, it is also to a discernible extent the product of a distinctive personality. It is both a satiric norm which guides or confirms the directions of the satire and occasionally a *direct* satiric voice.

Given, then, that there are distinct elements of presentation which allow us to have some vague idea of an individual, rather than an allegorical figure or one-dimensional *type,* that the style may to some limited extent *be* the man, then it is possible that the Parson is not only a satiric norm and occasionally a direct satiric voice, but is also slightly, delicately satirized through his style. The most obvious feature of the style is, of course, its dullness, which has been labelled "un-Chaucerian." Given Chaucer's intense awareness of style, sufficiently evident in the variety of *The Canterbury Tales,* his evident ability to vary the narrative mode and create distinctive speaking voices for his characters, can we not assume that this is what he intended? Can we not assume that, when the priest's rather pedantic enumerations become a trifle tedious, we are responding not irresponsibly, as Baldwin [in his *The Unity of the Canterbury Tales*] would have it ("It is dull only to those who regard the posing and discussion of such questions as the sport of, in Bacon's phrase, *sectores cymini,* as a sophistry"), but naturally, as the style directs us? Is it not special pleading to suggest that we find it dull only because we, mistakenly, find the matter dull; or to go further and speculate that Chaucer may have intended to rework it. Is it not more likely that Chaucer is here employing his acknowledged art quite deliberately to create a style which is peculiarly appropriate to the Parson?

The Parson as ideal is full of good sentence, but the Parson as a representative type is also rather pedantic, more concerned to propound his dogma than vivify it, and hence not infrequently tedious. While his sermon obeys the recommendations to quote *auctoritee,* it is difficult to avoid noticing the immense accumulation of authorities in the passage dealing with the third cause of contrition. Apart from a section of exegesis of a quotation from Job, the whole lengthy passage is composed of a massive sequence of quotations: "For, as Seint Jerome seith . . . as Seint Poul seith . . . and seith Seint Bernard. . . . And therfore seith Salomon. . . ." This super-abundant pastiche of authorities reminds one of Chauntecleer's quotation of authorities on and examples of dreams, because stylistically it can only be adjudged bad art or deliberate parody. The **"Parson's Tale,"** then, is full of worthy matter, occasionally enlivened by direct denunciation expressed in terms of basic human functions and betraying more than a little disgust with human sexuality, but for the most part notable for pedantic *longeurs* which, while not destroying the moral worth of the matter, serve to render the presentation more complex and remind us that the Parson is a part of the drama, a character like the others—not the direct moral voice of the poet, nor a judicial Duke Theseus. None of this should, of course, be taken as suggesting that the Parson is the object of satiric attack, or that Chaucer was a secret unbeliever, but it seems to suggest that perhaps we should be less ready to see the Parson simply as a personification of certain ideals and his sermon as "a peroration of that sermon of which the tales and the connectives may be said, loosely, to constitute an exemplum," and more ready to admit that he has certain distinctive personal traits which also render him subject to judgment, as the Host perceived: "I smelle a Lollere in the wynd." (pp. 94-116)

John Finlayson, "The Satiric Mode and the 'Parson's Tale'," in The Chaucer Review, *Vol. 6, No. 2, Fall, 1971, pp. 94-116.*

Patricia Anne Magee   (essay date 1971)

[*In the following excerpt, Magee argues that the Wife of Bath is a "challenge-prone" character who really desires male dominance.*]

In his essay on "Chaucer's Discussion of Marriage" [in the 1911-12 *Modern Philology*], George Lyman Kittredge complained that "we are prone to read and study the *Canterbury Tales* as if each tale were an isolated unit and to pay scant attention to what we call the connecting links,—those bits of lively narrative and dialogue that bind the whole together." However just Kittredge's complaint may have been in 1911, it is evident that later criticism on the *Canterbury Tales* swung in the opposite direction. In part through the influence of Kittredge, many modern critics placed such emphasis on the "dramatic realism" or "roadside drama" aspect of the *Canterbury Tales* that it became the individual tales themselves which came to receive the "scant attention." A few critics have recently attempted to turn the tide again, away from the "dramatic realism" concept, the main weakness of which was that it gave the "followers of Kittredge . . . every inducement to discuss the drama and every excuse for ignoring the tale," thus submerging the narrative problems in the problems of drama. This paper is concerned with a single teller, the Wife of Bath, and with a single problem which dominates her prologue and tale: the problem of mastery.

On the surface, the Wife of Bath is more of a caricature than a character. She seems to embody just about everything that the Middle Ages traditionally held to be typically female and also everything that was opposed to the tra-

ditional, orthodox view of marriage. Concerning her portrayal as a typical female, she is shrewish and a nag; she
is unscrupulous and wily; she is unfaithful and deceitful;
she has no devotion to the four husbands she ruled; she
is extremely sensuous. . . . Regarding her several violations of the rules of orthodox marriage, she has had a series of marriages, violating the medieval notion of "a clene
wydewe"; she insists on dominating her spouses, directly
contrary to the traditional medieval view of marriage as
a reflection of the relationship between Christ (husband)
and his church (wife); she is interested in fine clothes and
other worldly matters, an interest condemned by the Parson in his sermon; she states that sex is for pleasure as well
as for procreation, contrary to the orthodox idea that
"God made marriage in paradys . . . to multiplye
mankynde to the service of God," to replenish "hooly
chirche of good lynage"; she is loud and outspoken, the
opposite of the Parson's ideal wife. All of these traits
strongly suggest that the poet intended the Wife of Bath
to be the object of a humorous satire against women and
female mastery. In the course of her prologue, Alison
manages to allude to Theophrastus, Saint Jerome, Eustache Deschamps, Walter Map, and Jean de Meun—
authorities representing the classical anti-feminist tradition. It was truly a brilliant stroke on Chaucer's part to
write a piece of anti-feminist literature and put it all in the
mouth of a narrator who is an avowed feminist.

But is the Wife of Bath really a feminist? Obviously *she*
thinks she is, and indeed, on the surface she certainly appears to be one. Yet, any critic who is content simply to
label the Wife of Bath a feminist is ignoring a number of
important factors which complicate her personality.

Probably the most striking aspect of the **"Wife of Bath's
Prologue and Tale"** is the large number of contradictions
and inconsistencies which permeate them both. Here is a
woman who claims that women should rule their husbands, then goes on to demonstrate how unfit women are
to rule. In a tirade she scathingly condemns the anti-
feminist authorities, then shows by her actions and her account of her past life that she deserves their criticism. In
her prologue and tale, she claims that women desire mastery, and yet she readily admits that she loved most and
was happiest with her fifth husband, who dominated her.
She says that she advocates female mastery as the proper
marriage relationship, and yet, in the account of her marriage to Jankyn and in her tale, she recounts the stories of
happy marriages in which the wife was "obedient," devoted, and "trewe."

Was Chaucer merely being inconsistent in his portrayal of
the Wife of Bath? Certainly inconsistency is possible; the
notion of inconsistency as a fault is part of the modern sensibility. But perhaps there is another, more satisfactory,
answer to the problem. Perhaps Chaucer was not inconsistent at all in his portrayal of the Wife of Bath, but, on the
contrary, endowed her with one consistent personality
and view of marriage of which she is evidently unaware
but which she states and demonstrates repeatedly in her
prologue and tale.

I contend that the whole question of female mastery for
its own sake is really unimportant to the Wife of Bath. Her
apparent desire to dominate is merely a result of a much
deeper motivation, an understanding of which helps to explain the apparent inconsistencies and contradictions in
her point of view. The Wife demonstrates in [the **"Wife
of Bath's Prologue and Tale"**] that (as she explains in her
account of her marriage to Jankyn)

> I trowe I loved hym (Jankyn) best, for that he
> Was of his love daungerous to me.
> We wommen han, if that I shal nat lye,
> In this matere a queynte fantasye;
> Wayte what thyng we may nat lightly have,
> Therafter wol we crie al day and crave.
> Forbede us thyng, and that desiren we;
> Preesse on us faste, and thanne wol we fle.
> With daunger oute we al oure chaffare;
> Greet prees at market maketh deere ware,
> And to greet cheep is holde at litel prys:
> This knoweth every womman that is wys.

What lies at the heart of the Wife's desires is not mastery,
but simply *that thing which she does not have,* that thing
which presents her with the greatest challenge. As a
woman living in a male-oriented society and a woman
whose life revolves around relationships with men, the
biggest challenge she can face is an open confrontation
with male mastery. And so she takes on the male-
dominated society. That it is the challenge of fighting for
something which she does not have (rather than the actual
desire for female mastery) which is most important to her,
is demonstrated in her prologue and tale. Before elaborating on this point, I want to make another assertion, which
I will attempt to prove with the same evidence that supports the first point. My second assertion is that the Wife
of Bath, contrary to her openly stated views, actually
wants to be dominated.

As she states in her prologue, the Wife had mastery over
her first four husbands, and yet she was less satisfied with
them than she was with the fifth husband who dominated
her. She was intrigued with the first several husbands as
long as she was still trying to get mastery over them (and
they were, therefore, a challenge), but as soon as she had
them under control, she lost interest in them:

> Me neded nat do lenger diligence
> To wynne hir love, or doon hem reverence
> They loved me so wel, by God above,
> That I ne tolde no deyntee of hir love!
> A wys womman wol bisye hire evere in oon
> To gete hire love, ye, ther as she hath noon.
> But sith I hadde hem hoolly in myn hond,
> And sith they hadde me yeven al hir lond,
> What sholde I taken keep hem for to plese,
> But it were for my profit and myn ese?

Yet, describing her marriage to Jankyn, she relates:

> And yet was he to me the mooste shrewe;
> That feele I on my ribbes al by rewe,
> And evere shal unto myn endyng day.
> But in oure bed he was so fressh and gay,
> And therwithal so wel koude he me glose,
> Whan that he wolde han my *bele chose,*
> That thogh he hadde me bete on every bon,
> He koude wynne agayn my love anon.
> I trowe I loved hym best, for that he
> Was of his love daungerous to me.

In this marriage she was clearly dominated, both psychologically and physically, and she loved it. But since she did not have mastery, she was determined to get it. The violent argument over Jankyn's anti-feminist book provides her with the opportunity to frighten him into giving her "the bridel of myn hond, / To han the governance of hous and lond, / And of his tonge, and of his hond also." Yet, as soon as she has won the battle with Jankyn's verbal promise of obedience, she becomes a devoted wife:

> After that day we hadden never debaat.
> God helpe me so, I was to hym as kynde
> As any wyf from Denmark unto Ynde,
> And also trewe. . . .

Clearly, it was the attainment of something that she had lacked, and not the desire for dominance for its own sake, which motivated the Wife of Bath. And it seems equally clear that once she had won the challenge, she was quite content to become a devoted wife in the tradition of orthodox marriage.

That the Wife of Bath seems to be intrigued with the idea of a challenge and that she actually desires to be dominated is also demonstrated by her in her tale. Her story is of an old hag who converts a knight into accepting the idea of female mastery and then promptly transforms herself into a beautiful ("she so fair was, and so yong therto") and obedient ("And she obeyed hym in every thyng / That myghte doon hym plesance or likyng") wife. The parallels between this tale and the Wife's account of her conversion of Jankyn are obvious, and they reinforce my two-fold thesis concerning the Wife of Bath. The hag is a woman who takes on the challenge of getting a rather haughty young knight to submit meekly to her will. It is significant that Chaucer's hag differs from most of the old women in the various analogues, who are victims of an evil spell which can only be broken if they can get a young man to submit to them. Chaucer's hag, according to the text, is acting independently; no outside supernatural force should, therefore, be considered her motivation. Indeed, the fact that Chaucer noticeably left out any reference to the hag being the victim of a spell suggests that he had some other purpose in mind in depicting her as he did. The old hag in Alison's tale is very much like the Wife of Bath herself. She does not *need* the knight's promise of obedience to dispel some evil charm, as the hags in the analogues do. She seems to have no other motivation than her evident desire to accept the challenge of transforming an arrogant rapist into a meek and subservient husband. And once she has succeeded in getting a verbal promise of obedience out of the knight—

> "My lady and my love, and wyf so deere,
> I put me in youre wise governance;

> . . .

> For as yow liketh, it suffiseth me."
> "Thanne have I gete of yow maistrie," quod
>   she,
> "Syn I may chese and governe as me lest?"
> "Ye, certes, wyf," quod he, "I holde it best"—

she immediately turns right around:

> "Kys me," quod she, "we be no lenger wrothe;

> For, by my trouthe, I wol be to yow bothe,
> This is to seyn, ye, bothe fair and good.
> I prey to God that I moote sterven wood,
> But I to yow be also good and trewe
> As evere was wyf, wyn that the world was newe.
> And but I be to-morn as fair to seene
> As any lady, emperice, or queene,
> That is bitwixe the est and eke the west,
> Dooth with my lyf and deth right as yow lest."

> . . .

> And she obeyed hym in everythyng
> That myghte doon hym plesance or likyng.

The knight's words of submission and the hag's subsequent behavior towards him so closely parallel the Jankyn-Alison situation that they seem purposely to be intended to echo the first incident, thus reinforcing its significance. The pattern repeats itself. Again we are presented with an incident involving a woman who successfully meets the difficult challenge of achieving mastery in a male-dominated world, and then promptly becomes a devoted and obedient wife. Again the desire for female mastery is important, not for its own sake, but because it represents the most difficult challenge that a woman in a male-oriented society can face. Once the challenge is met, the transformed hag, having won the battle for supremacy with a verbal promise of obedience, becomes a model wife in the orthodox marriage tradition, just like the Wife of Bath.

In attempting to prove that the above pattern is the key to understanding the Wife of Bath, I have relied on five important pieces of textual evidence: the Wife's own statement that she, like all wise women, desires most whatever is denied her; her relative dissatisfaction with the four husbands she dominated (which contradicts her stated desire for mastery); her happy marriage to the husband who dominated her (the same contradiction); her argument with Jankyn in which she feigned injury to get him to submit verbally to her, then promptly became a "trewe" and devoted wife; and her tale of a hag who repeats the pattern of winning a promise of servitude and becoming an obedient wife. I submit not only that my thesis is valid, but that it is the most acceptable of theses since it legitimately resolves the puzzling contradictions and apparent inconsistencies that fill the Wife's prologue and tale. Other theories on the Wife of Bath have not satisfactorily resolved this problem, or have simply not addressed themselves to it at all. Certainly no one of these five textual references standing alone would be very convincing proof of this theory. Yet it seems evident that these major textual passages, taken together, reinforce each other and serve as convincing evidence to support my position.

Once the theory of a challenge-prone Wife of Bath who really desires male dominance is accepted, another aspect of Alison's personality takes on new significance. In her prologue the Wife makes reference to the astrological situation at the time of her birth:

> For certes, I am al Venerien
> In feelynge, and myn herte is Marcien.
> Venus me yaf my lust, my likerousnesse,
> And Mars yaf me my sturdy hardynesse;

Myn ascendent was Taur, and Mars therinne.

This passage has commonly and quite validly been interpreted as an indication of the Wife's combined sensuousness and open aggressiveness. One can, with equal validity, shift the focus slightly and view the Mars aspect of the Wife's personality as not merely general aggressiveness, but also the more specific desire to take on a challenge—to want to fight for "wayte what thyng we may nat lightly have." Also, the Wife's extreme sensuality, which she repeatedly and proudly refers to throughout her prologue, suggests that, at least physically, she wants to be dominated, since the "traditional," medieval female role in sex is essentially passive, while the male is active and aggressive. Indeed, as she explains in the important account of her marriage to Jankyn, his main attraction for her was that "in oure bed he was so fressh and gay," and "he / Was of his love daungerous to me." It was Jankyn's sexual aggressiveness which most pleased her. He obviously controlled their sex life, and this is the first thing she mentions when she recalls their happy marriage. Thus, when Alison's vital sexual nature is taken into account, it becomes easier to understand why she is happier when she is being dominated.

The Wife of Bath emerges, then, as a psychologically complex character. Chaucer's interest in psychology is certainly exceptional in medieval literature; it is obviously present in his portrait of the Wife of Bath. The inconsistencies which permeate her prologue and tale strongly suggest that there is a discrepancy between what the Wife thinks she wants and what she "really" wants. Obviously *she* intended her prologue and tale to be strongly feminist in tone, yet it seems clear that both are otherwise. Hopefully, the view of the Wife of Bath as a challenge-prone woman who really desires to be dominated explains the apparent inconsistencies in her desires, and reveals that, although the Wife of Bath is presented as a self-contradicting character, the poet who created her had one consistent characterization in mind. (40-5)

> *Patricia Anne Magee, "The Wife of Bath and the Problem of Mastery," in* Massachusetts Studies in English, *Vol. 3, No. 2, Fall, 1971, pp. 40-5.*

James Winny (essay date 1971)

[*Winny is the author of* Chaucer's Dream Poetry *(1973) and the editor of numerous editions of individual tales from the* Canterbury Tales. *In the excerpt below, he provides an introduction to the "Miller's Tale," emphasizing its comic aspects.*]

To all appearances **"The Miller's Tale"** is thrust upon the Canterbury pilgrims uninvited, against the Host's intention to present the tales in an orderly sequence determined by the social standing of each narrator. The company has just heard and applauded the first of the tales, told by the Knight after the oddly fortunate outcome of the Host's lottery; and when the Monk is invited to take his turn next it seems that the 'gentils' are to be given precedence over their humbler companions. But the Miller disputes this arrangement, and is undeterred when the Host reminds him of his lowly status:

> Abyd, Robin, my leeve brother;
> Som bettre man shal telle us first another.
> Abyd, and lat us werken thriftily.

Fortunately for the design of **The Canterbury Tales** the Miller is both too surly and too drunk to accept this amiable rebuke. He refuses to give way, frustrating a plan which seemed likely to segregate one genre of tale from another; and at last the Host ungraciously allows him to tell his scandalous tale. When the Reeve replies to the Miller's gibe against carpenters in a third tale, a random order of story-telling has been established; and the other pilgrims play their parts without much regard for social precedence.

Evidently the Host's reluctance to let the Miller tell his tale was not shared by Chaucer, for otherwise the Monk would have followed the Knight. None the less, the narrating poet does show some embarrassment at admitting such a tale to his collection, and tries to make it clear that he is not responsible for the offence which this scurrilous story may cause. His defence is that he is obliged to repeat the tales verbatim, whether decorous or not; and readers who prefer to avoid coarse language and vulgarity are advised to choose some other story, 'that toucheth gentillesse'. This disclaiming of responsibility is a joke typical of Chaucer, who pretends on other occasions to be nothing more than a peripheral figure reporting other men's stories and conversation; but the joke has its serious aspects. One reason why **"The Miller's Tale"** might require an apologetic preface is that it deliberately affronts the code of manners and the courtly standards respected throughout **"The Knight's Tale."** So long as we accept the make-believe situation that assigns one to the gentlemanly Knight and the other to the boorish Miller, the incompatibility of the two stories offers no difficulty; but when we reflect that in fact both tales are Chaucer's we appreciate why he might have felt some awkwardness in making one follow the other. Yet clearly his purposes required this—to an extent which is perhaps suggested by the Miller's aggressive determination to be heard, whatever objections are raised. In **"The Miller's Prologue"** a masterful impulse is seen elbowing its way to the front, and silencing the poet's misgivings by the kind of thrusting energy described in the portrait of the Miller, which speaks of his ability to break down doors 'at a renning with his heed'. An imaginative impulse of the same force appears to be driving Chaucer from the closed world of courtly ideals towards the lively informality of middle-class affairs and its graphically expressive language.

This development might have been foreseen from the beginning of Chaucer's poetic career, for even in the dream-poems of that early period he shows a wide-awake concern with the realities of common life, and makes some experiments with vernacular speech. These interests eventually found an important place in the design of **The Canterbury Tales,** where the master of ceremonies is a man of the people who judges the stories and their narrators from the standpoint of his own broad experience and common-sense. His comments in the links between the tales, as he praises one pilgrim or demands a story from another, keep us in touch with the unsophisticated terms of everyday life, and bring as contrast to the literary style adopted by some pilgrims a rough-textured idiom of spoken English. His rebuke to the Reeve, who seems disposed to ruminate and moralise instead of starting his tale, is characteristic of his vigorous forthrightness:

> Whan that oure Hoost hadde herd this sermon-
>   ing,
> He gan to speke as lordly as a king,
> And seide, 'What amounteth al this wit?
> What shul we speke alday of hooly writ? . . .
> Sey forth thy tale, and tarie nat the time;
> Lo, Depeford! and it is half-wey prime.
> Lo, Grenewich, ther many a shrewe is inne!
> It were al time thy tale to biginne.'

The references to Deptford and Greenwich and to the time of day—half-past seven in the morning—show Chaucer's imagination working inside the field of actual experience: a setting markedly at odds with the idealised background of courtly romance. A lively interest in the figures and happenings of the workaday world dominates Chaucer's poetry during the final phase of his career, superseding the absorption in courtly behaviour and literary conventions which had previously held him. The churlish Miller's insistence on being heard, and the challenge which his fabliau presents to the lofty assumptions of **"The Knight's Tale,"** symbolise the change of imaginative outlook so strongly registered in the earthy directness of the story which follows.

This final development of Chaucer's art does not involve a complete repudiation of courtly romance tradition. Some of its conventions are recognised in **"The Miller's Tale"**, most obviously in Absolon's affected wooing of Alison. But now the familiar conventions are being used satirically, partly to make Absolon more ridiculous and partly to show the comic incongruity of his genteel manners in the rough-and-tumble world of carpenters and cuckolds. Chaucer does not dissolve his longstanding attachment to courtly literature simply in the greater interest of describing common life, but in order to realise his remarkable gift as a comic writer. As we recognise from **"The Knight's Tale,"** the ideal of gentillesse, constancy and devoted service which courtly romance holds up invites serious respect from poet and audience alike. In such a rarefied atmosphere laughter would be out of place. That response is encouraged by the popular tales and anecdotes which propose no ideal standards, but describe life and human behaviour from a realistic viewpoint which accepts the indignities, farcical accidents and shameful misdemeanours which are part of common experience. When Chaucer's dreamer describes the elaborately figured gates of the House of Fame, refusing to give any detailed account of the beauty 'of this yates florisshinges',

> Ne of compasses, ne of kervinges,
> Ne how they hatte in masoneries,
> As corbetz, ful of imageries

the reader must feel awed and astonished; but the mention of the pop-hole for the cat in **"The Miller's Tale"**,

> ful lowe upon a bord,

> Ther as the cat was wont in for to crepe,

rouses amusement by its homely familiarity, and by the intrusion of something so everyday into the supposedly reserved enclosure of art. Before Chaucer's comic genius could fulfil itself, he had to part company with the courtly world and its unique, unearthly figures and move to the plane of humdrum actuality represented by such commonplace objects as ladders, coulters and kneading-tubs; where 'breed and chese, and good ale in a jubbe' stand on the tables, and where women—no longer etherealised and remote—are as physically tangible and appetising as a hoard of apples, 'leyd in hey or heeth'. A glance at some of the domestic terms used in **"The Miller's Tale"**—*barmclooth, kimelin, piggesnie, chiminee, viritoot*—suggests how far Chaucer has moved from the literary tradition of his courtly poems, to give the world of plebeian affairs its appropriate language.

This interest carries Chaucer much further. At several points of the story he brings in proverbial remarks, sometimes through the mouths of his characters. 'Men seyn thus', Nicholas reminds the carpenter as he concludes his instructions,

> 'Sende the wise, and sey no thing.'

Another proverb, quoted with the same prefatory comment, explains how Absolon's hopes of winning Alison are dashed by the fact that Nicholas lives under the same roof as she:

> Men seyn right thus, 'Alwey the nie slie
> Maketh the ferre leeve to be looth.'

These proverbial sayings do not in themselves indicate the growth of a new interest in Chaucer, for sayings of this kind can be found in most of his earlier poems. Like the comic tendency in the work of the same early period, this use of proverbs shows how the courtly Chaucer was drawn towards their pithy colloquial phrases and to a practical wisdom which bears little relevance to the outlook of high life. In the fabliaux of *The Canterbury Tales* this longstanding interest is given free rein, to be realised not only in proverbial sayings but in a much greater number of popular idioms and expressions, which give Chaucer's writing a particular energy and directness. So, in the futility of his efforts to win Alison, Absolon 'may blowe the bukkes horn'. He refuses to answer the smith's enquiry because he has 'moore tow on his distaf' than Gervase can guess; and he cares 'nat a bene' for the smith's teasing. The carpenter breaks into Nicholas' room to find his lodger sitting 'ay as stille as stoon', and gaping upwards

> As he had kiked on the newe moone.

In his tub 'the dede sleep' falls on the carpenter: when he wakes and cuts the rope holding him in mid-air, 'doun gooth al'. We hear of wafers 'piping hoot out of the gleede', and of a night 'derk as pich, or as the cole'. Alison makes Absolon 'hire ape', and when she hears of the threatened flood she acts 'as she wolde deye'. The humiliated Absolon weeps 'as dooth a child that is ybete', and his rival Nicholas promises himself a night of love 'if so be that the game wente alright'. Such idiomatic phrases and comparisons are a prominent feature of Chaucer's style in **"The Miller's Tale."** We cannot be certain that they are all taken from popular speech, though it seems unlikely that such expressions as 'what wol ye bet than weel?' 'be as be may', or 'him fil ne bet ne wers' were not in common use. Where Chaucer did not use proverbial or traditional forms of speech, he appears to have improvised phrases and idioms in keeping with their terseness and pungency. There is nothing patronising in the concern with common life which the tale requires of Chaucer, but to the contrary an enthusiastic adoption of a vernacular style which gives his work its final achievement.

But Chaucer does not abandon the serious and thoughtful interests which appear in his poetry from the first. It is clear that he was an enthusiastic reader, for few of his poems do not digress from the story to summarise or discuss another book or learned topic. **"The Nun's Priest's Tale"** is repeatedly interrupted by such digressions, and the Wife of Bath's racy anecdotes about her married life are mixed with arguments about religious doctrine, and accounts of her fifth husband's nightly readings from a 'book of wikked wives'. However deeply Chaucer becomes involved in the comedy of ordinary life, he does not forget the reserved and scholarly part of himself dedicated to the world of books—a figure whom he himself satirises more than once. It should not surprise us to discover that the setting of **"The Miller's Tale"** is a university town, and that one of its main characters is—like the Wife of Bath's fifth husband—a scholar. We are told that Nicholas' studies have taken a turn towards astrology, a subject of considerable interest to Chaucer, several of whose tales contain long references to astrological lore. This feature of the hero's character allows Chaucer to comment on Nicholas' astrolabe, his augrim stones and his copy of the *Almagest,* and to describe the kind of astrological forecast which Nicholas is able to provide. But these scholarly abilities also play an important part in the story. The outwitting of the simple carpenter, who considers himself a more discerning person than the study-crazed Nicholas, represents the triumph of scholarly subtlety over bourgeois native wit, and in this respect offsets Chaucer's imaginative commitment to common life. Moreover, the idea of foretelling the future is a vital comic theme of the tale, hinted at in the Miller's prefatory remarks about being 'inquisitif of Goddes privetee' and most immediately taken up in the account of Nicholas' powers as an astrologer.

Oxford, the amorous scholar, and the theme of astrological forecasting, are elements of **"The Miller's Tale"** which Chaucer added to the fabliau whose main idea he followed. [In *Sources and Analogues of Chaucer's Canterbury Tales*] Stith Thompson lists ten analogues of the tale, in German, Italian, Flemish and English, and concludes that the story was part of an oral tradition during Chaucer's lifetime. One of the most suggestive of the written analogues, dating from the fourteenth century, is told of Heile of Bersele. Unlike Alison in **"The Miller's Tale,"** the heroine is a courtesan whose favours are sought by three men; a miller, a priest, and a smith. She arranges for each of them to visit her at a different time during the same night: the miller first, followed by the priest at the ringing of the sleep-bell, and by the smith as soon as the thief-bell is rung—divisions of the night which perhaps correspond in

Chaucer's story to curfew-time, lauds, and first cock. The first client duly arrives, and later in the night is disturbed by the priest's plea to be admitted. The miller wishes to hide, and Heile advises him to conceal himself in a trough suspended from the rafters by a rope. When he is hidden, Heile lets in the priest, who also proceeds to enjoy himself; though subsequently he lapses into remorse and begins to quote from the scriptures, foretelling God's punishment of man by fire and water, and concluding that all mankind will be drowned. Sitting above in his trough, the miller reflects that this may well be. Now the smith arrives, but Heile pleads indisposition and refuses to admit him. As he begs for a kiss, Heile persuades the priest to put his buttocks out of the window to be kissed in mistake for her mouth. The trick works all too successfully, and realising how grossly he has been abused the smith runs back to his forge, heats an iron and returns to Heile's window. There he implores her for a second kiss, and when the priest repeats his trick he receives a shocking burn from the smith's red-hot iron. Hearing him screaming for water, the miller supposes that the great flood must already have come, and decides to launch himself in his wooden vessel. He cuts the rope by which the trough is suspended, and crashes to the floor, where he breaks an arm and a thigh. The priest thinks that the devil has burst in upon him, and in his frenzy he falls into the privy. He returns home painfully burned and befouled from his night's adventure, to be put to scorn and shamed.

The family resemblance of **"The Miller's Tale"** to this Flemish fabliau is obvious enough. The trough hanging from the rafters, with its occupant fearing the flood; the rejected lover's misplaced kiss, and the revenge he takes with the red-hot iron, are major features of both. But in his handling of the tale Chaucer has reshaped the material to his own design, sharpening the comedy of the story by a much subtler treatment of its situations, and refining some of its coarser elements out of existence. The heroine of his tale, described in one of the most evocative of his many character-portraits, is an eighteen-year-old wife whose eager vitality and freshness associate her with the lively young animals of an English countryside. Her husband, a stock figure of ridicule in taking a wife so much younger than himself, forfeits more sympathy by attempting to confine her wild beauty; and when Alison surrenders herself to a lover of her own age and spirit she invites no moral censure. Rather it is her husband the carpenter who continues to attract ridicule, by the fear and credulity which lead him so easily into Nicholas' snare, and which lead to his uncomfortable night in the kneading-tub while Nicholas occupies his bed. The carpenter, who corresponds to the first of Heile's clients in the Flemish analogue, is transformed by Chaucer into a much more comic figure; who is tricked into taking refuge in the wooden tub not to avoid being seen by the priest, but to escape the second flood forecast by Nicholas, and who is cuckolded into the bargain. (pp. 1-10)

Much of the immediate comedy of **"The Miller's Tale"** lies in the central episode, lines 315-502, to which nothing in the Flemish analogue corresponds. The passage describes how, when the carpenter has broken into Nicholas' chamber to rescue him from his petrified 'agonie', he is gradually prepared for the disclosure of the great secret discovered by Nicholas; and then brainwashed to the point where he can be persuaded to regard a domestic tub as a sea-going vessel in which he may embark 'as into shippes bord'. Few things in Chaucer have the sustained ironic comedy of this impudent hoaxing of a suspicious husband, who is so distracted by fear of the impending flood that he cannot scent a plot, even when Nicholas gravely warns him that he and his wife must occupy separate tubs, hanging far apart,

> For that bitwixe yow shal be no sinne.

The whole of this richly comic sequence stems from the single innovation of giving Nicholas—the counterpart of Heile's remorseful priest—the ability to predict a great flood, not while he is in bed with the heroine but as the means of bringing about their stolen night together. The change of character from priest to scholar-astrologer does not involve any great alteration of circumstances, but its effect on the tale is a striking increase of narrative compactness. Chaucer's instinctive recognition of the improvement which this change would produce is typical of the imaginative leap which enables a great poet to connect and knit together the elements of his work into a strong, coherent design.

The hoaxing of the carpenter is not the only consequence of introducing the theme of astrology. Belief in prediction and foreknowledge is treated as a theme of **"The Miller's Tale,"** with its centre in the episode describing Nicholas' warning of the great rain that is to fall 'a Monday next, at quarter night'. Before this point of the story the theme is expressed with heavy irony when the carpenter, supposing that Nicholas has driven himself mad with his studies, makes a plain man's comment on the foolish impracticality of the scholar's life, and singles out astrology for special ridicule. 'So ferde another clerk with astromie', he tells his servingman,

> He walked into the feeldes, for to prye
> Upon the sterres, what ther sholde bifalle,
> Til he was in a marle-pit yfalle;
> He saugh nat that.

Initially the joke is on the carpenter, whose simpler intelligence will not prevent his falling into the snare which Nicholas has prepared for him and is waiting to spring. As he discourses about the general superiority of men 'that swink' or work honestly with their hands, the carpenter is about to become the blindly credulous victim of a scholar whose ingenuity lies beyond a simple man's grasp. But the final episode of the story suggests that the carpenter is right after all; for like this other clerk, Nicholas fails to foresee or to avoid his own immediate fate when he tries to repeat the indignity just practised upon Absolon. Painfully burned and outwitted by his rival, he might echo Absolon's cry of regret, 'Allas, I ne hadde yblent!' but swept along by unthinking impulse, neither Nicholas nor the carpenter has considered taking precautions. In consequence, each of these characters is precipitated into a form of personal disaster which might have been foreseen, but which comes as a totally unexpected and humiliating shock. In the pitch-dark night Absolon obtains his long-desired kiss from Alison, but immediately realises that he

has defiled himself by an unmentionable contact: Nicholas thinks to crown his daring achievement but is caught by the vengeful Absolon with his coulter; and the carpenter awakes from his fantasy of Noah's Flood to discover that the real purpose of his vigil in the kneading-tub was to allow Nicholas to cuckold him, and that his anxious precautions have had the wrong object. (pp. 11-14)

The Miller's use of the phrase 'Goddes privetee' [in his prologue] is unexpected, since nothing in his previous conversation looks towards this idea; but clearly Chaucer's mind is beginning to work upon an important concept of his tale. The wifely secrets referred to in this passage concern her sexual life, into which a husband should not enquire too closely if he wishes to remain contentedly assured of her fidelity. The carpenter might have need of the Miller's advice, especially since he shares the Miller's views about the foolishness of prying into God's secret acts and intentions; and even more since his wife is young and desirable. The association of wifely secrets with divine ones in the Prologue has a special interest, for here Chaucer plainly admits a comic purpose which in the tale itself is never more than implicit. There the two kinds of 'privetee' are linked only through a narrative connection: the fantastic story which the carpenter is induced to regard as a divine secret being in fact the means by which Nicholas and Alison will consummate their 'deerne love'. In this consummation wifely 'privetee' of another kind will play an indispensable role. Chaucer's readers are not allowed to overlook this tacit pun, for at the comic climax of the tale Absolon, whether fortunately or not, makes physical contact with this secret, which is described in one of the broadest lines of Chaucer's outspoken story.

This comically indecent allusion, with other words and phrases which reflect the Miller's taste for 'harlotrie', might make it seem hard to justify a claim that Chaucer has refined the cruder elements of the original fabliau out of existence. Any version of the tale which retains the crucial episode of the misdirected kiss, treated as frankly as Chaucer has chosen to do, must invite the kind of censure which he tries to side-step in his apology for the Miller's vulgar manners. What excuses the realistic bluntness of Chaucer's language at this point of the tale is the moral justice of Absolon's humiliation, which is brought home by the use of such downright terms as this prim and fastidious character might himself find shocking. The transformation of Heile's third client into this provincial amorist and fop is the most remarkable of the changes which the three figures of the fabliau have undergone in Chaucer's re-working of the story. By the alteration Chaucer loses a convenient feature of the traditional story, in that being a smith the insulted third customer can fetch a red-hot iron from his own forge; but this is a small price to pay for so great an increase in comedy. Where the smith of the fabliau becomes a comic figure only through his repulse at the window, Absolon is from the first an absurdity whose fashionable affectation cries out for the reversal that will bring him to his senses. Chaucer makes him a parish clerk who also functions as barber, lawyer and public entertainer in the taverns; proud of his ability to 'casten to and fro' with his legs in dancing and to pleyen songes on a smal rubible;

and prouder still of his fine head of hair, which like his modish costume he keeps immaculate and trim. His obsessive neatness, his perfumed breath and the scrupulous delicacy which makes him 'somdeel squaymous of farting', combine to present an effeminate figure who is comically out of place in the robust plebeian setting of the story. This absurdity is increased by his anxiety to win popular approval by a variety of useful services, and by his painstaking efforts to play the lover with a sensitive refinement which might interest the Prioress. His wooing of Alison begins, significantly enough, immediately after the direct sexual assault by which Nicholas secures her promise of love 'at his comandement'; and so Absolon's case is lost even before he opens it. His technique and outlook as a lover attract only ridicule from Alison, who like Chaucer's reader sees in Nicholas the standard of a more manly determination and ardour. He tries to impress Alison by acting Herod in a Miracle play, by serenading her in his high-pitched voice, and by sending her every kind of present; and to prove his courteous regard for women he refuses to accept her religious offerings, as though they were intended as a gift for him. But despite his declarations of passionate love for Alison, and the lovesick looks which he bestows upon her in church he seems careful to avoid any direct approach to her, and he does not venture any boldly physical contact. By carrying out most of his wooing through intermediaries—an accepted tradition of *fine amour*—he satisfies appearances and provides a convenient cover for his disinclination to become involved in a purposeful liaison. He prefers to play a self-indulgent game of romantic love for the pleasure of admiring himself in the pathetic role of neglected suitor. 'No wonder is thogh that I swelte and swete', he tells Alison in an effort to melt her very proper scorn,

> I moorne as dooth a lamb after the tete.
> Ywis, lemman, I have swich love-longinge
> That lik a turtel trewe is my moorninge.
> I may nat ete na moore than a maide.

His account of himself is doubly foolish, in its unmanly comparisons and in the self-pitying commentary that accompanies his description. Absolon is sufficiently detached from his 'moorninge' to offer suitably touching analogies with his dejected condition. The falsity of his performance is exposed when he is allowed to take a kiss from Alison, in the state of spiritual exaltation required of a courtly lover, and realises what his mouth has actually touched. His frantic attempts to scrub away the sense of a shameful contact,

> With dust, with sond, with straw, with clooth,
>   with chippes,

reveals a general abhorrence of physicality, and the insincerity of his appeal for Alison's sexual interest. Her practical joke acquaints Absolon with the actuality which his elaborately showy courtship has been careful to avoid—the fundamental truth about his 'sweete cinamome', who is now shown to be the creature of animal appetites and functions whom Nicholas has never treated otherwise. The need to shock Absolon out of his romantic delusion explains why, in Chaucer's version of the story, it is not one of the heroine's lovers but she herself who receives the misdirected kiss. His comic reversal goes further than curing Absolon of what Chaucer rightly calls his 'maladie'. It drives him to the opposite extreme of hating and reviling women—a transformation which discloses the deep-rooted fear of sexuality previously disguised by his imposture as a gay and impetuous lover.

The sense of moral purpose behind this discrediting of a romantic fake justifies Chaucer's use of expressions which otherwise might seem outrageous. In the whole context of **"The Miller's Tale"** such occasional outspokenness is less shocking, for it springs naturally from the poem's close contact with the habits and circumstances of common life. We are not committed simply to a world of bumpkin clumsiness and vulgarity, for Chaucer's images repeatedly evoke impressions of delectable tastes and perfumes—liquorice and ginger, honey-sweetened bragget, mead, spiced ale and wine, cardamom and cinnamon—which give the poem something of their own delicacy. But the story also brings us into imaginative contact with simple, solid, coarse-grained reality, and with everyday physical objects that can be seized and put to use: a great measure 'of mighty ale', the ladders which the carpenter contrives,

> To climben by the ronges and the stalkes
> Into the tubbes hanginge in the balkes;

the leather purse hanging from Alison's girdle,

> Tasseled with silk, and perled with latoun,

and her own body, slim and sinuous as a weasel's. This could not be an environment hospitable to Absolon's affected manners, which call for rebuke not only from Alison but from the poet whose outlook is given form and substance by **"The Miller's Tale."** His description of the heroine tells us most of what we need to know about the nature of the world which his poem creates:

> Ful smale ypulled were hire browes two,
> And tho were bent and blake as any sloo.
> She was ful moore blisful on to see
> Than is the newe pere-jonette tree,
> And softer than the wolle is of a wether.

(pp. 15-20)

The portrait of Alison characterises the qualities of imaginative directness and honesty of writing found throughout **"The Miller's Tale"** where Chaucer exploits the simple strength of vernacular English. Here at least there is no need for the pilgrim narrator to apologise for the uncouth style of the story which he repeats, for writing could hardly be more open and unforced. Nicholas' directions on boat-building typify this entirely natural style:

> Anon go gete us faste into this in
> A kneding trogh, or ellis a kymelin,
> For ech of us, but looke that they be large,
> In which we mowe swimme as in a barge,
> And han therinne vitaille suffisant
> But for a day: fy on the remenant!
> The water shal aslake and goon away
> Aboute prime upon the nexte day.

This is not a particularly important section of the poem, but even here the language and expression have the compact soundness of a good apple. It is by the standard of such integrity, whether of writing or of human character, that Absolon is shown to be an impostor and exposed to ridicule. The physical liveliness which gives him a superficial likeness to Alison is merely an outward habit: his gaiety is a feverish sham, not springing from an abundance of natural energy but devised to draw attention to himself. His imposture serves the needs of the comic tale, but it also helps to identify the quality which Chaucer's writing acquires in this final phase—truth of substance. It is by this standard that **"The Miller's Tale"** as well as Absolon deserves to be judged.

The comic spirit of the tale has the same genuineness. It depends in some part upon farcical characters and incidents, in particular perhaps upon the reduction of the credulous carpenter to a distracted and trembling figure who, once installed in his makeshift boat, collapses exhausted and snores out the night of his cuckolding. But comedy is not simply a matter of funny scenes and circumstances. It involves an attitude to life prompted by vitality, assurance, and a sense of exuberant pleasure not in themselves amusing, but essential to the comic spirit. We recognise this positive and excited response in Chaucer's writing even in passages of **"The Miller's Tale"** which have no immediate comic intention, such as the account of Nicholas' chamber:

> His Almageste, and bookes grete and smale,
> His astrelabie, longinge for his art,
> His augrim stones, layen faire apart
> On shelves couched at his beddes heed;
> His presse ycovered with a falding reed.

There is nothing to make us laugh here, but a sense of delighted enumeration in the cataloguing of wonderful things—'His Almageste . . . His astrelabie . . . His augrim stones . . . his beddes heed, His presse'—which represents the narrator's enthusiasm in a very contagious form. A similar kind of delight is felt in the remark about the personal attractiveness of Nicholas:

> And he himself as sweete as is the roote
> Of licoris, or any cetewale.

A more complex comic response is evoked by Nicholas as he envisages to the carpenter their meeting on the morning after the great disaster:

> Thanne shaltow swimme as mirie, I undertake,
> As dooth the white doke after hire drake.
> Thanne wol I clepe, 'How, Alison! how, John!
> Be mirie, for the flood wol passe anon.'
> And thou wolt seyn, 'Hail, maister Nicholay!
> Good morwe, I se thee wel, for it is day.'

In predicting their cheerful greetings across the flood water, Nicholas implies that he and the carpenter are simple, guileless men in a world whose charming innocence is aptly symbolised by the white duck. This is obviously comic; but it is impossible to read his speech without also sensing the hilarious enjoyment which Nicholas derives from the complete success of his hoax, which has now reduced the carpenter to a state of mindless compliance with his plot. He must not betray this pleasure; but the story which he is telling the carpenter allows him to express his own high-spirited jubilation through the excited shouting

of the three survivors. The words which he puts into the carpenter's mouth,

> 'Hail, maister Nicholay!
> Good morwe, I se thee wel, for it is day'

represent his own exuberance, not at survival but at the triumphant proof of his ingenuity and daring. Alison is as good as won.

The jubilant feelings which Nicholas ascribes to the speakers in this forecast characterise the comic spirit of **"The Miller's Tale"**, and not just his own crazily improbable story. Like many of Chaucer's figures, Nicholas is here functioning as a story-teller within the bigger tale to which he belongs. This initial likeness to his own creator is enhanced by the inventiveness he displays in contriving his plot, and by his ability to talk the carpenter into treating his fantastic prediction as serious truth. His inventiveness is of course Chaucer's, whose re-shaping of fabliau material proves his instinctive feeling for a well-knit story; and so too is the persuasiveness which induces us, as readers, to accept its make-believe happenings and figures. But Nicholas is most like Chaucer in the self-confidence and buoyancy of spirit which he reveals in his story-telling. If Nicholas can feel jubilant at the success of his undertaking, so can Chaucer in his greater achievement; and evidence of this elation shows itself in the unclouded joyousness of **"The Miller's Tale."** Those who follow the apologetic advice of the pilgrim narrator and 'chese another tale' may find greater morality and courtesy elsewhere, but not a poem more clearly marked by the satisfaction of putting so masterful a creative gift to work. The farcical events of the story account only partially for the exultant comic spirit of **"The Miller's Tale."** The rest is explained by a characteristic activity of the poet's imagination, which reflects in what it creates the exhilarating pleasure of his task. (pp. 22-5)

> *James Winny, in an introduction to* The Miller's Prologue & Tale from the Canterbury Tales *by Geoffrey Chaucer, edited by James Winny, Cambridge at the University Press, 1971, pp. 1-25.*

Thomas W. Ross (essay date 1972)

[*Ross is an American scholar who has edited Thomas Kyd's* The Spanish Tragedy *(1968) and the "Miller's Tale" for the* Variorum Chaucer *(1983). In the following excerpt, he discusses the use of bawdy language in the* Canterbury Tales.]

Chaucer called a "queynt" a "queynt," but only when there was a good reason to be blunt. In all his works, there is hardly a word of bawdiness for its own sake. When he mentions sex or excretion, he almost never excites disgust or prurience.

Chaucer uses risqué words for one major purpose: to delineate comic characters and thus to make us laugh. Having said this, however, we have not really provided a meaningful assessment of the poet's methods. We need to distinguish and to judge his various devices, including the use of bawdy language for comic effect. Admittedly, in pious tracts like the **"Parson's Tale,"** the poet uses sex for homiletic purposes, not for laughs. Much more common, however, is his use of bawdry in the portraits of the Friar and the Monk (for instance) in the **"General Prologue"** to the *Canterbury Tales.* They derive their humorous qualities in large measure from Chaucer's indecent innuendos.

A widely respected critic [Haldeen Braddy in her 1966 *Southern Folklore Quarterly* article "Chaucer's Bawdy Tongue"] has stated—more unequivocally than I would dare—that in Chaucer's poetry "the speech always fits the speaker." There are occasional surprises. For instance, Chaucer gives the smug and sober Merchant one of the most ribald tales. Usually, however, where we anticipate bawdiness, we find it. There are some Chaucerian characters for whom lewdness is singularly appropriate. We expect to hear forthright language from Alison of Bath, and we are not disappointed. Some critics speak of her as if she were the real narrator of [the **"Wife of Bath's Prologue and Tale"**]. To counteract this sort of sentimental interpretation, we need to remind ourselves that Chaucer himself is ultimately responsible for the words his personages utter—even when he explicitly denies that responsibility. It is sometimes hard to judge the poet's tone when he forestalls possible charges of purveying scurrility. His customary trick is to claim that he is simply reporting others' words: the drunken Miller is a "cherl," as everybody knows. *He* said those words—not *I*, Geoffrey Chaucer.

Is the poet making a serious apology here, hoping to avoid the label of "foulmouthed" Chaucer, or is this another of those postures which, like self-deprecation, medieval authors assume? It is no doubt naïve to take Chaucer at his word in every passage where he makes these disclaimers. But, on occasion, he seems to be utterly serious. The "retractions" are the most familiar of these *mea culpa* apologies for smuttiness. He is ashamed, he says, of certain of the tales—"thilke (those) that sownen into (tend toward) synne." On the other hand, he is proud of his (clumsy and uncertain) translation of Boethius and of the saints' legends, which most modern readers find dull. In a very real sense, the pathological asceticism of the **"Second Nun's Tale"** is more offensive than are the Wife of Bath's terms for her wondrous vulva.

The Wife's "queynt" was probably as taboo in mixed company in the fourteenth century as is its twentieth-century counterpart "cunt." Alison uses the term without a blush; she is very much aware of what she is doing. She also varies her terms nimbly enough with "quoniam" and "bel chose," both pseudo-learned circumlocutions. It is amusing that she knows so many synonyms for her prized private part. The richness of the Wife's vocabulary tells us as much about her, indeed, as does her account of her five husbands in her prologue.

Chaucer often has no "persona" between himself and his readers or listeners. Most of us take at face value his remarks at the beginning of the *Book of the Duchess* that he has suffered from love for eight years. Huppé and Robertson [in their *Fruyt and Chaf*] claim that the whole thing is a Christian allegory and that Chaucer is not talking about *real* love—sexual, physical, secular love—but about Christian $\alpha\gamma\alpha\pi\eta$. I doubt if these scholars have

persuaded any but their most devoted acolytes. The lovesickness of Chaucer is quite in tune with the amusing pose assumed in the *Parliament of Fowls,* where Scipio perceives that the poet has lost his taste for love:

> But natheles, although that thow be dul,
> Yit that thow canst not do, yit mayst thow se.
> For many a man that may nat stonde a pul,
> It liketh hym at the wrastlyng for to be,
> And demeth yit wher [whether] he do bet or he.

The encouragement of voyeurism is tempered by the wonderfully appropriate wrestling metaphor and by the notion that though Chaucer may have passed his prime, he is still experienced enough to judge lovemaking like a connoisseur.

This is not to commit the heresy of reading literature as if it were veiled autobiography. We cannot legitimately interest ourselves in the question of whether Chaucer was *actually* a voyeur; neither is it the critic's concern to try to guess whether in real life the poet satisfied his wife Philippa in bed, or whether his "rape" of Cecily Chaumpaigne involved forced entry or simply kidnaping.

The interesting thing about Chaucer's "direct" or "personal" comments is their literary effect, not any imagined betrayal of the secrets in the poet's heart. If in a story about love a writer comments on the nature of the emotion, without using the intermediary of invented dialogue or the interior monologue of a character, his remarks will modify the significance of the erotic events in the narrative. In the **"Merchant's Tale,"** the old lecher Januarie tells his young wife May to strip, since "hir clothes dide hym encombraunce," and she obeys. Chaucer interrupts to comment:

> But lest that precious [prudish] folk be with me
>   wrooth,
> How that he wroghte, I dar nat to yow telle.

Is this simply the common rhetorical flourish called *occupatio*—feigned inability to describe something, usually because of its complexity or grandeur? Or is the pose of pudicity a subtle way of suggesting that it is best not to describe such a grotesquely mismatched coupling?

The poet continues:

> Or wheither hire thoughte it [it seemed to her]
>   paradys or helle.
> But heere I lete hem werken in hir wyse
> Til evensong rong, and that they moste aryse.

We know perfectly well, because Chaucer gives us plenty of hints, that May does not find it "paradys" in the arms of bristly old Januarie. And we savor the suggestion of effort that "werken" elicits. Even if this *is* merely the rhetorical trick called *occupatio*, it functions very well indeed.

Later on in the **"Merchant's Tale,"** Chaucer chooses to be direct when describing the sexual act. It is entirely proper that he should make this shift in style here, since he wants us to understand the coarse vigor of young Damyan's lovemaking, together with the bitch-in-rut pleasure that May takes in the union. The poet begins with an apology to the ladies; but this time, claiming rudeness of education and sensibility, he proceeds:

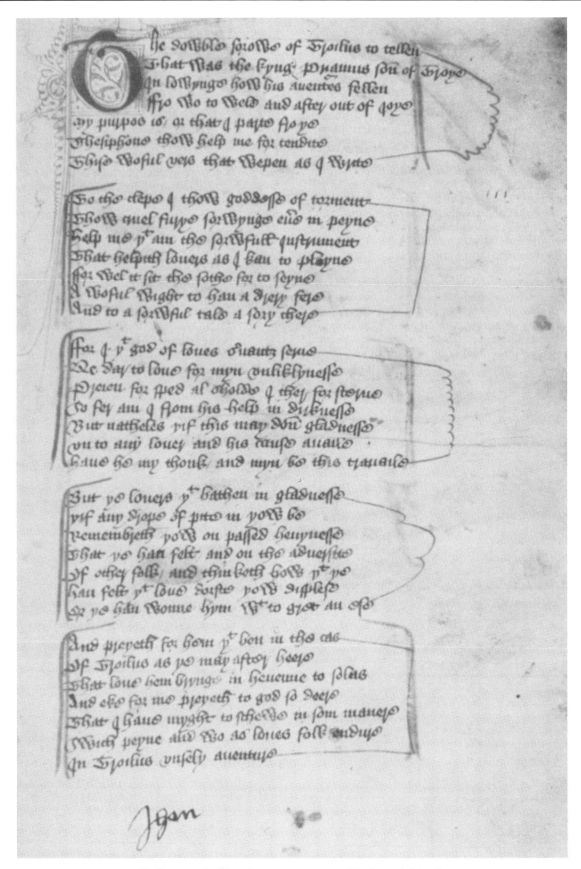

The first page of a fifteenth-century manuscript of Troilus and Criseyde.

Ladyes, I prey yow that ye be nat wrooth;
I kan nat glose, I am a rude man—
And sodeynly anon this Damyan
Gan pullen up the smok, and in he throng.

The deliberate pleonasm "sodeynly anon" makes Damyan's haste very clear: "throng" is indeed rude—deeper and more violent than "thrust."

Then Chaucer reassumes his posture of pudicity. His reluctance to describe what he has already portrayed, in vivid terms, is very funny. Januarie's blindness has been miraculously cured and he suddenly can see what the squire Damyan is doing to his wife May aloft in their "nest." The young stud has "dressed" May:

In swich manere it may nat been expressed,
But if I wolde speke uncurteisly.

The prim disclaimer comes too late, like an "Oh, excuse me, please!" after a particularly noisy and aromatic breaking of wind.

Chaucer thus uses various shades of comic sexual allusion and description to expose the coarseness of May and Damyan; to remind us of the senile stupidity of Januarie; and to present himself in an ironically and deliberately inconsistent light—now prudish, now forthright indeed.

But isn't it the Merchant, not Chaucer, who is at one moment rude and demure the next? Possibly the poet wants us to imagine that when there is commentary in the tale, we are "overhearing" the voice of the putative narrator—the Merchant, a henpecked husband unhappily married to a "shrewe at al." If it is this "persona" who so slyly reveals the vixenish crudity of the young wife May, then he (the Merchant) is avenging himself, by means of the tale, on womankind in general and more particularly, though in absentia, on his own nagging wife.

This additional level of narrative subtlety is not necessary, however, for an appreciation of the bawdy humor of the **"Merchant's Tale."** Indeed, many readers would deny that the "persona" device functions at all in this particular story. Chaucer could have assigned the *fabliau* to several of the other Pilgrims with equal appropriateness. The bond between tale and teller is not strong, particularly when contrasted with the links between Friar, Summoner, Miller, or Reeve and their tales.

Shakespeare's characters show a wider range of concern with sex than do Chaucer's. Hal's boisterous reference to the hot wench in flame-colored taffeta and Falstaff's boast about frequenting bawdy houses *are* like Chaucer's lubricious humor. But Lear's disgust over the simpering dame whose face between her forks presages snow; his Fool's sad little song about the codpiece; and Thersites' "greasy" talk about lust and venereal disease—these things are quite alien to Chaucer.

There are two reasons that this is true: Chaucer writes no dark comedies and no tragedies in the Shakespearean sense, and therefore references like Hamlet's bitter "nunnery" (which had a second meaning—brothel) and *country* matters" are not appropriate in his works. Second, and perhaps of equal importance, syphilis was unknown in fourteenth-century England. The horrors of the pox and

the futile treatments of the disease made a deep impression on Shakespeare's audience, and his characters frequently refer, directly and obliquely, to these ghastly matters.

It is therefore odd, perhaps, that some of Shakespeare's contemporaries found Chaucer shocking. In his *Apologie of Poetrie* (1591), Sir John Harington condemned the **"Miller's Tale"** and the **"Wife of Bath's Tale"** (by which he doubtless meant her prologue) and berated Chaucer for his "flat scurrilitie." Harington's prudery is particularly ironic, since he is probably best known today as the author of the *Metamorphosis of Ajax,* a cloacal and coprophiliac treatise on the water closet. The title itself contains a Rabelaisian pun on "a jakes"—a privy.

Throughout the sixteenth and seventeenth centuries, indeed, "Chaucer's jest" meant something indecent and disgusting, and "Canterbury Tale" was a term of contempt, "meaning either a story with no truth in it, or a vain and scurrilous tale."

Of course, Shakespeare, Spenser, and other Elizabethans revered Chaucer too—as the well of English undefiled, the first great name in English poetry. Side by side with the encomiums, however, there were expressions of prim distaste throughout the seventeenth, eighteenth, and nineteenth centuries. In her *Unfinished Sketches* (1713-14), Lady Mary Wortley Montagu found fault with Chaucer's "ribaldry and rhyme," reminding us again that during the Renaissance, Englishmen had lost the key to Middle English pronunciation and prosody. In his *Imitations of Horace* (1737), Pope published his often-quoted epithet for Skelton, the sixteenth-century Poet Laureate; few remember that it was coupled with an attack on Chaucer:

Chaucer's worst ribaldry is learn'd by rote
And beastly Skelton Heads of Houses quote.

The couplet is a satirical thrust at the evils of Pope's times, of course, not at Dan Geoffrey. Wrongheaded as it may seem today, it is at least testimony that the Augustans still read Chaucer, though "misread" might be more appropriate.

With all their reverence for native "antiquities," the Romantics persisted in expressing shock at Chaucer's bawdiness. In 1807, Byron wrote that he found the poet "obscene and contemptible." Four years later in his "Hints from Horace," he linked "Chaucer and old Ben" [Jonson], calling them "quaint and careless, anything but chaste." In his notes for a lecture written in 1818, Coleridge paired Chaucer with Boccaccio, finding both guilty of "gross and disgusting licentiousness." And as late as 1856, Edward Fitzgerald, the translator of the *Rubaiyat,* could still call him "licentious."

Victorian prudery, that familiar and often unjustly maligned whipping boy, was probably also one of the reasons that nobody has made a systematic study of Chaucer's "harlotrye," his indecorous words and innuendos. His first great modern editor was a Victorian clergyman, the Reverend W. W. Skeat, D.D., who was also a professor at Oxford. As was the custom among scholars at the end of the last century, when they were obliged to explain something indecent, they used Latin. The ladylike, of both sexes, found Skeat's Latin euphemism *pudendum* (literally "the shameful thing") less offensive than "vagina." The medical term is actually a metaphor, meaning "sheath" (for a sword). In our time, Skeat's two great followers, F. N. Robinson and A. C. Baugh—enlightened, liberal, American, Ivy-League professors and editors—still gloss "queynte" by calling on Skeat's Victorian Latin word.

Even today, Chaucer's marginal glossers and translators have trouble with the bawdy bits. For instance, the Wife of Bath tells one of her husbands that he has nothing to complain about:

> Ye shul have queynte right ynogh at eve.

In the modern "ponies," this becomes "tail"; "can have all you can take when day is done"; "have intercourse"; "you can have me all you want at night"; "evening rations"; and "i.e., lovemaking." The range is amusing; from the pompous-clinical to the military, with some boys' latrine terms thrown in. These (understandably) pusillanimous paraphrases remind us again that poetry is untranslatable, and that Chaucer's comic obscenity can be appreciated only in Middle English.

In Skeat's time, scientific lexicography was just beginning: the monumental *Oxford English Dictionary* had just begun its publication, which was not completed until the 1930s. Even this great scholarly work does not include the commonest four-letter word for intercourse, "fuck." Chaucer's "swyve" is there—perhaps because the editors thought *it* could be printed with a plain (and proper) mark *obsolete*.

In the 1950s, Hans Kurath and his fellows at the University of Michigan began publication of the *Middle English Dictionary*, less than half of which has appeared. The *MED* editors were precise, comprehensive, and not squeamish. Nonetheless they, like the *OED* staff, were not always sensitive to possible double entendres. Dictionary-makers *should* be suspicious of such things, no doubt, since many of Chaucer's suspected innuendos cannot be proved with scientific lexicographic precision. Therefore many of the entries in my study cannot display an *imprimatur* like "cited in *MED*" or "supported by contemporary quotation from *OED*." I must resort to terms like "possible," "likely," and "probable—especially in this context."

Between the appearance of the *OED* and the first fascicles of the *MED*, there developed three new kinds of scholarly approach, all important to the study of Chaucer's "harlotrye": first, Partridge's studies of slang (however much they owe to Henley and Farmer) and his seminal *Shakespeare's Bawdy;* then the work of the critics who study Chaucer's use of rhetorical devices; and, third, the emergence of "patristic exegesis," led by D. W. Robertson, Jr.

Partridge's candid study of Shakespeare's indecent words and innuendos is an urbane, if not always critical, analysis. I have imitated its format in this book. It revealed for the first time to a popular audience the thread (warp? woof?) of "low" references that runs throughout English speech and throughout the works of England's greatest poet.

We owe Partridge an immense debt. But for him, we would miss (for instance) the obscene fun hidden, like a wickedly gleaming golden filament, in the secondary meanings of "die" in Shakespeare's day (e.g., Enobarbus on Cleopatra). Neither Partridge nor any other critic can *prove* that "die" meant to have an orgasm, but he can persuade us that in certain contexts this meaning is very likely.

Even Partridge, overzealous as he sometimes is, misses some things. He seems not to have been familiar with the popularity of rhetorical devices in the Middle Ages of Renaissance. If one knows that the puns in Chaucer (or in Shakespeare) were a "flower" of rhetoric called *paranomasia,* one need not go through the tedious business of arguing against the half-literate superstition that the pun is the lowest form of wit. Had Eric Partridge known the work of scholars like E. R. Curtius, who described the medieval and Renaissance admiration for such rhetorical devices, he would doubtless have detected many more of Shakespeare's paranomastic bawdy references.

Almost twenty years ago, Helge Kökeritz, perhaps our foremost philologist in Middle and Early Modern English, wrote a revolutionary essay ["Rhetorical Word Play in Chaucer" *PMLA*, 1954] in which he identified the link in Chaucer between rhetoric and puns. In it he traced the amusing story of how it slowly dawned on the experts that medieval poetry owed something to paranomasia. Kökeritz began with Thomas R. Lounsbury, who found only two puns in Chaucer in 1892; F. N. Robinson identified nine in 1933. This was "before readers became aware of Chaucer's indebtedness to the precepts of medieval rhetoric," particularly to tropes like *traductio, adnominatio,* and *significatio*—the last a variety of equivocation. Native poetry adopted these figures from Latin. Kökeritz found a large number in Chaucer, both innocent and bawdy.

More recently, readers have not only identified a great many more Chaucerian puns but have begun to distinguish subtle differences among their effects. As Norman D. Hinton puts it [in his 1964 *American Notes & Queries* article "More Puns in Chaucer"], the puns

> are not simply the result of a superabundant sense of humor, nor a 'low' mind, nor even the result of a mixed style. . . . Most of the puns tend to complicate the thing which is being said. I do not want to claim that this makes Chaucer a more 'ironic' writer, or a composer of verse with 'levels of meaning' (which is too often taken to mean that the verse in question exists in separate layers, like a Viennese torte). It does suggest, however, that Chaucerian verse is more intricate than many critics have been willing to admit—that Chaucer is saying more than one thing at a time in more places than where previously suspected.

At about the same time as the revival of interest in medieval rhetoric—together with the recognition of the intricacy of Chaucer's poetry—there emerged the neo-exegetes. They are a group of erudite specialists whose findings run counter to, but also support, a study like this one, which depends to a considerable degree upon multiple meanings in Middle English poetry. D. W. Robertson, Jr., and Bernard Huppé are the most distinguished of these critics; they insist that Christian ethical concepts of *cupiditas* and *caritas* run through all medieval works of art. Sometimes a work that on the surface appears to encourage lovemaking ("swyvynge," as Chaucer might have called it), like the extremely popular *Le Roman de la Rose,* is discovered, by the exegetes, to have a second "truer" level: it is really a kind of anti-erotic jeremiad.

Understandably, the modern exegetical school has no central interest in Chaucer's bawdiness. The exegetes do insist, however, that what appears to be a perfectly plain meaning on the surface will turn out, upon closer inspection, to have a second, third, and even a fourth stratum of significance. Chaucer is not, they assure us, a naïve artist; on the contrary, as a learned medieval writer, and as a pre-Romantic, he was *compelled* by his own *Zeitgeist* to provide us with complex, sophisticated double meanings. He could not have written otherwise.

It is not quite fair of me to enlist the Robertsons and the Huppés in my camp, quite unbeknownst to them. They admit, of course, that there are comic passages in Chaucer. But when they explain Middle English humor, the exegetes sometimes make the jests sound like Sunday School teachers' jokes.

There are those for whom the exegetical way of reading Middle English poetry is uniquely stimulating, delightful—and useful. It restores to Chaucer the high seriousness that Matthew Arnold denied him long ago [see excerpt dated 1880]. For such readers, a disquisition on the obscenities in Chaucer will seem misguided, if not outright distasteful. The exegetes should *not,* however, find my study farfetched, in view of their own methods.

We are ready for a new "marriage" in Chaucer studies: the old, the new, the borrowed, and (of course) the blue. With the *OED* and the *MED;* with Partridge's example to guide us; with the new awareness and information from the rhetoricians; and with something borrowed from the exegetical critics—we are ready to begin our examination of Chaucer's "harlotrye." Our contemporary literature has been "liberated" legally for about a generation, since Judge Woolsey found *Ulysses* an acceptable import. We can now read without a blush Molly Bloom's soliloquy, with its reference to Stephen Dedalus' cock. We no longer need to ship copies of Henry Miller's schoolboy fantasies home from Europe in false-bottomed trunks. John Barth and John Updike and Allen Ginsberg and LeRoi Jones can publish four-letter words as part of their natural artistic vocabulary, using the blunt terms for comic or, more often, for emetic purposes.

Chaucer views copulation with healthy and effervescent good humor. The "swyvynge" that goes on in the **"Miller's"** or the **"Reeve's Tales"** is supremely good fun for those involved directly. In the latter narrative, the daughter and the wife enjoy immensely their (respective) fornication and adultery. We readers, the indirect participants, enjoy the comic ribaldry too.

Where there is adultery, there must be cuckolds. In Chaucer, they deserve their fates: they are stupid, suspicious, jealous, dishonest, and anti-intellectual. Only in Chaucer,

perhaps, is the last of these shortcomings grounds for cuckoldry.

On the morning after his delicate young wife has betrayed him, the carpenter-cuckold in the **"Miller's Tale"** falls from the ceiling and breaks his arm. Sentimental readers feel a twinge of pity for the victim of this gratuitous violence, but the sympathy does not endure. John's arm will mend, we know, just as we are sure that the "hurt gags" in movie cartoons will not result in permanent injuries to Sylvester the cat.

When Nicholas' scorched "toute" heals, he and the inventive Alisoun will find another occasion to repeat their lovemaking. They will hoodwink the stupid husband again and again, but from us he will never elicit any lasting sense of outrage or pity. Chaucer keeps the whole affair good-humored and comic.

Direct terms for sex (the act and the equipment) are actually not very common in Chaucer. He usually prefers double entendre, which will be discussed later, to the forthright "swyve" and "dight." The Middle English predecessor of "fuck" does not appear. "Swyve" is derived from a word meaning to sway and is related to "swivel." It is thus analogous to Modern English "screw" and to Italian "chiavare," to turn a key in a lock. "Dight" in the sense of "to swyve" is part of a vague verbal complex meaning generally to bring something about; it was also used in Middle English for the act of donning clothing.

"Queynte" is rare, too, compared with substitute metaphors or circumlocutions that Chaucer uses much more commonly for the vagina. He seems to have had no correspondingly direct word for the male organ. "Yerde" (yard, as in yardstick) later became the commonest term for the penis, but Chaucer used it but once or twice in this sense, and even these passages are doubtful.

Taboo words submerge and reappear, dolphin-like, as the centuries pass. Neither of Chaucer's words for intercourse is now current. But, who knows? Either "swyve" or "dight" may be resurrected.

Sometimes a perfectly innocent word may attract an indecent connotation. (Is the flies-to-honey proverb appropriate here?) Take "occupy," for example, which for a decade or so in the sixteenth century meant "swyve" (2 *Henry IV*) and then underwent amelioration, as semanticists say, and was reestablished in our neutral and unblushing vocabulary. "Quim" and "quiff" are old words for the female organ that never caught on. Nor does "spend" now compete with "come" for seminal emission, though in our grandmothers' time it was the common term.

Technical or unambiguous terms for excretion are also relatively uncommon in Chaucer's works, but when he chooses to use them, he does so without embarrassment. In the fourteenth century, "dong" and "pisse" surrounded one in the city streets and, of course, in the barnyard. You could use the "pryvee"; if the word was too euphemistic, you could call it the "gong" (i.e., "gang," the place where you *go*), a rougher word than "pryvee" in Chaucer. The fastidious Prioress calls it the "wardrobe," a hypereuphemism anticipating the modern powder room and comfort station. *Why* the Prioress uses this superpolite term should engage our critical attention. As a matter of fact, the purpose of this book is to make precisely such judgments.

Excretion was an accepted and semipublic event that Chaucer rarely uses for comedy. In the last century, these body functions have become rites performed in the shamefast privacy of a closed room, the excreta being immediately laved away by sparkling rivulets, to be seen and smelled no more. Because the act is now hidden, it is once again a source of humor. But to us, as to Chaucer, it is not so interesting or so funny as is copulation.

As there are secondary sexual characteristics, so are there secondary excretory phenomena—belching and farting. Eructation is a rare subject for jest in Chaucer. Breaking wind, on the other hand, is commoner and funnier. An entire tale among those of the Canterbury Pilgrims is built around the problem of equitable fart-division (the **"Summoner's Tale"**). Those who, like Absolon in the **"Miller's Tale,"** are squeamish about this act, will not find the exercise in arithmetic very funny. . . . I would guess, however, that the ranks of such squeamish clerks are diminishing, even among American coeds. They laugh (or titter), at least to themselves, when "Chaucer intrepidly joins sex with scatology in the **'Miller's Tale,'** " linking concupiscence with the "carminative faculty."

Direct allusion to excretion is uncommon in Chaucer's poetry; so too are the innuendos, metaphors, and puns related to these functions. Polite euphemisms like "passing wind" or "manure" are later inventions. In the fourteenth century, "manure" carts were filled with "dong" (what else?). "Shit(en)" occurs rarely and seems to have been confined to the barnyard or sheepcote. Although Chaucer does not often exploit this vein of humor, he has amusing disquisitions on the "reverberacioun" and "soun" of farts, and his "buf " is a precise echoic word for a belch.

When we enter the realm of paranomastic expressions for sex in Chaucer, we are in the richest lode in his mine of comedy. It is also the most hilarious and the most hazardous. We must be cautious, or we will begin to see covert sexual allusions in almost every line. I hope that I have "reformed that indifferently with us" (as the Player says to Hamlet), if not reformed it entirely. I am candidly uncertain about the innuendos that I suggest for "stonden in his lady grace," but where the phrase (or its variants) occurs, it must be discussed. The suggestion of a secondary erotic meaning for such a line is not purely whimsical or subjective; as the reader will see, there is a basis for the notion. But I confess that I cannot demonstrate it by citing dictionaries or contemporaneous works. An analyst of connotations in poetry can express opinions, guided by contexts and the scholar's critical apparatus, and he can suggest the likelihood of indecent innuendo. But, in the end, the reader, with the proper experience in analyzing this kind of literature, must decide for himself whether a naughty overtone can be heard. Like a musician who can train himself to hear high frequencies, inaudible to the layman, the reader of Middle English poetry can sensitize himself to the possibilities of sexy double meaning. However, just as the musician does not want to subject himself too often to frequencies that hurt his ears, so too the reader should not try to find scurrilities lurking behind every final *-e.*

The sources for copulation metaphors are as diverse as the Bible ("dette") and the arts ("daunce"). A phenomenon that surprised me is Chaucer's demonstrable habit of thinking in clusters of ambiguities. This is partly due to the demands of rhyme, especially in stanzaic poetry where rhymes are at a premium: "serve" will almost inevitably produce "sterve." But the prosodic requirements of rhyme royal in *Troilus and Criseyde,* for instance, will by no means explain all the clusters. "Lust-hunt-pleye" recurs often—naturally enough, since "pleye" has as its innocent meaning "divert," and "lust" could mean simple pleasure of any kind. The "pleye" of the "hunt" was for the fourteenth-century courtier one of his greatest "lusts." When, however, females like Dido are involved, the cluster takes on a blushing glow. "Pleye" is part of two other common nodules of allusion: with (1) "pryvetee" and "queynte" and (2) "jouste" and "daunce." "Pryve" seems to suggest to Chaucer "place" and "grace"; and "serve" (or "service," "servant") goes with (1) "grace," "holly"; (2) "hol," "plesaunce"; or (3) "sterve," "deye." If one is uncertain whether a word has a palimpsest of secondary sexual meaning in a particular passage, the sudden surge of clusters of associated words will often provide mutual reinforcement and heightened probability.

Derivatives must not be forgotten, though even the most perceptive analysts of Chaucer's style have generally ignored them. For instance, Kökeritz saw that the congruence of "mayden" and "hede" was suggestive. But no one has observed that "acqueyntaunce" often suggests the "queynte" referred to so shamelessly and directly by Alison of Bath.

We should also be alert to changes of tempo. In the **"Shipman's Tale,"** the movement from andante to presto is reinforced by the cluster that Chaucer assembles with ever-increasing rapidity: the wife appears pale because her husband has "laboured" her all night; then come references to love; a kiss (ostensibly symbolic of innocent agreement); love again; and "deere love." By this time, the bold Daun John is practically in the wife's lap and bosom—which the Middle Ages confused linguistically, if not anatomically. . . .

Deviant sex does not seem to have interested Chaucer's audience much. When the poet suspects it, he expresses disgust—for instance in the **"General Prologue"** when he gives us directly his own opinion of the Pardoner's effeminacy. Thopas' unmanliness seems to amuse him, however; at any rate, it amuses *us*—especially in view of the scholarly debate that it has aroused. . . .

Many of Chaucer's bawdy words exhibit marked semantic change. "Queynte" (quaint) and "luxurie" have now lost their sexual connotations: they have undergone amelioration. A word like "corage" could mean valor in the Middle Ages, but it also meant the capability to achieve and maintain an erection—the act of valor peculiar to the bedroom. The "good" sense of "courage" alone persists today. The opposite kind of semantic shift also occurs: "bawd(y)," "harlot," "lewde," "ravysshed," and "sluttish," which had relatively innocent meanings (along with secondary indecent ones) in Chaucer's day, have undergone pejoration. All are "impolite" terms in Modern English.

In shaping his sources, Chaucer sometimes adds bawdy material, sometimes omits it, and sometimes retains it: compare Boccaccio, *s.v.* hol, and Vergil, *s.v.* husbonde. A systematic listing of what he does in each case would be tedious. However, it should be noted that in the French *fabliau*—the narrative form that he used so often for his indecent tales—the indecent diction is much like Chaucer's. That is, direct terms for sex are rare, while metaphors are plentiful. Among the former, four words make up the bulk of the references in the extant *fabliaux: foutre* (fuck, for which the seventeenth century substituted the euphemism *ficher,* common today); *con* (cunt . . .); *coille* (testicle . . .); and *vit* (penis).

Much more common in these French tales are circumlocutions: *acoler* (embrace), *baisier* (kiss), *deduit* (amusement), *delit* (pleasure), *dosnoier* (strip, remove clothing), and *envoiseure* (frolicking sex, or organ that produces such). Lovers perform the *jeu d'amour* (game of love) or *le jolif mestier amourous* (the merry business of love); they do *lor bon* or *lors bons* (their "good"[s]) or *leur volonte* (their will); their *talant* or their *plaisir.* They *gesir* (lie) or *gesire entre les bras de* (lie in the arms of) someone. Chaucer uses many metaphors like these—sometimes translated directly from the vocabulary of the *fabliau.*

If the **Romaunt of the Rose** is Chaucer's, his practices are similarly consistent. Of the passages from the **Romaunt** that I have chosen to include in this study, almost all have a direct, bawdy source in the French. See gay, for instance, where the Old French words corresponding to the Middle English "gaye and amorous" are *gais e amoreus.* For "aqueyntaunce," *Le Roman de la Rose* has *acointance . . .* which plays on the word *cointe* in much the same way as does the Middle English upon queynt.

Chaucer ends the **Canterbury Tales** with an apology for his indecencies. . . . He asks forgiveness for those tales that are suggestive of sin and begs to be remembered for things like his "legendes of seintes." I too would like to voice a "retractation." I trust that I am not guilty of seeing bawdiness where it is not; on the other hand, I cannot claim to have unearthed ("laid bare" might be a better metaphor) all of Chaucer's double meanings of a sexual or scatological sort. I have often included words and passages that are only "possibles"; but when the possibility is there, the reader should be made aware of it.

Chaucer's poetry is delightful to read. I hope that this book will make it more pleasurable. To understand that he uses bawdry as a major comic device is important; despite his own "retractations," I think the poet himself would agree. (pp. 1-24)

> *Thomas W. Ross, in an introduction to his* Chaucer's Bawdy, *E. P. Dutton & Co., Inc., 1972, pp. 1-24.*

Stephen A. Barney   (essay date 1973)

[An American medievalist, Barney is the author of such

works as Word-Hoard: An Introduction to Old English Vocabulary *(1977), and* Allegories of History, Allegories of Love *(1979); he is also the editor of* Chaucer's Troilus: Essays in Criticism *(1980). In the excerpt below, Barney discusses the "Pardoner's Tale," praising its imaginative power.]*

> For though myself be a ful vicious man,
> A moral tale yet I yow telle kan,
> Which I am wont to preche for to wynne.
> Now hoold youre pees! My tale I wol bigynne.

With these words the Pardoner completes his boastful and cynical account of the art of preaching for money. The tale which follows, and the more cynical demand for money which follows the tale, exemplify the Pardoner's art. If the tale is not precisely one of the Pardoner's sermons, it can be taken as a comparable piece of artifice, modified to suit the circumstances of the Canterbury pilgrimage and of Chaucer's reading or listening audience. The Pardoner's claim that "I stynge hym with my tonge smerte / In prechyng" is a claim likewise made on his audience and Chaucer's audience. Does his tale sting? Has it the power to move its audience? There seems to be a universal accord in the affirmative. Just as a corrupt priest can administer valid sacraments, so this bad man can tell a good tale. Criticism since Kittredge has offered subtle and ingenious readings of the tale and its surrounding material as *expression,* as a mode of characterization of the Pardoner himself, but little has been written about the quality of the tale itself—its interior harmonies and its capacities to elicit powerful response—beyond acknowledgement that it is good.

Several reasons may account for this silence, a silence we do not find in criticism of the **"Knight's Tale"** or the **"Nun's Priest's Tale"** or the **"Clerk's Tale."** It may be thought that everyone can see why the tale is good. Critics may find the tale too short and simple to undergo their hard eye. Most important, the tale seems to have a source—and widespread analogues—but the exact source is unknown, so that Chaucer's unique contribution is impossible to assess. This last difficulty, with the exception of a few guesses, I have waived as, after all, not so considerable. The tale's virtues exist, no matter who is responsible for them, and Chaucer included it in the **Canterbury Tales** so that we may be permitted to view the tale in its significant context.

I propose that the **"Pardoner's Tale"** is good because it is eloquent, intelligent, significantly expressive, unified, and instructive. It is eloquent because it maintains an ethos and a style which gather forces and affect us throughout the tale; it is intelligent because it distinguishes things which ought to be distinguished and combines what ought to be combined; it is significantly expressive because the character of its narrator and the circumstances of its setting add to its meaning; it is unified in a strict sense in that it is disposed in an orderly fashion, and all its parts correspond and contribute to a single effect; and it is instructive because it commands its audience to look at themselves and their world in a new light.

Eloquence. The effect of the Pardoner's rhetoric can best be seen in its dynamics—in the way the orator moves from topic to topic. The reader of Chaucer commonly discovers that elements of the poems which at first seem to be super-fluous are in fact rhetorically strategic. Perhaps the best-known case is the series of exempla: at first these strings of old stories are lovable but dull, then they seem funny, then thematically interesting, and finally, under the closest and most learned reading, and under the broadest com-parative view, they seem of the quintessence of Chaucer's art. The principal excrescence in the manuscript fragment which contains the **"Pardoner's Tale"** is the **"Physician's Tale"**; the second 'problem' is the homiletic proem on the tavern sins.

The **"Physician's Tale"** concerns a young lady, Virginia, who chooses death rather than forced unchastity. The tale is horrible in two senses: because it is badly told, and be-cause it is gratuitously ugly in content. There is no telling what Chaucer had in mind while he worked up the tale, presumably with Livy and the *Romance of the Rose* before him, laboring to increase the pathos of the heroine's plight much as he had done in the **"Clerk's Tale"** and the **"Man of Law's Tale."** Whatever Chaucer's initial opinion of his work, when he included it in the *Canterbury Tales* he used it much as he had used other tales, which I shall call 'anti-tales,' either as foils for adjacent tales or as general paro-dies of certain literary excesses of his time. The anti-tale is merely a special case of the 'requital' principle in the *Canterbury Tales,* by which the Knight's tale, for exam-ple, is answered by the Miller's. The best example of the foil arrangement is the **"Monk's Tale,"** interrupted and sharply criticized on non-aesthetic grounds by the Knight and the Host, and followed by the **"Nun's Priest's Tale,"** Chaucer's best, in which the tragedy of fortune, so crudely handled by the Monk, is rendered in high, comic, and ulti-mately more serious fashion by an intelligence of the first order.

The **"Pardoner's Tale"** echoes the **"Physician's Tale"** at several points, as we shall see; and I think there is little doubt that the pair are best viewed together. The case I want to make here is that the Pardoner has seen and makes use of the two major faults of the preceding tale. The first is the imbalanced use of narrative materials. The Physician elaborates at relatively great length on the vir-tues of Virginia, and on the virtue and necessity of preserv-ing innocent chastity itself, but leaves at the periphery of the tale the really interesting matter: the character of her father, and the operation of the legal system and its rela-tion to the public. A glance at Livy shows how, especially with regard to the latter material, the story might better be told. In the Physician's version, the intervention of "a thousand people" who burst into court and save the father immediately after he has beheaded his daughter is gratu-itously shocking. The auditor cannot help asking where were those people a few moments before? Why did Vir-ginius fail to appeal to them before? Of course, this is melodrama and presumably an intentional effect of the story; but I think it must render an audience speechless. Livy had not presented this problem; Chaucer created it.

The second flaw in the **"Physician's Tale"** is the conclu-sion. Surely the pathos of the tale, especially in this ver-sion, is for Virginia and the trial of her virginity. Yet she

is not mentioned in the closing lines. Instead we are told "how synne hath his merite!" To our surprise, the final judgments on the villains, Apius and Claudius, turn out to be the 'moral' of the tale, and not the conflict between evils with which Virginia and her father wrestle. Beware, the Physician warns, and forsake sin, for no man knows when God will smite, nor how the "worm of conscience" will recoil from wicked life. This is conspicuous irrele-vance, which the Pardoner notices and uses to his own ends.

I said the **"Physician's Tale"** would leave its audience speechless, but I spoke of normal natures. Harry Bailly is a critic especially capable of powerful emotional response and rapid, nearly simultaneous articulation of his feelings. The first words after the **"Physician's Tale"** are, "Oure Hooste gan to swere as he were wood; / 'Harrow!' quod he. . . . " There follows a shotgun blast of critical com-mentary. The falsity of Apius and Claudius are berated; the cause of Virginia's death is ascribed to the "yiftes of Fortune and of Nature," her beauty; the tale is "pitous" (we have "pitee," "pitous," and "pitously" in twenty-odd lines) so that the Host must hear a merry tale or else his "herte is lost." We might imagine the Pardoner thinking that pity runneth soon in Harry's heart. The Host con-cludes with a request for entertainment to the Pardoner, whom he calls "beel amy," with a not so subtle glance at the Pardoner's effeminacy. The gentles, fearing that the Pardoner will continue acting out his obviously assumed mask of ribaldry, demand that he tell "som moral thing."

I hope that this brief treatment of the matter which pre-cedes the **"Pardoner's Tale"** in the manuscript fragment shows how the Physician and the Host 'set up' the Pardon-er and provide the initial grounds for his eloquence. The sensitive audience has been affronted in various ways by the Physician's literary failures, and the Pardoner has been especially affronted by the Host's slur. He takes up the attack and does as well as a man in his condition can do, even though the Host ultimately silences him; and the Knight, who seems to represent "thise gentils," has to help the Pardoner reassume his composure.

The Pardoner responds to the **"Physician's Tale"** both by what he does and what he does not do in his own tale. I shall need to anticipate some arguments in order to sum-marize how he does so. First, as to motive: the Physician says "the feend into his [Apius'] herte ran" and taught the judge the trick he needed to obtain Virginia; the Pardoner says of the third rioter, "atte laste the feend oure enemy, / Putte in his thought that he sholde poyson beye." It need scarcely be argued that the introduction of the fiend as motive in the **"Pardoner's Tale"** is superfluous after all that has been said about the deadly effects of vice. Apius, however, has been smitten by Virginia's beauty as sudden-ly as Troilus by Criseyde's, and it apparently never occurs to him to behave by any other counsel than the fiend's, who gets to his "herte" first, for reasons which never come out. Secondly, we learn from the Physician that Virginia was wont to flee the bad company who were "likely . . . to treten of folye"; the Pardoner gives us the bad company itself and thus avoids meeting the problem of poetic jus-tice. Third, Virginia twice refers to "grace" as she contemplates her dilemma, asking if there will be "no grace . . . no remedye" for herself, and reminding her father that "Jepte" gave his daughter grace (here, time) to make her complaint before he slew her. We shall see that the Pardoner mingles the themes of grace and death more skillfully. Fourth, the Physician begins his description of Virginia with a curious prosopopoeia, having Nature personified speak boastfully of her shaping and painting of Virginia. This is the gift of Fortune and of Nature to which the Host attributes the cause of Virginia's death. Again, we shall see how the Physician's clumsy grasp of the truth about creaturely benefits—especially clumsy since the Doctor's knowledge of causes is singled out for special praise in the **"General Prologue"**—is transformed by the Pardoner into an important theme of his tale. Fifth, the Physician's conclusion that no one knows whom God will smite, rather stupid in its context, is made the very occasion of the **"Pardoner's Tale,"** as the rioters learn of the "privee theef men clepeth Deeth." Sixth, the Physician's moral, that "Heere may men seen how synne hath his merite," so hideously inappropriate to a tale of innocence destroyed, has become the essential structural principle of the **"Pardoner's Tale."**

Finally, as far as I have seen, there is the matter of different uses of rhetoric. The Physician had claimed of Virginia that "no countrefeted termes hadde she." The Host, producing an absurd list of pseudo-medical terms in the link (urynals, jurdones, ypocras, galiones, letuarie, cardynacle, triacle), says, "I kan nat speke in terme." We know from elsewhere in Chaucer of a distrust of jargon as part of a generalized antipathy toward fancy ideas and clericalism, as, for instance, in the prologue to the **"Clerk's Tale."** The Host has told the Clerk, as later he tells the Pardoner, to tell a merry tale and has warned him from using "Youre termes, youre colours, and youre figures." Nature's speech is the principal 'rhetorical' ornament of the **"Physician's Tale,"** in medieval terms, being an extended figure of personification, and even including classical allusions. The Physician seems rather proud of it, ending it plumply with "Thus semeth me that Nature wolde seye." It contains the terms "countrefete" (twice), "colour," and "figures." Nature uses these terms to describe her own work in creating as God's "vicaire general," but the terms are all, as we see, especially rhetorical jargon, a point which I first noticed because of the close proximity of the phrase "countrefeted termes" to describe Virginia's speech. In brief, my conjecture is this: the Physician accidentally connects Nature's skill at shaping with the skill of an orator, in a passage which is rhetorically deficient. The Host reemphasizes the issue with his parody of medical jargon in the link. The Pardoner then picks up the theme, but subtly. He uses Latin "to saffron with" his preaching; he has his bulls, his sealed patent, his allusions to popes, cardinals, patriarchs, and bishops, and especially his relics and his silver tongue—he is a kind of walking embodiment of rhetoric, the trappings and ornaments of his profession performing the functions of authorization and persuasion that terms and figures perform for an orator. As a speaker can use his craft to wrong effect, so can a pardoner use his office to wrong effect. The Pardoner's assertion that "I wol noon of the apostles countrefete" indicates a rhetoric of behavior rather than a rhetoric of language. This is part of the

reason why the Host's brutal response to the Pardoner's final offer is so effective: this Harry Bailly who so distrusts "termes" has seen through the Pardoner's superficies and has returned to the state of the purely physical such things as relics and masculinity, which are not purely physical when they are involved in the delicate magic of the Pardoner's art. The joke is that once the Pardoner finally launches into the tale proper he uses almost no fancy rhetorical devices, with one exception, a personification, of which I shall make much later.

The first aspect of the Pardoner's eloquence, then, is his skill at listening. He seems to have caught in detail the flaws of the preceding tale and the inner meaning of the Host's response to it and to have turned them all to his own purposes. His confession of his methods, with its blunt exposure of the inner and outer motives of his preaching, comes as a shock after the fatuity and moral blindness of the **"Physician's Tale."** In the Pardoner, the Canterbury pilgrims must see that if they have to deal with vice, it will no longer be in the form of stupidity.

The prologue to the **"Pardoner's Tale"** is eloquent in a different sense: it has the art of truth. No matter that we may see the Pardoner's avarice as an audacious attempt to conceal his sexual inadequacy, he is still avaricious. Chaucer knew as well as Paul that sin is sin. As many have observed, truth so baldly put is just as much an ornament as rhetorical lying. Again, at the end, the Pardoner's audacity is stripped away.

Finally, having looked under the rubric 'eloquence'—the eloquence of responsiveness and the eloquence of truth—we should turn to the eloquence of assertion within the tale itself. The tale is structured in two ways which are characteristic of Chaucer. First is the bipartite structure, or pace, of the tale, which might be labelled 'auctoritee' followed by 'plot machine.' The Wife of Bath's prologue, which she calls a tale, and her tale are the most famous examples of this scheme; but we also find it in the talky beginnings and swift, eventful endings of other tales: the **"Miller's Tale,"** the **"Summoner's Tale,"** the **"Merchant's Tale,"** the **"Nun's Priest's Tale,"** and the **"Physician's Tale"** being outstanding examples—and they include some of Chaucer's finest work. The second structural characteristic is the efficiency of the plot machine, a device which works so well for Chaucer that one might guess that he was drawn with special delight to sources which contain this mechanism.

We expect the homily which fills the first part of the tale to be funny yet serious (like the Wife of Bath's prologue) and to bear an indirect but important relationship to the tale. We are disappointed. We might think that the exempla of Attila, Stilboun, and Demetrius, or the interpretation of the original sin or the very energy devoted to the lesser sins, are funny; but we know that it is the special kind of humor contemporary readers of Chaucer respond to with guilt, feeling fairly certain that Chaucer would not have seen the joke. The homily is pious and deadly serious. There are signs of care in its composition as the Pardoner turns from theme to theme, saying, "And now that I have spoken of glotonye, / Now wol I yow defenden hasardrye" and "Now wol I speke of othes false and grete." The movement into the homily is artful, as the pronouns of reference quietly shift from the "they" of the rioters to the "we" and "you" of a preacher and his audience, somewhere between lines 476 and 501. There is a little 'box' structure of the sort we find elsewhere in Chaucer, in which the Pardoner opens and closes a predicatorial topic on drunkenness with the words "Sampsoun, Sampsoun!" This parallels in small the large 'box' of the Pardoner's prologue, the phrase, "Radix malorum est Cupiditas."

But the real force of the homily is its energy, its Chaucerian plenitude and strenuousness. The images of vice the Pardoner chooses show men distorted and strained by evil effort:

> How greet labour and cost is thee [wombe] to
>   fynde!
> Thise cookes, how they stampe, and streyne, and
>   grynde,
> And turnen substaunce into accident,
> To fulfille al thy likerous talent!
>
> A lecherous thyng is wyn, and dronkenesse
> Is ful of stryvyng and of wrecchednesse.
> O dronke man, disfigured is thy face . . .

The most striking device of the first, more energetic part of the homily is the one-line catalogue, the device which Milton and Pope use to similar effect, to suggest surfeit and chaotic bustle (*Paradise Lost* 2.948-50; *Rape of the Lock* 1.138). Chaucer's most famous example describes the materials that Absolon in the **"Miller's Tale"** used to clean his mouth: "With dust, with sond, with straw, with clooth, with chippes." Aside from the lines quoted in the first passage above, the Pardoner gives others. . . .

It may be granted that the Pardoner's homily on the tavern sins is a tour de force of ordered disorder, urging the unattractiveness of sin, and by no means funny. Its relation to the rioters' plot is unusual. We and the pilgrim audience surely anticipate an indirect, and very likely comic connection. Instead, we have the simple arrangement: these men are vicious; here is the end of vice. The Pardoner keeps his eye steadily on the subject and even introduces into the homily some at first inexplicable references to death which serve to anticipate his plot: "Of whiche the ende is deeth, wombe is hir god!"; "he that haunteth swiche delices / Is deed"; "For dronkenesse is verray sepulture / Of mannes wit"; "Hasard is verray mooder of . . . manslaughtre"; "This fruyt cometh of the bicched bones two, / . . . homycide." These last three especially look odd until we reach the end, as we ask what have the tavern sins to do with homicide? But in spite of these overt connections, the homily is not a *sine qua non* for understanding the plot proper; it does not lay out themes like sovereignty and age (Wife of Bath) or scholarship and determinism (Nun's Priest) which open up the tale's significance. The relation, I think, is ethical only: the homily establishes an atmosphere and tone of disgust for vice and contempt for the vicious. The plot proper, astonishingly, comes as a considerable relief. We scarcely notice the dark setting, "this pestilence," but of course it is there.

The eloquence of the plot is its elegance; it is plain and efficient and operates on life and truth like Occam's razor. It turns on two points: dramatic irony and ineluctable symmetry of judgment. The former I wish to treat later. The symmetry of judgment consists in the generation of one motif out of another—hence plot 'machine'—as stupid drunkenness begets a quest for death which begets greed for gold which begets accidental revenge which begets death found. It is the mechanism primarily characteristic of the fabliaux: the cry "Water!" in the **"Miller's Tale,"** the "white thyng" in the moonlight in the **"Reeve's Tale,"** the earnest oath in the **"Friar's Tale,"** the blindness in the **"Merchant's Tale,"** the boastful, freeing word in the **"Nun's Priest's Tale."** An apparently extraneous but interesting element of plot comes suddenly as if by magic to be essential, and theme (here, being death-bound in avarice) becomes action (death in avarice). Inventing plots with this device requires a special kind of imagination, that of a Fielding or a Dickens. It was the imagination of the author of Genesis, who made the act of eating the fruit of the Tree of Knowledge the knowledge itself. I think there is no evidence that Chaucer was good at making up these stories, but he was clearly interested in them, translating and rewriting and weaving them into the texture of his *Canterbury Tales.* These plots behave as the world properly behaves *sub specie aeternitatis,* turning intangibles into tangibles and rendering justice at the end of time. I have called this kind of plot 'magic,' but of course from the authorial point of view it is that controlled magic which is better called intelligence.

Intelligence: this was our second reason for thinking the **"Pardoner's Tale"** a good tale. We have noticed that the tale is eloquent, in its response to the preceding tale, in the strikingly direct truthfulness of its prologue, in the assertive rhetoric of the homiletic proem and the elegant plot. The second pivot of the plot, its dramatic irony, I have reserved for treatment until now, although this and all the other 'beauties' of the tale contribute in a general way to its eloquence.

We know more than the rioters do. We have seen the tavern vices linked three times to death, and three times to homicide. We know that death is not a person living in a village over a mile away or under a tree in a grove. We know that the gold will not put the rioters "in heigh felicitee." We know, if we are clever, just before the end, what the end will be. The Pardoner lends us, through his art, the power of intelligence to discriminate between what the rioters see and what is truly to be seen. When the worst of the rioters speaks after they find the gold, and says, "My wit is greet," we laugh. The rioters are so incapable of understanding real value that they are glad of the sight of the gold "For that the floryns been so faire and brighte." We are, in fact, maneuvered into a double vision of the events of the tale, whereby we see what the rioters see but also see, from something like a doomsday perspective, how things really are. Our double vision operates in detail to unfold the meaning of the tale. The play on Eucharistic transubstantiation in the lines already quoted about the cooks who "turnen substaunce into accident" in their cooking may be taken as the key to this aspect of the tale: we are in a position to see things substantially while the rioters see accident only. The first figure of speech in the tale provides a correlative pair of terms: the rioters "doon the devel sacrifise / Withinne that develes temple, in cursed wise." This figure may derive from the puns in some medieval Latin verses on *taberna* (tavern) and *tabernaculum* (temple). To extend the metaphor, if the rioters' tavern is the devil's church, their whole vision of things is the devil's vision.

A telling distinction between the rioters' knowledge and ours lies in the accidental use of Biblical allusions by the characters in the tale. A rioter swears that "we wol sleen this false traytour Deeth," and the narrator, in case we have missed the point, reiterates:

> And many a grisly ooth thanne han they sworn,
> And Cristes blessed body al torente—
> Deeth shal be deed, if that they may hym hente!

We should here remember God's promise in Hosea 13:14, "I will deliver them out of the hand of death. I will redeem them from death: O death, I will be thy death; O hell, I will be thy bite"; and also Paul's use of the same logion: "O death, where is thy victory? O death, where is thy sting?" (I Cor. 15:55—Douay translation). But the rioters are killing Christ, the agent of life's victory, even as they set out to make death dead. A second allusion refers to the same chapter of Corinthians. Paul writes scornfully of those who do not believe in the resurrection, quoting Isaiah (22:13): "Let us eat and drink, for tomorrow we shall die" (I Cor. 15:32). The two rioters, having killed their companion, seem to echo these words: "Now lat us sitte and drynke, and make us merie, / And afterward we wol his body berie." The drink, of course, is poison.

Chaucer may also be recalling here a curiously analogous passage in the Book of Wisdom. The author is treating the themes of justice and death, and he quotes wicked men who do not reason right. They are aware of the brevity of life and say, "Come therefore, and let us enjoy the good things that are present, and let us speedily use the creatures as in youth. Let us fill ourselves with costly wine. . . . Let us . . . not . . . honour the ancient gray hairs of the aged." They are angry at the just man: "Let us therefore lie in wait for the just, because he . . . upbraideth us with transgressions of the law. . . . Let us condemn him to a most shameful death. . . . These things they thought, and were deceived: for their malice blinded them. . . . But by the envy of the devil, death came into the world: And they follow him that are of his side." My elliptical quotation has improved my case, but even so this looks like the **"Pardoner's Tale"** if we substitute both the Old Man and the third rioter for the just man. In any case, the first chapters of Wisdom provide an apt commentary on our tale.

The other two accidental Biblical allusions lend an apocalyptic cast to the 'substance' of the tale. The first, which is not certain, was noted by Robert Miller (*Speculum* 30 [1955]: 180-99). The Old Man wants death since he cannot have youth and complains, "Ne Deeth, allas! ne wol nat han my lyf "; during the locust plague of the fifth angel in the Apocalypse, John tells us, "And in those days men shall seek death, and shall not find it: and they shall desire to die, and death shall fly from them" (Apoc. 9:6). The second, which I think more likely, is the tavern boy's statement that "Ther cam a privee theef men clepeth Deeth." This alludes to the famous group of apocalyptic logia

which speak of the coming of the Son of Man as a thief in the night: "For yourselves know perfectly, that the day of the Lord shall so come, as a thief in the night." If the rioters had grasped these allusions, they might have known that judgment is at hand and that they are in the situation modern Biblical critics call realized eschatology.

The joke which begins the plot proper of the **"Pardoner's Tale"** is one of Chaucer's favorites, which might be called 'characterization by failure of imagination.'

The tavern boy explains to the rioters that an "old felawe" of theirs was slain by Death in the night. He warns the company to "be war of swich an adversarie," as his "dame" had taught him. The taverner himself, misapprehending the statement, proceeds to generalize his sense that many have died recently during "this pestilence" and concludes that Death's "habitacioun" must be in the great village over a mile from the tavern. One of the rioters, in his cups, responds to this news as if it were a challenge— his bravado is the sole motive for the plot at this point— and says, "Is it swich peril with hym for to meete?" The progression is from the dame's Christian lesson to the boy's possible misunderstanding to the taverner's utter misunderstanding to the rioters' action based on misunderstanding. What they misunderstand is the nature of personification, which is that the *accident* of the *substance* signified, in this case the *word* for *death,* can behave *in language* as if it were the substance itself, but not in reality. Personal names, "theef," "adversarie," "traytour," are apposed to the name, "Deeth," and the rioters assume the name is a person.

Their confusion, which Chaucer probably found in his source, cuts in two ways. First, obviously, it characterizes the rioters and taverner as stupid. The Pardoner, who surely takes pride in his intelligence, may well be glancing at the offending taverner, Harry Bailly, in his present company. The other angle of incision, however, derives from a favorite medieval paradox, the basis of much classical allegory, that personifications like this one are real. The rioters do meet Death, not because it is a person, but because on a level of reality of which they are unaware, Death is victorious over them. Bertrand H. Bronson speaks of the movement into the tale and the rioters' misapprehension of death's nature as a movement toward miracle drama and allegory (*In Search of Chaucer* [Toronto, 1960], 101-03). The landscape changes from the local and specific to the abstract and significant. The meeting point between the two worlds is the stile which the rioters are about to step over when they meet the Old Man; they enter just such a 'middle space' as Spenser's characters sometimes inhabit (as in *Faerie Queene*) in which moral states become physical actualities.

Finally, the tale's intelligence extends to the use of two terms, 'fortune' and 'grace.' The rioters address the Old Man, "What, carl, with sory grace!", here an expletive of contempt; but later the same phrase describes the rioter who poisons his fellows. The Old Man complains that mother earth "wol nat do that grace" to give him death and burial. The rioter whose "wit is greet" says that "This tresor hath Fortune unto us yiven," and, who would have thought "Today that we sholde han so fair a grace?" The rioters act without grace but think they have found it, as in fact they have—but it is the Old Man's version of grace. That gold is the gift of fortune is true, just as Virginia's beauty was the gift of Fortune and Nature in the Host's comment on the **"Physician's Tale."** Yet the Pardoner is not telling a tale of Roman history but a moral tale. In his tale the scheme is providential, not fortunate. The rioters' apprehension of these terms corresponds to their apprehension of the value of gold, the meaning of the crooked path and the tree, the Biblical allusions, and the personification, Death. The tale works in a way analogous to the method of satire. When we are shown failure of imagination and insensitivity to large perspectives, we readers perforce assume the large perspective ourselves and become, while we partake of the tale, instruments of divine vision and justice. We are Providence, and we keep watch for the thief who comes suddenly in the night.

The **"Pardoner's Tale"** is significantly expressive. Whatever the Pardoner's physical condition, his fellow pilgrims treat him as effeminate. In place of the obvious signs of masculinity, the Pardoner has his tongue, which goes "yerne," which is "smerte" in stinging, which spits out venom, and which the narrator describes as 'well-filed' in the **"General Prologue"**; he has also his wallet stuffed with relics and "bretful of pardoun," mentioned three times in the **"General Prologue"** and once in the epilogue to the tale. His tongue and wallet, the tools of his trade, behave like phallic symbols. The figure derives from *The Romance of the Rose,* where *bourses* (wallets) are euphemisms for scrotums, and *coillons* are associated with *reliques* (ed. Langlois, 7081-82, 7143). When the Pardoner invites the Host to kiss his relics and suggests that he "Unbokele anon thy purs"—for money, not, as usually, for a tale—Harry's references to the Pardoner's "breech" and "coillons" show that he responds to the Pardoner in these sexual terms. The Host is the very figure of masculinity which the Pardoner envies. His wish that the Pardoner be castrated is the final blow, and the Pardoner's tongue emphatically ceases its work:

> "Lat kutte hem of, I wol thee helpe hem carie;
> They shul be shryned in an hogges toord!"
> This Pardoner answerde nat a word;
> So wrooth he was, no word ne wolde he seye.

As long as Chaucer's work survives, the Pardoner will be "This" Pardoner at the end of his tale, a man set at a distance from us, and the word "word" will be associated with him through its rhyme, "toord."

The Pardoner offers first his tale, then his relics; from his point of view they are gifts of the same order. He gives as best he can the impression that *he* can see beneath the accidents of narrative art and sacred object to the real substance, his desire for gain. The Host's criticism of the tale is for once forestalled by the Pardoner's rapid patter. He can only reply to the relics, obviously specious, with proper disgust and anger.

It remains to determine our final response to the tale. One way to consider this question is to consider the fourth excellence of the tale, its unity. This is comprised of the elaborate scheme of corresponding duplicities which the tale and its teller present. The Physician tells his tale, which

fails to penetrate to true causes, with good intentions; the Pardoner tells his more penetrating tale with bad intentions. The Pardoner confesses to avarice and blindness to the final judgment; his tale condemns avarice and opens our eyes to the end of things. The Pardoner fills his audience with disgust for vice in his homily; he fills them with disgust for his vicious person in the epilogue. The tale carefully distinguishes accidental value from substantial value, irate, avaricious and gluttonous language from Biblical language, personification from spiritual reality; but the Pardoner in himself confuses all things, as liar and truth-teller at once. Very different are the analogues to the tale, in which saintly or divine figures of high authority provide the framework of meaning.

There are many ways of looking at these fusing, paralleling, contradicting, complicated relationships. Harry Bailly's way is to reduce all to a turd; the Knight's way is to insist on the continuance of the game. I think Chaucer is very serious in providing these more or less limited judgments from fellow pilgrims. The poet poses a question which—as the prologue and epilogue to the **"Parson's Tale"** show—was on his mind: whether this business of writing good literature, or telling good tales, makes any sense at all from the doomsday perspective or the perspective of natural reason. The Pardoner is an example of a literary artist who uses his craft according to the mutable realm of Fortune, with his eye cast to the earth.

The **"Pardoner's Tale"** is instructive. If we have any imagination, any power to make distinctions and draw analogies, we must look at last at ourselves when we finish reading the tale and wonder what we have been doing. If the tale alone is a true analogy to the world, then the rhetoric of art will be duplicated in the history of events, and our fictional experience of vitality and justice will be made real. If the tale in its setting, in the mouth of the Pardoner in the *Canterbury Tales,* is true, we may be exercising our imagination to no end or, like the Pardoner, to mean ends. All that beauty and energy, of the Pardoner's and maybe of Chaucer's, is for nothing. The magical things which can happen in a tale may have no counterpart in the world. The tale is a trial of faith. (pp. 83-95)

Stephen A. Barney, "An Evaluation of the 'Pardoner's Tale'," in Twentieth Century Interpretations of 'The Pardoner's Tale': A Collection of Critical Essays, *edited by Dewey R. Faulkner, Prentice-Hall, Inc., 1973, pp. 83-95.*

A. V. C. Schmidt (essay date 1974)

[*In the excerpt below, Schmidt examines the "General Prologue" of the* Canterbury Tales, *focusing on a variety of elements which contribute to its realism.*]

No less impressive in Chaucer's mature work than his feel for atmosphere and mood, his rhythmic sensitivity and verbal 'tact', is his sense of *structure*. From the taut, streamlined narrative of the **"Pardoner's Tale"**, to the astonishing twelve-hundred line 'frame-story' which holds the [*Canterbury Tales*] together (the story of the Pilgrimage), he reveals a complete control of his material which never degenerates into manipulation. Chaucer's characters have not only vitality but freedom. The Wife of Bath in her prologue threatens to burst the narrative framework almost as Falstaff does that of *Henry IV, Part I.* But the 'threat' is never realized: Chaucer's thematic concerns confine (without frustrating) the Wife's uninhibited self-expression. Her prologue and tale both accordingly take their place in a larger pattern of tales exploring the themes of marriage and true nobility, and Chaucer's creative energies issue not in anarchy but a more complex order.

If the *Tales* throw up a wide range of life-like characters—Dorigen, Simkin, Alison, January (from the [**"Franklin's Tale"**, **"Reeve's Tale"**, **"Miller's Tale"**, and **"Merchant's Tale"** . . . respectively])—characters scarcely less real than the pilgrims in whose tales they appear—they are equally varied in their setting, intention and form. The best poems of a Milton, Wordsworth or Pope all bear a generic resemblance to one another—which perhaps suggests the limitations of these undoubtedly great poets. But the emotional range Chaucer spans—from the highly amusing comedy of sex of the **"Shipman's Tale"** to the subtle exploration of moral crisis in a supposedly ideal marriage of the **"Franklin's Tale"**—is exceeded only by Shakespeare and equalled by no other English writer. Just as striking as the polar contrasts of literary genre within Chaucer's oeuvre are the varieties of *comedy* in the *Tales.* Nine of these are comedies in the usual modern sense—light-hearted stories which make us laugh (the *medieval* sense of 'comedy' was 'any story which *ended* happily')—and yet only the **"Reeve's Tale"**, a direct reply to the Miller's, closely resembles the mode or method of any of the others. The variety of Chaucer's treatment of his materials is such that readers are sometimes surprised to discover that a work like the **"Merchant's Tale"** is at once a handling of the stock *fabliau* theme of the old husband married to a young wife and cuckolded by a young man, and a mirror-image, however distorted, of the **"Franklin's Tale"**, a deeply serious poem untouched by the slightest levity. The comic tales (with which, in this respect, the **"General Prologue"** ought to be placed) abound in satire—of knights and squires, alchemists and their dupes, merchants, clerics, students and women. It is usually good-natured and often *dramatic* satire—that is, directed by one pilgrim against another or another's profession, sex or class through the tale he or she tells. For Chaucer's own attitude we need to turn from the *Tales*, to the **"General Prologue"** and the Frame-story.

The **"General Prologue"** is at once a great poem in its own right and a perfect introduction to medieval English literature. Chaucer wrote in the East Midland dialect of English, which was spoken at the court in Westminster, in the city of London and in the universities. This dialect, from which the English we speak descends, makes him easier to read than many of his contemporaries, some of them great poets, who wrote in more Northern or Western dialects. Chaucer's English is an earlier form of Shakespeare's, not a foreign tongue requiring "translation'. We sometimes have to paraphrase to bring out what is compressed or implicit in the original, but much of Chaucer is as clear as if written yesterday, like these lines describing the Summoner:

> A fewe termes hadde he, two or three,
> That he had lerned out of som decree—
> No wonder is, he herde it al the day . . .

In that Chaucer's pronunciation . . . differed from our own, he *does* resemble a foreign writer; but it is still arguable that for all his (now) obsolete words and idioms, Chaucer's poetry is in some ways actually easier to understand than much of Shakespeare or Milton. . . .

Chaucer probably wrote the **"General Prologue"** in about 1387, before most of the *Tales.* Its length and elaboration indicate that he regarded it as rather more than a mere introduction, like the Prologue to the work of his contemporary William Langland, *Piers Plowman* (c. 1362-90). Chaucer's prologue can be read as a self-contained poem, and though it initiates the frame-story, it does not depend on what follows to be understood and appreciated. In this it resembles the prologue to Chaucer's earlier collection of tales (never finished), *The Legend of Good Women* (?1386), a poem of over 550 lines which has an interest independent of and indeed surpassing that of an introduction to the individual legends. Chaucer's purpose seems to have been to create a living portrait-gallery of contemporary humanity as he knew it and to provide a faithful record and interpretation of the colourful and bustling life of his age. In spite of his pervasive moral interest and clear-cut moral standpoint, Chaucer's portraits do not illustrate a moral or philosophical thesis as do those of Pope, say, in his *Moral Essays.* Their contemporariness is as important as their timelessness. The **"General Prologue"** has always been valued for the light it throws on English society in the late fourteenth century. The older critics admired the depth of its human insight, but only more recently has attention focused on the subtleties of its consummate art.

Chaucer describes the progress of the pilgrims from Southwark to Canterbury in a series of passages known as 'links' which act as a kind of *frame-story* around the individual tales. Because Chaucer died before finishing the poem, some of the links are incomplete or missing, and because of variations between the MSS of the poem, the exact order of the tales is uncertain. All scholars divide them into ten groups, numbered A to I, with the group called B having two parts, B^1 and B^2. A widely accepted view, based on the internal evidence of the poem rather than on the authority of any MS or group of MSS, places the groups in the order: A, B^1, B^2, D, E, F, C, G, H, I, differing from that of the standard modern edition of Chaucer's *Works* (Robinson's), which follows the ordering of the Ellesmere manuscript.

Two tales are left *unfinished*, the **"Cook's Tale"** and the **"Squire's Tale"**. The former is a fabliau in type and only about a hundred lines were written. The latter gets further, but Chaucer may have become bored with it or else not known how to finish it. Two other tales are *'fragments'* but not unfinished, the **"Monk's Tale"** and Chaucer's tale of **"Sir Thopas"**. These were deliberately designed to be interrupted, the one by the Knight (who finds the Monk's recital of gloomy 'tragedies' too depressing for the occasion) and the other by the Host (on the ostensible grounds that the *rhyming* 'is nat worth a toord'). Of the completed tales two have long 'autobiographical' Prologues (Wife of Bath, Pardoner) and in a third (Canon's Yeoman) Prologue and Tale are scarcely distinguishable. . . . Other tales also have 'autobiographical' passages in their Prologues (e.g. the Reeve's and Merchant's, dealing respectively with the miseries of old age and unhappy marriage). These 'prologues' are in many cases identical with the Links.

The *Tales* cover a wide range of literary types and sum up the poetic achievement of the Middle Ages. This makes them an ideal introduction to medieval literature as a whole (although Chaucerian narrative, it is worth remembering, is always a highly sophisticated development of what is elsewhere a naïve or even crude genre). Of the two least attractive tales, both in prose, the Parson's is a sermon-treatise on the Seven Deadly Sins, and though not dull is mainly of historical interest, while Chaucer's own semi-allegorical tale of **"Melibee"** again appeals to the specialist rather than the general reader. **"Sir Thopas"** is a brilliant parody of bad popular romance, the first great parody in English. The Prioress and Second Nun tell tales of Christian martyrs and the Physician a tale of a pre-Christian 'martyr' in the cause of virtue. The Clerk and Man of Law tell tales about women whose patience and endurance are tested under extreme conditions. Together these five tales of *hoolynesse* constitute the least realistic group in the collection. Though very good of their kind, they are not the most accessible of Chaucer's works. The tales of the Manciple and Nun's Priest are both about animals, the one brief and terse, the other (a moral fable) developed with great richness and comic detail. The tales of the Knight, Franklin and Wife of Bath are generally classed as 'courtly romances', though each has a strong philosophical tinge and a moral intensity unusual in romance. The **"Wife's Tale"** uses a traditional story of the folk-tale type as a peg from which to hang a disquisition on the nature of true nobility (*gentillesse*), while the **"Knight's Tale"**, a brilliant *tour de force,* is a simultaneous celebration and critique of courtly-chivalric existence. The **"Franklin's Tale"** is a highly dramatic *nouvelle* about love, marriage and knightly ethics and (once again) the nature of true *gentillesse,* placed in a fantastic romance setting in which magic plays an important part. The **"Shipman's"**, **"Miller's"** and **"Reeve's Tales"** are fabliaux of great inventiveness and wit; the **"Summoner's Tale"** represents the simplest and coarsest variety of the type, while the **"Merchant's Tale"** can be called without exaggeration the apotheosis of the genre. No less impressive are two other comic works, the **"Wife of Bath's Prologue"** and the **"Canon's Yeoman's Prologue and Tale"**, which are wholly original and fit into no category, though they have affinities with the fabliau in mood and tone. Finally, the tales of the Friar and Pardoner are triumphant examples of the type of ironic narrative which is peculiarly Chaucer's own. . . . The humour of Chaucer's comic tales is by turns sardonic, boisterous and lighthearted, now punctuated by pathos, now by horror. The romances differ from most specimens of the genre and illustrate Chaucer's tendency to make every literary form he adapts more witty, learned and humane, imbued with the distinctive colouring of his mind and personality. Like Shakespeare with the chronicle-history, revenge-tragedy and comedy of in-

trigue, Chaucer transforms existing literary types rather than consciously creates new ones.

The *Tales* are generally well-suited to the tellers, though there are a few cases of inconsistency due to lack of final revision. Thus the Man of Law promises a tale in prose but in fact tells (in rhyme royal) the story of Constance, which is not unsuited to him but which may originally have been intended for another pilgrim (the epilogue to the tale does not indicate its teller). Some tales have more than a 'general' appropriateness (i.e. one of tone, content and style) to the teller; they may also be *dramatically motivated*—that is, they may spring out of one pilgrim's reaction to a preceding tale or to the character of the teller. Thus the Miller sets out to 'quyte' (pay back) the Knight's tale with a story which travesties the refined love-situation of the courtly romance. Here we see Chaucer brilliantly contrasting different literary genres, with their widely divergent attitudes and ethos. At the same time, the tale has another function in the whole, for in telling it, the Miller deliberately satirizes an old carpenter, who is cuckolded in the story by an Oxford student. The Reeve, who was 'a wel good wrighte, a carpenter', takes offence and revenges himself by telling an equally gross and violent tale which exposes a *miller* to yet greater discomfort, humiliation and shame. In the same way, a quarrel develops between the Friar and the Summoner that issues in either pilgrim's telling a tale which fiercely attacks the other's profession and character. 'Motivation' is a method which helps Chaucer to make his satire impersonal, and so more effective and convincing. The Summoner and his profession suffer far worse damage at the hands of the Friar than they would if subjected to a direct satirical onslaught from the author. . . . Again, in the **"Shipman's Tale"**, a monk (a very 'manly' one, at that) is shown as insinuating himself into the household of a merchant and seducing his wife; but in this instance Chaucer does not exploit the possibility of motivation, for the tale is neither provoked by the Monk's insulting the Shipman, nor does it provoke the Monk to reply. (Perhaps, considering that the monk in the tale is not in fact *discomfited,* the pilgrim-Monk would have regarded the Shipman's offering as a compliment rather than an insult!) More generally, 'motivation' enlivens the individual tales by giving them a further significance as parts of a dramatic whole, helps to weld together the pilgrims, the frame-story and the separate narratives, and contributes to the creation of areas of local unity within the total pattern. Thus the Wife of Bath, the Clerk, and the Franklin and Merchant all tell tales which have as their *subject* marriage (and particularly the questions of obedience, 'sovereignty' (or supremacy) in marriage, and adultery) and as their pervasive *theme* the definition of nobility or *gentillesse* in its ambiguous and shifting relations to character and social station. These tales accordingly make up a 'Marriage Group' which is perhaps the most complexly organized 'act' within the whole drama of the tales.

Chaucer does not achieve unity in the *Tales* through forcing a mechanical scheme upon an intractable body of mixed material. The 'unity' is rather something organic that grows from an imaginative absorption in the reality of his creations. Its very appearance of untidy, irregular

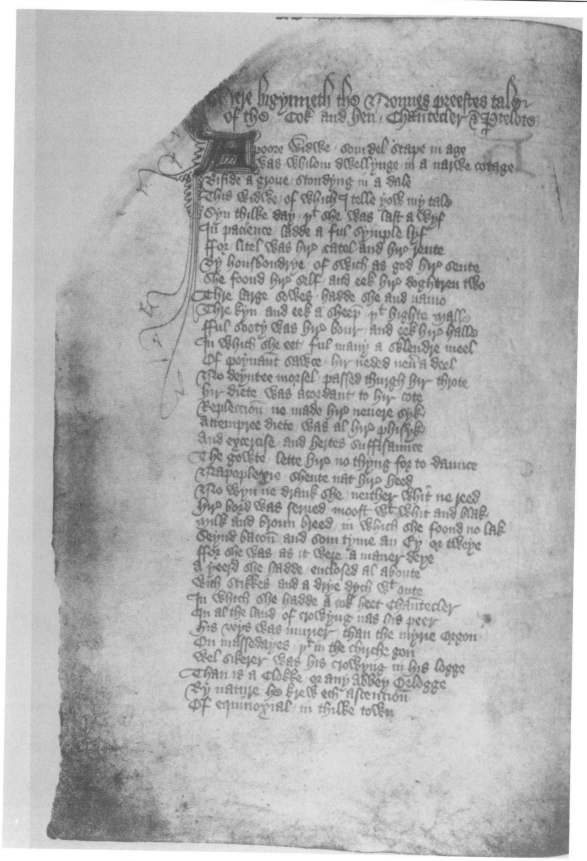

The beginning of the "Nun's Priest's Tale" from the Hengwrt manuscript.

spontaneousness makes the poem rather like a great medieval cathedral: at first sight so much rich colour, light and shade, and confusingly detailed carving in wood and stone, yet revealing on closer study a structural framework as clear and solid as it is complex and delicate. Yeats's lines about Homer in his poem *Ancestral Houses* apply equally aptly to Chaucer, who

> had not sung
> Had he not found it certain beyond dreams
> That out of life's own self-delight had sprung
> The abounding glittering jet . . .

Life, abundance and *self-delight* are the leading features of Chaucer's art. What is the relationship of this art to the life on which it draws?

Chaucer drew widely on literary sources as well as direct observation of life in creating the portraits of the pilgrims. . . . But although he may distort for the sake of emphasis (as in the caricature of the Miller's portrait) his usual method differs from the medieval *grotesque* of a writer like Langland or a painter like Hieronymus Bosch. Chaucer's avowed aim was to register *his impression* of reality—

> . . . al the condicioun
> Of ech of hem, *so as it seemed me* . . .

and even if this 'reality' was a construction of the mind, the poem was intended to seem the record of an actual pilgrimage Chaucer had been on himself. This is why in reporting the pilgrims' appearance and words he was unwilling to

> telle his tale untrewe,
> Or feyne thing, or finde wordes newe

or, as he says in the **"Miller's Prologue"**:

> . . . I moot reherce
> Hir tales alle, be they better or werse,
> Or elles falsen som of my mateere.

Realism is perhaps even harder for a narrative poet to sustain than it is for a dramatist. But Chaucer's realism is not an unselective, 'total' transcription of actuality. He isolates details and varies his method so as to bring out both the individuality and the typicality of his characters, and this means their moral as well as their social representativeness. In the ***Tales*** themselves the degree of realism fluctuates greatly, but in the **"General Prologue"** and the Links (which consist of dialogue and action rather than description) there is a fairly uniform level of realism within the given (non-realistic) convention of verse. The portraits move from the minute notation of physical features—

> Upon the cop right of his nose he hade
> A werte, and theron stood a toft of heris . . .

to summarizing comment on moral qualities—

> He was a verray, parfit, gentil knight.

Few of the portraits are composed entirely of physical details, nor are these chosen simply to reveal typifying traits. In this respect Chaucer's method differs from that of seventeenth-century 'character-writers' like John Earle

(*Microcosmographie*) or La Bruyère (*Caractères*) but is nearer to that of Dryden in his Achitophel or Zimri (*Absalom and Achitophel*), which are portraits of real people. Whether or not Chaucer drew partly on observation of actual contemporaries, his portraits in the **"General Prologue"** are nearest to those like Pope's portrait of 'Atticus' in his *Epistle to Dr Arbuthnot* (a portrait based on Addison but crystallizing the character and behaviour of the 'literary dictator' as a type). With a few exceptions, they are, as 'types', moral, social and psychological (which for medievals often meant *physio*logical) rather than professional. The exceptions are the Yeoman and Squire, who *are* more 'professional' types than anything else. The Parson and Plowman are embodiments of *ideal* concepts, as are, to a slightly lesser extent, the Knight and the Clerk. In the case of the latter, peculiarly medieval in their singleminded pursuit of one form of excellence (so different from the Renaissance idea of the complete man), it is difficult to disentangle the typical from the ideal, but for all this both men are wholly *credible* as 'people'. The other sixteen pilgrims who are fully described, together with the Canon and Yeoman who arrive towards the end of the journey, make up together the earliest collection of convincingly 'real' characters in English literature—'earliest' if, that is, we leave aside Pandarus, Criseyde and Diomede in ***Troilus and Criseyde*** (c. 1383-5).

Troilus and Criseyde provides a convenient point of departure for considering how far Chaucer's realism is a matter of *concreteness* of presentation. These lines describe Criseyde as the Trojan prince Troilus sees her in a temple and falls in love with her:

> She was nat with the leste of hir stature,
> But alle hir lymes so wel answeringe
> Weren to wommanhod, that creature
> Was nevere lasse mannyshe in semynge.
> And ek the pure wise of hire mevynge
> Shewed wel that men mighte in hire gesse
> Honour, estat, and wommanly noblesse.

Compare lines 151-6 from the Prioress's portrait:

> Ful semely hir wimpel *pinched* was,
> Hir nose tretys, *her eyen greye as glas,*
> Hir mouth ful smal, and thereto *softe and reed;*
> But sikerly she hadde a fair forheed—
> It was almost *a spanne brood,* I trowe—
> For, hardily, she was nat undergrowe!

The first passage relies on generalized assertion. The opening line politely indicates that Criseyde was tall and the remainder tells us that this did not detract from her femininity: she was wholly graceful and elegant as a woman should be. The italicized phrases of the Prioress's description show by contrast how specific the latter is. Even the conventional 'grey as glass' gains a new vitality in the context and becomes as 'real' as the Monk's 'eyen stepe, and rollinge in his heed', while the details of forehead, mouth and wimple concentrate (as the Commentary points out) a wealth of meaning. The *Troilus* passage is not bad writing, but it belongs to an altogether more formal 'courtly' mode. It is not, for that matter, wholly typical of the poem, but it does illustrate a type of writing Chaucer increasingly abandoned in the latest of his tales (the

"Canon's Yeoman's Tale" is an example). The important point is that the heroine's *exact appearance* is left for the reader's imagination to fill in, rather as in the novels of Henry James, for **Troilus and Criseyde** is largely concerned with the inner life of the protagonists. The **"General Prologue"**, by contrast, exemplifies an intensely *visual* mode of writing, deliberately cultivated as it were in rivalry to the minute realism of the late Gothic painters whose work culminated in the *Très Riches Heures* of the Duc de Berry. . . .

Apart from concreteness, what gives the poem its general air of reality is the *device of the pilgrimage* in which the author claims to have participated. Many medieval poets declare that their story is something they heard or read, and this is often the case. Others, like the authors of dream-vision poems such as *Piers Plowman* or *Pearl,* seem to be relating their own experience—and this is true in that the visions 'took place in' (i.e. were invented by) their imagination rather than being borrowed from a written source. But Chaucer vouches for the truthfulness of his first-person narrative in a way which both obliges him to write realistically and serves to excuse him when doing so leads to possible offences against taste:

> But first I pray yow, of your curteisye,
> That ye n'arette it nat my vileynye,
> Thogh that I pleynly speke in this matere,
> To telle yow hir *wordes* and hir *cheere,*
> Ne thogh I speke hir wordes properly.

The concluding words of this 'Apology' (which is really more of a covert manifesto) are also noteworthy, though not usually quoted as illustrating Chaucer's realism:

> Also I pray yow to foryeve it me,
> Al have I nat set folk *in hir degree*
> Here in this tale, *as that they sholde stonde* . . .

For although the **Tales** begin with one told by the pilgrim of highest social rank, they soon proceed without regard to hierarchical decorum. When after the Knight's tale the Host turns to the *Monk* for a story he is rudely interrupted by the drunken *Miller,* who insists on having his way and telling a tale to 'quyte' [answer] that of the Knight. The excuse Chaucer gives (ironically, one need hardly say) for flouting decorum both in his **"General Prologue"** and in the body of the work ('this tale') is his artistic naïveté:

> My wit is short—ye may wel understonde.

What we 'may well understand' is, however, that the Miller's abrupt intrusion makes the movement from the first tale to the second much more graphic and transforms what could have been an awkward transition into a scene of strong dramatic interest. Other writers who used frame-stories before Chaucer failed to exploit their full dramatic potential and left them as somewhat artificial devices for holding together what was virtually an anthology. But Chaucer seizes triumphantly on the opportunity of confronting one who

> nevere yet no vileynye ne sayde
> In al his lyf, unto no maner wight

with a 'churl' who

was a jangler and a goliardeys

Such dynamic oppositions would have been ruled out if his prime concern had been to 'set folk in their degree'. The essence of dramatic realism is to do the unexpected and yet make it seem, once it is done, the inevitable. Chaucer's whole conception in the **"General Prologue"** enables him to bring together characters with widely divergent attitudes and outlooks who could not have met one another in a work that fitted into any existing medieval literary genre. Part of the prologue's originality is that it creates a new genre in itself. George Crabbe, in the Preface to his **Tales** (1812), declared that 'to have followed the method of Chaucer might have been of use' but he did not attempt to do so because of its 'great difficulty and hazard'. It is a measure of Chaucer's achievement that he makes us forget the latent improbability of a 'colloquial and travelling intimacy' (in Crabbe's phrase) arising between such different and contrasting personalities. The realism of Chaucer's *art* makes us accept as probable (and therefore realistic) what is at best only possible.

While the Links sustain the general method of the **"General Prologue"**, the tales themselves vary from the rhetorical artifice of the Squire's offering to the down-to-earth directness of the Shipman's. The stylistic conventions of the tale's genre and the character of the teller partly determine the quality of the language and style. The Links are the extension of the prologue into the body of the work, presenting as actors in a living drama what we have hitherto seen as static images. The Links are if anything even more strikingly original than the prologue. The actual idea of a pilgrimage had been previously used in the *Novelle* of Giovanni Sercambi (1385), a work which Chaucer could have known, but the **Canterbury Tales** develop the device in an altogether new and unpredictable way (e.g. in the case of the 'Marriage Group' or the tales of the Miller and Reeve, and the Friar and Summoner, the most remarkable examples of a close dramatic relationship between frame-story and individual tales). In the Prologue to *Piers Plowman,* too, Chaucer would have found a visionary panorama of medieval society 'working and wandering as the world asks'; but he has also chosen his characters for the dramatic possibilities they offer as well as their social representativeness. Though Chaucer omits the highest and lowest ranks of society (barons and bishops; hired labourers) he nevertheless manages to include *tales* which deal with the life of the higher classes (e.g., the **"Knight's"**, **"Squire's"** and **"Man of Law's Tales"**). At the other extreme, with the exception of characters like the old widows in the **"Nun's Priest's Tale"** and the **"Friar's Tale"** or old Janicula in the **"Clerk's Tale"**, the life of the medieval poor is never presented with the immediacy and power of Langland, say. The sufferings of the poor never enter Chaucer's poetry as material for protest. Even when he is writing satire, his primary aim is to entertain, and when a tale ceases to be entertaining, Chaucer will arrange to have it interrupted—even if it is the tale he has given himself.

The author's own dramatic presence is above all what makes the device of the pilgrimage realistic. In connexion with his own tales of **"Sir Thopas"** and **"Melibee"** Chaucer contrives to poke fun at 'himself' by creating a fictional counterpart, 'Chaucer the Pilgrim', as E. T. Donaldson has usefully called him, who must have provided a very amusing contrast (all the funnier for the real similarities) to the self known to his patrons and friends. This character is not a new one, however: Chaucer is dramatically present in nearly every one of his earlier poems, and the main lineaments of the **Canterbury Tales** figure are already present in the 'Geffrey' of the **Hous of Fame.** Nevertheless, even this fact should not make us assume that a *wholly* fictional dramatic mask or *persona* is present in the **"General Prologue"** from the start, as well as in the body of the poem, in the section where 'Chaucer the Pilgrim' tells his tales. It is quite possible that the idea of exploiting the humour inherent in the discrepancy between his real and fictional selves only occurred to Chaucer after he had written the prologue. At any rate, nothing in the prologue itself demands to be read as coming from Chaucer the Pilgrim. A line like

> My wit is short—ye may wel understonde

need not be taken as a 'dramatic' statement coming from a 'naïve' pilgrim-narrator but may be only the conventional medieval expression of modesty used by innumerable writers. In fact, the mode of realism of the Links is rather closer to reportage than that of the **"General Prologue"** (which reveals, for example, knowledge of the pilgrims' life and characters which could have been acquired only *during* the pilgrimage, not *before* it). There is thus good reason for taking statements by the speaker in the prologue as coming 'straight' from the author. This point becomes important when we attempt to gauge Chaucer's moral standpoint in the prologue and his attitude to the pilgrims he satirizes. It is hard not to be aware of an element of caricature in many of the prologue-portraits, and because Chaucer's satirical intentions often require him to *distort* in the interests of greater vividness his 'portrait-realism' must never be confused with 'historical fact'. The descriptions themselves do not constitute documentary evidence for historical generalization and, indeed, have no value at all as such until they have been analysed and understood as *poetry*. The effect of historical allusions in the portraits is therefore somewhat confusing since they may have revealed to the original audience a level of *intention* (which is a part of *meaning*) not susceptible to modern critical analysis.

References and allusions to real places and people certainly occur in the **"General Prologue"**. Thus two characters who are not actually named until the **"Cook's Prologue"** appear to have been modelled on living contemporaries— Roger of Ware (the Cook) and Harry Bailly (the Host). Behind the Merchant's portrait may lie the figure of Gilbert Maghfield, a contemporary London merchant, and behind that of the Man of Law the Lincolnshire lawyer Thomas Pynchbeck. . . . The topical significance of the portraits probably added an extra touch of realism for the original audience but today the allusions are almost an encumbrance, and certainly a distraction. Rather more interesting than the hypothetical contemporary 'source' of the Merchant is the fact that Chaucer abstains from naming him and, further, draws attention to the fact:

> But (soth to seyn) I noot how men him calle
> (284)

—a line deftly suggesting the man's secretiveness. The fact that the *majority* of the characters are, as it happens, given no name, points to Chaucer's desire to emphasize their typicality as well as their individuality: 'Knight', 'Squire', 'Yeoman', 'Ploughman'. Like the portraits of Titian and Rembrandt, they are, as Blake called them, 'universal'.

Some portraits may appear more realistic than others, even where this is not just due to greater physical detail. Thus the whole descriptive *mode* of the Squire's portrait strikes us as 'conventional' and designed to evoke the image of the typical young squire. His total appearance (*cheere*) is an *outward expression* of his role in life. By contrast, the other youthful member of the company, the Pardoner, is described in terms which have nothing to do with his profession or social role: the dishevelled hair, beardless face and high-pitched voice express his character as an individual (or, at best, a *Physiological* 'type')—although Chaucer no doubt made him physically repulsive because he disliked Pardoners rather than *vice versa*. The amount of physical detail varies according to whether the idea or the image is dominant. Thus the *Manciple* is an embodiment of native 'wit' (as opposed to the kind acquired by learning, like that of his masters). In his portrait no details of looks appear and he is realized solely in 'ethical' terms—only his moral character and way of life are described. At the other extreme is the *Miller:* two lines describe his clothing, nine lines his success at wrestling and doorbreaking, his bawdiness, his dishonesty and his musical abilities; the rest of the portrait (ten lines) presents with grotesque precision the colour and shape of his beard, his nose and his mouth. For Chaucer, the Manciple's 'reality' consists in his cunning *mind* (to look at, the man is nondescript, perhaps), whereas the Miller, important as his crookedness and obscenity may be, impresses primarily as grossly *animal.*

Physical details are also expressive of *character.* The Summoner's 'narrow' eyes (for which there are good physical causes) and the glaring hare-like eyes of the Pardoner fitly express the lecherous character of both men. In a more learned and allusive way, the Wife of Bath's widely-spaced teeth 'express' her hyper-active sexuality, for the medieval physiognomists thought such teeth a sign of a bold, lascivious nature—an observation supported by the Wife in [the **"Wife of Bath's Prologue"**]. . . . Elsewhere physical details only *suggest* character, though the role of suggestion is vital in creating the total picture and illuminating particular lines. Thus the description of the Prioress's mouth as 'very small, and also soft and red', by stressing size, feel and colour, reinforces the implications of her name and contributes to the ambiguity of her brooch-motto. Further details strengthen this impression:

> She leet no morsel from hir *lippes* falle . . .
> Hir over *lippe* wyped she so clene . . .
> That of hir *smyling* was ful simple and coy . . .

The epithets 'humble' and 'shy' (*simple and coy*), applied somewhat unexpectedly to her *smiling,* are especially striking. Like the Prioress's *mouth,* the Pardoner's *hair* is emphasized: very long, waxy-yellow, smooth and thin, it suggests effeminacy so strongly as to render Chaucer's explicitness in line 691 otiose. These physical details also support the punning innuendo in line 673:

> This Somnour bar to him a *stif burdoun*

which is further reinforced by the insistence on the *smoothness* of the Pardoner's 'surface'. This quality makes him a fitting compeer to the Summoner, who is so *rough* that he cannot remove his 'whelks' and 'knobs'. These contrasts of surfaces reveal the portrait-artist's feel for *texture* in a surprisingly literal sense for one whose medium is not paint but words.

Words—those of the pilgrims themselves—also help to create an indelible impression of character. It may be a *Latin tag* unforgettably associated with a pilgrim—the Prioress's *Amor vincit omnia,* or the Friar's *In principio,* or the pathetic *Question quid iuris* parroted by the Summoner in his cups. Or it may be the name of an *authority*—the Doctor's fifteen physicians, the Franklin's 'Epicurus' (an ironic Chaucerian compliment: the Franklin's 'philosophy' of food is certainly not learnt from books!), the voluminous Aristotle of the Clerk. Elsewhere, the *names of places* illustrate the range of the three most widely-travelled pilgrims—the Knight's sieges and battles—Alisaundre, Algezir, Lyeys, Lettow; the Shipman's havens—from Gotland to Finistere; the Wife of Bath's shrines—in Italy, France, Germany, Spain and the Holy Land. Other names mainly pinpoint the essential interests and concerns of the pilgrim in question—the Merchant's ports of Orwell and Middleburg, the Man of Law's 'Parvys', the Clerk's Oxford, the Ypres and Gaunt whose weavers the Wife surpassed in skill. The 'world' of the pilgrims varies from that of the Knight, who had seen places which were *only* 'names' to Chaucer and his audience, to the Parson's, small enough to traverse on foot in journeys more purposeful than the Wife's 'wandring by the weye' (a phrase which implies triviality as well as street-walking).

The variety of the innumerable aspects of contemporary social reality that crowd into the **"General Prologue"** is nowhere better exemplified than in the *clothing* of the pilgrims and their equipment, especially their horses. The Doctor's deep red and blue contrasts with the Shipman's drab 'falding' gown, the Wife's semi-symbolic scarlet contrasts with the sober black the Parson must be imagined as wearing. The Prioress and Monk embody respectively ecclesiastical elegance and ecclesiastical luxury, the one bending her Rule by pleating her wimple, the other contemptuously flinging his out of the window by flaunting the most expensive fur on his sleeves. The two hypocrites, Friar and Merchant, are fittingly juxtaposed, and their clothing manifests their sense of self-importance (*solempnetee*). Contrasting with the portly Friar (who *should* be poor) is the Clerk in his threadbare 'courtepy'. He in turn is placed next to another learned pilgrim, the Man of Law, whose dress ('homely medley') is a compromise between the Clerk's unselfconscious shabbiness and the imposing opulence of the third learned pilgrim, the Doctor. (The Sergeant has spent his money not on books [like the Clerk] but on real property; of the Physician we are told that he was slow to *spend* the gold acquired from 'treating' victims

of the plague, but 'kept' it and 'loved' it.) The strongest contrasts in clothing occur in the first group of father, son and servant, who ride together in, respectively, a stained tunic, a flowery robe in the latest style, and a functional costume of woodland green. There is something almost emblematic about these pilgrims, as if we were meant to guess their role in life at a glance. . . . Not all the pilgrims' horses (sure indexes of social station) are specifically mentioned, but there is variety enough among those that are: the Clerk's horse resembles its owner in its leanness, the Plowman's mount is the humble mare, the Monk's horse is in 'great estate', as we would expect from one who had 'full many a choice horse' in his stables; the Merchant's way of sitting his mount ('high on horse') reflects his sense of his own dignity, while the Shipman, so skilful in his own element, is not at ease on his nag and rides 'as best he could'. Echoes, parallels and contrasts could be pursued through the complexions, features, attitudes and mannerisms of the pilgrims. Their rich multiplicity is captured no less in the sounds of their conversation and music-making—from the terse, pithy utterance of the logic-trained Clerk ('souning in moral vertu') to the solemn 'resouns' of the money-fixated Merchant ('souninge alwey th' encrees of his winning'). A profound contrast in values is underlined by the use of the same word ('souning'). No less effectively, the graceful, refined existence of the Squire is evoked by his fluting, just as the Miller's bagpipe conjures up the coarse energy of the man.

The **"General Prologue"** spans the social world of medieval England—from the relaxed, leisured milieu of the real and would-be courtiers to the hard-working existence of the labourers on whose efforts *all* the estates relied for their bodily needs. The 'fresshe floures, whyte and rede' cannot grow unless the soil is manured by the 'fother' of 'dong'. The pilgrimage at once asserts the reality of classes and exposes the irrelevance of class from the standpoint of ultimate values. But Chaucer seems to say that class-distinctions serve a useful purpose here and now, even if the enormous middle class reveals the obsolescence of the old classifications, and there is comedy in the efforts of the 'fringe' pilgrims such as the Prioress, who

> peyned hire to countrefete chere
> Of court, and been estatlich of manere

and the Monk, who devoted himself to the aristocratic sport of hunting and

> was a prikasour aright

(like the monk aptly summed up by Langland as riding 'with a heap of hounds at his arse, *as if he were a lord*'. *Snobbery* rings out in the indignant repetitions which seem to record the Friar's own phrases:

> It is nat honest, it may nat avaunce,
> For to delen with no swich poraille

and appears in the Merchant's attempts to conceal his true position with an 'estatly governaunce', in the Sergeant's undermining of his *genuine* learning, success and efficiency by trying to seem 'bisier than he was', in the Wife's anger if any woman in her parish took precedence over her at the mass-offering, and, finally, in the uniformly clothed and wived Gildsmen, the epitome of the new London bourgeoisie of the day.

Strongly contrasted with the class-conscious members of the middle ranks of society are the 'churls' who form a group towards the end. Three characters who do not fit neatly into any social group are the Manciple, the Shipman and the Franklin. The first is placed after the Miller in the churls' group, but by coming next to the Reeve illustrates a distinction between two kinds of cunning. Chaucer admires the Manciple but scorns the low and shady methods of the Reeve. One line

> They were adrad of him as of the deeth

serves to link the latter with the Summoner

> Of [whose] visage children were aferd

but the Reeve merits no softening touch of sympathy even in the midst of repulsion like the line declaring that the Summoner

> was a gentil harlot and a kinde.

The Shipman is another example of cunning (and worse) but he is not included among the churls and takes his place between Cook and Physician (both 'skilful' men, though Chaucer seems surer of the Shipman's maritime and the Cook's culinary than the Doctor's medical expertise). The Franklin, whose social position at this period would have been at the top of the middle class and just below the Knight, is not a man of skill but, in the full sense of the word, an *amateur*. Critics often note 'autobiographical' touches in this portrait, and was not Chaucer himself an amateur in all he attempted (except, of course, his poetry)? The **"Franklin's Tale"**, too, with its concern to distinguish the social and ethical meanings of *gentillesse,* coincides with Chaucer's own ideas on the subject as summed up in his Balade on *Gentillesse.*

In his attitudes to his characters Chaucer may show whole-hearted respect (Knight, Parson, Plowman), sympathetic delight in a single virtue (the Franklin's hospitality), general admiration for a kind of excellence (Squire, Clerk) tempered by humorous criticism of the excess that may go with it, plain appreciation of a job well done (Yeoman, Cook—with, in the latter case, a meaningful shudder . . .), or admiration for the skills of the churls (without this detracting from their 'churlishness'):

> A baggepype *wel* coude he blowe and sowne
> (Miller)

or

> He was a *wel good* wrighte, a carpenter (Reeve)

In all these cases Chaucer's attitude is *simple.* Complexity enters with the first touch of irony:

> He yaf nat of that text a pulled hen,
> That seith that hunters ben nat holy men . . .
> And I seyde, his opinioun was good (Monk)

or

> He was in chirche a noble ecclesiaste (Pardoner)

More subtle are the ironies of the Prioress's portrait, some

of which depend on historical information that we do not fully possess (her French and her brooch-motto are discussed in the Commentary). But a larger uncertainty perplexes our understanding. We know what the medieval ideal of a nun was and how Madame Eglentyne falls short of it, but did Chaucer judge her by this standard? Does he judge his characters at all?

While it is a fact that Chaucer never calls any pilgrim 'bad' he does call one of them 'good'. The line

> A good man was ther of religioun

is not merely praising the Parson for being 'good of his kind' or 'good at his job', any more than the comparative form in

> A bettre preest I trowe ther nowher noon is.

The Parson's portrait is notably explicit: he is 'riche in holy thoght and *werk*', 'holy' and 'vertuous', just as his brother the Plowman is not merely 'a trewe *swinkere*' but *lives* 'in pees and parfit charitee'. *Holiness, virtue* and *charity* represented the highest medieval values: they served to set standards, they could not be qualified by reference to higher criteria. From the standard established for *all* the pilgrims (but especially the clerical ones, who had a particular calling to virtue, charity and holiness) by the Parson's portrait, can we see whether Chaucer is judging the Prioress?

Chaucer states that he aimed to tell us

> *al the condicioun*
> Of ech of hem . . .

as well as

> Th'estat, th'array, the nombre, *and eek the cause*
> Why that assembled was this compaignye.

The 'condicioun' of the pilgrims and the 'cause' of their assembling may be connected, if we take *cause* as including not only 'purpose' (to go to Canterbury) but also 'motive' (reason for going). Does each pilgrim's 'total condition' ('*al* the condicioun') include his moral and spiritual state as well as (in the more obvious sense of the word) his appearance, 'image' and social position? If so, each pilgrim's attitude to the pilgrimage itself becomes a relevant consideration. As few as four of the pilgrims (the Parson and Plowman certainly, the Knight and Clerk almost as certainly) seem to be going to the shrine of St Thomas for *religious* reasons (*penitential,* as with the Knight, a man of war seeking to make satisfaction for his sins, or more generally *devotional,* as with the other three). The others have a variety of dubious motives and some are grotesquely out of place. It would seem that Chaucer's concern with realism has resulted in fundamentally undermining his story's credibility—for in choosing a pilgrimage as the means of assembling a varied collection of characters, he has forgotten that some of them would scarcely be there in the first place. The Wife of Bath no doubt found it a good way of meeting a potential sixth husband, but would the *Shipman* choose a pilgrimage as the best way to beguile his time (assuming that *he* is not impelled by devotional urges?) The questions are awkward, but it is the very realism of the poem that is responsible for raising them. And it is here that the realism of the **"General Pro-logue"** can be seen as limited and qualified by a further purpose or interest of Chaucer's. This is the symbolic or moral significance of the pilgramage as an *idea:* that is, to keep before the reader (at however great a distance) the Christian conception of human life and the values on which it is built. We may not be *invited* to judge the pilgrims, but we are certainly given a standard by reference to which they *can* be judged. Interestingly enough, there is one other character who *does* seem to be going on pilgrimage for religious reasons: this is Chaucer himself, who started out 'with ful devout corage' (22) and whose attitude is thus nearest to that of the Parson and the other three.

This conclusion will appear objectionable only if we base our idea of Chaucer's moral standpoint on the *conclusion* of the **Canterbury Tales** (the heavily didactic treatise on sin which constitutes the **"Parson's Tale"** and the so-called **"Retractions"** that follow, in which the author 're-nounces' or 'retracts' all those of his works which are 'conducive to sin' (*sownen unto sin*)—including most of his early works and the bulk of the **Tales**!). But this final or 'deathbed' attitude, which is narrow and negative, is strikingly at variance with the attitude which pervades the **Tales** as a whole—a warm, charitable love of humanity together with an acute sensitivity to moral evil and good. In the **"Parson's Tale"** and the **"Retractions"** we see Chaucer as the *mere* moralist—rather like Tolstoy in his old age, when he denied the worth of much of his greatest work from a standpoint of puritanical harshness. Chaucer's work displays almost everywhere a deep love of human nature in all its richness and poverty, and his creations are (in John Bayley's phrase) 'characters of love', sensed as *real* and *other* in the way we sense the reality and otherness of people we love. This 'love' is an act of the imagination distinct from the minor artist's 'affection' for the whimsical creations of his fancy which resemble aspects of himself. It is as free from sentimentality as the *charitee* of the Parson, who

> was to sinful men nat despitous

but strove

> To drawen folk to hevene *by fayrnesse,*

although

> were any persone obstinat,
> What so he were, of heigh or lough estat,
> Him wolde he snibben sharply . . .

Chaucer avoids the sentimentalist's error of glamorizing vice and the cynic's error of thinking all virtue hypocrisy. There is no sharper critic of vice (especially the vice of hypocrisy) and no warmer advocate of virtue and (for he was a medieval Christian, not an agnostic humanist) *holynesse.* However, Chaucer (and the Parson in the prologue-portrait) lacks the inhuman rigidity of the medieval religious outlook which moderns tend to think typical. The dominant feature of *Chaucer's* outlook is *fayrnesse*—connoting both 'justice' and 'gentleness' (or 'pleasantness'). Like the *charitee* of the Parson and Plowman, Chaucer's 'love' is *parfit* (complete, total). Part of such love is severity towards intransigent or cynically hardened

vice, and Chaucer can 'snibben sharply' characters who are not humanly weak but villainously corrupt. . . . Not all the pilgrims are 'characters of love' in the sense that the author would have liked them had they really existed; but none are 'characters of hate' created solely out of an urge to annihilate them in a destructive rain of satire.

Chaucer, in a word, has the power to endow his creations with a larger life than their function in the narrative strictly requires. His art penetrates more deeply than that of Pope, say, because his love for his characters (that is, his sense of their *reality*) is more intense than his desire to correct their faults. Pope's genius, which created both Sporus and the Man of Ross, might have been able to give us the Friar and the Franklin, but not the Prioress. Yet her portrait is 'complex' without this being due to Chaucer's 'ambivalent' (contradictory) feelings about its subject. The Prioress is, at the same time, more than an 'embodiment' of false courtliness or self-delusion. She exists as a rounded personality because she springs not from the moralizing intellect but the deepest creative imagination, which enables the artist to *realize* a character and also to offer the character for judgment, without actually passing judgment himself. That the achievement should be possible in *non*-dramatic poetry like the **"General Prologue"** is all the greater testimony to Chaucer's wonderful humanity. There is perhaps an element of paradox here: Chaucer is at once not a moralist and yet has a clear and unconfused moral outlook. The presence of bawdy fabliaux in the **Tales** does not of itself mean that Chaucer was 'trying to have it both ways'. Taken in isolation, the fabliaux may seem to be amoral—ebullient and seductive images of 'natural man' which *sownen unto sin,* or, at the very least, fail by the criterion established by Chaucer in his **"Retractions"**: ' "Al that is writen is writen for oure doctrine (to instruct us)"—and that is myn entente'. But taken in context they can be seen as, morally, the 'partial evil' which contributes to the 'universal good' of the **Tales** as a whole. Chaucer's wish to be true to reality required him to give *harlotries* to the churls, and, to do him justice, he never leaves his stories as the crude, perfunctory things that (to judge by the analogues) they originally were. (The 'justification' of his *realism* is fundamentally the justification of the freedom of the artist and the autonomy of the work of art and cannot be discussed here.) There is nothing cheap, mechanical or sensational about Chaucer's treatment of sex. Whether the fabliaux can be called 'bawdy' but not 'obscene' is a difficult question to be definite about. What *is* certain is the impossibility of dismissing such magnificent works of art as *generically* inferior or worthless. Literary criticism, rather than a 'permissive' attitude to sex, tells us that the fabliaux, from the **"Miller's Tale"** to the **"Merchant's Tale"** are, far from being embarrassing, an extraordinary achievement of unselfconscious and completely assured genius, springing from an integrated vision of life the leading feature of which is, in Chaucer's own fine word, *fayrnesse.* (pp. 4-24)

A. V. C. Schmidt, in an introduction to The General Prologue to The Canterbury Tales and The Canon's Yeoman's Prologue and Tale, *edited by A. V. C. Schmidt, University of London Press Ltd., 1974, pp. 1-44.*

Gloria Cigman   (essay date 1975)

[*In the excerpt below, Cigman provides an overview of the "Wife of Bath's Prologue and Tale."*]

The **"Prologue to the Wife of Bath's Tale"** is conspicuously longer than that to any of the other twenty-three *Canterbury Tales.* It is, in fact, as long as Chaucer's **"General Prologue"** to the entire collection, in which he gives us portraits of most of the pilgrims. Some of these portraits are more detailed than others and in the links between some of the *Tales* Chaucer adds to his initial characterizations here and there. But the Wife of Bath emerges as the pilgrim who is most fully portrayed, through the autobiographical form of her prologue which has a directness and intimacy that make her the most rounded character of them all.

The Wife of Bath is one of a group of pilgrims consisting entirely of men, except for the Prioress and her companion nun, and she has to hold her own as a woman without either the protection of a husband or the inviolable sanctity of a religious calling. Some readers regard her as coarse and vulgar, others see her as endearingly direct and honest; some regard the Prioress as trivial and hypocritical, while others see her as sheltered and refined. The Wife's attitude to men is far from deferential or respectful, but with her lively tongue, her sense of humour, and her open manner, most of her fellow-pilgrims would certainly have found her a welcome companion.

If we look at the portraits in Chaucer's **"General Prologue"**, we find that the dominant element is *vocation.* The pilgrims are drawn from a wide cross-section of society in late fourteenth-century England. The traditional three divisions of medieval society are represented: knights, clergy and labourers; the rulers and defenders, the spiritual leaders, and the cultivators of the land. In addition to these, there are representatives of the merchants, landowners, administrators and craftsmen who constitute the rising middle class. Casting his net across the clerical and secular life of his time, Chaucer brings together a wide variety of types and shows us extremes of corruption and hypocrisy on the one hand, and piety and virtue on the other, with, between the two, a range of neither wholly good nor wholly bad characters who have the foibles and defects of average humanity.

Where does the Wife fit into Chaucer's general scheme? The occupations of some of the other pilgrims carry certain moral obligations, violations of which serve as pointers to their characters. But the Wife of Bath's occupation as a cloth-maker is given only passing mention in the **"General Prologue"**. Instead, the emphasis in the initial portrait of this pilgrim, as in her prologue and her tale is on marriage.

It is to this question of marriage that we must look for understanding of the Wife's place in the scheme of *The Canterbury Tales.* In the midst of the lively and varied group of pilgrims assembled by Chaucer, she represents, quite simply, Woman. She is medieval woman at her most eloquent and her most basic. Despite her rather startling matrimonial score, she is essentially a conformist. Her behaviour may seem spectacular, but her needs and aspirations are really quite run-of-the-mill: she likes men, and she does not like sleeping alone. She is assertive and calculating in satisfying these needs but, as far as we are able to tell, she seems to have remained faithful to each husband while he was alive. She flirts and enjoys an easy familiarity with men but, whatever she may have done *in youthe* or later, she nowhere actually advocates sex outside marriage. Her prologue is an impassioned and persuasive defence of her point of view.

> Experience, though noon auctoritee
> Were in this world, is right ynogh for me
> To speke of wo that is in mariage;

The first part of the **"Wife of Bath's Prologue"** takes the form of an exposition. The Wife's views on marriage and sexual morality are elevated to the level of doctrine and, as such, are presented largely according to the common conventions of Chaucer's time. Medieval thought was eclectic: most thinkers drew on all the ideas accessible to them to formulate, expand or endorse their own views. A serious work of exposition would embody an encyclopaedic range of borrowed and adapted material, and most of the sources were acknowledged. The Wife of Bath accordingly supports her arguments throughout with references to respected authorities. In the first part of her prologue, her authorities are the Bible, and folk-commonsense presented in the form of proverbs and axioms.

But the opening words of the prologue make it clear that the Wife is defying convention in putting *experience* on a par with *auctoritee* as a teacher. She means, of course, her *own* experience, although she does not begin to develop this aspect of her discourse until after line 193. Until then, she states her point of view by means of generalized assertions, strengthened by external references meant to serve as evidence of objectivity. Nevertheless, however scholarly she may try to appear, her irrepressible confidence in her own experience is never far from the surface and finds expression from time to time.

In fact, the Wife utilizes both experience and authority in the course of her prologue. She draws upon about fifty authorities of varying stature, using examples from the Bible and references to Greek and Latin sources. . . . They reveal considerably more learning than might be expected in a woman of her social class—but she has, after all, travelled very widely and would have met and talked with many educated people; moreover, her fifth husband was a scholar who liked to tell her about what he read.

The Church was the dominant moral and spiritual authority in medieval England. It is therefore significant that before the Wife launches into the extended account of her marriage experiences she establishes very firmly her opposition to some of the prevalent attitudes of the Church to the subjects of marriage and sex.

The popular writings and preaching of the Church at this time were concerned first and foremost with virtue and sin. The Seven Deadly Sins included Lechery. The religious instruction familiar to Chaucer's pilgrims was continually urging men and women to curb their sexual appetites. Whatever the actual practice may have been, the stated ideal of the religious orders was celibacy. Marriage, although one of the sacraments of the Church, was viewed as greatly inferior to the state of virginity, in which spiritual and physical energies were directed entirely towards Christian devotion and pious living. But, given that most human beings could not achieve this spiritual ideal, the sexual relationship in marriage was seen as divinely ordained, its aim being procreation and not physical pleasure.

The first part of the **"Wife of Bath's Prologue"** is not merely a fierce attack on these attitudes, it is also a defence of robust sensuality. Her chief method of justification is that of the Church's own teachers: reference to Scriptural authority. But, characteristically, the Wife of Bath moves rapidly from theory and authority to experience, and reiterates her delight in sensuality in very personal terms.

> As taketh nat agrief of that I seye—
> For myn entente nis but for to pleye.

With these words the Wife of Bath ends her opening discourse on marriage, chastity and sex, and prepares to embark on the lengthy reminiscences which make up the rest of her prologue. She is to offer her companions the sort of personal revelations which modern journalese might describe as 'frank and fearless', in informal, colloquial language. And yet the Wife's account of her five marriages is not intended as mere gossip or chit-chat; it is a means of passing on what she regards as serious truths about marriage.

Most of the Wife's prologue, from line 196 on, is a narrative of her marriages, with examples from many authorities to support her conclusions and observations. One aspiration evident in each relationship is also the dominant theme of the **"Wife of Bath's Tale"**: the desire (which she attributes to all women) for mastery over their husbands:

> An housbonde I wol have, I nil nat lette,
> Which shal be bothe my dettour and my thral.

Ultimately, her prologue and tale are to reveal a surprisingly idealistic view of marriage, embodied in a paradox which will be discussed later in this introduction. First, however, she must establish her status as an authority on the subject. She sets about winning the respect of her audience by appealing to recognizably authentic experiences.

The level of experience farthest removed from that of the more devout pilgrims emerges in the imagery in which she likens sex in marriage to the world of commerce. A man must pay his debt to his wife; the sexual bond in marriage is a contractual obligation involving sustained toil. At times, this imagery is used as a form of euphemism, as when she speaks of her three elderly husbands:

> Unnethe mighte they the statut holde
> In which that they were bounden unto me—
> Ye woot wel what I meene of this, pardee!
> As help me God, I laughe whan I thinke
> How pitously anight I made hem swinke!

She argues that sexual love and desire are determined, like the value of commodities in a commercial market, by supply and demand:

> Forbede us thing, and that desyren we;

> Preesse on us faste, and thanne wol we fle.
> With daunger oute we al oure chaffare;
> Greet prees at market maketh deere ware,
> And to greet cheep is holde at litel prys;

The Wife, however, is not inhibited by any arch coyness and at times calls a spade a spade in a way which has only recently become acceptable again in 'respectable' literature:

> Have thou ynogh, what thar thee recche or care
> How mirily that othere folkes fare?
> For, certeyn, olde dotard, by youre leve,
> Ye shul have queynte right ynogh at eve!

The Wife knows how to utilize the persuasive power of laughter for her own ends (a device familiar to us through satire which attacks social, political or moral attitudes by means of exaggeration, caricature and parody). Her assertion that cloistered scholars are incapable of speaking well of any women except saints will eventually prompt the gentle Clerk of Oxenford to tell a tale of a woman totally unlike the Wife of Bath—but that comes later. Here, her scornful dismissal of the alleged anti-feminism of *clerkes* serves to ridicule all such scholars and, in so doing, win support for her own view:

> The clerk, whan he is old, and may noght do
> Of Venus werkes worth his olde sho,
> Thanne sit he doun, and writ in his dotage
> That wommen kan nat kepe hir mariage.

By inducing the audience to laugh at her taunting of her three elderly husbands, the Wife enlists their support against these feeble men who are pathetically ill-equipped to cope with her:

> Goode lief, take keepe
> How mekely looketh Wilkin, oure sheepe;
> Com neer, my spouse, lat me ba thy cheke;

The Wife seeks further support by using self-parody in her lengthy imitation of her own nagging of the unfortunate old husbands, a passage of 140 lines beginning:

> herkneth how I saide:
> 'Sire olde kaynard, is this thyn array . . . ?'

In her accounts of her own behaviour, the Wife consciously exposes the dishonesty of her own motives and thus precludes the stern condemnation which can arise when such dishonesty is exposed by others. She thus makes accomplices of those who laugh with her at the expense of her miserable victims.

Eventually, the humour of the Wife's prologue turns out to be largely at her own expense, although she never realizes this. Her cynical insistence on mastery in marriage is a damp squib, for the only husband she really loved beat her and treated her with disdain. Her account of how she eventually mastered him leaves the reader wondering whether it was the acquiescent and dutiful Wife or Jankin who really had the upper hand!

> After that day, we hadden never debaat.
> God helpe me so, I was to him as kynde
> As any wyf from Denmark unto Ynde,
> And also trewe; and so was he to me.

(pp. 1-7)

In her prologue the Wife of Bath puts her views about marriage before her audience at great length and in such lively anecdotal form that she might well be regarded as having made a most satisfactory contribution to the general entertainment before she reaches her tale. We can imagine that just a few of her fellow-pilgrims would have remained aloofly unamused by the prologue—the Parson, the Clerk of Oxenford, the Knight, the Prioress—but the rest would certainly have thoroughly enjoyed what the Friar calls her *long preamble*. Nevertheless, the Wife does go on to tell a story and she chooses one which is very different in mood and tone from her prologue.

We do not know the exact order of *The Canterbury Tales.* Here and there, links between the tales, in the form of comments by the Host or other pilgrims, indicate immediate sequence. The entire project remained far from complete, but it should be observed that *The Canterbury Tales*, as far as they go, form a varied collection of narrative types. Some are *Romances,* embodying such idealized human values as honour, loyalty, and the most elevated view of erotic love. Some are bawdy *Fabliaux,* amusing stories with a theme of coarse sexuality, but perhaps containing a moral view no less profound and significant than that found in the *Romances.* One type of *Fabliau* is the scurrilous tale which denigrates and ridicules a human type or human activity energetically disliked by the narrator. A fourth distinctive type of tale is the *Exemplum,* so called because it exemplifies, in the form of a story, a moral lesson of some sort. Features of these different types often co-exist in a single tale, and the categories can be further subdivided on the basis of such elements as the *miraculous,* manifested through divine intervention and *magic,* and the quality of *fable* in which (as in Æsop) animals assume human characteristics. This brief summary, oversimplified as it is, will indicate to the reader the possible range of expectations of the assembled pilgrims as they wait for the Wife of Bath to tell her tale.

There is some evidence that Chaucer originally intended what is now **"The Shipman's Tale"** to be told by the Wife of Bath. That racy story (of an unfaithful wife who not only sells her sexual 'favours' to her husband's best friend, but also makes her husband foot the bill) is certainly in keeping with the personality that emerges from the Wife's prologue. Nine lines, near the beginning of **"The Shipman's Tale"**, are not appropriate for the Shipman-narrator; these lines strongly support the view that the tale was intended for the Wife:

> The sely housbonde, algate he moot paye,
> He moot us clothe, and he moot us arraye,
> Al for his owene worshipe richely,
> In which array we daunce jolily.
> And if that he noght may, par aventure,
> Or ellis list no swich dispence endure,
> But thinketh it is wasted and ylost,
> Thanne moot another payen for oure cost,
> Or lene us gold, and that is perilous!

However, the story that the Wife tells in *The Canterbury Tales* as we have them begins:

> In th'olde dayes of the King Arthour

—and with that opening phrase the Wife moves suddenly

from the immediate present to some remote past; a past which is firmly associated, in medieval literary convention, with the Romances, with their elevated ideals, magic and fantasy.

The contrast between the tone of the Wife's prologue and the opening of her tale is like that between close and distant landscape: the one sharp, vivid and knowable, the other hazy and distant, an unfamiliar setting in which anything might be happening. The Wife's tale transports us into the realm of the fairy story, but the world of the medieval fairy story is no closer to childhood than are the worlds of the coarse *Fabliau* or the devout *Exemplum;* it is simply one of several possible vehicles for the expression of a theme.

The Arthurian reference at the beginning of her tale would have aroused in the Wife's audience the expectation of a world of sharply defined values and beliefs, where good is upheld and evil is condemned without compromise, and where the inhabitants are noble men and women who share a conviction that any deviation from their ideal morality must be corrected or the wrong-doer destroyed. This, then, is the setting of the Wife's tale. But she cannot simply get on with telling her story as a detached narrator; her own personality pushes through the formal structure from time to time. Very early in the narrative she returns suddenly to the present with an ironic aside at the expense of the mendicant friars. A little later, she interrupts the argument on the desires and aspirations of women which is an integral part of the story by adding vigorous observations based on her own experiences, supporting them with authoritative 'evidence' in the form of a story from Ovid. Even in the midst of the narrative, she cannot resist stepping forward again, this time to explain why there is to be no elaborate account of the wedding of the knight and the old woman. However, the Wife's direct involvement in her tale is not *merely* the result of her desire to assert herself: her personal interpolations are meant to endorse the *truth* of what she is relating.

It may perhaps seem strange that Chaucer should give the Wife a tale like this, instead of a robust and realistic story. But the stylized characterization of Arthurian Romance, and the fantasy and magic of an old folk story suit her purposes very well. The Arthurian knight epitomizes forceful and vigorous young manhood, but qualities which are strengths in a crusading warrior become moral defects when expressed in the rape of a defenceless girl. Such is the man, strong but culpable, whose act of rape symbolizes the ultimate mastery of woman by man, who is to be tamed in the Wife's tale. The hideous hag, the antithesis of youth and beauty, is the ultimate negation of desirability in woman. Such is the woman, totally lacking the sensual and erotic qualities by which women are traditionally believed to entice men, who is to win mastery over the virile knight. The knight's journey in search of the answer to the Queen's question is a variant of the quest in many Arthurian legends in which failure means death or disgrace. Answering the question in this tale wins the knight his life and eventually (though unexpectedly) leads him to perfect happiness and fulfilment. The narrative elements of the story can thus be seen clearly in relation to the Wife of Bath's philosophy of life.

One substantial element in the **"Wife of Bath's Tale"** remains to be discussed here: the moral debate which is introduced through the old woman's lengthy discourses on *gentillesse* and poverty. Some modern readers mistakenly regard these passages as a digression from the story and are impatient to return to the simple narrative thread, i.e. the sequence of events. This reaction is understandable, but inappropriate when applied to medieval literature. In order to understand this we must examine some of our assumptions about literature. When we encounter a long passage of moral argument in a nineteenth-century novel we are irritated, since we expect the writer of what we classify as 'fiction' to confine himself to situation and character, description and dialogue. As we move into twentieth-century literature we come to accept what has been described as 'internal monologue'—sustained passages which express not events but the thoughts and feelings of a character or of the author—but most modern readers are reluctant to move any further away from their concept of fiction. Reasoned argument is assigned a different place altogether, in the formal essay or treatise ('non-fiction'). There are many reasons why we have separated discursive writing from imaginative literature, but it must suffice here to say that for the Wife and her audience the discourses on *gentillesse* and poverty within the tale would not seem extraneous, because they regarded moral instruction as an integral part of the function of narrative literature, sometimes implicit and sometimes (as here) explicit.

The old woman who utters these discourses is, it must be remembered, reacting to her new husband's impassioned rejection of her. Although the knight has not explicitly mentioned by name either *gentillesse* or poverty, she interprets his reference to her descent from *so lough a kinde* ('such low origins') as referring to both. Her discussion is concerned with profound moral questions beside which (as the knight ultimately comes to see) his objections to her ugliness and poverty seem superficial. She urges him to examine his arrogant assumptions about his own superiority:

> Looke who that is moost vertuous alway,
> Pryvee and apert, and moost entendeth ay
> To do the gentil dedes that he kan:
> Taak him for the grettest gentil man!

True *gentillesse* is nobility of *spirit;* it inheres in moral qualities, not in social rank. The old woman points to the divine source of true nobility:

> Crist wol we clayme of Him oure gentillesse

and supports this scriptural allusion by a quotation from Dante:

> for God, of His goodnesse,
> Wol that of Him we clayme oure gentillesse

In the light of such fundamental moral values, poverty not only ceases to occasion shame, it is elevated by the precedent of Christ and by the many qualities it bestows on the poor:

> The hye God, on Whom that we bileeve,
> In wilful poverte chees to live His lyf

Eventually, the knight learns moral wisdom, relinquishes all claims to social superiority and suppresses the erotic desires which make the hideous hag so loathsome to him. Yet by giving way to his wife completely the knight finds that, far from being in an intolerable situation, he has attained everything he could want. Like the Wife of Bath's fifth husband, he achieves the gratification of all his wishes by first substituting his wife's will for his own. This culmination, which parallels that of the Wife's prologue, takes on a different form in the tale. The state of marital happiness which is simply described in the **"Wife of Bath's Prologue"** is heightened in the tale by the dramatic episode in which the hideous hag is suddenly transformed into a desirable young girl: the change from the jarring discord of conflict to the delight of harmony is enacted in a visible change from ugliness to beauty.

"The Wife of Bath's Tale" ends, as the prologue did, with a reassertion of her doctrine of mastery of husbands by wives. But, as in her prologue, there is a clear disparity between the proposition as she formulates it and the experience as she demonstrates it. The subservient husband of the tale, like Jankin in the prologue, finds the demanding woman transformed into a docile, compliant and obedient wife:

> And she obeyed him in every thing
> That mighte doon him pleasance or lyking

Who then has *maistrie* in this marriage? Or is the truth simply that by each seeming to give up mastery to the other both partners get their own way in everything? (pp. 8-14)

> *Gloria Cigman, in an introduction to* The Wife of Bath's Prologue and Tale and The Clerk's Prologue and Tale from The Canterbury Tales *by Geoffrey Chaucer, edited by Gloria Cigman, University of London Press Ltd., 1975, pp. 1-27.*

Donald R. Howard   (essay date 1976)

[*Howard is an American educator, translator, and author whose works of medieval scholarship include* The Three Temptations: Medieval Man in Search of the World *(1966) and* The Idea of the Canterbury Tales *(1976). In the following excerpt from the latter, he examines Chaucer's major work as a "human comedy."*]

In the mid-1380s, probably about 1386-87, Chaucer completed **Troilus and Criseyde** and turned his attention to **The Canterbury Tales.** For the rest of his life he gave his major efforts to this work, leaving it unfinished at his death. Except for **The Legend of Good Women** (whose prologue he revised in the early 1390s) and some short lyrics, it was, as far as anyone knows, the only poem he worked on in those years. He completed its beginning (the **"General Prologue"**) and its end (**"The Parson's Tale"** and **"Retraction"**) but not its middle: there are only twenty-three intervening tales, four unfinished. If Chaucer meant to do what he has the Host propose—have each pilgrim tell two tales on each leg of the journey—we have less than a fourth of the projected work. But if he meant to do what he did—ignore the return trip and have each pilgrim tell one tale—we have all but the tales of the Yeoman, Guildsmen, Plowman, and (if he was meant to tell a tale) the Host. Chaucer put the **"Knight's Tale"** first and linked most tales one to another; the order of the remaining un-linked tales or groups of tales is not always clear. Still, we have enough of the work to be able to say quite a few things about it. And the first thing we need to say is what kind of work it was meant to be.

There are not, as with modern poets, any journals, notes, letters, or drafts to clarify the poet's idea or its later muta-tions. We know Chaucer had an "idea" of the work be-cause he suggested one in the **"General Prologue"**. This idea doubtless changed somewhat as he wrote. Almost all the real evidence about the work is in the work itself, but I want to examine first some clues which come from out-side it. I find only three:

1. Chaucer, apparently referring to *The Canterbury Tales* (in *Troilus*), called it "some comedye."

2. Chaucer dedicated the *Troilus* to John Gower and al-most certainly alluded to Gower in the **"Man of Law's Prologue"**; in both passages morality is brought up. Con-temporary documents show that he and Gower were friends. Gower was working on the *Confessio Amantis* at the same time Chaucer was working on *The Canterbury Tales,* so it is probable that the two poets compared notes. Their two works are similar in plan and kind, though worlds apart in execution.

3. Chaucer appended to *The Canterbury Tales* a retrac-tion in which he revoked those of the tales that "sownen into sinne." In the same sentence he revoked other works, stating the title of each with the formula "The Book of. . . ." He did not apply this formula to *The Canter-bury Tales.*

These scraps of evidence can fairly be called "extrinsic." The rest of this chapter will consider what they mean.

Most critics in recent years have eschewed biographical evidence and tried to determine everything from "the text itself." Biographical evidence inferred from the author's works has in particular been reckoned fallacious or hereti-cal. But criticism of "the text itself," especially with older poets, almost always ends appealing to "the background." To explicate a text we must dredge up contemporaneous meanings of words, analogous forms or conventions, ico-nography, topoi, motifs, even here and there a real live his-torical event. This kind of "objective" criticism leaves one with the impression that "the background" gets silted into poems by natural erosion, though I doubt any critic be-lieves it. Almost everyone feels or senses an author's unique mind present in and behind his work—not just when, as with Chaucer, we know the canon of his works, but even when we read an anonymous poem like *Pearl* or *Sir Gawain.* This is not a matter of biography in any nar-row sense, for a writer gets some part of what is in his mind from other writers or their works, or from the cul-ture they share. Work, style, and mind are inseparable; we never confront the one without confronting the others.

But to get inside the mind of Geoffrey Chaucer in the mid-1380s, we have to acknowledge the difficulties. These are grave but not insurmountable.

First we have to face the reasons why no real biography of Chaucer has ever been written or can be written. We do not know enough. To have a biography, even a "por-trait," we need to know about a man's family and educa-tion, his marriage and domestic life, his beliefs, his atti-tudes, his friends, his work and amusements. With Chau-cer we have to throw up our hands in almost all these mat-ters. We know nothing about the personalities of his moth-er or father or the quality of his home life; we are not sure how many siblings he had, or, if he had a sister Katherine, whether she was younger or older; we do not know for sure where he got his early education, or when his wife died. We know who some of his friends were but do not know how intimate he was with them. We know a fair amount about his employment as a civil servant but can only guess how he viewed this position. We know he wrote poems for the king's court and was under the "patronage" of John of Gaunt, but we do not know the character of these acquaintanceships. From his works we can surmise a great deal about his learning and reading, yet scholars go on arguing about the gravity of his religion and about his tastes in reading or his understanding of what he read. Even the way he conceived of a poet's work or of poetry itself is the subject of a controversy. We get an impression of his personality from his writings, but knowing he was an ironist we cannot fully trust this impression. Any biog-raphy of Chaucer, trying to supply this missing evidence, must boggle in literary analysis and social history: we would be back again with the works and their "back-ground."

And then, even if the skeletal idea of *The Canterbury Tales* can be pieced together from a few odd bones, we can never be sure what Chaucer did with it. We know too little about his habits of composition. About half his longer works as they come down to us from fifteenth-century manuscripts are unfinished. But we cannot be sure he left all of them so—his own drafts could have been complete, the endings never revised, or left off in copying. We know he did revise: there are earlier versions of the prologue to *The Legend of Good Women,* of the **"Knight's Tale"**, and (some think) of the *Troilus.* We know he changed his mind in some matters: it appears, for example, that the **"Ship-man's Tale"** was first meant to be told by a woman and the **"Second Nun's Tale"** by a man. We even know he had a scribe named Adam who copied, or miscopied, the *Boece* and the *Troilus,* and perhaps other works; from the same short poem addressed to this scribe we learn that Chaucer proofread these copies, rubbing and scraping er-rors and correcting them. He says he worried about the accurate preservation of his work when copied: he was aware that English was spoken and written variously in various parts of England and that this could result in mis-takes of words or meter. It looks as if he set many works aside before completing them or considering them com-plete: several of the Canterbury tales seem to be works first written in the 1370s, and at least two of the tales are unfin-ished. He evidently worked on several jobs at once: while writing *The Canterbury Tales* he wrote *A Treatise on the*

Astrolabe, parts of *The Legend of Good Women,* perhaps other translations and poems. He says he read a great deal, and speaks so lyrically of books that we must believe him; besides, vast reading is revealed in his work. He says he had trouble getting to sleep, but always says this when he is writing a dream-vision, so it is not necessarily factual; and he mentions once that he looked "daswed" from reading late into the night, a fact perhaps confirmed by early portraits of him. But we do not know what his handwriting, drafts, or fair copies looked like, or how much revision he normally made in his poems. We are uncertain, and still debate, how much he got his ideas from literary models and how much from life. We know the man almost entirely through his works, and what we learn of him this way is not "extrinsic" evidence in the way Keats's letters or Shelley's drafts are. But then, such evidence, when it *is* available, is almost always used on the assumption that a work can be explained by tracing the process of its composition; and there are better ways of explaining literary works. They only begin, but do not live, in the workroom.

Finally, because **The Canterbury Tales** was not finished, we can never know the idea in its final embodiment. This is a fact. There is no getting around it. It is not, however, such a grave or special problem as it seems. There is much to admire and say about many unfinished works—we read the *Summa theologica* or *The Fairie Queene* without thinking them the less imposing or the more inexplicable. The history—and the esthetics—of unfinished works would furnish an ambitious author with a promising topic. With all works of art there is a sense in which even "finished" ones are unfinished. Henry James in his later years undertook to improve the style of his works; are we to take the earlier published works or the later revised ones as "finished"? The poems of Yeats and Auden, both tireless revisers, present even more complicated difficulties. Anyone who has edited a text, even of a comparatively recent writer, knows that twilight zone where the author's corrections to copy and proofs, or to succeeding printings and editions, shade off into the manhandling of editors, proofreaders, and typesetters. And can we be sure that an author's last-minute alterations represent the final embodiment of his idea? Might they not rather be blunders and losses of nerve made in the last moments of stagefright? Might not a work get finished out of impatience to "slay the beast" (as Winston Churchill put it) "and fling it abroad to the public"? The unfinished character of **The Canterbury Tales** is a more dramatic instance of the imperfect character of art, but the problems it raises are not of a different order: "Between the conception and the creation. . . . Falls the shadow."

When I talk about the unfinished character of **The Canterbury Tales** I have in mind the handful of missing and unfinished tales, some possible missing links between tales, and a few passages which might seem to call for revision. I do not have in mind another tale for each pilgrim on the way to Canterbury and two more for each on the return. By the time the Host is ready for the Franklin he is saying that each must "tellen atte lest / A tale or two," and outside Canterbury he declares "Now lacketh us no tales mo than oon." This is generally taken to mean that Chaucer changed his idea of the plan; yet it is the Host whose idea

changes. What Chaucer's idea was *at first* we cannot know. Perhaps he meant to identify it with the Host's suggested plan in the **"General Prologue"**; if so, he ended up revealing a grandiose plan unfulfilled and his own control unsustained, which could be Chaucerian self-humor. The *fact* stated in the **"Parson's Prologue"** as the pilgrims approach their destination is, only one tale remains to be told.

With all this talk just outside Canterbury about knitting things up and making an end, one assumes the work is over. Here there are strong reasons for saying that Chaucer, far from having "changed his mind," never had any idea for depicting the return journey. The one-way "pilgrimage of human life" was a conventional metaphor and topos, and would have been an effective frame for the work. Still, what he wrote is not an allegory like the *Pélerinage de la vie humaine* but a fictional account of a real pilgrimage. He chose to treat not the allegorical pilgrimage to the heavenly Jerusalem, nor the great pilgrimage (of which all others were mere types or imitations) to the Holy Land, but the familiar national pilgrimage to Canterbury. Moreover, he chose to depict the pilgrims busy with the very activity against which moralists always cautioned pilgrims: *curiositas.* He depicted a tale-telling game, squabbles, practical jokes, "quitting" (getting even with), bawdry. Emphasis falls on the amusement of the trip.

This may seem like an original stroke on Chaucer's part. The pilgrimage setting and the way tales characterize their tellers make **The Canterbury Tales** unlike the *Decameron* or Sercambi's *Novelle* (which, incidentally, did not depict a pilgrimage). Yet there was another tradition of writings against which **The Canterbury Tales** is never compared—the large number of guidebooks and realistic prose accounts of the Jerusalem pilgrimage. But even those which focus on sightseeing and curiosity do not ever depict the return journey. Probably the first author who found any intrinsic interest in the return and the homecoming was Friar Felix Fabri, who wrote his long account in the 1480s. The first fictional account of a pilgrimage—like Chaucer's, drawn from books—was *Mandeville's Travels* (1356), a work widely read in Chaucer's time which I believe Chaucer knew; but even Mandeville does not more than mention the return journey. Some accounts do not even do that. In fact the custom was to declare the Jerusalem pilgrimage finished at the destination. The pilgrims, those who had survived the perilous journey, often went their separate ways rather than return as a group. We must conclude that medieval pilgrims conceived of and experienced a pilgrimage as a one-way journey; the return was a mere contingency. This was not a metaphor or topos, but the source of the metaphor and topos: it was their *idea* of a pilgrimage.

That idea of a pilgrimage is part of the idea of **The Canterbury Tales.** Of course Chaucer might have meant to depart from this tradition of travel writings and this habitual way of experiencing a pilgrimage, but the weight of evidence is against it. All the other parts of the Host's plan are violated too; neither narrator nor poet ever suggests he anticipates more tales on the return; and the **"Parson's**

Prologue" outside Canterbury says the end is there. The pilgrimage, so conceived as a one-way journey, gave *The Canterbury Tales* an over-all unity, a "frame." It is a work, not "works"—disjointed, various, unaccountable, it still has a consistency of tone, of style, of tact, of mind. This conception and these arrangements were immanent in medieval culture and convention; they are preserved in the text of the work; but they *happened* in the mind of Geoffrey Chaucer in the 1380s and 1390s. If at some point during those years Chaucer had a bright vision, what he left us are shadows on the wall of a cave. But we will have to contemplate these, for they are all we have.

At the end of the *Troilus* Chaucer promised a future work:

> Go litel book, go, litel myn tragedye,
> Ther God thy makere yet, ere that he die,
> So sende might to make in some comedye.

This is surely a reference to *The Canterbury Tales.* The only other possibility would be a work he wrote which has not survived or one he planned but did not write. He could not have meant *The Legend of Good Women,* for he would have called it, as he did, by the generic term legend; besides, its subject matter is far from comedy as Chaucer would have understood the term. *The Book of the Lion* which he mentions in the **"Retraction"**—if indeed he wrote it and if it was, as is generally thought, an adaptation of Machaut's *Dit dou Lyon*—could not be called a comedy. So if we knew what Chaucer meant by "comedy" we would know something important about *The Canterbury Tales.* It is, by the way, the only time he ever used the word.

The passage sets "comedye" against "tragedye" with such emphatic parallelism as to suggest they are opposites, and that was the medieval view. There was, after all, no classic form of medieval comedy, as there was of tragedy. To know what tragedy meant one can examine collections of *de casibus* narratives and even quote the definition Chaucer put in the mouth of the Monk; since Chaucer knew this definition of tragedy, he likely knew the traditional definition of its opposite. That of Evanthius (who died ca. 359) was quoted in editions of Terence and used in glosses and encyclopedias, and Professor Cunliffe [in his *Early English Classical Tragedies*] points especially to the influence of this sentence:

> Inter tragoediam autem et comoediam cum multa tum inprimis hoc distat, quod in comoedia mediocres fortunae hominum, parui impetus periculorum laetique sunt exitus actionum, at in tragoedia omnia contra, ingentes personae, magni timores, exitus funesti habentur; et illic prima turbulenta, tranquilla ultima, in tragoedia contrario ordine res aguntur; tum quod in tragoedia fugienda uita, in comoedia capessenda exprimitur; postremo quod omnis comoedia de fictis est argumentis, tragoedia saepe de historia (*sic*) fide petitur.

> (Between tragedy and comedy there is, among other things, this principal difference, that in comedy there are insignificant fortunes of men, small forces of danger, and happy outcomes of actions; but in tragedy everything is the contrary—there are great personages, momentous

fears, and disastrous outcomes. In comedy things begin in turbulence and end in tranquillity; in tragedy things happen in the opposite way. Furthermore in tragedy the type of life to be avoided is represented, in comedy the type of life to be espoused. Finally, every comedy is about subjects which are invented, whereas tragedy is often taken from actual history.)

Here tragedy deals with significant "fortunes" of great men faced with great dangers, begins in tranquillity and ends in turbulence, treats historical subjects, and depicts a life to be fled. The *Troilus* fits this definition of tragedy nicely: it deals with significant fortunes (the Fall of Troy), involves great dangers and important figures, ends in disaster, and is taken from history. It does, to be sure, depict a "type of life to be espoused" in Book III; but it shows that life dissipate into a miserable one which the hero does indeed seek to flee. Troilus's laughter on the eighth sphere does suggest a kind of tranquillity; but the dominant movement rather than the ending itself is what the definition fastens upon, and Chaucer saw the dominant movement of the whole as "Fro woe to wele and after out of joye" according to the movement of Fortune's wheel, a tragic rather than a comic movement.

If the *Troilus* (which Chaucer called a tragedy) fits the old definition, one might expect *The Canterbury Tales* (which Chaucer called a comedy) to fit it too. *The Canterbury Tales* deals with less significant fortunes: pilgrims gather in an inn and tell tales as they ride, and most (but not all) tales treat ordinary affairs of ordinary men. The pilgrims are from all walks of life, but most are from the "commons" and none from the rank of princes. It begins in a sort of turbulence and ends with the Parson's words which may be thought tranquil. It treats for the most part invented subjects, though the author claims the pilgrimage really took place and the pilgrims often claim their stories really happened—a not unusual claim for storytellers. Whether it depicts "the type of life to be espoused" depends on the meaning of that phrase. Tragedy depicted a life falling into misery, a life to be fled, and so one to be held in contempt; comedy depicted its opposite. Perhaps *capessenda* here has a neutral connotation—not "enjoyed" or even "espoused" but only "entered into" or "taken up"; however you translate it, it refers to espousal of the world rather than contempt of it. And surely the initial concerns of *The Canterbury Tales* are worldly—the pilgrimage as it starts out at the Tabard is very much of this world and so are most of the tales. The work contains pathetic tales and tragedies, but the whole does not seem pathetic or tragic. Finally, the definition seems to suggest a distinction of social class. In tragedy the personages are *ingentes;* in comedy men's fortunes are *mediocres.* The mention of fortunes suggests the fickle goddess and her wheel, which involved a movement toward and then away from "high estate." That men's fortunes in comedy are *mediocres* could mean we are turning our attention to the domestic and private cares of nobles rather than to their more significant public cares; but it probably means we are turning our attention to the lower classes who do not properly *have* public cares. The *Troilus* is about great nobles but about their private cares; *The Canterbury Tales* is chiefly about ranks of society beneath that of great nobles, and chiefly about private cares.

The Canterbury Tales squares with this medieval definition of comedy enough to convince me that Chaucer initially thought of it as that kind of work and said so at the
end of the ***Troilus;*** but at this stage it was doubtless a
vague idea—ask any author to describe the book he is
going to write and you will get a lot of hemming and haw-
ing. This vagueness is expressed by the phrase "some comedye." "Some" used with a singular noun can mean "one
or another" (as in "lest they diden some follye," *LGW*) or
"a quantity of" (as in "some mirth or some doctrine"
CT), or "a kind of" (as in "ye han some glymsyng"
"Merch. T"), or "a certain" (as in "of some contree / That
shall not now be told for me" *HF*). These usages are on
occasion hard to differentiate—when Pertelote recommends "some laxatif" she might mean any of them; when
the Pardoner promises "some moral thing" he could mean
"a certain" or "a kind of," but the other uses do not fit.
At times, though, the sense can be narrowed: in the **"Miller's Tale"**, "In some woodness or in some agony" must
mean "a kind of" because the speaker's casting about
among various terms rules out the chance of a delimited
notion in the speaker's mind, which the other uses seem
to imply. "Some" was, and still is, a convenient obfuscat-
ing word. In the present line Chaucer meant either (1) a
certain comedy already in mind which he would not reveal, or (2) a kind of comedy, something like or in the nature of a comedy, which he had not yet clearly framed.
The line tells us he had chosen a genre, but it obscrues the
specific matter or form.

"To make in some comedy" is a puzzling phrase, and it
is still more puzzling that editors have not commented on
it. Why "in"? Possibly it means "with respect to" (as when
we say "succeed in business") or "in the realm of" (as
when scholarly foundations announce awards for "creative writing in poetry"). The line could be paraphrased
imaginatively "to compose in the manner (or, genre) of a
certain (kind of) comedy." Skeat paraphrased it "to take
part in composing some 'comedy.'" I do not find that

Chaucer used "in" this way anywhere else with "make,"
and rarely with any other verb. These difficulties have led
one commentator to suggest that "make" is an early instance of its use in the old sense "to match"; Professor
Robinson, abandoning his usual caution, accepted this
suggestion. The lines would then mean "wherefore may
God yet send your author the power, before he die, to
match (it) in some comedy" or "to do equally well in some
comedy." But "make" in this sense was a rare usage recorded only in the late fifteenth and early sixteenth centuries, and Chaucer used it nowhere else. These troubles
could be erased if the line read "to maken some comedye,"
and this reading, which occurs in one manuscript, was
nervously offered by Skeat in his textual notes with a question mark. The usual reading, "make in," is a more vague
(or cautious) utterance: it is one thing to say you will write
a comedy and another to say you will write in the *realm*
of comedy.

There is a reason why Chaucer might have preferred the
more cautious utterance: "comedy" suggests Dante's
Commedia. We must therefore ask whether in 1386-1387
Chaucer had in mind a poetic conception comparable to
Dante's.

Chaucer had read the *Commedia,* and it is possible he had
read as well the letter to Can Grande in which "comedy"
is defined. The definition does not add much to Evanthius's: it repeats the notion that comedy begins in harshness
and ends happily, but does not mention the stature of the
personages, the gravity of their fears, or the kind of life depicted, and does not say whether its matter is invented or
historical. It adds a fanciful etymology after the medieval
fashion (*comus,* village, and *oda,* song; hence village song)
without explaining what assistance this bit of intellection
has to offer. It also adds a detail very pertinent to Chaucer—that the fashion of the speech in this comedy is
"meek and humble, being the vulgar tongue" and that
even females communicate in it. One thinks at once of the
Reeve's dialect or the Wife of Bath's monologue.

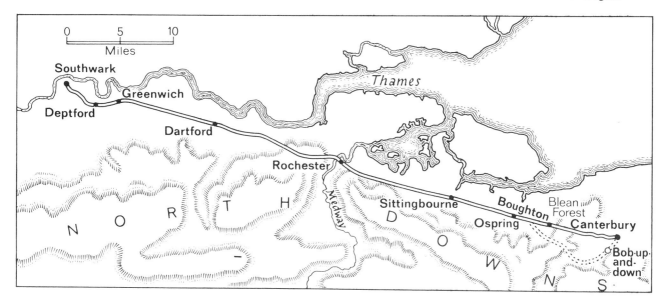

The path of Chaucer's pilgrims.

That Chaucer could have received much edification from Dante's letter seems dubious, but from the *Commedia* itself he received, or so it is usually thought, the most startling impression. It was Dante's use of the word *Commedia* as the title of his masterpiece, rather than his definition of it, which would have given it some ring of awe when it fell from Chaucer's tongue. But here again we stumble into the thicket of our ignorance. We know Chaucer made two, and perhaps three, journeys to Italy. The doubtful one was in 1368 when he left the country long enough and with enough money to get to Italy; but there is no evidence where he went and no suggestion of Italian influence on his work. He would have been about twenty-five. On December 1, 1372, he did go to Italy—we have documentary evidence of this—returning on May 23, 1373; he was then about twenty-nine. He spent a bit more than three months there, at Genoa (where his business was probably to negotiate the use of an English port by the Genoese) and at Florence. His reason for going to Florence is not known, but—for whatever reason he went—he would have returned with literary rewards and, very likely, an armload of books: there was an active cult of Dantisti there even then, it was the native town of Boccaccio, and it was a great cultural center. From this trip scholars have always dated an Italian influence upon Chaucer's writings and so an "Italian period." The influence shows up first in **The House of Fame;** the "period" fades into the larger scope of his later works. In 1378 he went abroad from May to September, this time to Lombardy for perhaps a month's stay, probably on matters touching the war with France. He was then about thirty-five.

Italy did make its mark on the young poet. There are indisputable influences and borrowings from Dante. And he was much taken with Boccaccio and Petrarch. True, he altered what he found in the great Tuscans. The **Troilus** and the **"Knight's Tale"** are brought within French traditions—are "medievalized," in C. S. Lewis's phrase, and have as much in common with the *Roman de la Rose* as with the *Filostrato* or the *Teseida*. That he knew, or knew about, the *Decameron* is more probable than was once thought, and its similarity to **The Canterbury Tales** has not escaped notice—though there are differences too. Where Chaucer imitated (rather than revised) Boccaccio was in the "collections"—in the **"Monk's Tale"**, an English counterpart to *De casibus virorum illustrum,* and in **The Legend of Good Women,** an English counterpart to *De claris mulieribus.* In these he was imitating the grave, the scholarly Boccaccio—that later, reformed Boccaccio who was to be praised in the next century as a man learned in divine and humane letters who had "also written one hundred stories in the vulgar tongue." And even toward them we find an ironic and humorous skepticism. In **The Legend of Good Women** we hear the poet's voice groaning under the burden of condensing the "legends"; the hapless Monk has to be stopped in his "tragedies" and charged with dullness.

To talk about this Italian influence on Chaucer we must remove from our minds our own enthusiasms—for the Renaissance, for humanism, for the bawdy younger Boccaccio, for the "dawning" and the vivacity we are accustomed to see there—and try to imagine Chaucer's actual experience of Italy. If we had even a single letter, even a sentence or two of explicit comment from him, it might offer us a clue. The best we have are these lines, which the Clerk speaks in the **"Clerk's Prologue"**:

> I wol you tell a tale that I
> Lerned at Padwe of a worthy clerk,
> As preved by his wordes and his werk.
> He is now deed and nailed in his cheste,
> I pray to God so yeve his soule reste!
> Fraunceys Petrak, the lauriat poete,
> Highte this clerk, whose rhetorike sweete
> Enlumined all Itaille of poetrie,
> As Linian dide of philosophie,
> Or law, or other art particuler;
> But deeth, that wol nat suffre us dwellen heer,
> But as it were a twinkling of an eye,
> Hem both hath slain, and alle shul we die.

In the **"General Prologue"** Chaucer presented the Clerk as an admirable young man, and it is reasonable to assume that he shared the feeling expressed here. If so, what this scrap points to is an admiration for the learning, the scholarship, the bookishness of the Italians, for the names of the great men themselves, for their poetry and rhetoric, for science, and for law. He shared the spirit of early humanism in its essential form, which was an enthusiasm for books. The most important Italian influence on Chaucer was upon his reading: beginning with his "Italian period" we discover in him an interest in classical literature. He likes to mention the works and names of classical authors, and it is clear he read them. The humanists parted company with him, though, when they edited ancient texts or imitated Cicero's Latin; by way of such scholarship he chose works to translate or adapt, and chose medieval ones. Still, in other ways the Italian humanists were more medieval than he—they wrote in Latin, they were dreadfully bookish, and they were (as the Italians say) *molto della chiesa.* What marks them as humanists is their fads—vernacular poetry, the love of learning, the discovery and preservation of ancient texts, accurate handwriting. All this we do find in Chaucer: he wrote *only* in the vernacular; translated what he thought were important Latin works; was steeped in book learning; scolded his scribe for copying badly and begged copyists to take care.

Beyond this scholarly bent, the Italian humanists were given to notions of idealized love and to aspirations for fame. In this they were emulating the fashions of aristocrats, for they were, like Chaucer, from the "middle class"—Petrarch the illegitimate son of a notary, Boccaccio a moneylender's son. Courtly love and the writing of love poems had been an aristocratic accomplishment for two centuries; and the love of fame, the "glory" of a good name which conferred an earthly immortality, had been a major preoccupation of knights since early feudal times. The humanists claimed a right to these aristocratic interests for their nobility of mind, their *virtù,* rather than for inherited family ties, and it is hard to escape a suspicion of class consciousness among their motives. In Chaucer, we find an interest in idealized love—he was indeed the poet of love in his youth—but he views it with irony, with self-humor about his own "unlikeliness," and, in the **Troilus,** with the noble dubiety of a religious and philosophical perspective. So with fame: in **The House of Fame** we see him preoccupied with the idea of reputation, but he views fame in medieval fashion as a thing made of hot air, bestowed capriciously. At the end of the **Troilus** he hopes modestly for fame, but nowhere in his works claims to have made a monument more perdurable than bronze or to have bestowed fame on others. He always dons the mask of a modest, useful fellow quite without pretensions—a humorous exaggeration, of course. We never find him, though, proclaiming a noble passion for a highborn lady as Boccaccio and Petrarch did, or hoping for fame except with conventional medieval modesty.

Chaucer caught the spirit of incipient Italian humanism, liked it, and shared many of its interests; but he was conservative in following its fads, viewed them with ironic disinterestedness, humor, and tolerant skepticism. He was never really interested in Italian literary *forms* like the sonnet or the "renaissance epic"; where he used them he made them palatable to English or French ears. The matter is important because Italian literary circles of the fourteenth century, the circles in which we find the beginnings of Renaissance humanism, doted upon Dante. Can it be that Chaucer viewed Dante as he did the other enthusiasms of the Italian *literati,* with irony, with skeptical good will, with amused English detachment?

It is not a palatable notion. We, if we read Dante at all, can never read him without astonishment and reverence, and an earlier generation of scholars projected this fact upon Chaucer, very reasonably. Surely he would have admired the magnificent conception of Dante's *Commedia,* its vast learning, and its poetic excellence. We catch in his work enough echoes of Dante to know he read the *Commedia* with care, whether or not he read Italian well. But we forget that he would not have come to the *Commedia,* as we do, with a running directory of medieval Florentines at the bottom of the page. The contemporary and parochial references in the *Commedia* are something every reader has to come to grips with, and I have heard respected Dantisti recommend they be ignored. But they are easier to ignore when we know we *can* identify names if we choose to. For Chaucer, it would have been a puzzle to find names of the poet's enemies mixed in Hell among the ancients, and one can imagine his curiosity turning to amusement as he saw what Dante was doing. He might well have fancied similar treatment for a few Londoners. Exactly such an interest in one's surroundings, in one's contemporaries and in one's own city, was an interest Chaucer shared with Dante. But Chaucer had a different temperament and a different experience of life. Dante was a disillusioned idealist; he was bitter, and an exile. Chaucer, though not without idealism, adopted an ironic view of the world; and, far from being an exile, he was a dutiful member of the establishment. Dante in exile looked at his contemporaries and saw the meaning of their lives from the viewpoint of eternity; Chaucer looked at his contemporaries close at hand with a certain even-tempered detachment. Dante's *Commedia* and Chaucer's "comedy" are miles apart in this respect, and almost the moment in Chaucer's early poetry where that parting took place, and the way it took place, have been isolated by Professor Fisher [in his *John Gower*] in a passage which I can do no better than to quote in full:

Dante had responded to . . . artistic dissatisfaction with his early lyrics by spiritualizing courtly love in the *Vita Nuova* and *Divine Comedy.* Chaucer acknowledged this solution (in **The House of Fame**) by having Geffrey rescued from his wasteland in perhaps the noblest and most genuinely sympathetic echoes of Dante in all his poetry. "O Christ!" he prays, "Fro fantome and illusion / Me save." Suddenly above him appears the eagle that had carried Dante's body to the first terrace of Purgatory: "In dream I seemed to see an eagle with feathers of gold poised in the sky, with its wings spread, and intent to stoop. And I seemed to be there where his own people were abandoned by Ganymede, when he was rapt to the supreme consistory" (*Purgatorio*). This image is fused with that of Beatrice gazing at the sun: "I saw Beatrice turned to her left side and gazing upon the sun: never did an eagle so fix himself upon it. (Inspired by her example) I fixed my eyes upon the sun beyond our wont. . . . Not long did I endure it, nor so little that I did not see it sparkle round about, like iron that issues boiling from the fire. And on a sudden, day seemed added to day, as if He who has the power had adorned the heaven with another sun" (*Paradiso*). In this context, Chaucer's dreamer becomes aware:

> That faste be the sonne, as hye
> As keene myghte I with my yë,
> Me thoughte I saugh an eagle sore,
> But that hit semed moche more
> Then I had any egle seyn.
> But this is sooth as deth, certeyn,
> Hyt was of gold, and shon so bryghte
> That never sawe men such a syghte,
> But yf the heven had ywonne
> Al newe of gold another sonne.

Had Chaucer been able to sustain this note, he would have been a different poet. But we prefer to have him Chaucer, as he evidently preferred to be, for in the first ten lines of Book II, he rejected the mystical way out of the wasteland, employing the homely touches and incongruities of sound and situation of which he was already such a master to reduce Dante's divine bird to the slightly ridiculous, very human mentor who spoke, "In mannes vois, and seyde, 'Awak!' "

There we see Chaucer's withdrawal from Dante. True, **The House of Fame** shows the influence of the *Commedia;* but the eagle borrowed from it is a funny eagle, the visit to a world beyond is a comic visit, and that world is an absurd world. It is not meant to discredit Dante—the highest praise one can give an author is to parody him, so the maxim goes. But it reflects one side of Chaucer's response to Dante. The other side, which we encounter only at the end of the **Troilus,** is serious: in its noble ending there are unmistakable echoes of the *Commedia.* But that is almost the only place in Chaucer where eschatological matters are raised. Chaucer mentions Dante in five places, never without reverence and twice in the same breath with Vergil. It may amuse us that the Wife of Bath has the hag in her tale quote Dante's *Convivio,* but the incongruity strikes us this way precisely because Dante's sentiments are so elevated. When we call Dante the poet of the secular world, we mean that he saw that world bound in the *saeculum,* an historical age which would end and be subsumed in eternity—"an earthly reality preserved in transcendence, in a perfection decreed by divine judgment." Chaucer was no less a poet of the secular world, but he fastened attention on the *saeculum* as it is known to us in this life; what lies beyond it, its ultimate reality, he does not explore. Between man's life in the secular world and the vast hierarchical design of eternity lie those acts of the human will which determine whether a man be saved or damned. In the secular world, the way to the eternal one is penance, and Chaucer fastens upon penance as the subject of the Parson's address at the end; a pilgrimage itself was, officially, a penitential act. Beyond penance, this worldly means to eternal grace, Chaucer does not venture. Dante saw the secular world approaching its ultimate perfect state when it would be ordered for all eternity. Purgatory and Earth are transient, Heaven and Hell eternal. Chaucer limited his view to Earth, to the world of disorder, temporality, memory, and story.

When Chaucer announced that he would write a comedy, he meant, then, a work notably different from the tragedy of *Troilus,* one which would deal with ordinary men, with everyday cares, and with story rather than history. It would treat a life to be espoused and so treat the problem of living aright in the world. With Dante's poem it had in common a concern with the secular world and a movement from turbulence to tranquillity. He arrested the idea of his work upon that element in *The Divine Comedy* which looks backward to the experience of secular life; if we could extrapolate from Dante the characters who were his contemporaries, the stories people told him, his memories, his observations, his concern for politics and ethics, we would have the stuff of *The Canterbury Tales*—but it would certainly not be *The Divine Comedy.* When Chaucer announced "some comedye," he must have had in mind this limitation to the experienced world of memory and story. There is not a scrap of evidence that he had any notion of treating things eschatological or arranging things in a symmetrical design; there is abundant evidence that his interests and gifts narrowed upon the experienced world. There is evidence, too, that he had among his drafts during the years he worked on *The Canterbury Tales* serious Christian works which focused not on eschatology or spirituality, but on the world itself, on the way a Christian must come to terms with the world—works like Pope Innocent III's "Wrecched Engendring of Mankind," the life of St. Cecilia (which was to become the **"Second Nun's Tale"**), "Origines upon the Maudelayne," Guillaume Peraldus's *Summa de viciis,* Raymond of Pennaforte's *Summa Casuum Penitentiae* or Frère Lorens's *Somme des Vices et des Vertus* (these last were to become the **"Parson's Tale"**). Chaucer, like Dante, was a Christian poet, but he was a poet of the secular world in a narrower sense—possibly a stricter sense—than Dante was; his comedy leaves out the eschatological side of Christianity which makes all life a comedy and which makes all that happens happen for the best. From this larger point of view we might say Chaucer showed things more nearly at their worst, that he was a gloomier poet than Dante. That greater eschatological vision which Dante wrote about must be implied or understood in *The Canterbury Tales,*

for it was prominent enough in people's thoughts; but it is not expressed. (pp. 21-45)

> *Donald R. Howard, "A Book About the World," in his* The Idea of the Canterbury Tales, *University of California Press, 1976, pp. 21-74.*

Derek Pearsall   (essay date 1984)

[*An English medievalist, Pearsall has contributed to numerous works concerning medieval poetics and is the author of* Old English and Middle English Poetry *(1976). In the following excerpt from his Variorum edition of the "Nun's Priest's Tale," he provides an interpretation of the tale which is founded on the premise that "to recognize that the tale has no point is the start of understanding."*]

There has hardly been a time when **"The Nun's Priest's Tale"** has not been appreciated as one of the wittiest and most accomplished poems in the English language. Readers have been delighted by its inexhaustible ingenuity and inventiveness and by its irreverent mockery of the solemn apparatus of human learning and rhetoric; they have warmed to its generous portrayal of the all-too-human foibles and weaknesses of its barnyard hero. If one were looking for Chaucer's most perfect poem—not the one with the loftiest ambitions but the one that most fully achieves the ideas implied in its form—it would certainly be a serious rival to Coleridge's choice, **"The Miller's Tale."** It is a tale also of hidden depths, shoals for the unwary, unplumbable abysses of multiple signification. The development in recent years of more sophisticated techniques of literary analysis has been notable for the light it has thrown on this most sophisticated of Chaucer's poems, but it is likely to remain elusive. Elusiveness is indeed its character, and the life and wisdom it contains are of a kind that must necessarily defy formulation. It is not always easy to resist the temptation to substitute an interpretative paraphrase for one's lived experience of reading a work of literature. **"The Nun's Priest's Tale"** in fact, offers us an explicit invitation to do just that ("Taketh the moralite . . . "). But the effect of accepting the invitation is not merely to miss the joke but to become the butt of it. As in all the best comedy, there is a sharp edge for all pretense and affectation in the midst of the warmth and gaiety. (p. 3)

The existence of the two forms of the *Monk-Nun's Priest Link . . .* can serve to introduce a discussion of the interpretation of the poem. There is no doubt that the existence of the two forms of the link has provided excellent opportunities for the elucidation of Chaucer's developing intentions in fragment B². The role of the tale as the climax to the longest integrated sequence of tales in the whole of *The Canterbury Tales* can be shown to be thereby reinforced, and a further interest added to the tale in terms of its place in the framework of the *Tales.* In particular, the expansion of the link gives added point, in the Knight's remarks (the original short form was designed for the Host alone), to the emphatic contrast between **"The Nun's Priest's Tale"** and **"The Monk's Tale."** This contrast is, in any analysis, an important part of the full meaning of **"The Nun's**

Priest's Tale" and the Knight's observations hint, without any laboring of the point, at the laughable inadequacy of "tragedy," at least as it is conceived of in **"The Monk's Tale"** and prepare us for the wise and humane accommodation of comedy, as it is evidenced in **"The Nun's Priest's Tale."**

It is necessary to stress, however—and this is the first of a series of objections to a mode of reading now unfortunately all too current—that the primary effectiveness of the contrast between the two tales is in the juxtaposition of the tales as tales, and not in any dramatically conceived confrontation between the Monk and the Nun's Priest as characters. It is possible to see that Chaucer intends us to derive some amusement from the contrast between the Monk and the Nun's Priest, especially the contrast between their horses (the only thing he specifically tells us about the Nun's Priest is that he rides "a jade . . . bothe foul and lene"), but to see **"The Nun's Priest's Tale"** as a satire on **"The Monk's Tale,"** directed personally by the Nun's Priest against the Monk and prompted by outrage at the latter's ostentation, jealousy of his high position in the ecclesiastical establishment, or contempt for his stupidity, is to deny the essential quality of the tale's humor. To see **"The Nun's Priest's Tale"** further, as the outcome of the Nun's Priest's desire to please the Host or to annoy the Prioress is to make it merely trivial. The humor of the tale, its raison d'être, resides in the "incompetent" mode of narration, in the superb display of irrelevant skills. It can hardly delight us in this way and at the same time be working toward a satirical objective planned and directed by the Nun's Priest as narrator. Even if the two ways of reading the tale are considered to be not completely incompatible, there is no doubt that the latter pales into insignificance compared with the former; it is, indeed, banal. The satirical objectives in the tale are Chaucer's, and the Nun's Priest is his stalking-horse. It could have been anyone, or it could have been, if this were not *The Canterbury Tales,* no one—in other words, that familiar figure, Chaucer-the-Narrator. Any interpretation of the tale that puts the Nun's Priest in the foreground, instead of leaving him in the background, where Chaucer put him, has lost touch with the important matter of the poem.

As far as the "dramatic" reading of *The Canterbury Tales* is concerned, **"The Nun's Priest's Tale"** is not an extreme or exceptional case, but rather an exceptionally clear demonstration of the norm. Chaucer contrived the scheme of *The Canterbury Tales* because he wanted it, and he seizes joyfully on the opportunities of dramatic interchange offered by the framework and the links. But he rarely pursues such matters much beyond the opening lines of a tale, and no sensible reader would want to pursue them for him, without prompting. For Chaucer it is sufficient to have created successfully the illusion that the narration of a tale is someone else's responsibility. That is the source of his freedom in the *Tales,* and the secret of the artistic energy released there. The return to the pilgrimage framework at the end of a tale is most often like the awakening from a dream, or, to be more exact, like the return to an illusion of reality after the experience of a superior reality. It is true that there are occasions in some of the tales when a shadowy projection of the narrator and his character

and circumstances becomes momentarily visible. There is such a moment in **"The Nun's Priest's Tale"** when the narrator hurriedly disclaims any intention of dispraising women: it seems highly unlikely that we are not here invited to recall the Nun's Priest and his relation to the Prioress. But that is as far as it goes, a sauce to the meal; to pursue interpretation beyond that would be to mistake the sauce for the meal.

The proliferation of "dramatic" interpretations of the tale and the prodigious ingenuity of speculation which has gone to the making of them are not the products of mere perversity. They have to do with a modern preoccupation with "character" in literature, and especially with that kind of interest in character which uses literary texts as a point of departure for groundless speculation about what fictional persons would have been doing if the author had remembered to tell us. Such readings are very easy to manufacture, since all they need is an elementary knowledge of human nature and some interest in mild personality disorder. They need none of the hard work on text, tradition, and genre that might enable us to glimpse, however briefly, the authentic meaning of a poem.

The "dramatic" interpretation of **"The Nun's Priest's Tale,"** however, receives so strikingly little sustenance from the tale itself that a further explanation of its popularity seems to be called for. It might be regarded as a simple refuge from the bewilderment created by the dazzling and many-faceted brilliance of the tale, but it has much to do, I think, with a misconceived interpretation of the role of the "incompetent" narrator. The tale evidently has an "incompetent" narrator, but to associate this incompetence with the intentions, achieved or unachieved, of a dramatically conceived "character" is to wreck the whole design of the poem.

To speak of the "incompetence" of the narrator in the tale may seem a dangerous game to play, since there could be nothing more tedious than a genuinely incompetently told tale. What we have in **"The Nun's Priest's Tale"** is rather a superbly competent narrator who is telling the wrong tale, or at least telling the right tale the wrong way. It is like a fireworks display that has got into the hands of a pyromaniac. It is very important to stress this quality of misdirected competence in the tale, since a number of mistakes have been made in the interpretation of it by readers who are unfamiliar with the techniques of burlesque or the mock-heroic. A case in point is the brief discourse on predestination and free will with which the narrator embellishes his story of Chauntecler's fall. This discourse, often described as confused and tortuous by critics, is in fact extremely clear and succinct, a model précis of current views on the theology of predestination. It could hardly have been better done. What has us helpless with laughter is that it should be done at all, in relation to a cock and fox. The narrator does not, and must not, realize how funny he appears if the comedy is to remain buoyed up; he must have no intention but to tell the tale to the best of his ability. Frequently his sententious itch is his undoing. As he continues after the last passage referred to, for instance, he has an irresistible urge to moralize on the misfortunes that await a man if he takes a woman's advice. The shadow of the Fall descends on the sunlit farmyard, and the prognosis for Chauntecler, it seems, is gloomy. But, of course, the narrator has misinterpreted his own story (and has been followed up the same blind alley by a number of equally sententious modern interpreters), for Chauntecler's problems are caused not by taking woman's advice but by not taking his own, and what sways him from his own good judgment of the matter is Pertelote's beauty, not her advice. His tale is a truer analogy for, and a more truly comic distortion of, the story of the Fall than he thought, just as his jokes (as about the book of Launcelot) are funnier than he realizes.

In much of this there are striking parallels between the narrator and his chief character, Chauntecler. Chauntecler is a superbly competent cock, though no songster, and he is an excellent scholar. His analysis of the oracular and significative power of dreams is a model of scholarly discourse, complete with full illustration, citation of authority, and judicious balancing of the evidence. It is not only persuasive but true—true in terms of the weight of medieval authority on the subject and true in the event. Within his discourse two exempla are told that demonstrate the art of laconic narrative at its most starkly portentous, especially the tale of the murdered man in the dung cart. We are close here to the excellences of the Pardoner's exemplum. Pratt has shown clearly how Chaucer has adapted his sources here to reinforce Chauntecler's theme of oracular premonition in dreams and his polite repudiation of Pertelote's view of the "vanite" of dreams. It is all very much to the point, and those critics have missed the point completely who complain that Chauntecler is rambling on aimlessly or that he has forgotten his argument in stressing the theme of "Mordre wol out" or, worse, that the Nun's Priest is satirizing the presence of this theme in the tale of his Prioress. It is essential to the story, on the contrary, that Chauntecler should be doing what he does to the top of his bent; only if this is recognized is the full comedy of the situation released, which is that Chauntecler, for all his eloquence, takes no notice at all of what he says and that furthermore, of course, he could not possibly be saying it (being a cock). Chauntecler's jokes, too, like the narrator's, misfire. He is very pleased with himself for getting the better of Pertelote with a polite mistranslation of an antifeminist tag, and he shares with us a patronizing snigger, but what he does not realize is that his mistranslation is really a true translation: woman is man's confusion *because* she is his joy and bliss.

What I have outlined so far are some of the basic requirements of burlesque or mock-heroic, which I take to be the genre of the tale. The mention of the allusion to the Fall, however, is a reminder that many modern interpreters would regard laughter as a very poor reward for the effort expended in reading the tale. Starting from the narrator's own injunction to "take the moralitee," they have subjected the tale to moralistic interpretation or even to systematic allegorical interpretation in the endeavor to extract a lesson that will confirm a certain set of moral and religious values. That the tale is shot through with allusion to serious matters is something no one could deny, and I shall argue presently that the tale has a serious (though very funny) meaning. But the determination of modern inter-

preters to bend the tale to the exemplification of a single moral or allegorical intent is destructive of its very fabric and has led to some excesses of overinterpretation which are as preposterous as the tale itself. The basic objections to such methods of interpretation have been often rehearsed, but they need restating briefly. Systematic allegorization of secular literature creates a common dead level of expectation in which all that literature does is demonstrate in more or less arcane form the truth of truths already known to be true from other sources (especially scriptural exegesis): it denies to the writer all individuality of imaginative activity, it denies the power of literature to disclose unperceived reality or to enhance understanding in unconceived ways, and it denies the nature and very mode of operation of imaginative writing.

With all this said, it must be recognized that moral and allegorical interpretation of **"The Nun's Priest's Tale"** has contributed significantly to the fuller understanding of the tale. Those critics, for instance, who have analyzed the aptness of the portrayal of Chauntecler as an image of male vanity, or of the triumph of the lower nature of man over his higher, have certainly recognized an important element in our enjoyment of the tale. The consistent, witty, and generous humanity of the tale is one of its characteristically Chaucerian marvels, but there is no lesson to be learned from this, no little nugget of "moralitee" which we can hoard away for our better edification. For one thing, Chauntecler escapes from the plight his folly has brought him to by the exercise not of his higher reason but of his low cunning, of a technique of flattery that he has learned from his deceiver. There is no lesson to be learned from this, except by animals. Likewise, the presentation of Chauntecler's folly is not true satire, since it is not done from the point of view of a standard of moral values that could be called normative. Moralistic interpreters often comment on Chauntecler's uxoriousness and his fondness for nonprocreative love play as the cause of his downfall. It will be seen, however, that there are no standards by which we can judge of this matter in relation to cocks and hens—a reasonably continent cock would be no cock at all. Here, as often in the tale, Chaucer employs the juxtapositions of beast fable, the constant switching from awareness of the animals as human to ludicrous awareness of the animals as animal, to deflate pompous interpretations and snag morality. The embarrassing surfeit of "morals" we are offered at the end of the tale hints at the inadequacy of easy moralizing.

Moralistic interpreters of the poem may be said to have missed its point, but with nothing like the resounding finality with which it has been missed by the exegetical interpreters. At the same time, exegetical interpretation has been valuable in alerting us to allusions and levels of meaning that do indeed need recovery. The idea of the cock as preacher, or of the fox as diabolical seducer, is certainly present in the tale by implication, as is the explicit series of allusions to the Fall. The effect of this, however, is not to set out for us a diagram of salvation but to take us deeper into the comedy of the tale, and particularly to allow us to enjoy the rich humor of the comedy of survival converted to the comedy of salvation. The inspiration for Chaucer's laughter here has long been neglected but has recently been exposed in a number of essays on Chaucer's debt to the preachers' use of beast fables. It is only in the knowledge of this characteristically medieval exemplary material that we can appreciate how exactly Chaucer caricatures the absurdities of allegorized fable, the joyful irrelevance of stories that have no point matched with allegories that do not work.

To recognize that the tale has no point is the start of understanding. I do not mean by this that it lacks the power to satisfy certain basic appetites that we expect to have satisfied in traditional narratives. In this tale that appetite is satisfied by the theme of reversal, or "the biter bit." But this is a fact of life, not a *point.* At the same time, we cannot feel entirely content with a recognition that the tale has no point, and we can perhaps express something more of our response to it by saying that the fact that the tale has no point is the point of the tale. The edifice of human understanding is a noble thing, and the arts of language and rhetoric and learning that bring it into being are noble arts. But man has a tendency to skulk inside this edifice, to mistake it for the reality of his observed world instead of a man-made model of that reality. In the tale Chaucer takes a few bricks out of the building and allows it to drop around our ears, laughing uncontrollably meanwhile. In so doing he restores a pristine and uncolored quality to our perception of the nature of language and rhetoric and learning and enables us to see the tricks that we play with them to preserve our high opinion of ourselves. He does so by means of a trick. This surely is a point worth taking, and one specially to be taken by a generation of critics and interpreters who are as fond of telling us what is good for us as were any of Chaucer's preachers. (pp. 3-13)

Derek Pearsall, in an introduction to The Nun's Priest's Tale *by Geoffrey Chaucer, edited by Derek Pearsall, University of Oklahoma Press, 1984, pp. 3-124.*

David Aers   (essay date 1986)

[*Aers is an English academic and the author of* Piers Plowman and Christian Allegory *(1975),* Chaucer, Langland and the Creative Imagination *(1980), and* Chaucer *(1986). In the excerpt below from the latter work, Aers examines Chaucer's portrayal of society.*]

Society was traditionally and authoritatively represented as a body organised in three estates: massive differences in power, access to resources, and status were allegedly in everyone's interest, the 'common profit'. Those who worked to sustain the basic life processes of the community (the lowest estate), those who were said to defend (= police?) the community (the knightly estate), and those who prayed (the clerical estate, bringing the community and God together), comprised the static, harmonious organism created by God. In it, all individuals should unquestioningly accept their inherited occupation and place. This dominant social ideology generated a mass of writings encouraging people to see themselves according to some version of its basic model and the values it carried. These writings presented the established division of power, wealth, work and knowledge as so 'natural' that any oppo-

sition to it must seem 'unnatural', monstrous. This is, of course, always one of the chief functions of social ideology sponsored by dominant classes. Human identity becomes defined in its terms—'There be in þis world þre maner of men, clerkes, knyytes, and commynalte.'

However, this ideology faced substantial anomalies by Chaucer's time, and well before then, in fact. Increasing social complexity, emerging social groups (especially with the great urban developments of the thirteenth-century), sharp social conflicts, the development of a profit economy, diversification of political theory and even the articulation of competing ideologies, constituted a world intractable to received frames of reference. Chaucer's writing is marked by an openness to many of the contradictory forces in this fluid situation.

About the time of the great, popular English rising of 1381, Chaucer wrote the ***Parliament of Fowls,*** a multifaceted, energetic poem which includes a representation of society and social ideologies. In this poem Nature, a personified metaphysical concept, supports a traditional perception of the community as a stable hierarchy. In isolation, this would look like the traditional authoritarian move whereby existing social order is made 'natural' and hence unquestionable, eternal. But the text offers us, against this, a figuration of conflict and violently egotistical behaviour, with each competing group presenting its own views as disinterested concern for 'commune profyt'. The leading groups are named first in a pointed manner:

> That is to seyn, the foules of ravyne
> Weere hyest set, and thanne the foules smale
>   . . .
> Ther was the tiraunt with his fetheres donne
> And grey, I mene the goshauk, that doth pyne
> To bryddes for his outrageous ravyne.

The dominant and powerful are thus presented as predators, tyrants and perpetrators of 'outrageous ravyne'. Through his explicitly social categories (the birds' language, the political form of a parliament), the poet invites the reader to take this as a gamesome model of the society she or he inhabits. The aristocratic birds, speaking a distinctly courtly language, monopolise the assembly and make the needs of other groups in the community quite invisible, literally unspeakable. Talk of common profit from such emphatically class-bound leaders is made rather ironic. Nor, significantly, are the lower orders, the creatures of the third estate, at all impressed. Instead of deferential respect, they burst into a very different language from the courtly figures, one expressing direct antagonism to the upper classes. The text creates conflicting forms of social life which involve conflicting perspectives and values:

> . . . 'Have don, and lat us wende!'
>   . . .
> 'Com of !' they criede, 'allas, ye wol us shende!
> When shal youre cursede pletynge have an ende?
>   . . .
> The goos seyde, 'Al this nys not worth a
>   flye! . . .'

This explosion challenges the upper-class monopoly of Parliament, power and speech. It works as a characteristically Chaucerian image of what Rodney Hilton has described as, 'The loss of plebeian respect for the traditional élites' in this period, an image of social energies recreated in a very different mode by Chaucer's contemporary, Langland. Not that the privileged Chaucer saw the lower social groups as carrying more admirable values. He has the lower-status cuckoo invoke the notion of common welfare only to disclose that here too self-interest underlies the rhetoric of charitable intervention. His poem displays competing versions of what is 'commune profyt' in a complex and divided society such as his own. It unveils the highly partial perspectives informing the language of 'common welfare' and 'unity', while it blocks off any attempt to escape to some transcendental solution.

A similar approach to his social world and its language is evident in *The Canterbury Tales.* Its recognition should be prominent in our readings of that fragmentary, carnivalesque and unfinished work. The **"General Prologue"** alludes to traditional ideology of the three estates through the figures of Knight, Priest and Ploughman-Peasant. But it does so in a context which dissolves the estates ideology, within a literary form well suited to figure forth a mobile, dissonant social world penetrated by market values and pursuits—very familiar to its author, a wealthy vintner's son who spent his life in a major urban economy, moving as easily with wealthy bourgeoisie as with courtiers and urban intellectuals. Chaucer represents this society in a manner which encourages critical reflection on the relations between its official ideology, languages and practices, while discouraging simple traditional judgements. It is a mode which could help us take a striking question in the **"General Prologue"** as far more than a jibe at the Monk: 'How shal the world be served?' In the poem's representation of social being this becomes deeply problematic.

Here, there is only space to illustrate this mode in the **"General Prologue"** by taking one figure, the Monk. Jill Mann [in her *Chaucer and Medieval Estates Satire*] has described the way Chaucer evokes traditional stereotypes of the corrupt monk only to refine the conventional judgements these carried. Certainly, the Monk is allowed to dismiss traditional rules and their attempts to confine monks to monastic cells:

> Ther as this lord was kepere of the celle,
> The reule of seint Maure or of seint Beneit,
> By cause that it was old and somdel streit
> This ilke Monk leet olde thynges pace,
> And heeld after the newe world the space.

Monks, like Chaucer, *did* inhabit 'the newe world', and the forces of 'the newe world' shaped religious practices and individual consciousness. As for the old proverbs asserting that monks out of their cloisters were like fish out of water:

> thilke text heeld he nat worth an oystre;
> And I seyde his opinion was good.

Readers should not take the assent here as simple sarcasm, whether they attribute it to Chaucer or the fictional pilgrim-narrator on whom so many words have been bestowed. For 'thilke text' had long since been made a dead letter, not by a few deviant, 'bad' monks, but by the development of monasticism within medieval society and its economy. The same applies to the comments that the Monk was an 'outridere', 'a lord ful fat' enjoying an aristocratic life-style, a 'manly man' and hence ideal for promotion within the religious establishment to the post of abbot. Monks, and especially their leaders, were drawn from the upper and middle classes, while the expansion of monasticism had been inextricably bound up with its economic foundations, practices and worldy success as a powerful landlord producing for medieval markets. Chaucer's art engages with this situation. Instead of writing a satire which lampoons 'worldly' monks as individual deviants from an unquestionable moral order, it discloses traditional ideology as made anachronistic by the practices and new language of thriving Christian institutions in 'the newe world'. The poetry figures decisive social forces which shaped contemporary and future human practices in directions quite alien to received ideology and the estates satire this sponsored. We are shown some of the implications of the monastic economy which the historian Lester Little [in his *Religious Poverty and the Profit Economy*] recently described in these terms:

> They [the Cistercians] did not slip casually into the profit economy, as had the black monks before them; instead—even if for the most part unintentionally—they plunged headlong into it. Their staying so far away from towns and their brilliant economic success together indicated how thoroughly the profit economy had permeated the countryside.

In such circumstances the reiteration of traditional rules and moral outrage (perhaps congruent with an earlier feudal order?) was, Chaucer's art suggests, rather shallow. By his time, there was nothing 'unintentional' about monks' economic commitments.

Throughout the **"General Prologue"** we encounter a world in which moral vocabulary and judgements become terms to depict success and respectability in a world where the market is central. The Wife of Bath, a successful 'clooth-makyng' member of the bourgeoisie, is called 'a worthy womman'; the Merchant, necessarily concentrating on 'th'encrees of his wynnyng' and representing the bourgeois life preoccupied with the market, its values and financial dealing, is called, 'a worthy man'; the Knight fights 'in his lordes werre', but as he fights for both officially Christian employers and heathens he too seems a 'worthy man' in the sense that he is a successful operator in the same social world and discourse as the other pilgrims. In these and similar cases it is a crude misreading to assume that 'really' Chaucer is being sarcastic at the expense of his 'persona', the fictional narrator mentioned above. Such misreading assumes that the text invites simple moral condemnation from a simply anti-mercantile position. Nobody had been more severely treated by traditional precapitalist moralists than the merchant. The thirteenth-century theologian, St Thomas Aquinas, [in his *Summa theologiae*] was conventional enough when he asserted that 'trade, in so far as it aims at making profits, is most reprehensible, since the desire for gain knows no bounds but reaches the infinite.' But the art of the London tradesman's son encourages no such moralisation. Rather, as Jill Mann has shown, the **"General Prologue"** stresses how 'worth' is defined according to professional criteria; it withholds any sense of that benevolent and organic interaction of estates so central in traditional social ideology. Chaucer's poetry dramatises the way a market society dissolves such traditional ideology and its ethical discourses while it shapes human relationships around the exchange of commodities. His work evokes human agents for whom traditional ideas of community and common profit are irrelevant anachronisms. The world emerging in the fiction is not unrelated to the 'newe world' Chaucer inhabited, one experiencing the substantial activity of mercantile capital and the historical consequences this held for human consciousness and relations.

Let us consider one of the less discussed *Canterbury Tales*—the **"Shipman's Tale."** Like so many others of the tales, this plunges us into a world in which market relations are the norm. Marriage, marital sex, extramarital sex, all are for sale, all absorbed into the cash nexus. This state of affairs is encapsulated in the final pun on 'taille' in the wife's comment, 'score it up upon my taille'— genitals are account-books, sex is a commodity, marital sex the balancing of financial accounts. As the Wife of Bath is made to show, 'al is for to selle.' These are matters returned to . . . [later]: here I wish to point out some of the more subtle ways in which Chaucer's text shows a market society affecting language, values and historical development. As in the **"General Prologue,"** words which are major terms in moral discourse becomes terms merely reflecting position and purchasing power in the economic market: 'wys' is a measure of 'wealth'; 'wys' human activity is defined as successful transactions on the international market, as is 'prudent' activity. Similarly, the key word 'good' loses any peculiarly ethical import and becomes a counter for signifying material possessions and their conventional value. Again, as in the **"General Prologue,"** 'worthy' takes on a purely professional and economistic frame of reference; so does the word for generosity, 'free.' It is also striking that the word 'noble' is applied to success in the market, something Gower observed and complained about in his *Miroir de l'omme.* There he asserted that, by the 1370s, 'the chivalric aristocracy is being replaced by a financial aristocracy: knights have become greedy for money, now fight only for ransom and engage in trade rather than seeking military prowess.' Similarly, in *Vox Clamantis,* he complained that, 'Arms are more of a business now than a mark of nobility, as a result, the tailor's boy now goes about in a helmet.'

Chaucer himself represents the merchant's life as one quite uninhibited by any sense of the traditional religious guilt about this vocation. It is shown as founded on an utterly individualistic pursuit of wealth through market transactions in which rational calculation and credit is a key to success. What becomes of traditional Catholic Christianity in such a way of life? Chaucer's text includes an astonishingly resonant answer. During the visit of the merchant's friend, the monk, the host withdraws from the festivities:

> The thridde day, this marchant up ariseth,
> And on his nedes sadly hym avyseth,
> And up into his countour-hous gooth he

> To rekene with hymself, as wel may be,
> Of thilke yeer how that it with hym stood,
> And how that he despended hadde his good,
> And if that he encressed were or noon.
> His bookes and his bagges many oon
> He leith biforn hym on his countyng-bord.
> Ful riche was his tresor and his hord,
> For which ful faste his countour-dore he shette;
> And eek he nolde that no man sholde hym lette
> Of his acountes, for the meene tyme;

As this merchant 'up ariseth' on 'the third day' the religious and moral *potential* of this passage should be registered. For example, the potential echo of Christ's resurrection on the third day, with its traditional moral allegorisation as the rising from sin demanded of all people in Christianity; the traditional religious and ethical potential of the emphatically solitary ascent into an upper room for scrupulous introspection and meditation ('To rekene with himself, as well may be . . . how that it with hym stood' and with his 'good'). Once we register this religious and ethical potential, we are well placed to understand the significance of the fact that far from being actualised the potential is stunningly transformed. For what Chaucer figures here is the way that such mercantile dedication to the market involves a psychological state which transforms traditional religious orientations in a manner that can be described as worldly asceticism. This impression is strengthened by the juxtaposition of the merchant's solitary withdrawal on the third day with the monk's gregarious and festive presence in the worthy house. The merchant's retreat replaces the traditional retreat of monasticism, and with this, of course, the old goals. Instead of the monastic cell, the *counting house;* instead of the Bible and saints' lives, *accounting books;* instead of monastic withdrawal to undertake scrupulous introspection in the pursuit of the love of God and the heavenly treasures of supernatural salvation, the merchant withdraws from the festivities to undertake meticulous, systematic calculations in the pursuit of monetary profit and the accumulation of very material '*good*' and '*tresor*'. Nor is his daily practice unaffected by this withdrawal. We find him travelling to Flanders and working in Bruges,

> faste and bisily
> Aboute his nede, and byeth and creauncheth.
> He neither pleyeth at the dees ne daunceth . . .

As his business succeeds, he thanks God who has apparently graced his buying and selling. Religion thus sanctifies a life centered on the individualistic and socially irresponsible pursuit of economic profit while the social milieu allows this, favours it, and even seems to take it for granted.

What then of the representative of the traditional pursuit of holiness, 'daun John' the monk? Like the Monk of the **"General Prologue,"** he has come out of his cell and into the world as an 'officer' licensed by his abbot to pursue the economic interests of his monastery, 'To seen hir graunges and hire bernes wyde' and to engage in market transactions to support the material foundations of a traditional religious order. Chaucer displays the contradictions between the original spiritual basis of monastic vocation and its social, economic and religious outcome, a matrix referred to earlier . . . . In contrast to the merchant, the business monk is quite free of ascetic tendencies. Like the Monk of the **"General Prologue,"** he enjoys the traditional pleasures of the landed upper classes with a relish which Chaucer's poetry conveys in a manner and context which leaves little space or language for traditional moral judgement.

In summary, then, Chaucer's work represents society as a composite of *inevitably* competing groups motivated by individualistic forms of material self-interest, and mediated through access to a market which he saw as encompassing and profoundly affecting most human relationships. In this vision all claims to be pursuing an allegedly *common profit* are exposed to a sceptical examination which subverts the very notion of a unified society and a harmonious common profit. With this goes a critical reflexivity which de-sublimates all attempts to erect ideologically secure, impersonally authoritative discourses. His texts continually return such discourses to the social processes within which they are generated and to which they contribute. Contrary to the dominant ideology, his work represents long-term *antagonism* between social groups as an altogether predictable, even inevitable state of affairs, while the literary modes he constructs subvert attempts to impose traditional social ideology and moralisations on what is exhibited as intractable material.

I shall now turn to the figuration of lordship, institutionalised secular authority, in two of Chaucer's most widely-read poems, the **"Knight's Tale"** and the **"Clerk's Tale."** Contrary to much academic wisdom, which seems to have enlightened our sixth forms, the **"Knight's Tale"** is not an unequivocal celebration of Theseus as the principle of law and order we are to worship. It is a critical, often highly ironic, exploration of secular rule, its forms of power and its uses of language.

Theseus represents the successful 'lord and governour', a 'worthy duc'. The **"General Prologue,"** as we saw, shows what words like 'worthy' signify in the current culture of discourse, and by its usage here we understand that Theseus is an expert ruler, remembering how the Merchant, the Wife of Bath and the Friar are also all 'worthy' professionals. What kind of order such 'worthy' and heroic military rulers propagate is made a major topic for reflection in the poem.

As soon as Chaucer introduces Theseus he makes the basis of his government clear—military domination. His 'wysdom and his chivalrie' are concentrated on wars of imperialist expansion which have an explicit economic motive: 'riche' countries are violently conquered to feed Theseus's 'wele' and his 'pride.' The poem's opening thus displays the foundation of the honour and aristocratic life so celebrated in conventional romance literature. It also emphasises that Theseus is a worshipper of Mars. The implications of this are drawn out in an extremely powerful passage, the depiction of Mars' temple and the ways of life pursued by that god's worshippers. The writing here evokes the human misery produced by violent aggression and it works in a manner whose critical bearings are not widely appreciated. The text displays the *common ground* between the 'tiraunt with the pray by force yraft', leaving

the 'toun destroyed', and the 'tresoun of the mordrynge in the bedde'; between the 'open werre' with masses 'slayn', the organised violence initiated by national rulers and the 'smylere with the knyf under the cloke'. The poetry persuades us to see *continuities* between supposedly different forms of violence. The ruling classes, however, strive to distinguish their own violence, which they glorify and aestheticise, from the violence of others, which they condemn. Contemporary Anglo-American scholars have tended to overlook the critical dimension of the **"Knight's Tale"** here. Yet even orthodox Christians have not always been blind to the disturbing continuities the text depicts. St Augustine himself [in the *City of God*] likened the order of kingdoms to that of robber bands, asserting that the only difference between them is the impunity of official rulers. Nor should we overlook the fact that having presented Theseus as the most successful conqueror of his era, riding under the banner of Mars, Chaucer now includes the image of 'Conquest, sittynge in greet honour' in this grisly temple of dehumanising violence. The passage concludes with another allusion to Theseus's Martian banner where the 'rede statue of Mars' shone in glory. Now the 'statue of Mars' is more closely described. We learn that the god Theseus worships seems insane, while

> A wolf ther stood biforn hym at his feet
> With eyen rede, and of a man he eet;

Such is the 'glorie' of Mars and his followers critically placed by Chaucer. The passage justly conveys the destructive contempt for humanity in the forms of law, order and life cultivated by rulers who exalt armed 'force', 'glorie' and 'honour'.

Given this, it should not be surprising that the poem shows how, when rulers of armed states accuse each other of tyranny, the accusations tend to lack political self-awareness even if they are not—as they mostly are—cynical propaganda. In the **"Knight's Tale,"** Creon is accused of 'tirannye' and Theseus promises to ride out as a 'trewe knyght' to smash this tyrant. But the poem conveys the self-interest and self-aggrandising motives in this righteousness. It follows Theseus's liberation of Thebes from the tyranny of Creon by giving us another decisive insight to the form of law and order the 'worthy' duke represents. Having killed Creon, he assaults Thebes, 'And rente adoune bothe wall and sparre and rafter.' This act of wanton violent destruction is a 'worthy' one for a follower of Mars in whose temple the destruction of civilian homes is figured. After this, Theseus 'dide with al the contree as hym leste'. Palamon's complaint about Theseus's 'tirannye' is not at all foolish. Indeed, at this point Chaucer adds a passage not in his Italian source to bring out still more sharply the implications of law and order as understood by the world's Theseuses:

> To ransake in the taas of bodyes dede,
> Hem for to strepe of harneys and of wede,
> The pilours diden bisynesse and cure
> After the bataille and disconfiture.

The scene takes us to the core of militaristic cultures, just as it focuses on the essential economic groundwork—ground so assiduously obscured by official pomp, pageantry and glorifications of war. The mentality which fosters any form of militarism culminates in an easy willingness to turn the vitally alive into dead bodies, ransacked for the victors' economic profit and their rulers' 'mooste pride'. The passage creates a memorable image of cultures which transform humans into objects, things, profitable dead things.

Some readers take Theseus's organisation of the tournament in which Arcite is killed as as sign of benevolent rule. Yet the poem hardly encourages a totally unironic response. True enough, the ruler does separate Palamon and Arcite, those emblems of a 'chivalrie' whose knightly ideals turn them into forms of life depicted in animal images such as 'wood leon', 'crueel tigre' and 'wilde bores' that 'frothen white as foom.' But Theseus controls them because they threaten his lordship, his own monopoly over the means and deployment of violence. As soon as he hears who they are, he announces that he need not torture the Thebans but can kill them immediately, 'by mighty Mars the rede.' The courtly ladies intervene successfully at this point and Theseus relents. Nevertheless, his 'pitee' is still quite explicitly part of a political calculation. It is also a peculiarly Martian version of 'pitee'. He could, after all, have settled the question of who, if anyone, should marry Emily in a host of non-violent ways—heresy of heresies, he could even have followed the lead of Nature in the **Parliament of Fowls** and allowed the female some choice! Instead, he centralises and increases the violence by ordering each of the two Thebans to bring another hundred armed knights who will fight until one of the leaders is killed or defeated. Later, Theseus does decide to limit the instruments of violence to lances, long swords and maces to protect the shedding of 'gentil blood', the blood of his own class. However, he still exhorts the armed knights to 'ley on faste', to fight their fill. The text then depicts the ensuing violence as bloody and animalistic. Simultaneously, in a profoundly illuminating juxtaposition, it shows the ruler who has organised the dehumanising violence surveying the scene as a spectacle while he sits above it, 'Arrayed right as he were a god in trone.' Such is still the custom of the lords of violence. As for the tournament, after the intervention of the culture's appropriately vicious gods, it ends in the miserable death of Arcite described in a mode which decisively resists all idealisation and glorification.

With this in mind it is worth recalling Chaucer's **"Tale of Melibee."** This includes a critique of conventional 'machismo' and upper-class aggression. It argues that war should not be glorified and must be avoided, stressing 'the grete goodes that comen of pees, and the grete harmes and perils that been in werre.' The work, itself conventional enough, is a salutary check on certain current myths about what 'the medieval mind' must have thought about war. With it one does well to recall the writing of Chaucer's close friend, the Lollard knight, John Clanvowe. In his treatise on *The two ways* he remarks that conventional defence and glorification of war may be antithetical to God's judgements, for unlike God:

> þe world [his class?] holt hem worsshipful þat
> been greet werreyours and fiyteres and þat dis-
> troyen and wynnen manye loondis, and waasten
> and yeuen muche good to hem þat haan ynouy.

And also þe world worsshipeþ hem muchel þat woln bee venged proudly and dispitously of euery wrong þat is seid or doon to hem. And of swyche folke men maken bookes and soonges and reeden and syngen of hem for to hoolde þe mynde of here deedes þe lengere heere vpon eerth.

Clanvowe, however, insists that 'God is souuerayn treuþe and a trewe iuge þat deemeth hem riyt shameful byfore God and alle þe compaigne of heuene'. The lucidity with which he identifies and condemns the ideological dimensions of romance is striking, setting himself (and his God, of course) in opposition to a matrix in which practice and discourse are inseparable. Chaucer's **"Melibee"** and his friend's tract offer a medieval perspective too often ignored. It is far closer to the informing critical vision of the **"Knight's Tale"** than those perpetuated by the commentaries emerging from the Anglo-American community of 'medievalists' which make the poem a hymn in honour of Theseus and his values.

The **"Knight's Tale"** concludes with a long parliamentary oration in which Theseus seeks specific *political* gains. The text is quite unequivocal about this:

> Thanne semed me ther was a parlement
> At Atthenes, upon certain pointz and caas;
> Among the whiche pointz yspoken was,
> To have with certein contrees alliaunce,
> And have fully of Thebans obeisaunce.
> For which this noble Theseus anon
> Leet senden after gentil Palamon

Theseus's motivation is plainly political self-interest perceived through that will for dominion which becomes so basic to those leading a society's ruling class. (Indeed, the speech is explicitly an expression of the ruler's 'wille'.) Here the leader and his Parliament determine a foreign policy which includes total control of those whose city they had earlier destroyed, tearing down 'bothe wall and sparre and rafter'. Through the speech itself, Chaucer shows how theological language can serve those in power. It enables them to present thoroughly limited class and nationalistic self-interests as universal ones dictated by a transcendental being to whom they have special, indeed monopolistic, access. Wonderful to say, this being never criticises the basic activities or views of the ruling class and never, never supports its opponents! Chaucer has sharpened the irony in this political oration by having the very worldly, militaristic Theseus, whose speech culminates in an order for a very worldly, wealthy and merry upper-class marriage, plunder bits and pieces from one of the poet's favourite texts, the *Consolation of Philosophy*. Boethius wrote this as part of an attempt to cultivate stoical detachment from the kind of world to which Theseus is so totally devoted: and he did so while awaiting execution decreed by his own worthy ruler.

Not surprisingly, Theseus transforms the *Consolation of Philosophy* into a *Consolation of Political Authority*. His oration, purportedly a rhetorical elaboration of the banal observation that all things must die, actually aims to persuade us that whatever is, is right. Indeed, the present social order is naturalised, eternalised and given divine rather than human and historical foundations. Theseus's message is one we have become accustomed to hearing from our political leaders who represent the chief beneficiaries of the social and economic order which sustains them:

> Thanne is it wysdom, as it thynketh me,
> To maken vertu of necessitee,
> And take it weel that we may nat eschue,
> And namely that to us alle is due.
> And whoso gruccheth ought, he dooth folye,
> And rebel is to hym that al may gye.

This is a highly partial and impoverished idea of human 'wysdom', but its political uses are hardly obscure. The discourse of authority would persuade us that its truncated version of reality is definitive. The slightest complaint against the current order is construed as madness, a madness which turns the protestor into a 'rebel' against God with whom the secular powers and their order are now conveniently merged. This is the context in which he pronounces it wisdom 'To maken vertu of necessitee', a context in which his own rule and its contingent social order are claimed as 'necessitee'. Richard Neuse is right to remind us how Milton placed such language in *Paradise Lost*:

> So spoke the Fiend, and with necessity,
> The tyrant's plea, excused his devilish deeds,

The meaning of 'love' in the speech undergoes as characteristic a reduction as 'wysdom'. It becomes a merely controlling and limiting force supporting the present order and its ruler. All elements in the oration converge in a sacralisation of Theseus's secular authority. We now see the full meaning of Theseus presenting himself 'as he were a god in trone'—visual image, state pageantry, theology and the language of political control fuse. It is salutary to remember that for such sacralisation of his own authority, King Richard II, was finally deposed and killed by the man Chaucer lauded as 'verray kyng'.

The **"Clerk's Tale"** is my second example of Chaucer's treatment of lordship. The critical power of this poem has been too often obscured by medievalists who seem to identify with Walter. This would hardly have surprised Chaucer, for he anticipated the likelihood of absolutist misreadings, mockingly placing them in the mouths of the Host and the Merchant. He also acknowledges that 'som men' will praise Walter's subjection of Griselda, but has the narrator make his own condemnation of such readers quite unequivocal.

In fact, the text's condemnation of Walter could not be more direct. His actions are described as evil ('wikke') and his purpose as 'crueel'. Walter is presented as a lawful ruler consumed by an insatiable lust for absolute dominion. Indeed, the word most frequently associated with him, from the opening description of him as one for whom 'his lust present was al his thoght', is the word 'lust'. His statement to Griselda's father illustrates assumptions about lordship common enough among authoritarian rulers: 'al that liketh me, I dar wel seyen / It liketh thee'. It is the ideal he proposes to Griselda:

> I seye this, be ye redy with good herte
> To al my lust, and that I frely may,
> As me best thynketh, do yow laughe or smerte,

> And nevere ye to grucche it, nyght ne day?
> And eek whan I sey 'ye', ne sey nat 'nay',
> Neither by word ne frownyng contenance?
> Sware this, and heere I swere oure alliance.

This is the ideal of all tyrants, whether domestic, in the world of work, or in the formally political sphere. Just as Theseus claimed that 'whoso *gruccheth* ought, he dooth folye, / And rebel is', so Walter demands that his subject never 'grucche it'. While her father stood before Walter 'al quakyng', so Griselda listens 'quakynge for drede'. Not suprisingly, she assents. This is a disturbing image of authority and obedience—nor is it one cherished by many late medieval people in practice or theory.

From here the poem displays the effects of such a political relation (for 'personal' relations are also 'political', and vice versa). The lord indulges in a rule of absolute and totally irresponsible sovereignty, driven on by a compulsive will over which he is shown to have no control. He becomes an example of a man overwhelmed by what St Augustine had called 'the love of ruling' which 'lays waste men's hearts with the most ruthless dominion'. But it is not only the ruler's moral state that is perverted in such a relation. The moral life of the obedient subject is also corrupted. Chaucer depicts this through the sergeant. Committed to 'feithful' service and unquestioning obedience, 'swich folk', the poet writes, will carry out 'thynges badde' if they are ordered to. The sergeant's view is that men *must* obey their rulers' 'lust', 'ther is namoore to seye'. This is the subject's version of Theseus's instruction to suspend all critical reflection or dissent, to accept the existing state of affairs as 'necessitee' and to make a 'vertu' of capitulation to it. (Such ideas did not offer any protection for the followers of Richard II executed in 1388.) Griselda's attitude is no different from the sergeant's, and no less culpable. In her servile obedience to her ruler, she renounces all responsibility, moral or religious. The terrible consequences of such subjection are made clear. It actually encourages vicious tyranny and it leads the subject into unambiguously evil actions. Griselda assents to the murder of her children without any attempt to protect them and without any protest or attempt to reform her vicious lord. Theseus's or Walter's ideal subject, she accepts the authoritarian ruler's self-deification, an acceptance the text treats with critical penetration. The deification of a 'cruel' and 'wikke' secular order is, if we wish to use theological terms, idolatry.

The poem is thus a powerful dramatisation of the effects of absolutism on both the ruled and the ruler. Its meaning should also be viewed in its own contexts—the contexts of Richard II's reign with its sharp and, for some, fatal, political and ideological conflicts. In these the distinction between legitimate rule and arbitrary absolutism, or tyranny, had become a live issue which Chaucer knew and experienced at first hand. These conflicts were only to be resolved with the overthrow of Richard. This was chiefly justified in the 1399 Articles of Deposition on the grounds that the ruler had become a tyrant exercising arbitrary will in the mistaken assumption that law resided in his own breast. He had, that is to say, become a Walter. But his Griselda rebelled.

Chaucer's text does include an alternative, if rather abstractly idealistic model of political authority to Walter's, and we should not overlook it. In Walter's absence Griselda becomes ruler. Her renunciation of the lust for power enables her to mediate between competing and conflicting groups, introducing judgements not of arbitrary will but of 'greet equitee'. She thus earns the trust and voluntary cooperation of the community. This is presented as an ideal and contrasts starkly with Walter's practices, as with all the absolutist ideologies he represents. It certainly matches the model expressed in Chaucer's *Legend of Good Women:*

> This shulde a ryghtwys lord han in his thought,
> And not ben lyk tyraunts of Lumbardye,
> That usen wilfulhed and tyrannye.
> For he that kyng or lord is naturel,
> Hym oughte nat be tyraunt and crewel,
> As is a fermour, to don the harm he can.
> He moste thynke it is his lige man
> And that hym oweth, of verrary duetee,
> Shewen his peple pleyn benygnete,
> And wel to heren here excusacyouns.
> And here compleyntes and petyciouns

This matrix is part of a development in late medieval political theory which presented the ruler's authority as derived from the community, the ruler as servant of the community, and the end of monarchy the well-being of human individuals, rather than of corporations or grand platonic abstractions. Chaucer's text supports a vision of limited monarchy, a secular power which is avowedly secular and should be exercised within limits determined by the divided community of individuals for whose interests the ruler exists. It is a vision quite in accord with the poetry's characteristic subversion of cognitive totalitarianism and dogmatic authority. It also accords with the writing's strikingly individualistic version of society. And here we meet one of the horizons of Chaucer's social imagination, for (in contrast to Langland's *Pier's Plowman*) it tends to abandon all ideas of fraternity, social justice and the social embodiment of charity, foreshadowing an ideological position that would become commonplace with the triumph of bourgeois individualism in the later seventeenth and eighteenth centuries. (pp. 14-36)

> *David Aers, in his* Chaucer, *Humanities Press International, Inc., 1986, 121 p.*

Martha Fleming   (essay date 1986)

[*In the following excerpt, Fleming examines the patterns of thematic repetition in the "Wife of Bath's Tale," maintaining that the tale "is not about marriage."*]

Much nonsense has been written about the Wife of Bath. She is held up as the model of the bad wife, her testimony that of the bad marriage; she is put forth as a feminist, her views evidence of Chaucer's feminist sensibilities; and she is reproved as a monster, an unnatural woman who does not wax and multiply. Certainly I am not the first to point out that she is none of these things, that were she transferred to a 19th century novel, the limits of her characterization would be all too evident. But the fact remains, she appeals to our imagination, and we readers see what we want to see. As Hugh of St. Victor wrote [in his *Didascalicon*], "imagination . . . is sensuous memory made up of the traces of corporeal objects inhering in the mind; it possesses in itself nothing certain as a source of knowledge."

I am interested in pursuing the connections between the **"Wife of Bath's Tale"** and the **"Wife of Bath's Prologue."** One of my assumptions is that we as critics have made too much of the notion that the Wife is the fictional maker of this tale, that she is the painter of this particular lion. We have been taken in by Chaucer's proficiency at "authenticating realism," to use Bloomfield's terms and by Chaucer's capacity for calling into play "sensuous memory," and thus we have been seduced by this appearance of verisimilitude into asking the wrong questions. We have been preoccupied with suiting the tale to the teller. The Wife as fictional maker of the tale is in fact the maker of the tale only superficially, simply enough to keep the dramatic frame in place. All the efforts to make the tale suit the teller, discussions of "unimpersonated artistry" and the like result from our inability or unwillingness to accept the insubstantial nature of the frame. The use, for example, of the grammatical "we," "we wives," "we wommen," the jibes at limatours which so suit the Wife's persona—women have nothing to fear any longer of faeries and elves but only of friars behind the bushes—the masterful use of dialogue at the end of the pillow lecture when the knight begs the hag "taak al my good, and lat my body go," show Chaucer's skill for establishing the dramatic possibilities the frame allows with a minimum of detail.

Because, however, we so often do read the prologue literally and because we take the tale to be supremely suited to the teller, the tale is most often read as an exemplum: a happy marriage results from female dominance. Donaldson suggests [in *Chaucer's Poetry*] it is the Wife's tribute to the woman's ability to accomplish good if she is allowed to dominate. He also suggests there is a parallel between the hag and the Wife in that both wed younger husbands. The hag is able to regain her beauty: "in her story the Wife is able to make the rules that govern the world, as she has not been able to do in her life." Whether we read this exemplum of the results of female dominance in marriage as an example of the happiness that ensues or as an example of the bad marriage as some critics do is really beside the point.

One of my starting points is Mary Carruthers' provocative discussion of the **"Wife of Bath's Prologue"** [in her 1979 PMLA article "The Wife of Bath and the Painting of Lions"], her convincing demonstration of the relation between love and economics, and her conclusion that happiness in marriage is based on economic equilibrium. Carruthers describes Alisoun's sentimental, romantic love for her fifth husband and her ill-advised handing over of her estate to him. When the Wife recovers her estate and the economic mastery that is due her because of it, domestic bliss ensues. Where I take issue with Carruthers is in her analysis of the **"Wife of Bath's Tale"** and its relation to the prologue. Carruthers writes, "painting her own lion becomes an occasion for her to reveal the sentimentality, the romance, involved in any idealistic painting." The Wife's intention then is parodic and comic, an attempt to show that only in fairy stories, only in the legendary days of King Arthur does an old, ugly, poor woman of undistinguished background find happiness with a handsome young knight of a class far removed from hers—and only then because she possesses magic rather than money. Certainly such things do not happen "biside Bath," as Carruthers points out, in the Wife's mercantile, economically defined world.

My point is that the tale says very little about the Wife of Bath; the tale in fact restores and contrasts the perspective of the other romances of the *Canterbury Tales,* in particular that of the **"Knight's Tale."** The devices used to "authenticate realism" create the illusion the tale is told by the Wife, but it is a very fragile illusion. As the tale unfolds, what we see is the restoration of order in this lusty bachelor's world, a definition of his proper role, a tale only incidentally about marriage, and, most importantly, a tale in which key terms, "mastery" and "sovereignty," are left open to misinterpretation. What we have in the *Canterbury Tales* are many variations on a theme or rather amplifications of an image set forth in the **"General Prologue,"** an image of a group on pilgrimage to Canterbury. With each tale part or parts of the image are elaborated upon, the perspectives slightly altered as we see the world defined and redefined in the play of tale, much in the fashion of the playful improvisation on an initial theme so characteristic of jazz compositions.

I will draw attention to three kinds of evidence, three patterns of repetition to construct my own improvisation on this theme: (1) the relation between the structure of romance narrative and ethics and the need to view the actions of characters as exemplars of behaviors to be praised or blamed; (2) repetition of the terms "mastery" and "sovereignty" in the Wife's prologue, the tale, and in analogues to the tale; (3) patterns of thematic repetition, particularly between the **"Knight's Tale"** and the **"Wife's Tale."**

The relation of fiction to ethics has been widely observed by the modern reader of medieval commentary and accessus. Two recent books, drawing rather different conclusions, Judson Allen's *The Ethical Poetic of the Later Middle Ages* and Glending Olson's *Literature as Recreation in the Later Middle Ages,* illustrate that like the Wife of Bath we critics know how to pick and choose our authorities. Even fictions read for enjoyment, for *delectio,* for *solaas,* are read for recreation so that the reader can return refreshed to more serious matters. Medievals seem very much aware of the danger of unrelieved work, even unrelieved meditation, and there are a number of exemplative stories which make this very point. By and large, however, readers were advised to read fictions in the spirit of Gregory the Great's advice [in his *Moralium libre*], in order "to transform what was read into our very selves, so that when our mind is stirred by what it hears, our life may concur by practicing what has been heard" and fictions, like Sacred Scripture itself, hold "a kind of mirror to the eyes of our mind that our interior face may be seen in it. There we recognize what is shameful in ourselves, what beautiful . . . " and by so doing are moved to moral behaviors.

Hugh of St. Victor describes in the *Didascalicon* the knowledge to be obtained by reading as fourfold, encompassing the four parts of philosophy: theoretical, ordered to truth; practical, ordered to virtue; mechanical, ordered to the relief of physical existence; and logical, the nature of true and correct discourse, the use of words. Each of these divisions contains further divisions. The practical, subdivided into the solitary, private and public or ethical, economic, and political, included ethics, the morality of private behavior, the governing of the self, the ethics of domestic behavior, that is, behavior within the family and the household in general, and ethical behavior in the public world.

Although Hugh never discusses "literature" as such, it is clear from his general discussion on the relations of fictions to the arts that in addition to the restorative powers inherent in such fictions, there was an advantage to the mixture of *sentence* and *solaas,* as readers were more likely to be influenced by praiseworthy behaviors if they were being pleased and instructed by example at the same time. Recent researches by Georges Duby [in his *The Chivalrous Society*] and others have indicated the possibility of more specific reasons for considering the romance as both entertainment and exemplar of ethical behaviors. There is a connection between the large numbers of unmarried men in the courts in the heyday of the romance and the custom of conserving the patrimony for a single heir, that is not dividing the family holdings among all the heirs but keeping them intact for a single heir. The younger sons, called "youths" from the time they were dubbed knights to the time they became heads of household, found themselves in a much protracted youth-time. It seems entirely possible that courtly entertainments and romances evolved at least in part as a response to the need to define or reflect on these youths' place in society, to define praiseworthy behavior between these youths and the rest of the public world as well as the women they wooed but could not marry. For these younger sons could not marry unless they married an heiress, for fear of establishing too many ancillary lines to the main patrimony. As long as marriage was out of the question, unless the lady was both free and an heiress, the courtly routines made adultery look attractive to the lady and covered up an essential misogyny on the knight's part, who knew very well that marriage was out of the question. Love's mastery was more illusory than real. Once estates became routinely divided among heirs, at least on the continent, younger sons married earlier and their youth was not extended so long.

And, as Allen and others have pointed out, the most literal representation of the shame culture, in its medieval form, is the romance. The characters in the stories are constantly concerned with appearing well, for avoiding occasions of shame. Who is to be praised, who blamed, for what, and why? Certainly in the **"Wife of Bath's Tale,"** the knight is blamed at the beginning for his rape of the young woman, a shameful act, a wrong use of love, a wrong use of the things of this world, and, more importantly, a violation of vows made as a knight.

Part of the problem for us as readers of this tale is that we have difficulty deciding what is beginning and what is end. Is the **"Wife of Bath's Prologue"** a beginning to the whole story unit, prologue and tale together, or is the prologue a beginning to an even larger unit? Judson Allen makes the interesting point, if in the end unverifiable, that the Wife herself announces the divisions of the story, that is, the woes that are in marriage, and he divides the story into four parts: glossing on Scripture, autobiography, the loathly lady story, and the pillow lecture. One could argue a variety of divisions to such a subject. I rather think the sequence exists only on the literal narrative level and like the frame is a fragile illusion. Each story unit is a gloss on what comes before; the units are additive rather than logical or sequential; each unit adds to the unit which precedes it, provides another example, moves to the large or to the small, proves, refutes, illustrates, enlarges. The **"Wife of Bath's Tale"** is not about marriage; the meanings are to be found in the behaviors themselves.

If such is the case, what we have in the Wife's prologue and in the tale is a gloss on interpretation and misinterpretation. From a clerk's point of view the Wife is misinterpreting Scripture, interpreting it for her own use as all glossators have done, including the clerk. Then the Wife's prologue and the tale are part of a larger semantic game of interpretation and misinterpretation of the "rules of the game," in the game of story telling and in the larger game of defining the world and how it is to be served. If we view order in the romance not as essentially sequential, that is, leading to a climax and denouement—either logical or chronological—but as additive, we have eliminated some of the difficulties for us as modern readers. This view is a critical commonplace for reading romance but not for reading the *Canterbury Tales.*

Elaboration is only one form of repetition. How are the terms "mastery" and sovereignty" defined in the Wife's prologue and in the tale. The traditional interpretation is that what woman want is mastery, that is dominance over men in marriage, and yet it is only too obvious in the prologue and in the tale that it is only a token mastery the Wife expects. In both instances the woman chooses not to exercise mastery once it is attained. In all her marriages the Wife worked to establish economic independence. She traded what she had, the favors of her sex, for financial security, and, in the last analysis, identity in male terms. She marries her fifth husband for love or for lust and, in her only romantic and sentimental gesture, gives over administration of her property and goods to him and loses in the gesture her authority, her independence, and maybe her identity. She recovers authority when she recovers or takes back mastery over her own goods and equilibrium within the marriage is established.

Part of the difficulty in interpretation lies in the words "mastery" and sovereignty" themselves. Commonly they are translated as simple dominance, devoid of merit or skill. Yet as others have pointed out, "maistrye," "Maister," "maistresse" make it clear that in Middle English "maistrye" "connotes skill and the authority deriving from that skill or superior ability rather than the idea of simple dominance" without realizing fully the implications for the **"Wife of Bath's Tale."** Parenthetically it cannot be simple coincidence that the glossing friar first accepts then rejects the title of "maister" in the **"Summon-**

er's Tale,"** for the word had specific connotations in the antifraternal controversy. In the **"Wife of Bath's Prologue,"** the Wife is simply recovering what is hers, authority over her goods, her material estate which she has assembled over the course of four marriages. It is this authority she wants and not simple dominance. This view makes more sense of the ending of the prologue:

> And whan that I hadde geten unto me,
> By maistrie, al the soveraynetee
> . . . . .
> After that day we hadden never debaat.
> God helpe me so, I was to hym as kynde
> As any wyf from Denmark unto Ynde,
> And also trewe, and so was he to me.

That is, by *maistrie,* superior ability and experience, she gets authority, *soveraynetee:* what I take unto myself by virtue of superior ability and experience is the authority over my own goods and all the *soveraynetee,* rule and control, which such authority allows. There is no further mention of crude dominance but rather equilibrium, harmony, and restoration of order. I was true to him and he to me.

In the analogues to the **"Wife of Bath's Tale,"** particularly in the Irish predecessors and analogues so thoroughly described by Eisner [in his *A Tale of Wonder: A Source Study of the Wife of Bath's Tale*], "sovereignty" meant sovereignty over the nation. The lady was a symbol of the royal rule of Ireland, and acceptance of her terms and her loathliness was the last in a series of tests leading to the identification of the knight who was to become king. The knight who won her favors became king. In what are called the English variations, the meaning of the word changed from royal rule to mastery over a husband, and Eisner is concerned with the point at which this change takes place. Yet the heroines of the English versions are also associated with kings and with succession if not so obviously and so directly. Her enchantment is an intrinsic part of the loathly lady's allegorical role. Marriage is not at issue.

In the so-called English variations, the ballad, the *Marriage of Sir Gawain,* and the romance, *Dame Ragnell,* it is Arthur himself who commits the shameful act of killing the hart. In both he is held to account by a man, not a woman, as it turns out by the loathly lady's brother. The loathly lady is promised the hand of the foremost knight in Arthur's court, of Gawain in *Dame Ragnell,* a motif found often in the early romances as Gawain is singled out among the knights of the Round Table. The lady is imprisoned in the hag's body and can only be released by the kiss of the hero. But in each case, it is not simply the solving of the riddle, the answering of the question, "what is it wommen most desiren" that is important but the complications which arise because of the vow made to the loathly lady either by Arthur or by Gawain or by Arthur for Gawain. In each of these instances, succession to Arthur is important. Each narrative begins with a shameful act, a violation of vows made, a violation of order; each narrative hinges on the fulfillment of a new vow undertaken, the necessity for this vow's being honored. Once the vow is honored, order is restored and harmony results.

Chaucer's portrait in the National Portrait Gallery, London.

As again I am sure I am not the first to point out, promises made and given, vows made, troths plighted, are motifs returned to again and again in the *Canterbury Tales.* In a world still not fully a contract society, vows and a consen-

sus of what constituted proper relations between people took the place of contracts. The betrothal vow and the dowry contract were equally binding.

In the **"General Prologue,"** the Knight draws the cut and needs to tell the first story, "as he that wys was and obedient / To kepe his foreward by his free assent." He agreed to keep his promise to play the game the Host had described and all had assented to. Assent is repeated in the link before the **"Man of Law's Tale"** when the Host reminds the Man of Law that he submitted by free assent to the arrangement that he will tell a tale and that his tale will be judged in the competition by the Host. "Ich assent. To breke forward is not myn entente," the Man of Law responds.

Taught to read in this way we can see that in the **"Wife of Bath's Tale"** what matters are the behaviors: the shameful act, a violation of the knight's vow to protect women, his new vow to the loathly lady, and the requirement that this time he keep his vow, that he honor it. To the hag in the story is due authority not only because of her age and experience and her allegorical role as a teacher (*maister*) and because on the literal level she has the answer which will save the knight's life, but because the knight freely gives her his promise. He vowed his "trouthe" to her. The "mastery" and "sovereignty" mentioned in the answer of the quest do not stand in isolation. The words take on meaning from the framework into which they have been put, by the behaviors of which they are a part, and by the resonances they call up.

In the **"Wife of Bath's Tale"** it is clear that the knight is to be blamed at the beginning of the tale just as he is to be praised at the tale's end. The hag requires neither praise nor blame, since she is simply the agent of the knight's instruction. In Chaucer's version, her enchantment and/or release from enchantment do not depend on the knight. In other words she does not need the kiss or marriage. She is free to release herself and is in fact the knight's reward for keeping his vows. The pillow lecture on the proper use of this world's goods defines his relation to society at large. His lesson is not the answer to the question "what wommen most desiren" but to keep the vow he has freely made to the hag when he learns from her the answer which is to save his life.

A brief look at the **"Knight's Tale"** reinforces this reading of the **"Wife's Tale."** The **"Knight's Tale"** follows the familiar outline of the guide for princes: the good prince is one who rightly rules himself, his family, his kingdom. The trappings of courtly love and courtly romance are distracting to the modern reader as we are led to ask, who is the more worthy of Emily's love, Arcite or Palamon? When marriage does ensue, however, it is for political, public reasons, to cement a political alliance, to bring peace to the two cities. Theseus calls Palamon and Emily together, describes the need for alliance, then following the speech on divine order, Theseus asks Palamon and Emily for assent and blesses their assent with his assent and thus the bond was made betwixt them. Right behavior in all three of the traditional categories is illustrated in this tale and in the pattern of vows made and broken. Love's mastery is subordinate to right rule of self, right relations between individuals, and right relations between groups. Marriage is part of the larger political, economic, and moral order. It was no accident that courtly love traditions existed outside marriage, for it was inevitable from the beginnings of these traditions that such must be the case.

These patterns of repetition, then—elaboration or amplification as repetition, verbal repetition, thematic repetition—all inform our reading of the **"Wife's Tale"** and as well the meanings of the behaviors. The tale is not *about* marriage, and certainly its lesson is not that happiness ensues from female dominance in marriage. The meaning lies in the behaviors themselves and in how they are perceived by the audience who is within the *Tale* as well as without.

The narrator's response when the Host allows the Miller to tell his tale out of order is pertinent here. If the reader finds a tale not to the liking, the narrator advises,

> Turne over the leef and chese another tale;
> For he shal fynde ynowe, grete and smale,
> Of storial thyng that toucheth gentillesse,
> And eek moralitee and hoolynesse.

And, as I have shown elsewhere [in *The Late Middle Ages*], much of Chaucer's *sentence* is implicit rather than explicit. The reader can see in the behaviors, behaviors to blame and behaviors to praise. The *solaas* of eloquence and wit refreshes so that the pilgrims can renew their vows, private, social, and public for the right "walken by the weye." Amid the sensory delights of this world called from memory, right reason guides them to pick and choose as they are faced with the multiplicity of authorities and experiences, definitions and redefinitions, interpretations and misinterpretations. (pp. 151-60)

> *Martha Fleming, "Repetition and Design in the 'Wife of Bath's Tale',"* in Chaucer in the Eighties, *edited by Julian N. Wasserman and Robert J. Blanch, Syracuse University Press, 1986, pp. 151-61.*

Edward C. Schweitzer   (essay date 1986)

[*In the excerpt below, Schweitzer examines the "Miller's Tale" in light of medieval thought concerning the cure for a lover's malady.*]

The Miller himself draws attention to the elaborate correspondences of shape, diction, and detail between his tale and that of the Knight, declaring that he knows "a noble tale" with which to "quite the Knyghtes tale," itself just acclaimed as "a noble storie" by "al the route . . . / And namely the gentils everichoon." And those correspondences, in general, are well known. But probably the most important and the most emphatic single correspondence between the first two *Canterbury Tales* has hardly been noticed, and its implications have been ignored, though they bring out a pattern in the fabric of the **"Miller's Tale"** making it indeed a trenchant commentary on the action narrated by the Knight: Absolon, like Arcite, suffers from "the loveris maladye / Of Hereos," a disease of the brain widely discussed by medieval physicians, one in which the

lover is so obsessed with the image of the beloved in his imagination that he cannot eat or sleep and becomes pale, tearful, hollow-eyed, and given to wild outbursts of emotion—all symptoms the Knight catalogues in Arcite, and the most conspicuous of which are likewise displayed in the Miller's Absolon. But while both Arcite, and Absolon suffer from that disease, Absolon, unlike Arcite, is cured—cured by the misdirected kiss at the climax of the **"Miller's Tale,"** cured in just the way medieval physicians prescribe. And both the diagnosis of Absolon's malady and its cure through the misdirected kiss point to the self-delusion that Absolon and Arcite have in common. Together the disease and its cure in the **"Miller's Tale"** point to the mistaken choice of goods that is the subject of the *Consolation of Philosophy* (evoked so often and with such pointed irony in the **"Knight's Tale,"** to what Boethius sees as the folly of seeking felicity in creatures rather than in their creator, to a figurative and philosophical malady mirrored in the literal and physical malady of *hereos*.

This crucial correspondence between Absolon and Arcite is emphasized by two verbal parallels between the tales. Once Absolon realizes how Alisoun has tricked him, the Miller tells us,

> His hoote love was coold and al yqueynt;
> For fro that tyme that he hadde kist hir ers,
> Of paramours he sette nat a kers;
> For he was heeled of his maladie.
> Ful ofte paramours he gan deffie,
> And weep as dooth a child that is ybete.

Since the "maladie" of which Absolon is "heeled" is equivalent to "his hoote love," now "al yqueynt," and since the first sign of its cure is that he rejects love *paramours,* Absolon's "maladie" is unmistakably "the loveris maladye," from which Arcite suffered without being cured. And the point is sharpened by the echo of a second passage in the **"Knight's Tale"**: when Arcite was thrown from his horse at the end of the tournament deciding which lover should win Emelye, everyone expected "he shal been heeled of his maladye"; but Arcite, of course, was *not* healed of that second malady any more than he was of his first, thought Absolon *is*, unexpectedly, "heeled of *his* maladie." This verbal parallel is especially telling, like the contrast it re-emphasizes between Absolon and Arcite, because the course of Arcite's fatal injury in Athens virtually re-enacted the progress of the *amor hereos* from which he suffered in Thebes: Arcite died, unable to expel the corrupting blood from the region around his heart, just as in Thebes, heartsick in another sense, he could not expel Emelye's image from his "celle fantastik." And, of course, Arcite would never have been injured in the first place if his passion for Emelye had not twice brought him back to Athens.

The correspondence is crucial because the Miller, it seems clear, intends to "quite the Knyghtes tale" precisely by emphasizing through his own tale the self-delusion of the Knight's lovers and by implying something like it in the Knight himself. The theme of not only absurd but pathological self-delusion (epitomized in the Miller's reference to the "maladie" from which Absolon is "heeled" is, accordingly, central to the **"Miller's Tale"** and figures even in the other half of its plot, where old John imagines he can see "Noees flood come walwynge like the see / To drenchen Alisoun his hony deere" and where the Miller, pointing to the same psychological process through which the symptoms of *hereos* are produced and at which any cure must be directed, exclaims of John's delusion,

> Lo, which a greet thyng is affeccioun!
> Men may dyen of ymaginacioun,
> So depe may impressioun be take.
> Hym thynketh verraily that he may see
> Noees flood come walwynge as the see
> To drenchen Alisoun, his hony deere.

The imaginative power of the soul may be equally obsessed with an image either supremely delightful or supremely terrible, and John's fear is like Absolon's desire (and Arcite's) not only in its psychological effect but also in its ultimate cause, for John fears the flood because, like Absolon, he desires Alisoun, whom he calls "his hony deere" just as Absolon, less than a hundred lines later, calls her his "hony-comb, sweete Alisoun, / . . . faire bryd . . . sweete cynamome." But while John hardly seems about to "dyen of ymaginacioun," *amor hereos is* a potentially fatal disease of the imagination, occurring when the lover is obsessed with the image of the beloved fixed in his imagination ("so depe may impressioun be take") and judges her the only true good, the only source of happiness, with the result that he can think of nothing else and the normal operations of his body break down. So in another Middle English narrative, in language recalling the Miller's reference to the fatal consequences of imaginative obsession, John Lydgate describes how one of two merchants fell in love with the other's bride-to-be and nearly died of "amor ereos":

> The roote wherof and the corrupcioun
> Is of thilke vertu callid estimatiff,
> As yif a man haue deep impressioun
> That ovirlordshipith his imaginatif.

In Absolon, of course, the lover's inability to eat or sleep seems mere comical pretense, but Arcite in Thebes was so ravaged by the lover's malady that he *was* in danger of death, and though he did not there "dyen of ymaginacioun," he died in Athens of the injury he suffered because he could not forget Emelye, an injury strikingly parallel in its effect to the lover's malady from which Arcite suffered first.

Like both the diagnosis of Absolon's malady and its cure, then, the Miller's remark that "men may dyen of ymaginacioun, / So depe may impressioun be take," looks through the action of his own tale to the parallel action of the Knight's and brings out the common role of image and imagination in John's deluded fear and Absolon's and Arcite's deluded love.

In the **"Miller's Tale"** the entire episode of the misdirected kiss emphasizes just his self-delusion in Absolon, dwelling throughout upon the absurdly exaggerated expectations of delight that distinguish Absolon's lovesickness from the simple passion of his counterparts in the tale's analogues. Absolon is so comically deluded, so much a victim of his expectations, his judgment so overpowered by his imagination, that he cannot fully comprehend

the trick played upon him until Alisoun laughs, " 'Tehee!' . . . and clapte the wyndow to," even though (the Miller reports) he

> thoughte it was amys,
> For wel he wiste a womman hath no berd.
> He felte a thyng al rough and long yherd,
> And seyde, "Fy! allas! what have I do?"

Hilarious as this emphasis on Absolon's delusion is, it prepares for the Miller's reference to the lover's malady as well as its cure and ironically re-views Arcite's (and Palamon's) love for Emelye.

Indeed, it is a remarkable fact that only the Miller's version of the famous misdirected kiss *could* have cured Absolon of his and Arcite's malady. In all the analogues of the **"Miller's Tale,"** wherever the cast of characters includes two rival lovers, Absolon's counterparts kiss the successful lover's rump, not the woman's. For Absolon's fantasy of "sweete Alisoun" to be shattered, however, Absolon must kiss not Nicholas but Alisoun herself. While Absolon's counterparts, accordingly, learn only that they have been tricked, the Miller makes Absolon, kissing Alisoun, learn that and more: Absolon learns the folly of love *paramours*—something about which the Miller himself and all those equally churlish smiths in the analogues can never have had any illusions.

Proving that a woman is not an angel, the misdirected kiss is thus linked to the **"Knight's Tale"** not only as the cure for Absolon's and Arcite's malady but also as the climax of the Miller's demonstration that the courtly ideal of beauty and conduct is mere affectation, a demonstration begun in the Miller's initial descriptions of his characters, for in Alisoun the ideal beauty of the ladies of lyric and romance is only artificial; her forehead shines, like theirs, but only because she has just washed it. Alisoun may sing "as loude and yerne / As any swalwe sittynge on a berne" while Emelye sings "as an aungel hevenysshly," but the misdirected kiss reminds us that Emelye and Alisoun are no different under their clothes.

The misdirected kiss, then, epitomizes the conflict of character between the Miller and the Knight and the contrast between their tales. But the kiss and its effect on Absolon do more than simply confirm the Miller's incorrigible coarseness, leaving the Knight's aristocratic enthusiasm for love *paramours* untouched—for it is a remarkable fact that Absolon is cured of his love-sickness in just the way medieval physicians prescribe for the most extreme cases: shocking the lover with the physical reality of sex in order to destroy the idealized fantasy by which he is obsessed.

The closest parallel in a medical text to Absolon's cure through the misdirected kiss, not only "amusing" but telling apt, is the cure for *heroes* recommended by Bernard of Gordon, one of the Physician's authorities in the **"General Prologue"** [in his *Lilium medicinae*]:

> Finally, when we have no other recourse, we implore the aid and counsel of old women, to slander and defame the beloved as much as they can. . . . Therefore, seek out a most foul-looking old woman, with large teeth and a beard and with foul, vile clothing, and have her carry

a menstruous rag in her bosom; and when she approaches the lover, have her begin to slander his beloved, explaining that she is bony and drunken, that she urinates in bed, that she is epileptic and shameless, and that there are huge stinking excrescences on her body, and all the other enormities about which old women are well instructed. If the lover will not relent on account of these persuasions, have her suddenly take out the menstruous rag before his face, holding it up, saying and shouting, "Such is your love, such!" If he does not relent on account of these things, he is not a man but a devil incarnate. His folly will be with him finally in perdition.

Bernard's cure, however, is conventional, unique only in its vivid narrative detail. Avicenna recommends, more generally, exactly the same cure. And Arnald of Villanova, Chaucer's "Arnold of the Newe Toun," describing that cure more generally still [in his *De amor heroyco*], makes clearer than either Bernard or Avicenna why it should be effective:

> Since this madness, and its formal cause, is intense thinking about something delightful with the confidence of obtaining it, the remedy and contrary corrective will be not to think about this delightful thing and not to hope in any way to obtain it. These ends will be accomplished effectively by whatever distracts the lover from this thought to another one, in whole or in part, through the representation of its forms in the imagination—for example, forms of things making the desired object hateful, such as showing the shameful actions of the thing to the eye or recounting them in words, and so on.

And so Absolon is "heeled of his maladie" ("fro that tyme that he hadde kist hir ers") by just such a sensible demonstration of the vileness of the object in which he has sought all delight.

Other cures for the lover's malady—the love of other women, conversation with friends, music, beautiful landscapes, travel—all aim at distracting the lover from his obsession with the unreal image of his "perfect" love. As the physician Valescus of Tarenta explains [in his *Philonium*], "all the cure consists in distracting the imagination; if therefore this false opinion or imagination is removed, all the sickness is removed also." But only this most radical cure accomplishes its end by revealing the falseness of the image, the imperfection of the beloved, insisting as Bernard's old woman does, brandishing that menstruous rag, "Such is your love, such!" Such, Absolon discovers to his comical dismay, is Alisoun. And the Miller might have cited good authority for the view implied in his tale that a similarly "misdirected" kiss in the **"Knight's Tale"** would have spared Arcite suffering and death.

Absolon, of course, is comically naive, as the Miller implies the Knight and his courtly lovers also are. But for the Miller to present the misdirected kiss as a cure for *amor hereos* suggests in Absolon the more general self-deception that is the subject of the *Consolation of Philosophy*, a self-deception that informs the **"Knight's Tale"** and creates much of its irony. This is a self-deception more

philosophical than sexual and one that John and Nicholas share, seeking felicity in a woman, as they all do. And it is a self-deception the Miller obviously cannot comprehend. But just as obviously the Miller's comical reprise of the Knight's romance cannot simply jettison its burden of philosophical allusion. According to Lady Philosohy, the appearance of misfortune and injustice in the world is an illusion that follows from seeking in creatures the true good and true happiness found only in their creator. And that idea, so crucial to the **"Knight's Tale,"** figures also in the **"Miller's Tale,"** not only because its action mirrors the action of the **"Knight's Tale"** but also because *amor hereos* epitomizes just such confusion: the lover, deluded by his senses and overpowered by his imagination "to trowe a wiht for love mor fayr or pure, / Than evir hym ordeyned hath God or nature," expects to find perfect happiness in a woman of flesh and blood. Since the physical malady of *hereos* thus displays outwardly the spiritual malady resulting from a mistaken choice of goods, Absolon, like Arcite, is doubly ill. And because he is, it is appropriate in a way the Miller certainly cannot comprehend that he should be "heeled" by the misdirected kiss, which reveals the inherent corruption of the flesh and of fleshly delights. As Lady Philosophy teaches Boethius, the gifts of Fortune, however beautiful they seem, are not only "brutel" and "transitorie;" there is nothing in them that "nys fowl, yif that if be considered and lookyd perfitly. . . . Whoso lokide thanne in the entrayles of the body of Alcibiades, that was ful fair in the superficie withoute, it schulde seme ryght foul." Given the correspondences and connections between the **"Miller's Tale"** and the **"Knight's,"** between the **"Knight's Tale"** and the *Consolation,* and between Boethius's spiritual malady and "the loveris maladye / Of Hereos," it does not seem too much to say that the misdirected kiss allows Absolon to look "in the entrayles of the body of Alisoun, that was ful fair withoute." Absolon, to be sure, weeps at his misfortune, as Boethius wept at his, but Boethius learned, and Chaucer learned from him, that bad Fortune was really good because it revealed the worthlessness of earthly goods.

It is no coincidence, then, that Dante's dream of the Siren in Canto XIX of the *Purgatorio* should also dwell upon the power of imagination to deceive, turning the ugly into the beautiful, since Dante's Siren embodies the common perversity of avarice, gluttony, and lust, all of which love the world's goods; and it is no coincidence that the imagination's illusion and the Siren's consequent power to seduce should be destroyed, like Absolon's illusion, when Virgil strips away the Siren's garments to reveal her belly and its stench. All this accords perfectly with themes of the *Consolation* that figure so largely in the **"Knight's Tale,"** with the disordered imagination and consequent error of judgment in *amor hereos,* and with the cure of that malady already described—especially Bernard of Gordon's recourse to an ugly hag who reveals to the lover the true nature of his love. The dream of the Siren thus confirms the traditional and philosophical implications of the misdirected kiss in the **"Miller's Tale."** For that kiss, like the Miller's allusions to the Song of Songs, reveals how misdirected Absolon's love has been—and not only his but also Palamon's and Arcite's, Nicholas's and John's. And from the perspective of the *Consolation,* it is only just that the fastidious Absolon should be punished with the misdirected kiss and a fart in the face, the lecherous Nicholas with a branded *toute,* and the jealous and avaricious John with a broken arm, while Alisoun escapes unscathed. She, after all, is the good they have chosen, as innocent in herself as gold or rich food or drink. The choice, not the object chosen, is punished. (pp. 223-30)

> Edward C. Schweitzer, "The Misdirected Kiss and the Lover's Malady in Chaucer's 'Miller's Tale'," in Chaucer in the Eighties, *edited by Julian N. Wasserman and Robert J. Blanch, Syracuse University Press, 1986, pp. 223-33.*

Mark Amsler   (essay date 1987)

[*In the excerpt below, Amsler finds that the "Wife of Bath's Tale" develops a "domestic critique of the post-feudal state."*]

In Chaucer's writing, the characterization of the Wife of Bath poses a peculiar yet pervasive problem. The Wife is one of only three women on the Canterbury pilgrimage, and the only female among the lay, urban, or middle-class pilgrims. Given the fact that Chaucer does not depict the higher lay nobility or the lowest peasant ranks among the Canterbury pilgrims, the Wife of Bath is the lone secular female among the large middle range of English society which was becoming increasingly mobile and, in Du-Boulay's terms [from *An Age of Ambition*], "ambitious." This class movement was especially marked in the aftermath of the first plague [1348] and in the subsequent shift in the labor/wage scale and the relation between tenants and entrepreneurs reflected in Edward III's Statute of Laborers [1351]. The liquidity of capital produces and is produced by the liquidity of social status. But the Wife is more than, as R. A. Shoaf puts it [in *Dante, Chaucer, and the Currency of the Word*], "a figure of the commercial idiom and the commercial imagination." First of all, the Wife of Bath often functions more like what Barthes [in his *S/Z*] calls a figure than a character. She is dispersed throughout Chaucer's writing like no other textual figure besides the Geoffrey persona, in the **"General Prologue,"** **"Gentilesse," "Merchant's Tale," "Clerk's Tale,"** and **"Lenvoy de Chaucer a Bukton."** Second, that the wife is a wealthy widow endows her with a power—sexual, economic, textual, and political—which is peculiar to England and the fourteenth century. Third, inscribed within the figure of the Wife of Bath are a specifically female (that is, gender specific) performance code and textual code which interrupt the cliche interpretation of the Wife as a self-destructing female. Rather the text deploys the Wife as a bourgeois, urban critique of women's sexual, textual, and political autonomy in the fourteenth century.

Like other texts of Chaucer's, the **"Wife of Bath's Prologue and Tale"** threatens to disperse itself into a network of citations, authorities, and sources. The Wife is an intertextual network, a proper name intersected by adjectives, attributes, texts, connotations, and historical reference. But by also keeping Alisoun close to the social and economic context of wealthy women in the fourteenth century, Chaucer constructs a text which reveals how that social and economic situation is contradictory and self-destructing for her as a female. Just as the text of the Wife of Bath includes but supersedes the fabliau cliche (women are lecherous, lying, ostentatious, and self-destructing), so it reproduces but ironizes the socioeconomic situation of women's power.

The Wife's ambivalent textual character is intertwined with the ambivalent social character of late medieval women and money. Since the relation between women and wealth was produced primarily as a response to the question of marriage, we need first to rethink some of our received ideas about the so-called marriage group in the **Canterbury Tales.** Many of the historical materials about the Wife's economic status and marriages have been available in local analyses of Chaucer's work and medieval culture. But they have not always been theorized within an account of Chaucer's textual strategies. As we shall see, the text of the Wife of Bath becomes the site where various fourteenth-century social conflicts regarding the status of women, the power of literacy, and the value of money are at once reproduced and critiqued. In the **"Wife of Bath's Prologue and Tale,"** history and cliche are mediated as text.

Georges Duby, in his work on sex and family structures in twelfth- and thirteenth-century France, [*Medieval Marriage* and *The Knight, the Lady, and the Priest*], distinguishes between the lay aristocratic and the ecclesiastic models of marriage. With some adjustments, these models can also apply to England during the later Middle Ages, as H. A. Kelly's survey of primarily ecclesiastic marriage theories [*Love and Marriage in the Age of Chaucer*] demonstrates. Prior to the eleventh century women often were designated as co-owners of land and possessions. But in the aristocratic model after the first half of the eleventh century, a marriage was legitimated as part of the more general feudal strategy to maintain landholdings within families or to strengthen a lord's position by controlling the marriages of his vassals' children, especially daughters. Aristocratic women, especially childless widows, could accumulate property through inheritance and dowers, but they had little control over the property and possessions which came to them in such marriages, although a widow could pay a fee to her lord to buy back her right to choose whom she wanted to marry or to permit her to remain unmarried. Unmarried widows, however, were suspect because they destabilized the political economy of feudal marriage. The aristocratic bias against matrilineal inheritance is indicated by the practice of allotting a marginal portion of the patrimony (acquisitions rather than principal inheritance) to the women of the family to be handed down from female to female.

In the aristocratic model, the often early betrothal (*desponsatio*) constituted the marriage agreement, while the partners were chosen by the feudal lord with the consent of the parents and guardians, a political strategy which many kings of England successfully exercised. The English situation in the later Middle Ages requires some adjustments in Duby's models. In England the Magna Carta (1215) was designed to limit the power of the monarchy (including the king's control of marriages) and simultaneously give individual lords more control over marriages while reserving for widows more autonomy to choose for themselves whether or not they wanted to remarry. The procedure prior to Magna Carta is exemplified in Glanville (ca. 1187), who wrote: "Lords have full powers during wardship over the persons and possessions of heirs of their men—for example, in granting churches which are part of the fief, or in marrying off girls who are in wardship. . . . Even if a female heir is of age, she shall remain in the wardship of her lord until she is married according to the desire and with the consent of the lord. . . . And if a girl . . . marries without the consent of her lord, by the just law and custom of the realm she shall lose her inheritance."

By contrast, in the ecclesiastic marriage model a marriage was legitimated primarily by the consent of the two parties involved or, after the twelfth century, by their consent, the exchange of vows in the presence of a priest, and in most cases married sexual intercourse. By the mid-twelfth century marriage "had come to be sacralized without being disincarnated," and so the two models had reached a compromise solution. By the thirteenth century, the aristocracy and the church, as a result of the church's challenge to feudal marriage, had divided the spheres of influence in marriage. A husband had authority over his wife and property, while the church had authority over the laity in matters of marriage and the spirit. This position, formulated primarily by John of Paris and Bracton and constituted in the so-called Alexandrian synthesis of 1163, interrupted the feudal family marriage strategy and supported the church's authority in marriage contracts. It also helped constitute the autonomy of children against their parents and lords as well as the autonomy and mobility of the growing urban and middle-class population for whom the possession of real estate and moveable property were concerns of the individual or the nuclear family rather than part of the extended blood or feudal family. Similarly, by the thirteenth century, canon law had formulated a rather ambivalent position regarding sexuality in marriage, which nonetheless reveals the interconnections of sex and wealth in medieval society. The canonists deployed a debt model of married sexual relations and affirmed the principle of mutual consent in order to protect the "marital rights" of both partners.

The English context during this period suggests some other important revisions in Duby's formulation. The ecclesiastic model as described by Duby and others can be linked to the economic and social status of later medieval peasants and middle classes, as is suggested by Alan Macfarlane's work on individualism in England [*The Origins of English Individualism*]. English aristocratic and peasant families both depended on arranged marriages, the one to preserve landholdings, the other to maintain a stable work force. But at least since 1250, English society had been oriented less toward family and more toward individual ownership. According to Macfarlane, England ceased to be a peasant society long before the fourteenth century. In other words, changes in marriage and family inheritance in later medieval England involved not only the aris-

tocracy but also the developing bourgeoisie and the individual landowners among the lower classes.

Reading the *Canterbury Tales* with these two models in mind, we can construct a somewhat different marriage group from the one George Kittredge described [in his *Chaucer and His Poetry*]. In my rereading, marriage in the *Canterbury Tales* not only reflects historical conditions, but also reflects on those conditions. The historical situation of the text of the Wife of Bath becomes the intertextual context. For instance, the **"Knight's Tale"** is the principal tale of aristocratic marriage; for all of Palamon and Arcite's wooing and warring, the chosen partners are appropriate for the kingdoms' political ends, the betrothal after the tournament legitimates the marriage, and the lord's conquest (*raptus*) of the woman (whether by Theseus or Arcite) signifies the male-dominated feudal marriage strategy. The **"Clerk's Tale,"** based on Petrarch's and/or Boccaccio's narrative, describes a limited aristocratic (monarchal?) marriage: Walter asks Griselda's father for her hand, receives her consent to do her lord's will, and then announces to his worried people, "This is my wyf." The question of succession dominates the **"Clerk's Tale"** in the people's anxiety about Walter's heirs, in the fact that Walter carefully protects the two children, and in the textual game of a possible incestuous marriage. The **"Second Nun's Tale"** which is about St. Cecilia, presents a radical version of the ecclesiastic marriage model wherein a virginal marriage between consenting adults is not only legitimated but also represented as an explicit act of piety. (The Wife of Bath is distinctly represented as orthodox in linking sex and marriage, whereas in the later Middle Ages virginal marriages were usually associated with heretics.) Within the **"Knight's Tale,"** Emily implies that the aristocratic and ecclesiastical models are mutually exclusive and that she cannot control her own marriage as a member of the aristocracy. Describing betrothal, intercourse, and childbearing as kinds of violation, she prays for a celibate life but is bestowed in marriage anyway. The list of entries in the marriage group now grows very large: the **"Man of Law's Tale," "Merchant's Tale," "Franklin's Tale," "Tale of Melibee"** and so on.

Between the aristocratic model and the radical ecclesiastic model is what I call the secular version of the ecclesiastic marriage model, characterized by the consent of the partners and legitimated by sexual intercourse but capitalized by the economic and social context of medieval marriage. I read the **"Wife of Bath's Prologue and Tale"** as a secular version of the ecclesiastic marriage model which opposes the aristocratic model and the radical ecclesiastic model in terms of property inheritance, the person's sexual nature, and female readers. The text of the Wife of Bath also challenges the argument that women are a separate estate or class which derives its status solely from sex and marriage. Thus the narrative performance of the Wife of Bath, the only secular female on the pilgrimage, marks the textual space of the urban and commercial bourgeoisie whose power and autonomy are defined largely by lay literacy, economic mobility, revised inheritance laws, consensual marriage, and religio-political reform in the fourteenth century. The text of the Wife's performance deploys this critical strategy as a series of readings and glosses on social and textual authority. Besides the Wife's portrait in the **"General Prologue"** and her tale, the [**"Wife of Bath's Prologue"**] is customarily divided into her sermon on men and virginity, her account of her first three husbands, and her description of her fourth and fifth marriages. Interrupting the fabliau cliche encoded in her portrait in the **"General Prologue"** the intertextual character of the Wife reveals the underlying interconnections between the control of textual interpretation, the control of land rights and property, and the control of one's body. These interconnections include but rewrite the relations within fabliau between language, money, and sex. In this respect, the Wife of Bath as part of the text of the ***Canterbury Tales*** does not automatically reflect an historical reality nor repeat a narrative cliche. Rather, the text negotiates the problem of understanding the relation between history and cliche as two types of texts. Moreover, the text of the Wife of Bath exemplifies the general problem of representation and authority in the ***Canterbury Tales.*** The seemingly iconic "portraits" of the pilgrims can only predict in a limited way the discursive performances of those pilgrims. The pilgrimage drama of the ***Canterbury Tales*** is textual, not referential. And perhaps there is no shrine for this pilgrimage.

In her countercommentary on the Pauline theory of marriage, the Wife is critical of expert knowledge and displaces the authoritative and antifeminist reading of the Bible by uncovering what God or St. Paul really meant. That so many readers and critics have focused on the way the Wife misinterprets or twists the scriptural passages to suit her own arguments indicates how the Wife's performance has so often been read as a failed male or ecclesiastic performance. True, the Pardoner refers to the Wife as a "noble prechour." But as a female lay preacher, the Wife's performance derives in part from the genre of the parodic sermon and is explicitly located at the margins of authoritative interpretive discourse. In the text of the Wife of Bath, the Wife's countercommentary is the figure for all marginal reading.

The public preaching and interpretation of the Wife derive from a more general increase in the range and depth of lay literacy in the later Middle Ages. Medieval literacy and textuality have become increasingly central to medieval studies, and I want to mention a few points here to indicate the social complexity of the Wife's countercommentary. For a member of the laity in the late Middle Ages, learning to read produced a certain freedom of interpretation, the possibility of construing a text without or instead of the controlling commentary and authoritative interpretation. Studies . . . have shown how lay literacy was often (rightly) associated with heretical movements like the Cathars or the Lollards. In England, the Lollards cultivated a book-conscious form of ecclesiastical rebellion wherein the knowledge really worth having was derived directly from the text by the pious reader. Among the Lollards, and to a lesser extent among the commercial or trade schools of the later Middle Ages, women like Alisoun or the real-life Alice Colyns were often, though not always, encouraged to learn to read. And one of the so-called Lollard heresies was that women were allowed, even encour-

aged, to preach. Lollard book production and Bible translation, along with the English tradition of vernacular preaching and commentary, broadened the access to scripture and commentary among new literates from England's peasant and urban populations. According to the *Chronicon* of Henry Knighton (1390), John Wycliffe translated the Gospel from Latin into English so that it was available to laypeople and ignorant folk, including "women who know how to read," whereas previously the scriptures and their interpretation had been more within the restricted domain of "well-read clerks of good understanding." A similar case can be made for the increased literate access to the common law system with the regularization of pleas, writs, and formulae during the thirteenth century. According to Eileen Bentsen and Sally Sanderlin [in their paper "A 'Soverane Teaching' of the Profits of Marriage in Late Medieval Scotland" read at the conference on Women and Power], William Dunbar, in *The Tretis of the Tua Mariit Wemen and the Wedo* (ca. 1508), specifically makes the widow an expert on the legal and economic aspects of marriage in order to ensure the inheritance through her own line.

When the Wife of Bath preaches about what the scriptures really mean regarding marriage and sex, she deliberately challenges the church's and the antifeminists' interpretive authority in a lay sermon whose propriety is determined by the particular system of norms and beliefs within which it is interpreted. Either the Wife is exemplifying the power of grace to reveal divine truth through the pious lay female Christian, or her performance is interpreted by the fabliau cliche that women can't be trusted, that when they try to play the man's or clerk's game they are self-destructive because they are morally corrupt or intellectually incompetent. However, the Wife's readings do not differ procedurally from certain orthodox scriptural interpretations. It is interesting in this respect to read contemporary interpretations of the text of the Wife of Bath which describe her performance as "digressive" or "easily sidetracked," even though she deploys standard medieval homiletic strategies of text, gloss, dilation, and exemplification. The Wife herself draws a parallel between her motivations and those of the clerks she opposes when she describes the origin of antifeminist texts in the intentions of sexually frustrated clerks. Such a leveling of intentions does not elevate the Wife above the clerks, but rather establishes the space for the multiplication of interpretations, the start of any epistemological crisis. In the fourteenth century, a woman's access to power was primarily through her increased access to traditionally male sources of power: literacy, the economy, and the law. But as the examples of the historical Margery Kempe and female entrepreneurs indicate, the increased access to male sources of power was not always sanctioned by those in power. For instance, more women were theoretically eligible to become citizens than were actually granted such status, while Margery Kempe secured her power through private mysticism. So, paradoxically, the Wife enters the commentary game and interrupts its male-dominated discourse, but she is in turn written by the masculine language of antifeminism. The intertextuality of the Wife of Bath reveals the masculine politics of crossdressing, Chaucerian impersonation, interruption, and glossing.

Nonetheless, in itself, the Wife's parodic sermon represents the power of a literate laity, especially the female literate laity. In the later Middle Ages, the state was more and more constituted by the ability of its individual members (male and female) to gain access to its apparatus through literate procedures, which in England included reading and interpreting the scriptures as well as using the system of common law pleas. The growing role of the laity in the affairs of state also altered the relation between state and church with respect to the individual. By interrupting the authority of the church to speak unilaterally on lay affairs, the Wife's performance marks the textual space of the temporal and the natural in human affairs as separate from the space of the eternal and the supernatural. Her much discussed "naturalism," then, is imbricated in a more general political discourse. If a woman's sexuality is part of her human nature, then the church can counsel her on her actions but it cannot presume to speak with unquestioned authority.

The Wife's sexuality is implicated not only in her textuality, cliched characterization, and lay literacy, but also in the contradiction between her economic status as a member of the state (though not a citizen) and the fabliau cliche which controls her representation. On the one hand, the autonomy of the Wife of Bath depends a great deal on the independence she exercises when she controls her land and property. On the other hand, her acquisition of land and property depends on the way she uses sex as a weapon and as a medium of exchange equivalent to money. (Recall that the **"Shipman's Tale,"** a fabliau which directly and systematically exchanges sex for money, may have at one time been assigned to the Wife of Bath.) Over and over, the text of the Wife of Bath exchanges money for sex: Alisoun accuses her jealous husbands of wanting to lock her body in their moneychests, while she also asserts that they must exchange one for the other ("Thou shalt nat bothe, thogh that thou were wood, / Be maister of my body and of my good." The text also presses the other side of this fabliau coin when the Wife equates virginity with pious poverty and so dismisses the celibate life as without profit.

Once again we find that the Wife's power and control are linked to a set of social conditions which do not directly correspond to the textual types regulating her characterization. Her individual autonomy and her exemplification of the deceiving fabliau woman both derive from her economic position in the text. According to Adorno [in his *The Philosophy of Modern Music*], "knowledge, like its object, remains bound to the contradiction defined." We can rewrite Adorno's analysis intertextually and say that the Wife's critique of domination and her false identity as a fabliau cliche are both generated by a textual economy. Furthermore, the economic subtext in the Wife's performance indicates how the well-known parallel between Alisoun and La Veille in the *Roman de la Rose* can be misleading. While La Veille dwells on deceit in love, she does not accumulate wealth through marriage. In fact, her discourse is about love and sex, but not at all about marriage. She laments that she squandered men's gifts and has now grown old, poor, and unmarried, although wise. In Chaucer's text, Alisoun has married more profitably.

In her account of her first three marriages, the Wife describes how her husbands "hadde me yeven al hir lond," a fact which she links to her sovereignty over them. These three give her both wealth and sexual service. The upshot of these marriages is that the Wife is three times widowed and a rather well off middle-aged woman. I take Chaucer quite literally on this point about the Wife's inheritance. She retains the property of her first three husbands, their real estate, which earlier in the Middle Ages and especially among aristocratic and bourgeois households would usually have reverted to the husbands' families, along with their moveable goods, which the Wife claims she and her husbands hold in common. As we saw, the Wife equates her body and her goods, so that she "owns" both and therefore can exercise some control over them in marriage. Between the twelfth and fourteenth centuries, widows and unmarried women among the nobility, middle classes, and peasants increasingly inherited property and moveable goods, sued and were sued, pleaded in court, and managed income on a par with men. In both England and France, society was more and more characterized by small fiefs and landholdings and by a more individualized social order. But the power of money could also support traditional forms of domination, and land and power could be accumulated by a few great lords who could buy out smaller owners. Individualization, then, did not necessarily mean the constant multiplication of owners.

Similarly, the absence of children in the Wife's discourse about her marriages radically interrupts the aristocratic marriage model which ensures proper and continuous succession within the family. This is no false problem, like "How many children had the Wife of Bath?" In the text of the Wife of Bath, sex and words are metaphorically coined, and words substitute for sexual relations. The Wife, then, heeds the biblical command, "God bad us for to wexe and multiplye," but she multiplies sexual experience, marriages, husbands, and textual meanings, not children. Solely for herself, the Wife accumulates sexual experience, scriptural interpretation, and property, and the text generates no one to inherit the products of her economic and sexual sovereignty. (Contrast the pregnant May at the end of the **"Merchant's Tale,"** the mirror text of the Wife of Bath's performance.) As a narrative strategy, Chaucer deprives the Wife of children in order to focus squarely on the marital relationship and the role of the archwife. In this respect, the text of the Wife of Bath reproduces as a discursive strategy the domestic crisis and social sterility which Wit describes in Langland's *Piers Plowman:* "In gelosie joyeles and janglyng on bedde / Manye peire sithen the pestilence han plight hem togidere. / The fruyt that thei bringe forth arn manye foule wordis; / Have thei no children but cheste, and choppis hem betwene." Paradoxically, the Wife's lack of children signals both a thwarted sexuality and an intense individualism. By representing Alisoun as taking and keeping all she can, the text of the Wife of Bath asserts her autonomy but prohibits her from passing on the means for that autonomy. But in her tale, she is figurally forever young and regenerating, a bourgeois version of the courtly fantasy of social stability, the never-changing, always desirable female. Again, the Wife's interruption of aristocratic and ecclesiastic authority is wrapped in a social contradiction.

That the Wife's inheritance motivates her social position, sexual value, and textual performance is further demonstrated when she describes her marriage to her fifth husband, the antifeminist clerk Jankyn. She describes how they wed "with greet solempnytee; / And to hym yaf I al the lond and fee / That evere was me yeven therbifoore." This property transfer initiates a rapid-fire series of events in the Wife's narration, all of which indicate that the Wife effectively gives up her control in the marriage:

> But afterward repented me ful soore;
> He nolde suffre nothyng of my list.
> By God! he smoot me ones on the lyst,
> For that I rente out of his book a leef,
> That of the strook myn ere wax al deef.
> Stibourn I was as is a leonesse,
> And of my tonge a verray jangleresse,
> And walke I wolde, as I had doon biforn,
> From hous to hous, although he had it sworn;
> For which he often tymes wolde preche,
> And me of olde Romayn geestes teche.

The Wife's account of her marriage to Jankyn, his antifeminist exempla, his famous Book of Wicked Wives, and her tearing of the book bring together the various strands of power, sexuality, and textuality which I have been spinning out thus far. As head of the household to whom she gave all her land and fee, Alisoun's clerkly husband (whom she refers to as "our sire") reads nightly to her from his anthology of domestic behavior. This practice, common among aristocratic and especially middle-class families in the thirteenth and fourteenth centuries, maintains the concept of descending literacy whereby the dominant male/ecclesiastic disseminates the text and its *sentence* to the subordinate members of the family. The Wife in her narrative challenges this practice by arguing that gender determines the ethos of the text: "Who peyntede the leon, tel me who? / By God! if wommen hadde writen stories, / As clerkes han withinne hir oratories, / They wolde han writen of men moore wikkednesse / Than al the mark of Adam may redresse." The Wife recovers the origin of antifeminist texts in the scene of sexually frustrated male clerks taking their revenge on the women they can no longer possess sexually. In her countercommentary, she reverses the genders but still reproduces the abstract power relation in the text. As Robert Burlin has argued [in his *Chaucerian Fiction*] "When the Wife of Bath attacks Jankyn's book, which is both her enemy and the source of her being, it is as if she were usurping the role of creator, destroying the 'original' so that she might recast herself in her own image." But that image of herself, Chaucer's impersonation, turns out to be very much a repetition of domination. The text of the Wife of Bath is generated in part as Alisoun's Boke of Wikked Housbondes. Just as she did in her first three marriages, the Wife uses her sexual power and her victimization to reverse the power relation which subjugates her. She rips apart Jankyn's book, plays dead when he clobbers her on the side of the head, and gains the *maistrie* (power) she seeks. Like other sexual/textual exchanges in the poem, the transfer of power in her marriage is marked in the text by the transfer of her property and sexuality back to her own control and by the censorship of a certain kind of reading: "But atte laste, with muchel care and wo, / We fille acord-ed by us selven two. / He yaf me al the bridel in myn hond, / To han the governance of hous and lond, / And of his tonge, and of his hond also; / And made hym brenne his book anon right tho." Alisoun's romantic account of her relation with Jankyn—she says she married him for love, not money—is yet one more version of the general textual strategy whereby sex is exchanged for love by economic power. This romantic economy in her narrative is embellished by the echo of a religious fraternity of social equals when the guilt ridden Jankyn calls out "Deere suster Alisoun" to the woman he has just beaten. But these idealized relations are qualified by the economic and political implications of the Wife's sovereignty and power in marriage, as emphasized by her only semifarcical exclamation after her husband has beaten her: "And for my land thus hastow mordred me? / Er I be deed, yet wol I kisse thee'." Whatever equality and autonomy the Wife gains in the text are countered by the economic and sexual inequality of the textual exchanges.

These interruptions and rewritings of both the aristocratic and the radical ecclesiastic marriage models in terms of sexual, textual, and political autonomy are continued in the Wife's Arthurian tale about a rapist knight who must search out what women desire most in order to preserve his life. Many critics have remarked how the romantic, idealized tale is a wish fulfillment and a projection of the Wife's anxiety about her age. In an appropriate turnabout, the Wife has spent her youth in small change but she cannot reap any dividends. But about half the tale is taken up with the Hag's curtain speech, in fact her counsel, on the nature and origin of true *gentilesse*. The Hag repeats the Wife's performance in the **"Wife of Bath's Prologue"** by explicitly interrupting the aristocratic marriage model. In a textual game of autoexegesis and autocitation, she "quotes" Chaucer's own **"Gentilesse"** (just as other characters in the *Canterbury Tales* quote the Wife of Bath as an authority), while Chaucer cites Boethius, Jean de Meun, and Dante in his lyric. The Hag denies that blood relations determine one's character or legitimacy. Extending the Wife's critique of aristocratic privilege based on inherited wealth, the Hag legitimates other bourgeois social values (autonomy, privacy, the individual) derived not from inherited or preordained status but from one's individual actions which can only be judged in terms of their virtue in the eyes of God. Coming as it does at the end of the Wife's performance, the Hag's speech argues not for ecclesiastic sovereignty and female dominance in marriage, but for the responsibility of each individual for his or her own actions as controlled by the pious interpretation of God's text and the desire to enhance the common profit. God is the origin of property, virtue, and textual meaning. The Hag's counsel provides the rationale for the Wife's narrative of an aristocratic queen who acts as a justice on behalf of a raped peasant girl, a narrative exchange in which all women in the state are equal under the female law. The reform of the English economy, the renewal of public and private morality, and the dispersion of literate practices and texts are part of a more general religio-political reform movement in the fourteenth century, for which the Wife of Bath as a secular female is an important sign. However, as a critique of domination, the **"Wife of Bath's Tale"** also reproduces a dominant ideology by substituting genders while leaving *maistrie* firmly in place as the basis of social relations. In the Wife's performance, women desire what men desire. Moreover, the young knight in the tale does not seem to have engaged the Hag or any other woman as an other in a hermeneutic dialogue. Rather, he simply reverses the social hierarchy, gives *maistrie* to his new wife, and finds out that he has not paid as dearly as he feared for the knowledge of what women desire most.

In the **"Wife of Bath's Prologue and Tale"** a woman's autonomy in society is achieved in two contradictory ways. On the one hand, the archwife schemes, deceives, bullies, harangues, and sexually abuses her men in order to gain the *maistrie* in her marriages. In this role, Alisoun is the *lex animata* (the living law) of the antifeminist cliche about women. On the other hand, the Wife inherits and retains property through her own line as a widow, does not lose part of her wealth to her children after her husbands die, retains control of her body and social position as long as she has "land and fee," and challenges the male-dominated textual system by interrupting the privilege of male-oriented reading and writing. I have concentrated here on this second aspect of the Wife's performance in the **Canterbury Tales** because the first account so often dominates the interpretations of the **"Wife of Bath's Prologue and Tale."** We see, then, how Chaucer's text rather than reflecting social conditions, represents them so as to expose an aspect of their contradiction. Textualized history is not mimesis but irony.

The Wife's performance reproduces the argument in the later Middle Ages for the autonomy not only of females but of the laity as a whole. Marsilius of Padua, in *Defensor pacis,* described the state as that natural political unit constituted by the will of all the citizens, whose laws are enforceable in so far as they are willed by the sovereign people. The state marks the domain of the temporal, the human, and the relative, as opposed to the church, which marks the domain of the eternal, the divine, and the absolute. Along side the violence of her marital struggles and deceptions, the text of the Wife of Bath asserts that sexuality is a part of one's nature, that sexual and textual experiences are relative to intentions and interpretive contexts, and that social and economic practices (such as inheritance) capitalize and determine the values of individuals. In this way, the text of the Wife of Bath transforms history and fabliau cliche into a textual idiom. In Chaucer's verbal portrait of the Wife of Bath, the contradictions in the Wife's situation, her economic and textual autonomy, her capitalizing of the body, and her repetition of the fabliau cliche about women, mark the ambivalence about women and the fear of women in power during the later Middle Ages. The text of the Wife of Bath interrupts a dominant concept of women and marriage, formulated primarily by aristocratic economics and social practices, with a countercommentary generated by the marginal reading of women as literate property owners. As intertextual characterization and figuration, the text of the Wife of Bath poses the question of authority and dominance in marriage. Like Chaucer's **"Melibee"** and **"Clerk's Tale"** and Langland's *Piers Plowman,* Alisounian textuality develops a domestic critique of the postfeudal state, that marriage

of not so equal individuals for the not always common profit. (pp. 67-81)

Mark Amsler, "The Wife of Bath and Women's Power," in Assays, *Vol. IV, 1987, pp. 67-83.*

Helen Cooper   (essay date 1989)

[*An English medievalist, Cooper is the author of* Pastoral: Mediaeval Into Renaissance *(1978) and* The Structure of the Canterbury Tales *(1984). In the following excerpt, she provides an overview of the "Parson's Tale."*]

The theme of the **"Parson's Tale"** is Penitence, and it is treated under the three main heads of Contrition, Confession, and Satisfaction: of being sorry, making a formal confession to a priest, and making amends. The moves from one to another are indicated by subheadings in the manuscripts. The three topics are compared to a tree, Contrition being the root, Confession the trunk from which spring various branches and leaves, and Satisfaction the fruit.

The clarity of this outline is somewhat blurred by a mass of smaller subdivisions, and in particular by the large proportion of the **"Parson's Tale"** taken up by the analysis, in the course of the Confession section, of the seven deadly sins and their remedial virtues. The image of the tree is repeated for the sins: pride is the root, the other six the branches, and each of these branches in turn produces its smaller branches and twigs.

Contrition, Confession, and Satisfaction are themselves subdivisions within the framing scheme of the treatise. It opens, sermon-style, with a text: 'Stondeth upon the weyes, and seeth and axeth of olde pathes (that is to seyn, of olde sentences) which is the goode wey'—the good way, which will lead humankind to 'Jerusalem celestial', being the way of Penitence. The Parson then announces the different aspects of Penitence he will discuss, and the rest of the treatise more or less fulfils these divisions. The first is 'what is Penitence'. Next comes the etymology, 'whennes it is cleped Penitence': this is not given a separate discussion, but it is covered by implication in 86, where the English, 'a man that *halt* hymself in sorwe and oother *peyne* for his giltes', disguises the Latin *poena* and *tenere*. The third and fourth divisions are, 'in how manye maneres been the accioun or werkynges of Penitence', and 'how manye speces ther been of Penitence'. The next section, 'whiche thynges apertenen and bihoven to Penitence', namely Contrition, Confession, and Satisfaction, forms the bulk of the treatise, and is discussed further below. The last section, 'whiche thynges destourben Penitence', is dealt with much more briefly. The final 'fruyt of penaunce' is described in the last few lines: this is the 'endeless blisse of hevene' promised in the opening exposition of the text, a goal reached through 'mortificacioun of synne'.

Contrition itself is divided into four main heads. First is 'what is Contricioun'; next 'whiche been the causes that moeven a man to Contricioun', discussed in turn in six parts—remembrance of sin, disgust at sin, fear of Judgement and hell, sorrow for good not done, the recollection of the Passion, and hope for forgiveness, grace, and glory. The third head is 'how he sholde be contrit', the fourth 'what Contricioun availeth to the soule'.

Confession is still more complicated. The Parson announces a three-part division: 'what is Confessioun, and wheither it oghte nedes be doon or noon, and whiche thynges been convenable to verray Confessioun'. Confession is defined as a true showing of one's sins to the priest with all their circumstances; this in turn requires an exposition of the sources of sin, how they grow, and what they are—whether venial or deadly, with their appropriate remedies. The circumstances of a sin are explained in 960-79. The treatise then returns more briefly to the other two divisions of Confession, whether it is necessary (without any textual indication of the new section), and what is necessary for a true confession (Chaucer announces a four-part treatment of this, but the numbering system becomes incoherent after the first two).

The origin of this material, in the penitential literature that sprang up in response to the decree of 1215 that required regular confession, explains some features of the treatise that might otherwise appear strange. The much greater emphasis on sin than on virtue and grace, for instance—an emphasis that has been estimated to give a ratio of fourteen to one of vice to goodness—is inevitable in writings of this kind: penitents have to learn to recognize what their sins are before they can make a full confession or properly repent. It does all the same make for a very negative view of humankind. The remedial virtues get little space, and are sometimes hurried over (as witnessed by Chaucer's drastic cutting of his original for these sections, or his passing mention of 'mo speciale remedies' that get minimal elaboration). Sometimes, too, these sections are partly taken up with further discussions of sin—a third of 'misericorde and pitee', the virtue counterbalancing Avarice, is devoted to 'fool-largesse, that men clepen wast', which is itself damnable.

The penitential treatise is an appropriate form to give to the Parson, in terms of both dramatic and rhetorical decorum. His portrait in the **"General Prologue"** stresses his teaching by example rather than by precept, but his tale does both at once: it is a set of instructions, but he also puts into practice a storytelling of 'vertuous mateere' that shows up the moral shortcomings of most of the other tales as strikingly as the goodness of most of the other pilgrims. The **"Parson's Tale"** shows him ready to 'snybben' sinners sharply where appropriate, but with the emphasis on castigating the sin rather than the sinner (cf. 'nat wrooth agayns the man, but wrooth with the mysdede of the man'). The fit of the tale to the **"General Prologue"** portrait is closer than for many of the pilgrims: a fact which makes the treatise one more tale among the many that are filtered through a narrator distinct from Chaucer, and at the same time privileges it by relating it to so explicit an ideal of the Christian life as the Parson represents.

By the time the **"Retractions"** are reached, Chaucer and the Parson are speaking with a single voice; and this makes it especially hard to be sure of the status of the narrating voice within the tale. Most of it is written in the voice appropriate to a preacher. There is a liberal sprinkling of exclamations—'lo', 'allas!', 'certes'—and the standard transition formulae are used for new sections, 'Now wol I speken of—'. Problems in identifying the narrator come when the authority of the preacher gives way to expression of uncertainty or inability. He says of unwilled sins of pride that they may be grievous but 'I gesse that they ne been nat deedly'; of the fruit of virginity, 'I ne kan seye it noon ootherweyes in Englissh, but in Latyn it highte *Centesimus fructus*'; he apologizes for not including a discourse on the ten commandments, 'but so heigh a doctrine I lete to divines'. Neither the Parson nor Chaucer is a professional theologian, and all such expressions can be paralleled elsewhere in the *Tales;* but they still suggest that the dramatic voice has not yet been abandoned completely.

The Parson is the last of a number of pilgrims who have not only told stories but have given their own discursive expositions of Scripture or of Christian doctrine to the assembled company. Their preachings were, however, very differently motivated from the Parson's. The Wife of Bath is concerned to justify her own way of life; the Pardoner is out to fill his pockets. Within the stories told, characters such as the Summoner's friar likewise exploit Scripture for their own ends. Other uses of the Bible inside the tales serve all kinds of worldly purposes: the Song of Songs becomes a lecher's seduction platform, Old Testament narratives prove to the Monk the dominance of Fortune. Only the **"Parson's Tale"** consistently expounds the Word of God for the sole end of bringing its hearers to salvation. In contrast to the Pardoner, he will not let souls go blackberrying if he can prevent them. His allusions in his prologue to the Second Epistle to Timothy serve to confirm his office as a true preacher, in contradistinction to the vicious man who can yet tell a moral tale.

It is impossible for the descendants of Adam and Eve to live without venial sin: 'this thyng may nat faille as longe as he lyveth'. A penitential treatise is in effect a compendium of human actions, for all actions performed in the world and for the world are tainted by the Fall. The treatise therefore inevitably overlaps with the earlier tales, and with the pilgrims themselves. The penitential stress on sin connects with the rest of the *Tales* most closely at those points where the various characters have stepped out of the 'good way' to heaven.

This does not mean that the **"Parson's Tale"** was deliberately written to show up such errors, nor that the earlier tales were written as exampla of the various ways of sinning. The aim of both the tales and the treatise is encyclopaedic; the viewpoints on life offered by the individual stories are as many and various as the pilgrims, but the whole *Canterbury Tales,* like the **"Parson's Tale,"** is concerned with the process of living in the world. As a *summa* in miniature, the **"Parson's Tale"** in one sense encapsulates the various *moralitees* of the whole work into a single treatise, just as the tale of the other priest on the pilgrimage, the Nun's Priest, encapsulates the aesthetics of all the tales, their styles and genres. The **"Nun's Priest's Tale"**, however, preserves the variety of the complete work, its interplay of voices and styles, its refusal to stand still. The

"Parson's Tale" pins every attitude, every action, into a fixed place on the various twigs of the branches of his tree of Penitence.

Not all of what Chaucer says in the **"Parson's Tale"** is critical of what he has said elsewhere: there is indeed as much reinforcement of moral messages already given as there is reappraisal of the amoral or immoral. That sinners should 'forlete synne er that synne forlete hem' (93) is the same moral as the Physician had thrown in to his tale; that one should not trust in fortune or riches is a theme first sounded by Arcite and repeated constantly; that *gentrie* comes from virtue and not birth, and that patience enables people to live in harmony with each other and to withstand the adversity contingent on living in an unstable world, are two of the key ideas of the whole *Tales.* That one should do good to one's enemies is the message of **"Melibee"**; that 'the roote of alle harmes is Coveitise' is as clear to the Parson as to the Pardoner. In both approval of virtue and castigation of vice, the **"Parson's Tale"** can endorse what has gone before.

It can also, of course, criticize. It would be possible to arraign a good many of the pilgrims under one form or another of sin—the Wife with her insistence on precedence, the Monk with his gay bridle, the Franklin's interest in food (though the elaboration of feasting described by the Parson goes beyond the Franklin's practices). The content of many of the stories is also put in a new light by the rigorous appraisal of sinful behaviour, which includes just about every form of sexual activity—among them, the procreation of children, and being raped. On the status of women, the treatise is not quite as patriarchal as it at first appears. It insists, as the whole culture requires, that women should be subject to their husbands, but it insists too that Eve was made from Adam's rib, and not his head or his foot, to show that 'womman sholde be felawe unto man'. The treatise has harsh words for the 'desray' visible 'day by day' that results from the woman's having the *maistrie;* and it notes the fallacy of wives' pretending they can please their husbands by 'queyntise of aray'—both closely relevant to earlier parts of the work, and both apparently Chaucer's own additions. Most of the variations on the sources that have to do with lechery and its corresponding virtue are inversely paralleled in the **"Merchant's Tale"**, in January's views on sex; much of the Parson's lengthy discourse on the subject could indeed serve as a commentary on January's delusions.

The treatise insists, however, on its generality. Just as it reserves its anger for the misdeed and not the man, so only a tiny fraction of its teaching bears any close relevance to the rest of the *Tales.* For every opportunity taken, Chaucer lets pass a dozen others: 'espiritueel marchandise', for instance, is limited to simony, and not extended to the Pardoner's malpractices; the section on the sins of the tongue, assembled from various points in the sources, never meshes closely with the Manciple's condemnation of loose speech or the Parson's own insistence on truth-telling. The *Tales* offer an abundance of qualifications that the Parson overlooks—reluctance to sleep with one's husband, for instance, is scarcely a virtue where May is concerned; Cecilia's spiritual authority over her husband is in no sense sin-

ful; Chauntecleer's preference for delight over procreation, and his readiness to mate with his sisters, invites a reading of the anthropomorphic condition not quite covered by the Parson's dismissal of the incestuous as 'lyk to houndes'. The treatise's flat condemnation of all questioning of divine Providence does not provide any answer to the questions posed by the **"Knight's Tale",** or by any of those tales that concern themselves with the suffering of the innocent, beyond its insistence on the value of patience.

The bulk of the treatise is taken up with matters that have only an oblique application to the rest of the work, or none at all. Its focus is different from that of the *Tales* at large, and if in most respects it is narrower—in its condemnation of most human activity, its refusal to admit any aesthetic or literary values, its joylessness—in other ways it looks more widely, to the world rather than the *Tales* alone. The **"General Prologue"** offered a cross-section of society, of the different estates representing earthly institutions and ranks of all kinds, each embodied in a distinctive individual. The **"Parson's Tale"** turns away from both individuality and social and professional distinctions; for him all men are descendants of Adam, and difference of estate lies in the eyes of God.

> Certes the estaat of man is in three maneres. Outher it is th'estaat of innocence, as was th'estaat of Adam biforn that he fil into synne . . . Another estaat is the estaat of synful men, in which estaat men been holden to laboure in preiynge to God for amendement of hire synnes . . . Another estaat is th'estaat of grace, in which estaat he is holden to werkes of penitence.

These estates are not the contingent professions of a society in flux, where rank and wealth and self-esteem struggle for dominance, but God-given conditions through which humankind can rise. Innocence may be less possible to regain even than a society in perfect hierarchical order, but the way from sin to grace is an open one, and the Parson is the spiritual guide.

The **"Parson's Tale"** is the last word of the *Canterbury Tales;* it is not the only word. Its timelessness, paradoxically, has stood the test of time worse than those distinctively fourteenth-century figures of the crusader Knight, the well-mannered Prioress, and the Pardoner of St Mary Rouncesval. Modern taste ranks the literary dazzle and the wit of the Nun's Priest above the scholastic moralizing of the Parson. To Chaucer, both were valid. We live in a world that allows for beast-fables and the Wife of Bath, but that has little time for saints' lives and penitential treatises. The narrowing is ours, not Chaucer's.

'I wol nat glose', the Parson declares in his prologue, and he is true to his word. The treatise is relentlessly expository, with none of the evasion of awkward prescripts that the glossing friar John of the **"Summoner's Tale"** specializes in, none of the self-serving selection from Scripture of the Wife of Bath, none of the rhetorical fireworks of the Pardoner. The Parson rejects fables as untruthful, and so rules out one of the main devices of the preacher to hold his auditors' interest. The play of voices found everywhere else in the *Tales,* including the dialogue of **"Melibee"** here comes down to a single voice of authority.

The **"Parson's Tale"** is not so consistently drab as this might make it sound, however. The Parson does not scorn quoting 'thilke newe Frenshe song' to drive a point home; and one exemplary tale does manage to creep in, in the shape of the child who reproves his master for losing patience. There are some striking similes, some already present in Chaucer's models, but which lose nothing in the translation: external pride as a sign of spiritual pride, 'right as the gaye leefsel atte taverne is signe of the wyn that is in the celer'; tight hose looking from the rear like 'the hyndre part of a sheape in the fulle of the moone'; Envy as a blacksmith, who 'holdeth the hoote iren upon the herte of man with a peire of longe toonges of long rancour'; old lechers past the age of performance like a hound, 'whan he comth by the roser or by othere (bushes), though he may nat pisse, yet wole he heve up his leg and make a contenaunce to pisse'; that the chaste should avoid company that might tempt them to sin, for a wall can be blackened by a candle though it may not itself catch fire. Such imagery is always closely integrated with the message of the treatise. Sin is associated with the dominance of the flesh over reason, as wine and drunkenness overcome rationality, or as animals lack the godlike faculty of intellect; it is a foretaste of the burnings of hell, and substitutes darkness for light.

The treatise is written in the plain style appropriate to exposition, where understanding is more important than persuasion. In keeping with the emphasis on sin as the subordination of reason, the appeal is to the intellect, not the emotions. This accounts in part for the emphasis on enumeration and subdivision. It may hinder the reader's being moved, but it serves as a kind of mnemonic structure, and moreover it reflects the order of God:

> God hath creat alle thynges in right ordre, and
> no thyng withouten ordre, but alle thynges been
> ordeyned and nombred.

There are however a few moments where the language becomes more highly charged, and where Chaucer's prose can briefly take its place beside that of that later master of religious rhetoric, Donne. On the Passion,

> Thanne was he byscorned, that oonly sholde han
> been honoured in alle thynges and of alle
> thynges. Thanne was his visage, that oghte be
> desired to be seyn of al mankynde, in which vis-
> age aungels desiren to looke, vileynsly bispet.
>
> (pp. 402-08)

Helen Cooper, "The Parson's Tale," in her The Canterbury Tales, Oxford at the Clarendon Press, 1989, pp. 395-409.

FURTHER READING

Allen, Judson Boyce. "The Old Way and the Parson's Way:

An Ironic Reading of the 'Parson's Tale'." *Journal of Medieval and Renaissance Studies* 3, No. 2 (Fall 1973): 255-71.

    Uses Boethian and Aristotlian philosophies to justify an ironic reading of the "Parson's Tale."

Arathoon, Leigh A., ed. *Chaucer and the Craft of Fiction.* Rochester, Mich.: Solaris Press, 1986, 430 p.

    Collection of fourteen examinations of Chaucer's narrative art.

Barney, Stephen A., ed. *Chaucer's Troilus: Essays in Criticism.* Hamden, Conn.: Archon Books, 1980, 323 p.

    Reprints seminal essays on *Troilus and Criseyde.* This collection also includes three original pieces.

Beichner, Paul E. "Chaucer's Pardoner as Entertainer." *Medieval Studies* XXV (1963): 160-72.

    Argues that the Pardoner's intent is to entertain, not to raise funds from the other pilgrims, as some critics have claimed.

Bennett, H. S. *Chaucer and the Fifteenth Century.* Oxford: Clarendon Press, 1947, 326 p.

    Presents an overview of Chaucer's time and literary accomplishment.

Bennett, J. A. W. *The Parlement of Foules: An Interpretation.* Oxford: Clarendon Press, 1957, 217 p.

    Illuminating examination of the poem's sources and literary traditions.

Benson, C. David. *Chaucer's Troilus and Criseyde.* London: Unwin Hyman, 1990, 226 p.

    Discusses the major topics of the poem, using prior criticism to illustrate the work's multiplicity of meaning.

Birney, Earle. *Essays on Chaucerian Irony.* Toronto: University of Toronto Press, 1985, 162 p.

    Collection of previously published essays, with an additional essay on irony by Beryl Rowland.

Boitani, Piero and Mann, Jill, eds. *The Cambridge Chaucer Companion.* Cambridge: Cambridge University Press, 1986, 262 p.

    Collection of fifteen essays for the "student approaching Chaucer for the first time," covering the major works and providing some historical context.

Brewer, D[erek] S., ed. *Chaucer and Chaucerians: Critical Studies in Middle English Literature.* University: University of Alabama Press, 1966, 278 p.

    Collection of nine important essays by prominent Chaucer scholars.

————. "Honour in Chaucer." *Essays and Studies* 26 (1973): 1-19.

    Illuminates the concept of honor as portrayed in Chaucer's works.

————, ed. *Geoffrey Chaucer.* Athens: Ohio University Press, 1975, 401 p.

    Collection of twelve essays on Chaucer's background and sources.

————, ed. *Chaucer: The Critical Heritage.* 2 vols. London: Routledge & Kegan Paul, 1978.

    Contains excerpts of significant criticism from Chaucer's time to 1933. This selection is less comprehensive than that of Spurgeon [see below].

————. *An Introduction to Chaucer.* London: Longman, 1984, 263 p.

Concise, readable overview of Chaucer, based on Brewer's highly regarded *Chaucer* (1953) and *Chaucer in his Time* (1963).

Brooks, Douglas, and Fowler, Alastair. "The Meaning of Chaucer's 'Knight's Tale'." *Medium Ævum* XXXIX, No. 2 (1970): 123-46.

Interprets the "Knight's Tale" as an expression of a later stage of the author's life.

Cawley, A. C., ed. *Chaucer's Mind and Art.* Edinburgh: Oliver & Boyd, 1969, 210 p.

Contains six reprints and four new essays intended to serve as an introduction to those aspects of Chaucer named in the title.

Chesterton, G. K. *Chaucer.* New York: Farrar & Rinehart, 1932, 310 p.

General appreciation which stresses Chaucer's underlying Christian humanism.

Cooper, Helen. *Oxford Guides to Chaucer: The Canterbury Tales.* Oxford: Clarendon Press, 1989, 437 p.

Provides a summary of criticism about the *Canterbury Tales* in easily accessible sections.

Dean, Christopher. "Salvation, Damnation and the Role of the Old Man in the 'Pardoner's Tale'." *The Chaucer Review* 3, No. 1 (1968): 44-49.

Claims that the Old Man represents two aspects of God: mercy and justice.

Dinshaw, Carolyn. *Chaucer's Sexual Poetics.* Madison: University of Wisconsin Press, 1989, 310 p.

Feminist analysis of Chaucer's poetry which finds Chaucer noteworthy for "the thoroughness, flexibility, and variety of his engagement with and exploration of traditional [gender] formulations."

Economou, George D. "Januarie's Sin Against Nature: The 'Merchant's Tale' and the *Roman de la Rose.*" *Comparative Literature* 17, No. 1 (Winter 1965): 251-57.

Reveals how the mirror imagery from the *Roman* functions in the tale.

Eldridge, Laurence. "The Structure of *The Book of the Duchess.*" *Revue de l'Université Ottawa* 39, No. 1 (January-March 1969): 132-51.

Elucidation of the symmetry of the work and its effectiveness.

Faulkner, Dewey R., ed. *Twentieth Century Interpretations of the Pardoner's Tale: A Collection of Critical Essays.* Englewood Cliffs, N.J.: Prentice-Hall, 1973, 123 p.

Collection of new and reprinted essays concerning the major critical views of the "Pardoner's Tale."

Fichte, Jeorg O. "*The Book of the Duchess*—A Consolation?" *Studia Neophilogica* XLV, No. 1 (1973): 53-67.

Determines that this work is a tribute to Blanche and serves as a lasting consolation for John of Gaunt.

Frank, Robert Worth, Jr. "Structure and Meaning in the *Parlement of Foules.*" *PMLA* 71, No. 3 (June 1956): 530-39.

Examination which reveals that the poem reflects courtly love conventions in unconventional ways.

Gordon, Ida L. *The Double Sorrow of Troilus.* Oxford: Clarendon Press, 1970, 154 p.

Determines, through emphasis on the work's ambiguities and complexities, that it can be dubbed "modern" due to the contemporary application of its philosophy of love and Chaucer's skillful use of language.

Haller, Robert S. "The 'Knight's Tale' and the Epic Tradition." *Chaucer Review* 1, No. 2 (1966-67): 67-84.

Examines the tale in terms of the classical epic and argues that love takes the place of politics at the center of the work.

Haymes, Edward R. "Chaucer and the English Romance Tradition." *South Atlantic Bulletin* XXXVII, No. 4 (November 1972): 35-43.

Examines the influence of English poetical tradition on the poet.

Hill, Betty. "On Reading Chaucer." *Proceedings of the Leeds Philosophical and Historical Society* 14, Part 6 (June 1971): 209-20.

Brief examination of Chaucer's poetics which reveals that he used the inherited characteristics of oral poetry and foreign literatures in his native tongue to create a masterful ouevre.

Hodgson, Phyllis. "Chaucer's English" and "Versification." In *General Prologue: The Canterbury Tales,* by Geoffrey Chaucer, edited by Phyllis Hodgson, pp. 148-73. London: Athlone Press, 1969.

Provides an introduction to Chaucer's language, versification, metre, and syntax.

Hoffman, Richard L. *Ovid and the Canterbury Tales.* n. p., 1966, 217 p.

Presents evidence of Ovidian influence in fifteen of the tales.

Howard, Edwin J. *Geoffrey Chaucer.* New York: Twayne Publishers, 1964, 219 p.

Concise overview of the poet's time and works.

Huppé, Bernard F. *A Reading of the Canterbury Tales.* Rev. ed. Albany: State University of New York, 1967, 245 p.

Interprets the work as a Christian allegory, following the conclusion of Robertson [see below].

————, and Robertson, D. W., Jr. *Fruyt and Chaf: Studies in Chaucer's Allegories.* Princeton: Princeton University Press, 1963, 157 p.

Allegorical interpretations of the *Parlement of Foules* and the *Book of the Duchess.*

Jones, George Fenwick. "Chaucer and the Medieval Miller." *Modern Language Quarterly* 16, No. 1 (March 1955): 3-15.

Provides background on the social status of medieval millers and discusses the tradition of satire concerning them.

Kellogg, Alfred L., and Haselmayer, Louis A. "Chaucer's Satire of the Pardoner." *PMLA* LXVI, No. 2 (March 1951): 257-77.

Provides historical background on pardoners.

Kittredge, George Lyman. *Chaucer and His Poetry.* Cambridge: Harvard University Press, 1915, 230 p.

Somewhat dated, but still valuable, seminal study.

Koban, Charles. "Hearing Chaucer Out: The Art of Persuasion in the 'Wife of Bath's Tale'." *The Chaucer Review* 5, No. 3 (1970-71):225-39.

Examines the tale in light of oral delivery techniques.

Lawlor, John. "The Pattern of Consolation in *The Book of the Duchess*." *Speculum* XXXI, No. 4 (October 1956): 626-48.

Examines the pattern of consolation within the tradition of courtly love evident in the work.

Lenaghan, R. T. "Chaucer's 'General Prologue' as History and Literature." *Comparative Studies in Society and History* 12, No. 1 (January 1970): 73-82.

Examines the viability of reading the "General Prologue" as history, finding that it provides a credible model of fourteenth-century English society.

Levy, Bernard S., and Adams, George R. "Chaunticleer's Paradise Lost and Regained." *Mediaeval Studies* XXIX (1967): 178-92.

Illustrates how Chaucer used biblical and patristic material to create a comic version of the Fall of Man, in the "Nun's Priest's Tale."

Lewis, C. S. "What Chaucer Really Did to *Il Filostrato*." In his *Selected Literary Essays*, edited by Walter Hooper, pp. 27-44. Cambridge at the University Press, 1969.

Shows how, in *Troilus and Criseyde*, Chaucer used rhetoric, the courtly love tradition, and the idea of *sentence* to return the Renaissance essence of Boccaccio's original to its medieval roots. This seminal essay was originally published in the 1932 *Essays and Studies*.

Leyerle, John, and Quick, Anne. *Chaucer: A Bibliographical Introduction*. Toronto: University of Toronto Press, 1986, 321 p.

Annotated compilation for readers who are relatively unfamiliar with the mass of criticism surrounding Chaucer and his works.

Long, E. Hudson. "Chaucer as a Master of the Short Story." *Delaware Notes* 16 (1943): 11-29.

Applies modern short story theory to the *Canterbury Tales* and finds Chaucer a master story teller.

Lumiansky, R. M. "Chaucer's *Parlement of Foules*: A Philosophical Interpretation." *The Review of English Studies* XXIV, No. 94 (April 1948): 81-89.

Interpretation of the poem as an inquiry into true and false felicity.

McAlpine, Monica E. *The Genre of Troilus and Criseyde*. Ithaca: Cornell University Press, 1978, 252 p.

Examines the *Troilus* as a tragedy in the Boethian sense, where tragedy is a device to reveal rich depictions of human reality rather than an organizational device to shape the representation of human experience.

McCall, John P. "The Harmony of Chaucer's *Parlement*." *The Chaucer Review* 5, No. 1 (1970-71): 22-31.

Claims that the poem is a conscious intermixing of conflicting elements and ideas.

McDonald, Charles O. "An Interpretation of Chaucer's *Parlement of Foules*." *Speculum* XXX, No. 3 (July 1955): 444-57.

Suggests that the work is a survey of the various kinds of love and that it is unified by the figure of Nature.

Mehl, Dieter. *Geoffrey Chaucer: An Introduction to his Narrative Poetry*. Cambridge: Cambridge University Press, 1986, 243 p.

In this revised translation of a 1973 German book, the critic provides a lucid introduction to Chaucer's major works and discusses the relationship of the author to the narrator and the author/narrator to the listener/reader.

Moorman, Charles. " 'Once More Unto the Breach': The Meaning of *Troilus and Criseyde*." *Studies in the Literary Imagination* IV, No. 2 (October 1971): 61-71.

Maintains that the poem deals with the influence of irrational, uncontrollable forces upon the actions of men.

Morgan, Gerald, ed. Introduction to *The Franklin's Tale from the Canterbury Tales*, by Geoffrey Chaucer, pp. 1-47. New York: Holmes & Meier, 1980.

Overview which stresses the thematic structure in the tale.

Owen, Charles A., Jr., ed. *Discussions of the Canterbury Tales*. Boston: D. C. Heath and Co., 1961, 110 p.

Contains short excerpts from important critical studies.

Payne, Robert O. *The Key of Remembrance: A Study of Chaucer's Poetics*. New Haven: Yale University Press, 1963, 246 p.

Places Chaucer's poetics in the context of rhetorical tradition.

Reid, David S. "Crocodilian Humor: A Discussion of Chaucer's Wife of Bath." *The Chaucer Review* 4, No. 2 (1969-70): 71-89.

Rejects the standard interpretations of the Wife and argues that she is a "stock figure and an absurdity."

Richardson, Cynthia C. "The Function of the Host in the *Canterbury Tales*." *Texas Studies in Literature and Language* XII, No. 1 (Spring 1970): 325-44.

Suggests that, for Chaucer, Harry Bailly represents the superficial and uncritical audience.

Robertson, D. W., Jr. *A Preface to Chaucer: Studies in Medieval Perspectives*. Princeton: Princeton University Press, 1962, 519 p.

An important and controversial study which argues that all medieval poetry, including Chaucer's, was intended to be interpreted allegorically, like the *Bible*.

Robinson, Ian. *Chaucer and the English Tradition*. Cambridge: Cambridge University Press, 1972, 296 p.

Assessment of Chaucer's native English qualities and comparision with his contemporaries. "Chaucer is the father of English literature not by begetting it or influencing it but by creating its form."

Root, Robert Kilbourn. *The Poetry of Chaucer: A Guide to Its Study and Appreciation*. Rev. ed. 1921. Reprint. Glouchester, Mass.: Peter Smith, 1957, 306 p.

Dated but still valuable introduction to the study of Chaucer.

Rowland, Beryl. "Chaucer's Blasphemous Churl: A New Interpretation of the 'Miller's Tale'." In *Chaucer and Middle English Studies in Honour of Rossell Hope Robbins*, edited by Beryl Rowland, pp. 43-55. London: George Allen & Unwin, 1974.

Interprets the "Miller's Tale" as a satire of mystery plays.

————, ed. *Companion to Chaucer Studies.* London: Oxford University Press, 1968, 409 p.

>   Invaluable collection of critical articles concerning many aspects of Chaucerian scholarship. Each essay contains its own bibliography.

Ruggiers, Paul G. *The Art of the Canterbury Tales.* Madison, Wis.: University of Wisconsin Press, 1965, 265 p.

>   Examination of the structure of the *Canterbury Tales* which finds Chaucer's view of humanity comprehensive and sympathetic.

Schoek, Richard J., and Taylor, Jerome, eds. *Chaucer Criticism, Volume II: Troilus and Criseyde & the Minor Poems.* Notre Dame: University of Notre Dame Press, 1961, 293 p.

>   Reprints seventeen important essays.

Severs, J. Burke. "The Sources of *The Book of the Duchess.*" *Mediaeval Studies* XXV (1963): 355-62.

>   Provides evidence for the anonymous French *Le Songe Vert* as a source of the poem.

————. "Chaucer's Self-Portrait in the *Book of the Duchess.*" *Philological Quarterly* XLIII, No. 1 (January 1964): 27-39.

>   Contrary to common critical opinion, the critic argues that Chaucer presents himself in the poem as a detached non-lover.

Slade, Tony. "Irony in the "Wife of Bath's Tale'." *The Modern Language Review* 64, No. 2 (April 1969): 241-47.

>   Reveals the ironic touches in the tale.

Spearing, A. C., ed. *The Knight's Tale,* by Geoffrey Chaucer, pp. 1-83. Cambridge: Cambridge University Press, 1966.

>   Comprehensive introduction which provides a thematic background to the tale.

Spurgeon, Caroline F. E. *Five Hundred Years of Chaucer Criticism and Allusions 1357-1900.* 3 vols. Cambridge: Cambridge University Press, 1925.

>   Collection of the majority of references to Chaucer through the nineteenth century.

Steinberg, Aaron. "The 'Wife of Bath's Tale' and Her Fantasy of Fulfillment." *College English* 26, No. 3 (December 1964): 187-91.

>   Finds that the tale is an exemplar of Chaucer's psychological insight.

Tatlock, J. S. P. "Chaucer's 'Merchant's Tale'." *Modern Philology* 33 (May 1936): 367-81.

Examination of characterization, emphasizing the tale's cynical bitterness.

Ten Brink, Bernhard. *The Language and Metre of Chaucer,* 2nd edition. Edited by Friedrich Kluge. Translated by M. Bentinck Smith. London: Macmillan and Co., 1901, 280 p.

>   Definitive study of Chaucer's versification and poetics.

Tupper, Frederick. "Chaucer and the Seven Deadly Sins." *PMLA* 29 (1914): 93-128.

>   Argues that the "Parson's Tale" is the fruition of the organizational motif of the *Canterbury Tales*—the seven deadly sins.

Tuve, Rosemond. *Seasons and Months: Studies in a Tradition of Middle English Poetry.* Paris: Librarie Universitaire S.A., 1933, 232 p.

>   Traces the literary precedents for the description of the seasons in Chaucer's work.

Uphaus, Robert W. "Chaucer's *Parlement of Foules:* Aesthetic Order and Individual Experience." *Texas Studies in Literature and Language* X, No. 1 (Spring 1968)

>   Attempts to account for the poem's intentional ambiguity by establishing a distinction between the level of discourse and the level of art.

Wagenknecht, Edward, ed. *Chaucer: Modern Essays in Criticism.* London: Oxford University Press, 1959, 413 p.

>   Reprints twenty-six distinguished essays by major Chaucerians.

Wimsatt, James. *Chaucer and the French Love Poets.* Chapel Hill: University of North Carolina Press, 1968, 186 p.

>   Traces the influence of the poetry of Guillaume de Machaut, the poems of Jean Froissart, and the *Roman de la Rose* on the *Book of the Duchess.*

Woolf, Virginia. "The Pastons and Chaucer." In her *The Common Reader,* pp. 13-38. New York: Harcourt, Brace and Co., 1925.

>   Stresses that Chaucer should be read as a whole, not in select pieces taken out of context, to fully appreciate his art.

Woo, Constance, and Matthews, William. "The Spiritual Purpose of the *Canterbury Tales.*" *Comitatus,* No. 1 (December 1970): 85-109.

>   Presents evidence for considering the poems primarily spiritual in intent and purpose.

Fifteenth-Century English Literature

"The fifteenth century," wrote Denton Fox, "is the *terra incognita* of English literature. It has long appeared on at least the cruder maps as a vast emptiness, labelled simply 'desert'." Sterility, repetitiveness, and unoriginality are attributes often used by traditional scholarship in assessments of late medieval literature, particularly poetry. Indeed, the fifteenth century lacked poets of Chaucer's stature, but poetry, despite the lassitude of courtly poetry, remained an important genre. Counterbalancing the decadence of courtly poetry, popular genres, such as ballads and carols, as well as non-courtly poetry in general, flourished. Prose, already mirroring the gradual shift from Middle to Modern English, thrived as an instrument of literary and scholarly expression, its increasing sophistication attested to by masterworks such as Sir Thomas Malory's *Le Morte d'Arthur* (1470).

The poetry of the period generally betrays a mood of spiritual fatigue, as critics have asserted, exemplified by imitation and the subordination of poetic inspiration to formulaic schematism. "The poetry of the fifteenth century," wrote Johan Huizinga, "often gives us the impression of being almost devoid of new ideas. The inability to invent new fiction is general. The authors rarely go beyond the touching up, embellishing or modernizing of old subject-matter. What may be called a stagnation of thought prevails, as though the mind, exhausted after building up the spiritual fabric of the Middle Ages, has sunk into inertia. The poets themselves are aware of this feeling of fatigue." In addition, court poets sometimes worked under constraints which hampered their talent. For example, John Lydgate, whose case Robert Graves calls "instructive and exceptional," produced an extraordinary quantity of poetry to please his superiors, including works such as the *Troy Book* (1412-20), a translation of Guido delle Colonne's 30,000-line *Historia Troiana* (1287), *The Pilgrimage of Man* (1426-30), a translation of Guillaume de Deguileville's 20,000-line *Pèlerinage de la vie humaine,* and *The Fall of Princes* (1431-38), a translation of a French version of Giovanni Boccaccio's 36,000-line *De Casibus Illustrium Virorum* (1355-1374?). Critics have also attributed the formalism of fifteenth-century courtly poetry to Chaucer's supposedly excessive influence. While Thomas Hoccleve and Lydgate in England, and the Scot William Dunbar openly acknowledged their debt to the poet of the *Canterbury Tales* (1386-1400), the issue of just how Chaucerian fifteenth-century poets truly are remains unclear. According to Fox, it is necessary "to determine when the fifteenth-century poets were influenced by Chaucer and when they simply shared with him a common background." For example, as this critic observed, "Chaucer used to be held responsible for the constant recurrence in fifteenth-century verse of such larger rhetorical elements as the spring opening, or the poet's insincere protestations of incompetence. But it has now become clear, especially since the publication of E. R. Curtius's *European Literature and the Latin Middle Ages,* that such *topoi* are part of the very fabric of medieval verse: Chaucer's contribution here was only to reaffirm patterns which already existed. It should be remembered, too, that these patterns are not necessarily pernicious: tedious in the hands of a bad poet, they can be filled with new life in such a poem as *The Kingis Quair*." Another reproach to fifteenth-century poets concerns their alleged inability to understand and reproduce Chaucer's versification, as a result of a confused perception of certain phonetic changes in late Middle English. It "seems incredible," Fox has remarked, "that the disappearance of the [syllabic final] -e, a very gradual phenomenon, could have caused Lydgate, who was born some thirty years before Chaucer's death, to become confused about Chaucer's versification." According to this critic, however, the incongruities of Lydgate's style are not necessarily unintended. An additional argument has been proposed by John Stevens: "It was, surely, absurd to imagine that courtly versifiers lacked even the elementary craft shown in popular 'metrical' poetry like the carol. Wyatt's ballets scan quite effortlessly; the different rhythms encountered in his translated sonnets and psalms cannot, then, be the result of incompetence."

While fifteenth-century poetry remained in the symbolical, allegorical, and stylistic context of medieval literature, it exhibited what some critics view as an unmistakable modern quality. Thus C. S. Lewis, arguing that Lydgate is a more modern love poet than Chaucer, declared that it "is hard to find in Chaucer so near an approach to the lyrical cry as we find in these neglected lines: 'And as I stoode myself aloone upon the Nuwe Yere night/ I prayed unto the frosty moone, with her pale light,/ To go an recomaunde me unto my lady dere./ And erly on the next morrowe, kneeling in my cloos/ I preyed eke the shene sonne, the houre whane he arros,/ To goon also and sey the same in his bemys clere'." Non-courtly poetry is represented by devotional verse, carols, ballads, and popular romances. Some of these forms blend poetry and music, attesting to the glory of fifteenth-century English music, in which Continental writers discerned a characteristic mellifluousness which they termed *contenance angloise*. A typical example is the carol, which truly flourished in the fifteenth century. Often devotional, but not necessarily a Christmas song, the carol, as R. L. Greene defined it, is actually "a song on any subject of uniform stanzas and provided with a burden," or refrain. "The carols," D. J. Grout added, "were not folk songs, but their fresh, angular melodies and lively triple rhythms give them a distinctly English quality." Inspired by the timeless lore of oral poetry, ballads, also enriched by musical accompaniment, retell old stories, usually of a dramatic and romantic nature. Especially popular in the fifteenth century were Robin Hood ballads, which continued a tradition which probably originated in the previous century, and *The Nut Brown Maid,* an outstanding poem celebrating a woman's constancy in love. Less important from a literary point of view but significant as historical documents were the numerous ballads which commemorated battles and various political events.

Drama in the fifteenth century continues the medieval tradition of the allegorical morality, mystery (inspired by Scripture), and miracle play (based on the lives of saints). The morality is the preeminent dramatic form of this period. "While the great wealth of medieval lyric can be drawn on to illustrate moments in the church year and the existence of the individual in it," Stephen Coote has written, "Morality Plays such as the incomplete *Pride of Life, The Castle of Perseverance* (c. 1405-25), *Mankind, Wisdom* (both c. 1460-70) and *Everyman* (c. 1500) present right conduct through dramatized allegory. This takes the form of a *psychomachia* or battle of the vices and virtues, a mode of fundamental importance to the medieval mind." *The Castle of Perseverance* dramatizes humankind's struggle against sin, while *Mankind,* a play known for its popular style and remarkably obscene language, addresses the subject of sloth, or *accidia. Everyman,* inspired by a Dutch morality play, is an allegorical pilgrimage to God, suggesting that only good deeds can assure an individual's salvation after death.

Critics agree that the greatest prose writer of the fifteenth century is Malory, whose prose romance *Le Morte d'Arthur,* derived from French Arthurian romances and the fourteenth-century English alliterative *Morte Arthure,* is an eminently readable retelling of the story of King Arthur. For Graves, Malory's work "remains an enchanted sea for the reader to swim about, delighting in the random beauties of fifteenth-century prose rather than engrossed by the plot." The elegance of Malory's style reflects the maturity of Middle English prose, which had attained a remarkable level of sophistication in the thirteenth century, as evidenced by the writings of Richard Rolle and John Wycliffe. Another key characteristic of fifteenth-century prose is its versatility—attested to by the proliferation of historical, philosophical, scientific, legalistic, and epistolary writings. Though usually devoid of literary value, epistolary prose, exemplified in this period by the *Paston Letters,* is of vital importance to anyone attempting to reconstruct medieval life. Written between approximately 1420 and 1505 by members of a prosperous bourgeois family, the *Paston Letters* faithfully document the vicissitudes of everyday life in a century of violence and political turmoil. Historical prose is represented by John Capgrave, whose *Chronicle* of England up to the year 1417 has been praised for its direct and clear style. Conversely, Reginald Pecock, a theologian, cultivated a labyrinthine style replete with lexical innovations—exemplified by his polemical work *Repressor of over much Blaming of the Clergy* (1455). If "Pecock's style is not an easy one," as R. W. Chambers has written, "there is justification for this want of ease. Pecock's work is a raid into new territory: he strives to conduct in English that kind of philosophical discussion for which Latin had hitherto been regarded as the only proper medium." Sir John Fortescue, the seminal legal and political theorist of fifteenth-century England, also used his native language as an instrument for theoretical discourse, traditionally the domain of Latin, but his prose, unlike Pecock's, is considered a model of clarity.

A period of momentous literary, linguistic, and cultural change, the fifteenth-century was also a time of ambivalence. No one, it seems, expresses this ambivalence more clearly than William Caxton, who literally brought modernity to medieval England by his introduction of printing in 1476, yet nostalgically championed the literature of a bygone era. It is significant, therefore, that Caxton, who published Malory's *Le Morte d'Arthur* on 31 July, 1485, claimed, as Graves has noted, "to be acting on the plea of many nobles and gentlemen who thought that 'King Arthur should be remembered among Englishmen before all other Christian kings'." Indeed, Caxton's enthusiasm for medieval romances symbolizes a desire to immortalize the waning Middle Ages. And if the fifteenth century, to use Huizinga's expression, is the autumn of the Middle Ages, a period presaging a new era, it is also the recapitulation of an enduring tradition. According to Emile Legouis, "In producing prose renderings of the medieval romances, [Caxton] followed the example of the French of the fifteenth century. He thus ensured a longer survival and wider popularity to these romances, which made them accessible to all men. In English, verse had hardly ever embellished them, and, had it not been for the minstrels, they would have fallen into neglect. Prose secured that the stories they enclosed became known. . . . In the chap-books of the Elizabethan period, they kept romance alive in the minds of simple people, awoke those dreams of extraordinary adventure to which many dramatists of the Renascence appealed. . . . By means of these compilations, the Middle Ages were kept from dying altogether, and sank, instead, to deeper and deeper strata of consciousness. Whatever may have been the value of the new works which sprang of the Renascence, the old stories still made the first and the favourite appeal to popular imagination."

BACKGROUND

David Daiches   (essay date 1960)

[A distinguished critic and literary scholar, Daiches wrote numerous studies, including Literature and Society *(1938),* Stevenson and the Art of Fiction *(1951), and* A Critical History of English Literature *(1960). In the following excerpt from the last-named work, he offers an overview of English literature and culture at the end of the Middle Ages.]*

The English literary scene after the death of Chaucer is not inspiring. The fifteenth century, though it saw a significant increase in lay literacy and marked an important stage in the rise of the middle class, suffered from the confusions and demoralization of the long reign of Henry VI and of the Wars of the Roses which followed it. Significant new forces were indeed working in the national culture;

the victory of English over French was now clear and complete, a new class of readers was slowly developing, the new movement of Humanism was beginning to awaken English interest, and social and economic changes were bringing about the transformation of the feudal system into a freer society based on a money economy; but it was some time before these changes were reflected in any important new movement of the mind or the spirit. At the beginning of the fifteenth century it was clear that none of Chaucer's followers had his technical brilliance, his imagination, or his understanding of men, and there was none who could combine the courtly and the bourgeois tradition as Chaucer had done. Fifteenth-century courtly poetry sometimes uses the old modes with a certain freshness: *The Flower and the Leaf*, long wrongly attributed to Chaucer, uses traditional material with charm, giving a new twist to the handling of tapestry figures of allegorical significance by having the narrator a woman and by having the two opposing sets of characters (worshipers of the flower and of the leaf, the idle and the faithful) treat each other with gentle friendliness; and other works of the "Chaucer Apocrypha" have their own appeal, though none is as fresh as *The Flower and the Leaf. The Cuckoo and the Nightingale* is a *débat* using familiar properties; *La Belle Dame sans Merci* (which gave Keats a title) has a lover pleading in vain with a lady whose matter-of-fact indifference to his love almost breaks out of the whole courtly love tradition; *The Assembly of Ladies* tells in heavy allegorical detail of pleadings before the Lady Loyalty. We see here a tradition working itself out.

Thomas Hoccleve and John Lydgate are the best known of Chaucer's followers in England; their lives overlapped Chaucer's, and Hoccleve apparently knew the master personally, yet they seem to belong to a different age. Hoccleve wrote less than Lydgate, but he is the more interesting, for, though there is little to choose between the two on grounds of poetic merit (or lack of it), there are realistic and autobiographical touches in Hoccleve's work that help to enliven it for us. He was a minor civil servant, a connoisseur of London night life and a tavern hunter, perpetually in need of money, seeking noble patrons and writing them begging verse letters. His *Mâle Règle* tells the story of his misspent life and ends with an appeal to the Lord Treasurer to pay him his overdue pension. There are some fairly vivid touches:

> Wher was a gretter maister eek than y
> Or bet aqueyntid at Westmynstre yate
> Among the taverneres namely   [especially]
> And cookes? Whan I cam, eerly or late,
> I pynchid nat at hem in myn acate,   [purchasing]
> Wherfore I was the welcomer algate
> And for a verray gentil man yholde.

And there is the well-known line

> Excesse at borde hath leyd his knyf with me.

His longer works are mechanical and tedious. They include many translations, among them the *Regement of Princes,* compiled from a variety of sources. His religious and didactic works have little value as literature, though they seem to reflect a genuine piety, for all his love of tav-

erns. Technically, his verse is extraordinarily unaccomplished: he is content if he produces the requisite number of syllables in the line, paying no attention to how they are stressed (while Lydgate, on the other hand, is happy if he has the requisite number of stresses and does not seem to care how many or what kind of unstressed syllables he has). He had a genuine admiration for Chaucer, and introduced into the *Regement of Princes* stanzas in praise of him:

> O mayster deer and fadir reverent,
> My mayster Chaucer flour of eloquence,
> Mirrour of fructuous endendement,
> O universel fader in science . . .

Elsewhere he hails him as

> The firste foundere of oure faire langage.

Chaucer, it is clear, became a legend soon after his death; but this does not mean that any of his English admirers had the ability to follow in his footsteps.

Lydgate is almost universally written off as a bore, and though he has occasional felicitous touches there is little reason to disagree with this verdict. Unlike Hoccleve, Lydgate led a cloistered life as a monk, mostly at Bury St. Edmunds, and though this did not prevent him from managing to see a good deal of men and affairs—and certainly did not prevent him from reading widely, for the library at the Benedictine Abbey at Bury was one of the best-stocked in England—he had nothing of Chaucer's gift of turning both his reading and his experience to lively account in his own writing. Over one hundred forty-five thousand lines of his verse survive, including the mammoth *Fall of Princes* (from a French prose version of Boccaccio's *De Casibus Illustrium Virorum*), the almost equally lengthy *Troy-Book* (from Giudo delle Colonne's *Historia Troiana*), several lives of saints (done for different patrons), several translations from the French, and many miscellaneous shorter poems, both secular and religious in subject. There is a deadening lameness in his versification, together with a syntactical looseness, which makes the reading of his longer didactic works a severe penance. Lydgate's were the routine didactic interests of the unadventurous spirits of his time, and we can at least console ourselves with the thought that his work illustrates the early fifteenth-century English mind. He contributed something, too, both to the themes of English literature and to the vocabulary of English. His *Fall of Princes* is the first full-dress collection of "tragedies" (in the medieval sense of stories of falls from high to low estate) of the many that were to influence English thought and literature up to Shakespeare's *Richard III*. His *Dance Macabre* introduced to England (from the French) a theme of great significance in medieval thought and art of the period: Death the leveller, who addresses in turn all classes of men, Pope, Emperor, cardinal, king, and so on down the scale to laborer, friar, child, clerk, and hermit, points the grim moral of a common mortality which is found so often stressed in the fifteenth century. Lydgate added many new words to the English vocabulary, though he rarely employed them with much sensitivity or poetic force; they are mostly polysyllabic words from Latin or French, such as "inexcusable," "credulity," "tolerance," and "adolescence." But what the reader is most conscious of is his frequent use of tag phrases—"sothly to telle," "ther nis namor to say," "as to myn intent," "yiff I shal not lye," et cetera.

Lydgate is at his best in his shorter poems, and in those where the demands of the narrative compel him to some liveliness of detail (and it might be added that his feeling for small children has been noted in his favor). A good example is his tale, "The Churl and the Bird," rendered from the French. The churl has caught the bird and put it in "a praty litel cage"; the bird speaks:

> . . . And though my cage forged were of gold
> And the penacles of byral and cristal,
> I remembre a proverbe said of olde
> Who lesith his fredome in faith he lesith al,
> For I had lever upon a branche smal
> Merely to sing amonge the wodes grene
> Thenne in a cage of silver bright and shene.
>
> Songe and prison han noon accordaunce;
> Trowest thou I wol synge in prisoun?
> Songe procedith of ioye and of pleasaunce
> And prison causith deth and distructioun . . .

But even emotion seeks, in Lydgate, to express itself in didactic or proverbial form.

The professions of literary incompetence made by so many of these fifteenth-century poets represent doubtless a mere fashion; but they spoke more truly than they knew. Among the little surviving verse of Benedict Burgh is a short poem of compliment to Lydgate which begins in this common self-deprecatory vein:

> Nat dremyd I in the mownt of Pernaso,
> ne dranke I nevar at Pegases welle,
> the pale Pirus saw I never also
> ne wist I never where the muses dwelle . . .

John Walton, whose translation of Boethius into English verse shows better metrical control than most of his fifteenth-century contemporaries, begins his prologue in similar strain:

> Insuffishaunce of cunnyng & of wyt,
> Defaut of langage & of eloquence,
> This work fro me schuld have withholden
>   yit . . .

The anonymous author of *The Court of Sapience* (he may have been Stephen Hawes), a long allegorical, didactic poem in two parts, the first dealing with the dispute between Mercy, Peace, Righteousness, and Truth concerning the fate of man and the second a conducted tour of medieval learning, varies the formula somewhat and speaks in livelier accents. He asks Clio to "forge my tonge to glad myn audytours," professing his own deficiencies:

> I knowe my self moost naked in al artes,
> My comune vulgare eke moost interupte,
> And I conversaunte & borne in the partes
> Wher my natyf langage is moost corrupt,
> And wyth most sondry tonges myxt &
>   rupte . . .

The Court of Sapience dates from about 1470: it is more vigorous in expression and competent in metrics than any-

thing by Lydgate, but in theme it represents the uninspired development of the allegorical didactic tradition.

It seems as though the simple story romance, so popular with an earlier generation of Englishmen, had been pushed out by allegory and didacticism. And, with the decay of feudalism and the slow but steady rise of a realistic and iconoclastic bourgeoisie, there was no new source of idealism to revivify the increasingly uninspired and conventional didactic allegory. But by a fruitful coincidence, the last flare-up of chivalry in the courts of Europe, a last Indian summer of knightly ideals in the earlier manner, occurred at the same time that printing came in. Caxton, who had been in Burgundy witnessing this revival at the French-speaking court of the Duke of Burgundy, brought with him (from the Low Countries) the art of printing on his return to England. The revival of interest in the chivalric story romance which accompanied chivalry's final fling was just in time to take advantage of Caxton's imported art; which accounts for the fact that some of the first works printed in England were chivalric stories of the older kind. This revival of interest in romance, though influential, was brief; it was killed in the sixteenth century partly by the new movement of Humanism, which in England in its early phase took a narrow view of romantic tales and, with Roger Ascham, protested against idle stories of chivalry, and partly by the growing bourgeois taste for a more realistic, picaresque kind of story.

The attenuated courtly tradition; satirical, topical, and political verse of little literary merit but of considerable historical interest; didactic, moralistic, and religious writing: these were the three main categories of fifteenth-century English literature, and the third is the largest. The religious lyric, following the types discussed in chapter three, flourished during the period: indeed, most of what has been said of the fourteenth-century lyric applies to the fifteenth century also, though new themes and attitudes begin to make their appearance as the century advanced, and will be discussed later.

That the fifteenth century was a period of transition in England is obvious enough to the political and economic historian. The Wars of the Roses, where the nobility destroyed each other and the middle class rose steadily; William Caxton's introduction of printing into England (Caxton's translation of Raoul Lefèvre's *Le Receuil des Histoires de Troye,* printed by him as *Recuyel of the Histories of Troye* at Bruges in 1474, was the first printed book published in English, and his return to London in 1475 was followed by his printing in 1477 of *Dictes and Sayings of the Philosophers,* the first book printed in England); the gradual impact on English thought of the Humanism of the Renaissance; the establishment of the Tudor monarchy in 1485—these are obvious and significant marks of change. In the literature of the period, however, we see for the most part simply the progressive exhaustion of earlier medieval modes. Yet much that appears at first sight merely to exhibit this exhaustion can be seen on a closer view to be influenced in some degree by new ways of thinking. Stephen Hawes' allegorical romance, *The Pastime of Pleasure,* dedicated to Henry VII in 1506, continues the lame versification and the mechanical allegorizing of Lydgate, with even less notion of the true nature of allegory than his immediate predecessors:

> The light of truoth, I lacke cunnyng to cloke,
> To drawe a curtayne, I dare not to presume
> Nor hyde my matter, with a misty smoke
> My rudenes cunnyng, dothe so sore consume
> Yet as I may, I shall blowe out a fume
> To hyde my mynde, underneth a fable
> By covert coloure, well and probable.

It is a curious view indeed that the function of allegory is to obscure truth. Yet this "smokey," didactic, allegorical romance, telling (in first person narrative) of the pursuit and eventual attainment by the hero, Graunde Amour, of La Bell Pucell shows some interesting new features. The hero, encouraged by Fame (a lady) and accompanied by Governaunce and Grace (two greyhounds), receives an elaborate education in the Tower of Doctrine before engaging on the knightly adventures which culminate in his marriage to La Bell Pucell. Here we have the union of the active life and the contemplative life, which had hitherto been sharply distinguished in medieval thought, following St. Augustine's influential statement in *The City of God* that "the study of wisdom is either concerning action or contemplation, and thence assumes two several names, active and contemplative, the active consisting in the practice of morality in one's life, and the contemplative in penetrating into the abstruse causes of nature, and the nature of divinity." The knight and the clerk are united in Graunde Amour, representing a new ideal of lay education; further, the hero's love for La Bell Pucell is chaste and Christian and leads to marriage—something quite impossible in the earlier courtly love tradition. The interest—one might say the obsession—with education is characteristic of the age; the combination of the didactic romance with the romance of knightly adventure in a context of education looks forward to Spenser's *Faerie Queene*. And at the end, after the hero has married and lived happily ever after, he addresses the reader from the grave in the one memorable stanza of the poem:

> O mortall folk, you may beholde and se
> How I lye here, somtyme a myghty knyght.
> The ende of Joye and all prosperite
> Is dethe at last through his course and myght;
> After the day there cometh the derke nyght,
> For though the day be never so longe
> At last the belles ryngeth to evensonge.

The Seven Deadly Sins, and Fame, Time, and Eternity, all play their part in the final pageant, which shows a certain grandeur of conception in spite of the technical inadequacy of the verse.

How dismal—to the point of being positively comic—the verse can become is illustrated by the following passage, describing the hero's education in grammar at the hands of Dame Doctrine:

> . . . To whom she answered, right gently agayne,
> Saiyng alwaye, that a nowne substatyve
> Might stande without helpe of an adjectyve.
>
> The latyne worde, whiche that is referred
> Unto a thing, whiche is substantiall

For a nowne substantive is well averred,
And with a gender is declinall.
So all the eyght partes in generall
Are latyn wordes, annexed proprelye
To every speache, for to speake formally.

This intolerable doggerel is representative of a whole area of late medieval English didactic verse. Yet not only does *The Pastime of Pleasure* have its moments of perception and even of eloquence; it is also a work of considerable historical importance in that it illustrates an attitude toward love, education, and the relation of the active to the contemplative life which foreshadows both the courtesy books of the Renaissance and the use of romance made by Spenser. Hawes saw himself, however, as a follower rather than as a pioneer, and he mentions Gower, Chaucer, and Lydgate (in that order) as his masters, listing the major works of the latter two. He seems utterly unaware of Chaucer's superiority to the other two, and Lydgate is especially praised for his eloquence:

> O master Lydgate, the most dulcet sprying
> Of famous rethoryke, wyth ballade royall,
> The chefe originall of my learnyng,
> What vayleth it, on you for to call
> Me for to ayde, nowe in especiall,
> Sythen your bodye is now wrapte in chest.
> I pray God to give your soule good rest.

Hawes' other allegorical-didactic romance, *The Example of Virtue,* is shorter and less interesting, and few other late medieval exercises in this mode have any special appeal. William Nevill's *Castell of Pleasure* (1518) is worth mentioning only because its printer, Robert Copland, himself (like Caxton) a translator and dabbler in letters, introduces a dialogue between the printer and the author at the beginning of the poem, and because, in its mechanical use of the allegorical formulas, it sinks to probably record depths of dullness. Nowhere is the popular medieval *ubi sunt* theme handled so flatly:

> Where is Tully, whiche had pryncypalyte
> Over all oratours in parfyte rethoryke?
> Where be all the foure doctours of dyvynyte?
> Where is Arystotyll for all his phylosophy & logyke?

Alexander Barclay (*ca.* 1475-1552) is a transitional figure of some importance. His *Ship of Fools* (1509) provided a new metaphor for English satire. It is a rendering of the *Narrenschiff* of the German Sebastian Brant through the Latin translation of Locher, a Swiss, but Barclay's own comments expand the poem to many times the length of his original. Satire, of course, was not unknown in the earlier Middle Ages; the *fabliau* tradition, as we have seen, is largely satirical, and Jean de Meun, Chaucer, and Langland have each his own satirical vein. The conception of the important people of the world as a collection of fools—courtiers, ecclesiastics, scholars, and merchants alike—seems to have become popular in the later Middle Ages, and Brant's idea of putting them all in a boat sailing off to Narragonia gave a new liveliness to the whole conception. It is a development of the older handling of the seven deadly sins, and the shift of attention from moral evil to intellectual folly is significant of a new temper in European civilization. *The Ship of Fools* looks forward to Erasmus' *Praise of Folly* as much as it looks backward to the theme of the seven deadly sins. Its interest is more in the contemporary social scene than with moral types, and this again marks an important development. Barclay's rhyme royal stanzas are pedestrian enough in movement, but the self-characterization of the representatives of different kinds of folly provides some vivid glimpses of the society of the time. Satire, so long directed against ecclesiastical abuses, is beginning to turn to wider themes, including life at Court (increasingly important with the establishment of the new national state with its centralized monarchy) and intellectual fashions. The satiric stream widens and deepens after Barclay, with Skelton's *Bowge of Court* and *Speak, Parrot* concentrating on the contemporary scene. The changes which Renaissance Court life and the first effects of Renaissance Humanism brought with them stimulated conservative minds to angry satire, and while the attack on folly is itself a Humanist theme, attacks on Humanism as well as on other novelties are made by angry conservatives. Indeed, angry conservatives have always produced the greatest satire, from Aristophanes to Swift, and while neither Barclay nor Skelton can be regarded as a great satirist they do share the great satirist's sense of outrage at what contemporary man is making of himself.

The pastoral also becomes at this time a vehicle for satire in English; it comes to replace the dream as the commonest kind of machinery for satirical as well as many other purposes. Barclay produced five eclogues, three translated (with many expansions) from the *Miserae Curialium* of Pope Pius II (Aeneas Sylvius Piccolomini) and two from the late fifteenth- and early sixteenth-century Italian poet, Baptista Mantuanus, known as Mantuan in England where he was much admired for his Latin pastorals in the sixteenth and seventeenth centuries. Thus a new breath from classical literature comes, though indirectly, into English literature, the first of very many such. The use of the pastoral for satire of Court life, urban life, ecclesiastical corruption, and other abuses of the time, as well as to discuss literary questions, established itself early in the Renaissance; Barclay is the first English writer to use a device, already common in Italy, which was to be developed significantly by succeeding generations of English poets, notably by Spenser in his *Shepherd's Calendar*. And as *The Shepherd's Calendar* is in some sense both the manifesto and the first-fruits of the "new" English poetry, the pastoral tradition is clearly of prime importance in English literature. . . . (pp. 128-36)

John Skelton (ca. 1460-1529) is the most interesting and original of all the transitional poets who, while considering themselves in the tradition of Chaucer, Gower, and Lydgate, are in fact Janus-faced, looking both toward the medieval past and to the Renaissance future. As a satirist, Skelton attacks the abuses of courtly life, new fashions in thought, religion and behavior, personal enemies, Scots, and aspects of the contemporary scene which he found annoying. *The Bowge of Court* is a satire of Court life in the traditional rhyme royal stanza, combining traditional medieval allegorical figures with the ship of fools device, the characters being sometimes allegorical personages and sometimes lively representatives of the contemporary scene. Less traditional in form and content is *Speak, Par-*

rot, a bubbling satirical piece mostly in rhyme royal but with some parts in other meters; the poet speaks through the bird in a characteristic mixture of bitterness and clowning. But *Colin Clout* and *Why come ye not to Court* represent his most characteristic and original satirical vein. The verse here is that short two-beat line which has become known as "Skeltonics"; the poems move with breathless abandon from point to point, highly personal in tone, deliberately discursive in progression, mingling fierce abuse, clowning humor, and bitter irony. Latin tags and even whole passages in rhymed Latin couplets, echoes or parodies of the Church liturgy or of the arguments of the schoolmen, are sprinkled freely among the wild and whirling verses. The life, the abandon, the high spirits, the reckless vitality of these pieces make them utterly unlike anything that English literature had yet produced. In *The Book of Philip Sparrow* he uses a similar technique to lament the loss of a young girl's pet sparrow: the lament is put into the mouth of the girl, and ends with Skelton's own tribute to the girl's charm and beauty. Its parody of the Office for the Dead and other aspects of the Latin liturgy of the Church is done with a cheerful recklessness reminiscent of the goliardic literature of the Middle Ages. The verse itself is crudely accentual—whether it derives from the breakup of a longer line or from medieval Latin poetry or from another source cannot be precisely determined—but it moves with extraordinary speed and vigor:

> Somtyme he wolde gaspe
> Whan he sawe a waspe;
> A fly or a gnat,
> He wolde flye at that
> And prytely he wold pant
> Whan he saw an ant;
> Lorde, how he wolde pry
> After the butterfly!
> Lorde, how he wolde hop
> After the gressop!
> And whan I sayd, Phyp, Phyp,
> Than he wold lepe and skyp,
> And take me by the lyp.
> Alas, it wyll me slo,
> That Phillyp is gone me fro!
>   *Si in-i-qui-ta-tes,*
> Alas, I was evyll at ease!
>   *De pro-fun-dis cla-ma-vi,*
> Whan I sawe my sparrowe dye!

The color and life of Skelton's most characteristic verse is perhaps best seen in *The Tunning of Elinor Rumming*, a remarkable description of an alewife and the goings-on in her alehouse:

> Come who so wyll
> To Elynour on the hyll,
> Wyth, Fyll the cup, fyll,
> And syt there by styll,
> Erly and late:
> Thyther cometh Kate,
> Cysly, and Sare,
> With theyr legges bare,
> And also theyr fete
> Hardely full unswete;
> Wyth theyr heles dagged,
> Theyr kyrtelles all to-iagged,
> Theyr smockes all to-ragged,

Wyth tytters and tatters,
Brynge dysshes and platters,
Wyth all theyr myght runnynge
To Elynour Rummynge,
To have of her tunnynge:
She leneth them of the same,
And thus begynneth the game.

His *Garland of Laurel* is an elaborate set piece in praise of himself: Fame and Pallas discuss his qualifications; Gower, Chaucer, and Lydgate hail him; a group of noble ladies make a laurel wreath with which to crown him. The incidental lyrics addressed to these ladies are in a new vein of lyrical tenderness, notably that addressed to Margery Wentworth:

With margerain jentyll,
  The flowre of goodlyhede,
Enbrowdred the mantill
  Is of your maydenhede . . .

Magnificence is a morality play with allegorical characters, showing how Magnificence is deceived and undone by vices, conquered by Adversity, and finally redeemed by Goodhope and Perseverance. It is aimed at Wolsey, but also has its general application.

Skelton moved in a Humanist atmosphere without fully realizing it; his attire was conservative in intention but in fact revolutionary in unconscious implication. His fiercely individual temperament, the vigor which he infused into his rough accentual verse, his ambiguous relation with the courts of Henry VII and Henry VIII, his attacks both on Church abuses and on radical reformers like Wyclif and Luther, his bitter feuds with so many of his contemporaries, his strange mixtures of anger and tenderness, of self-conceit and moral indignation, of prophetic elevation and low abuse, show a highly individual temperament coping in a strongly individual way with some of the bewildering crosscurrents in the civilization of his day. His lively and unpolished verse and his violently personal manner attracted English poets in the 1920's and 1930's who were looking for a style in which to express similar reactions, and Pope's verdict of "beastly Skelton" has in recent times been enthusiastically reversed.

Meanwhile, the revival of interest in feudal ideals which, paradoxically but understandably, accompanied the final decay of feudalism in England, produced in the prose Arthurian tales of Sir Thomas Malory the greatest of all its monuments. Malory, who appears to have been a mid-fifteenth-century knight of lawless behavior who wrote his stories in prison, turned, first the English alliterative romance known as *Morte Arthure,* and then a variety of French romances about Arthur's knights, into a series of tales of Arthur and his knights in which the ideals of practical chivalry replaced the sentimental and doctrinal elements which figure so prominently in his French sources. He cut his way through the tangle of complexly interwoven tales, fitted together in pieces like a Chinese puzzle, with which his originals so often presented him, and, to use Caxton's term, "reduced" his material to a coherent group of related stories in which incidents followed each other with less interruption and the emphasis was on action and motive rather than on sentiment or doctrine.

Caxton published the work in 1485, giving it a false unity by applying the title of the last group of stories—"The Morte Arthure Saunz Gwerdon"—to the whole collection. The discovery in 1934 of the Winchester MS of Malory's stories makes it clear that "Le Morte Darthur" is Caxton's title for the whole, not Malory's. (pp. 136-39)

Malory's prose style, which moves with a simple cogency always perfectly adapted to the narrative line which he is developing, is not easily placed in the history of English prose. He is outside the tradition of English devotional prose which continues from Anglo-Saxon times to the Tudor and Elizabethan translations of the Bible. He begins by capturing something of the rhythms, and using some of the alliterative devices, of Middle English alliterative verse as represented by the verse romance *Morte Arthure;* he simplifies, tightens up, adds weight and precision and, at the same time, a conversational flow. He learns as he writes, and the later books show a fine ease in dialogue together with a dignity and eloquence which derive at least in part from the heroic element in the *Morte Arthure.* The flow is simple enough, marked by such conjunctions as "and," "for," "but," "then," and "therefore." The underlying rhythms provide a quiet emotional ground swell to the narrative; the dialogue is lively and often captures the individual quality of a character; the accounts of action rise and fall with a restrained epic movement which has quiet gravity without magniloquence. The result of it all is an impressive summing up of the "Matter of Britain" as seen through the perspective of the Indian summer of the Age of Chivalry; excessive sentiment, the pure devotional note, and over-abundant narrative complication are equally pruned away, and Malory gives us the Arthurian stories set to an uncomplicated chivalric morality. But the epic note does not really belong to these nostalgic stories of a lost way of life; the defects of the code are manifest in the actions which are based on it, and in the end the heroic key is modulated into elegy.

It is paradoxical that William Caxton, who brought the art of printing to England, should have been so interested in chivalry and old romance. But the late fifteenth and early sixteenth century was a transitional period in which all sorts of paradoxical things were likely to happen. The work of Barclay and Hawes showed both old medieval modes and new Humanist influences. Humanism itself was one element in that complex movement we call the Renaissance, a movement whose reality has recently been questioned but which certainly was real, though its manifestations were not as sudden nor its causes as simple as was once thought. The world of medieval Christendom, set against the militant Moslem world, which bounded it on the south and east, had a significant religious and cultural uniformity; its intellectual and imaginative boundaries were limited, the scholar moving within the limits of "Latinitas," the philosopher and the scientist working deductively on truths taken from authority, the poet rendering his vision of past and present through notions of order and significance common to the whole of medieval Europe. The Holy Roman Empire, we know, was never more than an ideal, but the ideal represented a view of history and of society that lay behind most of the superficially differing attitudes which intelligent men in the Middle Ages expressed. The shift from the view of the Roman Empire as divinely ordained machinery for the Christianizing of the Western world to a view of the pagan culture of Greece and Rome as something more civilized, more splendid, more fully illustrative of what man can make of himself by cultivation of the arts and sciences than any subsequent phase of history, represented a real revolution in thought. And while it would be wrong to see this shift as simply the rapid result of the fall of Constantinople to the Turks in 1453, with the consequent emigration of Greek-speaking Christians from the Eastern Empire to Italy—for it was a slow process that had been going on since long before 1453—it would be ridiculous to assert that because the movement was gradual it did not take place. (pp. 141-42)

Medieval Christendom established itself in the chaos that followed the collapse of the Roman Empire; it took over what it could from the Roman world, compromised where it had to with both old pagan and new barbarian, and achieved a synthesis in which the thought and institutions of the classical world played a certain limited part. Humanism, that movement which represented the desire to recover the purest ideals of Greek and Latin expression and to assimilate the most civilized aspects of classical thought, was essentially an attempt to get behind the medieval synthesis, to approach the original sources of classical culture directly, not through the medium of clerical "Latinitas." Italy had known this movement since the fourteenth century, and long before it reached England it had exerted its influence on Italian literature. North of the Alps the Humanist movement became more directly involved in religious and moral questions. The ambitious and ubiquitous machinery of the medieval Church was ceasing to function effectively; satire of clerical abuses, amusedly ironical in Chaucer, soon swelled to an angry and bitter chorus, and this in turn encouraged the *avant garde* to turn to the secular thought of the classical world for guidance and enlightenment. That secular thought, touched with the moral earnestness of Christian protest against abuses of Christian institutions, produced a school of Christian Humanists which was to include reformers who remained within the Roman Catholic fold as well as Protestants. It must be remembered, too, that the "New Learning," as it was often called in the sixteenth century, encouraged the study of Hebrew as well as of Latin and Greek, and that the great German Humanist Reuchlin was even more important for the development of Hebrew studies in Europe than the great Dutch Humanist Erasmus was for the study of Greek. Hebrew and Greek, the languages of the Old and New Testaments respectively, were essential tools in any new approach to the Bible. If pre-Protestant reforming thought demanded vernacular Bible translation, it was the new scholarship of the Humanists that eventually made that translation possible from the original sources. Thus Humanism in spite of itself was drawn into new religious movements. (p. 143)

The political genius of Henry VII, whose accession to the throne in 1485 after his victory over Richard III brought to an end the Wars of the Roses and ushered in the new Tudor despotism, enabled him to win the loyalty of merchant, professional man, gentry, and nobility alike and so to maintain a political stability in the country of which it was in desperate need, and at his death to leave a secure throne to his son. Henry VII thought of himself as a medieval monarch, re-establishing a medieval monarchy, and did not see the implications of his own reign. He was no friend to Humanists. But with the accession of Henry VIII in 1509, the Humanists in England had their chance, and the early years of his reign were years of promise and excitement for English culture. The scene changed in the latter part of Henry's reign, when Henry's insistence on divorce from Catherine of Aragon, his break with Rome, his suppression of the monasteries and the consequent destruction of so many English art treasures, and his assumption of the supreme headship of the English Church lost him the approval of such a moderate Catholic Humanist as Sir Thomas More, whose execution for high treason in 1535 marks the end of Henry's alliance with the most attractive elements of contemporary Humanism and arrested the Humanist movement in England for a generation. More, scholar, statesman, diplomat, political theorist (the ideal commonwealth described in his Latin work *Utopia* represents a Humanist rather than a Christian conception of the state), and patron of the arts, represented all that was best in the new ideal of culture. His piety led him to seek to purify, rather than radically to reorganize, the Church, and he remained devoted to papal supremacy; like Erasmus, he wished to remove corruption without changing theological doctrine or ecclesiastical structure, but unlike the Dutch Humanist he became involved in practical affairs to his own undoing. He remains the glory and the tragedy of Henry VIII's reign.

The "New Learning" had made itself felt in England as early as the fifteenth century, but these early manifestations left no permanent mark. John Tiptoft, Earl of Worcester, William Grey (later Bishop of Ely), John Free of Balliol College, Oxford, and John Gunthorpe (later Dean of Wells) all visited Italy in the latter part of the fifteenth century and returned with Latin manuscripts which they left to Oxford college libraries. But it was not until the introduction of Greek learning into England that a more permanent enthusiasm for classical scholarship was aroused. Thomas Linacre, William Grocyn (who returned from Italy in 1490 to teach Greek at Oxford), and William Latimer, put Greek studies on a firm footing at Oxford, while at Cambridge the teaching of Greek by Erasmus from 1510 to 1513 gave a great impetus to Greek studies. John Colet, who had studied in Paris and Italy and was a friend of Erasmus, lectured on the New Testament at Oxford at the turn of the century and in 1510, then Dean of St. Paul's, endowed the Cathedral school of St. Paul's to bring the "New Learning" into secondary education. Richard Croke, who had studied Greek at Oxford with Grocyn and then studied at Paris and lectured at several continental universities, returned to Cambridge in 1518, where, the following year, he was appointed reader in Greek. He was succeeded by Sir Thomas Smith, and in 1540, when five new regius chairs were founded by Henry, Smith got that of civil law, while Sir John Cheke became professor of Greek. Cheke (hailed by Milton in one of his sonnets as having "taught Cambridge and King Edward Greek") later became tutor to the young King Edward VI: he did more than any other single person to make Greek studies popular in England.

The history of scholarship becomes important for the history of literature at this time because the new classical scholarship meant the establishment of direct contact with the achievements of classical culture and this in turn meant not only new ideals in literary style but new concepts of civilization and a sense that the Middle Ages had represented a vast deflection of progress of the arts and sciences off their true course. Further, the recovery of Greek science—which was one of the great achievements of Humanism, far too little realized—meant that Renaissance science could begin where Greek science had left off. Astronomy, physics, and medicine profited by this renewed contact with Greek thought: the scientific discoveries of the sixteenth and seventeenth centuries were made possible by the work of the fifteenth-century Humanists. In the Middle Ages, Greek science (and, indeed, much Greek philosophy) was only available in fragmentary and often distorted form through Latin translations from the Arabic, for the Moslem world were earlier heirs of Greek thought; now it became freely and directly available. No wonder that Renaissance thinkers came to regard the Middle Ages simply as an obstacle standing between them and the pure knowledge of the classical world. The ages of "Gothic superstition," which was all the seventeenth and, still more, the early and middle eighteenth century could see in the Middle Ages, were so regarded because they blocked the light of classical culture. (pp. 144-45)

David Daiches, "The End of the Middle Ages," in his A Critical History of English Literature, Vol. I, *The Ronald Press Company, 1960, pp. 128-45.*

Emile Legouis   (essay date 1924)

[*Legouis was an eminent French historian of English literature whose books include* Geoffroy Chaucer *(1910;* Geoffrey Chaucer, *1913),* Edmund Spenser *(1923;* Spenser, *1926), and the acclaimed* Histoire de la litterature anglaise *(1924;* A History of English Literature, *1926), written with Louis Cazamian. In the following excerpt from the last-named work, Legouis provides a concise synopsis of English literature in the period between Chaucer's death and the Renaissance.*]

England took two centuries to produce a poet worthy to rank with Chaucer. Nothing better proves his genius than the powerlessness of the succeeding generations to equal or even to understand him, a fact the more striking because all the poets knew him and rendered him homage. When, however, they believe themselves to be imitating him they do no more than follow his inferior work, in which he does not surpass the average level of his time. They leave on one side the poems in which he rose above his contemporaries. Most of them barely reach the plane of Gower. Criticism in the fifteenth and even in the sixteenth century was so incompetent that it constantly placed Chaucer and Gower together, and Lydgate, that retrograde and prolix disciple of Chaucer, beside the two of them.

The years from 1400 to the Renascence were a period disinherited of literature. Several causes of this destitution may be discovered, but none which is satisfying save the fact that no writer of genius was born during these long years. The only excuse for the poverty applies to poetry alone. It is that, in the transition to the analytical modern English which was in course, the last inflections were disappearing. The result was that Chaucer's accurate and sure versification ceased to be understood soon after his death. When the final *e* had become entirely mute, Chaucer's line, badly read and transcribed, and later badly printed, seemed to be variable and irregular, to contain a differing number of syllables and irregularly distributed accents. His successors, whose ear was imperfect, were not offended by this lack of rhythm, but felt that it authorised them to licence in their own versemaking. The English verse-form was thrown off its balance, and definitely recovered a sure rhythm only with Spenser.

This cause of decline was one which an harmonious poet would have charmed away, as indeed the poets of Scotland did exorcise it. Other causes of decadence, drawn from history, might be revealed by diligent search. The fatal effects on art of the Wars of the Roses (1454-83) might, for instance, be exaggerated, although this terrible civil conflict covered only a fourth of the vast desert space of time. Before this war, England under Henry V. experienced a time of military glory which recalled and exceeded the victories of Edward III., and the finest works of the fourteenth century had appeared during the deplorable and humiliating reign of Richard II. But it came to pass that neither triumphs nor disasters could inspire literature. Miserly Nature created only imitators and reiterators of outworn themes. The sense of the beautiful seems to have died with the sense of life and of reality. Contact with the continent, once so fruitful, could not revive the flagging literary impulse. Contact hardly existed except with France, herself disabled. Italy, which Chaucer had revealed, remained forgotten for a whole century.

England suffered not only checked progress, but also retrogression. Literature resumed its course as though the *Canterbury Tales* had never been written. The decline was immediate. Its signs appeared even in those who knew Chaucer, were near him and called him master, in Occleve and Lydgate.

Both were aware of his superiority. It is touching to see how Occleve represents himself as the stupid scholar of an excellent master:

> My derë maister,—God his soulë quyte,—
> And fader, Chaucer, fayne wold have me taught,
> But I was dulle, and lerned lyte or naught.

Occleve, dull indeed, saw in Chaucer only an all-wise philosopher, a pious poet, almost a saint. Chaucer's humour escaped him. Lydgate is more discriminating, for while he agrees with Occleve that no poet was left "that worthy was his ynkehorne for to holde," he was conscious of Chaucer's wit, and shows his indulgence, not unmixed with scepticism, for verses submitted to him by his youthful disciples. But neither Lydgate nor Occleve was capable of continuing Chaucer's work.

Thomas Occleve (1370?-1454?) is the author of a *Letter of Cupid* long ascribed to Chaucer. It is a translation of the *Epistre du Dieu d'amours* of Christine de Pisan, which was a reply to Jean de Meung's sarcasms against women. It recalls the *Legende of Goode Women* in theme, but it substitutes reasonings for imagination, humour and life.

In his *La Male Règle de T. Occleve,* which is a sort of confession, the poet informs us that he led a debauched youth, and that none was better known than he to the keepers of taverns and cook-shops in Westminster. The story of his irregularities entails some descriptions of London which are historically interesting although they have no value as poetry.

His principal work is the *De Regimine Principum,* written in 1411-12 to win the favour of the Prince of Wales, afterwards Henry V. It is a series of lessons on conduct, imitated from the Latin work of the same name which the Roman Ægidius wrote for Philip the Fair. Dissertations, historical examples and tales are used to inculcate the lessons. The whole is clear, fluent and sufficiently correctly versified, but the intellectual and artistic weakness is reminiscent rather of the didactic Gower than of Chaucer.

John Lydgate (1373?-1450?) has the distinction of being the most voluminous poet of the fifteenth century and even of all the Middle Ages in England. About 140,000 lines of verse, authentically his, are extant. This Benedictine monk of Bury St. Edmunds was principally an indefatigable translator and compiler. His longest poems are the *Storie of Thebes* and *Troye-Book,* which retell the famous romances, the *Falls of Princes,* adapted from the Latin of Boccaccio, the *Temple of Glas,* a heavy allegory of love, the *Pilgrimage of the Life of Man,* translated from Guillaume de Deguileville, and some lives of saints, those of Saint Edmund, Saint Margaret, Our Lady and others.

Lydgate's retrograde tendency is striking. He reverts in his *Troye-Book* to the original story, whence Boccaccio and Chaucer, in *Il Filostrato* and *Troylus and Criseyde,* had extracted the dramatic essence. He has forgotten that Chaucer took the best of his *Falls of Princes* for his Monk's Tale, and ironically ignored the rest, that Chaucer caused a Nun to relate the life of a saint with all its marvels, and thus disclaimed responsibility for it, and that he wearied of the allegory of his *Hous of Fame,* much as it exceeded the *Temple of Glas* in animation and picturesqueness. But no example could stay Lydgate's flow of words.

With Lydgate decomposition overtook English verse. He admits that he "toke none hede nouther of shorte nor longe," that is of accentuated and unaccentuated syllables, a candid confession which excludes the possibility of blaming copyists for the irregularities of his verse.

Much read and much admired by his contemporaries, who were grateful to him for telling so many stories, and telling them with a certain briskness, it is long since Lydgate has been disturbed except by courageous specialists. The small number of his verses which are still read are those extracted, as in an anthology, by Warton from his *Lyf of Our Lady,* or a few short pieces, religious and secular, a few fables, and, especially, *London Lickpenny,* which hymns with some liveliness the griefs of a countryman suing for justice in London. Unfortunately Lydgate's authorship of this, the most popular of the poems ascribed to him, is uncertain.

Here and there, especially in the most Chaucerian of his poems, the *Complaint of the Black Knight,* there are pleasant descriptions, but in spite of them we ask whether this Benedictine ever had time to lift his eyes from his books and papers and look at nature. It is certainly from books that he seems to have taken all his verses which speak of nature.

Much more attractive than the works of Occleve and Lydgate are certain short poems of which the authors are unknown or uncertainly known, and which were long attributed to Chaucer, so that they are included in many editions of his works. A study of their versification and language has, however, proved that they belong to the fifteenth, a few of them even to the sixteenth, century.

A translation of Alain Chartier's *Belle Dame sans Merci,* made by Sir Richard Ros about 1450, is negligible. It dilutes the French octosyllabic lines into the heroic metre, filling them out with expletives and padding, and the result has no merit but correctness of rhythm. *The Cuckoo and the Nightingale* (1403), now restored to Sir Thomas Clanvowe, who knew Chaucer, is, however, an agreeable poem, gracefully relating an argument between the two birds. Its rhythm is light and rapid, and its well-turned and pure language recalls both the *Parlement of Foules* and the prologue to the *Legende of Goode Women.* It is true that the charm of these three hundred lines is in the detail, for the conception—the debate between love and chastened experience—is not new. It goes back to the thirteenth-century debate between the *Owl and the Nightingale.*

The prologue of the *Legende of Goode Women* also inspired a charming allegory, the *Flower and the Leaf,* which was modernised by Dryden, who took it for Chaucer's. But Chaucer certainly did not write these disjointed verses, and they are now admitted to be the probable work of an unknown lady of the middle fifteenth century. The author reproduces the debate between the flower and the leaf to which Chaucer made only passing allusion.

The Leaf symbolises work and the serious and useful life, the Flower frivolous leisure. It is, however, possible to disregard the moral of this poem, and be charmed by the delicious opening descriptions of spring and nature, richer and less restrained than those of Chaucer. There are pretty effects of light and shade in the oak-wood to which the lady who cannot sleep resorts one spring day. There she sees appear, first the ladies and knights of the Leaf, dazzling in their pearls and ornaments or clad in gilded armour, and all crowned with laurel chaplets, who seat themselves beneath an oak. From another side there enter an equally sumptuous company of knights and ladies wearing flowery chaplets, who engage in a merry dance. It is all artificial, but the colour and brilliancy are delightful. A storm supervenes, and the followers of the Flower are drenched, their adornments spoilt. The queen gives them shelter and restores their beauty, and then all disappear.

This poem, like the one noticed before it, marks if not an advance on Chaucer's work, yet a difference from it. It is less substantial, real and humorous, but it has some added lightness, agility and airiness, and a new dewy quality. Although the fiction of a dream has been abandoned, the poem is more purely dreamy than its predecessors. This is, assuredly, the most exquisite product of the fifteenth century.

The *Court of Love* is a less freshly coloured poem, but one which is more mischievously witty, shows greater power of characterisation and has a surer rhythm. It is the one of these poems which might best be claimed for Chaucer, had it not the "gilded" style which hints at "rhetoriqueurs." It is, in point of fact, the furthest removed from him in date, recent criticism having ascribed it to the first half of the sixteenth century. The author, who calls himself "Philogenet, of Cambridge Clerk," loses his way in the palace of Cytherea, where Admetus and Alcestis are vice-regents. Philabone, a lady of the court, informs him of the rules of the place, and shows him the persons who have obeyed or broken the laws of love. Among the latter are such as have deliberately refused to love and are now tormented by regrets. The poet enters the service of the fair Lady Rosial, who at first treats him harshly, but becomes gracious at the entreaty of Pity. The poem is concluded by a choir of birds, of whom each one intones a beautiful hymn of the Church.

Were this poem not too imitative, and did not "Philogenet" rather preserve acquired qualities than add to them or transform them, the fifteen hundred lines of his *Court of Love* would redeem the sterility of this impoverished time.

To imitate was then the rule. Langland's imitators matched Chaucer's. As early as the extreme end of the fourteenth century, an unknown author wrote the *Crede of Piers Plowman,* a vigorous satire against friars of all orders. At an unknown date the Ploughman's Tale, which Chaucer had not time to write, was annexed to the *Canterbury Tales,* serving as a vehicle for the grievances of some Lollard. There is a whole series of fairly mediocre poems, alliterative or other, which are evidence of the continued popularity, well into the sixteenth century, of the great fourteenth-century satire.

They occur both before and after the Wars of the Roses. When, after this long period of sanguinary civil conflict which suspended all literary activity, poetry reappeared in the reign of the first Tudor sovereign, Henry VII., its languor and weariness and its unrhythmic verse are strangely reminiscent of Occleve and Langland. Yet, when the nausea produced by the repetition of so many old characteristics and old faults has been overcome, it is possible to discern in it vague signs of the coming Renascence.

The mediocre poet Stephen Hawes (1475-1530) illustrates this point. He is yet another of the allegorists, but, while he is too much an echo of the past, he also feebly heralds Spenser. When the Wars of the Roses destroyed almost the whole of English chivalry, they relegated the old chivalrous poetry to a dreamlike past. The attempts to revive it which were made at court did no more than reconstruct an empty show, for the soul of this poetry had gone. It had become imaginative material, almost as unreal as allegorical scenes and personages. In compensation, however,

chivalry had acquired the prestige which belongs to the remote, and the melancholy which attaches to regret, both elements of romanticism. It is only this vaguely romantic atmosphere which gives some interest to the languishing platitudes and uncadenced verses of Hawes. He complains that no one but himself in his generation cultivated true English poetry. So neglected was it that his king, Henry VII., reverted to an old precedent, and made a Frenchman, Bernard André of Toulouse, his poet laureate. Hawes, who acknowledged as his masters the trinity of Gower, Chaucer and Lydgate, and especially Lydgate, is like a ghost from the past. He writes allegories according to the formula of the *Roman de la Rose,* and, like Spenser, complicates it by the addition of chivalrous elements. Learned and didactic, he rejects all poetry which does not enclose a lesson.

He anticipates Spenser in that the subject of his principal works is the fashioning of man, by discipline, to an ideal of virtue. In his *Example of Vertu* (1503-4), he relates the allegory of a youth led by Discretion or Reason who finally marries fair Purity, the daughter of the King of Love. So long is the road he travels, so many his obstacles and so fearful the monsters he must slay, that he is sixty years old when he reaches his goal, and there is nothing better left for him to do than to ascend straight to heaven with his beloved.

Hawes's chief work, the *Pastime of Pleasure,* or *Historie of Graunde Amoure and La Belle Pucel* (1505-6), has a like plan. His aim in it is to exemplify a transcendent education, to show by what degrees of study and prowess perfection can be reached.

Graunde Amoure, the hero of the poem who tells his own story, relates that after falling asleep in a flowery valley he sees the Lady Fame appear to him. She tells that La Belle Pucel dwells in the magic tower of Music, but that giants bar the way thither. After serving a long apprenticeship to Ladies Grammar, Logic and Rhetoric, who constitute the Trivium, and Arithmetic, Music, Geometry and Astronomy, who are the Quadrivium, and after having slain the giants with his sword Clara Prudence, Graunde Amoure finally attains to La Belle Pucel, marries her, grows old and dies. Time writes his epitaph in the only lines of Hawes which still live in men's memory:

> For though the daye be never so long,
> At last the belle ringeth to evensong.

In general, Hawes's style, sometimes aggrandised by Latinised words, sometimes entangled by awkward constructions, is among the worst known to English poetry. Never did poetry in English sink to lower depths of the prosaic than when Lady Grammar explained the nature of a noun to her pupil. The verses on the garden of Greek roots and on cooking recipes are much better than these.

Barclay and Skelton, the two last writers of verse who are in the mediæval tradition, at least show some novelty of subject or manner.

Alexander Barclay (1474-1552), a Dominican, careful of doctrine, morals and orthodoxy, and a good Latinist, is hardly more than a translator, yet a free translator who adds matter of his own to his original. He is also the first of his nation to have come across a subject of German origin. His *Ship of Fools* is a translation made in 1509 from the Swabian poet Sebastian Brant, not directly but through the medium of a Latin and a French translation. This fiction of a ship in which all fools are invited to embark, so that the author is able to review every kind of folly and insanity provided by mankind, had a great success in England as on the continent. Barclay did not miss his opportunity of adding some peculiarly English types to the crew.

He was also the first to introduce the eclogue to his fellow-countrymen. In his youth he had written five eclogues, which he published in 1514, two of them imitations of Mantuanus, who was to be one of the classic Latin authors of the Renascence. They have nothing of the idyll, but are moral satires, discussions between a townsman and a countryman, between a poor poet and a rich miser, an exposition of the miseries of a courtier's life.

Barclay chose his models well, and he has the merits of sincerity of speech and a realism sometimes racy, but his style lacks ductility, his language is rude, and his verse suffers from the general lack of rhythm.

John Skelton (1460?-1529) is a fantastic personage, hard to classify or define. As a learned humanist who won praise from Erasmus, an Oxford laureate famous for his Latin verses and known as a grammarian, he belongs to the Renascence. He is very well acquainted with ancient poets and mindful of the mythology of antiquity. His occupations were serious, for he was tutor to the future Henry VIII. and rector of Diss in Norfolk. But he writes verses like a buffoon, in many respects like a man behind his times. He is faithful to satirical allegory, and sets fine order and classic nobility and elegance at naught. He found heroic verse debased, and, instead of attempting to reform it, most often abandoned it in favour of a short irregular line and rhymes multiplied until a dozen of them sometimes follow each other. His verses might have been improvised by some untiring tavern poet. He deliberately turns his back on beauty, is fully aware of what he is about, and acknowledges that his only aim is to strike hard and straight:

> Though my rime be ragged,
> Tatter'd and jagged,
> Rudely raine-beaten,
> Rusty and moth-eaten;
> If ye take wel therewith,
> It hath in it some pith.

The pith is mostly satire. In this age of dull repetitions Skelton pleases because he is brutal and coarse. No one has handled prelates more roughly, not even the Protestants among whom he is not numbered. Of his numerous poems, many of which are lost, the most interesting are the *Bowge of Court,* the *Boke of Colin Clout* and *Why Come ye not to Court?*

The first of these (1509?) is an allegory which recalls the *Ship of Fools.* The poet is on board a magnificent ship which is to take him to the land of Favour, and his voyage is troubled by the intolerable company of Fortune's friends, Favell or Flattery, Suspecte or Suspicion, Disdain and Dissimulation. They conspire against him, and he is about to throw himself into the sea in order to escape them, when he awakes—all has been a dream. How familiar is every one of these allegorical figures! Yet never, perhaps, have they been as living and as busy as in this poem. Exceptionally it is written in the stanza of seven heroic lines called Chaucerian.

Colin Clout (1519) is a peasant, another Piers Plowman, who like him chastises the vices of the clergy. With disorderly energy Skelton poses as the mouthpiece of popular wrath.

The last of these three poems, written in 1522, is a violent indictment of Cardinal Wolsey, the all-powerful minister of Henry VIII. It includes a stinging description of the terror in which he was held by the noblest of the kingdom.

Although Skelton's habitual tone is satirical, and he uses complacently the coarsest insults and worst indecencies, he yet showed himself capable, on occasion, of feeling and even of a certain grace, as in his *Boke of Philipp Sparowe* (1503-7), an elegy on the death of a sparrow who belonged to fair Jane Scroupe. It echoes the little poem of Catullus, with the difference that the Latin poet's eighteen lines have become 1382 lines of Skeltonic verse. It is a hotchpotch of reminiscences and buffoonery, alternating with passages full of freshness and charm. There is something of everything in John Skelton, that first rough sketch for Rabelais. Taken all together, however, his poetry represents rather the last stirrings of the dying Middle Ages than the first signs of life of the Renaissance.

. . . . .

There is pleasure in passing from the English to the Scottish poetry of the fifteenth century. It is not that the matter of poetry had been renewed in Scotland. North as south of the Tweed, the allegorical school was dominant and Chaucer's personal influence reigned. The Scots had, however, kept the artistic sense and a line which had an assured rhythm, and they had a vitality which contrasted happily with English languor. This is the most glorious period of all their old poetry.

The patriotic impulse which had caused Barbour to write his *Bruce* in the previous century had almost ceased to be felt. The only poem which matches *Bruce* is *Wallace,* written about 1461 by the minstrel called Blind Harry. He differed from Barbour, who related the comparatively recent exploits of the Bruce, for he went back to an earlier hero whose date was a hundred and fifty years before his own. The fabulous element looms much larger in *Wallace* than in *Bruce.* Wallace's exploits are magnified and multiplied. But the two poems tell their tale with the same naked simplicity. Barbour's prosaic quality is even intensified in Blind Harry, who is platitudinous. He is devoid of poetry, merely amasses detail, and his substitution of decasyllabic couplets for Barbour's eight-syllable verses only protracts the line awkwardly and increases its monotony.

This poem is isolated, and it heightens, by contrast, the ornate, even exaggeratedly brilliant, character of other Scottish verse in this century.

The first in date of the poets of Scotland who were influenced by Chaucer is King James I. (1394-1436). Doubts have been thrown on his literary claims, but they have not seriously shaken the beautiful and touching tradition that the *Kingis Quair* expresses in verse a romantic incident of his life which he himself commemorated.

At eleven years of age he was taken captive by the English, together with the ship which was carrying him to France, and, in spite of the truce between Scotland and England, was kept a prisoner for nineteen years, but honourably treated and carefully educated.

During this captivity he fell in love with Lady Jane Beaufort, niece to Henry IV., whom he married in 1424.

His poem describes his love, and is a graceful medley of allegory and reality. Chaucer's work must have been much read by the young prisoner, for the *Kingis Quair* is full of Chaucerian reminiscences. Especially James remembers the charming passage of the Knightes Tale in which Palamon and Arcite see, from the window of their dungeon, the fair Emely walking in the garden, and at once fall in love with her. He had read and re-read Chaucer's translation of the *Roman de la Rose* and the love-scenes in *Troylus and Criseyde,* particularly that in which the lovers first meet, and his head was filled with the poems in which a dream leads to a marvellous allegorical vision. His poem is inspired from all these known sources, but because he himself had partly lived through the traditional fictions, there is a freshness in his imitations which is quite personal, and more than once his stanzas surpass their models in emotion.

His complaint on his long captivity, his contemplation of the "gardyn faire" "fast by the touris wall" of his prison, the birds' song, "so loud and clere," which stirs him to love—all this is the most natural prelude to the appearance of the girl:

> For quhich sodayn abate, anone astert
> The blude of all my body to my hert.

The sight of her is such that—

> My hert, my will, my nature and my mynd,
> Was changit clene ryght in another kind.

He recovers enough to gaze at the fair vision, to note her features and ornaments, and especially the heart-shaped ruby:

> That, as a spark of lowe, so wantonely
> Semyt burnyng upon her quhytë throte.

There was in her—

> Beautee eneuch to mak a world to dote.

This prelude has so much charm and emotion that we willingly follow the poet through the dream which leads him from the palace of Venus to those of Minerva and of Fortune. Others have taken us thither before, but James can often point out a graceful or brilliant detail. And throughout the fantastic journey suspense reigns as to the outcome of a passion we know to be sincere:

> O besy goste! ay flikering to and fro,
> That never art in quiet nor in rest.

It is easy for us to share his joy when he wins to the "presence suete and delitable" of his mistress:

> And thankit be the fair castell wall,
>   Quhare as I quhilom lukit forth and lent,
> Thankit mot be the sanctis marcial,
>   That me first causit hath this accident.
>   Thankit mot be the grenë bewis bent,
> Throu quom, and under, first fortunyt me
> My hertis hele, and my comfort to be.

This royal pupil, who commends his book to Gower and Chaucer, his "maistiris dere," is a correct and harmonious versifier. His dialect is tempered by his assiduous reading of English models, and exempt from the difficulty increasingly felt in the poetry of his successors.

These, on the other hand, have more raciness, for they had not spent their youth in the English court. One of the most interesting of them is the Dunfermline schoolmaster, Robert Henryson (1425-1500), who evinces a real independence even when he is imitating Chaucer.

He had read and admired *Troylus and Criseyde,* but his moral sense was shocked by the conclusion of the story. How could the faithful Troylus be killed and the fickle Criseyde be happy with Diomede thereafter?

> Quha wait gif all that Chaucer wrait was trew?

Henryson, one cold day in Lent, set himself to recast the conclusion of the story and write the *Testament of Cresseid.*

His Diomede soon deserts Cresseid, who becomes a light-of-love among the Greeks, and in punishment is afflicted by Heaven with leprosy. Then "with cop and clapper" she goes begging from door to door. One day Troylus, who is not dead, is returning from a glorious expedition and passes near the place where she sits. Not recognising her, yet reminded by her "of fair Cresseid, sumtyme his awin darling," he gives her a generous alms:

> For knichtlie pietie and memoriale
> Of fair Cresseid.

When he has gone, and she learns from the other leper folk who he is, she falls to the ground. Before dying, she writes her testament, bequeathing her body to the worms and toads, and all her goods to the lepers, save a ring, set with a ruby, which is to be carried to Troilus after her death. When he receives it and hears her story—

> For greit sorrow his hart to birst was bown.

He causes "ane tomb of merbell gray" to be raised above her grave.

Henryson seems to have been guided by his sense of reality at least as much as by a moral aim. He thinks this miserable end the most probable for the Cresseids of this world. Chaucer, in pity, had drawn a veil over the life of his heroine after her fall. Henryson is no less pitiful: his heart aches for Cresseid even while he is describing her horrible chastisement. His morality is penetrated with sympathy and humanity. His *Testament of Cresseid* has been accepted as the natural sequel to the romance. It is written in the same stanza as Chaucer's poem and is as correct and harmonious.

Henryson was no mere sentimental moralist. His moral fables show him in more homely guise, capable of mischievous energy. He tells us that he has had a vision of an old man,

> The fairest man that ever befoir I saw,

who declares that he is a Roman and named Æsop. This Roman Æsop without a hump—how remote we still are from the Renascence!—can tell a good story, with a mischievous smile, and the thirteen fables he dictates to Henryson—*The Cock and the Jasp, The Uplandis Mous and the Burges Mous, Schir Chantecleir and the Fox, The Lyoun and the Mous, The Wolf and the Lamb,* and the others—are among the best fables ever told. The matter is commonplace and everything is in the manner. They are not epical fables, such as Chaucer wrote, when jestingly and in heroic tones he sang the adventures of the cock and the fox, but they are copious, crowded with detail and with notes of customs or characteristics, abundantly picturesque, much more extensive than those of La Fontaine. What life and go there is in the most celebrated of them, which is imitated from Horace, *The Uplandis Mous and the Burges Mous!* How amusing the contrast between the rural mouse in her "sillie scheill" (poor hut),

> Withouten fyre or candill birnand bricht,

and her sister, the burgess mouse, whose dwelling is a larder in a rich man's house, and who says to the other:

> My Gude Fryday is better nor your Pace!

All this is told with a swing and with fine humour, in the seven-lined Chaucerian stanza, and with sympathy for the animals brought on the scene. Happily the moral is placed by itself, so that nothing spoils or hinders the pleasure of the story.

Other qualities are revealed in Henryson's other short poems. *Orpheus and Eurydice,* founded on Boethius, has a pathetic lyricism, and *Robene and Makyne,* which is half-way between a *pastourelle* and a pastoral, is ingeniously constructed. Makyne has vainly sighed for Robene for "yeris two or thre," but he cares nothing for her, thinks only of his sheep, and repels her harshly. Hardly has she left him than he regrets her, and it is then his turn to beg and implore. But she reminds him of his hardness, laughs at his sighs, and bids him adieu:

> Makyne went hame blythe anewche
>   Attour the holtis hair.
> Robene murnit, and Makyne lewche;
>   Scho sang, he sichit sair:
> And so left him bayth wo and wrench,
>   In dolour and in cair,
> Kepand his hird under a huche
>   Among the holtis hair.

The *estrif* or *disputoison* is recalled, save for the fresh country air that blows through the poem. Of all the Scottish poets of this time, Henryson has most rustic realism and savours most of the soil.

The one of this remarkable group who is justly reputed the greatest is, however, William Dunbar (1460?-1520?). This churchman, first in Franciscan habit, then unfrocked, at one time a wandering preacher, at others sent by James IV. on embassies to London and Paris, became in some sort the poet laureate of Scotland. Some hundred of his poems are extant. Nearly all of them are short, but their variety of subject and versification is surprising. Dunbar's prolificity has nothing in common with the flat long-windedness of a Lydgate. He is an artist, even, in some respects, a great artist. It is true that there is nothing new in his thought or feeling. He does not abandon the mediæval frames; both his allegories and his satires keep to the traditional grooves. Nor does he ever, like Villon whose verses he knew, thrill with a personal and vibratingly emotional note. He is without Chaucer's and Henryson's fine gifts of observation. But he has to a rare degree—one never reached before him and seldom since—virtuosity of style and versification. No one hitherto had put so much colour in pictures; no one, above all, had given such a swing to lines and stanza. It matters little that Dunbar has not much to say which touches the heart or the mind. He dazzles the eyes and ravishes the ears.

It is brilliancy which is especially remarkable in his official allegories, for instance *The Thrissil and the Rois* in which he symbolises the marriage in 1503 of James IV. to Margaret Tudor, daughter of Henry VII., that union of Scotland and England. Dunbar has recourse to the convention of a vision during sleep, but what a wealth of coloured words he uses, how rapidly the allegories, usually so slow, unfold themselves in his hands! His flamboyant style can doubtless be criticised, yet artifice is in place in such occasional verse. Poetry of this kind, in which conventionalised and highly coloured heraldic figures are substituted for real beings—the lion, the eagle, the thistle, the rose—is surely suited to the celebration of a marriage between two countries. The very violences of the style are those of an artist whose effects are new, as when he speaks of birds singing—

> Amang the tendir odouris reid and quhyt.

He goes farther in his *Goldyn Targe,* in which he uses unremittingly a nine-line stanza having two rhymes. Nothing in this allegory shows an advance on the *Roman de la Rose.* There is yet another dream and description of a day in May; the white sail appears of a ship from which seven ladies "in kirtillis grene" are landed. The poet is accused by Dame Beauty and defended by Reason, who shields him with a golden targe or shield, so that his enemies are powerless against him until Presence blinds Reason by casting a powder in his eyes. The poet is then held prisoner until he awakes.

Certainly Dunbar does not wish to be taken seriously, but he gives the reader the pleasure of dazzling decoration and of a freedom of movement which, for once, keeps at bay the tedium which threatens all allegories. Can this rainbow-hued country, in which all the colours of precious stones—rubies, beryls, emeralds, sapphires—radiate together, be grey Scotland? It would be easier to believe ourselves transported to the kingdom of a Haroun al Raschid. The oriental imagination of this northerner is astonishing.

The natural must not be expected of this great decorator, nor mystical and fervent piety of this Franciscan. It occurred to him, one day, to bring the seven deadly sins on to his stage, but for no graver purpose than to set them spinning in a wild, macabre dance. We have enough edifying pictures of these sins to allow us to thank Dunbar for treating them as no more than the pretext for a mad whirligig. His *Dance of the Sevin Deidly Synnis,* written in lyrical twelve-lined stanzas, is perhaps the most characteristic of his poems. We do not seek in it either justice of detail or religious horror of vice. It has instead the marks of a strange coarseness, and is fuller of buffoonery than of edification. It ends with a rough jest against the Highlanders whom Dunbar held in derision. But the verbal swing and the giddy liveliness of these ten stanzas are marvellous.

Dunbar was a master of satire, especially of the jovial invective and repeated and unbridled insults which Scots call "flyting." Rabelais himself could hardly have held his own with him in this field, in which his vocabulary positively seems to be drunk, so dizzy is the play of rhymes and alliterations.

It should be added that Dunbar was ingenious in his choice of themes for his satires and framework for his mocking invective. Now he sees in a dream a demon in the guise of St. Francis who brings him the habit of his order, and to whom he explains why it does not please him to resume it (*How Dunbar was desired to be one freir*). Now he makes a pretended apology to the corporation of tailors who have complained of his ridicule, which he is thus enabled to repeat with more sting than ever (*The Tournament*). Or again, in order to mock a charlatan who has tried to fly on wings of his own making and has fallen and broken his leg, Dunbar pictures him attacked by all the fowls of the air when he takes his flight (*The Fenyeit Freir of Tungland*).

In every verse-form he excels. He uses Langland's alliterative line with as much success as the Chaucerian metre. He unites the metres of both masters when, with extraordinary cynicism, he relates the fable of *The Two Mariit Wemen and the Wedo,* whose scabrous conversation he overhears, as they sit in their garden after some hearty drinking. The remarks on the obligations of matrimony which, in alliterative verse, he puts in their mouths would have brought blushes to the cheek even of the Wife of Bath.

On occasion, however, he is capable of a higher lyricism. There is a note of melancholy in his *Lament for the Makaris,* in which he names the poets of his country and of England who have died. It recalls Villon's enumeration of the illustrious ones whom death has ravished. The Latin refrain, "Timor mortis conturbat me," sounds in these short stanzas the knell of the departed. But they have not Villon's sober exactness nor his intimate thrill. The effect produced is more external, and is due, above all, as it always is in Dunbar, to astonishingly skilful rhythm.

The fact that Dunbar's merits may, in the last analysis, be summed up as mastery of form, does not impugn his right to a place of honour. For with him there is no question of inert perfection, but of intense life such as belonged to

Illustration for a fifteenth-century poem in which a king, a "clerk," and a knight are carried off by Death.

none of the *rhétoriqueurs* whose contemporary he was. Far from bending beneath the load of his rich vocabulary, he carries it easily. He has dash, and this is to say that he is half-way to lyricism.

Very different from this frequently coarse Bohemian was the high-born Gavin Douglas (1475?-1522?), a churchman who became a bishop, and whose personal history mingled with that of Scotland when, after the disaster of Flodden in 1513, he was drawn into politics. While he hardly corresponds to the usual idea of a prelate, he was yet a man of heart and of honour, and also a man of letters who first gained distinction in the field of traditional poetry, and ended by showing himself almost a precursor of the humanism of the Renascence.

In his youth he began with allegory. At twenty-six he wrote the *Palice of Honour* (1501) in which he imitates Chaucer's *Hous of Fame.* The difference between the subjects of the two poems is reflected in their titles. It is the House of Honour which this poet enters in his dream, where dwell illustrious men who in their lives have followed the laws of truth and loyalty. Douglas modestly declares that he can find no place there for himself. In the course of the dream he mixes the sacred and the profane, moral allegory and mythology. The nymph Calliope explains the redemption of man to him, at his desire. There is a scholar as well as a moralist behind these puppets.

Later Douglas wrote *King Hart,* in which he shows much maturer psychological power. His great model is still the *Roman de la Rose,* but he also knows the *Séjour d'Honneur* of Octavien de Gelais whom he had already imitated in his earlier poems, and he has felt the influence of the morality plays which were then supreme in the theatre.

There is a constant mingling of humour and melancholy in this allegory. King Hart, or Heart, is made captive by Dame Pleasance, and delivered by Dame Pietie, then marries the charming enemy who has overcome him. But, after seven years, Age knocks at the gate of the palace of Pleasure, and all the young and flighty courtiers, who once had surrounded her, flee, and are at last followed by the dame herself. Reason and Wit then warn the king to return to his own castle, where he is ere long assailed by the hideous army of Decrepitude. Before he dies he makes an ironic testament.

The scene of the arrival of Age, most unwelcome of visitors, is full of life, and there is much graceful melancholy in the king's farewell to Youth:

> Sen thou man pas, fair Youth heid, wa is me!

In spite of their merits, these poems have too little novelty to have ensured Douglas's renown by themselves. He has another claim to fame in that, first in Great Britain, he translated Virgil into verse (1512-13). Before him, only Chaucer had rendered a few fragments of the Latin poet, and in such reedlike tones that he seemed to be writing a parody. Caxton, the first printer, had published a prose version made from a pretended French translation which was really a mediæval romance and of which Douglas says that, although Caxton had called it "Virgill in Eneados,"

> It has na thing ado tharwith, God wait,
> Ne na mair lyke than the devill and Sanct Aus-
>   tyne.

Douglas aimed at translating exactly, word for word, but need for comprehension and the imperfection of his language often led him to render one word or one line by several. He retains something of the Middle Ages and travesties characters, as when he makes a nun of the Sibyl or a gentle lord of Æneas.

He translates into heroic couplets in which he uses more licence than in his other poems. Altogether this is an interesting work, energetic and sometimes brilliant.

Its most curious part is the prologues which precede each book. These contain the most original and most Scottish verses of the poet. In them Douglas writes as his fancy bids him, of himself or of the season. In a description of winter which begins the seventh book, and one of spring which opens the twelfth, he may be said to have anticipated by two centuries his fellow-countryman Thomson, of *The Seasons,* for he is as faithful to nature and prodigal of detail. His exuberance is especially striking, his abundant colours, scents and sounds. He is like a Dunbar striving for realism. But in the long run his scene is felt to be crowded: mind wearies and eyes ache. His language is moreover the most difficult of the period because of the number of the learned and popular sources whence it de-

rives. An Englishman is unable and a Scot hardly able to read Douglas without a glossary.

In his prologues he allows himself full rein, for he writes them only for his own pleasure. In that to Book XII. he would merely have us know how the singing of the birds woke him at four in the morning and he resumed his translating. Sometimes his readers share the diversions of a humanist, as when he adds to Virgil a thirteenth book translated from the Italian Maffeo Vegio. Its prologue informs us that in a dream the writer is charged by Vegio to make this translation. He at first refuses, pleading unfitness, but Vegio insists that he who has translated the poem of a pagan is far more bound to do this service to a Christian, and finally the Italian poet prevails by the argument of twenty blows with a cudgel.

These particularities of his Virgil show, almost as much as his earlier allegories, that Douglas was not in the full stream of the Renascence. He stood on its brink, marking the transition from one age to another.

We have still to speak of his countryman Sir David Lyndsay, who poetically was even more attached than he to the past. Lyndsay's life was, however, a long battle which coincided with the Reformation, and he definitely belongs to the sixteenth century.

. . . . .

The works we have reviewed constitute, in Scotland as in England, the official poetry of the fifteenth century. This is far from being all the poetry of the period. There were also anonymous popular verses, both ruder and more truly alive, which often cannot be localised or dated with any precision. They cannot all be claimed for the fifteenth century, for poems of the sort must have had an earlier beginning and certainly were produced until a later time, but the impulse to make them seems to have been particularly active in this century, to which, moreover, the oldest extant specimens belong.

The word ballad, vague as it is, denotes them best. But they must be in no way identified with the courtly ballade, which was fixed in form and peculiarly learned and artificial. The two words doubtless share a derivation from *baller,* to dance, and the ballad and ballade both originated in the poetry which accompanied dancing and implied musical declamation with a collective refrain. But hardly more than the traces of this prototype remain. When the popular ballad of Great Britain emerges from the shadows it retains no more of its primary form than warrants a presumption, more complete than for other kinds of poetry, of cooperation between the poet and his audience. It has even been supposed that a ballad is the spontaneous and joint composition of a group of people. Reflection shows, however, that this theory has little plausibility. There could be agreement for the purposes of poetry among a number of people only in the sharing of a passion, and the work of an artist or several successive artists has to be recognised in a ballad of any length. It was artists, however primitive, who interpreted the multitude. Once a ballad existed, the public did in some sort collaborate in its making, for memory altered, modified or suppressed, and new circumstances suggested opportune additions. Oral tradition changed the form of the poem. Like money in circulation, it lost, little by little, its imprint; its salient curves were blunted; and long use gave it a polish it did not have originally. The exact fact to which it owed its birth grew misty in retrospect, and from being, in a humble way, historical, the ballad became romantic and acquired the prestige of the remote.

Perhaps, therefore, it is time rather than the mode of their making which gives ballads their special character. They differ from other poems because we never, or hardly ever, hear them as they were originally. At some moment of its life, already, it may be, a long one, a ballad becomes public knowledge, and the subtle effect of the human emotions excited while it has been endlessly repeated may indeed have given it the value of a collective work.

It may be said that this is equally true of the old songs which were not written down for many years. But a ballad is not a song. Usually it holds a story: it is the fragment of an epic; sometimes it is plainly the summary of old chivalrous poems of which only the essence has been kept for the purposes of a short recitation and to make a rapid impression on simple minds. Or else the ballad relates for a district a glorious or ill-omened incident which is known to all and has familiar heroes, so that, however allusively the poet expresses himself, he is sure of being understood even by the most ignorant.

The ballad exists everywhere in Europe, but is most copious and lively in the outlying regions, in Spain in the south and in Scandinavia in the north. Great Britain, insular and isolated, produced many ballads, especially on the Border, the scene in old days of so many sanguinary encounters of Scots and English.

We have spoken of the popular rhymes, dating from the fourteenth century, on Robin Hood, bowman and outlaw, but the ballads, a whole cycle of them, which are consecrated to his exploits do not go back further than the sixteenth century. While the existence of numerous ballads in the fourteenth and fifteenth centuries may be conjectured, there are only two which can certainly be placed before the Renascence: *Chevy Chase* and *The Nut-brown Maid*.

Chevy Chase is the oldest and the finest of the epical ballads. In theme and sentiment it is akin to *Roland* or *Byrhtnoth*. It is at least half-historical, its subject the struggle between Percy of Northumberland and the Douglas of Scotland at the beginning of the fifteenth century. The manners it reveals are at once violent and chivalrous, a love of battle combining with generosity to enemies. But that which in *Byrhtnoth* has an epic swing is here lyrical. This ballad is a sung recitation, a sort of melopœia. Already it has the metre which was to be pre-eminently that of the ballads, the seven-accented line in two divisions ($4 \div 3$) and the rhymes in couples. The division is so fixed that the couplet can be considered as a quatrain:

> The Persé owt off Northombarlonde
>   An avowe to God mayd he
> That he wold hunt in the mountayns
>   Off Chyviat within days three.

The division often leads to the rhyming of the first and third sections, giving quatrains with cross-rhymes (*abab*). The tendency to regularise rhythm also has the effect in the later ballads of making the lines syllabic, that is to say alternately of eight and six syllables. In *Chevy Chase* the verse is primitive in its rudeness and has the minimum of ornament.

There is in this ballad a manifest basis of realism. It tells an incident all too truly characteristic of life on the Border, where there was little distinction between warfare and brigandage. Percy wishes to hunt in enemy country, less for love of the deer than to provoke his adversary. He rejoices greatly when, after the hunt, the Douglas arrives and the battle begins. Yet these wild opponents have the spirit of chivalry: the Douglas, in order to spare "guiltless men," proposes to Percy to meet him in single combat. But the ardour of Percy's followers, who would think it shame to leave all the danger to their chief, cannot be restrained, and the fight is general. When the Douglas is slain, Percy, who a minute before had been drunk with battle, gives rein, before the body of his enemy, to artless grief and sincere admiration:

> The Persé leanyde on his brande, and sawe the
>   Duglas de;
> He tooke the dede man be the hande, and sayd,
>   Wo ys me for the!
> To have savyde thy lyffe I wold have partyd with
>   my landes for years thre,
> For a better man of hart, nare of hand, was not
>   in all the north countrè.

The minstrel who so vigorously sings the fine sword-play is mindful of the evils to which such violence will give rise:

> The chyld may rue that ys un-borne, it was the
>   more pittè.

Sincere emotion is betrayed by these very contradictions. The poem wins us by the truthfulness of its feeling as of its restrained decoration and its details. Whether or not the details be strictly historical, we follow the vicissitudes of the conflict, the part played by the English bowmen, the tactics of the Douglas when he caused his men to advance in scattered formation, the hand-to-hand struggle.

There is a sort of Homeric impartiality in this war ballad. The Percy and the Douglas show equal heroism, although their virtues are opposed like those of an Achilles and a Hector. The poet's English patriotism is clearly discovered only at the end. When he hears that the Douglas is slain, the king of Scotland is in despair, but Henry IV., learning Percy's death, is undismayed in his pride:

> God have merci on his soll, sayd kyng Harry,
>   Good Lord, yf thy will it be!
> I have a hondrith captayns in Ynglonde, he
>   sayd, as good as ever was hee:
> But Persè, and I brook my lyffe, they deth well
>   quyte shall be.

He then despatches an army which wins the victory of Humbledon.

It is almost impossible to exaggerate the importance of this short literary epic. Its success was not confined to the people, but extended to men of letters and poets. Sir Philip Sidney wrote of it about 1581:

I never heard the old song of Piercy and Douglas, that I found not my heart more moved than
with a trumpet; and yet it is sung buy by some
blind crowder with no rougher voice than rude
stile; which being so evil apparelled in the dust
and cobweb of that uncivil age, what would it
work trimmed in the gorgeous elegance of Pin-
dar?

As though to obey Sidney's wish, a poet of the first years
of the seventeenth century gave to the ballad, without de-
forming it overmuch, a correct form, modernised language and regular rhythm. Addison, in the full stream of
the classical period, read it in this version, which yet
seemed to him ancient, and praised it discriminatingly in
the *Spectator.* He realised the ballad's Homeric qualities,
and used it as a text to preach that the beautiful is the simple. He loved it as Molière loved the "old song of Henry
IV. of France" and for the same qualities, just style and
natural feeling. Finally Bishop Percy (1765) inserted the
oldest text in his *Reliques,* and *Chevy Chase* was one of the
mediæval poems which induced romanticism. Soon the
very irregularity of its verses was found to have a special
charm, and this rudeness inspired Coleridge to give a new
harmony to his *Ancient Mariner* and, above all, to his
Christabel. It is sincerity of tone, like that of *Chevy Chase,*
which, down the ages and among extravagances and artifices, brings back to natural truth the poetry which has left
nature too far behind.

Such fine romantic ballads as *Sir Patrick Spens, Clerk
Saunders* and *Child Waters* cannot be certainly ascribed
to the fifteenth century, for the versions of them which
have reached us are all of later date. But a poem of a special kind, which encloses the elements of a simple ballad
in the framework of a courtly *disputoison,* may be claimed
for this century.

A lady is represented as using the story of *The Nut-brown
Maid* to free women of the reproach of inconstancy constantly levied at them by men. The dark maid, who is a
baron's daughter, is visited by her lover whom she believes
to be a squire of low degree, and who comes to bid her
farewell because he has killed a man and must hide in the
woods as an outlaw. But neither his picture of a life of
pains and peril, nor even his avowal that he has another
mistress, can bend her from her will to follow him for
love's sake. He has but proved her, as Griselda was
proved, and, sure of her heart, he reveals himself as an
earl's son who will make her lady of his heritage in West-
morland.

There cannot here be question of a popular composition.
Nothing could be more artistic than these thirty six-lined
stanzas with their alternating refrains. Each stanza has
lines of seven accents, divided in $2 \div 2 \div 3$, and a system
of multiplied rhymes puts very severe constraint upon the
poet. Yet the simplicity of style and sincerity of tone do
not at all suffer. While the lady, who may be supposed to
be the author, plays the part of the Nut-brown Maid, the
other speaker takes that of the outlaw. There is a dialogue,
each of them in turn speaking a stanza with its refrain. The
dramatic interest and liveliness thus given to the little
poem cause its thesis to be forgotten in its story. The unadorned stylistic fabric, which admirably renders emo-

tion, does not lack broad images, such as those in the first
answer of the enamoured lady when her beloved announces his crime and banishment to her:

> O lord, what is this worldys blysse that changeth
>   as the mone!
> My somers day in lusty may is derked before the
>   none.
> I here you say, farewell: Nay, nay, we départ nat
>   so sone.
> Why say ye so? wheder wyll ye go? Alas! what
>   have ye done?
> All my welfare to sorrowe and care sholde
>   chaunge, yf ye were gone;
> For in my mynde, of all mankynde I love but
>   you alone.

If this poem be not a popular ballad but the work of a
courtly poet, it does but show the degree to which even the
learned poetry of the time could absorb popular songs and
be inspired by them. In this echo of some humble love-
ballad there is not one false note. Whoever can bring himself to read the lamentable imitation of it which Matthew
Prior made in the beginning of the eighteenth century, and
in which everything is falsified, both style and sentiment,
will recognise that the essence of poetry existed in this disinherited fifteenth century as it did not in the classical period. The *Nut-brown Maid,* which was printed in 1502, belongs incontestably to the reign of Henry VII.

. . . . .

It is with the drama as with the ballad. It cannot be said
to have been either created or fully developed in the fifteenth century. But this was the period in which most of
the cycles of the Christian theatre were compiled and in
which the miracle plays, not yet subject to competition
from dramatic performances of a more modern kind,
reached their apotheosis. It is therefore fitting to determine the characteristics of the mediæval dramatic art of
England in this rather than in another century.

Such characteristics are, in point of fact, few in number.

The religious theatre is an institution of Christianity
which had the same origin and a like evolution in all the
Christian countries of Europe, so much so that it is seen
wrongly or out of perspective if it be studied in one country alone. In that great common fatherland which was
Christendom in the Middle Ages, nations were, from the
spiritual point of view, hardly more than are to-day the
provinces of a centralised state. Therefore to relate the history of the Christian drama of England is, in many respects, little more than to repeat what is known of that of
France. It is thus possible to deal with the subject allusively and rapidly.

Everyone knows that this drama was an offshoot of the liturgy, which, with its solemn staging, lent itself well to dramatic development. The germs of the drama were in the
offices of the Church, in the chants alternating between the
priest and the congregation or the choir which represented
it, the recitative passages, the plastic decoration, the pro-
cessions, the ritual of movement and gesture. It was in the
form of "tropes," or declamation in dialogues, that drama
made its first appearance. Two tropes of the Easter office,

which were declaimed in England in the tenth and eleventh centuries, before as well as after the Norman Conquest, have been preserved, and make it almost certain that, with or without the Conquest, religious drama would have evolved in England as in every Christian country.

First given within the church and declaimed in Latin, these dialogues developed into small dramas when they left the church and were played in the porch and when they exchanged Latin for the vernacular, two conditions essential to the needed liberty. The best-known example of a transitional play of this kind is *Adam,* which was written in French, but by a Norman or Anglo-Norman of the twelfth century, and which seems to have been performed not in France, but in England. Very interesting because of its place at the origin of two great dramatic literatures, it is so also intrinsically. Restrained, even a little bare, but grave in thought, its sentiments just, decided and precise, and its language vigorous, it has a real value. It comprises three parts—the fall of Adam and Eve, the death of Abel, and a procession of the prophets who announce the coming of the Redeemer. The scene of Eve's temptation by the devil shows a certain refinement and some poetic grace. Almost all and the best characters of the religious drama are to be found in this old Anglo-Norman play.

But it was necessary for this drama to emancipate itself completely from the Church. It had to leave the church precincts for the highways, to take up its station in the market-place or the streets. Moreover, before the plays could be popular, they had to abandon not only Latin, as in France, but French also. It was essential that their language should be English.

Dramatic progress is connected with the development of the fairs, the increase of wealth, the rise of the burgher class, the prosperity of corporations, and finally the emancipation of the vulgar tongue. Little by little drama severed its connection not only with the Church, but also with the clergy, who at first provided all the actors. Not without resistance from the clerks, the mendicant friars and the Franciscans, who lost their monopoly, the actors came to be laymen. As a rule, henceforth, the clergy were no more than the playwrights. This change became marked and was accelerated from the second half of the thirteenth century onwards. The first plays in English were performed under Henry III., and at the same time a certain realism was introduced upon the stage.

In this reign also the great cyclical representations had their beginning, those in which the sacred history relating to an annual feast was depicted in successive scenes on the holiday. The Easter and Christmas cycles were the first in date, but the institution in 1264 of the feast of Corpus Christi and its generalisation early in the next century gave this day pre-eminence. The Easter and Nativity cycles, hitherto distinct, were united and were performed together on Corpus Christi day, which was less crowded with other events than Christmas and Easter day and which fell in the summer. All Holy Writ was thus staged at the same time and place, all the great facts of religious history reproduced in sight of the people. In some places, as in Chester, the performance was on Whit-Sunday rather than on Corpus Christi day.

Some towns, because of the fame of their fairs or the powerful organisation of their gilds, became celebrated for these representations, and the English miracle-plays we now possess are named after the places in which they were given. The cycle, embracing the whole of sacred history, is always the same, but differs locally in detail, mood, language and versification, its tone being more dignified or homelier in one place than in another. The plays of Chester and Coventry—Shakespeare may, as a child, have seen these last—those of Woodkirk Abbey, near Wakefield, called the Towneley Plays, and those of York have been preserved, as well as fragments of the Digby, Newcastle and Dublin plays. Other towns had cycles which have been lost.

The cycles were first compiled in the fourteenth century, but we possess them only as they were rearranged in the fifteenth, or even the sixteenth, for some were played until the theatre of the Renascence was nearing its apotheosis.

The popularity of the miracle-plays in the fourteenth century is attested by Chaucer, who relates in his Miller's Tale of Absolon, the merry clerk, that

> Sometyme to shewe his lightnesse and maistyre
> He playeth Heródes on a scaffold hye;

and who, in the play of the Flood, shows the Miller himself to be well informed about Noah's quarrels with his wife. Langland gives a yet more significant proof of the influence of the theatre, for he has cast more than one scene of *Piers Plowman* in the mould of the miracle-plays.

We can picture one of these immense representations, for instance that at York on Corpus Christi day. Every gild in the town contributed to it, and the festivities included forty-eight plays which comprised the whole of Scripture. We know not only the order of the plays, but also the gild responsible for each of them, appropriately chosen as far as possible. To the Armourers fell the expulsion from Paradise (the flaming sword), to the Shipwrights the building of the Ark, to the Fishermen and Mariners the Flood, to the Chandlers the shepherds following the star, to the Goldsmiths the adoration of the Magi, to the Bakers the Last Supper, to the Pinners and Painters the Crucifixion, to the Butchers the Mortification of Christ, to the Scriveners Doubting Thomas, and so forth.

An idea of the staging can be had if the meaning of pageant, a word of uncertain etymology, be understood. It sometimes referred to the platform on which a play was given, sometimes to the representation itself. Some platforms were fixed in a particular place, and the audience went from one to another of them, following the series of the plays. But elsewhere the pageant was mounted on wheels and movable, and the spectators stayed in one spot while these stages on wheels successively paused before them, gave their performance, and passed on to another point where the performance was repeated. Most of the gilds had their own pageant. Sometimes the action made several pageants necessary for one play, for instance one for Paradise, one for the earth and one for Hell. Each included, beneath the stage, a room in which actors spent the intervals between their appearances and properties were kept.

The duration of the performances varied with the number of the plays, but was always several days. In Chester, where the series included only twenty-four plays, it took three days. The nine first were given on Whit-Monday, nine more on Whit-Tuesday and the six last on the Wednesday.

What we know of the English theatre in the fifteenth century shows that it was very powerfully organised, that the gilds took an important part in its development, and that there was long local resistance to the engrossing of the plays by professional actors. In fact, its vitality and popularity were such as were surpassed nowhere. The number and diversity of the provincial centres, particularly in the north and the west, prove how widespread was the passion for the theatre.

Two points in which the English differed from the French drama must be noted. In England, although all the plays of the period are generally called miracle-plays, there are hardly any traces of what the French call *miracles,* that is plays concerned especially with the Virgin and the saints, as distinguished from the *mystères* which were founded on Holy Writ. All the cycles preserved in England are of scenes from the Bible. Secondly, the growth of the religious theatre was less disturbed in England than in France, and its development checked less early. It continued to flourish when the Renascence was in full swing, so firmly was it established in local custom and popular favour.

The extant English cycles offer another advantage to modern students. While the French mysteries in the collection compiled by the Brothers Greban are, on the whole, mediocre and monotonous, there is in the very various English plays a dignified emotion or a homely swing which sometimes makes itself felt through the awkwardness and rudeness of the style. It may be said that these plays, in the form in which they have reached us, prove that great artistic effort, no less real where it was mistaken, went to their making. They are almost all written in complicated and difficult stanzas, which have the fault that they are apt to sacrifice dramatic quality to lyricism. There are stanzas which multiply their rhymes and unite lines different in measure—as *aaabab* or *aaabaaab* or *aaaabcccb, b* standing for a short two-accented line among others usually of four accents. But while the stanza is learned, the rhythm is, as a rule, unformed and metrical padding abounds. The principal defect is due to the unfitness of such stanzas to render dramatic movement or easygoing dialogue. The difficulty of finding a metre appropriate to drama was the great obstacle to dramatic progress until nearly the end of the sixteenth century. The unknown authors of the miracle-plays are not poets enough to animate their awkward stanzas. Yet they are, at moments, capable of pathos, and more frequently there is full-flavoured comedy in their scenes.

As elsewhere, the religious drama had a value due to the simple grandeur of the total conception, and the artlessness of the means used to call up the whole of Scripture before the people is disarming. The poets effaced themselves before their subjects. They had no freedom of invention, hardly of composition, were debarred from discover-

ing motives for action except within strict limits. Since the stories were known to everyone, the principal interest was in the spectacles. Only here and there and accidentally does the author himself intervene, analysing passions or sentiments.

This happens in the play *Abraham and Isaac,* which was written in the fifteenth century and belongs to an unknown cycle. It has one scene of two hundred lines, than which nothing could be more pathetic. It is that which depicts the conflicting sentiments of the father who has the will to obey God, but is stayed by love for his child, and of the son divided between submission to his father and fear of death. Little Isaac trembles before the gleaming sword, thinks of his mother in grief, asks for the fatal stroke yet would avert it. The *Iphigenia* of Euripides has not more feeling, nor Shakespeare's *King John* when little Prince Arthur implores his executioner. We are irresistibly moved to tears; moral emotion and physical suffering are mingled. The only defect of this touching scene is its slowness, which has a slightly monotonous effect. The succeeding scene, in which Isaac, saved from death, expresses his childish joy and tenderly thanks the ram sacrificed in his stead, is very charmingly artless.

It is, however, in comic passages that the English playwrights show most go and originality. Comedy in the Middle Ages often mingled, in varying proportions, with solemn themes, in concession to a public condemned to listen to many and edifying declamation. Comedy of this sort has never been more developed than in certain English cycles. We have spoken of the fortunes of the *fabliau* in Great Britain, its progress in the hands of Chaucer, and the part it assigned to nature and observation. It has also an important place in some of the English plays, especially the Towneley Plays, which are more rustic than the others. In these, the *fabliau* is not in the unfinished state of a rough sketch, but has been retouched, again and again, and betrays a long experience of scenic effects. The complicated stanza which contains it, to which we have already alluded, is proof of real artistic labour.

It was only in the comic parts of the plays that their authors were fully independent, in the passages which owed nothing to Holy Writ saving the scenes in which they could safely be introduced. Sometimes the playwright enlivened secondary biblical characters; sometimes he entirely invented characters in order to provide comic relief where the gloom was heaviest. Thus a dramatist cheered the first human tragedy by the gift of a servant named Garcio to Cain, while others gave realistic vigour to the detractors of the Blessed Virgin, to the soldiers sent to kill the Innocents, to the Pharisees who brought before Christ the woman taken in adultery, to the beadle of Pontius Pilate, to the workmen who set up the Cross, to the soldiers who watched by Christ's sepulchre. There was nothing to prevent them from lending the manners and speech of the common people they knew to these supernumeraries. Shakespeare and his rivals did exactly the same thing, kept the tragic central pattern of their source often intact, and added to it a comic border of their own.

Of the English comic scenes, two took up more space than others in the Towneley Plays, those concerned respectively with Noah's wife and with the shepherds who followed the star.

Noah's quarrels with his wife, when he has to make her enter the ark, are very lively. He is most respectful of the divine injunction, but cowed by his mate, who is the typical scold of the *fabliaux,* shrewish, contradictious, stormy, giving blow for blow. Frightened as she is of the Flood, the arrangements of the ark do not please her, and she has barely entered it when she takes herself off to spin alone in a corner. Her husband and her sons and daughters implore her vainly: she will not budge. But no sooner does Noah tell her to do just as she likes than she changes her mind and comes on board. She is still, however, in a bad temper, and Noah has to beat her soundly before things are in train. From the moment of her beating Mrs. Noah is appeased and becomes a charming travelling-companion, helping to navigate the ark and send forth the birds, all her talk good sense and kindliness.

The broad comedy of this character in no way lessens the piety of the play, and occurs amid such artless simplicity that it is hardly discordant. Goodman Noah conversing with the Lord, monologuing as he builds the Ark, describing what he does as he goes along and complaining of his stiff back, and the concluding ingenious dialogue which suggests the various incidents of the voyage: all this makes a homely, cheerful whole, in which the buffoonery is not out of place.

The same mingling of simple piety and farce goes to make the nativity-play, but here the farce is more developed and almost constitutes an independent comedy in rustic northern dialect.

With the honest shepherds, who appear telling the troubles of their life—hard winters, the oppression of gentlemen—or who complain of the cantankerousness of their wives, there mingles a certain Mak, a cunning scamp, almost a precursor of the Shakespearian Autolycus. The action of the farce is that he steals a sheep from the others and conceals it, and that his theft is discovered. The sheep is put in a cradle, and Mak's wife, on her bed, groans as though she were just delivered of a child. When one of the good shepherds wants to give the baby a sixpence, the trick is exposed. And no sooner has Mak been tossed in punishment than the angel begins to sing "Gloria in Excelsis," and the good shepherds, led by the star, set out for the Crib, discoursing on the angel's beautiful song and on the prophecies. Before the Crib their demeanour is the same as before the cradle of the sham baby. They are touched by the infant's charm; they bring him simple presents, one a bird, another cherries—at Christmastime!—the third a ball to play at tennis. Their words of adoration alternate with their pity for the frailty and tininess and the poverty of the Divine Child.

It is very remarkable that in these two plays, *Noah* and the *Nativity,* the very brisk and copious comic element does not clash with the religious sentiment. This is due to the heartiness of the comedy, which has neither reservations nor irony. It does not imperil the dignity of the play to which it belongs. It is not destructive. It can be reconciled with faith and tender emotion. It is at once bold and art-

less. We shall see that, for like reasons, the comic blends easily with romantic or tragic elements in the best of the Renascence dramas. On the other hand, the cynical realism of *Maître Patelin,* also a fifteenth-century work, would be hard to imagine in a religious frame. *Maître Patelin,* with a theme somewhat analogous to the Mak episode, is markedly superior to the artless Towneley Play in refinement of analysis and pointed wit, but has a fundamental harshness, a certain dryness and cruelty. Nor is the French play in any sense rustic: it does not breathe the healthy country air which surrounds the shepherds of the *Nativity* and good-for-nothing, sheep-stealing Mak. In differences of this kind, rather than in a diversity of theory, the profound causes are to be discerned for the eventual triumph in English drama and rejection by French drama of the mingling of the tragic and the comic.

The earliest moralities preserved in England also belong to the fifteenth century. Later born than the mysteries, which are linked up with the epical period of the Middle Ages, the moralities are a product of the allegorical period. To the plays taken from the Bible, they are as is the *Roman de la Rose* to the old epics. For the characters of sacred history they substitute abstractions, vices or virtues. They are at their origin as much penetrated as the miracle-plays with Christian teaching, but they have a more intellectual character. While a miracle-play is essentially a spectacle, appealing primarily to the sight, a morality demands greater attention to the spoken word. Its text is more important than its scenery.

Although generally, as we pass from the miracle-plays to the moralities, we seem to go from the greater to the less great, to what is less alive and more coldly and artificially constructed, the morality must none the less be recognised to mark a necessary stage and, in a sense, a considerable advance in the progress towards the modern drama. The author of a morality can arrange his subject freely, attempt construction and unity. He is led to analyse human qualities and defects, to emphasise psychological characteristics. Miserliness, for instance, cannot be presented without study of the character of a miser. In this way the morality, even the religious morality, prepared drama for emancipation from religion. Its theme is the struggle of the forces of good and evil which contest for the human soul. This problem continued to confront the poet who was no longer inspired by the Christian faith. The permanent basis of every dramatic work had been discovered.

The material conditions of the theatre were transformed. Instead of multiplied, often movable pageants, the morality used a single, unchanging stage. In the earliest extant English morality, the *Castell of Perseverance* (middle fifteenth century), the unchanging scene showed a castle in its center, and in its corners scaffolds for the World, the Flesh, the Devil, and God. As the miracle-plays led to the numerous and changing scenes of historical drama, so the moralities prepared the way for tragedies restricted to one plot.

The exact date at which the morality had its rise is unknown. It was doubtless not later than the middle of the fourteenth century, not far removed in time from Langland's great religious satire which was so filled with animated, almost scenic moral allegories. Allegories were early introduced into the miracle-plays. In the Coventry cycle there are such characters as Contemplation, Calumny, Detraction, Truth, Justice, Peace, Death, and, in the Digby Mysteries, especially in the play on Mary Magdalene, the World, Luxury and Curiosity figure, as well as the Seven Deadly Sins.

In the *Castell of Perseverance,* the oldest and longest of the moralities, the reign of allegory is undisputed. "Humanum genus," placed between his good and his bad angel and long the slave of Pleasure and Folly, takes refuge in the Castle of Perseverance with the Christian virtues. He is seduced by Covetousness, who makes his way into the castle and prevails on him to leave it. But before his death, as his soul is about to be carried to hell, he is saved by the intervention of Peace and Mercy.

An analogous conception recurs in the shorter moralities, *Mankind,* approximately of the same date, and *Mundus et Infans* and *Hyckescorner,* which belong to the early sixteenth century. These plays are, however, less tensely grave and have comic passages. In *Mankind* it is the demon Tityvillus whose jokes give the comic relief, while in *Hyckescorner* the scamp who names the piece plays malicious tricks with his companions in debauchery, Free Will and Imagination.

These moralities, by turns cold and scholastic or comic in a very mediocre degree, have little merit. But another of the same period is really impressive and might well be called the masterpiece of its kind, the play of *Everyman.* For long it was believed to have originated in Holland, having been printed in Dutch as early as 1495 and before any edition of the English text. To-day, however, the dominant opinion is that the play was born in England, where certainly it seems to have been very popular down to the Reformation.

The tragedy is that of Christian death, and it is staged with poignant restraint and force. God sends Death to summon Everyman, and he, in anguish, implores a respite, and obtains only a few hours to gather together the friends who shall go with him on his supreme journey. Everyman appeals vainly to Fellowship, his boon companion, to Kindred and to Goods. None of them will hearken to him. Then he remembers Good Deeds, whom he has long abandoned, who is lying on the ground, weak and miserable, but who hears his prayer, helps him, and recommends to him her sister, Knowledge. Knowledge sends him to Confession, and Everyman, shriven of sin, is ready to meet God. At the moment at which he reaches the grave, Beauty, Strength, Discretion and Five-Wits depart, in spite of their promise to follow him. Knowledge would go with him but cannot. Only Good Deeds is left; she alone is not vain and will plead for him. Everyman dies pure of sin and forgiven.

The conception is simple and enthralling. There is here no classical influence, and yet nothing could be more classically constructed. The beauty of the work is its sincerity. There is an inevitability in the subject. In a sense, every dramatic work, whether ancient or modern, seems frivolous by the side of this essential tragedy. It has recently

been revived in Great Britain and the United States and has made a profound impression on its audiences. All the moralities, all controversial works which followed *Everyman,* have something small and ephemeral as compared with it. It would be a complete masterpiece were its form less naked, less dull, less devoid of brilliancy. The artistic impulse seems wholly to have exhausted itself on the construction, which is itself no more than a severe staging of the transcendent message of Christianity.

After the fifteenth century the miracle-plays were still performed, but their form had been fixed and was not changed henceforth. The morality, on the other hand, had an active life, and was used by the dramatists of the Renascence and the Reformation as a means to their ends.

. . . . .

English prose of the fifteenth century amounts to little if the name be reserved for writings which have originality and some artistic value. There was the same reason for inferiority as in the preceding period: Latin still attracted writers whose purpose was not strictly utilitarian or who were more than mere translators. The bold movement of Wyclif and his partisans had, moreover, been checked. The first half of the fifteenth century was a period of narrow orthodoxy in which the cruelly persecuted Lollards were reduced to silence. Only in the second half of this century did a few rare works which deserve notice appear in English prose. It would, however, be wrong to conclude from this dearth that the spread of reading and learning had been arrested. Education made its way in spite of foreign and civil wars and was diffused. The number of persons able to read and write increased and the first epistolary collections were made. The lateness of English as compared to continental prose is principally due to the fact that it was still poorly provided, and was too easily able to enrich itself by translations of numerous foreign and especially French books which continued completely to satisfy the reading public. In this century men had not yet abandoned the paths of the Middle Ages. Literary sentiment was still not national, which is to say that there was as yet no artistic ideal.

It was the desire to bring the last Lollards back to orthodoxy which decided the learned Reginald Pecock (1395?-1460?) to write in English. This Welshman, who had taken orders and become bishop, first of St. Asaph and then of Chichester, was, as early as 1447, disquieting the clergy by the arguments he used to defend them, and he put the finishing touch to their indignation in 1455 by his *Repression of Overmuch Blaming the Clergy,* in which he defends images, pilgrimages, the temporal goods of the Church, the hierarchy, the papacy, the friars and the monks, but founds his argument only on reason. He puts natural law above Scripture and the sacraments. He has recourse only to logic and does not defer to the principle of authority.

To Wyclif and his disciples, who founded all their faith on Holy Writ, he retorted by invoking, as superior to the Scriptures, "the boke of lawe of kinde writen in mennis soulis with the finger of God." The words of Scripture ought, he says, to be "interpretid and brought forto accorde with the doom of resoun in thilk mater; and the doom of resoun oughte not forto be expowned, glosid, interpretid and broughte forto accorde with the seid outward writing in Holi Scripture."

To establish these principles in the vulgar tongue was in those days to create a scandal among the orthodox, the very class whom Peacock professed to champion. It was criminal to reason about religion with so much independence, to argue with heretics, to bring the people into these disputes by speaking to them in their own language.

Summoned to disown his book or go to the stake, Pecock chose disavowal, and not he, but his book, was burnt.

This logician, as intrepid as indiscreet, stands in isolation, and was afterwards mistaken by the Protestants for an adherent. He was understood neither by his own nor by the following century.

His prose shows a marked advance on that of his predecessors. He had clarity, the gift of choosing homely examples, and a wealth of words. His vocabulary was even excessive: drawing on its double source, English and French, he is tautological and redundant.

Sir John Fortescue (1394?-1476?) was a lawyer who wrote mainly in Latin. Like Pecock, he based his arguments on the law of nature, for instance in his *De Natura Legis Naturæ,* but his object is to establish the right to the throne of Henry VI., the grandson of the Lancastrian usurper. He premises that there are three kinds of government—absolute and monarchical, republican, constitutional and monarchical. The Lancastrians are legitimate kings because of the English constitution. Fortescue was the first to admire the constitution of his country, which he praises in his *De Laudibus Legum Angliæ* (1468-70).

When the Lancastrian cause was lost, Fortescue went over to the Yorkists and wrote, this time in English, his little treatise of forty pages on the *Gouvernance of England.* He had stayed in France with Henry VI. when this king was a fugitive, and he takes France as the type of an absolute, England as that of a limited, monarchy. This writer affords the first example of national political pride. He admires his own country, as compared with France, for its greater liberty and more abundant riches, his patriotism leading him so far that he celebrates the outstanding valour of his compatriot highwaymen. The French, he says, are, like the Scots, too cowardly to steal. "Ther is no man hanged in Scotland in vii yere to gedur ffor robbery. . . . But the Englysh man is off another corage. Ffor yff he be pouere, and see another man havynge rychesse, wich mey be taken ffrom hym be myghte, he will not spare to do so."

The *Paston Letters,* the correspondence of the Paston family, are interesting rather to the historian than to the student of literature. While scholars, clerks and nobles still wrote in Latin, the middle class was taking to English. The letters have been preserved of three generations of the Pastons, a well-to-do Norfolk family, and they give much intimate and curious information about English life from 1422 to 1509. Passages are not lacking which suggest the barbarism of the period, but the picture as a whole is of a very modern middle-class society, much engrossed by money matters, leases and the letting of land, the management of property, lawsuits, home comforts, domestic cleanliness. We learn what men read in those days and how severely they brought up their children. Dame Agnes inquires if her son Clement be working well at the Inns of Court, and begs his tutor that otherwise "he wyll trewly belassch hym, tyl he wyll amend, and so ded the last maystr, and the best thet ever he had, att Caumbrege." There is a sure and serious affection between husband and wife and they work together to establish the family fortunes. The wife shows great courage when the house is attacked by a band of enemies during her husband's absence.

There is nothing literary in these letters about business, all of them utilitarian, and they cannot be said to show that their writers used the English language easily and fluently. They managed to understand each other, nothing more.

English prose was still formless and indefinite, distributed among numerous local ways of speech, when in 1474 the first English printer began his work. William Caxton (1421-91) has himself told how hampered he at first was by the anarchical state of his language. The unity constituted by the King's English in the fourteenth century had as yet been realised only in poetry. Evolution was, moreover, still in course, so that in his sixtieth year Caxton found the language very different from that spoken in his childhood. He asked himself how he could please everyone. To make himself more certain of being understood he sometimes places the French beside the English word, as *chasse* and *hunt.* He wrote as he habitually spoke, avoiding too rustic terms, aiming at the comprehension of clerks and gentlemen, having his books revised by Master John Skelton, poet laureate of Oxford University. He thus succeeded in being intelligible, and he hardly went beyond this modest ideal. He is a mediocre translator and the best of his prose occurs in his explanatory prefaces, in which he shows himself a good fellow and a man of cheerful disposition.

It is usual to number the discovery of printing among the causes of the Renascence. By helping the spread of knowledge it certainly favoured the great literary revolution which was at hand. But it is possible, at least in England, to ask whether its first effects were not to fortify and prolong the Middle Ages. To draw up a list of the books issued from the English printing presses during almost fifty years is to cast up the balance-sheet of the past. It is barely possible to discern, here and there in such a list, a book which heralds the new age.

Caxton himself had nothing of the humanist. He was a Kentishman, a member of the Mercers' Company, who at twenty years old left England for the Low Countries. He settled in Bruges and there acted as a consul responsible for the trading interests of his fellow-countrymen. His stay in Flanders acquainted him with the most civilised court in Western Europe, that of the Dukes of Burgundy, to whose dominions Flanders belonged. In this court, although a great appetite for art and learning was manifest, letters were still confined in the mediæval frames. It was with French literature that Caxton came to be impregnated, and to its propagation that he devoted his energies as translator and printer. Bruges was one of the first towns to take advantage of Gutenberg's invention, and Caxton, having been initiated by the printer Colard Mansion, finished an incomplete translation of the *Receuil des Histoires de Troye* by Raoul Lefèvre, chaplain to the Duke of Burgundy, and published it at Bruges in 1474. It was the first printed English book. The second was the translation of another French work, a moral and allegorical treatise on the game of chess.

When more than fifty years old Caxton returned to England, in 1476, and established the first English printing-press near Westminster Abbey. Amid much encouragement and protected by Earl Rivers and by the Duke of Gloucester, afterwards Richard III., he worked there until his death in 1491.

What is interesting is his choice of books for printing. He has right neither to the glory of having discovered printing, which belongs to Gutenberg and Schoeffer, nor to the glory of erudition won by the Aldi of Venice and the Etiennes of France, nor even to that of producing beautiful volumes. He was essentially a practical man, on the look-out for books likely to please, and also a man whose personal tastes were determined by his long sojourn on the continent and by his age. But although his title to represent his nation has been questioned, it is impossible not to be struck by the fact that the library he formed is very like that of the Paston family. It contains the same mixture of poetry, chivalrous romances, moral allegories and books of devotion.

He was a great admirer of Chaucer and printed the *Canterbury Tales* (1478) and *Troylus and Criseyde,* but he also found room for Lydgate and Gower.

He preferred prose, however, as a medium for the translations of French chivalrous romances which he made or had made—the *Recuyell of the Historyes of Troye,* the *Boke of Histories of Jason,* the *Lyf of Charles the Grete,* the *Morte d'Arthur,* the *Foure Sonnes of Aymon.* It was also into prose that he translated the *Historye of Reynart the Foxe* from the Dutch.

Among works of piety issued from his press were the Hours of the Church, a life of Christ, and a translation of the *Golden Legend* which had the largest circulation of all his publications.

Nothing shows the mediæval character of his reading and his mind better than the *Æneid* he published in 1490, which is translated not from Virgil but from a baroque romance of the Middle Ages.

If it be remembered that Caxton's immediate successors, Wynkyn de Worde, Richard Pinson and the others, did not notably deviate from his lead in their choice of publications up to 1530, it becomes clear that the English Renascence began amid a considerable body of books which were penetrated by the mediæval spirit. It might even be thought, so nearly complete is the absence of the books properly called classical, that the country remained outside the current along which Europe was being swept towards Greek and Roman antiquity. But in justice it should be said that the English found it more convenient to procure books of the newer kind from continental publishers,

and to keep their own presses, still few in number, for popular books written in their own language.

What is most remarkable, from the literary point of view, is the development of English prose for which Caxton, a mediocre writer, was responsible. French prose, of which he definitely perceived the qualities, was his ideal. He admired "the fair language of French, which was in prose so well and compendiously set and written, which methought I understood the sentence and substance of every matter" (*Recuyell of the Historyes of Troye*). He himself aimed at a like clarity and like ease.

In producing prose renderings of the mediæval romances he followed the example of the French of the fifteenth century. He thus ensured a longer survival and wider popularity to these romances, which he made accessible to all men. In English, verse had hardly ever embellished them, and, had it not been for the minstrels, they would have fallen into neglect. Prose secured that the stories they enclosed became known. In more or less shortened form, these romances passed from hand to hand, the principal one of the wares the pedlar bore in is pack. In the chapbooks of the Elizabethan period, they kept romance alive in the minds of simple people, awoke those dreams of extraordinary adventure to which many dramatists of the Renascence appealed and which others of them mocked. By means of these compilations, the Middle Ages were kept from dying altogether, and sank, instead, to deeper and deeper strata of consciousness. Whatever may have been the value of the new works which sprang of the Renascence, the old stories still made the first and the favourite appeal to popular imagination. They shared the rôle with the ballads, which were multiplied in the same period as they, and which often epitomised in a few verses stories like theirs.

Among the prose versions of old romances published by Caxton there was, however, one which was to be not only food for the people but also a feast for the fastidious. Caxton was well inspired on the day he printed Sir Thomas Malory's *Morte d'Arthur.* He tells us that when he had published the noble feats of Hector, Charlemagne and Godfrey of Bouillon, he was "instantly required" by "many noble and divers gentlemen" also to imprint those of Arthur who belonged to the realm of England. In reply, he pleaded that "divers men hold opinion that there was no such Arthur," yet allowed himself to be persuaded. The translation he used was ready to hand, having been made by Thomas Malory, knight, member of parliament and Lancastrian, who shared the misfortunes of his party and died in 1471. His translation was complete in 1469 and published in 1484.

Malory represents himself as translating a French book. In truth he seems to have had recourse to many books, so that his *Morte d'Arthur* is a compilation. He has brought together scattered romances and co-ordinated them, without eliminating the traces of disparity. In spite, however, of the immense parentheses which recount the separate adventures of Sir Balin, Sir Pelleas, Sir Palomides, Sir Bors, the history of Tristram and Isoud, we can distinguish in his work the lines of a dominant story, that of Arthur, which is logically followed by the tale of the Sangreal. Malory tells of Arthur's triumphant reign, the unfaithfulness of his wife Guenever who takes Launcelot for her lover, Launcelot's punishment by the failure of his quest of the Sangreal, the finding of which is reserved for the purer Galahad. He shows the knights disaffected to the king because of Guenever's sin, and relates Mordred's revolt and Arthur's death. The book ends religiously, for Guenever becomes a nun and Launcelot a hermit. Romantic though it be, we feel that it bears a relation to actualities. The painter of the evils of civil war in this legendary kingdom was a victim of the Wars of the Roses, and the fact sometimes brings a moving gravity and melancholy into his pages.

But both this application to the author's own time and the moral lesson which unites the adventures are uncertain, vague and hesitating in Malory's work. Even the moral is inconsistent, for Launcelot and Guenever in their sin are cited as an example to true lovers. Hence the Puritan reproach, formulated by Roger Ascham: "the whole pleasure of whiche booke standeth in two speciall poyntes, in open mans slaughter and bold bawdrye." In fact, this over-loose compilation lacks unity both of thought and of plot.

It has, however, another unity, that of manner, tone and atmosphere. Malory transports us to a strange country in a distant world, unreal, impossible and yet imaginatively coherent—a country where all is tourneys and battles, where the only dwellings reared are castles, a country without agricultural life or trade, a region of mirage in which the marvellous is at home and fantastic personages are plausible.

It is the evocation of a vanished epoch, of a sort of golden age, a story of the Round Table written during atrocious civil conflict. It is a refuge, beneath hovering and all-diffused melancholy, from the hardships and crudities of the present.

The narrator of these fanciful tales found a style which fits them well—simple, even childish, monotonous, but harmonious and having poetic cadences. A clear, transparent and smooth style which does not date. It breathes a soft archaic odour. It betrays neither labour nor culture. The charm of this prose is that it is made up of poetic reminiscences inherited from a long line of earlier poems. The style is that of the fairy-tales which are told to little children, and makes a Frenchman think of Perrault's stories, but it is the product of a period which was less wise than Perrault's and of a narrator less self-conscious than he. It is delicious prose of a particular kind, although unfit for other than its own purpose, as is apparent when the author attempts to reason. But when he relates he reaches excellence. An artist like Tennyson could do no better than translate almost literally Malory's story of Arthur's death and of the colloquy between him and Sir Bedivere. There are even good judges who prefer Malory's simple prose to the too elaborate verses of the Victorian poet.

The literary importance and influence of this collection cannot be exaggerated. It is England's first book in poetic prose, and also the storehouse of those legends of the past which have most haunted English imaginations. It is the

work which kept the chivalrous spirit alive among the literate, the poets and the gentry, while the people were fed by the chap-books. Whether such a book would have met with a like fortune in France is doubtful. The author does not sufficiently dominate his material for a French audience. He is incapable of making an explanation or giving a sign of self-consciousness. He repeats his tale like a marvelling child trying to tell faithfully what it has heard and not entirely understood. He gives a wide field to the imagination and does not trouble himself about the intelligence.

The second important prose work that appeared after Malory's was another translation from the French. It was Froissart's *Chronicles,* translated by John Bourchier, Lord Berners (1467-1533) and published in 1523-5. Lord Berners's excellent prose, as animated, lively and highly coloured as his original, yet represents a return to the fourteenth century, as does also his other book, *Huon of Bordeaux,* which contains the story of the dwarf Auberon. These books appeared when the humanist movement had begun, and the first troubles of the Reformation were manifesting themselves. Without abandoning French, writers were about to add to it the direct study of Latin or even Greek, and on occasion to prefer to it the southern languages. The same Lord Berners was a pioneer of the new prose and a precursor of the Euphuists in his translation of the *Golden Book of Marcus Aurelius* from the Spanish of Antonio de Guevara. He is the connecting-link between the two ages in prose, as Skelton and Douglas, on very different grounds, are in poetry. (pp. 99-126)

Emile Legouis, "The Fifteenth Century—From the Death of Chaucer to the Renascence (1400-1516)," in his A History of English Literature: The Middle Ages & the Renascence (650-1660), Vol. I, *translated by Helen Douglas Irvine, J. M. Dent & Sons Ltd. 1926, pp. 99-126.*

POETRY

H. S. Bennett   (essay date 1947)

[*An English literary scholar, Bennett wrote* England from Chaucer to Caxton *(1928) and* Chaucer and the Fifteenth Century *(1947), which forms part one of the second volume of* The Oxford History of English Literature. *In the following excerpt from the second-named work, he provides an exhaustive survey of fifteenth-century poetry, discussing all the varieties of the genre.*]

[Fifteenth]-century literature is deserving of far more respectful attention than it has received from literary historians in the past. . . . In verse the emphasis in literary histories has been on 'courtly' poetry, and Lydgate and his followers—the so-called 'Chaucerians'—have had most of the critical attention, while the whole body of writers of 'non-Chaucerian' verse have been fobbed off with a few condescending paragraphs of mild commendation. Dr.

A. W. Pollard has been an honourable exception here: as early as 1903 he was calling attention to the mass of poetry of a 'non-Chaucerian' or 'non-courtly' nature that was available, and after quoting some verses from the *Nut-Brown Maid* declares: 'to say that English poetry was dead when verse like this was being written is absurd. It was not dead, but banished from court.'

Anyone who follows the advice implicit in this statement soon comes to realize that there is a great body of fifteenth-century verse available. Some of this is purely religious: indeed Professor Carleton Brown tells us in his Introduction to *Religious Lyrics of the Fifteenth Century* that 'the volume of extant fifteenth-century religious poetry, contrary to the impression which one receives from handbooks of literature, is many times larger than that of the preceding century'. Not only religious poetry, but political, satiric, and occasional verse of many kinds was being produced—most of it mediocre, but generally bearing about it something lacking in the 'courtly' poetry—a something which we may conveniently summarize as a lively contact with life. This is the vital dividing line between the two great streams of fifteenth-century poetry, and we must distinguish sharply between them. Throughout much of the century there was still a demand for the old 'courtly' type of poetry, a demand encouraged by the chivalric renaissance of the court of Edward III. (pp. 124-25)

The demand for 'courtly' poetry . . . encouraged many poets to fashion their verses in the old tried forms, and to elaborate themes which had been old centuries before. Gradually a crushing weight of tradition was created which no 'courtly' poet was strong enough or audacious enough to defy. The two leaders of poetry in the early decades of the century were Lydgate and Hoccleve, who untiringly acknowledged their indebtedness to Chaucer and their determination to follow in his footsteps. But who can draw the bow of Ulysses? Both these writers could only take over the verse-forms, the diction, and the conventions used by Chaucer, and in their turn hand them on to their successors and pupils. The degradation of verse which was brought about by this progressive in-breeding can be estimated by reflecting on the implications of Hawes's profession that he tries

> To folowe the trace, and all the perfitnes
> Of my master Lydgate.

Whatever vitality Chaucer had imparted to his themes and metrical patterns was utterly exhausted during the century, for unless constantly renewed their strength rapidly becomes formalized and emptied of delight. This was the history of the ambitious 'courtly works' of the fifteenth century. It was the hey-day of the poetaster, who, with little feeling for verse and no intellectual powers of any consequence, beat out his numbers with growing incompetence.

These writers slavishly followed traditional forms and themes, and clutched eagerly at any device which they thought might help them. Hence they took over ready-made the dream-convention, and began their poems by dozing over their books, or by allowing the author to read and to fall asleep over his book; or by a description of the time of year, in imitation of Chaucer's *Prologue;* or by a prologue explaining their deficiencies and how they came to write at all. They exploited every technical device, such as telling of their story by 'cloudy figures', or by 'veiled discourse', or by the elaborate use of the 'rhetorical colours', or by a reliance upon allegory. They employed the metres, forms and diction which had descended from the time of Chaucer, and hoped by so doing to merit for themselves the title of poet.

To illustrate all this in detail would be tedious, but an understanding of what was wrong with this 'courtly' poetry depends upon a realization of how widespread the canker of servile imitation had become. Take, for example, the idea of prefacing a work by a prologue. We have plenty of examples in Chaucer's work, or in the *Confessio Amantis,* or the *Parliament of the Three Ages* to remind us how effective this device may be. It is otherwise with many fifteenth-century prologues. In the general prologue to his *Legends of Holy Women* Bokenham follows scholastic tradition with his careful statement of the four causes of his work: material, formal, final, and efficient. Fortunately, in the prologues to the separate legends he gives a more lively and gossipy account of their origin, and despite much conventional self-abasement, his prologues remain the most readable part of his work. Other writers use the prologue to excuse themselves or to put in a claim for the indulgence of their readers or their patron. Lydgate luxuriates in these introductory grovellings, which at times he couples with entreaties for money. Walton apologizes for his 'Insuffishaunce of cunnyng and of wit, Defaut of language and of eloquence'. The anonymous translator of *Palladius on Husbandry* devotes a prologue of 128 lines to the praise of the patron, Humphrey of Gloucester, while Ridley dedicates his *Compound of Alchemy* to Edward IV in an introduction of 240 lines. Hawes is little briefer in the *Pastime of Pleasure,* where he apologizes to his 'Ryght myghty prynce and redoubted souerayne' Henry VII because his work is 'opprest with rudenes Without rhetoryke or colour crafty'.

The 'colours' of which Hawes speaks were among the technical devices used by all medieval poets. In the pseudo-Ciceronian treatise *Ad Herennium* will be found a list of the various *exornationes* of formal speech. Later writers enlarged on these, and Brunetto Latini in his *Livre dou Trésor* lists Ornament, Circumlocution, Comparison, Exclamation, Fable, Transition, Demonstration, and Repetition as 'colours' or embellishments of style. (pp. 125-27)

Fifteenth-century poets expected more, perhaps, from these 'rules' than it was possible to obtain, and they are constantly pleading their inability to conform to the rules, or to the practice of great followers of the rules (as they thought) such as Chaucer. But here they misunderstood what had happened. Chaucer began by being the servant of rhetoric but ended by being its master. No fifteenth-century 'courtly' poet laughed at 'Gaufred, deere maister soverayn'; yet no poet could profit from works like Geoffrey's *Nova Poetria* who took them too seriously and regarded rhetoric as an end in itself. Thus the author of the *Court of Love* apologizes for his work, since in it 'Ne craft of Galfrid [Geoffrey] may nat here sojorne', while *La Belle*

Dame sans Merci, its author tells us, 'Standeth ful destitute Of eloquence, of metre, and of colours', whereas it ought to be written, as Walton regrets he cannot write, 'With wordes set in colour wonder wel, Of rhetoryk endited craftily.'

Despite such disclaimers, most authors endeavoured to use the rhetorical 'colours' so far as they could, since they enabled the writer to exhibit his *expertise,* and powers of amplification. But they were a double-edged weapon, which had to be used with a clear knowledge of the effect they were designed to obtain. Used clumsily, or excessively, they only resulted in boring or annoying the reader; and in the main, fifteenth-century writers used these devices in a lifeless, unenterprising way.

Even with such aids, these poets never tired of proclaiming their own incompetence. One and all they repeat with wearisome unanimity that they never slept on Parnassus nor drank of the Muses' well, have never been inspired by Clio, or Melpomene, or Calliope, and have failed to garner any wisdom from Tully, Quintilian, Virgil, or other 'laureate clerks'. Benedict Burgh's comprehensive disclaimer may well illustrate this trick:

> Of tullius frauncis and quintilian
> fayne wolde I lere. but I not conceyve can
> The noble poete virgil the mantuan
> Omere the greke and torqwat sovereyne
> Naso also that sith this worlde firste began
> the marvelist transformynge all best can devyne
> Terence ye mery and plesant theatryne
> porcyus lucan marcyan and orace
> stace Juvenall and the lauriate bocase.

Their timidity of outlook and lack of enterprise also betrayed itself in the way in which they clung to forms, such as allegory. Where Langland had used it as a vital part of his poetic method and as a means to an end, a host of lesser writers found in it an end in itself. Hence much fifteenth-century verse is disfigured by allegorical conceits which lie heavy and lifeless upon such ideas as the poets have. To men who had laughed at the 'churls' tales' of Chaucer, with their homely realism and frank acceptance of men as men, the insistence on allegorical interpretations, on personified abstractions, and the continual emphasis on moral and philosophical considerations rapidly became tedious. Some men might still be willing to work their way through such instructive works, but long before the end of the century it became clear that this form of poetry was losing its appeal. Men were no longer content to accept the medieval, Christian view, that for poets, 'Ther chieff labour is vicis to repreue With a maner couvert similitude'. By the end of the century Hawes reiterates this as the proper doctrine, but is forced to admit that

> rude people, opprest with blindnes
> Against your fables, will often solisgise
> Suche is their minde, such is their folishnes
> For they beleue, in no maner of wyse
> That vnder a coloure, a trouth may aryse
> For folyshe people, blynded in a matter
> Will often erre, when they of it do clatter.

'Courtly' poets were also servile in their use of stanza forms and in their diction. This may be seen by noting the volume of verse written in Chaucer's rhyme royal. Hoccleve and Lydgate also use rhyme royal, though Lydgate especially makes use of other metres. Many a later writer, however, uses rhyme royal for the most unlikely purposes—in a treatise on agriculture, or one on alchemy, or to introduce one on economic policy—as well as for poems of a more traditional kind, such as *The Pastime of Pleasure, The Ship of Fools,* or *The Garland of Laurel.* It is perhaps worth noting that Skelton realizes the unsuitable nature of the stanza for his *Garland,* and in places bursts out into a tripping, singing measure that offers the reader much needed relief. For even with Chaucer's verses before them as a model, the work of these poets is void of metrical pleasure. There is a prosodic incompetence about it which is well nigh omnipresent. A few writers show some feeling for verse—the anonymous writers of *Palladius,* or of the *Lover's Mass,* for example—but for such writers as Lydgate, Hawes, and Barclay we can only regret that they were misguided enough to think that they could use Chaucer's verse form. A reader who tries to read them aloud halts and stumbles as he endeavours to make the lines scan or run with any ease. The incompetence of these poets cannot be entirely explained in terms of the elimination of the final *e* and other changes in syntax and pronunciation which were in process at the time. Hoccleve and Lydgate were both men of thirty and over when Chaucer died, and were both admitted followers of Chaucer, yet their verses are halting and rhythmically insensitive to a degree. In common with their contemporaries and successors, Hoccleve and Lydgate failed to understand what constitutes easy-moving verse. The ordinary laws of scansion hardly obtain in many places, and words are stressed or coined to suit the author's purpose in a most unexpected fashion. Lydgate must bear much of the blame for the disastrous example he set, and much of what has been said above will be illustrated in detail in a consideration of his work.

Their diction is as lacking in freshness and enterprise as their use of verse forms. 'So all my best is dressing old words new', writes Shakespeare, but these writers use old words without making them new. Within some fifty lines the author of the *Court of Sapience* uses *heavenly* to help describe *sound, a wood, a voice, colours,* and *paradise.* Words such as 'golden', 'sugared', 'angelic', 'lusty', and many others are worked to death and there is a resulting flatness and lack of originality. As offensive is the 'aureate' language which more and more came to be thought necessary, so that Hawes could declare it to be the poet's duty to tell

> the tale in termes eloquent
> The barbary tongue it doth ferre exclude
> Electynge wordes whiche are expedyent
> In latyn or in englysshe after the entent
> Encensynge out the aromatyke fume
> Our langage rude to exyle and consume.

The best examples of 'courtly' poetry in fifteenth-century England are to be sought among those poems for long accepted as the genuine works of Chaucer. The ascription of these poems to Chaucer, and their inclusion in the Chaucer canon, gave to them a wider publicity than they have had since Skeat and other editors consigned them to the Chaucer apocrypha. Dryden modernized *The Flower and the Leaf* and Wordsworth *The Cuckoo and the Nightingale,* Keats borrowed a title from *La Belle Dame sans Merci,* and Hazlitt in his lecture on 'Chaucer and Spenser' quoted nine stanzas from *The Flower and the Leaf* to illustrate the gusto of Chaucer's descriptions of natural scenery. 'They have a local truth and freshness, which gives the very feeling of the air, the coolness or moisture of the ground. Inanimate objects are thus made to have a fellow-feeling in the interest of the story; and render back the sentiment of the speaker's mind.'

The earliest of these poems is *The Cuckoo and the Nightingale,* written about 1403 by Sir T. Clanvowe, a member of a Herefordshire family, and well known at the court of Henry IV. It follows the familiar pattern in which the poet, after reflections on the power of Love and the influence of May upon lovers, leaves his sleepless bed and wanders into the fields to hear the nightingale. Soothed by the song of birds, and by the running water, he falls asleep, and in his dream hears the debate of a nightingale and a cuckoo. The cuckoo laughs at Love and its victims, and makes light of the nightingale's praise of Love's gifts to men. . . . There is little here that is new, and the poet excites little surprise by his handling of the theme. His five-line stanza is not very firmly controlled: 'headless' lines are comparatively frequent, while there are a number of lines with faulty metrical patterns. There is, however, a certain freshness in the way that the poet extols the May morning

> whan they mowe here the briddes singe,
> And see the floures and the leves springe,
> That bringeth into hertes remembraunce
> A maner ese, medled with grevaunce,
> And lusty thoughtes fulle of greet longinge.

The country-side is 'a launde of whyte and grene' in which the birds sing and debate, and leave far behind them a world in which Love and the troubles of lovers have to be dealt with in more business-like ways. While we read the poem we are still in that well-known country so favoured by the 'courtly' poet, and known for centuries as his homeland by 'every wight that gentil is of kinde'.

The strong hold which this 'courtly' poetry had is shown by the way it persisted through the century. Throughout the period of the Wars of the Roses every now and then someone thought it worth while to commission, or to get copied out for themselves, one of these poems. *La Belle Dame sans Merci,* for instance, belongs to the middle years of the century and is a translation by Sir Richard Ros of a poem by Alain Chartier written about 1424. The core of the poem consists of a long debate between a lover and a lady. He is ardent, she is cold. Her matter-of-fact replies to his enthusiastic outbursts are an interesting commentary on how *amour courtois* was regarded by some fifteenth-century people. To the lover's assertion that 'Who sonest dyeth, his care is leest of alle', she answers: 'This sicknesse is right esy to endure, But fewe people it causeth for to dy', and says plainly, 'Who secheth sorowe, his be the receyt!' She concludes by telling the lover that:

> My hert, nor I, have don you no forfeyt,
> By which ye shulde complayne in any kynde.
> There hurteth you nothing but your

conceyt . . .
> Ye noy me sore, in wasting al this wynde.

Against such a matter-of-fact attitude the lover can make no progress. He states his case with zeal and orthodoxy. 'Resoun, counsayl, wisdom, and good avyse Ben under love arested everichoon', he cries, but it is all of no avail. The lady is adamant, and the poet departs: 'And in himself took so gret hevinesse, That he was deed, within a day or twayne.'

Though the matter is translated and conventional there are some noteworthy things in the poem. As in *Troilus and Criseyde,* the courtly dialogue had an interest of its own for a contemporary audience. There is the medieval delight in the pursuit of a word, and one speaker often takes up a word or phrase coming at the end of the previous stanza and makes it the subject of his new utterance. There is a skill in this word-play that was fascinating to the original readers of the poem. We, unfortunately, feel but little of this. The word-spinning nature of the dialogue requires a leisure and a sympathetic understanding of conventions which are very remote to us. *La Belle Dame,* therefore, refuses to come to life, although the poet is well in command of his form, and handles his eight-line stanza with fluency and ease:

> In-to this world was never formed non,
> Nor under heven crëature y-bore,
> Nor never shal, save only your persone,
> To whom your worship toucheth half so sore,
> But me, which have no seson, lesse ne more,
> Of youth ne age, but still in your service;
> I have non eyen, no wit, nor mouth in store,
> But al be given to the same office.

Perhaps the best-known poems of a 'courtly' nature written in the fifteenth century are *The Flower and the Leaf* and the *Assembly of Ladies.* They both belong to the second half and probably to the end of the century. Scholars have been unable to agree as to their authorship: Skeat thought they were both by one author—a woman—but his conjecture has not been accepted, nor have those guesses which attribute *The Flower and the Leaf* to Lydgate, or even to Chaucer. The unknown writer of *The Flower and the Leaf,* however, was a poet of distinction: . . . Hazlitt used a passage from this work to illustrate Chaucer's outstanding merits, and the whole poem is gracefully contrived. It tells how the poet, a woman, unable to sleep, wanders afield and takes up her station in an arbour from where she can see and hear the nightingale and the goldfinch. After a time a 'world of ladies' and of knights and men at arms, all in white garments, appear. These are the followers of the Leaf, who worship the laurel. Another band of lords and ladies arrive, clad in green, who dance, and then kneel in praise before the daisy—the followers of the Flower. While the former party rest in the shade of a laurel tree, the company of the Flower suffer from heat, are buffeted by hail and rain, and present a bedraggled appearance to those beneath the laurel. The latter succour them, anoint their blistered limbs, and provide them with 'plesaunt salades', and in good time

> They passed al, so plesantly singing
> That it would have comforted any wight.

The poet asks a conveniently belated member of the Leaf party to explain the meaning of all she has seen. The followers of the Leaf, she is told, are those who have been chaste, brave, and steadfast in love, while the followers of the Flower are those who have loved idleness, and cared for nothing but hunting, hawking, and playing in meads. The party of the Leaf are led by Diana, of the Flower by Flora.

The value of this poem cannot arise from any novelty of subject-matter. All its concomitants—the orders of the Flower and the Leaf, the white and green costumes, the cult of the daisy, the astronomical reference, the spring setting, and the rest—can be traced to one or more earlier poems in French or English, but the poem's distinction lies in the ease and grace with which they have been adapted to the author's purpose. For unlike its models, *The Flower and the Leaf* is no straight-forward example of the ordinary 'courtly' type. The chaste, brave, and constant in love are set against the idle, frivolous, and casual. The knightly amusements of the chase or the pleasuring with ladies 'down by the river or up in the forest' are pastimes of the party of the Flower, which wilt and suffer under the blasts of everyday life. The life of devotion and restraint is opposed to one of pleasure and indulgence. Yet both are so much a part of life as we know it that the poet, while expressing a preference for the Leaf, does not exile the Flower, and the story ends with the departure of the two parties to sup together. The whole is a pleasing little morality: the blacks are not really very black, while the whites are not too self-conscious of their own virtues. It marks the beginning of a change: the appeal seems no longer to be to ecclesiastical or 'courtly' standards, but rather to a common-sense morality which might commend itself to the changing age it sought to amuse and instruct.

The instruction is half-concealed, partly by the allegory of the Leaf and the Flower, and partly by the graceful accomplishment of the verse. Although much of the imagery and diction are conventional, the poet gives us many charming pictures of the goldfinch on the medlar, or the entry of the supporters of the Leaf with 'so greet a noise of thundring trompes blow', or of the ladies with their chaplets of 'leves fresh and grene'. Bright, clear colours abound: the greens of the 'benched arbour' or the robes of the Knights of the Flower are contrasted with the white surcoats and horse-harness of the Knights of the Leaf. Country sights and sounds are with us throughout, and the simple cadences in which the poet describes the scene and its action make a harmonious accompaniment which allows us to enjoy this unforced contribution to the allegory of Love. Among all fifteenth-century poems written in this genre it well deserves the high place it has held since its earliest appearance in print in 1598.

The *Assembly of Ladies* belongs to this group of poems. Skeat's view that it was by the same author as *The Flower and the Leaf,* although of a later date, has not been strongly supported, for much of the material that is common to the two poems is the stock-in-trade of the 'courtly' poet. Allegory has laid a heavy hand on the *Assembly;* and, in place of the charming groups which gathered about Flora and Diana, we are confronted with such stock characters as Perseveraunce, the usher; Countenance, the porter; Largesse, the steward; Remembrance, the chamberlain; and many others who are servants to the Lady Loyalty, dwelling at Pleasant Regard.

The story is simple and inconclusive. The narrator and four of her friends are summoned to appear before the Lady at her council, and there to present their petitions. We follow their preparations to this end, and finally find ourselves in the presence-chamber of Loyalty, who receives the petitions, and then adjourns the sitting, postponing her answer till 'within short tyme our court of parliment Here shal be holde', when their grievances shall be remedied. All this is a dream which comes to the writer (supposedly a woman) and is as unsatisfying as dreams often are. The machinery has creaked and groaned to no purpose. The writer clearly makes use of the allegorical form because it is there at hand, and is the conventional method of expressing one's ideas. But Perseveraunce, Loyalty, and all the rest are very shadowy figures: Loyalty never comes to life, and never assumes any individuality of her own. She is fully described: her beauty is such

Sir John Fortescue

> That, in ernest to speke, withouten fayl,
> For yonge and olde, and every maner age,
> It was a world to loke on her visage.

Even so, both she and her court remain but lay-figures.

What life there is in the poem comes from the writer's frank interest in the ceremonial of princely courts, the behaviour of cultured people, and the conversation that such places and people implied, and the fresh simplicity of the writing.

Thus the opening stanzas are admirable in their economical description of the garden and of the conversation between the lady and a knight:

> He asked me ayein—'whom that I sought,
> And of my colour why I was so pale?'
> 'Forsothe', quod I, 'and therby lyth a tale.'
> 'That must me wite', quod he, 'and that anon;
> Tel on, let see, and make no tarying.'
> 'Abyd', quod I, 'ye been a hasty oon,
> I let you wite it is no litel thing.'

Throughout the poem there are constant touches which enliven the dull wastes of the allegorical landscape: the description of Pleasant Regard ('a very paradyse'); the asides or last-moment thoughts of the characters, as when the dreamer remarks that 'long to sewe, it is a wery thing', and asks her friend if her gown is becoming: 'It is right wel', quod she, 'unto my pay: Ye nede not care to what place ever ye go'—an opinion which is enforced later by the tribute of Diligence: 'Sister', quod she, 'right wel brouk ye your new'. The etiquette and intrigue of courts are cleverly suggested in a few phrases, and the reader is constantly aware of the bifocal vision of the author. At moments we are asked to see at long distance (as it were) the movement of the story and characters as parts of the allegory: at other moments at short distance, and much more clearly, we get touches of life or of lifelike material. Hence the poem cannot be considered a success: the handling of the fable is uncertain, and is not redeemed by any poetic vision of life, or by any mastery of technique. Despite some memorable passages, much observation and a sense of dialogue, the *Assembly* remains a museum piece.

Few medieval institutions have excited more speculation than the so-called Courts of Love, said to have been held by such ladies as Eleanor of Aquitaine or Marie of Champagne. Their fame and influence early became a matter of first-rate importance to poets, for the decisions of these courts, and the rules of love on which they were based, are at the root of most courtly poetry. The action of the lovers in *Troilus and Criseyde,* or of the lover in *La Belle Dame,* as we have already seen, is in conformity with the classic rules of love as stated by Andreas Capellanus, and as interpreted by the Courts of Love. Consequently it is no surprise to find among 'Chaucerian poems' one entitled the *Court of Love.* Its author and the date of its composition are unknown. It exists in one manuscript only, said to be of the early sixteenth century; its use of some linguistic forms show that they are archaisms and that it was written at a period when the final -*e* was seldom sounded. We may reasonably consider it to be the work of a writer well read in Chaucer and Lydgate, and fully conversant with the body of poetry, both French and English, which made use of all the paraphernalia of courtly love.

The poem tells how Philogenet appears at the Castle of Love, is sent by Admetus and Alceste into the temple where the oath of allegiance and of obedience to the twen-

ty commandments of Love (which are recited in full) is administered. Philogenet is introduced to the Lady Rosiall, who in due course confesses her love for him and tells him he may stay until the first of May, when the festival of Love is celebrated. The poem concludes with this festival, when the birds sing the praises of the god.

This poem serves as a good example of the debilitating effect of a tradition that has lost its vigour. All the materials common to the type are here. The twenty statutes of Love and their discussion take us back to Andreas Capellanus, while the detailed description of Rosiall and of her dress, the May-day song of the birds, the numerous allegorical figures, the court of Admetus and Alceste—all these had flourished for centuries, but had little importance at a time when Henry VII and Henry VIII were fashioning the new Tudor England. The poet of the *Court of Love* is skilful, ingenious, and a versifier of some power: he has some pretty fancies, is fluent, and carries us along with the buoyant enthusiasm of his 'little Philobona' and the ardent lover; the dialogue in places is well contrived and managed with great skill. If we have to class this poem with the *Assembly of Ladies* as a *tour de force* we must again remind ourselves that a good deal of poetic talent is here stultified, because it is content to pad round in the traces of a thousand predecessors, and has not courage and strength enough to break away and risk failure in new unaccepted forms.

From these 'Chaucerian' poems we turn to scrutinize the works of others who called Chaucer their master, and at their head stand Lydgate and Hoccleve. An examination of their poems will emphasize what has been said in the opening paragraphs of this [excerpt], and will explain why many critics after reading in their works have impatiently pronounced a general condemnation of the poetry of the century. (pp. 127-37)

We know little of [Lydgate's] early life, but he tells us himself how he entered the abbey of Bury St. Edmunds while still a boy, and was a novice there, passing his days idly and little inclined to listen to his teachers, or to abstain from 'ryot or excesse', until in his fifteenth year

> holdyng my passage
> Myd of a cloyster, depicte upon a wall,
> I saugh a crucifix, whos woundes were not
>   smalle,
> With this word 'Vide', wreten there besyde,
> 'Behold my mekenesse, O child, and leve thy
>   pryde.'

From that day he dated his real conversion, and the rest of his life was spent mainly in the cloister at Bury or nearby at Hatfield Broadoak. Life passed him by while he spent endless hours in the scriptorium turning out verses on very many subjects, so that, despite the inevitable losses, there still remain 145,500 lines of verse to testify to his energy.

While his energy cannot be gainsaid, the value of his work as poetry has been a matter of much dispute. Ritson, *more suo,* speaks of him as 'a voluminous, prosaic, and drivelling monk', and one of his recent editors tells us that 'it cannot be too clearly asserted that as poetry Lydgate's works are absolutely worthless'. From this we may pass to the opposite point of view strongly advanced on several occasions by Churton Collins that Lydgate was a poet of genius, most musical, with a style and verse of exquisite beauty at its best, and great powers of pathos.

Before surveying his work we must admit that its volume raises doubts concerning its quality, and the fact that so much of it was written to order adds to our uneasiness. The long poems on which his contemporary reputation was based were all commissioned work, as was also much of his occasional verse. To whatever demands were made on him Lydgate willingly responded, and his prodigious output has been a heavy legacy for generations of students. (p. 138)

An early piece from his pen, *Reason and Sensuality,* a poem in octosyllabic couplets, was written about 1408, and is one of the more readable of Lydgate's works. It is translated from the French *Les Échecs Amoureux,* and its theme is chastity. Here is much of the familiar apparatus of the allegorical convention: Spring, gardens, Nature, the Goddesses, together with the Forest of Reason and the Garden of Pleasure. Having reached the Garden of Pleasure the poet watches a game of chess, and then begins one himself with a fair maid; but before they have got far the poem breaks off. There is some freedom in Lydgate's use of his octosyllabics, despite much tiresome padding, and he has not yet lapsed into his practice of over-lengthy description and trite moralizing.

A few years later Lydgate began one of the longest of his compositions—*The Hystorye Sege and Dystruccyon of Troye,* as Pynson styled his edition of 1513, or the *Troy Book* as it is more generally called. . . . It consists of decasyllabic couplets, with a prologue and epilogue in addition, and follows closely the version of Guido delle Colonne's *Historia Troiana.* Few readers will have patience to read much of this uninspired translation: here and there, however, the social historian will find full-length descriptions of medieval life, such as the account of the workmen and of the building of New Troy, or that describing the powers of the 'nigromancer'. There are also occasional poetic moments when Lydgate describes the Spring, or strikes out lines such as 'With swiche colour as men go to her graue', or 'And saue the eye atwen was no message'. While still working on the last stretches of the *Troy Book* Lydgate put in hand his *Siege of Thebes.* It may, perhaps, be regarded as his tribute to his master Chaucer. Written in the autumn of 1421, or early in 1422, it is composed in decasyllabic couplets. The story has been adapted from an unknown French prose romance—itself a redaction of the verse *Roman de Thèbes*—with garnishings from the writings of Boccaccio added by Lydgate. The *Siege of Thebes* is the most readable of Lydgate's epics, since here he has not indulged unduly in his characteristic enlargements and adornings. Even so, it is far too long: the preparation for the siege takes up three-quarters of the poem, and although the poet has the fortunes of Oedipus at his disposal, we are never absorbed by the story. The most interesting part of the poem in every way is the prologue, in which Lydgate represents himself as joining the pilgrims at Canterbury, and being invited to ride with them towards London, and to tell a tale. Here Lydgate appears 'almost as Chaucer's ape', writes Ten Brink, and we have only to read the two prologues side by side to realize the gulf between master and pupil.

A few years after he had completed his *Troy Book* Lydgate was at work again on another lengthy enterprise, *The Pilgrimage of the Life of Man.* . . . The original of Guillaume de Deguilleville, entitled *Le Pèlerinage de la Vie Humaine,* and Lydgate's version are of a monkish, allegorical, and didactic nature, which Lydgate's stylistic limitations do nothing to make more palatable. Mr. C. S. Lewis has remarked that 'the poem is unpleasant to read, not only because of its monstrous length and imperfect art, but because of the repellent and suffocating nature of its content'. We share with him 'a heartfelt relief' in turning to other work even of Lydgate.

The longest of Lydgate's commissioned works was the *Fall of Princes.* This was composed between 1431 and 1438 for Humphrey, Duke of Gloucester, and is mainly written in rhyme royal. It is a translation, based on Laurent de Premierfait's second and enlarged version of Boccaccio's *De Casibus Virorum Illustrium,* and is a long-winded affair in which Lydgate embroiders at will on the French rendering, and there is much in his version that is alien to Boccaccio's work. Lydgate sees in the Fall of Princes material from which he can draw clearcut moral lessons. Wickedness is punished here and now; tragedy results from the evil-doing of men, for poetic justice overtakes them. 'Remembreth pleynli, yif ye be vertuous, Ye shal perseuere in long prosperitie' is his constant theme. Yet at the same time, Fortune is playing her incalculable part;

> Fortunis wheel by reuolucioun
> Doth oon clymbe up, another to discende.

Lydgate shares with many medieval writers a belief in the 'unwar strok' which may fall on even the most innocent. Arthur, bravest and most famous of men, was destroyed by Fate and Fortune, and so were Alcibiades, Hector, and scores of others. The monk in Lydgate wallows in relating these woes, and sees no hope for men unless they retire from the world and its mutable affairs. Lydgate's treatment of his material is almost unbearably prolix, and the modern reader will find that much judicious skipping is necessary if he wishes to reach the end.

These are large-scale works, and a reader interested in statistics may like to know that *Reason and Sensuality* runs to 7,042 lines, the *Troy Book* to 30,117, the *Siege of Thebes* to 4,716, the *Pilgrimage of the Life of Man* to 24,832, and the *Fall of Princes* to 36,365 lines, so that these five works contain nearly three-quarters of the surviving verses of Lydgate. In addition he wrote many shorter poems on religious and didactic themes. He tells us that the chief office of poets is 'vicis to repreue', and whatever they write they should always 'on vertue ay conclude'. With this in mind he wrote such poems as his versions of Aesop's *Fables,* or the tales of *The Horse, Goose and Sheep* and *The Churl and the Bird. London Lickpenny,* a vivid and satirical commentary on London life and on lawyers, is now generally denied to Lydgate. The current taste for saints' lives was gratified by his *Life of St. Margaret,* and later by the *Lives of St. Edmund and St. Fremund.* These now rank among the most lifeless of his works. His religious lyrics have more to be said for them—especially the *Testament of Dan John Lydgate*—for in these his real religious fervour gives some excitement to his verse.

This vast volume of work was not written without the author having some sense of its imperfections. Despite the high esteem in which Lydgate was held by his contemporaries, almost every poem of any length warns us that he is aware of his feeble poetic powers. He bemoans his dullness and the fact that the Muses did not preside at his cradle. He laments that he never slept on the hill of Parnassus, and that he is ignorant of the flowers of Tully and that he lacks metrical skill. These things soon become apparent to the reader. The plain grammatical meaning of passage after passage only becomes clear on a second or third reading, and then often only at some violence to syntax or grammar. At the same time the reader finds himself in the midst of a spate of words which seem to be doing very little, while the development of the argument or the narrative appears to be in abeyance. A closer scrutiny reveals various reasons for this. First, we may notice Lydgate's own views on narrative technique, expressed fairly late in his career in the General Prologue to the *Fall of Princes.* There he writes:

> Ffor a stori which is nat pleynli told,
> But constreyned vndir wordes fewe,
> Ffor lak of trouth, wher thei be newe or old,
> Men be report kan nat the mater shewe.
> Thes ookes grete be nat downe ihewe
> Ffirst at a strok, but bi longe processe;
> Nor longe stories a woord may nat expresse.

In his comments on this passage Thomas Gray said:

> These 'long processes' indeed suited wonderfully with the attention and simple curiosity of the age in which Lydgate lived. Many a 'stroke' have he and the best of his contemporaries spent on a sturdy old story, till they had blunted their own edge and that of their readers; at least a modern reader will find it so: but it is a folly to judge of the understanding and of the patience of those times by our own. They loved, I will not say tediousness, but length and a chain of circumstances in a narration. The vulgar do so still: it gives an air of reality to facts, it fixes the attention, raises and keeps in suspense their expectation, and supplies the defects of their little and lifeless imagination; and it keeps pace with the slow motion of their own thoughts. Tell them a story as you would tell it to a man of wit, it will appear to them as an object seen in the night by a flash of lightning; but when you have placed it in various lights and in various positions, they will come at last to see and feel it as well as others.

This is well said, but we must not impute the whole of Lydgate's long-windedness to the 'spirit of the age'. The root fact is that Lydgate was a man with a timid, limited, unenterprising mind. His life in the cloister did nothing to bring out other qualities which may have been latent in him, and his knowledge of men and women was sadly handicapped through lack of personal contacts. Even the little he knew of life was coloured by his ecclesiastical prejudices; and, as a result, his work is almost entirely derivative, often no more than direct—if diluted—translation. Unfortunately, the limitations of his mind were coupled with an overwhelming facility of utterance and a very imperfect understanding of the problems of form and style.

Lydgate's limited poetic gifts show most clearly in his diction and the use he makes of words and phrases. An examination of Chaucer's diction [shows] us how we must look at the medieval poet's use of language, and in Lydgate even more than in Chaucer we shall find that words have but a limited associative value, and are not rich in 'overtones'. Phrases like 'her sonnysh hair', or the 'restless stone' of Sisyphus, are rare: Lydgate uses them in the strict sense of the language from which he takes them— generally French or Latin. He extends our vocabulary of abstract terms—dismay, infallible, solicitude, tolerance— but he does little to use language in an imaginative or stimulating fashion. This comparative 'deadness' of language is to be found everywhere in Lydgate: he had little feeling for the poetical value of words. The *mot juste* meant nothing to him. Indeed the most outstanding feature of his style is repetition—both of word and phrase. He sought to obtain his effects, not by selecting the most suitable word or phrase, but by heaping up a series of synonyms and relying on their cumulative effect. Thus he writes 'synge and make melodye'; 'for veray joye and gladnesse', 'ruthe and pitie'. Simple adverbs such as 'nowhere' are evaded by phrases: 'neither in borgh or toun', or 'withinne nor withoute'. Phrases or sentences are even more full of potentialities for him: 'Pertynent to thy voyage' is followed by 'And nedful to thy pylgrimage'; while 'In al hast when I was clad' he thinks requires 'And redy eke in myn array' to make it clear. This itch for repetition is carried to greater excess, as in:

> Thorient
> Which ys so bryght
> And casteth forth so dire a lyght,
> Betokeneth in especiall
> Thinges that be celestiall
> And thinges, as I kan diffyne,
> That be verrily dyvyne.

Wherever we turn this verbiage is to be seen: in pleonasms—'togedir yferre'; 'suffise enowgh'; in periphrases— 'thy hevenly emperesse', 'this noble goddesse honurable'; in a delight in intensives for their own sake—wel, passingly, pleynly, sothely; or in the constant use of rhyme tags and padding formulae.

All medieval poets are fond of verbal formulae, but with Lydgate they are carried to outrageous lengths and are an outstanding feature of his style. They have been classified as 'those which make some appeal to, or assertion of the good judgement and intelligence either of the reader or of the poet, such as "As thou wel wost", or "as to myn intent". Secondly, phrases that are strongly confirmative of some preceding point—"It is no doubt", or "yiff I shal not lye". Thirdly, those that contain reference to authority— "as the phylisofre seyth", or "as clerkys teche". Fourthly, such expressions as, "In substaunce", or "shortely to specefye", and lastly, certain adverbial expressions of place and time—"erly and late", "both este and weste" or "at eve and eke at prime".' We may classify these things, but that does not justify their use, nor does it illustrate fully 'the deep damnation of their taking off'. Phrases like 'Ther nis namor to seye', or 'In al the haste he may', are constantly used by Lydgate to fill up his lines, and he will go even farther, so that 'in al the haste he may' in one line can provoke the equally feeble 'withoute more delay' in the next. 'Yf I shal nat feyne' is not to be taken at its face value, but as a convenient line-filler to be followed by 'They be set lyk hornes tweyne', and this principle leads to such couplets as

> I am the same, thys the cas,
> Off whom that whylom wrote Esdras

or

> That Malebouche, yt ys no lye
> Ffledde ffyrst out off Normaundye.

This slackness of control and inability to resist the easy, empty tag or phrase or rhyme is characteristic of Lydgate's work. In the face of tens of thousands of lines disfigured by such blemishes, the limited number of lines where Lydgate rises above correctness to something nearer poetry cannot be considered as sufficient to justify the claims made by Churton Collins and others on his behalf.

But it is not on these grounds alone that any such claims must be resisted. Lydgate's sense of syntax was as uncertain as his feeling for words. He has no rules to guide him in the construction of the sentences; indeed he often seems to start out with no clear idea of where his sentence will lead him. Clauses and phrases in apposition are frequent, the main thread is picked up again with 'I mene', or some such phrase, only to be followed by many qualifying phrases and dependent sentences. 'His clauses run headlong, shuffling and entangled in proportion as the idea is intricate.' And as with the smaller units, so with the greater. The verse, the paragraph, the section—these were but dimly apprehended units to Lydgate. He seldom looked far ahead, and had little notion, apparently, of the relation between the parts and the whole. Size was to him what it is to a child with a box of bricks—the larger the better. So his works ramble on with little attempt to tell their story clearly and economically. Even when he is translating, he finds it necessary to expand his original to inordinate lengths. His mind is at the mercy of innumerable side issues, any one of which may start him off on a heap of verses which have little connexion with his theme. The mention of the gods, of the heroes of antiquity, of the saints, or of any one of the many stock subjects of the Middle Ages elicited from him a stock response which often meant the pouring out of all his knowledge and miscellaneous reading, or gave him an opportunity for trite and dreary moralizing with a seemingly unending series of examples. The 'catalogue method' of describing a woman's charms or the beauty of a May morning had no more determined adherent than Lydgate, while the unending line of historical personages, such as we get in the *Fall of Princes,* fascinated him, and encouraged the production of his monumental series of 'tragedies'—a poetic blunder realized by Chaucer when he left part told the *Legend of Good Women* or interrupted the Monk's 'tragedies' with the Knight's 'good sire, namoore of this'. These many weaknesses are made the more exasperating by Lydgate's

peculiar versification. While it may be untrue to say that he cannot write three consecutive lines without offending the rules of metre, the fact remains that even with the best modern 'edited' texts the scansion of innumerable lines of Lydgate is performed only with difficulty. Professor Schick adopted for Lydgate's decasyllabic line a scheme whereby he divided the lines into five principal types, differentiated according to the number of their syllables. Whatever merits this scheme may have for reducing Lydgate's prosodic practices to some system, it does little to make his lines more tolerable to the eye or ear. More recently Mr. C. S. Lewis has invited us to overcome these difficulties by reminding us that Lydgate was 'comparatively heedless of the number of syllables and generally attentive to stress', and that Chaucer's tradition of writing in true decasyllables was very soon lost. It was therefore possible for Lydgate to write lines many of which can be tortured into a decasyllabic pattern of sorts, but which in reality are what Mr. Lewis calls 'fifteenth-century heroics'—that is a series of lines 'each divided by a sharp medial break into two half-lines, each half-line containing not less than two or more than three stresses'. Many of Lydgate's lines can be read as four-stress lines with a movement like that of the fables in the *Shepherd's Calendar,* in which critics have supposed Spenser to be imitating the 'riding rhyme' to Canterbury. Even if all could be so read, the necessity of emphasizing the stresses and slurring the intermediate syllables breeds, in a poet with no gift for rhythm and musical phrasing, an unbearable monotony. But many cannot be so read, and the ear dithers between two or more systems of versification and rests in none.

Even if we admit that Mr. Lewis is Lydgate's Tyrwhitt, there remain the many weaknesses when some larger unit than the line is considered. Where we saw Chaucer working by the large paragraph unit, with a full understanding of 'the perpetual conflict between the law of verse, and the freedom of language', Lydgate moves forward hesitantly line by line, and frequently his metrical peculiarities only serve to direct our attention to words that have no claim to special consideration. When Chaucer writes: 'Tróuthe and honóur, frédom and cúrteisie', the stresses are so placed as to bring out the force of the four stressed words. When (following his master) Lydgate writes: 'Pées and qúyete, cóncorde and vnyte', the stresses only serve to draw attention to the tautologous nature of the coupled terms. When Lydgate tries to use the larger paragraph there results a lamentable confusion in which sense and rhythm are both swept away. A good example may be seen in the prologue to the *Siege of Thebes,* where Lydgate opens his poem with a sentence of 78 lines modelled on the *Prologue* to the *Canterbury Tales.* But where Chaucer controls his paragraph with reiterated *Whan* followed in due course by 'Than longen folk . . . ', Lydgate begins, then begins again and accumulates a series of clauses and phrases for at least 78 lines without reaching a principal verb, while his versification also is lacking in Chaucerian suppleness and rhythmic flow.

To turn from Lydgate to his contemporary Hoccleve is to turn from the cloistered tranquillity of Bury St. Edmunds to the bustle and movement of London. The recluse gives way to the man of the world, and the larger part of the interest that Hoccleve has for us comes from the social rather than poetical reason that his many autobiographical passages recreate in vivid fashion the London of his day. There apparently he lived throughout his working life, and much of his poetry is the direct result of his experiences as a clerk in the Privy Seal office by day and a 'man about town' by night. (pp. 138-47)

His works . . . are much more limited in character than those of Lydgate. They are in the main of a moralizing, didactic nature, plentifully interspersed in the large works by refreshing personal anecdotes and reflections. We are always in touch with the poet: we do not feel that his poems are mechanic exercises, but the reflection of the poet's own ideas and personality. That does not give his verses value, for on the whole Hoccleve has not a sensitive alert mind. He is an egoist, and the naïve outpourings of his own hopes and fears are presented to us in all their crude immediacy. What his mind thought his pen set down without much preliminary attempt to control or refine his matter in a clear picture: yet his dialogue gives the illusion of life: we feel something of the give and take of conversation in such passages as:

> 'The book concludith for hem is no nay,
> Vertuously my good freend dooth it not?'
> 'Thomas, I noot, for neuere it yit I say.'
> 'No, freend?' 'No, Thomas.' 'Wel trowe I, in fay;
> Ffor had ye reed it fully to the ende,
> Yee wolde seyn it is nat as ye wende.'

This immediacy gives what little value may be found in Hoccleve's work. He does not pierce far below the surface, nor has he a very poetic view of life, but his poems move to their conclusions without the padding and syntactical confusion of Lydgate. Hoccleve never rises to any heights—even such a passage as Lydgate's verses on his conversion is beyond him, and he has no feeling, or liking, apparently for nature. Fortunately he never tries to cover up his poetic weaknesses by the use of 'aureate' language, but is content with a limited vocabulary which he occasionally uses to good effect by the inclusion of some colloquial phrase, such as 'ryse up and slynge hym down', or 'I told him so'; or by a striking line—'Excesse at borde hath leyd his knyf with me', or 'For rethorik hath hid fro me the keye', or 'There never strode yet wyse man on my fete'. His control of rhythms and the verse forms which he adopts is very imperfect, but at times he gets beyond a mechanical counting of syllables and marking of stresses. On the whole, however, the Chaucerian music, which he tried to imitate, eluded him completely. He has every reason to ask his friends to correct his work

> If that I in my wrytynge foleye,
> As I do ofte, (I can it nat withseye,)
> Meetrynge amis or speke vnfittyngly,
> Or nat by iust peys my sentences weye,
> And nat to the ordre of endytyng obeye
> And my colours sette ofte sythe awry.

Hoccleve, then, cannot claim any high place in the poetic heavens. Indeed, this 'crimeless Villon', as Saintsbury calls him, survives mainly for two reasons. First, because his devotion to Chaucer endears him to all lovers of poetry. He rises to something near eloquence when he speaks of

his 'master deere and fadir reuerent' who 'fayn wolde han me taght, But I was dul, and lerned lite or naught', and tells how he has had Chaucer's likeness painted in the manuscript of his *Regiment of Princes:*

> That hei that haue of him lest thought and
>   mynde,
> By his peynture may ageyn hym fynde.

Secondly, Hoccleve's work is full of interest for the student of social history. The extravagant costumes of his time; the debauchery and riotous behaviour of the 'man about town'; the starvation endured by those broken by the wars; the decay and partiality of justice; pluralism and absenteeism; the abuses of child-marriages—these and many another topic find expression in the pages of Hoccleve, and help to create the picture of the world in which the poet lived, and in which poetry could hope for but a casual and fugitive hearing among the many distractions of the times.

Hoccleve and Lydgate were only two of the many writers of long religious or didactic poems in this century. Devout authors tried to interest and instruct at the same time, and improving narratives in verse, or saints' lives, or portions of the Psalms, were produced from time to time. There is nothing surprising in this: the Church was still immensely powerful, and a concern for things spiritual was ever close to men's thoughts whenever they paused from their getting and spending of things material.

A typical example is Brampton's *Seven Penitential Psalms.* This is a competent piece of versifying, but is uninspired and contains nothing that cannot be paralleled in many a poem written by Lydgate and his followers, and well represented in Carleton Brown's *Religious Lyrics of the Fifteenth Century.* The lives of a number of saints or legends of holy women by Osbern Bokenham are of greater interest. . . . He was born about 1392, and died in or just before 1447, and his *Legends* were 'doon wrytyn in Canebryge by his soun Frere Thomas Burgh'. He translated his *Legends* from various Latin sources, and kept closely to his text. In common with many others he was a great admirer and disciple of Chaucer, and like them seems forced to write in verse, despite his limitations. He apologizes from time to time for his lack of skill, and asks his friend not to mention his name in Cambridge, 'where wythys be manye ryht capcyous and subtyl'. He composed at a good speed when in the vein, for he tells us that he wrote the life of St. Katherine, which runs to 1,064 lines, in five days. His method of translation was that commonly adopted by medieval writers, namely to follow his author not word by word but sentence by sentence. The most pleasing parts of his work are the introductory and connecting passages, where he prattles away about the reasons for undertaking the work or indulges in 'poetical' passages, such as that in the Prologue to the life of St. Mary Magdalene, where the date is indicated in a sentence of twenty-three lines. He betrays his naïve pleasure in his own powers, in spite of his conventional outcries that he lacks the 'cunnyng and eloquens' of Gower, Chaucer, and Lydgate; and 'as euere crystene man owyth to do', he utterly rejects the elaborate eloquence of some writers, and cries for help to Christ and not to the Muses. His telling of the saints' lives never reaches any distinction: when he is held by his source material he is able to control his verse better than when he is free to go his own way. He uses the staple measures of rhyme royal and decasyllabic couplet in the main, although some of his prologues and the stories of Christina and Elizabeth employ an eight-line stanza, and generally he confines himself to the accepted vocabulary of his age. His narrative lacks individuality or even the well-mannered ease of much of Gower; and if read continuously the seemingly endless barbarities and cruelties which confronted these holy women become unendurable.

One of the most learned men of his day, John Capgrave, also turned from his voluminous prose works in English and Latin to write the *Life of St. Katherine* in verse. He tells us that the work is a translation from the Latin, just made by an English priest, but that it was not easy to understand because of the 'derk langage' that he used. Capgrave rewrites it to make it more plain, and after a confused appeal to God, Apollo, and Saint Paul begins his poem. This consists of 8,372 lines in rhyme royal. Dr. Furnivall speaks of the poem as 'worthless', and this is very nearly the truth. Capgrave's work, like many other lives of the saints, has little to commend it as poetry. It might equally well (or better) have been written in prose, for its slow-moving pedestrian verse does nothing to reconcile us to the *longueurs* of the narrative, the credulous recital of the impossible, and the long-drawn-out descriptions of torture and mutilation, in spite of Capgrave's plea:

> And if ye dowte, ye reders of þis lyffe,
> Wheyther it be southe, ye may well vndyrstande:
> Mech þing hath be do whech hath be ful ryue
> And is not wretyn ne can neuer to our hande,
> Mech þing eke hyd in many dyuerse lande;
> Euene so was þis lyffe.

The writing of saints' lives represents one side of didactic versification in this century. Another is admirably illustrated by the works of John Walton, Canon of Osney, who in 1410 translated into verse the *Consolations of Boethius,* and from the comparatively large number of surviving manuscripts (twenty-three in all) it is clear that his version provided his readers with an acceptable account of this work which so fascinated the medieval mind. The interest of Walton's work to modern students, however, is not so much in his restatement of Boethius' ideas as in his skilful management of his materials. Chaucer had attempted a version in prose: Walton uses an eight-line stanza for his first three books, and rhyme royal for the last two. Both writers lose by abandoning the plan of their original, for Boethius alternated his prose sections with lyrical passages, thereby giving relief and variety to his reflections. Walton undoubtedly had Chaucer's version before him, but makes his own translation and exercises a good control over his matter, and at times is as astonishingly successful in reproducing the ideas of Boethius—no easy task for a poet, especially when it is remembered that Walton's endeavour was to keep to the words of his original 'as neigh as may be broght where lawe of metyr is noght resistent'. His abandonment of the eight-line stanza at the end of Book III is evidence of his tact. Walton must have realized that the rhyme requirements of his stanza invited padding, for when he comes to deal with the problems of

Fate and Providence, of Destiny and Free Will, he eliminates one line of his stanza, and so tightens his verse unit and rids himself of the extra rhyme. Even so, he feels that

> Lo of so hye a matre for to trete
> As aftir þis myn auctour doth pursue
> This wote I well my wyttes ben vnmete
> The sentence forto saue (in) metre trewe
> And not forthi I may it not eschewe.

Walton's translation lacks much of the conciseness of his original, but it is a workmanlike, honest attempt to render his author in a readable and flowing verse, as shown in the following passage:

> Bot here þou makest this obieccioun:
> 'If goddes science may be changed so
> Right as myne owne disposicioun,
> And when I now this and now þat m[ay] do,
> Than may I enterchaungen to and fro
> His hye science be stoundes of my wille?'
> 'Nay, nay, forsothe, þat myght þou not be skille,
>
> For-why þe knowynge of devyne sight
> It goth bifore þat þing þat schall be-falle,
> And right before his propre presence right,
> Lo of his knowyng he retorneth all
> That euer was or ben here-after schall.
> Ne as þow wenest he alterneþ noght
> His presence be stoundes of þi þoght,
>
> As now þis þing and now þat þing to knowe,
> Bot he, beholdyng euery wyt, compaseth
> The chaunginge of þi þoghtes all arowe.
> With o syght all at ones he enlaceth;
> He goth also before and all embraceth.

Another aspect of didactic poetry in its most forbidding form is found in the *Court of Sapience,* a poem of about 1470. Its authorship is still in dispute: it was long attributed to Lydgate, but critical opinion now is more in favour of Hawes, although his claims have not been fully established. Whoever wrote it was a man well versed in medieval education and theology, and his learning is poured out in a fashion little to the modern taste. The work is in two books. In Book I we read of how the fate of man is debated and disputed by the Four Daughters of God— Peace, Mercy, Righteousness, and Truth—and is decided by the taking of human form by Christ. This leads to the reunion of the Four Daughters, and is related by Sapience to the author. (pp. 149-54)

Despite the heavily didactic nature of this poem, the reader is lured on by the considerable skill with which the writer uses the rhyme royal. He has a real feeling for verse; and occasional phrases, such as 'she gan unlace her tressyd sonnysh here', or 'the swerde of sorow ran oute thurgh myne hert', are attractive. Certainly the author is here far more capable than Hawes in the *Pastime of Pleasure,* or any late fifteenth-century writer in this genre, to express himself clearly, although his story is greatly overladen with detail and digression. Contemporary readers would find in it a convenient epitome of much current knowledge and belief, and were not deterred by the unpoetical way in which this was expressed.

At any rate these limitations did not deter Stephen Hawes from taking a good many hints from the *Court of Sapience* when he was composing the *Pastime of Pleasure.* In it Hawes attempts to give new life to two outmoded and decaying expressions of medieval thought—chivalry and scholasticism. He obstinately clings to both of these, although he wrote after the Wars of the Roses and in the first great days of the New Learning. The poem is a depressing specimen of very early sixteenth-century versifying, and what interest it has is more for the student of literary history than for the lover of poetry.

There is satirical and controversial verse as well as devout. The vigour and excitement generated by such poems as Hoccleve's *Reproof to Oldcastle,* or the anonymous *Against the Lollards,* testify to the zeal of their authors even though they add little to their reputation as poets. There is but little poetry in the diatribe known as *Jack Upland* and its accompanying pieces. *Jack Upland* is a vigorous (not to say violent) attack on the friars, which is answered by the *Reply of Friar Daw Topias,* and followed by Jack Upland's *Rejoinder.* Only the *Reply* is really in verse, and its writer is capable of a crude alliterative line (modelled perhaps on *Pierce the Ploughman's Crede*), but attempts to find a metrical system for the other two have not succeeded. The real interest of all these works (apart from their importance as documents in religious controversy) lies in their use of popular and alliterative phrases and snatches of proverbial wisdom. We hear of 'that wicked worm Wyclif' from one who himself is spoken of as 'lewed as a leke', and who in turn tells Jack Upland that 'thou wost no more what thou blaberist than Balames asse'. Jack likens him to 'blynde Bayarde (that) berkest at the mone, or as an old mylne dog when he begynnith to dote'. We learn that 'on old Englis it is said unkissid is unknown, and many men spekyn of Robyn Hood ond shotte nevere in his bowe'.

Side by side with the 'courtly' poetry there was a growing output of verse written to satisfy the demands of a new reading public. Chaucer's 'churls' tales' to some extent reflect his response to this demand, but its growth made poetry, long the handmaid of the Church and the nobility, also the maid of all work for those who wished to inculcate manners, amusement, instruction, popular wisdom, and the like in a palatable form. 'How the Wise Man taught his Son', or the *Libel of English Policy,* are poor enough stuff as verse, but are precious indications of a growing determination to induce poets to write on themes other than those hallowed by centuries of use. Naturally the nobility and the clergy still exercised a considerable control, but the pressure of the fifteenth-century *bourgeoisie* may be said to have brought to an end an era in which literature had so limited a contact with any readers except a privileged minority.

It is not surprising, therefore, that social behaviour rather than religious belief is the theme of much minor verse of the fifteenth century. From its opening years we have a series of poems which set out correct behaviour in some detail, and instruct the young in matters of ceremonial and etiquette. Even now manuscripts containing such poems survive in considerable numbers, and they must have circulated widely throughout the fifteenth century. Their merits as poetry are non-existent: verse is used merely as a convenience to throw into story and couplet instruction often taken from a Latin or French source. In the main they are undoubtedly meant for the 'bele babees' of the aristocracy and the well-to-do. These are admonished not to imitate the uncouth manners of the rustic 'felde men', and when at table to sit where they are told. 'To embrace thi jawis with bred, it is not dewe', says one manual, and adds 'pyke not thi tethe with thi knyfe, ne spitte thou not over the tabyll'. They learn how to enter and leave a chamber, and how to behave while there; how to walk in the streets, to avoid scandal, and not to be 'to noyous, ne to nyce, ne to new fangylle'.

More elaborate treatises, such as John Russell's *Book of Carving and Nurture* (*c.* 1440) explain to the pupil in considerable detail the duties of a butler, pantler, chamberlain, and carver. Russell had been 'sum tym seruande with Duke Umfrey of Glowcetur, a prynce ful royalle, with whom uschere in chambur was y, and mershalle also in halle', and his book is a mine of detailed information, invaluable to those who would know what is meant by Chaucer's commendation of Harry Bailly as one fit 'for to have been a marchal in an halle'. Other books of a similar nature, such as the *Book of Courtesy* (*c.* 1460) or Hugh Rhodes's *Book of Nurture* (*temp.* Henry VII), help to fill out the picture.

Another series of poems concern themselves more with the relations between people than with table manners and the like. One of the most popular of these was 'How the good wife taught her daughter'—a work full of practical wisdom concerning the getting and keeping of a husband, the treatment of strangers and of her own children and household. At home, at church, in the street, or in the alehouse, decorum is advocated: 'if thou be ofte dronken, it fallith the to grete schame'. The work is an epitome of common sense, and may be paralleled by 'How the Wise Man taught his Son' (*c.* 1430) in which similar good advice, but of a more general nature, is given, or by 'A Father's Counsel to his Son', 'A Father's Instructions to his Son', or 'A Good Wife's Counsels to her Daughter'. A short work in alliterative alphabetical verses, known as *Aristotle's ABC,* epitomizes a great deal of worldly wisdom and advice:

> To Amerous, to Aunterous, ne Angre the nat to
>   muche;
> To Bolde, ne to Besy, ne Bourde nat to large;
> To Curteys, to Cruelle, ne Care nat to sore;
> To Dulle, ne to Dredefulle, ne Drynke nat to
>   offte; . . .

This work is sometimes attributed to Benedict Burgh, but it was actually written by a certain Benedict of Norwich. A version of the *Disticha Catonis,* an ever popular work in the Middle Ages, was made by Benedict Burgh. It is in two parts: 'Cato Major' in 111 stanzas, and 'Cato Minor' in seven stanzas, both of rhyme royal. It has little merit as verse, but gives a convenient summary of precepts:

> Sith manys liff is fulle of miserie,
>   Whilom in mirthe and aftir in myscheef,
> Now in the vale, now in the mont on hihe;
>   Now man is poore and eft richesse releffe;
>   The shynyng morwe hath ofte a stormy eve—

> To this policie take heed and entend:
> Look thou haue lucre in thy labours eende.

Yet another series of these little verse treatises deals with matters of bodily health. Lydgate's *Dietary* was the most popular of them all, and survives in forty-six manuscripts. Other widely circulated works were little books on bloodletting, or of medical recipes in couplets, or a series of versified herbals which gave simple advice to the layman.

At the other end of the scale in length stands Peter Idley's *Instructions to his Son*. This is a long work of 1,108 stanzas of rhyme royal written between 1445 and 1450. It is almost entirely derivative—a fact which commended it to the age, for not only does it incorporate the kind of advice given in many of the short treatises mentioned above, but it also draws its material from two longer works by well-known authors. Book I is based on the Latin treatises of Albertanus of Brescia entitled *Liber Consolationis et Consilii* and *De Amore et Dilectione Dei*. In this book Idley sets out a collection of instructions on a miscellany of subjects. It is full of worldly wisdom—much of it highly unsuitable for the boy of six to whom it was ostensibly addressed. In Book II 'the counsels of the world' give place to 'the exhortations of the Church' and Idley uses Mannyng's *Handlyng Synne* and Lydgate's *Fall of Princes* as a supplementary source of information, and begins a detailed exposition of the usual kind—the Ten Commandments, the Seven Deadly Sins, and so on.

No doubt when manuscripts were expensive and learning difficult to come by, Idley was very much to the taste of some sober spirits of the time, but he makes dull reading now. Idley had little skill as a versifier ('I have non vteraunce for this cheffare Sauffe oonly nature whiche doith me leede'); he seems unable to decide whether the staple line is one of eight or ten syllables, and even when we have allowed for this difficulty, the lack of rhythmical movement makes the reading of his verses a tiring, vexatious feat. His diction, also, is contaminated with 'floresshed eloquence', so that he turns the simple English of Mannyng's 'To thefte wyl y neuer go' into 'That occupation shall I never assent unto', or 'Abraham ne graunted hym noght' into 'Abraham wold not enclyne to his peticioun'.

The subject-matter is equally unrewarding. We have read it all before done by more accomplished writers. The interest of Idley resides in the personal touches in his work which reveal something of the man and something of his times. He advises his son to 'ride on the right of a stranger bearing a spear: on his left if he wears a sword'; regrets that 'a man shall not now kenne a knave from a knight', and still worse, that it is hard to tell 'a tapester, a Cookesse, or a hosteller's wife fro a gentilwoman', since they are all so painted, and 'with wymples and tires wrapped in pride'. . . . As with all moralists, Idley looks back to the Golden Age when true religion flourished, and God and the king were honoured as they should be. (pp. 155-59)

Idley is of interest to us also as one among many laymen who were working quietly in their several spheres to educate their children and friends—often from worldly motives it is true, but also with a deep conviction of the part each of them had to play in the service of the Church and the State. Peter Idley's *Instructions* are the verse analogues

of innumerable passages in the letters of such typical fifteenth-century characters as the Stonors and the Pastons, and his latest editor, Miss Charlotte D'Evelyn, does well to remind us that Idley's work can be compared

> with that most poignant of fatherly instructions, the letter written by the first Duke of Suffolk to his son on the eve of his banishment, April 30, 1450. Composed under circumstances so different and written in a compass so much more compact, the letter is nevertheless an epitome of his counsels. Dread of God, knowledge of his laws and commandments, loyalty to the King, respect for his mother, caution in the choice of counsellors: these are the subjects of the Duke's farewell admonitions.

To fifteenth-century fathers these were still the all-important subjects of paternal advice.

One other work of advice requires brief mention, the *Libel of English Policy*. It is a work of some 1,200 lines of verse which set out the author's view of 'the trewe processe of Englyshe polycye'. This is, in brief:

> Cheryshe marchandyse, kepeth amyralté
> That we bee maysteres of the narowe see.

The author gives an account of the commodities and exports of various countries from the Mediterranean to the Baltic and argues that the true interests of England lay in developing this trade and in ensuring permanent supremacy at sea.

> Kepe than the see, that is the wall of Englond,
> And than is Englond kepte by Goddes sonde.

The English domination of the Channel is essential: secure that, says our author, and all nations, including the troublesome Flemings, will be forced to cultivate our friendship if they wish to pass through English waters. As poetry the work has no merits: as a vigorous patriotic outpouring of one desperately anxious to uphold his country's prestige (and trade) it is an interesting and significant work. To students of literature perhaps its greatest importance is in the evidence which it furnishes of the fifteenth-century tendency to use verse for works of information, whether on politics, husbandry, etiquette, travel, or alchemy.

As we look back on Idley's moralizings and most [fifteenth-century verse] we may well cry, 'Not here, O Apollo, are haunts meet for thee!' and turn to the lyrics and popular verse of the century. Lyric poetry of this period is not so devoid of interest as many writers have suggested. True it has lost the first freshness of 'Lenten is come with loue to toun', but in place of that it has acquired control over form, ability to use technical devices, and a considerable metrical agility. It avoids the use of 'aureate' diction for the most part, and at its best is capable of outstanding works which reach their height in *Quia amore langueo* or 'I syng of a mayden', or 'Adam lay i-bowndyn, bowndyn in a bond'.

The religious lyric still predominated, and poems on many phases of Christian life and faith were composed for the edification of the ordinary worshipper. They generally reach no great heights, but present in an attractive and easily followed form songs to the Blessed Virgin, to the Trinity, or for the various Church seasons. Others again tell of man's mortality: 'Farewell, my frendis! the tide abideth no man: I moste departe hens and so shall ye', or lament the untimely death of youth:

> Of lordis lyne and lynage sche was, here sche
>   lyse!
> Bounteuus, benigne, enbleshed wyth beaute,
> Sage, softe and sobre an gentyll in al wyse,
> fflorishyng and fecunde, with femenyn beaute,
> Meke, mylde and merciful, of pite sche bar þe
>   prise.

The carol also comes to its fullest perfection in this period. As well as the work of old blind Awdelay, who wrote

> As I lay seke in my langure
> In an abbay here be west,

or of the Franciscan, James Ryman, there is that of many anonymous authors. The carols, with their characteristic refrains—'Hey now, now, now', or

> Now let us syng and mery be,
> For Crist oure Kyng hath made us fre,

—and their fresh, singing note won a wide popularity. There were carols not only for Christmas, but for many other moments in the Christian year. There were also the secular carols, the combats between the Holly and the Ivy, the ceremonial entry of the boar's head, or the convivial and amorous carols. The secular lyric was far from dead. The *Nut Brown Maid* is the best-known and perhaps the finest of these fifteenth-century lyrics, but it had many companions of merit. Love-songs predominate, though the border-line between earthly and heavenly love is often extremely hard to define. They range from the sophisticated to the simple, and express the courtier's ardours as well as the homely realistic passion of the countryman.

Other lyrics come closer to the ordinary people. They tell of everyday affairs, and express the homely wisdom, shrewdness, fears, affections, and amusements of the folk. *London Lickpenny* with its caustic refrain 'For lack of money I myghte nat spede' has its counterpart in a series of poems on the same theme expressed more tersely. The amorous songs and love plaints are replaced by the caustic realism of the husband's cry, 'I dare not seyn, whan she seith "Pes"!' The life of the tavern is re-created in songs with the refrain:

> Brynge vs home good ale, ser; brynge vs home
>   good ale,
> And for owre dere Lady love, brynge vs home
>   good ale.

Other events have their chronicles in verse as is seen in the realistic account of the pilgrim's sea voyage to St. James of Compostella in Spain:

> Men may leve alle gamys
> That saylen to Seynt Jamys,
> Ffor many a man hit gramys,
>   When they begyn to sayle;
> Ffor when they have take the see
> At Sandwyche or at Wynchylsee,
> At Brystow, or where that hit bee,
>   Theyr hertes begyn to fayle.

> Anone the mastyr commaundeth fast
> To hys shypmen, in alle the hast,
> To dresse hem sone about the mast,
>   Theyr takelyng to make;
> With 'Howe! hissa!' then they cry;
> 'What, howe! mate, thow stondyst to ny,
> Thy felow may nat hale the by';
>   Thus they begyn to crake . . .

> 'Hale the bowelyne! now, vere the shete!
> Cooke, make redy anoon our mete;
> Our pylgryms have no lust to ete,
>   I pray God yeve hem rest.'
> 'Go to the helm! what, howe! no nere!'
> 'Steward, felow, a pot of bere!'
> 'Ye shalle have, sir, with good chere,
>   Anon alle of the best . . . '

> Then cometh oone and seyth: 'Be mery,
> Ye shall have a storme or a pery.
> 'Holde thow thy pese! thow canst no whery,
>   Thow medlyst wondyr sore.'
> Thys menewhyle the pylgryms ly,
> And have theyr bowlys fast theym by,
> And cry after hote malvesy:
>   Thow helpe for to restore.

> And som wold have a saltyd tost,
> Ffor they myght ete neyther sode ne rost;
> A man myght sone pay for theyr cost,
>   As for oo day or twayne.
> Som layde theyr bookys on theyr kne,
> And rad so long they myght nat se.
> 'Allas, myne hede wolle cleve on thre!'
>   Thus seyth another certayne . . .

> A sak of strawe were there ryght good,
> Ffor som must lyg theym in theyr hood:
> I had as lefe be in the wood,
>   Without mete or drynk.
> For when that we shall go to bedde,
> The pumpe is nygh oure beddes hede;
> A man were as good to be dede
>   As smell therof the stynk!

Works of 'Mirthe and solas' also claimed the attention of poets. Such writings were popularized in hall and market-place by a host of professional minstrels who had at their finger-tips a vast and highly variegated repertoire. They could tell a devout story, or narrate the affecting details of some saint's life, but they could also reel off coarse *fabliaux* or the more decorous romance. The fifteenth century still found people eager to listen to the romances which had been composed in earlier centuries, and also to hear any new ones which the minstrel could recite. Among such new works were *Sir Triamour, Sir Torrent of Portugal, The Squire of Low Degree, Parthenope of Blois*.

We can sympathize with these fifteenth-century authors who came into the field so late in the day, and who must have felt that all the best material had been used. They could only take the French romances and give them a new English form, sometimes by cutting out much introspection and conversation (*Life of Ipomadon*), or by giving them a strongly didactic note (*Le Bone Florence, Parthenope*). Often, however, they took the easiest course, and piled incident upon incident without much thought of structure (*Generydes, Sir Triamour*), so that long, rambling narratives resulted which relied on picturesque incident or elaboration of detail for their main effects (*Le Bone Florence, Sir Cleges,* the *Squire of Low Degree*). In a few romances there is a good sense of narrative (*Le Bone Florence, Life of Ipomadon*) or of dialogue (*Sir Gawayne and Dame Ragnell, Sir Triamour*), but on the whole, the romance form was living on its past.

All this body of verse has been preserved in a wealth of manuscripts, some of them handsome presentation copies, the work of highly trained scribes and illuminators, some of them good workmanlike 'shop' copies, varying in quality according to their price, and some of them cheaply made or amateur productions. All helped to make known the variety of contemporary verse, and to encourage the making of collections of favourite pieces in 'commonplace-books' by enthusiasts. These 'commonplace-books' or scrap-books are revealing evidence of personal likes and interests. The well-known British Museum MS. Egerton 1995 is a good example. This was written about 1470-80, and consists of some fifteen items of a very diverse nature. Romance is represented by the *Seven Sages of Rome;* history by Lydgate's *Chronicle of the Kings of England,* the *Siege of Rouen,* and the prose chronicle of a citizen of London, William Gregory. Advice on health is given in a number of little treatises like Lydgate's *Sapientia phisicorum* or 'directions for blood-letting'. Etiquette is dealt with in the *Book of Courtesy,* and hunting in two treatises setting out the names of hawks and the terms of venery. Miscellaneous information on the assize of bread, the names of the Bishops of England, and of the London churches, prognostications in Latin, and some gnomic verses *Erthe upon Erthe* complete the volume. Here in some 450 pages its owner had a 'library' *in parvo,* and many fifteenth-century lovers of letters had similar volumes, as for instance that now in the National Library of Scotland (Advocates, 19.3.1). This is a volume of 432 pages mostly written down by a John Hawghton. It contains much religious poetry: carols, Lydgate's *Life of Our Lady* (Books V-VII), the *Trental of St. Gregory,* Lydgate's *Stans Puer ad Mensam* and a prose *Life of St. Katharine.* Romance is represented by *Sir Gowther* and *Sir Isumbras.* There is much miscellaneous material: poems on 'marvels' and deceit; prognostics on thunder; medical and alchemical receipts; 'Proper terms' for game, &c.

To turn from English to Scottish poetry is not to move into a very different world. It has been asserted, with some justice, that there is no need to differentiate sharply between the two literatures before the mid-fifteenth century. In the first place, little is known about the Celtic influences on such few writings as have come down to us from before the early fourteenth century. Secondly, writings after that date follow lines familiar to the student of English medieval literature. The fourteenth century saw little Scottish literature save Barbour's *Bruce* and the works of Huchoun, and well into the fifteenth century the writing of poems and chronicles enshrining the adventures of national heroes and outlining the course of Scottish history occupied the attention of native poets. Andrew of Wyntoun's *Original Chronicle of Scotland* (c. 1424) is the link between the earlier work of this kind and the *Acts and Deeds of the Illustrious and Valiant Champion, Sir Wil-liam Wallace* (c. 1482), by Henry the Minstrel, or Blind Harry, as he is sometimes called. This kind of poetry slowly gave place to a more sophisticated and literary genre which made use of the common stock which Chaucer in England and his contemporaries in France had made so popular. Scottish poetry in the fifteenth century slowly passes from the octosyllabics of heroic declamation and nationalistic fervour to enjoy the many forms and measures and the subject-matter which were available in the poetry of Chaucer, Machaut, Deschamps, and others. Only when this was accomplished towards the end of the fifteenth century could Scottish authors fully assert their individuality. To label them 'Scottish Chaucerians' is to single out one element only in their poetic equipment, and to disguise the fact that, like Chaucer, they look to France for much that gave form and style to their writings. In addition to this body of writers, there was also the alliterative variety of verse, steadily losing ground but not yet extinct, and as we can see from the Bannatyne and Maitland collections lyric poetry was being written to edify, amuse, and instruct. A few words about Barbour's *Bruce* are necessary, although the poem was finished by 1375, for it marks a decisive moment in Scottish literature. The long struggle waged by Scotland for her independence made itself felt in literature for a long time, and here in the *Bruce* Scottish themes and personages are the life of the poem. Barbour writes more as an historian than as a teller of romance, and his object is to preserve for posterity the exploits and patriotism of Bruce and of those who fought with him for Scotland's freedom. The aggressive spirit of the English is contrasted with the defensive attitude which animates the Scots, and Barbour infuses into his poem the temper which went to the making of Bruce's Scotland. Thus it is that the poem is a strange amalgam of the old *chanson de geste* and the chivalric romance. The actions of the hero are often as bloody and violent as those of earlier warriors such as Gautier d'Arras or Raoul de Cambrai. The heroic element is stressed: Bruce is as sagacious in council as he is unmatched in the field, while Douglas exhibits even more of the primitive hero. He is harder and more determined than his leader, since his personal wrongs have inflamed him more fiercely against the English. It is the national cause, however, rather than individual wrongs that animates Bruce and most of his followers. A sense of responsibility controls their actions; loyalty to Scotland, not as in chivalric romance to a lady, or a king, or to a remote ideal.

Not that chivalry is absent. Throughout the poem much is done that would have been left undone but for the ideals which animated knights at their highest moments. There is no senseless denigration of the enemy's merits. The valour of the 'douchty lord Douglas' is equalled by the 'high prowess' of Sir Ingram de Umfraville, while Barbour stays to laud the action of Sir Giles de Argentine, who bade King Edward 'gud day' when he saw him turn to fly while he himself rode forward

> And in that place than slayne wes he.
> Of his ded wes rycht gret pite
> He wes the thrid best knycht, perfay,
> That men wist lyfand in his day.

These lines are characteristic of a chivalric temper which

pervades the poem alongside a fiercer, more violent note, for much of the poem is taken up with violent action—single combats or the encounters of army with army are fully and vigorously described. The noise, excitement, and movement of fighting fill Barbour's pages, and culminate in the classic description of the fight between Bruce and De Bohun at Bannockburn. The fights are not described merely for the pleasure their hearing would give to an audience, but as part of the daring struggle against the English invader. Behind the whole poem is the feeling so memorably expressed by Barbour in his famous apostrophe:

> A! fredome is a noble thing!
> Fredome mayss man to haiff liking;
> Fredome all solace to man giffis,
> He levys at ess that frely levys!
> A noble hart may haiff nane ess,
> Na ellys nocht that may him pless,
> Gyff fredome failyhe; for fre liking
> Is yharnyt our all other thing.

The *Original Chronicle of Scotland,* by Andrew of Wyntoun, is a work of some merit as a chronicle-history, but it is poor poetry. Andrew is animated by the desire to make his listeners aware of their heritage, and although his chronicle is ostensibly a history of the world from its earliest (original) times, its main purpose is to emphasize the claims of Scotland to an independent existence. From the eighth century, therefore, he makes Scottish history his main theme, and tells his story in detail. He relies on a variety of sources for his material up to the time of Bruce, and from then onwards his own account is a valuable authority.

Wyntoun's circumscribed life as a cleric did little to develop any poetic powers he may have had. He uses the octosyllabic couplet in a dull, mechanical fashion and little would have been lost could he have written in prose. His greatest importance, perhaps, is as an indication of how deep-felt was the patriotic feeling against the English. Wyntoun extols the bravery of the Scot and shows a bitter hatred of the English. He has no doubt as to King Edward's fate:

> The sawlys that he gert to slay down thare
> He sent quhare his sawl nevyrmare
> Wes lyk to come, that is the blys
> Quhare alkyn joy ay lestand is.

This vigorous patriotic note is also sounded with great emphasis by the author of the *Wallace.* His identity has been the cause of much dispute. John Major, the author of *Historia Majoris Britanniae,* asserted that the work was written by 'Blind Harry' or Henry the Minstrel as he is sometimes called, and that it was composed during Major's infancy (c. 1460). . . . (The sole surviving manuscript was written by James Ramsay in 1488.) 'Blind Harry the Minstrel' has also come in for some heavy criticism, and it is hardly too much to say that we are now uncertain whether he was blind or called Harry or a minstrel. Major, however, spoke of him as blind from birth and existing by reciting in the halls of lords (*coram principibus*) as a wandering minstrel. From this critics have found it an easy step to think of him as going from hall to hall, picking up new

items for his repertory the more readily because his blindness had accustomed him to rely on his ear. Thus, like Blind Homer, he recited the deeds of heroes and their descendants in the defence of their country. It is a charming story, but there is little to show that it is true. Indeed, much of the evidence points to a contrary conclusion. Henry, it is true, proclaims himself 'a burel (ignorant) man', who writes 'a rurall dytt' (a rustic song), but this is but 'common form', as we have seen in English poets of this age. The metres he uses—the couplet and the nine-line stanza—do not bear out his depreciatory statements, nor do the descriptions of natural scenery, the many classical allusions, nor the 'aureate' terms. The author of the *Wallace,* whoever he was, cannot be thought of as ignorant or uncouth. To turn to the poem itself: it is a production in which everything is sacrificed on the altar of patriotism. The author does not allow himself to be hampered by considerations of historical accuracy. Fact and fiction are inextricably mingled as a glowing picture of Scotland's fight for freedom is created. The story is told so as to exalt Wallace as a national leader. No exploit is too daring for him, no odds too great. He kills armed men although himself unarmed; he is the equal of Hector and Achilles combined; 'Awful Edward durst nocht Wallace abid, In playn battaill for all England so wid'. Wallace is the avenger, the scourge of the English, so that 'It was his lyff, and maist part of his fude, To see thaim sched the brynand Southroun blude'. The tone of the whole work is suggested by the opening lines:

> Our ald ennemys cummyn of Saxonis blud,
> That neuyr yeit to Scotland wald do gud,
> Bot euir on fors, and contrar haile thair will,
> Quhow gret kyndnes thar has beyne kyth thaim
>   till:
> It is weyle knawyne on many diuers syde,
> How thai haff wrocht in to thair mychty pryde,
> To hald Scotlande at wndyr euirmair.

A strong hatred of England and of the English permeates the poem. There is a savage element in Wallace and his followers, and they burn and kill without mercy. Many descriptions are given of such scenes, of Wallace's superhuman strength, and of 'acts of prowess eminent'. It is the story of a barbarous chieftain of barbarous times, and we must accept this and all that flows from it, just as we must accept the grotesquely false historical background against which the action takes place. This falsification of history reaches its height in an episode in which romance and wish-fulfilment take the place of fact. Wallace is said to have reached as far south as St. Albans, and an ultimatum sent by him to Edward, cowering in the Tower, is finally replied to, but 'No man was thar that durst to Wallace wend'. At this juncture the queen volunteers to take the message, and the poem goes on to describe her arrival at St. Albans and her reception by Wallace in terms more suitable to a romance than to an heroic chronicle. Despite the queen's blandishments ('Wallace', scho said, 'yhe war clepyt my luff') Wallace refuses to treat with her, and although he shows her every courtesy, insists on his country's demands. It is with a jolt that we remember that history tells us how Wallace never penetrated farther south than Newcastle and that Edward was known as *malleus Scotorum.*

In short, our pleasure in the poem comes not from its tone but from the skill with which the minstrel tells his tale. He is a facile artist, and moves easily in the decasyllabic couplet, well aware of its possibilities, and well instructed in the use of rhetorical figures. Thus he pictures Wallace lamenting the death of Sir John de Graham as follows:

> He lychtyt doun, and hynt him fra thaim aw
> In armys up; behaldand his paill face,
> He kyssyt him, and cryt full oft; 'Allace!'
> My best brothir in warld that euir I had!
> My a fald freynd quhen I was hardest stad!
> My hop, my heill, thow was in maist honour!
> My faith, my help, strenthiast in stour!
> In the was wyt, fredom, and hardines;
> In the was trewth, manheid, and nobilnes;
> In the was rewll, in the was gouernans;
> In the was wertu with outyn warians . . .

The chronicle poets, however, belonged essentially to a fast dying state of society. While it was laudable to commemorate in song the exploits of past heroes, much that was of interest lay outside this field, and here the powerful influence of Chaucer and his disciples was of great moment. Both in matter and form English poets were laid under contribution, and outstanding among poems written in the 'Chaucerian' tradition is the *Kingis Quair*. That its author owes much to a study of Chaucer cannot be doubted. In places Chaucer's situations are closely copied, in others it is Chaucer's phrasing that is followed. The Chaucerian seven-line stanza (which takes its name 'rhyme royal' from this poem) is adopted, and the poem concludes with a recommendation of the work to 'my maisteris dere, Gowere and Chaucere'. Gower's influence is less marked, but that of Lydgate's *Temple of Glass* is clear enough at times. More important still, the whole work is an allegorical love poem, complete with dream, with interviews with Venus, Minerva, and Fortune, and tricked out with much well-known detail made familiar by the *Romance of the Rose*. In spite of all this it is an original work. In taking over all these stock elements the author has refused to be overcome by them. He uses them for his own purpose and often as freshly as if they had never been used before. The all-important moment of the first sight of the beloved has never been more admirably stated than in the poet's words:

> And therwith kest I doun myn eye ageyne,
>> Quhare as I sawe, walking under the toure,
> Full secretly new cummyn hir to pleyne,
>> The fairest or the freschest yong floure
>> That ever I sawe, me thoght, before that houre,
> For quhich sodayn abate, anon astert
> The blude of all my body to my hert.

It is also an original work in its attitude to its subject-matter. Here the lover's suit to the lady finds its consummation in marriage, not in 'courtly love'. The lover is closely questioned by Minerva, who agrees to help him only when he has convinced her that 'in vertew [his] lufe is set with treuth', and that it is 'ground and set in Cristin wis'. Although the poet makes use of a well-worn literary form, he gives it a life of its own because he uses it to tell (or seem to tell) his own story. From the moment he sets out to obey the injunction 'Tell on, man, quhat the befel',

the poem has a personal note, and the verses often have an intensity of feeling rarely met with in medieval poetry. The poet is an artist in words. He piles up his adjectives and nouns but makes them effective:

> With new fresche suete and tender grene,
> Oure lyf, oure lust, oure governoure, oure quene.

He uses the artifices of the rhetoricians with skill, as in the lines above, and as in:

> My wele in wo, my frendis all in fone,
>> My lyf in deth, my lyght into derkness,
>> My hope in feer, in dout my sekirness,
> Sen sche is gone: and God mote hir convoye,
> That me may gyde to turment and to joye!

At times he falls back on a cliché: 'the colde stone', 'the rokkes blak', but he is capable of 'a turtur quhite as calk', or of speaking of the fish 'with bakkis blewe as lede', and comparing their bright scales to the glitter of a suit of armour ('That in the sonne on thair scalis bryght As gesserant ay glitterit in my sight'). The management of the stanza and the lyrical quality of many passages denote the work of one who has studied his masters with attention and has gone on to strike out his own music.

Who wrote the *Kingis Quair*? The scribe who finished copying the unique manuscript now in the Bodleian (MS. Arch. Selden B. 24) wrote at the end of the poem 'Quod Jacobus Primus, Scotorum Rex Illustrissimus', while on a blank space opposite the third stanza of the poem a different hand from any in the manuscript has written: 'Heirefter followis the quair Maid be King James of Scotland ye firft callit ye Kingis quair and maid q^n his Ma. was In Ingland.' The writer of this second note gives us the title of the poem, which is not stated elsewhere, and also says that it was composed by James while in England. James I of Scotland was a prisoner in England for many years, and the story of the poem parallels in many ways his wooing of Joan Beaufort and marriage. Although attempts have been made to find an author for the poem other than James, these have not been generally accepted. The case for King James has recently been strengthened by Sir William Craigie, who has argued convincingly that the Scottish linguistic features were probably added by scribes, such as the writer of Selden B. 24, and that the poem was originally written in post-Chaucerian Southern English by an author in close touch with the language which he wrote and able to use it correctly. It is highly unlikely that this would have been possible to anyone whose connexions and training were purely Scottish. On the other hand, as Sir William says, 'accepting King James as the author, everything becomes normal and natural; eighteen years' residence in English surroundings, added to an acquaintance with the works of Gower and Chaucer, and no doubt of contemporary English poets, would be amply sufficient to qualify him as a competent maker of poetry after these models'.

The other outstanding 'Scottish Chaucerian' is Robert Henryson, generally identified with 'the scholemaister of Dunfermeling', one who deserves a high place among Scottish medieval poets. His work is more insular than that of Chaucer or of his contemporary Dunbar, but it has

John Lydgate at his desk.

an originality and ease of expression which give it distinction. Henryson is rooted in his Scottish world, for as Allan Ramsay observed of these early Scottish poets: 'Their Poetry is the Product of their own Country. . . . Their Images are native, and their Landskips domestick; copied from those Fields and Meadows we every day behold. The Morning rises . . . as she does in the Scottish Horizon. We are not carried to Greece or Italy for a Shade, a Stream or a Breeze . . . the Rivers flow from our own Fountains, and the Winds blow upon our own Hills.' So Henryson draws his imagery from freshly observed every-day events and scenes. He observes the 'fronsyt face', 'runclit beik', 'hyngand Browis, and hir voce so hace' of the Frog with 'hir logrand leggis, and hir harsky hyd'. Here his observation is exact and detailed as compared with much of the stock material commonly used by English poets of this time. He sees the labourers

> Sum makand dyke, and sum the pleuch can
>   wynd,
> Sum sawand sedis fast from place to place,
> The harrowis hoppand in the saweris trace.

He delights in homely phrases and in alliterative jingles drawing strength and colour from these popular elements. Similarly the humour of the folk plays throughout his work, especially in the *Fables,* while the movement of the verse with its frequent alliteration often emphasizes the movement of his narrative in the happiest fashion. Take for example the meeting of the town mouse with her sister the country mouse:

> The hartlie joy, God! geve ye had sene,
> Beis kith quhen that thir Sisteris met;
> And grit kyndnes wes schawin thame betwene,
> For quhylis thay leuch, and quhylis for joy thay
>   gret,
> Quhyle(s) kissit sweit, quhylis in armis plet.

A warm humanity infuses all his work. The cry of Orphe-

us 'Quhair art thow gane, my lufe Euridices?' and the superscription Troilus placed over the grave of Cresseid:

> Lo, fair Ladyis, Crisseid, of Troyis toun,
> Sumtyme countit the flour of Womanheid,
> Under this stane lait Lipper lyis deid.

express his graver emotions, but he could also delight in the antics and feelings of the animals in the *Fables,* as he sees their likeness to humans, and records their failings and their activities. Thus, gorged with the stolen kid, the Fox seeks a resting-place, and

> Unto ane derne for dreid he him addrest,
> Under ane busk, quhare that the sone can beit,
> To beik his breist and bellie he thocht best;
> And rekleslie he said, quhair he did rest,
> Straikand his wame aganis the sonis heit,
> 'Upon this wame set wer ane bolt full meit.'

Henryson's output was not large, but he essayed many forms. His shorter poems are unimportant, although the vigour of his alliterative verses in his extravagant *Sum Practysis of Medecyne* is worthy of remark. *Orpheus and Eurydice* tells of the quest of Orpheus as he proceeds 'by Watlingis Street' to seek out his lady in the realm of Pluto. The story is well told, and is interspersed with lyrical passages and some vivid descriptions as when Orpheus reaches Eurydice, and finds her

> Lene and deidlyk, and peteouss paill of hew,
> Rycht warsche and wane, and walluid as the
>   weid,
> hir Lilly lyre wes lyk unto the leid.

In *Robene and Makyne* Henryson gives us one of the earliest forms of the *pastorelle* that was to have so great a vogue. This charming piece of rustic wooing, with its *moralitas,* 'The man that wilt nocht when he may Sall have nocht when he wald', is played out by Robene and Makyne on 'a gude green hill' amid the flocks feeding in 'a full fair dale', and ends with the solitary Robene left

> In dolour and in care
> Keepand his hird under a huche
> Amangis the holtis hair.

Henryson manages the narrative with skill. The background, the characters, and the interplay of grave and gay are all expressed in brief but telling lines.

In the *Testament of Cresseid* the 'scholemaister' in Henryson is in the ascendant. He adds a pendant to Chaucer's poem which drives home with unrelenting emphasis what happened after the parting of 'fals Cresseid, and trew Knicht Troilus'. Henryson pictures Cresseid stricken down with leprosy, living out her life with 'cop and clapper' in the Spital House 'at the tounes end'. As she begs for alms one day Troilus and his company come her way

> Than upon him scho kest up baith hir Ene,
> And with ane blenk it come into his thocht,
> That he sumtime hir face befoir had sene.
> Bot scho was in sic plye he knew hir nocht,
> Yit than hir luik into his mynd it brocht
> The sweit visage and amorous blenking
> Of fair Cresseid sumtyme his awin darling . . .

> Ane spark of lufe than till his hart culd spring

> And kendlit all his bodie in ane fyre

and he throws down to her a princely alms. Cresseid learns that it was Troilus who passed, whereupon she makes her testament and dies. A fellow leper takes her ruby ring to Troilus, who

> Siching full sadlie, said: 'I can no moir,
> Scho was untrew, and wo is me thairfoir.'

Henryson tells his story with dignity and poignancy. The pauses for the great 'set pieces', depicting Saturn, Jupiter, Mars, and others, or the 'Complaint of Cresseid' give richness and detail, but do not unduly delay the action. The versification has much of Chaucer's felicitous power of varying the stresses so that monotony is avoided, while a rich vocabulary is aptly but not extravagantly employed to give life and colour to the verse. The *Testament* forms a not unworthy pendant to Chaucer's poem.

The death of Henryson (*c.* 1508) came at a moment when his contemporary Dunbar (*c.* 1460-*c.* 1530) was pouring out his astonishing variety of poems. In him Scottish poetry finds a champion who can use all the forms, knows all the traditions, and can extoll or laugh at them as the mood takes him. Once his work has been read it is impossible to think of Scottish poetry as 'provincial' or 'Chaucerian': it stands on its own merits. (pp. 159-76)

> *H. S. Bennett, "Fifteenth-Century Verse," in his* Chaucer and the Fifteenth Century, *1947. Reprint by Oxford at the Clarendon Press, 1958, pp. 124-76.*

C. S. Lewis (essay date 1936)

[*Lewis is considered one of the foremost Christian and mythopoeic writers of the twentieth century. An acknowledged master of fantasy literature, he was also an authority on medieval and Renaissance literature. In the following excerpt, he discusses fifteenth-century English poetry, discerning instances of greatness, and tracing "the process whereby the erotic and homiletic allegories. . . were fused together to produce something that anticipates* The Faerie Queene. . . . "]

In many periods the historian of literature discovers a dominant literary form, such as the blood tragedy among the Elizabethans, or satire in the eighteenth century, or the novel of sentiment and manners in the last age or in our own. During the years between Chaucer's death and the poetry of Wyatt allegory becomes such a dominant form and suffers all the vicissitudes to which dominant forms are exposed. For it must be noticed that such dominance is not necessarily good for the form that enjoys it. When every one feels it natural to attempt the same kind of writing, that kind is in danger. Its characteristics are formalized. A stereotyped monotony, unnoticed by contemporaries but cruelly apparent to posterity, begins to pervade it. . . . In the second place, a dominant form tends to attract to itself writers whose talents would have fitted them much better for work of some other kind. . . . Thus in the fifteenth and sixteenth century we have the *Assembly of Ladies* written by a poet who has no better vocation to allegory than that of fashion. And thirdly—which

is more disastrous—a dominant form attracts to itself those who ought not to have written at all; it becomes a kind of trap or drain towards which bad work moves by a certain 'kindly enclyning'. Youthful vanity and dullness, determined to write, will almost certainly write in the dominant form of their epoch. It is the operation of this law which has given later medieval allegory—and hence allegory in general—a bad name. A recognition of the law will perhaps liberate our critical faculties to distinguish between good and bad work—between the poetic use and the fashionable abuse.

But there is yet another 'accident' to which dominant forms are liable, and it is one which much concerns the historian. Often, though not always, we can detect under the apparent sameness of such productions the burgeoning of new forms, and find that a tradition which seemed most strictly bound to the past is big with the promise, or the threat, of the future. . . . It is therefore unwise to neglect the adventures of a dominant form, for in so doing we run the risk of misunderstanding its successors. There are few absolute beginnings in literary history, but there is endless transformation. Some of the allegories [which I will discuss] are, perhaps, mere continuations of the past; but others look to the future, and all alike tell us something of taste and sentiment in the period which produced them. The story is a complex one. In order to understand it, we must divide it, and here, with some reluctance, I will abandon a chronological arrangement. Lydgate's *Pilgrimage of the Life of Man* may have been written before *La Belle Dame Sans Merci,* and if I wrote as an annalist I should deal with it among the Chauceriana. But it belongs to a totally different order and illustrates another, and far more important, metamorphosis of the dominant form. I shall not scruple, therefore, to reserve it for treatment along with the work of Hawes and Douglas in the last of the groups into which I am dividing the subject. It must be understood from the outset that the sameness of these later allegories is deceptive. Under the common name of allegory things of quite different natures are concealed.

Before approaching the allegories themselves, however, there is a question which ought to be faced. In the *Confessio Amantis* we found naturalistic presentation of the lover's life in many places emerging from the allegory, and in *Troilus* we found allegory abandoned altogether in favour of a direct delineation of love. For Chaucer (and in a less degree for Gower) the long allegorical discipline has done its work. If this interpretation is correct, we might well hope to find among their successors both the impulse and the power to paint the inner world without the help of allegory. It would be too much, indeed, to demand, as of right, a copious and brilliant production of unallegorical subjective poetry. If we have fallen on an age poor in genius, it will be more likely that this new impulse and new power will continue, in its timidity, to manifest itself in the guise of allegory—a guise which will henceforth be a defect because it is unnecessary. But one or two unambiguous attempts in the direction I have suggested would be a welcome confirmation of our view. Fortunately they are to hand.

The first of them, as the reader will have guessed, is *The*

Kingis Quair. The importance of this poem does not lie in the fact that it introduced the Chaucerian manner into Scotland. Its importance lies in the fact that it is a new kind of poem—a longish narrative poem about love which is not allegorical, which is not even, like *Troilus,* a romance of lovers who lived long ago, but the literal story of a passion felt by the author for a real woman. It is true that the poem contains a dream, and even an allegorical dream; but the difference between a dream framed in a literal story and an allegorical story framed in a dream is of considerable importance. What makes the novelty even more surprising is the fact that the author seems to be well aware of what he is doing. Careless reading has obscured the fact that the poem opens with what is really a literary preface. The author, after reading Boethius too late at night, falls into a meditation upon Fortune, and reflects

> In tender youth how sche was first my fo,
> And eft my frende . . .

and well he might, if, as the story tells us, he was once a solitary prisoner, and is now a free man and an accepted lover. It is at this point that a brilliantly original idea occurred to him, a novelty that struck with such unpredicted resonance on his mind that the easiest imaginative projection sufficed to identify it with the matin bell striking that same moment in the objective world. As he says

> me thocht the bell
> Said to me, *Tell on man quhat thee befell.*

In our own language, the author, who had long desired to write but spent much ink and paper 'to lyte effect', had suddenly perceived that his own story, even as it stood in real life, might pass without disguise into poetry. He had heard the same voice that called Sidney 'Fool!', bidding him 'Look in thy heart and write'; and making a cross in his old manuscript to distinguish the new dispensation from all his previous attempts, he sat down to write what most emphatically deserves to be called 'sum newe thing'. The authorship of the poem has been disputed, but the dispute need not concern us. Whether the story is taken from the poet's life or from the life of another, the originality of thus telling it at all remains. It is true that the inspiration fails before the end, but the poem is full of beauty and the passage in which the lady is seen from the window is at least as good as its analogue in the *Knights Tale.* The differences between the two are significant. When Palamon sees Emelye his hue becomes 'pale and deedly on to see', and he complains that he has a hurt 'that wol his bane be'. The Scottish poet, in the same predicament, is equally 'abaisit', but he explains that it is because his

> wittis all
> Were so overcome with plesance and delyte.

Again, though both lovers become equally the captives of their ladies, it is only the Scot who says

> sudaynly my hert became hir thrall
> For ever, of free wyll.

In this beautiful oxymoron we see how nature has taught the poet to feel and to express both sides of the complex experience where Chaucer wrote in a tradition that invited him to see only one of them. And so also, even where the two poets approximate most, Palamon cries merely 'as though he *stongen* were unto the herte', and the image is one of pain; the later prisoner says

> anon astert
> The blude of all my body to my hert

recording with singular fidelity that first sense of shock which is common to all vivid emotions as they arise and which transcends the common antithesis of pain and pleasure. In a word, Chaucer for the moment is not looking beyond the lachrymose and dejecting aspects of love which the tradition has made so familiar; the Scottish poet, here far more realistic, telling 'what him befell', recalls us to the essential geniality, the rejuvenating and health-giving virtues of awakened passion, and having thus first presented them directly, goes on to give them that symbolic expression which they demand, in his lyrical address to the nightingale,

> lo here thy golden houre
> That worth were hale all thy lives laboure.

Chaucer himself, and all medieval love poets, had excelled in painting the peace and *solempne* festivity of fruition: but it needed this later and minor poet to remind us that Aphrodite even in her first appearance, when all the future is dark and the present unsatisfied, is still the golden, the laughter-loving goddess. Such is the reward of his literalism, his Scotch fidelity to the hard fact. And this fidelity has another, perhaps a stranger, result. As love-longing becomes more cheerful it also becomes more moral. His Aphrodite loves laughter, but she is a temperate, nay a christened, Aphrodite. There is no question in his poem of adultery, and no trace of the traditional bias against marriage. On the contrary, Venus refers the poet to Minerva, and Minerva will not help him without the assurance that his love is grounded in God's law and set 'in cristin wise'.

About the absolute merits of this little poem we are at liberty to disagree; but we must not misunderstand its historical importance. In it the poetry of marriage at last emerges from the traditional poetry of adultery; and the literal narrative of a contemporary wooing emerges from romance and allegory. It is the first modern book of love.

The other production which I wish to mention in this context is, in a way, more interesting precisely because it is not concerned with love at all. I am referring to the earlier parts—especially the first sixteen stanzas—of Hoccleve's *Regement of Princes.* Here we have a description, much infected with allegory but still unallegorical, of a sleepless night. The cause of Hoccleve's insomnia is by no means erotic: it is what we call Worry, and what Hoccleve calls simply Thought. Hoccleve's means are small and uncertain and he does not see how he is going to make both ends meet. Now it is doubtless impossible to prove that Hoccleve could not have written this passage unless the erotic allegories had been written first; but I question whether any reader who comes to it after studying the subject matter . . . will fail to detect some influence. For if we may make a distinction between writing about one's poverty and writing about the state of mind which reflection on one's poverty produces, then certainly Hoccleve does the second. He analyses the state of his emotions during that wakeful night just as the love poets had analysed the state of the sleepless lover; and Thought personified—as he might be in any erotic allegory—is recognized as the immediate enemy, while the objective circumstances which give rise to Thought are thrust into the background. The result, however it came about, is a piece of very powerful writing; and every one, unhappily, must recognize its truth. The 'troubly dremes, drempt al in wakynge', and the grim generalization (so curiously anticipating Keats)

> Who so that thoghty is, is wo be-gon,

deserve to be better known. But there are finer things than these. What balm for all our anxieties there is in the beggar's invitation to the anxious man, to 'Walke at large out of thi prisoun'! And though it may seem absurd to mention Aeschylus in connexion with Hoccleve, could Aeschylus himself have written much better of Thought than thus?

> That fretynge Adversarie
> Myn herte made to hym tributarie
> In sowkynge of the fresschest of my blood.

Do not the lines cry out to be re-clothed in sesquipedalian iambics?

As a poet of courtly love Lydgate bears a double character. In his style, and in the construction of his poems, he is the pupil of Chaucer. His conception of poetical language, and sometimes his achievement, are based on that way of writing whose slow, triumphant development [can be discerned] within Chaucer's own work. . . . In this respect Lydgate claims a place in the high central tradition of our poetry and at times (I fear I cannot say often) he makes good the claim.

> And with thy stremes canst every thing discerne
> Thurugh hevenli fire of love that is eterne . . .
>
> Redresse of sorrow, o Cithéria . . .
>
> A world of beaute compassid in her face
> Whos persant loke doth thurugh min herte
>   race . . .

Such passages are on the main line of development that runs from Chaucer to Spenser, and beyond him to Milton, to Pope, and to the Romantics. In his conception of allegory, again, Lydgate hardly modifies the practice of Machault and Chaucer. He is rather inclined to go back behind Chaucer, or at least to go back to Chaucer's earliest work. He uses allegory merely as a frame-work for effusions which are unallegorical or which, at the most, reintroduce allegory only in the form of rhetorical personifications. The amorous complaint, or letter, or prayer, is the form in which he is really most at home. Thus in the *Black Knight* the spring morning and the bird-haunted garden serve only to introduce the Knight's soliloquy which constitutes the real body of the poem. In the *Flour of Curtesye* they are merely the setting for the poet's letter. In both poems, indeed, it might be argued that there is no allegory at all: the landscapes probably have a *significacio* in fact, but it is unimportant and uncertain. In the *Temple of Glas,* again, we are brought 'ful fer in wildirness' to a 'craggy roche like ise ifrore', not mainly that we may witness an allegorical action but that we may hear the long solilo-quies and conversations of the Lady, the Lover, and the Goddess. And Lydgate was wise to concentrate on these; for nothing is more striking in this poem than the superiority of the stanzaic speeches and dialogues over the poet's own narration in couplets. Nearly all that is of value is in the former. No doubt with Lydgate, as with most minor poets, the choice of a metre almost determines the quality of the work: the couplet offers no obstacle to his fatal garrulity (the first sentence of the poem lasts for nine, the third for eighteen, lines) while the stanza compels him to 'grow to a point'. But the difference of metre goes with a difference in content. The slow building up and decoration, niche by niche, of a rhetorical structure, brings out what is best in the poet.

But in his conception of love Lydgate is more modern than Chaucer: he ranks with the author of the *Kingis Quair* as one who helped to make the old, wild Provençal tradition more possible and more English. In the *Black Knight,* I confess, he has a conceit sufficiently outrageous, when he says of Vulcan, that is, of Venus' lawful husband, that

> The foule chorl had many nightes glade
> Wher Mars, her worthy knight, her trewe man,
> To finde mercy, comfort noon he can.

Cuckolds have often been ridiculed; but it seems very hard that they should be thus scolded as well. The passage, however, is far from being typical of Lydgate, and in the *Temple of Glas* we are moving towards a less wilful conception. In this poem it is easy to miss the importance of the passage where the unhappily married, and those who have been forced into the cloister as children, complain piteously to Venus. It seems natural to us that these two classes of people should complain. But Marie de Champagne would have laughed and so would Andreas. Lydgate regards the matrimonial, or the celibate, vow as a cruel obstacle to the course of true love; but in the original tradition such vows, and the breach of such vows, were so far taken for granted that married people and clerks, or even nuns (in the *Concilium*) were the typical lovers. Plainly, when we reach this passage, we have turned a rather important corner. But the poet does not again speak so clearly, and as we proceed we find interesting ambiguities. The heroine of the poem is certainly married, and not married to her lover; and so far the tradition is preserved. But then her marriage is the heroine's chief grievance (it had not troubled Guinevere) and seems to be regarded as an insurmountable obstacle to her desires,

> My thoght goth forth, my body is behind.

When Venus replies to this complaint, she promises that the Lady will one day possess her lover 'in honest maner without offencioun'. I am not sure what Lydgate means by this. He may mean no more than that time and place will so agree that the Lady can fulfil the code of courtly love without detection and therefore without objective 'dishonour'; but equally he may mean that she can remarry. No less ambiguous is Venus' charge to the lover:

> But understandeth that al her cherishing
> Shal ben groundid upon honeste,
> That no wight shal thurugh evil compassing
> Demen amys of hir in no degree;

For neither merci, routhe, ne pite
She shal not have, ne take of the non hede
Ferther then longith to hir womanhede.

We are even left in doubt as to the conclusion of the whole story. When Venus has finally brought the two lovers together, the Lady warns the knight,

Unto the time that Venus list provide
To shape a wai for oure hertes ease,
Both ye and I mekeli most abide.

But what are they waiting for Venus to do? That they are waiting is apparent, for they merely kiss and praise the relevant deities, and there is no suggestion that their love is consummated. The most natural explanation certainly is that they are 'meekly abiding' until Venus 'shapes a way' not to adultery but to marriage. As the euphemism goes, 'something may happen' to the undesirable husband,

For men by laiser passen many a mile,
And oft also aftir a dropping mone
The weddir clereth.

It may well be that Lydgate himself was not quite certain how his story ended; but the uncertainty itself would be significant.

In the poem as a whole this new direction of the sentiment produces an increase of pathos. The lot of the unhappily married becomes more significant for poetry if they assume that the marriage vow must be kept; and the heroine of the *Temple,* even through the medium of Lydgate's imperfect art, moves me more than Chrétien's Guinevere. And when Lydgate pleads, in lines I have already mentioned, for the young girls forced into marriage to mend their father's estates, and for the yet younger and more deeply wronged oblates, snatched from the nursery to the cloister for the good of their fathers' souls,

In wide copis perfection to feine
And shew the contrari oitward of her hert,

he rises to true poetry. Probably no reader comes upon the opening words of this passage ('I herd othir crie') without remembering the *voces vagitus et ingens* in Virgil's hell, or without reflecting that Lydgate all too probably spoke from his own memory of the secret tears and homesickness of monastic childhood.

Lydgate's best work lies outside his allegories of courtly love, and some of it we shall happily have occasion to study. . . . But I cannot forbear, though it carries us for a moment outside our subject, to remind the reader how much better Lydgate can be, even as a love poet, than these slight allegories suggest. It is hard to find in Chaucer so near an approach to the lyrical cry as we find in these neglected lines:

And as I stoode myself alloone upon the Nuwe
   Yere night,
I prayed unto the frosty moone, with her pale
   light,
   To go and recomaunde me unto my lady dere.
And erly on the next morrowe, kneling in my
   cloos
I preyed eke the shene sonne, the houre whane
   he aroos,

To goon also and sey the same in his bemys clere.

The little anthology of love poems by obscure or unknown authors, which the old editions included with the work of Chaucer, has had a curious fate. There is a great deal of chance in literary history. If these poems had never been associated with the name of Chaucer, if they had slumbered in manuscript until the last century and then been released only to the half-waking existence conferred by some learned society's publication, it is doubtful whether the historians would now treat them more kindly than the known works of Lydgate and Hawes. An accident—or something not unlike an accident—has scattered a knowledge of them broadcast, and thus secured for them the justice which is not done to other poems of the same kind and the same age. Thus Milton does not disdain to borrow a phrase from the *Flour of Courtesye* and a conceit from the *Cuckoo and the Nightingale:* thus Dryden, Wordsworth, and Keats translate or praise poems vastly inferior to *Reson and Sensualite* or the *Palice of Honour.* Favour intrudes itself even into the text and format of the books. Lydgate is sent to press with all his imperfections on his head, his margin defiled with jocular (and erroneous) scholia, and his text ugly with diacritics: the *Flower and the Leaf* is cleansed 'by sheer editing' (in Saintsbury's phrase) from its metrical and grammatical blemishes and printed on a clean page. With such adventitious aids it is not surprising that a poem should outstrip in popular estimation works at least as good as itself. It is high time that criticism should redress the balance. It is not, perhaps, to be desired that we should admire the 'Chauceriana' less; but we must discount the accidental element in their fame in order to admire some other allegories more. The best of these favoured pieces deserve their popularity, and the whole collection is a charming formal garden, on a small scale, where lovers of antique sentiment do well to linger. But it contains none of the greatest work in this kind, and it contains little promise for the future.

The *Cuckoo and the Nightingale* is perhaps the earliest of these poems. It is a bird debate of the familiar kind, written in an unusual rhyme scheme, and pleasantly full of country sights and sounds. The vernal love-longing,

that bringeth into hertes remembraunce
A maner ese, medled with grevaunce.

is well expressed. The reader will notice that the precision and felicity of the last line are of a kind as proper to prose as to verse. This is no reproach, for poetry is not necessarily at its best when it is most unlike the other harmony; but it serves to distinguish this author's talent from Chaucer's. We find in him neither the merits nor the defects of the high style. Despite his airy subject he remains, as a stylist, on the ground: he has not caught from Chaucer the new richness and sweetness of speech, and the effect is usually that of one who talks and not of one who sings.

This quality—I hardly call it a defect—is well brought out by the contrast between the author of the Cuckoo poem and the author of *La Belle Dame Sans Merci.* The very first lines of the latter,

Half in a dreme, not fully wel awaked,

The golden sleep me wrapped under his wing

give us at once what we have missed in the *Cuckoo and the Nightingale,* and give it triumphantly; and they also introduce us at once to the real importance of the *Belle Dame.* It is as an admirable exercise in poetical style (and I use the word 'exercise' in no derogatory sense) that this poem concerns us. It is a translation from the French of Chartier, and the content is of no great significance. It is not an allegory, but a poem in which some preliminary adventures lead up to a long dialogue between a lover and his mistress—the merciless and immovable mistress who gives her name to the poem. The theme suggests the sentiment of the piece, which consists in a continued emphasis on what I venture to call (but 'let rude ears be absent') the masochistic element in the attitude of the courtly lover. The author is not morbid; he remains everywhere within the bounds of the healthy and normal, but he is playing with shades of feeling which need very little more encouragement to pass those bounds and to become a recognizable perversion. Certainly his picture of the mistress, though well suited to this turn in the sentiment, is poetry, not pathology, and deserves to be quoted:

> In her fayled nothing, as I could gesse,
> O wyse nor other, prevy nor apert.
> A garnison she was of al goodnesse
> To make a frounter for a lovers hert—
> Right yong and fresshe, a woman ful covert,
> Assured wel her port and eke her chere,
> Wel at her ese, withouten wo or smert,
> Al underneth the standard of Daungere.

But however we define the sentiment, it would be misleading to regard it as the main thing in the poem. The main thing is the dialectic of the conversation between the lady and her lover, and it is doubtless on the subtlety of her answers, and on the recurrent intellectual suspense between each question and each answer, that Chartier chiefly relied for keeping up the interest of his readers. To us, who have separated our sentimental and our intellectual games so widely, it is not very interesting; and unfortunately it is in these passages that the English translator breaks down. I am not sure that he was a perfect master of the original; and certainly his version of the dialogue contains obscurities. But of English his command is perfect; and throughout the poem—but specially in the earlier stanzas before the dialogue begins—we see an essentially second-rate theme redeemed by sheer good writing. We have to reconsider our whole conception of the culture of the fifteenth century when we read such an accomplished stanza as the following:

> To make good chere, right sore himself he
>   payned
> And outwardly he fayned greet gladnesse;
> To singe also by force he was constrayned
> For no plesaunce, but very shamfastnesse;
> For the complaynt of his most hevinesse
> Com to his voice alwey without request,
> Lyk as the soune of birdes doth expresse
> Whan they sing loude in frith or in forest.

In this, as in the previous extract, it will be seen that we have to deal not with mere writing in stanzas, but with that very different thing, really stanzaic writing. The last

line is felt throughout the whole grave minuet which words and sense go through in order to reach it; and when it comes, there is a full close for ear and mind, and a concluding tableau for the inner eye. The thing is difficult to do, and even Chaucer and Spenser do not always succeed. There are single lines, too, in the poem, which tempt me to quotation; but its real quality lies, not in occasional 'beauties' that can be pencilled, but in its *aureum flumen*—the rich, even, melodious continuity of the whole.

The *Flower and the Leaf*—a much later work by an unknown hand—belongs to a different world. Its author is less accomplished and more original, and the poem is, in some respects, of more historical importance. It represents, in a very mild form, that fusion of the courtly and the homiletic allegory of which there will be more to say in a later section. The story is probably familiar to every reader. The author—who represents herself as a woman, and must therefore be assumed to be a woman, by the principle of Occam's razor—wanders into a forest where she witnesses the revels of two parties of mysterious beings, who are distinguished as the company of the Leaf and the company of the Flower. The latter are afflicted by excessive heat and violent showers, while the former remain in comfort under the shade of a 'fair laurer'. When the storm is over, the servants of the Leaf, cool, dry, and comfortable, offer hospitality to the wet and blistered followers of the Flower, and prescribe 'plesaunt salades'

For to refresh their greet unkindly heet.

Finally an unnamed lady (who is rather artlessly introduced) explains to the authoress the meaning of the vision. The Queen of the Leaf was Diana, and the Queen of the Flower, Flora. Their two companies consisted entirely of ghosts—the ghosts of virgins, true lovers, and valiant knights following Diana, while Flora's retinue consisted of those who had loved idleness and found no better occupation than 'for to hunt and hawke and pley in medes'. This is the surprising conclusion of a poem which began with all the air of an allegory of courtly love. From the courtly tradition it has borrowed the idea of an *exercitus mortuorum*. From the same source it has borrowed the conception of a future reward and punishment which have no connexion with Christian eschatology. But then it allots these rewards and punishments on a purely moral basis: there is no hell for cruel beauties, and if true lovers are rewarded they are rewarded along with virgins. Love and valour and virginity find themselves ranged together and opposed to idleness, frivolity, and inconstancy. The antithesis is purely moral, and the morality is that of modern life. At the core of this little poem—which looks, at first sight, so like *La Belle Dame* or the *Parlement of Foules*—we find a moral allegory on the lines of the choice of Hercules, a little psychomachia of Virtue and Vice. It is, in fact, a hybrid—a moral allegory wearing the dress of the Rose tradition. It is not, indeed, probable that the authoress is consciously drawing upon the homiletic allegory; and perhaps she is not conscious, either, of any call to reform the erotic tradition. One suspects that she knows the more perverse expressions of the latter to be 'only poetry' and is not interested: while the fierce monotony, the unreal black and white, in which the contemporary pulpit painted the *bellum intestinum* leaves her respectfully unmoved. 'She was ful mesurable, as wemen be.' She allegorizes a world she knows: a world in which the more terrifying virtues and vices do not appear, but in which, nevertheless, she is conscious of a better and a worse, a protective leaf and a soon withering flower. As a moralist she stands nearer to Addison than to Deguileville. She too would enlist fancy and fashion on the side of virtue—a virtue pictured in such homely, urbane, and practicable colours as startlingly anticipate our eighteenth-century Whig literature. Hence, though she deals with the moral choice, her treatment of it 'turns all to favour and to prettiness'. Only the most lenient virtues and the most pardonable vices appear, and the contention between them is one of courtesy. It ends with the Virtues inviting the Vices to a picnic and helping them to dry their clothes. In all this we may, if we please, detect a ladylike ignorance of the heights and depths: nor will I plead (though the thing is arguable) that the behaviour of these Virtues is, in a sense, more worthy, because more Christian, than that of Deguileville's Gracedieu. I do not pretend that the authoress was thinking on so grave a level. But if she does not look very deep, at least she looks with her own eyes: she allegorizes life as it appears to comfortably circumstanced people of good breeding and good will, and not as any convention, homiletic or erotic, would have it appear. If she cannot claim wisdom, she has a great deal of good sense and good humour, and is guided by them to write a poem more original than she herself, perhaps, suspected. A similar merit, and a similar limitation, appear in her execution. Her language is fresh and genuine, but never reaches the last felicity. She describes what interests her, selecting rather by temperament than by art; and she finds considerable difficulty in getting the right number of syllables into each line.

The *Assembly of Ladies* is also put into the mouth of a woman, and critics, anxious to economize hypotheses, have suggested that it is by the same hand as the *Flower and the Leaf.* If this is true—a question which we shall probably never be able to answer—she was a remarkable woman; for the *Assembly* represents a wholly different, and, in some ways, a not less interesting modification of the tradition. Taken as an allegory, it is as silly a poem as a man could find in a year's reading. A number of ladies are summoned to a 'counsayl' at the court of Lady Loyalty; they arrive and present their petitions; Loyalty postpones her answer till her next 'parliment' and the dreamer wakes. As a story, and still more as an allegorical story, this is clearly of no value. The poem belongs to that class in which the allegorical pretence is assumed only at the bidding of fashion. What the writer really wants to describe is no inner drama with loyalty as its heroine, but the stir and bustle of an actual court, the whispered consultations, the putting on of clothes, and the important comings and goings. She is moved, by a purely naturalistic impulse, to present the detail of everyday life; and if her poem were not hampered by being still attached—as with an umbilical cord—to the allegorical form, it would be an admirable picture of manners. Indeed, if only the first four stanzas survived, we might now be lamenting the lost Jane Austen of the fifteenth century. They read exactly like the beginning of a novel in verse; and in them we have the rare priv-

ilege of listening to an ordinary conversation, as opposed to a wooing, between a well-bred man and woman of that age. The dialogue is admirable, and perhaps better than Chaucer's earliest attempts. Nor does this realism fail when the lady begins to tell her dream. We soon forget that it is a dream, or an allegory. The messenger from the court of Loyalty delivers her summons and is already departing when she turns back to say 'I forgot: you must all come in blue'. The heroine, arriving at the court, begs one of the ladies in waiting 'helpe her on with her aray'. An official stands her friend, pulls wires on her behalf, and tells her whose ear she must gain. A cry goes down the presence chamber, 'Voyd bak the press up to the wal'. The waking from the dream is eminently natural; and so is the conclusion of the whole poem,

> Now go, farwel! for they call after me.

We cannot call the piece satisfactory as a whole: for the fatal discrepancy between the real and the professed intention is felt at every turn. To read it is to learn why some critics hate allegory; for here the *significacio* is—what some suppose it to be in all allegories—a chilling and irrelevant addition to the story. But the detail of the poem shows powers akin to genius, and reveals to us that much neglected law of literary history—that potential genius can never become actual unless it finds or makes the Form which it requires. 'Materia appetit formam ut virum femina.' In the *Assembly* a great deal of good 'matter'—kindly satire, lively dialogue, a shrewd eye—remains fruitless.

The reader will have observed that all the Chauceriana, with the possible exception of the *Flower and the Leaf,* display a weakening of the genuinely allegorical impulse. The trappings of allegory are retained but the true interest of the poets lies elsewhere, sometimes in satire, sometimes in amorous dialectic, and often in mere rhetoric and style. Before we can proceed to the true allegories of this period in which the impulse is by no means decadent and is indeed preparing itself to pass on to the new triumphs of *The Faerie Queene,* there are a number of other poems to be considered which fall into the same class with the Chauceriana.

Dunbar is, perhaps, the first completely professional poet in our history. Versatile to the point of virtuosity, he practises every form from satiric pornogram to devotional lyric and is equally at home in the *boisteous* language of his alliterative pieces, the aureation of his allegories, and the middle style of his ordinary lyrical poems. His content is everywhere as central and obvious, as platitudinous if you will, as that of Horace; but like Horace he is such a master of his craft that we ask nothing more. His allegories are not of historical importance. They have no purpose in the world but to give pleasure, and they have given it abundantly to many generations. The *Thistle and the Rose* is an allegorical epithalamion after the manner of Chaucer's *Parlement,* though any comparison between the two is rather unfair to Dunbar. Into the *Parlement* Chaucer has put the whole of his early strength and made a paradise of tenderness and fun and sublimated sensuality. Dunbar's poem does not aspire to be more than a festal exhibition of fine language adding a new touch of magnificence to a royal wedding and strictly comparable to the court dresses of its first hearers. As such it is a brilliant success, but it yields to the *Golden Targe*. In the *Targe* the language is more splendid, the stanza more adapted to support such splendour, and the images more dazzling. To notice the abundance of such words as 'crystalline', 'silver', 'sperkis', 'twinkling', and the like is to indicate sufficiently the quality of the poem. And this peculiar brightness, as of enamel or illumination, which we find long before in *Gawain* and *Perle* and again in Douglas, is worth noticing because it is the final cause of the whole aureate style—the success which enables us to understand the aims of all the poets who did not succeed. And when the thing is successful it silences all *a priori* objections (such as the Wordsworthian heresy) against artificial diction: when the thing is well done, it gives a kind of pleasure that could be given in no other way. From our own point of view the poem might almost be classified as a radical allegory. It has an intelligible allegoric action: the poet's mind, though long defended by reason, becomes at last the prisoner of beauty. But this action is so slight and degenerates so often into a mere catalogue of personifications (which is the only serious fault of the *Targe*) that we are right to neglect it. The real significance of the poem lies elsewhere: in it we see the allegorical form adapted to purposes of pure decoration, as the Pastoral form was adapted by Pope or the elegiac by Matthew Arnold—we might add, by Milton. For this also is one of the things that happens to a dominant form.

A much less happy example of such decorative allegory occurs in Skelton's *Garland of Laurel*. That Skelton could write genuine allegory when he chose we know from the admirable *Bouge of Court*. The purely satirical content of this poem puts it outside my province; and I suppose that no reader has forgotten the vividness of its characters or its nightmare crescendo from guilelessness to suspicion, from suspicion to acute nervousness, and thence to panic and awakening. The experience of a young man during those painful years in which he first discovers that he has entered a profession whose motto is *Dog eat Dog,* could hardly be better described. But the *Garland* is not, in this sense, an allegory at all. Allegory in it is merely a pretext or a succedaneum—a blank wall on which tapestries of various kinds may be hung. Of such 'tapestries' the lyrics are of course the loveliest; but there are good things even in the Rhyme Royal stanzas, as this, of Phoebus embracing Daphne:

> the tre as he did take
> Betwene his armes, he felt her body quake.

In Dunbar and Skelton the decay of true allegory is redeemed by beauties of another kind—beauties so great that we forgive the false form of the poems for their sake. But in the work of William Nevill we reach the nadir of the whole genre. The *Castell of Pleasure* illustrates the unhappy operation of a dominant form in making mediocrity vocal. The author was a very dull young man; but he might have carried the secret to the grave with him if the whole recipe for making poems of this kind had not lain so fatally easy to his hand. The plot of the poem is a debate between Beauty, Pity, Disdain, and Desire framed in a dream journey to a castle of Pleasure. The ingredients are familiar, but this would not prevent the dish being palat-

able; the real trouble is that the cook is naught. The debate might have represented—like the dialogue of Pity, Shame, and Danger in the *Roman*—a real psychological process in the heart of the heroine, or, failing that, might at least have had the dialectical charm of the *Belle Dame Sans Merci*. But Nevill makes it predominantly juristic, and most of the arguments are not even tolerable conceits. The only good turn is the unexpected thesis of Pity that love of *effeccyon* (that is of passion and psycho-physical 'affinity') is really more stable than love grounded upon *condicyons*—as we should say, on community of tastes and interests, and companionship. The journey to the Castle, again, in better hands might have proved full of beauty and wonder; but in Nevill we get only one good picture,

> I was ascendynge a goodly mountayne
> About the whiche the sonne over eche syde did
>   shyne,
> Whereof the coulour made my herte ryght fayne
> To se the golden valeyes bothe fayre and
>   playne . . .

—where the landscape, though not the metre, is alive. The thought—for even William Nevill will have his thoughts—is banal. He, too, is aware of a choice between the life of love and another life, and the poem is prefaced by a dialogue between the author and the printer on this very subject, to which we return later at the gate of the castle. The alternative is that between love and money. In the prologue he is afraid (or his publisher is afraid) that the public will be more interested in books telling them how to make a fortune than in books of love: at the gate of the castle he finds twin inscriptions in letters of 'golde' and 'yndye blewe' informing him that he must here choose between the road to worldly wealth and that to 'beauties hygh estate'. The reader will remember how the authoress of the *Flower and the Leaf* had softened the old stern theme of the *psychomachia* into a gentle play between the mildest virtues and the most venial faults. Nevill's choice—which he does not hesitate to compare with the choice of Hercules—illustrates the merely bathetic side of the same process. Her antithesis was, at worst, pretty and unimportant: his is irredeemably commonplace and yet by no means universally valid. The two together are a timely reminder how far we have travelled from the real Middle Ages. The great and true antitheses with which the older poets were concerned—the eternal conflict between Venus and Diana or Venus and Reason, or the subtle discrimination, possible only to a civilized society, between Venus and Cupid—these have sunk out of sight. Something of magnanimity and something (in the deeper sense) of realism seems to be lost as the Middle Ages draw to a close: a great tide of the prosaic and the commonplace seems to be rising and carrying old landmarks away. We many, if we please, describe it as a return to nature, but only if we remember that 'spiritual' and 'civil', as well as 'artificial', are the opposites of 'natural'. And even if mere nature is to be endured when she is humble and naïve, as she is in the ballads, or even as she is in the *Flower and the Leaf,* nature pretentiously tricked out in the robes originally devised for rarified and arduous sentiment, is intolerable. The earlier poets used allegory to explore worlds of new, subtle, and noble feeling, under the guidance of clear and masculine thought: profound realities are always visible while we read them. But who can endure letters of gold and azure over a castle-gate to symbolize a worthy young blockhead's decision between the richer and the prettier of two neighbouring heiresses?

For indeed this is all that Nevill means. The love which he celebrates is a perfectly respectable love, ending in marriage, and opposed to the acquisition of a competence only by accident, if at all. It is this, indeed, which constitutes his chief interest for us as historians: we must place him along with Lydgate, King James, and Hawes, as an indication of the way the wind is blowing. In one respect he goes farther than they. He does not hesitate to show us the reversal of the lovers' relations which marriage will effect, by which the 'servant' becomes the master.

> I wyll moreouer be subdued to your correccyon
> Yf it like you to mary me and haue me to your
>   wyfe.

It is remarkable that this change in the real theme leaves unchanged certain characteristics of the old love poetry which, logically speaking, ought henceforth to disappear. Thus Nevill warns lovers to be 'secret', not noticing that there is now nothing to be secret about. Thus, again, he ends, after awakening from his dream, on a note of disillusion and quotes *omnia vanitas*. He does not repent, for he has nothing to repent of; but I cannot help suspecting behind this passage the influence of the old palinode, as in Chrétien, Chaucer, or Gower—as I suspect it also behind the far better close of the *Pastime of Pleasure*. What was originally a moral necessity is becoming a structural characteristic.

I have spoken hardly of Nevill, and it would be unfair to conclude without mentioning his merits. These are not to be found in his style, which varies between excessive aureation ('precyous pryncesse of preelecte pulcrytude' or the like) and the verbose, shuffling, pseudo-logical or legal prolixity which the earlier Chaucer found it so hard to escape from. His merits are two. The less important is a dash of that graphic power which we detected in the *Assembly of Ladies:* the comings and goings on the poet's way to the presence of Beaute are sometimes lively enough. But his real strength, such as it is, lies in his eye for natural appearances, and this sometimes sets us wondering what he might have done if he had lived in an age of descriptive poetry. The best passage, though it has been quoted before, is still so little known as to deserve transcription:

> The nyght drewe nye, the daye was at a syde.
> My herte was hevy, I much desyred rest
> Whan without confort alone I dyd abyde,
> Seynge the shadowes fall frome the hylles in the
>   west.
> Eche byrde under boughe drewe nye to theyr
>   nest;
> The chymneys frome ferre began to smoke;
> Eche housholder went about to lodge his gest;
> The storke, ferynge stormes, toke the chymney
>   for a cloke.
> Eche chambre and chyst were soone put under
>   locke;
> Curfew was ronge; lyghtes were set up in haste.

> They that were without for lodgynge did
>   knocke. . . .

And here a man would willingly break off and conceal the fact that Nevill, having written this, sees fit to conclude the paragraph with the line—

> Which were playne precedentes the daye was
>   clerely paste.

We are accustomed to anonymity in medieval poetry, but few poems are so deeply anonymous as the *Court of Love*. Its style and metre are not those of any known period in our literature; and it is difficult to guess who this author was or when he wrote a poem which scans perfectly provided you make every final -e mute and also sound the -e in every plural and genitive in -es. Fortunately, it is not part of my undertaking *tantas componere lites;* but even the content of the poem presents us with similar problems. When the poet explains that Nuns, Hermits, and Friars are among the courtiers of Love—for 'there is non ex
cion made'—we seem to be back in the ages before Lydgate and King James and Nevill; but then the language of the poem suggests a date so much later that we wonder whether the author can really know the old tradition; whether it is not more probable that he writes from a Protestant dislike of celibacy. So, again, the pedantic enumeration of Love's twenty statutes carries us back to the world of Andreas, and the beautiful matins and lauds sung by the birds at the end of the poem belong to an early stage of the tradition; but the name, and perhaps the character, of 'little Philobone', sound more modern. Most probably we have here to do with a poet who had read widely in the literature of courtly love, with the detachment of one studying a mode that has almost passed away, and who then used a whimsical eclecticism in building up his own poem, which is predominantly satiric. It is a lively piece, full of movement and gaiety; and once at least it strikes the note of rapture:

> O bright Regina, who made thee so fair?
> Who made thy colour vermelet and white?
> Where woneth that god? How far above the air?
> —Great was his craft and great was his delight.

(pp. 232-57)

Hitherto I have been following the story of a death, or something as near a death as we ever reach in the history of literary kinds; and the reader may pardonably feel that this particular form of allegory—the form which descends from poets like Machault and Chartier—has taken an unconscionable time to die. It is with relief that I turn to that much more interesting branch of my subject which concerns the vital development of allegory in our period, the transformation by which we pass from the *Romance of the Rose* to works within measurable distance of *The Faerie Queene*. In order to understand this transformation we must [refer to an earlier period]. . . . It will be remembered that allegory originally disengaged itself as a literary form under the pressure of a strongly ethical interest. Virtues and Vices were its first *dramatis personae,* and the moral conflict its first theme. The oldest kind of allegory is the moral or homiletic allegory. . . . [The] same age which saw the rise of the *Roman* saw also a rich development of the homiletic kind in such works as the *Songe d'Enfer,* the *Voie de Paradis,* and the *Tornoiement Ante-crist.* On allegory of this kind, though it was the parent stem, it was natural that the *Roman* itself should exercise an influence. Great allegories of the moral type were produced by moralizing poets in answer to the libertinism of Guillaume de Lorris and Jean de Meun; but to answer is to be influenced. Personifications and themes from the culprit work were naturally borrowed by the works that reproved it: they appeared in order to be rebuked, but they appeared. And thus insensibly a new kind of allegory arises. To set Virtue and Venus in action within a single poem is also to transcend the narrowness both of the strictly homiletic and the strictly erotic allegory, and to come a step nearer to a free allegorical treatment of life in general; and with this enlarging of the subject-matter there comes inevitably a complication and variety which were lacking before. A closed battle-field served Prudentius, and a closed garden Guillaume de Lorris. But if the hero is to be subjected to the appeals both of the false gods and the true, some sort of visionary geography at once becomes necessary, and some amount of journeying. And when a poet has reached this stage it is impossible that he should not begin to incorporate into his allegory certain elements from the romances where the journey with adventures is already the norm; and before he has finished he will find himself making an imaginary country whose allegorical pretext justifies it in being rather more imaginary than the countries in romance, being grounded not in Britain or France or even Alexander's East but in the much wider and more indefinite realities of inner experience. Once again, as long before in Claudian, allegory liberates the mind for free excursions into the merely imaginable: a 'world of fine fabling' becomes accessible and we are in sight of *The Faerie Queene.*

It will be noticed that this account of the matter distinguishes two things: the homiletic allegory pure and simple, and the homiletic allegory influenced by, and usually hostile to, the *Romance of the Rose.* The homiletic type in its purity is represented in England by the *Assembly of Gods*—an allegory so purely moral that it hardly falls within the scope of [our study]. It may be briefly described as a *psychomachia* with trimmings. These trimmings—the complex fable in which the battle of Virtue and Vice is set—are by no means without merit. The visit of *Attropos* to the assembled gods faintly anticipates the ascent of *Mutabilitie* in Spenser's poem; and the final agreement of the Rational and Sensitive souls in their common fear of Death is well conceived. The execution displays most of the typical vices of second-rate medieval literature; the phrase is prolix, the language undistinguished, catalogues and commonplaces are frequent. Yet some of the characters are painted lively enough; and if we may bring out by a typographical device the real nature of the rhythm (which is that of *Pease pudding hot!*) the following may please:

> So thedyr came Diana
>   Caried in a carre,
> To make her compleynt
>   As I told you all;
> And so did Neptunus
>   That doth both make and marre,
> Walewyng with his wawës

And tombling as a ball.

Or the entry of Vice—

> On a gliding serpent
>   Riding a great pas,
> Formed like a dragon,
>   Scalyd hard as glas;
> Whose mouth flamëd
>   Feere without fayll,
> —Wingis had hit serpentine
>   And a long tayll.

Such merits as the work has, turn mainly on this kind of vivacity. The strife between moral personifications has something of the stir of a real battle. The battle-field is described, almost in the Anglo-Saxon spirit, as the place 'where sorrow should awake'; the Vices cry 'On in Pluto name! On, and all is oure'; Vertew, coming to succour his men

> Caused hem be mery
>   That long afore had mornyd,

and as he advances 'his pepyll set up a gret shout. . . . A Vertew! A Vertew!' This manly strain helps us to forgive the clumsy, honest poet; who was certainly not Lydgate if we judge by his metre.

The *Court of Sapience,* though it should be mentioned here, is not so pure an example. Indeed it comes into this class at all only because of its introductory digression. The core of the poem is a modest little encyclopedia in verse which covers jewellery, physics, botany, the liberal arts, and elementary religious knowledge. One is reminded of a sampler; and the author, who may well have been young, seems to have written more for his own pleasure than for that of any reader. But such is the influence of the dominant form that he has seen fit to connect his catalogues on the thin thread of narrative provided by a visionary meeting with Sapience and a journey to her house; and this again gives rise to the matter of his first book where Sapience describes the greatest feat she has performed—that of devising the means to man's Redemption. This passage is homiletic allegory; and, what is more, it is certainly good, arguably great, poetry. The allegory is not original; and the theology turns on a crudely 'substitutional' view of the Atonement. But this does not prevent the poet from rising at this point to almost mythopoeic heights. The whole of the first Book should be familiar to every English lover of poetry. Langland himself has nothing more sublimely imagined than the scene in which Peace turns away from Heaven to voluntary exile, or better expressed than her valediction:

> Farewell Mercy, farewell thy piteous grace,
> So wellaway that vengeance shall prevayle:
> Farewell the beamyd lyght of hevyns place,
> Unto mankinde thou mayst no more avayle;
> The pure derknesse of hell thee doth assayle.
> O lyght in vaine! . . . the clyps hath thee incluse,
> Man was thy lord, now man is thy refuse.
> O Seraphin, yeve up thyne armony,
> O Cherubin, thy glory do away,
> O ye Thronys, late be all melody,
> Your Jerarchy disteyned is for ay.
> Your maisteresse, see, in what aray

She lyth in soune, ylorene with debate.
—Farewell, farewell, pure household desolate.

To remember what Dryden, and even Milton, have made of similar themes, is to have a measure of this old poet's tenderness and majesty. And in this same book he gives a beautiful illustration of the homiletic allegory's debt to the poets of courtly love. Our Lord is imagined as a knight who takes Mercy for His lady, and promises her (surely an exquisite transmutation of the old knightly and heroic *bēōt*),

> Full manfully I shall my payne comport
> And thynke on you as on my own lady.

And when His adventure is achieved, He returns to her with the words,

> Have here yowre man; do wyth him what ye lyst.

This introductory allegory, I confess, is the only reason for mentioning *The Court of Sapience* at this point; but I find it hard to leave. There is something in the hero's journeyings with Sapience among the flowers and trees and precious stones which defies analysis. It is very absurd that a critic should (apparently) be found who thought that Milton's description of Eden owed something to this obscure poem; absurd, yet after all significant. For I must confess that more than once as I progressed slowly through these brightly coloured and indistinctly shaped landscapes, half pleased and half tired with the names of Asteryte, Charbuncle, Crisopras, and Auripigment (or else of dolphin, cokadryll, efemeron, or coryaundre, plantane, and amomum)—more than once I found myself reminded of Milton. It is very unlikely that the explanation lies in any real similarity of poetic art: it is of Milton's theme, not of his style, that we are reminded. He wrote of Paradise; but the old poet seems rather to have written *in* Paradise, to be himself paradisal in his piety, his cheerful gravity, his childlike love of matter. For the rest, he uses a moderate degree of aureation and has some talent for what Dryden called the 'turn'; he can contrive a conceit; and save in some incorrigibly scientific passages he is hardly ever prosaic.

From such homiletic allegories I must now turn to those which illustrate the fusion of the homiletic and the courtly types. This stage in the history of our subject is represented by the two great allegories which Lydgate translated from the French, the *Pelerinage de la Vie Humaine* and *Les Echecs Amoureux*. Both are of great importance, and the second, though almost universally neglected, is a delight.

Deguileville's *Pelerinage* was an early fourteenth-century poem, somewhat longer than the *Roman de la Rose*. When I speak of it as a 'fusion' of the two kinds of allegory, I do not mean that there is any fusion of erotic and moral sympathies in the author's mind. His intention is purely homiletic, and the fusion is a purely artistic one. But on this level it is well marked. A student of homiletics might take it for an ordinary versified sermon, employing the common allegorical method of the pulpit, and borrowing from the erotic convention. A student of courtly allegory might equally well take it for a true scion of the *Rose* badly inoculated with homiletics.

Its homiletic characteristics are obvious. The author is not only more anxious to teach than to delight, but also more anxious to teach by direct statement and exhortation than by poetic suggestion. Hence his narrative, especially in the earlier parts of his poem, often stands still while long passages of unmitigated doctrine are uttered by such characters as Grace Dieu and reason. The positions advanced are those of an orthodox monastic of that age. The degrees of humility are cited from Benedict and Bernard. Heresy is condemned, and the fact that she will

> Hardyd with obstynacye
> Continue til the ffyre be hoot

is mentioned without qualm. The voluntary poverty of monks is praised in a passage of real beauty; but we also learn that monasteries lose their wealth only as a punishment for corruption. Ordinary poverty, on the other hand, seems to have lost its gospel blessing, and we hear only of *Poverte Impacyent,* figured as a foul, old woman unfit to appear among the lady Virtues. *Religioun,* in the technical sense, is the only ark of safety in the troubled sea of the present world. The founders of monastic life are pictured as powerful friends who help their clients 'by ful gret subtylyte' to climb into heaven over the wall, or pull them up by ropes, while ordinary people have to take their chance of being admitted at the gate. The author was far from foreseeing a famous chapter in *The Water Babies.*

But the influence of the *Roman* is equally marked. It is explicitly mentioned for reprobation—for the *Pilgrimage* is a religious counterblast to the profane allegory—but the author has also learned from his adversary. His picture of Reason descending from her high tower, and again of Reason offering herself to the Dreamer as his paramour, recall famous passages in the *Romance*. More important, both to the critic and to the historian, is the figure of Nature, to whom Deguileville allots perhaps the most obviously beautiful lines in his poem:

> I make alday thinges newe,
> The olde refreshing of her hewe.
> The erthe I clothe yer by yer,
> And refresshe hym of hys cher
> Wyth many colour of delyte,
> Blewh and grene, red and whyt,
> At pryme temps, with many a flour,
> And al the soyl, thorgh my favour
> Ys clad of newe; medwe and pleyn . . .
>
> The bromys with ther golden floure,
> That winter made with his shour
> Nakyd and bare, dedly of hewe
> With levys I kan clothe hem newe;
> And of the feld the lyllyes ffayre.

The origins of this speech are obvious. But Deguileville by no means leaves the goddess Natura as he found her; and for the most part his treatment of her, if less beautiful than this, is more original. His conception of religion is fierce, colourless, and sincere. He is more concerned to exclude than to draw in; and one of the most important parts of his poem is the debate in which Grace Dieu overthrows first Nature, and then the human reason, which is represented by Aristotle. Natura thus becomes one of the enemies, and Deguileville sets about her in a manner which is sufficiently surprising. Her antiquity, which had charmed poets as long ago as Claudian's day—*vultu longaeva decoro*—is shamelessly twisted into a charge against her. As Grace Dieu drily observes

> ye wite wel
> Offte sithe ryot and age
> Putte folkys in dotage,

and the rest of her speech is in keeping with the taunt. She rates Nature without mercy, extorts her abject submission, and sends her away with a harsh warning to mind her own business and not to repeat her impertinence. Since the subject under discussion is the miracle of the sacrament, the allegorical intention is obvious, and perhaps unexceptionable. But what is interesting is the poet's handling of it. He is entirely in agreement with Grace Dieu and represents Nature, at her first entry, as a mere bustling and scolding old woman. The comic effect of the passage is almost certainly intended, for the homiletic tradition by no means excludes buffoonery, and, after all, the poet is attacking the *Romance of the Rose* and wishes to blacken one of its heroines:

> And thanne anon upon the pleyn
> I sawh a lady of gret age
> The which gan holden hir passage
> Towardys Grace Dieu in soth,
> And of her port irous and wroth,
> And her handys eek of pride
> Sturdily she sette a syde . . .
> She was redy for to strive,
> For anger did her herte ryve
> Atweyne.

The conception is ignoble, and perhaps absurd; and I am inclined to distrust that species of respect for the spiritual order which bases itself on contempt for the natural. Deguileville's doctrine that the soul is 'buried quyk' in the body looks back, in the long run, to pagan rather than to Christian sources; and is of a piece with his assertion that nature herself, as opposed to sin, ordained that flesh and spirit should be at strife. After this we are not surprised to learn that Music is born of Pride and is inimical to virtue. But these are questions of doctrine, and they should not blind us to the vigour of his execution. His picture of Nature is alive.

It is harder to defend the structural vices of the poem. Its theme is substantially the same as that of the *Pilgrim's Progress,* and every comparison between the two serves but to emphasize the greatness of Bunyan and the weakness of Deguileville. Bunyan opens with a picture which prints itself upon the eye like a flash of lightning; and in a few pages he has his pilgrim started upon a journey as enchanting as any in romance. In Deguileville, of the twenty-four thousand odd lines which make up the poem, ten thousand have already passed before the pilgrim is allowed to set out. This monstrous delay is occupied by instruction and preparation, and is allegorical only in so far as much of it is put into the mouths of personifications. It is not true allegory, and might as well have been uttered by the poet in his own person. His characters, like those whom Aristotle condemns, utter 'not what the tale, but what the poet, desires'. And even when we are at last launched upon the spiritual journey, we travel towards an anticlimax. The pilgrim is kidnapped, dragged in the mire, bound, beaten, and left clinging to a rock in the midst of the sea: it is here that Grace Dieu appears as the *deus ex machina* and takes him on board her ship of 'religioun'. With this rescue the poem ought to have ended. Unfortunately the poet continues to describe the pilgrim's career after his rescue, and makes it plain that the ship is unseaworthy and the rescue ineffective. The ship may bear him to a Cistercian 'castle'; but what awaits him there is rough handling from Envy and her crew, who succeed in breaking all his limbs, which is more than the vices of the outer world ever did to him. Since all associations of human beings are imperfect, this picture of cloistered intrigue and corruption may not be a very strong practical argument against monasticism as an institution; but it is a fatal aesthetic argument against monasticism as the climax of a poem.

In the technique of allegory Deguileville is in places the worst writer with whom the present study will have to deal. Nothing is easier or more vulgar than to make allegories, if we are content with purely conceptual equivalences and do not care whether the product will satisfy imagination as well. But when they are made they are monstrosities, and of such monstrosities the *Pilgrimage* is guilty. Penance is represented with a besom in her mouth, or the Pilgrim is made to pluck out his eyes and put them in his ears. When we read such things, we can almost excuse the last century of criticism for rejecting allegory root and branch as a mere disease of literature; but if we persevere we shall find even in Deguileville passages that restore our faith. The Pilgrim, newly clad in the armour of righteousness, finds that

> Yt heng so hevy on my bak
> I wolde fayn have lett yt be.

and presently complains, from the interior of his suffocating panoply:

> Myn helm hath rafft me my syyng
> And take away ek myn heryng . . .
> Thes glovys binde me so sore,
> That I may weryn hem no more
> With her pinching to be bounde.

Finally he is allowed to have his armour carried behind him in a cart while he himself walks free, in the hope—a hope which, of course, deceives him—that he will find time to put it on when the enemy appears. (pp. 259-69)

The poet is so fierce and gloomy a man that we should look in vain in his work for any presentation either of the beauty of holiness or of the pleasures of sin. The severity of the one and the foulness of the other are his natural subjects, and the only relief he allows us is his grim humour. It is, indeed, on this limitation that the quality of his poetry depends: for he also has something of his own—a flavour or an atmosphere which is recognizable, though by no means ever present. The reader who wishes to taste this flavour, to know, as we say, 'what Deguileville is like', should read the central portion of the poem, where the Pilgrim contends with the seven deadly sins and the Devil himself. Here he will find no Spenserian seductions on the one hand, and no Miltonic loftiness on the other. He will meet Venus, not in her youth and beauty, but old and crone-like and masked, riding on a sow. Venus and Gluttony together will knock him down and drag him in the mire, tied to that sow's tail. Pride will come to their aid, not 'tricked and frounced' as she is wont in other allegories, but as a hag riding pick-a-back on Flattery her subject-hag, and both 'ful owgly of ther syht'. The Pilgrim lies helpless while the whole chorus of witches—aged, obscene shapes, all female and all monstrous—stand over him and plot his death. Nothing is more characteristic of Deguileville's imagination than his continued insistence on the old age of these nightmare shapes. Well may he exclaim:

> Allas! what hap have I or grace!
> All they that I meet in this place
> Ben olde, echon.

There is no effort to illustrate the subtleties of evil; but there lies over the whole passage a heavy squalor, a strangeness without glamour, and a disordered variety which somehow contrives to be monotonous. We have no doubt of the author's desperate sincerity. But there is power also in his unrelieved picture of evil, of bewildered degradation, of nausea. Milton's or Dante's hell, superior as they are by innumerable degrees in art, yet do not come so near to the worst we can imagine. There we have grandeur, fortitude, even beauty; but Deguileville's vision is of the last evil—of something almost omnipotent yet wholly mean; and ultimate deformity. From this point of view (though of course from no other), if I had to mention a modern poet who affects us in something the same way as the blackest parts of Deguileville, I think I should choose Mr. [T. S.] Eliot. (pp. 270-71)

The poem is unpleasant to read, not only because of its monstrous length and imperfect art, but because of the repellent and suffocating nature of its content. Yet in a way it is freer than the *Romance of the Rose,* in so far as the moral point of view is an abstraction less rigid than the erotic. It brings in more of our experience. And this widening in the allegorical subject is reflected in the literal content of the story. Dark as the world of the *Pilgrimage* is, it is at least a world in which we can go to seek adventures. We are not confined endlessly to the garden: the road and the resting-places, woods, seas, ships, and islands, distant cities and wayside meetings—these are the great contribution of Deguileville's poem.

It is, nevertheless, with heartfelt relief that we turn to *Les Échecs Amoureux,* or, as Lydgate's version is called, *Reason and Sensuality.* A better antidote to Deguileville could hardly be devised, for here, while we find once more the new variety of incident and increased romanticism of plot which are proper to the fused allegory, we find also what the reader who has just finished the *Pilgrimage* so badly needs—sunshine and charity.

The story is as follows. As the poet lies between sleep and waking on a spring morning, Nature in all her brightness appears before him, filling his bedchamber with the smell of amber and rose, and thus addresses him: 'Arise and betake yourself to virtuous activity. Prove all my works and see if there be any flaw in them—yet all this beauty was

made for you alone. Be worthy, Man, of your dominion.' And he asks, 'Where shall I go?' 'Learn,' says Nature, 'that there are two roads. The road of Reason, beginning in the east, runs westward all about the world and so returns again to the east; but that of sense rises in the west, and though it leads eastward, to the west it comes again at last. To follow the first of these is the prerogative of man who alone among the beasts

> hath intelligence
> To make his wit to encline
> To knowe things that be divine,
> Lassting, and perpetual,
> Hevenly and espirituel,
> Of heven and of the firmament
> And of every element;
> Whos wit is so clere yfounde,
> So perfyt pleynly and profounde
> That he perceth erthe and hevene
> And fer above the sterris sevene.

With these words the goddess vanishes, and the dreamer rises and goes out into the spring morning, where he soon loses his way. So indeed does the author, and wantons in descriptions which might be called prolix if the theme itself, the relaxed and boundless sweetness of vernal nature 'wilde above rule or art', did not condone and invite delay. The thing, so often well done in medieval poetry, has never been done better, and the reader pauses gladly to notice how

> The freshnes of the clere welles
> That fro the mountes were descended,
> Which ne mighte be amended,
> Made the colde silver stremes
> To shine ageyn the sonne bemes;
> The rivers with a soote soune
> That be the wallys ronne doune . . .

It seems but natural, not only to those who love Plato but to those who love poetry also, that the young man, so solicited by ear and eye, should forget the high pre-natal charge of *Natura,*

> That al my lyf which passed was
> Was clene out of my remembraunce.

As he wandered, four celestial shapes approached him. Mercury was the leader, who came on an errand from Jove, presenting Minerva, Juno, and Venus for his judgement, as once he had done to Paris. Though Minerva offered him wisdom and Juno wealth, he gave the prize to Venus, and forthwith found himself alone with her; for Pallas and Juno incontinently vanished, and Mercury, observing with a shrug that 'al this worlde goth the same trace', shook his wings and was off. What follows marks well the difference between a purely decorative allegory and an allegorical picture of real life. Venus is ready enough to promise the youth a mistress as fair as Helen, but the youth remembers Nature's bidding sufficiently to be uncomfortable. As he explains to Venus, he is not quite his own man. He has promised Nature to travel by the road of reason and to fly sensuality. But he would not disoblige Venus either,

> And for that I am lothe toffende
> To you or hir by displeasaunce,

I hang as yet in ballaunce.

—an admission which leaves to Venus the obvious reply that she is Nature's most intimate friend and indispensable ally, and that no question of divided loyalties need arise. In the end the dreamer becomes 'her man', and the reader begins to feel some apprehension lest once again the commandments of Love are to be enumerated. But the poet knows better. His Venus, instead of commandments, has good news of a far country to deliver, and tells him of the goal to which he must set out—the garden of her two sons, Cupid and Deduit. The passage is interesting as an interpenetration of courtly and homiletic allegory, with the happiest results. The lover, like the Christian, becomes a traveller, and Love's garden, like the Celestial City, comes at the end of his story instead of the beginning. Before she leaves him, Venus fixes the right direction by pointing out to him the battlemented tops of Cupid's castle in the distance—a graphic touch not unworthy of Bunyan.

The young man has not gone far on his journey before he enters a large forest; a place 'wonder fair and delytable' where the tall trees send forth a wholesome smell and golden fruit hangs beneath their unwithering foliage. It is the home of Diana, who at first refuses to speak to him because he is Venus' servant, but presently relents and warns him of the dangers of his enterprise. 'You have been duped by that goddess', she says, 'whose very name means venom,

> For thou hast noon experience
> Of hir large conscience!

The garden to which she is leading you is full of perilous sirens, and of beds more enchanted "than was the bed of Launcelot". There are trees yonder whose shadow kills a man, and wells where he can drown like Narcissus. Turn back. Enter it not,

> But abyde and make arest
> Her with me in my forest
> Which hath plentevous largesse
> Of beaute and of fairenesse;
> For shortly through my providence
> Her is noon inconvenience,
> No maner fraude, deceyt, nor wrong
> Compassyd by Sirens songe . . .
>
> And ther thou shalt no welles fynde
> But that be holsom of her kynde,
> The water of hem is so perfyte
> Who drinketh most hath most profyte.
> Eke in thys forest vertuous
> No man taketh hede of Vulcanus.

The Diana of this poet is a complex, as well as a gracious figure, of closer kin to Spenser's Belphoebe than to the abstract 'Chastity' of the pulpit. Virginity, indeed, is her profession; but she can also praise faithful loves, and it is part of her complaint against Venus that love nowadays is not as it was when Arthur reigned, when famous warriors loved gentlewomen of high degree 'nat but for trouthe and honeste', and for their sakes put life in jeopardy in 'many unkouth straunge place'. Yet her Hesperean forest, in the poet's main intention, probably symbolizes the conventual life, and his hero condemns it as being, for all its beauty, too 'contemplatyfe'. If so, it is a lesson in allegory to compare this representation of 'religioun' with that of Deguileville. There we have a castle, in which we meet such characters as Lady Lesson and Wilful Poverte: here, a pagan goddess, with bow and quiver, stands in glittering attire amidst a forest out of fairyland, and discourses upon heroes of old romance. In the prosaic sense it is obvious that Deguileville's picture is very like the thing symbolized, while that in *Reason and Sensuality* is, in the same sense, not like it at all. But if we look deeper, if we attend, as in poetry we always should attend, not to the objects mentioned in the passage but to its quality and atmosphere, its immediate flavour, so to speak, upon imagination's palate, we see that Deguileville has effected nothing, where his rival has called up for us the eternal appeal of virginity, retirement, and contemplation. The one deals with a doctrine, a superficies; the other with a spiritual solid.

To the speech of Diana the traveller retorts by quoting Nature's original command 'go, se the world', and will not heed the reply that he has misunderstood it. The phrase is happily chosen, for it is made clear that the young man wishes to 'see the world' in many senses. As this poet's Diana is something more than chastity, so his hero is more than an abstract lover. He is obstinate youth in all its aspects, and love, though his chief, is not his sole, preoccupation. He feels the thirst that Marlowe's heroes were to feel, and longs for

> the knowleching
> Of the heven and his meving
> And also of the salte see,
> And eke what thing it mighte be,
> Why the flood, as clerkys telle
> Folweth with his wawes felle,
> And after that the ebbes sone
> Folweth the concours of the Mone.

His final rejection of Diana, when, beaten out of all his guards yet impenitent, he determines to see the garden of Deduit for himself, is expressed in terms exquisitely natural:

> Thogh yt were as mortal
> As horryble and foule also
> As is the paleys of Pluto,
> And as ful of blak derkenesse,
> Of sorwe, and of wrechchidnesse,
> Yet finaly, how ever it bee
> I shal assayen and go see . . .
> It semeth a maner destiny.

The verse (which, after all, is Lydgate's) may halt, and perhaps the images are ready made; but the psychology is excellent.

At this profession of invincible secularity, Diana 'took the thykke of the forest' and was seen no more. The hero, full of 'joy and pleasaunce' continued his journey to the walls of the happy garden, where the poet pauses to praise the *Romance of the Rose* as an incomparable work of 'philosophie' and 'profounde poetrie'. The figures on the Wall, the portress, and the beauties of the garden are described, and the rest of the poem, so far as Lydgate has translated it, is occupied with an allegorical game of chess. The poem at this stage is still readable, but the inspiration of the earlier parts has disappeared. There is much satire on women here, which depends on the simple device of attributing to them all those virtues which tradition notoriously denies them; whether it is Lydgate or another who made assurance doubly sure by adding *cujus contrarium est verum* in the margin, I have not been at the pains to inquire.

This poem, in its truncated English form, is one of the most beautiful and important pieces produced between Chaucer's work and Spenser's. The historian will notice that it represents a far fuller and happier fusion of the moral and the courtly allegory than Deguileville. The author is not partisan; he gives us a balanced, even a detached, picture of the mingled yarn of human experience. The allegory, in his hands, is beginning to forget its origins in the pulpit and the courts of Love, and to feel its way towards the treatment of 'general nature'. The aesthetic critic may care nothing for tendencies and influences; but he too should remember the poem, for the unearthly freshness of Diana's forest, and for the shining and exuberant vitality of those early passages where the earth

> made him faire and fresh of hewe
> As a mayde in hir beaute
> That shal of newe wedded be,

and perhaps even more for the lofty platonizings in this description of Nature's robe,

> Ther was wrought in portreyture
> The resemblaunce and the figure
> Of alle that unto God obeyes,
> And exemplarie of ydeyes
> Full longe aforn or they weren wrought
> Compassed in divine thought;
> For this Lady, freshest of hewe,
> Werketh ever and forgeth newe
> Day and night in her entent
> Weving in her garnement
> Thinges divers ful habounde,
> That she be nat naked founde.

The *vis medicatrix* of Nature herself has passed into the poet's imagination. He pipes as if he would never be old, and his lines are a sovereign antidote either to Renaissance fever or modern discouragement.

In both these poems we trace the beginnings of a new kind of allegory. When I say that this impulse is continued in the work of such poets as Hawes and Douglas, I do not mean that I can prove an 'influence' or draw up a list of 'parallels'. It is not a question of a literary school, of models and imitations, but of an unconscious tendency, given no doubt in the whole state of mind at that period rather than in its literary ideals, whereof all these later allegories are in varying degree symptomatic. (pp. 271-78)

The first of these authors with whom I shall deal is Stephen Hawes; and Hawes for our purpose means the *Pastime of Pleasure* and the *Example of Virtue*. The *Pastime* is a difficult work to judge. Read it conscientiously from cover to cover, and you will conclude that it is the heaviest of tasks; but then from such a reading something will cling to your memory—odd lines, odd scenes, a peculiar flavour—till you are driven back to it, to find that its faults are just as grievous as you first supposed but that its merits are greater. No poem gives us the impression of so wide

a gap between its actual achievement and the thing it might have been. There is a kind of floating poetry in the author's mind but not in his grasp. He seems ever on the point of becoming much better than he actually is. Nor is it very wonderful that this should be so, for Hawes, stumblingly and half consciously is trying to write a new kind of poem. He himself believes that he is trying to revive an old kind: the praise of Lydgate is often on his lips, and he deplores the direction in which poetry is moving in his own time:

> They fayne no fables pleasaunt and coverte
> But spend their tyme in vainfull vanyte
> Makynge balades of fervent amite.

Like Caxton, he wishes to revive the 'floure of chyvalry' which 'hath be longe decayed'. But this illusion, whereby the mind posits in the past the desired thing which is really still in the future, is not unnatural, and its working explains the early history of Romanticism in the eighteenth century, when men like Walpole and Macpherson not only sought, but even invented, in the past, faint images of the poetry which was really to be written in the nineteenth century. The combination of allegory on the large scale and chivalrous romance which Hawes wants to revive, could not be revived because it had not existed. There had been some approach to it in Deguileville: but Hawes carries it much further, and we shall not find the thing in perfection till we reach *The Faerie Queene*. Hawes in the meantime moves about in worlds not realized. He has very little art and his poem is dark and tortuous, but a fitful wind of inspiration stirs in the darkness. He so misunderstands the original of allegory that he thinks its purpose is to hide the subject—'to blowe out a fume' are his own words; but one of the reasons why he thinks so is his native and by no means unpoetic bent for the indefinite and the allusive—in a word for the romantic vague. Before his pilgrim finishes his journey and wins La Bell Pucell we have that journey so frequently predicted that all suspense is lost; but then suspense is not part of his aim, and this constant pressure of the remote and unattained—this continual hinting and casting forward (*ripae ulterioris amore*)—is of the very nature of one kind of romance.

> By the way there ly in wayte
> Gyauntes grete dyffygured of nature—
> But behonde them a grate see there is
> Beyonde which see there is a goodly lande
> Moost full of fruyte, replete with Joye and
>   bliss—
> Of ryght fyne golde appereth all the sande.

So speaks Lady Fame to the youthful Graunde Amour, and the lines are good poetry because they lead the mind on and open the doors of the imagination: and good allegory, because to be young and to look forward is, after all, very like hearing what Graunde Amour heard. And if the same journey is foretold again a couple of hundred lines later—this time the hero sees it pictured on a wall—even this has its own sense of mysterious fatality and its own truth to life. As we proceed the allegory becomes more difficult. I have not been able to find the *significacio* in the repeated partings of the hero and heroine, and perhaps there is none. Perhaps Hawes himself would have been neither able nor willing to throw much light on the deeper

For I wote wel, of what someuer condicion Women ben in
Grece, the Women of this contre ben right good, wyse, play
sant, humble, discrete, sobre, chast, obedient to their husbon-
dis, trewe, secrete, stedfast, euer besy, & neuer ydle, Attempe
rat in speking, and vertuous in alle their werkis, or atte
leste sholde be soo, For whiche causes so euydent my sayd lord
as I suppose thoughte it was not of necessite to sette in his
book the saiengis of his Auctor socrates touchyng Women
But for as moche as I had comandement of my sayd lord
to corecte and amende Where as I sholde fynde faulte, and
other fynde I none sauf that he hath left out these dictes &
saynges of the Women of Grece, Therfore in accomplisshtg
his comandement for as moche as I am not in certayn whe-
der it was in my lordis coppe or not, or ellis perauenture
that the wynde had blowe ouer the leef, at the tyme of tras
lacion of his booke, I purpose to wryte the same saynges
of that Greke Socrates, whiche wrote of the Women of
grece and nothyng of them of this Royame, whom I sup
pose he neuer knewe, For if he had I dar plainly saye that
he wolde haue reserued them inespeciall in his sayd dictes
Alway not presumyng to put & sette them in my sayd lor
des book, but in thende aparte in the rehersayll of the werkis
humbly requiryng al them that shal rede this lytyl rehersayll that yf they fynde ony faulte tarette it to Socrates
and not to me Whiche wryteth as here after foloweth

Socrates sayde That Women ben thapparailles to
cacche men, but they take none but them that wil
be poure, or els them that knowe hem not, And
he sayde that ther is none so grete empeshement vnto a man

A page from Dictes and Sayeings of Philosophers, *printed by William Caxton in 1477.*

obscurities of his poem. He loves darkness and strangeness, 'fatall fictions', as he says, and 'clowdy fygures' for their own sake; he is a dreamer and a mutterer, dazed by the unruly content of his own imagination, a poet (in his way) as possessed as Blake. It is at once his strength and his weakness that he writes under a kind of compulsion. Hence the prolixity and frequent *longueurs* of his narrative, but hence also the memorable pictures, whether homely or fantastic, which sometimes start up and render this dreariness almost 'a visionary dreariness'.

> I sawe come rydynge in a valaye ferre
> A goodly lady envyroned aboute
> With tongues of fyre as bryght as ony sterre.
>
> I came to a dale.
> Beholdynge Phebus declynynge low and pale,
> With my grehoundes in the fayre twylight
> I sate me downe,
>
> And on his noddle derkely flamynge
> Was sette Saturne pale as ony leed.
>
> Eternity in a fayre whyte vesture. . . .
>
> We came unto a manoyr place
> Moted aboute under a wood syde.
> 'Alight', she sayd, 'For by right longe space
> In payne and wo you dyde ever abyde;
> —After an ebbe there cometh a flowynge tyde.'

Indeed, all the resting places on the journey of Graunde Amour are good; and all the roadside twilights and dawns,

> Whan the lytell byrdes swetely dyde synge
> Laudes to theyr maker erly in the mornynge.

Much that he describes does not interest us, but he describes nothing that he has not seen, whether with the inner or the outer eye. He has noticed the morning sky coloured like curds, and the 'bypaths so full of pleasaunce,' the little images of gold moved with the wind on the top of the tower of Doctryne, and the sun shining, as a man wakes, in the mirror of a strange bedroom. Some medieval writers have little feeling for the difference between combat with a man and combat with a monster; but when the three-headed giant crosses the path of Graunde Amour

> My greyhoundes leped and my stede dyde sterte,

and he is as meticulous as Spenser in telling us how many cartloads the giant's corpse measured. So clear is his vision, so perfect his poetic faith in his own world, that the poem ought to be good; but his incapacity to select, his stumbling metre, and his long delay in the tower of Doctryne, have condemned him to not undeserved obscurity.

The *Pastime* is not exclusively an allegory of love, but of life as a whole, with special emphasis on love, education, and death. The educational sections in which Hawes vainly endeavours to rival the allegorico-encyclopaedic work of Martianus Capella or Jean de Meun, are the dullest part of the poem. With the possible exception of the fine passage on grammar

> (By worde the worlde was made oryginally:
> The Hye King sayde: it was made incontinent).

none of his presentation of the liberal arts deserves to be re-read. Much more interesting is his treatment of love. No poet whom we have considered is more homely—if you insist, more Victorian—than Hawes, in the context which he imagines for the passion. Not only does Graunde Amour look forward to marriage as the only conceivable form of success: he even hesitates over the inequality in wealth between himself and his mistress, and is reassured by *Counseyle* (who here fills the role of Frend, or Pandarus) that 'she hath ynoughe . . . for you both'. The Lady, on her part, answers to his suit that she is 'sore kept under' by her 'frendes' who 'wolde with me be wrothe' if they heard of his proposal. This is the work-day world with a vengeance, and it might seem that we were within easy distance of the commonplace of Nevill; but then the Lady's very fear that her relatives will lead her 'to a ferre nacyon' (*ferre* is a key-word in Hawes) and his answering promise that he will follow

> And for your sake become adventurous

are essentially romantic. And if Hawes is prosaic in the context of his love, on the subjective side he is all on fire, 'wrapped,' as he says, in a 'brennynge chayne'. He is far indeed from the unambiguous desire of Guillaume de Lorris, or the heroical passion of Troilus: the fire of his love is a dim fire, charged with sentiment and imagination, a thing much more ambiguous and brooding, in a word more romantic, than that of older love poetry. It is a cloudy ecstasy, love veritably in a mist, a dream or a glamour and none the less for that reason a reality; and he writes of it lines which are irreplaceable in the sense that no other poet has struck just the same note.

> She commaunded her mynstrelles ryght anone
> to play
> *Mamours,* the swete and the gentyll daunce.
> With La Belle Pucell, that was fayre and gaye,
> She me recommaunded with all pleasaunce
> To daunce true mesures without varyaunce.
> O Lorde God! how glad than was I
> So for to daunce with my swete lady!—
>
> For the fyre kyndled and waxed more and more,
> The dauncing blewe it with her beaute clere.
> My hert sekened and began waxe sore;
> A mynute six houres, and six houres a yere
> I thought it was.

But it is Hawes' treatment of his third theme, the theme of death, which is most remarkable. Critics have been found to whom it is merely ridiculous that a narrative written in the first person should continue after the narrator is dead and thus permit him to describe his own decease. But the convention whereby the dead are allowed to speak, or the living to assume the person of the dead, is surely not a very difficult one: the Greek anthology, and the first country churchyard you turn into, will supply precedent. And if you object that dead men do not really talk—and I can see no other objection—you will be well advised to study any subject rather than poetry, where the naïve realist can never succeed. So much suspension of disbelief as this device demands, is our debt to every poet; and to Hawes, for a special reason, the debt is very easily paid. For even from the outset—perhaps because his imagination is so earnest and his conscious skill so weak—the good passages have had this peculiar quality, that they seem to come from nowhere, to be a disembodied voice, not always a perfectly articulate voice, coming to us out of a darkness; so that when, at last, it comes to us admittedly from the grave, it at once compels belief.

> O mortall folk, you may beholde and se
> How I lye here, somtyme a myghty knyght.
> The ende of Joye and all prosperite
> Is dethe at last through his course and myght;
> After the day there cometh the derke nyght,
> For though the day be never so longe
> At last the belles ryngeth to evensonge.

Every one knows this stanza: but few know that it comes at the end of a dirge sung by the Seven Deadly Sins in which the reiteration of a single phrase ('erthe of erthe') has all the brutal insistence of a bell heard from within the church, and that dirge and epitaph together are merely the starting-point for one of the most nobly conceived passages in any allegory. For when his hero lies dead and the poem might be expected to end, Hawes does a most surprising thing; he rolls up curtain after curtain of his cosmos, as the successive backcloths roll up in the transformation scenes of the old pantomime, or as the planes of time disclose themselves in Mr. Dunne's serial universe. *Remembrance* has hardly finished the epitaph over the grave of Graunde Amour when Dame Fame enters the temple to enroll him among the Worthies, and to conclude with her vaunt

> Infenyte I am. Nothing can me mate.

and here again we suppose we are at the end: it is a familiar consolation at the funerals of great men. But no—on the heels of Fame comes another shape, the same on whose 'noddle' the dark flame of Saturn was set, and whom we quickly recognize by the horology in his left hand, and who proclaims himself,

> Shall not I, Time, dystroye bothe se and lande,
> The sonne and mone and the sterres alle?

But Time is wiser than Fame and boasts less, and comes confessedly but as the usher of Eternity—Eternity who ends the poem, appearing in her white vesture and triple crown,

> Of heaven quene and hell empres.

If the execution of this whole passage had been equal to the conception, it would have been among the great places of medieval poetry. It is not; but we must still say (more reasonably I hope than Goethe said of another poem) 'how nobly it was all planned'.

His other allegory, *The Example of Virtue,* for some reason lacks the faint, peculiar appeal of the *Pastime.* It is a simpler and shorter poem in which Youth, after some good adventures, but also after assisting at a very dull *débat* between Nature, Fortune, Hardiness and Wisdom, changes his name to Virtue and marries Cleanness. Perhaps the most interesting character in the poem is this lady's father, the King of Love. His name prepares us for a picture of Cupid and Cupid's court: but the old Cupid could hardly have had Chastity for his daughter. And as we approach his castle and find that we are cut off from

it by a swift river spanned with the traditional perilous bridge—'not half so broad as a house ridge, and that this bridge bears the legend

> No man this bridge may overgo
> But he be pure without negligence
> And stedfast in God's belief also.

we begin to doubt whether he is not meant for the King of Love in a very different sense. Cleanness appears on the far side of the river encouraging the hero much after the style of *Perl.* But when at least we meet the King,

> (At the upper end of the hall above
> He sat still and did not remove,
> Girded with willows),

he turns out to be very like Cupid after all—blind, winged, naked, and armed. But when he tells the wooer that none shall have his daughter's hand who does not 'scomfit the dragon with heads three', (which are the World, the Flesh, and the Devil), and when the wooer arms himself for this adventure in the Pauline armour of a Christian man, then again we are thrown back on some celestial Cupid. The truth is that we have reached a point at which Hawes does almost unconsciously what Dante or Thomas Usk did by an arduous conceit; the sort of unification or ambiguity (it is not a mere critic's business to decide) on which Spenser's sixty-eighth sonnet is based, has already become natural.

Two passages in the poem are memorable. The first is the poet's shocking interview with Nature:

> Methought she was of marvellous beauty
> Till that Discretion led me behind,
> Where that I saw all the privity
> Of her work and human kind;
> And at her back I did then find
> Of cruel Death a doleful image.

This is not merely a conventional exercise in late medieval gloom, for in the same passage the poet forces us to attend also to Nature's beauty and fecundity.

> a fair goddess
> All things creating by her business

and working 'withouten rest or recreation. Either side of the picture, alone, would be a commonplace; the synthesis of the two awakes a much deeper response. The second passage is a lovely example of the convincingness of Hawes. After a night journey in a great wilderness the traveller finds himself in a desolate place full of wild beasts. Any allegorist might have done this, but perhaps only Hawes, or only one of those far greater poets who share Hawes' matter-of-fact faith in their imaginary worlds, would have added that he knew by the sweet smell that there was a panther somewhere near.

Gavin Douglas is so much of an individual, and so much more of an artist than Hawes, that I do him some wrong in citing him as the illustration of a general tendency at all. But though his allegories are distinctly his own and need no historical significance to recommend them to the lover of poetry, they have in common with their period the widened scope and the increasing imaginative liberty. Their great distinction is the artistic control, the disciplined splendour of style, the proportion and balance, in which the medieval Scottish writers so often excel the English. *King Hart,* especially, is an admirably ordered little work which ought to rejoice the heart of a French critic. Its content represents the fusion of erotic and homiletic allegory to perfection. The real theme is that of Youth and Age, and the fable tells how the Soul, long captive to beauty and pleasure, is at last awakened by age, deserted by the brisk companions of its youth, forced to return to its own long-abandoned dwelling-place, and finally defeated by death. The poem thus has an obvious affinity with the *Confessio Amantis,* and a more recondite and subtle affinity with *Beowulf*—which is well brought out when the poet, describing the foul water of Corruption in the moat of King Hart's castle which is rising and lapping upward 'gre by gre' against the walls, adds the fact that

> thai within maid sa grit melody
> That for thair reird thay micht nocht heir the
>   sound.

It is, of course, a theme which easily becomes platitudinous; but good allegory (next to the style of Johnson) is the best way of reviving to our imaginations the grim or delightful truths which platitude conceals, and the whole of this poem marches impressively, in the words of a later poet,

> To the small sound of Time's drum in the heart.

As in *Beowulf,* the end is felt from the beginning, and the very brightness of the first stanza gives us the disquieting sense of weather that will not last:

> So semlie was he set his folk amang
> That he no doubt had of misaventure,
> —So proudly wes he polist, plane and pure
> With youthheid and his lustie levis grene,
> So fair, so freshe, so liklie to endure—

The adventures of King Hart during his long sojourn in the castle of the Lady Pleasance are good radical allegory of love, and truer to the original *Rose* pattern than anything we have met since the fourteenth century. Hart and his companions are thrown into a dungeon with Danger for their jailer, and there

> Full oft thai kan vpone Dame Pietie cry,
> 'Fair thing, cum doun a quhyle and with vs
>   speik!'

and it is only when Danger sleeps that Pity is able to grant their request, and thus to make Hart in the end the master of his captor. But the whole of this traditional passage is new-coloured because it is set between Hart's gay, unsuspecting youth in his own castle and the hour when Age arrives:

> Ane auld gude man befoir the yet was sene
> Apone one steid that raid full easelie.
> He rappit at the yet but courtaslie,
> Yit at the straik the grit dungeon can din

The contrast between the gentle knocking (the *small* sound of Time's drum) and its appalling repercussions is a fine specimen of the complex appeal of good allegory. Without its *significacio,* taken as a purely magical event in a romance, it is already the kind of contrast that calls

to something deeply lodged in our imagination, and is always potent, whether for laughable or horrifying effects, when used on the stage. Add the *significacio,* by remembering the vast emotional disturbances which that small sound has sometimes produced in your own experience, and its potency is doubled: and then go on to remember (as poetry of this kind will force you to do) the innumerable experiences of quite different kinds in which the same small knocking without produces the same convulsions within, and you will find that this seemingly facile piece of allegory is a symbol of almost endless application, to use which is to come as near as our minds can to the concrete experience of a universal. The same may be said of the scene in which Hart returns to his own deserted castle. How well the image fits the experience of coming back to a man's own interests and earliest bent of nature after the long constraint imposed by some passion! But the passion need not be love, the return need not be repentance; the symbol, consciously intended for one kind of return, fits all, and gives *in concreto* a characteristic of our life so fundamental that if you try to conceive it (instead of imagining it) it will escape you by its very abstraction. *King Hart* is not a good poem for a sick or sorry man to read, but if any one dismisses it as a frigid or conventional work he must have little feeling for reality. It strikes home where the screaming exaggerations of Blair (dare I add, of Donne?) on the same theme, go harmlessly over our heads.

The Palice of Honour is a much more elaborate, and also a more cheerful, poem. The theme, if I have understood it aright, may be expressed in Milton's words (Fame is no plant that grows on mortal soil, &c.) and the poet would set before us the mild paradox that so seemingly mundane a good as Honour can be conferred in its true form only by God and enjoyed only in eternity. The *Anagnorisis,* so to speak, of the allegory, comes at the moment when the palace of Honour, long heard of and sought for, turns out to be the dwelling-place of God; and the whole point of this passage depends, oddly enough, on the language Douglas used. When the pilgrim is allowed to peep through the keyhole of Honour's hall (like the page at the 'whummil bore' in the ballad) he sees, seated bright amidst the almost unbearable brightness of the place 'ane god omnipotent'; modern English, compelled to choose between the rendering *one God* and *a god,* inevitably destroys the careful equivocation, a kind of intellectual pun, on which the force of the original depends.

This conceit, though perhaps not very profound, is the nerve of the whole allegory, and it is enough to show that the *Palice,* even from the strictly allegorical point of view, is by no means contemptible. But unless the *significacio* throughout has escaped me, the poem as a whole illustrates the furthest point yet reached in the liberation of fantasy from its allegorical justification. Douglas is no dreamer like Hawes, for he is not the servant of his dream, and he writes with a clear head and a learned and practised pen; but what he describes is sheer wonderland, a phantasmagoria of dazzling lights and eldritch glooms, whose real *raison d'être* is not their allegorical meaning, but their immediate appeal to the imagination. The success of the poem depends on his poet's privilege of being awake and asleep at the same time, drawing on the dreaming mind for his material without for one moment losing his power of selection or the matter-of-fact realism which compels our acceptance. In the midst of the ominous wood he tells us that 'the stichling of a mouse out of presence' would have terrified him. Caught by Venus' courtiers, and mindful of other goddesses who have punished their victims by turning them into beasts, he tells us how

> Oft I wald my hand behald to se
> Gif it alterit, and oft my visage graip.

The horses 'shynand for sweit as they had been anoynt, the sea-nymphs 'dryand thair yallow hair', and the Muses 'yonder, bissie as the beis' in their garden, are admirable examples of this mixed fantasy and realism. But this liveliness is never allowed, as it sometimes is in Chaucer, to extinguish mystery and glamour. The very opening of the dream ('Out of the air come ane impressioun') is an invitation to enchantment. The howling wilderness beside the river, where the fish 'yelland as elvis shoutid', into which the poet wakes in his dream, may represent the dangers and desolation of man's birth into the world of nature; or again, it may not. But who cares? To miss such a point in the *Romance of the Rose* would be to miss nearly all; but in this poem the shouting fish and the wood full of decaying trees and 'quhissilling wind' really exist in their own right. The weird energy of the description—rattling with broad Scots words of the *boisteous* style—and the careful contrast between this and the spring morning described in the Prologue, satisfy us completely. The inconsequence of the figures hithering and thithering as the narrative proceeds hits off exactly the sense of freedom combined with uneasiness which is proper to such dreams; and the sense of space, almost of infinity, which they bring, is well evoked by the words which Sinon and Achitophel shout over their shoulders to the poet as they pass,

> To the Palice of Honour all thay go;
> —Is situat from hence liggis ten hunder,
> Our horsis oft or we be thair will founder.
> A dew! we may na langer heir remane.

The catalogues, no doubt, are an obstacle to the modern reader's enjoyment: but such obstacles will be found in all works outside our own period—slaughters in Homer, ritual in Ovid, vocal gymnastics in the old operas, which time has dulled for us. Their most profitable use is when they set us speculating which features in contemporary masterpieces are likely soonest to become similar deadweight.

Douglas, in one sense, is not nearly so close to Spenser as Hawes is. The quality of his fancy is at once brighter and more terrifying. He is 'eldritch' where Spenser uses a solemn gloom, and full of hard light where Spenser is voluptuous. The whole difference between the air of Edinburgh and the air of Southern Ireland divides them. But if we are classifying by degrees of merit, then doubtless the *Palice* is much nearer to *The Faerie Queene* than Hawes' work is to either.

[This essay] would be incomplete without some reference to a follower of Douglas, John Rolland. His *Court of Venus,* printed in 1575, is a book which has had few readers. Its 'haltand verse' (which the author twice acknowl-

edges) and its excessively dull prologue, are likely to deter any student who is not supported by some historical interest. To recover, at this time of day, the taste for its peculiarly Scottish and medieval blend of gallantry, satire, fantasy, and pedantry is all but impossible; and a full enjoyment of it presupposes that familiarity with legal technicalities which was for so long an essential part of Scottish culture. Our best chance of approaching it with sympathy is to imagine how the Baron of Bradwardine might have enjoyed it: for if the Baron, why not Scott?—and from Scott it is no long journey to ourselves. As an allegory it is nearer to Guillaume de Lorris than to Machault or Chartier in so far as the core of it is an allegorical action and not a mere complaint. It opens indeed with a debate, such as we have learned to dread, between Esperance and Desperance; but this only leads up to the moment at which Esperance faints at the arguments of his companion and thus exposes the latter to the wrath of Venus. The goddess appears, revives her champion, and on the advice of her 'greit advocat' Themis instructs Nemesis to serve Desperance with a summons. The second book is occupied with Desperance's attempts to get counsel to defend him and his final success in retaining Vesta. The third and fourth give us the trial, in which he is convicted but finally pardoned and re-converted to the service of Venus. The allegory is coherent and reasonable, but even this abstract is enough to show that it is slight: and if the poem, despite its faults, has a certain interest, this is once more because the interest lies in other things for which the allegory is only the pretext. The first of these is the realistic presentation, in some degree satiric, of the contemporary legal world; and in this respect the *Court of Venus* is a close parallel to the *Assembly of Ladies.* The passage in which Nemesis presents poor Desperance with his summons is lively and obviously true to life. He wants a copy of it for his own use: and Nemesis would be quite prepared to give him one *gratis* if he were not

> repugnant
> To Venus Quene and to hir court obstant.

As it is, he can have one only by paying for it: and they fail to agree on the price. The trial scene is naturally more difficult to a layman: but all of us can relish Vesta's objections to the jury, and still more the picture of the jury retiring 'Richt stupefact cause the mater was hie'. When they got to their room,

> First doun they kest Moyses Pentateuchon
> With his storyis, and Paralipomenon

and so forth for twenty-five lines.

The other interest I should venture, once again, to call that of romance, if the word were less ambiguous. The presence of this element in Rolland is much less certain than in Douglas and Hawes, and many readers might deny it altogether. Perhaps fantasy or extravaganza would be a better word. Certainly, by whatever name we call it, there is something in Rolland's second book which brings us near sometimes to *The Faerie Queene* and sometimes to *The Water Babies* or to *Alice in Wonderland.* Here, as in Douglas, we have a widening and deepening of the allegorical *terrain*—a tendency, still faint, but recognizable, to shift the interest from the personifications to the whole world in which such people and such adventures are plausible. The second book of the *Court of Venus* is, as it were, a land with an air of its own which we remember, and which we should recognize if we met it again in a dream or in another book. What complicates the issue—though it also improves the book as literature—is the fact that in this passage the interest which I am finding it so hard to define is inextricably mixed with the other satiric and realistic interest. Desperance successively applies for legal assistance to the Seven Wise Men, the Nine Muses, the Nine Worthies, the *Ten Sibillais,* the Three Fates (or 'weird sisteris' as Rolland calls them), the Three Graces, and Vesta. The deepening despair of the unfortunate suitor and the cold comfort with which each of these authorities, except the last, sends him on to the next, make a picture which every one can recognize. This is what happens when poverty or unpopularity seeks assistance against enemies whose star is in the ascendant: every one drops his business like a hot potato. Equally true, and more entertaining, is the picture of Desperance hesitating outside the door of the Nine Worthies—whose very aspect terrifies him—and almost deciding to pretend that he has come on some quite different errand:

> Best is to say I am ane chirurgiane . . .
> Best is to say that I covet service.

But in one of the old allegories all these different figures would have appeared as they were required with no more sense of distance or wandering than we have on a chessboard. In Rolland we are never allowed to forget the journeys in between,

> Throw Mos and Myre and mony hie Montane,
> Half wo begone allone all solitair
> Throw wildernes in woddis and greit dangeir.

We are even made to feel the passage of time and to watch the traveller, who was in good point enough when first we met him, becoming

> Daglit in weit—richt claggid was his weid
> In stormis fell and weder contagious,
> In frost and snaw.

In the end these journeys cease to be mere connecting links. One of them extends itself to some eighty lines, and these lines breathe a spirit quite unknown to the old allegory, and take us to the Caucasus 'most heich in Scithia' and 'excandidate with snawis fell', where the sun is above the horizon for twenty hours out of the twenty-four. There the traveller lies down to sleep upon 'ane merbill stone' and receives comfort in a dream, and wakes to lament: but afterwards meets the sender of the dream.

For the rest, Rolland is a very minor poet. He has a command of that pungent vigour which we find in all the Scottish writers of the Middle Ages; and the conclusion of his poem, where he unexpectedly introduces himself at the feast in Venus' court and identifies himself with *Eild*— thus becoming one of the personifications in his own allegory—is, so far as I know, original and is certainly very effective. Nor must it be supposed, because I have here dwelt on other aspects of his work, that he is deficient in truly allegorical power. The tournament in the fourth book, when once its *significacio* has been seen, can hardly

be quoted without indecorum, but it is a masterpiece: for it is a very good realistic description of a tournament, and yet at the same time a close parallel to the real subject. I do not expect to make many converts to Rolland: and I myself have not obeyed his request that the poem should be read more than once.

> For anis reading oft tyme it garris authoris
> Incur reprufe be wrong Interpretouris.

But authors not obviously better than he, who write in easier language and more popular forms, are daily read for pleasure and mildly praised in books of criticism. Certainly there is real poetry in the words of Desperance as he hears the song of the Muses:

> God! gif it war my fortoun, than said he,
> My fatall weird and als my destenie,
> I war convert into the may Echo
> That I micht bruik this greit quotidian joy.
>
> (pp. 278-96)

> C. S. Lewis, "Allegory as the Dominant Form," in his The Allegory of Love: A Study in Medieval Tradition, *Oxford at the Clarendon Press, 1936, pp. 232-96.*

Charles Lethbridge Kingsford   (essay date 1913)

[*Kingsford was a historian whose writings include* Henry V, The Typical Medieval Hero *(1901) and* English Historical Literature in the Fifteenth Century *(1913). In the following excerpt from the last-named work, he reviews ballads and satirical verse inspired by political events.*]

The fifteenth century was peculiarly favourable to ballad literature. True ballads are in the first instance circulated orally; thus some perish, and others are varied in the process of transmission, and gradually put on a more modern dress which conceals, if it does not destroy, the historic value of the original. But some have the good fortune to be committed to writing at a date early enough to prevent the loss of their most valuable characteristics. For the fifteenth century we have examples both of original and transmitted ballads. Those of the former class, though they can be only a small survival of the fittest, are numerous enough to be of great value to the historian; if it is only seldom that they preserve facts which would be otherwise unknown, they are nearly always of interest as an expression of popular opinion. Since, however, ballads are only produced on some sufficient occasion we cannot look for any continuous history; it is natural that the ballads of the fifteenth century should centre round certain marked events, and fall into well-defined groups.

At the beginning of the century the warfare on the Scottish March and in Wales must have furnished the balladmakers with many admirable themes. But there is no ballad on Homildon, or on the exploits of the Umfravilles, to compare with the late fifteenth-century ballads on Otterburn and the mythical Chevy Chace. Of the Welsh war we know from Adam Usk that 'the wonderful deeds of Edmund Mortimer were told at the feast in song'; but no example of any such ballad has survived.

Thus Agincourt and the French campaign of 1415 furnish us with our first group of ballads. The chief is the long *Battaile of Agincourt* attributed incorrectly to Lydgate, which is preserved in two versions. Of these one, which is the ruder, shorter, and apparently the older, was printed by Hearne in the Appendix to his edition of the Pseudo-Elmham's *Vita Henrici Quinti* from Cotton. MS. Vitellius D xii; this manuscript was entirely destroyed in the fire of 1731. The other version was printed in Nicolas and Tyrrell's *Chronicle of London* from Harley MS. 565, the date of which can be fixed precisely to 1443-4. The longer version contains three 'Passus': the Siege of Harfleur; the Battle of Agincourt, and the Triumph at London. The shorter version lacks the third 'Passus', and the first six stanzas of the first 'Passus'; but has about seventy additional lines in the second 'Passus'; the greater part of this additional matter consists of a list of the prisoners. There are also numerous textual variations. The theme for the first 'Passus' is of the Dauphin's scornful present of tennis-balls, and how Henry with his great guns played tennis at Harfleur. The idea appears in other places, notably in the *Brut,* but it is nowhere developed so fully as in this poem. The second 'Passus' describes the march to Agincourt and the battle on much the same lines as the *Brut* with additional detail of a more or less poetic character; but the debate of the French princes before the battle is peculiar, and is given most fully in the older version; the list of prisoners in that version comes no doubt from the same source as those in one version of the *Brut* and in the Cleopatra Chronicle of London. The third 'Passus' probably follows the official programme of the Triumph, though a stanza describing how the French lords wondered at the swarm of citizens, 'England is like an hive within', seems to be an addition by the poet. The *Battaile of Agincourt* and the *Brut* are no doubt closely related, though it would be rash to argue too certainly as to their relative originality. This much, however, is clear, namely, that the prose narrative of the *Brut* is in part at least derived from ballad sources. Such phrases as 'the King . . . cast down both tower and town, and laid them unto the ground: and there he played at Tennis with his hard gunstones', and 'when they should play, they [the citizens] sang welaway and alas that ever any such tennis-balls were made', have an unmistakable ring of verse. But these phrases are not paralleled exactly in the *Battaile of Agincourt,* and the *Brut* would appear to preserve traces of some other ballad now lost. The narrative in the *Brut* was probably written before 1430, and in its original form perhaps a dozen years earlier. It does not seem possible to fix the date of the *Battaile* more precisely. Dr. Oskar Emmerig has argued that in the *Battaile* we have the original of the tennis-ball story; but the evidence of Elmham, Otterbourne, and Strecche is conclusive for its currency in other quarters. The *Battaile* itself is, as it stands, probably a comparatively late production made up of earlier half-popular ballads.

The *Battaile* was certainly not the only ballad of the time relating to Agincourt. Later sixteenth-century ballads may preserve somewhat of the contemporary poems, and possibly of the originals of the *Brut.* But the most strictly contemporary in its present form of all the Agincourt poems is the ballad which is in part paraphrased and in part preserved in the Cleopatra Chronicle of London. This is a finer production in a literary sense than the *Battaile,* and also gives the impression of being more genuinely popular. If it does not add anything material to our knowledge, it is certainly the best and most spirited of the Agincourt poems.

The Pseudo-Elmham, amplifying a curt and rather obscure sentence of Tito Livio, states that Henry V, when he made his triumphal entry into London, would not suffer any songs to be made in his praise. There is, however, extant a poem ["Our King Went forth to Normandy," quoted in Nicolas, *Battle of Agincourt*] which professes to have been written and sung on this occasion; if its internal evidence is accepted it must at all events have been written in Henry's lifetime. It is interesting for its character and quality, if not remarkable for its contents.

It is difficult to suppose that no later incident of the French war in the reign of Henry V, or in the early years of Henry VI, attracted the ballad-makers. Nevertheless, we do not meet with any contemporary ballad till we come to the siege of Calais in 1436. The defection of Philip of Burgundy in 1435 had stirred English national feeling to its depths, and revived the old commercial hatred for the Flemings. The defence of Calais in the following year was assuredly a fine achievement. After Philip and his Flemish army had departed from Calais, with great shame, disworship, and loss, many rhymes of the Flemings were made amongst Englishmen. Of these ballads four specimens have been preserved, two in versions of the *Brut* and two elsewhere. Two are strictly narrative, and the other two are rather satirical on the treachery and discomfiture of Duke Philip. All four appear to be in the fullest sense contemporary. Of the narrative pieces the first is perhaps the best and most spirited of all the fifteenth-century ballads:

> Remember how ye laid siege with great pride and boast
> To Calais, that little town; the number of your host
> Was a hundred thousand and fifty to reckon by the polls,
> As it was that same time founden by your rolls;
> And yet for all your great host, early neither late
> Calais was so feared of you, they shut never a gate.

Both this and the other narrative ballad, which comes from Cotton. MS. Galba E ix, are full of graphic and interesting detail of real value. The early date of the second of these narrative ballads is proved by the quotation of the final lines in the *Libel of English Policy.*

Of the two satirical ballads, one which begins

> Thou Philip, founder of new falsehood,
> Disturber of peace, captain of cowardice,

is imperfect. It may have been written in 1435 on the occasion of Philip's abandonment of the English alliance; or it may have gone on to describe the siege of the following year. It is certainly very similar in character to the fourth ballad, which is said to have been written on the latter occasion, 'in despite of the Flemings', but is rather aimed at Philip himself, and ends scornfully:

> What hast thou won with all thy business,

> And all thy tents to Calais carried down,
>
> . . . . .
>
> Thy cowardly flight, cockney of a champioun,
>   Which durst not fight, and canst so well
>   maligne.

The French war gave no further occasion for triumph. The next incident for the ballad-maker was the downfall of Eleanor Cobham. The *Lamentacion of the Duchess of Gloucester* appears in the commonplace book of Richard Hill, which was written much later; but the poem itself may be of contemporary date. With this may be coupled the poem on *The Mutability of Worldly Changes,* which moralizes on the fates of Eleanor Cobham, John Beaufort, Duke of Somerset, and Humphrey of Gloucester; this also exists only in a sixteenth-century copy, but seems to have been written about 1460; it gives a dubious story as to the grounds of the charge against Gloucester. Both these pieces are rather literary exercises than political poems or ballads. Their historical allusions are only incidental, and they are more interesting than important.

The only other political poems of the fifth decade are Lydgate's verses *On the Prospect of Peace,* and *On the Truce of 1444.* Probably they were written to order in support of the foreign policy of the Court party. They certainly do not reflect any strong public opinion. It was the mismanagement of the war, and not its continuance, which stirred popular feeling.

The next group of poems (they are rude satires, not ballads) centre round the loss of the English possessions in France and the downfall of Suffolk and his unpopular colleagues. Most of them come from a Collection made by a London citizen in or about 1452. The earliest of the series is in the form of an attack on William Boothe, Bishop of Lichfield, who was Chancellor to Queen Margaret, and is said to have owed his advancement to Suffolk. Boothe is accused of having obtained his see by simony: Suffolk is elsewhere charged with having disposed of bishoprics from corrupt motives. Whilst the main subject of this poem is the attack on Boothe, and the corruption of the government, other ministers are also censured: Trevilian for his falsehood, and Suffolk for his ambition:

> The Pole is so parlyus men for to passe,
>   That fewe can escape it of the banck rialle.
>   But set under suger he shewithe hem galle:
> Witness of Humphrey, Henry and Johan,
> Whiche late were on lyve, and now be they goon.

These lines refer to Humphrey of Gloucester, Cardinal Beaufort, and John Holland, Duke of Exeter (a grandson of John of Gaunt), who all died in 1447. Boothe was consecrated in July of that same year. The poem may be as early as 1448, or even as the autumn of 1447.

The second of the series in point of time is the *Warning to King Henry.* Suffolk is accused of having sold Normandy; if the commons do not help the King, he will bear the crown. The King is warned against his ministers, and in particular against Daniel and Saye; the traitors will never be true, they are all sworn together to hold fast like brothers. They had impoverished him for their own profit:

> So pore a kyng was never seene,
> Nor richere lordes alle bydene.

Henry himself seems to be excused: 'the King knoweth not alle.' The date was probably the end of 1449.

The *Verses against the Duke of Suffolk* belong clearly to the same time. He must go, or the land is lost:

> Hong up such menne to oure soverayne lorde,
>   That ever counselde hym with fals men to ac-
>   corde.

So also do the *Verses on the popular discontent at the disasters in France,* which begin, 'The Rote is dead.' From the reference to the loss of Rouen they must be later than October 1449. The lines

> And he is bouden that oure dore should kepe,
>   That is Talbot our goode dogge,

no doubt allude to the fact that Talbot had been given as a hostage to the French when Rouen was surrendered. The various personages of the time are satirized or described by their cognizances. The final lines, which refer to Richard of York, show to what direction popular opinion was turning:

> The Faukoun fleyth, and hath no rest,
>   Tille he witte where to bigge his nest.

The lines 'Now is the Fox driven to hole' must have been written after Suffolk's arrest on January 28, 1450; and since he was still in the Tower, before his removal to Westminster on the 9th of March. The writer rejoices that Suffolk (the Fox of the south) is in the Tower, 'if he creep out he will you all undo'; it was he who with his clog had tied Talbot our good dog, and who at Bury slew our great gander. Suffolk was popularly accused of the death of Humphrey of Gloucester, though his enemies did not venture to include the charge in the formal indictment.

The final, most vigorous and virulent poem of this series is not included in the Cottonian Collection. Suffolk left England on May 1, was intercepted by the Nicholas of the Tower in the Channel, and executed on the following day. A poet of the popular party hailed the event with savage glee: all the dead man's friends were bidden to come and assist in performing

> For Jack Napes soule, *Placebo* and *Dirige.*

It is an extraordinary demonstration of the depth of political hatred, though in a narrower way it is chiefly useful as a list, with some pungent personal touches, of the adherents of the Court party. In [the Lambeth MS. 306] it is described as made by the commons of Kent at the time of Cade's rising.

The early years of the Wars of the Roses have left us no popular poetry except some pieces which comment in a general way on the abuses of the time, the evils of maintenance, the prevalence of violence and disorder, and the miscarriage of justice. A poem of this description with the refrain 'For now the bysom leads the blind' was certainly written before August 1456, but is probably not much earlier. Another poem of similar date attributes all the evils to 'Meed'. Others satirize extravagance, and the 'many laws and little right'. But it is impossible to date such productions precisely.

The great reconciliation of 1458, when the King and Queen and Yorkist leaders all joined in a procession of thanksgiving at St. Paul's on March 25, gave a London poet the opportunity to rejoice at the prospect of peace. His verses may afford some evidence of the existence of Lancastrian sympathies in the capital. Another poem, which belongs to the same year, strikes a stronger note. It is remarkable as the only poem definitely on the Lancastrian side which has been preserved. In its form it is an allegory on *The Ship of State,* and is of more than usual literary merit. The King is the ship, and the various Lancastrian leaders are described as the parts of the ship: thus the Earl of Shrewsbury is called the top-mast 'who keepeth the ship from harm and blame'.

> Steer well the good ship, God be our guide,
>
> . . . . .
>
> This noble ship made of good tree,
> Our sovereign lord King Henry,
> God guide him in adversity
> Where that he go or ride.

The Ship of State was written when the prospects of Lancaster were most hopeful. The events of 1460-1, which culminated in the triumph of York, produced a series of poems on the other side. This series begins with two pieces, which were probably intended to prepare the way for the return of the Yorkist leaders in July 1460.

In the early summer of 1460 the Earls of March, Warwick, and Salisbury, who were at Calais, entered into communication with their friends in Kent, and when they knew the true hearts of the people determined to cross over to England. Shortly before their coming there was a *Ballad set upon the gates of the City of Canterbury.* The writer takes for his text the words of Isaiah, 'the whole head is sick and the whole heart faint.' England was divided against herself, and being brought to destruction. King Henry was impoverished, and his rule could not endure; he had banished his true blood. All England mourned for those that were hence.

> Send home, most gracious lord Jesu most be-
> nign,
> Send home thy true blood unto his proper vein
> Richard, Duke of York, Job thy servant insign,
> Whom Satan not ceaseth to set at care and dis-
> dain.

The writer prays also for the return of the Earls of March, of Salisbury, and of Warwick, 'shield of our defence'. He hints that Henry's son was a false heir, born in false wedlock; a venomous slander, which Warwick had fostered. It is probable enough that this ballad was inspired by the Yorkist leaders as part of their propaganda.

Another piece, of the same date but of London origin, describes how the writer walking down Cheapside saw a woman embroidering letters, which he proceeds to expound:

> Y. for York that is manly and mightful

> . . . . .
>
> W. for Warwick, good with shield and other de-
> fence,
> The boldest under banner in battle to abide.

The glorification of Warwick in the poetry of this time is very apparent. He is, with the Earl of March, the hero of the ballad of *The Bearward and the Bear,* which celebrates the Yorkist victory at Northampton. The framework of the ballad is allegorical. The Bearward (Edward, Earl of March) and the Bear (Warwick) went to chase the Dogs (Shrewsbury, Beaumont, and Egremont) and the Buck (Buckingham).

> The game was done in a little stound,
> The Buck was slain and borne away;
> Against the Bear there was no hound,
> But he might sport and take his play.

The Bear and Bearward save The Hunt (King Henry), and beg him not to take their act unkindly. The Hunt replies that the Buck and the Dogs had brought him into distress: 'I followed after, I wist not why.' Then the Hunt is brought reverently to London, over which the Eagle (Salisbury) had meantime hovered watchfully. Herein we see the desire of the Yorkist leaders up to this point to preserve the semblance of loyalty, and to dissociate Henry from his advisers. The poem ends with a prayer that God may 'bring home the Master of this Game, the Duke of York . . . Richard by name'. From this it is clear that the ballad was written before Richard came over from Ireland in October. The recognition of Richard as Protector seemed to confirm his triumph, but a Yorkist poet warned his leaders not to be too trustful; for those who now spoke fair, were as false as ever:

> They say in their assemble, it is a wonder thing
> To see the Rose in winter so fresh for to spring;
> And many barked at Bear that now be full still,
> Yet they will him worry, if they might have their
> fill.

The terror in London after the victory of the Lancastrians, with their northern army, at St. Albans on Shrove Tuesday, February 17, 1461, the relief with which Edward was welcomed and acknowledged as King, and the triumph of the Yorkists at Towton inspired another fine ballad, *The Rose of Rouen.* The writer was clearly a Londoner:

> Upon a Shrove Tuesday, on a green leed
> Betwixt Sandridge and St. Albans many man
> gan bleed:
> On an Ash Wednesday we lived in mickle dread;
> Then came the Rose of Rouen down to help us
> in our need.

These last three pieces are all of a high degree of merit, and have a certain similarity of form which suggests that they may be the work of one writer.

> Some pleasant verses of the same date, which
> begin
> Sithe God hathe chose the to be his knyght,

are noteworthy only for their expression of thankfulness for Edward's victory.

It was a less practised hand than the author of the *Rose*

of Rouen who a little later reviewed the whole situation from the point of view of the successful party in a piece, which Wright styled *A Political Retrospect*. The dethroning of Richard II, whose reign was 'abundant with plenty of wealth and earthly joy', is described as a great wrong. Henry of Derby won the crown by force and perjury; he killed Scrope 'the blessed confessor', and by the judgement of God was smitten with leprosy. Henry V, though he reigned unrightfully, was the best of his line and upheld the honour of England. Henry of Windsor by great folly brought all into languor. In his days through false treason the good Duke of Gloucester was done to death; since which time there had been great mourning in England, with many a sharp shower. Woe unto the land where the King was unwise or innocent! Queen Margaret had endeavoured to rule all England, and would have destroyed the right line: she would have brought the country to confusion, not scrupling in the pursuit of her ends to make use of the help of foreigners. King Edward had appeared to be England's comforter, and banish the black clouds of languor. His threefold victories at Northampton, Mortimer's Cross, and Towton, were a sign of God's favour. In the support of his right the Earl of Warwick, 'lodestar of knighthood,' had ever been foremost. This is an excellent statement of the interpretation put upon the history of the previous sixty years by the bias of the Yorkists.

Ten years later *The Recovery of the Throne by Edward IV* describes at length the return of the King, his march to London, and victory at Barnet. The battle of Twekesbury is passed over, and the poem ends with a detailed account of the defeat of the Bastard of Fauconberg's attack on London, which is the most useful part of it. The writer was no doubt a London citizen. Though the poem adds little to the official narrative of *The Arrival,* it is interesting for some personal touches. Earl Rivers, by his share in the defence of London, 'purchased great love of the commons'. Richard of Gloucester, 'young of age and victorious in battle,' was the chosen husband of fortune. Hastings, the Chamberlain, had 'failed his master neither in storm nor stour'.

The later years of Edward IV furnished the ballad-makers with no suitable themes. Under Richard III the fate which overtook William Collyngbourne for the couplet which he posted on the doors of St. Paul's

> The Cat, the Rat, and Lovel our dog
> Rule all England under a hog—

would be a warning to other versifiers. But Richard's downfall was naturally attractive to writers of the early Tudor period. Their productions, which were probably not committed to writing till long after the date of their original composition, have survived only in late and altered copies. But even in their present form they preserve genuine contemporary material.

The earliest as regards the date of its subject is a ballad on the *Betrayal of Buckingham by Banister*. Its description of how Banister lived to an old age of misery and shame points to its original composition having been as late as the early part of the sixteenth century; on the other hand, it is not likely to have been much later.

Of more interest are two ballads which were originally composed by minstrels in the service of the Stanleys. *The Rose of England* is put in an allegorical form so similar to that of the ballads of 1460-1 as to justify the belief that at all events it preserved the same literary tradition. Since it praises Sir William Stanley, it is not very likely that its original composition was later than Stanley's execution in 1495. England is described as a fair garden with a beautiful red rose-tree. There came a beast called a Boar, who 'rooted this garden up and down', and tore the rose-tree asunder. But a sprig of the Rose (Henry Tudor) was preserved, and returning to England with the Blue Boar (the Earl of Oxford) sent for help to the old Eagle (Lord Stanley). Together they won the victory, the Earl of Oxford being in particular distinguished for his skill in manœuvring Henry's army:

> The Blue Boar the vanward had,
> He was both wary and wise of wit;
> The right hand of them he took
> The sun and wind of them to get.

This is an historical touch which we do not get elsewhere. Another is the story of Master Mitton, the bailiff of Shrewsbury, who refused to admit Henry, but was pardoned by him for his loyalty to his charge.

A much longer and more important piece is *The Song of the Lady Bessy,* which has survived in several versions. The variation of these versions is probably due to the fact that the poem had been long current before it was put in writing. The *Song* is poetical both in its construction and its development, and much of the idea and the detail is due to the author's imagination. As a literary work it is 'well constructed, vivid, dramatic, and marked by an epic breadth of treatment'. Still, underlying its poetic form, there is a solid base of fact, though it is not always easy to disentangle the truth. From the part which Humphrey Brereton plays in the story it has been conjectured that he was the actual author. In any case the *Song* was certainly the work of some one who had a good knowledge of the events which he describes. At the latest the original must have been composed in the early years of the sixteenth century.

The Lady Bessy is Elizabeth, daughter of Edward IV. The song begins by describing how she was importuned by her uncle Richard to become his Queen. But Richard had murdered her brothers, and rather than wed with him she would be burnt on Tower Hill. She would marry no one but the Earl of Richmond. In her trouble she appeals to Lord Stanley, who is by an anachronism called Earl of Derby. Stanley at first refuses to help her: King Richard was his lord, and they would both be undone if they were discovered. Elizabeth then declares that she knew that the tyrant intended to destroy the Stanleys, as he had destroyed Buckingham. Still Stanley is obdurate. But at last he is overcome by her distress and manifest sincerity. Then Elizabeth and Stanley together plan a great conspiracy: the Princess writes letters to their friends at Stanley's dictation, and Humphrey Brereton, an old servant of King Edward, is sent to deliver them. The conspirators meet at Stanley's house in London, and Brereton is chosen to take their message to the Earl of Richmond. Brereton does not know the earl, but by good fortune a fellow countryman from Cheshire was porter at Beggrames Abbey, where Henry then dwelt. The porter tells Brereton how to recognize the Prince of England, who, dressed in black velvet, was shooting at the butts with three of his lords; the Prince had a long pale face, with a wart a little above the chin:

> His face is white, the wart is red,
> Thereby you may him ken.

This and other minute details as to Brereton's errands seem to bear the stamp of personal knowledge, and furnish the ground for the suggestion that he was the author of the *Song.* Certainly they leave us in no doubt as to the good quality of the material on which it was based. The principal share which the Lady Bessy is made to take in organizing the conspiracy is an obvious poetical invention. But our other information is so scanty that we cannot tell exactly how much truth there may be in the story.

To return to the *Song* Henry sends back word that he will cross the sea for the Lady Bessy. He lands at Milford Haven, is joined by the Stanleys, and marches to Bosworth. Lord Stanley had, however, been forced to leave his son, Lord Strange, as a hostage with the King. Strange is in danger of his life, and is only saved at the last minute by the imminence of Richard's own peril, which compels him to postpone his vengeance. The battle is won by the help of the Stanleys:

> There may no man their strokes abide,
> The Stanleys' dints they be so strong.

Richard is urged to take horse and flee, but makes answer:

> Give me my battle-axe in my hand,
>   And set my crown on my head so high,
> For by him that made both sun and moon,
>   King of England this day I will die.

This is an historic touch, but the concluding scene is happily apocryphal. When Richard's dead body is brought naked to Leicester, the Lady Bessy meets it with bitter reviling:

> How like you the killing of my brethren dear?
> Welcome, gentle uncle, home!

The Song of the Lady Bessy is very interesting as an example of how early ballads are compacted of truth and fiction; and also as showing, through its varying versions, how ballads composed for recitation and transmitted from mouth to mouth are changed in the process before they are set down in writing. Of the extant copies of the *Song* the oldest is no earlier than the reign of Elizabeth, and one is as late as that of Charles II. It is further of interest as an early specimen of the work of a professional minstrel in the service of a great feudal family. The Stanley cycle of ballads did not of course stand alone. As another instance we have a Percy cycle, including the famous though unhistorical *Chevy Chace.* A poet in the employment of the Percy family, though he was not a ballad-maker, was William Peeris. He was secretary to Henry, fifth Earl of Northumberland (d. 1527), for whom he wrote a metrical *Chronicle of the family of Percy.* Its interest is, however, chiefly genealogical, and it contains nothing of importance for general history. (pp. 237-52)

Charles Lethbridge Kingsford, "Poetry and Ballads," in his English Historical Literature in the Fifteenth Century, *Oxford at the Clarendon Press, 1913, pp. 228-52.*

Gustave Reese   (essay date 1959)

[*A noted historian of music, Reese wrote* Music in the Middle Ages *(1940),* Music in the Renaissance *(1959), and* The Commonwealth of Music *(1965). In the following excerpt from the second-named work, he comments on the main characteristics of the carol in the fifteenth century.*]

As the 1400's reached midpoint, England was one of the leading musical nations, owing largely to insular traits best exemplified in the music of Dunstable, who himself introduced them to the continent. Somewhat later, composers of English birth—e.g., Morton—were active in the music-making of the Burgundian court. However, English composers on the continent represented but one aspect of 15th-century English music. Their works survive chiefly in continental MSS, while few of their names appear in the largest early 15th-century source of native English music, the Old Hall MS. Moreover, while a man like Morton was to become rather French in outlook, the composers not known to have left England seem to have been little affected by musical developments across the Channel. Instead of following the "modern" styles of Ockeghem or Busnois, the English after the mid-century tended increasingly toward an insular conservatism, remaining less touched than continental musicians by the forces that were preparing for the appearance of a composer of the stature of Josquin. That this situation was recognized in the 15th century itself is evidenced by the writings of Tinctoris, who regarded Dunstable, Dufay, and Binchois as the teachers of the Ockeghem generation and who regretted that, while much that was new was being discovered, the English "continue to use one and the same style of composition, which shows a wretched poverty of invention." The gradual decline of the prestige of English music abroad is borne out by the contents of the Trent Codices: English music is well represented in the earlier MSS (those from c. 1420-1440), while less and less appears for the middle decades of the century, and for the period c. 1460-1480 no English works seem to be included at all. The conclusions suggested by this evidence have often been questioned. But investigation has not yet revealed a "missing link" that will provide really great music for the period between Dunstable and Fayrfax. English music isolated itself from the trends of late 15th-century Europe, developing an estimable—sometimes a highly estimable—but conservative school of composers. The persistence of conservatism in Late Renaissance English music, though with certain notable exceptions, will necessitate our proceeding further chronologically in England than on the continent to cover comparable developments. Fortunately, this persistence did not in the least prevent the production—mainly, to be sure, by the exceptional composers—of music that provides the Late Renaissance with some of its crowning glories.

Our knowledge of English music—as compared, for example, with that of Franco-Netherlandish music—is fairly sketchy from approximately 1450 to the closing years of the century, when the first sources of Tudor music begin to appear. However, [the Egerton 3307 MS], probably dating from c. 1450 or a little earlier, is one of the sources affording some idea of developments at about this time. Copied out at Meaux Abbey, Yorkshire, especially known for interest in the arts, the MS contains sixteen hymns and versicles, a Mass, two settings of the Passions, twelve carols, twenty-two Latin *cantilenae,* and a drinking song. (pp. 763-64)

With the carols of Egerton 3307, we approach the popular realm of English music, although such pieces could be inserted in the liturgy. . . . Pieces of the type in question are peculiar to England. Nevertheless, the English did not confine the texts of the carols to their own language. Included in the Egerton MS, for example, are carols with completely English texts, with English stanzas and Latin burden, with macaronic texts of English, Latin, and French, and with entirely Latin texts, pieces of the last type being usually called *cantilenae.* In his definitive work on English carol texts, R. L. Greene [see Further Reading] defines the carol before 1550 as "a song on any subject, composed of uniform stanzas and provided with a burden," emphasizing that "the burden makes and marks the carol." To the extent that the burden is meant to be sung after each stanza, it is a refrain. Sometimes, however, a refrain has already appeared at the end of the stanzas, as an integral part of them. The burden, on the other hand, is "a self-contained formal and metrical unit." For ease of reference, therefore, it is better to limit the term "refrain" to the material recurring at stanza-closes. The term "chorus" sometimes appears in the MSS, applied to second settings of the burden "(and certain parts of the stanza also)." Apparently, if nothing was indicated to the contrary, a polyphonic carol was to be sung by a group of soloists. Consequently, if a second setting was provided with the indication "chorus," the first setting, sung by a group of soloists, was presumably followed by the second setting, sung by a choral group.

To differentiate the carol from the ballad, the other English literary-musical form employing a refrain, Greene points out, among other things, the dependence of the popular ballad on oral tradition for its transmission and the essentially narrative character of its texts. Both ballad and carol derive ultimately from the dance, as may be seen in their alternation of stanza and burden. However, about 1400 the carol ceased to be danced, at least in cultivated society, and became a simple polyphonic form. The ballad, however, remained a popular form, essentially monophonic, though undoubtedly at times associated with improvised instrumental accompaniment.

The popular nature of the carol (popular "by destination" rather than "by origin") is suggested by several facts. The basic form of the carol (though it is more a type than a form)—*ABcdeb* (or *a*) *AB*—is related to other "popular" forms found on the continent at the same time: the *lauda, ballata, villancico,* forms derived ultimately from medieval dance, from solo-chorus performance, and in the Renaissance associated with the social life of court and town and

with religious groups. The carol structure is intimately related also to the processional hymn with its *repetenda*. It is significant that the Franciscans, who had utilized the primitive *lauda* in order to further their essentially folk-like religious ideas, were among the best-known English authors of 15th- and 16th-century carol texts. These religious men made deliberate use of the popular carol to spread their teachings, and this use may in turn have shaped and developed the carol itself (especially in regard to text): five of every six surviving carol texts are of a religious or moralistic character and many carol texts incorporate fragments of religious verse (both liturgical and non-liturgical), often using the original melody, in an ornamented form, in one of the parts.

The carol before 1480 is set in triple measure, *a 2* or (less expertly) *a 3,* the parts often moving in parallel thirds or sixths, recalling the earlier gymels. Either superius or tenor may be the leading voice or the parts may be of equal importance. After 1480 there is a tendency to add variety to the musical texture of the carol, and, in the early 16th-century Eton MS, carols with smooth-flowing polyphony in duple measure and with pairing of the voices show the influence of the Tudor motet style. About 1515, carols written in imitative counterpoint appear in the works of Richard Pygott and others, a style that leads directly to the carol motets of Byrd.

Like other forms of popular art, the carol is found current in higher social levels. Court records give us an occasional glimpse of court entertainments, such as that on Twelfth Night, 1488, when "at the Table in the Medell of the Hall sat the Deane and thoos of the kings Chapell, whiche incontynently after the Kings furst Course sange a Carall." Under the Tudor monarchs such holidays were to be the occasion for dramatic entertainments by the Chapel choir. (pp. 765-67)

Gustave Reese, "England: Music from c. 1450 to c. 1535," in his Music in the Renaissance, *revised edition, W. W. Norton & Company, Inc., 1959, pp. 763-814.*

DRAMA

Richard Axton   (essay date 1982)

[*Axton is a literary scholar, editor, and translator whose writings include* European Drama of the Early Middle Ages *(1974). In the following excerpt, he discusses the most important dramatic works of fifteenth-century English literature:* Everyman, The Castle of Perseverance, *and* Mankind.]

Everyman was printed (the first English morality to be so) for private reading four times between 1510 and 1525. It is quite short (921 lines) and has seventeen parts, playable by ten actors doubling. Described by the printer as 'a treatyse . . . in maner of a morall playe', it sets out as an allegory the medieval Christian doctrine concerning Holy Dying. The dramatic interest comes from development of Everyman's first moment of recognition, 'O Deth, thou comest whan I had thee leest in mynde!' as a series of encounters in which he discovers which parts of his nature are friends unto death. The allegory of death as a pilgrimage gives the mind an image of action in a play that would otherwise be very static. It also puts a veil between Everyman and the prospect of death, a veil such as we normally hold there, in order to keep removing it. Recognition is made more sobering by the dramatization of man's evasions, which first take the form of proverbial self-comfort (Everyman pitifully hopes that Good will help him make his 'reckoning', 'For it is sayd ever among / That money maketh all ryght that is wronge'). In the climactic moment Everyman reaches his destination accompanied by Strength (shown here as one of the champions of Christendom) and Beauty. The chilling force of his discovery is the greater because the spare, unemotional quality of his language contrasts so well with Strength's ironic boasts and Beauty's proverbial bustle. The language insists on both the physicality of experience and the negativeness of death;

STRENGTH.
    Everyman, I wyll be as sure by thee
    As ever I dyde by Iudas Machabee.

EVERYMAN.
    Alas, I am so faynt I may not stande;
    My lymmes under me do folde.
    Frendes, let us not tourne agayne to this lande,
    Not for all the worldes golde;
    For in to this cave must I crepe
    And tourne to erth, and there to slepe.

BEAUTE.
    What, in to this grave? Alas!

EVERYMAN.
    Ye, there shall ye consume, more and lesse.

BEAUTE.
    And what, sholde I smoder here?

EVERYMAN.
    Ye, by my fayth, and never more appere.
    In this worlde lyve no more we shall,
    But in heven before the hyest Lorde of all.

BEAUTE.
    I crosse out all this. / Adewe, by Saynt Iohan!
    I take my tappe in my lappe and am gone.

The spareness of the language is notable. A. C. Cawley comments [in the introduction to his 1961 edition of *Everyman*], quoting T. S. Eliot on poetry and drama: '. . . the freely rhythmical verses of *Everyman* harmonize inconspicuously with its neutral style, so that we find ourselves "consciously attending, not to the poetry, but to the meaning of the poetry".'

In the final sequence Everyman commends his spirit into God's hands and Knowledge describes his passing. The soul is carried to the upper storey of the House of Salvation, where it is welcomed in marriage as God's 'electe spouse', having now become female. This sequence forms the only real spectacle in *Everyman*, which in some ways

resembles the oldest Christian ritual drama: a procession to a sacred place to witness a miracle. In the *Visitatio Sepulchri* man witnessed the miracle of Christ's resurrection. In *Everyman* man himself is transformed at the House of Salvation. This property marks the goal of Everyman's journey and occupies the centre of the acting place.

In *The Castle of Perseverance,* a colossal East Anglian morality dated *c.* 1425, the image of the house of the soul is elaborated to explore psychological allegory and develop dramatic action. Mankind's whole life is shown as a kind of journey, but the central action of the play is a siege of the castle itself; this provides many opportunities for vivid conflict between the virtuous occupants of the castle and their besiegers. Allegorical castles are sometimes described in medieval homiletic writing as an aid to memorizing moral truths; what distinguishes the dramatic use of the castle is, of course, the occupation of an actual play castle by live actors. The form of the play's action, reduced to its simplest dimension, is that of many children's games. Mankind must journey to his goal without being captured; he has a home-base where he is safe and has a team to protect him; outside this base he is hunted by the enemy. In the courts of medieval Europe elaborate siege games were known, mostly, it seems of an erotic kind: a lady or ladies were besieged in a model castle, known in England as the 'maydens castle', and might protect themselves from capture by amorous knights by showering the besiegers with flowers and sweets.

According to the staging plan in the Macro manuscript, the *Castle* was played, like several other East Anglian plays, 'in the round'. The acting circle has scaffolds at its perimeter to raise the chief characters to the audience's view: God, the Devil, Flesh, World, and Covetousness. At the centre is the castle itself, a two-storey building, open at ground-level to show the bed where Mankind will die, and with an upper gallery for the embattled Virtues. The castle is surrounded by a ditch with 'water abowte the place'; alternatively it is to be 'strongly barred al a-bowt' against the enemy—and inquisitive audiences. This splendid arena accommodates thirty-six actors and embodies the whole world of man, both macrocosm and microcosm. The audience can see invisible moral and spiritual process-

John Lydgate presenting his Troy Book *to King Henry V.*

es happen before their eyes: vices and virtues strive for man's company and for his body; at the body's death the soul is 'born', emerging as a child actor from under Mankind's bed, to be carried physically by the Bad Angel to Hell and finally snatched back for God by the troupe of motherly Daughters of God. The castle, then, directly represents the psychological and metaphysical space that man inhabits; it is not an image of something physical (as might be the case in a play about the Siege of Jerusalem); rather, it projects into three-dimensional space and time those elements in man which we could not otherwise see.

An audience's need for spectacle and for conflict is well catered for. In the siege, which occupies a third of the playing time, each of the three captains of vice leads his troops and war machines against the castle and is repelled; there are also individual combats across the moat between the female Virtues protecting Mankind and their opposite Vices outside. Analysis of the cast list reveals matched 'teams' of good and evil figures who struggle sixteen-a-side for possession first of Mankind's body, then his soul. (This principle of matching 'friend' and 'foe' is even extended to Heaven, where the 'older' two of God's daughters want to damn Mankind and two 'younger' to save him.) The siting of 'camps' by points of the compass makes visible many elemental conflicts: God (East) is confronted by both the Devil (in the 'nip of the North' as was traditional) and by World (West), so that the contrasts of salvation/damnation and immortality/mortality are ever present. Flesh rules over his trio of Gluttony, Lechery, and Sloth in the warm South. In the frosty North-East there is a scaffold specially for Covetousness, who has particular power over Mankind in old age. There is also an opposition of male vices (all but Lechery) and female saving virtues.

The play's meaning is conveyed mainly by spectacle and movement. Consequently, speech is of secondary importance, though the verse is lively and well crafted. The speeches enliven the action and interpret the moral and theological point of the visual images. Thus Sloth uses a spade to dig through the bank of the castle moat to let out the water of Grace, and he hyperbolically urges 30,000 of the audience to join in the assault. But he is soundly beaten by his busy female opponent and finds himself appropriately suffering from the symptoms of Sloth and burning from his association with Lechery, so that he must call for water:

ACCIDIA.

> Out, I deye! Ley on watyr!
> I swone, I swete, I feynt, I drulle!
> Yene qwene, with hir pityr-patyr,
> Hath al to-dayschyd my skallyd skulle!
>
> It is as softe ass wulle.
> Or I have here more skathe,
> I schal lepe awey, by lurkinge lathe;
> There I may my ballokys bathe,
> And leykyn at the fulle.

The Vices are defeated when the Virtues in the tower drop roses on them, emblems of Christ's Passion. This emblematic action is doubly allegorical, showing the triumph of Christian virtues over vice and also the historical battle of

the Passion, which is related. Patience responds to Wrath's abusive speech with an account of Christ's own patience:

PATIENTA.

> Fro thy dowte, Crist me schelde
> This iche day, and al mankinde!
> Thou wrecchyd Wrethe, wood and wilde,
> Paciens schal thee schende!
> (*Quia ira viri justitiam Dei non operatur.*)
> For Marys sone, meke and milde,
> Rend thee up, rote and rinde,
> Whanne he stod meker thanne a childe
> And lete boyes him betyn and binde.
> Therfor, wrecche, be stille!
> For tho pelourys that gan him pose,
> He myth a drevyn hem to dros;
> And yit, to casten him on the cros
> He sufferyd al here wille.

The pattern of man's individual life coincides with that of Christian history in the conclusion, when God the Father 'sitting in judgement' speaks of doomsday 'whanne Mihel his horn blowith at my dred dom' and delivers the same warning to the audience as concludes . . . *Everyman:*

> Thus endith our gamys.
> To save you fro sinninge,
> Evyr at the beginninge
> Thinke on your last endinge.

Whereas the *Castle of Perseverance* has 3,648 lines and is constructed on an epic scale, demanding four or five hours playing time and relying on spacious explanation of allegorical action, *Mankind,* in the same Macro manuscript but dating from about 1465, is altogether different: it offers slick theatrical entertainment and brilliant verbal comedy in 914 lines (about seventy minutes playing). It seems to have been designed for touring by a company of six in East Anglia between Cambridge and King's Lynn, playing in manorial halls (some local gentry are named in the dialogue) as well as at inn yards and in the canvas-covered 'game-places' found in fifteenth-century East Anglia.

In *Mankind* there is no symbolic structure to house the protagonist; nowhere he is safe from his worldly enemies, who come at him from the audience with boasts of thievery and violence. In this portable drama Mankind has only a spade with which to demonstrate man's lot since the Fall of Adam and to use eventually as a sword; the vices have a mere rope halter with which to urge him to suicide. Life and death are thus economically suggested in this contest. The teams in this Shrovetide 'game' are unevenly matched: on one side Mankind and his father confessor Mercy; on the other Mischief, foreman of a foul-mouthed, rough-and-tumbling trio, Nought, Nowadays and Newguise, and their diabolic master Tityvillus 'that goth invisibele'. The Lenten virtues of prayer, abstinence, and hard work are set against the grosser attractions of carnival riot and licentious speech.

The image of Mankind digging the earth and planting his corn connects a complex of themes ingeniously developed through dialogue in the lively manner of a popular sermon. Mankind's spiritual adviser Mercy preaches on the Last Judgement, when 'The corn shall be savyde, the chaffe shall be brente', warning the vices that 'such as they have sowyn, such shall they repe', and these texts are imprinted in the audience's minds even as they are mocked by Mischief ('Misse-masche, driff-draff, / Summe was corn and sume was chaffe', 'Corn servit bredibus, chaffe horsibus, straw firybusque') who cheekily offers himself as a 'winter corn-thresher'. Mankind's strenuous labouring at his 'earth' contrasts with the mockery of idlers who make fun out of the conventions of the play, drawing attention to the size and unpromising nature of the hall floor as a corn field.

A second Shrovetide theme is the conflict in man between soul and body ('my soull, so sotyll in thy substance', 'my flesch, that stinking dungehill'). Mankind's predicament is graphically suggested in the excremental language and threats of the vices. (Nought suggests that if Mankind wants a good crop: 'If he will have reyn, he may overpisse it; / Ande if he will have compasste, he may over-blisse it / a lityll with his ars'.) Mercy warns,

> Ther is ever a batell betwix the soull and the
>   body:
> *Vita hominis est militia super terram.*

The Old Testament text (*The life of man on earth is a battle*) connects Mankind himself with Job, sitting (as the Vulgate Bible has it) on a dung heap, patiently refusing to speak evil of God. Mankind must imitate 'the grett pacience of Job in tribulacion'; he sits upon the earth, having hung about his own neck a motto from *Job*:

> *Memento homo, quod cinis es, et in cenerem reverteris.*
> (*Remember, O man, that you are dust and to dust you will return.*)

This penitential text belongs to Ash Wednesday, the beginning of Lent and end of the carnival season which lasted from Christmas to Shrove Tuesday. (There is some evidence from the later Middle Ages that plays were prohibited during Lent.) While Mankind digs earnestly, the vices create a carnival atmosphere and teach the audience a 'Cristemas songe', taking delight in excremental parody of the *Sanctus* of the Mass. With the obscene gusto of Swift's Yahoos they discover the bodily meaning lurking within the word 'holy':

> *Cantant Omnes:* Hoylyke, holyke, holyke!
> Holyke, holyke, holyke!

By such 'idle language' and 'delight in derision' the three N's show themselves 'wers then bestys'. Indeed, at their first entrance Nought is made to dance to music by being beaten by the other two as if he was a performing bear, and the suggestion of a recent editor that the actor should inhabit a bear-skin makes good sense of the comic lines in which the bear-head is removed to address the audience. The temptations of his enemies finally turn Mankind himself into a beast; leaving aside his spade and prayers, despairing of Mercy, he is sworn into the fraternity of rioters; his jacket is removed and cut so short that it no longer covers his body and, when Mercy approaches to reclaim him, Mankind is driven like an animal to the tavern to cries of 'Hay, doog! hay, whoppe! whoo! Go yowr wey lightly', and 'lende us a football'. When Mischief threatens

to defile the audience, their disenchantment with vice should be complete. Mercy is left to mourn for Mankind's unnaturalness ('Man on-kinde') and to think of death as a comfort.

The apprehension of death which is central to many plays in the morality tradition is not of final importance in *Mankind*. This may be because the playwright concentrates on life itself as a battle in which the inevitable descent into sin should lead to contrition (Mankind is ashamed to be 'so bestially disposyde'), confession, and mercy in the course of everyday living. Another reason is that the play's comic action is developed along lines from the old folk drama. In the following sequence Mankind's spade is used in a mock-beheading/castration (Newguise sits on Nowadays' shoulders). The vices then prime the audience for the appearance of Tityvillus. They will only show him if the audience will pay:

NEWGUISE.
> Alasse, master, alasse, my privite!

MISCHIEF.
> A wher? Alake, fayer babe, ba me!
> Abide! Too sone I shall it se.

NOWADAYS.
> Here, here, se my hede, goode master!

MISCHIEF.
> Lady, helpe! Sely darlinge, *vene, vene!*
> I shall helpe thee of thy peyn:
> I shall smyte off they hede and sett it on again.

NOUGHT.
> By Owr Lady, ser, a fayer playster!
> Will ye off with his hede? It is a schrewde
>   charme!
> As for me, I have none harme—
> I were loth to forbere mine arme.
> Ye pley: *In nomine patris,* choppe!

NEWGUISE.
> Ye shall not choppe my jewellys, and I may.

NOWADAYS.
> Ye, Cristys crose! Will ye smight my hede awey?
> Ther, wher, on and on? Oute! Ye shall not
>   assay—
> I might well be callyde a foppe.

MISCHIEF.
> I kan choppe it off and make it again.

NEWGUISE.
> I had a schrewde *recumbentibus,* but I fele no
>   peyn.

NOWADAYS.
> Ande my hede is all save and holl again.
> Now, towchinge the mater of Mankinde,
> Lett us have an interleccion, sithen ye be cum
>   hethere.
> It were goode to have an ende.

MISCHIEF.
> How, how? A minstrell! Know ye ony ought?

NOUGHT.
> I kan pipe in a Walsingham whistill, I, Nought,
>   Nought.

MISCHIEF.

>Blow apase, and thou shall bring him in with a
>flowte.

TITYVILLUS.

>I com, with my leggys under me!   [*off stage*]

MISCHIEF.

>How, Newguise, Nowadays, herke or I goo:
>When owr hedys wer together, I spake of *si de-
>dero*.

NEWGUISE.

>Ye, go thy wey, we shall gather mony onto—
>Ellys ther shall no man him se.

>[*To the audience*]

>Now gostly to owr purpos, worschipfull
>soverence.
>We intende to gather mony, if it plesse yowr
>negligence,
>For a man with a hede that is of grett omnipo
>tens—

As happens in the mummers' plays, the collection develops a life of its own, with the actors commenting on their
takings. In return for gold and silver (Tityvillus 'Lovith
no groats') they will 'bring in' the devil-with-the-great-
head. The collection gives the actor who plays Mercy time
to change into this 'abhominabull presens'. The players
make sure they are paid and take the opportunity to chastise stinginess.

The theatrical sophistication of *Mankind* depends on skilful professionals harnessing the energies of popular carnival plays within a framework of moral homily: a joining
of 'sermon' and 'game'. . . . This was an effective pattern
interlude which would be acceptable to all kinds of audience, and playable by small travelling troupes during the
later fifteenth century. These companies, often the liveried
servants of nobles, thrived by offering a different sort of
theatre from the large-scale spectacular outdoor miracle-
play cycles produced by amateur communities. Increasing
private patronage and professional rivalry stimulated dramatic experiment; the possibility of printing play texts
gave playwrights new scope and prestige. From the turn
of the fifteenth century playwrights are no longer anonymous: we know of Henry Medwall, who wrote interludes
for performance in Cardinal Morton's household, where
Thomas More grew up, and of John Skelton, John Rastell
and John Heywood. The early Tudor playwrights found
fresh inspiration for their interludes in humanist debate,
French farce, and Spanish novel, but the morality tradition remained strong. Dramatists were still little interested
in 'story', preferring to conceive plays as conflicts between
vice and virtue. Man is at the centre, he chooses his company, is tempted, resists, falls, repents, and starts anew.
The same pattern of action that conveyed sacramental and
penitential wisdom was adapted for political analysis
(Skelton's *Magnificence, c.* 1520, Lyndsay's *Satire of
Three Estates, c.* 1540), for educational allegory (Red-
ford's *Wit and Science, c.* 1535), and for popular scientific
instruction (Rastell's *Four Elements, c.* 1518). Some of the
interludes were acted for élite audiences at court, in
schools and colleges, and at the private houses of humanist
scholars; but they did not lose touch with the popular the-

atrical tradition. They were didactic but they were
'merry'. The dramatic models based on the popular games
of the Middle Ages remained potent into the age of Marlowe and Shakespeare. (pp. 342-51)

>*Richard Axton, "The Morality Tradition," in*
>Medieval Literature: Chaucer and the Alliter-
>ative Tradition, Vol. I, *edited by Boris Ford,
>revised edition, Penguin Books, 1982, pp. 340-
>52.*

Stephen Coote   (essay date 1988)

[*A scholar and editor, Coote has written widely on English literature. His publications include* The Penguin
Book of Homosexual Verse *(1987), which he edited,
and* English Literature of the Middle Ages *(1988). In
the following excerpt from the last-named work, Coote
analyzes some general trends in fifteenth–century
drama, providing historical background and discussing
several plays.*]

While the great wealth of medieval lyric can be drawn on
to illustrate moments in the Church year and the existence
of the individual within it, Morality Plays such as the incomplete *Pride of Life, The Castle of Perseverance (c.*
1405-25), *Mankind, Wisdom* (both *c.* 1460-70) and *Everyman (c.* 1500) present right conduct through dramatized
allegory. This takes the form of a *psychomachia* or battle
of the vices and virtues, a mode of fundamental importance to the medieval mind.

The manuscript in which *The Castle of Perseverance* is
preserved also contains a much-disputed plan of the staging. This suggests the presence of five scaffolds grouped
around a large circle. The eastern scaffold is God's and lies
in the direction of the holy city of Jerusalem. The western
scaffold represents Mundus, or the World. In the north is
the home of the Devil, while the south is the location of
the Flesh. Finally, in the north-east—and so between the
Devil and salvation—stands the scaffold devoted to Avarice. In the centre of the circle made by these five scaffolds
stood a single tower or castle. This was open at its base and
in it stood a deathbed with a cupboard at its foot. The
tower—a conventional image of spiritual security—was
also surrounded by a ditch full of water. The audience
grouped itself around these fixed points across which the
action was then played out.

That action took the form of a journey which symbolized
a spiritual sequence of great and long-standing importance. Here we might turn to a sermon attributed to St
Bernard in which we are shown the life of man from youth
to age. In the weakness of his youth, man wanders from
the paradise of Good Conscience into sin. This state he
briefly relishes until, guided by Hope and Fear, he journeys to the Castle of Wisdom where he is prepared for his
reunion with God. At the end of the sermon, St Bernard
summarizes the four stages of this journey:

>First man is needy and foolish, then headlong
>and heedless in prosperity, then anxious and
>fearful in adversity; lastly he is foreseeing, in-
>structed and made perfect in the kingdom of
>Charity.

This sequence of innocence, temptation, fall, the life of sin, and then of realization and repentance leading to salvation, is found in many works. For example, it underlies Deguileville's *Le Pèlerinage de la Vie Humaine* (which Lydgate translated in 1426 as *The Pilgrimage of Man*) and it recurs in the construction of the first book of Spenser's *Faerie Queen* (1590). It also lies at the heart of *The Castle of Perseverance.*

At the start of the play proper, the figures of the World, the Flesh and the Devil boast of the powers with which they threaten man. Humanum Genus, Mankind himself, then appears, 'ful feynt and febyl'. His Good and Bad Angels attend him while he makes his journey towards Mundus. This suggests Mankind's spiritual journey towards sin. Backbiter then lures Mankind towards the scaffold of Avarice—a figure of central importance to the play—where he is joined by the remaining Deadly Sins, each of which describes himself with great vigour. Here is part of the speech of Invidia or Envy:

> Whanne Wrath gynnyth walke in ony wyde
> wonys,
> Envye flet as a fox and folwyth on faste.
> Whanne thou steryst[e] or staryst[e] or stumble
> up-on stonys,
> I lepe as a lyon; me is loth to be the laste.
> Ya, I breyde byttyr balys in body and in bonys,
> I frete myn herte and in kare I me kast.

wyde wonys: abroad, about *balys:* torments *steryst[e] or staryst[e]:* stir or stare about

Since the Seven Deadly Sins play so prominent a role in medieval literature, a brief account of their origins and function may be useful. Such an account will also help to illustrate how *The Castle of Perseverance* stands in the main tradition of the popular Christian doctrine it is concerned to illustrate.

The most widely accepted hierarchy of the Seven Deadly Sins was that suggested by Gregory the Great in the late sixth century, which placed pride at the root of wrath, envy, avarice, sloth, gluttony and luxury. This is the list and—substantially—the order that Chaucer adopted when he included a treatise on the Sins in *The Parson's Tale.* In *The Castle of Perseverance,* we have seen that avarice has taken the initiative from pride. This was a fairly common change in the late Middle Ages, and it may perhaps be connected with the move away from a society described according to the strict hierarchy of feudalism to one where money was attaining an importance verging on that of inherited rank. However that may be, the Seven Deadly Sins continued to provide a most influential way of describing sinful man's behaviour and so urging on him the importance of confession and penance. St Thomas Aquinas, for example, considered the Deadly Sins to be among the final causes which give rise to all mankind's other errors. As the Parson declares: 'been they cleped chieftaines for-as-muche as they been chief, and springers of alle othere sinnes'. They are thus the fundamental errors which, in the familiar pattern, pervert the will away from what the reason knows to be man's proper good and incline it instead to something which only appears to be good—worldly pride or sexual indulgence, for example.

Such things are sinful because they place earthly pleasure before obedience to God.

The concept of the Seven Deadly Sins was a popular and effective means of analysing man's conduct, and the Church required that it should be widely disseminated. The result was a profusion of imagined recreations of the Sins and a concern with them that entered deep into the popular imagination—so deep, in fact, as to give the Sins an importance perhaps greater than their position in theology truly warranted. In *The Castle of Perseverance* they hold Mankind in thrall, and we see him getting ever more self-indulgent and aggressive, ever more mean, as he shows himself 'headlong and heedless in prosperity'. Finally, his Good Angel asks for the help of Confession and Penitence. The latter strikes him with a lance and makes him descend from the scaffold of Avarice. 'A seed of sorrow is in me set,' Mankind declares. When he has been shriven he enters the castle itself, and is attended by the Seven Virtues: Humility, Patience, Charity, Abstinence, Chastity, Solicitude and Liberality, each of whom delivers a sermon on the proper way of avoiding the appropriate vice.

Mankind has passed through innocence, temptation, his fall and the life of sin, to realization and repentance. Now when he is apparently ensconced with the Seven Virtues, his castle is attacked by the forces of the World, the Flesh and the Devil. This second section of the play is essentially a spectacle. Flesh, for example, enters on horseback along with the Sins, while Humanum Genus and the Virtues prepare themselves in the castle. The Good and Bad Angels look down on the scene and, as the lively siege takes place with plenty of physical contact and the loud, comic lament of injuries, so there are no less than twenty-two actors on the stage. Mankind is still in his vigorous middle years, however, and he and the Virtues eventually win the day by showering their opposites with rose petals. But Avarice has one last trick.

Humanum Genus has at last grown old, and Avarice plays on what was conventionally seen as the money-loving vices of the aged. True to type, Mankind descends from the castle (despite the protests of the Virtues) and, when he takes money from Avarice, falls into his power.

The scene now moves to the deathbed at the foot of the castle. Death himself enters and, in a tableau of great power, strikes Mankind to the heart. Man calls on the World to help him, but Mundus only sends his sinister servant Garcio who, with savage glee, deprives Man of his goods. As Humanum Genus dies, his soul is about to be snatched to Hell by his Bad Angel. Damnation as the reward of sin seems assured. But, at the last, Man calls on God for mercy:

> Now my lyfe I have lore.
> Myn hert brekyth, I syhe sore.
> A word may I speke no more.
> I putte me in Goddys mercy.

Such a cry does not go unheard. Pity, Truth, Justice and Peace—the four daughters of God—go to their Father's scaffold and discuss the fate of Man's soul. In other words, they institute a debate on justice and mercy. God finally decides in favour of Man and the four daughters save his soul from the Devil's scaffold and bring it to God's. Salvation—the purpose of life's pilgrimage—has thus been achieved.

The Castle of Perseverance shows the whole life of man against the dramatized forces of sin and redemption. In its far smaller compass, *Everyman* presents a tableau of the preparation for death. Death himself appears to the hero and summons him before God to make a reckoning of his life and account for the use he has made of the goods that have been lent him. Accounting terminology characterizes much of the language of the play and is given emblematic form in the account-book itself which Everyman carries. Like the servants in the parable, Everyman is going to be obliged to render an account of what he has made of his 'talents'. At first, Everyman turns fearfully to the things of this world for support, but, as Felawship, Kynrede, Goddes (i.e. 'Worldly Goods' or 'Possessions'), Beauty, Strength, Discrecyioun and Five Wittes desert him, so we feel his intense isolation and the heavy burden of moral responsibility. His 'pylgrymage' to God becomes an awesome matter indeed and in the end, when he has received instruction and confessed, only his Good Dedes can help him. These are the true fruits of the talents that have been lent him. At the close, Everyman commends his soul to God in perfect faith and in the wish to die. He begs to be saved and is received into Heaven at the last:

> Come excellente electe spouse to Jesu!
>   Here above thou shalte go,
> Bycause of thy synguler vertue.
>   Now the soule is taken the body fro
> Thy rekenynge is crystall clere;
> Now shalte thou into the hevenly spere,
> Unto the whiche all ye shall come
> That lyveth well before the daye of dome.

The great cycles of Mystery Plays conform explicitly to the Christian pattern of history from the creation of the world, through Old Testament events that prefigure those in the New, and on to the Gospels and Doomsday. In an age when the study of the Bible text was deliberately restricted, the Mystery Plays were designed to make all sections of the laity re-experience emotionally what intellectually they already knew of the Christian story. Just as carvings and windows in cathedrals and greater churches told sermons in stone and stained glass, so the Mystery Plays told biblical truths in verse and action. In addition to a number of fragments, four major English dramatic cycles survive more or less intact: Chester (*c.* 1375), York (before 1378), the Towneley plays from Wakefield (mss. *c.* 1450), and the so-called 'N-Town' plays (mss. 1468) once wrongly ascribed to Coventry. Each has its origins in the ecclesiastical Feast of Corpus Christi which thus provides an essential background.

The Feast of Corpus Christi is of French origin. It was extended to the whole Church in 1264, but only became fully effective by a decree of the Council of Vienne in 1311. The Feast was designed to focus special devotion on the eucharist, on the events that led up to and followed from its institution, and on the majesty of the risen Christ. The invitatory for the matins of the Feast has a repeated refrain that brings these ideas together: 'Let us adore Christ the King, ruler over the nations; he has given richness of spirit to those who consume him.' In other words, the risen Christ offers his saving body in the communion and is King over the universe. For the Old Testament past he provided earthly rulers who imperfectly prefigured his own embodiment of kingship, shown living obediently under divine law in the New. For succeeding times—our times, in fact—his Word is the ultimate law, giving to the one universal community of mankind its various places in a hierarchy of obedience. To contravene this is to sin. Sin may be forgiven through Christ's sacrifice, while the risen Christ as both King and Judge asserts his authority over the unrepentant at Doomsday.

It is with such a vision that all the cycles close. We see the damnation of the wicked and the salvation of what St Augustine called, in a passage used as one of the Corpus Christi lessons, 'that very society of saints in which there will be peace and full and perfect unity'. While the audience watch this vision, so as individuals they are drawn into the whole progress and final end of history. They are shown their place in the community of mankind, the body of believers. This is literally the Church and typologically the body of Christ. By presenting the universal history of mankind—often with a full awareness of comedy—and by making each spectator feel more fully a part of the Church and Christ, the Mystery cycles augment the Corpus Christi devotion. We watch the creation and fall of man, the corruption of Old Testament society, the life of the Redeemer and the end of all. As we do so, we come to see the overwhelming importance of Christ's sacrifice and the 'precious, awesome and unspeakable mystery' of the communion by which we can share in the benefits derived from that sacrifice. Finally, we tremble at the wrath of God, remember our sins and are grateful for the body of Christ through which these can be absolved. As with the lyrics, the very powerful artistic effects achieved in many of the plays are not ends in themselves but a means of bringing faith alive.

While the theological background to the presentation of the Mystery Plays is clear—we will see later how individual works fit into the cycles as a whole—the manner of their staging is less certain. Most were performed by local guilds or associations of craftsmen (a 'mystery' is another term for a skilled trade) which also charged a levy of between a penny and fourpence on their members to cover costs. This was known as the 'pageant silver' and was entrusted to annually elected pageant masters. Sometimes the pageant masters were also required to assess the qualities of aspiring actors. At York, this duty was supervised by the town council.

The action of the plays took place in the open air, on and around raised stages (the *loci*) which were either stationary scaffolds or moveable wagons known as 'pageants'. A description of the pageant used by the Norwich Grocers is particularly useful here: 'a Pageant, yt is to saye, a House of Waynskott paynted and buylded on a Carte with foure whelys . . . A square topp to sett over ye sayde House.' When the action did not take place on this—as is implied, for example, by the famous stage direction: 'here

Erode ragis in the pagond and in the strete also'—then such an unlocalized area was given the Latin name *platea*.

The greatest problem about the staging of the Mystery Plays—and one that has not been conclusively solved—is whether the pageant carts were rolled past a stationary audience or (and this seems certain in at least some cases) whether they were grouped, most probably in circles, around a central *platea*, the audience moving from one group of *loci* to the next. The latter was evidently the form of staging adopted for *The Conversion of St Paul* since, just before Saul sets out on the road to Damascus, a figure called Poeta announces:

> ffynally of this stacyon thus we mak a con-
> clusyon
> besechyng thys audyens to folow and succede
> with all your delygens this generall processyon.

Riding into the *platea* of the succeeding group of *loci*, Saul is struck blind. His followers then 'lede forth Sale in-to a place' or *locus* where he receives his baptism from Anani-as. Since the play is referred to in the text as a 'pro-cessyon', it was evidently the audience and the actors who processed rather than the individual pageants. (pp. 302-08)

Christ as the Lamb of God is . . . the central image of what is perhaps the greatest of the Mystery dramas: *The Second Shepherds' Play* from the Towneley cycle. This is the work of an unnamed reviser from the first half of the fifteenth century who also worked on *Cain and Abel, Noah, The First Shepherds' Play, Herod* and the *Coliphiza-cio* or 'Scourging of Christ'. His skill with the nine-line alliterative stanza, with characterization, with varied dramatic effects, and—above all, perhaps—his truly inventive use of scriptural exegesis have earned him his name as the 'Wakefield Master'. He is one of the geniuses of English drama.

The subject of *The Second Shepherds' Play* is, of course, the adoration of the baby Jesus by the shepherds. What is particularly remarkable about the piece is the way in which the shrewdly observed realism of the work is related dramatically to the interpretation of the incarnation of Christ as both the Good Shepherd and the Lamb of God. Christ is the Saviour who, typologically, is the fulfilment of the shepherds' own craft. By virtue of this role, the shepherds—as the earliest Christian believers—become his sheep. Christ is also the sacrificial Lamb who offers redemption and so gives purpose to the shepherds' lives. Further, through the excellently constructed, farcical incident of Mak the sheep-thief, these Christian themes are placed in the context of the devil's power to steal and corrupt the goodness of the world. The biblical text which brings this sequence of imagery together comes from the tenth chapter of St John's gospel: 'The thief comes only to steal and kill and destroy; I come that they may have life, and have it abundantly. I am the good shepherd. The good shepherd lays down his life for the sheep.'

Let us see how this works. The play begins in the world of the three human shepherds: Coll, Gyb and Daw. Each has an extended, powerful soliloquy which shows the harshness of the life of the poor in the fallen world:

> Lord, what these weders ar cold! And I am yll
> happyd.
> I am nere hande dold, so long have I nappyd;
> My legys thay fold, my fyngers ar chappyd.
> It is not as I wold, for I am al lappyd
> In sorow.

Here is an existence apparently without human or divine relief, where 'thys gentley men' oppres the overtaxed agricultural labourers and 'wo is hym that grefe or onys agane says'. This is the substance of contemporary 'complaint' poetry cast in the idiom of the people. The second and third shepherds repeat its tone. The ungratefulness of human life is their subject, too. Gyb then laments the pains of marriage in terms derived from conventional medieval anti-feminism, while Daw sees life and the world passing 'ever in drede and brekyll as glas'. Though formal and conventional in content, the direct and sharp observation of these soliloquies brings them vividly to life—a suffering, hard-done-by, timeless existence. Daw, the youngest of the shepherds, now tells us he is hungry. He protests against the conditions of his employment but gains no sympathy from the others. There is not a trace of sentimentality here. Coll and Gyb are hard but not unkind men in a hard and unkind world. All three have the relief of their music, however—the part-song which they now perform. While music helps structure the play (in this case rounding off the first section), we shall see that it also has a far deeper significance.

Mak the sheep-stealer now enters in disguise, complaining not of his earthly master but about God and the insupportable burden of God's bounty revealed to him in the form of his large family. Though the shepherds immediately see through his disguise, Mak maintains his ridiculous and arrogant pose as the 'yoman' of a great king. By his disdain, he becomes the antitype of the charitable angel of the Nativity sent by the King of Kings. As the wary shepherds compare Mak with the devil, we begin to see something of the range of associations that gather about him. Mak eventually lies down in feigned sleep among the shepherds, then, drawing a circle round them and muttering an incantation, he goes to steal a sheep—a parodic image of the Lamb of God. Beneath the comic action, the diabolic suggestions already touched upon begin to build up as the audience is led to compare Mak's theft to the devil stealing grace from mankind. For the very human and hungry Mak, however, his theft is a form of worldly salvation. He and his large family will be able to eat and sustain their wicked selves through a stolen physical lamb rather than nourish their spiritual selves through the spiritual Lamb of God offered in the eucharist.

On his return home, Mak's quick-witted wife Gyll realizes the danger that the theft has put them in and suggests a stratagem which—like the other Mak episodes—is at once a farce and a parody of Christian imagery. The couple will bind the feet of the sheep, place it in a cradle, and, if the shepherds come searching for it, pretend it is another child newly born to them. By placing the stolen lamb with its bound feet in the cradle, the couple at once suggest the image of the lamb with bound feet that conventionally symbolized the Crucifixion and also the Nativity of Christ in the humble stable at Bethlehem. In each case, their wicked yet farcical actions are a hollow parody of the divine.

As we have seen, it is fundamental to Christian thought that sin can achieve nothing of itself and can only parody the spiritual. It is so here. His loot apparently secure, Mak returns to the shepherds, pretends to be asleep among them and then, when they have woken up, wanders home. His alibi, it seems, is sound. On his return, his wife—once again reinforcing the diabolic imagery—calls him 'Syr Gyle'.

Needless to say, the shepherds discover that one of their sheep is missing and hurry, distraught, to Mak's house. He at once starts singing a grotesque lullaby—it is perhaps meant to remind us of the hymns of the Nativity and is certainly the lowest musical point in the play, the one furthest away from the divine harmony of Heaven. His wife meanwhile feigns the agonies of childbirth. Even this grotesque incident can be made into a parody of the eucharist:

> A, my medyll!
> I pray to God so mylde,
> If ever I you begyld,
> That I ete this chylde
> That lygys in this credyll.

Having failed to find their sheep, the disappointed shepherds eventually leave with their apologies. Then they remember their charity. They have given nothing to the newborn child and so return to Mak's cottage. Through the exercise of charity, they discover the truth—their lamb in Mak's cradle. The alleged human baby, they find, has a 'long snoute' like a devil's child, but when Mak claims it has been enchanted into the form of a sheep, we are intended to see this as a parody of the spiritual miracle by which Christ became the Lamb of God. The good shepherds then retrieve their lost sheep from the image of the devil's lair and signify their triumph over Mak by tossing him in a blanket.

Having won a victory over this farcical image of the devil, the shepherds sleep once again. The angels now appear to them, singing *Gloria in excelsis* with a music whose complexity—so much greater than the shepherds' own and so wholeheartedly approved of by them—we should understand as the heavenly harmony itself descending to these poor men in the Yorkshire dales. They at once obey the angels' command and hasten to Bethlehem. As they present the true Lamb of God with the most touchingly simple presents, a 'bob of cherys', a bird and a ball—presents symbolic of the incarnation, Resurrection, and Christ as King over the orb of the world—so they are drawn into the true spiritual mystery, and away from the discouraged worldly suffering of their opening soliloquies. (pp. 315-18)

> *Stephen Coote, "Medieval Drama," in his* English Literature of the Middle Ages, *Penguin Books, 1988, pp. 302-20.*

PROSE

H. S. Bennett   (essay date 1947)

[*In the excerpt below, Bennett traces the development of English prose in the fifteenth century, noting a gradual shift from stylistic variety to formal coherence.*]

Fifteenth-century prose has not been well treated by literary historians. Indeed, much of it has scarcely received more than a bare mention in accounts which have lavished space upon Pecock, Fortescue, Malory, and Caxton. Pecock and Malory, in particular, have interested critics, yet neither of them had much influence on English prose. While attention has been thus diverted, the main movement of prose writing has been missed. If we wish to know what was done for prose in this century we shall find it best to give only limited attention to the four authors we have mentioned and to concentrate far more than has been the fashion on the many writers—known and unknown—who took over from the fourteenth century an inheritance which they fostered and developed with zeal and success.

The preliminary requisite for any successful development of an English prose style had been secured when English gained the upper hand over French or Latin as the normal vehicle for written communications between Englishmen. It was a difficult matter for those educated to write in French to accustom themselves to the use of English, and sometimes we find a letter in which both languages struggle for supremacy. (p. 177)

Once this linguistic struggle was over, the way was clear for the next development. Put in the broadest terms there were two schools of prose usage open to writers from Chaucer's time onwards. When a clerk found himself asked to write in English, the most obvious thing for him to do was to make use, as best he could, of the constructions, phrasing, and rhetorical figures to which he was accustomed in Latin. Similarly, the scholar was likely to write English in a way that approximated as closely as possible to the Latin which was his daily reading. There was, however, another way. Even as early as the latter part of the fourteenth century men had realized that there was something alien to the English of everyday speech in the form which prose was taking. In 1387 Usk says that he will ignore the 'queynt knitting coloures' (i.e. curious fine phrases, that 'knit' or join words together) and use 'rude wordes and boystrous, to maken the cacchers ther ben the more redy to hente sentence'. About the same time Wyclif was declaiming against the 'pomposam eloquenciam' of many preachers, advocating a plain, direct method of speaking, and an avoidance of the use of rhythmical ornament and other rhetorical devices. *Nude et apte* was his formula for good prose. Lastly, John of Trevisa had discussed a similar problem with his lord when, about 1387, he asked Sir Thomas of Berkeley whether he should write in verse or in prose. He was told: 'In prose, for comynlich prose is more clere than ryme, more esy, and more playn to knowe and understonde.' English prose during the fifteenth century had to decide between these issues.

It must be remembered that prose had an ever-widening field before it. All available knowledge was rapidly becoming its province; for much that hitherto had been written in Latin began to take on English dress, while new opportunities for the use of the vernacular were arising. To some extent these varying matters required varying styles. 'Heigh stile, as when Kings endite' was evidently in the minds of the city of London, when, encouraged by the king's example, it began to write letters such as:

> Right high, right myghty, and right honurable Prince, we recomaunde vs un-to your Lordly excellens in the most humble and seruisable maner that we can best ymagine and deuise, Thankyng lowly your noble grace of the gracious lettres in makyng gladsom in vndyrstandyng and passyng confortable in fauoring of our pouer degrees Whyche you liked late to send vs from Craille vpon case in Normandie . . . whyche hath made vs notable report and right comfortable exposicion of thestate and tidinges of that lond, blessed be god.

This is only an English version of the stock pattern to be found in the medieval books of *dictamen*. Its 'humble and serviceable', 'imagine and devise', 'notable report and right comfortable exposition', &c., follow a pattern, and are an attempt 'to embellish, ornate and make fair our English'—an attempt which had its dangers. It led to a prose analogous to that elaborate type of poetry practised by Lydgate and his followers, who developed an aureate use of language and an ability to 'cloke in subtle terms, with colour tenebrous' what little they had to say, to the detriment of both prose and verse.

The cultivation of the *florida verborum venustas,* as Professor E. F. Jacob has shown, flourished in the fifteenth century, and writers in Latin, such as John Whethamstede, favour the 'recondite and precious, or an impressive rotundity. The influence of Cicero is yet to come, and the medieval as opposed to the renaissance attitude still holds sway.' This may be seen both in poets and prose writers. Lydgate, Hawes, Dunbar, and Barclay follow the medieval tradition: Wyatt and Surrey, the humanist. Not until late in the fifteenth century does a new sense of the use of language begin to show itself. 'Enlarged and adorned' prose, therefore, had a powerful ally in some of its Latin models, and much official and clerical prose was composed in this fashion. . . . (pp. 178-79)

Latin was also, in varying degrees, at the back of much religious and homiletic prose. It may be allowed that this did not imply mere slavish imitation: the great fourteenth-century writers—Rolle, Hilton, and even Wyclif—had shown otherwise. Often when the writer had the advantage of a Latin version (or a French translation of the Latin) before him, his work achieved a tautness and coherence that was frequently lacking in contemporary original prose. An outstanding writer, such as Nicholas Love, used his Latin originals so skilfully that he produced a translation of the *Meditationes Vitae Christi* which gives us some of the most beautiful prose of the century—a prose ordered and controlled by a clear grasp of its underlying sequences of thought and argument and by the use of many of the devices of the rhetoricians.

It is prose of this kind (though not often of this quality)

which gave grounds for R. W. Chambers's claim that the continuity of English prose is to be found in the sermon and in every kind of devotional treatise. While there is much truth in this, prose was also continuing to develop along simpler and more conversational lines. Men who owed little or nothing to French or Latin were constantly attempting to put down their thoughts in a clear and unornamented fashion. They have little to offer the seeker of 'fine prose'; their only endeavour was to state their ideas in a straightforward fashion, almost as simply as if they were talking. English was used in a thousand petty ways which helped to give men a better control of the medium. In civic affairs the London guilds make it serve their purpose: letters from the corporation, ordinances and proclamations, proceedings in the mayor's court are written in English. Men make wills, write letters, attempt little treatises on hawking or fishing, set down medical or herbal recipes, or note what seasons or days are fortunate—all in English.

Prose had almost everything to learn and there were no great writers whose influence was all-pervasive, so that prose in this century developed by much trial and error and owed much to 'unprofessional' as well as to professional writers.

To take the prose written by ordinary men first. Here we are fortunate, for the fifteenth century is the century of the Pastons, the Celys, and the Stonors—to name only the three greatest known families of letter-writers of this period. Here, as perhaps nowhere else, can we see what powers of handling the language were possessed by all that variety of men and women who used the pen mainly or solely to state their own business or pleasures. Naturally no thought of publication was ever in the writers' minds—indeed they frequently exhort their correspondents to burn their letters when read—and their writings reveal the ability of many to write straightforward unaffected prose. Every kind of topic is dealt with: descriptions of riots, forays, and executions; requests for money, books, cooking materials, or wives; accounts of legal proceedings and unsuccessful bribery; of attempts to hold courts, execute distraints, engage servants; descriptions of possible brides, of weddings, of feasts, of illnesses—in short, everything that formed part of the fabric of medieval life. A correspondent, describing the execution of the Duke of Suffolk in a small boat at sea, apologizes for blurs in his letter because 'I am right sorry of that I shalle say, and have soo wesshe this litel bille with sorwfulle terys that on ethes ye shalle reede it'. This personal, direct note marks the whole series of letters. To illustrate the straight-forward homely clarity of this way of writing we may turn to a vivid account given by an eyewitness of a manor court held by the Duke of Suffolk, at Hellesdon, in 1478.

He tells us that the duke was full of spleen against Sir John Paston, and at

> hys beyng ther that daye ther was never no man that playd Herrod in Corpus Crysty play better and more agreable to hys pageaunt then he dud. But ye schall understond that it was after none, and the weder hot, and he so feble for sekenes that hys legges wold not bere hyme, but ther was ij men had gret payn to kepe hym on hys fete;

and ther ye were juged. Som sayd, 'Sley'; some sayd, 'Put hym in preson.' And forth com my lord, and he wold met you with a spere, and have none other mendes for the troble at ye have put hym to but your hart blod, and that will be gayt with hys owen handes.

One more example may be taken from a letter written from Calais in 1476 by Thomas Betson to Katherine Ryche, the eldest daughter of Elizabeth Stonor by her first husband, when Katherine was little more than a child. Betson writes a long amusing letter to her, his bride to be, bidding her to overcome her dislike of meat, and 'evene as you loffe me to be mery and to eate your mete lyke a woman'; he tells her to 'grete well my horsse', and goes on:

> I praye you, gentill Cossen, comaunde me to the Cloke, and pray hym to amend his unthryffte manners: ffor he strykes ever in undew tyme, and he will be ever affore, and that is a shrewde condiscion. Tell hym with owte he amend his condiscion that he will cause strangers to ad-voide and come no more there. I trust to you that he shall amend agaynest myn commynge, the which shalbe shortely with all hanndes and all ffeete with Godes grace. . . . And Almyghty Jhesu make you a good woman, and send you many good yeres and longe to lyveffe in helth and vertu to his plesour. At great Cales on this syde on the see, the ffyrst day off June, whanne every man was gone to his Dener, and the Cloke smote noynne, and all oure howsold cryed after me and badde me come down; come down to dener at ones! and what answer I gaveffe hem ye know it off old.

Letters like these are proof enough that before the end of the century a tradition of what constituted good prose had been created. The prose of Sir Thomas More descends from the wit and grace of this kind of writing as well as from the tradition of devout prose. These letter-writers are drawn from various stations of life, and the ease of a Thomas Betson in writing playfully to his little friend is matched by the dramatic description of the Duke of Suffolk's behaviour or by other passages which might be taken from fifteenth-century letters. Here we are dealing with writings put together with no thought of their literary quality: we could not have a better opportunity of assessing the ordinary person's ability to use his pen or of the plain style which he affected. Some of his fellows, however, while they would not have claimed more than an amateur status, undoubtedly wrote for a wider circle of readers, and we might well expect their work to show a greater control over their medium.

This is exactly what we find in the writings of William Thorpe, the Lollard, and of Margery Kempe, the mystic. Thorpe's writing is in the main an account, written down many years after the event (and slightly modernized by Tyndale), of his examination for heresy before the Archbishop of Canterbury in 1407. It gives a clear and vivid account of the interview, and sets out in dialogue form the thrust and parry of the disputants. Thorpe's command of prose is shown in the careful expositions of his theological position and belief. Here the utmost nicety of expression was essential if he was to save his life, and Thorpe's En-

glish comes out of the ordeal most successfully. For example:

> And the Archbishoppe asked me, 'What was holye church'. And I said, 'Syr I told you before what was holye churche: but since ye aske me this demaunde: I call Christe and his sayntes holye church'. And the Archbishop saide vnto me, 'I wotte wel that Christ and his saintes are holy church in heauen, but what is holy church in earth'. And I said, 'Sir, though holy church be euery one in charity, yet it hath two partes. The first and principall part hathe ouercomen perfectly all the wretchednesse of this life, and raigneth joyfully in heauen with Christe. And the other part is here yet in earth, besily and continually fighting day and night against temptacions of the fiend, forsaking and hatyng the prosperity of this world, despising and wythstanding their fleshly lustes, which only are the pilgrimes of Christ, wandering toward heauen by stedfast faithe, and grounded hope, and by perfect charity.'

(pp. 180-83)

Margery Kempe of Lynn was illiterate herself, as far as we can tell, but there can be little doubt that her autobiography was taken down at her dictation and conveys her own way of expressing herself. In common with those of her time and class, she used a homely, vivid style and made use of phrases such as 'that wicked worm, Wiclif', or proverbs such as 'many men spekyn of Robyn Hood, and shoote neuere his bowe', or in speaking of an opponent she tells him that 'thou wost no more what thou blaberest than Balamis asse'—all phrases and proverbs, as we have already seen, used by her contemporaries. The following passage illustrates how close to actual speech her language could be, and how clearly her narrative reveals its teller:

> Than went þis creatur forth to London wyth hir husbond vn-to Lambhyth, þer þe Erchebisshop lay at þat tyme. And, as þei comyn in-to þe halle at aftyr-noon, ther wer many of þe Erche-bysshoppys clerkys & other rekles men boþe swyers & yemen whech sworyn many gret oþis & spokyn many rekles wordys, & þis creatur boldly vndryname hem & seyd þei schuld ben dampnyd but þei left her sweryng & oþer synnes þat þei vsyd. & wyth þat cam forth a woman of þe same town in a pylche & al for-schod þis creatur, bannyd hir, & seyd ful cursydly to hir in þis maner, 'I wold þu wer in Smythfeld, & I wold beryn a fagot to bren þe wyth; it is pety þat þow leuyst.' Þis creatur stod stylle & answeryd not, & hir husbond suffred wyth gret peyn & was ful sory to heryn hys wyfe so rebukyd. Than þe Erchbusshop sent for þis creatur in-to hys gardeyn. Whan sche cam to hys presens, sche salutyd hym as sche cowd, prayng hym of hys gracyows lordshyp to grawnt hir auctoryte of chesyng hyr confessowr & to be howselyd euery Sonday, yyf God wold dysposen hir þerto, vndyr hys lettyr and hys seel thorw al hys prouynce. & he grawnt it her ful benyngly all hir desyr wyth-owtyn any syluer er gold, ne he wold latyn hys clerkys takyn any-thyng for wrytyn ne for see-lyng of þe lettyr. . . .

There were not many Thorpes or Kempes writing in the fifteenth century, it is true, but wills, civic records, books of the chase, of gardening, and the like, all show that English prose could express the everyday commonplaces, desires, and requirements of most people. Such prose reached out to no great heights, but was content with stating its matter in simple, but often vigorous and dramatic language. It knew little of cadence or of striking phrases, yet at times it achieved something of both by its unaffected use of homely speech rhythms which were native to fifteenth-century people of ordinary education and breeding.

But prose had to give expression to something more than these straightforward practical matters. It had to convey the religious, didactic, philosophical, and scientific ideas of the age. This was a heavy burden for a prose which was still far from fully developed, but a laudable attempt was made to meet these various demands. Religious and homiletic themes found expression in such works as Nicholas Love's *Mirror,* or Capgrave's *Life of S. Gilbert,* or in collections of pious tales and *exempla,* such as the *Gesta Romanorum,* or the *Golden Legend,* or the *Book of the Knight of La Tour Landry,* or *Jacob's Well.* Learned argument and exposition are to be found in the works of philosophical interest of Pecock: past and contemporary English history in the *Brut* and in Capgrave's *Chronicle,* while Fortescue's treatise on the *Governance of England* sets out a philosophy of political ideas. Scientific treatises, such as translations of Lanfranc's *Science of Cirurgie,* or John of Bordeaux's plague pamphlet, put new problems before the prose writer. Add to these, tractates on the *Craft of Numbering,* the keeping of horses, hawking, hunting, and fishing; on travel and pilgrimages; or huge tomes such as Trevisa's translation of Bartholomew's *De Proprietatibus Rerum,* and something of the volume of prose that the century produced will be evident.

These works bring us into contact with the 'professional' writers, who hoped that their work would have as widespread a circulation as medieval conditions made possible. A strong didactic purpose informs many of these, of which the *Gesta Romanorum* may serve as an excellent example. It was one of the most famous compilations of the Middle Ages. Originally compiled in Latin, probably in England late in the thirteenth century, this collection of tales was greatly in demand among preachers and moralists, and in the fifteenth century was given an English form. . . . The wide range of stories which it contains are all told in simple, straightforward language, and include all those elements dear to the medieval mind. Here are to be found 'nigromancers' and other workers of magic; dragons and loathly worms; beautiful princesses and gallant youths; tyrants and fiends. Deeds of daring are the results of wagers; prisons, pits, and fetters fail to hold men, despite magic rings and pursuit by unicorns. Yet much homely detail keeps these stories within bounds: men go by ways that are 'stony, thorny and scraggy', or watch the catchpoles dragging men at the tail of a string of horses; the watchmen disturb the silence of the night by their horns and the nightingales 'synge wondir swetly'. The ease and simplicity with which the several stories are told may be seen from the following extract:

Polemius was an Emperoure in the cetee of Rome, þe whiche hadde iij sonnes, that he moche lovid. So as þis Emperoure laye in a certeyne nyght in his bedde, he thowte to dispose his Empir, & he thought to yeve his kyngdome to the slowest of his sones. He called to him his sonnes, & saide, 'he that is the sloweste of yow, or most slewth is in, shall have my kyngdom after my discese'. 'þenne shall I have hit', quod the Eldest sone, 'for I am so slowe, & swiche slewthe is in me, that me hadde lever late my fote brynne in the fyr, whenne I sitte þer by, than to withdrawe, & save hit'. 'Nay', quod the secounde, 'yet am I mor worthi thanne þow; for yf case that my necke wer in a rope to be hongid; & yf þat I hadde my two hondes at wille, and in on honde þende of þe rope, and in that oþer honde a sharpe swerde, I hadde levir dye and be hongid, þan I wolde styr myn arme, and kitte þe rope, whereby I myte be savid'. 'Hit is I', quod the thirde, 'that shalle regne after my syre, for I passe hem bothe in slewthe. Yf I lygge in my bedde wyde opyn, & þe reyne reyne vppon boþe myn yen, yee, me hadde leuer lete hit reyne hem oute of the hede, than I turnid me oþere to the right syde, or to the lyfte syde'. Þenne the Emperoure biquathe his Empir to the thirde sone, as for the slowist.

Even more popular than the *Gesta Romanorum* was the *Legenda Aurea.* This work, by Jacobus de Voragine, was translated into English about 1438 in a version of 179 items of the original cycle. These simply-told stories of the lives of the saints were immensely popular. They instructed and entertained at the same time, and were compounded of a mixture of the credible and incredible so dear to the medieval mind. Another good example of the way in which English was being used for homiletic purposes may be seen in Mirk's *Festial.* This was a collection of sermons with *exempla* attached, written for the aid of such priests as those who 'excuson hem by defaute of bokus and sympulnys of letture'. It contained sermons for various feast days throughout the year, and each of these made considerable use of *exempla* to drive home their points by means of homely, lively incident, or relation of some exciting story, or account of the supernatural. All this matter was conveyed in such a way that a simple priest, and a still simpler congregation, could understand it without difficulty, by the use of language such as the following:

Then þe fende operyd yn syght of all þe pepull lyke a man of Inde, blak altogedyr as pich, wyth a sharpe nase and a lodely face, wyth a berde down to his fete, blake as soote, wyth een brennyng as doth yern yn þe fyre sparklyng on yche syde, and blowyng flamys of brennyng fure, wyth hys hondys bownden byhynde hym wyth chaynys brennyng.

Here is a prose admirably suited to its audience. The writer appeals to the sense of colour and of drama inherent in simple folk, and in his clear language pictures in their imaginations the Devil, as they had often seen him in the religious plays, black and beast-like as possible, and as the stage direction says, 'with gunpowder burning in pipes in his hands, and in his ears'. His comparisons have the air of being proverbial ('as black as pitch' or 'black as soot') and refer to homely, everyday things. A rather more secular note is struck in the *Alphabet of Tales* and in the *Book of the Knight of La Tour Landry,* both translated from the French. The *Alphabet* is a handy work of reference, for the preacher had but to turn to Abstinence, Accidia, Adulation, &c., for *exempla* upon these themes. The knight's book was written—with the aid of two priests and two clerks—for the edification of his daughters, and was translated into English first about 1450 by an author who for the most part kept closely to the original. The subject-matter conveyed instruction under the guise of a series of stories. . . . As a source book of medieval life and thought this book takes a high place: wherever we open it we find stories—and conclusions drawn from them—which throw a flood of light on contemporary conditions. A few lines from the prologue show the translator at his best, for he is here translating into prose the verse prologue of the original.

> As y was in a gardin, al heui and full of thought,
> in the shadow, about the ende of the monthe of
> April, but a littell y rejoysed me of the melodie
> and song of the wilde briddes; thei sang there in
> her langages, as the thrustill, the thrusshe, the
> nytinggale, and other briddes, the which were
> full of mirthe and ioye; and thaire suete songe
> made my herte to lighten, and made me to
> thinke of the tyme that is passed of my youthe,
> how loue in gret distresse had holde me, and
> how y was in her seruice mani tymes full of
> sorugh and gladnesse, as mani lovers ben.

Prose was to be put to more severe trials, however, than were placed on it by the moralists and tellers of didactic stories. The growing ability to read in the vernacular was considerable enough by the second quarter of the century to compel attention from those who hitherto had confined their views and arguments to readers able to read and think in Latin. Now it was becoming necessary for scholars to step down into the arena where ordinary laymen, in such intervals of leisure as came to them, were demanding information and instruction in matters formerly only interpreted to them orally by priests and clerks. Hence, despite the fact that 'langagis ben not stabli and foundamentali writen', vernacular exposition of the Faith was growing, and a prose had to be formed which would convey the niceties of argument, illustration, and philosophical reasoning. This was attempted on a large scale by Reginald Pecock, Bishop of St. Asaph and later of Chichester.

This scholarly and pugnacious man set himself to meet by argument the teaching of the Lollards and other 'Bible men'. Instead of invoking the powers of the statute *De Heretico Comburendo,* Pecock invoked those of reason—and of reason in the vernacular. He had a fanatical belief in 'the doom of reason' and in the use of the syllogistic method, for as he says:

> so stronge and so mygti in al kindis of maters,
> that though al the aungels of hevene wolden seie
> his conclusions were not trewe, yitt we schulde
> leeve the aungels seiyng, and we schulden truste
> more to the proof of thilk sillogisme than to the
> contrarie seiyng of alle the aungels in hevene, for
> that alle Goddis creaturis musten nedis obei the

doom of resoun, and such a sillogisme is not ellis than doom of resoun.

In keeping with this view, Pecock proceeded to confute his opponents by argument, and to instruct them and all the faithful by a series of philosophical disquisitions on many matters of faith and doctrine. He writes in English, he tells us, to instruct and to inculcate the love of God, and uses 'the common peplis langage' for this purpose, just as the preachers use it for their sermons. But while Pecock could talk of writing in the ordinary man's language, he rapidly found that such a language had none of the resources of vocabulary or expression which would convey abstract philosophical ideas. Pecock, therefore, was forced to invent words. This he did with great energy, yoking together English and foreign elements, and often producing strange and uncouth results. Part of our difficulty in reading Pecock to-day arises from this. His pages are disfigured with such words as 'agenvnstondabilnes' (unchangeableness), 'knowyngal' (pertaining to knowledge), 'vntobethoughtvpon' (unconsidered), 'neperte' (inferiority), or 'outdroughte' (extract). Technical words new to English (tropology, anagogy) are used; suffixes in *-al* or *-ioun* are tagged on to existing words; foreign words are anglicized or translated into their nearest equivalent, and so on. Pecock was determined to make the truth as he understood it known and if possible clear to all men, and if the language was not there to help him, he was prepared to help the language. It is this deep-felt anxiety to make himself clear which renders much of Pecock's writings nearly unreadable to-day. We are spared nothing. The schoolman's delight in distinctions almost for the sake of distinctions, the logical reduction of every aspect of the point at issue to its ultimate terms, the scrupulous effort to leave no loophole or ambiguity—all these habits of mind are seen in the laboured, overelaborated prose of Pecock. His habit of inversion, of the use of synonym, of finishing his sentence with a verb, does not make it easier to know exactly where we are in any of his arguments, and although there is almost invariably a clear logical thread running throughout all that he writes, it is not always apparent on a first reading. (pp. 184-91)

[His style makes] it impossible to keep Pecock where it has been fashionable to place him since Babington's edition of the *Repressor* in 1860. He is not one of the glories of fifteenth-century prose, nor can we accept the implication that he is of great importance in the development of English prose style. Pecock remains a lonely phenomenon.

His insistence on the 'doom of reason' was the outstanding feature of his teaching. 'Reason' he declared to be 'more necessarie to Cristen men, and . . . more worthi than is the outward Bible and the kunnyng therof.' By reason man can guide his conduct and build his institutions, religious and temporal. Virtue, he argued, is dependent on the free will, and grace is given to assist the religious man. Virtuous deeds are necessary to fulfil man's potentialities and thus to fulfil God's purpose, and eventually to bring man to heaven. These virtuous deeds are necessarily based on reason: there is no virtue in unreasoning ignorance. Pecock's Four Tables, which are explained at length in the *Donet,* the *Follower to the Donet,* and the *Rule of Christian Religion,* all rest on reason and faith, with reason predominating. These Four Tables set out the 'menal virtues' which are the means leading to the 'eendal virtues', and Pecock constantly refers to them as the outline of his philosophical system.

For reason to have its fullest scope it was necessary that man's knowledge should be as accurate and all-embracing as possible. Hence Pecock was a strong advocate for the active testing of doctrine and historical writings by the light of reason. The authority of Aristotle or of the Fathers should be questioned if the matter was one that allowed of reason, for he declared that 'Aristotil made not philosofie' but was 'a laborer to knowe the trouthis of philosofie as othire men weren'. In holding such ideas he was clearly ahead of his time, and that immense confidence which marks all his writings at last carried him too far, and gave opportunities to his ecclesiastical enemies which led to his ruin. Although he says in *Folewer* that 'y neuer bowid yit in wil neither in word, ond with goddis grace neither y schall in tyme comyng' in the maintenance of truth, yet the day was to come when he was forced to say: 'I am in a strait betwixt two, and hesitate in despair as to what I shall choose. If I defend my opinions and position, I must be burned to death; if I do not, I shall be a byeword and a reproach.' In the end he retracted, handed the executioner some fourteen of his works for public burning, and spent the rest of his days in close confinement in the remote Fenland Abbey of Thorney. He was allowed 'no books to look on, but only a portuous, a mass-book, a psalter, a legend and a Bible: nothing to write with; no stuff to write upon'. The 'pestiferous virus' of his writings, of which Edward IV complained, had but little chance to spread after this, and the fifteenth century rapidly forgot him. It was not until the present century that any determined attempt was made to print his extant writings.

The death of Pecock, about 1461, came at a time when another thinker was beginning to put into writing the ideas which a lifetime of busy, anxious experience had engendered in him. Lawyer, negotiator, politician, administrator, Fortescue learnt political and constitutional wisdom by experience. His legal *dicta,* however, are not remarkable, for it was not when he was presiding in his court that he showed at his greatest or most original. His present reputation rests on his exposition of political theory; first in his Latin works, *De Natura Legis Naturae* and *De Laudibus Legum Angliae,* and his English work *On the Governance of England.* The first two of these works do not concern us deeply, but they set out in some detail Fortescue's ideas on the nature of the monarchy and on the conduct of princes. Many of these ideas are given an English form in the *Governance of England,* where for the last time Fortescue explains his political theory. There are two kinds of kingdom; the first the *dominium regale*—absolute monarchy—he rejects in favour of the *dominium politicum et regale*—a monarchy both politic and royal, for he argues that the absolute monarch possesses nothing which is denied to the politic king save the power to do wrong. He is concerned to show how a political monarch can best serve the State, and after a long discussion of the economic resources of the realm, the relation between the commons and their rulers, and the dangers of over-mighty subjects, he proceeds to discuss the appointment and composition

of a body which will help the king to exercise his functions, always bearing in mind that the King of England has no power to alter the law, for a politic king can only change the law by the consent of his people expressed in Parliament. The Council, as Fortescue conceived it, was to be partly administrative, partly advisory—an executive which would put forward proposals for the consideration of Parliament. Such a scheme, Fortescue believed, would preserve parliamentary rights, while helping the day-to-day conduct of affairs, and would relieve the king of much dangerous responsibility. Fortescue's theory is based on experience: he is cautious, limited in his suggestions; and it must be admitted vague on important points such as the method by which the Council should be chosen, or the way in which the various estates should be represented in Parliament.

His treatment of his subject shows the man. He is strongly influenced by his studies: biblical references abound, while quotations from classical and ecclesiastical authors (whether of his own finding or from a convenient 'commonplace book') are frequent. There is much of the medieval scholar about his method. Yet he is capable of leaving his book learning and making use of what he has seen with his own eyes and learnt from his long sojourn in foreign countries, especially in France. Thus, in a famous passage, he contrasts the French commons with the English, and refers scornfully to the cavern nature of the French, 'wherfore it is right selde that Ffrenchmen be hanged ffor robbery, ffor thai haue no hartes to do so terable an acte. Ther bith therfore mo men hanged in Englande in a yere ffor robbery and manslaughter, then ther be hanged in Ffraunce ffor such manner of crime in vij yeres'. He states his views in an admirably clear terse English. Where in Pecock we are struggling with the pattern of a long, complicated sentence of many words, Fortescue expresses his ideas with point and clarity. So he opens his work: 'Ther bith ij kyndes off kyngdomes, of the wich that on is a lordship callid in laten *dominium regale,* and that other is called *dominium politicum et regale.* And thai diversen in that . . . ' His illustrations, as shown above, are clear and concrete, and of a homely nature. . . . Fortescue writes clearly because his mind works within narrowly defined limits. He will speculate only so far as his experience as a lawyer and an administrator will serve to guide him, and will furnish him with materials. So he conducts us from one part of his argument to another by a series of closely related facts or ideas. Illustrations of these are allowed, but not abused, and each sentence is taut and forms an integral unit in the structure which he is building. In common with other fifteenth-century writers, Fortescue is not capable of writing a highly complex prose, but what straightforwardness, simplicity, and clear thinking could accomplish may be seen on almost any page of the *Governance of England.*

Apart from the narrative and exposition, prose had much to accomplish in other fields. Scientific writings in the vernacular were wellnigh unknown before 1400, but throughout the fifteenth century they steadily increased in number and variety. Treatises dealing with special diseases abound. We have works on stone or gout, or on the diseases of women, as well as John of Bordeaux's *Tractatus de morbo epidemiae*—the most popular of plague pamphlets, of which over forty manuscripts have survived. Even more popular was the little manual sometimes entitled the *Judgment of Urines.* Nearly seventy manuscripts (mostly of the fifteenth century) still exist of this popular work. Writings of this kind are couched in simple direct English, generally for the use of laymen, as is clear from the heading of one of these tracts in the Cambridge University Library: 'Tractatus . . . composuit breviter in lingua materna magis plane ad intelligentiam laicorum.' Surgical works, both large and small, also appeared. John of Arderne was the most famous English surgeon of his day, and translations of various of his works appeared after 1400. Vernacular renderings of other surgical works, like that of the great French surgeon, Guy de Chauliac, or those of William of Saliceto, or John of St. Paul, may also be noted. There are individual tracts on special topics, and it is clear that works in the vernacular on medicine and surgery of every description were in circulation in some numbers during the fifteenth century.

Allied to these were writings on plants, herbs, and herbal remedies. Such works begin to appear in a vernacular form in the fourteenth century, but their number is trebled or quadrupled in the next century. . . . Not only medical but natural science flourished in this period. The most valuable indication of the knowledge of natural science at this time is afforded by the great encyclopaedia of Bartholomeus Anglicus. Trevisa's translation of his *De Proprietatibus Rerum* was completed on 6 February 1398, and for long remained a standard work. It circulated in its full form and in an abstract before an abridged edition was printed by Wynkyn de Worde in 1495 and by Berthelet in 1535. It was reissued with some additions by Stephen Batman, under the title of *Batman upon Bartholomew,* in 1582. Perhaps it was optimistic on Thomas East's part to think that his contemporaries would be satisfied with information first compiled over 300 years earlier, but there can be no doubt that it was still considered a trustworthy source in the fifteenth century. . . . The pursuit of knowledge was a difficult matter in medieval times, and fifteenth-century inquirers were ready enough to read in Trevisa's version of how elephants could be captured by the singing of maidens in the Ethiopian desert, or of how cinnamon was shot from the phoenix's nest with leaden arrows. They learnt that the 'men of Ireland be singularly clothed and unseemly arrayed and scarcely fed; they be cruel of heart, fierce of cheer, angry of speech, and sharp'; that 'the bear bringeth forth a piece of flesh imperfect and evil shapen, and the mother licketh the lump, and shapeth the members with licking', and that 'by the spleen we are moved to laugh, by the gall we are wroth, by the heart we are wise, by the brain we feel, by the liver we love'.

Many of the topics in Bartholomew were taken up and developed by later writers. There are numerous tracts dealing with the nature and influence of the planets and with the signs of the zodiac and their effects on human bodies. There are also treatises on the significance of the months and days in the lives and fortunes of men, while the science of alchemy was popularized by tractates in English which were constantly being written and circulated. Many other little treatises dealt with more practical matters and made

further demands on prose writers. A number of manuals of arithmetic appeared, while others dealt with the keeping of horses, hawks, fish, or doves. Hunting was one of the commonest of aristocratic recreations, and the second Duke of York's translation of Gaston de Foix's *Livre de Chasse* under the title of the *Master of Game* was very popular. Smaller treatises on hunting also appeared, and in particular works on hawking, in which information on the care and training of hawks is set out in a clear and workmanlike fashion. The subject was still of sufficient importance in 1486 to warrant the publication of the *Book of St. Albans,* reputed to be the work of Dame Juliana Berners, but much of it is taken from Twici's *L'art de venerie* (*c.* 1320) and from other treatises which have not been traced. The edition of 1496, by Wynkyn de Worde, was memorable for its inclusion of 'a treatise of fishing with an angle'. In this, we learn that if the fisherman fail of one fish,

> he maye not faylle of a nother yf he dooth as this treatyse techyth: but yf there be nought in the water. And yet atte the leest he hath his holsom walke and mery at his ease, a swete ayre of the swete sauoure of the meede floures: that makyth hym hungry. He hereth the melodyous armony of fowles. He seeth the yonge swannes: heerons: duckes: cotes and many other foules wyth theyr brodes. Whyche me semyth better than alle the noyse of houndys: the blastes of hornys and the scrye of foulis that hunters: fawkeners & foulers can make.

The writer of this passage knows what he wants to say, and says it with some felicity of phrasing and a delight in outdoor sights and scenes rarely met with in medieval literature. The author of the *Anatomy of Melancholy* swept this passage with his dragnet to the confusion of those who quote it as an example of Burton's own style. Although Burton probably took the passage from an Elizabethan intermediary, his version differs hardly at all from the original.

For those who wished to be more venturesome than these sportsmen, and to embark upon real or imaginary journeys, instructive manuals were prepared. The outstanding work, of course, was the well-known *Travels of Sir John Mandeville,* the author of which need have been no traveller himself as his information has been traced to earlier sources. This purports to be a guide-book for travellers to Jerusalem, but is also an account of the wonders of the East in the realms of the Great Cham. It was in great demand and translated into many languages. At least four versions of the original (which scholars are now generally agreed was in French and written about 1356) were in circulation during the fifteenth century, and over thirty manuscripts in English have survived. It is written in a simple style, and the paragraph is built up of a series of loosely related sentences:

> And all be it þat men fynden gode dyamandes in Ynde, yit natheles men fynden hem mor comounthe myne of gold is. And þei growen many togedre, on lytill, another gret. And þer ben . . . And þei . . .

(pp. 192-99)

That the writer gave the public something they wanted is

clear from the several versions in English and the large number of existing manuscripts. The subject-matter, besides being intrinsically interesting, is treated in a way that cannot fail to hold the reader's attention. The author combines truth and fiction, and gives so many vouchers of time and place and numbers—or even more engagingly writes: 'Of Paradys can I nought speke properly, for I hafe noght bene thare'—that we are forced to believe what he says, and his simple way of writing only serves to reinforce the air of perfect honesty and good faith which it is his desire to create.

Other works of travel of a less ambitious and more practical nature were produced. There is an anonymous 'hand book' for travellers across Europe by the Lowlands to Venice and so to the eastern Mediterranean and home through the Straits of Gibraltar. This gives much advice on practical matters: guides and their habits, the choice of travelling impedimenta, hints as to weather and 'the usaunce of the hote lands', and how to conduct oneself, for our author tells us that 'englissh men have but little love in meny parties, but yet hit be for their money, or the better of gouernaunce'. Other accounts of the pilgrimages both to Rome and Jerusalem also survive as, for example, that of John Capgrave, whose work the *Solace of Pilgrims,* written about 1450, gives an account in great detail of the topography, legends, and buildings of the Holy City.

While the majority of writers of the fifteenth century were busy endeavouring to make use of prose for new ends, here and there we meet with a writer who holds firmly to the old ways. Such a one was Sir Thomas Malory. In one of the most fortunate moments for English literature, he decided to make use of his tedious leisure as a prisoner of Edward IV by reading and reducing into English the vast compilation of stories about Arthur which he found, in the main, in his 'French book'. . . . As Sir E. K. Chambers has said, he came late to his high theme. By the fifteenth century whatever had existed of the chivalric life mirrored in the *Morte Darthur* had long since passed away. The age of Malory was no fruitful soil in which to replant the ideal of chivalry; his own experiences in the Wars of the Roses must have taught him that. Occasionally he exclaims against the times, but for the most part he retires into a world of long ago. It is a world of heroes—and one into which few but heroes are admitted. It is unconcerned with getting and spending. Kings and knights serve queens and ladies in court or in the field in an unending series of settings designed for the most part to show them to advantage. It is a world wherein the ordinary sordid affairs of business and politics are not allowed to intrude. Many battles are fought: many quests undertaken. Love and war are the twin poles of men's existence. In the course of relating much concerning these matters Malory also contrives to tell some of the greatest stories of the world, and in one of them—that of Lancelot and Guenevere—rises to the height of his great argument. Malory's conduct of the final books of the *Morte* has long been recognized as a masterpiece of story-telling. The movement is splendidly controlled and maintained, while the figures of Arthur, Lancelot, Gawaine, and Guenevere move in and out ineluctably pressing forward to the great final scenes and the

break-up of the Round Table and of all Arthur's dreams. (pp. 199-201)

In the Prologue of his edition of 1485 Caxton wrote what is still the best tribute. He has printed the book, he says,

> to the entente that noble men may see and lerne the noble actes of chyualrye / the Ientyl and vertuous dedes that somme knyghtes vsed in tho dayes / by whyche they came to honour / and how they that were vycious were punysshed and ofte put to shame and rebuke / humbly besechyng al noble lordes and ladyes wyth al other estates of what estate or degree they been of / that shal see and rede in this sayd book and werke / that they take the good and honest actes in their remembraunce / and to folowe the same / Wherein they shalle fynde many Ioyous and playsaunt hystoryes / and noble & renomed actes of humanyte / gentylnesse and chyualrys / For herein may be seen noble chiualrye / Curtosye / Humanyte / frendlynesse / hardynesse / loue / frendshyp / Cowardyse / Murdre / hate / vertue / and synne / Doo after the good and leue the euyl / and it shal brynge you to good fame and renommee.

Caxton printed the *Morte Darthur,* so he tells us, after he had 'accomplysshed and fynysshed dyuers hystoryes as wel of contemplacyon as of other hystoryal and worldly actes of grete conquerors & prynces / And also certeyn bookes of ensaumples and doctryne'. (p. 203)

As our first printer Caxton is worthy of our undying regard. The sneers of Gibbon and Disraeli, and any modern attempts to write down his services to English literature, must be regarded as ignorant and unworthy. Except that he omitted to print *Piers Plowman,* Caxton showed a real understanding of what was best in the available literature of his time. The printer of the first editions of the *Canterbury Tales, Troilus and Criseyde, Confessio Amantis, Morte Darthur,* to say nothing of various smaller works of Chaucer and Lydgate, deserves our warmest praise. But Caxton's services to literature were not confined to one class of writing. He showed an admirable catholicity of taste, while retaining a preference for certain kinds of books. The works of the great writers of antiquity he did not attempt to print in their original languages. That was being done by countless continental presses, and Caxton preferred to translate afresh, or use the translations of others. (pp. 205-06)

Caxton is very modest about his abilities, both as a translator and as a writer of English. With regard to the first, we need not take his protestations too seriously. His school and commercial education had given him a sound working knowledge of the languages which he used, and while he was not a finished scholar, the imperfection in his translations may often be ascribed to haste rather than to ignorance. His knowledge of French, in practice, was good. . . . (pp. 208-09)

Any discussion, however, of his merits as a translator must involve the wider consideration of his merits as a writer of English. In forming a judgement we have, in addition to his translations, the invaluable prologues and epilogues which he attached to some of his works, and these

Shepherds presenting their gifts to the infant Christ, from a late fifteenth-century Horae.

give many precious indications of his hopes and fears as a writer. 'Rude and simple' is his favourite way of describing his powers of writing English, and almost every piece of original work by him harps upon his ignorance, inexperience, and lack of skill. To some extent these protestations were common form, but Caxton was genuinely concerned about his limitations as a writer. To begin with he lacked any training in the use of 'the art of rhetoric or of gay terms'. Eloquence he regarded as 'soo precious and noble that amooste noo thyng can be founden more precious than it'. In common with most people of his time, he sincerely believed in the 'polysshed and ornate termes' for which he praised Skelton, and made attempts to follow what he thought to be the most elegant current English. But innumerable difficulties beset him, for he could get no one to advise him where the best English was to be found. Almost at the end of his life we find him still uncertain. (pp. 209-10)

We must allow that Caxton lacked any sensitive feeling for prose, and only stumbled on a good sentence by accident. The reader of Caxton is fortunate if he does not find himself in difficulties on every page, difficulties which arise from an inability to see how the sentence is planned. It is

not that his prose has an archaic flavour which is unpleasing, but rather that it is often involved and confused in sentence structure. (p. 211)

The history of printing in England before 1500 is so much the history of Caxton's press that we are apt to forget his companions in the art. The earliest press set up during his lifetime was one at Oxford in 1478, while another commenced to print at St. Albans in 1479. Both were mainly concerned in the publication of works in Latin for scholastic use. At Oxford only one book was published in English, Mirk's *Festial* (1486). At St. Albans two vernacular works came from the press, but both of considerable interest. *The Chronicles of England* (1485) was not a mere reprint, but in addition to Caxton's text (1480: 1482) included a history of the popes and other ecclesiastical information. The other was the so-called 'Book of St. Albans', *The Book of Hawking, Hunting, and Blasing of Arms* (1486).

Apart from these two presses which published nothing after 1486, the only other press of note was that of John Lettou, founded in 1480, and merged into a joint venture by Lettou and William de Machlinia in 1482. This press was mainly engaged in the publication of works in Latin on ecclesiastical matters, or in legal texts and year-books up to 1483, when de Machlinia became the sole proprietor. After this date and before 1491 he issued some twenty volumes, but only six of them were in English, and none of outstanding importance.

The death of Caxton in 1491 left only two printers at work—Wynkyn de Worde, who succeeded Caxton at Westminster, and Richard Pynson at London. Wynkyn de Worde published very little for the first few years after Caxton's death, contenting himself almost entirely with reprints. In 1495 he issued the *Vitas Patrum,* a translation by Caxton, finished according to de Worde on the last day of Caxton's life. The same year saw the publication of another large new work, Trevisa's translation of Bartholomew's *De Proprietatibus Rerum.* The next year was a notable one, for de Worde published seven new works, seven reprints, and the *Statutes of the Realm* for five separate years. The most interesting of the new works was the treatise on fishing attached to his edition of the 'Book of St. Albans'. He continued to publish new books and reprints until the end of the century. Many of them are of little interest now, but we owe to him the first editions of such famous works as *Robin Hood* (1500), *Bevis of Hampton* (1500), *Sir Eglamour* (1500), Lydgate's *The Assembly of the Gods* (1498) and *The Siege of Thebes* (1500?) and the first published work of Skelton, *The Bowge of Court* (1499?).

Richard Pynson, a graduate of Paris, early in his printing career published an edition of the *Canterbury Tales* (1490); on the whole he was content to publish reprints, and has to his credit a bare dozen books hitherto unprinted in his first ten years as a printer (1490-1500). Most of these are of small moment, but we are indebted to him for the first editions of Mandeville's *Travels* (1496) and *Guy of Warwick* (1500).

A survey of the work of the printers between 1477 and 1500 reveals the strength of the demand for religious and didactic works. Caxton, de Worde, and Pynson all devoted something like half their output to meeting this demand. Once that was satisfied, they turned to other needs. Literature of information and instruction received about the same attention from Caxton as did the romances and poems. Both de Worde and Pynson, however, apparently found the former a better market, for de Worde published some 28 works of information and instruction to 18 of a more literary nature, while Pynson increased this disparity still further by publishing 41 of the former to 18 of the latter. In all this, as might be expected, prose works predominated, but much of Chaucer and Lydgate, as well as some verse romances got into print. Further, some 80 per cent. of the prose was translation, much of it dating from about 1470 onwards.

As we look back at the prose of the fifteenth century we see (as did Caxton) that a variety of styles were practised. There were writings in 'ouer curyous termes', and writings in 'old and homely termes', while others were more readable since they were 'not over rude ne curyous but in suche termes as shal be vnderstanden'. Gradually a prose was being formed which had not surrendered its native characteristics in order to acquire greater flexibility and power. It remained an English prose, just as the Anglo-Saxon Chronicle, or the *Ancren Riwle,* or the writings of Wiclif were English prose, and it assimilated foreign words and constructions by adapting them to English patterns and rhythms. Thus, despite the overwhelming importance attached by Latin writers to the ordering of the sentence and the nice use of the *cursus,* little of this can be seen in English prose of the period. The insistence on throwing the accent on the penultimate syllable, and of avoiding the accented monosyllable which was so important to Latin writers, failed to secure acceptance. What Professor Saintsbury calls the 'trochaic hum' prevailed, and prose had to wait until the sixteenth century, and until the Ciceronian influence was stronger, before the effects familiar to us in the cadences of the Collects and the Book of Common Prayer became naturalized.

Prose written under the influence of medieval Latin in the fifteenth century, such as that of Lydgate, Pecock, the City Fathers, or the University of Oxford, made but limited headway. The majority of writers did not accept this way of writing, and what this meant may be seen by comparing the two following passages, each of them translations of the *De Imitatione Christi.* The first, dated about 1460, is by an anonymous writer and runs:

> Trouþe is to be sought in holy writings, & not in eloquence. Every holy writing owiþ to be radde with þe same spirit wherewiþ it was made. We owin in scriptures raþer to seke profitabilnes þan highnes of langage. We owe as gladly to rede simple and deuote bokes as hye bokes and profounde sentences.

This is rendered by William Atkynson about 1504:

> The principall thynge that we shall inquyre in scripture is charite & nat elygance in speche, & we shuld endeuoure our selfe to rede the scripture with as great fervour of spryte as it was receyued firste. And wisdome wolde we shude fo-

lowe these auctors and bokes where we may haue moste swete & profitable fedyng for owre soule. The fame of sotell phylosophers, the knowlege of poetes & retoricke, as a smoke or fume vanissheth awey: but the trouthe of god abydeth without ende.

Atkynson's version of the passage, especially of the third sentence, with its 'phylosophers, . . . poetes & retoricke', together with its image of 'smoke or fume', is a movement towards a richer, more cadenced prose, it is true, but also towards a prose more verbose and pretentious in manner, and one which was to lead to the excesses of Tudor prose. The 'aureate' language, the over-latinization, the constant use of Latin or French constructions, the flamboyance accompanying an enthusiastic use of rhetorical 'colours'— all these, on the whole, are kept at bay by most writers, and prose acquired a certain flexibility, and within limits pursued a straightforward path. A more skilful use of Latin was made by many writers who, following St. Jerome and current tradition, had endeavoured 'non verbum e verbo, sed sensum exprimere de sensu'. One such writer, a Carthusian monk of Beauvale, in Nottinghamshire, wrote in 1411: 'Ne I translate not þe wordes as þei bene wrytene, one for a noþere, þat is to seye þe englische worde for þe latyne worde', for he says that many Latin words are not understandable in English, and so he will put the matter in such a way that it will be clearly understood without serious alteration of his original. This he does, keeping pretty closely to the Latin for the most part in thought, but using a variety of English constructions which are syntactical equivalents of the Latin. By so doing he gives a clear exposition of Suso's *Horologium Sapientiae,* and a lively and realistic account of the lives of St. Elizabeth of Spalbeck and St. Mary of Oignies. Another translator from the Latin, Nicholas Love, while less faithful to the original in his *Mirror of the Blessed Life of Jesus Christ,* at the same time composed what was perhaps the most popular book of the century. His prose is so singularly easy and natural that Professor R. W. Chambers may well have been right when he claimed that Love did more than Hereford or Purvey's rendering of the Scriptures in providing a model for future writers of English prose. For example:

> Thus standen they to gidre, etyng and spekyng, with grete ioye to hem of the blessed presence of hir lorde: but neuertheles with grete drede and turbulance of his aweie passyng: and no wonder, for thei louede hym so tenderly that they myghte not with esy herte bere the wordes of his bodily departyng from hem, and namely oure lady, his blessed moder, that louede him passynge all othere. We mowe wel suppose that sche, touchede and stired souereynly with the swetnesse of moder loue, as she satte nexte hym at the mete, leyde doun her hede swetely, and restede vpon his blessid breste, as seynt John dide bifore in that forseide and moste worthy sopere.
>
> And so with swete teres sighynge, sche spak to hym in this manere preienge: My dere sone, if thou wilt alway go to thy fader, I preie the lede me with the. And oure lorde confortynge her seide: I pray the, dere moder, take not heavily my goynge for the, for I goo to the fader for thy

beste, and it is spedeful that thou dwelle her yit awhile to conferme him that schulle trewely byleue in me: and after I schal come and take with me into everlating blisse. And then sche seide: My swete sone, thy wille be done.

Translation indeed played a most important part in the development of our prose. Translations from the Latin and the French form a considerable section of the prose literature of the century, and the form and coherence of the English sentence was often largely dependent on the quality of the original. As time went on, 'an increased recognition of both the mechanical and the logical processes of structure, if not in many cases a capable control over them' was manifested, and readers were encouraged to expect and welcome technical accomplishment and the production of a prose 'clear, easy and plain'. This was not brought about in a day, nor everywhere at the same time, but throughout the century writers were slowly learning to write sentences in which the parts were grammatically combined: the old enemies of anacoluthon, pleonasms, synthetic verbs, and the like were in retreat. A wide variety of constructions begins to give life and variety to prose, and an effort is made to achieve a structural coherence of sentence and paragraph. The way forward to a more developed and cadenced prose has been attained. (pp. 213-17)

H. S. Bennett, "Fifteenth-Century Prose," in his Chaucer and the Fifteenth Century, *1947. Reprint by Oxford at the Clarendon Press, 1958, pp. 177-217.*

FURTHER READING

Bennett, H. S. "The Fifteenth Century." In his *Chaucer and the Fifteenth Century,* pp. 96-104. Oxford: Clarendon Press, 1947.

A concise historical and cultural overview of fifteenth-century England.

Brown, Carleton. *Religious Lyrics of the Fifteenth Century.* Oxford: Clarendon Press, 1939, 394 p.

A collection of fifteenth-century religious verse including dialogues, laments, prayers, songs, and hymns.

Bukofzer, Manfred. "Holy-Week Music and Carols at the Meaux Abbey." In his *Studies in Medieval and Renaissance Music,* pp. 113-75. New York: Norton, 1950.

Includes a detailed analysis of the musical structure of the English carol.

Chambers, E. K. *English Literature at the Close of the Middle Ages.* Oxford: Clarendon Press, 1945, 247 p.

An authoritative and detailed review of late medieval drama and fifteenth-century popular poetry.

Chambers, R. W. *On the Continuity of English Prose from Alfred to More and His School.* 1913. Reprint. Oxford: Oxford University Press, 1966, 174 p.

Contains an analysis of the principal features of fifteenth-century century prose, documenting the use of the vernacular for theoretical discourse, traditionally reserved for Latin.

Fox, Denton. "The Scottish Chaucerians." In *Chaucer and Chaucerians: Critical Studies in Middle English Literature,* edited by D. S. Brewer, pp. 165-200. University: University of Alabama Press, 1966.

A concise critical study of late medieval Scottish poetry, with particular emphasis on William Dunbar, Gavin Douglas, and Robert Henryson. Fox argues that it is somewhat tautological to call Scottish poets "Chaucerian," given Chaucer's critical influence on English poetry as a whole.

———. "Chaucer's Influence on Fifteenth-Century Poetry." In *Companion to Chaucer Studies,* edited by Beryl Rowland, pp. 395-402. Toronto: Oxford University Press, 1971.

Posits that the figures, motifs, topoi, and rhetorical characteristics of fifteenth-century English poetry which critics have traditionally attributed to Chaucer's influence actually stem from the common heritage of European medieval literature.

Graves, Robert. "The Crowning Privilege." In his *The Crowning Privilege,* pp. 13-36. Harmondsworth, England: Penguin Books, 1959.

Includes a discussion of John Lydgate's career as a court poet.

———. Introduction to *Malory's Le Morte d'Arthur,* translated by Keith Baines, pp. xi-xx. New York: Mentor/Penguin Books, 1962.

Characterizes Malory's prose work as an example of stylistic elegance.

Gray, Douglas. "Later Poetry: The Popular Tradition." In *The Middle Ages,* rev. ed., edited by W. F. Bolton, pp. 313-37. London: Sphere Books, 1986.

Includes a discussion of fifteenth-century courtly poetry.

Greene, R. L. *The Early English Carols.* Rev. ed. Oxford: Clarendon Press, 1977, 517 p.

Regarded as the seminal work on the carol as a genre; includes a collection of religious and secular carols.

Grout, D. J. "Medieval to the Renaissance: English Music and the Burgundian School in the Fifteenth Century." In his *A History of Western Music,* rev. ed., pp. 146-71. New York: Norton, 1973.

Includes a discussion of the English carol.

Huizinga, Johan. *The Waning of the Middle Ages.* London: E. Arnold, 1924, 328 p.

A translation of Huizinga's seminal 1924 work *Herfsttijd der Middeleeuwen,* an indispensable introduction to fifteenth-century studies.

Jusserand, J. J. *A Literary History of the English People from the Origins to the Renaissance.* New York: G. P. Putnam's Sons, 1895, 545 p.

Includes an engaging and informative discussion of English literature in the late Middle Ages.

Ker, W. P. "Chaucer and the Scottish Chaucerians." In his *Form and Style in Poetry,* pp. 49-91. London: Macmillan, 1928.

Explains the characteristic expressiveness and vitality of fifteenth-century Scottish poetry in terms of the specific features of Scottish English.

Lewis, C. S. "The Fifteenth-Century Heroic Line." In his *Selected Literary Essays,* edited by Walter Hooper, pp. 45-57. Cambridge: Cambridge University Press, 1969.

> Refutes, with the help of metrical analysis, the "commonplace of literary history that English metre is bad from the age of Chaucer to the age of Surrey."

MacDonald, George. "The Fifteenth Century." In his *England's Antiphon,* pp. 44-54. London: Macmillan, 1868.

> A brief discussion of fifteenth-century religious poetry.

Pearsall, Derek. "The English Chaucerians." In *Chaucer and Chaucerians: Critical Studies in Middle English Literature,* edited by D. S. Brewer, pp. 201-39. University: University of Alabama Press, 1966.

> Emphasizes the importance of fifteenth-century English poetry, observing that "we should not let our admiration for Chaucer . . . blind us to the real qualities of the English Chaucerians," especially their "appropriation to the tradition of new modes of thought."

Schirmer, Walter. *John Lydgate: A Study in the Culture of the XVth Century.* Translated by Anne E. Keep. Berkeley and Los Angeles: Univesity of California Press, 1961, 303 p.

> An exhaustive and richly documented study of John Lydgate's life and works.

Stevens, John. *Music and Poetry in the Early Tudor Court.* London: Methuen, 1961, 483 p.

> Includes many references to fifteenth-century poetry.

Workman, Samuel. *Fifteenth Century Translation as an Influence on English Prose.* New York: Octagon Books/Farrar, Straus and Giroux, 1972, 210 p.

> An extensively-documented study on the impact of translated works on the structural and narrative features of English prose. Includes a list of fifteenth-century English prose translations.

Yaeger, Robert F., ed. *Fifteenth-Century Studies: Recent Essays.* Hamden, Conn.: Archon Books/Shoe String Press, 1984, 364 p.

> A collection of scholarly articles on fifteenth-century English literature. Contributions include linguistic studies, textual criticism, reviews of scholarship, and essays on the dominant literary themes of the period.

Stephen Hawes

1475?-1523?

English poet.

Remembered almost exclusively for his allegorical narrative *The Pastime of Pleasure,* Hawes represents a transitional era in English poetry. While he repeatedly acknowledged his debt to his medieval predecessors Geoffrey Chaucer, John Gower, and especially John Lydgate, some elements of *The Pastime* presaged Edmund Spenser's Renaissance allegory *The Faerie Queene.* Hawes viewed himself as "the only faithful votary of true poetry," which for him meant the medieval tradition of didactic allegory. His major works illustrate the pilgrimage of life in allegorical terms: a man seeks to attain such goals as love and virtue, prevailing over numerous obstacles in the process. Although many critics assert that the significance of his works is mainly historical, others find them to contain passages of descriptive beauty and inspired imagination.

Very little is known about Hawes's life. He was born in Suffolk around 1475, was educated at Oxford, and subsequently travelled in Europe, particularly France. His familiarity with French culture, in addition to his witty conversation and excellent memory, aided him in procuring a position in 1502 as Groom of the Chamber in the court of Henry VII. Nothing has been documented about the actual duties this position involved, but critics speculate that the honor was bestowed upon Hawes as a reward for his literary skills. During his association with the court of Henry VII, Hawes wrote most of his poetry: *The Pastime of Pleasure,* which contains a lengthy dedication to the king; *The Example of Virtue,* which depicts the quest of Youth for virtue and purity; and *The Conversion of Swearers,* a verse sermon. He further honored the crown with *A Joyful Meditation of the Coronation of Henry the Eighth.* Hawes's last known work, *The Comfort of Lovers,* is thought to be autobiographical and recounts a personal hardship the nature of which is indefinite. All of Hawes's works were published by Wynkyn de Worde, a major English printer; some poems were reprinted several times, indicating a continuing demand for them. John Bale, one of Hawes's successors, called "his whole life . . . an example of virtue." Biographers generally cite 1523 as the year of Hawes's death.

The Pastime of Pleasure was popular with contemporaries of Hawes, and today his critical reputation is largely based on this single work. One of the main reasons for continuing interest in this narrative is its role in literary history as a transitional work from medieval to Renaissance poetry. Although Hawes did not make a great departure from medieval poetic forms, he did occasionally display a new approach to them. The expression of life as a pilgrimage was an established medieval convention to which Hawes added an element of adventure. In this respect, *The Pastime* resembles the heroic poetry of the Renaissance. Hawes believed that all poetry is allegory, a literary form he considered the ideal vehicle for educating the reader. In the course of his journey, the hero of *The Pastime,* Grand Amour, receives instruction from allegorical representations of the Seven Liberal Arts: Grammar, Logic, Rhetoric, Arithmetic, Geometry, Music, and Astronomy. In addition to instructing the reader in these subjects, Hawes indicated the necessity of a practical education to Grand Amour's quest for knighthood and true love. In Hawes's view, education was more valuable for its moral instruction and spiritual enlightenment than for its purely intellectual reward. Arthur B. Ferguson has explained that, for Hawes, "the final end of the seven sciences is to lead the soul to heaven," and Hawes chose to cloak his messages in these "clowdy figures" of allegory. While his didactic stance is distinctly medieval, certain aspects of his instructive narrative—allusions to classical literature and the emphasis on pragmatic education—indicate a shift toward Renaissance thought. Many critics argue that the Renaissance elements in Hawes's poetry are unintentional reflections of subtle changes in cultural attitudes at the time, and that Hawes revered the poetry of Lydgate and other predecessors too much to desire poetic innovation. In his introduction to the 1928 edition of *The Pastime,* William Mead describes Hawes as a romanticist whose "imagination was stirred by the ideals of an earlier day." Indeed, his treatment of such themes as chivalry and courtly love, as well as the lack of logic and precision in the plot, all reflect typical traits of medieval poetry.

For the most part Hawes has been critically dismissed as a minor poet. Many critics assert that Hawes possessed poetic potential that he never fully realized. C. S. Lewis suggests of *The Pastime* that "no poem gives us the impression of so wide a gap between its actual achievement and the thing it might have been." Even critics who praise *The Pastime* agree on its defects, particularly noting its inconsistent, sloppy meter and faulty plot construction. Hawes outlines the plot in the fourth of forty-six chapters, removing all suspense for the reader—and then, as if realizing his error, he deviates from the outline. He has also been criticized for his excessive use of aureate diction, a poetic device he borrowed from Lydgate. Hawes believed lofty concepts such as truth, love, and virtue should be written of in lofty terms, so he used ornate Latinate words to ennoble his poetry. The result, commentators observe, is an often confusing work cluttered with words that are used more for decoration than to illuminate meaning. Seth Lerer describes Hawes's "defense of aureation [as] a meager excuse for verbosity." Nevertheless, most critics concur that *The Pastime* is not without merit and contains passages of beauty and passion. Hawes also displays a keen awareness of the world around him, specifically the conventions and mores of courtly society.

Although *The Pastime* is not generally cited for its literary value, its significance is unquestionable, as stated by

Mead: "Hawes, more than any other writer of his time, represents the most characteristic features of the rapidly disappearing Middle Ages and embodies them in the one work by which his memory is kept alive in our day."

PRINCIPAL WORKS

The Conversion of Swearers (poetry) 1509
The Example of Virtue (poetry) 1509
A Joyful Meditation of the Coronation of Henry the Eighth (poetry) 1509
The Pastime of Pleasure (poetry) 1509
The Comfort of Lovers (poetry) 1515

Thomas Warton (essay date 1778)

[*Warton was an English critic, literary historian, and poet. His three-volume* History of English Poetry from the Close of the Eleventh Century to the Commencement of the Eighteenth Century *(1774-81) is widely considered the most significant literary history published in the eighteenth century. Along with Warton's critical works on John Milton and Edmund Spenser, this work helped revive interest in medieval and Elizabethan literature and promote the study of literature as an art. In the following excerpt from a reprint of the second and third volumes of the first-mentioned work, he unconditionally praises Hawes's* The Pastime of Pleasure.]

The only writer deserving the name of a poet in the reign of Henry VII., is Stephen Hawes. (p. 459)

Hawes's capital performance is a poem entitled The Passe-tyme of pleasure, or the Historie of Graunde Amoure and La Bal Pucel: contayning the knowledge of the seven sciences, and the course of man's lyfe in this worlde. Invented by Stephen Hawes, groome of kyng Henry the seventh hys chambre. It is dedicated to the king, and it was finished about the beginning of the year 1506.

If the poems of Rowlie are not genuine *The Pastime of Pleasure* is almost the only effort of imagination and invention which had yet appeared in our poetry since Chaucer. This poem contains no common touches of romantic and allegoric fiction. The personifications are often happily sustained, and indicate the writer's familiarity with the Provencal school. The model of his versification and phraseology is that improved harmony of numbers, and facility of diction, with which his predecessor Lydgate adorned our octave stanza. But Hawes has added new graces to Lydgate's manner. Antony Wood, with the zeal of a true antiquary, laments, that "such is the fate of poetry, that this book, which in the time of Henry the seventh and eighth was taken into the hands of all ingenious men, is now thought but worthy of a ballad-monger's stall!" The truth is, such is the good fortune of poetry, and such the improvement of taste, that much better books are become fashionable. It must indeed be acknowledged, that this poem has been unjustly neglected. . . . (p. 465)

The reader readily perceives, that this poetical apologue is intended to shadow the education of a complete gentleman; or rather to point out those accomplishments which constitute the character of true gallantry, and most justly deserve the reward of beauty. It is not pretended, that the personifications display that force of colouring, and distinctness of delineation, which animate the ideal portraits of John of Meun. But we must acknowledge, that Hawes has shewn no inconsiderable share of imagination, if not in inventing romantic action, at least in applying and enriching the general incidents of the Gothic fable. In the creation of allegoric imagery he has exceeded Lydgate. That he is greatly superior to many of his immediate predecessors and cotemporaries, in harmonious versification, and clear expression, will appear from the following stanza.

> Besydes this gyaunt, upon every tree
> I did see hanging many a goodly shielde
> Of noble knygtes, that were of hie degree,
> Whiche he had slayne and murdred in the fielde:
> From farre this gyaunt I ryght wel behelde;
> And towarde hym as I rode on my way,
> On his first heade I saw a banner gay.
>
> (p. 477)

Thomas Warton, "Section XXVIII," in his The History of English Poetry from the Eleventh to the Seventeenth Century, *1778. Reprint by Alex Murray and Son, 1870, pp. 459-79.*

William Edward Mead (essay date 1928)

[*In the following excerpt, Mead examines the literary strengths and weaknesses of* The Pastime of Pleasure.]

A just appraisal of [*The Pastime of Pleasure*] in our own day is peculiarly difficult, since our modern ideals of life and literature are so different from those of the early, and even the later, sixteenth century; for not until a generation after the time of Hawes was England swept into the full current of the Renaissance, and the difference between the Elizabethan time and our own is startling. In our study of the sources we have found that allegorical compositions with their troops of vague and lifeless characters largely dominated the time when Hawes wrote; and we need hardly remark that however eager sixteenth-century readers may have been for the allegorical feast spread in *The Pastime*, later generations have manifested no great appetite for such entertainment.

When *The Pastime* was first published, some two and a half centuries had already passed since the appearance of the first part of the *Roman de la Rose*, and much that was fresh and appealing in the middle of the thirteenth century had, by continual repetition, become conventional and commonplace. Saturated as Hawes was in the work of his adored master Lydgate—to say nothing of earlier allegorical poetry—he could perhaps hardly be expected to escape following the fashion. But it cannot be denied that allegory protracted through nearly six thousand lines, as it is in *The Pastime*, puts a severe strain upon the average modern reader, and certainly does not irresistibly draw him on. Even the *Faerie Queene*, exquisitely beautiful as it is, has long been more praised than read, and that, too, although in Spenser's great poem the allegory can be in a measure forgotten.

Not so in *The Pastime.* The poet is never weary of forcing his 'cloudy figures' upon the reader's attention. But the crowning defect of most allegories, and certainly of *The Pastime,* is that the pale, bloodless figures encountered at every turn lack human interest. No one can view with affection beings who are only personifications or types, and such are the chief characters of the poem.

In attempting to write a romance of adventure and to clothe it in the garb of allegory Hawes disregarded the fact that by the end of the fifteenth century the old machinery of romance was practically worn out, and that his chief work when finished was already in some sense a survival. For although Malory's *Morte d'Arthur* continued to be the most popular book after the Bible throughout most of the sixteenth century, and the lower classes still cherished the memory of Guy of Warwick and Bevis of Hampton, the growing strength of the Puritan temper, the bitterness of religious controversy, and the contempt of the classicists for the Middle Ages tended to brush aside everything which, like *The Pastime,* so uncompromisingly represented the spirit of an age that no longer made a living appeal. In still greater measure the prevailing spirit of the seventeenth century and most of the eighteenth was far removed from that of *The Pastime,* for the poem is so saturated with the old science, the old scholastic philosophy, and the old conceptions of religion, of society, of life, that it is a veritable epitome of the Middle Ages. And this medievalism is the more striking since *The Pastime* was written at a time when already for some two generations or more Italy had been in an intellectual ferment and actively discussing problems that in comparison make the sketchy outline of the Seven Arts in *The Pastime* appear strangely jejune and antiquated, and when at Rome, Florence, Bologna, and other intellectual centres, the leaders in art, architecture, and literature had turned away from the Middle Ages as a time of semi-barbarism. Even Ariosto, though he makes free use of medieval romantic machinery, treats it very lightly, and easily makes the exploits of his heroes an excuse for a jest.

In developing his theme Hawes is inspired with a high and serious purpose. He is not content to be merely entertaining; he wishes to teach, and in his zeal for teaching he loses sight of the fact that certain topics are by their very nature unsuited to poetical treatment. Not even the most ardent admirer of Hawes can find a trace of poetry in such lines as the following:

> And dysposycyon / the trewe seconde parte
> Of rethoryke /doothe euermore dyrecte
> The maters sounde / of this noble arte
> Gyuynge them place / after the aspecte
> And oftyme / it hathe the inspecte
> As frome a fayre parfyte narracyon
> Or elles by a stedfaste argumentacyon
> The whiche was constytute / by begynnynge
> As on the reason / and yf apparaunce
> Of the cause / than by outwarde semynge
> Be harde and dyffyculte / in the vtteraunce
> So as the mynde / haue no perceyueraunce

> Nor of the begynnynge / can haue audyence
> Than must narracyon / begynne the sentence.

His English, regarded as a vehicle of literary expression, may be taken as fairly representative of the language of his time, when usage had not yet been authoritatively determined and much was left to personal preference. But Hawes seems to have no desire to be an innovator. He is evidently much concerned to do the proper thing if he can learn what it is. His chapters on Rhetoric, the most elaborate of all in his exposition of the Seven Arts, clearly indicate the importance that he assigns to correct and well-balanced speech. In discussing choice of diction he somewhat awkwardly presents his thought as follows:

> So that elocucyon / doth ryght well claryfy
> The dulcet speche / frome the langage rude
> Tellynge the tale / in termes eloquent
> The barbary tongue / it doth ferre exclude
> Electynge wordes / whiche are expedyent
> In latyn / or in englysshe / after the entent
> Encensynge out / the aromatyke fume
> Our langage rude / to exyle and consume.

Unfortunately, he so keenly feels the defects of his native English that whenever he assumes the mantle of the teacher he smothers his thought under heavy latinized diction. A fairly representative passage is the following:

> For though a man / of his propre mynde
> Be inuentyf / and he do not apply
> His fantasye / vnto the besy kynde
> Of his connynge / it maye not ratyfye
> For fantasye / must nedes exemplyfy
> His newe inuencyon / and cause hym to entende
> With hole desyre / to brynge it to an ende
> And fourt[h]ely / by good estymacyon
> He must nombre all the hole cyrcumstaunce
> Of this mater / with breuyacyon
> That he walke not / by longe contynuaunce
> The perambulat waye / full of all varyaunce
> By estymacyon / is made annuncyate
> Whether the mater be longe or breuyate.

The very nature of didactic poetry puts a severe handicap upon the poet. Hawes not only labours under it but makes his readers labour too. He had a genuine poetic nature which could and often did express itself simply and exquisitely. But along with this he had the conventional university education, with its ponderous latinized vocabulary, and as soon as he began to reflect and choose his words with deliberation he was too likely to smother his thoughts, to say nothing of his poetry, under a blanket of pedantic verbiage.

To be both entertaining and instructive is given to but few. And Hawes attempts to combine a romantic love-story with a course of scholastic training. This compels him to follow a thorny path, for he soon faces a serious dilemma. If he allows himself to develop the didactic portion of the poem so as to make a useful treatise, he may reduce the love-story to a mere appendix to his treatise; if the story is the main thing, the utility of an elaborate work of erudition is not too obvious. Hawes manfully tries to be just both to the demands of the story and to his supposed duty as a teacher. He calls his poem *The Pastime of Pleasure,* but he is really bent upon something beyond mere pleasure, and in many passages offers little more than a sermon or something like a dull lecture, with the result that at times one loses sight of the lover altogether. The poet is evidently somewhat overcome by his plan, and, having determined to give his hero a course in the Seven Arts, he feels compelled to carry the instruction through more than a thousand lines, many of them strangely incongruous with the temper of an impassioned lover. And, what is worse, there is nothing to indicate that the scholastic training which Graunde Amoure receives materially furthers his wooing of La Bell Pucell. Moreover, the very fact that as a rule the poet merely outlines the course of study makes many passages about as poetical as a college catalogue. In some way he might, it should seem, have indicated that his hero had received the normal university training without, for example, incorporating into his poem a futile treatise on rhetoric far too detailed for a romance and far too brief and vague for a text-book. The poet himself appears to have realized the impossibility of converting the technique of syllogistic reasoning into poetry, and he wisely compacts his utterances into a few lines. As for the disquisition on the Direct Operations of Nature, or on the Five Internal Wits, or on the High Influences of the Supernal Bodies, they add nothing poetical to **The Pastime** and they would afford relief if omitted.

Not merely the selection of his material but the development of his narrative appears to have given the poet some difficulty. Already in the nineteenth chapter La Bell Pucell has yielded and promised her love to Graunde Amoure. But in order to protract the poem the hero must not only finish his course in the Seven Arts and be made a knight, but also enlist the aid of Venus in winning the lady already won, and fight a giant with three heads, then a giant with seven heads, and a monster made of seven metals. These useless combats, we need hardly remark, awaken no apprehension in the reader, for he realizes that the victory of the hero is inevitable.

It is indeed obvious that Hawes finds great difficulty in moulding large masses of material and fitting them with due subordination into his general scheme. Skill in narration requires that the reader's curiosity shall be continually stimulated and not too suddenly satisfied. But in **The Pastime** interest is dulled almost at the outset by the presentation of a detailed outline of what is to be expected later on. More than once also in subsequent passages the poet indicates what is soon to happen, so that the reader is repeatedly confronted with a twice-told tale. Furthermore, in many passages the incidents do not appear as an inevitable sequence of what precedes them but rather as arbitrary inventions, with the result that not infrequently the poem lacks spontaneity and progress and impresses many readers as being at least a third too long. But even they may well consider to what length **The Pastime** would have extended if it had been the work of the indefatigable Lydgate.

Notwithstanding its obvious shortcomings, the romantic part of the poem is not without interest. The plot, indeed, is not notably original—though doubtless every true lover regards his own romance as something new and wonderful. But Graunde Amoure is not unworthy of the lady

whose love he seeks, and she is not lacking in charm. Some of the wooing, it may be admitted, is of the strictly conventional type, but more than once there is a burst of genuine passion which atones for much that is artificial.

In the treatment of his theme Hawes almost inevitably adopted a literary fashion that began long before his time and persisted some three centuries or more after his work ended—the fashion of making free use in poetry of the names of the gods of Greece and Rome and of classical names for winds, seasons, and so on. Like Chaucer, he calls the west wind Zepherus, the sun Phebus, the moon Diana, the dawn Aurora. He brings in Cupid, Ercules, Esperus, Flora, Jason, Pegasus. All these, by the way, are found in Lydgate's short poem, *The Complaint of the Black Knight*—681 lines—and Hawes has many more in reserve.

But we need not dwell longer upon features of the poem that must be sufficiently obvious. Hawes may be at times merely a dull versifier, but he has nevertheless the soul of a true poet.

In the course of the story he finds frequent occasion for introducing descriptions which to most readers are probably the most attractive portions of **The Pastime.** He takes obvious delight in various aspects of nature and describes them with zest. None of his descriptions touch the highest levels, for Hawes lacks the magic gift of Shakespeare or Milton or Wordsworth, but in them he reveals a nature keenly sensitive to the beauty of the morning, to the delights of a medieval garden, and to the splendour of a medieval castle.

A few passages will illustrate his method. Identifying himself with his hero awaking out of slumber, he says,—

> I loked aboute / the nyght was well nere paste
> And fayre golden Phebus / in the morowe graye
> With cloude[s] reed began / to breke the daye.

On another morning,—

> Auroras beames
>
> Gan for to sprede / aboute the fyrmament
> And ye clere sonne / with his golden streames
> Began for to ryse / fayre in the oryent
> . . . . .
> And the lytell byrdes / makynge melodye
> Dyde me awake / with theyr swete armonye.

And yet again,—

> Thus all in comunynge / we the nyght dyde
>   passe
> Tyll in the ayre / with cloudes fayre and rede
> Rysyn was Phebus / shynynge in the glasse
> In the chambre / his golden rayes were sprede
> And dyane declynynge / pale as ony lede
> Whan the lytell byrdes / swetely dyde synge
> With tunes musycall / in the fayre mornynge.

Hawes evidently admired these lines and considerably later in **The Pastime** he repeats a part of the stanza:

> Ryght in the morowe whan Aurora clere
> Her radyaunt beames began for to sprede
> And splendent Phebus in his golden sper

The crystall ayre dyde make fayre and rede
Derke Dyane declynynge pale as ony lede
Whan the lytell byrdes swetely dyde synge
Laudes to theyr maker erly in the mornynge.

Hawes would doubtless have been ill at ease amid wild and rugged scenery such as stirred Wordsworth and Coleridge to enthusiasm, but he could fully appreciate the elaborate medieval garden with its flowers, its arbour, its trees trimmed in the form of dragons and peacocks, and its marvellous fountain,—

Of golde and asure / made all certayne
In wonderfull / and curyous symylytude
There stode a dragon / of fyne golde so pure
Vpon his tayle / of myghty fortytude
Wrethed and skaled all with asure
Hauynge thre hedes / dyuers in fygure
Whiche in a bath / of the syluer grette
Spouted the water / that was so dulcette.

Following the lead of the medieval romancers, who quite outdo themselves in painting the splendour of castles and palaces, Hawes revels in the beauty of the gorgeous apartments that he depicts. In the temple of Music,

to a chambre /full solacyous
Dame musyke wente / with la bell pucell
All of Iasper / with stones precyous
The rose was wrought / curyously and well
The wyndowes glased / meruaylously to tell
With clothe of tyssue / in the rychest maner
The walles were hanged / hye and cyrculer
There fate dame musyke / with all her mynstral-
sy.

Less happy is his description of the Tower of Doctrine, though he succeeds admirably in giving a vivid impression of its magnificence:

And after this / ferder forthe me brought
Dame countenaunce / in to a goodly hall
Of Iasper stones / it was wonderly wrought
The wyndowes clere / depured all of crystall
And in the rose / on hye ouer all
Of golde was made / a ryght crafty vyne
In stede of grapes / the rubyes there dyde shyne
The flore was paued / with berall claryfyed
With pyllours made / of stones precyous
Lyke a place of pleasure / so gayly gloryfyed
It myght be called / a palays gloryous
Somoche delectable / and solacyous
The hall was hanged / hye and cyrculer
With clothe of aras / in the rychest maner
That treted well / of a full noble story.

When Graunde Amoure arrives at the palace of King Melyzyus, where he is to be knighted, he is met by Minerva and conducted

Into an hall of meruaylous facyon
Ryght strongly fortysyed of olde foundacyon
The pyllours of yuory garnysshed with golde
With perles sette and broudred many a solde
The flore was paued with stones precyous
And the rose was braunched curyously
Of the beten golde both gay and gloryous
Knotted with pomaunders ryght swetely
Encencynge out the yll odours mysty
And on the walles ryght well dyde appere

The fege of Thebes depaynted fayre and clere.

From the hall he is taken up a stairway and entrusted to Truth, the guardian of the door of the king's chamber,—

And than the good knyght trouthe incontynent
In to the chambre so pure / soone me lede
Where sate the kynge so moche benyuolent
In purple clothed set full of rubyes rede
And all the flore on whiche we dyde trede
Was crystall clere and the rose at nyght
With carbuncles dyde gyue a meruaylous lyght
The walles were hanged with clothe of tyssue
Broudred with perles and rubyes rubyconde
Myxte with emeraudes so full of vertue
And bordred aboue with many a dyamonde
An heuy herte it wolde make Iocunde
For to beholde the meruaylous ryches
The lordeshyp / welthe / and the grete
worthynes.

Lastly, we note the stanza with the famous couplet at the end, doubtless the most frequently quoted lines in the entire poem:

O mortall folke / you may beholde and se
How I lye here / somtyme a myghty knyght
The ende of Ioye / and all prosperyte
Is dethe at last / through his course and myght
After the day there cometh the derke nyght
For though the day be neuer so longe
At last the belles ryngeth to euensonge.

By various writers much has been made of **The Pastime of Pleasure** as a forerunner of Spenser's *Faerie Queene*. Elizabeth Barrett Browning is especially enthusiastic [see Further Reading], though not at all critical, and considers **The Pastime,** along with *Piers Plowman,* the *Hous of Fame,* and the *Temple of Glas,* as 'one of the four columnar marbles, the four allegorical poems on whose foundation is exalted into light the great allegorical poem of the world, Spenser's *Faerie Queene*'. Since her day industrious students have assembled various passages showing points of resemblance which clearly indicate that both Hawes and Spenser worked to some extent with similar material and in the same cycle of ideas.

If, now, it could be proved that Hawes was the only writer who had treated the themes common to **The Pastime** and the *Faerie Queene,* the indebtedness of Spenser to his sixteenth-century predecessor might be readily granted. But for practically every situation cited as evidence of the indebtedness of the *Faerie Queene* to **The Pastime** we are able to point out earlier possible antecedents, and in view of Spenser's vast range of reading there is no reason to suppose that sources open to Hawes were not equally open to him. We may safely assume that Spenser was acquainted with **The Pastime,** as with other notable English poems before his day, and there is little objection to the supposition that from it he may have got some hints for his ampler work.

But to single out items that almost inevitably recur in any treatment of similar themes as evidence of direct indebtedness appears far beside the mark. Situations and forms of expression that were common literary property in the medieval period are an ever-present pitfall against which the

Woodcut of the figure of Death from the 1509 edition of The Pastime of Pleasure.

student of literary origins must be on his guard. That Hawes used various literary motives which to some extent appear also in the great work of Spenser, more than five times as long as *The Pastime,* is not at all surprising, for both poets had gleaned in the field of medieval romance. Further than this we can hardly go with safety.

From what has been already adduced it is obvious that with our modern outlook we are not prepared to give unqualified praise to *The Pastime.* Ours is a bustling age; and *The Pastime* was not written for readers in a hurry. But those who have the time and the patience to follow the hero through his course of training in the Seven Arts and his long wooing of La Bell Pucell will find numerous passages that suggest what exquisite work the poet might do were he not ensnared in the meshes of allegory and medieval conventionality. In these passages the verse is delightfully fresh and charming. It breathes the air of the sweet English landscape in the spring when fields are green and birds are bursting into song. Many of the situations in *The Pastime* are indeed well-worn features of medieval romance, but along with the banalities and extravagances there is a strong personal feeling struggling for utterance—the sort of emotion that does not find full expression until the coming of Sidney and Marlowe and Spenser and Shakespeare.

No competent critic would now venture to rank *The Pastime* along with the great works of the Elizabethan age. But to the contemporaries of Hawes who had traversed the barren wastes of fifteenth-century literature it may well be that *The Pastime of Pleasure* seemed like the dawn of a new day. Modern readers inevitably view it with less enthusiasm, but if they judge it fairly they must recognize it as a notable outgrowth of types of composition that had long dominated the nations of Europe and as an historic landmark in the evolution of English literature. (pp. c-cxiii)

William Edward Mead, in an introduction to The Pastime of Pleasure *by Stephen Hawes, 1928. Reprint by Kraus Reprint Co., 1971, pp. xiii-cxiv.*

C. S. Lewis (essay date 1936)

[*Lewis is considered one of the foremost Christian and mythopoeic authors of the twentieth century. Indebted principally to George MacDonald, G.K. Chesterton, Charles Williams, and the writers of ancient Norse myths, he is regarded as a formidable logician and Christian polemicist, a perceptive literary critic, and an accomplished writer of fantasy literature. Lewis served on the English faculty at Oxford and Cambridge, where he was an authority on medieval and Renaissance literature. A traditionalist in his approach to life and art, he opposed the modern movement in literary criticism toward biographical and psychological interpretation. In place of this, Lewis practiced and propounded a theory of criticism that stresses the importance of the author's intent, rather than the reader's presuppositions and prejudices. In the following excerpt, Lewis offers a general appraisal of* The Pastime of Pleasure, *focusing on themes of education, love, and death.*]

[*The Pastime of Pleasure*] is a difficult work to judge. Read it conscientiously from cover to cover, and you will conclude that it is the heaviest of tasks; but then from such a reading something will cling to your memory—odd lines, odd scenes, a peculiar flavour—till you are driven back to it, to find that its faults are just as grievous as you first supposed but that its merits are greater. No poem gives us the impression of so wide a gap between its actual achievement and the thing it might have been. There is a kind of floating poetry in the author's mind but not in his grasp. He seems ever on the point of becoming much better than he actually is. Nor is it very wonderful that this should be so, for Hawes, stumblingly and half consciously is trying to write a new kind of poem. He himself believes that he is trying to revive an old kind: the praise of Lydgate is often on his lips, and he deplores the direction in which poetry is moving in his own time:

> They fayne no fables pleasaunt and coverte
> But spend their tyme in vainfull vanyte
> Makynge balades of fervent amite.

Like Caxton, he wishes to revive the 'floure of chyvalry' which 'hath be longe decayed'. But this illusion, whereby the mind posits in the past the desired thing which is really still in the future, is not unnatural, and its working explains the early history of Romanticism in the eighteenth century, when men like Walpole and Macpherson not only sought, but even invented, in the past, faint images of the poetry which was really to be written in the nineteenth century. The combination of allegory on the large scale and chivalrous romance which Hawes wants to revive, could not be revived because it had not existed. There had been some approach to it in Deguileville: but Hawes carries it much further, and we shall not find the thing in perfection till we reach *The Faerie Queene.* Hawes in the meantime moves about in worlds not realized. He has very little art and his poem is dark and tortuous, but a fitful wind of inspiration stirs in the darkness. He so misunderstands the original of allegory that he thinks its purpose is to hide the subject—'to blowe out a fume' are his own words; but one of the reasons why he thinks so is his native and by no means unpoetic bent for the indefinite and the allusive—in a word for the romantic vague. Before his pilgrim finishes his journey and wins La Bell Pucell we have that journey so frequently predicted that all suspense is lost; but then suspense is no part of his aim, and this constant pressure of the remote and unattained—this continual hinting and casting forward (*ripae ulterioris amore*)—is of the very nature of one kind of romance.

> By the way there ly in wayte
> Gyauntes grete dysfygured of nature—
> But behonde them a grate see there is
> Beyonde which see there is a goodly lande
> Moost full of fruyte, replete with Joye and
>   bliss—
> Of ryght fyne golde appereth all the sande.

So speaks Lady Fame to the youthful Graunde Amour, and the lines are good poetry because they lead the mind on and open the doors of the imagination: and good allegory, because to be young and to look forward is, after all, very like hearing what Graunde Amour heard. And if the same journey is foretold again a couple of hundred lines later—this time the hero sees it pictured on a wall—even this has its own sense of mysterious fatality and its own truth to life. As we proceed the allegory becomes more difficult. I have not been able to find the *significacio* in the repeated partings of the hero and heroine, and perhaps there is none. Perhaps Hawes himself would have been neither able nor willing to throw much light on the deeper obscurities of his poem. He loves darkness and strangeness, 'fatall fictions, as he says, and 'clowdy fygures' for their own sake; he is a dreamer and a mutterer, dazed by the unruly content of his own imagination, a poet (in his way)as possessed as Blake. It is at once his strength and his weakness that he writes under a kind of compulsion. Hence the prolixity and frequent *longueurs* of his narrative, but hence also the memorable pictures, whether homely or fantastic, which sometimes start up and render this dreariness almost 'a visionary dreariness'.

> I sawe come rydynge in a valaye ferre
> A goodly lady envyroned aboute
> With tongues of fyre as bryght as ony sterre.
>   . . . . .
>
> I came to a dale.
> Beholdynge Phebus declynynge low and pale,
> With my grehoundes in the fayre twylight
> I sate me downe,
>   . . . . .
>
> And on his noddle derkely flamynge
> Was sette Saturne pale as ony leed.
>   . . . . .
>
> Eternity in a fayre whyte vesture . . . .
>   . . . . .
>
> We came unto a manoyr place
> Moted aboute under a wood syde.
> 'Alight', she sayd, 'For by right longe space
> In payne and wo you dyde ever abyde;

> —After an ebbe there cometh a flowynge tyde.'

Indeed, all the resting places on the journey of Graunde Amour are good; and all the roadside twilights and dawns,

> Whan the lytell byrdes swetely dyde synge
> Laudes to theyr maker erly in the mornynge.

Much that he describes does not interest us, but he describes nothing that he has not seen, whether with the inner or the outer eye. He has noticed the morning sky coloured like curds, and the 'bypaths so full of pleasaunce,' the little images of gold moved with the wind on the top of the tower of Doctryne, and the sun shining, as a man wakes, in the mirror of a strange bedroom. Some medieval writers have little feeling for the difference between combat with a man and combat with a monster; but when the three-headed giant crosses the path of Graunde Amour

> My greyhoundes leped and my stede dyde sterte,

and he is as meticulous as Spenser in telling us how many cartloads the giant's corpse measured. So clear is his vision, so perfect his poetic faith in his own world, that the poem ought to be good; but his incapacity to select, his stumbling metre, and his long delay in the tower of Doctryne, have condemned him to not undeserved obscurity.

The **Pastime** is not exclusively an allegory of love, but of life as a whole, with special emphasis on love, education, and death. The educational sections in which Hawes vainly endeavours to rival the allegorico-encyclopaedic work of Martianus Capella or Jean de Meun, are the dullest part of the poem. With the possible exception of the fine passage on grammar

> (By worde the worlde was made oryginally:
> The Hye King sayde: it was made incontient).

none of his presentation of the liberal arts deserves to be re-read. Much more interesting is his treatment of love . . . Not only does Graunde Amour look forward to marriage as the only conceivable form of success: he even hesitates over the inequality in wealth between himself and his mistress, and is reassured by *Counseyle* . . . that 'she hath ynoughe . . . for you both'.

The Lady, on her part, answers to his suit that she is 'sore kept under' by her 'frendes' who 'wolde with me be wrothe' if they heard of his proposal. This is the work-day world with a vengeance, and it might seem that we were within easy distance of the commonplace of Nevill; but then the Lady's very fear that her relatives will lead her 'to a ferre nacyon' (*ferre* is a key-word in Hawes) and his answering promise that he will follow

> And for your sake become adventurous

are essentially romantic. And if Hawes is prosaic in the context of his love, on the subjective side he is all on fire, 'wrapped,' as he says, in a 'brennynge chayne'. He is far indeed from the unambiguous desire of Guillaume de Lorris, or the heroical passion of Troilus: the fire of his love is a dim fire, charged with sentiment and imagination, a thing much more ambiguous and brooding, in a word more romantic, than that of older love poetry. It is a cloudy ecstasy, love veritably in a mist, a dream or a glamour and none the less for that reason a reality; and he writes of it lines which are irreplaceable in the sense that no other poet has struck just the same note.

> She commaunded her mynstrelles ryght anone
>   to play
> *Mamours,* the swete and the gentyll daunce.
> With La Belle Pucell, that was fayre and gaye,
> She me recommaunded with all pleasaunce
> To daunce true mesures without varyaunce.
> O Lorde God! how glad than was I
> So for to daunce with my swete lady!—
> For the fyre kyndled and waxed more and more,
> The dauncing blewe it with her beaute clere.
> My hert sekened and began waxe sore;
> A mynute six houres, and six houres a yere
> I thought it was.

But it is Hawes' treatment of his third theme, the theme of death, which is most remarkable. Critics have been found to whom it is merely ridiculous that a narrative written in the first person should continue after the narrator is dead and thus permit him to describe his own decease. But the convention whereby the dead are allowed to speak, or the living to assume the person of the dead, is surely not a very difficult one: the Greek anthology, and the first country churchyard you turn into, will supply precedent. And if you object that dead men do not really talk—and I can see no other objection—you will be well advised to study any subject rather than poetry, where the naïve realist can never succeed. So much suspension of disbelief as this device demands, is our debt to every poet; and to Hawes, for a special reason, the debt is very easily paid. For even from the outset—perhaps because his imagination is so earnest and his conscious skill so weak—the good passages have had this peculiar quality, that they seem to come from nowhere, to be a disembodied voice, not always a perfectly articulate voice, coming to us out of a darkness; so that when, at last, it comes to us admittedly from the grave, it at once compels belief.

> O mortall folk, you may beholde and se
> How I lye here, somtyme a myghty knyght.
> The ende of Joye and all prosperite
> Is dethe at last through his course and myght;
> After the day there cometh the derke nyght,
> For though the day be never so longe
> At last the belles ryngeth to evensonge.

Every one knows this stanza: but few know that it comes at the end of a dirge sung by the Seven Deadly Sins in which the reiteration of a single phrase ('erthe of erthe') has all the brutal insistence of a bell heard from within the church, and that dirge and epitaph together are merely the starting-point for one of the most nobly conceived passages in any allegory. For when his hero lies dead and the poem might be expected to end, Hawes does a most surprising thing; he rolls up curtain after curtain of his cosmos, as the successive backcloths roll up in the transformation scenes of the old pantomime, or as the planes of time disclose themselves in Mr. Dunne's serial universe. *Remembrance* has hardly finished the epitaph over the grave of Graunde Amour when Dame Fame enters the temple to enroll him among the Worthies, and to conclude with her vaunt

> Infenyte I am. Nothing can me mate.

and here again we suppose we are at the end: it is a familiar consolation at the funerals of great men. But no—on the heels of Fame comes another shape, the same on whose 'noddle' the dark flame of Saturn was set, and whom we quickly recognize by the horology in his left hand, and who proclaims himself,

> Shall not I, Time, dystroye bothe se and lande,
> The sonne and mone and the sterres alle?

But Time is wiser than Fame and boasts less, and comes confessedly but as the usher of Eternity—Eternity who ends the poem, appearing in her white vesture and triple crown,

> Of heaven quene and hell empres.

If the execution of this whole passage had been equal to the conception, it would have been among the great places of medieval poetry. It is not; but we must still say (more reasonably I hope than Goethe said of another poem) 'how nobly it was all planned'. (pp. 278-85)

> C. S. Lewis, *"Allegory as the Dominant Form," in his* The Allegory of Love: A Study in Medieval Tradition, *Oxford at the Clarendon Press, 1936, pp. 232-96.*

Arthur B. Ferguson   (essay date 1960)

[*Ferguson is a Canadian educator and critic. In the following excerpt, he examines Hawes's emphasis on education in* The Pastime of Pleasure.]

[Hawes] made the problem of education a main theme of his allegory, ***The Pastime of Pleasure.*** Although written ostensibly as light reading for a gentle public, it was in the best tradition of medieval didactic literature. Hawes despised "ballads" and "trifles without fruitfulness." But he wore his didacticism with a difference. It is necessary to remember that his unusual combination of love allegory and chivalric romance was set within the larger pattern of the "pilgrimage of the life of man," and that his representative man is a member of the knightly class. So it is really an allegory of chivalric life. Considered in this context Hawes's opinions on education become very valuable to anyone seeking among the sparse and equivocal documents of the period a clue to the chivalric mind in transition.

I should like to emphasize the medievalism of this context. Not only did Hawes draw the principal ingredients of his poem—the allegory of love, the chivalric romance, and the pilgrimage theme—from the most familiar of literary traditions, the education he prescribes for the man aspiring to the status of knighthood is essentially scholastic. It is the well-worn formula of *trivium* and *quadrivium.* Moreover, the final end of the seven sciences is to lead the soul to heaven. Before he is finished, Hawes has rung in the seven deadly sins, an echo of the Dance of Death, and the admonitory commonplace that earthly fame is soon dissipated in the spiritual vastness of eternity. His single-minded admiration for "his master," John Lydgate, "flower of eloquence," "the chief original of my learning," may or may not indicate an equally strong link with the culture of medieval England, depending on how one interprets the mind of that tedious, but erudite, genius. It is, I think, fair enough to say that, but for a more comprehensive familiarity with classical authors and themes than was common among fifteenth-century English poets, and a sensible, though not at all necessarily humanistic, regard for the English language, Lydgate was likely to have bequeathed to his younger admirer little that would help him cross the threshold of Renaissance culture.

Even that legacy of familiarity with classical authors is, however, important. If it failed to make a humanist of Hawes in the way that More, for example, was a humanist, it gave him the raw materials of humanism to work with, and may well have accounted for his undeniably fresh handling of old themes. It also made it possible for him to enter the circle of classicists employed at court. It was from that group, more probably than from his legacy of medieval classicism, that he derived the high regard for rhetoric as a practical instrument for life in the world of affairs that constitutes the most extensive as well as the least medieval part of an otherwise quite traditional treatment of education.

"Cunning" is for Hawes a thing not only pleasant but fruitful; and rhetoric is the discipline through which it achieves its fruitfulness. It is the instrument through which "poets," who are the custodians of practical wisdom as well as artists in words, must make their contribution to society. It is through them and their study of the "fatal problems of old antiquity" that justice was established. To use a term not yet current, it was they who led mankind from the state of nature into civil society and the rule of law.

> Before the law, in a tumbling barge
> The people sailed, without perfection,
> Through the world all about at large.
> They had no order nor no steadfastness
> Till rhetoricians found justice doubtless
> Ordaining kings of right high dignity,
> Of all commons to have the sovereignty.
> The barge to steer with law and justice
> Over the waves of this life transitory,
> To direct [correct] wrongs and also prejudice;
> And those that will resist a contrary [wrongful-
>   ly]
> Against their king, by justice openly
> For their rebellion and evil treason
> Shall suffer death by right and reason.
> O what laud, glory and great honor
> Unto these poets shall be notified.
> The which distilled, aromatic liqueur
> Cleansing our sight with order purified,
> Whose famous draughts, so exemplified,
> Set us in order, grace and governance
> To live directly [in orderly manner], without en-
>   cumbrance.
> But many one, the which is rude and dull,
> Will despise their work for lack of cunning.
> All in vain they do so hayle and pull [harass and
>   criticize]
> When they thereof lack understanding.
> They grope over where is no feeling;
> So dull they are that they cannot find
> This royal art for to perceive in mind.

In short, poets, by the discipline of rhetoric, are able to point their fellows "the ways of virtue, wealth and stableness." And the matter they interpret for the rest of their society is the history and literature of ancient Rome, where the "noble paynims" labored disinterestedly for the profit of "the comyn welthe."

Thus spoke Stephen Hawes. And if the words have a medieval ring, the spirit is that of Tudor humanism, pure and simple. It falls far short of the realistic discussion of public issues that marks so much of the work of the humanists in the third and fourth decades of the century. *The Pastime of Pleasure* had, indeed, scarcely received its first printing before Thomas More had followed the New Learning far beyond the naïve faith of Hawes in the "fruitfulness" of rhetoric to a newly realistic appraisal of contemporary England. But it represents nonetheless a development in the history of chivalric thought of considerably greater import than its contribution to the history of *belles lettres*. For it must always be borne in mind that Hawes addressed the English aristocracy and gentry ("O ye estates surmounting in nobleness"), that the education he described in such detail was clearly and specifically a prelude to knighthood, and, as for the successful suitor in Tiptoft's dialogue, the way to advancement.

Hawes's treatment of book learning indeed quite overshadows his description of the hero's training in the military skills and the chivalric principles that were the very essence of the traditional manuals of knighthood. Unless we read into the word "rebels" a hint of the seditious risings that so frequently had challenged Henry VII's title to the crown, and therefore find Hawes enlarging the protective function of knighthood to include support of the "new monarchy," there is nothing new in it at all. The novelty arises rather from the interlocking assumptions underlying the whole allegory, namely, that the knight is a soldier in only one aspect of his activity, that he is a person who owes a primary duty to the whole commonwealth simply as a member of the governing class, and that learning, even of the most traditional kind, is essential to the proper fulfilment of that duty. He even recognizes as a fact—not a very praiseworthy one, but a fact nonetheless—that the knight is also a person with economic interests. It was a fact few apologists for the chivalric ideal cared to contemplate and some, the authors of *The Boke of Noblesse* for example, heartily deplored. The hero's anticlimactic decision in his less passionate years to devote himself to making money is as accurate sociologically as it was contrary to all the prejudices of medieval knighthood. (pp. 209-13)

> *Arthur B. Ferguson, "Chivalry and the Education of the Citizen," in his* The Indian Summer of English Chivalry: Studies in the Decline and Transformation of Chivalric Idealism, *Duke University Press, 1960, pp. 182-221.*

Florence W. Gluck and Alice B. Morgan   (essay date 1974)

[In the following essay, Gluck and Morgan evaluate Hawes's minor poems in terms of meter, grammar, syn-

tax, and diction, as well as the literary tradition and conventions they follow.]

Hawes's metrical usage is the clearest index of his position as one of the pre-Renaissance poets, from whose pedestrian verse the productions of the 'new courtly makers' were such a dazzling departure. Among these writers, he has been especially singled out for hostile criticism, but the general consensus about Tudor metrics is firmly stated by Tillyard [In his *The Poetry of Sir Thomas Wyatt, A Selection and a Study*], who emphasizes the lack of any 'unifying pattern' to sequential lines.

This problem is most evident in the **Example of Virtue,** where lines may have four, five, or six stresses, and anywhere from six (l. 812) to fourteen (l. 1398) syllables. (The usual range is from seven to twelve.) Such latitude is not of itself a fault: it is not the variations from a norm which offend, so much as the absence, in general, of any norm at all. The effect may be seen in the first stanza of the **Example of Virtue.** The opening two lines may be read as pentameter, when the emphasis on the rhyming syllable is accepted. They are followed by a verse of seven syllables and four stresses. Line 4 is again pentametric (with the first foot a trochee), but line 5, while having eleven syllables, is pentameter only with the reader's active collaboration, so that the rhythm has been lost again before the final pentameter verses. Even if one abandons the arbitrary 'norm' of pentameter, no pattern reveals itself in these lines. The reader can develop no justifiable aural expectation, and no effect is achieved, no aspect of meaning underlined, by the awkward sequence of metres. Since this stanza is fairly typical, any attempt to classify Hawes's metre seems doomed to failure. The later poems offer greater regularity, but not enough to warrant the view that Hawes had a specific verse pattern in mind, as Pyle claims, for example, for Barclay.

Hawes is not alone in his difficulties with metre. His predecessors Hoccleve and Lydgate, and Barclay and Skelton, his contemporaries, have related problems. The general level of metrical competence in the early Tudor period is notoriously low, and various theories have been offered to explain this situation. The matter is complicated by the fact that there are good metrists at this time, and that a writer like Hawes, with all his overt incapacity, uses a complex metrical form successfully with no apparent effort.

The traditional view of the situation is stated by A. W. Pollard in his introduction to the Roxburghe Club edition of the *Castell of Labour* (Edinburgh, 1905). The poem, then thought to be by Barclay, poses metrical problems of the same sort as occur in Hawes's works. Pollard notes that only two generations after it was written, Chaucer's verse was no longer a succession of decasyllables, but a sequence of lines with varying metre, some with ten syllables, others with fewer, owing to loss of final -e and of inflectional syllables. Barclay, Pollard goes on, 'normally uses lines of four accents, but mixes with them . . . others of a slower movement with five . . . this is what Barclay found when he read Chaucer . . . and I believe that he accepted these alternations as a beauty, and one which should be imitated'. This explanation, which has been widely accepted, emphasizes both contemporary linguistic chaos and the forces of a metrically anarchic authority. Poets who might have written reasonably regular verse would tend not to do so because their poetic model had (apparently) not done so. And thus the misunderstood metre of Chaucer would beget the poor metre of Hoccleve and Lydgate, which in turn would lead to that of Hawes and Barclay.

This formulation of the process of decay has not gone unchallenged. In 1938 C. S. Lewis, in an article entitled 'The Fifteenth-Century Heroic Line', offered a metrical pattern of two half-lines with from two to four stresses in each as an explanation of the incompetent pentameter of the period. He suggested that this varying pair of half-lines, rather than Chaucer's decasyllabic line, was the model for the fifteenth-century poet, and offered several examples from the works of Lydgate and others of how the poetry was to be read. The main flaw in this theory, as he himself admits, is that the metre is so flexible that virtually anything, including prose, can be fitted to it. Lewis returns to this subject in *English Literature in the Sixteenth Century* (Oxford, 1954), where he omits any discussion of his heroic metre, but does restate the considerations that led him to reject the traditional explanation:

> . . . the poets were not trying to write Chaucer's metre. To explain their departures from it by the loss of final -e is to presuppose the metrical ignorance which this theory attempts to explain. If men understand metre, that understanding itself reveals to them that pronunciation has changed . . . If [hypothetical alternate metres] are both rejected, then the true state of the case is that early sixteenth-century England witnessed a poetical barbarism in which rhyme itself became the only constant characteristic of verse . . . and that the causes of this barbarism are unknown.

It will be seen that in both the traditional view and Lewis's original alternative, poets at this time were trying to write something other than regular iambic pentameter. The difference between the two positions concerns the nature of the model: a debased Chaucer or a hypothetical metre based upon a half-line structure. Pyle, in his article on Barclay's metre, offers other such patterns for Barclay's verse. An extension of this alternative challenges the usual reading of Chaucerian verse itself, claiming that Chaucer was not writing iambic pentameter either. It seems, then, that the attempt to explain the state of Tudor prosody has led to theories that challenge the accepted view of both Chaucerian metre and the verse of Wyatt. Since no consensus has yet been reached on these issues, one may simply observe that the recent tendency to accept metrical norms which appear idiosyncratic may eventually alter our view of the disorderly prosody of the fifteenth and early sixteenth centuries. It seems unlikely, however, to change radically the reader's general discomfort with most of this verse, because the rehabilitations depend largely on allowing the verse to create its own patterns. There is thus little use of what John Lawlor has isolated as having 'from the greater Elizabethans to the early Georgians dominated English verse-making—an organization which turned upon the possibility of intimate contrast between the run of speech and a measured norm'. Thus it is likely that the verse of Hawes and most of his contemporaries will continue to appear metrically deficient, even if the blame does not fall, as in Lewis's second treatment of the problem, squarely on the poets themselves.

In Hawes's case, there is considerable improvement between the *Example of Virtue* and the later poems, and even in the *Example of Virtue* there is effective use of syllabic variation. Line 8, 'I now symple and moost rude', has only seven syllables, but can be read as a five-beat verse with the first two words each representing a foot. This unusual line gives emphasis in accordance with meaning, and provides a good start for the stanza. Moreover, the pentameter rhythm has not been totally lost, and is reasserted in the line that follows. While any of the poems will provide examples of disorder, the interesting point is that there are cases of proper metrical usage and of effective use of pattern and variation. The most obvious of these is the *tour de force* in the *Conversion of Swearers,* ll. 113 ff. This is a tail-rhyme inset in which the four-line stanzas, rhyming in pairs (aaab cccb), begin with lines of one syllable, increase the number to six, and then decrease again to one. Hawes accomplishes this with only the latitude of pronouncing the plural *-es* as a separate syllable, and it seems obvious that the stringency of the form has brought out all his metrical skill. In the same poem the long lines 323-4 (and cf. 1. 111) with their shifting rhythm represent very well the emotional character of Christ's complaint. Similarly, the movement in ll. 50-6 to the long and heavily weighted final couplet is very expressive, even though none of the lines is very good metrically. The poetry of Hawes, then, provides some evidence for the view that stresses the poetic models and poetic expectations of the Tudor period. However the metrical laxity began, it seems clear that Hawes could, had he wished, have written much better metre than he did, and that the generally low standards must bear part of the blame here. In his handling of metre, as in his use of syntax or his treatment of allegory, Hawes was willing to do only enough to place himself in the already accepted tradition.

Since the reader cannot rely upon the aural pattern of Hawes's verse to direct, emphasize, or clarify, he must seek such organization in other aspects of the poetry. It is unfortunate that the poems' statements also lack firm pattern, so that instead of structure there is only confusion.

English grammar was, in the early sixteenth century, an informal and imprecise study, not recognized as independent of grammar *per se* (that is, the study of Latin). Any piece of contemporary literature will provide errors of the sort Hawes makes; the difference is one of degree only. In the poetry we are considering, grammatical disorder is sufficient to make the reader uncertain where he is in the progression of thought. This result is achieved by a variety of techniques which fall, generally, into two large categories: the thought is either interrupted by some other, related idea; or its expression involves a confusing welter of referents. In both cases the subject is effectively lost.

In the first group we find the parenthetical clause or state-

ment, which separates two sections of another sentence, and renders both unclear. Since the parenthesis is not marked by punctuation, the confusion is considerable. Instances include *Example of Virtue,* ll. 954, 1053, 1391. Closely related to this technique, in that one construction is halted while another intervenes, is *Example of Virtue,* ll. 423-7:

> For who that from his rome remoueth
> He is often full gretely to blame
> And medeleth with other in theym lame
> As no thynge connynge nor expert
> They may hym say syr malapert

If 1. 424 is omitted, and 1. 426 is considered as an amplification of *in theym lame,* the result is still anacoluthon, but it is perfectly comprehensible. With 1. 424, however, there are essentially two sentences, each having as subject '[he] who' of 1. 423, but concluding differently and making different statements. Either sentence is acceptable, but Hawes tries to give us both and destroys them in the process. *Comfort of Lovers,* ll. 519-21 is a similar case.

The interruption may act to destroy the original construction, or it may merely interpose so effectively between parts of that construction that the effect is equivalent to destruction. A typical example of the extended interruption is the long complex sentence, with a perfectly correct syntactical skeleton, that opens the *Example of Virtue.* The model here is the first sentence of the *Canterbury Tales,* and it is instructive to compare Lydgate's attempt at this construction at the start of the *Siege of Thebes,* an attempt which ends in total disaster. Hawes has the correct framework (as he has in *Comfort of Lovers,* ll. 29-36, or, in a more complicated case, *Example of Virtue,* ll. 29-46). Unfortunately, he has thoroughly disguised and vitiated this framework by trying to do too much, grammatically, in the course of the sentence. Between ll. 1-2, 'Whan I aduert in my remembraunce / The famous draughtes of poetes eloquent', and 1. 14, 'It fereth me sore for to endyte', Hawes characterizes the poets, their works, their times, and himself. He then returns to the independent clause his dependent ones are introducing. Each of the intervening subjects is tied in to some preceding part of the sentence, but the ties are not compatible. While the result is comprehensible, especially if taken clause by clause, it is neither good grammar nor good poetry.

This brings up the next major category of disorder: that of clausal progression. Frequent difficulty seems to stem from Hawes's failure to recall his immediate referent. An instance in which there is, finally, no sentence at all may be found in the *Example of Virtue,* ll. 1163-9:

> So forth I went walkynge my iournay
> Metynge a lady olde and amyable
> Syttynge in a castell both fressh and gay
> On an olyphauntes backe in strength so stable
> Whiche it to bere was good and able
> Hauynge in her hande a cup of golde
> Sette with perles ryght many afolde

It is easy to see what happened: Hawes begins with himself as the subject, and *Metynge* in 1. 1164 refers to him. Then, desiring to characterize the lady further, he employs another participle to do it, and this time it refers to *lady* in

1. 1164, as does *Hauynge* in 1. 1168. But with the loss of the original subject, the sentence is lost, and Hawes compounds his felony by introducing *Whiche* in 1. 1167, with yet another antecedent, and then going on to describe the gold cup in 1. 1169. The description may succeed, but the syntax fails.

This sort of construction, in which similar grammatical forms appear with different referents, is common in Hawes's work, and is nearly always unsuccessful. 'Whiche', 'that', and participial forms occur over and over again, attached to any part of a preceding clause, and giving an entirely unwarranted appearance of grammatical continuity. Syntactical sense may be made out of almost any such construction if it is taken in isolation; but coming one after another, as they do, they discredit each other. Instances abound: *Example of Virtue,* ll. 540-6, 869-77, 1927-37; *Comfort of Lovers,* ll. 519-22. Sometimes the problem stems from Hawes's tendency to build his clause out of a word which should not be the antecedent of a pronoun. In the *Example of Virtue,* ll. 869 ff., for example, the normal referent of the lengthy clause, 'Whiche . . . shyneth' is either *Sapyence* or *counsayll,* not *kynge:*

> I Sapyence am of the kynges counsayll
> Whiche is clothed with purple that sygnyfyeth
> The grace and the pulcrytude . . .
> . . . that in hym shyneth

Another example of the way in which Hawes creates considerable ambiguity by deviating from normal English order in rather long and complicated constructions is to be found earlier in the poem:

> Whan he the sone of god on hy
> That is his brother agayn wyll crucefy
> Yf he had power . . .
>
> (ll. 788-90)

He, the subject, which refers to *man* (last mentioned in 1. 786), is followed by the object rather than the verb, and the object has an appositive, moreover. Again, Hawes will occasionally introduce into a line a construction quite unrelated to the one governing the preceding words. The new construction is usually suggested by a word somewhere in the preceding phrase, which is then treated as if it were an entire phrase in itself. Example will make this clearer:

> . . .your gardeyn gloryous
> Vnto whiche now fayne wolde I go
> There for to dwell and you also
>   (*Ex. Ver.,* ll. 1875-7)

The last three words of 1. 1877 make grammatical sense only if we expand the lines before them to something like 'fayne wolde I that I (and you also) go there for to dwell'. Or consider:

> Commaundynge me . . .
> To drawe this treatyse for to enlumyne
> The reders therof by penytencyall pyte
> And to pardon me of theyr benygnyte
>   (*Conv. Swearers,* ll. 53-6)

In this case the subject of the final line is *reders* (the antecedent of *Commaundynge* is singular). The idea is that the readers are to pardon the author; the grammatical construction is nil, depending on an imaginary expansion: 'to

enlumine the readers, who are to pardon me . . . ' *Example of Virtue,* ll. 1469-71 may be similarly reconstructed.

The destructive effects of such writing may be best appreciated when they are set against proper techniques of statement and organization. Hawes's poetry offers several instances of the successful application of his havourite devices. In the *Example of Virtue,* ll. 2053-9, the suspended sentence, with intervening modifying phrases, is used to excellent effect. Here the subject is *floure* throughout, and the slow progress to the happy conclusion is perfectly suited to the subject of the stanza, the long period that elapsed before Henry VII was able to attain the throne. Similarly successful, but in quite a different way, is the stanza from the *Conversion of Swearers* (ll. 99-105) in which Christ pleads with man to refrain from swearing, and the rapid alternations of subject, first Christ (ll. 99, 100, 104), then man (ll. 101-3, 105), are well managed and effective. In such passages, Hawes accepts the authorial burden of indicating to the reader where he is going, and how, in his assertions. There is no groping for direction, for subject, for statement. Such control may be evident even when the grammar is not technically correct. In the *Comfort of Lovers,* ll. 757-63, Pucell never quite completes the *yf* clause of 1. 758, but the import of the stanza is clear; her maidenly confusion, since she suspects that she is the object of Amour's passion, is well conveyed by the fragmentary grammar. Here, as in his use of metre, Hawes reveals a competence that is too often negated. Direction and emphasis in his poetry must therefore come from techniques whose normal function is clarification and ornament.

With the larger structures blunted or diffused, the smaller ones, such as images, phrases, and single words, become more central to Hawes's poetry. The weakness and conventionality of his poetic figures, however, further detract from a style already enervated by lack of technical strength.

Hawes's typical image in the *Conversion of Swearers* is the appropriate, but standard, reflection of the theological context. Christ is meek as a lamb (1. 97), hearts are hard as stone (1. 231), and the joys of the world pass like snow melted by the sun (ll. 312-13). The allegorical figures of Mercy, peace, Truth, and Righteousness appear, as does the Devil with his snares and nets. There are images of Grace curing the poet of the sin of idleness (ll. 50 ff.), and of the sheltering wings of the sovereign, heavenly and earthly. Most of these images are to be found in Scripture.

Similarly, the only poetic images in *A Joyful Meditation* are centred on the red and white roses of Lancaster and York, represented by Henry VII and his queen, and on their son, Henry VIII, whose coronation is celebrated in the poem. There are a royal tree and flower, drops of golden dew, and a dew of Grace and Joy. Katherine of Aragon, Henry's wife, appears as a fair flower of virtue.

It may be seen that nothing in this array of images is likely to arrest the reader. All are so appropriate to their context as to be almost inherent in it. In the *Example of Virtue* there are, of course, more figures, and these are more varied. Many similes, however, are exceedingly well worn.

Hardynes is a 'shynynge sterre' (1. 694); Sapience is the 'lode sterre of heuenly doctrine / The sprynge of comfort Ioye and solace' (ll. 772-3); the Virgin is a 'sterre' (1. 780) and 'chosen vessell' (1. 782); Clennes is the 'sterre of excellence' (1. 1253) and 'flour of complacence' (1. 1255); the young prince is a 'sterre of humylyte' (1. 2098). Justice is true as steel, marble black as jet, windows clear as crystal; love burns hot as fire; the world turns like a ball. There are the conventional astrological and architectural descriptions, and the conventional allegorical figures of Pride, Sensuality, Fortune, Justice, Courage, Nature, Wisdom, Charity, Love, and a host of others more minor. All of the above are, again, perfectly suitable and totally undistinguished. It is therefore all the more surprising to find, in the **Comfort of Lovers,** some deviation from this pattern.

The **Comfort of Lovers** repeats some figures of the earlier **Joyful Meditation.** Pucell is a 'gentyll floure' (1. 296), a 'floure of Ioye and grace' (1. 302). She is also, as in the **Example of Virtue,** a 'holsome sterre of lyght' (1. 91) and fair as 'the bryght daye sterre' (1. 610). Her neck is white as a lily (1. 729) and her beauty pierces with a dart (ll. 296-7). One of the mirrors into which Amour looks is as bright as the sun (1. 349). The chess figure in the poem (ll. 652-3) is a common metaphor in medieval poetry.

Hawes does, however, develop more emphatic and striking images in the **Comfort of Lovers,** largely derived, it appears, from the book of Psalms. Many concern animals, and metaphors of snaring appear more than once. Colloquial figures, perhaps based on proverbs, occur, like the narrator's statement that he has caught cold, or the lines (176 ff.) that show the sweeping broom as a symbol of destruction. Because Hawes reaches out of the immediate literary context for his images, he is more successful in their use in this poem. While occasional impressive or suggestive figures give the **Comfort of Lovers** considerable interest, they are not sufficient to create a sense of organization or to make clear the obscure problems which are the poem's subject.

Excessive use of tags and fillers further vitiates Hawes's style. In addition to tags familiar from the works of other medieval writers, there are certain ones peculiar to Hawes, usually phrases that serve no function in the line except that of the very vaguest emphasis. These include *without resystence, without corrupcyon, withouten jeoperdye, by ryght excellent courage, by ryght good knowledgynge,* and others. Unnecessary adjectives and adverbs are frequently used merely to lengthen the line and not for emphasis. Examples are *ryght, eke, anone, moost,* and *full.* A phrase like *full ryght sore* (*Ex. Ver.,* 1. 1498) can result. Another common filler is the expletive verb. Line after line is reinforced with *do* or *dyd* and occasionally *gan.* Whole lines can be emptied of meaning by the use of a combination of these devices. Note, for instance, the **Comfort of Lovers,** 1. 530, 'Yet moreouer / as I do well reherce'.

The adjectival poverty of Hawes's verse also contributes to its lack of colour. Stanzas containing only one or two adjectives can be culled from all the poems in this volume. In the **Conversion of Swearers,** for example, the stanza beginning 1. 99 has, out of a total of fifty-nine words, the one

adjective 'swete'; in the **Comfort of Lovers** the stanza beginning 1. 813 contains only the adjective 'harde'. Of a sample of nearly 500 lines of the **Example of Virtue** (1051-1549), fewer than one in twelve, or about 8 per cent, of the total words are adjectives. Of these, more than one-fifth are occurrences of *great, fair,* or *good,* and other 'idealizing' adjectives (the term is [Derek Pearsall's]) like *bright, pure, virtuous, noble, clear, marvellous, dear, royal, precious* make up a large portion of the rest. The overuse of such words, employed 'to idealise rather than to record reality, to excite admiration rather than to define', results in vagueness and imprecision, and imparts an unreal, detached quality to Hawes's poetry. Descriptive adjectives which differentiate and distinguish stand out because of their scarcity. These include *stynkynge, infernall, agast, blo, troublous, mysty, venymous,,* and the aureate words such as *fulgent, dyuynall,* and *depured* (all ten of which, incidentally, appear in our sample).

The verb usage, too, appears to be conservative. In the same sample, about one in seven, or about 14 per cent, of the total words are verbs. These figures may be compared with those of Miles (*Eras*) which yield, for 900 lines of the **Pastime of Pleasure,** proportions of nine adjectives to eight verbs (to thirteen nouns) in ten lines. It will be seen that our sample yields far fewer adjectives in proportion to verbs than does Miles's. This may be one reason why the **Pastime of Pleasure** is Hawes's best poem. Of the total number of verbs in our sample, more than half are past participles or forms of 'to be', 'to have', 'to come', 'to go', 'to say', static or unpictorial forms against which a few lively words like *marched, strykynge, plucked,* and *mured* (all from our sample) stand out. Thus we have in Hawes's work a style heavily dependent for brilliance upon the nouns, often grand and weighty concepts like *grace, mind, love, power,* and *truth.*

The carelessness with which Hawes treats both the large and small aspects of technical organization may be contrasted with his evident concern over one particular variety of word usage. It is not surprising that his name, more than any other poet's, has been linked with the phenomenon of aureate diction: this aspect of his style is the one on which his poetical faculties were concentrated. In his many discussions of poetry, aureation and the veiled colours of allegory are the inevitable constants, and his work bears out his precepts most clearly in the former instance.

Hawes's most eloquent exposition of the art of aureate diction appears in the **Pastime of Pleasure:**

> Connynge is lyght / and also pleasaunt
> A gentyll burden / without greuousnes
> Vnto hym / that is ryght well applyaunt
> For to bere it / with all his besenes
> He shall attaste / the well of fruytfulnesse
> Whiche Vyrgyll claryfyed / and also Tullyus
> With latyn pure / swete and delycyous
> From whens my mayster Lydgate deryfyde
> The depured rethoryke / in englysshe language
> To make our tongue / so clerely puryfyed
> That the vyle termes / shoulde nothynge arage
> As lyke a pye / to chattre in a cage
> But for to speke / with Rethoryke formally
> In the good ordre / withouten vylany.

(ll. 1156-69)

In these lines the Latin models are clear, as is the recognition of Lydgate's role in transmitting the high style. . . . Hawes reiterates his opposition to 'vyle termes' a few stanzas later, where he goes so far as to declare that a noble matter cannot redeem a lowly formulation:

> For thoughe a mater be neuer so good
> Yf it be tolde / with tongue of barbary
> In rude maner / without the dyscrete mode
> It is dystourbaunce / to a hole companye
> For to se them / so rude and boystously
> Demeane themselfe / vtterynge the sentence
> Without good maner / or yet intellygence
>
> (ll. 1198-1204)

In Hawes's work aureation provides relief from nebulosity and an indication that he was concerned about the effect of his work on the reader, in one area at least. It suggests again, as does an occasionally felicitous use of metre and of grammatical structure, that he could direct his language and make coherent choices when he perceived the necessity of doing so.

Hawes's verse provides both precept and example for many of the major elements in the transition from medieval to Renaissance in England. To a reader aware of the direction of poetry at that time, Hawes may appear to be a forerunner of later and greater poets, a man consciously altering his verse to meet new challenges and to attract new audiences. But this view, however tempting, lacks convincing support, and it is more accurate to see him as a traditional poet, following models of the two preceding centuries, using medieval forms, subjects, and rhetorical devices. Hawes himself provides the best evidence for such a view: there is no extant poem in which he does not assert his literary dependence on the examples of Chaucer, Gower, and especially Lydgate.

His debts to the Chaucerian tradition are obvious. In the larger area of genre, he is persistently medieval. His poems include a verse sermon, two allegories, a congratulatory poem on Henry VIII's coronation, and a consolatio-debate. Within these structures Hawes relies heavily on the favoured devices of Lydgate and his predecessors: the astronomical periphrasis, the modesty prologue, the 'go, litel boke' envoi, the lapidary decorations. In matters of poetic technique he is further allied with the fifteenth century; at the same time, it is possible to find portents of the future in most of Hawes's poems, although he himself never seems to see his work as innovation. The most important such instance, in the light of later English literature, is undoubtedly the use of a knight as the travelling hero in the *Example of Virtue,* repeated in the *Pastime of Pleasure.* While the use of knights in symbolic quests is not at all unusual, the less complex and commoner form of the allegorical motif was that of the pilgrimage, as used by Deguilleville, translated into English prose and verse (the latter by Lydgate) in the fifteenth century. Instead of Deguilleville's pilgrimage, Hawes's knights embark on chivalric excursions. They are thus free of the overtly religious (perhaps even Catholic) implications of pilgrimage, and represent more readily a view of life which is centred in activity in the world. Whether or not Spenser owed his decision to use the chivalric allegory to Hawes's example, the combination was important for the increasingly secular, active world view of Hawes and his audience. Chivalric achievement was a characteristic metaphor for successful activity in the world, as the many splendid tournaments of Henry VIII suggest, and as Spenser's use confirms. A further aspect of Hawes's allegory involves the role of education, which is given humanistic emphasis. Even spiritual achievement is largely the result of human effort and activity.

Other cases of Hawes's literary prescience occur. He abandons his usual rhyme-royal only three times in 10,000 lines. An eight-line stanza in the *Example of Virtue* gives emphasis to the armour of salvation, and the tail-rhyme inset in the *Conversion of Swearers,* with its unusual technique of lengthening and then contracting verses, shows a surprising concern with form. At this point in the poem, Christ is speaking, reminding man of His Passion. The mixture of a highly emotional appeal and a rigid syllabic pattern was a technique that was to become very popular, especially in the sixteenth and seventeenth centuries when it was used by Browne, Herrick, Traherne, Herbert, and others. In the *Pastime of Pleasure* couplets are used to characterize the rude clown Godfrey Gobelive: this and the tail-rhyme inset reveal Hawes's occasional interest in technical decorum.

Hawes shares, in addition, the general Renaissance concern for the defence of poetry and for the definition of its functions and the explanation of its fictional surface. In his last poem, the *Comfort of Lovers,* this concern is mingled with pressing personal difficulties, amatory and political, to produce a poem intensely personal, dramatic, and colloquial, albeit obscure. These cases stand out against the duller background of traditional attitudes and usages. Hawes's work offers us most clearly evidence of the need for the new forms and new ideas which he himself, occasionally, supplied.

Hawes's difficulties with some of the small conventions of medieval poetry provide insight into the larger problems. Many of the familiar, indeed mandatory, poetic devices of allegory or dream vision are, in Hawes's poems, extraneous or ornamental. In the case of the seasonal or astrological setting at the opening of the *Example of Virtue,* we find that he has borrowed outright lines from both *The Assembly of Ladies* and *The Bowge of Courte.* Moreover, there is no real reason for the poem to start in autumn, and no astrological information is conveyed by the introduction, apart from the time of year. This and similar references suggest that while Hawes may have been conversant with astrological principles, he is not here invoking them. The heavenly bodies are used ornamentally, because they are stylistically appropriate, like the jewels that fill the descriptions of the various castles. Occasionally a gem appears in connection with its proper 'virtue', but this occurs only often enough to assure us that, had he wished, Hawes might have made all his lapidary references significant. Instead they are embellishment, heightening the material of the poem as the aureate style heightens its vocabulary. Other commonplaces are similarly treated: windows, walls, and tapestries are decorated with the stories of Troy or Thebes, but they are just that—decorated. No narrative or atmospheric point is made with the decoration; the story is not rehearsed as an example, an introduction, a contrast.

An indication of Hawes's attitude toward these traditional materials is the kind of repetition they entail. Thus in the many castles (***Pastime of Pleasure,*** ll. 361-4, 2556-62; ***Example of Virtue,*** ll. 211-24, 246-8; ***Comfort of Lovers,*** ll. 65-71, 216-45) there are always gold, glass-like crystal, towers or turrets, 'knottes'; favourite terms are *goodly, marveylous, solacyous, craftely;* the décor includes a plenitude of precious stones. Nor is such repetition confined to descriptive passages. The device of anaphora, a medieval favourite, is heavily used by Hawes. In three poems (***Pastime of Pleasure, Conversion of Swearers, Example of Virtue***) he bases extended sections on the phrase 'wo worth'. These passages are often so lengthy that their original point is obscured: they serve as a rhetorical flourish rather than as part of the poem's statement. Again, when Hawes apologizes for his poetic ineptitude, he repeats words, phrases, and entire lines exactly. Certain concatenations of idea and phrasing are introduced whenever they seem appropriate. This saves thinking, obviously, but at a high price. In addition to producing some very tedious verse, it unfits Hawes for dealing with a particular convention when he wants to use it in a new way to make a new point.

As an example of this we may consider Hawes's theory of poetry. Comparing the subject in its appearances in the poems, we find a great deal of repetition. Words and phrases reappear, not necessarily applied to the same subjects, or making the same points, but as if the whole matter called forth a given vocabulary. The standard treatment draws heavily on the following: *fatall fyccyons, clowdy fygures, olde antiquite, craftely, cloke, coloured, sentence, sentencyously, scryptures, expert, endyte, auctorite, moralyte, trouthe, memoryall, fruytfull.* After reading two or three of the passages, one tends to lose interest in Hawes's theory of poetry, which appears to involve only the greatness of past writers and the importance of an unspecified variety of artifice. When, however, this theory intrudes into the ***Comfort of Lovers*** in a most significant way, it becomes far more noteworthy. In lines 281-94 of that poem Hawes seems suddenly to take literally the notion of 'fatall'—that is, prophetic—poetry. In his distress, the narrator derives comfort from the poems of earlier writers, which indicate that he and his beloved will eventually come together (and compare ll. 635-7, 797-8). What poems are meant, and how they can foretell the future, are not explained; and the obscurity is deepened by the lines that follow. Since the ***Comfort of Lovers*** is partly about Hawes's own role as a poet, and also partly about false and true prophecy, the predictive capacity of poetry is decidedly relevant. Faced with the need to make clear his meaning and its connection with the rest of the poem, Hawes resorts to the same vague declarations he used in the more conventional passages. The underlying idea does not receive adequate statement, and the theory of poetry remains imprecise in itself, with only the faintest narrative and thematic relevance. Having always used conventions

for matters already fully known, Hawes cannot now use them to convey original ideas.

An analogous situation is present in the larger areas of subject and form. In his two shortest poems, Hawes is successful with the forms he has chosen. The praise of Henry VIII in ***A Joyful Meditation*** and the invocation of the planets, with their standard associations, are straightforward and suitable. In the ***Conversion of Swearers*** Christ speaks of the Passion of the Crucifixion, and compares it with the torment inflicted on Him by blasphemers. The assumptions underlying the association of these two passions are real to Hawes, and the poem succeeds accordingly. But the allegories are another matter altogether. In them, Hawes appears ill at ease both with the content and with the form he has chosen to embody it.

To begin with, Hawes has yoked together two traditions which were moving in opposite directions. The romance in England was a dying genre, either fully decadent, as in the typical *Squire of Low Degree,* or consciously nostalgic, as in Malory. The allegory, on the other hand, was growing steadily more secular, political, and realistic. The traditional spiritual journey was becoming a journey to wealth, to power, to wordly security; the conflict of vice and virtue was seen in a courtly or political arena. The best

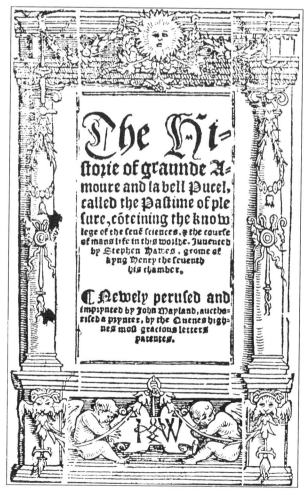

Title page of the 1554 edition of The Pastime of Pleasure.

Tudor allegories are frankly secular: in the *Bowge* Skelton pits the narrator against an unholy seven who are specifically social evils, and in *Magnificence* the happy end entails the recovery of the power of the title character, an earthly monarch. Curious mixtures of the spiritual and the secular are common: the *Castle of Labour* shows the hero, beset by the horrors of poverty, achieving his goal with the help of reason. The goal itself is both financial and spiritual success: it is attained by the rejection of Sloth and the pursuit of Diligence, and on the way each of the deadly sins must be overcome. Another mixture, relying rather more on the tradition of the *Romance of the Rose,* is the *Castle of Pleasure,* in which Desire must follow either Beauty or Worldly Riches (that is, marry either for Love or for Money), and in which he finally wins Beauty despite the interference of Disdain. Here the already secular goal is brought further into the world of every day, just as the spiritual journey becomes a voyage to a worldly haven.

It was this changing allegorical mode which Hawes combined with the fantastic world of the romance, and his use of the combination attests to the unconsciousness of his transitional pose. His first essay in this genre was the *Example of Virtue.*

The poem consists of three sections. In the first, the narrator, in a typical dream vision encounter, meets Discretion, who conducts him to a series of castles and finally to an island where he hears a debate among Hardiness, Fortune, Nature, and Sapience. This portion of the adventure corresponds to Book I of the *Court of Sapience,* where the narrator sees Sapience mediate the quarrel of the four daughters of God. It is the judgement of Sapience that leads to the redemption of mankind by Christ, thus satisfying the demands of Truth and Righteousness. Hawes has adopted the debate form and several peripheral features (four women debating, a female judge, a question relating to dominance over man), but the central concern of the episode is quite distinct from the overall pattern of the poem—that is, from the transformation of Youth into Virtue. Comparison with Lydgate's *Pilgrimage of the Life of Man,* which Hawes probably used as a model for his allegorical journey, shows that all of the many debates in that poem serve to educate the pilgrim by illuminating various doctrinal issues. Hawes seems to have felt that debates were a part of his poetic convention, but to have failed to see their function in a narrative. The *Example of Virtue's* debate is interesting for its eclectic use of traditional materials, as the Classical virtue Hardiness combats the ancient goddesses Fortune and Nature, in combination with the Christian Sapience. The subject, which of these forces is most dominant over man, is treated with a neutrality characteristic of the debate tradition. Judgement is often suspended (as in *The Owl and the Nightingale*) or conciliatory (as in *The Court of Sapience*). Here it is the latter, and the debate serves merely to display some personifications and to provide edifying discourse. It is, however, allegorically irrelevant to Youth's education and adventures.

In the second major division of the poem, the hero makes an allegorical journey, meeting and overcoming various obstacles. The action is simple and unambiguous, but not convincing. The fundamental justification for allegory, that within a man there may be disparate or conflicting elements, is not recognized by Hawes. The guide, the hero, the challenges, are discrete poetic creations, entirely in their author's control. The tale recounts the overcoming of external difficulties, and Hawes must constantly remind the reader and, one feels, himself, that another, implicit, story is being told. A pause for signification, however, is not enough: it does not help to know that the forward lady on the goat represents Sensuality, or that the three-headed monster is the World, the Flesh, and the Devil. Hawes neglects the spiritual action, for which the physical is merely an analogue. Thus, when Youth spurns temptation by walking away from the lady on the goat, there is no drama to suggest renunciation. When he fears to cross the narrow bridge, Youth fears a physical danger; his love for Cleanness overcomes his fear. Potentially, this is good allegory; but it must carry an emotive force that suggests a different fear and a less common compulsion. The failure is more than a technical one: it is a fundamental misapprehension of the purpose of allegory.

In the last section of the poem, a third traditional genre, the vision of heaven and hell, appears. Visions are often introduced into large allegorical narratives; the narrator views both regions in Douglas's *Palace of Honor,* a poem similar in many ways to Hawes's two allegories. But in the *Example of Virtue* Hawes has introduced the vision without considering its implications, with the result that Virtue and Cleanness are said to die before they see the afterworlds. Surely this cannot imply spiritual death, as that would mean damnation. In an allegory they ought not to die in a physical sense—and yet they do. The poem has two consummations, the marriage and the ascension to heaven, and they are not allegorically compatible.

What has happened is simple and not really surprising. Hawes has ceased to write allegory, and is now proceeding as if he were dealing with real people. He allows himself the licence of a voice after death, but for a Christian such a voice is closer to realism than traditional allegory. All the events of the final section are possible: nothing represents anything else. Even when writing traditional homiletic allegory, Hawes fails to understand its function, and in the end he loses track of it altogether.

Compared with the earlier *Example of Virtue,* the *Pastime of Pleasure* shows considerable technical advance. Much more is attempted, and the means of organization is better. The long section on the Seven Arts and the Godfrey Gobelive interlude are both attached to the motif of the hero's education, as the debate in the *Example of Virtue* is not. The final exaltation by Fame is an apotheosis which is allegorically consistent with Grande Amour's progress, while Virtue's ascension to heaven makes sense only outside its allegorical context. The theme, worldly education and artistic rather than spiritual success, seems to have been more appealing to Hawes. But the poem has some new faults, chief among them its great length. Whole sections are exceedingly tedious: the new interest in education is served with more than a thousand lines of monologue which temporarily destroy the narrative movement. The action is largely repetitive: there are numerous battles against similar monsters. Most of all, however, the theme creates difficulties. In order to deal with the allegorical material, Hawes tries to bring the techniques and details of homiletic allegory into the realm of worldly knowledge, worldly progress, and worldly fame. This turns out to be an awkward enterprise.

Hawes wishes to show his hero's developing perfection in love and knowledge: he both wins Labell Pucell and achieves Fame. Two great Renaissance themes are thus invoked, and Grande Amour ought to be the first of those carefully formed gentlemen the Renaissance was so anxious to create. To treat the progress toward the two separate goals was not, however, a simple matter, and Hawes never thinks about the consistency of his hero's adventures. Thus in the Tower of Doctrine, Grande Amour learns what he would at a university, and at the Tower of Chivalry he learns to handle arms. He then fights a sequence of strictly allegorical monsters in order to attain his beloved. Was his education in chivalry allegorical as well? Did it teach him, not actual battle techniques, but ways to achieve honest love? And if this is the case, thus making the hero's training in arms consistent with his use of them later in the poem, what about the Tower of Doctrine? What is the reality corresponding to its curriculum? Some things, in short, are more allegorical than others.

In adapting the spiritual journey to a new territory, Hawes made a number of incomplete transfers, which interfere with his new message by suggesting the more traditional one. The *Example of Virtue's* three-headed monster, the World, the Flesh, and Devil, becomes in the *Pastime of Pleasure* a giant whose heads are Falsehood, Imagination, and Perjury, vices of the lover. The sevenheaded giant of the later poem represents sins of love, but necessarily recalls the frequently depicted dragon whose heads stand for the seven deadly sins. The monster of seven metals, helpless before a special ointment, and the great serpent with the head of a woman, also betray their origins in Christian iconography. Hawes's emphasis on the satisfactory active life is forward-looking, but traditional medieval formulations suggest themselves throughout the poem.

It is possible to find difficulties or failures in Hawes's use of allegory in both the *Example of Virtue* and the *Pastime of Pleasure.* Nevertheless, the over-all messages of the poems are clear, and the very simplicity of content is partly responsible for revealing the form as inadequate or imperfectly handled. In the *Comfort of Lovers* the situation is very different. The form is perhaps the clearest aspect of the poem: it is a visionary *consolatio,* in which Hawes meets his beloved and persuades her to consider his suit. The décor appropriate to such a poem is in evidence: a castle, a garden, two consoling women, extensive use of the lover's plaint, magical mirrors, and special objects of *virtu* are some of the features. So far one can go with reasonable certainty. But this leaves a great deal uncertain, and it is hard indeed to state firmly what the other elements in the poem are, and what they mean. Hawes is apparently protesting not only his affection for his lady, but his loyalty to the Tudor court, while making his own imputations of disaffection. His enemies, moreover, are in some way involved with *calculacyon*—that is, astrological divination; and much of the poem is given over to warnings against

this enterprise, and praise of the truly prophetic character of those inspired by God. There is a strong sense of personal involvement, even urgency, in the *Comfort of Lovers.* It has its aureate moments, and its conventional decoration, but it also shows an extraordinary reliance on colloquial diction, on homely metaphor and forthright assertion. Hawes, speaking of his enemies, declares, 'Aboue .xx. woulues / dyde me touse and rent . . . ' When the attempt to injure him by rumour fails: 'Nought was theyr besom / I holde it set on fyre . . . ' The lady, finding him depressed and solitary, approaches him with, ' . . . me thynke ye are not well / ye haue caught colde / and do lyue in care'. At times only the colloquialism and vigour are apparent, and the meaning is not:

> . . .I suffred well the phyppe
> The nette also dydde teche me on the way
> But me to bere I trowe they lost a lyppe
> For the lyfte hande extendyd my Iournaye
> (ll. 890-3)

Such passages occur in the midst of more conventional descriptions, of lovelorn complaint, or of poetic theory. The more typical themes and diction lie beside these new, pressing concerns, and are never effectively mingled with them. Perhaps Hawes was actually altering a simple love poem to incorporate some new themes in more immediate language. We do have, in a sixteenth-century manuscript, a perfectly coherent love poem made up of stanzas of the *Comfort of Lovers* (see above, p. xxi). All references to enmity and calculation, and all the narrative detail, are omitted. Whether the poem itself once had this form, or whether the compiler of the manuscript was himself responsible for it, it reveals how easily the *Comfort of Lovers* could be divested of its personal and colloquial elements. It is probable that Hawes wrote the poem to express his position as a lover, as a poet, and as a political individual, all at once. No doubt these matters were related in fact: since, however, there were standard methods of revealing love in poetry, and since Hawes was familiar with them, he chose to rely on these techniques for this aspect, while attempting new ones to express his other ideas.

The *Comfort of Lovers* represents a political challenge of some sort, and may also display a real affection, although this seems doubtful. What is clear, in any case, is the new role poetry is to play in the world of the poem. Hawes tells us that his love poems were addressed to the lady of *Comfort of Lovers,* that he stopped writing them for three years under political pressure, and that his poetry has been attacked as disloyal to the Tudor throne. In the debate which concludes the poem, he is Amour and the lady is Pucell (cf. Grande Amour and Labell Pucell of *Pastime of Pleasure*), and the debate itself has many features, even some lines, in common with those in the *Pastime of Pleasure.* The difference is that in the *Comfort of Lovers* the dialogue moves back and forth from the conventional postures associated with the form to personal ones relevant only to Hawes's immediate situation (ll. 820-924). Moreover, Hawes seems to have been aware that he was treating poetry in a new way, finding in it a new specificity. The fables which cloak moral truth, in his view of his predecessors' works, become here veritable predictions, offering comfort to Hawes in his various distresses (ll. 282-7).

If one considers the ***Comfort of Lovers*** simply as a poem of consolation, it is not very compelling. The causes of the poet's unhappiness remain uncertain, and the reason for the lady's capitulation is equally uncertain. The narrative section, in which the hero sees mirrors of past, present, and future, and receives tokens of his worth, is unconnected with the encounters which precede and follow it, except in so far as the poet's possession of the magical items attests to his gentility and prowess. The themes of calculation, true prophecy, and political hostility have no clear place in the pattern of the dream vision as it here appears. If, however, one sees in the ***Comfort of Lovers*** an attempt at intimacy, at personal revelation, at coping with large problems both personal and political within the inadequate framework of the conventional *consolatio,* then the poem becomes both important and exciting. In it Hawes is grappling with a set of difficulties common to the developing Renaissance: the use of convention for public poetry, the relation between artifice and personal utterance, the special role of the poet in relation to the ideal world and the world of political action. Just as the general atmosphere of Tudor England led him to move from spiritual to secular allegory, so his personal position forced him to try to extend the traditional form into new areas, to make it do new things. He was not entirely successful in this endeavour, partly because he seems to have been unaware, much of the time, of what he was trying to do.

Hawes was, as he so often declares, anxious to follow in the steps of Lydgate. He wanted to write as the great medieval triumvirate had written, or as he thought they had. This desire led him to choose enervated forms, into which he was incapable of infusing full poetic life. But while his poetry shows how traditional modes were becoming inadequate, it also indicates the terms of that inadequacy. Despite his conscious stance of looking backward, Hawes was inevitably moving forward, urged on by pressures to which he responded, it would seem, quite unconsciously.

It is not possible to claim with any certainty that Hawes was specifically influential. Attempts have been made to show that Spenser was indebted to him, and certainly the chivalric allegory of Hawes's poems may have suggested the use of this form to Spenser. No definite evidence can be adduced to support this conjecture, and every close reader of both poets will surely doubt a significant relationship. The only other specific influence which has been postulated for Hawes is that of the ***Pastime of Pleasure*** and the ***Comfort of Lovers*** on the *Castle of Pleasure.* The connection here, if indeed it exists, is strictly conventional and very minor. Feylde, who imitates Hawes in the prologue to *Lover and Jay,* imitates the Hawes who is imitating Lydgate.

In Hawes, then, we see a literary conservative, content with the traditional forms of his art, who yet exemplifies the trends which would ultimately alter those forms. He is a splendid representative of the transitional quality of the early Tudor period: his work displays the insufficiencies of the medieval conventions and the unconscious attitudes which led to the innovations of the Renaissance. The poet of the ***Comfort of Lovers,*** beset by difficulties he cannot render into verse, seeking some security in an irrele-

vant convention, epitomizes Hawes's literary position and suggests the typical problems of his era. (pp. xxiii-xlvii)

Florence W. Gluck and Alice B. Morgan, in an introduction to Stephen Hawes: The Minor Poems, *edited by Florence W. Gluck and Alice B. Morgan, Early English Text Society, London, 1974, pp. xxiii-xlvii.*

Frank J. Spang   (essay date 1975)

[*In the following excerpt, Spang discusses the style and major themes of Hawes's allegorical poetry and the reasons for the largely unfavorable critical reception of these works.*]

Despite a fair amount of acclaim in his own time, posterity and critical opinion have not been kind to Stephen Hawes. His name and a number of his poems have survived but neither seems to have been enhanced by time. One of his love allegories, ***The Pastime of Pleasure,*** has often been cited as a probable influence on Spenser's *Faerie Queene.* In itself, however, it has been faulted as a basically tedious poem with a few memorable lines and its popularity in the first half of the sixteenth century attributed to a reading public weaned on bad verse. More recently, Hawes has been seen as the last notable practitioner of the medieval poetic genre which involved the allegorical treatment of love in a highly stylized way. This view has the tradition beginning in France with *The Romance of the Rose,* being translated and developed in England by Chaucer, and reaching a dead end by the early sixteenth century when Hawes finally falls heir to the tradition. By this time, according to this view, it is a thoroughly burnt out poetic tradition having been labored over by a hundred years of poets with neither talent nor vision. It is unfortunate that Hawes's poetry appears at the time that it does because it almost inevitably must be seen as the sort of bad poetry which the Renaissance was to sweep away. If Hawes's poetry is taken within the context of the poetic tradition of the earlier century it appears far more successful than when compared with what followed after.

Whatever Hawes's reputation has been, it has been based on one poem, ***The Pastime of Pleasure,*** which in his time and in ours has been his most frequently reprinted and discussed poem. It went through at least five editions between 1510 and 1555 and has a modern edition by W. E. Mead in the Early English Text Society series. Because of its position at the beginning of the sixteenth century, it is often mentioned in studies of the period and included in anthologies as typical of the poetry of the period. However, the Hawes canon runs to more than just this one poem and places him as a poet who should be of more than passing interest. In addition to ***The Pastime of Pleasure,*** four poems which are clearly by Stephen Hawes have survived. These are two somewhat shorter love allegories, ***The Comfort of Lovers*** and ***The Example of Virtue*** as well as a coronation poem for Henry VIII called ***A Joyful Meditation of the Coronation of Henry the Eyght,*** and an attack of blasphemy in royal courts entitled ***The Conversation of Swearers.*** None of these works has had anything but marginal attention, and ***The Comfort of Lovers,*** which survives in only one copy, has been totally unavailable in any form. (pp. vii-viii)

On one level all of Hawes's love allegories are about the education of rulers. **The Pastime of Pleasure** contains a rather detailed formula for this process. La Graunde Amoure, the central figure of the poem, does become a king after going through instruction by the seven liberal arts. In **The Comfort of Lovers,** the hero is presented with a flower, a shield, and a sword; each of which is carefully labeled as royal.

Hawes's concern with the education of a king not only links him with the concerns of the Tudor family but places him in opposition to the representatives of the "New Learning" who were also pedagogues at heart and interested in the education of kings but in a totally different way than Hawes was. . . . Hawes's educational system is characteristically medieval and in opposition to many of the new ideas. The early sixteenth century was a period of change both politically and intellectually. Hawes's identification with the past rather than the future in the terms of both could not serve him well. The new ideas were not really so new but the perception of them at that time was that they were. Like John Skelton he was largely out of step with the times, but unlike Skelton he had neither position in the church nor a strong satiric bent to carry him through. While Skelton appears to mount a radical attack on the immorality of the new ideas, Hawes appears to be merely old-fashioned. Even though Hawes himself seems to have been the subject of Skelton's furious satire both often take the role of embattled defenders of orthodoxy.

Though change was in the wind in the early sixteenth century, the Renaissance and the new learning do not come upon England and English literature like a thunderbolt. Chaucer had used and modified Petrarch's material but now medieval patterns and forms were beginning to yield to new ones which we see as characteristic of the Renaissance. English poets were starting again to look to the Continent for models in French and Italian poetry and to classical antiquity for theories to support this literature. This is most notable in terms of genre. At this time many of the characteristically medieval and English types of poetry became extinct. At the same time experimentation began on new types of metrical frameworks for these borrowed genres. These changes, however, are not evident in Hawes's poetry. Hawes continued to write love allegories and continually declared his indebtedness to Chaucer, Gower, and Lydgate, the three great worthies of earlier English poetry. Of these three, it is obviously John Lydgate, Monk of Bury, who is most important to Hawes. His devotion to Lydgate personally as well as to Lydgate's type of poetic craft is acknowledged over and over again in his poems. Each long poem is literally framed by Hawes's assertion of Lydgate's superiority as a poet. Characteristically, the last stanza of the prologue to **The Example of Virtue** reads,

> O prudent Gower in language pure
> Without corrupcy on moost facundyous
> O noble Chauser euer moost sure
> Of frutfull sentence ryght delycyous
> O vertuous Lydgat moche sentencyous

> Unto you all I do me excuse
> Though I your connynge do now use.

and the prologue to **The Comfort of Lovers,**

> Fyrst noble Gower / moralytees dyde endyte
> And after hym Chaucers / grete bokes delecta-
>   ble
> Lyke a good phylosophre / meruaylously dyde
>   wryte
> After them Lydgate / the monke commendable
> Made many wonderfull bookes moche profyt-
>   able

Hawes's admiration and emulation of Lydgate places him nearly as the end of a group of mainly fifteenth-century poets who are generally labeled the Chaucerians. This group included Thomas Hoccleve, Robert Henryson, James I of Scotland, and William Dunbar as well as most of the poets who wrote in the century immediately following the death of Chaucer. Of this group, it is the Scotsman, Dunbar, who is often considered the best poet. The Chaucerians saw themselves heirs to the immensely successful and popular poetry of Chaucer. Modern critics have tended to see them as sterile imitators of Chaucer's least comprehensible poetry. It is important to remember that, for the most part, the Chaucer that we admire is not the one which was most admired in the fifteenth and sixteenth centuries. Modern readers of Chaucer tend to focus on the poetry which appears to be psychological while neglecting that which is moral. In terms of his own times, Chaucer's best poetry was his love allegories. These were his most frequently praised and imitated works. The fact that modern readers do not especially care for this sort of poetry is not particularly germane to the question of quality. Lydgate, Hawes, and the other Chaucerians were genuinely popular serious poets who dealt with moral and ethical norms in a form which has its own merits. The major elements in this form are its development of allegory and its use of a particular poetic diction.

Hawes's plots are straightforward allegorical lessons where a character moves through a series of clearly defined situations which are designed to teach him right conduct. In a sense Hawes's plots bear a strong similarity to those of morality plays. The lessons that his heroes receive are always clear to the reader as well as to the hero even though he may diverge from the straight and narrow as Graunde Amoure does in **The Pastime of Pleasure** when he falls in with Godfrey Gobylyve. Unlike Chaucerian allegory, Chaucerian poetic diction is obscure. These poets used what they called rhetoric in order to mask meaning and produce poetic effects. This effect has been called aureation but might be better seen as an elaborate poetic diction much like that which the eighteenth century derived from Milton. The language of poetry is never the same as that of everyday speech. At various times the distance between the two is a great one. In the fifteenth century the distance is great for a number of reasons. It is a fact that the English language changed markedly in a short period following the death of Chaucer. Vowel values changed and the stock of grammatical inflections was reduced, making it difficult to use Chaucer's metrics and diction in a "natural" way. The Chaucerian poets derived a formalized poetic diction which was based on Chaucer's.

Made up of a combination of ink-horn terms and elaborate circumlocutions, Chaucerian diction fulfills one of the main precepts of medieval aesthetics. Chaucerian diction obscures meaning in order to give the reader an opportunity to exert his intelligence in a positive act in order to understand the essential meaning of the poem and thus to reap the pleasure of having solved a complex problem. In **The Pastime of Pleasure** Hawes states,

> The Lyght of trouthe / I lacke connynge to cloke
> To drawe a curtayne / I dare not presume
> Nor hyde my matter / with a mysty smoke
> My rudeness connynge / doth so sore consume
> Yet as I maye / vnderneth a fable
> By conuert colour / well and probable

In the first stanza of **The Comfort of Lovers,** he picks up on this theme and blends it with the love allegory tradition,

> The gentyl poets / vnder cloudy fygures
> Do couche a treuth / and cloke it subtylly
> Harde is to construe poetycall scryptures
> They are so fayned / & made sentencyausly
> For some do wryte of loue by fables pryue
> Some do endyte / vpon good moralyte
> Of chyvalrous actes / done in antyguyte

Thus the subject matter of Hawes's love allegory is the chivalric acts of long ago and the manner of presentation is through the use of rhetorical devices ("cloudy fygures" or "couert colour") in order to create "poetycall scryptures." These "poetycall scryptures" are actually moral and ethical messages which are congruent to those available in Holy Scripture and which are subject to the same kinds of interpretation when they are obscure.

It is notable that Graunde Amoure, the hero of **The Pastime of Pleasure,** receives his formal education in the Tower of Doctrine and the largest section describing his education is devoted to the instruction given by the personification of rhetoric. In sum total, the education that he gets is that which was thought necessary to interpret scripture. The relationship between scripture and literature is one which was seen frequently in the Middle Ages. The main difference between the two is that the literary one is built on the sacred one and must not contradict it. Dante's Letter to *Can Grande Della Scala* provides an ideal tool for explicating poetry such as Hawes's.

The messages of Hawes's allegories are, for the most part medieval commonplaces such as the variability of fortune, the neccessity of good works, and the value of humility. One unusual point in his allegories is his focus on the sin of sloth. **The Pastime of Pleasure** seems to be devoted to this. On the surface, it appears strange that a rather long work of an elevated nature should be devoted to avoiding a vice which might be construed as a minor sin. If, however, the opposite of sloth—Christian industry—is considered, Hawes's purpose is clear. Christian industry, from Hawes's perspective, is an important virtue in a king who is responsible for the well-being of his people. The relationship between the educational theme and the vice of sloth is clear. Hawes is not talking about mindless activity when he deals with the avoidance of sloth but with the absolute necessity that a ruler avoid the indolence which

leads to misrule. Hawes never mentions this corollary virtue to the vice of sloth in **The Pastime of Pleasure** but it becomes clear from the education and adventures of the hero that this is the essential meaning of the poem. Hawes's treatment of blasphemy in royal courts in **The Conversion of Swearers** displays the same concern with the responsibilities of rulers.

Hawes's poems are always in some sense political in that they deal, either in the text or in prologues and epilogues, with the responsibilities of rulers and ruled. Hawes responds to the typical English concern with misrule which grew out of the political chaos of the Wars of the Roses. In this way he is typical of many other Tudor apologists even though the use of the love allegory framework is atypical. (pp. x-xvi)

> *Frank J. Spang, in an introduction to* The Works of Stephen Hawes, *Scholars' Facsimiles & Reprints, 1975, pp. vii-xvii.*

John N. King   (essay date 1978)

[*King is an American educator and critic. In the following excerpt, he discusses Hawes's use of allegory as a means of illustrating the transition from medieval to Renaissance poetic forms.*]

An important example of the transition from medieval to Renaissance, the **Pastime** looks backward to the contemplative traditions of the Middle Ages and forward to the increasingly secular world of the Elizabethans. In literary history, the **Pastime** is significant as the first English exemplar of a new kind of heroic allegory that ultimately flourished in Edmund Spenser's *The Faerie Queene*. Like its successors, Hawes's **Pastime** weighs the relative merits of the active and contemplative lives by means of the ancient iconographic pattern of the choice of Hercules. Instead of the more traditional medieval allegory in which the life of man is figured as a pilgrimage, found in such works as Guillaume Deguileville's *Pèlerinage de la vie humaine* (ca. 1331), Hawes's hero, Graunde Amour, sets forth on a series of chivalric adventures. Although the description of Graunde Amour's quest takes up the greater part of this very long poem, only in his conclusion (ll. 5383-5795) does Hawes make explicit the moral significance of Graunde Amour's quest, Hawes concludes with a quickly paced and exciting series of emblematic tableaus. These allegorical pageants assimilate the rich iconographic tradition of Petrarch's *Trionfi* into English verse, thus placing Hawes's encyclopedic allegory of human life in the universal context of eternity.

The following analysis of the narrative strategy and ending of **The Pastime of Pleasure** seeks to demonstrate the allegorical symmetry of Hawes's poem as a coherent whole, and in the process to offer an insight into the origins of the English literary Renaissance. Following the Lydgate tradition of chivalric romance, Hawes focused the **Pastime** on Graunde Amour's quest for La Bell Pucell. Equating the life of man with this search, the poet uses the narrative as a framework for an allegory on the various ages of man, ranging from sensual youth to self-controlled adulthood. At the outset of the poem, Graunde

Amour comes to a fork in a road marked by a marvellous signpost pointing out two different ways, the active and the contemplative life. After weighing the relative advantages of the two paths, he chooses that of the active life leading to La Bell Pucell. The knight's quest for La Bell Pucell, representing the search of the active man for pleasure in life, comprises the narrative action of the poem. The reader eventually learns that what Graunde Amour thought to be ideal beauty turns out to be only earthly pleasure in its evanescence.

Hawes repeatedly interrupts his story with long intellectual digressions presented in the form of visits to allegorical towers along the roadside. Graunde Amour first meets Lady Fame, riding on horseback and enveloped in flaming tongues. A symbol of worldly reputation, Lady Fame directs the knight to the Tower of Doctrine, where he is instructed by the Seven Liberal Arts who live in emblematic chambers in the tower. During the course of his instruction, Graunde Amour actually meets La Bell Pucell, the object of his quest. But the brief encounter leads only to La Bell Pucell's announcement that she must leave for a foreign land and that Graunde Amour must undergo testing before they may be reunited. After completing his tour of the Tower of Doctrine, which represents the completion of the youth's bookish education, the knight goes on to the Tower of Mars, where he is promised assistance in chivalric combat. After learning the principles of knightly courtesy in the Tower of Chivalry, Graunde Amour finally dons the whole armor of God (Ephesians 6:10-20). Proceeding then to the Temple of Venus, the knight receives promises of assistance in love and undergoes a series of ordeals, including combat with a three-headed giant representing Falsehood, Imagination, and Perjury, and with a seven-headed dragon whose heads represent various impediments to winning one's love. Finally, after an appropriate greeting from Perseverance, Graunde Amour is reunited with La Bell Pucell and they marry on the following day.

Hawe's narrative provides a framework for didactic episodes about the development of an ideal knight who seeks as his reward what he considers to be the embodiment of ideal beauty. The first part of the *Pastime* functions as a courtesy book designed to produce a carefully trained, complete gentleman. In deliberately drawing out Graunde Amour's quest for La Bell Pucell, Hawes leads his reader to expect a resolution in the lovers' marriage. Throughout the poem, their union is anticipated as the source of all pleasure and joy for Graunde Amour. The word "joy" occurs repeatedly, in almost every case connoting earthly pleasure. When the lovers are united, Hawes explicitly identified this "joy" with La Bell Pucell, who greets Graunde Amour with "all solempne Joye" (1. 5192). But the *Pastime* is not conventional romance, and the lovers' reunion and life together are described in a relatively brief passage of fewer than two hundred lines (ll. 5187-5382). And instead of enjoying his long-sought-for reward, Graunde Amour sickens and dies.

An explanation for this surprising shift from romance to tragedy may be found in Hawes's fusion of two motifs that were familiar in various forms of Renaissance iconograph-

ic art: the traditions of the Herculean Choice and the pageant allegory for the ages of man developing from Petrarch's *Trionfi*. During the Middle Ages, Hercules had been gradually transformed from the superhuman but morally flawed demigod of the Greeks, who was remembered chiefly for his twelve great labors, into a symbol for Christian excellence. Graunde Amour's choice of life would have implicitly reminded the educated Tudor reader of Hercules's archetypal choice between two roads joined together at a fork. According to the moralized legend, two spokesmen urged upon the hero the respective merits of the two paths of Virtue and Pleasure (or sometimes Vice). Because he chose the path of Virtue, Hercules developed into an example for moral heroism in overcoming the temptations of physical desire through rational control. Hawes's *Pastime* sets a precedent to be followed in succeeding heroic poetry; noting how all of Spenser's heroes in *The Faerie Queene* face the Herculean dilemma, Hallett Smith observes [in his *Elizabethan Poetry: A Study in Conventions, Meaning, and Expression*] that "the Renaissance heroic poem ideally presented a solution to the problem of the relative claims of contemplation and action." Although the *Pastime* looks forward to *The Faerie Queene*, Hawes remained essentially medieval in one very important respect. Unlike the Protestant Spenser, who gave the active life a role that is at least equal to the way of contemplation, Hawes advocated the contemplative life. Hawes's conclusion explains that Graunde Amour's life went astray in his original choice of the active over the contemplative life.

The moralization of Hercules as the exemplar of heroic virtue was elaborated and completed during the Renaissance in mythographic commentaries such as Boccaccio's *Genealogia Deorum Gentilium,* Natalis Comes's *Mythologiae,* and the works of their English followers. In explaining the fictional surface of literature, both Hawes and the mythographers shared in the prevalent Renaissance concern with the defense of poetry. Responding to the moral ambiguity of the classical myths and epics, the mythographers justified these sources against the attacks of Christian moralists by demonstrating how they contained an allegorical core of abstract morality. Boccaccio outlines this allegorical theory of poetry in the fourteenth and fifteenth books of *Genealogia Deorum Gentilium,* a text widely read in Tudor England. He defends fiction against the perennial charge that it is worthless and corrupt on the ground that it contains valuable truths concealed by an allegorical veil:

> . . . fiction is a form of discourse, which, under guise of invention, illustrates or proves an idea; and as its superficial aspect is removed, the meaning of the author is clear. If, then, sense is revealed from under the veil of fiction, the composition of fiction is not idle nonsense.

Hawes similarly defines poetry in terms of the concealment of allegorical truth through the use of "cloudy figures":

> Yet as I maye I shall blowe out a fume
> To hyde my mynde underneth a fable
> By convert [sic] colour well and probable . . .
> For under a colour a truthe may aryse

As was the guyse in olde antyquyte
Of the poetes olde a tale to surmyse
To cloke the trouthe of theyr infyrmyte
Or yet on Joye to have moralyte. . . .
(ll. 40-42, 50-54)

Appearing thus for the first time in English, this allegorical definition of poetry becomes integrally associated with the heroic poetry of the English Renaissance, culminating in the great native epic, *The Faerie Queene.* In the commentaries to their translations from classical and Renaissance poetry, George Chapman, George Sandys, and Sir John Harington all treated the allegorical pattern of the Herculean Choice between virtue and pleasure as the moral center of heroic poetry.

Hawes resolves the competing claims of the active and contemplative lives through his concluding series of emblematic tableaus, thereby conflating the Herculean Choice with the tradition of Petrarchan pageant allegory [The critic explains in a footnote: "Citing as an example the opening tableau of *The Faerie Queene* in which Una leads 'in a line a milke white lamb' (I.i.4.9), C. S. Lewis defines pageant allegory as a 'procession or group of symbolical figures in symbolical costume, often in symbolical surroundings' (*Spenser's Images of Life,* ed. Alastair Fowler)"]. Hawes could have picked up his ideas and images from any of several possible sources stemming from and including Petrarch's *Trionfi,* a series of triumphal pageants allegorizing six consecutive states of the human soul. Although the entire first part of Hawes's ***Pastime*** bears a general resemblance to Petrarch's initial triumph of Love, none of its episodes corresponds to the triumph of Chastity. But in presenting exactly the same conquests in the same order, Hawes closely links his concluding tableaus of Death, Fame, Time, and Eternity to Petrarch's visions. At the court of Henry VIII, Petrarch would not yet have attained the cult status that he acquired during the 1590's vogue for Sir Philip Sidney's *Astrophil and Stella.* The *Canzoniere* were relatively unknown at the dawn of the English Renaissance, and Hawes would have known Petrarch through his Latin works and the *Trionfi* as the Christian humanist and moral philosopher who also happened to be a poet and lover of Laura. Since the *Trionfi* was first published in England during the reign of Queen Mary in Baron Morley's translation (ca. 1553-56), Hawes would have known Petrarch's successive triumphs of Love, Chastity, Death, Fame, Time, and Eternity through Petrarch's Italian text, Sir Thomas More's "Pageants" (ca. 1503), or through an iconographic intermediary. Pervading the graphics arts of the fifteenth and sixteenth centuries, the contents of the *Trionfi* appeared in countless tapestries, frescoes, paintings, and other forms of pictorial art.

The use of woodcuts to accompany the text stresses the emblematic nature of Hawes's conclusion. The entire poem is richly illustrated, but most of the earlier woodcuts are generalized and bear little direct relation to the text. Hawes's printer, Wynkyn De Worde, took most of these woodcuts from a variety of earlier publications, including medieval romances, the *Ars Moriendi,* and Hawes's own *Example of Vertu.* Although approximately one-half of the woodcuts are linked to the text, it cannot be deter-

mined whether they were specifically commissioned for the first edition of ***The Pastime of Pleasure.*** But eight woodcuts fit the text closely, and these include the illustrations for the concluding pageants. The final lines of the episode involving Godfrey Gobelyve and the ill-favored maid ("Lo here the fygures of them both certayne / Juge whiche is best favoured of them twayne") seem to indicate that Hawes collaborated with his printer both in writing and in illustrating his poem. The concluding illustrations are so closely tied in to the text that it appears that either the woodcuts were produced to the specifications in Hawes's text or that Hawes wrote with them before him. These woodcuts function as a pictorial extension of the text, very much in the manner of Andrea Alciati's *Emblematum liber* (1531) and later English emblem books by Geoffrey Whitney, George Wither, and Francis Quarles. Hawes's ***Pastime*** is an early antecedent of the later vogue for emblem literature in Renaissance England.

The woodcut for chapter forty-one depicts the grinning figure of Death, armed with spear, mattock, and spade, emerging on horseback from a hell's mouth. Facing Death is the figure of Graunde Amour, illustrated by the same woodcut used earlier to accompany the knight's life of pleasure. Filled with disemboweled corpses and skulls, a woodcut of a charnel house illustrates the knight's burial in chapter forty-two. The winged figure of Lady Fame, clothed in flaming tongues, introduces chapter forty-three. In chapter forty-four, the winged figure of Time, armed with a spear and clothed in the sun, moon, planets, and stars, bears a burning flame in his right hand and a horologe in his left. The double crown of the empress of heaven and hell and simple white vestments adorn the figure of Dame Eternity as she emerges from her temple in the final illustration in chapter forty-five.

Hawes shifts to Petrarchan pageant allegory at the arrival of Age. At that point Graunde Amour turns away from physical pleasure and begins to find "joy" only in wealth. Death follows Age, the logical conclusion of an allegory of the life of man. But the knight's soul survives the burial of his body by Dames Mercy and Charity, and he overhears the composition of his epitaph by Remembrance. She moralizes Graunde Amour's life as an example of the brevity and insignificance of earthly pleasure (ll. 5418-24). Hawes has led his reader to expect a conventionally happy ending, but the knight's death serves as a moral *exemplum* in the manner of medieval *de casibus* tragedy, one demonstrating the fragility of human wishes in the face of death. Human hopes and desires cannot survive in a world governed by mortality—Death triumphs over life spent as a pastime of pleasure. In developing this theme, Hawes embarks on an eloquent flight of meditative verse; in contrast to the stiff personification allegory of the romance quest, this passaage constitutes the most beautifully sustained and exciting part of the entire poem. Reminding the reader of the Christian doctrine of the immortality of the soul, the procession of emblematic figures universalizes Graunde Amour into a representation of the life *and afterlife* of every man. With its refrain of the medieval *topos* of "erthe on erthe," a phrase that echoes the service for the burial of the dead, the epitaph discusses life in terms of the seven deadly sins. This obvious *memento mori* places wordly pleasure in an eternal perspective that had been missing during the earlier chivalric adventures. Graunde Amour concludes his own epitaph, which in its continual repetition of the phrase "erthe on erthe" has created a dirge-like impression nicely complementary to the episode itself:

> o mortall folke you may beholde and se
> How I lye here somtyme a myghty knyght
> The ende of Joye and all prosperyte
> Is dethe at last through his course and myght
> After the day there cometh the derke nyght
> For though the day be never so longe
> At last the belles ryngeth to evensonge.
> (ll. 5474-80)

Only now does Hawes explain the true significance of the word "joy," which he has repeated so often during the poem, as he instructs the reader that the only end of worldly pleasure is death. Comprehending the insignificance of the active life spent in pursuit of pleasure, Graunde Amour prays for salvation in the terms of the traditional *de contemptu mundi* motif:

> That after your lyfe frayle and transytory
> You may than lyve in Joye perdurably.

For the first time, the knight understands that the proper goal of man is heavenly rather than earthly "joy." In shifting from the microscopic detail of his encyclopedic survey of the life of man to a universal vision of heavenly bliss, Hawes makes his Christian morality explicit. Of the many works in the *de contemptu mundi* tradition, one close to Hawes's pageant of Death is the contemporary Tudor morality *Everyman* (translated from the Dutch, ca. 1500). But what in Hawes's poem is only one of several concluding themes is the main theme in *Everyman:* the inevitability of death and man's unwillingness to prepare for his end.

The concluding pageants are not isolated and static. Just as Death triumphed over life, Lady Fame returns to console Graunde Amour with the knowledge that he has achieved immortality through fame ("In brennynge tongues he shall be parmanente") and thus has joined the company of the Nine Worthies. Just as Death succeeded the knight's lifelong quest for pleasure, Fame now transcends Death through the traditional heroic consolation of posthumous recognition. Her promise of enduring praise ("Yet my renowne sholde reygne eternally") offers assurance of stability in a world of change.

Although Lady Fame appears to have had the last word, her definition of "joy" is as incomplete as La Bell Pucell's, and the winged figure of Time quickly supplants Fame. He protests Fame's violation of the temporal law that all mortals must die. The sweeping perspective of Time encompasses the central events of Christian history: the fall of Adam and Eve; Christ's incarnation, crucifixion, and resurrection; and the Last Judgment (ll. 5698-5746). Time is the relentless devourer of all worldly things, the Ovidian destroyer lamented in so many medieval and Renaissance works. The pageant of Time in chapter forty-four is the most swiftly moving section of the poem, and Hawes himself calls attention to its brevity:

> And as dame fame was in laudacyon

> In to the temple with mervaylous lykenes
> Sodaynly came tyme in brevyacyon. . . .

This striking contrast to the tedious amplification of the first part of the *Pastime* provides a stylistic example of the relativity of time. Hawes shares Petrarch's obsessive concern with the swiftness of time and brevity of life. Petrarch anticipated Hawes's backward perspective in a letter to Phillip of Cavaillon, in which he commented on how all the dilated events of life shrink away in the face of Time: " 'Thirty years! How time stealthily slips away! If I cast a glance backward, those thirty years seem so many days, so many hours.' " The pageant of Time reflects a sense that time is a valuable commodity that should be conserved carefully:

> Whan erthe in erth hath tane his corrupte taste
> Than to repente it is for you to late
> Whan you have tyme spende it nothynge in
>   waste. . . .

Some intellectual historians argue that this conception of time was absent during the Middle Ages and provides one test for determining the beginning of the Renaissance: "Only now was formulated the new interpretation of time which saw it as a value, as something of utility. . . . It was realized that time was always short and hence valuable, that one had to husband it and use it economically. . . . Such an attitude had been unknown to the Middle Ages. . . . It became so only when regarded from the point of view of the individual who could think in terms of the time measured out to him."

Unlike Death and Fame, figures presented as if complete in themselves, Time announces the arrival of Eternity, who will govern after the dissolution of Time through the Apocalypse. Like Petrarch, Hawes accepts the philosophical distinction between time and eternity made by St. Augustine and Boethius. He opposes the material world dominated by change to the stability of the timeless world of eternity. Although the pageant of Time is incomplete in itself, together with the pageant of Eternity it forms a complete whole. In looking backward at the life of an individual man, Hawes's pageant of Time has affinities with late moralities such as *Mankind* and *Everyman*. But as a complement to the pageant of Eternity, Hawes's vision of Time looks forward to later works such as Spenser's *Cantos of Mutabilitie,* Donne's *Anniversaries,* and Sir Thomas Browne's *Hydriotaphia* and *Garden of Cyrus.* Of the many Elizabethan successors to the *Trionfi,* an untitled allegorical vision by William Smith is closest to Hawes's pageant of Time. In each of these later works, a destructive vision of time and change is transcended by a sequel describing the attainment of true "joy"—the triumph of eternity. Andrew Marvell's "To His Coy Mistress" follows the same basic pattern as the *Pastime,* except that Marvell inverts the theme of *tempus edax* with his final return to the body.

In urging man to abandon life spent as a pastime of pleasure and to look to the health of his eternal soul, Dame Eternity delivers Hawes's *moralitas:*

> In heven or hell as he dothe deserve
> Who that loveth god above every thynge
> All his commaundementes he wyll then observe
> And spende his tyme in vertuous lyvynge

Ydlenes wyll evermore eschewynge
Eternall Joye he shall then attayne
After his laboure and his besy payne
O mortall folke revolve in your mynde
That worldly Joye and frayle prosperyte
What is it lyke but a blaste of wynde
For you therof can have no certaynte
It is now so full of mutabylyte
Set not your mynde upon worldly welthe
But evermore regarde your soules hetlhe [sic].

Hawes goes far beyond Petrarch's simple and unadorned vision of eternity. The *Trionfi* concludes with a tranquil elegy on Laura. Hawes, on the other hand, closes anxiously with an apocalyptic vision. The **Pastime** concludes with a eulogy of the contemplative life and a prayer to the Virgin Mary for intercession:

Now blyssed lady of the helthe eternall
The quene of comforte and of hevenly glorye
Pray to thy swete sone whiche is infynall
To gyve me grace to wynne the vyctory
Of the devyll, the worlde and of my body
And that I may my selfe well apply
Thy sone and the to laude and magnyfy.

Far from being a source of "joy" and pleasure, the world is now seen to be the enemy of man's soul. Hawes anticipated this conclusion in originally clothing Graunde Amour with the whole armor of God, which St. Paul described as the best means of defense in the Christian's warfare against the infernal triad: the world, the flesh, and the devil (Ephesians 6:11-17). Hawes shares this orthodox morality with rigorist works as diverse as *Piers Plowman* (B.8.38-44 and B.16.25-52), "Satire III" (ll. 33-42) by John Donne, and John Bunyan's *Pilgrim's Progress*.

The concluding pageants of Hawes's **Pastime** arrive unexpectedly and transcend the earlier action of the poem. The impact of the ending by far exceeds that of Graunde Amour's episodic quest. It would verge on sophistry to argue that Hawes was a good poet who wrote intentionally bad poetry to frustrate the reader in order to teach him the irrelevance of earthly pleasure. By such an argument, repetition, vagueness, superficiality, and utter tediousness would become sophisticated rhetorical devices calculated to punish the reader for expecting to enjoy the poem and to lead him to the realization that he is better off dead. But one is left with the critical problem of accounting for the success of Hawes's conclusion. It seems that at Hawes's hands medieval personification allegory in the Lydgate tradition would inevitably ramble on for hundreds of stanzas of flaccid rhyme royal. But his naive shift to the newer Renaissance mode of emblematic pageant allegory led, almost by accident, to a surprisingly emphatic conclusion. This strangely perplexing poem captures the moment of transition to a new Renaissance mode of allegorical patterning. (pp. 57-67)

John N. King, "Allegorical Pattern in Stephen Hawes's 'The Pastime of Pleasure'," in Studies in the Literary Imagination, *Vol. XI, No. 1, Spring, 1978, pp. 57-67.*

Frances McNeely Leonard   (essay date 1981)

[In the following excerpt, Leonard describes Hawes's failure to explore comic possibilities inherent in the allegory of The Pastime of Pleasure.*]*

Hawes's concept of comedy seems rigidly limited to one kind of action only: a refractory mocking that is ended by drastic punishment. [In his *European Literature and the Latin Middle Ages*] Ernst Robert Curtius points out that this pattern was frequently used in medieval saints' lives, where the mockery had the effect of blasphemy. So too in **The Pastime of Pleasure,** where the fool's indecency makes the hero seem saintly. Hawes intends to be entertaining, but he serves up a scarcely palatable pottage of physical ugliness and spiritual doltishness in the figure of Godfrey Gobylyve. Godfrey is a professional fool, a "folysshe dwarfe" with a hood, bell, foxtail, and bag, the emblems of his occupation, but Hawes turns him into a buffoon, literally one who *is* fooled. The formal entertainment that Godfrey offers is two fabliaux that center upon the undignified behavior caused by love and climax in cruel practical jokes. Love-besotted Aristotle lets a woman ride him publicly for a horse; an equally drunken Virgil is hung in a basket by his Lady but repays her by lodging a blazing coal in her nether parts and sending the citizens to light candles thereat. Godfrey is more pleasantly entertaining, though no less doltish, when he devotes himself to parody of courtly manners. In identifying himself, he mocks the traditional respect paid to noble ancestry; his noble sires are Peter Prate Fast, Sym Sadle Gander, and Davy Dronken Nole. At the Court of Venus he burlesques the love judgment by describing a witch and demanding to be told that she is uglier than he. When last he is seen, imprisoned in the dungeons of Correction and scourged for being "False Report," he is suffering the fate of all blasphemous mockers. Aesthetically, his punishment seems entirely justified, for his entertainment, like himself, has been dwarfish and ugly.

Hawes is not devoid of a modest comic talent, despite the deficiencies of Godfrey Gobylyve, but he does seem incapable of distinguishing between comedy and what his source books must have identified for him as comedy. At least twice before the Godfrey interlude he verges upon comedy, but the blunting of these passages, coupled with the clear example of Godfrey, suggests that he stumbled toward comedy without really knowing it. When he has Graunde Amoure's pandering friend Counseyle compare the lover to Troilus and Priam, Hawes strikes a vein of irony that is left unmined, possibly because he meant these comparisons to be seriously heroic.

Again, in relating an argument between Mars and Fortune, Hawes sets in motion a vigorous comic action but abandons it halfway, as soon as he has fulfilled his plan to provide information for the moral allegory. The argument takes place atop the wheel of Fortune located in the Temple of Mars, adjacent to the Tower of Chivalry. As one of the secular forces propelling the lover forward, Mars promises him victory in his forthcoming battles. Fortune interrupts sharply, "Aha!" and accuses Mars of presumptuousness. She is his superior, she claims, ordained by the high God to keep the world unstable so that man will not trust in himself alone. Her motivation, however, is not to define God's working in the world but to arrogate divinity unto herself, and so, she concludes, Graunde Amoure "must pray to me." Now Mars says "Aha!" with bellicose force, accusing her of claiming divine powers when in reality she is nothing but a figure made up by poets to express how man creates his own welfare. If man were to pray to her, he would but pray to himself.

The course is clearly marked: the divine forces are on a banana-peel slide from godliness to mindless brawling; but Graunde Amoure, sorely amazed, turns away to his nobler interests. The comic pattern is visible in the fragment, but Hawes's treatment of the scene indicates that he is either unaware of or else uninterested in comedy here. His development is governed by his ideological scheme of providing a definition of the role that Fortune plays in any human pilgrimage. That done, he returns his attention to the lover's progress and so leaves the potential comedy perpetually paralyzed, forever unfulfilled. (pp. 118-20)

[In *The Pastime of Pleasure,*] the hero is not a comic figure. Hawes presents Graunde Amoure with consistent sympathy, something like the Creator's love of man that springs from his awareness of man's fallibility. Hawes stresses that his hero is not only liked but *well liked* by the powers that it pays to have on one's side. He is, from the beginning, assured and reassured of success at frequent enough intervals to remove any suspense from his perilous trials. Upon departing from the garden of innocence and choosing the path of Beauty and La Bell Pucell, he is greeted by Fame, who tells him how to win the Lady. When he arrives at the Tower of Doctrine, he reads on the arras the prophecy of his quest, and he is thereafter promised success or assistance to success by such figures as Mars, Venus, and Pallas, as well as the ladies who come from La Bell Pucell to attend him unto her. In accordance with their prophecies he proves himself an apt student, a competent knight, and a successful lover and husband. Hawes's gentle treatment of the lover arises, however, not from admiration at his achievements but from sorrow over his error. The poem expresses a profound pity for the man whose devotion to earthly glory teaches him to love only earthly things and thereby earns a rebuke from Eternyte (lines 5780-81):

> Set not your mynde upon worldly welthe
> But euermore regarde your soules helthe.

By repenting before his death, the pilgrim has made sure that after purgation his soul will enter heaven, but he has irrevocably wasted his life. The seriousness of his error is reflected by Hawes's treatment of him and his journey. Out of the character of the pilgrim arise the several figurative lines of narrative that enlarge the scope of the poem from personal to universal significance. Literally, he is the hero of a romance, the knight on a quest that requires him to undergo self-examination and correction and to slay giants and dragons before he can enter into his destined paradise. His quest differs from the usual knightly adventure, however, in that it is not designed for anyone else's benefit. He is indulging his own desires by undertaking the perilous adventure, and it is he himself who is gratified by it.

On an equally important narrative plane, he is the Lover in search of the Rose, here represented by La Bell Pucell—literally, the beautiful statue. When he first sees her in the chamber of Music (at the Tower of Doctrine), he is enthralled by love and despair alike, until finally he meets her at a fountain in a garden at sunrise. Their interview is as patterned and slow as a minuet, he pleading and she refusing until pity intervenes and grants him her assent. Even then their love is not consummated, for she retreats and lets Disdain and Strangeness discourage her from loving him. He follows after her, sore of heart, lamenting his estate at every feasible opportunity, and overcoming all obstacles until she admits him into her court, where they are wed by *Lex Ecclesie*.

The perils that he faces enroute to his Lady are traditional emblems of evil, giants and dragons, but each wears banners that identify it as being no universal evil but only an emotional difficulty between lovers. As a result, the knightly quest seems to function like a "clowdy figure cloking the trouthe" of the love story that motivates the quest. Of this double narrative, which so often stumbles and overlaps itself, C. S. Lewis provides a provocative explanation [see excerpt dated 1936]:

> . . . Hawes, stumblingly and half-consciously is trying to write a new kind of poem. He himself believes that he is trying to revive an old kind . . . [But] the combination of allegory on the large scale and chivalrous romance which Hawes wants to revive, could not be revived because it had not existed.

As a result, Lewis continues, Hawes moves about in the darkness of worlds not yet realized. He has neither the verbal facility nor the narrative inventiveness to let the knightly quest run freely, nor can he be at ease with the love story. His basic intention, to prove the error of the lover's choice, seems to nag at him always, making him scant art in favor of doctrine.

In the moral allegory of the poem Graunde Amoure is the student—the philosopher-king—learning all that he can about order, propriety, and harmony as they exist in ideal worlds. In the Tower of Doctrine, he is taught by the seven sciences, the trivium and quadrivium of medieval education, that all knowledge is morality. Dame Grammar welcomes him into her chambers to tell him that verb tenses exist to remind man of the brevity of existence ("all that is / shall be tourned to was," line 560), while the function of the "nowne substantyue" is to name accurately all the phenomena of existence. Out of the word, she concludes, the world was made: "The hye kynge sayde / it was made incontynent" (line 604). Dame Logic assures him that the utility of her science is learning "to deuyde the good / and the euyll a sondre" (line 632). From Rhetoric, in an extremely detailed and tedious interview, he learns that the study of rhetoric enables a poet to write fables that teach truths. In the chamber of Geometry he learns that geometry is the science of measure, or, to be more precise, of moderation and temperance, the basic rule of conduct in an ethical world. Astronomy teaches him the moral orderliness of God's world, laying particular stress upon man's intelligence, which enables him to perceive, estimate, and bring into balance his knowledge of the world.

Woodcut of Graunde Amour from
The Pastime of Pleasure.

It is against this reality, against morality at last, that the pilgrim is judged. At the end of his journey he learns that he has been ignorant, and therefore immoral, in failing to despise "The bryttle worlde so full of doubleness / With the vyle flesshe" (lines 5489-90).

As regards the specifically Christian level of allegory, Graunde Amoure is designated as the Christian knight, dressed in the whole armor of God and trying to do battle against the sins of the world. After he has completed his training in the Tower of Chivalry and has been knighted by King Melyzyus, he is dressed in proper attire (lines 3375-81):

> For fyrst good hope his legge harneys sholde be
> His habergyon of perfyte ryghtwysnes
> Gyrde fast with the gyrdle of chastyte
> His ryche placarde sholde be good besynes
> Braudred with almes so full of larges
> The helmet mekenes / and the shelde good fayth
> His swerde goddes wordes as saynt Poule sayth.

So outfitted, he belongs to the tradition of Sir Gawain with his Pentangle shield, while he particularly presages Spenser's Red Cross Knight. (Hawes is traditionally listed as one of the primary English influences on Spenser, and certainly he was, although essentially as suggesting things that a great poet could do better and not in the sense of a master leading his pupil). Hawes stresses also the role that Christian tradition plays in his knight's quest: he meets the Lady at Pentecost; they are wed by *Lex Ecclesie*. Graunde Amoure seems to spend his life in properly Christian pursuits, but in his death he recognizes how badly he has failed the Christian ideal. Although his soul goes to Purgatory, he laments the expense of spirit that results from not having chosen the pathway to Contemplation.

Ultimately Graunde Amoure is a redeemed man, destined to be a resident of the New Jerusalem, but there is so strong a denunciation of the misspent life that the concluding note is more hellish than joyous. Running from the report of the epitaph through the speech of Eternyte, there is so heavy an emphasis upon sin and loss that it takes a conscious effort to recall that the soul is being purified for entry into Paradise. What Hawes does in the conclusion is reject the secular life as a valid alternative to the religious, for it leads only to debasement of the spirit. Out of this conviction he ends his poem with a prayer (lines 5789-95):

> Now blyssed lady of the helthe eternall
> The quene of comforte and of heuenly glorye
> Pray to thy swete sone / which is infynall
> To gyue me grace to wynne the vyctory
> Of the deuyll / the worlde and of my body
> And that I may my selfe well apply
> Thy sone and the to laude and magnyfy.

By critical consensus Hawes's use of allegory has been termed "old-fashioned" or "thoroughly medieval." Such phrases are generally meaningless, except that they imply a value judgment of bad or dull. There is much about the poem that is dull, and occasionally some passages are downright bad, especially the inset lyrics praising measure ("Mesure / mesurynge / mesuratly taketh") and lament-

Of this journey through the seven liberal arts it is difficult to be tolerant, let alone enthusiastic. Hawes provides some small variety by giving Arithmetic short shrift and interrupting Music with the full account of the meeting and parting of the lovers, but he yields to an impulse to dilate the role of those sciences that interest him, while at the same time he is intent upon stating the precise moral utility of them all. He has, Angus Fletcher comments [in his *Allegory: The Theory of a Symbolic Mode*], entered upon a structural scheme that demands being completed, no matter how dull the product may be.

Other passages devoted to didacticism and morality manage to be more dramatically educational—for example, the argument between Mars and Fortune or the hero's epitaph, which becomes a figurative procession of the seven deadly sins to whom man gives hostel. Even Godfrey Gobylyve serves a moral end, for he provides a direct, if ill-spirited, criticism of Graunde Amoure's pilgrimage. Despite seeming almost sacrilegious at the time, his mockery of love proves a truer vision than the hero's. His function in the poem may be aptly summed up by Northrop Frye's theory that the dwarf in romance represents "the shrunken and wizened form of practical waking reality."

ing pain in love ("Wo worthe my loue"), which indicate that Hawes understood lyricism to be repetitious chanting. The weakness of the poem must be ascribed, however, not to "medievalism" nor to medieval allegory nor even to the pernicious theory that allegory was dead by the time Hawes wrote, but finally to the limitations of Hawes's poetic faculties. Hawes's allegory is not so much dead as it is weakly and mechanically realized. C. S. Lewis has advanced the theory that Hawes completely misunderstood the medieval practice of allegory: whereas the medieval poet used allegory to give voice to the speechless and body to the impalpable—to *reveal*—Hawes defines it as a process of cloaking truth with cloudy figures. Lewis interprets Hawes's intention as being the reverse of traditional procedure, but Lewis errs by setting the two in opposition. In using the simile of the cloak, Hawes is concerned with neither revealing or concealing; what he does is justify the use of fiction by describing it as the outer covering of a moral lesson. Like the medieval poets he is providing both fruit and chaff in order to entertain and instruct his audience at the same time.

Providing the fruit of instruction is indisputably his primary interest, while the narrative exists fundamentally to exemplify what he is teaching. It is the moral lesson that links the Court of Love and the knightly quest so tightly together; it is the lesson that carries the pilgrim beyond the wedding and into Purgatory. It is the metaphor of the pilgrimage, however, that ties the units together and gives shape to the Christian argument of renunciation and purification. Among the happier choices that Hawes made in creating his poem, the best was his selection of the pilgrimage to represent the social and spiritual progress of the Dreamer. (pp. 120-25)

> *Frances McNeely Leonard, "The Pilgrimage of Love," in her* Laughter in the Courts of Love: Comedy in Allegory, from Chaucer to Spenser, *Pilgrim Books, Inc., 1981, pp. 105-32.*

A. S. G. Edwards   (essay date 1983)

[*In the following excerpt, Edwards provides a retrospective of Hawes's critical reputation and discusses the value of his works as indicators of the transition from medieval to Renaissance poetry.*]

A couple of tendencies can be seen running through critical commentary on Hawes's poetry from the latter part of the nineteenth century onward. In the first place, there has been general criticism of his metrics—the view first enunciated by Henry Morley [see Further Reading] that Hawes was "held by his ears when he was dipped in Helicon." This has become a commonplace of criticism of Hawes's verse.

It is beyond dispute that Hawes's versification is erratic. His intermittently successful metrical effects, as in the *Conversion of Swearers,* have to be set against his halting rhyme royal and clattering couplets. But having conceded this, any accusation of metrical ineptitude on Hawes's part needs some qualification; needs to be set clearly in perspective. It is relevant here to recall that it is possible to overes-

timate his degree of metrical incompetence when seen in relation to other contemporary poets. Fitzroy Pyle, in an interesting study, ["The Barbarous Meter of Barclay," *Modern Language Review* (1937)], has argued that the **Pastime of Pleasure** "shows a greater approach to metrical consistency than most fifteenth-century works in this kind [of metre]. . . . I should say that 60 per cent of the lines are ten-syllabled heroics and a larger proportion five-accented." Later he contends that "there is a greater proportion of impeccable ten-syllabled heroics in the **Pastime of Pleasure** than in perhaps any other poem written in the conventional 'mingled' mode." [In his *Chaucer's Prosody*] Ian Robinson has also briefly affirmed—and disapproved of—what he terms Hawes's "deadly balanced pentameters," which he feels constitute a slavish imitation of Lydgate's own metrical regularity. But, in fact, Mead's demonstration of the variation and flexibility of Hawes's pentameter suggests that the degree of opprobrium his meter has received is excessive. While his control lacks absolute confidence and can be maladroit, it would seem that it was probably better than that of any post-Lydgate poet in its use of rhyme royal.

The other general notion about Hawes is harder to respond to since it is less clearly defined. This is the idea that he is a "potential poet," one whose conceptions are not generally matched by his execution. This idea has been enunciated by a number of critics, most notably by C. S. Lewis [see excerpt dated 1936]. Once again, it has an element of justice. There is, at times, a gap that can become an unbridgeable abyss between intention and execution in Hawes's poetry. We often find an accumulation of heterogeneous materials, drawn from different modes and genres, which are placed in conjunctions which appear highly perplexing for a modern reader, in particular because of the narrative discontinuities these occasion. The intrusion of the Seven Liberal Arts into the **Pastime of Pleasure,** the extended debate in the first half of the **Examples of Virtue,** and the episode of the three mirrors in the **Comfort of Lovers** are all instances where Hawes's use of such materials leaves a modern reader at best uncertain of his bearings, if not wholly confused. (pp. 102-03)

Hawes does have much more of a controlling sense in his use of such materials than may be immediately apparent. But such a controlling sense is not consistently apparent even to the most sympathetic attempt to explicate his works, and there remain aspects, of varying importance, that resist all but the most tentative of conjectures. To this extent it is valid to see Hawes as a potential poet, all of whose works are, to a greater or lesser degree, flawed by failures or execution. But such a view, however valid, is not by any means the whole story.

In the first place, it is worth stressing that Hawes is remarkably interesting as a transitional poet, existing in a relationship both to earlier, medieval English traditions of verse writing and also a part of a milieu in which such traditions were being reworked or superseded. The designation "transitional" has become something of a cliché with respect to English poetry of the fifteenth and early sixteenth centuries, a way of accepting and justifying its badness rather than seeking its merits. But in Hawes's case the term does have a validity that can, properly applied, afford some insight into his poetic achievement.

Thus we perceive in his work a use of medieval poetic traditions and resources. He looks to medieval allegories of love, to the exposition of the Seven Liberal Arts, and to such conventional topics as the Nine Worthies, the Seven Deadly Sins, and complaints against swearers for his poetic materials. He draws in style and attitude from his mentor Lydgate. And he shows a generalized consciousness of earlier literary traditions as providing models for his own activities.

Often, however, his themes seek to deploy these debts to medieval tradition in new ways. For example, his stress on pragmatic, practical education for the nobility in the *Pastime of Pleasure* has been seen as "one of the most original" of his achievements, giving "a fundamentally medieval tradition a peculary Renaissance twist" [Arthur B. Ferguson, *The Indian Summer of English Chivalry*]. Similarly, his discussions of aspects of rhetoric in the same poem break new ground and anticipate directions in Renaissance thought. . . . (pp. 103-04)

But in much broader ways his use of his medieval poetic resources is strikingly innovative. . . . [Much] of his poetry appears to draw its impetus from contemporary events and circumstances. His shorter poems, the *Conversion of Swearers* and *A Joyful Meditation,* are clearly personal responses to contemporary circumstances or events. *The Example of Virtue* and *Pastime of Pleasure* seem to be controlled to a greater or lesser extent by attempts to make their materials applicable to contemporary circumstances. The *Comfort of Lovers* remains so obscure for modern readers because of its texture of occasional and autobiographical allusiveness.

What we find is that Hawes is at pains to maintain, both overtly and allegorically, a connection between the content of his writings and the contemporary, courtly world of which he was a part. His cumbersome medieval poetic resources are given a new orientation, if not a new impetus. The observation of [Gluck and Morgan (see essay dated 1974)] about the *Comfort of Lovers* has a wider applicability than they suggest:

> Just as the general atmosphere of Tudor England led him to move from spiritual to secular allegory so his personal position forced him to try to extend the traditional form into new areas, to make it do new things.

Two of these "new things" are particularly important. The first is Hawes's evident sense of the role of the poet, particularly within a courtly society. He sees his function clearly as an admonitory, didactic one. The role of the poet becomes that of critic, guide, and reformer, providing more or less under the veil of allegory a commentary on contemporary conduct, particularly among the ruling class. He provides not so much a series of injunctions on proper conduct as a series of allegorical homilies that modulate between the general and the particular but always retain at least some broad applicability to the circumstances of Hawes's court circle and especially to Henry VII. The willingness to give his poetry such a contemporary appli-

cability indicates a degree of personal courage and integrity when one considers the degree to which personal well-being, prospects of advancement, and even life itself were, in Hawes's case, dependent upon royal favor. Hawes's poetry often reflects the attempt to walk a narrow line between offending his betters and articulating principles and beliefs in accord with his notions of moral integrity.

The delicacy of his position provides a partial justification for the cumbersomeness of much of his poetry. The lumbering allegorical machinery he employs does seek to make traditional poetic forms do new things. Allegory becomes not simply didactic, but admonitory, moving from generalized sentiousness to particular application. And at the same time Hawes's frequent expressions of admiration for literary tradition—Chaucer, Gower, and especially Lydgate—provide a justification for his choice of forms. Thus he is enabled to preserve a delicate balance between discretion and admonition.

It is, however, the fact of his situation that focuses the other important "new thing" in Hawes's poetry. For Hawes remains clearly very conscious of his own situation vis-à-vis the court circle in relation to what he is trying to say in his poetry. This consciousness makes him arguably the first English poet to attempt, on any scale, to turn autobiography into the subject matter of his poetry. This is particularly evident in his final, most cryptic work, *The Comfort of Lovers,* although his sense of a relationship between his writings and his personal identity is evident in some of his other poems. But in the *Comfort* we see Hawes striking a new vein of personal complaint that is unusual if not unprecedented in English verse. It has "a strong sense of personal involvement, even urgency" [Gluck and Morgan] and seeks to give poetic form to harrowing personal experience. If the poem itself cannot be adjudged a success—it remains too inaccessible and the relationship between form and content too unclear—it does suggest a way in which Hawes was capable of channeling his poetic concerns in new ways. The problem is, once again, the failure in execution of an unusual conception.

A similar problem dogs another aspect of Hawes's innovativeness. He is the first English poet to combine allegory and romance, as he does in both the *Example of Virtue* and *Pastime of Pleasure.* Once again, we see him as an anticipator of modes of verse writing which were, in more skillful hands, to be explored with a fuller sense of their potential. His poems are in this respect curiously anticipatory analogues of Spenser's *Faerie Queene.* But Hawes's use of romance motifs is never integrated into a coherent design with his allegorical concerns as Spenser's is. For the quest is never a central aspect of such concerns. He remains much more interested in his static, allegorical, expository set pieces than in any combination of allegory and romance that would yield incremental or evolving significations for his poem. His essentially medieval sensibility severely circumscribes the potential of his innovative technique.

In at least one other respect Hawes can be seen as a harbinger of the Renaissance. This is his sense of the potentially fruitful relationship between words and images in his poetry. . . . [There] were evidently careful, highly deliberate efforts made by Hawes and his publisher de Worde to insure a significant correlation between text and woodcut in the *Example of Virtue* and the *Pastime of Pleasure.* They evidently perceived the complementary nature of the two forms and sought to exploit this perception. Such curious innovativeness can be seen as an extension of the expository, didactic element in Hawes's poetry, prompting him to seek to have rendered in dramatic, visual terms what he was trying to express in his verse. In this respect he anticipates the emblem writers of the later sixteenth and seventeenth centuries, who rediscovered and redeveloped what Hawes had earlier perceived about the fruitful links between word and image.

In such respects it is possible to claim Hawes as an innovator, an anticipator of new and fruitful developments in English literary history. But it is not possible to claim any direct influence on later and/or more gifted writers except in the limited terms I have indicated. Hawes constitutes virtually an historical dead end. Later writers were to proceed by different routes to arrive at the point he had reached and then perceive a clear direction forward.

The nature of Hawes's failure becomes clearer when contrasted with the work of his contemporary or near contemporary fellow poets. He lacks any evident inspiration from humanist or classical writings of the sort that can be found in the poems of Wyatt or Surrey in, for example, the former's translations from Petrarch or the latter's rendering of Vergil's *Aeneid.* Even such a limited poet as Alexander Barclay proved sufficiently sensitive to the new cultural climate to produce the first English eclogues. But Hawes set his face firmly against such tendencies, preferring to seek his inspiration in the native traditions of verse writing, looking back to the triumvirate of Chaucer, Gower, and Lydgate, and drawing on an ill-digested stock of conventional formulae and topics. He embodies a cultural last stand, remaining resolutely parochial at a time when more astute and gifted writers were already sniffing the winds of change.

His style is equally limited. It draws once more, in language and technique, upon the past: his erratic rhyme royal, his leaden couplets, his stock phrases all bespeak lessons learned diligently from his predecessors, but learned without understanding. A comparison with his fellow courtier John Skelton is relevant here. Both began their poetic careers in about the same relationship to earlier poetic traditions. Skelton's first major poem, *The Bouge of Court,* was a dream allegory in rhyme royal. But whereas Hawes never really moved stylistically beyond this, we see Skelton advancing to develop new poetic techniques, such as his use of Skeltonics, which enabled him to refine characteristically medieval forms like complaint and satire to give them new vitality and urgency. Hawes's own complaints remain stifled by their allegorical apparatus much of the time, even though he seems to care as urgently as Skelton about aspects of the contemporary political scene and court life. Skelton can find new and appropriate poetic modes for voicing his concerns. Hawes cannot.

But Hawes is not to be disparaged or ignored on these grounds. Rather, he is worth reading because he reveals the problems of an aspiring poet in early Renaissance En-

gland. We see how a commitment to earlier modes and styles of verse writing serves, in effect, to thwart the full expression of a genuine poetic talent. If Hawes's execution does not match his conception, then the reasons why this is so tell us a great deal about the cultural and social situation of Hawes's time and place.

Hawes, then, is an interesting minor poet. He is of less significance, historically or intrinsically, than his contemporaries Skelton or Wyatt. But he is still worth our attention, for he marks a watershed, the last fling of an outmoded medieval poetic, which he was already reshaping to serve new purposes and occasions. He did not live to complete this task. But he has left, particularly in his most important poem, *The Pastime of Pleasure,* and his most enigmatic, *The Comfort of Lovers,* abundant evidence to justify his claims to serious, sympathetic response from modern readers. (pp. 104-08)

> *A. S. G. Edwards, in his* Stephen Hawes, *Twayne Publishers, 1983, 128 p.*

Seth Lerer   (essay date 1985)

[*In the following excerpt, Lerer discusses Hawes's use of the fifteenth-century poetic device of aureate diction as a means of creating distinctive works and thus attempting to secure a high position in the history of English literature.*]

One tends to think of aureate diction as an embarrassing experiment in the history of English literature. Ever since Lewis labelled it a feature of the "Drab Age," critics have seen aureation as the product of fifteenth-century misreadings of Chaucer and as evidence of the warped aesthetics of John Lydgate and his followers. In this spirit Alice Miskimin, in her recent book [*The Renaissance Chaucer*], considers Stephen Hawes's *Pastime of Pleasure* (1509), "one of the most crippled and myopic of early sixteenth century allegorical poems." Readers have found in Hawes little else but slavish imitation of the already derivative Lydgate, and have seen in his defense of aureation a meager excuse for verbosity. I would argue, however, that Hawes differs significantly from his fifteenth century predecessor in his theory of poetry and his practice of aureation. For Lydgate, words such as "enlumyn," "aureate," and "goldyn" signify the poet's power to reform and beautify his world. The "sugrid aureat licour" which falls from the Muses—or from God—inspires the poet to write. *Endyting* for Lydgate presupposed a two-fold process of illumination: while the poet received divine enlightenment in order to write, his task was to *enlumyn* his readership.

While Lydgate's aureate terms were designed primarily to communicate a sense of inspiration, Hawes's aureation had a much different purpose. Lydgate was interested in the processes of poetry writing—in the relationship between God and the Muses and the poet. Hawes was interested in the effects of poetry—in the relationship of the poet and his reader. If Lydgate was fascinated with problems of inspiration, Hawes was possessed by problems of preservation. He developed an aureate diction which stressed the preserving power of poetry, its ability to make a poem's subject memorable and its author immortal.

Two historical events separated Lydgate and Hawes and were responsible for this shift. One was the discovery of complete texts of Cicero's philosophical works, and the ensuing humanist preoccupation with public service and literary fame. The second, complementary development was the invention of printing. What Hawes did was to incorporate Cicero's psychological and artistic metaphors for creation and perception into the technical language of book making. He developed a language of "impression," a language which linked remembering, writing, and printing as physical processes which could preserve a poet's work and ensure his fame. It is this term "impression" which Hawes would have also found in Chaucer, and which would have given him an insight into Chaucerian poetic and psychological theory denied to Lydgate.

The language of impression developed well before the advent of movable type. To Cicero, patterns of understanding were impressed on the mind as notions or concepts. To John of Salisbury (*ca.* 1115-1180), the images of things were, in effect, impressed on the soul; in this way, sensation produced imagination. This imagery was also to be found in Boethius' *Consolation of Philosophy*, and it no doubt entered the English language through Chaucer's *Boece*. In Book V, metrum 4 of the *Consolation* Boethius restates Stoic perception theory. The Stoics held that the mind was passive, merely receiving impressions from outside as a wax tablet receives printed words. In Chaucer's translation, the Stoics,

> wenden that ymages and sensibilities . . . weren enprientid into soules from bodyes withoute-forth . . . ; ryght as we ben wont somtyme by a swift poyntel to fycchen lettres enprientid in the smothness or pleynesse of the table of wex. . . .

In the *Merchant's Tale*, this psychology explains January's thoughts on his impending marriage: "Heigh fantasye and curious bisynesse / Fro day to day gan in the soule impresse" (1577-1578). It explains how Criseyde's image remains fixed in Troilus' mind: "That in his hertes botme gan to stiken / Of hir his fixe and depe impressioun" (*Troilus and Criseyde*). The imagery appears repeatedly in that poem to offer a coherent psychological vocabulary for experience and sensation.

Hawes develops these metaphors to explain everything from the workings of memory to the aesthetics of poetic diction. It is with human and artistic memory that Hawes is fascinated throughout the ***Pastime of Pleasure.*** In his extended treatment of the five parts of classical oratory, the first such treatment in English, he devotes great length to *memoria.* But Hawes is apparently not interested in ordinary remembrance—what classical theory called "natural memory"—but rather in mnemonotechnics, the art of memory celebrated by Cicero and Quintilian and explained for modern readers by Frances Yates [In her *The Art of Memory*]. Here, physical *loci* are used to retain parts of a speech or order an argument. Hawes integrates the technical mnemonic language into his larger metaphorical structures. He sees the memory as a *grounde* on which *ymages* are placed, and these words translated the *loci* and *imagines* of the *ad Herennium.* His concern is not with fo-

rensic oratory but with poetic narrative. Each image is a *sygny fycacyon* (1255) of both narrative and its moral import. Implicit in this theory is the view of literature as a storehouse of moral exempla; recollection is thus imbued with deep ethical significance.

In his explanation, Hawes preserves the imagery of writing and impressions:

> So is enprynted / in his propre mynde
> Euery tale / with hole resemblance
> By this ymage / he dooth his mater fynde
> Eche after other / withouten varyaunce
> (1261-1264).

The mind becomes a piece of paper or an engraver's plate on which images, like words, are inscribed. When the poem's hero, Grande Amoure, beholds the vision of his lady, he notes:

> But with my heed / I made her a token
> Whan she was gone / inwardly than wrought
> Vpon her beaute / my mynde retentyfe
> Her goodly fygure / I graued in my thought
> (1505-1508)

Her image remains "registered well in my remembraunce" (1753), like an entry in a log. He repeatedly notes how her "goodly countenaunce and fayre fygure" remain "engraued" in his mind (3881-3882). Later in the poem, Grande Amoure describes the Tower of Chivalry,

> That all of Iasper full wonderly was wrought
> As ony man can prynte in his thought
> And foure ymages aboue the toure there were
> (3000-3002)

This passage states a central tenet of Hawes's aesthetic theory and his justification of aureation. Poetry and memory function as engravings or paintings, for they all store visual images. He notices golden images of lions on shields, whose pictures, like the explanatory "scrypture" beneath them, are "grauen" (4287-4290). As "symylytudes" (939, 985), poems and pictures represent figures, stories, or ideas. The figure of Atlas, in one case, "exemplifies" certain moral virtues. But more importantly, it is the story of Atlas, preserved in poetry, which provides that example. Hawes's defense of exemplary fable shares with Cicero a common critical vocabulary in which the terms of artistic representation describe literary processes.

Cicero employed the terms of art and art criticism to characterize a variety of literary and rhetorical concepts, from the principles of poetic imitation and pedagogic instruction to a defense of literature itself. In *De Oratore* he has Antonius express the growth and development of the novice orator in words taken from the techniques of the plastic arts. The teacher molds the pupil as a sculptor works clay or casts bronze, and his words, *limare* and *adfingere,* refer to the processes of filing away irregularities in metal or of shaping a sculpture by adding clay. But, from the student's viewpoint, Antonius shows how he must portray the model through practice, and the words *exprimere* and *effingere*—die casting or hand-shaping in wax—bring out the implicit associations of rhetor and artist Cicero had maintained throughout his writings. Familiar to a Renaissance readership, and cited by Skelton, is the famous association of the sculptor Zeuxis with which the young Cicero opened Book II of *De Inventione.* Elsewhere, poetry is defended in the terms of artistic imitation. Literature offers models of virtue, and readers may emulate literary ideals to formulate their own notions of character. "How many pictures of high endeavor," he argues in *Pro Archia,* "the great authors of Greece and Rome have drawn for our use, and bequeathed to us not only for our contemplation, but for our emulation." Literature, he concludes, surpasses the plastic arts, for a statue offers only a likeness (*imagine*) of the body, not of the soul. A great man should prefer to be remembered through writings, rather than portraits, for, "How much more anxious should we be to bequeathe an effigy of our minds and characters, wrought by supreme talent." In the recently reconstructed *De Officiis,* fifteenth-century readers would have found Cicero's defense of exemplary fable also couched in these terms. Hypothetical narratives, he asserts, present *exempla* of moral conduct. Human laws, too, appear in this language: "We possess no substantial, lifelike image of true law and genuine justice." All we are capable of is a mere outline sketch which imitates models presented by nature and truth. Philosophical fables and human laws thus share an essentially imitative purpose and can be characterized in the language of artistic replication.

Hawes was clearly alive to the resonances of this artistic vocabulary when pressed into the service of literary criticism. The very title of his *Example of Vertu* plays off the old, Ciceronian sense of an *exemplum* as a literary representation, and the opening lines of Hawes's prologue reinforce the associations of moral literature, imitation, and book-making. When, in the *Pastime of Pleasure,* he considers the purpose of poetry as "moralyzing the symylytude," he also focuses on artistic replication and interpretation. Poems are like pictures for both make resemblances. To take one brief case, Hell is presented "in terryble fygure" (1010). Cerberus survives in literature as the "deflouered pycture" (1013). Myths and texts are "fatall pyctures" (1028), and poets "depaynt" (1045) character and narrative. In an extended passage, Hawes links poetry and painting with history, using a classical example received, no doubt, through Chaucer.

> By the aduertence / of theyr storyes olde
> The fruyte werof / we maye full well beholde
> Depaynted on aras / how in antyquyte
> Dystroyed was / the grete cyte of Troye.
> (1077-1080)

These theoretical concerns explain one repeated narrative feature of the *Pastime.* Everywhere he goes, Grande Amoure encounters painted towers, walls, or objects. Again and again, gold towers "enameled aboute / With noble storyes / . . . do appere without" (272-273). He sees a "famous story / well pyctured . . . / In the fayre hall / vpon the aras" (475-476); or "lytell turrets / with ymages of golde" (365). The Tower of Chivalry is

> Gargylde with beestes in sundry symylytude
> And many turrettes aboue the toures hye
> With ymages was sette full meruaylouslye.
> (2959-2961)

When he enters the tower, Grande Amoure sees, "of golde

so pure / Of worthy Mars the meruaylous pycture / There was depaynted all aboute the wall" (3023-3025). What Hawes may have found in Chaucer's *Knight's Tale* (with its painted temples), in his *Book of the Duchesse* (with the room painted with scenes from the *Roman de la Rose*), or in the towers of the earlier English romances *Sir Orfeo* and *Floris and Blauncheflour,* he has transformed into a statement about narrative and poetry. Grande Amoure has become a reader of images and signs. He is forced to interpret: "Whan I the scrypture ones or twyes hadde rede / And knew therof all the hole effecte" (4298-4299). In addition to his didactic instruction at the hands of the Liberal Arts, and on top of his education in the field of battle, the protagonist is confronted with narrative images which he must decipher. The brilliant gold and enamel imagery of these pictures echoes the same vocabulary Hawes had used to describe poetic diction. His language is "Depaynted with golde / harde in construccyon" (912). Like Lydgate, Hawes has literalized the *colores* and *flores rhetorici* into literal colors and images. But unlike Lydgate, who had considered the poet's purpose "to adourne and make fair . . . peint and florishe," Hawes has gone a step further. Painting and poetry share a common aureate quality. In a deep sense, both arts have a single purpose. They are recepticals of history and fame. The destruction of Troy painted on the Tower of Chivalry depicts "noble actes to reygne memoryall" (3027). In the encapsulated biographies of great heroes at the poem's end, Hawes stresses how their deeds survived in written books and shared oral history: "I spred his dedes in tonges of memory," Fame says of Judas Machabee (5543).

For Hawes what makes aureate diction a suitable vehicle for poetry is both its luster and its physical hardness, and I want to explore one specific case of this theory in action. In the Godfrey Gobelive section of the poem, Hawes dramatizes the distinctions between the language of poetry and that of the common man. The grotesque dwarf Godfrey joins Grande Amoure after his excursion from the Tower of Chivalry. From his head to his toes, Godfrey is a figure of vice and corruption according to the standard iconographies (3494 ff.). When he addresses the knight, he spouts forth in the rude accents of his native Kent:

> Sotheych quod he whan I cham in kent
> At home I cham thogh I be hyther sent
> I cham a gentylman of moche noble kynne
> Thogh Iche be cladde in a knaues skynne.
> (3510-3513)

This bit of philological naturalism, on a part with Chaucer's *Reeve's Tale,* reifies the theoretical statements about language Hawes makes through Lady Rhetoric. Godfrey's rude provincialisms stand in sharp contrast both to the courtly discourse of Grande Amoure and the aureate diction of the poem's narrative. Godfrey's dialect becomes a skin of language far more revealing than the "knaues skynne" which he claims shields his gentlemanliness. As an allegorical figure of "false report," Godfrey represents an impediment to the knight's achievement of love and fame. But as a physical embodiment of a mundane language, the dwarf's appearance reveals the linguistic impediments to decorous communication in society.

Woodcut of Lady Fame from The Pastime of Pleasure.

Faced with such language in everyday speech, Hawes seeks throughhis poetry to refine and purify diction. His statement that aureate diction works by analogy, "As we do gold / from coper purify" (916), also returns us to the concrete nature of his imagery. In fact, Hawes seems possessed by the physicality of writing: by the feel of the pen, the touch of an engraving, or the weight of a book. Such an attitude informs his transformation of the tropes of rhetoric into palpable entities. Hawes turns the *loci* of invention into the places along Grande Amoure's pilgrimage; he turns the *sedes* of argument into the thrones on which Lady Rhetoric and Grammar sit. By making the world of words a world of things, Hawes suggests that allegorical poetry, like allegorical painting, is a process of making the imaginary real. He transforms the mental activity of education into the physical motion of the hero's journey, and in this respect the goals of his enterprise dovetail with the theories of "place logic" which developed towards the end of the fifteenth century. Ong has described in detail the ways in which this theory of argument spatialized thought. Mental activity became transformed into physical motion, as the act of finding an argument (*inventio*) became a physical search. In the same year that Hawes published the **Pastime of Pleasure** a Strassbourg printer brought out Murner's "Mnemonic Logic," a student handbook which presented on the page physical systems of reasoning and remembering. The student would move through various places of argument, progressing by steps to mastery of the topics. Ong has characterized Murner's text in words which, I think, pointedly apply to the movement of Hawes's poem.

> Murner's allegory itself is not pure allegory but a device for fixing his symbols in mnemonically servicable space. . . . The chief psychological implement is a sense of diagrammatic structure, strongly influenced by the mnemonic tradition

which is evident from . . . his thinking of his whole book as a series of places moved through by steps.
> [Walter Ong, *Ramus, Method and the Decay of Dialogue*]

The progress of the student mirrors the progress of Hawes's lover. The various places to which Grande Amoure arrives become, in this schema, imaginative seats of thought and argument. The literalizing of rhetorical method, the concretizing of aureate terms, and the attention given to mnemonic theory all point to Hawes's preoccupation with the spatial nature of thought. The experience of vision fixes everything literally on the page and figuratively in the book of memory.

By turning poetry into a seen thing, Hawes restates a fundamental link between literary activity and the pursuit of fame. With the advent of printing, his structures and metaphors are given new immediacy. The meaning of *impression* now moves from the psychological to the typographical. While the *OED* cites a 1508 quotation as the first use, in English, of "impress" meaning "to print," the Latin word *impressor* was early on used to characterize printers. Fifteenth-century colophons record *impressit* as the word for "printed." For Hawes, "impressions" become literal when, at the **Pastime**'s end, he echoes the envoi at the close of Chaucer's *Troilus*. Here, the poet fears not the misapprehensions of scribes, but, for the first time (*OED, s.v.* impression, 3), the typographical errors of printers:

> Go lytel boke I pray god the saue
> From mysse metrynge by wronge Impressyon.
> (5803-5804)

The implications of this rewriting signal an important shift in English literary attitudes. No longer are we in the manuscript culture of a Chaucer or a Petrarch, who could complain of scribal infidelity. Their texts, as Gerald Bruns acutely observes, remain "open" in that they are constantly subject to the vagaries of copyists. In print culture, though, texts end firmly and insistently "closed": once the author has approved their form, they may be reduplicated intact. [In her *The Printing Press as an Agent of Change*] Elizabeth Eisenstein summarizes this new development from one very specific point of view: the idea of the errata sheet. She notes "a new capacity to locate textual errors with precision and to transmit this information simultaneously to scattered readers". Hawes thus calls attention to two key features of print culture and its impact on literary dissemination. First, books can be standardized and reproduced at will; corruption, when it does occur, results not from scribal diversity but from uniformly reprinting a single error.

Second, there is the preserving power of print. Hawes seeks to make "grete bokes to be in memory" (5815) like those of his master Lydgate. He attempts to preserve poetic fame not simply through writing but through publishing; and if he wishes to remain famous with Chaucer, it will be "in prynted bokes" (1337). His arguments counter the stance of his contemporary Johann Tritheimus, who in the last decades of the fifteenth century was busy praising scribes at the expense of the new print technology. Tritheimus claimed that manuscripts on vellum would last one thousand years, while paper books would survive a mere two hundred. But in lauding manuscript culture, Tritheimus misses the point, and he offers a convenient foil for Hawes. The point, of course, is not the survivability of a single book but the reduplicability of that book. Hawes recognizes that in replication lies immortality, and it is in this concept that the old Ciceronian model dovetails with the new technology to speak directly to the Humanists' renewed sense of the pursuit of personal distinction. The greatest guarantee of posthumous honor is literary achievement. The imagery of concrete artifacts appears in Vergerius's *Ingenius Moribus,* in a passage which addresses Hawes's own central metaphors: "With a picture, an inscription, a coin, books share a kind of immortality. In all these, memory is, as it were, made permanent."

The advent of printing could only reinforce this cultural predisposition. Eisenstein has suggested that "the drive for fame itself may have been affected by print-made immortality". What she labels the "duplicative powers of print" are at the fore of Hawes's restatement of heroic fame at the end of the *Pastime.* Hector lives "in full many bokes ryght delycyous" (5527); Joseph's reputation is written down, "To abyde in bokes without ony fayle" (5534); King Arthur's worthy acts are "Perpetually for to be commendable / In ryall bokes and lestes Hystoriall" (5570). Finally, Lady Fame will "cause for to be memoryall" the pilgrimage of Grande Amoure (5586 ff.), and as she calls Dame Remembrance forth, it is clear that this allegorical figure represents not merely memory, but poetic writing.

> Commaundynge her ryght truely for to wryte
> Bothe of my actes and my gouernaunce
> Whiche than ryght sone began to endyte
> Of my feates of armes / in a shorte respyte
> Whose goodly storyes in tongues seuerall
> Aboute were sente for to be perpetuall.
>
> (5594-5599)

In the end, the goal of Grande Amoure's journey, and of Hawes's energies, is the production of a text. We have witnessed the hero of the *Pastime* progress as a student and as a reader, and with our reading, ideally, we too should grow. The inescapable fact that Hawes writes to be printed and read, that he inscribes his imaginary reader in his own texts, leads me to conclude on a speculative note. Summarizing the developments of fifteenth-century humanism, Eisenstein implies that much of Renaissance activity was fundamentally concerned with the recovery of texts and the restructuring of educational systems around reading and writing. The place of printing in such a self-consciously literate environment is thus vital to its success. In turn, any arguments about Cicero's place in this study may devolve not simply to the recovery of his texts in the early fifteenth century or the frequency of their publication at the century's close. They may also involve claims for a post-Petrarchan attempt to recapture something of the essence of "antiquity," a word which Hawes himself uses with great reverence when discussing the production and reproduction of literature. There are, perhaps, two implications to this view. First, as books became staples of pedagogy, education became an instruction in the arts of reading. Grande Amoure is thus a revealing

transitional figure in the history of education: one of the last to sit at his masters' feet and learn by hearing; one of the first to read the signs and inscriptions which write the progress of his growth. Second, Hawes articulates for vernacular literature an attitude already established for the classics. We find at work in his contemporary Politian a new historical awareness: a growing sense of the need to preserve classical texts in classical forms and to edit the text into an edition of historical viability and authenticity.

At the very least, however, we may find in Stephen Hawes a poet preeminently concerned with the concept of literary fame and with his own posthumous reputation. His central metaphors of printing and impression reinforce the idea of printed books as repositories of the memory of the poet's name. His long excurses on the triumvirate of English literature, Chaucer, Gower, and Lydgate, do more than comment on early Tudor reading tastes. Hawes attempts a fundamental statement about the canon of English literature and his own desire to be canonized. For aureate diction to become the rhetoric of fame, it was essential that Hawes find in the newly recovered works of Cicero and in the printing technology of his own day a vocabulary of replication and preservation. If his method and technique still firmly place him in the Drab Age, they also create the environment in which a Sidney or a Spenser could look upon this brazen world and turn it gold. (pp. 169-80)

Seth Lerer, "The Rhetoric of Fame: Stephen Hawes's Aureate Diction," in Spenser Studies: A Renaissance Poetry Annual, *Vol. V, 1985, pp. 169-84.*

FURTHER READING

Browning, Elizabeth Barrett. *Essays on the Greek Christian Poets and the English Poets.* New York: J. Miller, 1863, 233 p.

> Contains praise of *The Pastime of Pleasure,* including a description of the narrative as one of "the four columnar marbles, the four allegorical poems, on whose foundation is exalted into light the great allegorical poem of the world, Spenser's *Faery Queen.*"

Chew, Samuel C. *The Pilgrimage of Life.* New Haven: Yale University Press, 1962, 449 p.

> Study designed as "[narrative] of man as pilgrim through life, in the world of time and fortune," with scattered references throughout to *The Pastime of Pleasure* and *The Example of Virtue.*

Courthope, W. J. "The Progress of Allegory in English Poetry." In his *A History of English Poetry, Vol. I: The Middle Ages,* pp. 341-92. 1895. Reprint. London: Macmillan and Co, 1919.

> Summarizes the plot and suggests literary sources of *The Pastime of Pleasure.*

Ellis, George. "Reign of Henry VII." In his *Specimens of the*

Early English Poets, Vol. I, pp. 377-416. London: Longman, Hurst, Rees, Orme, and Brown, 1811.

    Examines structural and stylistic flaws in *The Pastime.*

Howell, Wilbur Samuel. "The Five Great Arts." In his *Logic and Rhetoric in England, 1500-1700,* pp. 66-115. New York: Russell & Russell, 1961.

    Discussion of rhetoric in *The Pastime* as it applies to poetic theory.

Lewis, C. S. "The Close of the Middle Ages in England." In his *English Literature in the Sixteenth Century, Excluding Drama,* pp. 120-56. Oxford: Clarendon Press, 1954.

    Brief evaluation of Hawes's poetic skill.

Minto, William. "Stephen Hawes." In his *Characteristics of English Poets, From Chaucer to Shirley,* pp. 91-3. Boston: Ginn & Co., 1904.

    Negative assessment of *The Pastime.*

Morley, Henry. "Stephen Hawes." In his *An Attempt towards a History of English Literature, Vol. VII: From Caxton to Coverdale,* pp. 71-83. London: Cassell & Co., 1891.

    Biographical and critical essay.

Murison, William. "Stephen Hawes." In *The Cambridge History of English Literature, Vol. II: The End of the Middle Ages,* edited by A. W. Ward and A. R. Waller, pp. 254-71. New York: G. P. Putnam's Sons, 1908.

    Focuses on flaws in the style and structure of *The Pastime.*

Rubel, Veré L. "Skelton, Hawes, and Barclay." In his *Poetic Diction in the English Renaissance, From Skelton through Spenser,* pp. 31-46. London: Oxford University Press, 1941.

    Technical discussion of Hawes's use of aureate diction and other poetic devices in his works.

Saintsbury, George. "The Successors of Chaucer." In his *A History of English Prosody from the Twelfth Century to the Present Day, Vol. I: From the Origins to Spenser,* pp. 218-45. London: MacMillan and Co., 1923.

    Analysis of the meter of Hawes's *The Conversion of Swearers* and *The Pastime.*

Smith, G. Gregory. "England: The Chaucerian Tradition." In his *Periods of European Literature, Vol. IV: The Transition Period,* edited by George Saintsbury, pp. 24-6. Edinburgh: William Blackwood & Sons, 1927.

    Discussion of Hawes's "historical position, in his relation to the earlier allegorical mood of the century and to the later mood of the *Faerie Queene.*"

Snell, F. J. "The Spenserian Vanguard." In his *The Age of Transition, 1400-1580, Vol. I: The Poets,* pp. 112-47. London: G. Bell and Sons, 1931.

    Biographical and critical essay, emphasizing Hawes's position as a link between Geoffrey Chaucer and Edmund Spenser.

Southey, Robert, ed. *Select Works of the British Poets.* London: Longman, Rees, Orme, Brown and Green, 1831, 1016 p.

    Comments that "*The Pastime of Pleasure . . .* is the best English poem of its century."

Ten Brink, Bernhard. "The Renaissance up to Surrey's Death." In his *History of English Literature,* edited by Alois Brandl, translated by L. Dora Schmitz, pp. 93-121. London: George Bell & Sons, 1902.

    Critical overview of *The Pastime.*

Woolf, Rosemary. "Complaints Against Swearers." In her *The English Religious Lyric in the Middle Ages,* pp. 395-400. London: Oxford University Press, 1968.

    Includes discussion of *The Conversion of Swearers.*

Ivan IV

1530-1584

(Born Ivan Vasilovich.) Russian czar and epistler.

Known by the popular epithet *grozny* ("the Terrible"), Ivan IV was the first grand prince of Moscow to be officially crowned Czar of Russia. The epithet, widely misunderstood to connote "cruel" or "atrocious," in Russian actually means "dreadful" or "awe-inspiring." Historical study of Ivan is difficult because many of Moscow's historical archives were destroyed during invasions by the Crimean Tartars in 1571, the Poles in 1610-12, and Napoleon's forces in 1812. Copies of two lengthy letters attributed to Ivan remain, however, and are considered of great importance to understanding the czar. Ivan wrote these invective-filled, passionate epistles to Andrei Mikhailovich Kurbsky, an exiled Russian prince, defending his stand on the need for autocratic rule in Russia, his harsh brand of justice, and the reasons for his reign of terror. The first literary effort by any Russian ruler, these letters breathed new life into the Russian language by juxtaposing lofty biblical allusions and coarse vernacular expressions.

Ivan was born in Moscow to the grand prince Vasily III and Elena Glinskaya. His father's death in 1533 and his mother's in 1538 left the young heir alone at an early age to face eight years of fierce power struggles among the boyars, or ruling noble class. During this time, as Ivan claims in his letters, he suffered scorn and degradation at the hands of the boyars, who many times neglected to give him food and clothing. Ivan suspected, as do some historians, that members of this class poisoned his mother, a speculation which, combined with the difficult years of his childhood, helps to explain the deep hatred of the boyars evident in the czar's letters and political policies.

Crowned Grand Prince of Moscow in 1546 at the age of sixteen, Ivan gave himself the title Czar (from the Latin "Caesar") one year later, the first Russian ruler to do so. That same year he married the first of his seven wives, Anastasia Romanovna Zakharina Yurleva. Reform and expansionism characterized the early portions of Ivan's reign. Through force of arms, Russia's borders were extended east to Kazan in 1552 and south to Astrakhan in 1556. Possession of these two territories gave Russia full control of the Volga River and facilitated trade to the Caspian Sea. Aside from military victories, Ivan addressed domestic issues, calling the first national assembly, or *zemski sobor,* in 1549. The assembly, intended to serve the czar in an advisory capacity, comprised several elected members. Ivan also sought to protect the interests of the gentry, awarding them land and money in an attempt to create a class indebted and loyal to the czar. He reorganized the military command, providing for appointments based not only on noble birth but also on merit. Scholars point out that such reforms foreshadow Ivan's more radical policies aimed at complete destruction of the boyars.

Historians generally agree that a major shift in Ivan's reign occurred in 1560. That year, the death of his first wife, who may have been poisoned by the nobility, combined with disputes with his advisers on the direction of a new campaign intended to open routes to the Baltic Sea and increase trade with the West, markedly aggravated Ivan's suspicions of treason in his top officials. His fear of treachery reached new heights in 1564, leading to his abdicating the throne and leaving the Kremlin with his family, refusing the pleas of the people of Moscow to return without the boyars' approval of his establishing an *Oprichnina,* or independent state, within Russia. (As the head of this state, the czar would have the right to imprison, execute, or seize the property of any traitors within its borders. Ivan's proposed *Oprichnina* constituted about one-half of the Muscovite state and contained the rich lands of many of the wealthiest, strongest boyar families.) After the boyars accepted his plan he returned to power, but continued to see treason everywhere, using his *Oprichniki* or 6,000-

man praetorian guard to execute many of the *Oprichnina* boyars. Noble families were not the only ones to suffer the czar's fearsome wrath; believing the city of Novgorod to be the seat of treason, Ivan ordered the massacre of nearly all the inhabitants, with the total number of deaths estimated at 27,000 to 60,000.

Ivan's violent temper and fear of betrayal are legendary. One victim of the czar's wrath was his twenty-seven-year-old son and heir, the czarevich Ivan, who was mortally wounded in 1581 when, suspecting him of treason, his father struck him with his trademark iron-pointed staff. Ivan also employed the aid of his *Oprichniki* in an attempt to eliminate the boyars, whom he detested. Yet these atrocities and others do not constitute a complete picture of his thirty-seven-year rule. As early as 1553, after English merchants arrived in Moscow, Ivan proceeded to establish diplomatic and trade relations with England, thus gaining access to modern weapons normally denied to Russia by Europe and neighboring states because of fears of the czardom's growing strength. Trade with England continued, though somewhat unsteadily, for thirty-one years until Ivan's death. Under his direction, Russia expanded its borders to the south, east, and north, annexing Siberia in 1560, and becoming more administratively and culturally centralized than at any other point in its history before Ivan's time.

Ivan's short-lived literary career was occasioned by the defection of his respected and victorious general, Kurbsky, who, fearing the czar's wrath following his division's disastrous defeat by Polish troops at the battle of Nevel, escaped to Lithuania in 1564. He wrote to Ivan from exile, accusing the ruler of killing his military leaders and of torturing many of his subjects. Ivan's initial reply was a 28,000-word epistle, so full of historical and biblical allusions, so picturesque in its language, and so diverse in its rhetorical devices that, as many critics agree, it establishes Ivan IV as one of the most erudite persons of his day. Scholars note that with the responsibilities of consolidating a new, larger realm and simultaneously conquering additional territory, it is surprising that the czar took the time to write such lengthy and detailed responses to the exiled general's complaints. His two letters to Kurbsky, written between 1564 and 1579, manifest a rich pool of knowledge, gained from wide reading in his youth. In his later years, however, Ivan focused his studies more narrowly, concentrating only on works that would support his concept of the autocrat. His main source was the Bible, specifically the Old Testament and the Epistles of St. Paul, which he quoted to argue for Russia's need of autocracy, harsh and unyielding justice, and a ruler unafraid to implement them. The style and language of the letters have been called revolutionary, exemplifying several aspects new to Russian literature: frequent biblical allusions and lofty literary diction combined with coarse vernacular and expletives; a conversational tone which many times addresses and questions the reader directly; attempts at plays on words, and many other variations in prose style. Ivan also used invective, historical disquisition, satire, and various other rhetorical forms excluding poetry. Of his two letters to Kurbsky, the more important is the first, a long epistle containing colorful and often violent language. Pe-

riodically, Ivan's hot temper appears to cause his syntax to slip, the composition losing its sense of sequential arrangement and falling into a haphazard diatribe. But the majority of the writing is so powerful that some critics have called his letters masterpieces; their forceful language, diversity of style, and vigorous expression of the czar's convictions combine to make them, as Richard Lourie suggests, an imperative in any collection of old Russian literature.

The Ivan-Kurbsky correspondence did not receive much critical attention until the early twentieth century. No original manuscript is known, and the letters exist only in copies dated from 1620 and later. Although it is believed that Ivan and Kurbsky corresponded by publishing their letters for all to read, English explorers, traders, and ambassadors who wrote of their experiences in Russia in the mid to late sixteenth century make no mention of the correspondence. Complete editions of the letters were printed in Russian in the early nineteenth century and have been anthologized in readers for Russian schools since the 1850s. Little criticism by Russian scholars concerning the correspondence has been translated into English, however. Most of the existing criticism began to appear in early biographies of Ivan, usually with one chapter devoted to the "Ivan-Kurbsky affair" and some mention made of the literary value and distinctiveness of the correspondence. In addition to literary scholars' evaluation of the correspondence, historians have traced the altering perceptions of Ivan as a ruler; his portrayal has ranged from autocratic despot to, after the Russian Revolution and above all during Joseph Stalin's regime, the heroic precursor to the Soviet state who helped eliminate Russia's boyar class in favor of a more egalitarian society. Articles and even a full-length book appeared during the mid twentieth century noting pronounced parallels between the autocratic rule of Ivan and that of Stalin. Later biographies have searched for a balance between Ivan the autocratic, monstrous tyrant and Ivan the military expansionist and political reformer. Critics have asserted that Ivan saw himself as necessarily both a monster and a saint whose love of country and the Russian people forced him to commit atrocities in order to safeguard and increase Russia's greatness. Some have argued that he was a Renaissance ruler who found himself the head of a barbaric kingdom still remote from the humanistic advances of the West. Taking a different approach to the study of the correspondence, Edward L. Keenan attempted to disprove Ivan and Kurbsky's authorship of the letters, and to demonstrate that their authors' arguments are unclear and illogical. Most critics, however, accept the correspondence as authentic and point to it as a priceless document in the study of sixteenth-century Russian literature.

As some critics claim, Ivan's two long letters lack discernment in their excessive digressions and quotations and their arguments, intended to refute Kurbsky's accusations, and they appear at times less than convincing. But other scholars praise the correspondence, applauding Ivan's effective satire and diverse prose styles which are unique in sixteenth-century Russian literature. The letters also serve as a chronicle of this period's conflict between the autocracy of the czar and the conservative views of the boyars, a contest which fueled much of the political drama of the time. As Jean Koslow writes, in the two epistles, Ivan "revealed himself as both a person and a Czar as no other Russian ruler, with the exception of Catherine the Great, has ever done in the history of Russian czardom. As a source of enlightenment on the attitudes and goals of Ivan the Terrible the correspondence is invaluable."

PRINCIPAL WORKS

The Correspondence between Prince Kurbsky and Tsar Ivan IV of Russia (letters) 1955
*The letters were written between 1564 and 1579.

Ivan IV   (letter date 1564)

[*In the following excerpt from his first letter to Andrey Kurbsky, Ivan justifies his political atrocities by listing examples of powerful biblical and historical leaders who ruled through fear and suppression. For Kurbsky's reply, see the following excerpt.*]

[How] could you fail to understand . . . that it is unbefitting for rulers either to rage like wild beasts or in silence to abase themselves? In the words of the apostle: "And of some have compassion, making a difference: and others save with fear, pulling them out of the fire." See you then how the apostle bids "save with fear"? Thus will you find even in the days of the pious tsars much still fiercer torment. How then, according to your mad reasoning, can a man be tsar in one manner only, and not in accordance with (the demands of) the present day? Are then brigands and thieves to be absolved of torment? But cunning schemings are a worse evil than these! (If such crimes are allowed to go unpunished), then all kingdoms will come to ruin in disorder and fratricidal strife. Is this then the duty of a shepherd, that he should have no care for the disorders wrought by his subjects?

How is it that you feel no shame when you call the evil-doers martyrs without considering the reason for the suffering of any of them? Yet the apostle cries out: "If a man be tormented for his transgressions (*lit.* unjustly), that is to say not for his faith, he is not crowned." And the divine Chrysostom and the great Athanasius say in all their teaching (*lit.* confession): "Thieves and brigands and evildoers and adulterers shall be tormented; for such are not blessed, since they shall be tormented for their sins and not for the sake of God." And the divine apostle Peter says: "For it is better that ye suffer for well doing, than for evil doing." Can you see, that nowhere men extol the torments of evil-doers? But you, like in your devilish manner unto the serpent, belch out your poison, taking into (no) account (such things as) the penitence of men, the transgression of laws (or) the times (we live in), trying with your devilish scheming to cover up your wickedly cunning treachery by means of flattery.

Is this then "contrary to reason"—to live according to (the demands of) the present day? Recall to memory Con-

stantine, mighty even amongst the tsars; how he killed his son, begotten by him, for the sake of his kingdom. And how much blood was spilt by your forefather, Prince Fedor, in Smolensk at Easter! Yet they are numbered among the saints. And David, who was found pleasing to God in heart and will—(do you remember) how even David ordered that "each man smite a Jebusite . . . and the lame and blind and them that hate David's soul", for they received him not into Jerusalem—how then will you number them amongst the martyrs for not wishing to receive the tsar given to them by God? How is it that you have not reflected on this, that a tsar of such piety (i.e. David) showed his strength and wrath even against his weak servants? Or then is the evil committed by the traitors of today less than (*lit.* unequal to) (that committed by) them (i.e. the Jebusites)? Nay, far greater and more evil! For they (the Jebusites) merely hindered his entrance (into the city of Jerusalem) and achieved nothing. But these (the traitors of today), by breaking their oath to the tsar, rejected him who had been accepted by them, who had been given them by God and who had been born to rule in their land, and they perpetrated as much evil as they could, in every manner, by word and by deed and by secret schemings; why then should they (the Jebusites) be more worthy of the fiercest penalties than these (the traitors of today)? Should you say "that is manifest, but this is hidden", then in this is your devilish habit the more evil, for your "goodwill and service" are clear to men, (but) from your hearts there issues forth scheming and evil-doing, mortal destruction (which leads) to ruin; "with your mouth do you bless, but you curse with your heart". Many other things too will you find in the reigns of the tsars. They have restored the kingdom in its times of trouble and they have frustrated the thoughts and ill deeds of the wicked. And (therefore) is it ever befitting for tsars to be perspicacious, now most gentle, now fierce; mercy and gentleness for the good; for the evil—fierceness and torment. If a tsar does not possess this (quality), then he is no tsar, for the tsar "is not a terror to good works, but to the evil. Wilt thou then be not afraid of the power? Do that which is good. But if thou do that which is evil, be afraid; for he beareth not the sword in vain,—but to revenge evil-doers and for the praise of the righteous." If you are righteous and just, why, when you had a burning flame in your council, did you not extinguish it, but instead kindled it? Where you should by the counsel of your understanding have torn out the counsel of evil, there rather did you sow (*lit.* fill with) tares. And there came to pass on you the words of the prophet: "All you that light a fire, walk in the light of the flame of your fire which you have kindled." How then will you now (not) be considered as the equal of Judas the traitor! For just as he for the sake of riches raged against the common Lord of all men and delivered him to murder, dwelling with the disciples and yet rejoicing with the Jews—so too did you, dwelling with us, eating our bread and agreeing to serve us, store up in your heart all these evil things against us. Is it thus that you have kept your oath on the Cross—your oath to wish us well in all things without any cunning? And what could be more evil than your wickedly cunning schemings? As the wise man said: "there is no head above the head of a serpent"; nor is there any evil worse than your evil. (pp. 37-41)

Spiritual authority is one thing—the rule of a tsar is another. To abide in fasting is like being a lamb which offers resistance to nought or "the fowl(s) of the air which sow not neither do they reap, nor gather into barns". But in the communal life, even if one has renounced the world, one still has regulations and cares, and likewise punishments too. For if one does not heed these things, then will the communal life be destroyed. For spiritual authority, because of the blessed power within it, calls for a mighty suppression of the tongue, of glory, of honour, of adornment, of supremacy, such things as are unbefitting for monks; but the rule of a tsar, because of the folly of the most wicked and cunning men, (calls for) fear and suppression and bridling and extreme suppression. Consider then the difference between the life of fasting and the coenobetic, between priesthood and royal power. And is this befitting for a tsar: when he is struck on the cheek, for him to turn the other cheek? Is this then the supreme commandment? For how shall a tsar rule his kingdom if he himself be without honour? Yet this is befitting for priests—consider then in this light the difference between priesthood and royal power! Amongst those who have renounced the world you will find many punishments (inflicted), and although (these do) not (include punishment) by death, yet they are exceeding grievous. How much more befitting, then, for royal authority to punish evil men! (p. 59)

> *Ivan IV, in a letter to A. M. Kurbsky in July, 1564, in* The Correspondence between Prince A. M. Kurbsky and Tsar Ivan IV of Russia, 1564-1579, *edited and translated by J. L. I. Fennell, Cambridge at the University Press, 1955, pp. 37-41, 59.*

Andrey Kurbsky   (letter date 1565?)

[*In the following excerpt from his reply to Ivan, probably written in 1565, Kurbsky criticizes Ivan's first letter and defends himself against Ivan's accusations of treason.*]

I have received your graniloquent and big-sounding screed, and I have understood it and realized that it was belched forth in untamable wrath with poisonous words, such as is unbecoming not only to a tsar, so great and glorified throughout the universe, but even to a simple lowly soldier; and all the more so, (as) it was composed of many sacred words (i.e. quotations)—and those (were used) with much wrath and fierceness, not in measured lines or verses, as is the custom for skilled and learned men, should it occur to anyone to write about anything, enclosing much wisdom in short words; but beyond measure diffusely and noisily, in whole books and parœmias and epistles! And here too (there are passages) about beds, about body-warmers, and countless other things, in truth, as it were the tales of crazy women; and so barbarically (did you write) that not only learned and skilled men, but also simple people and children (would read your letter) with astonishment and laughter, all the more so (as it was sent) to a foreign land, where there are certain people who are learned not only in grammatical and rhetorical (matters), but in dialectical and philosophical matters as well.

But in addition to all this you threaten and menace me so ominously and bombastically before the judgment of God—me, who have humbled myself to extremity in my wanderings, who am much insulted and driven out without justice, who, even though a great sinner, nevertheless have a sensitive heart and a not untrained tongue. And instead of consoling me in my many sorrows, how does your majesty visit me, guiltless in my exile, with such (words) in the place of comfort, as it were having forgotten the prophet and swerved from him ("do not offend", he said, "a man in his distress", for sufficient [is his misfortune] to such a man)! May God be your judge in this! And so bitingly you gnaw behind my back (*(lit.* eyes) at me, a guiltless man, who from my youth on was once your true servant! I do not believe that this would be pleasing to God.

And I do not understand what indeed you want from us. Already you have killed with various forms of death not only princes of your family, who trace their descent from the great Vladimir, and (you have robbed) (not only) their movable and immovable possessions, such as your grandfather and father did not plunder; but also—I may speak with boldness according to the word of the Gospel—our last shirts have we not forbidden your haughty and royal majesty (to take). And I wanted to answer each of your words, O tsar, and I would be able to in a choice manner, for, thanks to the grace of my Christ, I am master of the tongue of our fathers, instructed according to my abilities, even if I have learned this here in my old age. But I have restrained my hand with the reed for this reason: as I have already written to you in my former epistle, entrusting all this to God's judgment, I have reflected and considered it better here (on earth) to remain silent, but there (in heaven) to speak out before the majesty of my Christ with boldness, together with all those massacred and persecuted by you, as indeed Solomon said: "Then shall the righteous stand before the face of such as have afflicted them"—then, when Christ shall come to judge, they will speak forth with much boldness with their tormentors or offenders, where, as even you yourself know, there will be no respect of persons (at that judgment), but each man's justice of heart and cunning will be disclosed. Instead of witnesses (there will be) each man's own conscience crying out and bearing witness. And there is yet another point—(namely that) it is not befitting for chivalrous men to wrangle like servants, and furthermore it is very shameful for Christians themselves to belch forth unclean and biting words from their mouths, as I have many times said before; better, I thought, to put my hope in almighty God, glorified and worshipped in three persons, for he is the witness for my soul, that I do not feel myself guilty in aught before you. So for this reason let us wait a little; for I believe that near at hand, on the very threshold of the porch of our Christian hope, is the coming of Our Lord God and Saviour, Jesus Christ. Amen. (pp. 181-85)

> *Andrey Kurbsky, in a letter to Ivan IV in 1565? in* The Correspondence between Prince A. M. Kurbsky and Tsar Ivan IV of Russia, 1564-1579, *edited and translated by J. L. I. Fennell, Cambridge at the University Press, 1955, pp. 181-85.*

George Turbervile   (essay date 1568)

[*Turbervile accompanied England's ambassador to Russia on a diplomatic mission to that country in 1568. During his time there, he wrote letters to various friends describing the realm and its people. In the following excerpt from one of Turbervile's letters, he relays his views regarding the power of Ivan IV.*]

[Thou] weart better farre at home, I wist it well,
And wouldest be loath among such lowts so long
a time to dwell.
Then judge of us thy friends, what kinde of life
we had,
That neere the frozen pole to waste our weary
dayes were glad.
In such a savage soile, where lawes do beare no
sway,
But all is at the king his will, to save or els to
slay.
And that sans cause, God wot, if so his minde
be such.
But what meane I with Kings to deale? we ought
no Saints to touch.
Conceive the rest your selfe, and deeme what
lives they lead,
Where lust is Lawe, and Subjects live continually in dread.
And where the best estates have none assurance
good
Of lands, of lives, nor nothing falles unto the
next of blood.
But all of custome doeth unto the prince re-
downe,
And all the whole revenue comes unto the King
his crowne.
Good faith I see thee muse at what I tell thee
now,
But true it is, no choice, but all at princes pleasure bow.
So Tarquine ruled Rome as thou remembrest
well,
And what his fortune was at last, I know thy
selfe canst tell.
Where will in Common weale doth beare the
onely sway,
And lust is Lawe, the prince and Realme must
needs in time decay.
The strangenesse of the place is such for sundry
things I see,
As if I woulde I cannot write ech private point
to thee.

(pp. 106-07)

George Turbervile, in a letter to Edward Dan-
cie in 1568, in The Principal Navigations,
Voyages, Traffiques & Discoveries of the English Nation, Vol. 2, *by Richard Hakluyt,*
1907. Reprint by J. M. Dent & Sons Ltd.,
1926, pp. 99-107.

Giles Fletcher   (essay date 1591)

[*Fletcher was an English diplomat under Elizabeth I. He was trained as a lawyer, served in the English Parliament, and participated in embassies to Scotland and Hamburg. When sent to Russia on a diplomatic mission in 1590, he kept a journal describing the country, its peo-*
ple, and its leaders, forming the basis for his book Of the Russe Commonwealth *(1591). In the following excerpt from that book, Fletcher notes an example of Ivan's cruel version of justice.*]

To make of these officers (that haue robbed their people) sometimes a publike example, if any be more notorious then the rest: that the Emperour may seem to mislike the oppressions done to his people, & transferre the fault to his ill officers.

As among diuers other, was done by the late Emperour *Iuan Vasilowich* to a Diack in one of his Prouinces: that (besides many other extortions, and briberies) had taken a goose ready drest full of money. The man was brought to the market place in *Mosko.* The Emperour himselfe present made an Oration. These good people are they that would eate you vp like bread, &c. Then asked hee his *Pola-chies* or executioners, who could cut vp a goose, and com-maunded one of them first to cut off his legges about the middes of the shinne then his armes aboue his elbowes (asking him still if goose fleshe were good meate) in the ende to choppe off his head: that he might haue the right fashion of a goose readie dressed. This might seeme to haue beene a tollerable piece of iustice (as iustice goeth in *Russia*) except his subtill end to couer his owne oppres-sions. (p. 42)

Giles Fletcher, "Of the Emperours Customes
and other Reuenues," in his Of the Russe
Commonwealth, *Harvard University Press,*
1966, pp. 36-45.

K. Waliszewski   (essay date 1904)

[*In the following excerpt, Waliszewski notes the impor-tance of the Ivan-Kurbsky correspondence and summa-rizes Ivan's achievements and failures in the context of Russian history.*]

[In Kourbski's] pleadings we find more rhetoric than truth, less reason than passion. He enumerates his services and the ill-treatment he has endured; he vents impreca-tions on the Tsar's crimes and his abuse of power, on his dissolute life and the unworthiness of his new favourites— such men as Basmanov and Maliouta-Skouratov, de-bauchees or bloody ruffians. Copiously and laboriously, he exhausts all these facile themes, yet never lays a finger on the heart of the question, the complex and deep-seated causes of the disagreement between the Sovereign and the portion of society which refused to accept the master's will.

This fact diminishes the historical value of the document. But that its author should have been able to sting the Tsar of all the Russias into taking up the gauntlet and entering on a literary duel; that he should thus have made his own disgrace and rancour echo far and wide, and drawn the an-cient struggle between past and future, between the parti-sans of the old and new system, between the two rival branches of the house of Rurik, into these narrow lists, is in itself a great matter, and marks an epoch of capital im-portance in the national history. It is an eloquent affirmation of the entrance of the great Northern Empire upon the track of modern life.

By his rank, Ivan might have scorned the offered provocation, and his overweening pride would have seemed to make such a course most probable. But his own temperament, and, added to that, his modern instinct, gained the day, and to this circumstance we owe, not only a most precious historical document, but a remarkable writer. I do not refer to Kourbski. His style is diffuse, confused, and dull. Ivan's is more prolix still; he sheds no light on the dispute, and shows no more anxiety than his opponent to bring it back to its proper limits. His pleading, like Kourbski's, is all one-sided, and he limits his replies and his own attacks to facts and interests of quite secondary importance. Did he have such a boïar killed in church or in his dungeon? Did he or did he not attempt Kourbski's life? All this is not really important. But, still, the Tsar invests his arguments, in part at all events, with that which the other never succeeded in putting into his. Not style indeed—Kourbski's style is bad, but Ivan has no style at all—but spirit, vehemence, sustained energy, words that tell, phrases that hit the mark like an arrow from the bow. 'You who call yourself just and pious, how came you to fear death so much that you sold your soul to save your body?' And he proves his learning, too—gives us bits of Scriptural exegesis. This is a controversy between two learned men! Kourbski has quoted Scripture to prove that a monarch ought to listen to his counsellors. Has he forgotten Moses, then? He has denounced the executions ordered by Ivan as crimes. And how about King David? As to the right of departure, put into practice by the noble fugitive, as to the other privileges claimed by him and his adherents, not a word. The sole political theory the meaning and formula of which the Tsar condescends to evoke and set forth, is that of the absolute power. 'We are free to punish and to reward as it seems good to us, and no Russian Sovereign has ever given an account of his actions to anyone on earth.'

I have already pointed out, and shall again have to show, in the political history of the Moscow of that period, a sort of tacit agreement whereby realities were concealed under appearances, and which sometimes ended by completely disguising facts and persons, and the parts these persons played. These two adversaries, though they crossed pens in public, as I have said, were to observe an agreement of this kind, and, to the very end, to avoid tearing the veil asunder, though under its shadow they dealt each other mighty blows. To defend himself against the mass of quotations with which the Tsar sought to crush him, Kourbski appealed to the superiority of his own literary education. 'You ought to be ashamed to write like an old mad woman, and send so ill-composed an epistle into a country full of people who know grammar and rhetoric, dialectics and philosophy!' the allusion to the publicity of the controversy is clear enough here. But both parties continued to shirk the pith of the question. (pp. 232-34)

Kourbski gained [many advantages] in his newly-chosen fatherland, after having dreamed at Moscow, if not of recovering the appanage of his ancestors—and yet one of his peers, Chouïski, when he ascended the throne soon after-

wards, was to claim exactly similar rights—at all events of protecting what remained of his inheritance against the encroachments of the State, and increasing it at the State's expense; of defending his right to sit on his master's councils, too, and make himself heard there, as well as his claim to yield him just so much obedience as might suit his own convenience. Thus, partisan of progress though he may have been, he remained a laggard, dallying behind his time, amidst the formal traditions of bygone centuries. He had an ideal, no doubt—the political ideal, though he did not dream it, perhaps, of the hospitable country he despised and detested, even though he had come to break bread at her board. But this ideal, anarchical enough in its own birthplace, dangerous and even fatal, was not susceptible of transportation to Muscovite soil. Once across the frontier, it collided with different conceptions and habits, it was transformed into a mere negation—refusal of service, desertion, treachery. And thus it comes about that in the popular legend, and in spite of all the exile's pains to endue him with that appearance, Kourbski's crowned adversary is not, and never has been, the persecutor of innocence oppressed. He is, and always has been, 'the destroyer of treason on Russian soil.' That is the one thing the Russian people has perceived and understood in the drama in which itself played the part of the ancient chorus, together with the fact that when the Tsar massacred or ill-used his boïars he did it in defence of the humble and the weak.

This needs explanation, and for that purpose, Kourbski's career may serve. Most of Ivan's historians have refused to admit that the people sided with the despot. What did he offer the mass of the peasants, husbandmen yesterday, half-serfs to-day, and soon to be utterly enslaved—to these beings whose backs were bent in never-ending labour, bound to the soil, and more and more ground down, more mercilessly cheated, as the needs of the State increased? Yet the facts speak for themselves. Ivan has been sung, lauded, extolled, by the population of helots whose slavery and misery he deepened. When suffering has reached a certain pitch, any change, even if it should increase the torture, is a benefit. In 1582, the peasants of one of the Polish properties bestowed on Kourbski made a complaint against their new master. They had known others, who had not made their life any too easy, but this one they could not endure! The complaint was admitted to be well founded, and my readers may imagine in what fashion Kourbski had been in the habit of treating the unhappy *moujiks* on his Russian *vottchina*. There were thousands of Kourbskis in Russia, and this one was a liberal, a man of progress! The hatred all these men inspired built up Ivan's popularity. (pp. 235-36)

.   .   .   .   .

It is not surprising, considering the lack of affection, and even of kindness [Ivan experienced in his youth], and the perpetual terrors he had to endure, that he should have contracted a timidity which sometimes took the form of want of confidence in himself, and sometimes that of physical collapse in the face of danger. But the man who held his own for twenty years against all the Kourbskis in his Empire was no coward. From the same source, thanks to those who brought him up with an equal care to flatter his worst instincts and offend his best feelings, he drew that scorn of men in general which accident transformed into downright hatred. Taube and Kruse both speak, as men who know, of his *listiges krokodilisch Herz*. Cunning he was, indeed, and cruel. He had been ill-treated and scoffed at in his youth, and all his life long he seems to have sought impossible revenges. He seems to have felt a passionate need of jeering at men, when he could not or did not desire to make them suffer otherwise; a bitter pleasure in putting them in the wrong, and taking advantage of it; an utter and absolute lack of sympathy and pity. This last feature he possessed in common with Peter the Great, and it had its roots in the same cause. Read these lines addressed to Kourbski after a victorious campaign: 'You have complained that I sent you to distant towns, as though you were in disgrace! With God's help, we ourselves are now much farther off. . . . And where did you expect to find repose after such great fatigues? At Wolmar? We are there now, and you have had to flee whither you did not expect to go!' . . . And remember the story of the favourite *Opritchnik* Vassili Griaznoï, who was taken prisoner by the Tartars. Did his master pity him, and take compassion on his fate? No, indeed!

> 'You should not have gone into the infidels' camp for no reason at all, Vassiouchka, or, having gone there, you should not have slept like a top according to your usual habit! You thought you were out hunting with your hounds, and would have caught your hare, and instead of that the Tartars have caught you in your form, and tied you up to their saddlebow! . . . These Crimean fellows do not snore, like all of you, and they understand how to humble you, pack of women that you are! . . . I wish they were like you! Then I should be sure they would not dare to cross the river, and still less should I have to fear I should see them appear at Moscow! . . . '
>
> (p. 382)

Some people have regarded Ivan's propensity to confess his crimes, and even exaggerate them, . . . as a sign of mania or neurosis. This, as it seems to me, is merely a symptom of the actor's temperament, frequent in the case of men who, having every other passion likewise, have that for showing themselves off, attracting onlookers' attention, even to their own disadvantage. Look at Luther, amongst the Tsar's own illustrious contemporaries. He carried his mania for this sort of thing beyond all the limits of decency. And, in this matter, Ivan proved how modern he was. None of the Sovereigns of ancient Russia had felt his need or possessed his gift of speaking, discussing, either *vivâ voce* or in writing, on the public square or between four walls, with a fugitive boïar or a foreign envoy, ceaselessly, unrestingly, without decency, too; for on these occasions he undresses his soul as he might undress his body; he strips it naked, he shows all his sores and all his warts, and cries, 'See how ugly I am!' He exaggerates them, writing to Kourbski, 'Though I am still alive, I am nothing in God's eyes, thanks to my vile actions, but a corpse, unclean and hideous. I have done worse than Cain, the first murderer; I have imitated Esau's shameful excesses; I have been like Reuben, who soiled his father's bed!'

Which does not prevent him from thinking and saying that the man to whom he confesses himself guilty of so many shameful acts is quite in the wrong as to the disagreement between them. But if he cannot make himself admired, he is quite willing to inspire horror, so long as people notice him and pay attention to him. Jean Jacques Rousseau must surely have been trained in the self-same school. (p. 384)

[Ivan] knew many things, drawn from his wide reading, but he was incapable of understanding them thoroughly, or setting them in clear order in his mind. During the first years of his reign, when, the government being in the hands of the boïars, he had long hours of leisure, and was driven to commune with himself in savage loneliness, he read everything that fell into his hands and roused his curiosity—sacred history, Roman history, Russian and Byzantine chronicles, the works of the holy Fathers, and menologies. His memory retained many passages, and by preference he chose those that seemed to him applicable to his own person, his position in the world, and the part he desired to play in it. His correspondence with Kourbski gives us a sort of inventory of the knowledge he thus acquired, and also some idea of the use to which he knew how to put it. It constitutes a pamphlet in two parts against the boïars, combined with a treatise on the absolute power, both of them elaborated by means of quotations which are certainly from memory. In most cases, indeed, the words are not exactly quoted, though there is nothing to indicate any intentional alteration. Gregory of Nazianzus and St. John Chrysostom, Moses and Isaiah, the Bible and the Greek mythology, the 'Iliad' and the legends of the Siege of Troy, which have been incorporated into the ancient literature of Russia, have all been laid under contribution, and present us with an extraordinary mixture, in which we come on names which must be astounded to find themselves in such close proximity—Zeus and Dionysius along with Abimelech and Gideon, Æneas beside Genseric, King of the *Sauromates* (*sic*)—Ivan writes his name *Zinzirikh*—swarming with the most improbable anachronisms, and in which the boldest political aphorisms rub shoulders with the most unexpected philosophical considerations. And yet, in spite of Kourbski, who calls all this literature 'old woman's talk,' this confused tumult of memories and impressions, this chaos of imagery and confusion of ideas, forms a solid whole, bound together, evidently, when we look at it closely, by a thin but always visible thread, which connects it all with one sole and only object, the theory of sovereign power as the author conceives it—supreme and absolute, Divine in its origin and superior in its essence. And little does it matter, in all truth, that the self-taught writer confuses dates and events, talks of the division of the Empire under Leo the Armenian, makes a mistake of two centuries as to the period of the conquest of Persia by the Arabs. His trumpery barbarian's learning is a thing of nought. It is the ideas and feelings that live in it and use it which are important, and when we see the fiery despot juggling with things of which his father and grandfather knew nothing at all, and turning them into arguments in favour of a theory of which they never dreamt, or to which, at all events, they never gave a thought, we realize that a new world has come into being, and that to have been conscious of that fact is in itself sufficient to make the glory of the extraordinary man who, in spite of his lack of modern science, was the first, in his own country, to acquire the instinct, the taste, the passion, for modern progress.

On this impressionable nature, indeed, memories acted like events. To such an extent did they take hold of Ivan's thought and rule his speech that the erudition he had gathered up so confusedly in his mind was a law to him as much as it was his servant; it dragged him perpetually from one subject to another; it suggested the most unforeseen digressions to him, and at the same time the eagerness he threw into everything, like the rage that almost always shook him when he was writing, rendered him incapable of using his knowledge with discernment, weighing the elements he drew from it, and considering how he should employ them.

And though he may be fond of showing off what he knows, or fancies he knows, he is, speaking from the literary point of view, above all things a controversialist, wordy and prolix to excess, but skilled, amidst all his digressions and circuitous ways, in finding out his opponents' strong and weak points, and bent, most especially, on striking home. Kourbski, according to the fashion of those times, was a learned man—in other words, a man of wide reading—and the Tsar breaks him down with his own booklore, convinced, and rightly so, no doubt, that the other will be quite incapable of verifying the accuracy of his quotations. But, knowing him as religious as he is lettered, he does not forget to address himself to this weak point, and we find him calling up a picture of the fugitive boïar helping the Poles to destroy the Orthodox churches, trampling the holy ikons underfoot, and presiding, like a second Herod, over massacres of innocent children. . . . He weeps over the victims and their executioner, for he loves the lyric, and by no means despises the pathetic. Kourbski has said something about the blood he has shed in the Tsar's service. 'And I,' replies Ivan, 'have I not shed my blood too? If not from wounds made on my body, at all events in the tears of blood your treacheries have drawn from my eyes! . . .'

We may agree with Monsieur Klioutchevski (*Course of History,* i.) that this rhetoric betrays more artifice than conviction, more phosphorescent brilliance than heat; but it is an anachronism to seek in the sixteenth century, close to the Scholastics, all the sincerity and emotion the modern soul has learnt, since those days, to put into its external manifestations. As for taking the Tsar's letters to be a collective work in which his favourites were his collaborators, this conjecture, borrowed by Monsieur Mikhaïlovski, an acute but biassed critic, from the author of an inferior novel (*Prince Kourbski,* by Fédorov, 1843), will not bear even a superficial examination of the document, in which Monsieur Mikhaïlovski himself recognises the existence of a perfect unity of style and composition, and in every line of which the author's hall-mark, his personal touch, is evident.

Ivan certainly does not hold the first place in the intellectual movement of the period, and the part he played in the struggle then going on between the moral idea elaborated in the hermitages of the north, and the coarse corruption

prevalent among the great majority of Russians, was neither the best nor the worst. This conflict had brought two eccentric types face to face and into bitter conflict. There were solitary ascetics on one side and heroic bandits on the other, and both classes lived on the outer margin of society. Ivan remained in the middle. Highly gifted as he was, his mind was not sufficiently ripened by study, nor, above all, was his soul so filled with generous impulses, as to enable him to represent the noblest tendencies of a chosen few. He went to the *Stoglav* firmly intending to support the reform party, and he failed to adhere to his intention, less from lack of energy than from want of conviction. In religious matters he continued, at heart, to belong to the old school, in which the wearing of the full beard and of the *odnoriadka*—a garment recently recalled to honour— were matters of doctrine. Nil Sorski's teachings glided over his intelligence, but never reached his conscience. And, on the other hand, he possessed no means of initiating himself into the wider intellectual currents of Europe, whether in the domain of science or in that of art. Europe was still too far away, and Russia too far behind the West. Ivan turned his mind to the most pressing matters, and those easiest of accomplishment. What he asked his neighbours to give him was *results*—engineers, artisans, printers. This is the course generally pursued by backward peoples anxious to make up for lost time. Look at Japan. In this fashion, too, artificial and superficial civilizations are attained. Modern Russia is an example of this even in the present day.

The detractors of Ivan the Terrible have gone the length of refusing him any originality at all, declaring all he did was to walk, and rather clumsily at that, in the rut his grandfather had cut for him, defend old theories against literary attack on the part of the opposition party, and turn over ideas drawn from the books he had read. The historic prerogatives of the *Boïarchtchina* were already broken down, the appeal to the new strata of society had begun, the attempts to reorganize the communes on the autonomic principle were nothing but a return to the older form of these institutions, and Ivan, even in his conception of the part he was personally called to play, simply drew his inspiration from the teachings of Holy Writ. These over-severe judges seem to me to forget that it takes something to make anything, and that Napoleon did not find the elements of his Code in his own brain. Besides, they graciously grant the great value of the reforms carried out in the early years of Ivan's reign, though they give all the credit for them to the men who were about the Sovereign. Have they taken the trouble of reading the thirty-seven proposals as to the reorganization of the Church, and the ten proposals or rough drafts of laws, for the organization of the State? If so, they should have realized that the man who wrote these pages was the man who corresponded with Kourbski at a period when Adachev and Sylvester were both far away. In both cases the spirit and style are identical, and that style is most personal in its nature. Adachev, Sylvester, and Kourbski certainly had no hand in the *Opritchnina,* and yet the *Opritchnina* and the reforms of the year 1551 together form one complete whole. . . . And it is because Ivan's biographers could not understand what the *Opritchnina* was that they have refused to grant him what they have granted to his fellow-workers. Peter the Great was never deceived in this matter.

Ivan was the first of the Russian Tsars, not only because he was the first to assume the title, but also and especially because he was the first to comprehend the realities corresponding with it. The theory was there, no doubt, and had been worked out, ever since the fifteenth century, in the literature of the country. But neither to Vassili nor to Ivan III.—the Great—had it occurred to lay hold of the concrete meaning of that theory—the idea of a Sovereign whose power came to him from God, and who was responsible to God alone for the way in which he used it, unaided, as the sole representative of the Divine will and the Divine wisdom, on whom no human assistance could be imposed, and who could not accept any control whatever.

To this theory Ivan added a personal commentary of his own of which none of his predecessors had thought, and which none of his successors were to adopt. Peter the Great was to regard himself merely as the first servant of the State; Ivan regarded the Sovereign's person as a kind of Divine essence, and boldly set it far above the State. 'We know,' he writes, after pouring abuse on Batory, 'what is due to the majesty of Princes. But the Empire is majesty, and above that majesty stands the Sovereign in his Empire, and the Sovereign is above the Empire!' (Note handed to Possevino in September, 1581, *Historical Documents,* x.). Poland had won the day, and Muscovy was forced into submission. But the Tsar set himself above this necessity—he hovered in higher space, where no such outrage could reach him. The idea is a subtle one, but it is a feeling rather than an idea. Ivan's ideas and feelings have often been confused together, and a short analysis must be devoted to them.

Ivan the Terrible went through a great deal of suffering, and these sufferings, which he exaggerated as he exaggerated everything, have been rightly ascribed to a twofold moral cause—to his very lively consciousness of all the faults and vices of the political and social organization over which he had been called to rule, and an equally painful consciousness of his powerlessness to apply any efficacious remedy to them. This painful sensation was repeated in his own consciousness, in the midst of the personal weaknesses of which he recognised the shamefulness, and the useless acknowledgment of which he was perpetually multiplying. But it is a mistake, in the first place, to take all this for an exceptional case of self-distrust. It is the eternal history of the human race before Medea's *video meliora proboque,* and after it, for ever and ever. Historians of the school of George Samarine are certainly mistaken when they take Ivan to be a man who lived lonely and misunderstood. He alone, according to their theory, recognised that the habits of his period were full of terrifying symptoms of decomposition and awful omens for the future, and, finding nobody would share his scorn and hate of all these things, he grew so bitter in his loneliness that he struck out blindly at everything around him, because he did not know how to separate the evil from the good, either in himself or his surroundings, and also because his will was not so strong as his intellectual superiority was great. This judgment wrongs the Sovereign and his period.

Ivan knew and frequented the company of men far more capable than himself of conceiving the necessity, and also the conditions, for a renovation of morals. In this particular the disciples of Nil Sorski aimed at a much higher ideal than his. On the other hand, the Tsar, in his struggle with his boïars, knew right well what he was doing, and the objects at which his blows were struck. To represent him, as Bestoujev-Rioumine has represented him, as a sort of Hamlet, constitutionally inclined to abstract reflection, and stumbling hither and thither at every step the moment he entered the world of realities, is an historical absurdity. The *Opritchnina* was not an abstract idea, and Hamlet would certainly have been quite incapable of playing the most delicate of games with the most finished diplomatists of his time.

Ivan had a will of his own. Some people have thought they perceived a proof of the weakness of his will in the instruments he chose to carry out his plans—instruments which he constantly destroyed because he could not find suitable ones, and which he nevertheless replaced, because, being himself unable to give form to his own ideas, he could not do without them—a man of meditation, not of action, a theorist, an artist too, who could conceive what was good and beautiful, but had not the skill to pass from conception to realities; and a man, also, who sought sensation and picturesque effect even in the horrors of the torture-chamber. . . . This is the theory put forward by Constantine Akssakov. It seems to admit the possibility, for the head of a State, of doing everything himself. In this even Peter the Great could not succeed, and he has been blamed, with some show of justice, for having lost himself in details. The great man could not find enough helpers. Ivan's helpers were inadequate, like Biélski, or vile, like Skouratov; but he set to work in his own person, and put his own hand to the task, oftener, indeed, than he should have done.

Like Peter the Great, again, he was a carrier on of a previous work. He followed in his grandfather's footsteps, and was, like him, the champion of similar interests—moral, intellectual, social, and more especially political—in the struggle between the future and the past. He brought in a few new ideas, but more particularly some new weapons, of his own. Ivan III. had fought in silence, with an axe. Ivan IV., true to his own period, did not, indeed, put the axe back into its bear-skin sheath, but he supplemented the labours of the executioner by the action of his economic reforms and of the power of speech. Was he not bound to speak, since men's tongues were wagging all round him? Silence was to fall once more, when the theory of the absolute and despotic power had triumphed, and the Empire was subject to its rule; and no faint echo of Kourbski's bold clamour was to rise till Europe witnessed the coming of another epoch of revolutionary disturbance, and heard the voice of Radichtchev. But Ivan, in the sixteenth century, could do no less than follow the impulse which prompted every intellectual being, even in Russia, to discourse.

Yet, contrary to the general opinion, he proved himself much stronger in practice than in theory; for though within the borders of his own country he maintained his adopted programme against every Kourbski of them, and carried it to its logical conclusion, and though, outside them, he yielded to nothing but Batory's genius and the good fortune which attended it, his ideas, both as to politics and religion, frequently strike us as vague, confused, and unsettled, and his powers of reflection by no means correspond with the power of his instinct, which is extraordinarily sure, as a rule. He is instinctively inclined to depend on the masses of the population, and yet he gives over his peasants to be squeezed by his 'men who serve.' Devout as he is—a fortnight after his marriage in 1547 he makes a pilgrimage to the Troïtsa, and goes the whole way on foot, in spite of the bitter cold—and deeply convinced of the excellence of his form of religion, as his discussions with Possevino and Rokita prove, he frequently gives vent to sallies savouring strongly of free-thought. On other occasions he shows a tolerance which does not seem to be founded on any principle, for it is intermittent and opportunist. The Protestants had an experience of this when they were first permitted to build two churches at Moscow, and then vilely maltreated after they were built. (pp. 386-92)

Ivan's exceedingly personal conception of his part and way of playing it, his impetuous vigour of action, his exuberant mimicry, his fulness of gesture and redundance of language, have built up the illusion as to his having been a sort of *hero-Cossack,* out of the cycle of Ilia of Mourom. It must be admitted, indeed, that this cycle was only definitely closed in Russia by the reforms of the eighteenth century, and that up till that date the existence of the race ruled by Peter the Great was spent in a series of exploits, and lulled by the harmonious chantings of its rustic bards. Ivan shares with Ilia of Mourom that quality of humour which still exists in the national temperament, and his fits of furious rage. But the Tsar's psychology is far the more complicated of the two. Behind the external mask which imparts a family resemblance to these figures, and in spite of the dreamy quality common to both, we note, in Ivan's case, a great depth of realism. After he passed away, leaving his iron sceptre in feeble hands, and carrying the secret of his all-powerfulness with him into his grave, his people was to sing on, and dream on, for another century. But he had shaken it rudely once, and his life had narrowed the space available for heroes who would not wake out of their dreams and take their place amongst realities, in the hierarchy, under discipline. Such as they had better flee to the Ukraine.

Imagination held a great place in the moral existence of the man we are now studying, and in this there is an essential difference between Ivan and Peter the Great, one of the most positive intelligences the world has ever known. He is also distinguished from his great successor by his very high opinion of his own powers, which is most curiously mingled with that distrust of himself and others of which he was never to rid himself. Peter, like that builder up of a colossal American fortune whom a reporter lately questioned as to the talents to which he owed his success, would have readily affirmed, 'Talents? I have none at all! I work—I work myself to death, and that is all!' Ivan thought he had a great many talents, if not every one. He represented a race of foreign conquerors, and in this very

fact of his origin he recognised an element of personal superiority. In Peter the Great we see the consciousness and pride of a *common* nationality strongly developed. As to certain sides of his temperament, the Reformer was of the populace, and was proud of it, and he would never have said, when handing over some ingots of gold to a foreign workman, 'See well to the weight, for all Russians are thieves!' Ivan frequently made speeches of this kind. (pp. 393-94)

The massacres ordered by Ivan have been notoriously exaggerated by his enemies and his detractors, the first egging on the second. Kourbski mentions the *entire destruction* of families—such as the Kolytchev, the Zabolotski, the Odiévski, the Vorotynski—all of which appear in the inventories of the following century. The gaps created in the ranks of the aristocracy by emigration were certainly much larger, and even so they were not entirely emptied. Ivan's conduct in this particular was not dictated by any fixed principle, and he himself endeavoured to ensure the future of three great houses—the Mstislavski, the Glinski, and the Romanov—whose fidelity seemed guaranteed by lack of connections in the country, by a material state of dependence, or by family relationships. The two first-named families had just arrived from Lithuania, and the last was related to the Sovereign's own house.

The principal factors in the weakening of the aristocratic element were economic causes and political measures. In the course of the sixteenth century, as a result of the condition of debt to which everybody had been reduced, landed property began to crumble away of itself in the boïars' hands. (pp. 394-95)

Now, this financial distress amongst the great families was the direct consequence of the new political system, and the obligations it had cast upon them. Universal service implied residence at Court, or near it, even if it did not imply active military service or the performance of some official function or other. When the nobles had lived on their family properties they had found it hard enough to draw a scanty income from them. Once they left them, they were very soon ruined. Thereupon came the *Oprichnina*—that is to say, wholesale dispossession . . .—and this dealt the position, economic and political, of the persons concerned its death-blow. Ivan's system of guarantees increased the effect of emigration twofold—nay, a hundredfold, seeing that for every fugitive there were from ten to a hundred persons who had to pay for him. Except for the Stroganovs, you will not find a single instance of a large fortune in the aristocratic class which escaped this other form of massacre. (p. 395)

And thus a class which already differed from the Western aristocracies, in that the feudal principle was entirely absent from it, was completely and democratically levelled. The hierarchy of the service did indeed create new titles and fresh prerogatives, guaranteed by the *miéstnitchestvo,* but these were not corporative elements in the Western signification of the term. They rather tended to break up the family and reduce it to atoms, on which the hold of the absolute power continued, and grew perpetually stronger.

This revolution, which had seemed destined to benefit the popular element, brought it nothing but the bitterest fruit. The new system was a house of two stories, both built on the same plan. The officials were upstairs, the serfs below, and slavery everywhere. But in this matter all Ivan the Terrible did was to complete or carry on that which had been the Moscow programme for two centuries past, and the *Oprritchnina* itself was no more than an extension of the policy applied by the Tsar's predecessors to all their conquered towns and territories. It was a sort of colonization backwards. As to colonization in the normal direction, it continued to depend on private enterprise; but Ivan opened a wider field for it.

Westwards his expansive policy failed. It would not be just to cast all the responsibility for this on him. If Peter the Great, when he took the same road 150 years later, had found his way barred by a man like Batory, instead of by a madman like Charles XII., the result of the Battle of Poltava might have been very different. Eastward, Kazan, Astrakan, and Siberia make up a noble score in Ivan's favour.

From the economic point of view, the conquest of Kazan did not result in the immediate advantages that might have been expected from it. The trade of that place, which the Tartars had exaggerated in their desire to induce the Sultan to retake possession of the town, was a disappointment to the English merchants. Ivan did not fail to seek compensation elsewhere. When he offered the Swedish traders a free passage through his dominions, even for going to India, he stipulated for a similar privilege for his own subjects, in their enterprises, existing or to be undertaken, with Lübeck and even with Spain. In 1567 the chroniclers mention the departure of Russian merchants for Antwerp and London, and in 1568 English authorities mention the presence on the banks of the Thames of two such Muscovites, Tviérdikov and Pogoriélov, who were taken to be Ambassadors. They performed both offices, no doubt, and devoted their endeavours partly to diplomacy and partly to mercantile affairs.

The development of industry in Ivan's time was rather superficial; the field was widened by the annexation of the eastern provinces. The acquisition of the Lower Volga favoured the development of fisheries. There were ninety-nine establishments of this kind at Péréiaslavl in 1562. After the occupation of the banks of the Kama by the Stroganovs, and the discovery of salt-mines near Astrakan, the salt-works there attained great importance.

Ivan's financial policy does not call for praise. It may be summed up as a series of expedients, all savouring more or less of robbery. Fletcher mentions several of these. Governors of provinces were treated with the utmost tolerance till they had gorged themselves with plunder, when they were forced to give up the spoil. The same system was applied to monasteries, which were allowed to heap up wealth in the same way. There were temporary seizures or monopolies of certain forms of produce or merchandise, thus made to bring in very large profits. Fines were imposed on officials for imaginary offences. The English diplomat tells an almost incredible story about a capful of *live flies* demanded in this way from the Moscow municipality.

The taxes themselves were managed in the most senseless manner that could have been devised. Generally speaking, every fresh need resulted in the imposition of a fresh tax, and there never was the smallest care as to fitting the burdens to the means of those who had to bear them, nor the slightest prudence as to killing the goose that laid the golden eggs. By the time the end of the reign was reached, the bird's laying-powers were very nearly exhausted.

The interests best served by the conquest of Kazan and Astrakan were those of the Church, whose borders were thus enlarged. Gourii, first Archbishop of Kazan, made a good many converts among the Tartars; but this triumph of orthodox proselytism was counterbalanced, till the close of Ivan's reign, by the prolonged resistance of the paganism still existing in the interior of his dominions, and especially in certain districts in the province of Novgorod. As to the Tsar's attempts at religious reform, which he soon abandoned or only carried on in a most perfunctory fashion, they produced no appreciable result at all, and the intellectual and moral condition of the clergy was in no way altered by them.

Yet, from a more general point of view, there was a visible increase in the intellectual life of the country. Though the schools planned in 1551 never were anything but plans, though printing did not get beyond the stage of rudimentary attempt, the author of the letters to Kourbski did none the less witness a certain upward trend of ideas, which took their flight out of the narrow walls of the cloister and the confined circle of religious discussion into the world of secular thought. This beginning of the secularizing process was one of the great conquests of Ivan's reign.

On the other hand, Ivan, even in his international dealings, could not or would not break with certain barbarous traditions which harmonized but ill with progress such as this. Just as in past times, envoys sent to his Court were often treated as if they had been prisoners of war, and the fate of his genuine prisoners of war continued to be lamentable. The happiest thing they could expect was to be sold or given to the monasteries as serfs. Occasionally they were simply thrown into the water. In 1581, Ivan gave orders that when the Swedish 'tongues'—in other words, the persons, belligerents or non-belligerents, taken with a view to obtaining information—had served their purpose, they were all to be killed. Polish and Swedish captives were used as current coin in the exchanges arranged by Tartar merchants on the Constantinople markets.

But as he stood, with all his faults and vices, his errors and his crimes, his weaknesses and his failures, Ivan was popular, and his was a genuine popularity, which has stood the twofold test of time and of misfortune. This, too, is a result. In the cycle of the historic songs of Russia, the Tsar holds the place of honour, and is shown in by no means repulsive colours; he is open to every feeling of humanity—severe, but just, and even generous. True, indeed, his sacerdotal majesty lifts him up so high and surrounds him with such an aureole of glory that no critic would dare to lay his hand upon him. But we feel that, in spite of that, all the popular sympathies are with him. When he indulges in savage orgies over the corpses of the vanquished Tartars, or hands one of his boïars over to the executioner on the merest hint of suspicion, the masses are on his side; they applaud the carnage, and rejoice in their master's joy. Even when they cannot applaud, they shut their eyes respectfully, religiously, and cast a mantle of decent fiction over that which makes their consciences revolt. (pp. 396-98)

This is the theory of morals peculiar to the period to which Ivan's name is attached. The ideal it evolves is one of material greatness and brute force—a twofold postulate to which the Russian race has proved itself ready to sacrifice everything else, though it has endeavoured to delude itself as to the value of the end pursued, and the extent of the sacrifice it has entailed. In this other dream, Tsar and people both had their part, and they were to make it a living reality on the day when Peter took Ivan's place, and completed the incarnation which gave birth to modern Russia. But when Ivan died, this work was in the embryonic stage. His labour had been one of destruction, more especially, and he had no time to build up again. Still less had he ensured the continuity of his effort. The legacy left his country by the luckless adversary of Batory, the murderer of the Tsarevitch, his own heir, was a war with Poland and a state of anarchy. The germ was there, too, of a fresh inroad by the rivals of the Slavonic West, destined, under the shelter of the false Dmitri, to reach Moscow itself, and of a triumphant return of the aristocratic oligarchy, which, favoured by the general crumbling of the unfinished edifice, was to recover its old advantages. This was to be the history of the seventeenth century. But Peter the Great was not to guard his inheritance any better against future risks; and yet, after a fresh eclipse, Catherine was to come, even as he had come. The strength was there still, increased materially and tempered morally—the imperishable pledge of a mighty future. (p. 399)

K. Waliszewski, in his Ivan the Terrible, *translated by Lady Mary Loyd, 1904. Reprint by Archon Books, 1966, 431 p.*

D. S. Mirsky   (essay date 1927)

[*Mirsky was a Russian prince who fled his country after the Bolshevik Revolution and settled in London. While in England, he wrote two important histories of Russian literature,* Contemporary Russian Literature *(1926) and* A History of Russian Literature *(1927). These works were later combined and portions were published in 1949 as* A History of Russian Literature. *In 1932, having reconciled himself to the Soviet regime, Mirsky returned to the U.S.S.R. He continued to write literary criticism, but his work eventually ran afoul of Soviet censors and he was exiled to Siberia. He disappeared in 1937. In the following excerpt, first published in* A History of Russian Literature, *Mirsky compares the effectiveness of Ivan's letters and those of his longtime correspondent Kurbsky.*]

Iván was no doubt a cruel tyrant, but he was a pamphleteer of genius. His epistles are the masterpieces of Old Russian (perhaps all Russian) political journalism. They may be too full of texts from the Scriptures and the Fathers, and their Slavonic is not always correct. But they are full of cruel irony, expressed in pointedly forcible

terms. The shameless bully and the great polemist are seen together in a flash when he taunts the runaway Kúrbsky by the question: "If you are so sure of your righteousness, why did you run away and not prefer martyrdom at my hands?" Such strokes were well calculated to drive his correspondent into a rage. The part of the cruel tyrant elaborately upbraiding an escaped victim while he continues torturing those in his reach may be detestable, but Iván plays it with truly Shaksperian breadth of imagination. Besides his letters to Kúrbsky he wrote other satirical invectives to men in his power. The best is the letter to the Abbot of St. Cyril's Monastery where he pours out all the poison of his grim irony on the unascetic life of the boyars, shorn monks, and those exiled by his order. His picture of their luxurious life in the citadel of asceticism is a masterpiece of trenchant sarcasm.

Iván's principal opponent, Prince Andréy Mikháylovich Kúrbsky . . . , was one of the most cultured and enlightened men in Muscovy. He played a prominent part in the administration and distinguished himself as a soldier at the siege of Kazán and in the Livonian war. In 1564, during the war with Lithuania, when Iván had instituted his reign of terror, Kúrbsky, fearing responsibility for a reverse of his army, deserted to the enemy. From Lithuania he wrote his famous epistles to the Tsar and a *History* of his reign. The latter work is pragmatic, not annalistic, and shows him a man of keen and constructive intellect. He deliberately exaggerates the crimes of his archenemy and is not to be trusted as impartial witness. His style is strongly infused with West Russian, Polish, and Latin influences. It does not reveal any original literary temperament. The same with his epistles: for all their sincere violence, just indignation, and forcible argument, as literature they are inferior to those of his opponent. (p. 21)

D. S. Mirsky, "The Literature of Old Russia," in his A History of Russian Literature from Its Beginnings to 1900, *edited by Francis J. Whitfield, Vintage Books, 1958, pp. 3-30.*

Hans Von Eckardt   (essay date 1941)

[*In the following excerpt from a biography originally published in German in 1941, Von Eckardt describes why and how Ivan replied to Kurbsky's initial reproaches and examines the historical importance of their correspondence.*]

Immediately after his flight, and on joining the Polish army, the voivode Prince Andrei Kurbsky addressed a letter to his sovereign from his safe refuge, in which, in the name of all those insulted and humiliated by Ivan, he uttered a solemn protest against the Reign of Terror. [His first letter runs:]

> Wherefore, O Czar, . . . hast thou destroyed the mighty in Israel? Wherefore hast thou delivered over to manifold kinds of death the voivodes given thee by God, and shed their victorious, sacred blood in the churches? Why hast thou devised unheard-of torments and persecutions and modes of death for the willing servants who pledged their souls for thee, falsely accused true believers of treason and sorcery and other

abuses, and endeavored in thy wrath to turn light into darkness and to call what is sweet bitter? Of what were they guilty before thee, O Czar, and in what have the leaders of Christendom provoked thee?

Kurbsky called upon the spirits of the murdered and bade them rise up against their persecutor:

> Delude not thyself, O Czar, neither think of us with thoughts of false wisdom, as though we, innocently slain, banished, and unjustly expelled by thee, were already rooted out. Boast not thyself of an empty victory, and rejoice not in it. Those whom thou hast slain plead for revenge before the throne of the Lord. We, who are banished and driven out from thee contrary to all right, cry out to God day and night from foreign soil. Though in this fleeting existence thou mayst plume thyself in thy pride upon devising instruments of torture for the Christian people, and outraging and trampling underfoot the monastic life, that angelic system, amid the appluase of thy flatterers, of these thy boon companions, the boyars with their everlasting quarrels, united on this one point alone, who have ruined thee both body and soul, who inflame thee with venereal lusts and use their own children worse than the priests of Kronos. . . .

This was the climax of his reproaches: that Czar Ivan had disgraced his own immortal soul and that of his people and loaded them with indelible guilt, because he had not held his hand before the divine institutions of the Church, but had added to his persecution of persons outrages upon institutions, sanctuaries, sacred shrines, and symbols of the world beyond and its everlasting peace.

It was not only Ivan's inhuman cruelty that had to be arraigned, but also the cynicism with which he utterly demoralized what had still survived as the last consolation of the people outside the direct scope of his power: the spheres of faith and conscience. Even the Tatars had not succeeded in doing this; and for this reason there were many to whom it seemed that the Orthodox Czar was setting up to destroy not only this world but the next as well. Blasphemy is very much more than a crime; to make inroads upon the world of a people's imagination is more disastrous than mass murder and violent deeds of destruction. "It is through this," runs a manuscript addition to this grandiose attack, "that he has outraged the angelic system. When he blazes up in wrath against this or that man, he has him forcibly tonsured as a monk, together with his wife and little children, and compels them to live the monastic life forever in fortified monasteries and gloomy cells. And thus, with the consent of a few wicked and crafty monks, he turns the holy places into dungeons of hell."

This was too much. By so doing, God's Anointed destroyed his own soul's salvation. But the Czar was the incarnation of Russia, God's earth. Should Antichrist have arisen, then, in his shape, what was to become of both land and people?

"Thinkest thou thyself immortal, O Czar? Or hast thou fallen into unspeakable heresy, as if thou alone wert not bound to appear before the incorruptible Judge?"

Kurbsky had no right, he said, to pass judgment on Ivan's policy. But he both must and should lament the sin committed by the Czar against his own salvation, and seek to set a check to it.

It was this point, and this point alone, to which Ivan Vasilievich replied. He could not swallow the accusation of heresy. And so he replied in words tumbling over one another and endless periods, with oaths, arguments, and learned historical and theological dissertations, overloaded with quotations. The Old Testament is cited at length thirty-one times, to illustrate his point, in this polemical document of Ivan's, and the New Testament no less than thirty-nine times. It was not he, but the fugitive Kurbsky, he said, who had sold his soul to the devil through his betrayal of the Czar, his perjury, and treachery to his country. The proof of this is conclusive: The powers that be are ordained of God. Kurbsky's defection from his sovereign is an act of apostasy from God. Ivan turns and twists this idea in all directions, constantly embarking upon endless digressions and then harking back to the point that, according to the teaching of the Holy Scriptures, perjury is the greatest crime in the world. In Moscow was preserved the "life-giving Cross," made out of the wood of the Cross of Christ, which the Byzantine Emperor Alexius Comnenus was supposed to have sent to the Grand Prince Vladimir Monomachos. Since then it had served for swearing in the army commanders. Whosoever broke this oath of fealty was guilty of a crime against the Cross (a *krestoprestupnik*), and had, as Ivan described it, "destroyed not only his own soul, but also those of his forefathers." Eternal damnation was the lot of the sinner, and nothing could ever free him from the curse. And besides, Ivan went on to argue, the fall of all the great empires of history was to be attributed to the treachery of renegade counselors and generals of the emperors and kings. For the rest, autocracy was the one and only solution for all political problems—all consultation of counselors and sharing of power was an evil.

Here they were on common ground, for Kurbsky, too, thought in terms of religion and authority. But, he maintained emphatically, there still existed a tradition that made it the Grand Duke's duty to listen to his Council of Boyars, the *sinklit.* "We do not desire any instruction from men," was the Czar's haughty reply, "nor is it befitting to ask others for the understanding necessary to rule over a number of people." Besides, the boyars of the Duma had already become renegades and traitors, all and sundry of them, like their fellow boyar Kurbsky. And that was what had made the institution of the ancient Duma of the Boyars impossible, as that of the Chosen Council had also become.

Thereupon in his next letter Kurbsky reiterated the accusation and justified his political position, denying that he had infringed his duty or the law; for it had been an ancient and well-authenticated prerogative of the Russian nobility to be allowed to change their suzerain. (pp. 318-21)

Engraving of the Novgorod massacre of 1570 by an unknown artist.

Ivan had let himself be carried away into answering [Kurbsky] at positively interminable length. His intention had been to justify himself, and for this reason he pondered deeply over his youth. For the purpose of proving the guilt of the boyars he had likewise scraped together every possible instance of how they had sinned against the State and himself. To this "verbose epistle of the Grand Duke of Moscow"—which has become a historical document of the highest importance to us, and also forms the basis of this sketch of the life of Czar Ivan—Prince Andrei sent only a brief reply [see excerpt dated 1565]:

> I have received thy boastful and clamorous letter and have understood and recognized that it is spat out with uncontrollable fury in venomous words, ill befitting not only so great a Czar, renowned throughout the whole world, but even a poor, simple warrior; especially since it is pieced together out of many sacred words, and that with much fury and ferocity, not in strophes or verses, as would have been customary with those skilled in art and learning, but diffusely and confusedly beyond all measure, out of many books, memorials, and *paroemiæ* (proverbs). Thou dost write of beds, fur garments, and countless other matters, forsooth, like crazy women's tales! And in such barbarous wise, to the amazement and derision not only of men skilled in learning and art, but also of simple folk and children. And what is more, thou dost send such things to a foreign land, where there are no small number of men experienced not only in

grammatical and rhetorical studies, but also in dialectical and philosophical ones.

Kurbsky well knew how to indulge in learned sneers—Kurbsky, who called himself "chivalrous," in Polish fashion, yet had so recently attained to this superior knowledge and bookish culture as an emigrant and a fugitive.

But bombastic invective was regarded as an art in itself, and was quite in keeping with the contemporary style of controversy. In this case it was not mere Muscovite barbarism, but that style of embellishment with inflated verbiage which was generally current. (pp. 323-24)

[Ivan] lived in Moscow, and could only have acquired the more refined manners, urbane quality, and good taste of the humanists of the day at second hand. Thus it was quite easy for Kurbsky, who had already grown accustomed to the polished forms of social intercourse of the Polish nobility, to make fun of Ivan IV's self-taught learning.

On this occasion Kurbsky wrote only a few lines, which, moreover, never reached him to whom they were addressed, since no further opportunity now existed of delivering his letter direct. The Russian realm, or, as Prince Andrei expressed it, "free human creatures," had been shut in and cut off by Ivan "as in a castle of hell." Anyone crossing the frontier was threatened with the death penalty, and since Lithuania returned tit for tat, there was, in point of fact, no further intercourse between the neighboring lands. Yet this unique correspondence did not cease. Thirteen years after his first letter Ivan sent Kurbsky another, which he gave to his envoy attending the peace negotiations with Poland in 1577. This time the Czar wrote from the conquered Livonian city of Valmiera, speaking solemnly and condescendingly and, in his own fashion, moderately and severely.

> Through the efficacy of the intervention of the almighty and all-preserving justice of God the Lord, who sustains the ends of the whole earth, and of our Redeemer Jesus Christ, to whom, with the Father and the Holy Ghost, be all glory and honor, it has pleased Him in His grace that we, His humble and unworthy servant, should hold in our hand the scepter of the Russian Empire and receive from His all-supporting justice the banner of the Cross—we, the Great Lord, Czar, and Grand Duke Ivan Vasilievich of all Russia, Vladimir, Moscow, and Novgorod, Czar of Kazan and Czar of Astrakhan . . . hereditary lord and owner of the Livonian land, ruler of the German Estates and the whole of the Siberian land and of the northern regions, we write these presents to our former boyar and voivode, the Prince Andrei Mikhailovich Kurbsky.

Then, after this great list of titles, there follows without any transition a typically Russian spontaneous confession. Ivan's love of theatricality and pomp, his craze for indulging in a histrionic display of himself, measuring the depths of his humility against the loftiness of his office and dignity, lead him away into fantastic exaggerations, which are more revealing than most of his other utterances. As yet he was by no means supreme over Livonia, Siberia, and the northern regions; but just as Orthodox priests were in the habit of putting a letter to St. Peter in the hand of the dead, telling the doorkeeper of heaven to open its gates to the true believer, so Ivan, too, had to demonstrate solemnly how great and mighty was the sinner who was here abasing himself. In the act of pardon the sinner himself was the determining factor. God had revealed Himself in the successes of Ivan's armies. And so it was for Ivan to set the tone. He compares his impious acts with those of Manasses in the Bible and tries to find words of repentance and self–accusation. After a long period of difficulties and reverses his armies had at last been successful. Ivan's headquarters was now established in the midst of the fortified cities of Livonia. No stratagems of war had been required. God Himself had given victory to his banner. And so, he concludes, God had also forgiven him his sins. And though these were like the sands of the sea in number, yet he had never abandoned God, nor had he ever doubted the mercy of the Lord. And so his readiness to repent had been rewarded . . . and thus his opponents and critics, the slanderers, renegades, and traitors, the enemies of his childhood and those who had opposed his government, had been proved, finally and once and for all, in the wrong. And now Ivan could no longer conceal his triumph. His faith was the true one, and therefore his understanding had been clear and pure. It was an indescribable delight to him to fling this, in so many words, in the teeth of him who had insulted him and once again to arraign Kurbsky and his party. And so he related all over again the occasions on which he had been injured and wronged, badly advised and provoked. It was as though he had at last emerged from the gloom of his forest residences and the silent Kremlin and exulted in his own eloquence, his burning, insulting, raging words, worthy of a Czar: "Prince, it is God's decree. God gives the power to him whom He has chosen."

Ivan felt himself justified on religious grounds. Fundamentally there was, indeed, only one unforgivable mortal sin: apostasy from God. Yet Ivan had never felt a single doubt. As Cæsar he had always had faith in God, and his invocation of divine grace had been the starting-point of his actions and thoughts. One who, like him, bears within him the destiny of a sovereign is conscious of justification through repentance and faith and may therefore pass lightly over his own failures and sins. Fervor, devout absorption, the sense of God's immanence, the knowledge of His commandments and teaching in every detail, compel a man to take sides for God. By this means everything is made clear, and everything, too, is preordained and expressly laid down. For now there are no more hesitations, no more problems, and no more bewilderment. . . .

A religious justification of history has always been attempted at all stages of culture and at all periods. Ivan the Terrible was not alone in the strange conclusions that he drew from his ideas. Even Bernard of Clairvaux had similar ideas, when he succeeded in influencing the history of Europe for centuries through crusades "ordained by God." The Maid of Orléans acted under a like inspiration; and Loyola felt himself to be God's partisan and champion no less than Philip II did.

Though Ivan did not know much about them and was conscious only of the differences in their beliefs, rather than of the similarity of their type of mind and conscience, he none the less resembled them. He, too, was forever brooding and restlessly seeking, but in an unswervingly direct line. To be on God's side, out and out on God's side! (pp. 324-27)

The survival and posthumous influence of Ivan's personality have been extraordinarily powerful. He felt this instinctively and for that reason was eager to say what he had to say. Prince Kurbsky was keenly conscious of the force with which he did so, and that is why he replied to the Czar over and over again. These further letters—which, unfortunately, have come down to us only in copies dating from the latter part of the seventeenth century, but which Kurbsky published abroad at the time in Poland and beyond with much sound and fury, and made use of for diplomatic purposes, reveal Kurbsky as on the same plane, with his realistic outlook and his feudal patriotism. But they made no further change in the balance of forces in this controversy. Kurbsky won over European opinion to his side; but Ivan achieved more than this. From the confessions contained in these writings the Russians gained a telling picture of his mission. Yet the line taken by the correspondence was quite unsatisfactory. Ivan IV was incapable of coining words and ideas of such a kind as to reveal his intellectual superiority. The Czar identified his mission with the State and the nation. The Czar rules exclusively by divine right. To be scandalized at him is apostasy and betrayal. Had the Czar only been able to add that no statesman could be expected to recognize the transference of allegiance to a national enemy, Kurbsky and all the others who had abandoned their nation and home and were fighting against them would have been confuted. But such words had not yet been thought of, and so the duologue plunged into the unfathomable depths of divergent interpretations of the word of God. And since the Lord God can have only one will, each declared the other to be a blasphemer and a heretic.

If Kurbsky failed to understand Ivan's revolutionary and national idea, it was not granted to Ivan to grasp the humanist world of ideas. Essentially Moscow knew nothing of humane culture, dignity, or civilization. The learned Greek monks' contribution to knowledge in former days had become accessible to the Russians only in a narrowly dogmatic and religious form and was never used as anything more than a means and mode of expression—not as having any meaning and never as having any worth in itself. Ivan, who was an inveterate and extremely thorough reader, was uncomfortably well informed; yet he did not realize the value of knowledge and had never had any experience of investigation and truth. Untrained in logic, devoid of any breath of skepticism or doubt, to believe seemed to him the sole task of the intelligence. Work undertaken for its own sake would have been quite as inconceivable to him as would have been the mere examination and understanding of mankind, its development and capabilities, and the formation of its character. All that had carried western Europe away like an intoxication since the Renaissance and helped it to its radiant *joie de vivre* and creative power, besides its discoveries and science, was still entirely strange to Moscow at the beginning of the seventeenth century.

But Prince Andrei had been in Livonia and now lived in Poland; he had learned Latin, and was familiar with artists, men of learning, books, and works of art. Thus he had obtained a notion of things the knowledge of which made a different and loftier view of mankind possible. In Old Testament style Ivan called Kurbsky a dog, a slave, a mangy beast. The boyars, he said, were his servants and serfs. In a land where freedom cannot even be conceived, there can be none but inferior creatures, or, at most, servants of God; but not men, in the sense of the antique world or of the consciousness of civilized Europe. Rejoicing in his new insight into things, Kurbsky, who was already educated and cultured, rose in his wrath and confronted the despot with a demand for human rights. " 'He in whom virtue abides never lacks a happy life'—from Cicero's most wise book, called the *Paradoxa,*" he quoted at length; and to score a further point and demonstrate his intellectual superiority, he added yet another passage from Cicero. Ivan must hear what the great Roman wrote and taught, and, by way of commentary, must at least be given to understand with what matters Kurbsky was now occupied and how bright and spacious was the world with which the deluded tyrant of Moscow was seeking to contend. These parts of the great polemical correspondence build up an antithesis of crushing weight. Ivan seems completely isolated, desperate, and defeated. Kurbsky tears off the Muscovite's cloak of pitiful religious learning and triumphs over the nakedness of this obscurantist, exposing him as a laughing-stock to the humanist—a triumph of unmasking. For now the great Czar is seen as no more than a tyrant and hence has no intellectual standing, but is only terrible as a tormentor of men and a senseless destroyer of life.

Ivan sent no further replies. But after all, this correspondence between Czar and emigrant, which lasted for fifteen years, from 1564 to 1578, was in no sense a literary event. The number of years which elapsed between the letters is alone proof of that. The men of those days, indeed, had a preternaturally lively memory. They felt ideas burning within them and forgot nothing that had been an experience to them. Thus in the year 1569 Ivan wrote to a renegade monk and soldier an answer to a letter of this fugitive's that had been addressed to one of his voivodes thirteen years before. For thirteen years he had restrained his anger, for thirteen years he had been thinking over this letter, bearing in mind all the renegade's phrases and sophistries, only to break out now and send his wrath after the man who had abandoned him.

In his correspondence with Kurbsky an additional factor played its part—namely, all that had happened while it was going on. The Livonian War dragged on, bringing with it victories and defeats, and ended in an utter fiasco for Russian policy. Ivan IV had made his notorious experiment in setting up within his empire a domain subject to his absolute sovereignty; he had systematically gone on with his persecution of the boyars, and had finally destroyed the ancient liberties of Novgorod, in order to carry out, on the *tabula rasa* wiped clean by his fury, the plans he had devised. Kurbsky followed the course of events from his safe distance and laid hold upon the outward symptoms, Ivan's fury and destruction. But he failed to see the historical achievement that was being carried out, nor did he understand how the developments which took place in the political situation from time to time were bound to react upon the autocrat of Moscow. After all, though Ivan had the makings of an intellectual, he was no debater, but a politician. He did not react to words, but to the events of the age; and if he felt his absolute form of government to be the only possible one, this was, in part, also due to the conclusions that he felt bound to draw from the destiny of the neighboring State. Thus the great debate between the Czar and the new feudatory of Poland became at the same time a commentary upon the matters at issue between the two hostile states. (pp. 330-33)

Hans Von Eckardt, in his Ivan the Terrible, *translated by Catherine Alison Phillips, Alfred A. Knopf, 1949, 433 p.*

Vera Alexandrova   (essay date 1943)

[*Alexandrova is a Russian-born American critic known for her studies of Russian literary history and analyses of contemporary Soviet literary and cultural developments. In the following excerpt, she suggests some reasons for the reevaluation of Ivan IV that began in Stalinist Russia in the early 1930s.*]

A revolution represents a most radical break with the past: a transformation of institutions, a rupture of age-old traditions, a revaluation of values. Why then in the face of the mighty successes of the Red Army are Soviet officials and intellectuals engaged in the glorification of the Russian past? Why are the heroes of the Civil War brushed aside in favor of ancient knights, generals, noblemen, landowners and tsars? This tendency has become ever clearer since the speech of Stalin on the anniversary of the October Revolution in the year 1941, when he called upon the Red Army to seek inspiration "in the courageous images of our great ancestors: Alexander Nevsky, Dmitri Donskoy, Kuzma Minin, Dmitri Pozharsky, Alexander Suvorov, Michael Kutuzov!" Since that day a completely favorable revision of the once rejected Russian past has brought the Soviet writers to a new milestone, to the revaluation even of Ivan the Terrible.

In no contemporary state (if we exclude, perhaps, those of Asia) does the historical past play so big and active a role in the formation of public opinion as in Russia. At the beginning of the Eighteenth Century when Russia as a result of the reforms of Peter the Great entered into the family of European nations, its historians and writers began to study Russia's past. In that past they found the answers to the burning problems of their time: With the aid of the ancient past they formed their esthetic, moral and political criteria. The greatest attention, naturally, was paid to the most critical epochs: The reign of Ivan the Terrible who with the aid of the *Oprichnina* created by him as an organ of terror, destroyed the feudal system; the "Time of Troubles"; the rise of the Romanov Dynasty; the Reformation of Peter the Great, etc. Precisely in such critical epochs do the lines and possibilities of development show themselves most clearly.

A second fact is no less noteworthy. Despite all their close and passionate study of these problems, never and nowise were the investigators able to establish a single opinion which would be accepted by all. Ivan the Terrible and Peter the Great had their warm defenders and no less vehement detractors. Thus Mikhailovsky, one of the outstanding democratic writers of the end of the nineteenth century, in his book, *Ivan the Terrible in Russian Literature* (1891) pointed out that the self-same traits of Ivan the Terrible, the same events of his reign, led investigators to directly contrary conclusions. Some pictured Ivan as a "fallen angel," others as a "pure devil." Mikhailovsky noted in passing a very interesting fact, namely that the apology for Ivan the Terrible started at the time of the Russian reaction of the thirties and forties of the Nineteenth Century. In these apologetics many progressive-minded intellectuals took part, "people who differed most completely in other questions" united to glorify him. Thus, we find a positive appreciation of Ivan the Terrible on the part of so sincere a democrat as the critic Belinsky; and along with him were to be found the Slavophile writers, the spokesmen of future Russian conservatism, who in all else quarreled with Belinsky. Mikhailovsky himself, by the way, avoided the errors of the majority of the investigators of Ivan thanks to the fact that he turned his attention to the pangs of conscience which tortured Ivan: "If Ivan the Terrible himself was visited by torments of conscience for the evil and mad things done by him, then why do the apologetic historians not heed the voice of their hero, why do they not in this case believe his better nature?" (pp. 318-19)

The Russian Revolution began as if it were determined to break with all the old traditions of historiography. The most influential Communist historian, Prof. Mikhal Pokrovsky, in his *Course in Russian History,* followed the method of a primitive abstract and oversimplified Marxism which almost dispensed with historical personages altogether. Pokrovsky and his followers concentrated all their attention on the study and clarification of social-economic processes. Tsars, military leaders, priests, heroes were filed in the archives. Russia appeared as a vast empty space with social forces and raging "class-struggles" but without human population. Russia's early history appeared as a struggle between the categories of princes and landowners, then between peasants and feudal lords, then between latifundists and small gentry; finally appeared upon the scene "merchant capital" followed by the industrial capital and the proletariat.

But in the journalism and literature of the first ten years after the Revolution matters were much more alive. Together with the victorious revolutionists there entered into letters new writers from the peasant and urban intelligentsia. They undertook to show in the Russian past the peasantry and town dwellers, who, always oppressed by the ruling classes, still carried on a struggle for a better future. In this conception were elements of a revolutionary democratic revision of the Russians past (Yessenin, *Songs of the Great Campaign, Pugachov;* Zamyatin, *The Flea;* Chapygin, *Stepan Razin;* Olfa Forsh, *Jacobin Yeast*).

But this progressive revision of Russian history did not meet with the approval of the official critics. Knowing that Russia was a land overwhelmingly peasant and petty bourgeois in which the working class up to recent times always constituted an insignificant minority, they had no taste for excursions into distant centuries. Moreover, such excursions were regarded as "a flight from the present," as a desire to call in question the very foundations of the "proletarian dictatorship."

The picture changed fundamentally at the beginning of the thirties with the first successes of the Five Year Plan. Then were heard the first faint hesitant notes of a discussion of the relations between *morality and progress.* The opinion prevailed that progress, even though realized by means of terror, is something positive in itself, carrying with it its own moral sanction. (pp. 319-20)

The limits of the present article do not permit us to follow all the stages of this remarkable transformation which began as we have seen long before the Russo-German war and which has led the writers at last to the feet of the statues of Russian antiquity. In all this revision of historical values it is however important to discover one thing: namely, why this revision occurred, what aspects and what personages of Russian history have again attracted the attention of these distant descendants?

The successes of Soviet industrialization were accompanied by one most significant sociological phenomenon: the growth and strengthening of the leading stratum of economists, engineers, administrators and officials. This layer comes from many social classes—peasants, intellectuals, workers and in no small degree children of the former ruling classes. This diversity of social origin carried with it the danger of difference and dispersion in all directions. Only a great common and unifying idea could give cohesion to this new ruling group and that idea could be either the Revolution or Russia's national Past. For reasons which can barely be touched on here, not the Revolution but the national Past prevailed.

Inevitably it carried with it the idea of the *primacy of the state* in the lives of the people and the land, because this very idea has been predominant throughout the entire history of Russia. The state was allpowerful, in the name of the state the heaviest sacrifices might be demanded, in the interest of the state the most frightful cruelty could be exercised. The interests of the state took the place of the interests of the people; the idea of the Revolution, that the state exists for the people, was reversed: the people once more existed for the state.

From this arose the need for re-examining Russian history and extracting from it the moments in which the energy of leaders devoted to this same idea of the primacy of the state saved Russia from foreign invasion and furthered its growth and strength. Thus arose out of the darkness of the centuries the figures of Alexander Nevsky, who in the twelfth century in the famous Battle on the Ice defeated the Teutonic knights, of the great prince Dmitri Donskoy who in the fourteenth century undertook his victorious revenge on the Tartars, and so on. Out of the same necessity arose the new conception of the personality and reign of Ivan the Terrible.

Professor Bakhrushin, in his *Ivan the Terrible* (1942),

gives in passing a summary and one-sided view of the attitude of former investigators of Ivan. He writes: "The reign of Ivan the Fourth (the title "the Terrible" is notably absent!) represents a necessary and extremely important stage in the history of the formation of the centralized state, which unified the Russian people in a strong political organization, capable not only of resisting invading enemies but also of realizing national aims in internal policy." This same idea pervaded all the art of the epoch of Ivan: "it splendidly asserted the idea of the strengthening of the centralized feudal state, which arose out of a complicated class struggle." At the same time from the political unification "arose a mighty and original national culture."

In the year 1941 appeared the first part of the Trilogy by Alexey Tolstoi, *Ivan the Terrible*. It did not satisfy the Soviet critics. But not long after in the weekly review *Ogonyok* ("Hearth") Tolstoi told his readers something about his intentions in the second part of the Trilogy: "The personality and deeds of Ivan the Terrible for many reasons were distorted by former historians. Only now, on the basis of recently discovered documents Russian historiography has returned to that epoch to illuminate it anew."

All the new demands were satisfied in the opinion of Soviet critics by the novel of Kostylyov likewise entitled *Ivan the Terrible*. The writer also conceived it in the form of a Trilogy. So far only the first part. *Moscow on the March* (1942) has appeared. It deals with preparations for war and the first campaign of Ivan in Livonia. Wherever the writer deals with the well-known traits of the Tsar's character, his rudeness, his capricious spirit, his despotism and sadism, Kostylyov employs the language of the period, enriching it with quotations from Ivan himself. But the writer attempts to show us an entirely different Ivan, that Ivan who was imagined by the first apologists for the Terrible Tsar, the Russian Slavophiles. Here, however, Kostylyov betrays his artistic instinct and begins to talk about Ivan in contemporary formulae in place of portraying him.

But when the writer ceases to devote himself to the task of discovering Ivan the national hero, he manages in some measure to give the feeling of a great epoch by other means; he succeeds in bringing to life the background of that period, troubled, filled with alarming rumors, fearful of the expectations of change, regarded by some with terror and hatred and by others—the common folk—with curiosity to see what would happen. Thus the daughter of a Mordvinian fisherman, Okhima, dreams of going to the Tsar to find out what has happened to her fiancé, who was taken prisoner by the Russians during the campaign in Kazan. On the road she meets Andrey and Gerassim—fugitive serfs. Together they go to Moscow, where they come under the eyes of the powerful Vaska Gryaznoy, the favorite of Ivan, who reports concerning them to the Tsar. Okhima is sent as a worker to the first printing plant in Russia, Andrey becomes a skilled worker in a munitions plant and Gerassim goes into the military service as a guard on the state frontiers. For all these people "the service of the state" is good fortune. Were it not for Ivan they would have finished their days in bitter slavery or been flogged to death by some cruel *boyar*. The parallel is obvious with the devotion of the new layer of "Stalinist promoted workers" to the "total state."

To what extent Soviet ideologists are attributing serious meaning to the new conception of Ivan is suggested by the fact that the famous film director, Eisenstein, who at the beginning of the revolution won fame by his creation of the revolutionary film *Potemkin,* is now engaged in the preparation of a picture whose hero will be *Ivan the Terrible.*

From *Potemkin* to *Ivan the Terrible,* from the glorification of the October Revolution to the Glorification of the Terrible Tsar—that is a long road. What profound doubts must have arisen in the justification of the dictatorship of the Communist Party, how shaken must be the faith in the liberating idea of the great Revolution, if in the ideological domain a retreat has been undertaken all the way to the foot of the ancient image of the *Leviathan State!* (pp. 320-23)

> Vera Alexandrova, "New Concepts of Ivan the Terrible," in Books Abroad, *Vol. 17, No. 4, Autumn, 1943, pp. 318-24.*

Jules Koslow   (essay date 1961)

[*Koslow is an American historian and literary critic. In the following excerpt, he analyzes the nature and style of Ivan's letters, praising the Czar's intellectual interests and affirming the historical value of his correspondence with Kurbsky.*]

At the time when Ivan was reaching a decision to sue for peace in Livonia, the Czar received his fifth—and last—letter from Kurbsky. Since 1564, when Kurbsky fled Russia and sought sanctuary in Poland, he had written Ivan a total of five letters. Ivan, in return, had written two to Kurbsky. In these two letters, the first one running to sixty pages, Ivan revealed himself as both a person and a Czar as no other Russian ruler, with the exception of Catherine the Great, has ever done in the history of Russian czardom. As a source of enlightenment on the attitudes and goals of Ivan the Terrible, the correspondence is invaluable.

Kurbsky's decision to go into exile was a most difficult one to make, and only a man with a profound grievance against his ruler and a deep-seated fear for his personal safety would have taken such a step. When he fled to Poland from his military post in Dorpat, leaving behind him his wife and son, who later were put to death by Ivan, he knew he was cutting off any possibility of ever again returning to Russia. For the rest of his life, Kurbsky carried on a campaign against the Czar and his policies to justify his running away.

As for Ivan, there was no one he hated more than Kurbsky after his self-imposed exile. He attacked him on every front, and called him every conceivable name from "vicious dog" to "cowardly traitor," even sneering at Kurbsky's complexion and the color of his eyes. "You value your face dearly!" Ivan wrote. "Who indeed wishes to see such an Ethiopian face? Where will one find a just man who has pale-blue eyes? For your countenance betrays your wicked disposition."

In 1564, when their correspondence began, Ivan was thirty-four, Kurbsky was thirty-six. Both men were at the height of their intellectual powers; their passions were strong, their ambitions great, and their hatreds deep. Both men had great pride, and their letters reflect the profound hurt each felt at the other's betrayal of his person and belittlement of his stature. (pp. 214-15)

Kurbsky's first letter was comparatively brief, running only a few pages. Ivan's reply, which he wrote shortly after receiving Kurbsky's letter, was extremely long; it makes up more than sixty per cent of the whole correspondence. The length of Ivan's letter and the manner in which it was written gives some credibility to the idea that not only were he and Kurbsky engaging in a personal debate but that their letters were intended for public consumption. This conjecture is further strengthened by the fact that even though Kurbsky had the earlier letters published in Poland and widely distributed, Ivan was still willing to carry on the correspondence, and wrote his second letter to Kurbsky as late as 1577.

In essence, Ivan's lengthy reply was his political treatise on the right—and duty—of the Czar to be an absolute monarch, free of any interference from any group and immune from criticism from any quarter, and a polemic against the boyars and their political claims to any position, except that which the absolute monarch deigned to assign them, in the government. In this regard, Ivan's letters are the first written expression in Russia until that time—and for years later, the fullest expression—of the divine origin of the Czar's supreme and absolute power. Thus, Ivan was the father of the theory of czardom as it existed in Russia in later centuries and, as the most extreme practitioner of that theory, the original model of the autocratic monarchs who ruled in Russia until 1917, as well as the traditional national model for the supreme leader of the Russian state, best exemplified by Stalin, that existed after the Revolution. (p. 218)

Ivan's letters to Kurbsky are filled with vainglory. Ivan cannot refrain from parading before Kurbsky as the greatest sovereign on earth. Even the pompous titles that other Russian Czars gave themselves pale a bit before the grandiloquent title Ivan used for himself in his second letter to Kurbsky. As if to further the great distance that separated him from Kurbsky, who responded sneeringly by addressing himself to Ivan as "the lowly Andrei Kurbsky, Prince of Kowell," Ivan began his letter:

> By the all-powerful and almighty right hand of Him who holds the ends of the earth, our Lord God and Saviour Jesus Christ, who, with the Father and the Holy Ghost in unity worshiped and glorified, by his mercy had permitted us, his humble and unworthy servants, to hold the scepters of the Russian kingdom, and from his almighty right hand has given us the Christ-bearing banners—so do we write, the great sovereign, Czar and Grand Prince Ivan Vasilievich of All Russia, of Vladimir, Moscow, Novgorod, Czar of Kazan, Czar of Astrakhan, Sovereign of Pskov and Grand Prince of Smolensk, Tver,

Yugra . . . , Perm, Vyatka, Bolgar, . . . and others, Sovereign and Grand Prince of Novgorod of the Lower Land . . . , Chernigov, Riazan, Polotsk, Rostov, Yaroslavl, Bieloozero, hereditary Sovereign and Master of the Livonian land of the German Order, of Udora . . . , of Obdoria . . . , Kondia . . . , and all the Siberian land and ruler of the Northern land—to our former boyar and voivode, Prince Andrei Mikhailovich Kurbsky.

When it suited his purpose, Ivan forgot his vainglory and had no hesitation in craftily seeking out a scapegoat upon whom to blame his shortcomings. For instance, he wrote to Kurbsky, who accused him of backsliding in spiritual matters, that "if there is any question of small sins to be imputed to me, then this is only because of your corruption and treachery. . . . " And then as if he realized he had been too blunt and direct in using Kurbsky for a scapegoat, he softened his accusation by adding this remark: " . . . still more so because I am only human; for there is no man without sin, only God alone."

Yet at another place he does not even bother to soften the accusation, and puts the burden of his lapses in religious matters squarely on others. Ivan wrote: "But if you consider that my observance of church ritual has been at fault and that games have been encouraged, then this is only the result of your cunning plans, for you tore me from a spiritual and a quiet life, and put upon me, in your pharisaical manner, a scarcely bearable burden and yourselves have not touched the burden with one of your fingers."

This self-pity that is so obvious here Ivan could not contain at any time in his life. He constantly answered attacks on himself by bemoaning his sad lot in life, the troubles he had to bear, the ill luck that was his, and the lack of appreciation everyone had for his noble and sincere efforts. To Kurbsky's charge that Ivan persecuted him, Ivan wrote: "You lay before us the charge of persecuting men—yet have not you together with the priest (Sylvester) and Alexei (Adashev) persecuted me?" (pp. 222-24)

Throughout the correspondence, Kurbsky raked up as much evil as he could about Ivan's personal life. For years, Feodor Basmanov had slept in the same room with Ivan, ostensibly to protect him against assassins, but Kurbsky, probably referring to Basmanov and others, wrote that "they defiled the temple of your body with various forms of uncleanliness, and furthermore practiced their wantonness with pederastic atrocities and other countless and unutterable wicked deeds." Previously, Ivan had executed an old boyar for telling Basmanov that "you serve the Czar for the infamous vice of sodomy, but I, descended from a noble family, serve the Czar, like my forefathers before me, for the glory and profit of the fatherland."

But if Kurbsky resorted to personal defamation, so could Ivan. In fact, the Czar in his letters was not content to accuse Kurbsky of treason and crimes but insisted on including his family, and even his ancestors, as state criminals. He wrote that Kurbsky's grandfather was guilty of plotting against Ivan the Great, and that Kurbsky's father plotted against his father, Vasili. He then began on Kurbsky's maternal side and made similar accusations against these ancestors, and finally concluded that Kurbsky was "born from a generation of vipers."

It was for Kurbsky himself, however, that Ivan saved his harshest language. The Czar was a master of invective, and some of his choicest abuse was used on Kurbsky. A random sampling of the invective, occurring throughout Ivan's letters, includes the statement that Kurbsky wrote his first letter "in an unseemly manner, barking like a dog or belching forth serpent's venom." In another passage, Ivan accuses Kurbsky of acting "in your houndish, treacherous manner," and in still another passage calls him "a stinking hound and evil, unjust traitor." To Kurbsky's charge that he is a sodomist, Ivan first sneers at Kurbsky for his assertion, and then labels him and others "traitors and fornicators." To Kurbsky's advice to Ivan to mend his evil ways, Ivan retorts that Kurbsky is a "cur," and that his counsel "stinks worse than dung."

Yet, brutal as Ivan's words could be, he had a gift for language that could reach poetic heights at times. In his second letter, Ivan spoke of the coming of Orthodoxy to Russia, and then noted, "And as the words of God encircle the whole world like an eagle in flight, so a spark of piety reached even the Russian kingdom."

Still, the most notable aspect of Ivan's epistolary style is not his invective or his occasional poetic phrases, but his use of innumerable quotations and passages from the historical and religious works that he had read. His memory was indeed prodigious, if inaccurate, and literally scores of quotations and short passages—many of them obviously from memory—were interpolated into the correspondence. The main source was the Bible, especially the Old Testament prophets and the Epistles of St. Paul. His use of facts left much to be desired, and he either twisted them because of faulty memory or distorted them to prove a point. Even in such a matter as the number of times Chancellor visited Russia, Ivan stated in a letter to Queen Elizabeth that Chancellor had visited his kingdom three times, when in fact it had been only twice. Most of his allusions to history were to the Byzantine Empire and the East, only rarely to the West. His knowledge of the Roman Empire was extensive for the period, and he seemed to have some knowledge of France, Poland, Lithuania, and Greece. (pp. 224-25)

For a sixteenth-century Muscovite, Ivan was extremely well read. His contemporaries referred to him as a "rhetorician of lettered cunning." Books were his favorite pursuit, and he had the best library in Russia. His interest in ancient manuscripts amounted to a passion, and, even though he was miserly, he spent a fortune in sending emissaries to all parts of Russia, especially the old intellectual center of Kiev, and to various countries in the Balkans and in Asia Minor to buy manuscripts. Besides the old manuscripts from Kiev, he inherited the manuscripts that his grandmother, Zoe Paleologus, had inherited from her uncle, John Paleologus, the last emperor in Constantinople before it fell to the Turks in 1453, and from her father, Thomas, as well as from his father, Vasili. (pp. 225-26)

Although in his younger days Ivan read because he was

intellectually curious, it appears that in his later days he read only those works that were pertinent to his own task of ruling and that he concentrated on remembering only those things that were applicable to himself, his position as Czar, and what could be of benefit to him in advancing his own ideas of czardom and the relation of ruler to ruled. His mind, to judge from the letters to Kurbsky at least, appeared to have retained from his reading an unsorted clutter of disconnected passages, phrases, and ideas from religious and historical works.

It is this clutter of information that Kurbsky could not refrain from commenting upon. Kurbsky in his third letter, written around 1578, wrote disparagingly of Ivan's writing ability and erudition. About Ivan's letters, he wrote that they were "astonishing and worthy of amazement and limping strongly on both hips and betraying the unseemly movements of the inner man. . . . Now you humiliate yourself exceedingly, now you raise yourself up without limit and beyond measure!"

Kurbsky's belittling of Ivan's knowledge and literary style was the result not only of Ivan's frequent lapses of recall and his habit of raking over his memory and throwing in quotations and passages whether they applied or not but also of Kurbsky's desire to preen himself before Ivan now that he was in a land of civilized men, not in the intellectual desert that Russia was at that time. (pp. 226-27)

However, Kurbsky is unjust in sneering at Ivan's literary style, which, though extremely rough and disjointed, had a vigorous, satiric ring that was extremely effective at times. The fact that his historical references, as well as his religious ones, were often inaccurate is understandable, since he quoted mainly from memory; the remarkable thing is that he was acquainted with history at all, considering the almost complete lack of books or intellectual curiosity that then prevailed in Russia. In his intellectual interests Ivan was in advance of his times. (p. 227)

Ivan's intellectual curiosity was great, and though he expressed it mainly by seeking out illustrious opponents for debates on religious topics, he also wrote many letters and briefs in which he expressed his views on Protestants, Jews, the Catholic Church, and other subjects. His support was asked by the few monks interested in doing translations of old manuscripts, and he usually gave it. In Ivan, Russia had for the first time a ruler who gave some thought and effort to affairs of the intellect and assistance in the dissemination of knowledge. He did this, however, not as a political or social move, for he was opposed as much as other Russian rulers to educating and uplifting the ignorant mass; he did so because of his great intellectual drive and curiosity.

He was a masterful orator, and he carried people away with his passionate delivery. He had the ability to speak from the very depths of his feeling, and the ring of sincerity and heartfelt emotion moved his audiences to anger or tears. In the deeply religious atmosphere of Russia, speeches and writings heavily weighted with Biblical allusions did not appear stilted, but full of meaning to every man. Some of his power can be felt in the following passage:

With what sins have I not offended against God between then and now! With what chastenings did He not visit us, that He might lead us to repentance! Over and over again we tried to avenge ourselves upon our enemies. Our efforts were in vain. We were not aware that our misfortune was a punishment of God and not a triumph for the heathen. These severe chastisements did not lead us to repentance; of our own accord we conjured up the horrors of a civil war, and the unhappy Christians were abandoned to every violence. And God in His mercy chastened our countless sins by floods, pestilence, and a thousand diseases. But even these punishments were in vain. Then the Lord sent us terrible fires. The treasure of my forefathers went up in flames. Fire destroyed God's holy churches, people without number were destroyed. Then terror entered into my soul, and fear seized upon my bones. My spirit humbled itself and was appeased, and I confessed my sins.

Ivan's emotionalism in his writing, to which he brought little restraint or organization, was sharply criticized by the more sophisticated Kurbsky. Sarcastically, he called Ivan's writings the gossip of a crazy old woman and said that Ivan was so unlearned that people in foreign lands would laugh at such an ignorant presentation. Kurbsky's words in the opening of his second letter read [see letter dated 1565]:

> I have received your grandiloquent and big-sounding screed, and I have understood it and realized that it was belched forth in untamable wrath with poisonous words, such as is unbecoming not only to a Czar, so great and glorified throughout the universe, but even to a simple lowly soldier; and all the more so, as it was of many sacred words—and those were used with much wrath and fierceness, not in measured lines or verses, as is the custom for skilled and learned men, should it occur to anyone to write about anything, enclosing much wisdom in short words; but beyond measure diffusely and noisily, in whole books and paroemias and epistles! And here too there are passages about beds, about bodywarmers, and countless other things, in truth, as it were the tales of crazy women; and so barbarically did you write that not only learned and skilled men, but also simple people and children would read your letter with astonishment and laughter, all the more so as it was sent to a foreign land, where there are certain people who are learned not only in grammatical and rhetorical matters, but in dialectical and philosophical matters as well.

Still, Kurbsky with his finish and polish could not measure up to Ivan in the power of phrase that Ivan could deliver so tellingly. In his first letter to Kurbsky, Ivan wrote:

> How much more does our blood cry out against you to God, our blood spilt by you yourselves, not in wounds nor in bloody streams, but in much sweat and a profusion of toil and senseless oppression caused by you, for in all too much were we oppressed by you beyond the limit of our strength! And because of your animosity and provocation and coercion, instead of blood there flowed many a tear of ours and there was much sighing and groaning of the heart.

In one area after another, Ivan wrote tellingly, and at times brilliantly.

On pride: "But I boast of nought in my pride, and indeed I have no need of pride, for I perform my kingly task and consider no man higher than myself."

On sin: "For a sin is not evil when it is committed; but when a man, after committing sin, has no perception and no repentance, then is the sin more evil, for transgression of the law is confirmed as law."

On piety: "I thank my God that I know how to maintain—at least partially—my piety, in as far as, thanks to the grace of God, I have strength."

On the hereafter: "I believe in the last judgment of our Saviour, when the souls of men together with the bodies with which they were united will be received together in one choir and will be separated into two, each man according to his deeds."

On each man keeping his station in life: "Rank shall not be turned against rank, but let each be in his rank and in his own service."

On war: "Now this is praiseworthy—to wage war willingly, of one's own accord."

On the qualities of Czars [see excerpt dated 1564]: "And it is ever befitting for Czars to be perspicacious, now most gentle, now fierce; mercy and gentleness for the good; for the evil—fierceness and torment. If a Czar does not possess this quality, then he is no Czar, for the Czar is not a terror to good works, but to the evil."

On obedience: "If a Czar's subjects do not obey him, then never will they cease from internecine strife."

On the role of the autocrat: "I endeavor with zeal to guide people to the truth and to the light in order that they may know the one true God, who is glorified in the Trinity, and the sovereign given to them by God; and in order that they may cease from internecine strife and a forward life, which things cause kingdoms to crumble."

The Ivan-Kurbsky correspondence, which lasted from 1564 to 1579, took place during a period of profound changes and of ambitious imperial designs. For all the petty personal backbiting and animosity, the correspondence reveals the temper of the times and the deep cleavage that existed within Russia between the Czar and his boyars. It reveals Ivan's ideas on the role of the autocracy and the relationship between the ruler and the ruled. And most important for an understanding of the terrible Czar, the correspondence reveals Ivan as a man as well as a Czar, a man who, though arrogant and cruel in the extreme, had a brilliant mind and a dynamic, forceful character. The correspondence helps to lay to rest the canard that Ivan was nothing but a vicious madman, and helps to restore him to his rightful place in Russian history as the originator of the ideology of Russian autocracy, the architect of the methodology of the totalitarian state, and the prototype of the all-wise, all-powerful leader. (pp. 227-30)

Jules Koslow, in his Ivan the Terrible, *1961. Reprint by Hill and Wang, 1962, 271 p.*

Ian Grey   (essay date 1964)

[*In the following excerpt, Grey compares the style and arguments of Ivan's epistles with those of Kurbsky, concluding that "Ivan was a tragic man, because he was unable to subdue his own egocentric nature."*]

Kurbsky wrote this first letter from Wolmar soon after his flight. He was to write several other letters as well as his damaging *History of the Great Muscovite Prince*. But the main importance of his letters and *History* now, four centuries after they were written, is that they prompted two lengthy replies from Ivan, which make this correspondence one of the most illuminating documents in Russian history.

Both men were ardent controversialists. Ivan was more learned and expressed himself more powerfully than his adversary. He had the further advantage of writing from sincere conviction, not from malevolence which led Kurbsky to lie and distort facts. Nevertheless, Kurbsky provided some insight into the discontent and opposition of the boyars, while Ivan's long letters, conveying vividly the gale-force of his anger, also revealed him as a monarch with a deep sense of responsibility and mission.

Kurbsky, in fact, had two purposes in writing his letters; he wanted to defame Ivan and at the same time to justify himself, for his defection had made a stir in Muscovy and in Eastern Europe. He referred to the "brilliant victories" that he had won for the Tsar's glory, to his labours and his wounds "inflicted by barbarian hands in various battles", but "to you, O Tsar, was all this as naught. . . . " And he exclaimed:

> What evil and persecutions have I not suffered from you! . . . But I cannot now recount the various misfortunes at your hands which have beset me owing to their multitude . . . of everything have I been deprived; I have been driven from the land of God without guilt, hounded by you!

His charges and complaints seemed to ring with truth, and all in Lithuania were ready to believe them. But they were in fact exaggerated and almost groundless. Ivan in one of the quieter passages of his reply wrote:

> Unjust evils and persecution you have not received from me; and ills and misfortunes we have not brought upon you; it was for your crime, for you were in agreement with our traitors. Falsehood and treacheries which you have not committed we have not imputed to you.

The letters indeed reveal that Kurbsky was ready to go to any lengths in distorting facts to serve his ends. Ivan, although eager to explain and justify himself, did not disclaim what he had done, but admitted and defended or excused his actions.

Kurbsky's malevolence sprang from personal hatred and from his opposition to Ivan's determination to rule absolutely and alone. The Grand Princes of Muscovy had always, he maintained, ruled with the advice and help of their boyars, and this had been the strength of Muscovy. The departure from this tradition had, he alleged, begun with the baleful influence of the Greek Princess, Sofia, wife of Ivan III and grandmother of Ivan, and had been continued by Ivan's mother, the foreigner, Elena Glinskaya. In his *History* he dwelt on the beneficent influence of the Boyar Council in the days when it had important advisory powers and shared in the rule of the country. But Kurbsky did not limit this function of advising and assisting to his own boyar class. He also extended it to include the people, and he evidently had in mind the Assembly of the Land (Zemsky Sobor), which had first been summoned in 1550.

Kurbsky thus declared himself in favour of the new state of Muscovy, united under the Tsar, and did not seek to revive the old independent principalities. His sole political objective was to restore the procedure whereby the Tsar would rule not alone but with the advice and help of his boyars and people.

In spite of his political ideas, as stated in his letters and his *History,* however, Kurbsky belonged emotionally to the time when Muscovy was split into independent principalities. He was at heart the ruler of a principality, his loyalty and interests concentrated in his petty domain. The union of Muscovy under the strong rule of the Grand Prince and the birth of the nation meant to him only the loss of his independence; it had not led him to acknowledge new loyalties. He had served only for personal honour and gain and, when these were threatened, he fled.

Such was the mentality of many of the boyars and princes whom Ivan mistrusted and feared. Neither as individuals nor as a class did they seek to overturn the existing regime. They had demonstrated this during the ten years of Ivan's minority when, ruling unchecked, they might have effected extensive changes. But they had changed nothing, and had merely by their incessant quarrelling reduced the government of the country to chaos. To Ivan, however, it was evident that the boyars were plotting to assassinate him and destroy the nation. Kurbsky's treason and his frantic efforts to attack him and reduce Muscovy to ruins seemed to provide dramatic proof of his gravest suspicions.

Ivan's immediate fury was, however, due more to Kurbsky's gross temerity in writing publicly and charging the Tsar with all manner of crimes and cruelties, and with failing in his responsibilities.

This was more than Ivan could endure. Normally he would have dismissed with contempt such a letter, written by a traitor. But this letter read like a summons to other boyars to follow his example, and its attempt to denigrate the Tsar and to show disaffection could not be ignored.

In a fury Ivan replied and his letter, in one edition taking up eighty-six pages, compared with just over four pages of Kurbsky's first letter, is a magnificent document. Composed in the white heat of anger, Ivan often breaks from one argument to pursue another. His letter is not easy to read, but it abounds in illuminating phrases and sentences.

It reveals his intimate knowledge not only of the history of his own people, but of ancient Greece and Rome, of Byzantium and Persia, and to him history was not the chronicle of long-dead events, but the vital living record of rulers and peoples who had faced trials such as he himself was facing. But the dominant influence in his letters was the Bible. He had read and studied it so intensively that it had dyed his mind and become a part of his thinking. Indeed the stark minatory style of many passages in his letters makes them resound like a book from the old testament.

Ivan opened his letter with a statement of his ancestry from which the autocracy "has come down even to us, the humble sceptrebearer of the Russian Tsardom". He then asserted the nature and source of his power and condemned Kurbsky for committing not merely treason, but apostasy.

> By the grace of God and with the blessing of our forefathers and fathers [he wrote], as we were born to rule, so have we grown up and ascended the throne by the bidding of God. . . . This is our Christian and humble answer to him who was formerly boyar and counsellor and voevoda of our autocratic state and of the true Christian faith, but who is now the perjurer of the holy and life-giving Cross of the Lord and destroyer of Christianity, the servant of those enemies of Christianity who have apostasized from the worship of the divine ikons and have trampled on all the sacred commandments and destroyed the holy temples and befouled and trampled on the sacred vessels and images, like Isaurian and the one who is called Putrefaction, and the Armenian . . . to him who has cast in his lot with all these, to Prince Andrei Mikhailovich Kurbsky, who with his treacherous ways wished to become master of Yaroslavl, let this be known!

Ivan then addressed Kurbsky direct. "Why have you set yourself up as a teacher of my body and soul? Who placed you as a judge or as one in authority over me?" he demanded. "What is it, you cur, that you write and for what do you grieve, having committed such evil? What will your counsel, stinking worse than dung, resemble?" The reason for Ivan's great anger on this score was less on the ground that he himself was the subject of accusations than that Kurbsky should dare to criticize anyone, for he had himself committed the greatest sin of all, apostasy. He had betrayed the Tsar, appointed by God, and so he had betrayed God.

Ivan's unwavering vision of the divine source of his power emerges strongly from his letters. The other factors which are shown to be dominant in his mind are the need of the young nation for a strong central rule and his duty to provide that rule. Kurbsky's references to the Tsar's "well-wishers", meaning Sylvester and Adashev, draws from Ivan furious disavowals that they were anything but evil counsellors, seeking to usurp his power and thereby to destroy the nation. He refers to the "devilish scheming" behind Kurbsky's deeds,

> since you took counsel with the priest [Sylvester]

that I should be sovereign only in word, but that in deed you and the priest should rule. . . . Bethink yourself: did God, having led Israel out of captivity, appoint a priest to command over men or numerous governors? No, he made Moses alone lord over them, like a Tsar.

Ivan was convinced that it was his holy duty to wield this tsarish power as, so he was persuaded, his forebears wielded it, for "from the beginning they have ruled all their dominions, not the boyars, not the magnates". He cited Greek and Roman history to show how quickly nations and empires fell from greatness, if not "under one authority".

In his reply Kurbsky attempted to dismiss the Tsar's letter as a "grandiloquent and big-sounding screed . . . belched forth in untamable wrath with poisonous words, such as is unbecoming not only to a Tsar, so great and glorified throughout the universe, but even to a simple lowly soldier" [see letter dated 1565].

Kurbsky's contemptuous strictures were, however, not unmixed with bravado. Like a man who opens a furnace door and is hurled backwards by the blast of heat, he was at first overwhelmed by the intensity of the Tsar's anger and the fury of his anathemas. But his strictures were not without some justification. Ivan had demeaned himself in answering, especially in such detail, Kurbsky's letter, and thereby bringing himself to the level of the traitor. Nevertheless he had written not only from anger, but also with a passionate sincerity, as though driven to explain himself and also to assert and explain his absolute power and his duty to wield it for Muscovy.

Ivan's second letter to Kurbsky was far shorter and quieter in tone. Written in 1577, after he had suffered betrayals and tasted despair, it expressed in its first pages the bewilderment of a man who cannot understand why he had been so deceived and beaten down by misfortunes. It was the mood of a man who saw himself as Job. The arrogant conviction of the divinely appointed Tsar had been mellowed by a greater consciousness of human frailty and in particular of his own frailty. In the war between arrogance and humility, constantly waged within himself, humility was more often gaining the upper hand, but it was always liable to be dissipated by his sudden unpredictable rages.

In his second letter strong recrimination gave way to complaint and even remorse. "And why did you separate me from my wife?" he asked, recalling the harmony of his first marriage and Anastasia's death seventeen years ago, which he had come to blame on Sylvester and Adashev.

> If only you had not taken from me my young one, then there would have been no 'sacrifices to Cronus'. You will say that I was unable to endure this loss and that I did not preserve my purity—well, we are all human. . . . If only you had not stood up against me with the priest! Then none of this would have happened; all this took place because of your self-willedness.

Ivan then renewed his imprecations, but he closed his letter with the injunction to Kurbsky, "Think on these things to yourself and unfold all these things for yourself. And we have written all this to you neither boasting nor puffing ourselves up—God knows—but to remind you to mend your ways, that you might think of the salvation of your soul." In this chastened mood, many years after the event, it was almost as though he might have received Kurbsky as a prodigal, had he dared to return to Muscovy.

In these two letters to Kurbsky, Ivan revealed something of the complexity of his character and of the conflicts within him. He strove after moderation and restraint, but they usually eluded him. He had a lofty sense of mission to Muscovy and of responsibility to his people, but at times it overwhelmed him and then, because he was merely human, he gave way to debauchery. His conviction of his divinely bestowed power made him arrogant, but then the enormity of this power made him humble. Storms of vindictive anger seized him and he regretted them and his furious anathemas. The more he suffered misfortunes, the more he was conscious of his burden of sin, for misfortunes were, he believed, punishments from God.

Ivan was a tragic man, because he was unable to subdue his own egocentric nature. The essence of his tragedy was that he was incapable of the complete dedication to his office which he knew it required of him, and that he was incapable of submitting before God with the humility which Job had demonstrated. (pp. 154-59)

> *Ian Grey, in his* Ivan the Terrible, *J. B. Lippincott Company, 1964, 258 p.*

Bjarne Nørretranders (essay date 1964)

[*In the following excerpt, Nørretranders explores the methods Ivan used in his letters to justify his ideas and to gather support for his arguments regarding the role of the ruler. This work was originally published in 1964 in Danish.*]

When the question arises, whether Ivan Groznyj had an ideology of a political kind, or at any rate, a set of clearly defined axioms, on which he based his exercise of power, it is natural to seek the answer in his correspondence with Prince Andrej Kurbskij. This document is the richest source for the elucidation of the Czar's personality and his way of thinking and expressing himself, and perhaps also for a knowledge of his convictions and the development of his ideas, but in any case, for ascertaining what he wanted the rest of the world to know or to think were his beliefs and his views.

In this connexion, the most significant part of the correspondence is the first message to Kurbskij, obviously written in July 1564—a couple of months after Kurbskij had gone over to the Polish King and six months before Groznyj's revolution. This paper, the prolixity of which provoked the receiver's scorn, resembles more a treatise then a letter. There has been some discussion on the question of whether the message was originally meant for Kurbskij alone or for a wider circle. In favour of the first view, there is its personal, often actually colloquial style: in favour of the second, its breadth and polemical aim. And yet it seems evident, even without deciding this question, that the message is the expression of a general clash and a programme with political aims—a clash with hitherto power-

ful forces in the Russian czardom, forces that are symbolized in Kurbskij's defection, and a programme that portends an intensified struggle against these forces, the struggle that began at the turn of 1564.

It is thus not only the extent and copiousness of the message that makes it an invaluable means of coming *in medias res.* According to the traditional interpretations of earlier Russian historians, the years from 1560 to 1564 formed a fateful period in Groznyj's life, during which he underwent a metamorphosis from a just ruler to a tyrant, from normal to abnormal. In this connexion, it is useful to note that Ivan's first message to Kurbskij was written in the closing stage of this period of metamorphosis, and that, in taking this message as the main source for the elucidation of Groznyj's views and the development of his ideas, one feels on more or less safe ground with regard to the general value of this source for the subsequent years also. It does not originate from a sane person who later went mad. If it marks the end of an epoch, it gives, at any rate, just as clear warning of a new one. The inclusion of Groznyj's second letter to Kurbskij, written thirteen years later, serves as further confirmation, for, in spite of slight differences, it is a repetition of the first.

The theory that Ivan Groznyj underwent a change in the course of those four years of crisis was first formulated by Andrej Kurbskij in the letter he sent to the Czar soon after his defection, which might be called a notice of renunciation of allegiance. It is addressed "To the Czar, exalted above all by God, and who appeared most illustrious, particularly in the Orthodox Faith, but who has now, in consequence of our sins, been found to be the contrary of this". The rest of the letter is in the main only a justification of this contention that the Czar is changed, with particular emphasis on what, for Kurbskij, was the most important consequence of the change, Ivan's liquidation of his magnates and army leaders "whom God has given him". In other words, Kurbskij admits that the Czar sits on his throne by the Divine will, but indicates at the same time that the change in the monarch is such as to lose him the Divine benevolence, and that consequently his subjects must be entitled to regard him with aversion. Moreover, he manages to limit his admission of Groznyj's divine authority by inserting the remark about the magnates and army leaders being given to the Czar by God, just as the throne was. The Czar is therefore not justified in treating them in an ungodly way, he implies. And now that he has, according to the writer of the letter, turned to this way, this is a fall from grace, which justifies Kurbskij's defection. If this letter is taken as notice of renunciation of allegiance, the analogy with feudal custom in Europe can be taken further, and its content called a portrait of a *rex iniustus.*

This was Groznyj's cue to define his attitude to this view of his authority, and in the moment of action, so to speak, to give his reply to posterity's theory of the change in him. It appears very clearly from Ivan's first letter, how anxious he was to repudiate and invalidate the allegation of a fall from grace.

In form, the introduction of the message is constructed in accordance with the scheme of the traditional intitulation and the devotional formula as it is found in the Czar's second letter to Kurbskij, and in most of his other letters. But it is quite obvious that the pattern is burst in the first message. The *dei gratia* of the devotional formula, usually expressed by *Boga milost'*, appears here in a couple of variants (*Božije izvolenije, Božije povelenije*) with an underlining of the Divine will and command, and as the framework of a full confession of faith, while the intitulation takes the form of a historical justification of the Czardom.

The bursting open of the introductory formula may probably be explained stylistically by the need for a fuller and more monumental exordium to this enormous letter than the usual one. This is scarcely an adequate explanation, however, in that it does not answer the far more important question of why the bounds of the epistolary style, as a whole, burst under the pressure of the content. The essential point, also in regard to the introduction, is undoubtedly an intention that exceeds the needs of the routine, official communication, and which, therefore, is not content with the conventional, official statement of the religious justification of the power of the Czar, but requires something more impressive and emphatic. The letter is a piece of psychological warfare. And since the war was about the very basis of the Czardom, Groznyj cannot be satisfied here with the official statement of this basis, but must plunge into defensive polemics at the very start.

In his introduction, Ivan attaches great importance to stressing that the Orthodox, well pleasing to God, dominion on earth begins with the Emperor Constantine the Great, and began in Russia with St. Vladimir when he Christianized the country. From that time, Ivan claims, the Orthodox autocracy was transmitted from monarch to monarch, and finally, by the will of God and by God's command—and thus not merely suffered to happen by God's grace or God's mercy—has been inherited by Ivan Groznyj himself. From this follows his claim that he exercises the autocracy, *samoderžanije,* by virtue of the Divine command and the right of inheritance. In other words, Groznyj repudiates the right of Kurbskij or anybody else to set up criteria by which the Czar's authority can be judged—it is nationally and religiously rooted—founded on the rocks of the nation and Orthodoxy, and cannot be shaken. The Czardom is one and indivisible, beyond human caprice. The Czar is not responsible to man.

This emphasis on the Czardom as an unlimited autocracy by the grace of God, is repeated later in the message with greater precision. Ivan replies to Kurbskij's reproaches for having exterminated the country's magnates with the sarcastic remark that he does not know whom Kurbskij is talking about, since the Russian realm is governed by God's mercy and the grace of the most pure Mother of God, the prayers of all the Saints, the blessing of all his parents and finally by Ivan himself, its sovereign—but not by magnates and army leaders, of whom, for that matter, by the help of God he has enough, even without defecting traitors. Otherwise, he reserves to himself the right both to punish and to reward his servants. It is right that a master should correct his servants, but not that the servant should call his master to account. No-one dared to reprove the ungodly Emperor Theophilos, in ancient Byzantium,

in the manner Kurbskij takes the liberty of reproaching a pious Czar—it is consequently not seemly for subjects to distinguish between just and unjust rulers. Even Constantine, most pious of Emperors, killed his own son for the sake of the Empire. The Czar will render his account only to God on the Day of Judgement, but in return he will also answer for the acts of his subjects, if any have sinned owing to the Czar's remissness. It is therefore impossible to accuse him, the Czar, of devising methods of torture against the Christian race, as Kurbskij claims he does. Ivan is ready to defend this people against all enemies, both with his blood and with his life. In other words, there is no basis for a right of resistance to the Czar: on the contrary, he is bound at peril of his salvation to prevent his subjects, whether they will or not, from going astray, and to keep the realm of Orthodoxy safe from enemies.

It is consequently not for his own pleasure that the Czar undertakes the punishment of disobedient servants. He must do so, since good must be rewarded with good and evil with evil. This does not mean that the Czar himself is without sin, for only God is without sin—all the more reason for subjects to avoid provoking the Czar to wrath, so that in his human weakness he might, perhaps, be led into sin. Such lapses on the part of the Czar, however, do not alter the main point, that God has enfeoffed him with the unlimited autocracy. It is precisely this that is the crucial difference between the truly Orthodox Russia and the impious nations—with which Kurbskij has been kind enough to compare the Czar—that these, characteristically enough, do not have rulers with sovereign power, but only monarchs who obey the orders of their servants. And, Groznyj adds, that just as the boyars and army leaders have no right to rebuke the Czar, neither have the clergy any such right. It is not the Lord's intention that priests should meddle with matters of government. It is one thing to save one's own soul, and quite another to have the responsibility for many souls and bodies. It is one thing to abide in fasting, but another to live in common with others. The spiritual authority of the church is one thing, to govern as Czar another. In communal life, there are supervision and rules and punishment, and if these are neglected, the life of the community breaks down.

According to Groznyj's definition, as it appears from the account given above, the ideal government—Orthodox Russia's *samoderžanije*—is a dominion exercised by the hereditary Czar over the subjects of the realm, without respect of persons, without responsibility to the church or any other earthly representative of the divine power, but responsible only to the Highest Judge at Doomsday. In life on earth, the Czar has the right and the authority to decide what is fidelity and what treason, good and evil, piety and sacrilege in relation to the Czardom.

It is obvious that this view of the state, in spite of its radical and sharp formulation, cannot be accepted as well defined without further consideration. It is so broad and so abstract in its formulation, that it is more axiomatic or dogmatic than definitive or of the nature of political science. Ivan's repudiation of Kurbskij's approach to the formulation of a right of resistance and renunciation of allegiance does not imply a clear position on the Czar's re-

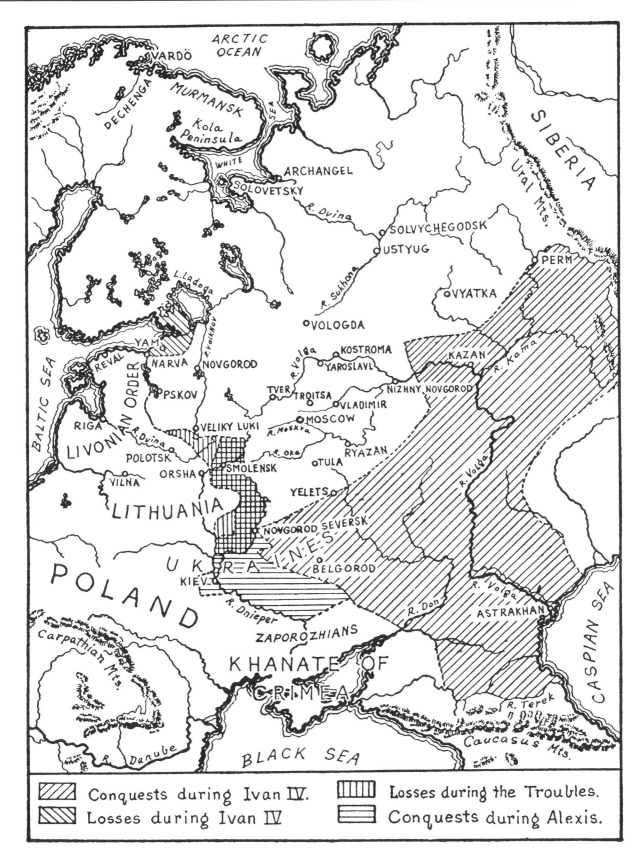

Map of Muscovy in the 16th and 17th centuries illustrating the conquests and losses of Ivan IV.

sponsibility to the rules he has himself dictated. By laying it down that in communal life there must be rules that must be maintained to prevent the life of the community from sinking into chaos, he has debarred himself from claiming the right to break or change quite arbitrarily the rules he himself has made—a point which Kurbskij has also taken up, as will be seen later. And by claiming for the Czardom an exclusively religious legitimation, he has simultaneously undertaken to show, at any rate, a steadfastness in piety that does not seriously offend against the general notions of piety. To Kurbskij he curtly declared that he was and would remain pious, unlike his Byzantine predecessor Theophilos. But he was unable to draw the logical conclusion and state that in cases where the spiritual and the temporal clashed, it would be the temporal power that would decide what was true piety.

Seen against the background of this capacious axiom, it is not surprising that Ivan Groznyj had to support his view still further by a series of reasons or proofs of various types, primarily, of course, biblical reasons, a *scriptural justification*. In continuation of what might be called the extended devotional formula, and because the church was in principle declared incompetent in temporal matters, the Czar turned to the Bible itself as the unshakable foundation—and, one might add, the long-suffering instrument—for the temporal power's claim to religious legitimation. The Pauline formulation of a theory of the state, which in the course of the centuries has played a much more fatal role than the much criticized realism of Machiavelli, forms the corner-stone of Groznyj's argumentation, and lies so close alongside his way of thinking and expressing himself that the quotations merge into the context. The sword here is not merely legitimized, it is legitimation itself. This authoritarian justification of the autocracy naturally does not make it more explicit or concrete, rather it assumes, to an even higher degree, the character of an axiom, firmly founded on the inappellable revelation. What this involves for Ivan Groznyj's argumentation will be discussed later.

In connexion with his religious proofs, the Czar also gives a *historical justification*, as already foreshadowed in the introduction to the message. Because of the nature of the situation, it was very natural that Groznyj should replace the traditional intitulational list of the actual extent of his dominion by a list of the ancestral gallery of the Russian autocracy. Historically, of course, this was quite unjustifiable, since the autocracy in Groznyj's sense had not existed in previous centuries. It was a postulate, of the same kind as the genealogies by which the Russian royal house—like the other potentates of Europe at that time—claimed descent from Caesar Augustus. Groznyj, however, had a more concrete form of historical justification, reference to previous cases illustrating the consequence of strong or weak rule in the ancient states.

The Emperor Augustus, says Groznyj, ruled over the whole world: all states were under the same rule up to and including the first Christian ruler, Constantine the Great. But after Constantine's sons had divided the Empire between them, power began to be divided and weakened. Small princes and governors began to establish their own

independent kingdoms—as the traitors to Ivan also dream of doing—and from that time order ceased in the Greek Empire, because every man interested himself only in power, glory and wealth, and it perished in political conflicts. Although the power of the Byzantine Empire steadily decayed, its magnates and councillors did not cease their egoistic intrigues and disruptive manoeuvres, but continued in their evil ways, closing their eyes to the threatening dangers. The end was inevitable under such conditions, and the unbeliever Mohammed destroyed the Greek Empire and like a storm-wind and a tempest, left no trace behind. Which shows how ill it goes with that kingdom which is characterized by the Czar's obedience to his magnates and councillors.

It is obvious that with this argumentation, Groznyj has crossed the boundary between the axiom based on religion and political theory. From a historical point of view, the justification of the autocracy lies in its importance for the existence, undivided and unimpaired, of the kingdom. Autocracy means order—aristocracy, chaos. Nationally, therefore, the Czar has a duty to keep the magnates under control, just as much as it is his religious duty to do so.

In the last resort, Groznyj's theory of history is a means of supporting what is actually and essentially a *political justification*. We have already seen how the Czar distinguishes sharply between the tasks of the individual in respect of his spiritual life, and the tasks of the Czar as the guardian of society. Spiritual authority must require a mighty suppression of the tongue, of glory, of honour, of adornment, of supremacy, which are all things unbefitting monks. But the Czarist system is compelled to use terror, repression and coercion, even the most extreme oppression, corresponding to the madness of the most evil and cunning men. To the Czar, not even the scriptural command to turn to other cheek applies—he must return the blow. If he does not, he will never be able to keep the kingdom safe, since without internal peace and order no kingdom can defend itself against external enemies, just as a tree cannot blossom if its roots are dry. In other words, the Czar's power rests not merely on divine grace, but also on the supreme *raison d'état*—not only on faith but also on reason.

It is not for his own pleasure or to enrich himself at the expense of his subjects that the Czar punishes and executes traitors. To wage effective war against the enemy, the Czar has need of many army leaders and assistants, and consequently no Czar in his right mind would begin to exterminate his assistants if it were not necessary. But traitors do get their well deserved punishment, as is the custom in other countries where government is not corrupted by the intrigues of the magnates. When Kurbskij had to reveal his traitorous sentiments, therefore, it did not surprise the Czar that he should choose to go over to the country hostile to Russia, where King Zygmunt August cannot exercise any rule, but is less then his lowest servant. It will soon appear that Kurbskij will find little comfort or support in such a place, where each thinks only of his own advantage. No, life must be lived in accordance with the requirements of the present day—for otherwise thieves and traitors will work their will and the kingdom perish in confusion, simply because its shepherd had no care for the disorders of his subjects. It is thus not merely the lessons of history that furnish the proofs of the indispensability of the autocracy for the kingdom and its vital interests, but also, unfortunately, the actual state of things.

It will be clear that while Groznyj is quite ready to accept the authority of the Bible when it is a question of the Pauline theory of the state, he did not consider the words of Jesus about turning the other cheek were of general application—the command does not apply to Czars. There are two necessities—one religious, one political. It might seem as though Groznyj was conscious of a choice between these two things should they come to clash—a choice which for him must quite obviously be the political necessity. He cannot declare himself clearly, and as a programme, on this point. This was partly because his period—in spite of approaches to political realism, such as Machiavelli's—was not favourable to secularization, and especially not in Orthodox Russia, and partly because Groznyj—bound as he was by the cultural situation in Russia—was scarcely able to make a fundamental analysis of this problem. None the less, there are certain hints in his polemical writing, besides those already mentioned, of what is perhaps an involuntary, perhaps actually unconscious, tendency to secularization.

One of Kurbskij's accusations, and the one to which Groznyj returns most frequently and with the greatest resentment, is that the change in him has caused him to forsake his former piety and to turn against the faith—that he has become "the opposite", *soprotiv*. It is obvious that Ivan feels the central significance of this accusation, and attaches corresponding importance to refuting it. It is quite extraordinarily striking, however, that though in his message he takes up this accusation no less than eleven times, he disputes against the word *soprotiv* in its original context, that is, with regard to orthodoxy, at only one of these places. In five other places, the connexion is not clear, though at any rate with more connexion with political than with religious questions. And finally, in the last five cases, he uses the word in a way quite different from Kurbskij's, in that he connects the word with the concept of reason, *razum*, instead of with orthodoxy, *pravoslavije*. In these last cases, he justifies his refutation clearly and unambiguously by political necessity and the Czar's responsibility for the unity and security of the kingdom. It is not contrary to reason that the Czar will not serve his servants, that he will rule as the time requires, that he will defend himself against opponents, that when he came of age he decided to make his formal mastery real, instead of allowing himself to be guided by the will of others.

In so central a question, then, Groznyj not only puts the main emphasis on interests of state and political motives when he wants to prove his adherence to the true faith, he actually, in the heat of action, makes a shift in his concepts, so that he comes to argue from a purely temporal criterion, that his actions are in agreement with political reason. It is difficult to explain this shift merely by the fact that Kurbskij in his letter brings in the concept of reason in the next sentence. Here it is a matter of such vital principles that Groznyj would hardly have made a contamination of the concepts unless he had had some deeper motive for doing so.

Further support is to be found for the conjecture that for Groznyj, the political motives dominated over the religious ones, by examining that part of his argument that may be called a *personal justification*. By this is meant his argumentation for his political views by means of examples from his personal experiences as ruler of the Muscovites—and they were abundant, since he succeeded to, or was put on, the throne at three years old, twenty-one years before he wrote his message to Kurbskij. This personal justification is a long, connected argument in the form of a sort of autobiography, and occupies a good fifth of the total text of the message. Here Ivan paints a sombre picture of political conditions after the death of Vasilij, that grew even worse after the death of his mother. The tendencies towards centralized government were energetically countered by the powerful boyar houses, which did not shrink even from attempting to promote their own interests by making agreements with the rulers of neighbouring countries. As to home politics, this was completely dominated by the struggle for power among the boyars, and their egoistic urge to enrich themselves. The regency during Ivan's minority assumes the character of a struggle, often bloody, with the supporters of the royal house. On several occasions, he saw these violent, and tumultuous events at close quarters, as when he was present at an attempt to murder one of his faithful boyars in the very dining chamber. In other ways, too, he could observe the hostility of the magnates and the regents, for both he and his brother were normally reduced to living as though they were foreigners or paltry serving boys. Irregular meals and inadequate clothing were the order of the day, just as the indignant boy had to look on while one of his regents sprawled comfortably on his late father's bed, without showing the boy prince either the kindness due to a child or the respect due to the sovereign of the country.

From his fifteenth year, the boy now tries to take control, but is met by intensified intrigues by the boyars, who, for example, try to exploit the great fire at Moscow to raise the people against the Grand Ducal house. And when the young Czar has taken his first steps in an independent exercise of government with the help of two new men in the administration, Aleksej Adašev and the priest Sil'vestr, he only finds that his two assistants ally themselves more and more closely with his enemies, and even that the priest, instead of devoting himself to the Czar's spiritual education, starts intriguing politically. Ivan is constantly excluded more and more from deliberations and decisions on matters of state. Should he contradict even an inferior servant, he is scolded for his bad behaviour, but if he himself was abused by a councillor, without respect or kindness, the councillor, on the other hand, is reckoned a pattern of good behaviour. Ivan's honourable supporters and followers are persecuted and martyred, but his enemies and opponents come to riches and honour. When he speaks, Adašev and Sil'vestr brush him aside with reproaches for his unreasonableness and his childishness—which he has in remembrance when he now reads Kurbskij's accusations.

The most incurable of the hurts in Groznyj's memories belong to his time of trial, when, in his twenty-third year, he lay on his death-bed, given up by all. His first and last thoughts were to secure the continuity of the Czardom, to prevent the work of reform he had started from coming to a standstill, and to ensure the continuation of the consolidation of the kingdom externally, so well begun with the conquest of Kazan' some months previously. He demanded that the boyars should swear fealty to his infant son, and thus guarantee his succession while he himself still lived. Instead, they prepared to make his cousin, the insignificant Vladimir Starickij, Czar, so that they could have free scope in the future. This plan failed only because Groznyj, by the grace of God, survived the crisis. This, and many other plots, caused Groznyj to take measures against the boyars and the councillors. At the beginning of this purge, the Czar's wrath, *gnev,* was administered with mercy, *milost'*. Nobody was put to death, but the worst opponents were banished from the court and council, and others were ordered to hold no communication with them. Not until this order was disregarded, and every means used to intrigue again, did Groznyj turn to the sterner measures for which Kurbskij now attacks him.

This autobiographical account cannot, of course, on the face of it be considered to be more in accordance with the truth than his historical justification. That does not matter, however, in this connexion, where the object is to ascertain what are the Czar's views and arguments, not to verify his evidence. Yet it is natural to note here two confirmatory circumstances. First, there is a clear difference between the basis and premisses of the historical justification and the autobiographical one. The historical justification partakes largely of the character of a myth which serves to render intelligible the Czar's political doctrine. Groznyj writes Russian and world history from his present standpoint, and adjusts it to this, which was not out of keeping with the custom of the time. The history of his own life, however, was still too recent to mythologize it. Secondly, the principal motif of his autobiographical review, the fundamental conflict of interest between the boyars and the Czar, was real enough. It is unnecessary to resort to psychiatric or psycho-analytical explanations to find meaning in Groznyj's argumentation, however great a part his autobiographical statements may have played in posterity's judgement on his mental state and constitution.

With every conceivable exaggeration, aberration of memory, suppression and perversion of facts . . . the autobiography is something other and more than an illustration of Groznyj's general political justification. It is an account of an extremely concrete and direct experience of life, which could find adequate, theoretical expression only in Groznyj's political formulations. This does not, however, answer the question of whether Groznyj wanted to force the conditions to take form according to his ideas, or whether he wanted to do the opposite. But it is clear enough that he has not reconstructed the story of his life to make it fit his ideas. He has constructed his autobiography in polemical form, it is true. But the ideas were taken from experience, not the other way round.

In the previous pages, it has been argued that Groznyj's

historical justification supports the political one, and that in the last resort, the political role plays a greater part for Groznyj than the religious one, at any rate, where the two clash. This last point seems to gain further confirmation from the study of Groznyj's personal justification, which to such a great extent centres in his experiences with his political opponents. His very sharp emphasis on the priest Sil'vestr's alleged misuse of his spiritual authority to meddle with temporal matters, and his disillusioned view of the ideal of piety of those around him as a cynical excuse for keeping him in tutelage—all this also points towards a tendency—conscious or unconscious—to *secularization* in Groznyj, simultaneously with his adherence to the axiom of Orthodoxy. This compound of religious dogmatism and political realism, of axiom and empiricism, must now be brought into the centre of observation, in the attempt to analyse the method in Groznyj's argumentation.

There may appear to be little justification for speaking of tendencies to secularization in Ivan Groznyj, when it is considered that he quotes from the Old and the New Testaments, the Church Fathers, and other Orthodox authorities to such an enormous extent that the quotations occupy about a quarter of the text. How quotations are used, however, is not without importance, a point of which Kurbskij also found occasion to make an acid comment.

In many places, it is striking to note with what casualness, almost even laxity, the Czar turns to account these ultimative sentences. We have already seen him appeal to St. Paul where St. Paul's words fit a ruler's hand like a glove, but reject like a challenge and without hesitation, Jesus' injunction to exercise patience. And he himself declares that he shall not be called to account till Doomsday, but in response to Kurbskij's declaration that he will appeal to the Supreme Judge against Groznyj, he replies that that is to blaspheme against the very words of the Saviour, who said, "Let not the sun go down upon your wrath". That the words are those of St. Paul is, of course, of less importance than the polemical aptness of the quotation in the debate. Kurbskij was not slow to make use of this weakness. When Groznyj wished to show that his defection was not only a betrayal of his father land but also a disregard of the words of Jesus—"If a kingdom be divided against itself, that kingdom cannot stand"—Kurbskij promptly replied with the just as authoritative "When they persecute you in one city, flee ye into another".

It is a trite observation, that Kurbskij's obvious repugnance to this duel with quotations is due to his humanistic education, very different from Groznyj's traditional Byzantinism. From the point of view of style, Kurbskij shoots with whetted arrows, while Groznyj hurls granite boulders. To Kurbskij, a quotation is a means of expressing much in a few words, as he says in his criticism of Groznyj's style. Groznyj, on the other hand, quite obviously quoted in order to express one and the same thought through as many impressive authorities as possible. He underlines their weight with such phrases as "as Gregory who is called the Theologian said, writing with solemn words", or "as the divine Gregory (Nazianzen) said to those that have confidence in their youth, and who at all times presume to be teachers", or "this was said by the divine (Dionysios the Areopagite) in his epistle", or the like. Groznyj's aim is not to spit his opponent on a well directed point, but to crush him under the massive weight of his authorities. It did not worry him, therefore, that the quotations sometimes grew so long that the starting-point is forgotten before the end is reached. Groznyj's cultural orientation and ideal were rooted in the Russian literature of translation, and through this to the Byzantine classics. The quotations undoubtedly show that in this field he was well read. And yet it does not seem possible to explain the use of the quotations simply by reference to the type of education the Czar had received, so different from Kurbskij's. Many of the quotations look as if they had been stuck on afterwards, caught by an association of ideas, under the need to find polemical ammunition.

In one single case, the first quotation from the letter to the monk Demophilos, traditionally ascribed to Dionysios the Areopagite, it is perhaps possible actually to get an insight into Groznyj's technique in preparing his propaganda piece. The word for word quotation—about the vision of the Blessed Carpos—is followed by some concluding remarks to Kurbskij, after which several manuscripts have a colloquial paraphrase of the same account, but now ascribed to Bishop Polycarp instead of to Carpos, and this again is followed by approximately the same concluding remarks to Kurbskij. Earlier conjectures of two different but extremely homogeneous accounts must be rejected, as does *J. S. Lur'je*. Instead, we must assume a tautological error in editing, committed perhaps by Groznyj or his assistants while actually drafting the text. It is very natural to take this idea a stage further, and to assume that the second version is one, dictated from memory, of the quotation Groznyj wanted his chancellery to produce for him, but which, either by a lapse of memory or by a misunderstanding, was not removed from the fair copy. Obviously, no-one minded this visionary tautology. The more, the better.

The second, very long extract from the epistle to Demophilos seems to have been seized on with joy in Groznyj's spiritual reading as a welcome proof of the universal validity of his idea of the state.

The gist of what is said here is that Demophilos has no moral or ecclesiastical right to exceed his competence by denouncing a superior in the ecclesiastical hierarchy. One cannot, on behalf of Our Lord, assume the right to change the divinely transmitted order. Disorder and laxity are aberrations from the divine commands and edicts. And apart from the fact that one cannot permit oneself to judge without having authority to do so, God's perfect justice will not tolerate that one should allow one's anger to infringe upon His clemency.

It is obvious that this quotation attracted Groznyj because of its emphasis on the unshakableness of authority. The requirement of clemency is onesidedly thrown over on Kurbskij, without Groznyj's realising that it could come back like a boomerang. He has simply not been interested enough in this idea to consider its possible relation to himself. From the observation of this to the conjecture of what it is that particularly struck Groznyj in reading this passage and fixed it in his memory it is only a step—it must

be just the comparison with worldly conditions: "And if someone were to take upon himself the government of a people without being commanded to do so by a king, justly would he be tormented. And what if anyone present of those who are subjected to a prince should dare to criticize that prince when he was acquitting or condemning anyone, to say nothing of vituperating him and driving him from power?" What is meant, in the epistle, to serve merely as an illustration of the spiritual order, to Groznyj is the main point, which is to be confirmed by this spiritual authority—which thus furnishes one more argument for his *groznoje povelenije,* his "terrible fiat".

This twisting of the real meaning of the quotations is revealed with absolutely sublime irony by the little quotation from St. John Chrysostom, where men are enjoined to refrain from strife: with men, one wins or loses on earth, with God one is in every case defeated. The quotation is aimed at Kurbskij, and is meant to prove to him that it is vain to resist Groznyj's spiritually and temporally rooted power, which, like the house Jesus spoke of, is founded upon a rock. Here the axiomatic compound of power and piety appears in its purest and clearest form, but expressed by the words of the very man whose efforts were concentrated on getting the theory of the state in the Epistle to the Romans accepted as meaning that though temporal authority as an institution (*to pragma*) was undoubtedly of God, the individual representatives of that authority (*hoi kath' ekaston arkhontes*) were not necessarily so—and who cited Jesus' house that was founded upon a rock in defiance of the omnipotence of the Byzantine Emperor. Even if Groznyj had been able to realise this, he would certainly have been quite indifferent. Here, the object is not logical or dogmatic proof, not a linking of his own thoughts with those of others, but exclusively the exploitation of the thoughts of others for his own purposes.

This—to use a word that Groznyj can hardly have known, but which was beginning to be really topical in the Western Roman Catholic world—was *propaganda*. Propaganda not for the Faith, but for the supremacy of the Czar. That Groznyj devoted so much of his polemical tract to religious evidences, was primarily due to the fact that Orthodoxy was the only common and accepted ground for Ivan, Kurbskij and the Russian people. It was the medium, so to speak, in which an argument could be carried on. This is not meant to imply that Ivan, purely privately, was indifferent to the Faith, and was simply using it as a political weapon. That he meant to do so seems to be fully shown by his argumentation, but at the present stage it is impossible to pronounce on his private faith—beyond the observation that he distinguished sharply between individual piety and the conditions of communal life, or, as it would now be put, between religion and politics. He was debarred, however, from carrying this point to its logical conclusion, and was compelled, instead, to carry on his political struggle with religious arguments, however difficult he might find it, consciously or unconsciously.

It can hardly be doubted that this dogmatic or axiomatic basis for Ivan's argumentation has had considerable influence on his thinking in concrete, political matters. He uses the description of Hellenistic heathendom from Gregory

Nazianzen—according to which men made themselves gods in the images of their passions, so that sin was held to be not merely innocent but divine, since responsibility was attributed to the gods they worshipped—to show that Kurbskij praises the Czar's enemies in agreement with his own treason. Whether or not Groznyj was right in this judgement of Kurbskij, this is one of the rare cases in which a quotation is used efficiently, that is to say, as a parallel that explains and characterizes, and even with a certain pungency in the point. Kurbskij would have been justified, of course, in replying that the Czar himself acknowledged the Trinity as an image of his own absolute power. What is more important, however, is that the quotation probably seems so effective because it is a direct and genuine expression of a phenomenon in Groznyj's argumentation that lies at the centre of his method.

It must be seen as the result of Groznyj's axiomatic way of thinking, that his political polemics take to such a degree the form of *collective identification.* By this is meant that he condemns a person—particularly Kurbskij, of course—by identifying him, by means of a special type of argumentation, with a group that is *a priori* condemned.

In the case just mentioned, Groznyj could have confined himself to using the vituperative word "traitor" to Kurbskij, which would not have seemed unnatural after Kurbskij had gone over to a hostile country. It would rather have seemed so obvious that it would have fallen rather flat. His Majesty would thereby have betrayed that he was offended or upset by the defection of a single man, which would have been incompatible with the contempt a ruler must feel for an individual of such a calibre. When Groznyj uses words of abuse in a quite primitive way, it serves to emphasise his boundless and subjective contempt for the individual as such—as, for example, when in the middle of a formal explanation he spits out a "cur" or "wretch" at Kurbskij, or congratulates himself that he no longer sees his "Ethiopian face". Kurbskij's individual act, his defection to King Zygmunt, is not worth calling treason, it only shows that Kurbskij thereby "completed his devilish, currish betrayal" and that "in his devilish, currish desire" he has gone to a master who will let him live on in his arbitrary obstinacy, "self-will", *samovolstvo.* Therewith, Kurbskij is characterized as an individual.

When, on the other hand, it is a matter of primary importance, the invective is qualified, so to speak, by being raised to the plane of general principle, as with the quotation from Gregory. There crime and treason became a cosmic principle—like the Devil as against God—and thus the evil complement to the justice and order of the autocracy. And when the moral scope and consequences of the act are designated simply "treason", without adjectives, then it is a question of a collective phenomenon, a conspiracy of menacing extent, a wide-spread net of intrigue, the object of which is to persecute the Czar and all who support him, both clerical and lay—a conspiracy that can be traced back in history and in all the troubles and frustrations that Groznyj has ever experienced. Not until he has been "placed" in this conspiracy is Kurbskij properly characterized.

It is difficult to say to what extent Kurbskij, from an objec-

tive point of view, had qualified himself for this collective identification. The previous history of his defection is unknown, except from hints by the parties to the case, and we do not know, therefore, whether he evaded by his flight Groznyj's anger and punishment for some act of political opposition. All that can be said is that he lays himself open to Groznyj's condemnation by his general expression of sympathy with the Czar's victims and by including himself in their number. It is quite obvious, however, that this did not imply any declaration of political relations with or collaboration with these people. By virtue of his high birth, his membership of the Select Council (*izbrannaja rada*), and his position as an army leader, Kurbskij must of necessity have known and been more or less familiar with the Czar's victims, but his horror at their fate seems to have been primarily a humane, not a political, reaction. He is more interested in the fates of the individuals than in the collapse of the boyars' policy.

Groznyj seems to have felt this, and occasionally argues on this basis, especially by pointing out to Kurbskij that his peers at home in Russia, in spite of their manifestations against the Czar, are still living in complete freedom (*svoboda*) and increasing wealth. Here Ivan argues on the individual plane: when Kurbskij now prefers to go his own way rather than submit to the supremacy of the Czar, and his equals, however, continue to enjoy their freedom in their own country—why, then, does he not stop making a nuisance of himself? Here, however, Kurbskij found no difficulty in replying. When Groznyj wrote again, thirteen years later, he was clearly suffering from pangs of conscience, and no longer mentions freedom. As early as 1567, he answered Zygmunt II August, who had accused him of violating the free nature of man, with a half-admission, that servitude prevailed everywhere, also in the realm of the Polish King himself. Kurbskij, on the other hand, spoke with renewed force of the victims of Groznyj's lawlessness (*bezzakonije*), of executions without law or justice (*bez suda i bez prava*), and said that Ivan had "shut up the kingdom of Russia, in other words, free human nature (*svobodnoje jestestvo čoloveče skoje*) as in a fortress of hell", and that he killed everyone that tried to escape. This is to argue on behalf of the individual against the terror, against insecurity and lawlessness in the Czardom, but not for any political alternative to the autocracy.

If Kurbskij to a high degree polemizes on behalf of the individual and in defence of the rights of the individual, Groznyj speaks almost everywhere on behalf of the state, and sees his opponents as the state's opponents. It is typical that Groznyj goes far towards obvious insincerity when, as in the case just cited, he speaks of the position of the individual in the state. There are other cases where he directly contradicts himself in this connexion, as when he declares at one moment that he has not persecuted and exterminated whole families, but in the next actually praise himself for not having made Sil'vestr's son pay for the sins of his father. Groznyj was not interested in the fate of the individual—as is shown even in his letter to his faithful servant, Vasilij Gr'asnoj, whom he would not ransom from the Tartars. He is uncertain in a discussion of this question, but all the more certain in his collective identification of the enemies of the state, of the traitors' interwoven and continuing net. What does interest him is to show the place of the individual mesh in the net.

This identification Ivan usually demonstrates by means of a type of argument that might be called *implicative characterization.* By this is meant that, on the basis of a specific resemblance between a phenomenon and a particular category, he identifies the phenomenon with the general characteristics of that category. It is consequently not a question of partial identification, as in applying the Aristotelean principle of subsumption.

Thus we already have an implication when Ivan counts Kurbskij among the traitors because he protests against Ivan's treatment of them, just as they themselves, of course, do. This example is not quite perfect, however, since in this connexion Ivan must have had in mind Kurbskij's defection to the King of Poland, even though he does not mention it. In many other cases, however, implication plays a predominant part, and especially where the conclusion follows from theological premisses.

The most peculiar case is the argument with which Ivan introduces his declaration that he must answer both for his own and his subjects' actions at the Day of Judgement. Here, he begins with an extremely ingenious double implication. Kurbskij's rhetorical question of whether the Czar believes himself to be immortal—which clearly means that Groznyj would hardly act as he has done if he expected to be answerable in the other world—Ivan takes as his starting-point for the accusation that Kurbskij is postulating that Ivan does not acknowledge that he has a soul which must answer, after death, for the acts done in life on earth, and that therefore Ivan is guilty of a heresy like that of the Saducees, who, of course, denied that the soul survived death. In other words, Ivan implies that Kurbskij implies heresy is Ivan. After which Ivan goes on to the second implication, in that he answers Kurbskij's postulated accusation of heresy by the assertion that Kurbskij himself is a heretic. The Manichees maintain that Christ reigns in Heaven, man on earth, and the Devil in Hell. Kurbskij talks of the coming judgement in Heaven, but condemns God's punishment on earth—i.e. the punishment administered through the Czar by the grace of God—therefore he is a heretic, as well as a maker of false accusations of heresy.

In a similar manner, Kurbskij also becomes a disciple of the Cathars, because like Novatian he does not accept repentance, but requires that men shall rise above their human nature, which is implied in his reference to Judgement Day. In a single instance, Ivan kills two birds with one stone: what Kurbskij reproaches him for, says Ivan, is that he will not give himself up to destruction at the hands of his adversaries; but Kurbskij himself has broken his oath of allegiance because he feared death at Ivan's hands—this is at once Novatianism and Pharisaism, the first because Kurbskij demands that men shall be superhuman, and the second because he does not himself act as he would have others act. Here, too, it is at bottom a question of a double implication, since the actual demonstration of Novatianism and Pharisaism is done by implication, and the basis for the demonstration is likewise implied: Kurbskij's defence of the boyars who have become

Ivan's victims is taken as an accusation against Ivan for refusing to become the boyars' victim.

Since Groznyj has adopted the Pauline theory of the state, it follows as normal logical sequence of thought for him to declare that Kurbskij opposes God in opposing the Czar, since the Czar's authority is of God. It is also consistent, logical thinking when Ivan claims that Kurbskij's heresy is so much the worse in view of the fact that Ivan succeeded to the throne without strife or bloodshed, and by inheritance, and consequently without any circumstance whatever that could cast a shadow of doubt on the Czar's authority. For Ivan, however, this is not enough. At the very beginning of his message, he hints at an implication that is to show Kurbskij in even darker colours— he, the former boyar, councillor and general for the autocracy and Orthodoxy, has now broken his oath of fealty, and has thereby become a direct destroyer of Christendom by going over to the service of the enemies of Christendom. This idea is extended a moment later. When Kurbskij now goes to the wars with the enemies of the Czardom, he will come to destroy churches, trample upon icons, murder Christians; the soft limbs of Russian youths will be crushed and maimed by the hoofs of the horses as the armies advance. And even though Kurbskij may perhaps refrain from active participation in such things, he will still contrive this evil work with the deadly poison of his thoughts. This is a line of thought that has a much longer perspective than Kurbskij's particular case. Here it is a matter of an implication that, when used by a ruler, is the most portentous of all, that a person's thoughts can make him the accessory to the acts of others and a sharer in the responsibility for them.

But the implication goes even further. The person's thoughts, in spite of everything, belong to his characteristics as an individual, just like his actions, and since they are under his control he is responsible for them, if not in a legal, yet in an intellectual and moral sense. This might be the unexpressed premiss for the implication just mentioned, even though it is scarcely probable. It is more difficult, on the other hand, to find such an immediately explicable premiss for the implication by which Kurbskij is identified collectively with his forefathers, and consequently with the legal obligations and crimes of his family. Here, the argument runs in two lines. On the one hand, by breaking his oath of fealty and joining the enemies of Christendom, Kurbskij destroyed not only his own soul but those of his forefathers, since his forefathers had sworn, for themselves and their successors, fealty to Ivan's grandfather, Ivan Velikij and his successors. On the other hand, Kurbskij is described as a traitor because he comes of a race of traitors, as a spreader of poison because he is born of a generation of vipers. His grandfather intrigued against Ivan Velikij, his father against Groznyj's father, Grand Duke Vasilij, and the same tradition appears on the mother's side. From this point of view, Kurbskij has committed treason in the hope of regaining the ancestral land of the princely house of Kurbskij, Jaroslavl', which had been incorporated into the Grand Duchy of Moscow a hundred years before.

It is consequently a double taint that Kurbskij bears in

consequence of his descent. By the breach of his oath, he has annulled the merits of his ancestors. And through his ancestors' crimes his own becomes the greater. It is conceivable, perhaps, that this reasoning reflects an ancient view of the solidarity of the family, transmitted in a vague and blurred form that approaches the popular belief of the kind that the apple does not fall far from the tree. The argument is more precise than it would have been had it been based merely on such a belief. This is shown not least by the reference to Jaroslavl'. But it shows, at the same time, a more primitive view of justice than Kurbskij's, who emphasises justice and judgement and free human nature as fundamental concepts. What probably decided Groznyj to use this argument, however, was that he found here yet another opportunity of classifying Kurbskij as an enemy of the Czardom. Both in thought and in act he shows himself to be a participant in the great treason plot, and by birth he is a member of the group that plots it, the boyars.

All these cases of implication have this in common, that they are deduced from religious premises—the political oath of allegiance is, of course, a religious act, as was evidenced by the kiss on the cross (*krestnoje celovanije*)—and they lead to a judgement that is of a markedly political character. This seems to confirm yet again that Groznyj's primary interest lay in ensuring the vindication of his political principles with every means at his disposal, and apparently it is also the clearest revelation of the line along which Groznyj's thinking assumes its axiomatic character. The religious axiom is secularized, but retains its character as an axiom whence proofs can be deduced.

[An] account has been given of Groznyj's conception of the autocracy by the grace of God, as an indivisible, religious-political whole, and of the just as indivisible, heretical-treasonable whole directed against the autocracy. Quite obviously, these ideas imply a highly axiomatic but loosely defined political programme, the concrete conditions and execution of which are not perceived or foreseen in detail. The question of whether Ivan Groznyj had a political programme is thereby answered with a simultaneous yes and no: yes, in the sense that there are clearly political intentions that are justified politically; no, in the sense of a later period's conception of a political programme as a fundamental charter issued by those exercising power, and conditioned by political empiricism. (pp. 20-40)

> *Bjarne Nørretranders, "Ivan Groznyj's Programme," in his* The Shaping of Czardom Under Ivan Groznyj, *translated by Harold Young, Variorum Reprints, 1971, pp. 20-40.*

Edward L. Keenan   (essay date 1971)

[*In the following excerpt from his full-length treatment of the Ivan-Kurbsky correspondence, Keenan argues against Ivan and Kurbsky's authorship and questions the clarity and justification of the arguments in the letters.*]

There are some particularly important features of [the] Ukrainian experience which must be considered in any discussion of the patterns of Muscovite culture in the six-

teenth and seventeenth centuries. First, it must be stressed that in the case of the Ukraine, we are dealing not with the simple transmission of early modern Western ideas, but with a bitter, life-and-death struggle for religious freedom and cultural integrity between the Ukrainian and Belorussian Orthodox establishment and the powerful forces of official counterreformation, in a context created by reformation ideas. It was here that the East Slavs threw up their first lines of defense against the encroachment of the Catholic West, here that Orthodoxy was reinfused with the cultural vigor required for the struggle, here that the first significant printing establishments appeared, and that the first attempt at an East Slavic vulgate Bible was made. And in this territory first appeared those traditions of polemical literature, based both upon interpretation of Orthodox tradition and scholarly analysis of Catholic and Protestant works, which were to prove so important for Muscovite cultural life in the seventeenth century.

In the late sixties and seventies of the sixteenth century, this ferment was well begun in the Ukrainian and Belorussian territories, but nothing comparable can be observed in Muscovy, which seems to have been untouched by all but the faintest echoes of the *Kulturkampf* which was convulsing Europe. Here doctrine was unchallenged (save for a few internal heresies) and polemics traditional. Here the genres, language, and content of the (predominantly religious) literature were quietly canonical, and the manuscript book was unchallenged by Ivan Fedorov's unsuccessful attempt to introduce printing.

The general features of this late sixteenth-century pattern are well known and indisputable; it may indeed be one of the sources of Muscovy's later strength that she was spared, at this stage of her development, the convulsions that generated the cultural efflorescence in the western parts of East Slavic territory. But can Ivan and Kurbskii and their **Correspondence** be placed within the context so defined? For these texts, and previous scholarly literature, ask us to believe that our correspondents were Renaissance men, keenly interested in the questions which were stirring all of Europe *except* Muscovy, well-versed in precisely the texts which were the marching chants of peoples *outside of* Muscovite territory, eager to refute heresies which had not yet challenged Moscow's Orthodoxy.

Can it be? Can we accept the notion, crucial to the traditional attribution, that Kurbskii composed or translated after his flight a number of polemical works, extremely topical for the time in his new home—some even credited as the first of their kind—and that no one in Lithuanian territory even knew about them, or at least mentioned them? Can it be that a layman of Muscovy's warrior class became in effect the teacher of the learned clerical defenders of Orthodoxy in the Polish-Lithuanian state? Can it be that Ivan, who in the **Correspondence** appears more ponderously erudite, if less versatile, than Kurbskii, was a Renaissance prince of a realm with no Renaissance—that he was decades ahead of his subjects in cultural development? No, if what we think we know of the cultural history and cultural patterns of East Slavic territory is to be credited, it cannot be.

It cannot be, that is, unless there exists some firm evidence that Kurbskii and Ivan were, indeed, exceptional within the general context of Muscovite culture and had somehow become particularly well-educated men. A considerable amount of biographical source material about Kurbskii, and rather less concerning Ivan, does exist, and we may turn to it now, with the hope of establishing some record of their literacy and literary education.

About Kurbskii's childhood there is no evidence. He first appears in our sources in 1550 as a warrior, and all of his activities before his flight to Lithuania were essentially military. After his defection, Kurbskii continued to distinguish himself primarily as a military man, and the documents make clear that he was a litigious adulterer, an accessory to murder, a thief, and a general blackguard. There is no evidence that he owned a single book. His will, which details his possessions with great care (he was apparently extremely avaricious), bequeaths to the well-known patron of early Ukrainian book publishing, his friend and executor, Konstantin Ostroz'kyi, not some prized incunabula, but a suit of armor!

There is, of course, nothing in the general run of human experience to indicate that a base adventurer cannot ipso facto be a man of some erudition. But given the traditions and techniques of education of Kurbskii's time, and the rigid differentiation of the roles of scholar and warrior characteristic of Muscovy, his imputed erudition must be considered highly improbable, to say the least.

One need hardly go into the contradictions of this nature in the case of Ivan, before whose exploits Kurbskii's adventures seem the peccadillos of *un homme moyen sensuel*. Concerning his education we possess, as in Kurbskii's case, no reliable information. Note should perhaps be taken, however, of the recurrent myth of the existence of a library of Latin and Greek books which presumably were Ivan's, and are thought by some to be buried to this day under the Kremlin wall. Proving that they are not buried there, or anywhere else is, of course, similar to proving that one is not a camel. The possibility that some trusting individual will someday uncover such a collection cannot be entirely excluded, but, within the limits of present knowledge and the parameters of normal logic, Belokurov long ago showed [in his *O Biblioteke*] that this library is the figment of a number of overheated imaginations.

Thus, to put the contradiction in its starkest form: if these letters are to be accepted as genuine, one must then also accept the compound paradox that the two most erudite authors of their age, who anticipated by two generations later formal and philosophical developments in Muscovite literary culture, whose careers are otherwise rather well illuminated in documentary sources, left no evidence of their literary activities, nor indeed of their functional literacy, aside from texts questionably attributed to them, and that their innovative and heroic intellectual achievements remained entirely unknown to their contemporaries.

A final comment about the content of the **Correspondence:** the main attention of scholars in the past has been attracted by the presumed political polemic conducted in these letters, in which Ivan has been assumed to be defend-

ing the absolute autocracy with which he is traditionally identified, while Kurbskii has been variously described as the representative either of the "old feudal order" or of a more modern oligarchic point of view. As Nørretranders has shown in his minute and thoughtful analysis of these letters [*The Shaping of Czardom under Ivan Groznij*], there is strikingly little basis for either of these views. Kurbskii, in particular, never really does make clear what he believes in, aside from his complaints against Ivan's personal tyranny, while Ivan, for the most part, is at pains to justify his own actions on personal and historical grounds, rather than by any consistent theoretical program. (pp. 57-60)

> *Edward L. Keenan, "The Pseudo-Ivan and the Pseudo-Kurbskii?" in his* The Kurbskii-Gronznyi Apocrypha: The Seventeenth-Century Genesis of the "Correspondence" Attributed to Prince A. M. Kurbskii and Tsar Ivan IV, *Cambridge, Mass.: Harvard University Press, 1971, pp. 47-72.*

Dmitri Likhachev   (essay date 1976)

[*Likhachev is the foremost contemporary Soviet scholar of old Russian literature. In the following excerpt, he explores the style of Ivan's letters as a manifestation of the czar's behavior.*]

Ivan the Terrible's oeuvres belong to an epoch when the individuality of statesmen and most of all that of Ivan the Terrible became already conspicuous, whereas the individual style of writers was still rudimentary and revealed itself but latently. The only exception is apparent in the style of Ivan the Terrible's works. How can one account for this? In the ensuing exposition, I shall endeavour to circumstantiate that the idiosyncrasies of Ivan the Terrible's individual style of writing are first and foremost a vision of his individual behaviour, a peremptory declaration of his attitude to life.

Ivan the Terrible's behaviour was characteristic of feigned self-abasement, sometimes concurrent with histrionics and dressing disguisedly. (pp. 1-2)

Ivan the Terrible's dresses were consonant with a specific semiotic system. There is every reason to believe Isaac Mass when he has the following to write about Ivan the Terrible, "When he was dressed in red he shed blood, when in black everybody was in for a spell of trouble and grief: people were drowned, throttled and plundered; and when in white, merriment was to be seen everywhere, yet not in a manner befitting a good Christian".

In his works Ivan the Terrible displays the same proclivity for "changing attire" and histrionics. He would either write on behalf of the Boyards or would invent a buffoon literary pseudonym . . . and constantly changes the tone of his messages ranging from an ornated and loquacious strain to a scoffing, servile and humble one.

By far the most characteristic feature of the style of Ivan the Terrible's Epistles is the simulated submissiveness and common parlance intermingled with high-flown and arrogant expressions, church Slavonic language and scholastic citations from the Apostles and great Greek doctors of the church. (pp. 2-3)

His irate epistle to Father-Superior Kozma of the monastary in Kirillo-Belozersk is interspersed with a crescendoingly self-humiliating cant. It is common knowledge that Ivan the Terrible was on the point of, or pretended to be on the point of taking the (monastic vows) in Kirillo-Belozersk. In his epistle to Father-Superior Kozma, he "enacts" a monk. . . . He calls himself "damned", "a vicious blackguard", "a sinful and vile scoundrel", "an infernal murderer steeped in vice", reckons himself among "the wretched in spirit and miserable beggars". His writing is defined as "idle talk". The humble and contrite cant is intermingled with fierce, haughty and solemn accusations against the monastic morals.

Ivan the Terrible's enactments of humbleness are never protracted. It was important for him to pinpoint the contrast with his real status of a sovereign vested with absolute power. Feigning modesty and humbleness was a way of scoffing at his victim. He was fond of impetuous wrath, unexpected and swift executions and murders.

Given the alternation of his position as a tzar and a subject, an absolute monarch and an abject petitioner, a sinful monk and a spiritual preceptor, it is but natural that the style of Ivan the Terrible's writing is characteristic of an interchange between the Church Slavonic language and the colloquial popular parlance at times degrading into expletives.

In his remarkable article [in *Acta Litteraria Academiae Scientiarium Hungaricae,* 1976] entitled "Notes on the language of Ivan the Terrible's Epistles," S. O. Schmidt points out that

> Ivan the Terrible is distinguished by a unique feeling for language, hence his literary style and vocabulary depended to a large extent upon the addressee and the nature of the epistle under consideration; thus, in the first part of the Epistle to the Monastry in Kirillo-Belozersk and in the brief edition of the First Epistle to Kurbsky the vocabulary predominantly consists of Church Slavonic words, in the letter to Vasyutka Gryaznoy there is an abundance of popular expressions, whereas in the epistles to Poland there recur Polish borrowings and words most often used in the Western regions of the Russian State. Being well-versed in officialese, Ivan the Terrible was superb in imitating the forms of various documents making good use of creative elements in the language of official papers.

In his article, S. O. Schmidt makes an attempt at a kind of explanation for this "imitativeness" of Ivan the Terrible's language and style. S. O. Schmidt has the following to say on the issue,

> From official letters and decrees adopted in accordance with the petitions, Ivan the Terrible seems to have also assimilated the wide-spread manner of answering the letters. The content of the document or part of the document to which the answer had to be composed and the decree adopted would be recounted at the outset. The exposition had to be brief, as close to the original

text as possible, at times even reiterating it word-for-word . . . The custom of reiterating some of the words or expressions of the addressee in the answers may account for the use of foreign words, namely Polish borrowings and Western-Russian dialectisms by Ivan the Terrible in his Epistles to the Polish-Lithuanian State, especially in the epistles to Stephan Báthory.

This observation is extremely interesting and partly explains the versatility of the language and style in Ivan the Terrible's epistles which has been accentuated many times by the investigators of his language. However, his partial explanation does not rule out the other elucidation, i.e. the dependence of Ivan the Terrible's style on his behaviour contingent incidentally on Ivan the Terrible's theatricality and specific buffoonery. In part, S. O. Schmidt has also taken notice of this by pointing out the influence exerted upon Ivan the Terrible's speech by folklore, "Evidence has been preserved of Ivan the Terrible's participation in popular ritual games, of his love for popular fairy tales and songs, of the omnipresence of folklore genres at his court . . . Ivan the Terrible's propensity for theatrical effects seems likely to have been shaped under the influence of popular stagings and religious festive occasions".

Mention recurs in the sources that Ivan the Terrible used to swear heavily. Bad language employed in his works was a mere transplantation of his behaviour into belles-lettres. It is characteristic that his profanities should be trite, and frequently reiterated. (pp. 3-5)

On the whole, it is to be emphasized that expletives constitute the most stable and typical lexical group in Ivan the Terrible's language.

There is an unexpected array of expletives only in his epistle to Polubensky. (p. 5)

This is an instance of an impromptu swearing. Polubensky is called by the names of all sorts of musical instruments . . . which were apparently used by the buffoons. The use of non-expletives to make expletive comparisons is sporadic and is fraught with offence in the very image, not in the verbal expression.

Very much like many emotional writers, Ivan the Terrible's style preserved the traces of verbal thinking. He wrote the way he used to talk. It is conceivable that he dictated his epistles. Hence not only the traces of conversationalism in his writing, but also of verbosity, frequent repetitions of thoughts and expressions, digressions and sudden alternations of topics, questions and exclamations, constant salutation of the reader as if he were his hearer which is characteristic of colloquial speech. He "holds his reader in leash" and would address him as his equal or even superior, or would strive to overwhelm him with his erudition, his high status, his high birth, his omnipotence and so forth.

In his epistle, Ivan the Terrible behaves very much as in life. He betrays more of his manner in treating his interlocutor than that of writing. In the background of his writing there always stands reality: real power, real cruelty, real mockery. Not only does he write but he also acts: he is in a position to carry out his threats, his wrath may give way to mercy, or mercy to wrath.

All these aspects of his writings mesmerize the reader, while the verbosity in his epistles is not so much mere garrulity as a way of enchanting and hypnotizing the reader, of affecting him emotionally, of oppressing or relaxing him. He is a tyrant in life as well as in his writings—the way an actor with elements of Ancient Russian buffoonery used to be.

In his epistles Ivan the Terrible constantly enacts somebody. Hence the multi-faceted style of his epistles.

It is common knowledge that Ivan the Terrible was fond of striking up verbal disputes on religion, on diplomatic issues with his equals as well as with his victims. He liked to substantiate his actions, to persuade and scoff, to triumph in altercations. The colloquial methods of holding disputes were transferred by Ivan the Terrible into his works. (pp. 5-6)

Ivan the Terrible had a very concrete picture of his opponent before himself while dictating or, as it were, putting down his colloquial speech. Therefore there occurs the inner dialogue in his epistles. He seems to say his opponents arguments after him, and then to smash them to pieces and triumph, writing ironically, mocking or pointing out that his opponent's argumentation and the opponent himself merit no more than ridicule. . . . (p. 6)

As to Ivan the Terrible, to jeer meant to annihilate the opponent spiritually. This is why in his works the argumentation of his opponents is refuted by being scoffed at.

In his inner dialogues, Ivan the Terrible displays superb showmanship. Not only does he exactly render his opponent's arguments, but he also seems to transcend into the position of his opponent and take account of his character. True enough, he simplifies and distorts his opponent's arguments, remaining at the same time within the boundaries of the possible and the probable.

The inner dialogue occurs in the epistles to Kurbsky, to Gryaznoy, to Polubensky and many others.

An opponent's imaginary counter-arguments are disguised in the form of questions which Ivan the Terrible poses as if on behalf of his opponent. Especially characteristic in this respect is the Epistle of Ivan the Terrible to Kurbsky. Kurbsky's argumentation which he used in an epistle to Ivan the Terrible is elaborated and augmented by Ivan the Terrible in the form of questions which one can hardly call "rhetorical" since they are associated so closely with his opponent's personality and psychology. . . .

Next comes a delineation of Ivan the Terrible's abject position in custody of the Boyards. He enumerates all the wrongdoings perpetrated on him by the Boyards, for example, the way he was separated from his young wife and puts forth a brave counterargument on behalf of his opponents right away, i.e. an accusation that he used to be unfaithful to his wife. He makes excuses by alluding to his human nature and takes the offensive by reminding Kurbsky of some sort of compromizing goings-on with a sol-

dier's wife. . . . The squabble with Kurbsky turns into digging up the wrongs done in the past, into a conviction of his behaviour, and into bragging of his victories in Lithuania which forced Kurbsky to flee from him farther on. . . . (p. 7)

So, Ivan the Terrible's epistles manifest his splendid talent of showmanship, his skill of alternating the style of exposition, imitating the role he assumes (that of a cringing petitioner, of a humble monk or an offended tzar), assuming the role of an imaginary author Parpheni the Ugly, or vividly conceiving his opponents by writing on behalf of the Boyards. He possesses striking skills for making use of inner dialogue by means of disguising his opponent's arguments behind questions posed to himself.

Nothing even remotely similar can be encountered in the whole Old Russian literature. Stylization is absent in the Old Russian literature. Imitation amounted only to borrowings and repetitions of the original. One can judge the immaturity of the attempts to imitate the nature of the original by the false correspondence between Ivan the Terrible and the Turkish sultan.

How can one account for the imitating talents of Ivan the Terrible as a writer? The underlying reason, I suggest, is that Ivan the Terrible's works were an inseparable part of his behavior. He "behaved" in his works very much the same way as in life, he wrote as he spoke, he turned to his adversaries in his writings as if they talked eyeball-to-eyeball, in his works he displayed his character, his talents

Portrait of Ivan IV from a wood engraving.

for the depiction and transformation into the personage on whose behalf he wrote, his proclivity to mock and ape, jeer and ridicule with amazing spontaneity.

However, many of Ivan the Terrible's works can be understood only in the given real context of life on the background of which they were written. Thus, for instance, Ivan the Terrible's epistle to Vasyutka Gryaznoy is written in the same tone of merry banter which was customary among them at table, yet the situation was entirely different from Gryaznoy's point of view (Gyraznoy was in captivity and his death sentence was imminent) which makes Ivan the Terrible's playful disposition sound ominously ironical. The irony is accentuated by the fact that Ivan the Terrible's epistle responded to a humble and abject petition from Vasyutka Gryaznoy. Ivan the Terrible is "lightly" facetious with a man whose appeal for pardon he resolutely turns down.

There are many examples in which Ivan the Terrible's real style of writing becomes manifest only with due consideration of his real actions. To accompany an execution with a joke, to jocularly reject an appeal for pardon, to kiddingly beg Simeon the pseudo-tzar the permission for carrying out one of the largest-scale executions . . . is, as a matter of fact, not so much a style of writing as a style of behaviour the literary oeuvres being but a part of an imaginary and at times enacted real situation.

Ivan the Terrible's salient style characteristics, his emotionalism and excitability, drastic alternations of lofty Church Slavonic language and the brusque popular speech are derived not so much from an adopted literary school or literary tradition as from his nature and are part of a parcel of his behaviour. They are pregnant with the traditions of buffoonery rather than elements of literary tradition.

It is easy to notice that Ivan the Terrible's behaviour was typically that of a despote. Depotism and showmanship are inseparable. Incidentally, it is also possible to discern the characteric parts to which the tyrant's actors aspire: these are the roles of simpletons.

Traits of showmanship were noticeable not only in Ivan the Terrible but also in Peter I, "monarch of half the world". There were element of showmanship in his dressing like a carpenter, a sailor (in Russia as well as abroad), in the low army rank of a bombardier which he conferred on himself, etc. His penchant for histrionics was also evident in the role which Peter enacted in. However, Peter's showmanship was not betrayed in his writings (although Peter used to write the scenarios of some jocular acts himself).

Napoleon was also a showman. In the entourage of kings, dukes and marshals at an extraordinary grandiose court he would make his appearance in "his gray army camp coat" which he could not button all the way up his little bourgeoise paunch.

There was a certain degree of showmanship also in the generals, say, in Suvorov. Being a man of refined Franco-Russian culture, Suvorov liked to play the role of a simpleton. His penchant for histrionics rarely tells on his numerous writings, yet in some of his speeches and military messages the style of buffoons keeps cropping up.

It would be conceivable to compose a fascinating book on the theatrical manifestations presented by the despotes, beginning with Nero, to their peoples, "The Theatre of Despotes". They all were similar, and yet different in their style of acting.

Ivan the Terrible's style of acting was that of buffoon's manifestations. (pp. 8-9)

> *Dmitri S. Likhachev, "The Histrionics of Ivan the Terrible: To the Question of the Farcical Style of His Works," in* Acta Litteraria Academae Scientiarum Hungaricae, *Vol. XVIII, Nos. 1-2, 1976, pp. 1-10.*

Francis Carr   (essay date 1981)

[*In the following excerpt, Carr summarizes the major basis of argument between Ivan and Kurbsky, and explains how the czar used biblical quotations to support his policy of terror.*]

In the opinion of J. L. I. Fennell, the translator and editor of Kurbsky's letters and of a brief history of Ivan written by Kurbsky, [the Ivan-Kurbsky letters] are 'of capital importance'. They give 'a strangely true and sober picture of the age'; they are written 'by a true Muscovite, with a large amount of factual detail, particularly as regards the lists of Ivan's victims'. They are in this respect comparable to Solzhenitsyn's *Gulag Archipelago.*

Kurbsky's letters and Ivan's replies are especially interesting since we have so few letters of any kind from the Tsar or his court. It is, however, this contrast between the paucity of Russian documents of literary value at this time and the unique quality of this royal correspondence that has led one American historian, Edward L. Keenan, to question its authenticity [see excerpt dated 1971]. It is, in his opinion, too good to be true. The letters, he thinks, were written some sixty to eighty years later. It is only in the last few years that anyone has doubted Kurbsky's and Ivan's authorship; Keenan's book was published in 1971. We are therefore confronted with a text which must carry conviction of its authenticity by its own merits. Each reader can judge for himself whether these letters come from Ivan himself and from his general, or whether they show signs of another hand. If they were not written until the following century, it would be a further indication of the intellectual backwardness of the Russian court at this time. All published correspondence has to be edited; these letters are no exception. However, the original manuscripts, or copies earlier than 1620, cannot be traced.

In essence the argument of both Tsar and general centres on the right of the subject to rebel. Ivan's main complaint is that Kurbsky has 'seized upon such evil thoughts, resisting in all things the Master given you by God'. Both antagonists strengthened their arguments with frequent quotations from the Bible; Ivan compared Kurbsky to Judas; Kurbsky compared Ivan to Saul, who consulted soothsayers. Ivan quoted extensively from Byzantine texts; Kurbsky sent the Tsar a translation of two chapters of Cicero's

Paradoxa Stoicorum (chapters 2 and 4). These passages contained the following statements:

> You know not, madman, what strength virtue possesses. You simply use the name of virtue; but you do not understand what virtue means. Your lusts torture you; you are in torment day and night; the conscience-pricks of your evil deeds goad you on; wherever you gaze your unjust acts encircle you like furies . . . You are out of your mind and mad . . . That horde of bandits . . . is that a state? See how I despise the weapons of your bandits. Nothing is mine that can be taken away, torn away or lost. If you had rent from me my mind, then I would admit having suffered an offence . . . You, in truth, are not even a citizen now, unless one can be an enemy and a citizen. You have caused a massacre in the forum; you held the temples with armed brigands; you burned the houses of private persons. All the evil men, whose leader you confess yourself to be, whom the laws wish to be punished with exile, are exiles, even if they have not left the land. When the laws ordain that you are an exile, are you not a traitor? By all the general laws you are a traitor.

These charges were made by Cicero against Antonius and Clodius, who exiled him from Rome.

Since many of Kurbsky's accusations can be directed with equal force against Stalin and the communist dictators, his letters have been wisely omitted by the Soviet educational authorities from their standard history text books, and Kurbsky himself is dismissed as an unreliable authority on Ivan's reign. (pp. 122-23)

Ivan's policy of *strux,* terror, or *schrechlichkeit,* succeeded in deterring the majority of his countrymen from open rebellion. It has also had another, more surprising effect, making some western historians a little too ready to minimise Ivan's atrocities, unconsciously subscribing to the theory of the divine right of kings to govern abominably. This readiness to genuflect is in fact a tribute to the intensity of the terror that Ivan generated. It is difficult to find another reason for this reluctance to criticise Ivan dispassionately. A good example of this reluctance, this desire to praise Ivan, in spite of all the evidence against him, is clearly shown in the following two remarks in a recent western study of Ivan:

> I have found Ivan far less terrible than the Tsar of legend. This does not mean that the savageries perpetrated in his reign can be denied or extenuated in any way . . . Ivan could be unexpectedly mild and forgiving, even towards individual boyars whose crime was treason. Suspecting Prince Ivan Belsky of planning flight to Lithuania, Ivan ordered him to swear on the Cross that he would not depart from the realm or from his principality. Further, twenty-nine men were required to act as sureties for him and 120 men to be sureties for them. Notwithstanding these extraordinary precautions, Belsky later in the same year pleaded guilty to treason in that he had sent messages to Sigismund Augustus, asking him for a safe conduct to Lithuania. Ivan nevertheless par-

doned him. Others enjoyed similar clemency from their unpredictable Tsar.

The reader is entitled to feel not a little confused by this, and remain unconvinced. All tyrants are guilty of occasional clemency.

The distinguished Russian historian Karamzin described Ivan as 'a horrible meteor' and 'a beast, a frantic bloodsucker'. In 1564, when Kurbsky deserted Ivan and fought against him with the Polish army, the Russians may well have hoped that this reverse would induce the Tsar to make their lives a little easier, their poverty a little less severe, their lives a little more secure, their deaths less painful. But this reverse was taken by Ivan as proof that all the boyars were his enemies, therefore enemies of the state, and that his people as a whole must be shaken still harder to convince them of the gulf that separated them, as miserable sinners, from their God-given, God-inspired leader, who could do no wrong. In his two letters to Kurbsky, he repeats over and over again the message that he was authorised by God to kill without mercy, with copious relevant and irrelevant quotations from the Old Testament. The Bible is quoted so frequently, especially in his verbose first letter, that the reader begins to wish that this ancient collection of Hebrew myth, legend and fact had never been brought to Russia. (pp. 135-36)

> *Francis Carr, in his* Ivan the Terrible, *David & Charles, 1981, 220 p.*

FURTHER READING

Backer, George. *The Deadly Parallel.* New York: Random House, 1950, 240 p.
   Examines the similarities between the tyrannical rules of Ivan the Terrible and Joseph Stalin.

Bobrick, Benson. *Fearful Majesty: The Life and Reign of Ivan the Terrible.* New York: Putnam, 1987, 398 p.
   A biography of the czar that relates the circumstances surrounding the Ivan-Kurbsky correspondence and illustrates, using excerpts from Ivan's letters, the czar's vision of his responsibilities.

Cherniavsky, Michael. "Ivan the Terrible as Renaissance Prince." *Slavic Review* XXVII, No. 2 (June 1968): pp. 195-211.
   Explores the significance of the epithet "the Terrible" in light of Ivan's own understanding of the responsibilities of a czar, and in the larger context of Renaissance ideas on the duties of a ruler.

Graham, Stephen. *Ivan the Terrible: Life of Ivan IV of Russia.* New Haven: Yale University Press, 1933, 335 p.
   An in-depth biography of the czar's life which contains a brief discussion of the contents and importance of the correspondence.

Grey, Ian. "Ivan the Terrible." *History Today* XIV, No. 5 (May 1964): pp. 326-33.

Discusses the origin of Kurbsky's correspondence with Ivan and comments on the themes and style of Ivan's letters.

Inge, William Ralph. "Ivan the Terrible." In his *A Pacifist in Trouble,* pp. 210-15. London: Putnam, 1939.
　　Compares Ivan's atrocities with those of the governments of Russia, Germany, and Spain in the mid to late 1930s.

Kurbsky, Andrey Mikhaylovich. *Prince A. M. Kurbsky's History of Ivan IV.* Edited by J. L. I. Fennell. Cambridge: Cambridge University Press, 1965, 314 p.
　　The first Russian historical monograph, this sixteenth-century work relates events from Ivan's reign between 1533 and 1570. Kurbsky attempts to influence public opinion in Lithuania-Poland and Russia against Ivan IV.

Marcu, Valeriu. "Ivan the Terrible and Stalin." *Current History* XLVIII, No. 5 (May 1938): 50-2.
　　Short essay on the similar personalities of the two autocrats.

Owen, Thomas C. "A Lexical Approach to the Kurbskii-Groznyi Problem." *Slavic Review* 41, No. 4 (Winter 1982): 686-91.
　　Traces biblical and historical references in the Ivan-Kurbsky letters to their possible sources in an attempt to date the correspondence accurately.

Payne, Robert. "A Man Like No Other." *The New York Times Magazine* (8 September 1963): 78-80, 82, 84.
　　Short biographical sketch of Ivan's life along with a favorable review of Sergey Eisenstein's film trilogy on Ivan.

Rowse, A. L. "Europe's First Glimpse of the Russians: Elizabeth I and Ivan the Terrible—A Study in Diplomacy." *Saturday Review* XLI, No. 23 (7 June 1958): 9-11, 34-5.
　　Narrates the history of trade and diplomatic relations between England and Russia from the mid-sixteenth century to Ivan's death in 1584.

Troyat, Henri. *Ivan the Terrible.* New York: E. P. Dutton, 1984, 283 p.
　　A critical biography that relates the circumstances surrounding the relationship between Ivan and Kurbsky and comments briefly on their correspondence.

Yanov, Alexander. *The Origins of Autocracy: Ivan the Terrible in Russian History.* Berkeley and Los Angeles: University of California Press, 1981, 339 p.
　　A study of Ivan that summarizes and comments on the idea that he and Kurbsky did not represent the "new state" and the status quo, respectively. Yanov argues that they fought for the same ideal, that is, the freedom "to show mercy and to execute whomever [one] like[s]."

Zenkovsky, Serge A. "Prince Kurbsky-Tsar Ivan IV Correspondence: Reflections on Edward Keenan's *The Kurbskii-Groznyi Apocrypha.*" *The Russian Review* 32, No. 3 (July 1973): 299-311.
　　Calls into question several aspects of Keenan's essay (see excerpt dated 1971), which indicates that an exiled Russian prince actually authored the entire correspondence between Ivan and Kurbsky.

Jean de La Bruyère

1645-1696

French philosopher.

La Bruyère was one of the great French writers of the seventeenth century. A moralist in the sense of one who observes and reflects upon human nature, he devoted his literary efforts to the development of a single work, *Les caractères de Théophraste, traduits du grec, avec les caractères ou les moeurs de ce siècle* (*The Characters, or Manners of the Age*), a collection of maxims, reflections, and portraits which was enormously popular during his life and continues to be regarded as one of the vital works of world literature. Seventeenth-century readers were particularly fascinated by the ostensibly fictional portraits in *The Characters,* which are composite sketches of well-known personalities of the day, predominantly those associated with the court of Louis XIV. *The Characters* remains important today for its detailed documentation of French society in the late seventeenth century as well as its psychological and social insight.

La Bruyère was born in Paris in 1645. He received legal training at the University of Orléans, but it is not clear if he actually practiced law. In 1673, with an inheritance from a relative, La Bruyère purchased the position of Treasurer General of Finances for the district of Caen. The practice of purchasing government positions was common at the time and provided a title and an income. La Bruyère continued to live in Paris despite his position in Caen, and in 1684 he joined the household staff of the Condé family as tutor to the grandson of Louis II, Duke of Enghien. Many critics have speculated as to why La Bruyère, a dignified and sensitive man, would have accepted a position as a servant; his income from Caen would have provided the independence he cherished, while as a domestic in the Condé household he was completely dependent and occasionally the object of ridicule. In any case, his position allowed him to spend the rest of his life unobtrusively observing life in the court, thus contributing to an important aspect of his work. After considerable hesitation, and what some critics speculate may have been close to ten years of preparation, La Bruyère published *The Characters* in 1688. This first edition was published anonymously, with La Bruyère's *Characters* presented as an appendage of his translation of the Greek philosopher Theophrastus's work of the same name. But it ultimately became apparent that the translation was merely a pretext for La Bruyère's original writing. *The Characters* was published in eight different editions over six years, and with each edition La Bruyère expanded the work, with the eighth edition containing almost three times as much material as the first.

Because *The Characters* contained inflammatory criticism of the French aristocracy and society of his time, La Bruyère acquired several powerful enemies who attempted to bar his acceptance into the French Academy. In 1693,

however, La Bruyère's equally powerful friends secured his election. His acceptance speech was far from humble, and his arrogance only fueled the anger of his detractors. La Bruyère continued to involve himself in controversy in the last years of his life; he wrote the *Dialogues posthumes du sieur de La Bruyère sur le quiétisme* on behalf of his friend Jacques Bénigne Bossuet, who was embroiled in a theological controversy with François de Salignac de La Mothe Fénelon. La Bruyère died of apoplexy in 1696.

La Bruyère's *Characters* is divided into sixteen chapters with broad headings such as "Of Women," "Of Mankind," "Of the Court," and "Of the Town." The work is loosely structured; some commentators criticize La Bruyère for lack of unity and coherence in his work, while others find in it a definite organization based on various structural designs. Part of the controversy regarding the structure of the work results from the fact that it comprises several literary genres, including maxims, portraits, and short stories. La Bruyère is best known for his portraits, some of which describe unique characters such as Gnathon the glutton, while others are more generic: "the courtesan" or "the financier." Discussions of La Bruyère often include a comparison to his contemporaries who also studied human nature, specifically François de La Rochefoucauld and Blaise Pascal—though La Bruyère insisted he was not influenced by these moralists. The moralists of seventeenth-century French literature, Odette de Mourgues explains, were writers who studied humankind "within the limitations of nature and reason." La Bruyère, writing at the end of this era, expanded the rationalist codes of the classicists by including observations of a metaphysical and theological nature in his study.

While La Bruyère expressed attitudes and insights on a wide range of subjects in *The Characters,* critics often concentrate on a few central themes of the work. La Bruyère, frequently described as conservative, even reactionary, objected strongly to what he viewed as the disintegration of French society. In particular he criticized the hypocrisy prevalent in the court, the unprecedented social mobility of the bourgeoisie, and the extravagant wealth of the country's upper class. Since the reign of Louis XIV was distinguished by a complete centralization of authority, the nobility, deprived of their usual power, jealously competed with one another to win favor from the king through flattery. The king's religious awakening resulted in a wave of religious hypocrisy, which La Bruyère treated with unyielding disdain. He also objected to the parvenus—members of the bourgeoisie who were able to purchase both property and titles, thus creating a new aristocracy in which noble lineage was irrelevant. Several critics have cited La Bruyère's treatment of the poor as graphic, sensitive, even revolutionary. He wrote of the harsh conditions of peasant life and the extreme disparity between the social classes. One passage in *The Characters* describes Champagne, a wealthy member of the new aristocracy. Sated from a sumptuous meal, he signs an order depriving the citizens of an entire province of their food supply. La Bruyère sarcastically excuses Champagne's behavior, commenting that it is difficult to understand starvation in the aftermath of a large meal. But in opposition to what some critics consider La Bruyère's sympathy with the poor, Roland Barthes has asserted that for La Bruyère the peasantry only existed as "that pure exterior without which bourgeoisie and aristocracy could not realize their own being." In general, critics contend that the conservative La Bruyère would never have advocated a social revolution. They maintain that when La Bruyère spoke of the dignity of the poor, he usually meant not the peasantry but those of noble lineage who had lost their fortunes. With increasing numbers of the bourgeoisie ascending to the rank of nobility, La Bruyère perceived a disturbing instability in the social structure, as noted by Barbara Woshinsky: "What can it mean to be 'noble' or to speak of 'noble sentiments,' if nobility, once a moral quality, has become a salable item?"

La Bruyère wrote only one major work, but its significance is such that he is considered among the classic writers in French literature. In his effort to create an accurate and detailed portrait of a particular time and place, scholars contend that La Bruyère created an enduring and universal work. As Edmund Gosse has asserted, La Bruyère's "great book remains eminently alive, and wields . . . a permanent influence."

PRINCIPAL WORKS

Les caractères de Théophraste, traduits du grec, avec les caractères ou les moeurs de ce siècle (philosophy) 1688
    [*The Characters, or The Manners of the Age,* 1699, also published as *Characters,* 1963, and *The Characters,* 1970]
Discours prononcé dans l'Académie française, par M. de La Bruyère, le lundy quinzième juin 1693, jour de sa réception (speech) 1693
Dialogues posthumes du sieur de La Bruyère sur le quiétisme (dialogues) 1699
Oeuvres complètes (philosophy, speech, dialogues) 1951

Jean de La Bruyère   (essay date 1694)

[*In the following preface to the eighth edition of* The Characters, *published in 1694, La Bruyère defends his work and explains his intent in writing it.*]

The subject-matter of this work being borrowed from the public, I now give back to it what it lent me; it is but right that having finished the whole work throughout with the utmost regard to truth I am capable of, and which it deserves from me, I should make restitution of it. The world may view at leisure its picture drawn from life, and may correct any of the faults I have touched upon, if conscious of them. This is the only goal a man ought to propose to himself in writing, though he must not in the least expect to be successful; however, as long as men are not disgusted with vice we should also never tire of admonishing them; they would perhaps grow worse were it not for censure or reproof, and hence the need of preaching and writing. Neither orators nor authors can conceal the joy they feel on being applauded, whereas they ought to blush if they aim at nothing more than praise in their speeches or writings; besides, the surest and least doubtful approbation is a change and regeneration in the morals of their readers and hearers. We should neither write nor speak but to instruct; yet, if we happen to please, we should not be sorry for it, since by those means we render those instructive truths more palatable and acceptable. When, therefore, any thoughts or reflections have slipped into a book which are neither so spirited, well written, nor vivid as others, though they seem to have been inserted for the sake of variety, as a relaxation to the mind, or to draw its attention to what is to follow, the reader should reject and the author delete them, unless they are attractive, familiar, instructive, and adapted to the capacity of ordinary people, whom we must by no means neglect.

This is one way of settling things; there is another which my own interest trusts may be adopted; and that is, not to lose sight of my title, and always to bear in mind, as often as this book is read, that I describe **The Characters; or, Manners of the Age;** for though I frequently take them from the court of France and from men of my own nation, yet they cannot be confined to any one court or country, without greatly impairing the compass and utility of my book, and departing from the design of the work, which is to paint mankind in general, as well as from the reasons for the order of my chapters, and even from a certain gradual connection between the reflections in each of those chapters. After this so necessary precaution, the consequences of which are obvious enough, I think I may protest against all resentment, complaint, malicious interpretation, false application and censure, against insipid railers and cantankerous readers. People ought to know how to read and then hold their tongues, unless able to relate what they have read, and neither more nor less than what they have read, which they sometimes can do; but this is not sufficient—they must also be willing to do it. Without these conditions, which a careful and scrupulous author has a right to demand from some people, as the sole reward of his labour, I question whether he ought to continue writing, if at least he prefers his private satisfaction to the public good and to his zeal for truth. I confess, moreover, that since the year MDCLXXXX, and before publishing the fifth edition, I was divided between an impatience to cast my book into a fuller and better shape by adding new Characters, and a fear lest some people should say: "Will there never be an end to these Characters, and shall we never see anything else from this author?" On the one hand several persons of sound common-sense told me: "The subject-matter is solid, useful, pleasant, inexhaustible; may you live for a long time, and treat it without interruption as long as you live! what can you do better? The follies of mankind will ensure you a volume every year." Others, again, with a good deal of reason, made me dread the fickleness of the multitude and the instability of the public, with whom, however, I have good cause to be satisfied; they were always suggesting to me that for the last thirty years, few persons read except for the pleasure of reading, and not to improve themselves, and that, to amuse mankind, fresh chapters and a new title were needed; that this sluggishness had filled the shops and crowded the world with dull and tedious books, written in a bad style and without any intelligence, order, or the least correctness, against all morality or decency, written in a hurry, and read in the same way, and then only for the sake of novelty; and that if I could do nothing else but enlarge a sensible book, it would be much better for me to take a rest. I adopted something of both those advices, though they were at variance with one another, and observed an impartiality which clashed with neither. I did not hesitate to add some fresh remarks to those which already had doubled the bulk of the first edition of my book; but, in order not to oblige the public to read again what had been printed before, to get at new material, and to let them immediately find out what they only desired to read, I took care to distinguish those second additions by a peculiar mark ((¶)); I also thought it would not be useless to distinguish the first augmentations by another and simpler mark (¶), to show the progress of my *Characters,* as well as to guide the reader in the choice he might be willing to make. And lest he be afraid I should never have done with those additions, I added to all this care a sincere promise to venture on nothing more of the kind. If any one accuses me of breaking my word, because I inserted in the

three last editions a goodly number of new remarks, he may perceive at least that by adding new ones to old, and by completely suppressing those differences pointed out in the margin, I did not so much endeavour to entertain the world with novelties, as perhaps to leave to posterity a book of morals more complete, more finished, and more regular. To conclude, I did not wish to write any maxims, for they are like moral laws, and I acknowledge that I possess neither sufficient authority nor genius for a legislator. I also know I have transgressed the ordinary standard of maxims, which, like oracles, should be short and concise. Some of my remarks are so, others are more diffuse; we do not always think of things in the same way, and we describe them in as different a manner by a sentence, an argument, a metaphor, or some other figure; by a parallel or a simple comparison; by a story, by a single feature, by a description, or a picture; which is the cause of the length or brevity of my reflections. Finally, those who write maxims would be thought infallible; I, on the contrary, allow any one to say that my remarks are not always correct, provided he himself will make better ones. (pp. i-v)

> *Jean de La Bruyère, in a preface to his* Characters, *translated by Henri van Laun, 1885. Reprint by Brentano's, 1929, pp. i-v.*

George Saintsbury   (essay date 1902)

[*Saintsbury has been called the most influential English literary historian and critic of the late nineteenth and early twentieth centuries. His studies of French literature, particularly* A History of the French Novel (1917-1919), *have established him as a leading authority on such writers as Guy de Maupassant and Honoré de Balzac. As a critic of poetry and drama, Saintsbury was a radical formalist who frequently asserted that subject is of little importance, and that "the so-called 'formal' part is of the essence." In the following excerpt, he assesses La Bruyère as a literary critic.*]

La Bruyère's contribution [to literary criticism] is contained in the opening section, "Des Ouvrages de l'Esprit," of his famous *Caractères.* It is not very long; it is—as according to the plan of the work it is not merely entitled but obliged to be—studiously desultory; and it is not perhaps improved by the other necessity of throwing much of it into portraits of imaginary persons, who are sometimes no doubt very close copies of real ones. But it contains some open and undisguised judgments of the great writers of the past, and a number of astonishingly original, pregnant, and monumentally phrased observations of a general character. In fact I should not hesitate to say that La Bruyère is, after Dryden, who had preceded him by twenty years, the first very great man of letters in modern times who gave himself to Criticism with a comparatively unshackled mind, and who has put matter of permanent value in her treasuries without being a professional rhetorician or commentator. We need not dwell on the famous overture *Tout est dit,* for it is merely a brilliant example of the kind of paradox-shell or rocket, half truth, half falsehood, which a writer of the kind explodes at the beginning of his entertainment, to attract the attention of his readers, and let them see the brilliancy of the stars that drop from it. But how astonishing is it, in the 17th section, to find, two hundred years and more ago, the full Flaubertian doctrine of the "single word" laid down with confidence, and without an apparent sense that the writer is saying anything new! No matter that soon after, in 20, we find an old fallacy, ever new, put in the words, "Le plaisir de la critique nous ôte celui d'être vivement touchés de très-belles choses." If criticism does this it is the wrong criticism—the criticism à la Boileau, and not the criticism after the manner of Longinus. A man may have spent a lifetime in reading "overthwart and endlong" (as the *Morte d' Arthur* says) in every direction of literature, in reading always critically, and in reading for long years as professional reviewer, and yet feel as keenly as ever the literary charm which age cannot wither nor custom stale,—the "strong pleasure" of the beautiful word.

But how well he recovers himself, among other things, with the remarks on the *Cid,* and the difference between the fine and the faultless at 30! with the declaration of independence immediately following in 31, and practically drawing a cancel through the whole critical teaching of Boileau! "Quand une lecture vous élève l'esprit, . . . ne cherchez pas une autre règle pour juger; il est bon." How delicate his remarks in 37 on the delicacy of touch, the illogical but impeccable concatenation, the justice of phrase, of the best feminine writing! Not a few of his observations are paraphrases or, as it were, echoes of Longinus himself, whom he has assimilated as Longinus' translator never could have done. And if some further remarks on criticism in 63 seem to regard rather the abuse than the nature of the art—if the famous "Un homme né Chrétien et Français se trouve contraint dans la satire; les grands sujets lui sont défendus," is half a political grumble and half a paralogism, which was to be accepted with fatal results in the next century—both this and other things are redeemed throughout by the general independence and freshness of the judgment, the vigour and decision of the phrase. In the judgments of authors above referred to (which begin at 38 and continue for some eight or nine numbers . . .), it is especially possible to appreciate La Bruyère's idiosyncrasy as a critic, the vivacity and power of his natural endowments in this direction, and his drawback, arising partly from sheer acceptance of prevailing opinion, and partly from the fact that he is merely coasting the subject on his way to others. (pp. 301-03)

On the whole, the only reasons for not ranking La Bruyère's criticism very high indeed are that there is so little of it, and that it is obviously the work of a man to whom it is more a casual pastime than a business—who has not thought himself out all along the line in it, but has emitted a few observations. Still, those which express his deliberate opinions are almost always sound, and only some of those which he has adopted without examination are wholly or partially false. (p. 304)

> *George Saintsbury, "From Malherbe to Boileau," in his* A History of Criticism and Literary Taste in Europe from the Earliest Texts to the Present Day, *1902. Reprint by William Blackwood & Sons Ltd., 1949, pp. 240-322.*

Edmund Gosse   (essay date 1918)

[*Gosse was a prominent English man of letters during the late nineteenth century. A prolific literary historian, biographer, and critic, he remains most esteemed for a single and atypical work:* Father and Son: A Study of Two Temperaments *(1907), an account of his childhood that is considered among the most distinguished examples of Victorian spiritual autobiography. He was also a prominent translator and critic of Scandinavian literature, and his importance as a critic is due primarily to his introduction of Henrik Ibsen to an English-speaking audience. In the following excerpt, he examines the reasons for the enduring popular and critical success of* The Characters.]

[*The Characters; or, the Manners of this Age*] was published in January 1688, but, as is believed, had been begun nearly thirty years earlier, and slowly finished, the final revision and arrangement dating from 1686 and 1687. The book, like so many of the world's masterpieces, is short, and a fashionable novelist of to-day could scribble in a fortnight as many words as it contains. But there is not a careless phrase nor a hurried line in the whole of it. I do not know in the range of literature a book more deliberately exquisite than the *Caractères.* It started, probably, with the jotting down of social remarks at long intervals. Then, I think, La Bruyère, always extremely fastidious, observed that the form of his writing was growing to resemble too much that of La Rochefoucauld, and so he began to diversify it with "portraits." These had been in fashion in Paris for more than a generation, but La Bruyère invented a new kind of portrait. He says, on the very first page of the *Caractères,* "you make a book as you make a clock"; he ought to have said, "I make *my* book," for no other work is quite so clock-like in its variety of parts, its elaborate mechanism, and its air of having been constructed at different times, in polished fragments, which have needed the most workmanlike ingenuity to fit them together into an instrument that moves and rings.

What perhaps strikes us most, when we put down the *Caractères* after a close re-perusal of one of the most readable books in all literature, is its extraordinary sustained vitality. It hums and buzzes in our memory long after we have turned the last page. We may expand the author's own image, and compare it, not with a clock, but with a watchmaker's shop; it is all alive with the tick-tick of a dozen chronometers. La Bruyère's observations are noted in a manner that is disjointed, apparently even disordered, but it was no part of his scheme to present his maxims in a system. We shall find that he was incessantly improving his work, revising, extending and weighing it. He was one of those timid men who surprise us by their crafty intrepidity. It was dangerous to publish sarcastic "portraits" of well-known influential people, and there are few of these in the first edition, but when the success of the book was once confirmed these were made more and more prominent. It was not until the eighth edition, of 1694, that La Bruyère ventured to print the following study of one of the most influential men of letters of that day, Fontenelle—

The Portrait of Cydias

Ascange is a sculptor, Hegion a bronze-founder;

Æschine a fuller, and Cydias a wit—that is his profession. He has a signboard, a workshop, finished articles for sale, mechanics who work under him. He cannot deliver for more than a month the stanzas which he has promised you, unless he breaks his word to Dosithée, who has ordered an elegy from him. He has an idyl on the loom; it is for Crantor, who is hurrying him, and from whom he expects a handsome price. Prose, verse, which do you want? He is equally successful with either. Ask him for letters to sympathize with a bereavement or to explain an absence, and he will undertake them. If you want them ready-made, you have only to enter his shop, and to choose what you like. He has a friend whose only duty upon this earth is to promise Cydias a long time ahead to a certain set of people, and then to present him at last in their houses as a man of rare and exquisite conversation; and, there, just as a musician sings or a lute-player touches his lute before the people who have engaged him, Cydias, after having coughed, and lifted the ruffle from his wrist, stretched out his hand and opened his fingers, begins to retail his quintessential thoughts and his sophistical arguments. . . . He opens his mouth only to contradict. "It seems to me," he gracefully says, "that the truth is exactly the contrary of what you say," or "I cannot agree with your opinion," or even "that used to be my prepossession, as it is yours, but now—!"

The idol of the gossips, "the prettiest pedant in the world," was thus paid out for his intrigues against La Bruyère in the French Academy.

There was great danger, or so it would seem to a timid man like La Bruyère, in affronting public opinion with a book so full of sarcasm and reproof, so unflinching in its way of dealing with success, as the *Caractères.* He adopted a singular mode of self-protection. That was the day of the mighty dispute between the Ancients and the Moderns, and La Bruyère, at all events ostensibly, took the highly respectable side of the Greeks and Romans. There had lived a philosopher in the fourth century B.C., Theophrastus, the successor and elucidator of Aristotle, who left a book of *Ethical Characters,* which had been introduced to the Western world by Casaubon at the end of the sixteenth century. For some reason or other, the greatest impression had been made by Theophrastus in England, where there appeared a large number of successive imitations or paraphrases of his *Characters.* In France, on the other hand, Theophrastus was still unknown to the vulgar, when La Bruyère took him up. It seems likely that his own collection of portraits and maxims was practically finished, when, as M. Paul Morillot has put it, he determined to hoist the Greek flag as a safeguard. He made a French translation of the sketches of Theophrastus, and he put this at the head of his book, waving it to keep off the public, as a lady unfurls her parasol at a cow whose intentions are uncertain.

The evidences of La Bruyère's extreme caution are amusing. He hesitated long, but in 1687 he submitted his MS to Boileau, who was highly encouraging, and to the poet-mathematician, Malizian, who said, "This will bring you

plenty of readers and plenty of enemies." Finally he determined to risk the dive, and he took the book to Michallet, the publisher, saying as he did so, "If it is successful, the result shall be your daughter's dowry," the said daughter being a little child who was then seated on La Bruyère's knee. The ultimate success of the book being prodigious, Mlle Michallet must, by the time she was marriageable, have become a remarkable *parti,* but the story is not one which commends itself to the Incorporated Society of Authors. **Les Caractères** was published in January 1688, and the critics, with the veteran Bussy-Rabutin at their head, welcomed it with shouts of applause. Bussy frankly said, "It must be admitted that having proved the merit of Theophrastus by his translation, he has obscured the fame of that writer by what he has done next, for he has penetrated, in his own portraits, deeper into the heart of man than Theophrastus did, and has penetrated with even greater delicacy and by means of more exquisite language." This must have been very gratifying from the survivor of the great school of Malherbe and Balzac.

At the age of forty-three, then, previously unknown in the world of letters, this shy and obscure gentleman-in-waiting to the Princes of Condé, rose into fame, and enjoyed the admiration or the envy of whatever was most prominent in Paris. The public which he addressed was one which we may pause a moment to contemplate. The authority of the Academic and noble *salons* was practically at an end, and intellectual culture had spread to a somewhat wider circle. Those who governed taste had thrown off many affectations of a previous generation, and in particular the curious disease of "preciousness." They were healthier, soberer and slightly less amusing than their forerunners. But they formed, in the heart of Paris, the most compact body of general intelligence to be met with at that time in any part of the world. They were certain, in their little sphere, of their æsthetic and logical aims. They were the flower of an intense civilization, very limited, in a way very simple; so far as the adoption of outer impulses went, very inactive, and yet within its own range energetic, elegant and audacious. To this world the **Caractères** was now offered, modestly, as though it were a summing up of the moralizations of the last fifty years. The author begins by deprecating the idea that he has anything new to impart. His trick is rather subtle; he concentrates our attention on the sayings of an ancient Aristotelian philosopher, and then, as if to fill up the time, he ventures to repeat a few reflexions of his own. These he introduces with the words: "Everything has been said, and we arrive too late into a world of men who have been thinking for more than seven thousand years. In the field of morals, all that is fairest and best has been reaped already; we can but glean among the ancients and among the cleverest of the moderns." In this insinuating manner, he leads the reader on to the perusal of his own part of the book, and soon we become aware how cold and dry and pale the Greek translation seems beside the rich and palpitating world of the new French morality.

Whether he perceived it or not—and I for one am convinced that he did perceive it—La Bruyère introduced a new thing into French literature; he opened out, we may almost say, a new world. The classical attitude of the great age had produced splendid manifestations of thought and form. However revolutionary it pleases us of 1918 to be, we cannot get away from the perfection of the age of Bossuet and Racine and La Fontaine and Fénelon. We come back to these solid and passionate writers after each one of our romantic excursions, not entirely satisfied with them, as our forefathers were, but with a sense of their solid glory, with a confidence in their permanent value in stimulating and supporting human effort. They may not give us all that they were once presumed to give, but they offer us a firm basis; they are always there for the imagination to start from. We must not forget, of course, that in 1688 in Paris these classics of the hour represented a great deal more than that; their prestige was untarnished. They so completely outshone, in cultivated opinion, all else that had been produced since the Christian era, that the Italy of Dante, the Spain of Cervantes, and the England of Shakespeare did not so much as exist. If the intelligence was not satisfied by Descartes, well! there was nothing for it but to go back to Plato, and if Racine did not sufficiently rouse the passions, they must be worked upon by Sophocles. In all this, the divines took a particularly prominent place because they alone presented something for which no definite parallel could be found in antiquity. It was the great theologians of the age with whom La Bruyère chiefly competed.

These theologians were themselves artists to a degree which we have now a difficulty in realizing, although in the seventeenth century the Church of England also had some great artists in her pulpits. If Jeremy Taylor had been a Frenchman, the work of La Bruyère might have been different. But the French orators lacked the splendour and oddity of the author of "The Great Exemplar," and we can feel that La Bruyère, who was instinct with the need for colour, was dissatisfied with the broad outlines and masses of character for which the French divines were famous; indeed, even Bossuet, to an English reader fresh from Fuller and Taylor, seems with all his magnificence too abstract and too rhetorical. La Bruyère determined to be less exacting and yet more exact; he would sink to describing emotions less tremendous and to designing figures of more trifling value, but he would paint them with a vivid detail hitherto unsolicited. The consequence was that the public instantly responded to his appeal, and we have continued to contemplate with reverence Bossuet's huge historical outlines, but to turn for sheer pleasure to La Bruyère's finished etchings of the tulipomaniac and the collector of engravings.

Everyone who approaches an analysis of the *Caractères* is obliged to pause to commend the style of La Bruyère. It is indeed exquisite. At the time his book was published our own John Locke was putting together his famous *Thoughts on Education,* and he remarked on the "policy" of the French, who were not thinking it "beneath the public care to promote and reward the improvement of their own language. Polishing and enriching their tongue," so Locke proceeds, "is no small business amongst them." It is perhaps not extravagant to believe that in writing these words the English philosopher was thinking of the new Parisian moralist. For La Bruyère was a great artist, who understood the moral value of form in a degree which

would peculiarly commend itself to the lucid mind of Locke. He says, early in his book, "Among all the different expressions which can render a single one of our thoughts, there is only one which is right. We do not always hit upon it in speaking or composing; nevertheless it is a fact that somewhere it exists, and everything else is feeble and does not satisfy a man of intelligence who desires to be understood." This search for the one and only perfect expression was an unfailing passion with La Bruyère. In another place he says: "The author who only considers the taste of his own age is thinking more of himself than of his writings. We ought always to be striving after perfection, and then posterity will render us that justice which is sometimes refused to us by our contemporaries." This is an ideal to which Locke, anxious to make disciples by his regular and sometimes racy use of language, never attained. La Bruyère, who did not address the passing age, so polished his periods that all successive generations have hailed him as one of the greatest masters of prose.

Voltaire's definition of the style of La Bruyère is well known, but cannot too often be repeated. He calls it "a rapid, concise, nervous style, with picturesque expressions, a wholly novel use of the French language, yet with no infringement of its rules." Fortunately, with all his admiration of others—and his great chapter "Des Ouvrages de l'Esprit" is one of the most generous and catholic examples of current criticism which we possess in all literature—with his modest and glowing appreciation of his famous predecessors, he did not attempt to imitate them in the grand manner. We are able to perceive that Bossuet, who was nearly twenty years his senior, to whom he owed his advancement in life, whose majestic genius and princely prestige were so well adapted to dazzle La Bruyère, remained his indefatigable patron and probably his closest friend. But we do not find in La Bruyère a trace of imitation of the great preacher whom he loved and honoured. If we think what the authority of Bossuet had come to be at the time when the *Caractères* was published, how hardly its evangelical science pressed upon the convictions of all Frenchmen, and particularly upon those of men who accepted it as unquestionably as did the author of that book, that there should be no trace of Bossuet on his style is a great tribute to the originality of La Bruyère.

"There is no pleasure without variety," this same mighty Bossuet had written in 1670, and his young friend had taken the axiom to heart. We find him pursuing almost beyond the bounds of good taste the search for variety of manner. He has strange sudden turns of thought, startling addresses, inversions which we should blame as violent, if they were not so eminently successful that we adopt them at once, as we do Shakespeare's. La Bruyère passes from mysterious ironies to bold and coarse invective, from ornate and sublime reflections to phrases of a roguish simplicity. He suddenly drops his voice to a shuddering whisper, and the next moment is fluting like a blackbird. The gaiety with which he mocks the ambitions of the rich is suddenly relieved by the dreadful calm with which he reveals the horror of their disappointments. He is never in the same mood, or adopting the same tone, for two pages running. It is difficult in a translation to give an idea of the surprising element in his style, but something of its oddity may be preserved in such an attempt as this—

> There are creatures of God whom we call men, who have a soul which is intelligence, and whose whole life is spent and whose whole attention is centred in the sawing of marble. This is a very simple, a very little thing. There are others who are amazed at this, but who themselves are utterly useless, and who spend their days in doing nothing at all. This is a still smaller thing than sawing marble.

English prose, which a century earlier had limped so far behind French in clearness and conciseness, was rapidly catching its rival up, and in the next generation was to run abreast with it. But if we wish to see how far behind the best French writers our own best still were, we need but compare the exquisite speed and elasticity of the **Caractères** with the comparative heaviness and slowness of a famous Theophrastian essay published in the same year, 1688, namely the "Character of a Trimmer." In the characteristics of a lively prose artist, we shall have to confess La Bruyère nearer to Robert Louis Stevenson than to his own immediate contemporary, Lord Halifax.

The surface of La Bruyère's writing is crisp and parched, but it is easy by careful reading to crack it, and to discover the coolness, the softness, the salutary humidity which lie beneath the satirical crust of his irony. He is primarily a satirist, dealing as he says with the vices of the human mind and the subterfuges of human self-deception. He lays bare "the sentiments and the movements of men, exposing the principles which actuate their malice and their frailty"; he aims at showing that such is the native evil implanted in their souls that "no one should any longer be surprised at the thousands of vicious or frivolous actions with which their lives are crowded." We note him at first as entirely devoted to these painful investigations, and we are apt to confound his attitude with that of La Rochefoucauld, the weary Titan, who sighs contemptuously as he holds up to censure the globe of human *amour-propre*. But we do not begin to understand the attitude of La Bruyère until we notice that there always is, in the popular phrase, "more in him than meets the eye." He is indeed a satirist, but not of the profound order of the Timons of the mind; his satire is superficial, and under it there flows a lenient curiosity mingled with a sympathy that fears to be detected.

There is a note of sadness, a mysterious melancholy, which frequently recurs in the **Caractères,** and this produces a constant variety in its appeal to the feelings. We find the author amusing himself by detailing the weaknesses of his fellow-beings, but the entertainment they offer him soon leaves him dissatisfied and sad. He is overheard to sigh, he is seen to shake his head, as he turns his clear eyes away from the self-humiliation of men. There is nothing of this in the hard superiority of La Rochefoucauld, and one of the most important things which we have to note is the advance in feeling which the later moralist makes, in spite of his extremely unpretentious attitude. La Bruyère attains to a reasoned tolerance which neither his immediate predecessor nor Pascal nor Bossuet reached or had the least wish to reach. In him we meet, not commonly nor prominently presented, but quite plainly enough, the modern virtue of indulgence, of tolerance. Here is a passage which could scarcely have been written by any other moralist of the seventeenth century:—

> It is useless to fly into a passion with human beings because of their harshness, their injustice, their pride, their self-love and their forgetfulness of others. They are made so, it is their nature, and to be angry about it is to be angry with the stone for falling or with the flame for rising.

Here is the voice of the man who had lived and who was still living in the house of that Prince de Condé of whom Saint Simon said that, "A pernicious neighbour, he made everybody miserable with whom he had to do." I like to imagine La Bruyère escaping from some dreadful scene where Henry Jules had injured his dependants and insulted his familiars, or had drawn out in public the worst qualities of his son, "incapable of affection and only too capable of hatred." I imagine him escaping from the violence and meanness of those intolerable tyrants up into the asylum of his own hushed apartment at Versailles; there flinging himself down for a moment in the alcove, on the painted bedstead, then presently rising, with a smile on his lips and the fright and anger gone out of his eyes, and advancing to the great oaken bureau which displayed his faience and his guitar. He would glance, for encouragement, at the framed portrait of Bossuet which was the principal ornament of the wall above it, and then, listening a moment to be sure that he was safe from disturbance, he would unlock one of the three drawers, and take out the little portfolio in which for years and years he had been storing up his observations upon society and his consolations in affliction. Presently, with infinite deliberation and most fastidious choice of the faultless phrase and single available word, he would paint the Holbein portrait of one of the prodigious creatures whom he had just seen in action, some erratic, brilliant and hateful "ornament of society" such as the Duke de Lauzun, and the picture of Straton would be added to his gallery:—

> Straton was born under two stars; unlucky, lucky in the same degree. His life is a romance: no, for it lacks probability. He has had beautiful dreams, he has bad ones: what am I saying? people don't dream as he has lived. No one has ever extracted out of a destiny more than he has. The preposterous and the commonplace are equally familiar to him. He has shone, he has suffered, he has dragged along a humdrum existence: nothing has escaped him. . . . He is an enigma, a riddle that can probably be never solved.

La Bruyère aimed at the improvement of human nature. La Rochefoucauld had said, "Don't be ridiculous—a blatant love of self is the only spring of your being." Pascal, less haughty but more overwhelming, had said, "Insect that you are, doomed to damnation, cease to strive against your own miserable impotence." La Bruyère's teaching was not so definite, partly because his intellect was not so systematic as theirs, but partly because he was more human than either, human with more than a touch of the modern democratic humanity. His attitude was the easier one implied in the sense that "there is so much that's good in the worst of us, and so much that's bad in the best of us" that there is room, even among moralists, for an infinite indulgence. His was, on the whole, and accounting for some fluttering of the nerves, a very tranquil spirit. He is much less formal and mechanical than La Rochefoucauld, and he seems to study men with less dependence on a theory. His own statement should not be overlooked; he says, very plainly, that he desired above all things to make men live better lives.

Boileau said that the style of La Bruyère was "prophetic," and I do not know that any one has attempted to explain this rather curious phrase. But we may adopt it in the light of more than two centuries which were unknown to Boileau. More than any other writer of the end of the seventeenth century La Bruyère prophesied of a good time coming. He did not speak out very plainly, but it is the privilege of prophets to be obscure, and their predictions are commonly not comprehensible until after the event. But we may claim for La Bruyère the praise of being a great civilizer of French thought; more than that, he widened human social intelligence throughout Europe. He is the direct ancestor of the Frenchman of to-day who observes closely and clearly, who has the power to define what he sees, and who retains the colour and movement of it. To this day, as may be amply seen in the records and episodes of the war, in the correspondence of officers at the front, in the general intellectual conduct of the contest, Frenchmen rarely experience a difficulty in finding the exact word they want. These men who arrest for our pleasure an impression, who rebuild before us the fabric of their experience, descend in direct line from La Bruyère. It was he who taught their nation to seize the attitude and to photograph the gesture.

La Bruyère's express aim is to clarify our minds, to make us think lucidly and in consequence speak with precision. We have already seen what value he sets on the right word in the right place. He is the enemy of all those who shamble along in the supposition that an inaccurate phrase will "do well enough," and that any slipshod definition is excused by our saying, "Oh, you know what I mean!" His own style is finished up to the highest point, and it is brightened and varied with such skill that the author never ceases to hold the attention of the reader. He reaches the very ideal of that elegant wandering art of writing which the Latins called *sermo pedestris*. Indeed, he gives so much attention to the perfect mode of saying things that some critics have brought it as a charge against him that he overdoes it, that in fact his style is more weighty than his subject. This, I think, is a very hasty judgment, founded a little, no doubt, upon a certain dread on La Bruyère's part of being commonplace. He was dealing, as every moralist is bound to deal, with ideas of a more or less primitive character, to which sparkle and force must be given by illustrative examples. These examples gave him his great chance, and he built them up, those exemplary "portraits" of his, with infinite labour, accumulating details to make a type; and sometimes, it is possible, accumulating too many. The result is that the *Caractères* are sometimes a little laboured; I do not know any other fault that can be laid to their charge.

One of the most important qualities of La Bruyère was that he prepared the popular mind for liberty. He is democratic in many ways, in his language, where he often borrows words from the *patois* of the common people; in his exposure of the errors of the *ancien régime,* its tyranny, its selfishness, its want of humanity and imagination; in his hatred of wealth, the scandalous triumph of which had already reached a pitch which the next generation was to see outdone. In all this, as cannot be too often insisted upon, it was essential for a reformer to be prudent. The People had no voice, and that their interests should be defended was inconceivable. In the next century, after the reign of Louis XV was over and speech had, in a great measure, become free, it was not understood how difficult it was under Louis XIV to express any criticism of the feudal order. For instance, there is a long passage at the end of the chapter "De la Ville," which scandalized the political reformers of the eighteenth century. It is that which begins, "The emperors never triumphed in Rome so softly, so conveniently, or even so successfully, against wind and rain, dust and sunshine, as the citizen of Paris knows how to do as he crosses the city to-day in every direction. How far have we advanced beyond the mule of our ancestors!" La Bruyère was charged, and even by Voltaire, with attacking the progress of civilization, and with preferring the rude subterfuges of Carlovingian times to the comforts of 1688. But he was really making an appeal for thrift and modesty of expenditure on the part of those bourgeois who had suddenly become rich, as a satirist of our own day might denounce the pomp of a too successful shopkeeper, without being accused of denying the convenience of motor-cars or desiring to stop the progress of scientific invention.

La Bruyère was the first effective moralist who realized what a monstrous disproportion existed between the fortune of the rich and of the poor. If we read the chapter "Des Biens de Fortune" we may be astonished at his courage, and we may see in him a direct precursor of the revolution which took a little more than a hundred years to gather before it broke on France. He describes the great of the earth with a savage serenity, and then he adds, "Such people are neither relatives, nor friends, nor citizens, nor Christians, nor perhaps even men. They have money." There are many such maxims in the chapter "De l'homme" which must have set people's thoughts running in channels which had before been wholly dry. La Bruyère was not a political reformer, and we must not exaggerate the influence of his charming book in this particular direction. But, as a popular imaginative writer, he took a long step in the democratic direction. Frenchmen were already touched in their consciences and beginning to examine the state of their souls with anxiety; but the teachers of the ascetic revival had been too uncompromising. Ordinary mortals could not hope to reach the ascetic ideal of Port Royal, they could only be discouraged by the savage attacks on *amour-propre,* while in the **Caractères** they met with a lay-preacher who was one of themselves, and who did not disdain to encourage moral effort.

It was a great advantage to La Bruyère, and a sign of his genius, that he was able to descend from the pulpit, and walk about among his readers with a smile, recognizing them as reasonable beings. He is persuasive; his forerunners had been denunciatory. He may be harsh and sometimes unjust, but he is never contemptuous to human nature. He feels that he is addressing a wide public of intelligent men and women, whom he would fortify against the moral tyranny of the violent and the rich. For this purpose, though he would tell them their faults, he would not shut the gates of mercy in their faces. But how admirably he himself puts it in his chapter "Des Jugements":—

> A man of talent and reputation, if he allows himself to be peevish and censorious, scares young people, makes them think evil of virtue, and frightens them with the idea of an excessive reform and a tiresome strictness of conduct. If, on the other hand, he proves easy to get on with, he sets a practical lesson before them, since he proves to them that a man can live gaily and yet laboriously, and can hold serious views without renouncing honest pleasures; so he becomes an example which they find it possible to follow.
>
> (pp. 66-87)

One last word about our amiable author. His great book remains eminently alive, and wields after two centuries and a half a permanent influence. When you refer to it, you must not expect a logical development of philosophical theory. We do not look to find a system in a book of maxims and portraits. La Bruyère was a moralist, pure and simple; he awakened sensibility, he encouraged refinement, and he exposed the vicious difference which existed around him—and which no one else had seemed to notice—that the possession of more or fewer pieces of money made between human beings otherwise equal. He had a democratic philosophy which is sometimes that of Mr. Micawber, "Celui-là est riche qui reçoit plus qu'il ne consume; celui-là est pauvre dont la dépense excède la recette." But he is seldom so prosy as this. Let us think of him as one who wished to turn his talent as a painter of still life to the benefit of his nation, and who succeeded in a degree far beyond his own modest hopes. (pp. 92-3)

Edmund Gosse, "La Bruyère," in his Three French Moralists and the Gallantry of France, *William Heinemann, 1918, pp. 55-93.*

Roland Barthes   (essay date 1963)

[*Barthes was among the most influential and revolutionary writers in modern critical thought. His importance derives less from persuasive illumination of his themes or from his introduction of certain nonliterary perspectives into his writing (he has at various times employed viewpoints adopted from Marxism, psychoanalysis, and structuralism), than it does from the insight that language—or any other medium of communication: painting, fashion, advertising—is a "system of signs." The aim of Barthes's method is to expose the "myths" of a specific sign system, revealing their origins in custom and convention, in order to practice what Barthes views as the only valid purpose of criticism: the observation of the inner workings and interrelationships governing a sign system to define the symbolic elements that constitute everything from a work of literature to an advertising billboard to a striptease act. In the following essay,* first published in 1963, Barthes explains why La Bruyère does not occupy a position of greater influence and significance in literary history.*]

La Bruyère occupies an ambiguous place in French culture: he is taught as a "major author"; his maxims, his art, his historical role are assigned as dissertation subjects; his knowledge of Man and his premonition of a more equitable society are extolled: *The notion of humanity,* Brunetière used to say, *dawns with La Bruyère;* he is made (O precious paradox!) at once a classic and a democrat. Yet outside our schools, the La Bruyère myth is a meager one: he has not yet been caught up in any of those great dialogues which French writers have always engaged in from one century to another (Pascal and Montaigne, Voltaire and Racine, Valéry and La Fontaine); criticism itself has scarcely bothered to renew our entirely academic image of him; his work has not lent itself to any of the new languages of our age, has stimulated neither historians nor philosophers nor sociologists nor psychoanalysts; in short, if we except the sympathy of a Proust quoting some penetrating maxim ("Being with the people one loves is enough; dreaming, talking to them or not talking to them, thinking about them or about indifferent things in their presence, it is all one." "Du coeur," No. 23), our modernity, though quite ready to appropriate classical authors, seems to have great difficulty recuperating him: though he stands with the great names of our literature, La Bruyère is nonetheless disinherited, one might almost say *deconsecrated:* he lacks even that final fortune of the writer: to be neglected.

In short, this glory is a little drowsy, and it must be admitted that La Bruyère himself is not a likely agent for great awakenings; he remains, in everything, temperate (Thibaudet used to speak of La Bruyère's *chiaroscuro*), avoids exhausting the subjects he initiates, renounces that radicality of viewpoint which assures the writer a violent posthumous life; close as it is to La Rochefoucauld's, for example, his pessimism never exceeds the prudence of a good Christian, never turns to obsession; though capable of producing a short, lightninglike form, he prefers the somewhat longer fragment, the portrait which repeats itself: he is a moderate moralist, he does not scald (except perhaps in the chapters on women and money, of an unyielding aggressiveness); and furthermore, although an avowed painter of a society and, within that society, of the most social passion there is, worldliness, La Bruyère does not become a chronicler, a Retz or a Saint-Simon; it is as if he wanted to avoid the choice of a specific genre; as a moralist, he persistently refers to a real society, apprehended in its persons and events (as the number of "keys" to his book testifies); and as a sociologist, he nonetheless experiences this society in its moral substance alone; we cannot really deduce from him the image of man's "eternal flaw"; nor can we find in him, beyond good and evil, the lively spectacle of a pure sociality; perhaps this is why modernity, which always seeks certain pure nutriments in the literature of the past, has difficulty acknowledging La Bruyère: he escapes it by the most delicate of resistances: it cannot name him.

This uneasiness is doubtless that of our modern reading of La Bruyère. We might express it differently: the world of La Bruyère is at once *ours* and *different; ours* because the society he paints conforms so closely to our academic myth of the seventeenth century that we circulate quite comfortably among these old figures from our childhood: Ménalque, the plum lover, the savage beast-peasants, the "everything has been said and we have come too late," the city, the court, the parvenus, etc.; *different* because the immediate sentiment of our modernity tells us that these customs, these characters, these passions even, are not ourselves; the paradox is a cruel one: La Bruyère is ours by his anachronism and alien to us by his very project of eternity; the moderation of this author (what used to be called *mediocrity*), the weight of academic culture, the pressure of contiguous readings, everything makes La Bruyère transmit an image of classical man which is neither distant enough for us to relish its exoticism, nor close enough for us to identify ourselves with it: it is a familiar image which does not concern us.

To read La Bruyère would of course have no reality today (once we have left school), if we could not violate that suspect equilibrium of distance and identity, if we did not let ourselves be swayed toward one or the other; we can certainly read La Bruyère in a spirit of confirmation, searching, as in any moralist, for the maxim which will account in a perfect form for that very wound we have just received from the world; we can also read him and underline all that separates his world from ours and all that this distance teaches us about ourselves; such is our enterprise here: let us discuss everything in La Bruyère which concerns us little or not at all: perhaps we shall then, at last, collect the modern meaning of his work.

And first of all, what is the world, for someone who speaks? An initially formless field of objects, beings, phenomena which must be organized, i.e., divided up and distributed. La Bruyère does not fail this obligation; he divides up the society he lives in into great regions, among which he will distribute his "characters" (which are, roughly, the chapters of his book). These regions or classes are not a homogeneous object, they correspond, one may say, to different sciences (and this is natural enough, since every science is itself a dividing up of the world); first of all, there are two sociological classes, which form the "basis" of the classical world: the court (the nobility) and the city (the bourgeoisie); then an anthropological class: women (a particular race, whereas man is general: he says *de l'homme* but *des femmes*); a political class (the monarchy), psychological classes (heart, judgment, merit), and ethnological classes, in which social behavior is observed at a certain distance (fashion, customs); the whole is framed (an accident, or a secret significance?) by two singular "operators": literature, which opens the work (we shall discuss, later on, the relevance of this inauguration), and religion, which closes it.

This variety of objects manipulated by La Bruyère, the disparity of the classes he has constituted as chapters, suggest two remarks; first of all: **Les Caractères** is in a sense a book of total knowledge; on the one hand, La Bruyère approaches social man from every angle, he constitutes a kind of indirect *summa* (for it is always literature's function to circumvent science) of the various kinds of knowl-

edge of the *socius* available at the end of the seventeenth century (it will be noted that this man is indeed much more social than psychological); and on the other hand, more disturbingly, the book corresponds to a kind of initiatory experience, it seeks to reach that supreme point of existence where knowledge and conduct, science and consciousness meet under the ambiguous name of *wisdom;* in short, La Bruyère has sketched a kind of cosmogony of classical society, describing this world by its aspects, its limits and interferences. And this leads to our second remark: the regions out of which La Bruyère composes his world are quite analogous to logical classes: every "individual" (in logic, we would say every *x*), i.e., every "character," is defined first of all by a relation of membership in some class or other, the tulip fancier in the class *Fashion,* the coquette in the class *Women,* the absent-minded Ménalque in the class *Men,* etc.; but this is not enough, for the characters must be distinguished among themselves within one and the same class; La Bruyère therefore performs certain operations of intersection from one class to the next; cross the class of *Merit* with that of *Celibacy* and you get a reflection on the stifling function of marriage ("Du mérite," No. 25); join Tryphon's former virtue and his present fortune: the simple coincidence of these two classes affords the image of a certain hypocrisy ("Des biens de fortune," No. 50). Thus the diversity of the regions, which are sometimes social, sometimes psychological, in no way testifies to a rich disorder; confronting the world, La Bruyère does not enumerate absolutely varied elements like the surveyor writers of the next century; he combines certain rare elements; the man he constructs is always made up of several principles: age, origin, fortune, vanity, passion; only the formula of composition varies, the interplay of intersecting classes: a "character" is always the product of the encounter of at least two constants.

Now this is a treatment of man which to us has become if not alien at least impossible. It has been said of Leibnitz, more or less La Bruyère's contemporary, that he was the last man able to know everything; La Bruyère, too, was perhaps the last moralist able to speak of *all* of man, to enclose all the regions of the human world in a book; less than a century later, this would require the thirty-three volumes of the *Encyclopédie;* today, there is no longer a writer in the world who can treat man-in-society by regions: not all the human sciences combined can manage to do it. To borrow an image from information theory, we might say that from the classical century to our own, the *level of perception* has changed: we see man on another scale, and the very meaning of what we see is thereby transformed, like that of an ordinary substance under the microscope; the chapters of **Les Caractères** are so many brakes applied to the vision of man; today we cannot stop man anywhere; any partition we impose upon him refers him to a particular science, his totality escapes us; if I speak, *mutatis mutandis,* of the city and the court, I am a social writer; if I speak of the monarchy, I am a political theorist; of literature, a critic; of customs, an essayist; of the heart, a psychoanalyst, etc.; further, at least half the classes of objects to which La Bruyère refers have no more than a decrepit existence; no one today would write a chapter on women, on merit, or on conversation; though we continue to marry, to "arrive," or to speak, such behavior has shifted to another level of perception; a new dispatching refers them to human regions unknown to La Bruyère: social dynamics, interpersonal psychology, sexuality, though these realms can never be united under a single kind of writing: narrow, clear, "centered," finite, obsessive, La Bruyère's man is always *here;* ours is always elsewhere; if it occurs to think of someone's character, we do so either in terms of its insignificant universality (the desire for social advancement, for instance), or of its ineffable complexity (of whom would we dare say quite simply that he is a *dolt?*). In short, what has changed, from La Bruyère's world to ours, is what is notable: we no longer *note* the world the way La Bruyère did; our speech is different not because the vocabulary has developed, but because to speak is to fragment reality in an always committed fashion and because our dividing-up refers to a reality so broad that reflection cannot accommodate it and because the new sciences, those we call the human sciences (whose status, moreover, is not clearly defined), must intervene: La Bruyère notes that a father-in-law loves his daughter-in-law and that a mother-in-law loves her son-in-law ("De la société," No. 45); this is a notation which would concern us more today if it came from a psychoanalyst, just as it is Freud's Oedipus who sets us thinking now, not Sophocles'. A matter of language? But the only *power* history has over the "human heart" is to vary the language which utters it. "Everything has been said now that men have been living and thinking for seven thousand years": yes, no doubt; but it is never too late to invent new languages.

Such, then, is La Bruyère's "world," accounted for by several great classes of "individuals": court, city, Church, women, etc.; these same classes can easily be subdivided into smaller "societies." Merely reread fragment 4 of the chapter "De la ville": "The city is divided into various societies, which are like so many little republics, each with its own laws, customs, jargon, and jokes . . . " One might say in modern terms that the world is made up of a juxtaposition of *isolates,* impermeable to one another. In other words, the human group, as La Bruyère sees it, is not in the least constituted in a substantial fashion; beyond the purely contingent way in which these little societies are filled with bourgeois or with nobles, La Bruyère seeks out some feature which might define them all; this feature exists; it is a form; and this form is enclosure; La Bruyère is concerned with worlds, with *the* world, insofar as they—and it—are closed. We are dealing here, poetically, with what we might call an imagination of partition which consists in mentally exhausting every situation which the simple enclosure of a space gradually engenders in the general field where it occurs: choice of the partition, different substances of *inside* and *outside,* rules of admission, of exit, of exchange—it suffices that a line be closed in the world for a host of new meanings to be generated, and this is what La Bruyère realized. Applied to the social substance, the imagination of enclosure, whether experienced or analyzed, produces in fact an object which is both real (for it can be derived from sociology) and poetic (for writers have treated it with predilection): this object is worldliness. Before literature raised the problem of political realism, worldliness was a precious means for the writer to ob-

serve social reality yet remain a writer; worldliness is indeed an ambiguous form of reality: committed and uncommitted; referring to the disparity of the human condition but remaining in spite of everything a pure form, enclosure guarantees access to the psychological and the social without passing through the political; this is why, perhaps, we have had a great literature of worldliness in France, from Molière to Proust: and it is in this tradition of an entire imaginary world focused on the phenomena of social enclosure that La Bruyère obviously takes his place.

There can exist a great number of little worldly societies, since they need merely be closed in order to exist; but it follows that enclosure, which is the original form of all worldliness, and which we can consequently describe on the level of infinitesimal groups (the coterie of fragment 4 of "De la ville," or the Verdurin salon), assumes a precise historical meaning when it is applied to the world as a whole; for what is then inside and outside it inevitably correspond to the economic partition of society; this is the case for the general worldliness described by La Bruyère; it has necessarily social roots: what is inside the enclosure are the privileged classes, nobility and bourgeoisie; what is outside are men without birth and money, the people (workers and peasants). La Bruyère, however, does not define social classes; he variously populates an inland and an outland; everything which occurs inside the enclosure is thereby called into Being; everything which remains outside it is rejected into nothingness; one might say, paradoxically, that social substructures are only the reflection of the forms of rejection and admission. The primacy of the form thus renders indirect the notations we would today call political. La Bruyère's democratic sentiments are often hailed, generally supported by fragment 128, "De l'homme," which is a grim description of the peasants ("Certain wild animals . . . are to be seen about the countryside . . . "). Nonetheless, *the people,* in this literature, has no more than a purely functional value: it remains the object of a charity, of which the subject alone, the charitable man, is called upon to exist; in order to exercise pity, there must be a pitiable object: *the people* obliges. In formal terms (and it has been said how much the closed form predetermined this world), the poor classes, enlightened by no political consideration, are that pure exterior without which bourgeoisie and aristocracy could not realize their own being (see fragment 31, "Des biens de fortune," in which the people watches the nobility live their emphatic existence, as though on a stage); the poor are the thing starting from which one exists: they are the constitutive limit of the enclosure. And of course, as pure functions, the men of the exterior have no essence. We can attribute to them none of those "characters" which mark the inhabitants of the interior with a full existence: a man of the people is neither a dolt nor absent-minded nor vain nor greedy nor gluttonous (greedy, gluttonous—how could he be?); he is merely a pure tautology: *a gardener is a gardener, a mason is a mason,* no more can be said of him; the only double quality, the only relation to Being which, from the interior and beyond his utensile nature (to tend the garden, to build a wall), he can occasionally be granted is to be a man: not a human being, but a male whom the women of the world discover when they are too sequestered ("Des femmes," No. 34): the questioner (the torturer who applies the question) is not a bit cruel (that would be a "character"); he is simply "a young man with broad shoulders and a stocky figure, a Negro moreover, a black man" ("Des femmes," No. 33).

The "character" is a metaphor: it is the development of an adjective. Forbidden definition (being merely a limit), the people can receive neither adjective nor character: therefore the people vanishes from discourse. By the very weight of the formal postulate which consigns what is enclosed to Being, all the writing of *Les Caractères* is focused on the interior plenitude of the enclosure: it is here that characters, adjectives, situations, anecdotes abound. But this abundance is, one might say, rare, purely qualitative; it is not a quantitative abundance; the inland of worldliness, though filled to bursting with Being, is a narrow and sparsely populated territory; there occurs here a phenomenon of which our mass societies are losing all notion: everybody knows everybody else, everyone has a name. This interior familiarity, based on an openly sociological circumstance (nobles and bourgeois were a small minority) suggests what happens in societies of minor demography: tribes, villages, even American society before the great immigration. Paradoxically, La Bruyère's readers could conceive the universal better than the anonymous: thus any description of a character coincides with the sentiment of an identity, even if this identity is uncertain; the many "keys" which followed the publication of *Les Caractères* do not constitute a paltry phenomenon which would indicate, for instance, contemporary incomprehension in the face of the book's general scope; it is perhaps indifferent that the glutton *Cliton* was actually Count de Broussin or Louis de la Trémouille; it is not indifferent that the "characters" were almost all drawn from a personalized society: nomination here is a strict function of enclosure: the worldly type (and it is here that it probably differs from the typical roles of comedy) is not born of abstraction, quintessence of countless individuals: the worldly type is an immediate unit, defined by his place among adjacent units whose "differential" contiguity forms the inland of worldliness: La Bruyère does not purify his characters, he recites them like the successive cases of one and the same worldly declension.

Enclosure and individuation, these are dimensions of a sociality we no longer know anything about. Our world is open, we circulate in it; and above all, if enclosure still exists, it is anything but a rare minority which is confined within it and emphatically finds its being there; on the contrary, it is the countless majority; worldliness, today, is normality; it follows that the psychology of partition has entirely changed; we are no longer sensitive to characters resulting from the principle of vanity (decisive when it is the minority which is associated with both Being and Having), but rather to all the variations of the abnormal; for us, characters exist only marginally: it is no longer La Bruyère who gives a name to men now, it is the psychopathologist or the psychosociologist, those specialists who are called upon to define not essences but (quite the contrary) divergences. In other words, our enclosure is extensive, it confines the majority. There ensues a complete reversal of the interest we can take in characters; in the past, the char-

acter referred to a "key," the (general) *person* to a (particular) *personality;* today, it is the opposite; our world certainly creates, for its spectacle, a closed and personalized society: that of the stars and celebrities which we might group under the name of modern Olympians; but this society does not yield characters, only functions or roles (the love goddess, the mother, the queen enslaved by her duty, the vixen princess, the model husband, etc.); and contrary to the classical circuit, these "personalities" are treated as persons in order that the greatest number of human beings can recognize themselves in them; the Olympian society we create for our own consumption is, in short, only a world set within the world so as to represent it—not an enclosure but a mirror: we no longer seek out the typical but the identical; La Bruyère condensed a character in the fashion of a metaphor; we develop a star like a narrative; Iphis, Onuphre, or Hermippe lent themselves to an art of the portrait; Margaret, Soraya, or Marilyn renew that of the epic gesture.

This "structural" distance of La Bruyère's world in relation to ours does not cause our lack of interest in his, but merely exempts us from trying to identify ourselves with it; we must get used to the idea that La Bruyère's truth is, in the full sense of the term, elsewhere. Nothing will prepare us to do this better than a glance at what we would call today his political position. As we know, his century was not subversive. Born of the monarchy, fed by it, entirely immersed within it, writers of the period were as united in approving the establishment as those of today are in contesting it. Sincere or not (the question itself was virtually meaningless), La Bruyère declares himself as submissive to Louis XIV as to a god; not that his submission is not experienced as such; simply, it is inevitable: a man born a Christian and a Frenchman (i.e., subject to the king) cannot, by nature, approach the great subjects, which are the forbidden subjects: nothing remains for him except to write well ("Des ouvrages de l'esprit," No. 65); the writer will therefore fling himself into the sanctification of what exists, *because it exists* ("Du souverain," No. 1); it is the immobility of things which shows their truth; the Siamese welcome Christian missionaries but refrain from sending theirs to Europe: this is because their gods are false and "ours" true ("Des esprits forts," No. 29). La Bruyère's submission to the most emphatic (and therefore to the most banal) forms of the royal cult is of course not at all strange in itself: every writer of his day employed this style; but all the same, there is one singularity about it: it suddenly reins in what today we would call a demystifying attitude: moralism, which is by definition a substitution of rationales for appearances and of motives for virtues, ordinarily operates like vertigo: applied to the "human heart," the investigation of truth seems unable to stop anywhere; yet in La Bruyère, this implacable movement, pursued by means of tiny notations throughout a whole book (which was the book of his life) concludes with the dullest of declarations: that the things of this world remain finally as they were, motionless under the gaze of the god-king; and that the author himself joins this immobility and "takes refuge in mediocrity" (*mediocrity* in the sense of the *juste milieu;* see "Des biens de fortune," No. 47): it is as if we were hearing a new profession of dharma, the Hindu law which prescribes the immobility of things and of castes.

Thus there appears a kind of distortion between book and author, a discrepancy at once surprising and exemplary; surprising because, whatever effort the author makes to submit, the book continues to ignite everything in its path; exemplary because by founding an order of signs on the distance between the witness and his testimony, the work seems to refer to a particular fulfillment of man in the world, a fulfillment which we call, precisely, *literature*. It is, finally, just when La Bruyère seems farthest from us that a figure suddenly appears who concerns us very closely and who is, quite simply, the *writer*.

It is not a question, of course, of "writing well." We believe today that literature is a technique at once more profound than that of style and less direct than that of thought; we believe that it is both language and thought, thought which seeks itself on the level of words, language which considers itself philosophically. Is that what La Bruyère is?

One might say that the first condition of literature is, paradoxically, to produce an *indirect* language: to name things in detail in order not to name their ultimate meaning, and yet to retain this threatening meaning, to designate the world as a repertoire of signs without saying what it is they signify. Now, by a second paradox, the best way for a language to be indirect is to refer as constantly as possible to objects and not to their concepts: for the object's meaning always vacillates, the concept's does not; whence the concrete vocation of literary writing. Now **Les Caractères** is an admirable collection of substances, sites, customs, attitudes; man here is almost constantly dominated by an object or an incident: clothing, language, movement, tears, colors, cosmetics, faces, foods, landscapes, furniture, visits, baths, letters, etc. Everyone knows that La Bruyère's book has none of the algebraic dryness of La Rochefoucauld's maxims, for instance, which are based on the articulation of pure human essences; La Bruyère's technique is different: it consists of *putting on record,* and always tends to mask the concept under the percept; if he wants to say that the motive of modest actions is not necessarily modesty, La Bruyère will produce a little story of apartments or meals ("The man who, lodged in a palace, with two sets of apartments for the two seasons, comes to the Louvre to sleep in a vestibule," etc. "Du mérite," No. 41); every truth begins this way, in the fashion of a riddle which separates the thing from its signification; La Bruyère's art (and we know that art, i.e., technique, coincides with the very Being of literature) consists in establishing the greatest possible distance between the evidence of the objects and events by which the author inaugurates most of his notations and the idea which actually seems to choose, to arrange, to move them retroactively. Most of the characters are thus constructed like a semantic equation: the concrete has the function of the signifier; the abstract, that of the signified; and between them comes a suspense, for we never know in advance the final meaning the author will draw from the things he treats.

The semantic structure of the fragment is so powerful in La Bruyère that we can readily attach it to one of the two fundamental aspects which Roman Jakobson so usefully distinguishes in any system of signs: a selective aspect (to choose a sign from a reservoir of similar signs) and a combinatory aspect (to connect the signs thus chosen within a discourse); each of these aspects corresponds to a typical figure of the old rhetoric, by which we can designate it: the selective aspect corresponds to *metaphor,* which is the substitution of one signifier for another, both having the same meaning, if not the same value; the combinatory aspect corresponds to *metonymy,* which is the shift, starting from a same meaning, from one sign to another; esthetically, a resort to metaphorical procedure is at the origin of all the arts of variation; a resort to metonymic procedure is at the origin of all the arts of narrative. A portrait by La Bruyère, then, has an eminently metaphorical structure; La Bruyère chooses features which have the same signified, and he accumulates them in a continuous metaphor, whose unique signified is given at the end; consider, for instance, the portrait of the rich man and of the poor man at the end of the chapter "Des biens de fortune," No. 83: in *Giton* are enumerated, one right after another, all the signs which make him a rich man; in *Phédon,* all the signs of the poor man; we thus see that everything which happens to Giton and to Phédon, although apparently recounted, does not derive, strictly speaking, from the order of narrative; it is entirely a matter of an extended metaphor, of which La Bruyère himself has very pertinently given the theory when he says of his Ménalque that he is "less a particular character than a collection of examples of distraction" ("De l'homme," No. 7); by this we are to understand that all the distractions enumerated are not really those of a single man, even one fictively named, as would occur in a real narrative (metonymic order); but that they belong instead to a lexicon of distraction from which can be chosen, "according to taste," the most significant feature (metaphoric order). Here perhaps we approach La Bruyère's art: the "character" is a false narrative, it is a metaphor which assumes the quality of narrative without truly achieving it (we recall moreover La Bruyère's scorn for storytelling: "Des jugements," No. 52): the indirect nature of literature is thus fulfilled: ambiguous, intermediate between definition and illustration, the discourse constantly grazes one and the other and deliberately misses both: the moment we think we perceive the clear meaning of an entirely metaphorical portrait (lexicon of the features of distraction), this meaning shifts under the appearances of an experienced narrative (one of Ménalque's days).

A false narrative, a masked metaphor: this situation of La Bruyère's discourse perhaps explains the formal structure (what used to be called the composition) of the **Caractères:** it is a book of fragments precisely because the fragment occupies an intermediary place between the maxim which is a pure metaphor, since it defines (see La Rochefoucauld: "Self-love is the worst flatterer"), and the anecdote, which is pure narrative: the discourse extends a little because La Bruyère cannot be content with a simple equation (he explains this at the end of his preface); but it stops as soon as it threatens to turn into a story. **Les Caractères** exploits, in fact, a very special language, one which has few equivalents in a literature so imbued with the excellence of determined genres, fragmented language (the maxim), or continuous language (the novel); yet we might cite precedents—a prosaic reference and a sublime one. The prosaic reference of the fragment would be what we call today the *scrapbook,* a varied collection of reflections and items (press cuttings, for instance) whose mere *notation* leads to a certain meaning: **Les Caractères** is indeed the scrapbook of worldliness: a timeless fragmented gazette whose pieces are in a sense the discontinuous significations of a continuous reality. The sublime reference would be what we call today *poetic language;* by a historical paradox, poetry in La Bruyère's day was essentially a continuous discourse, of metonymic and not metaphoric structure (to return to Jakobson's distinction); it has taken the profound subversion worked upon language by surrealism to obtain a fragmentary utterance which derives its poetic meaning from its very fragmentation (see for instance Char's *La Parole en archipel*); if it were poetic, La Bruyère's book would certainly not be a poem but, in the manner of certain modern compositions, a pulverized language: that the example refers us on the one hand to a classical rationality (characters) and on the other to a poetic "irrationality" in no way alters a certain shared experience of the fragment: the radical discontinuity of language could be experienced by La Bruyère as it is experienced today by René Char.

And indeed it is on the level of language (and not of style) that **Les Caractères** can perhaps touch us most closely. Here we see a man conducting a certain experiment upon literature: its object may seem to us anachronistic, as we have seen, though the word ("literature") is not. This experiment is conducted, one may say, on three levels.

First of all, on the level of the institution itself. It seems that La Bruyère very consciously worked out a certain reflection on the Being of that singular language which we now call *literature* and which he himself named, by an expression more substantial than conceptual, *the works of the mind:* in addition to his preface, which is a definition of his enterprise on the level of discourse, La Bruyère dedicates to literature a whole chapter of his work, and this chapter is the first one, as if all reflection on man must initially establish in principle the language which sustains it. No one at that time, of course, could imagine that *to write* was an intransitive verb, without moral justification: La Bruyère therefore writes in order to instruct. This finality is nonetheless absorbed in a group of much more modern definitions: writing is a métier, which is a way of demoralizing it and at the same time of giving it the seriousness of a technique ("Des ouvrages de l'esprit," No. 3); the man of letters (a new notion at the time) is open to the world yet occupies a place in it shielded from worldliness ("Des biens de fortune," No. 12); one engages in writing *or* in not-writing, which signifies that writing is a choice. Without trying to force the modernity of such notations, all this suggests the project of a singular language, distant both from the playfulness of the *précieux* (naturalness is a theme of the period) and from moral instruction, a language which finds its secret goal in a certain way of dividing up the world into words and of making it signify on the level of an exclusively verbal labor (which is *art*).

This brings us to the second level of the literary experiment, which is the writer's commitment to words. Speaking of his predecessors (Malherbe and Guez de Balzac), La Bruyère remarks: "Discourse has been given all the

order and all the clarity of which it is capable (which it can receive): it can now be given only wit." Wit designates here a kind of *ingenuity* between intelligence and technique; such, indeed, is literature: a thought formed by words, a meaning resulting from form. For La Bruyère, to be a writer is to believe that in a certain sense content depends on form, and that by modifying the structure of form, a particular intelligence of things is produced, an original contour of reality, in short, a new meaning: language, to La Bruyère, is an ideology in and of itself; he knows that his vision of the world is somehow determined by the linguistic revolution of the beginning of his century and, beyond this revolution, by his personal utterance, that ethic of discourse which has made him choose the fragment and not the maxim, metaphor and not narrative, the *naturel* and not the *précieux.*

Thus he affirms a certain responsibility of writing which is, after all, quite modern. And which leads to the third determination of the literary experiment. This responsibility of writing is not at all identified with what we now call commitment and what was then called *instruction.* Of course the classical writers could quite well believe that they were instructing, just as our writers believe they are bearing witness. But even though it is substantially linked to the world, literature is elsewhere; its function, at least at the heart of that modernity which begins with La Bruyère, is not to answer the world's questions directly but— at once more modestly and more mysteriously—to lead the question to the verge of its answer, to construct the signification technically without fulfilling it. La Bruyère was certainly not a revolutionary nor even a democrat, as the positivists of the last century used to claim; he had no idea that servitude, oppression, poverty could be expressed in political terms; yet his description of the peasants has the profound value of an awakening; the light his writing casts on human misery remains indirect, issuing for the most part from a blinded consciousness, powerless to grasp causes, to foresee corrections; but this very indirectness has a cathartic value, for it preserves the writer from bad faith: in literature, through literature, the writer has no rights; the solution of human misery is not a triumphant possession; his language is there only to designate a disturbance. This is what La Bruyère has done: because he chose to be a writer, his description of man touches on the real questions. (pp. 221-37)

Roland Barthes, "La Bruyère," in his Critical Essays, *translated by Richard Howard, Northwestern University Press, 1972, pp. 221-37.*

Jean Stewart　(essay date 1970)

[In the following excerpt, Stewart discusses La Bruyère as a moralist.]

Like other writers in the Classical tradition, La Bruyère looks beyond, or beneath, the manners and morals of his age (*les mœurs de ce siècle*) to the universal nature of man. He follows in a well-worn path; Montaigne, Descartes, Pascal, Molière, Racine, La Rochefoucauld had shown the way; ever since the *Essais* French literature had become, it has been said, 'a vast enquiry into human nature'

[G. Michaut, *La Bruyère*]. La Bruyère was well aware of his distinguished predecessors. '*Tout est dit,*' he begins his book, 'it's all been said before', but he will express his thought in his own way, '*comme mien*'.

All great writers of the time had this in common: they did not believe in the natural goodness of man—that was a myth for the next century to discover. They were deeply imbued with the concept of original sin, which indeed a look at the social scene only tended to confirm. Man, they held, is a prey to self-love, his heart an abyss filled by limitless passions, ephemeral and conflicting; he is unaware of his own motives, self-deceiving and yet seeking to deceive others; he is inconstant, shallow and vicious; his faults stay with him from childhood to the grave. The most relentless interpreter of this pessimistic view is La Rochefoucauld.

What's the answer? how can the human condition be made tolerable? La Fontaine takes a detached, ironic look at men-like-beasts, and with a shrug enjoys such pleasures as life offers. Molière's attitude seems closer to Philinte's disillusioned acceptance of human weakness than to Alceste's indignant denunciation of it. Pascal, in the Christian tradition, reveals the depths of man's misery without God in order to bring him to felicity *with* God. La Rochefoucauld's attitude is a complex one. He betrays occasional hankerings after the *morale héroique* of an earlier age, the Renaissance *virtù* ('*il y a des héros en mal comme en bien*'); he goes half-way to a Nietzschean overthrow of conventional ideals; but finally he opts for a provisional aesthetic code, that of the *honnête homme*. This attempt to compensate by nurture for the deficiencies of nature is one of the central issues of French seventeenth-century civilization. Superficially, the *honnête homme* means a well-bred man, a member of good society; the phrase was used by one Nicolas Faret in 1630 as the title of a popular treatise on correct deportment. It became the ideal of the *morale laïque,* morality divorced from religious belief, and was analysed by that freethinking man of the world, the Chevalier de Méré, Pascal's sometime friend. 'So many rare qualities are needed to become a perfect *honnête homme,*' he concludes, 'that it is easier to mention the things one must avoid than the things one must acquire.' And La Rochefoucauld summed it up briefly: 'The *honnête homme* is the man who prides himself on nothing.' The term implied qualities of modesty, rationalism, tolerance, politeness, consideration: the golden mean that was one of the aims of Classicism. But it implied also a considerable level of culture, of sensitivity in social and personal relations, in conversation and in writing. It was essentially an ideal of perfection within man's reach. La Bruyère had mixed with the best society of the time and was well aware of the charm of its intercourse. In Chapter V ('De la Société et de la Conversation') he provides his own manual of good social behaviour.

But by 1688 the ideal had begun to wear thin; and if in his earlier editions La Bruyère uses the term *honnête homme* in the accepted sense (e.g. II, 15; III, 13), by the fifth (1690) he strips it of its glamour. The *honnête homme* (XII, 55) stands midway between the *homme de bien,* the good man, and the *habile homme,* the clever opportunist;

he is merely a man who commits no obvious crimes, for whom respectability is identified with virtue.

La Bruyère's attitude, indeed, is basically different from the aristocratic intransigence of La Rochefoucauld; it is closer to the more humane view we sense in Molière, the 'knowledge of good-and-evil' in man's nature (to borrow E. M. Forster's phrase). La Bruyère does, indeed, at times, echo and paraphrase La Rochefoucauld's savage dicta; but he will not pursue to its bitter end the game of debunking 'virtues'. In his more deeply felt observations he admits the existence of such good qualities as modesty (for La Rochefoucauld merely 'the desire to be twice praised'), pity (for La Rochefoucauld 'a useless passion serving only to weaken a man's courage'), simplicity, sincerity, sympathy. He is not possessed by La Rochefoucauld's consuming destructive semi-nihilism. His stress is on *l'homme de mérite* rather than on *l'honnête homme,* and he thus looks forward to the bourgeois ideal of the eighteenth century.

If La Bruyère is less ruthlessly pessimistic than La Rochefoucauld, it is partly a matter of temperament and partly of social class, but also a result of his religious faith, which was genuine if not intense, calm and orthodox rather than fanatical, far removed from the burning asceticism or the sublimity of a Pascal. He admits the coexistence of vice and virtue in the human heart, but implies that there can be no real virtue without faith (Chapter XVI, 'Des Esprits forts'). (He was, needless to say, hostile to the growing spirit of scepticism and free inquiry which had already found expression in Pierre Bayle's *Pensées diverses à l'occasion de la Comète,* 1682, and in the *Entretiens sur la pluralité-des-mondes* of his literary enemy Fontenelle, 1686; such subversive thinkers would be included in the condemnation of free-thinkers along with the frivolous *libertins* of the aristocracy, and he may have discerned in these French representatives of a European movement the forerunners of 'that great battle which is being prepared against religion', denounced by Bossuet in 1687.) La Bruyère condemns hypocrisy ('*fausse dévotion*') the more vehemently because he believes in the possibility of true piety; he inveighs against showy and meretricious services and sermons, and self-seeking priests (Chapter XV, 'De la Chaire') because he has read the Gospel and listened to sincere 'apostolic' preachers. He thus in all sincerity, and not merely as a lightning-conductor, ends his survey of man's condition with an apology for religion. The pity is that these two final chapters come rather as an anticlimax. The study of pulpit oratory has little interest for us today, except in so far as this plea for simplicity and truth illustrates La Bruyère's general aesthetic and moral tenets; while the last chapter, 'Des Esprits forts,' shows him following a long way after Descartes in an elaboration of the *cognito ergo sum,* and a long way after Pascal in an attempt to prove the truth of Christianity by a demonstration of the wonders of nature and the 'two infinites'. We may indeed feel inclined to agree with Voltaire that 'when he meddles with theology he is even inferior to the theologians'.

There is one sphere, however, in which La Bruyère speaks with authority, and where his opinions are of the highest interest: that of literary criticism (Chapter I, 'Des ouvrages de l'esprit'). This chapter holds some of his most deep-rooted convictions; he found little to add to it in later editions. It is his professional credo, and his answer to all the vain, jealous and superficial critics at whose hands he has suffered.

It expresses the purest Classical doctrines, vivified by strong personal feeling: the concern for craftsmanship, the insistence on self-discipline, on self-criticism (and willingness to accept valid criticism from others), the search for the *mot juste,* the exact expression. All of these, though, are valueless without 'inspiration', and important as are the rules, writers of genius can rise above them; for, as Molière said, the greatest of all rules is to please. Yet, as has already been pointed out, for the Classical theorist the purpose of art is not only to please but to teach, to make man better by aesthetic means. There is no question of art for art's sake, or art for pleasure's sake. We find here that respect for the virtues of simplicity and harmony inherent in the art of Classical antiquity which made La Bruyère, like Racine and Boileau, a staunch defender of the *anciens* against such modernists as Fontenelle and Perrault in the notorious Quarrel. And we find, finally, the rationalist's distrust of 'imagination', which in that pre-Romantic era meant 'fancy'—of eccentric individualism as opposed to that profounder truth to universal human nature which is intuitively grasped by that indefinable faculty, taste—*le goût.* Indeed, the Classical equivalent to Keats's romantic dictum 'what the Imagination seizes as Beauty must be Truth' would be 'what Taste seizes as Truth must be Beauty'.

The question arises, of course, how far La Bruyère's practice conformed to his precepts. Undeniably his own style sometimes errs against the purest Classical canon; he is liable to strain the truth for the sake of wit or comic effect, he is given to occasional extravagance or over-refinement, for he is heir not only to the Classical tradition but also to those of Preciosity and Burlesque, both strong currents throughout the seventeenth century. And as though to compensate for this non-conformity, he shows, in his criticism, a breadth of mind, a historic sense (in this as in other fields) rare for his time. He can give generous appreciation to writers of a different age; he delights in Montaigne and Rabelais, and can even value Ronsard and Théophile. In that curious philological disquisition that concludes Chapter XIV he shows his concern for the richness and vigour of the language as well as for its elegance and purity; and his own style is not afraid of bold and racy expressions.

What has La Bruyère to say to us today, 270 years after? now that the social scene he satirized has vanished, the quarrels and controversies are forgotten, the personal references and topical allusions are of interest only to the specialist? The modern reader, aware that the seventeenth century did not have a monopoly of snobbery and affectation, self-interest and ambition, injustice and cruelty, must reinterpret La Bruyère's indictment in contemporary terms; he will relish, for instance, the analysis of diplomatic cunning and cannot fail to respond to the eloquent denunciation of war. And there remain, too, La Bruyère's own qualities: the clear-sightedness and compassion, the

courage and sensitivity; we value him not so much for his scathing picture of his age as for the generous indignation that called it forth; not so much for the wit and craftsmanship of his show-pieces as for the quiet penetrating truth of his personal observation. We must not expect from him any profound, original or systematic thought; in fact, to record all his borrowings from Montaigne, Pascal or La Rochefoucauld, to mention only the most famous names, would require a wealth of footnotes. . . . But when he is speaking of what he has felt, or seen, or discerned about personal or social relations, about friendship or love or suffering, he reveals a sensibility and a warmth that seem to overlap the centuries. (pp. 18-23)

> *Jean Stewart, in an introduction to* Characters *by Jean de La Bruyère, translated by Jean Stewart, Penguin Books, 1970, pp. 7-24.*

Raymond Picard   (essay date 1970)

[*In the following excerpt, Picard discusses the structure and principal ideas of* The Characters.]

The huge success of [the ***Characters***], despite its ill-defined scope and at times rather rambling pace, is due not only to the scandal arising from certain identifications but also and above all to the intense interest (going back half a century) of a whole section of the public in the study of psychology and conduct. The men of the age were convinced that behaviour was fundamentally intelligible. Despite its variety, its complexity and its contradictions, it constituted a stable and homogeneous field of study. It could be described; its manifestations could be classified, perhaps even form the basis for deduction. There were universal judgments, rules which were applicable to every possible case. The diversity of minds, feelings and attitudes could be reduced to general and constant patterns which it was possible to determine and in terms of which, with an adequate dose of subtlety, individual anomalies could be satisfactorily defined. In short, they practised what we would today call an *essentialist* psychology, and they disserted on friendship or vanity as if they were moral substances possessing specific properties. When publishing a collection of verse by different hands in 1665, a friend of Madame de Sévigné's felt that the most convenient way of listing the different forms of love was to put them in alphabetical order with a view, as he explained, 'to bringing some tidiness into such diversity'. The passages thus quoted were classified under clearly defined rubrics, and the reader moved from *Despite* to *Desire,* and then from *Disorder of the Heart* to *Discordance.* In a word, there was a sort of transcription of the moral world into spatial terms. . . . In the same way La Bruyère takes his reader through the maze of a psychological garden, describing and assessing the various clumps of shrubs and the innumerable species, passing from the gentleman (*honnête homme*) to the well-bred man (*l'homme de bien*), from the man of good sense to the man of good taste, and from the fool to the conceited fop.

But a careful distinction must be made between them. For it is important to identify those species which are so closely related as to be mistaken for each other, to separate what seems to belong together, and lastly to pinpoint differences which had only been vaguely noted. There is in La Bruyère a sort of naturalist who catalogues and observes the peculiarities of psychological life. And it is no accident that he has put himself under the patronage of Theophrastes. A disciple of Aristotle, the Greek philosopher was the author of treatises on botany, meteorology, physics and zoology, and in his treatise on **Characters** he applies the same method of classification and observation to the study of manners. The character is the distinctive mark which enables us to recognise a particular nature, which in effect characterises it. But at this point science becomes something of a sport. The identification of the decisive sign presupposed an effort to make distinctions which become more and more subtle as each analyst sought to outbid the other. For the tendency was to discover increasingly imperceptible variations and delicate shades. A survey of this kind naturally gave rise to a drawing-room diversion in which everyone was able to show off his ingenuity. The *portrait* which, by constant retouching, built up to a specific individuality and the *maxim* which brought out an illuminating and previously unsuspected connection between different concepts of conduct were genres which flourished in the salons and from there soon invaded the whole field of literature.

However, instead of degenerating into mechanical and conventional exercises, these analyses made possible, within clearly determined limits, a veritable campaign of psychological exploration. The inherent brevity of the maxim encouraged research into modes of expression. The selectiveness and the precision demanded by the portrait stimulated not only observation but a sort of algebra of concepts of behaviour. Strangely enough, it fell to La Bruyère in the quiet of his study to devote his efforts to these diversions which had so long been the preserve of society circles, to impart to them a high degree of variety, explaining the subject to be studied by, in turn as he puts it 'a definition, a maxim, an argument, a parallel, a straightforward comparison, a trait, a description or a painting' and to present his discoveries to the public under the title of **The Characters or The Manners of the Present Century.**

Can the work be regarded as a coherent whole with a logical structure? It certainly cannot. La Bruyère admits that he has studied man 'haphazardly, unmethodically, as and when the subject came up—by age, sex and station, and by the vices, foibles and ridiculousness attaching to each of them'. The order of the reflections is not often very enlightening and sometimes frankly capricious and arbitrary. Between one edition and the next, dozens of new pieces were inserted, while others were sometimes switched from one chapter to another. But, if there is little hope of ever deciphering a hidden or mysterious sequence which might explain the position of each of the 1,120 remarks, the fact remains that the ingredients of this carefully put together work are very far from random. La Bruyère, the least negligent of men, was at pains to achieve the desired effects of contrast and echo. It is obvious, to take only one example, that the opening remark in the first chapter 'Des ouvrages de l'esprit,' 'Everything has been said, and we come too late', corresponds to the last one

(69): 'Horace or Boileau said so before you. Yes, I take your word for it, but I have said it in my own special way'.

The first ten chapters study life, customs, institutions—the 'Ouvrages de l'esprit' first of all, since the contemporaries' interest in these was unbounded and since the writer was induced to reflect on his own undertaking in the process. Then follows 'Du mérite personnel,' of value only if it is based on the genuine qualities of mind and heart, though in real life this is never the case. Next there are two chapters on the fair sex and on the feelings which they inspire—one of the ruling powers in polite society, 'Des femmes' and 'Du coeur.' Chapter V—'De la société et de la conversation'—is devoted to society life. Lastly, five chapters review the five social categories whose role at that time was decisive and the principles underlying each of them—the world of money with its maniacs and its victims ('Des biens de fortune'); 'De la Ville,' that is, Paris society; 'De la Cour'; aristocracy and birth ('Des Grands'); and the monarch ('Du souverain ou de la république'). This social gradation culminates in the King, to whom La Bruyère erects a statue at the end of Chapter X. His survey then becomes less closely linked with the structure of the society of the age, less involved in history. It turns off sharply to concentrate on the study of man, as is fairly clear from the titles of the chapters—'De l'homme' (XI); 'Des jugements' (XII); 'De la mode' (XIII); 'De quelques usages' (XIV). By a natural transition, it ends on religion as it is preached ('De la chaire') and as it is lived ('Des esprits forts'). The first fifteen chapters have shown the ridiculousness, the void and the absurdity of man. They prepared the way for the sixteenth and last chapter in which man turns to God.

This progression, consciously slanted but extremely subtle, is admirably suited to a student of human behaviour who detests the systematic approach. Despite his preference for universals, La Bruyère is not a philosopher in the modern meaning of the word with a comprehensive and integrated interpretation of man, or of his powers and his position in the world. Nor, despite his naturalist's attitude, is he a scholar concerned with complete enumerations *à la Descartes.* Certain general ideas emerge from his book—of the vanity (i.e. the unsubstantiality, the emptiness) of man, the predominance of personal interest, egoism and self-love, and hypocrisy. But the ideas are not original, since they immediately remind one (and indeed reminded the author himself) of Pascal's *Pensées,* La Rochefoucauld's *Maximes* and Molière's comedies. Above all, he is content to prove their existence by reference to real life, without attempting to make a more thorough analysis or founding a real science of man on it. He is bitter and disillusioned, but his lucid, detached pessimism prompts him to make ill-tempered sallies and not to preach a philosophy of despair.

'A man who is Christian and French by birth', he noted, 'has his hands tied when it comes to satire. He is forbidden to deal with the major topics.' (I, 65). A student of human nature is bound to feel the same embarrassment (and for the same reasons) as a satirist. Devout Christian as he was, La Bruyère did not suffer too much from the restrictions that a state religion imposed on freedom of expression where religion was concerned. His social and political criticism, on the contrary, was undoubtedly influenced by the fact that, as a Frenchman, he lived under the Absolute Monarchy. His daring was great, but it was always slightly muted. He did not go to the bitter end. If he was hard on the grandees and poked fun at the courtiers, it was simply the better to sing the king's praises—or at least to extol the royal dignity. He has forceful pages on the absurdity of war. 'If you were told that all the cats in a great country assembled on a plain', he writes, 'and that, after having mewed to their hearts' content, they fell at each other furiously, and wielded both tooth and claw, that this encounter cost both sides nine or ten thousand cats dead on the field, who infected the air ten leagues round about with the stench . . . [and if these cats] told you that they loved glory, would you conclude that they sought it by assembling at this fine tryst, by destroying each other in this way and wiping out their own species?' (XII, 119). But in another passage he criticises the generals for dining too lavishly during their campaigns—as if there were anything in common between this fairly minor abuse and the catastrophic institution of war. The fact is that La Bruyère, in his inventory of habits and customs, makes no attempt to see the objects he is examining in perspective or to assign these their respective importance in the universe which they combine to form. He is content to let his eye dwell on them for a time. Then he passes by, and we pass by with him.

If he has not sought to carve out and construct an organised world, that does not make him a mere chronicler of day-to-day events, or a purveyor of anecdotes. On the contrary, he is always anxious to rise above the particular, to extract the typical, significant aspects from the individual person or case. True, his taste for the concrete seems to become more marked; from one edition to the next, the number of portraits increases considerably. It rises from a dozen in 1688 to about a hundred and forty in 1694. But, even when he has a living model, what he sees in that model is above all the psychological, moral or social species to which it belongs, and his painting is equally valid for other members of the same species. It is easy to understand why his contemporaries suggested so many *keys* for the portraits in which everybody could recognise himself. *Menippus* is perhaps the Marshal de Villeroy, but he is also the vain and insignificant man of the world. At Versailles such men were legion, and each of them could imagine—unless his friends imagined it for him—that La Bruyère had him in mind. People recognised *Hermippus* as the Count de Villayer, but in reality the type of behaviour in question is to be met with in every century. He is the type who loves to potter about and to have his comforts. In any case, the writer often proceeds by juxtaposing characteristics drawn from a number of individuals, and out of these he composes a sort of generic image. For example, in the case of *Menalcus,* the typically absent-minded man, details are piled on so thick that the portrait becomes completely unconvincing. 'This', he was to note, 'is less a particular character than a collection of facts about absent-mindedness.' The truth is that the reader is almost always confronted not with real portraits, but with what artists today call composite works. La Bruyère, then, is as far (or almost as far) removed from the immediate data of life as

from philosophical thought. He moves in the world of conduct which is in between, but is closer to the anarchy of the world than to a transparent and orderly cosmos. His unflagging curiosity for people, for their relationships, for the life they lead is precisely what for two centuries (i.e. up to the *Physiologies* of 1840-2, up to Balzac) gave rise in France to a whole literature of psychological analysis in which we find the same sense of observation, occasionally the same humour, the same concern for precise detail, the same predilection for classifications, the absence, too, of great ideas and of systems, the same rejection of synthesis—a literature which rises above the day-to-day recording of facts, but does not soar into the thoroughly suspect empyrean of doctrine.

In any case, La Bruyère realises that he is not a profound or original thinker. But, since 'everything has been said', the writer can at least strive to put in a striking formula what has already been said. In a slightly modified form, Valéry's dictum 'doubt leads to form' is applicable in this context. Since he will not or cannot be a philosopher, the author of the **Caractères** becomes a stylist. He chooses his terms, polishes his sentences, constructs his paragraphs with meticulous care, makes his effects converge on the objective. This kind of studied effort must occasionally leave traces of stiffness or constraint. The analyst is also a man of letters, and it is no coincidence that his first chapter is devoted to the 'Ouvrages de l'esprit.' This feeling of definitive form which he often gives readers is due as much to the perfection of his style as to the accuracy of his aim, and it is hard to say whether the felicity of his touch belongs to the domain of language or to that of psychology. A concerted and many-faceted work, the **Caractères** are both a collection of documents and a repertory of literary exercises. It is the society of Louis XIV seen through the eyes of a man of letters, but in the perspective of eternal man and of eternal literature. (pp. 26-33)

> *Raymond Picard, "Religion, Philosophy and Psychological Analysis," in his* Two Centuries of French Literature, *translated by John Cairncross, Weidenfeld and Nicolson, 1970, pp. 12-33.*

Odette de Mourgues   (essay date 1978)

[*In the following excerpt, Mourgues examines* The Characters *in terms of its style and structure.*]

It is . . . very difficult to come to a definite judgement of value on the **Caractères** taken as a whole. Our own century is particularly hesitant, and this hesitation to commit ourselves to a definite appraisal of the book tends to keep La Bruyère in a respectable but rather dull place by-passed by the great movements of revaluation. Julian Benda's attack—unfair and illuminating at the same time—failed to dislodge La Bruyère from his too-secure niche in a dead end or to bring him nearer to us, for better or for worse. Roland Barthes speaks of the *malaise* of the modern reader confronted in the **Caractères** with a picture of the world which is both familiar and alien [see essay dated 1963]. One of the most recent studies, *Les Caractères de La Bruyère, bible de l'honnête homme,* by André Stegman seems in its sub-title to confirm the traditional image of innocuous respectability, but, after a remarkably thorough analysis of the work, the author ends on a non-committal note, and chooses as a final qualification of the book the ambiguous adjective *singulier:* original? strange? or a mixture of both?

There is a fascinating quality about the work which even the most tepid admirers acknowledge and try to sum up by saying that whatever reservations they may have about La Bruyère he was one of the greatest 'stylists'. This concern for 'style', for the problems facing the writer, is undoubtedly an important aspect of the **Caractères.** But to call La Bruyère a stylist is not, in itself, a satisfactory explanation. Style does not exist in a vacuum. A certain way of saying things corresponds to a certain way of seeing them, and the fascinating quality of La Bruyère's writing may well reside in the way—or ways—he chose to look at men and at life: the curious angles of vision, the parcelling out of topics, the unexpected and puzzling shifting of the camera, from the close-up to the panoramic scene, from earth to heaven.

I say puzzling, and some would add irritatingly so; for the almost universal reproach directed against **Les Caractères** has been the apparent untidiness of the work, its lack of unity, its lack of pattern.

A great variety of subjects is grouped somewhat loosely under a number of headings: 'Du Mérite Personnel', 'De la Cour', 'De l'Homme', and so on, and the observations made by the author do not always have an obvious link with the heading. In the course of the various editions La Bruyère moved some paragraphs from one section to another without the reason for the move being very clear in some cases.

The form adopted by the writer varies from the epigrammatic maxim to the short story, such as the tale of Emire at the end of the chapter 'Des Femmes'. Even if we think of the portrait as being La Bruyère's most typical form of expression, it is difficult at times to decide what is a portrait and what is not. La Bruyère may be concerned with a particular individual to whom he gives a name; such is the portrait of Straton ('De la Cour', 96) which stresses very individual characteristics. But a name may equally apply to a type of man, to the allegory of a vice (Gnathon, the glutton).

Very often there is no name attached to the portrait: 'le courtisan', 'le financier'. Even the precarious individualisation given by the definite article tends to vanish: 'un homme de mérite', 'un bel esprit', 'une femme de la ville'. More than once what is portrayed is not one man but a group of men: 'les grands', 'le peuple'. The dividing line between the portrait and the general remark is not clearcut. A paragraph may start with a portrait which becomes by almost imperceptible degrees an abstract statement about mankind, or the other way round.

Moreover, and this is perhaps more upsetting, there is no real coherence of thought in the book. Critics have had a happy time collecting the contradictions they have found in the course of their reading. Was La Bruyère aware of these inconsistencies? In the fifth edition of the **Carac-**

tères, after noting how a man's good qualities are seen as bad ones as soon as he falls out of favour, the passage ends rather abruptly with the following paragraph:

> Je me contredis, il est vrai: accusez-en les hommes, dont je ne fais que rapporter les jugements; je ne dis pas de différents hommes, je dis les mêmes, qui jugent si différemment.

It is not very clear whether this remark is aimed at public opinion, the vagaries of which he has just stressed, or whether he includes himself among the men he criticises.

Should one suppose that the conflicting opinions expressed by La Bruyère are to be cancelled out by a unifying process, by the intention, on the part of the author, to give a definite shape to the succession of his 'caractères de ce siècle' and to the order of the chapters? La Bruyère hinted at a *plan d'ensemble* in one of his prefaces to the book and was even more specific in the Preface to his 'Discours de Réception à l'Académie Française' where he states that the first fifteen chapters of the **Caractères** are destined to make man realise his vices and follies and to lead to the sixteenth chapter where atheism is attacked and the Christian ideal offered as the wisest attitude. As Robert Garapon remarks [in an introduction to the **Caractères**], this borrowing of Pascal's plan for his apology is very much an afterthought used for self-justification.

A few critics have, however, tried to discover a coherent pattern in the book and none with such care, patience and finesse as André Stegman, who has examined more particularly La Bruyère's remodelling of his work in order to achieve a more satisfactory grouping and progression of topics. His demonstration is attractively presented. But one is perhaps more tempted to admire the critic's own remodelling of the **Caractères** into a complex architecture than to be altogether convinced by his arguments.

Whatever La Bruyère's assertions and his attempts to give more unity to his work, our doubt persists. The best way to look at the book, as far as its overall shape is concerned, may be, I think, to consider it as a kind of diary which spread over twenty years of the author's life and where he noted at different times in different ways the different topics which interested him at a given moment.

Besides, trying to find a close structure for the **Caractères** is perhaps the wrong approach. To look for some kind of 'architecture' which would give the work a harmonious form is to look for something uncompromisingly static, and it can be argued that La Bruyère does not anyhow need such a justification.

The lack of unity, the variety of subjects treated (literary criticism, fashions, politics, metaphysical problems, psychology of children) need not be explained away as the apparently negative features of an untidy literary work. They have a positive significance and can help us to see what kind of a moralist La Bruyère is.

An important part of his book is certainly inspired by the moralist's purpose, which is to study man within the limitations of nature and reason. A fair number of remarks, of maxims, even, remind us of La Rochefoucauld, and we find there the same clear insight into the human condition and into the working of the human mind. But, if we [have] a slight hesitation in using the term moralist in its strict connotation in the case of La Rochefoucauld, when we come to La Bruyère it is obvious that the author of the *Caractères* does not confine himself to the carefully circumscribed universe of the moralist. Something seems to happen to that near perfect sphere which was the world of La Fontaine, La Rochefoucauld, Racine or Madame de Lafayette. The centre tends to shift away from its formerly stable position; under the pressure of those eccentric impulses the sphere bursts and La Bruyère's investigations shoot out in all directions in a kind of centrifugal movement.

This may be viewed as a historical phenomenon. La Bruyère was thirty years younger than La Rochefoucauld, and the *Caractères* may be considered, and have been considered, as marking the beginning of the disintegration of French classicism. But it may equally well be a personal choice, the product of an original mind, of a restless intelligence impatient with limitations, ambitious and passionately inquisitive. The two explanations are not mutually exclusive.

I would venture to say that the most interesting aspects of the work—and some of its shortcomings too—are highly significant of this 'explosion' of the moralist's universe. (pp. 95-9)

> *Odette de Mourgues, "The Eccentric Moralist," in his* Two French Moralists: La Rochefoucauld & La Bruyère, *Cambridge University Press, 1978, pp. 95-113.*

Jacques Barzun   (essay date 1986)

[*Barzun is a French-born American scholar whose wide range of learning has produced distinguished works in several fields, including history, culture, musicology, literary criticism, and biography. Barzun's contribution to these various disciplines can be noted in such modern classics of scholarship and critical insight as* Darwin, Marx, Wagner *(1941),* Berlioz and the Romantic Century *(1950),* The House of the Intellect *(1959), and the recent biography* A Stroll with William James *(1983). Barzun's style, both literary and intellectual, has been praised as elegant and unpretentious. In the following excerpt, Barzun presents an overview of* The Characters.]

La Bruyère is the author of only one work, called *Characters.* [In a footnote, the critic explains: Whether or not one takes the *Dialogues on Quietism* for authentic, they are unfinished and unrevised as well as unread. The inaugural speech to the Academy is important but not "a work" in the accepted sense.] Of that work, the part that educated people remember or recognize at sight is the first sentence: "Tout est dit, et l'on vient trop tard depuis plus de sept mille ans qu'il y a des hommes, et qui pensent." This remark suggests from the outset that the author belongs to the school that pretended to believe that no modern writer could equal or outdo the ancient Greek and Latin classics. In the famous quarrel of his time between the Ancients and the Moderns, he is an ancient, one who proffers his

work as a late variation or adaptation of an old model. Accordingly, La Bruyère's *Characters* was published as a sort of appendix to his translation from the Greek of a book of the same title by the philosopher Theophrastus, a younger contemporary of Aristotle's.

The pretence of being only an imitator accounts for the designation of "neo-classical." It is a mere device—I have called it a pretence—which was extraordinarily astute, though it had, like all good pretences, some slight basis in fact. The men of the 17th century were bred on the ancient classics and admired them sincerely. But playing the role of translator and adapter to current taste was a wonderful protection: a writer could say, "You are not criticizing me, but Euripides or Seneca or Theophrastus." A further advantage, the best of all, was the insinuation, "Look at what I have been able to do with an old battered subject." In La Bruyère the triumph is manifest. Whereas Theophrastus's thirty characters consist of simple enumerations of human traits, those of La Bruyère are portraits of individuals in action; and these are merged, not to say submerged, in a vast depiction of an entire society, its cultural types, professions, customs, intellectual and ethical beliefs, its vices and other passional tendencies. The book is the mirror of an age and a place, including those whom the age despised and degraded.

Take a look at the large divisions of the work and their titles. The treatment of persons comes under the headings: Personal Merit, Women, the Heart, Conversation, and Advanced Minds. The classes are dealt with in: Wealth, the Great, the Town, the Court, the State, and the Clergy. Manners and morals, La Bruyère takes up in: Judgment, Fashion, Customs, and Works of the Mind, as well as Man in general. To be sure, all the topics overlap, and La Bruyère is not so foolish as to segregate his living sketches of persons in a few categories. The description of behavior, plain or satirical, occurs throughout, although it follows the varying intention of each large subject. We are far from the static gallery of monochrome features offered by Theophrastus or his other imitators, from Joseph Hall and Quevedo to Addison and Steele and the Comtesse de Genlis.

But has La Bruyère's social panorama a form? At first, the sixteen parts or chapters look as if thrown together helter-skelter. Rereading and reflection show the logic of the sequence as well as the artful return of themes. There is the outline of a circle, closed by an ingenious last link: the first chapter is about the works of the mind; the last is about "advanced minds," that is, the anti-religious, and this final topic grows naturally out of the one just preceding, which is "The Clergy." At every turn, our author draws consecutive contrasts within and between the species, which converts description into drama and contiguity into irony.

In his own time and since, La Bruyère has been blamed for not tying together his observations into a smoothly continuous whole. He gives us "characters," dialogues, meditations, aphorisms, anecdotes, in paragraphs that range from two lines to four pages. Why not stuff the cracks with transitions? One answer is: he was an artist and also a moralist. Moralists looking at society are bound to think in fragments, for persons, and classes, and social habits are conglomerates, not systems. Transitions among such units would be artificial and repetitious and therefore dull. From La Rochefoucauld through Vauvenargues and Joubert down to Nietzsche and Oscar Wilde, the true artists have seen that maxims and vignettes are the proper form of moral thought. True, some satirists in verse give the impression of continuous discourse, but that is an illusion: their fragments are only held together by meter and rhyme.

There was perhaps one way in which La Bruyère could have made his work not more unified, for it is that already, but more unitary in appearance: he could have written a picaresque novel. In that genre, the vagabond hero roams up and down the layers of society and meets a mixed bag of characters. In between, he utters home truths about persons and institutions—just like La Bruyère. One might say that he wrote a "potential" novel. He reminds us often of Le Sage and even of Balzac and Proust, with their frequent dissertations on topics now left to social-science professionals.

Take for example La Bruyère's treatment of the court and the great. It is so detailed, so "fouillé" as to motives, so thoroughly organized and explained that it transcends the simple gallery one might have expected and been content with. What is this marvelous institution led by the Sun King? The nearest analogue is Hollywood in its heyday—brilliant, extravagant, polished, conceited, hypocritical, cruel, sycophantic, vicious, and neurotically anxious in its unending struggles for prestige, power, and money. At the same time we know that art, wit, elegance and literature did grow out of that unlikely soil.

Supposing that the idea of a story with such ingredients had occurred to La Bruyère, one sees why he did not write it. The novel was not a genre in much esteem. The pastoral kind was popular but silly; the picaresque was narrow and scanty until Le Sage expanded the form; besides these, there was but the solitary example of another type which Furetière gave in *Le Roman bourgeois* (1666). Even if *Gil Blas* had existed in 1688, when La Bruyère published, its scope was still restricted by the need to supply, over and over, narrative links about inns and horses and incidents of the road. The novel as a genre has been characterized—and hampered—by this matter-of-fact filler, which many writers in our time have tried to get rid of. The psychological novel, first, and later the "nouveau roman," have rejected all furniture and most connectives in favor of states of mind and anecdotes. Some of these works remind us of nothing so much as La Bruyère's. This ancient turns out a modern.

He is a modern also in his language. More perhaps than any of his prose contemporaries and like *our* contemporaries, he is obsessed with style. The changes he made in the nine successive editions of his book show this preoccupation as much as his increasing boldness of utterance. He improves his text not by greater correctness but by further nuance. Some critics have blamed him for that concern and prefer Saint-Simon, and Mme de Sévigné, because they are "more natural." The comparison is not just: neither of these admirable writers was writing for publication and La Bruyère was. His sense of the obligation thereby

imposed is shown in his criticism of Molière, who, he thinks, "n'a manqué que d'éviter le jargon et le barbarisme, et d'écrire purement." That, too, is unjust, because Molière knew his business when he made his characters speak the vernacular at its most colloquial, even in verse.

La Bruyère believed in being "natural" too, but he knew that a work on his chosen scale needs variety, which means suiting the diction to the different subjects and providing changes of pace; it forbids rattling on spontaneously. His awareness shows both in the text and in his apologia for it in the preface. I translate his words, to let our more familiar terms give his credo its full force: "Even if in one's work some ideas and reflections have slipped in that are less striking, less neatly turned, less vivid than others, and that seem to have been put in so as to relax the mind and enable it to be once more pulled together and alert to what follows—unless these expressions turn out to have a familiar, touching, and informative air, suited to the common reader, whose interest a writer must never overlook—[in these conditions] the critical reader is free to censure such expressions and the author should have kept them out—that is the rule." This is surely the loveliest, as it is the most sudden, turn of irony in all French literature: the author describes his admirable method and the reasons for adopting it, then invites the reader to disallow it, "because of the rule." Clearly, not all the neoclassicists were as obedient as one tends to believe.

Part of the modernity one feels in La Bruyère's prose is not wholly his doing but that of the French authors who, for the last half century or more, have affected archaism and reinstated some of the ways of 17th-century grammar and syntax. Writers such as Gide, Valéry, Abel Hermant, André Beaunier, François Mauriac, in reacting against both the Symbolist and the Naturalist prose of the Goncourts, Zola, or Huysmans, have resorted to the dry, abstract, and colorless diction, and sometimes also to the loose constructions, of the classic century. Reading La Bruyère reminds one of these authors, for he has their complexity as well as their studied simplicities. Notice, for example, the use of *ne* without a following *pas* or *point;* the placing of the personal pronoun object of an infinitive before the verb on which the infinitive depends ("ceci me pourrait faire penser"); the tolerance for the asymmetrical pairing of a noun and a clause as direct objects, for unattached participles, and for *cascades de qui et de que;* the preference for *quoi* over *lequel* and *laquelle* as a relative; and for *soi* over *lui* after prepositions; the choice of uncommon ones after verbs—*aimer de* instead of *à,* and so on. The net result is to make La Bruyère much less quaint to present-day readers than he was to a student who attended the lycée before 1920. (pp. 16-21)

From the passage on "The Great," it is clear that La Bruyère, although dependent on their bounty, had a low opinion of them. He had no choice but to be, in the language of his time, a "domestic." He lived in the house of the princely family of Condé, was fed and protected by it, and esteemed by at least one of its members. But tradition has it that he was also ridiculed and roughly used by some others. Hence some lines about the nobles' native malignity suggest autobiography and tell us two other things: La

Bruyère did not take these insults as a matter of course and he had the courage to depict the ignoble traits of the nobles. It was courage, for he cannot have supposed that his book would not be read and understood by his patrons. (p. 23)

All that La Bruyère says about rank and power has raised the question whether he was a democrat—an early and rebellious one. The question is meaningless. Democracy as we use the word is a notion that did not exist till the middle of the 19th century. What should be said of La Bruyère's politics is that he saw the evils of an aristocracy deliberately rendered idle by a court, and that his faith in the stability of monarchy had been shaken by the English revolution of 1688. He had no illusions about social classes: "Le peuple n'a guère d'esprit, et les grands n'ont point d'âme. . . . Faut-il opter? Je ne balance pas, je veux être peuple."

Within the large class he called the people he was open-eyed enough to see two groups that had no rights, and he took pains to describe them. By now, his sketch of the French peasantry is fairly well-known: "L'on voit certains animaux farouches, des mâles et des femelles, répandus par la campagne, noirs livides, et tout brûlés du soleil, attachés à la terre qu'ils fouillent et qu'ils remuent avec une opiniâtreté invincible. Ils ont une voix articulée; et quand ils se lèvent sur leurs pieds, ils montrent une face humaine; et en effet ils sont des hommes. Ils se retirent la nuit dans des tanières, ou ils vivent de pain noir, d'eau et de racines; ils épargnent aux autres hommes la peine de semer, de labourer et de receuillir pour vivre, et méritent ainsi de ne pas manquer de ce pain qu'ils ont semé."

The other group is—children. They are ruled by their passions: ils sont déjà des hommes. The growth of reason augments their powers and perceptions: they see all the defects and vices of their masters the grownups, and soon use their knowledge for their own ends. Their life in common is at first a sort of anarchy; it turns monarchical in deference to the superior strength or skill of one of them.

In view of La Bruyère's political and social insights, one may be surprised to find Roland Barthes trying to explain La Bruyère's low reputation among intellectuals by the fact that the continuing "dialogue" with the past, that is, the unbroken currents of thought among great writers, have not included La Bruyère [see entry dated 1963]. His fame, says Barthes, has been kept alive only by academics. This is very likely true. Among educated readers, **Les Caractères** is not a "livre de chevet" like La Rochefoucauld, and except for the opening sentence and the portrait of the peasant, the common run of authors do not quote or cite La Bruyère as they do Molière, La Fontaine, Sévigné, Boileau, and the rest. But Barthes's explanation itself needs to be explained, for it is obvious that La Fontaine and Sévigné do not belong to a continuing line of thought either.

What Barthes might better have said is that La Bruyère does not satisfy the public demand for concentration, for specialization. He cannot be classified by means of one clear tendency, or the mastery of one clearcut form. La Fontaine means fables (delightful); Sévigné means letters (vivacious); Bossuet means funeral orations (tremendous);

Molière means comedies (hilarious). Please note how these impeccable judgments quietly suppress other works or aspects of each great master: La Fontaine wrote erotic tales; Bossuet, who disliked funeral orations, wrote histories; Mme de Sévigné was often neurotically depressed; and Molière, besides the hilarious, had a strong vein of the tragicomic.

In France, artists not reducible to formula fare poorly. They dazzle by their ceaseless variety, and what is dazzling leaves an after-image that is indistinct, hence not easily or pleasantly memorable. On this account, Diderot, for example, was neglected or undervalued until the middle of this century. Rabelais exists in public opinion only as boisterously obscene; his extraordinary range of thought and artistry is virtually unknown. In La Bruyère as in these writers (or in Berlioz or Delacroix), there is a superabundance of genius, coupled with an amplitude of form. Both features disconcert; their appreciation requires re-reading, rethinking many times, to make up for the steady novelty within the work. The repetition that the author does not supply must come from the beholder. (pp. 23-6)

Jacques Barzun, "Introducing La Bruyère," in Papers on French Seventeenth-Century Literature, *Vol. XIII, No. 25, 1986, pp. 15-26.*

FURTHER READING

Berk, Philip R. " 'De la ville xxii': La Bruyère and the Golden Age." *The French Review* 47, No. 6 (May 1974): 1072-80.
    Focuses on the final entry in the chapter on city life in *The Characters,* placing it "among the most skillful, original and witty adaptations of the Golden Age theme in the French tradition."

———. "La Bruyère and Juvenal." *Classical and Modern Literature* 4, No. 3 (Spring 1984): 131-41.
    Examines La Bruyère's debt to Roman satirist Juvenal.

Borgerhoff, E. B. O. "La Bruyère." In his *The Freedom of French Classicism,* pp. 212-20. New York: Russell & Russell, 1968.
    Considers La Bruyère's work as it pertains to a concern among French authors of the classical period with the "indefinable and inexplicable."

Campion, Edmund J. "Rhetorical Theory in *Les Caractères.*" *Papers on French Seventeenth-Century Literature* VIII, No. 15, 2 (1981): 227-38.
    Discussion of La Bruyère's concept of rhetoric as demonstrated in *The Characters.*

Chamard, H. "La Bruyère." *The Rice Institute Pamphlet* 18, No. 1 (January 1931): 31-43.
    Discusses La Bruyère as "neither entirely a philosophical moralist, nor altogether a religious moralist. He is rather a social moralist; therein lies his originality."

Harth, Erica. "Classical Disproportion: La Bruyère's *Carac-*

tères." *L'Esprit Créateur* XV, Nos. 1-2 (Spring-Summer 1975): 189-210.

Describes the "disproportion" in the portraits of *The Characters* as a quality arising from conflicts peculiar to French society of the time.

Hewlett, Maurice. "La Bruyère." In *Last Essays of Maurice Hewlett,* pp. 191-210. London: William Heinemann, 1924.
Descriptive overview of *The Characters.*

Horowitz, Louise K. "La Bruyère: The Limits of Characterization." *French Forum* 1, No. 2 (May 1976): 127-38.
Focuses on four chapters of *The Characters*—"Of the Town," "Of the Court," "Of Women," and "Of Mankind"—as a means of illustrating the difficulty inherent in La Bruyère's attempt to define human nature.

———. "La Bruyère." In her *Love and Language: A Study of the Classical French Moralist Writers,* pp. 145-60. Columbus: Ohio State University Press, 1977.
Compares La Bruyère's attitudes toward love with those of his literary predecessors.

Knox, Edward C. *Jean de la Bruyère.* New York: Twayne Publishers, 1973, 140 p.
A biographical and critical study intended "to demonstrate the cohesion of [*The Characters*], its unity, and its variety."

Koppisch, Michael S. "On Three Texts of La Bruyère." *Papers on French Seventeenth-Century Literature* VIII, No. 15, 2 (1981): 201-09.
Focuses on the portrait of Pamphile, a character who illustrates La Bruyère's views on the court and the town.

———. *The Dissolution of Character: Changing Perspectives in La Bruyère's Caractères.* Lexington, Ky.: French Forum, 1981, 127 p.
Outlines the shift in La Bruyère's assessment of humankind throughout his lifetime. Koppisch finds that early editions of *The Characters* portray the individual as independent and self-determined, while later editions indicate the conclusion that human beings rely on the opinions of others for a definition of self.

Kra, Pauline. "Jean de La Bruyère." In *European Writers: The Age of Reason and the Enlightenment,* Vol. 3: *René Descartes to Montesquieu,* edited by George Stade, pp. 229-60. New York: Charles Scribner's Sons, 1984.
Provides a comprehensive outline of *The Characters,* explaining the rationale behind La Bruyère's system of organization.

Krailsheimer, A. J. "La Bruyère." In his *Studies in Self-Interest: From Descartes to La Bruyère,* pp. 196-208. Oxford: Clarendon Press, 1962.
Assesses La Bruyère's literary strengths and weaknesses in comparison with those of his contemporaries, including François de La Rochefoucauld and Blaise Pascal.

Moore, Will G. "The Soul of Wit." In his *French Classical Literature,* pp. 132-35. London: Oxford University Press, 1961.
Praises La Bruyère as "a great satirist, . . . [and] a master of brevity."

Potts, Denys C. Introduction to *Characters,* by Jean de La Bruyère, translated by Henri van Laun, pp. vii-xi. London: Oxford University Press, 1963.
Addresses La Bruyère's treatment of the underprivileged in *The Characters.*

Strachey, Lytton. "Two Frenchmen." In his *Characters and Commentaries,* pp. 67-73. New York: Harcourt, Brace and Co., 1933.
Describes La Bruyère as "one of the great writers of the world" and criticizes Elizabeth Lee's translation of *The Characters.*

Turner, Margaret. "The Influence of La Bruyère on the *Tatler* and the *Spectator.*" *Modern Language Review* XLVIII, No. 1 (January 1953): 10-16.
Demonstrates the extent to which Joseph Addison and Sir Richard Steele were influenced by La Bruyère's *Characters.*

Wadsworth, Philip A. "La Bruyère Against the Libertines." *The Romanic Review* XXXVIII, No. 3 (October 1947): 226-33.
Focuses on the treatment of religion in *The Characters,* maintaining that the devout Christianity professed by La Bruyère is sincere.

Wardman, H. W. "On Defining Character in *Les Caractères.*" *Essays in French Literature,* No. 11 (November 1974): 1-13.
Synthesizes several critical approaches to *The Characters.*

Woshinsky, Barbara R. "Shattered Speech: La Bruyère, 'De la Cour,' 81." *Papers on French Seventeenth-Century Literature* VIII, No. 15, 2 (1981): 211-26.
Focuses on a passage in *The Characters* to exemplify "the relation of language to ideology in the text."

Yarrow, P. J. "La Bruyère." In his *A Literary History of France,* pp. 369-82. London: Ernest Benn, 1967.
Cites "penetrating reflections on life, human nature, and society, shrewd advice, a sane philosophy, [and] amusing portraits" as "some of the things that have kept La Bruyère's book alive."

Paston Letters

English family correspondence.

Written between approximately 1420 and 1505, the *Paston Letters* reflect the lives of three generations of a wealthy Norfolk family. Often compared to such important document collections as the *Cely Letters* and the *Plumpton Correspondence,* the *Paston Letters* are recognized by historians as valuable sources of information regarding the social condition and traditions of England during the era of the Wars of the Roses. The *Paston Letters* also provide scholars with a reference point for determining the stability and dynamics of the English language during and since the fifteenth century. As literary critic Richard Garnett stated, "There is no such testimony anywhere to the social condition of England . . . as is afforded by the *Paston* correspondence."

The Paston family came into prominence in the early fifteenth century in the figure of William Paston, justice of the common pleas. John Paston, his son, was the first member of the family to collect both the letters he received and copies of those he sent to other people. It is John Paston's family's correspondence that comprises the bulk of the *Paston Letters;* the correspondence virtually ends with the death of William's youngest son, also named John, in 1503. It was not until 1787, however, that the Norfolk antiquarian John Fenn published the collected letters under the title *Original Letters, Written during the Reigns of Henry VI. Edward IV. and Richard III.* Historians believe that these records were kept for purely practical reasons. The social turmoil of the age left any successful family and their holdings under the daily threat of attack by angry or jealous groups; aside from petty warfare among the gentry, litigation was the primary means of protecting and retaining property. The letters provide a chronicle of social and political events to substantiate legal claims, and for this reason they are invaluable to historians.

While legal and political events of great interest are reported in the *Paston Letters,* historians are also intrigued by their importance as documents revealing the course of everyday affairs in fifteenth-century England. Admitting that the life reflected in the *Paston Letters* may not be representative of all of English society, scholars believe that the papers accurately depict the circumstances of most English landowners during this time. Legal papers, valentines, household accounts, and marriage arrangements are among the diverse contents of the collection. Historian Maurice Keen noted that "if every now and again [the *Paston Letters*] illumine some great event and bring it close to us, the general tone of the letters is in a minor key. If they can be at their most useful when they throw light on the incident of politics, the bulk of them do far more to enlighten us about social and economic history, the story of the everyday life of men and women."

Linguists have also noted the importance of the *Paston*

Letters in tracing the history of the English language through the fifteenth century, a transitional period in which modern syntax and spelling gradually developed. Noted scholar Norman Davis remarked that "many of [the *Paston Letters*] are informal, written to other members of the family on current business, so that they seldom pretend to grace of style or originality of thought. Apart from the conventional opening and closing phrases, and many obvious echoes of legal phraseology, they must often present an only slightly formalized version of the speech of the writers. They are therefore a much better guide to the real state of the spoken language than any literary work, conscious of tradition and seeking special effects, can ever be."

The historical value of the *Paston Letters* has been recognized by scholars since their first appearance in 1787. As James Westfall Thompson wrote, "the student of economic and social history, the purely political historian, the genealogist, and the antiquarian will all find a mine of profitable study in these pages, which so conclusively prove that history is not the study of dead peoples but the mirror of humanity."

PRINCIPAL WORKS

Original Letters, Written during the Reigns of Henry VI., Edward IV., and Richard III. 5 vols. (letters) 1787-1823

The Paston Letters, 1422-1509 (letters) 1872; enlarged edition, 1904

Paston Letters (letters) 1958

Paston Letters and Papers of the Fifteenth Century, Part 1 (letters) 1971

Paston Letters and Papers of the Fifteenth Century, Part 2 (letters) 1976

Alexander Ramsay (essay date 1849)

[*In the following excerpt, Ramsay examines the content of the* Paston Letters, *commenting that "the chief interest of this collection will be found in its domestic and social character." In support of the* Letters' *authenticity, he quotes extensively from an earlier introduction by John Fenn, the first editor of these papers.*]

The *Original Letters written during the reigns of Henry VI., Edward IV., and Richard III.,* are not those of statesmen or mere politicians, but of men and women occasionally of course mixed up with public affairs, but treating of them only as affecting their private interest. "The artless writers of these letters," says Sir John Fenn, the editor of these papers, "here communicate their private affairs, or relate the reports of the day; they tell their tale in the plain and uncouth phrase of the time; they aim not at shining by art or eloquence, and bespeak credit by total carelessness of correction and ornament." Indeed we have probably in no books so detailed and wholly unprejudiced a description as in these of the national domestic and social manners and modes of action and thought, together with the semi-public relations of the people, which, too minute for the notice of history, are even on that account the more popularly interesting, developing as they do the feelings and state of the most numerous classes in the country, and explaining and illumining incidentally much of the cause and course of many historical events. In many of these letters we see, or think we see, much of the peculiar principles which have distinguished us as a nation both before and since their date, and which, constantly instilled, have been constantly perpetuated:—untiring activity, indomitable resolution, and confident self-reliance, united to a full sense of the power and advantages of co-operation, producing a willingness to submit to the most implicit subordination for the attainment of a desired object, provided that object is kept steadily in view; and a readiness, if left alone, to act alone. In this collection we see how mothers thought there were things more to be dreaded for their sons than death; who "had leu (*rather*) they wer fayr beryed than lost for defaute;" and it was doubtless from such sources that our forefathers were enabled to show "the mettle of their pasture," and that they "were worth their breeding," alike in the bloody conflicts of Agincourt, Trafalgar, or Waterloo, and in the civil contests of the time here spoken of, as in the more peaceable but not less arduous struggles for freedom in the houses of parliament and the courts of law. There was then as now the strong practical common sense, sometimes expressed, we hope and believe, more harshly in words than in acts. For although in the letters every marriage is made to rest upon the sole basis of property, we have little doubt that then, as now, this was only pursued in part so far as to ensure independence and comfort, and that the feelings of the parties were rarely if ever violated: although law-suits were prosecuted with great eagerness, and in cases of disputed title, with great violence, and all parties complain of delay, and injustice, and oppression, and corruption, yet the complaints seem generally to be, as now, the common language of all litigants, particularly of defeated ones: although men here avowedly change their political sides because they think they shall benefit themselves thereby, and seem more openly to consult prudence than principle, yet on the whole they seem as now to make their interests and principles usually to agree, and the letters being confidential, may account for the occasional openness and bluntness of expression.

It may be remarked that these letters afford little direct information as to the means of internal communication. Journeys appear to have been made usually on horseback and written communications were sent either by special messengers, or entrusted to persons about to travel, letters being then immediately written in haste to such acquaintance or friends as might chance to reside near to such places as the traveller passed, or to which he was ultimately destined. We find many allusions in the letters here published to such opportunities having been embraced. Great care, however, seems to have been taken to preserve the integrity of the letter. It was carefully folded, and fastened at the end by a sort of paper strap, upon which the seal was affixed; and under the seal a string, a silk thread, or even a straw was frequently placed running around the letter. (pp. xiv-xv)

As of course all the value of such a collection depends on its authenticity, we shall quote as much as may be necessary from Sir John Fenn's own account of them in his introduction to the first volume.

> It will now be necessary to satisfy the reader of the authenticity of the letters here laid before him, by presenting him with a pedigree of their descent, accompanied with such observations as have arisen in the mind of the editor, from an accurate examination of every one of them.
>
> These letters were most of them written by, or to particular persons of the family of Paston, in Norfolk (who lived in the reigns of Henry VI., Edward IV., Richard III., and Henry VII.), were carefully preserved in that family for several descents, and were finally in the possession of the Earl of Yarmouth [their lineal descendants, with whom the male line of the family terminated]; they then became the property of that great collector and antiquary Peter le Neve, Esq., Norroy; from him they devolved to Mr. Martin, by his marriage with Mrs. le Neve, and were a part of his collections purchased by Mr. Worth, from whom, in 1774, they came to the editor.
> The hand-writing in some of the letters is, though black and thick, very true and legible; in others, the decyphering of it has been attended with much trouble and difficulty.
>
> The thought of transcribing [or rather translating] each letter, according to the rules of modern orthography and punctuation, arose from a hint which the editor received from an antiquary, respectable for his knowledge and publications; whose opinion was, that many would be induced to read these letters, for the sake of the various matter they contain, for their style, and for their curiosity, who, not having paid attention to ancient modes of writing and abbreviations, would be deterred from attempting such a task, by their uncouth appearance in their original garb.
>
> (pp. xv-xvi)
>
> [The paper] on which they are written is of different degrees of fineness; some sheets being rough, and, what we now call very coarse, while others are perfectly smooth and of a much finer texture; these different sorts, however, must have been all of foreign manufacture, since the art of paper-making was not introduced into England before the reign of Henry VII.
>
> The size of the whole sheets of paper varies from ten to twelve inches in length, as the writing runs, and from about sixteen to seventeen, or eighteen inches in depth.
>
> The various sizes of the letters themselves are from ten to twelve inches in length, to three, six,

eight, ten, or twelve inches, or more in depth, according to the quantity of the matter written.

Most of the letters have been neatly folded up in different shapes, from three to four inches in length, and from one and an half to three inches in breadth, having either a hole cut by a knife, and a piece of paper put through it; or threads drawn through by a needle, and brought under the seal, by which they were fastened.

Many of the seals are so far perfect as to discover the impressions of arms, crests, letters, heads, or some other devices; some of them have likewise a braid of string, or straw twisted round the impression, and fixed when the wax was warm.

The dates are sometimes, though seldom, fully expressed in the letters, except in some of those of particular writers, as Sir John Fastolf and Sir John Paston; the day of the month only, or the saint's name, to whom the day is dedicated, being generally all the date they have.

The editor has taken some trouble to supply these defects, and to fix the exact dates of the letters from calendars, from some fact mentioned, or other *data* in the letters themselves, and by these means to place the different letters in chronological order. In this his success has in a great measure answered his own expectations, and he hopes those of his readers will not be disappointed, since they may not be aware how much time and trouble the ascertaining of the date of a single letter has sometimes cost him.

It is proper here to observe, that the date of the year is always supposed to commence on the 25th day of March; and that the full dates are always placed at the end of the transcribed letters; where, notwithstanding all the endeavours of the editor, some still remain uncertain as to the exact year, &c.

(pp. xvii-xviii)

But, after all, the chief interest of this collection will be found in its domestic and social character. We see the modes of living, of dress, of educating the sons and daughters of the middling classes; we are told of the little transactions that enliven or distract the quietude of private life, the quarrels with neighbours, the slanders of enemies, of marriages, deaths, the making and executing of wills, and incidentally of the commerce and manufacturers of the country. We discover that the people were not so priest ridden as has been asserted and believed; and that priests were by no means above the law; though their superior education and abilities made them useful and therefore influential; and we have a specimen of the style of popular preaching. We are shown also the great extent of parental authority, and the lowly and submissive style used by children to and of their parents, and by the wife to the husband, which will not fail to be noticed by the reader; as also the extreme respect and formality with which all correspondents address each other. In all such points we have no record so complete and so satisfactory in any other period of our history. (pp. xix-xx)

Alexander Ramsay, in an introduction to Pas-

ton Letters, *edited by John Fenn, revised edition, Henry G. Bohn, 1849, pp. xiii-xxiv.*

Herman Merivale   (essay date 1865)

[*In the excerpt below, Merivale challenges the authenticity of the* Paston Letters.]

It is not without feelings of compunction amounting almost to a consciousness of sacrilegious boldness, that I venture to lay before the readers of the *Fortnightly Review* what I will by no means call a disproof of the authenticity of the famous **Paston Letters,** but some reason at all events for entertaining doubts of their genuineness. Not that there is anything new or singular in the suspicion. The question has been propounded—I will not say agitated—by various sceptics, but the investigation has never been followed up; while by almost all our historical writers their authenticity has been assumed without the slightest hint of a suspicion. Hallam, Lingard, Turner use their contents freely, both to illustrate the manners of the age and to establish historical facts; and refer to them without any note of suspicion as being (what, if genuine, they undoubtedly are) the most remarkable, if not exactly valuable, monument which we possess of an age peculiarly barren of written relics,—that of the Wars of the Roses. Reinhold Pauli, our latest historian of those times, possessed as he is of all the critical acumen of a German, mentions and uses them as amply as his predecessors, and, like them, without any suggestion of a doubt. Mr. Charles Knight, who has drawn on them largely, and terms them in his *Pictorial History of England* an "invaluable record of the social customs of the fifteenth century," has lately in his own genial and unsuspecting way, bestowed on them a characteristic eulogium.

"I have," he says,

> a great affection for the Pastons. They are the only people of the olden time who have allowed me to know them thoroughly. I am intimate with all their domestic concerns; their wooings, their marriages, their household economics. I see them as I see the people of my own day, fighting a never-ending battle for shillings and pence; spending lavishly at one time, and pinched painfully at another. I see them, too, carrying on their public relations after a fashion that is not wholly obsolete; intriguing at elections, bribing, and feasting. I see them as becomes constitutional Englishmen, ever quarrelling by action and writ; and, what is not quite so common in these less adventurous times, employing the 'holy law of pike and gun' to support the other law, or to resist it. I see them, in their pride of family, despising trade, and yet resting upon its assistance. I see the young ladies leading a somewhat unquiet and constrained life till they have become conformable in the matter of marriage. This is all very edifying; and I am truly obliged to this gracious family, who, four hundred years ago, communicated with each other and their friends in the most frank manner upon every subject of their varied lives.

We must, indeed, all participate in the gratitude which

Mr. Charles Knight considers himself to owe to this "gracious family" if the correspondence which passes under their name is really genuine. I do not mean partly genuine; of this there can be little doubt; but entirely genuine, without adulteration by modern hands. Whether it is so or not, is the question which I wish to place before my readers as clearly and circumstantially as I can.

The ***Paston Letters*** were given to the public at intervals. The first two volumes appeared in 1787, with a rather long and pompous title-page beginning "Original Letters written during the reigns of Henry VI., Edward IV., and Richard III., by various persons of rank or consequence." And the following is the account which Mr. (afterwards Sir John) Fenn, the editor (of whom a good deal more will be said presently), gives of the originals, from which he professes to have taken them:—

> These letters were most of them written by, or to, particular persons of the family of Paston, in Norfolk, who lived in the reigns of Henry VI., Edward IV., and Richard III., were carefully preserved in that family for several descents, and were finally in the possession of the Earl of Yarmouth.

There were two Pastons of that title: the first, famous for having been "shot at in his coach," died in 1685; the second in 1732, when his estates were sold, and passed to the Ansons; but which of them parted with the papers does not appear.

The papers "then became the property of that great collector and antiquary Peter le Neve, Esq., Norroy; from him they devolved to Mr. Martin" (of Palgrave, in Suffolk). This last gentleman was born in 1697, admitted a fellow of the Antiquarian Society in 1718, died 1771: an antiquarian of repute in his neighbourhood, whose collections, after his death, were sold by his administratrix, for £650, to Mr. Worth, an apothecary and chemist, at Diss, in Norfolk. Mr. Worth purchased these collections with an intention of arranging and selling them to the best advantage. He was elected a fellow of the Antiquarian Society in 1771; "and before he had completed the sale of his collections, died suddenly on the 8th of December, 1774." "From Mr. Worth," adds Sir John Fenn, "they came to the editor." In what way they "came," whether by purchase or otherwise, is not further explained.

It must certainly be at once admitted that a more meager and unsatisfactory account of the pedigree of papers, of which the authenticity is matter of question, can hardly be imagined. No legal claim, for instance, could possibly be rested on documents which had passed through so many hands, and been subject to the chance of so many careless or intentional tamperings. At the same time, those who maintain that authenticity are fully entitled to the benefit of the simple and undoubting manner in which Sir John tells the story: had he been either cognizant or suspicious of forgery (they will of course argue), he would have taken care to place himself more on the defensive, and recount his tale with more of particulars.

Sir John goes on to give a very detailed account of the peculiarities of the autographs of the original letters, the water marks on the paper, and so forth; all which I pretermit as unimportant: for the fictions, if such they are, probably rest on the basis of a certain number of really original papers. He then gives details respecting the transcription, and informs the public that the while of this labour was performed by himself at his own residence (East Dereham, in Norfolk). And although he records his thanks "for the assistance which he has received from the honourable Horace Walpole, the reverend Sir John Cullum, Bart., and Edward King, Esq., men who are so well known in the world of literature that their names (wherever they are permitted to be used) will stamp a value upon any work which they may honour with their approbation," yet there is no evidence in the Preface to show that these distinguished persons, or any one else, had ever cast eyes on the originals themselves. Nor is there a word—a point which we beg our readers to bear especially in mind—to announce to the public that the bulk of the originals were not published, or that the editor had still any portion of consequence in his hands. Nay, more than this, he seems to say that it had occurred to him to print only "a select number of the letters," but that he thought it better to give the whole.

A "second edition" of the two first volumes was, however, called for with the most unprecedented rapidity. If the editor is to be believed, the whole first impression was disposed of within a week of publication! In the advertisement to this so-called second edition, he informs the public, *for the first time,* that he has more treasures in reserve to communicate to them. "As this work has been so very favourably received, the editor is preparing for the press a *further* selection of letters and papers, written during the reigns of Henry VI., Edward IV., and Richard III., to which he intends adding such as are in his possession which were written in the reign of Henry VII." Accordingly, in 1789, the public were favoured with the promised additional remains, in the form of a third and fourth volume. "Several of the first characters for literary productions had expressed their wishes that the editor should proceed to publish the original manuscripts still remaining in his possession," says the preface to these volumes.

Let us now see what became of these and the former originals after publication. We must have recourse again to the preface to the third and fourth volumes, just cited.

> After the publication of the first and second volumes of these letters, the editor, in his advertisement to the second edition, informed the public that the original manuscript letters were lodged for a time in the library of the Antiquary Society, for general inspection. During their continuance in that repository, it was intimated to the editor that the king had an inclination to inspect and examine them. They were immediately sent to the Queen's Palace, with a humble request from the editor, that if they should be thought worthy a place in the Royal Collection, His Majesty would be pleased to accept them. To this request a most gracious answer was returned, and they are now in the Royal Library.

And yet, strange to say, after all this parade of minute information, these manuscripts, thus solemnly announced and described, have never been discovered; the most persevering researches have failed to ascertain either their present whereabouts, or their past history. They are not in the British Museum, nor in any other repository possessing parts of George the Third's library. Not only have they disappeared bodily themselves, but, as far as I am aware, there is no record or mention that they had ever been seen, in the king's library (while it subsisted) or anywhere else, by any single individual.

To which this may be added. The Antiquarian Society, particularly in its early days, was in the habit of publishing a rather copious list of articles exhibited at its meetings, with discussions which ensued thereupon. I have searched in vain the volumes of the "Archæologia" for any notice of the deposit of these alleged originals, or for any mention of them whatever, although the publication of the two first volumes is duly recorded in its place, as an event of interest.

Such are the facts; but it is of course open to the defenders of the genuineness of the letters to argue, with much reason, that it is scarcely possible so circumstantial a story as that of the exposure of these volumes at the Antiquarian Society, and their deposit in the Royal Library, could have been invented by the boldest forger. I do not profess to solve the problem. I only place the two suppositions in face of each other.

The mystery respecting the originals, however, does not end here. Sir John Fenn died in 1794. His death appears to have interrupted the design (already announced in his second preface) of publishing a fifth volume. His widow died in 1814: and on her decease his manuscripts passed to the hands of her nephew, Serjeant Frere, of Downing College, Cambridge, an unexceptionable witness, it is needless to say, if his evidence bore at all on the authenticity of the letters, which it will presently be seen it does not. Serjeant Frere published the fifth volume, in 1823, *"from a copy prepared by Sir John for the press."* In this copy, says the Serjeant, in his advertisement,

> the original letters are transcribed almost entirely in the handwriting of Mr. Dalton, now of Bury St. Edmund's, who was, at that time, commencing the profession of the law at East Dereham, and had been engaged also by Sir John Fenn in transcribing many of those printed in the third and fourth volumes. The few letters in this volume which are not in Mr. Dalton's handwriting are in Sir John Fenn's, and all are revised and corrected by him. *The originals of the fifth volume I have not been able to find. Some* originals I have, which appear not to have been intended by Sir John Fenn for publication.

The general result, therefore, is, that not only have the originals, said to be in the King's Library, never been seen there by any one who has recorded the fact, but that those of the fifth volume—which, if they existed at all, one would have deemed that such an antiquarian as Sir John Fenn would carefully have preserved—never were discovered among his papers which came from the custody of his widow. It may be added, to complete this portion of our little history, that Mr. Dalton, the transcriber in question, is reported to have died in 1860, at the age of ninety-three.

Such are the circumstances on record—suspicious enough, it will readily be owned—respecting the custody and disappearance of the originals of these letters. But I should not be treating my readers fairly if I did not at this early stage of my inquiry give them notice that an antiquary of no less authority than Sir Frederic Madden, with all these facts fully before him, has nevertheless, very recently, pronounced his judgment in favour of their genuineness. For that judgment he gives, it is true, no reasons; but the name of Sir F. Madden, on such a question, is worth many reasons; and if any of my readers prefer to be guided by his decision, rather than follow the arguments which I shall endeavour to urge against it, I shall have no right whatever to complain of their partiality. The following letter was addressed by Sir F. Madden to the editor of *Notes and Queries* a short time ago (Second Series, vol. vii.):—"There can be no doubt whatever of the genuineness of these letters; but in regard to their subsequent history, after they left the hands of Sir John Fenn, something more definite may be stated." Sir Frederic then mentions their loss; disproves a report, which had found its way into *Notes and Queries,* that this loss could be traced to the Prince Regent; and cites the *Morning Chronicle* of 24th May, 1787, which informs the world as follows:

> Yesterday, John Fenn, Esq., attended the levee at St. James's, and had the honour of presenting to his Majesty, bound in three volumes, the original letters, of which he had before presented a printed copy, when his Majesty, as a mark of his gracious acceptance, was pleased to confer on him the honour of knighthood.

Sir Frederic Madden then proceeds as follows:—

> The real question now is, what became of these originals after George III. received them? Had they remained at Buckingham Palace, they would probably have accompanied the Royal Library to the Museum, in 1823. They did not, however, come with that collection; and the inference was, either that they had been taken down to Windsor by George III., or else kept back when the Royal Library was presented to the nation by George IV. The late Bishop of Llandaff (Dr. Copleston) was extremely anxious to ascertain the fate of these letters; and often consulted me on the subject about the years 1832-4. Repeated inquiries were made at that time and since of the librarians at Windsor, for the purpose of ascertaining whether these valuable letters were still in existence; but without any favourable result. From the *Morning Chronicle* we learn that they were bound in three volumes; and it seems in the highest degree improbable that they should have been wilfully or even accidentally destroyed. The only way to account for their disappearance is to suppose that they were lent by George III. to some person about the Court,*who forgot to return them.* Had they been stolen, they would long ago have turned up in some form or other, and even now I do not despair of seeing them come to light again some day, to the great joy of all true antiquaries.

It is obvious that Sir F. Madden's indulgent theory as to the mode of loss is open to precisely the same objections as those by which he combats other theories respecting the disappearance. The "person about the Court" who "forgot to return" these precious volumes must be dead long ago. Consequently the articles themselves must long ago have lapsed into the category of "things destroyed" or "things stolen;" both of which possibilities he dismisses as untenable.

This, however, is only by the way: however unsatisfactory Sir F. Madden's suppositions on this head may be, his authority, as I have said, is necessarily of great weight; and I feel myself, in pursuing this investigation, at the disadvantage of having his judgment already recorded against me. But I am also at a scarcely less disadvantage—and one which it is impossible for me not to regret—in having to support a case which rests, there is no use in disguising it, on a charge of literary mystification; and that, apparently, against a gentleman, long deceased indeed, but who passed through life with the repute of high respectability, and left it followed by the regret of many attached friends. This is a subject on which I will say but little, for every reader will appreciate at once the embarrassment of my situation. I write with no intentional disrespect to the memory of Sir John Fenn; but historical truth requires a fearless investigation of the genuineness of commonly received documents, even when it cannot be conducted without involving imputations of this class on those who can no longer defend themselves. For the rest, I fully allow that the deceased knight is entitled to all the benefit of character, even though his merits may militate against my theory. The memoir of him contained in Serjeant Frere's advertisement to the fifth volume, describes him as a country gentleman of liberal education, much respected in his country, entertaining a "sincere and disinterested attachment to monarchical government, and to the doctrines of the Established Church." Early in life he addicted himself to literary pursuits, particularly those of history, topography, heraldry, and so forth; and it is an amusing instance of his antiquarian zeal (and the only eccentricity which I have seen reported of him), that when Sheriff of Norfolk he is said to have insisted on reviving the venerable but somewhat painful usage under which that functionary was accustomed to attend at public executions. In short, never was there an editor, to all appearance, better qualified to vouch by sobriety and steadiness of character for the genuineness of his wares, or having less about him of the literary Bohemian. A strong contrast, certainly, to his unhappy contemporary, Chatterton. Nevertheless there is one passage in the Preface to the third volume—a passage which would pass unnoticed probably by the casual reader—which has a singular and somewhat ominous significance, when once the suspicion of fabrication has been raised in our minds. And I cannot do otherwise than extract it.

> The editor from his infancy was always particularly pleased with that paper in the *Tatler* where the merry meeting at the house of a friend was interrupted by the entrance of the sexton of the parish church in a sort of surprise, informing the company that as he was digging a grave in the chancel, a little blow of his pickaxe opened a decaying coffin, in which were several written papers; the curiosity of the party was raised, they

adjourned to the spot, and discovered a parcel of letters which had been deposited in the grave of a lady whose daughter was then present. *The letters contained in these volumes have, as it were, lain in the grave for centuries,*

&c., &c. Did the sexton really "disinter" them? Have we any clue here to the real mind of the highly respectable editor? The passion for the concoction of literary romances of this description is as congenial to some natures, as irresistible, and as fertile in its devices, as that kindred passion for personation and similar impostures which is known to take so strong a hold, particularly of the female disposition, and has found itself a way to the surface in such various and strange manifestations. I must not conclude this disagreeable part of my task, however, without noticing, in fairness, that the reader who cannot accept the entire genuineness of these letters is not therefore driven absolutely to the conclusion that Sir John Fenn was the party guilty of the imposture. They had been for a century in many hands. Le Neve, Martin, Worth the chemist, might just as well be cited to answer on affidavit in their defence as Sir John. Only it is impossible to avoid thus much of accusation; whatever amount of suspicion is deducible from the most untoward "disappearance" of the alleged originals, rests on Sir John, and on him alone.

And the impartial reader cannot really fail to find any such suspicions increased, and not abated, by the language of Sir John's two prefaces—studied and inflated, though not, perhaps, more so than might be expected from a provincial antiquary little conversant with the critics, but also full of mysterious reticences. As I have said, his first preface gave no indication whatever that any important portion of the correspondence remained unpublished. Nevertheless, the preface to the third volume begins as if the ground were entirely new, with a whole series of letters covering almost exactly the same ground as the first (Letters in vols. i. and ii., 1440 to 1483; in vols. iii. and iv., 1432 to 1470). He does indeed state that when "he (the editor) made his first arrangement, he chiefly selected those letters which treated of public affairs and of persons of consequence, conceiving, on the first production of this distant correspondence, that such were more likely to interest the reader in their favour;" but that having from his own taste added a few on private subjects, "some of his literary friends, and many learned individuals, have pressed him to form the remaining ones for the public on the same plan which he before pursued," and that, consequently, the present letters are "of a more private nature than those before given to the public." A suspicious account in itself, looking as if the demand created the supply. But in point of fact they are *not* of a more private nature; the second series seem to consist of documents bearing on public as well as domestic matters nearly as promiscuously as those in the former. The very first so-called "letter," for instance, **"Articles proposed by the Earl of Warwick to the lords and council for their approbation, as preceptor to King Henry VI."** is perhaps the most important historical paper (if genuine) in the whole work. What reason could the editor have had for not including it in the first series, and for placing it at the head of the second without any prefatory words whatever accounting for that omission?

The same question will occur to every reader, when his attention is once directed to the subject, throughout these third, fourth, and fifth volumes. Nothing more natural than their contents and arrangement, if the author of a clever literary romance, finding it successful, had tried his hand at a continuation. Nothing less so, in my opinion at least, if an intelligent antiquary were honestly arranging for public use a series of documents which had come into his possession, and which had employed and interested him during years of study.

Let us next see—continuing what I may term the extrinsic argument for or against the genuineness of the letters—what are the probabilities of the supposition, laid before us by the editor, of their collection and preservation.

The Pastons were a family belonging to what we should now term the "squirearchy" of a remote part of Norfolk. Their dignities culminated, in the seventeenth century, in a peerage—the earldom of Yarmouth—which did not remain long in the line. But at the time of this correspondence, they had nothing higher to boast of in their pedigree than a judge or two of the superior courts. They were undistinguished people, in arts and arms. Except from the circumstance that one of them was an executor of the renowned Sir John Fastolfe, and got involved in considerable trouble in relation to that executorship, even county history itself, with all its attachment to details, would have little or nothing to record respecting them beyond their marriages and descents.

The supposition which we are called upon to accept is, that the members of this family, for sixty or seventy years, including that dark period of the Wars of the Roses, were in the habit of constantly writing to each other; of keeping their correspondence; and, finally, of collecting it in some one repository. That this correspondence embraced all manner of subjects, precisely as the analogous remains of a worshipful family of the present day would do: matters of business, family rejoicings, family quarrels, lawsuits, debts, marriages, deaths, inheritances. That it included, also, the ordinary stuff of which daily life is made,—mutual expressions of affection, playful mystifications, coarse jocularity. That, in addition to all these common ingredients, the matter thus collected comprised public documents of considerable and varied interest: letters to and from great public characters, with discussions and suggestions on the events of the time, such as in many instances might have involved the writer in time of civil war in hostility to very important personages, possibly in serious peril.

Now the singularity of the circumstance that all this should have been done in an age commonly called illiterate, has indeed been often remarked on, even by casual readers who have not founded any scepticism thereupon. This, however, is an improbability on which too much stress must not be laid; at least as far as the mere composition of the letters is concerned. There can be no doubt that the writing of English letters, both business and familiar, was—notwithstanding the total absence of postal communication—very common in the fifteenth century. Sir Henry Ellis has pointed out the curious circumstance that there exist "complete letter writers," manuals of episto-

lary composition both in French and English, of the date of Henry the Fifth, though I am not aware that any of them have been printed. In point of fact, if the want of posts militated against letter writing, on the other hand the great difficulty of travelling, and the long absences which it engendered, must have made communication by writing, between people who *could* write, very essential, and, one would suppose, very usual, whenever they could find opportunities. But then one would naturally expect that letters depending on such rare opportunities would be comparatively few and long. On the contrary, nothing is more remarkable in the ***Paston Correspondence*** than the extreme and business-like shortness of most of them. They seem to anticipate the breviloquent era of Sir Rowland Hill. They do not in general exceed a few printed lines. The writers, as a rule, seem fully to appreciate the maxim of Chaucer's *Creseide:*—

> Th' entent is all, and not the letter's space,
> So fare you well, God have you in His grace!

And this is evidently not occasioned by any difficulty which they find in expressing themselves. One of their chief characteristics (as we shall perceive more distinctly by-and-by, when examining into their style) is, that they are remarkable for readiness and fluency of language. The inference which would be naturally drawn from them is, that writing was almost as common and easy then as in our days; which, *aliunde,* we should assuredly not conjecture.

But, passing by for the moment the improbability of such preservation of letters at all, let us attend to another very curious circumstance already suggested; namely, the extremely miscellaneous character of the letters thus preserved. Generally speaking, an individual who has the task of preserving letters, if merely as a man of business, keeps those addressed to himself, with *transcripts* of a few of his own which it may be important to preserve. In a literary age, and with a view to publication, the system adopted is of course more developed, and complete transcripts of the writer's own letters may be preserved with or without the answers, as was the case with those of Horace Walpole. But the ***Paston Correspondence*** is not the least like either of these. We have to believe that the whole Paston family or large parts of it, were in the habit, for about eighty years, of keeping almost every scrap of paper which came into their hands, and then that some one member of the family took the pains of collecting and preserving the whole mass of them. No matter how far the members are separated from each other, or where the epistles reach them, the documents find their way into the common portfolio at last. The bulk of the letters, it is true, are addressed to three individuals—John Paston, Esquire (born 1420, died 1466); Sir John Paston, his son, (born 1440, died 1479); John Paston, called of Gelston, brother of the latter (died 1503). But the exceptions are extremely numerous, and consist, first, of letters and miscellaneous documents addressed to and by sundry parties, sometimes scarcely connected with the Pastons in any way, on matters both of public news or importance, and of private interest; secondly (and this is still more singular), of letters addressed to *other* members of the family by these three John Pastons or by others; Sir John Paston to his mother Margaret;

John Paston, the younger, to the same lady; divers parties to Sir William Paston, and to Agnes Paston, and Margaret Paston; Agnes to Edmund Paston, and so forth; not letters of business only, but letters of mere news, gossip, quarrelling, banter. In the fifth volume both Sir John Paston and John of Gelston have a good deal of bickering, as well as business, with their mother Margaret; and the letters on *both* sides occur, apparently in regular series, in the correspondence; nor is there any mention of transcripts; all seem to be original. How got they all together? It is difficult to conjecture, on any theory involving the genuineness of the whole of them.

On the whole, therefore, in summing up this portion of the evidence, namely, the external characteristics of the ***Paston Letters,*** we can say with positiveness no more than this: If genuine, they constitute a perfectly unique phenomenon. Sir John Fenn, in his first preface, expresses a hope that owners of private collections would follow his example, and anticipates the happiness which society would derive from the publicity of many similar treasures, as yet buried in secret repositories. A vain expectation. Many such repositories have been greedily ransacked since his time, but nothing whatever has been disinterred at all resembling his compilation; nothing *simile and secundum;* nor, we may add, have contemporaneous excavations in France, Italy, or Germany produced any other result. There is no other monument of mediæval times at all resembling the ***Paston Letters.***

And now, in conclusion, let us examine how far the contents of the letters, from internal evidence, justify the supposition of their authenticity. This is an inquiry of much more difficulty, and to conduct which properly a much closer knowledge is required of English mediæval habits of thought and language than is commonly possessed, and certainly far more than I possess.

This much, however, may be remarked even by a superficial reader, that considering that these volumes contain the unpremeditated effusions of a series of writers who by their own account were in close connection with some of the leading spirits of English history during the Wars of the Roses, and personal observers of many of the remarkable events of the time, our first expectation of course would be that they would offer much that is new and interesting in the way of political disclosure. And such was seemingly the general anticipation at the time when they appeared. If so, never were hopes more disappointed. It is not saying too much to state that no addition whatever to our knowledge of the politics of that most obscure age has been made through the ***Paston Letters.*** A writer of the last century, observing on Mr. Fenn's careful annotation of his volumes, says that in a historical sense never was so much trouble in the way of marginal commentary thrown away on a subject of less value.

How does this deficiency of special information—of the communication of any knowledge of importance which may not be drawn from other sources—affect the question of the genuineness of the letters? Strangely enough, the editor himself seems to expect that his readers will receive this barrenness as a *proof* of that genuineness. He observes in the preface to his third volume that

every criterion of authenticity accompanies the original documents; *no novel or suspicious anecdote will stagger credulity;* no new hypothesis is to be established or even proposed; no inveterate faith in received history is to be shaken; no eccentric genius is to appear, and call for admiration of talents that exceeded his means of improving or displaying them.

Now the question is whether the impartial critic would not draw the very opposite conclusion from these facts; whether he would not infer from the general absence of novelty in the incidents, the cautiousness of an inventor who was unwilling to commit himself, and kept guardedly within the bounds of what was already known. This was one of the tests which Macaulay, in one of the earlier and not the least able of his writings, his review of Wordsworth's "Icon Basilike," applies to the once favourite problem (now, thanks mainly to him, quite obsolete) whether Charles the First was the author of that work. "It has," he says with truth, "no allusion to facts not accessible to any moderately well-informed man." The editor does, indeed, elsewhere say, "where these letters differ from our history, they give the report of the time;" but such instances are certainly very rare.

I will notice one example, indeed, of this servile adherence to authorities, which is peculiarly unfortunate, because it goes too far. The battle of Towton is described by John Paxton, the elder, in a letter in which he professes to transmit to his correspondent a copy of one written by Edward IV. to his mother about the same event. The battle of Towton was no doubt a very bloody affair; it lasted part of two days; 100,000 men are *said* to have been engaged, and great rancour was displayed in the contest. But the number reported to have been killed outright, varying in most accounts from 30,000 to 40,000, is simply absurd. According to all reasonable historical criticism such slaughter is only possible in one case,—when the defeated are surrounded and massacred, which was by no means the fact at Towton, where the Lancastrians had full opportunity to run away, and did so. Accordingly, our last historian, Pauli, treats the number in question as wholly apocryphal, and accepts the estimate of an otherwise indifferent authority enough, William Worcester, who speaks of 9,000 slain, as far more probable. Now, had the Paston writer only repeated the ordinary fable, this would have suggested no reasonable suspicion of fabrication. Unfortunately, he "lies with a circumstance." He makes Edward the Fourth say, that 28,000 dead, on the Lancastrian side only, were *counted by the heralds.* And this in a letter which reaches London only five days after the action. It never seems to have occurred to the writer to think how long it would have taken the "heralds" in question to count and certify 28,000 dead bodies, even were the story credible in other respects.

But a much closer and more important test of the truth, as regards these remarkable monuments whether of truth or fiction, is to be found in the language in which they are given to the public.

That this is easy, fluent, and free from archaic stiffness to a very extraordinary degree, is the common verdict of all the learned who have consulted them, without the slightest suspiciion of their genuineness. Hallam (speaking of the "old obsolete English" as having gone out of use about the accession of Edward the Fourth) observes that

> Lydgate and Bishop Pecock, especially the latter, are not easily understood by a reader not habituated to their language; he requires a glossary, or must help himself out by conjectures. In the **Paston Letters,** on the other hand, in Harding the metrical chronicler, or in Sir John Fortescue's discourse on the difference between absolute and limited monarchy, he finds scarcely any difficulty. Antiquated words and forms of termination frequently occur; but he is hardly sensible that he reads these books much less fluently than those of modern times (*Introduction to the Literature of Europe*).

Still more distinctly to the same effect speaks Reinhold Pauli: "How people wrote and spoke in the last decennia of the fifteenth century, is best shown by the letters of the Pastons." "In those letters," he adds elsewhere, "we have the autographs of old and young, men and women. They write for the most part with tolerable orthography, and, generally speaking, are able to express themselves with readiness and fluency" (*Geschichte von England*). Both these considerable authorities (and others might be cited to the same effect) speak with evident surprise of the literary proficiency of ordinary people, as shown by Sir John Fenn's discoveries. The possibility of those discoveries being after all fictitious suggested itself to neither.

"Harding's Chronicle," to which Hallam compares these letters in point of comprehensibility, is a long rhyming jingle, as easy to understand as ordinary ballads, but so exceedingly different in style and execution from these familiar letters that nothing is gained by their juxtaposition. Fortescue's style is more to the purpose, but it is very far from the Paston English after all; and so is the pleasing and almost melodious descant of "Morte Arthur." But since Hallam wrote, very valuable contributions have been added to our means of ascertaining the written and spoken language of our forefathers of the fifteenth century, especially in the publications of records under the authority of the Master of the Rolls. There we have the business English of the day in a variety of forms—sometimes in the stiff commonplaces of official circumlocution; sometimes in the briefer and more incisive language of plain men writing in earnest. And I think any one who makes a fair comparison between these and the Paston letters will be struck in particular with that specialty on which Pauli remarks—the infinitely greater fluency of the latter. Writers of that day always seem to be exercising their limbs in fetters; the fetters of an unformed language, in which they could not readily find means to express the various niceties of thought which recurred to them. They had plenty of words at their command, for they had the boundless resource of borrowing, as far as they pleased, from the mediæval Latin, or from the current French of the day; no dictionary-makers had as yet arisen to object to such importations; and the more a writer garnished his discourse with these fringes, the more he was pleased with himself, and the more admired by others. Every reader will remember the long-drawn Gallicisms with which Chaucer, genuine Englishman as he was, loves to conclude

his paragraphs and point his rhymes. "In the hundred years which followed Chaucer," says Archbishop Trench (*English, Past and Present*), "a large amount of Latin found its way, if not into our speech, yet at all events into our books. . . . A crop of words long since rejected by our language sprang up. . . . While other words, good in themselves, and which have been since allowed, were yet employed out of all proportions with the Saxon vocables with which they were mingled, and which were altogether overtopped and overshadowed by them. . . . "

But this unlimited free trade in words was of little value towards the great object of writing, namely, making the meaning clear and precise; for these imported words had no recognised, secondary, popular meaning in English mouths; consequently they made but a feeble impression on the reader. And hence, in part at all events—partly, no doubt, also from an imaginary sense of stateliness of diction—arose the lawyer-like habit, so marked in early English writing, of lavish tautology. Learned words were as yet little emphatic; the notion, therefore, was to obtain additional emphasis by coupling two or three of them together; which, of course, degenerated into a trick, and was employed in the most abundant and tedious manner. (pp. 129-43)

Now this is a peculiarity from which the Paston letters, except here and there an official document contained in them, are, I think, entirely free. There is no more of this sort of iteration in them than would be used by an ordinary English letter-writer in the present day. Of course the ready answer may be given, that these are familiar letters. True; but unfortunately they are the only familiar letters of the age extant; if therefore they are unlike all other existing monuments of the language, we cannot indeed receive this as proof positive against them, but we are absolutely without collateral proof in their favour.

And much the same result would probably attend our inquiries, if we were to pursue the subject on the ticklish ground of style in the closer sense. On this head, curious as it is, I must be brief; partly for want of space to do it justice, partly because I cannot myself profess that close familiarity with the English of the fifteenth century which is required of one who would speak with authority. Generally speaking, the result would seem to be this: if forgeries, these are very clever forgeries. And yet there is a modern air, by no means so easily described as felt, which pervades a great part—the really questionable part—of these compositions, in the use of words as well as in other respects. (p. 144)

As in the case of language, so in the case of the manners and customs depicted in these letters; it is extremely difficult to state exactly the grounds for the suspicion which they excite, and yet, when once raised, it is quite impossible to get rid of it. There is a vast deal of ordinary matter, such as might have occurred in the daily gossip of England in any age: the country gentleman grumbles and winces under his pecuniary difficulties, the mother is in despair at the flirtations of her daughters, the Lady Bountiful is earnest about her nostrums, the damsel about the stuff of her gowns—all this, no doubt, is natural enough, for squire, and dame, and miss were much the same by nature then as now, and not quite so different by education as is commonly supposed. Still our curiosity seems to require more than this. There must have been differences of habit and feeling between them and us, sufficient to produce some very marked divergencies in the tone of ordinary correspondence. When a really new discovery occurs, letting one deeply into the internal life of any past age—*a trouvaille,* such as that of the recovered "Diaries of Pepys and Evelyn" in England, the "Historiettes de Tallemant des Réaux" in France—although, in these instances, not older than two centuries ago—the first, and most natural, emotion of the reader is the interest which he feels in being introduced to people so similar to himself, and yet so very different; similar in so many general thoughts, tendencies, associations—utterly diverse in so many of the more minute characteristics of life.

The *dramatis personœ* of the Paston letters belong to a far more venerable age, before what is called social life began. They are the contemporaries of those who might have known Chaucer and Gower, who saw and shared in the incomprehensible fights of the Roses, who had thrown up their caps for the good Duke of York, or his son Crookback Richard, who had beheld Caxton at his printing-press, and the Lollards burnt, and Eleanor Cobham doing penance barefoot. And yet their records represent scarcely anything but the most common-place, ordinary, pale details, such for the most part as might have occurred in any worshipful family of any date. Now there is nothing impossible in this: people may have lived, and begotten children, and died, and disclosed in their epistles no more signs of the specialties of their age than the Pastons; yet it is singular, to say the least of it.

And when we descend to particulars, we are constantly provoked, just as in the case of the language, by little hints of manners and usages, having to the antiquarian reader the most modern air possible, and yet which cannot be convicted of rank modernism on the face of the document. Take the following, by way of a few instances, to illustrate my meaning. The Prior of Bromholm wants to go abroad (about 1449), and he asks John Paston's advice about various matters, particularly as to the best way of taking money with him. "Some counsel me to have a letter of exchange, though it were but of forty shillings or less." Now bills or letters of exchange were no doubt in use, between merchants and for their purposes, long before this; but surely they could not have become ordinary substitutes for coin. The first known precedent of a *lettre de change,* according to Nouguier, in his treatise on those instruments, bears date only in 1381; and it is a cumbrous affair. It was only in 1394 that the magistracy of Barcelona are said to have enacted that they should be paid within twenty-four hours after presentation. But it would be curious to ascertain how long, after the **Paston Letters,** the next traveller on the Continent is reported of as carrying a "letter of exchange" with him. So again, Margery Paston expresses (in 1484) her satisfaction that at Lady Morley's house the society is orderly; "there is none disguisings, nor harping, nor luting, nor singing, nor none lewd disports; but playing at the tables, or chess, *and cards.*" Was playing at cards the amusement of a country manor house in 1484? That they were invented by that time we know; and this prevents us again from obtaining a conviction for anachronism; but surely their use was as yet uncommon, notwithstanding the belief of our popular antiquarian, Mr. Wright to the contrary, which indeed is founded mainly on this very passage. (See his *Domestic Manners and Sentiments.*)

More remarkable than these instances is the extreme meagreness of those notices of the education of the age, which are scattered throughout the volumes. Walter Paston was a scholar at Oxford in 1478, and was also, as it seems, at Cambridge. There is a good deal of discussion between him and his family about his expenses and other matters; but there is nothing characteristic whatever,—literally nothing, which conveys an idea of the special student life of those days, or which might not have been written equally well—saving the different value of money, and the old spelling—by a youth about to take his degree in the present day. He becomes B.A. and "makes his feast," for which he expects presents of venison, but is disappointed. Now it is perfectly possible that a hearty B.A. of 1478 "made his feast," just as his successor in 1778 gave a supper; nevertheless it seems strange that so very commonplace an usage alone should be recorded, and everything characteristic of the time omitted. William Paston was at Eton in the same year. We are told he was then *nineteen* years of age,—an age at which men, in the time of the Roses, were heads of families, and commanded armies,—and he writes home about money for his "commons," and wants "to come with a friend *by water,* and sport me with you a day or two in London this term time," almost in the very language of a captain fresh from Salt Hill. He has to pay for his board to his "hostess,"—in better-known phrase his "dame." As Eton, even in those early days, did profess by her statutes to make some provision for the education of the *filii nobilium,* we are not entitled absolutely to deny the antiquity of these passages; but anything less like what we should have expected as a record of Eton, in the days when the robes of good King Henry's first seventy scholars had hardly lost their gloss, it is certainly difficult to imagine. To sum up the result of this class of evidence; the contents of the letters, so far as domestic manners are concerned, are very much such as a careful forger might compile, studious to keep on safe ground: very unlike, in my judgment, real effusions of their supposed times, in which one would almost unavoidably discover much more of what was not common both to that time and our own.

One characteristic detail, however, of the life of that age, to which a great deal of correspondence in the third and fourth volumes is devoted, has been not unfrequently cited as an instance on the other side, as containing a record of incidents utterly strange, and yet undoubtedly true—namely, the account of the mixed proceedings of law and fighting concerning the inheritance of Sir John Fastolf, ending with the siege of Caistor Castle by the Duke of Norfolk, in private feud with the Paston family and others, the deceased fat knight's executors. But the plain fact is, that all which is important in this narrative is contained in the *Itinerarium* of that enigmatical personage, William Worcester (the William Botoner of the letters), which was used by the compiler of the fifth volume of Blomfield's *Norfolk,* in 1775, and was at Sir John Fenn's hand as he wrote: and that (unless I am mistaken) the letters do not wander into a single important new particular, or important divergence of fact, from the story in the *Itinerarium*. With this clue in our hands, we shall, I think, perceive that the letters read very like a sample of flourishing historical romance, cleverly grafted on the shrivelled trunk of an old chronicle.

Such are the reasons which I venture to offer for considering these volumes, the favourites of so many eminent historical antiquaries, as liable to very grave suspicion. As I have said, the idea of a mere wholesale forgery is evidently improbable; but that large additions were made by some fabricator to existing originals—additions calculated to render them much more interesting and attractive, and which it is now quite impossible to unravel from what is authentic—is a far more credible supposition. I have endeavoured, nevertheless, fairly to lay before the reader such arguments as have suggested themselves to myself in passing in favour of the more orthodox conclusion. The suggestions which I have made are entirely my own; the subject has not been treated of, to my knowledge, by others, and I have too profound a distrust of my own antiquarian knowledge, not to believe it possible that superior knowledge may point out in what respects my suspicions are ill founded, and my instances valueless. And I can truly say, that it would give me great satisfaction to be persuaded that my own ingenuity was at fault; and that, although the authenticity of the **Paston Letters** cannot be established on positive ground (unless the lost originals should ever be discovered), yet we are entitled to use their curious and amusing, if not very important contents, as they have hitherto been used, in illustration of the most obscure period of English history since the Conquest. (pp. 145-49)

> *Herman Merivale, "Are the 'Paston Letters'*
> *Authentic?," in* The Fortnightly Review, *Vol.*
> *II, August 15 - November 1, 1865, pp. 129-49.*

James Gairdner   (essay date 1865)

[*In the following excerpt, Gairdner defends the* Paston Letters *against Merivale's charge of doubtful authenticity.*]

The first thing that must strike the reader on perusing Mr. Merivale's paper ["Are the **Paston Letters** Authentic?" See excerpt above] is, that his argument owes its chief weight to external evidence. The main point on which his suspicions turn is the one fact that the original letters are not now to be found. This fact cannot be disputed. Their disappearance is unsatisfactory in many points of view, and, it may be readily conceded, is quite a legitimate ground of suspicion if other evidences go to confirm the doubt. But if it can be shown that there is really *no* other evidence, that the whole circumstances of the publication of these letters, and everything we know about their hstory, their editor, and their presentation to the king, is quite consistent with the plain unvarnished tale their editor himself has given of them, and if, besides, it can be proved that they bear strong internal marks of authenticity, it would surely be idle to build much upon the mere fact of the MSS. being lost.

Now, as to the external evidence I do not feel it necessary to say very much. Mr. Merivale himself admits that Sir John Fenn's character, so far as known to us, does not warrant the suspicions he would attach to it; and I may add that we are equally without evidence that either he, Le Neve, or Martin of Palgrave (excellent antiquaries though they were), or Worth, the chemist, was possessed of such an extraordinary genius as to have deceived posterity to the extent Mr. Merivale supposes. But I must take notice of some statements touching Sir John's preface to the first two volumes. In that preface Mr. Merivale asserts, and calls special attention to the point, there is not a word to inform the public "that the bulk of the originals were not published, or that the editor had still any portion of consequence in his hands. Nay, more than this, he seems to say that it had occurred to him to print only 'a select number of letters,' but that he had thought it better to give the whole." Now if Mr. Merivale will read the preface a little more carefully he will see that it *does* contain pretty sufficient indications that the editor had more originals than he had printed, and that he nowhere says any such thing as that "he had thought it better to give the whole." He seems, in fact, to have been afraid to print too much, and to have published the first two volumes with some misgivings that a portion even of their contents would be pronounced not to have been worth publication. He declares apologetically that he "found great difficulty in judging what letter or part of a letter to omit when he thought it of no consequence; considering that though it might not appear to him to convey any information, yet that it might be useful to other antiquaries in their particular investigations." This consideration ought certainly to have led him to print the whole collection at once; but it is evident he did not, as he tells us "some are *inserted*" for their style, others to illustrate the mode of education, and so forth; and, again, that he had "likewise *inserted* two pieces of poetry of the times."

The passage which Mr. Merivale construes as meaning that the editor had dismissed the thought of making a mere selection is as follows:—

> Some readers, perhaps, may think that a select
> number only of the original letters, printed in
> their antique dress, would have sufficed as speci-
> mens to have gratified the taste of the antiquary.

This sentence certainly, in itself, is easy enough to misunderstand. It must be explained, however, that the editor merely intends to apologise for the form in which he has printed the collection. Each letter is given in duplicate, one copy on the left-hand page with the antique spelling, capital letters, general absence of punctuation, and other peculiarities of the original exactly reproduced, while on the other side is a transcript in modern orthography and intelligible punctuation, with here and there a parenthetical explanation of some obsolete phrase. It was because he had done this all through the work that the editor apprehended the objection of "some readers," who would have been satisfied with one or two letters in the antique spelling as specimens. "Let such, however, consider," he goes on to say, "that a faithful delineation of our language during a period of almost half a century. . . . is a matter not only of much curiosity, but of some use; and though this method of printing the letters has been attended both with additional trouble and expense, yet it is hoped that the purchaser will not think that too high a price has been set upon these volumes, as the editor assures him that if he be paid by the sale for his trouble and expenses attending the publication he shall be satisfied." These words show clearly that the previous sentence cannot possibly mean what Mr. Merivale has supposed.

Thus it cannot be said that the language of the original preface gives any colour to the suspicion thrown out that the editor was encouraged by the success of the first two volumes to fabricate three more. As to the argument which Mr. Merivale puts forward from the contents and arrangement of the documents, it seems to me to be a little overdrawn. He contradicts the statement of the editor that the documents in the third and fourth volumes had been reserved as being "of a more private nature than those before given to the public." This second series, Mr. Merivale declares, "consists of documents bearing on public as well as domestic matters, nearly as promiscuously as those in the former." They do not appear so to me. It is quite true that the first contains domestic matters as well as public affairs; the second public affairs as well as domestic matters; and it must also be admitted that there are a few documents in the third and fourth volumes of such remarkable historic interest that their omission in the first two could only be owing to their importance not having been then discovered. But it is nevertheless a fact, of which any reader can easily satisfy himself, that the great mass of documents in the third and fourth volumes have less bearing on great historical events, or, as the editor says, on "public affairs and persons of consequence," than those in the first and second. Nothing appears to be more natural than that a timid editor, uncertain of the interest the public would take in his materials, should have limited them at first to those contained in the first two volumes; nor is it at all surprising, when the labour of deciphering is considered, that even one or two important historical documents should have escaped his observation. But if we are to suppose, with Mr. Merivale, that Sir John Fenn was only "the author of a clever literary romance," who, "finding it successful, had tried his hand at a continuation," we must acknowledge that he worked very rapidly to have performed his task so well. The first two volumes were published in 1787, and a second edition, with some corrections, was issued in the same year. The third and fourth volumes appeared in 1789. Two years is little enough time for the fabrication of two quarto volumes of historical documents such as cannot even now be proved, but only suspected, to be forgeries.

And here I cannot pass over in silence Mr. Merivale's ungenerous sneer in speaking of the "so-called second edition" of the first two volumes. I have compared the two editions one with the other, and though the differences are not great, they are quite sufficient to warrant the editor's assertion that additional notes and corrections had been inserted; while even the pages that most exactly correspond show, on careful examination, such minute differences in what printers call "the make-up," as to prove that in no part could the two editions have been printed from the same types. There is, therefore, no ground even here

for suspecting Fenn's literary honesty. What more remains? Fenn says he placed the originals of the first two volumes for a time in the library of the Antiquarian Society; but the Proceedings of the Society itself take no notice of the circumstance. Fenn says he then presented the letters to the king; but "they are not in the British Museum, nor in any other repository possessing parts of George the Third's library." I do not profess to explain everything, and these things, I acknowledge, puzzle me; but I do not suppose Fenn would have publicly stated that he lodged the manuscripts for a time with the Society of Antiquaries if he had not actually done so. Nor can any one suppose that he told an untruth in stating (what is also mentioned in the *Morning Chronicle* of that date) that he had presented the manuscripts to George III. And if it be admitted as a fact that he did present three volumes, purporting to be the ***Paston Letters,*** to the king, I presume it will hardly be contended that they contained no such documents at all. Genuine or spurious, Sir John actually gave the letters away; and, unless he intrigued to get them back again and destroy them, it is hard to connect the mystery of their disappearance with a doubt of their authenticity. That this is possible, I do not mean to deny; but whether it be probable, I shall leave the reader to judge. Only, before he makes up his mind upon the subject, I shall request him to give due consideration to what I have to say concerning the letters themselves.

Mr. Merivale also finds some difficulty in crediting the preservation of such a correspondence. "We have to believe," he says, "that the whole Paston family, or large parts of it, were in the habit, for about eighty years, of keeping almost every scrap of paper which came into their hands, and then that some one member of the family took the pains of collecting and preserving the whole mass of them. No matter how far the members are separated from each other, or where the epistles reach them, the documents find their way into the common portfolio at last." Mr. Merivale half answers this difficulty himself by going on to remark that the bulk of the letters are addressed to three individuals—John Paston, Esq., who died in 1466; Sir John, his son, who died in 1479; and John Paston called of Gelston, brother of Sir John, who died in 1503. During the earlier period especially, almost every letter is addressed to John Paston, Esq., while there is only one written by him, except those addressed to his wife. That one, which is an answer to a very important proposal from a nobleman, is without signature, and was printed by the editor from a copy in Paston's own hand. The family certainly were good men of business, and understood the importance of keeping letters; but there is no need to suppose that any one of them took the pains to collect a scattered correspondence. The papers passed from father to son, and were filed, no doubt, as they accumulated. Many of them, it is true, are not addressed to members of the Paston family at all; and some are political, even of the nature of state papers. This shows that the Pastons were often entrusted by others with documents of great importance, but it is not in itself a thing altogether unaccountable.

Some have wondered that such a correspondence should ever have taken place in an age commonly regarded as illiterate; but Mr. Merivale does not press that objection, knowing that there is evidence enough that a good deal of correspondence did take place. He says, however, with some degree of truth, that the *Paston Letters* are a unique phenomenon. They are unique in the interest of their contents, but not so entirely in their character as Mr. Merivale seems to imply. *The Plumpton Correspondence,* published by the Camden Society, is not very dissimilar in its nature to that of the Paston family, and extends partly over the same period; nor do I think it any way inferior to the other in that fluency of style which Mr. Merivale considers so suspicious. The Talbot Papers, published by Lodge, date only from the beginning of Henry VIII.'s reign; but they too exhibit very much the same conciseness and ease of expression as the *Paston Letters*. If, however, a strictly contemporary test is wanted, I may refer to the portions of the Stonor Correspondence, in the reigns of Edward IV. and Richard III., which are published in the *Excerpta Historica*.

But I come now to the subject of internal evidence, which in cases of this sort is always the most important; for documents that have a suspicious history may bear in themselves the most convincing marks of genuineness, but if internal evidence be against them, the best vouched pedigrees are of very little use. And in the first place it must be owned that to forge five quarto volumes of correspondence is a task of pretty considerable difficulty. To impose a fabrication of this sort upon the world, even if only for a time, requires no ordinary ability; but to do it so successfully as not to be found out for generations after, is a feat, I will venture to say, quite unparalleled in literature. Nearly eighty years have elapsed since the *Paston Letters* were first published; during that time they have been used and quoted by every historian of the period which they illustrate; and great as has been the advance in historical criticism, not one anachronism has been discovered, not one irreconcilable discrepancy between the statements in the *Paston Letters* and our daily increasing knowledge derived from other sources. Mr. Merivale himself evidently feels the impossibility of the whole collection having been a forgery; for he more than once admits that "there can be little doubt" they are "partly genuine," and that "the fictions probably rest on the basis of a certain number of really original papers." This is a great concession. (pp. 579-84)

And really, if a part of the letters are genuine, why not the whole? Have the genuine and false originals been purposely destroyed together? But why should a collector, possessed of some real gems, purposely set false diamonds by the side of them? And if he had done so, would they not have been found out by this time? It is conceivable, of course, that a single document or two of no very particular import may have been fabricated and escaped detection; but what could have been the motive for an act that would have added nothing to the value of the other papers, and endangered suspicion being thrown upon the whole? And if the forgery was on a considerable scale, I really cannot see that there is *primâ facie* much more difficulty in the hypothesis that it extended to the whole collection. Those who see any weight in Mr. Merivale's suspicions will be apt, if I mistake not, to carry them further than Mr. Merivale. His guarded hypothesis has, however, this advan-

tage: it is almost impossible logically to disprove it. The strongest evidences will not serve you unless they are exhaustive; for even if you had positive and overwhelming proof that ten, twenty, fifty, nay, a hundred, documents were genuine, Mr. Merivale might say in answer, "That is just what I imagined; but what about the three or four hundred others?"

The presumptive evidence, however, against the whole series being a forgery is really quite as strong against any considerable part being so regarded. That Hallam, Lingard, Turner, Mr. Charles Knight, and Dr. Pauli, whose names Mr. Merivale himself refers to, should all have used this correspondence in the same "unsuspecting way," is surely a very strong argument in its favour. It may be presumed that these historians have examined it with as much care as Mr. Merivale; not to mention that it has probably engaged the attention of many a nameless student, who, if he had found one apparent anachronism or other insoluble difficulty, might have found a vent for his remarks in the pages of the *Gentleman's Magazine* or *Notes and Queries*. But no such difficulty has been found, even by Mr. Merivale himself, and the negative result of his search is in itself pretty considerable evidence against the conclusion he would draw. He criticises the language and the references to manners and usages, and finds instances in both which he thinks "have the most modern air possible, and yet which cannot be convicted of rank modernism on the face of the document." That is to say, Mr. Merivale has certain preconceived ideas about language and manners, what usages are ancient and what modern, and instead of testing the accuracy of these ideas by documents like the *Paston Letters*, he prefers to retain them till he meet with other evidence. Of course he is quite at liberty to do so. He ought not, however, to make his preconceptions stand in the place of evidence against the suspected documents, especially when he considers that genuine evidences are sure to interfere with some of our preconceptions. That the *Paston Letters* do so to some extent is really an argument in their favour, seeing that there is no single instance where they can be "convicted of rank modernism." But, further. If the *Paston Letters,* or, as before supposed, any considerable part of them (the evidence is precisely the same against either supposition), were a forgery, the form in which they were published appears to me quite unaccountable. I have already stated that each letter is printed in duplicate, the original spelling and punctuation being given on one page, and the modern on the page opposite. This plan was not only followed in the publication of the first two volumes, but was rigidly adhered to throughout the three remaining ones. Now it must be obvious to every reader that the only effect of such a mode of publication would be to invite the closest attention to the peculiarities both of the antique language and of the spelling. (pp. 584-85)

Would any fabricator have adopted such a plan? If so, I must again insist that it is most extraordinary he should have succeeded in deceiving, not merely his own age (which was not very critical), but every historical student down to the present day, with the sole exception, I believe, of Mr. Merivale. For even the spelling of the fifteenth century, though it owned no definite laws, followed certain usages; so that the spelling alone ought to have condemned the Rowley ballads of Chatterton at the very first blush as forgeries. To invite critical attention to the spelling of his text was certainly the very last course a judicious forger would have pursued. Yet Fenn did more than even this. Not content with having given as close an imitation of the originals as could be done in print, he all but placed the originals themselves under the eye of every reader; for the publication was accompanied by numerous facsimiles of the signatures, and even of the text, besides careful engravings of the water-marks of the paper and of the seals attached to the letters. The number of these illustrations is as follows:—For the first two volumes, 3 facsimiles of letters, 77 signatures, 45 paper-marks, 28 seals; in the third volume, 46 signatures, 18 paper-marks, 11 seals; in the fourth, 24 signatures, 15 paper-marks, 6 seals; and in the fifth, 40 signatures, 20 paper-marks, 11 seals. In all 3 facsimiles, 187 signatures, 98 paper-marks, and 56 seals. In short, it would appear that he engraved (or his nephew, Serjeant Frere, engraved from drawings prepared by him) every signature, seal, and paper-mark in the whole collection, except duplicates; so that there is not a single letter in all those five volumes (except one or two that are anonymous) of the handwriting of which we are not furnished with a specimen.

Now, the evidence of genuineness in the case of these facsimiles is, I will say, altogether irresistible. No person familiar with the handwritings of that age has ever discovered in them the smallest ground of suspicion; and I will venture to say that the greater his experience the less will any man be inclined to distrust them. Perhaps I may be believed in this when I state that for nearly twenty years it has been my constant duty to read, copy, or summarise documents of the fifteenth and sixteenth centuries; but the well-known name of Sir Frederic Madden will give, on this point, better assurance to the public. Sir Frederic had doubtless examined well the facsimiles before he wrote in *Notes and Queries* the opinion, "There can be no doubt whatever about the genuineness of these letters." So decided a judgment would certainly not have been pronounced without due consideration by the head of the MS. Department in the British Museum. And when it is considered that these specimens of handwriting not only in a general way resemble the characters of the fifteenth century, but that they contain well-known signatures and autographs, which have often, since the days of Sir John Fenn, been engraved from other MSS., but in those days had been seen by few, the public may partly appreciate the grounds of the palæographer's undoubting confidence. For among these facsimiles we find such signatures as those of kings and princes whose handwriting was little known in the last century, of Henry VI., Edward IV., Richard III. (as Duke of Gloucester and as king), of Richard Duke of York, father of the two sovereigns last named, of Elizabeth Woodville, Edward's queen, and of Henry VII. and his queen Elizabeth,—of lords and bishops, such as Humphrey Stafford, Duke of Buckingham, Cardinal Bourchier, Lords Cromwell, Scales, and Molyns, of the time of Henry VI.; Warwick the king-maker, and his father Salisbury, Archbishop Neville of York, that Earl of Oxford who was beheaded under Edward IV., that Lord Hastings who was beheaded by Richard III., that Duke of Suffolk who was murdered at sea, and that Duke of Suffolk who married Edward IV.'s sister, that Duke of Norfolk who fell at Bosworth, and that Earl of Surrey, his son, whom Henry VII. restored to confidence,—men whose signatures, for their curiosity, may now be seen in the British Museum and the Record Office, but were not in Fenn's days so easily accessible; not to speak of men like William Botonel, who made no figure in history, but whose handwriting may be equally well identified elsewhere.

And all this, if fabricated, was done in the retirement of East Dereham, in Norfolk, where, as the editor complains, he was at a distance from public libraries! Yet he also engraved the papermarks and seals of the letters, in the hope that they would prove "a means of ascertaining the dates of many old writings;" and in point of fact we have such paper-marks elsewhere, and such seals elsewhere. The inconceivability of forgery, as we take all these things into consideration, becomes almost inexpressible, especially when we know how little would have been required to impose on the easy faith of the eighteenth century. (pp. 586-88)

To sum up all in a few words, my argument is this. Ever since the *Paston Letters* came out they have excited much attention. The historian, the genealogist, the antiquary, the palæographer, and the philologist have each examined them with attention for illustrations of their respective subjects; but no one, except Mr. Merivale, has seen any reason to doubt their genuineness. Mr. Merivale himself cannot prove one anachronism, and none of the instances he has brought forward of what seem to him modern phraseology and manners are strong enough to justify suspicion. The only point involved in mystery is the disappearance of the original letters; and from this mystery and the circumstances attending it I by no means desire to withdraw attention. The question should be continually kept before the notice of all who by possibility may help to throw a light upon it, and no efforts should be spared in any quarter to ascertain what has become of the MSS. That they still exist there can be very little doubt, and their recovery would be most important. The *Letters* might then be edited anew in one complete chronological series, including all those omitted by Sir John Fenn, and the dates corrected by comparison with each other; for never until this is done shall we know the full value of this wonderful collection. Mr. Merivale will therefore have done excellent service if his observations lead to further inquiry. (p. 594)

> *James Gairdner, "Authenticity of the Paston Letters," in* The Fortnightly Review, *Vol. II, August 15 - November 1, 1865, pp. 579-94.*

Herman Merivale   (essay date 1873)

[*In the following excerpt from a review of James Gairdner's 1872 edition of the* Paston Letters, *Merivale briefly discusses their historical value.*]

On the infinite historical value of [the *Paston Letters*] it is quite unnecessary to dilate. They have furnished a mine of raw material, for these eighty years past, to our most industrious explorers. Probably, to those who have studied the correspondence in a general way, there are two features which have come most prominently into notice. The first is the fundamental likeness which they establish between the aspect of society in their age, and in our or any age. After all, the tastes, interests, family attachments, personal hopes and fears of men, 'quicquid agunt homines,' do not vary so much in the course of centuries as our first fancies would lead us to imagine. The metal is the same, the setting only different. In the *Paston Letters* we meet with personages of the better class in all periods of life. The Eton schoolboy, the anxious maiden, the match-making mother, the resolute woman of business, the poor cousin, the family counsellor, the chief of the house himself, full of party politics, but fuller still of plans of pecuniary gain and personal aggrandisement—are there, all busy as they on earth were busy, and as, with superficial differences only, their descendants of the twelfth generation are busy to this day. The lesson is a very obvious one, but it is not therefore the less strange to some of our preconceived notions, nor the less amusing. The other feature which we would notice is one in which the Paston times—the fourteenth and fifteenth centuries generally—did nevertheless exhibit characteristics somewhat peculiarly their own. It was an age in which the two great methods of enforcing claims and rights—private war and litigation—were mingled together, or alternated with each other, after a fashion scarcely comprehensible either in more civilised or in less civilised days. All the Paston family are deeply engaged in endless lawsuits. The progress of these suits, the hopes and discouragements of the parties, present a constant and somewhat wearisome store of family communication. But yet, at the same time, people were very far indeed from having renounced the earlier and more summary method of self-defence and retaliation. 'Why don't you take good cudgels, and settle it?' says Counsellor Pleydell to Dandie Dinmont, touching his march-suit with Jock of Dawston-Cleugh.

> 'Odd, sir! we tried that three times already; but I dinna ken; we're both gey good at single stick, and it could na weel be judged.' 'Then take broadswords, and be damned to yon, as your fathers did before you.' 'Aweal, sir, if ye think it wadna be again the law, it's all one to Dandie.'

'Social development,' in the Paston neighbourhood, had just reached the same point of ambiguity as among Scott's imaginary Liddesdale borderers. An instance or two, out of a great number, will illustrate our meaning. John Paston (1448) is disturbed in his claim to the manor of Gresham by Lord Molynes. His lordship 'listened to the counsels of John Heydon of Baconsthorpe, a lawyer, who had been sheriff and also recorder of Norwich, and whom the gentry of Norfolk looked upon with anything but good will.' Heydon persuaded Lord Molynes that his claim was good; and Lord Molynes, 'without more ado, went in and took possession.' To go to law with Lord Molynes, 'a powerful young nobleman connected with various wealthy and influential families,' was no light undertaking for an esquire. Paston first tried the intercession of the Church through the medium of Bishop Waynflete; but this also failed him. Then he resorted to reprisals. He

took and held possession of the mansion; and for

some time without opposition. But at last, while John Paston was away in the country on business, there came before the mansion at Gresham a company of a thousand persons, armed with cuirasses and brigandines, with guns, bows and arrows, and with every kind of offensive and defensive armour. They had also mining instruments, long poles with hooks, called cromes, used for pulling down houses, ladders, pickaxes, and pans with fire burning in them. With these formidable instruments they beset the house, at that time occupied only by Margaret Paston and twelve other persons; and having broken open the outer gates, they set to work undermining the very chamber in which Margaret was. Resistance under the circumstances was impossible. Margaret was forcibly carried out. The house was then rifled of all that it contained—property estimated by John Paston at 200*l.*— the doorposts were cut asunder, and the place was left little better than a ruin.

The war of the Roses would seem to have cut short the promising quarrel, *tam Marte quam Mercurio,* which the learned counsellor Heydon had started. The character of Sir John Fastolf, of Caistor Castle, the hero of so large a portion of the correspondence, evidences quite as forcibly this double characteristic of the times. He was constantly in arms for the Crown abroad, and occasionally in affairs of his own at home. Nevertheless, as Mr. Gairdner says, 'from the general tenor of his letters we should certainly no more suspect him of being the old soldier that he actually was, than of being Shakespeare's fat, disorderly knight.' Almost every sentence in them refers to

> lawsuits and title deeds, extortions and injuries received from others, forged processes altering property, writs of one kind or another to be issued against his adversaries, libels uttered against himself, and matters of the like description. Altogether the perusal is apt to give us an impression that Sir John would have made an acute and able, though perhaps not very high-minded solicitor . . . . The familiarity shown even by Fastolf with all the forms and processes of the law is probably due not so much to the peculiarities of his personal character as to the fact that a knowledge of legal technicalities was much more widely diffused in that day than in ours . . . . The *Paston Letters* afford ample evidence that every man had property to protect, if not every well-educated woman also, was perfectly well versed in the ordinary forms of legal processes.

Altogether, these disclosures to a certain extent remind us of the state of things of which some of us have made personal experience, and others have heard and read at secondhand, as prevalent in some of the Western States of America in recent or present days. The spirit of technical law, and the spirit of Lynch law, divide the sway between them. The lawyers have on the whole the best of it; they are the real masters of the situation; but their influence is largely assisted by that of the bowie-knife and the revolver. And one aftergrowth of this condition of society—a condition through which probably all communities must more or less pass—is the luxuriance of the great legal profession. Our English peerage offers abundant evidence of its aspiring tendencies, and at no period of our history, probably, have the foundations of great legal families been more extensively laid than in the fifteenth century. (pp. 5-7)

> *Herman Merivale, in an originally unsigned review of "The Paston Letters," in* The Edinburgh Review, *Vol. CXXXVIII, No. CCLXXXI, July, 1873, pp. 1-27.*

James Westfall Thompson   (essay date 1901)

[*In the excerpt below, Thompson comments on the value of the* Paston Letters *as sources of information on fifteenth-century English social customs.*]

The **Paston Letters** are far from being the annals of a quiet neighborhood, although the familiar correspondence of an English family whose position was originally that of small gentry. For their time is those eventful years in English history when the white rose of York and the red rose of Lancaster were dyed a common color on Wakefield Heath and Bosworth Field.

The intense human interest of these famous letters has commanded the admiration of readers ever since John Fenn edited them,—or, rather, those then known,—in 1787. It remained for Mr. Gairdner, in 1872-5 to give them to the world in what then seemed as complete form as could be hoped for, since some of them were supposed to be irretrievably lost. (p. 132)

Our knowledge of the social life of the men and women of the Middle Ages is not great; but so much is known that it is not for us to cast imputation upon either our forefathers' knowledge or their culture or their attainments in the fifteenth century. In an age of blood and iron, like our own, they yet felt that the essence of civilization was not in material invention or mere political achievement, but in the sway of principles of mind and heart. The amount of education possessed by the common people of England in that day was not slight. Mr. Gairdner truly observes that

> These letters show that during the century before the Reformation the state of education was by no means so low, and its advantages by no means so exceptionally distributed, as we might otherwise imagine. For it is not merely that Judge Paston was a man of superior cultivation, and took care that his family should be endowed with all those educational advantages that he had possessed himself. This was no doubt the case. But it must be remembered that the majority of these letters were not written by members of the Paston family, but were only addressed to them; and they show that friends, neighbors, lords, commoners, and domestic servants possessed the art of writing, as well as the Pastons themselves. No person of any rank or station in society above mere laboring men seem to have been wholly illiterate. All could write letters; most persons could express themselves in writing with ease and fluency.

In 1479, William Paston, a lad of nineteen, is at Eton "ver-

sifying" in Latin hexameters and sending his effusion to an elder brother for criticism, which implies a classical training in the latter also. Sir John Paston's library contained (and his letters show that he read them with pleasure) Chaucer's *Troilus and Cressida, The Legend of Good Women, The Parliament of Birds, La Belle Dame Sans Mercie,* and Lydgate's *Temple of Glass,* though the circumstances that one of the landed possessions of the family, the manor of Gresham, had been purchased from the son of the first laureate, may have increased Sir John's interest in that poet. The Shakespeare scholar will be even more interested in these letters, for in their pages Sir John Falstaff—or Fastolf, as the name is properly spelled—appears in veritable reality, not as a type of the pseudo-chivalry of the fifteenth century. Judge Paston was executor of Falstaff's will, and the latter left his fairest possession, Caister Castle, to him, with the understanding that the property be ultimately devoted to the founding of a college wherein were to be maintained "seven priests and seven poor folk." The spirit of the will was faithfully kept by his executor, who, finding it impracticable to found an independent institution in Norfolk, devoted Caister to the support of Magdalen College. If Shakespeare perverted Falstaff in order to point the moral of decadent feudalism, yet in one particular he was not altogether unfaithful to his character. Falstaff—yet Shallow more so—was fond of interlarding his conversation with legal terms. His numerous letters to Judge Paston regarding the execution of his will attest his familiarity with the intricacies of the law touching property.

The claims of property are continually thrust upon the reader of these letters. Betrothal or marriage where the question of dowry was not considered, even between those outside the aristocracy, were deemed scandalous, and the finer sensibilities of both men and women were singularly blunt. Yet they were not without sentiment. The love correspondence of John Paston and Margery Brews is a curious compound of sense and sentiment. The girl's father long held back with reference to the match. Writing to the elder Paston, he says:

> The cause of my wryting un to yow, at thys tyme is, I fele wele . . . that ye hafe undystondyng of a mater, whech is in commynicacyon tocyng a maryage, with Godds grace, to be concluded betwyx my saide cosyn yowr broder, and my doghter Margery, wheche is far commonyd, and not yyt concluded, ner noght schall ner may be tyll I hafe answer from yowe.

Margery was loyal to her father's wishes and the custom of the country, but her woman's heart was sad at times. "If that ye hade not halfe the lyvelode that ye hafe, for to do the grettest labur that any woman on lyve myght, I wold not forsake yowe," she writes on St. Valentine's Day, to "My ryght welebeloved Voluntyn."

The quality of the sentiment of the fifteenth century seems hard to us. We may admire more the simplicity and honesty of the people as a whole. One John Gywne, a servant, finds a purse on the highway near Cambridge, and sends it to his master at Trinity College to know if any of his knowledge, or any other, have lost such a purse, and that the tokens there of being told he shall have it again. An unknown man, evidently young, writes to his friend in Lincoln, who is of superior station, in a letter of straightforward friendship and manly purpose: "A man shall never have love of God, nor love nor dread of good men for miskeeping of much good as though it were his own; but where it is truly dealt with and goodly disposed then followeth both great merit and worship."

Space fails to tell of the minute things of interest in this correspondence. The student of economic and social history, the purely political historian, the genealogist, and the antiquarian will all find a mine of profitable study in these pages, which so conclusively prove that history is not the study of dead peoples but the mirror of humanity. (pp. 132-33)

> *James Westfall Thompson, in a review of "The Paston Letters," in* The Dial, Chicago, *Vol. XXXI, No. 365, September 1, 1901, pp. 132-33.*

Charles Menmuir   (essay date 1903)

[*In the excerpt below, Menmuir examines the social life and material welfare of fifteenth- and sixteenth-century England in a comparison of the* Paston Letters *with another collection of family papers, the* Cely Letters, *from the same period.*]

The England that the ***Paston Letters*** describe for us cannot remain an unknown land. Its men and women are flesh and blood, for these letters are as graphic as Pepys. (p. 327)

The two most important sources upon which we can draw for our information [about England during the Wars of the Roses] are the ***Paston Letters*** and the *Cely Letters.* A few words relating to their importance, as well as to their limitations, may not be out of place here, before any attempt is made to draw upon their contents for evidence of the statements that follow. Both books, if one may call them so, deal with the everyday life of a well-to-do family, not high enough to be exclusively concerned in affairs of state, nor low enough to be unworthy of any record whatever. Both series of letters were private and personal, but they dealt with facts of vital moment to the writers. In neither instance can we advance sufficient reason for not accepting the story they tell. They are artless, but they carry the conviction of sincerity, and within their limited range—the one deals with the life of a landed proprietor, the other with a family of wool merchants—they are to be regarded without reserve. The picture they paint is certainly not England at large, as they are extremely parochial in feeling, but the Norwich of the ***Paston Letters*** is on broad lines the microcosm of the England of that day, and there is no valid reason for refusing to admit George Cely's life in Calais as otherwise than typical of his contemporary in Bristol or Newcastle.

Stubbs, in his *Lectures on Mediæval and Modern History,* regards the ***Paston Letters*** as forbidden ground for all but the professed student of history. "Their language," he says, "their localised details, their minutiæ of family history and illustrations of manners are without any meaning

to nine people out of ten." To a large extent this may be so; they make hard reading, no doubt, to those who care for none of these things, but the learned historian's opinion seems unnecessarily emphatic, unless his "innermost ring of historic students" has a fairly ample circumference. Nevertheless, his belief must have due weight and consideration, for it may be best expressed by saying that care has always to be exercised in using details so local and petty for the establishment of a panorama of the general social condition of things. These details give us at most vivid glimpses of social life, but the haphazard way they present themselves to us forbids their having much value as a systematic record of social progress. And the same may be said of the *Cely Letters.*

Social history in its widest sense embraces more or less many forms of human activity. It views man in his contact with his neighbour, as friend and enemy, as citizen and as merchant; it has to consider his relations to church, and town, and household; it must not neglect his accomplishments in learning, nor the refinement of his manners, nor the attitude he adopts towards the Ten Commandments. In short, nothing that he strives after or fights against, nothing in his thoughts or his actions, but will leave its impress upon the society of which he is a member.

The beginning of the Wars of the Roses found England a country more suited for the training of the hardier virtues than for the development of the so-called finer graces that may adorn human life. A man, to hold his own, had more frequently than not to avail himself of rough and ready measures. He could not always afford to sit down and patiently wait until "the law's delay" was at an end, or until the "insolence of office" had condescended to consider him. Party spirit ran high, and turbulence was connived at by noblemen and country gentlemen. Innumerable passages in the ***Paston Letters*** confirm the existence of this lawlessness. (pp. 330-31)

Much has been said of the want of real domestic feeling during this period, but can we wonder at it altogether? The attitude of the members of the family circle towards one another is well painted in the documents we have at hand. It is pre-eminently a business one. The mainspring of action is regulated, more frequently than not, by questions of pounds, shillings, and pence, and the outcome is naturally productive of only a niggardly and selfish sympathy. Gairdner remarked that domestic life was tainted by the system of "wardship" which put the marriage of heirs under age at the disposal of their superior lords. But the evil was wider in its operation than this. A superior lord might almost be excused, from a business standpoint at least, if he considered himself to some extent in such a contingency. At any rate in many cases he could not be reproached on the score of selling his own kith and kin. In the ***Paston Letters,*** however, we have witness over and over again that a father or brother might exercise his power over daughter or sister for similar ends. Marriage was regarded almost solely as serviceable in strengthening financially or otherwise the status of the family. The natural feelings of the individual were ignored in the careful calculation of the pros and cons of the case. (p. 335)

There is not even an attempt at glozing over the sordidness

of it all. "Wardship" and its attendant evils did all the mischief that has been put to their discredit, but society was permeated with the same opinion in all directions, and in cases that lay altogether outside of the relations existing between superior and ward. Pecuniary considerations ruled in the legal aspect of the question, but they were also rampant within the home itself. They were of primary importance to men and women alike, at least to the latter after they had entered the bonds of matrimony and had presumably acquiesced in the barter of themselves. Paston's wife and his mother were every whit as good judges of an eligible party, from the standard then in vogue, as was John Paston himself or even the much-experienced Richard Cely.

Home life in other respects seems to have been of a harsh enough nature, and physical force was resorted to in circumstances that would now bring upon such conduct the verdict of brutality. Elizabeth Clere wrote to John Paston about his mother's Spartan views of discipline in reference to his sister Elizabeth, who had come to a marriageable age, and had evidently a will of her own. "And sche hath sen Esterne the most part be betyn onys in the weke or twyes, and som tyme twyes on a day, and hir hed broken in to or thre places." Old Mrs. Paston evidently was a firm believer in the doctrine of Solomon. She wrote of her son at Cambridge that she considered his last master the best he ever had, because his methods were based upon the primitive principle of the rod. Her counsel to Grenefeld, the lad's new master, is in a similar strain, and she asks him "to send feythfully word by wrytyn who Clement Paston hath do his dever in lernyng and if he hathe nought do well nor wyll nought amend prey hym that he wyll trewly belassh hym, tyl he wyll amend." In the same letter Clement's sister Elizabeth is warned that "she must use hyr selfe to werke redyly as other jentylwomen done, and sumwhat to helpe hyr selfe ther with."

Master and servant, as might be expected, were bound together by no less stringent measures. Paston, as landlord, seems occasionally to have got at loggerheads with his tenants, and, even if allowance is made for the pressure brought to bear upon the tenants by powerful neighbours—my Lord of Suffolk or my Lord of Norwich as the case might be—there is no reason to believe that Paston's attitude towards his inferiors was always one of a lenient nature. Richard Calle, his right-hand man of business, advocated drastic measures when trouble cropped up and the tenants had been forced into active resistance. In his letter to John Paston, junior, he writes of certain of these men: "they have enforced them as stronke as they kan and they have broken doune the brigge and have leide a planke over in cas that ye go theder ye may not come at Dale is howce in no waie." Sufficient evidence lurks between these lines to show that previous experience had given these men a knowledge of what would be forthcoming. Calle's letter finishes with the remark "but and ye wolde gete my Lords meane and pulle the knaves out be the heede it were weele done."

But, to be fair, there was sometimes a better feeling displayed. Sympathy with the poverty of dependents did now and again stir even the bosom of careful Mrs. Paston. In

1465 we find her writing to her husband about the grievous plight of some of their tenants, and urging him to allow certain measures for their relief. It is true that she is careful to explain that no great demands are to be made upon the husband's pocket, as "the wynfall wood at the manner," which she proposes to give them, is "of noo gret valewe." Still the kindly suggestion is there, and we can afford to ignore little details because of the pleasure there is in finding that a glint of charity is sometimes in evidence.

That there was need for such a feeling then can be little doubted. The poverty that was thankful for Mrs. Paston's "ruschis to repare with her howsys" was accentuated all too frequently by the visitations of sickness and plague. Ever since the Black Death of 1348-9 there had been a frequent recurrence of pestilence. (pp. 336-38)

No evidence of any kind is forthcoming in any of these records of much help of a practical kind. Crowds of pilgrims went to and fro, actuated mainly by a desire to escape the infliction, or, it might be, grateful for renewed health if they had been lucky enough to recover. In 1471, the year which Paston mentions as the worst in his experience, he wrote to his younger brother about a pilgrimage of this nature which the King and Queen undertook to Canterbury: "As ffor tydyngs, the Kyng and the Qwyen and moche other pepell ar rydden and goon to Canterbery, nevyr as moche peple seyn in Pylgrymage hertofor at ones, as men saye." But the numbers that went did not go from altruistic motives. Their object was to secure personal immunity, and their means of attaining this did not by any means further peace or security throughout the country. In fact, such individuals gave a large amount of unconscious encouragement to the robbery so prevalent at this time.

With regard to the direct means for staying the onrush of the plague, it may be surmised that these were of little or no value. It was an age when sorcery could still be used as a charge in 1470 against the Duchess of Bedford, and when licenses, as late as 1477 at least, could be obtained for the purposes of alchemy. An educated and intelligent set of people like the Pastons could only fight disease with these weapons. "My moder be hestyd a nodyr ymmage of wax of the wette of yow to oyer Lady of Walsyngham . . . and I have be hestyd to gon on pylgreymmays to Walsingham and to Sent Levenardys for yow." It cannot therefore be stretching a point very far if we believe that the medical skill of the age was not of a very advanced character, and, unfortunately for the case, a plague cannot be successfully stamped out by faith-cures or by Christian science treatment. Pest-houses were indeed found near most large towns, but the attempts at isolation could not have been in any way thorough, as there was no local authority to enforce even elementary precautions. Such plague-houses were attached to each of the leading Oxford Colleges, and the fellows evidently used them, not for the purpose of sending the sick there, but for their own habitation and retirement when "the sickness was hot under the shadow of St. Mary's spire."

In conclusion, the demoralising effects of all this upon the character of the people, when they were suffering under these visitations, must have been appalling. Paston's interest in the matter is confined, if we may judge him from his own words, to a fear for his friends and well-wishers. The pilgrimages were merely unadulterated proofs of individual selfishness and of childish terror. No evidence exists of co-operation to lessen the trouble. Evils were not faced, they were fled from. Social life almost ceased to exist whilst the plague stalked through the land; men grew more callous than even a callous age had made them, and six months of the plague would undo the progress of as many years' social prosperity.

So far our evidence has tended to show the manifold burdens under which life was led. The unsettled state of the country at large, the vagaries in the administration of justice, the frequent appeal to force, the frequent recurrence of much sickness, all tended to dwarf, if not to destroy, any efforts toward the evolution of those higher social virtues that so readily decay in a tainted atmosphere.

But, on the other hand, material welfare was slowly progressing in spite of and alongside of these drawbacks. England in the fourteenth century had been mainly engaged in exporting raw material, but by the close of the period we are now considering she had become a manufacturing centre, and that at the expense of the Flemish cities. The din of 40,000 looms had resounded through Bruges during the thirteenth century; at the end of the fifteenth she was ready to bestow her privileges for next to nothing. The population of Ypres had decreased from between 80,000 and 100,000 in 1408 to about 5,000 or 6,000 in 1486, and Ghent and other towns told a similar story of decay. This startling change stands as an indirect proof of the altered condition of affairs in England. (pp. 339-40)

Political proofs of a higher standard of comfort and of a more ambitious ideal in at least some of the external marks of social life are at hand in the Statutes of Apparel of 1463 and 1482, both of which were framed against an apparently universal extravagance in dress. . . . Furthermore, the Acts of the fifteenth century, directed against the giving of liveries, testify partly to the love of display among the upper classes at least, although the evil lurking behind this question may have been more of a political one from the point of view of the government.

In the **Paston Letters** we get a glimpse now and again of Mrs. Paston's desire to appear well before the world. Even she, with her full share of troubles, can find time to give her husband detailed orders in small matters that show she was not always burdened down by the fact that "there is grete prese of pepill and fewe frendes." So on occasion Paston's instructions run: "That æ wyld bye a zerd of brode clothe of blac for an hode fore me of xliiij d. or iiij s. a zerd." She smooths away possible objections by letting her husband know that "for the child is gwnys, and I have them, I wel do hem maken."

In the question of diet there is a strong likelihood that a somewhat like condition of things existed. The *Cely Papers* contain enough information for us to conclude that their class at least knew something of the fleshpots of Egypt. (pp. 341-42)

It was exactly this new class, of whom the Pastons and the Celys formed types, that had no legacy of tradition in the sphere of social life to fall back upon. They had to do more than combat evils adverse to their social advancement, for they were forced to create for themselves a standard of living. Trade had increased and was largely increasing the wealth of a large section of the community, and this class at least had begun to feel that they had claims upon an entrance into what was not only a position where a higher standard of comfort held good, but a position where more refined social ideals were eventually necessary. Many were rising in the world to an affluence which previously it was impossible for their fathers to attain. The Church was no longer the only door through which one of the masses might reach to eminence, even although she was still to show that an Ipswich tradesman's son could aspire by her aid to fill St. Peter's chair. And this new society, independent of and largely antagonistic to the Church, could not very well draw inspiration from thence for the formation of a social code. Neither could the moribund baronage give it any lessons, for sympathy with trade was as foreign to them as it was to the clergy. As a matter of fact, new condition had rendered many of the regulations of the Church, as well as of the nobility, ridiculous and incapable of acceptance on the part of a set of men whose very rise and existence were based on opposition to the old order of things. Nay, more, the new moneyed class had frequently the power of conferring favours upon instead of receiving them from the clergy and nobility alike. A nobleman might place in pawn to some merchant prince the heirlooms of his house, and the transaction placed the obligation at his door. (pp. 342-43)

The belief that money could stand by itself and was independent of all other aid, was certainly not so prevalent in this period as might be expected. Education, and the power with which it equips a man, were beginning to be regarded with an importance which previously had been confined to the Church alone. No doubt it was regarded as a means to an end, and that end did not imply a high standard of culture. In Caxton's *Book of Curtesye* we find the outlines defined for us in a few of the rhymes:

> It is to a godly chyld wel syttynge
> To use disports of myrthe and pleasure,
> To harpe or lute, or lustely to synge,
> Or in the prees right manerly to daunce. . . .
>
> Exercise your self also in redynge
> Of bookes enornede with eloquence.

The aim was essentially one of a practical nature, and, despite the above lines, confined more or less to a knowledge of legal matters. Nothing is more striking in a way than the display of this fact in the **Paston Letters,** or, as a matter of fact, in other documents as well. Both the **Paston** and the *Cely Letters* give abundant illustration of the state of education among at least the middle and upper classes. None of the letters betray the writer as totally unaccustomed to the art of correspondence. On the other hand, they very frequently prove him able to express himself with that ease and point which only come with frequent practice. Many of the letters in their way are models of terse expression and businesslike brevity. It must be remembered as well that they are not the production of a few highly trained or exceptionally gifted individuals. They are far more widely spread in their origin, as the greater number of the ***Paston Letters*** were written by people who only had business or family realtions with the Pastons: their superiors, it might be, in one case, their neighbours and equals in another, or frequently enough those merely in their employ. (pp. 346-47)

Within the Paston family circle there existed no undecided opinion as to the value of an educational training. Reference has already been made to Mrs. Paston's care for the upbringing of her son at Cambridge, and in 1460 she writes to her son Sir John: "Your fader, wham God assole, in hys trobyll seson set more by hys wrytyngs and evydens than he did by any of hys moveabell godys." Such an opinion leaves little doubt but that he would attach adequate importance to the cultivation of those faculties that would enable a man both to record and to use such "wrytyngs and evydens."

In the view held at that time regarding the purpose of education, the legal element continually intrudes. Gairdner, in his introduction to the ***Paston Letters,*** points out that a liberal education then invariably implied a good working knowledge of the law, and stern necessity no doubt compelled others to gain the same useful information by other and harder channels. The procedure of the courts and the technicalities of legal administration seem to have been well within the grasp not only of those who may have had

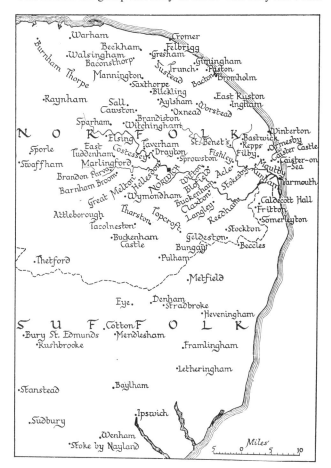

Map of the regions of Norfolk and Suffolk most closely associated with the Pastons.

a course of formal legal study, such as the universities could give, and such as we can imagine Sir John Paston or Sir John Fastolf to have had, but also of women like Mrs. Paston, or even, to some extent, of dependents. The contents of letter after letter bear out this statement. Agnes Paston writes thus to her son Edmund: "To myn well belovid sone, I grete you wel and avyse you to thynkk onis of the daie of your faders counseyle to lerne the lawe," and she continues, giving the very significant reason therefor, "for he sayde manie tymis that ho so ever schuld dwelle at Paston schulde have nede to conne defende hym selfe." I suppose this reason strikes at the root of that remarkably widespread acquaintanceship with the law that is so specially characteristic of these times. The legal officials who administered the law were evidently so seldom above suspicion—Paston is informed in 1451 "that the Sheriff is noght so hole as he was, for now he wille shewe but a part of his frendeschippe"—that the implicit trust which honourable dealing can sometimes foster would have spelt in such cases sheer madness. It was not always a wise course to imagine oneself thrice armed because of the justice of one's quarrel. At least from our evidence it would appear that some insight into ways and means, both honest and dishonest, was not at all a qualification to be despised or safely dispensed with. (pp. 347-48)

Our eyes must not . . . be shut to the evidence bearing upon the laxity of the moral standards then in vogue. Mention has already been made of the readiness with which men resorted to the use of force for the protection of their rights, and we have seen that the condition of the law to a certain extent framed an excuse for this, since force may well become almost a legitimate course of action, however much its employment may be deprecated. In the present instance, at least, its use cannot be very strongly condemned because it is practically certain that other means of redress were as a rule absent during these times.

The more questionable use of fraud, however, was prevalent enough as well, and its frequent occurrence lends far greater weight to the disapproval of the morals of that day than can ever be fairly given by the fact that men were more liable then than now to use the strong hand when an opportunity offered itself. Men of the standing of the Cely family were ready enough for a little sharp practice in business. Richard Cely writes in 1482 to his brother George: "Syr, I hawhe sowlde Py; I kon not get for hym byt V marke on my fathe, and zehyt he that has hym thynkeys hymselfe full begyllyd." Evidently horse-dealing was as full of pitfalls for the uninitiated of that day as it ever has been since. In their business as wool-traders they were equally ready to deviate from the paths of honesty. In 1487, September 12, their papers admit a case of their changing samples of wool, and no doubt the irksomeness of the subsidy upon wool led them when possible to avoid its payment.

Bitter complaints are continually to be found in the *Cely Letters* about the piracy that was so rampant upon the Narrow Seas. (p. 351)

The ***Paston Letters*** afford abundant evidence of a similar system of fraud, especially in legal matters. Bribery was regarded as a course almost necessary. It might be and it was objected to strongly enough by those whose pockets had to suffer, but the objection was not based upon ideas of right and wrong, but rather upon the fact that a gift had to be forthcoming. Paston on one occasion was unsuccessful in his suit for "an especiall assise," and the reason given to him shows that, even in the highest places, hands were not always clean.

> It shuld not like my Lord Chauncellor to graunt assise for als moche as the Lord Moleyns hadde sore be laboured in his cuntre to pees and stille the people, there to restreyngne them from rysyng, and so he was dayly laboured there about in the Kyngg's grace, and that considered he trusted veryly that there shuld non assise be graunted to your entent.

Even if we grant that Moleyns did all that this credits him with—and such an admission would be a rather hazardous one, as Letter 66 gives a very different picture of this noble lord:

> Also the Lord Moleyns wrott in his forseyd letter that he wold mytyly with his body and with his godis stand be all tho that had ben his frends and his wel willers in the matter touching Gressam

—still the amplest consideration of his services to the King cannot be accepted as a ground for refusing Paston fair treatment. Moleyns as the apostle of peace cuts a sorry figure as "the seid Lord" who "sent to the seid mansion [Paston's house] a riotous people to the nombre of a thousand persones." My Lord may have "dayly laboured there about in the Kyngg's grace;" but what of Paston "not abille to sue the commone lawe in redressyng of this heynos wrong for the gret myght and alyaunce of the seid Lord"? Letter 155 contains another reference to him. "Also the Shereffe enformed us that he hath writyng from the King that he shall make such a panell to aquyte the Lord Moleynes." It would be impossible for even the most lenient to see the presence of a high moral ideal in a tangle like this. Scandals as serious are the property, no doubt, of every age, and an age cannot be condemned on the ground that such things have happened among its contemporaries. The evil lies more in the fact that these are not isolated cases, but in the present case of common occurrence. It will be remembered that, in the petition of the town of Swaffham against Sir Thomas Tudenham, "imbraceryes," or attempts to corrupt a jury, are specially mentioned as one of their main grievances.

Paston's disputes with his neighbours show us what means of retaliation were usually employed. Writing to the Sheriff of Norfolk in 1452, he says:

> Plese yow to wete that Charles Nowell with odir hath in this cuntre mad many riot and sautes; and among othir, he and V of his felachip set upon me and mo of my servants at the Cathedrall chirch of Norwich, he smyting at me, whilis on of his felawis held myn armes at my bak . . .

Such glimpses impel one to rate the moral standard of the latter half of the fifteenth century anything but highly.

From this standpoint, indeed, its chief characteristics seem to have been little charity for your neighbour, small consideration for your relations, much selfishness, a liberal use of brute force, and bribery and fraud where force was futile.

In summing up, the first conclusion arrived at in our reading is that the times of the Wars of the Roses illustrate in a significant way the principle that the social life of a people may not advance *pari passu* with their material welfare. That welfare has always, indeed, a strong bearing upon social advancement, but still it may, for short periods at least, exercise a comparatively small influence. Great difficulties and great temptations no doubt existed even in connection with purely material progress. Law gave little of that security which such advancement demands, and trade, though prospering, was still to a large extent something of a gamble, for great risk in trade as in other things fosters unscrupulousness. Change of tillage land to pasture land brought additional evils to the front. England was suffering from a time of transition, just such as she was again to endure when machinery ousted the labour of the hand. Partly from this also it was a period of extremes. As one writer has put it, "there were probably more paupers in proportion to the population, but there was certainly less poverty." It was, moreover, a time when monopoly began to take a firm hold over this country. The statutes regulating the policy of the crafts were invariably based on a system of protection. The evils of the truck system had become so glaring that even in the reign of Edward IV. an Act had been passed to check them. (pp. 352-54)

Notwithstanding these drawbacks, however, it cannot be said that the England of that day had deteriorated from a material point of view. The opinion, so frequently met with, that the Wars of the Roses produced no very serious effect upon national prosperity, must be taken with a very considerable amount of reservation. Hallam, in maintaining this view, says of the wars of York and Lancaster: "Some battles were doubtless sanguinary; but the loss of lives in battle is soon repaired by a flourishing nation; and the devastation occasioned by armies was both partial and transitory." The facts of the case, however, appear in a very different light in the ***Paston*** and *Cely Letters,* which perpetually reiterate the protest of the people against the disorder arising from the war. As a matter of fact, the Wars of the Roses may not have been so national as the civil war of the time of Charles I., but that does not clear them from having had a deterrent effect upon social progress at least, if not so much upon material advancement. The period was certainly not, as some writers hold, one of peaceful development notwithstanding these wars. Development there undoubtedly was, but it was strenuously and not always scrupulously fought for. Philip de Comines's opinion, that these civil wars were not of a kind to touch the domestic peace and prosperity of the nation, is contradicted in numerous instances in the most trustworthy documents that refer to and show us only too well what that domestic peace very often was. As has been said already, it was a time of extremes, and it has perhaps not unnaturally given rise to opinions that verge on the extreme. Malden, in his introduction to the *Cely Letters,* refers to "the often-repeated fiction that the Wars of the Roses were hurtful only to the nobility and their retainers," and from a social point of view this is undoubtedly the truth. From the standpoint of material welfare their effects were perhaps of less consequence than might be expected from the general character of such wars. On the whole, the last half of the fifteenth century, as it appears in the light of original authorities, shows too unmistakably as a period of transition, of extremes, of monopoly, and of war. It was a time when the letter of the law was greater than the spirit, and when even the letter was too often misread; a time when many could well have said what Stow wrote of Henry VI., that they "enjoyed as grate prosperitie as favourable fortune coulde afford, and as great troubles on the other side as shee frowning coulde poure out."

From the social point of view it was also a period of transition and of tentative efforts towards the attainment of a sound practical, but narrow code of social conduct. The possibilities that lay in the hands of the people were wider and more powerful than they could fully or most advantageously make use of, as wealth and material prosperity had outstripped social ideals, since the former are often mushroomlike in growth compared with the far slower evolution of the latter. The "rough plenty" that Rogers claims as characteristic of the time fell into the lap of a people insufficiently advanced as a society to adapt that plenty to the refinement of their lives as members of society. To the idealist in social reform, England then may be an object of scorn, with the selfishness of its aims, the unscrupulousness of its methods, and the poverty of their results. But grant this, and there is still left the fact that the men and women of that generation could show, in their life at home and in the street, a vigour that was the practical outcome of their hard surroundings, and exert a practical outlook upon all things that refused to be bounded by any utopianism. And in judging that life we must be careful not to read too many modern social ideas into it. For one thing, the claims of local life were far more exacting then than now, and so the home—the true test of the social life of a people—was to a great extent sacrificed. Living, not necessarily more immoral, was certainly coarser and more brutal, and the finer shades of social life were at most and only rarely found in individuals specially favoured by circumstance or exceptionally endowed by nature. No class, high or low, could as a class claim such a possession, for environment rendered such a condition of things wellnigh impossible.

Shrewdness paid better than brotherly love, and accordingly it was the common motive that dictated action in all matters—in law and marriage, in home and business life. Certain phases of our conduct, we flatter ourselves, have been raised into a higher plane and are governed by loftier and more disinterested motives now. Taken in a wide sense, this is no doubt true, but in one respect that period can hold its own, inasmuch as hypocrisy is largely absent from its social life. One of the most outstanding features both of the ***Paston*** and the *Cely Letters* is their naïve outspokenness, the frank recognition of their writers of themselves as they lived and moved among their fellows. There is no decadent note in their strenuous grip of life, albeit their grasp of circumstance was not elevated. Men's views

of duty were narrow from the fact that they were more frequently, or at least more powerfully, brought into contact with the elemental forces underlying social life. They had to face more lawless times than ours. Should we wonder, then, if they fought more bitterly? They experienced greater hardships all round. Should we be surprised, then, if finer sentiments did not flourish apace? They were ignorant of many of our advantages and privileges. They might beg a favour where we might be strong enough to demand a right. Should we therefore condemn their contentment with a smaller share of the highest enjoyments in life? They were the explorers of the possibilities of modern social progress. Can we call them to account for not leaving us more than a rough outline?

And this period has been a pitfall for many a worker. It has bred pessimists and optimists in turn. It has had its vehement partisans and its scornful detractors. It is questionable if it has ever been tenderly and temperately surveyed. Comparatively little is known of these years; documents are scantier than some earlier ages can show, and "Tout comprendre c'est tout pardonner." Perhaps no time in our history demands more fully the exercise of historic sympathy. Lack of this has led many into one or other of the opposing camps. The time may be at hand when the meliorist will have his turn, and when larger truth and keener insight will give those who care for such things a more kindly and judicious outlook upon times that could well be blamed for Mrs. Paston's bitter cry, "God for hys merci send us a good world," or that could drive Paston himself to moralise because "Fortune with hyr smylyng coutenens, strange of all our purpose, may mak a sodeyn change." (pp. 354-57)

> *Charles Menmuir, "The England of the Paston Letters," in* The Gentleman's Magazine, *Vol. 295, October, 1903, pp. 327-57.*

Richard Garnett   (essay date 1903)

[*Garnett was an English literary critic. In the following excerpt from a study first published in 1903, he evaluates the literary merit of the* Paston Letters.]

No other nation has anything to vie with ***The Paston Letters.*** They are a perfect exhibition how life went on throughout the greater part of the fifteenth century in an English family of condition living in a state of constant warfare with grasping neighbours, not the less deadly for being mainly waged upon paper and parchment. As this state of affairs resulted in great measure from the dislocation of society in times of civil strife, the correspondence affords indirectly a valuable picture of the fallen condition of the country under Henry VI. and during the Wars of the Roses; while, nevertheless, the fermentation of the new is as visible as the decay of the old. Feudalism is passing away, and we assist at the birth-throes of the modern State. The letters which portray this striking scene are in general written by persons of good education for their times, but of no enlargement of mind, or any conception that they are making and recording history. They are in general the members of the Paston family in Norfolk, their lawyers, stewards, retainers, and other persons brought into connection with them. The letters are in the main on business, though domestic news and expressions of affection or the reverse are not wanting. Their unexpected recovery near the close of the eighteenth century may be compared to that equally unexpected recovery of papyri which has of late thrown such light on the social condition of Egypt under the Ptolemies and the Romans. The effect in both instances resembles the sudden opening of a window in a dead wall. The papyri, however, from their brevity and their mutilated condition, afford mere glimpses in comparison with the flood of light which the Paston correspondence pours upon the circumstances of the time. (pp. 250-53)

There is no such testimony anywhere to the social condition of England, ere records had been multiplied by the art of printing, as is afforded by the Paston correspondence; and the constant encounter with interesting and graphic particulars renders it most attractive reading. Of strictly literary merit the letters have little; yet the clearness and propriety with which the writers, belonging to diverse ranks and orders of society, manage in general to convey their meaning, show that the education of the day was really good and thorough as far as it went. They are in harmony with the literary tendencies of their time in being entirely utilitarian. Nothing else, it may be said, could be expected from family letters written on matters of business, but the writers make us feel that their interests are limited to the ordinary affairs of life. Save for one book-bill, there is no hint of the existence of such a thing as literature; no vestige of admiration for natural beauty; stirring events are narrated with cold formality; the dramatic vicissitudes of the day awaken no emotion of loyalty; and of patriotism there is not a trace. Society, left to itself, would be entirely anarchical; fortunately, the need for some judicial system is recognised in theory; and even when the central authority is in abeyance the gradual softening of manners indisposes to open violence, and inclines men to avail themselves of the quirks and quillets of the law. Nothing seems more remarkable than the general acquaintance of the laity with legal phraseology and technicalities; men have not yet reached the stage when their rights are safe from lawless encroachment, but they are in a stage of development when these can be successfully defended by pen and ink. The general sordidness of the picture is in some measure relieved by the vigorous portraiture of the leading personages: the elder Sir John Paston, shrewd and hard; his gay and careless successor, intent on horse and hound; the grim veteran Fastolf, slowly sinking like a battered ship, but with colours flying to the last; Dame Margaret Paston, a thoroughly lovable person, with her wifely duty to her husband, and a solicitude for her son's interests which lends force to her frequent chidings. The following portion of one of her letters will show that the English gentry of the fifteenth century could express themselves on paper with no inconsiderable vigour:

> I would ye should purvey for yourself as hastily as ye may, and come home and take heed to your own and to mine, thereto, otherwise than ye have done before this, both for my profit and for yours, or else I shall purvey for myself otherwise

in haste, so that I trust shall be more ease and avail for me and none ease nor profit to you in time to come. I have little help nor comfort of you yet, God give me grace to have more hereafter. I would ye should assay whether it be more profitable for you to serve me than for to serve such masters as ye have served afore this; and, that ye find more profitable thereafter, do in time to come. Ye have assayed the world reasonably, ye shall know yourself better hereafter. I pray God we may be in quiet and in rest with our own from henceforth. My power is not so good as I would it were for your sake and other; and if it were, we should not long be in danger. God bring us out of it, who have you in his keeping. Written with unheartsease the Monday next after Relic Sunday, By your Mother.

(pp. 255-56)

Richard Garnett, "The Fifteenth Century," in English Literature, An Illustrated Record: From The Beginnings to the Age of Milton, *Vols. I & II by Richard Garnett and Edmund Gosse, The Macmillan Company, 1935, pp. 238-73.*

The Edinburgh Review   (essay date 1908)

[*In the following excerpt from an unsigned review, the critic explores such diverse aspects of the* Paston Letters *as spelling constructions, historical content, and the tone of the correspondence between individual members of the Paston family.*]

Of what Poppyland now is, hundreds of weary Londoners make proof every summer; of what it will be when that threatened infantry division of the German Army has landed on the stretch of coast between Cromer and Yarmouth, and marched to Norwich, living the while on the country, those will know who live to see it; of what it was in scarcely happier times four or five hundred years ago—before, during, or just after the Wars of the Roses—those may form a fairly adequate idea who take the trouble to read the interesting volumes [of the ***Paston Letters***]. They form a new, enlarged, and practically complete edition of a work, well known, indeed, to students of history, which has been before the public for upwards of a century, though we believe we are right in saying that far more people know it by name than by perusal, and are contented in their ignorance. If, in explaining to our readers what it is, we induce them to cultivate a direct acquaintance with it, we shall have established a claim on their gratitude which will not lightly be set aside; for though it differs from the celebrated Diary of Samuel Pepys in almost every possible respect, and particularly in the general gravity of its tone and the moral purity of its pages, there is no book in the language with which it can more fittingly be compared, as giving us a peep behind the scenes of the society of a bygone age. The book, however, is not a diary, and does not lay bare the workings of the writer's mind or his private cogitations. It had, in fact, many writers; for it is simply, as its title indicates, a collection of letters and papers—some of public, but more of personal or local interest, and many on business connected with landed property or law suits—as made in the fifteenth century by a Norfolk family, which took its name from the place of its origin, Paston, a village on the coast, a few miles to the south-east of Cromer. (p. 390)

We are led to believe that this habit of preserving letters, once established, became the custom of the family; but, if so, the greater part of the collection has been lost. Some fragments of it are in the British Museum, but do not offer much of interest, though a fairly connected series of letters dated about 1680—before and after—might repay a careful examination. During the Tudor period there is practically nothing, which is the more to be regretted as there were then members of the family of whose career we would gladly know more. (p. 392)

But of the great bulk of these historical treasures all trace seems to be lost. We are thus compelled to fall back on the proverb which tells us that the best way to get what we want is to want what we can get; and as we can get these and no more, for these we are duly grateful. . . . (p. 393)

We have already spoken of the letters as better known by hearsay than by reading, and we are quite sure that a great number of would-be readers are deterred by the marvellous and utterly irregular aggregations of vowels and consonants which stand for familiar words, and are made more marvellous still by the desire to represent them by modern type, which necessarily seems to stand for the modern sound. The Middle English q and   were gutturals, the sounds of which are quite lost in the modern 'q' and 'z,' and x, as an initial, is certainly more correctly represented by the modern 'sh,' as is well illustrated by the change of the Spanish Xeres into 'sherry.' No one will doubt the importance of the old spellings to lexicographers and phonologists, their interest as guides to the old pronunciation, of the value of such a work as that of Dr. Neumann [in his *Die Orthographie der Paston Letters von 1422-1461*, 1904] on the spelling of the vernacular, as distinct from the formal or literary medieval English, which Mr. Gairdner's editions of 1872 and 1900 have alone rendered possible. But that being now on record and available for the students of language, we would strongly assert the claims of literary and historical students, in favour not perhaps of a modern, but certainly of a systematised spelling.

Anyone who attempted this would be at first astonished to find how often the modern spelling appears. The most frequent form of the second personal pronoun is 'yow'; but 'you' is very common, more so than the more conspicuous zow, zou, zu, zw, yw, meaning, no doubt, to represent the same pronunciation, but which, as printed, represent nothing human. The first word in a majority of the letters is 'Right,' a word, too, that is very common throughout the text; and this, in a large majority of instances, is spelt in the modern way. Next to that in frequency is 'ryght,' which may almost be counted the same, and then follow— more noticeable by their eccentricity—ryt, ryte, ryth, rythe, rytht, rytz, rygth, rygh, and probably others, all presumably standing for the same pronunciation, and only showing that the writer's idea of the phonetic value of letters was extremely vague; just as, even now, men often write 'yatch' for 'yacht,' without any design of miscalling the word.

Prominent at the beginning of a great many letters is the word 'worshipful,' a very common form being 'Right worshipful and entirely well beloved—husband, mother, brother, cousin, friend, servant, sir,' &c., and the most frequent spelling of this word is 'worshipful.' But the misspellings are numerous and fantastic, without, apparently, changing the pronunciation. The o becomes e, u, ou, or y; the i becomes e, o, u, or y; an e sometimes follows the p; the u sometimes, but rarely, becomes w; occasionally there is a final e. Of the consonants, the s is sometimes doubled; sh becomes ch, sch, and, though rarely, tsh; the p is doubled; the final l is generally, but not always, doubled. It sometimes seems as if the length of the word was extended in compliment to the dignity of the person addressed, so that we find such a form as 'wourschippfull.' To follow out these and all other words in the numerous changes which ignorant writers could invent, or modern readers can imagine, appears to us not only a waste of labour on the part of transcriber, compositor, and editor, but—and to a still greater degree—on the part of the reader, with no commensurate advantage, or indeed, with no advantage at all; and we would suggest that in any future edition the labour of correcting the press to ensure the accuracy and completeness of this useless tangle, should be spent rather in collating the doubtful words, or in annotating their meaning.

For, after all, the main interest of these letters is not the linguistic but the human. They tell us how dukes and duchesses, nobility and gentry, and persons of lower estate—average men and women—wrote to and dealt with each other five hundred years ago. Of history, in the text-book acceptation of the word, they have very little, and that little, as published by Fenn, has been long since gleaned 'for the use of schools.' The Introductions to the several volumes, which Mr. Gairdner wrote for the 1872 edition of the *Paston Letters,* he amalgamated in 1900 into what was, in many respects, the best history we have of this troubled time; and so it remains, without any disparagement of the fuller *Lancaster and York,* by Sir James Ramsay, or the excellent volume contributed by Professor Oman to the *Political History of England,* now being edited by Dr. Hunt.

But, though the *Paston Letters* scarcely mention the parliaments and the battles which fill such a large space in our histories, they are everywhere aglow with the sentiment of the times; and reading in them of the impeachment of the Duke of Suffolk, the rising of Jack Cade, the insanity of the king and his blind confidence in the Duke of Somerset, the insults offered to the Duke of York and his charges against his enemies, the story acquires a living interest which no text-book has ever yet given it; we begin to know the men and their surroundings, to understand their motives and their actions. More than all, we find in them the system of maintenance in full force, and learn the meaning of that terrible scourge which, more than anything else, gave the Tudors their semi-despotic power; for, as it is said the old Roman put it—

> In seasons of great peril,
> 'Tis good that one bear sway.

The evil which Henry IV and Henry V had tried to amend,

which under Henry VI had completely taken charge, and which set Edward IV and Richard III at defiance, yielded to the absolute power entrusted for that purpose to Henry VII. And as no one who has not read the ***Paston Letters*** can fully realise the magnitude of this evil, so no one ignorant of them can quite understand the necessity for that century of arbitrary government. (pp. 396-99)

We have in the ***Paston Letters*** frequent, though vague, mention of parliament; there is nothing definite. For any record of its methods and actions we have to go elsewhere. But what we do get is a very clear light as to the manner of an election. Two centuries later, it was very much the custom, in the political controversies of the day, to refer to the power, liberties, and privileges of parliament under the House of Lancaster, and especially in the time of Henry VI. The stress so laid on these, the importance attached to the precedent has very naturally permitted our histories to speak of that as the golden age of parliamentary representation, of free election, untrammelled by the power of the land, as in the eighteenth century, or of the caucus, as in the nineteenth. But the golden age, like rainbow gold, is always afar, and the ***Paston Letters*** enable us to appreciate this boasted freedom with some exactness. The return was decided by an order from the noble who had, at the time, the chief power in the district; an order none the less peremptory because given with a certain pretence of option. We have, for instance, the letter written by the Duchess of Norfolk, in the name of the duke, on the general election of June 1455. It was addressed to John Paston, probably because he had been spoken of as a likely candidate:

> Right trusty and well-beloved, we greet you heartily well. And forasmuch as it is thought right necessary for divers causes that my Lord have at this time in the Parliament such persons as belong to him, and be of his menial servants, wherein we conceive your good will and diligence shall be right expedient, we heartily desire and pray you that at the contemplation of these our letters, as our special trust is in you, you will give and apply your voice to our right well-beloved cousin and servants, John Howard and Sir Roger Chamberlayn, to be knights of the shire, exhorting all such others as by your wisdom shall now be behoveful to the good exploit and conclusion of the same. And in your faithful attendance and true devoir in this party, you shall do unto my Lord and us a singular pleasure, and cause us hereafter to thank you therefore, so as you shall hold yourself right well content.

A letter such as this is worth many pages of explanation of the constitution of 'the Good Parliament' of 1376, of John of Gaunt's Parliament of 1377, of 'the Merciless Parliament' in 1388, of the Parliament of Shrewsbury in 1398, or in fact of any of the parliaments whose acts are written large in our constitutional histories.

But, quite independent of their direct historical value, these volumes have an interest peculiarly their own in the glimpses they give us of the family and social life of the period. Marriage, it is familiarly known, was more openly and avowedly a matter of business then than it is now, per-

haps because the choice lay more directly with the parents or guardians than with the young people, who were expected and not unfrequently compelled to accept the will of their elders. It was, perhaps, unusual for a young woman of the better sort to have any say in the matter; and very commonly her first interview with the prospective bridegroom was after the engagement was definitely concluded. We have a pretty illustration of this in a letter from Agnes Paston to her husband, the judge, describing the visit of Margaret Mautby, who, it had been arranged, was to marry their son John.

> 'Blessed be God,' she wrote, 'I send you good tidings of the coming and the bringing home of the gentlewoman you wot of from Redham this same night, according to appointment. . . . And as for the first acquaintance between John Paston and the said gentlewoman, she made him gentle cheer in gentle wise, and said he was verily your son; and so I hope there shall need no great treaty betwixt them. The parson of Stockton told me if you would buy her a gown, her mother would give thereto a goodly fur. The gown needeth for to be had; and for colour, it would be a goodly blue or else a bright sanguine.'

Rather brilliant for a young girl's wedding dress according to modern ideas! but Margaret's tastes, apparently, ran to bright colours; elsewhere she writes of a gown of scarlet as her special fancy. John Paston was at this time about nineteen; the bride's age is not mentioned; presumably she was a year or two younger; but the marriage was not long delayed, and she at once settled down as a help meet for her husband. Till his death, twenty-six years afterwards, she acted the part of a careful housewife, attending to his interests both at home and abroad. Fortunately for us, John Paston was a good deal away, and his wife had to send him frequent reports as to business matters, or to ask for instructions. Her letters were thus necessarily, in the first place, letters of business. And the same may be noticed of most of the letters; paper was scarce, probably costly, and writing was an expenditure of both time and labour; people, therefore, did not write letters unless they had something to say; and in private life that something was generally matter of business.

But it has often been said that the letters—not Margaret Paston's only, but generally—are noticeable for their hard tone, their want of sympathy and family affection. This seems a mistake, due partly to not considering the usage of the time, partly to a misapprehension of the language, or of the conditions under which the letters were written. The usage of the age: for our ancestors did not carry their hearts on their sleeves or let their affections habitually gush over; and in writing held to the opinion which Mr. Kipling has attributed to the pen of a modern Indian prince: 'Between brother and chosen brother be no long protestations of Love and Sincerity. Heart speaks naked to Heart and the Head answers for all' ["Many Inventions"]. The language: for the formal phraseology of the fifteenth century was as much a matter of convention as that of the twentieth; and 'Right worshipful and entirely well-beloved,' or 'Right reverend and worshipful Sir,' was the ordinary and recognised equivalent of the modern 'Dear Sir,' which no one understands as necessarily implying any over-bubbling affection. Margaret Paston usually began 'Right worshipful husband,' and to her son a very common form was 'I greet you well and send you God's blessing and mine,' which would seem to be more than a mere convention. The son's reply was 'Right worshipful mother, I commend me to you and beseech you of your blessing and God's.' And similar words, 'Right worshipful,' 'Right trusty,' 'Right reverend,' and such like, applied to ordinary business correspondents must be taken as meaning very much the same as 'Your obedient,' or 'Your obedient, humble servant,' at the foot of an official letter of the present day.

And, finally, the conditions: a great many of the letters of Agnes and Margaret Paston were written by a casual secretary; the editor has not distinguished them, and this could now only be done by reference to the originals; but it may, perhaps, be laid down that those ending 'By your wife,' or 'By your mother,' were not written by the person indicated. It is this which gives Margaret Paston's letters their curiously irregular spelling; they had many different writers; and, after personal examination, we are able to say that those which abound in   , q, and x are in a masculine hand. William Lomner seems to have been so much in the habit of writing for her, that on one occasion, writing in his own name to John Paston, he ended the letter—'By yowr wyfe. W. L.' However much the poor woman, separated from her husband, wanted to express her yearning she might well shrink from dictating it to her amanuensis for the time being.

But, as a matter of fact which seems to have been very generally overlooked, there is a good deal of warm affection expressed in many of the letters, both from mothers and wives, husbands, sons, and brothers; and that without counting the now well-known letter from the Duke of Suffolk to his seven-year-old son, the exact authenticity of which may be doubtful, and which, in any case, must have been written for effect rather than for the infant to whom it was addressed. As a letter from a mother to her son, now grown up, with the cares of a wife, family, and estate on his shoulders, and perhaps also, as Mr. Gairdner suggests, some unnamed trouble, this seems to us to tell of the best type of affection. We give it verbatim, as illustrating the form as well as the matter:

> Son, I greet you well, and let you wit that forasmuch as your brother Clement letteth me wit that ye desire faithfully my blessing—that blessing that I prayed your father to give you the last day that ever he spake, and the blessing of all saints under heaven and mine might come to you all days and times; and think verily none other but that ye have it, and shall have it, with that that I find you kind and willing to the weal of your father's soul and to the welfare of your brethren. By my counsel dispose yourself as much as ye may to have less to do in the world. Your father said, In little business lieth much rest. This world is but a thoroughfare and full of woe; and when we depart therefrom, right naught bear with us but our good deeds and ill. And there knoweth no man how soon God will clepe him and therefore it is good for every creature to be ready. Whom God visiteth him he lo-

veth. And as for your brethren, they will, I know, certainly labour all that in them lieth for you. Our Lord have you in his blessed keeping, body and soul. By your mother, A. P.

Many of Margaret Paston's letters are touching in their yearning for her husband's home coming implied more frequently than directly expressed, but written plainly enough for any loving reader; and even her hard and prosaic husband occasionally breaks out with 'My own dear sovereign lady,' and ends with 'By your true and trusty husband, J. P.' Similarly, when Margery Paston wrote to her husband, the youngest John—'Myne owyn swete hert. . . . I mervell sore that I have no letter from you, but I prey God preserve you, and send me good tydinges from you and spede you well in your materes. . . . I have gotyn me another logyn felawe, the ferst letter of hyr name is Mastras Byschoppe'; it is difficult to see how a modern wife could write more tenderly or wind up with a little joke more up to date. But all Margery's letters are curiously modern in tone; her marriage, too, though arranged by her father, Sir Thomas Brews, on strictly business principles, seems to have been, on her part, a veritable love match. (pp. 405-10)

It would be easy to go on calling attention to points of interest; but there are six volumes, they are all interesting, and they cannot all be shot into the pages of the *Edinburgh Review;* so it is necessary to stop, with a recommendation to our readers to follow up the trail on which we have started them. And they need not fear. A very little perseverance will overcome the difficulties of the language, which are largely artificial, by reason of the irregular and often eccentric spelling, and will vanish in reading aloud. Once past these, it is astonishing how very modern are many of the ideas and even of the expressions, verging some of them on slang. (p. 412)

There is one thing further. It has been said by captious critics that the letters are coarse and often indecent: a most unjust charge, which can only mean—so far as it has any meaning at all—that some items of news are told with a directness which does not accord with modern usage. It was the custom for a man to say what he had to say, and in the simplest manner. If he wished to say that a woman named was 'with child,' he did not think it necessary to veil the fact in French, or to describe it as 'interesting.' It is not so now, but that does not make the old custom, in itself, coarse or indecent. And even so, the only letters that could be objected to for some such reason are some three or four—out of more than a thousand—between brothers—William and John, or the two younger Johns; and we may doubt if the letters of two brothers or two intimate friends at the present day are always more delicately worded. A fairly exhaustive study of the volumes permits us to say that there is not a line in them that savours of uncleanness; and that is far more than can be said of a majority of the novels which are every day freely circulated from the libraries. (p. 412)

"The Paston Letters," in The Edinburgh Review, *Vol. CCVII, No. CCCXXVI, October, 1908, pp. 390-412.*

Alice D. Greenwood   (essay date 1908)

[*In the excerpt below, Greenwood provides a concise introduction to several features of the* Paston Letters.]

The famous collection of letters and business papers preserved by the Pastons furnishes a detailed picture of three generations of a well-to-do Norfolk family, their friends and enemies, their dependents and noble patrons. At first John Paston and his devoted wife Margaret, afterwards their sons, are the leading correspondents, and the cares of property form the topic. John Paston inherited from his father, a worthy judge, considerable estates and was ambitious of acquiring more; but the cupidity of the nobles of the district kept him in continual difficulties. The old judge used to say that "whosoever should dwell at Paston should have need to know how to defend himself," and had placed his sons to study at the inns of court, since the only help against violence lay in the intricacies of the law, with which every age, class and sex was acquainted. The letters, accordingly, trace the endeavours of John Paston, and, after him, of his sons, to form such a combination of royal favour, local intrigue and bribery as to procure effective legal protection against those who seized their manors by armed force. This main thread of interest is interwoven with every sort of business. We should scarcely gather that the crown of England lay in the scales of civil war. What the correspondence reveals is a state of anarchy in which jurymen are terrorised, gentlemen of repute waylaid by ruffians after church or market, or even dragged from the Christmas dinner at home to be murdered by the wayside; when a sheriff professedly friendly dare not accept a bribe, because he cannot safely take more than £100 (*i.e.* over £1000 present value) and lord Moleynes (Paston's foe) is a great lord who can do him more harm than that; when the duke of Suffolk's retainers attack dame Margaret in her husband's house with bows and handguns, pans of fire and scaling ladders, break in the gates, undermine the house-front, cut asunder the great timbers and carry the courageous woman forth to watch them destroy it.

In the midst of such turmoil, business is conducted regularly. We see the squires and their stewards incessantly riding to and fro, letting farms and holding manor courts, attending markets or elections at Norwich, trying to curry favour at the court of the duke of Norfolk, complimenting the duchess or giving her waiting-woman a jewel, above all visiting London, where lawyers may be found and, possibly, the appointment of sheriff or under-sheriff manipulated. Letters come by messengers, with plate and money concealed in parcels; sometimes tokens are mentioned, for a seal might be stolen—"by the token that my mother hath the key but it is broken." Countless commissions are given for grocery or dress. Treacle "of Genoa" is sought whenever sickness is rife, cinnamon and sugar, dates and raisins, "of Coruns" must be priced to see if they be "better cheap" than in Norwich. If Paston once orders a doublet "all of worsted for the honour of Norfolk"—"which is almost like silk"—his wife prays that he will do his cost on her to get something for her neck, for she had to borrow her cousin's device to visit the queen among such fresh gentlewomen, "I durst not for shame go with my beds."

The family acts together, like a firm, against the rest of the world; husband and wife are working partners, mother and brothers can be counted on to take trouble; the confidential servants are staunch, and not one seems to have betrayed his master, though gratitude is not a marked trait of the next generation. Nor does it seem surprising that the daughter, Margery, neglected as her upbringing had been—Paston had grudged outlay on his elder children—should have fallen in love with the steward, Richard Calle, and, after two years of home persecution, insisted that she had betrothed herself to him and would marry him—"to sell kandyll and mustard in Framlyngham," as her angry brother cried. Her mother immediately turned her out of the house and left her to the reluctant charity of a stranger. Every relationship of life, indeed, was of the commercial nature: marriages were bargains, often driven by the parents without intervention of the persons concerned, as had been the case with John and Margaret. The wardship of children was purchased, as a speculation. "There is a widow fallen," writes one brother to another, or, "I heard where was a goodly young woman to marry . . . which shall have £200," or, "Whether her mother will deal with me." Paston's hard old mother, dame Agnes, sends to ask at the inns of court if her son Clement "Hath do his dever in lernyng," and, if not, to pray his tutor to "trewly belassch hym tyl he will amend, and so did the last maystr and the best that evir he had, att Caumbrege." The tutor's fee was to be ten marks. Several of the lads went to Cambridge, one to Oxford and one to Eton, where he stayed till he was nineteen; the inns of court came later, for some at least; then, one was placed in the household of the duke of Norfolk for a time, and another remained long in the service of the earl of Oxford, the one courteous nobleman of this correspondence.

Daughters were merely encumbrances, difficult to marry with little dowry, expensive to bring up in the correct way by boarding with a gentle family. Keeping them at home was a disagreeable economy. Dame Agnes so maltreated her daughter Elizabeth, beating her several times a week, and even twice in a day, forbidding her to speak to anyone, and taunting her, that her sister-in-law besought Paston to find her a husband. "My moder . . .wold never so fayn to have be delyvered of her as she woll now." Parental authority was so unquestioned that, years after Paston's death, his sons, grown men, and one, at least, married, were boarding with their mother and treated like children. Dame Margaret leaned on her chaplain, one James Gloys, and quarrels were picked to get John and Edmund out of the house. "We go not to bed unchidden lightly." "Sir James and I be tweyn. We fyll owt be for my modyr with 'thow proud prest' and 'thow proud sqwyer.' " The priest was always "chopping" at him provokingly, but "when he hathe most unfyttynge wordys to me I smylle a lytyll and tell hym it is good heryng of these old talys." Thus (1472) writes John, a husband and father, to his elder brother, also named John, a young knight about court in London.

With this younger generation a rather lighter tone becomes apparent in the letters. Sir John was of a somewhat shallow and unpractical character, his brother a man of high spirits and good temper; and it would seem as if after Towton field, the dead weight of terrorism had begun to lighten. The decade after 1461 was less anarchical than that which preceded it, and the young men sometimes have leisure for slighter concerns than sales and debts, lawsuits and marriage bargains. Sir John took an interest in books, his brother in hawking, and he merrily threatens his elder "to call upon yow owyrly, nyghtly, dayly, dyner, soper, for thys hawk," which he suggests might be purchased of a certain grocer "dwelling right over against the well with 2 buckets" near St. Helen's. When Sir John at length sends a poor bird, it is with admirable temper that the disappointed brother thanks him for his "dylygence and cost . . . well I wot your labore and trowbyll was as myche as thow she had ben the best of the world, but . . . she shall never serve but to lay eggys." Sir John had a better taste in the points, laces and hats about which his brothers and he were so particular. Their friendliness is the most amiable thing in the letters. The one sign of parental affection in them comes from the younger John, who was sent in the princess Margaret's train (1468) to the court of Charles the Bold. ("I hert never of non lyek to it save Kyng Artourys cort.") He is anxious about his "lytell Jak" and writes home "modyr I beseche yow that ye wolbe good mastras to my lytell man and to se that he go to scole." Humour was, apparently, invented in London, for the brothers and their town friends have many a jest, crude as these often are. Sometimes we have a touch of slang—"He wolde bear the cup evyn, as What-calle-ye-hym seyde to Aslake" (*i.e.* be fair). "Put in hope of the moon schone in the water." If the tailor will not furnish a certain gown, "be cryst, calkestowe over hys hed (? a double caul) that is schoryle (churl) in Englysche, yt is a terme newe browthe up with my marschandis of Norwych," says John the younger, who addresses his knightly brother as "lansmann" and "mynher," and jests on having nearly "drownke to myn oysters," *i.e.* been murdered. Many a good colloquial expression never found its way into literature; "to bear him on hand" is common for "to accuse"; "cup-shotten," "shuttle-witted" are good terms. (pp. 346-49)

> *Alice D. Greenwood, "English Prose in the Fifteenth Century," in* The Cambridge History of English Literature: The End of the Middle Ages, *Vol. II, edited by A. W. Ward and A. R. Waller, G. P. Putnam's Sons, 1908, pp. 326-52.*

Virginia Woolf (essay date 1925)

[*An English novelist, essayist, and short story writer, Woolf is considered one of the most prominent literary figures of twentieth-century English literature. A discerning and influential critic, Woolf began writing reviews for the* Times Literary Supplement *at an early age. Her critical essays cover almost the entire range of English literature and contain some of her finest prose. In the excerpt below, first published in her* The Common Reader (1925), *Woolf imaginatively reconstructs the passions and struggles of the people who composed the* Paston Letters.]

The tower of Caister Castle still rises ninety feet into the air, and the arch still stands from which Sir John Fastolf 's

barges sailed out to fetch stone for the building of the great castle. But now jacksaws nest on the tower, and of the castle, which once covered six acres of ground, only ruined walls remain, pierced by loopholes and surmounted by battlements, though there are neither archers within nor cannon without. As for the 'seven religious men' and the 'seven poor folk' who should, at this very moment, be praying for the souls of Sir John and his parents, there is no sign of them nor sound of their prayers. The place is a ruin. Antiquaries speculate and differ.

Not so very far off lie more ruins—the ruins of Bromholm Priory, where John Paston was buried, naturally enough, since his house was only a mile or so away, lying on low ground by the sea, twenty miles north of Norwich. The coast is dangerous, and the land, even in our time, inaccessible. Nevertheless, the little bit of wood at Bromholm, the fragment of the true Cross, brought pilgrims incessantly to the Priory, and sent them away with eyes opened and limbs straightened. But some of them with their newly-opened eyes saw a sight which shocked them—the grave of John Paston in Bromholm Priory without a tombstone. The news spread over the countryside. The Pastons had fallen; they that had been so powerful could no longer afford a stone to put above John Paston's head. Margaret, his widow, could not pay her debts; the eldest son, Sir John, wasted his property upon women and tournaments, while the younger, John also, though a man of greater parts, thought more of his hawks than of his harvests.

The pilgrims of course were liars, as people whose eyes have just been opened by a piece of the true Cross have every right to be; but their news, none the less, was welcome. The Pastons had risen in the world. People said even that they had been bondmen not so very long ago. At any rate, men still living could remember John's grandfather Clement tilling his own land, a hard-working peasant; and William, Clement's son, becoming a judge and buying land; and John, William's son, marrying well and buying more land and quite lately inheriting the vast new castle at Caister, and all Sir John's lands in Norfolk and Suffolk. People said that he had forged the old knight's will. What wonder, then, that he lacked a tombstone? But, if we consider the character of Sir John Paston, John's eldest son, and his upbringing and his surroundings, and the relations between himself and his father as the family letters reveal them, we shall see how difficult it was, and how likely to be neglected—this business of making his father's tombstone. (pp. 1-2)

The gigantic structure of Caister Castle was in progress not so many miles away when the little Pastons were children. John Paston, the father, had charge of some part of the business, and the children listened, as soon as they could listen at all, to talk of stone and building, of barges gone to London and not yet returned, of the twenty-six private chambers, of the hall and chapel; of foundations, measurements, and rascally work-people. Later, in 1454, when the work was finished and Sir John had come to spend his last years at Caister, they may have seen for themselves the mass of treasure that was stored there; the tables laden with gold and silver plate; the wardrobes stuffed with gowns of velvet and satin and cloth of gold, with hoods and tippets and beaver hats and leather jackets and velvet doublets; and how the very pillow-cases on the beds were of green and purple silk. There were tapestries everywhere. The beds were laid and the bedrooms hung with tapestries representing sieges, hunting and hawking, men fishing, archers shooting, ladies playing on their harps, dallying with ducks, or a giant 'bearing the leg of a bear in his hand'. Such were the fruits of a well-spent life. To buy land, to build great houses, to stuff these houses full of gold and silver plate (though the privy might well be in the bedroom), was the proper aim of mankind. Mr. and Mrs. Paston spent the greater part of their energies in the same exhausting occupation. For since the passion to acquire was universal, one could never rest secure in one's possessions for long. The outlying parts of one's property were in perpetual jeopardy. The Duke of Norfolk might covet this manor, the Duke of Suffolk that. Some trumped-up excuse, as for instance that the Pastons were bondmen, gave them the right to seize the house and batter down the lodges in the owner's absence. And how could the owner of Paston and Mauteby and Drayton and Gresham be in five or six places at once, especially now that Caister Castle was his, and he must be in London trying to get his rights recognized by the King? The King was mad too, they said; did not know his own child, they said; or the King was in flight; or there was civil war in the land. Norfolk was always the most distressed of counties and its country gentlemen the most quarrelsome of mankind. Indeed, had Mrs. Paston chosen, she could have told her children how when she was a young woman a thousand men with bows and arrows and pans of burning fire had marched upon Gresham and broken the gates and mined the walls of the room where she sat alone. But much worse things than that happened to women. She neither bewailed her lot nor thought herself a heroine. The long, long letters which she wrote so laboriously in her clear cramped hand to her husband, who was (as usual) away, make no mention of herself. The sheep had wasted the hay. Heyden's and Tuddenham's men were out. A dyke had been broken and a bullock stolen. They needed treacle badly, and really she must have stuff for a dress.

But Mrs. Paston did not talk about herself.

Thus the little Pastons would see their mother writing or dictating page after page, hour after hour, long long letters, but to interrupt a parent who writes so laboriously of such important matters would have been a sin. The prattle of children, the lore of the nursery or schoolroom, did not find its way into these elaborate communications. For the most part her letters are the letters of an honest bailiff to his master, explaining, asking advice, giving news, rendering accounts. There was robbery and manslaughter; it was difficult to get in the rents; Richard Calle had gathered but little money; and what with one thing and another Margaret had not had time to make out, as she should have done, the inventory of the goods which her husband desired. Well might old Agnes, surveying her son's affairs rather grimly from a distance, counsel him to contrive it so that 'ye may have less to do in the world; your father said, In little business lieth much rest. This world is but a thoroughfare, and full of woe; and when we

depart therefrom, right nought bear with us but our good deeds and ill.'

The thought of death would thus come upon them in a clap. Old Fastolf, cumbered with wealth and property, had his vision at the end of Hell fire, and shrieked aloud to his executors to distribute alms, and see that prayers were said 'in perpetuum', so that his soul might escape the agonies of purgatory. William Paston, the judge, was urgent too that the monks of Norwich should be retained to pray for his soul 'for ever'. The soul was no wisp of air, but a solid body capable of eternal suffering, and the fire that destroyed it was as fierce as any that burnt on mortal grates. For ever there would be monks and the town of Norwich, and for ever the Chapel of Our Lady in the town of Norwich. There was something matter-of-fact, positive, and enduring in their conception both of life and of death.

With the plan of existence so vigorously marked out, children of course were well beaten, and boys and girls taught to know their places. They must acquire land; but they must obey their parents. A mother would clout her daughter's head three times a week and break the skin if she did not conform to the laws of behaviour. Agnes Paston, a lady of birth and breeding, beat her daughter Elizabeth. Margaret Paston, a softer-hearted woman, turned her daughter out of the house for loving the honest bailiff Richard Calle. Brothers would not suffer their sisters to marry beneath them, and 'sell candle and mustard in Framlingham'. The fathers quarrelled with the sons, and the mothers, fonder of their boys than of their girls, yet bound by all law and custom to obey their husbands, were torn asunder in their efforts to keep the peace. With all her pains, Margaret failed to prevent rash acts on the part of her eldest son John, or the bitter words with which his father denounced him. He was a 'drone among bees', the father burst out, 'which labour for gathering honey in the fields, and the drone doth naught but taketh his part of it'. He treated his parents with insolence, and yet was fit for no charge of responsibility abroad.

But the quarrel was ended, very shortly, by the death (22nd May 1466) of John Paston, the father, in London. The body was brought down to Bromholm to be buried. Twelve poor men trudged all the way bearing torches beside it. Alms were distributed; masses and dirges were said. Bells were rung. Great quantities of fowls, sheep, pigs, eggs, bread, and cream were devoured, ale and wine drunk, and candles burnt. Two panes were taken from the church windows to let out the reek of the torches. Black cloth was distributed, and a light set burning on the grave. But John Paston, the heir, delayed to make his father's tombstone.

He was a young man, something over twenty-four years of age. The discipline and the drudgery of a country life bored him. When he ran away from home, it was, apparently, to attempt to enter the King's household. Whatever doubts, indeed, might be cast by their enemies on the blood of the Pastons, Sir John was unmistakably a gentleman. He had inherited his lands; the honey was his that the bees had gathered with so much labour. He had the instincts of enjoyment rather than of acquisition, and with his mother's parsimony was strangely mixed something of his father's ambition. Yet his own indolent and luxurious temperament took the edge from both. He was attractive to women, liked society and tournaments, and court life and making bets, and sometimes, even, reading books. And so life now that John Paston was buried started afresh upon rather a different foundation. There could be little outward change indeed. Margaret still ruled the house. She still ordered the lives of the younger children as she had ordered the lives of the elder. The boys still needed to be beaten into book-learning by their tutors, the girls still loved the wrong men and must be married to the right. Rents had to be collected; the interminable lawsuit for the Fastolf property dragged on. Battles were fought; the roses of York and Lancaster alternately faded and flourished. Norfolk was full of poor people seeking redress for their grievances, and Margaret worked for her son as she had worked for her husband, with this significant change only, that now, instead of confiding in her husband, she took the advice of her priest.

But inwardly there was a change. It seems at last as if the hard outer shell had served its purpose and something sensitive, appreciative, and pleasure-loving had formed within. At any rate Sir John, writing to his brother John at home, strayed sometimes from the business on hand to crack a joke, to send a piece of gossip, or to instruct him, knowingly and even subtly, upon the conduct of a love affair. Be 'as lowly to the mother as ye list, but to the maid not too lowly, nor that ye be too glad to speed, nor too sorry to fail. And I shall always be your herald both here, if she come hither, and at home, when I come home, which I hope hastily within XI. days at the furthest.' And then a hawk was to be bought, a hat, or new silk laces sent down to John in Norfolk, prosecuting his suit, flying his hawks, and attending with considerable energy and not too nice a sense of honesty to the affairs of the Paston estates.

The lights had long since burnt out on John Paston's grave. But still Sir John delayed; no tomb replaced them. He had his excuses; what with the business of the lawsuit, and his duties at Court, and the disturbance of the civil wars, his time was occupied and his money spent. But perhaps something strange had happened to Sir John himself, and not only to Sir John dallying in London, but to his sister Margery falling in love with the bailiff, and to Walter making Latin verses at Eton, and to John flying his hawks at Paston. Life was a little more various in its pleasures. They were not quite so sure as the elder generation had been of the rights of man and of the dues of God, of the horrors of death, and of the importance of tombstones. Poor Margaret Paston scented the change and sought uneasily, with the pen which had marched so stiffly through so many pages, to lay bare the root of her troubles. It was not that the lawsuit saddened her; she was ready to defend Caister with her own hands if need be, 'though I cannot well guide nor rule soldiers', but there was something wrong with the family since the death of her husband and master. Perhaps her son had failed in his service to God; he had been too proud or too lavish in his expenditure; or perhaps he had shown too little mercy to the poor. Whatever the fault might be, she only knew that Sir John spent twice as much money as his father for less result; that they

could scarcely pay their debts without selling land, wood, or household stuff ('It is a death to me to think of it'); while every day people spoke ill of them in the country because they left John Paston to lie without a tombstone. The money that might have bought it, or more land, and more goblets and more tapestry, was spent by Sir John on clocks and trinkets, and upon paying a clerk to copy out Treaties upon Knighthood and other such stuff. There they stood at Paston—eleven volumes, with the poems of Lydgate and Chaucer among them, diffusing a strange air into the gaunt, comfortless house, inviting men to indolence and vanity, distracting their thoughts from business, and leading them not only to neglect their own profit but to think lightly of the sacred dues of the dead.

For sometimes, instead of riding off on his horse to inspect his crops or bargain with his tenants, Sir John would sit, in broad daylight, reading. There, on the hard chair in the comfortless room with the wind lifting the carpet and the smoke stinging his eyes, he would sit reading Chaucer, wasting his time, dreaming—or what strange intoxication was it that he drew from books? Life was rough, cheerless, and disappointing. A whole year of days would pass fruitlessly in dreary business, like dashes of rain on the window-pane. There was no reason in it as there had been for his father; no imperative need to establish a family and acquire an important position for children who were not born, or if born, had no right to bear their father's name. But Lydgate's poems or Chaucer's, like a mirror in which figures move brightly, silently, and compactly, showed him the very skies, fields, and people whom he knew, but rounded and complete. Instead of waiting listlessly for news from London or piecing out from his mother's gossip some country tragedy of love and jealousy, here, in a few pages, the whole story was laid before him. And then as he rode or sat at the table he would remember some description or saying which bore upon the present moment and fixed it, or some string of words would charm him, and putting aside the pressure of the moment, he would hasten home to sit in his chair and learn the end of the story. (pp. 3-8)

So Sir John read his Chaucer in the comfortless room with the wind blowing and the smoke stinging, and left his father's tombstone unmade. But no book, no tomb, had power to hold him long. He was one of those ambiguous characters who haunt the boundary line where one age merges in another and are not able to inhabit either. At one moment he was all for buying books cheap; next he was off to France and told his mother, 'My mind is now not most upon books.' In his own house, where his mother Margaret was perpetually making out inventories or confiding in Gloys the priest, he had no peace or comfort. There was always reason on her side; she was a brave woman for whose sake one must put up with the priest's insolence and choke down one's rage when the grumbling broke into open abuse, and 'Thou proud priest' and 'Thou proud Squire' were bandied angrily about the room. All this, with the discomforts of life and the weakness of his own character, drove him to loiter in pleasanter places, to put off coming, to put off writing, to put off, year after year, the making of his father's tombstone.

Yet John Paston had now lain for twelve years under the bare ground. The Prior of Bromholm sent word that the grave-cloth was in tatters, and he had tried to patch it himself. Worse still, for a proud woman like Margaret Paston, the country people murmured at the Pastons' lack of piety, and other families she heard, of no greater standing than theirs, spent money in pious restoration in the very church where her husband lay unremembered. At last, turning from tournaments and Chaucer and Mistress Anne Hault, Sir John bethought him of a piece of cloth of gold which had been used to cover his father's hearse and might now be sold to defray the expenses of his tomb. Margaret had it in safe keeping; she had hoarded it and cared for it, and spent twenty marks on its repair. She grudged it; but there was no help for it. She sent it him, still distrusting his intentions or his power to put them into effect. 'If you sell it to any other use,' she wrote, 'by my troth I shall never trust you while I live.'

But this final act, like so many that Sir John had undertaken in the course of his life, was left undone. A dispute with the Duke of Suffolk in the year 1479 made it necessary for him to visit London in spite of the epidemic of sickness that was abroad; and there, in dirty lodgings, alone, busy to the end with quarrels, clamorous to the end for money, Sir John died and was buried at Whitefriars in London. He left a natural daughter; he left a considerable number of books; but his father's tomb was still unmade.

The four thick volumes of the *Paston Letters,* however, swallow up this frustrated man as the sea absorbs a raindrop. For, like all collections of letters, they seem to hint that we need not care overmuch for the fortunes of individuals. The family will go on, whether Sir John lives or dies. It is their method to help up in mounds of insignificant and often dismal dust the innumerable trivialities of daily life, as it grinds itself out, year after year. And then suddenly they blaze up; the day shines out, complete, alive, before our eyes. It is early morning, and strange men have been whispering among the women as they milk. It is evening, and there in the churchyard Warne's wife bursts out against old Agnes Paston: "All the devils of Hell draw her soul to Hell.' Now it is the autumn in Norfolk, and Cecily Dawne comes whining to Sir John for clothing. "Moreover, Sir, liketh it your mastership to understand that winter and cold weather draweth nigh and I have few clothes but of your gift.' There is the ancient day, spread out before us, hour by hour.

But in all this there is no writing for writing's sake; no use of the pen to convey pleasure or amusement or any of the million shades of endearment and intimacy which have filled so many English letters since. Only occasionally, under stress of anger for the most part, does Margaret Paston quicken into some shrewd saw or solemn curse. 'Men cut large thongs here out of other men's leather. . . . We beat the bushes and other men have the birds. . . . Haste reweth . . . which is to my heart a very spear.' That is her eloquence and that her anguish. Her sons, it is true, bend their pens more easily to their will. They jest rather stiffly; they hint rather clumsily; they make a little scene like a rough puppet show of the old priest's anger and give a phrase or two directly as they were spoken in person. But

when Chaucer lived he must have heard this very language, matter of fact, unmetaphorical, far better fitted for narrative than for analysis, capable of religious solemnity or of broad humour, but very stiff material to put on the lips of men and women accosting each other face to face. In short, it is easy to see, from the *Paston Letters,* why Chaucer wrote not *Lear* or *Romeo and Juliet,* but the *Canterbury Tales.*

Sir John was buried; and John the younger brother succeeded in his turn. The *Paston Letters* go on; life at Paston continues much the same as before. Over it all broods a sense of discomfort and nakedness; of unwashed limbs thrust into splendid clothing; of tapestry blowing on the draughty walls; of the bedroom with its privy; of winds sweeping straight over land unmitigated by hedge or town; of Caister Castle covering with solid stone six acres of ground, and of the plain-faced Pastons indefatigably accumulating wealth, treading out the roads of Norfolk, and persisting with an obstinate courage which does them infinite credit in furnishing the bareness of England. (pp. 15-17)

> *Virginia Woolf, "The Pastons and Chaucer,"
> in her* Collected Essays, *Vol. 3,* The Hogarth
> Press, *1967, pp. 1-17.*

Norman Davis   (lecture date 1954)

[*Davis, edited the Oxford editions of the* Paston Letters *(1958, 1971, 1976). In the excerpt below from a lecture delivered to the British Academy on 19 May 1954, he examines "some features of the language of the Paston family."*]

In the prologue to his translation of the *Eneydos,* printed in 1490, William Caxton wrote these familiar words: 'And certaynly our langage now vsed varyeth ferre from that whiche was vsed and spoken when I was borne.' It was the shifting currency of words that impressed him most: 'And thus bytwene playn, rude, and curyous, I stande abasshed; but in my iudgemente the comyn termes that be dayli vsed ben lyghter to be vnderstonde than the olde and auncyent Englysshe.' But he must have noticed also movements in pronunciation, in the spellings that represented it—for his treatment of which he has sometimes been unjustly censured—and in some of the few remaining inflexions. We know, in a general way, the directions in which these features of English were changing during the fifteenth century; but there is a great deal still to be learnt, by close study of dated and localized texts, about the speed and the distribution of the changes. How might the usage of each new generation differ from that of the earlier? How far could the language of a single individual develop during his adult life? How much might members of the same community differ from one another in the details of language? What was the 'social status' of particular forms of speech at different periods within the century?

It is with Caxton's words in mind—and so from a point of view a little different from that of earlier studies—that I wish to begin by examining briefly some features of the language of the Paston family as we find it in their surviving letters. The great collection of *Paston Letters* includes over 400 letters and memoranda written by or for members of the family, of which the earliest autograph document is credibly dated 1425, and the latest 1503. The collection thus covers a span a little longer than Caxton's life (c. 1422-91), and almost identical with it. The letters are good evidence, for we know something of most of the writers, and the dates can usually be fixed within at any rate a year or two. Many of them are informal, written to other members of the family on current business, so that they seldom pretend to grace of style or originality of thought. Apart from the conventional opening and closing phrases, and many obvious echoes of legal phraseology, they must often present an only slightly formalized version of the speech of the writers. They are therefore a much better guide to the real state of the spoken language than any literary work, conscious of tradition and seeking special effects, can ever be.

Only about half of the letters are in the handwriting of the authors. The earliest group of autograph letters, a small one, was written by William Paston of Paston in Norfolk, who lived from 1378 to 1444, and was a justice of the Common Pleas from 1429. He was survived by four sons, John, Edmond, William, and Clement, born in 1421, 1425, 1436, and 1442, letters from each of whom are extant. The judge's earliest letter is of 1425, his latest of 1442; the earliest of the new generation, a single letter written by Edmond, probably of 1447, so that the gap is only of some five years. Over thirty years pass before the last letter of the second generation, by William, in 1480. John, the judge's eldest son and heir, lived until 1466 and had five sons from whom letters survive: two named John, born in 1442 and apparently 1444, Edmond, Walter, and William, born in 1459. This is by far the best represented of all the generations that appear in the collection. There is no gap between it and the earlier generation: indeed, the two younger Johns' letters, beginning in 1461, overlap their father's by several years and their uncle William's by many years. The latest letter, written by the youngest John, is apparently of 1503. This John, who fell heir to his brother in 1479, had a son William, the fourth of that name, who is represented by only one short letter, of about 1495. Thus four generations of Pastons—though only three at adequate length—exhibit, in their own handwriting, the current usages of epistolary English.

And these are only the men. Three generations of women also appear: Agnes, wife of the judge; Margaret, wife of the first John, and Elizabeth, his sister; and Margery, wife of the third John. Some of the women's letters are among the most interesting and important of all, but they do not give as precise linguistic evidence as the men's; for it does not appear that any of them are autograph. Agnes must have employed several clerks: six of her seventeen letters are in one hand, two in another, and the rest in eight or nine more. Margaret's 104 letters are in an extraordinary variety of hands, some found in as many as twenty letters, many in only one. Margery's six are in four different hands; and Elizabeth's two are in different hands. It does not seem possible to prove that no single one of the hands that appear in the letters of Agnes or of Margaret is that of the author of the letter, though many of them can be identified; but neither is it possible to prove that any one

of them *is* that of the author. Certainly no considerable group can be shown to be autograph. The fact that both women employed so many clerks suggests that they could not write themselves, or at any rate did not find writing easy and did not like it. Margaret could perhaps read; but *schewe* in her son Sir John's injunction to his brother, 'I praye yow schewe ore rede to my moodre suche thynge as ye thynke is fore here to know' (1470) may mean only 'make known' (*O.E.D. show* v.23). It does not follow that she could write; and another indication that she did not may be seen in a suggestion made by the youngest John in 1477. He has prepared a draft of a letter to be sent in her name, and he introduces it thus: 'Wherfor, modyr, if it please yow, myn advyse is to send hyr answer a yen in thys forme following, *of some other manys hand.*' Both of Elizabeth's letters are certainly in secretaries' hands. Margery could write, but only just: three of her letters bear conventional subscriptions in the same tremulous, totally unformed hand, quite distinct from that of the body of each letter, and this must be her own. The letters of the women, then, cannot be taken as preserving the language of their authors undisturbed. They can probably be trusted, since they were presumably dictated, to preserve the words and even the syntax of the authors, but they cannot be trusted for the details of form, or for such limited information about sounds as spellings may reveal. (pp. 45-9)

This is not the place to discuss in detail minute differences of spelling, sounds, inflexions, and syntax. But I must offer some examples of the kind of variation that exists, and for this purpose I shall use only the writings of the men, and for the most part only a few critical features which provide a fairly clear series of comparisons: in spelling, the treatment of the final group of sounds in syllables that ended in -*ht* in Old English, as in 'right', 'thought', 'daughter'; in sounds, the lowering of *i* as shown by the writing of *e*, as *heder* 'hither', *wretyn* 'written', which, even if its interpretation is sometimes open to doubt, cannot be without phonetic significance; in forms, two points: first, in the pronoun of the third person plural, the alternation of the English *her* and *hem* in possessive and objective cases with the originally Scandinavian *ther* and *them*; and second, in the verb, the incidence of final -*n* in infinitive, present and past plural, and strong past participle.

The first William, the judge, as the sole representative of the first generation, must be the starting-point. His spelling was generally close to the practice of good manuscripts of his time, such as the Ellesmere Chaucer, and he always used -*ght* in words like 'right' and 'thought'. In words like 'written' he used *i*, not *e*. In the pronoun, he used only *here* and *hem* for 'their' and 'them'. In the verb, in infinitive and present plural he occasionally used -*n*, but markedly preferred endingless forms. A typical example of the mixture is the following, from a set of instructions for the building of a wall: 'and thenne Þo brode sawed stones shulde euere *stonde* in Þe werk betwen Þe seid weel bedde[d] stonys, Þat shuld *rise* but a fote in Þe walle and *ben* ankered iche of hem with other; and Þis werk shal *be* strong j nowe, as werkmen *seyn,* and *drawe* but litill cariage.' In the past participle, on the other hand, forms with -*n* strongly predominate—there are 11 with it against 2 without.

The judge's four sons all differ from their father in all these matters, but they differ among themselves as well.

Edmond's one short letter shows important changes from his father's usage, in spelling 'right' *ryth,* 'nought' *nowth,* and 'thought' *thowte;* in using *e* for *i* in *wrete, preuye, trenyte,* and with similar effect *wheche, meche;* and in using *-n* in verbs only in one plural *ben* and one past participle *seen:* 'for sche [his mother] woll tell persones many of her counsell this day, and to morwe sche woll sey be Goddis faste Þat the same men *ben* false. I haue *seen* parte of Þe euydence, and Þe maner hathe be purchasid. . . .' The ratio in the past participle, one *-n* form to 4 without, contrasts sharply with the judge's 11 to 2.

John—among whose forty-four documents, from about 1445 to 1465, only two complete letters and some brief additions and interlineations are autograph—has more variety than Edmond in the 'right' group, which mostly has *-gth,* but sometimes *-gt, ght,* as well as *-th;* but he treats the 'thought' group in the same way, with *-owth* and *-owt* about equal. His language is coloured by a preference for *e* instead of *i* in several classes of words: *wret(e),* the past participle, occurs nine times and is his only form, and— *heder, theder, leuyng, well* 'will', and probably *ded* 'did' are of the same type. The *e* in *deke* 'dike' and *lekith* 'likes' must be of similar origin. That in *besines* and *ken* (beside *kyn*) may well, but of course need not, be the same again. The prominence of *e* is further increased by *whech, sech, mech,* the usual though not exclusive forms of these words. In the pronoun, *her* and *hem* are much the commoner forms; *Þer* and *Þem* appear from about 1460, for the first time in the family letters, but only 6 times against 24 of the others. There is only one certain *-n* form in the verb, the past participle *don* found 3 times, compared with 28 participles without ending—a proportion of endingless forms much higher even than Edmond's, and indeed than that of any other of the correspondents. John's language seems to show no important or consistent development throughout his writings.

The second William's letters and papers run for nearly thirty years, from 1452 when he wrote from Cambridge, and they, too, are remarkably consistent for so long a period. William usually writes both 'right' and 'thought' groups with *-th(e),* occasionally with *-t* only, but never with *-ght.* He uses *e* for *i* in many words, such as *heder, pekyd, leke* (some half-dozen times), *tedyng; abedyn, redyn, wretyn; contenu, indeferent, parteculer, pete, qwett, sperituall; beryed, besy, ded.* On the other hand he favours *y* instead of *e* in some words: *frynd* (3 times), *pryste* (also *prist*), and *wyll, will* 'well' (9 times). He uses *e*-forms also in *qweche* and *meche,* but *much(e), moche,* and *myche* as well, and only *suche, soche.* In the pronoun, *hem* is the usual form, though *them* does occur; but the possessive *ther(e)* is commoner than *here.* In the verb, *-n* is not used in normal infinitives, but it appears in perhaps 4 present plurals and one past plural, and in 19 past participles (10 of them *wretyn*) against 18 without it. Some progression may be seen in this particular: though *wretyn* is regular from the first, it is only from 1459 onwards that other *-n* forms of the participle are frequent. It may not be irrelevant that in 1459 and 1460 William writes from London.

The youngest of the judge's sons, Clement, has left six letters from 1461 to 1466. He agrees with Edmond and William in spelling both 'right' and 'thougth' groups mainly with *-th(e)* and *-t(e).* But he differs from all his brothers in his very limited use of *e* for *i:* he has only *dede* 'did' and *wretyn* once, elsewhere writing *y,* however he pronounced it. His pronominal forms are too few to be significant. In the verb, he has no *-n* forms in infinitive or past plural, but 4 in the present plural (3 of them *ben*), and in the participle 21 forms with *-n* to 10 without.

In the participle the difference of practice among the brothers is striking: John and Edmond are very sparing of *-n;* Clement has it twice as often as not; William takes a middle position with numbers roughly equal.

In general, the two eldest brothers, John and Edmond, tend to agree, and to differ from William and Clement— William was eleven years, Clement seventeen years, younger than Edmond. The younger brothers share an important peculiarity of spelling: the use of *qw-* and *w-* instead of *wh-* in words like 'which', 'where'. There are some differences of treatment in particular words. In William, 'which' is only *qweche,* 'whether' only *weder;* 'where', 'what', 'when', and 'while' appear both with *qw-* and with simple *w-;* and 'squire' is *swyre.* In Clement, 'which' is *qwyche* but also *wych.* The alternation with *w-* is enough to show that the *qw-* form is purely conventional, and that the pronunciation was [w]; and this is confirmed by William's spelling of 'was' as *qwas.*

Clement alone spells 'shall' and 'should' *xall* and *xwld(e).* Both the *qw-/w-* and the *x-* spellings are highly characteristic of Norfolk writers, and it is remarkable that they should appear only in the hands of the two younger brothers. We hear something of Clement's education, some three years before the first of his surviving letters, in a memorandum of his mother's 'errands to London' in 1458: 'To prey Grenefeld to send me feythfully word by wrytyn who Clement Paston hath do his devere in lernyng. And if he hathe nought do well, nor wyll nought amend, prey hym that he wyll trewly bèlassh hym tyl he wyll amend; and so ded the last mayster, and ye best that euer he had, att Caumbrege.' Perhaps Norfolk spellings were accepted at Cambridge—William had also been there; but it is surprising that they should survive so stern a schooling in London as well.

In a few things, such as the appearance of *them* and *ther,* this generation shows some trends towards more modern usage than that of the judge; but in other ways—the common lowering of *i,* the confusion of spelling in the *-ght* words, and the instability of *-n* in the past participle— none of the sons is as near to the later literary language as their father had been. It is the younger brothers who favour the less orthodox spellings, and nobody changes his habits much in the course of time.

In the generation that follows—grandsons of the judge— the evidence for the usage of two of the brothers is extremely full. Sir John the elder has left 69 autograph documents, the younger John 74 written on his own account as well as 11 written for his mother Margaret and parts of three more for his father and others. Both series continue over many years, and change somewhat in language as time goes on. I must go into some detail here to show how the changes appear.

The eldest brother's first surviving letter is, I think, one which can be dated 1461. Some features of it do not occur again. Words like 'right', for example, are variously spelt: *rygth, mythg*; and 'writing' is *wrythgtyng*. Words like 'thought' are similarly unsettled: *nowgth, nogth, nowthg*, and also *thowt*. 'Much' is *myche*. There are eight reduced forms of *have* in compound tenses: *ye schuld a ben hurt, I schuld an had it*. The other autograph letters date from probably 1464 onwards, and in the interval John had been at court, had been knighted, and had evidently entered the king's service. In the latest letters the spelling *-ght* becomes virtually regular in the 'right' group, though in the 'thought' group there is no set form even in the latest: *thowt, thowght, thogt* (both with and without *-e*) all occur, but *-wt(e)* about twice as often as either of the other two. As soon as the *-ght* type establishes itself in words in which the spirant is historical, it appears also in words that never had the sound: the verb 'write' is nearly always *wryght*, and there are a few forms like *dowght*. 'Much' is nearly always *moche*, with *meche* perhaps twice; and compound tenses with *have* are fully written out. There is no change in the use of *e* for *i*, which is common—though not regular—throughout: *thedyr, whedyr* (but usually *hyddre*), *leuyd, wedowe; dreuyn, redyn, strekyn, wretyn; contenew, peler, preuy; besy, ded*. In the pronoun, *them* and *ther(e)* overwhelmingly predominate, with perhaps only three cases of *hem*. In the verb, no *-n* forms appear in infinitive or past plural, and only a few in the present plural(*be(e)n* six times, *seyn* once). In the past participle, on the other hand, they are well established from the first, and more or less consistent at different periods. There are about 330 with *-n* against 32 without—roughly 10 to 1. Those which are always without *-n* have stems ending in a nasal or *-nd*: *bonde, bownde, fonde, founde; bygonne, wonne*. (Yet *comen* is normal, occurring 27 times against only 2 of *com(e)*).

Sir John makes two new departures, though both remain very much in the minority. He uses *-ys* in the third person singular present indicative of verbs, only five times beside the immeasurably commoner *-yth*; and he once has *yow* instead of *ye* as a nominative. These exceptional forms are all in letters to his younger brother John, the *-s* forms in 1472-4, *yow* in 1477 (no. 306).

The youngest John's hand, the most fully represented of the whole family, first appears in a group of letters written on behalf of his mother, most of them between 1460 and 1462. In this group the spelling of words like 'right' is *-yth* six times as often as *-yt(e)*, and *-ght* is not used at all; in words like 'thought' *-wt(e)* is regular. Lowering of *i* is common: *hedyr, thedyr, levith, seth(yn); wretyn; dechys, lek; indeferent; ded*; but 'which', 'much', and 'such' all usually have *y: whyche (wyche, qwyche), myche, swyche (syche, siche, suche* twice). The plural pronoun is *hem* twice as often as *them*, but (though numbers are small) *ther* is commoner than *her*. In the verb, *-n* appears once in the present plural *ben* and once in the past plural *redyn*;

in the past participle less than one-third of the total of nearly 70 have *-n*.

John's own letters begin probably in 1461. At first his forms are in all important respects the same as in the letters he had written for his mother. (There are small differences of detail; e.g. *syche*, earlier rare, now becomes normal.) As the years pass, however, new spellings and forms appear, sometimes as alternatives but sometimes altogether displacing the earlier types.

This is especially well seen in the 'right' group. The usual spelling is *-yth*, with *-yt* rarely, up to 1466. *Myght* appears first in a letter apparently written early in 1467, and though there is a temporary reversion in 1468, *-ght* thereafter is unchallenged. The 'thought' group is less clear-cut, but the same in tendency: *-owght* begins to appear in 1467, the same date as *-yght*; but remnants of *-owt* survive sparsely until 1470, and from that date also *-ought* begins and gradually becomes commoner. Soon after the adoption of the new spellings they spread to words historically without the spirant, and *wryght* and *abowght* are John's usual forms after about 1469. In this matter the brothers agree fairly closely. Both begin by using *-yth* and *-owt*, and adopt *-ght* later, the younger man going further in finally making *-ght* his regular form after a back vowel as well as a front. The early spellings show that the spirant was no longer pronounced; and the extension of the new spellings to words with no etymological right to them proves that the change of spelling does not imply a change of pronunciation.

No such movement affects the use of *e* for *i*. The youngest John has most of the usual examples, though there are a few differences of detail: from 1467, for example, 'like' is nearly always *lyek*, not *lek*. *Whyche, syche, myche* unexpectedly regularly have *y*.

But the plural pronoun is complicated. Unlike his elder brother, the third John often uses *hem*, and occasionally *her*. Beside these stand *them* and *ther*, but the by-form—it may be only a spelling variant—*theym*, which appears first in 1467, is prominent enough to call for special notice. In all, *hem* occurs 58 times, *them* 36, *theym* 38; *her* only 3 times, *ther* and *thers* jointly 69. Thus the currency of the possessive *her*, compared with *ther*, is enormously less than that of the accusative-dative *hem* compared with *them* and *theym*. But the proportions change greatly within the series. Taking the ten autograph letters written up to 1467, *hem* is three and a half times as frequent as *them* and *theym* together; but in the 25 letters up to the middle of 1471, *hem* occurs 45 times out of its total of 58, *them* 29 out of its 36, but *theym* only 5 times out of its 38. There is, then, a strong increase in *th*-forms after 1467, and another strong increase of *theym*, largely at the expense of *them*, from 1471 onwards. *Her* is from the first so unimportant that its disappearance after 1472 is not surprising.

The history of *-n* forms in the verb is almost equally complicated. They occur, in normal use, only in the past participle. Over the whole series there are some 236 forms with *-n* to 70 without it-about 3.3 to 1, in contrast with the elder John's 10 to 1. But there are far fewer endingless forms in later than in earlier letters, and in particular there is a discernible decline from a letter dated 1475, and another apparent break from 1473. In the letters from 1473 to the end, the proportion of *-n* forms to endingless is 8.7 to 1; from 1475 to the end it is 11 to 1. After 1475 the only forms without *-n* in ordinary use are *be* (3 times beside *been* 18) and verbs ending in a nasal or *-nd*, which never have *-n*: *bond, bownde, com, fond*. Two minor observations may be made. The youngest John uses only *com* in the past participle, whereas his elder brother uses *comen* almost always. Two abnormal forms, the infinitive *doone*, the only *-n* form outside the past participle, and the past participle *shake*, without *-n*, have a special explanation: they are used in a poem, and in rhyme, *doone* rhyming with *soone*, *shake* with the infinitive *take*. This is a trifling but neat example of the way in which the demands of rhyme may force a versifier quite away from his usual linguistic forms.

Finally, the youngest John extends the *-s* ending in the present indicative somewhat beyond his brother's use. There are 15 examples, 8 of them *thynkys*, against Sir John's 5—a difference too great to be explained simply by the larger bulk of the younger man's writings. These forms do not begin until 1467.

It is noticeable that this is also the year that marks the first appearance of *-ght* spellings. The increase of *th-* forms of the pronoun begins in 1468, and 1473 and 1475 mark stages in the adoption of *-n* in the participle. Why 1467 should have seen such changes is not clear. The following year brought new experiences which may well have left their mark—John and his brother went to Bruges in the retinue of Princess Margaret, sister of Edward IV, for her marriage to the Duke of Burgundy. The later dates may also have some connection with events in his life. In 1473 he made plans to go on pilgrimage to Compostela, but there is no firm evidence that he went. In 1475 he records his return from a visit to Calais: 'I haue be seek euer sythe I cam on thys syd the see, but I trust hastyly to amend; for all my seknesse that I had at Caleys, and sythe I cam ouer also, cam but of cold. But I was never so well armyd for the werre as I haue now armyd me for cold.'

The next brother, Edmond, writes seven letters, or parts of letters, for his mother as well as six on his own behalf. He is in some ways more individual in his usage than either of his elders, especially in spelling 'shall' and 'should', in early letters for Margaret, with *x-*, as his uncle Clement had done. In other things he is like his brothers. He uses *e* for *i* in many words, and *them* as well as *hem* in the pronoun—*them* rather more commonly, especially later. In the 'right' and 'thought' groups he uses *-th(e)*, occasionally *-te*, until 1472, but, after a long interval, he adopts *-ght* in all but a few cases. In the verb, he has rare *-n* forms in the infinitive and the present and past plural, and in the past participle 24 *-n* forms against 2 (*com, woond*) endingless. He has 14 *-s* forms in the present indicative, in his own letters only, beginning in 1471—perhaps significantly, after living for a time in London.

The third William, eight of whose letters we have, has again characteristics of his own. He is like his elder brothers in using (*-ght* in the 'right' group (including 'to write'), but both *-wt* and *-wght* after back vowels; and *e* in *thedyr*,

mende, ded. But in the plural pronoun he is the first of the family to use exclusively *th-* forms—a total of 27. In the verb, he has *-n* forms only in the past participle, but his preference for them there is striking: of 31 examples 28 have *-n*, and the odd three are all *come*. But he does not use *-s* in the present. His greatest singularity is the representation of a diphthong in *cawlyd, gowld*, in two letters written from Eton, probably in 1478 and 1479. He once uses *yow* apparently as a nominative: 'as for hyr bewte, juge yow that when e see hyr.'

Walter is of special interest in that his three surviving letters where written at Oxford, where he took his degree in 1479. In the first of them, evidently comparatively early in his undergraduate career, he spells 'shall' and 'should' with *x-*, but in the others changes to *sch-*. The 'right' and 'thought' groups are poorly represented, but offer *nyth, mythy, rytgh, rygth,* and *thowth*. In the verb, *-n* appears only in the past participle *wretyn* three times, and endingless forms in *do, forgete, wryt*—a departure from the practice of the elder brothers by this date. Walter's greatest distinction is his frequent use of *yow* in the nominative—8 times in all, 6 of them in his last letter, against a total of 5 cases of *ye*.

The third generation carries further some of the tendencies which had begun in the second. *Them* and *ther* gain ground strongly. In the verb, *-n* endings decrease still more in parts other than the past participle, in which, on the other hand, they become almost general except in words with stems ending in a nasal or *-nd*. The spelling *-ght*, regular in the judge's writings but very infrequent in his sons', becomes common again; and in particular, it is preferred in the later letters of those writers who change their habits in the course of time. Some features are new. The *-s* ending in the present and the use of *yow* as nominative arise first in this generation, but remain only occasional. There is a good deal of variation among the different writers, but in some things, notably the widespread use of *e* for *i*, the judge's grandsons are farther from the central stream of development of English than he had been.

There remains the fourth William, the only representative of the fourth generation. Unfortunately his single letter is so brief that it offers too little evidence to be worth setting against the far fuller record of his ancestors.

From the great variety of usage revealed by this very limited study of a few points, it is obvious that no simple statement can answer the sort of question that I suggested at the beginning. Each new generation does, in broad terms, show some differences from its predecessor; but individuals go their own ways, and some change considerably in the course of years while others retain the habits of their youth. Perhaps the clearest result of the inquiry is the demonstration that in roughly the third quarter of the fifteenth century men of some education, of similar background and interests, could choose among so many 'permitted variations' that no two of them wrote exactly alike.

But there is, I think, more than this to be said. When all allowance for idiosyncrasy has been made, certain trends can be discerned. Some members of the third generation even though it worthwhile to alter some of their linguistic habits; those who did so all changed in the same direction, and it was the direction of the future literary language. It is especially interesting that the writers who—partly as a result of these changes—seem nearest to the general development of the language are not, as we might have expected, those educated at Eton or Oxford, still less the Cambridge men; but rather the courtier and soldier Sir John, and his younger brother who also became Sir John and the trusted servant of noble families. That such men thought it desirable to modify their English implies that they were conscious of a model worthy of imitation. Sir John the elder did not think highly of ordinary Londoners. He writes of his aunt: 'She is in many thyngys full lyke a wyffe of London and of Londone kyndenesse, and she woll needys take advise off Londonerys, wheche I telle here can nott advyse her howghe she scholde deele weell wyth any body off worshyp.' But it must have been from London—no doubt from Londoners 'off worshyp'—that he and some of his brothers learnt to adopt new forms and spellings; so that even at this date one type at least of London speech must have acquired something of the prestige of an incipient 'standard' language.

The linguistic behaviour of these brothers may also contribute something to the understanding of variations of scribal practice, or even of the spelling habits of early compositors. Clearly one man might in his time use many forms, sometimes changing them quite suddenly; and each so regularly that his writings could be placed in roughly chronological order on their evidence alone. If the youngest John's letters, say, had been copied by clerks or printed, we might be disposed to account for the different linguistic strata by assigning them to different writers; but his handwriting is happily unmistakable. (pp. 50-61)

> *Norman Davis, "The Language of the Pastons," in* Middle English Literature British Academy Gollancz Lectures, *edited by J. A. Burrow, Oxford University Press, Oxford, 1989, pp. 45-70.*

Norman Davis   (essay date 1958)

[*In the excerpt below, Davis discusses the tone and style of the* Paston Letters.]

In 1787 John Fenn, a Norfolk antiquarian, published under the title **Original Letters, Written during the Reigns of Henry VI. Edward IV. and Richard III. By various Persons of Rank or Consequence** a selection from a large number of manuscripts in his possession. They had come into his hands, through several intermediate owners, from the estate of William Paston, second Earl of Yarmouth, who died in 1732 and with whom the main Paston line became extinct. To the first two volumes three were later added. Even in Fenn's day—and indeed before his edition was published—the collection came to be called **The Paston Letters,** and it was under this title that James Gairdner began in 1872 to publish his new edition, much augmented from manuscripts that Fenn had not printed. This edition was further expanded in 1900, and finally revised in 1904. Most of the manuscripts had by then been acquired by the British Museum, but an important group

remained in private hands until 1935; a few are in other libraries.

The collection forms a fairly compact series of over a thousand documents from about 1420 until soon after 1500. Most of them are letters, about a third written by or for members of the Paston family and most of the others written to them by estate servants or friends. Their preservation we owe chiefly to John Paston I (d. 1466); for during his long absences from home, in his attempts to secure his title to property, his indefatigable wife Margaret managed the estates and wrote to him reporting what she had done and asking for advice and instructions. Many of these letters, and others like them from his clerks and bailiffs, John filed; and this careful habit was continued after his death by his widow and their sons. Thus, though letters written by John I himself are comparatively few, he long dominates the correspondence because while he lived most of the letters were written to him. After his death the proportions are much more even, for his two eldest sons, both named John, kept each other's letters as well as their mother's. After Margaret's death in 1484 there are relatively few family letters, and the series virtually ends with the death of John III in 1503. (p. vii)

Those writers from whom a number of letters survive have generally succeeded in leaving a strong impression of their individual characters and temperaments. Agnes, who has a keen ear for the sound of a quarrel—'I told hym if hys fadyr had do as he dede, he wold a be achamyd to a seyd as he seyd'—shows in her dealings with the villagers of Paston the sternness, tending to arrogance, that becomes tyrannous cruelty to her daughter who would not marry as she wished; yet she has softer moods, seen best in her advice to her insatiably acquisitive son: 'Be my counseyle, dyspose youre selfe as myche as ye may to have lesse to do in the worlde'. John's letters to his wife reveal a disposition that may well seem in need of such advice, though not very likely to heed it. He reproves Margaret and her officers for slackness in managing his property, and expels his eldest son from his house because he is 'as a drane amonges bees'. Once, and that in unpromising circumstances since he is in prison, he unbends so far as to write to his wife as 'myn owne dere sovereyn lady', and to end his letter with twenty lines of laboriously humorous doggerel. Margaret as a young woman is a more attractive person. She can be at once ironic and tender: 'I ham waxse so fetys that I may not be gyrte in no barre of no gyrdyl that I have but of on. . . .Ye have lefte me sweche a rememraunse that makyth me to thynke uppe on yow bothe day and nyth wanne I wold sclepe'. Concern with business soon brings an almost unrelieved earnestness, but she is always vigorous and competent. As the years pass, and the strain perhaps tells, she too becomes censorious, implacably banning from her house the daughter who insisted on marrying beneath her, often reproving her eldest son, and quarrelling with her second. Her elder sons disappointed her, and her better hopes of the young Walter were crushed by his early death. Despite the difficult moods that her sons complain of, she kept their devotion to the end: 'ther is neyther wyff nor other frend shall make me to do that that your comandment shall make me to do'.

John II appears as easy-going and likeable, well-meaning but often ineffectual. He is generally good-humoured, fond of a joke and not always particular about its refinement, yet with some appreciation of the subtleties of courtship: 'And bere yore selfe as lowly to the modere as ye lyst, but to the mayde not to lowly, nere that ye be to gladde to spede nere to sory to fayle'. His relations with John III are nearly always free and cordial, but he stiffens into unsympathetic formality over Margaret's gift of a manor to his brother on his marriage. During the siege of Caister he seems never to have taken the measure of the danger, and his negotiations for its relief came to nothing. By comparison John III is steady and circumspect, managing the property in his brother's long absences and much less concerned with courtly pleasures: 'I had lever se yow onys in Caster Halle then to se as many kyngys tornay as might be betwyx Eltam and London'. He drives a hard bargain for his marriage with Margery Brews, but he does not otherwise show his father's single-minded concern for profit. And he can be as agreeably light-hearted as his brother: '*Memento mei,* and in feythe ye shall not loose on it; nor yet myche wyne on it, by God, who preserve yow'. Less engaging than John II, he makes an impression of sounder qualities, and it is not surprising that he left the family fortunes in good case.

Of the persons less fully represented, young William III at Eton, with his interest in coming to 'sporte me wyth yow at London a day or ii thys terme tyme' in one letter, and, beside his Latin verses, in the nuptial prospects of the young Margaret Alborow, who is 'dysposyd to be thyke', in another, is pleasantly fresh and simple. But in the whole collection there is nothing to match the tenderness and charm of Margery Brews in her two 'Valentines' to John III. She begged him 'that this bill be not seyn of non erthely creature safe only your selfe'. It is our good fortune that he failed to take her at her word.

All but a handful of the letters are business letters, written quite unselfconsciously for private information or advice, and often written in haste. If they have any literary qualities it is for the most part by accident. Yet not entirely so; critics have too exclusively stressed the most conspicuous qualities of artlessness and directness. Most of the writers are rhetoricians enough to point their arguments with sim-

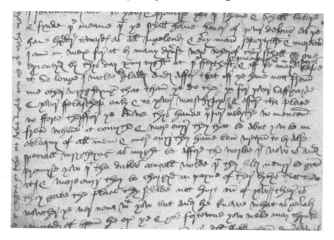

A sample from a letter written by John Paston II.

ile or proverb: 'the Duck of Suffolk ys abyll to kype dayly in hys hows more men then Dabeney hadde herys in hys hede'; 'my Lady Anne P. lappe, as white as whales bon'; 'it is but a sympill oke that is cut down at the firste stroke'; or to construct a balanced sentence: 'Thys mater is drevyn thus ferforthe wythowte my cowncell; I praye yow make an ende wythowte my cowncell. Iffe it be weell, I wolde be glad; iff it be oderwyse, it is pite'. On occasion the older women especially will use phrases or rhythms that can scarcely be other than reminiscences of what they have heard in church or from their chaplains: 'This worlde is but a thorughfare, and ful of woo; and whan we departe therfro, righth noughght bere wyth us but oure good dedys and ylle. And ther knoweth no man how soon God woll clepe hym, and therfor it is good for every creature to be redy'; 'Send me word how ye doo of yowyr syknes . . . , and yff God wol nowt suffyr yow to have helth, thank hym theroff and tak yt passhently, and com hom ageyn to me, and we shall lyve togeddyr as God woll geve us grase to do'. Sometimes the younger men allow themselves a flourish that has its origin in romance rather than religion: 'And they that have jostyd wyth hym into thys day have ben as rychely beseyn, and hym selve also, as clothe of gold and sylk and sylvyr and goldsmythys werk myght mak hem. . . . And as for the Dwkys coort, as of lordys, ladys, and gentylwomen, knytys, sqwyirs, and gentyllmen, I herd never of non lyek to it save Kyng Artourys cort'. That the women tend to use the simpler rhythms is no more accidental than that they employ amanuenses while the men usually write with their own hands. The more sophisticated grammar of the men comes from their advantage in education.

Overwhelmingly, it is true, it is 'the plain style' that everyone uses, aiming at conveying uncomplicated meaning in unvarnished words. They do not always succeed, and when they do not it is most commonly because their minds are too full of the jargon of the law: 'And the maire and comons of the said cite mad ther menys to have grace be Lord Montagu and Lord Barenars, whiche befor the Kyngys comyng into the said cite desyred hym of grace for the said cyte . . . '. Yet far oftener than their endowments, or their education, or their objects in writing would seem to justify our expecting, they do succeed. The prevailing tone is that of good speech. This does not mean that the writing simply follows the speaking voice, so far as writing can ever catch its rhythms and tones, hesitations and repetitions. Some quotations of direct speech, and some reports, come close to it: 'It fylle in hys brayne to come to Norwyche, and he in an angre wolde nedys to horse—he wolde non horsse litter, he was so stronge'. But this is not often appropriate. Most of the writing is colloquial in the sense that it is easy and unaffected, the sentences kept simple without being mere strings of primitive coordinate clauses.

It naturally varies in its degree of formality. It can be shaped and heightened for special effects without in any way losing its essentially practical and common roots: 'But, modre, I fele by yowre wryghtyng that ye deme in me I scholde not do my devyre wythowt ye wrot to me som hevye tydyngys; and, modre, iff I had nede to be qwykynyd wyth a letter in thys nede I were of my selfe to slawe a felaw'; 'I pray yow geve them ther thank, for by my trowthe they have as well deservyd it as eny men that ever bare lyve; but as for mony, ye ned not to geve hem wythowt ye wyll, for they be plesyd wyth ther wagys. . . . We wer, for lak of vetayll, gonepoudyr, menys hertys, lak of suerte of rescwe, drevyn therto to take apoyntement'. In this there is a sense of form that concentrates the inherent vigour of the thought; rhythms and patterns are briefly used to make a point, but never as mere ornament empty of sense.

There is not much literary antecedent in English to this kind of writing. It certainly does not derive from the kind of prose that Chaucer wrote, or yet from the cadenced prose of the celebrated devotional treatises of the fourteenth and fifteenth centuries. It comes so easily to so many people that it must have been common far longer than surviving documents allow us to observe. This, the practical writing of ordinary men and women, is the kind of language on which modern prose was built. (pp. xi-xv)

Norman Davis, in an introduction to Paston Letters, *edited by Norman Davis. Oxford at the Clarendon Press, 1958, pp. vii-xvi.*

Maurice Keen   (essay date 1959)

[*In the following excerpt, Keen discusses the value of the* Paston Letters *as historical documents and compares them with the collected letters of the Stonor and Shillingford families.*]

The fifteenth century is without any great chronicle; it has no Froissart, no Mathew Paris to tell its story once and for all. The chronicles of London or of the White Rose are disjointed and fragmentary; many of the most famous incidents of the Wars of the Roses are known to us only through the writings of the Tudor historians. But if chronicle histories are less numerous and less comprehensive than before, in the fifteenth century a new source for historical study becomes for the first time important—collections of private letters. The word private is important; letters have survived from earlier periods, but they are mostly of an official nature—the formal letters of public men about public business. Families like the Pastons and the Stonors, however, who now begin to leave us their correspondence, although locally people of wealth and weight, were not in the forefront of political affairs. They were well-established gentry, the middle people, for whom political events had their sometimes terrible consequences, but who were not themselves responsible for them. Their testimony is doubly interesting; not only are their letters a valuable record, they also give us a touchstone whereby to gauge the reaction of the ordinary, prosperous individual to contemporary events.

Moreover, even in the simple matter of events the letters can furnish us with valuable evidence. Among the *Paston Letters* there is one dating from 1440 that throws interesting light on the negotiations undertaken with France through the Duke of Orleans, who had been a prisoner in England since Agincourt, and on the Duke of Gloucester's opposition both to his release and to the policy of peace. "The Duke of Orleans hath made his oath on the sacra-

ment, never to bear arms against England, in the presence of the King and all the Lords, except my Lord of Gloucester, and proving my said Lord Gloucester never agreed to his deliverance, when the mass began he took to his barge." Throughout the letters, passages like this crop up, giving a sudden and more vivid glimpse of some event of the time.

The *Paston Letters* do not really become important for the political historian until about the time of the fall of Henry VI's favourite, the Duke of Suffolk. Although they had on occasion suffered at his hands, the Pastons were warmly on the side of their great neighbour; the articles of his impeachment were interesting enough to John Paston for him to preserve a copy of them, and this reaction of his is almost as interesting as the document itself. William Lomnour's letter to Paston—"a little bill so washed with tears that hardly ye shall read it"—is easily the best account of the Duke's cruel death on his way to exile, at the hands of pirates.

> In the sight of all his men he was drawn out of the great ship into the boat; and there was an axe and a stock, and one of the lewdest of the ship bade him lay down his head, and he should be fair fared with and die on a sword; and he took a rusty sword and smote off his head with half-a-dozen strokes; and they took away his gown of russet and his doublet of velvet mailed, and laid his body on the sands of Dover.

Again, among the Stonor letters there is an excellent account of the first battle of St. Albans, the first pitched battle of the Wars of the Roses, the most detailed record of it that we possess; while John Payn's letter to Paston, telling of his adventures at the time of Jack Cade's revolt, gives as clear an impression as any source of the hardships of that time and the miseries that the rebellion brought to many people of good standing who were involved. Perhaps as interesting and important as any of the letters is the one that his brother Clement wrote to John Paston on the eve of Towton in 1461, when the Pastons were on the Yorkist side—were, indeed, relying on its success for their good fortune in their litigation over the estate of Sir John Fastolf. "It is well do, and best for you," writes Clement, "that ye would come with more men and cleanlier arrayed than another man of your own country would, for it lieth more upon your worship and toucheth you more near than another man of that country, and also ye be more had in favour with my lords here." Throughout this period the letters, especially those of the Pastons, are of first-class importance in tracing its tangled history. There is little enough news, it is true, of battles or of fighting, but the regular bulletins from London relations and the general tone show how deeply even a moderate country family was certain to be involved in the struggles of political faction. Sometimes the letters become a primary authority; always they are invaluable in assessing the state of the country and the extent of disturbance.

Every now and again the letters bring us into direct contact with great figures or stirring events—into that kind of personal contact that no chronicle history can ever provide. One might instance the grumbling letter of an English soldier in France, impatient with Henry V's negotiations with the Dauphin in 1419: "Certes all these ambassadors be double and false. Pray for us that we may come soon out of this unlusty soldier's life into the life of England"—it brings suddenly home the familiar homesickness of the soldier abroad, and the human life and gossip of the camp in an army in times which, if romantic, are often too distant to come readily to life. Or there is the letter written by the Duke of Suffolk to his son "giving him very good counsel," the last letter that he ever wrote, and of which Paston kept a copy, a letter that brings us into touch with one of the greatest men of the time and that must sway any historian who attempts to pass judgment on him. "It is difficult to believe," as Lingard wrote, "that the writer could have been a false subject or a bad man." There is something pathetic in the ring of it; in the devotion to the monarch who had turned against him— "Above all earthly thing, be true liegeman in heart, in will, in thought, in deed, to the king our elder most high and dread sovereign . . . charging you, as father can and may, rather to die than to be the contrary, or to know anything against the welfare or prosperity of his most royal person, but as far as your body and life may stretch, ye live and die to defend it." Look, too, at the parting injunction, to live "in such wise that after the departing from this wretched world here, ye may glorify Him eternally among his angels in heaven. Written of mine hand the day of my departing from this land—your true and loving father, Suffolk." Little wonder that historians should call William de la Pole "one of the finest types of the old chivalry that was passing away"; his last words in his letter lay bare the tragedy of the servant loyal still in spite of exile and disgrace, a tragedy standing out in all its personal poignancy from the dusty records of faction and intrigue that seem so often to be the stuff of fifteenth-century history.

In quite a different spirit, the letter of Robert Wennington, the West Country pirate, which also comes from the Paston collection, brings us up against a personality; a pirate of the same bold, confident stamp as the adventurers of Elizabeth's time, Hawkins, Drake or Oxenham, who did not care overmuch for odds when booty was at stake. "I and my fellowship said, but unless he will strike down the sail, that I would oversail him by the grace of God, and God will send me wind and weather; and they bade me do my worst, because I had so few ships and so small, that they scorned me. And as God would, on Friday last was, we had a good wind, and then we armed . . . and made us ready to oversail them . . . and there yielded all the hundred ships to go with me to what port me list." It is only when one comes across such a letter as this that one is reminded that the Tudor age grew directly out of the fifteenth century; the spirit that brought it to its greatness was growing up in the years after Agincourt, the battle which more than any other event had awakened a new national consciousness.

Yet if every now and again they illumine some great event and bring it close to us, the general tone of the letters is in a minor key. If they can be at their most useful when they throw light on the incident of politics, the bulk of them do far more to enlighten us about social and economic history, the story of the everyday life of men and women. It would be hard to work up a romance out of the

Paston Letters; to make them the basis for a nineteenth-century novel of the good bourgeois brought up in comfort and in the most conforming of homes, yet every once in a while confronted with the horrid pains of life, mental and physical, face to face—this would be less hard. Their foci of interest are never earth-shaking. In the time of William Paston the main theme of the letters is the lawsuit between the old judge and the so-called Prior of Bromholm, John Worte. In the next generation, interest still centres very often in litigation; after the death of Sir John Fastolf in 1459, concern as to the disputes over his inheritance monopolizes more and more attention—indeed John Paston's interest in politics in this period is very largely governed by regard for his lawsuit. John needed to take good care for his own, especially in the ungoverned period of Edward IV's struggle with Warwick and the readoption of Henry VI—in 1469 the Duke of Norfolk, pursuing a claim to the Fastolf property, besieged Paston's castle at Caister with three thousand men.

Curiously enough, the other collections are less important for the political historian than the *Paston Letters.* The Stonors were bigger folk; one of them, John Stonor, had been Chief Justice of the Court of Common Pleas for more than twenty years under Edward III, while the last of them, Sir William Stonor, was with Lord Lovell one of the most important figures in Buckingham's rebellion against Richard III in 1483. Yet the majority of their letters relate to family affairs and business; the most interesting are those to and from a relative William, who was a merchant of the Staple in the years 1475 to 1480. The main matters of the Plumpton correspondence (the letters of an old Yorkshire family) are again lawsuits and family disputes. The Cely papers come from a family of London merchants and woolmongers; their greatest interest is for the light they shed on commercial relations with Flanders and on the garrisoning of Calais, where the Celys had a place of business. The letters of John Shillingford, the Mayor of Exeter, are entirely concerned with a suit between the citizens and Edmund Lacy, the bishop, which arose between the years 1447 and 1450. The round of everyday affairs and business is the main concern of all the important collections.

Even thus, out of the limelight, the letters bring the life of the times closer than mere records or accounts ever could, for the personal element is always there. The Celys lay aside affairs when the married merchants of Calais challenge the bachelors to a shooting match. "And it would please you for your disport and pleasure upon Thursday next coming to may with us . . . ye shall find a pair of pricks of length between the one and other 13 tailor's yards met out with a line; there we underwritten shall may with as many of you, and shoot with you at the same pricks for a dinner or a supper per 12d a man." These kind of details, almost modern in tone, abound; Margaret Paston writes to her husband that he will get the stuff for the child's gown cheapest at Hay's wife; Jane Stonor writes that she "would rather break up household than take sojournants, for servants be not so diligent as they were wont to be." On the other hand, there is an endless host of little items to testify to how different a world it was, and with what different assumptions. Shillingford writes home to his fellows, full of naïve and innocent exultation in his own good handling of the justices in their case—"as my lord Chancellor bade the justice to dinner against that same day saying that he should have a dish of salt fish; I hearing this, I did as methought ought to be done . . . and sent thither that day 2 stately pickerells and 2 stately tenches, which my lord Chancellor made right much thereof . . . for it came in good season, for my lords the Duke of Buckingham and the Marquess of Suffolk and other dined with my lord Chancellor that day." This is an unfamiliar way of administering justice, but to accuse the good Mayor Shillingford of corruption would be out of place.

Likewise, when we come to marriage, it may startle us for a moment to find Margaret of Anjou, as a girl of barely twenty, writing to Dame Jane Carew, a widow of thirty-six, "for as much as our trusty and well-beloved squire Thomas Burneby, as well for the great zeal, love and affection he hath to your person, as for the womanly and virtuous governance that ye be renowned of, desireth with all his heart to do you worship by way of marriage; we, desiring the furtherance and preferment of our said squire . . . pray you right affectuously that at reverence of us you will have our said squire towards his said marriage." There is plenty about marriage in the **Paston Letters,** but it is nearly always the economic side that looms largest; when Margery Paston married below her station for love, there was a family outcry and the Bishop of Norwich was even called in to dissuade her from this appalling mésalliance. One is glad to know that she won her battle in the end; her love letters are among the most appealing in the whole collection.

The arrangements for a normal marriage were endlessly complicated in the effort to secure the maximum advantage; a marriage agreement in the Trevelian papers even provided compensation in the case of the death of a party before full value had been obtained. "Furthermore provided if it hap the said Elizabeth to decease within twelve months next after the said marriage, that then the said Thomas (her father) shall repay to the said John (Trevelian) 100 marks." Even in the smaller, everyday things there is a strange unfamiliarity. Growing up was a much tougher process for children of both sexes than it has since been. Elizabeth Clere writes to John Paston of his young sister, "she was never in so great sorrow as she is now-a-days, for she may not speak with no man how so ever he come . . . and she hath since Easterne the most part been beaten once in the week or twice, and sometimes twice on a day, and her head broken in two or three places." Agnes Paston's delicate request to her son's tutor, "that he will truly belash him, till he will amend," is only less surprising. All these details, small as they are, remind us that we are moving in a world of quite different conventions; they help the historian to think himself back into a past that is gone beyond recall.

Much of the dead past lies embedded in the letters like fossils in the letters like fossils in the rock; yet, if there is one feature of them that must be stressed, it is their newness, for they are the first private letters of English people that have survived. This is important; it brings out a side of the century's history that is often enough forgotten. We are so accustomed to thinking of the middle of the fifteenth century as a period of wild political disorder that we are apt to assume automatically that the arts and learning were also in decline. This impression is quite contrary to the evidence of the letters. The far greater part of them are autograph, even those written by women; and they bear witness to a surprisingly high standard of literacy among the merchant classes and the country gentlemen. Excited by these suggestive facts Kingsford and others have brought together a clear body of evidence pointing to the steady spread of education, particularly among laymen, during the fifteenth century. It is the period of the foundation of numerous schools and colleges, of Eton by King Henry VI and of Magdalen by Waynflete. In 1446 an ordinance was passed in London limiting the licensed schools to five, but there were in fact many more, and the reason for the measure was the eagerness of parents to send their children to schools, regardless of whether the education they received there was good or bad. The universities of the fifteenth century have been called dead, but this seems to be very far from being exact; if an Italian visiting scholar in 1422 could write that Oxford scholars delighted more in scholastic disputation than in the new learning, and if to Walter Paston the most important aid to obtaining his degree should seem to have been that his guests were satisfied with the banquet that he provided for the occasion, one must not lose sight of men like Flemming of Lincoln or Sellyng, said to have been a fellow of All Souls, both diligent collectors of manuscripts of classical authors, or Thomas Chandler, the Warden of New College, who invited Cornelius Vitelli to come and lecture in Greek at Oxford. Grocyn, who was a student in the college under him, lived to be the friend of Colet, More and Erasmus.

Throughout the period of the Wars of the Roses, the seeds of English culture were growing; there was a new avidity for books in the English tongue. Trevisa's translation of the old Latin *Polychronicon* found a ready public; it is significant that most of the contemporary chronicles are in English. John Paston had a dozen or more books of romances, poetry and heraldry, together with the *De Senectute* and *Amicitia* of Cicero; even before the advent of printing many lay gentlemen had small libraries, while some, like Humphrey of Gloucester or Tiptoft, brought together large and valuable collections. The new literacy of the fifteenth century was to flower a hundred years later in the writing of the English renaissance in Elizabeth's time. Its own literary products, apart from Malory, are banal enough, it is true, but the seed time was necessary for the harvest.

Perhaps it is this attention they call to the fifteenth century as a germinal period that is the most important feature for the historian of the letters that have been here considered. They paint in the background of a period in which two civilizations overlap—a function the more important since if one looks only at the foreground the scene is still altogether medieval. Henry V, *sans peur et sans reproche,* gallant, pious, "and above all," says Chastellain, "the Prince of Justice," is the last great king of English chivalry, the pattern of all that was best in the medieval conception of the monarch. Henry VI, pious and often imbecile, is the last king-saint of our medieval history. The vassals, too, be they courteous and wise like Suffolk, or like Warwick, Kingmakers, are medieval figures. The letters show one what is going on beneath this surface; the rise in importance, in education and in ambitions of the smaller folk; their everyday life that continues, very little affected, while the wars rage in the land. The chronicles can spotlight for us the great political events, the falls of kings and princes. The letters do what neither chronicles nor accounts nor public records can do; they bring us into direct contact with the people. They are, in a sense in which the other sources are not, alive, because they are personal records. Whether it is the young Paston at Eton, writing to his elder brother that, "I may come and sport with you in London a day or two this term time," or Mayor Shillingford, writing to his fellows in the early morning, full of cheer as ever: "and I lying on my bed at writing of this right rarely, merrily singing a merry song"—whichever it be—it is part of the common human experience, and there is a kind of pleasure in reading it that is not to be sought in the chronicles, be they never so full of rhetoric or of gossip. They can describe the high deeds; but the letters bring ordinary men before us, face to face, for the first time. (pp. 352-58)

> Maurice Keen, "The First English Family Letters," in History Today, *Vol. 9, No. 5, May, 1959, pp. 352-58.*

Kirkland C. Jones   (essay date 1976)

[*In the essay reprinted below, Jones examines biblical allusions, especially to the Book of Proverbs, in the* Paston Letters.]

The Pastons of Norfolk were a family of substance who began early in the fifteenth century to collect private letters and other types of correspondence. These letters represent a variety of subjects and frequently reveal a remarkable fluency and epistolary alertness. The **Paston Letters** include more than 1000 original letters and documents extending over the period from 1422-1508. The earliest of these are from William Paston, known as the "Good Judge," born in 1378, and from Agnes, his wife. A great number were written either by or to John Paston of the Inner Temple, son of the judge and husband of Margaret Paston; and in addition, a substantial number were written to or by the sons of John and Margaret, namely John II, often referred to as "John the Eldest," and John III, his younger brother. Despite the unsettled orthography of the time, the **Paston Letters** are not exceptionally difficult to read and understand, for their language relates to common affairs of life and was, by and large, written as it was spoken by the people. The majority of these letters, then, are informal, written to other members of the family concerning matters of business and about social and political affairs. Nevertheless, as this paper reveals, these documents are not, as some scholars would asset, devoid of "grace of style and originality of thought."

Until very recently the **Paston Letters** have, by and large, been viewed, as has other private correspondence of the fifteenth century in England, as most illustrative of social, political, and linguistic history and as having little or no literary worth. In other words, the literary qualities of the **Paston Letters,** including the elements of proverbs and proverbial sayings, have been overlooked. Unfortunately, there are still those critics who labor under the mistaken pronouncements of earlier investigators, doubting that anything literary could have come out of the "unproductive" fifteenth century in England. But Charles J. Kingsford, in the "Preface" to his book on the intellectual milieu of fifteenth-century England [*Prejudice and Promise in Fifteenth Century England*, 1963], endeavors to clear up much of the prejudice and distortion of fact perpetrated by earlier critics. He observes that " . . . the truth about fifteenth-century England [has been] distorted through prejudice of chroniclers and Tudor historians;" and he goes on to state that ". . . the truth [can] only be discovered by the study from different sources of the Fifteenth Century as the seed time of the future."

The present writer has found that despite the apparent lack of formality and the relative absence of ornateness of expression that characterize the **Paston Letters,** they deserve more than just an examination of their sociohistorical and linguistic content. In fact, one may justifiably assume that in addition to matters of business and the element of gossip about contemporary events, these documents probably contain much, both in content and in form, that is inherited from the past and that represents a link in the chain of literary tradition. Owing to the fact that during the fifteenth century the conveyance of letters was difficult, letters were not often written on trivial occasions; on the contrary, they were concerned with business, or with urgent family affairs. It is only incidentally that allusions to other matters come in. But as it is not uncommon for intrusive, subsidiary elements to find their way into the major literary themes of even the most noted writers, so do literary expressions and forms find their way into the writings that are considered to be, at least in their author's intent, sub-literary.

The term "Age of Transition" has frequently been used as a polite way of saying that the fifteenth century in England lacks much literary interest. But the Middle Ages in England—many critics seem to have forgotten—thought differently of originality of content; the writer was praised who could take the materials of antiquity and adapt them to his own purposes. Admittedly, English prose of the fifteenth century possessed no formed technique, much less a philosophy of composition, as more than one modern critic would remind us. Yet the prose writings of a number of genres, including those of the chronicle and official and personal correspondence, experienced during this time a great shift, and a rapid one, to native prose as a medium of expression. These writings also endured a slow growth in sophistication of style, pointing towards a culmination in the highly stylized prose of the sixteenth and seventeenth centuries. Hence it is of the utmost importance, if one is to understand the literary prose of the English Renaissance, that he read the prose of this "Period of Transition" with the aim of appreciating and comprehending the typical literary experiences—in reading as well as in writing—of the average fifteenth-century Englishman. For this reason, then, publications on how the writers of the **Paston Letters** and other prose writers of the period made use of certain traditional materials and on how they were influenced by literary tradition and rhetorical teaching in terms of thought, taste and technique are long over due.

Moving toward the specific scope of this paper, this writer has found that in their use of proverbs and proverbial wisdom as counsel, various authors of the **Paston Letters** lean heavily upon language that is unmistakably Biblical in content as well as flavor. Not only does one find innumerable discussions of matters pertaining to God, Holy Church and Holy Writ—reinforced by myriad sprinklings of obviously Biblical phraseology such as, "beseeching Almighty God," "as touching," and so forth—but there are also a number of examples of exhortation and advice that call to mind one or more Biblical passages, some more familiar and more commonly used than others.

Agnes Paston, wife of William, "the Judge," writes after the death of her husband to one of her younger sons, reminding him to "thynkk onis of the daie of youre fadris counseyle." This phrase, as well as much of the instruction that the letter contains, calls to mind the entire fourth chapter of Proverbs that opens with an admonition to youth: "Hear, ye children, the instruction of a father, and attend to know understanding" (Prov. 4:1). And of similar meaning is this verse, "where no counsel is, the people fall: but in the multitude of counsellors there is safety" (Prov. 11:14). Speaking of "counsel" in a different sense, Margaret Paston in a letter sprinkled with motherly advice warns John, her second son (here-after referred to as "John the Youngest"), to "werk wysely and bewar wham that ye lete know your councell." Margaret, in another letter to "John the Youngest" in which she instructs him in certain matters of urgent business, also includes a brief bit of counsel with regard to his personal conduct, "and if ye wull have my good wille, eschewe such thyngis as I spake to you of last in owr parisch chirch." The word "eschew" calls to mind passages from both the Old Testament and the New (See Job 1:1; 2:3; I Peter 3:11, as examples). And much like the fervent, spiritually oriented epistles of St. Paul is the letter of parental instruction and counsel written by the Duke of Suffolk to his son. As this entire letter constitutes an exceptionally good example from this correspondence of the use of Biblical language and allusion for instructional purposes, and because it is similar to many shorter passages of its kind appearing in the collection, it shall here be quoted in full. Its headnote reads: "The copie of a notable Lettre, written by the Duke of Suffolk to his Sonne, giving hymn therein very good counseil":

> My dere and only welbeloved sone, I beseche oure Lord in Heven, the Maker of alle the world, to blesse you, and to send you ever grace to love hym, and to drede hym; to the which, as ferre as a fader may charge his chile, I both charge you, and prei you to sette all spirites and wittes to do, and to knowe his holy lawes and comaundments, by the which ye shall with his grete mercy passe alle the grete tempestes and troubles of this wrecched world. And that also, wetyngly, ye do no thyng for love nor drede of any erthely creature that should displese hym. And there as any freelte maketh you to falle, be secheth hys mercy soone to calle you to hym agen with re-

pentaunce, satisfaccion, and contricion of youre herte never more in will to offend hym.

> Secondly, next hym, above alle erthely thyng, to be trewe liege man in hert, in wille, in thought, in dede, unto the kyng oure alder most high and dredde sovereygne Lord, to whom bothe ye and I been so moche bounde to; chargyng you, as fader can and may, rather to die than to be the contrarye, or to knowe any thyng that were ayenste the welfare or prosperite of his most riall person, but that as ferre as your body and lyf may strecthe, ye lyve and die to defende it, and to lete his highnesse have knowlache thereof in alle the haste ye can.

> Thirdly, in the same wyse, I charge you, my dere sone, alwey, as ye be bounden by the commaundnesses and to beleve hyr councelles and advises in alle youre werks, the which dredeth not, but shall be best and trewest to you. And yef any other body wold stere you to the contrarie, to flee the councell in any wyse, for ye shall fynde it nought and evyll.

> Forthe[rmore], as ferre as fader may can, I charge you in any wyse to flee the company and counsel of proude men, of coveitowse men, and of flateryng men, the more especially and myghtily to withstonde hem, and not to drawe, ne to medle with hem, with all youre myght and power. And to drawe to you and to your com[any good] and vertuowse men, and such as ben of good conversacion, and of trouthe, and be them shal ye never be deseyved, ner repente you off. [Moreover never follow] Youre owne witte in no wyse, but in alle youre werkes, of such folks as I write of above, axeth youre advice a[nd counse]l]; and doyng thus, with the mercy of God, ye shall do right well, and lyve in right moche worship, and grete herts rest and ease. And I wyll be to you as good lord and fader as my hert can thynke.

> And last of alle, as hertily and as lovyngly as ever fader blessed his child in erthe, I yeve you the blessyng of oure Lord and of me, which of his infynite mercy encrece you in alle vertu and good lyvyng. And that youre blood may by his grace from kynrede to kynrede multiplye in this erthe to hys servise, in such wyse as after the departyng fro this wreched world here, ye and thei may glorefye hum eternally amongs his aungelys in hevyn.

> Wretyn of myn hand,
> The day of my departyng fro this land.
>   Your trewe and lovyng fader. Suffolk

This letter advises the son on a variety of subjects to which many Biblical and non-Biblical proverbs are applicable. The Duke's son (John de La Pole), who succeeded him as Duke, is advised to honor both his parents (Ephesians 6:2; Exodus 20:12; Deuteronomy 5:16); to flee the counsel of the evil man and to seek the company of the good and the virtuous (Proverbs, especially Chapters 2-7); to trust in the Lord, leaning not to his own understanding (Proverbs 3:5-6). For the reader the one Biblical passage that sums up in a nutshell the father's advice is "Render . . . unto

Caesar the things which are Caesar's; and unto God the things that are God's" (Matthew 22:21). Though this wisdom might have been derived otherwise—and there is no certainty that it was derived from Bible sources—they were the most accessible and the most likely origins of Biblical sayings, paraphrases and allusions in this correspondence and are therefore being considered here as the most plausible places from which these materials issue.

On the theme of constancy and perseverance in the face of difficulty, a favorite of the Middle Ages, Archbishop Warham writes to William Paston: "Cousyn Paston, I recommaunde me unto you and have received your letter, by the which I have understand of the deth of my cousyn your fader, whose soule Jesu assoile. I wol consaile and exhorte you to take it as wel and as paciently as ye can, seeyng that we al be mortal and borne to dey. . . .The meane season, loke that ye be of as confortable chere as ye can, exhorting my lady, your modre in lawe, to be in like wise, . . . " This passage bespeaks the wisdom of a number of Scriptural verses, including Job 5:7; 14:1; 15:14; 25:4, "man born to trouble"; Matthew 11:11, "man born of woman"; and on patience in adversity: Luke 21:19; Romans 5:3; Colossians 1:11; James 1:3; 5:10-11, among others. Margaret writes to her first son, "John the Eldest": "Send me word how ye doo of yowyr syknes that ye had on yowr hey eye and yowr lege; and yff God wol nowt suffyr yow to have helth, thank Hym thereof, and takyt passhently, . . . " And to her husband she writes: " . . . be of good comfort, and trost veryly be the grase of God that ye shall overcome your enemys and your trobelows maters ryght welle, yf ye wolle be of good comfort, and not take your maters to hevely that ye apeyr not your self, and thynke veryly that ye be strong inowe for alle your enemys be the grace of God." The sentiment of much of the exhortation and advice on this particular theme may be summed up by Proverbs 24:10: "If thou faint in the day of adversity, thy strength is small."

In a letter to John Paston, Senior, his cousin Elizabeth Clere alludes to the Bible's teaching about a wife's obedience to her husband: she should "rewle her to hym as sche awte to do." Titus 2:4-5 commands: " . . . teach the young women to be sober, to love their husbands, . . . (to be obedient to their own husbands." St. Paul, in the letter to the Ephesians, writes: "Wives submit yourselves to your husbands" (5:22); and in other passages we learn: "A virtuous woman is a crown to her husband" (Proverbs 12:4), for she obeys him and eats not the bread of idleness. Cecily Dawne reminds "John the Eldest" who, incidentally, never married, that he should choose "one . . . that wil drede and faithfully unfeyned love you above alle othir erthely creatures. For that is most excellent richesse in this worlde, as I suppose." In this same letter Cecily instructs her young friend with proverbial wisdom in much the same way that Pandarus instructs both Troilus and Criseyde in Chaucer's long, narrative poem (Pandarus's speeches in Books II and III); she even refers to herself as his "oratrix." The reader recognizes her allusion to the sentiment of more than one verse from the Book of Proverbs: a faithful wife is to a man great riches.

The element of counsel in the **Paston Letters** is not always

in the form of friendly advice, especially where parents are desirous of correcting their children. Margaret writes to her oldest son a letter that consists almost entirely of rebuke and verbal chastenings. After sarcastically reminding him of her displeasure at his having left home without her knowledge, she then admonishes him: " . . . that ye war (beware) of your expence bettyr and ye have be befor thys tyme, and be your owne purse berer, I trowe ye shall fyndyt most profytable to you." And in a mood of self-rebuke, Thomas Howes (sometimes spelled Howys) writes to John Paston, Senior, regretting that he (Howes) has entered into a faulty agreement concerning the wardship of Thomas Fastolf, for whom the two men were appointed guardians: " . . . be God, I shal trust no more no fayre wordes." Perhaps Howes recalled in this instance the exhortation of Solomon: "When he [the wicked man] speaketh fair believe him not: for there are seven abominations in his heart" (Proverbs 26:25).

In addition to the commonplaces of instruction covered by the preceding examples, the use of Biblical wisdom in the **Paston Letters** also covers a variety of other topics: How to live in fear and admonition of God; avoidance of evil fellowship; how to choose the good instead of the bad; letting one's deeds reflect love for God and charity to his neighbor; avoiding slander and gossip; the proper observance of times and seasons; wise use of time and talent; abstention from fleshly lusts ("Lollardy of fleshe"); against being overly wise in one's own conceit; against perjury and falsehood.

We are able to see demonstrated in the Biblical language and concepts of the kind discussed in this paper a fact reiterated by many critics of English, especially by those of the medieval period: the Bible naturally exercised a stronger influence on English than any foreign work, if, indeed, we can call a book foreign that was read—or at least quoted—in every household. For a view of the influence of Scripture upon the language and thought of fifteenth-century England, it is hardly necessary to do more than direct attention to a few of the Biblical proverbs and sentences that attracted the writers of the period in the same way as they had attracted Chaucer before them and Shakespeare who came after. Furthermore, the presence of these Biblical materials along with wise sayings of other types, reveals that in the fifteenth century the medieval love for moralizings of various kinds and the medieval appetite for the sententious still prevailed. The prevalence of ancient proverbial materials as well as of the anecdotes incorporated into the sermons of medieval homilists, demonstrates that the Church and the whole outlook of Her ministry and instruction were still predominantly universal. Moreover, the Bible itself, with its many parallels to myth and legend, not only provided for medieval audiences an exposure to the kind of knowledge found in books of ancient history, but it also presented sayings which represent, both in content and in form, a link in the chain of literary tradition. The preceding statement, of course, is not based on the traditional asumption that "literary tradition" must of necessity imply a conscious striving by the writer(s) for certain preconceived artistic effects. And even though these documents are not expected to produce much that is belletristic, these Biblical materials, as used in this correspondence, do produce a considerable amount of literary quality. (pp. 155-63)

> *Kirkland C. Jones, "Biblical Sayings, Paraphrases, and Allusions in 'The Paston Letters'," in CLA Journal, Vol. XX, No. 2, December, 1976, pp. 155-63.*

FURTHER READING

Duthie, D. Wallace. "The Women of the *Paston Letters.*" *The Nineteenth Century and After: A Monthly Review* 68, No. 402 (August 1910): 227-41.

　　Informal look at the representation of women in the *Paston Letters.*

Sykes, W. J. "The *Paston Letters.*" *The Dalhousie Review* XVI, No. 2 (July 1936): 157-70.

　　Surveys the social conditions of fifteenth-century England as revealed in the *Paston Letters.*

Trevor-Roper, H. R. "Up and Down in the Country: The *Paston Letters.*" In his *Men and Events: Historical Essays,* pp. 30-4. New York: Harper and Brothers, 1957.

　　Chronicles several important events in the history of the Paston family.

Turner, Charles W. "The *Paston Letters.*" *The Sewanee Review* V, No. 4 (October 1897): 425-37.

　　Explores the value of the *Paston Letters* as historical documents.

White, Beatrice. "Sundry Ways of Love, Medieval Style." *Essays and Studies* (1985): 1-11.

　　Brief examination of fifteenth-century marriage practices.

ISBN 0-8103-6116-7